CORSICA

EYEWITNESS TRAVEL GUIDES

FRANCE
BEST PLACES TO
EAT & STAY

EYEWITNESS TRAVEL GUIDES

FRANCE
BEST PLACES TO
EAT & STAY

Main contributors
NATASHA EDWARDS & SHARON SUTCLIFFE

LONDON, NEW YORK,
MELBOURNE, MUNICH AND DELHI
www.dk.com

PROJECT EDITOR Cécile Landau
ART EDITOR Janis Utton
WINE EDITOR Bill Evans
ASSISTANT EDITOR Jo Gardner
DTP DESIGNERS Jason Little, Conrad Van Dyk
CARTOGRAPHIC EDITOR Casper Morris
PICTURE RESEARCHER Brigitte Arora

MAIN CONTRIBUTORS
Natasha Edwards, Sharon Sutcliffe

WHERE TO EAT AND STAY
Compiled by The Content Works, London

PHOTOGRAPHERS
Andrew Holligan, Ian O'Leary

MAPS
Dominic Beddow, Simonetta Giori
(Draughtsman Ltd)

Reproduced in Singapore by Colourscan
Printed and bound by Graphicom, Italy

First published in Great Britain in 2004
by Dorling Kindersley Limited
80 Strand, London WC2R 0RL

Copyright © 2004 Dorling Kindersley Limited, London
A Penguin Company

**The information in this
Eyewitness Travel Guide is checked annually**.
Every effort has been made to ensure that this book is as up-to-date
as possible at the time of going to press. Some details, however,
such as telephone numbers, opening dates and prices, are liable to
change. The publishers cannot accept responsibility for any
consequences arising from the use of this book, nor for any material
on third party websites, and cannot guarantee that any website
address in this book will be a suitable source of travel information.
We value the views and suggestions of our readers very highly.
Please write to: Publisher, DK Eyewitness Travel Guides,
Dorling Kindersley, 80 Strand, London WC2R 0RL, Great Britain.

Bread on a Provençal market stall

CONTENTS

Chardenoux, a traditional
Paris bistro

Sunflowers, widely grown for their oil in southwestern France

Pike-perch, a popular fish of the Loire Valley

REGION BY REGION

Bauges cheese from the Alps

Grapevines in the Languedoc

Introduction

Whether you're self-catering with local produce, or dining in a grand restaurant, eating and drinking are among the great joys of foreign travel. Nowhere is this truer than in France where, even in the fast-food era, there's an unparalleled appreciation of the sheer sensual pleasure of a good meal.

The French love of food is proverbial; they simply do it better than most other nations. There are many reasons for this. A characteristically Gallic pleasure in the physicality of eating may be one. Then there's the fact that after the Revolution, many of the great aristocratic households downsized their kitchens, releasing a flood of skilled chefs into general society. Another factor is *terroir* – the almost mystical conjunction of soil, climate and agriculture that is said to determine the qualities of the produce.

The French have been great culinary inventors, too; restaurants are a case in point. The first public dining room opened in Paris in 1765, a modest establishment owned by a soup vendor named Monsieur Boulanger, who advertised his *restaurants* – or "restoratives" – on a sign above his door. The restorative power of good dining was not lost on the Parisian public and, by the early 19th century, the capital boasted more than 500 such places.

Walnut oil and walnuts

A couple of centuries later, the whole country is teeming with eateries from tip to toe. But if you want to eat well in France, it's essential to grasp that not all of them are good and, precisely because France is synonymous with good food, it can be more than usually disappointing to experience a substandard meal.

France: Best Places to Eat and Stay aims to save you that disappointment. Every restaurant, brasserie, bistro and patisserie in our selective listings excels in one way or another – whether for its classic French dishes, its regional specialities, or for straightforward good value.

Our accommodation suggestions are all tailored to good eating: some are hotels with fine restaurants; some offer no food themselves but are near a recommended restaurant; some are restaurants-with-rooms. All will allow you to savour a great meal and then to cap the experience with a comfortable night's sleep.

Left Garlic stall in Sarlat market **Above** Grape harvest in Provence

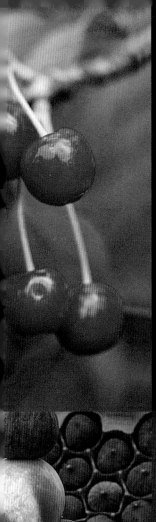

THE FOOD
& WINE
OF FRANCE

*Climates ranging from the maritime
and temperate to continental and
Mediterrean, across a landscape that
varies from arable plains to steep Alpine
pastures, allow an enormous variety of
produce to be grown, reared or fished in
France. Small-scale, family businesses
still thrive, with quality remaining of
prime importance. Travel in France
offers the chance of sampling the very
best of its superb food and wine.*

Regional Cuisine & Appellations

The French are proud of their regional identities, be they Breton, Béarnais or Auvergnat, and nowhere is this more evident than in their regional cuisine and produce. Many specialities are protected by AOC rules and top-notch produce may bear further special labels.

While some of France's high-quality meat, fruit and vegetables, charcuterie, cheeses, cakes and confectionery can be found in shops and supermarkets across the country, and sometimes abroad, many products remain essentially local and can only be found at shops, markets and restaurants in the region in which they are produced.

Alongside universally popular dishes, such as the adored *steak-frites*, one of the features of French cuisine is the range of distinct regional dishes you will come across in each area you visit. The *aligot* of the Massif Central, *choucroute garnie* of Alsace or Flemish *waterzooï* all point to the strength of different local traditions, though what you eat in restaurants

Camembert label

today is probably rather more refined than the thick bean soups, pork and cabbage stews or rustic crêpes that once sustained peasant life. Soups, such as the *garbure* and the *tourin* of the southwest that once formed a peasant staple, now tend to be only found in rustic restaurants. But there is also a growing trend for more gastronomic versions, from the luxurious *bouillabaisse* of Provence to a vast range of sophisticated creamed soups being presented by top chefs.

VARIATIONS ON A THEME

Pretty much every area seems to have a one-pot mixed meat and vegetable stew, called a *potée* in the Champagne, Limousin or Lorraine, a *hochepot* in the Nord and *kig ha farz* in Brittany. Fish soups and stews also vary according to the local catch and traditions – with or without the addition of shellfish, potatoes or *aïoli*. Coq au vin, although most often associated with Burgundy and Beaujolais, similarly exists in pretty much every region that produces red wines. Elsewhere, as in Picardy, you may also find variants made with beer.

Certain regional products, such as *magret de canard*, once almost totally restricted to the southwest, are now found all over

Moules marinières

France. Provençal style vegetable preparations and the use of olive oil and black olive tapenade have also been widely adopted, in part because of the move towards healthy eating. Conversely, certain traditions endure, such as the use of butter in the north, goose fat in the southwest and olive oil in the south.

EXTERNAL INFLUENCES

French cooking, however conservative its image, has always absorbed foreign influences. This includes the spread of the potato – introduced from America in the 16th century but only widely popularized by Parmentier in the 18th – and the more recent arrival of North African couscous and Asian seasonings.

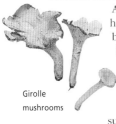

Girolle mushrooms

As a country which has extensive land borders and a long history of changing frontiers, France has also been influenced by its neighbours. Not surprisingly, the food and wine of Alsace shows strong Germanic overtones; the Nord shares many dishes with Belgian Flanders; Roussillon and the Pays Basque show the mark of the Catalan and Basque cuisines of Spain; while in Nice and Savoie, both part of Italy until 1860, many of the local dishes have a strong Italianate flavour.

NEW TRENDS

While some regional restaurants adhere firmly to dyed-in-the-wool traditions, many of today's young chefs are modernizing the repertoire by producing attractively presented, lighter dishes that still showcase the high quality of local produce but give it a creative spin. More recently, too, there has been a proliferation of fashionable culinary trends, such as the widespread use of fiery Espelette peppers as a seasoning.

Label Rouge chicken

SPECIAL DESIGNATIONS

AOC The *appellation d'origine contrôlée* (AOC) distinguishes both quality and regional authenticity of produce that typifies a particular *terroir* – a term that relates not just to an area of land, but also to its climate, culture and traditions. Qualifying items must adhere to a strict charter of quality. The largest number of AOCs concern wines and spirits, but there are 43 AOCs for cheeses and dairy products, including Camembert and Roquefort, butter from Charentes-Poitou and cream and butter from Isigny-sur-Mer. Twenty-two AOCs for other food products include olive oils, pine honey from Alsace and Bresse poultry.

Label Rouge The *label rouge or* "red label" distinguishes products of above average quality. It is generally applied to a group of producers that meet certain required standards and methods of production. Most have been awarded to meat and charcuterie, such as chickens from the Landes, milk-fed veal, Quercy lamb and Bayonne ham.

Label AB The AB *(agriculture biologique)* label identifies any organic produce.

Denomination Montagne A "mountain" label can be awarded to products such as *jambon de montagne* that are entirely produced in mountainous zones.

Provençal olive oil

Meat, Poultry, Game & Charcuterie

The quality of meat in France is usually very high, and many regions boast a number of renowned meat dishes. But such high standards are often best appreciated in a simple, lightly grilled steak, found on nearly every menu, from that of the grandest kitchen to the simplest café.

Regional cattle of Alsace

BEEF

Beef from cattle such as Charolais (Burgundy), Limousin, Salers and Aubrac (Massif Central), Maine-Anjou (Loire Valley), and Chalosse and Blond d'Aquitaine (Aquitaine) is particularly prized, as is that from the small black bulls of the Camargue (Provence). Some varieties, such as Salers and Maine-Anjou, are still largely restricted to their region of origin, though Charolais and Limousin cattle are now found all over France.

LAMB

The best-flavoured lamb often comes from mountain pastures, such as those of the Pyrenees, Sisteron (Provence), and the limestone plateaux of Lodève (Languedoc). Also worth seeking-out is the *pré-salé* lamb from animals raised on the salt marshes of the Baie de Mont-St-Michel (Normandy), the Baie de Somme (Picardy) and Pauillac (Aquitaine).

PORK

The days when every rural household kept a pig are long gone, but there is large-scale pig-rearing in Brittany, and they are often kept in dairy regions, where they are fed on whey, a by-product of cheese-making. Efforts are being made to preserve rare breeds, such as the cul-noir of Limousin (Massif Central), the Basque pig (Pyrenees) and the semi-wild Corsican pig, raised in natural conditions where it can feed on roots and nuts.

POULTRY

Poulet de Bresse (see p226) is the only chicken to have received an *appellation contrôlée (see p11)*, but good quality, free-range chickens, which have been

Bresse chickens

awarded *labels rouges (see p11)* are bred in many areas of France. These include *poulet Loué* from the Loire Valley, and chickens from Normandy, Licques (Le Nord), and the Landes (Aquitaine). Challans duck (Loire) is also highly regarded, as is the guinea fowl from Licques and the Drôme (Rhône Valley).

GAME

Hunting is popular in rural France and the game season is taken very seriously. From October, expect to see plenty of wild boar, venison, hare, pheasant and partridge hanging up in butchers and on menus. Rabbit, pigeon, quail and duck are now largely farmed, but you can sometimes find leaner, and tastier, wild specimens. Most game in France is not hung for a long period, as in Britain.

Regions noted for their game include Corsica, Massif Central, Périgord, the Ardennes (Champagne) and the forests of the Sologne (Loire Valley).

TRIPE AND OFFAL

Calves' liver, along with veal kidneys and sweetbreads all feature widely in classic French dishes, as does cows'

Morteauvian butcher

tripe, particularly in the cuisines of Normandy and the Lyon area (Rhône Valley). Strongly flavoured pigs' tripe and offal is mainly used for charcuterie, while sheep's feet and stomach feature in the diet of the Auvergne (Massif Central).

Foie gras, the specially fattened liver of corn-fed geese and ducks *(see p325)* is most often associated with southwest France, although it is also produced in parts of Alsace and Normandy.

CHARCUTERIE

Almost every part of the pig is used for charcuterie, from the ears to the trotters. Even the intestines are employed as sausage casings. The better cuts are made into ham, which divides roughly into two main types: cooked ham *(jambon cuit* or *jambon blanc)*, and cured ham *(jambon cru)*, which has been salted and then either air-dried or smoked for several months.

Pork meat is cooked for hours in its own fat and potted to make *rillettes*, while the liver features in terrines and pâtés, often combined with pork meat and sometimes game. Even pigs' blood is used – as the central ingredient in *boudin noir* (black pudding or blood sausage).

Areas noted for their fine charcuterie include Alsace, the Auvergne (Massif Central), Corsica, Franche-Comté, Lyon (Rhône Valley) and the Pays Basque (Pyrenees). Other regions, however are famed for just one or two select products: *andouillette de Troyes* (Champagne), *andouille de Vire* (Normandy), *andouille de Guémené* (Brittany), *saucisse de Toulouse* (Gascony) and the *rillettes de Tours* and *du Mans* (Loire Valley).

Fish, Shellfish, Frogs & Snails

Thanks to a long coastline and extensive inland waters, the variety of fish available in French restaurants and markets is enormous. Remember, however, that the same fish is often given different names in different regions.

Fishing boat at La Turballe

SALTWATER FISH

In France, fishmongers will indicate where fish originated, and if it was line-caught *(de ligne)* or farmed *(d'élevage)*. In good seaside restaurants, the fish may well be priced by weight, with a basket of whole, raw fish brought to your table for you to choose from.

The major fishing ports include Boulogne-sur-Mer (Le Nord), Dieppe and Fécamp (Normandy), Concarneau, and Guilvinec (Brittany), St-Jean-de-Luz (Pyrenees) and Sète (Languedoc). At these, the catch is auctioned off daily, but there are also many smaller fishing ports, where you may still be able to buy direct from fishermen.

Mackerel and flat fish, including sole and turbot, are a major part of the catch in Normandy, as are sardines and sea bass in Brittany and tuna and hake in St-Jean-de-Luz. Catches in Languedoc,

Provence and Corsica include monkfish, red mullet and sardines as well as the distinctly Mediterranean *rascasse*, a key ingredient of *bouillabaisse*.

In many ports, processing the catch is as big an industry as the fishing itself. Sardines are canned at Nantes (Loire Valley) and in Brittany. At Collioure (Languedoc), anchovies are still hand-salted, as they have been for centuries. Boulogne-sur-Mer is renowned for its herring smokeries, and is also a major centre for canning, freezing and salting.

FRESHWATER FISH

Trout, salmon, shad, pike and pike-perch are all at home in France's lakes and rivers. Brown trout are still common in fast-flowing mountain streams, though other trout, along with salmon, are now mainly farmed.

Carp and lake char are found in the alpine lakes, those of Alsace being famed for their carp. In the brackish, estuarine waters of the rivers Loire, Rhône and Somme, eels flourish. Lampreys are found in the river Gironde and are considered a delicacy in Bordeaux, though the river's sturgeon are now farmed – part of a resurgent caviar industry.

Freshly caught fish at St-Tropez market

Giant prawns for sale on a market stall

SHELLFISH

Huge brimming platters of shellfish are a regular feature on menus in many coastal regions, as well as of Parisian brasseries. Normandy and Brittany are the main regions for crabs, lobsters, langoustines, prawns, whelks, clams and scallops, and the Atlantic coast generally is important for mussel and oyster farms. The northern waters are also noted for tiny grey shrimps.

Mediterranean shellfish treats include langouste and sea urchins; you may even come across that rare delicacy, the violet or sea potato. When near inland waters, look out for freshwater crayfish on the menu, especially when in the Dombes area of the Rhône Valley.

SNAILS

Two types of edible snail are common in France: the *petit gris (helix aspersa)* found in Provence, Languedoc and Poitou and Aquitaine, and the larger *escargot de Bourgogne (helix pomatia)*, that is found in Burgundy. Snails are often associated with wine-producing areas, as they tend to flourish in the vineyards. However, most snails eaten in France today are raised on snail farms, where their diet can be carefully controlled, or imported from eastern Europe. They are either sold live or pre-cooked, ready to heat and serve – the most common way of eating them is from their shells with garlic butter.

FROGS' LEGS

Despite the cliché of the French as a nation of frog-eaters, frogs have become something of a rarity on restaurant menus, though you will find them in many grand restaurants and in areas with the damp pond and marsh habitats in which they thrive, such as the Dombes (Rhône Valley), the Jura (Franche-Comté), the Vosges (Alsace), the Vendée (Loire Valley) and the Somme (Picardy).

OYSTERS

France is by far Europe's largest producer – and consumer – of oysters. The native flat oysters *(ostrea edilis)*, known as *plates* or *belons*, are raised in Riec-sur-Belon and Cancale in Brittany, but are now becoming a rarity and have largely been replaced by the faster-growing, hardier, crinkle-shelled creuse oysters *(crassostrea gigas)* of Pacific origin. These are cultivated along the coast of Normandy, and at Arcachon and Marennes-Oléron (Poitou) and at Mèze (Languedoc).

Oysters are traditionally eaten in months with an "R" in them (between September and April), although modern refrigeration means that they are now available all year round. Many people, however, still prefer their cleaner, brinier, winter flavour to the *laiteuse* or milky quality they acquire in summer, when they spawn. The *iodé*, or salty-minerally, flavour of oysters will vary considerably, depending on where and how they are raised. Most seafood restaurants just serve oysters raw on a bed of ice, usually with a simple twist of lemon or a shallot vinegar, but some menus feature them cooked, frequently gratinéed.

Fruit & Vegetables

From the cool north down to the sun-kissed shores of the Mediterranean Sea, via land-locked plains and alpine pastures, ideal conditions can be found somewhere in France for growing most types of fruit and vegetables.

The variety of produce that can be grown on French soil is considerable, ranging from the chicory and root vegetables of the north to the olives, figs and citrus fruits of Provence and Corsica.

Artichokes are a speciality of both Brittany, where they come as large compact globes, and Provence, where you find the small violet variety with hardly any choke. Asparagus is grown pretty much anywhere with the right sandy soils that it likes – in particular in the Landes (Aquitaine) and along the

Le Garde-Freinet cherries

Languedoc coast, and Durance river (Provence), in the Lot (Quercy) and in the Sologne (Loire Valley).

Cantaloup melons are grown in a number of areas, notably around Cavaillon in Provence and in Poitou. The best strawberries come from Plougastel in Brittany, the Périgord and the Vaucluse. Renewed interest in different varieties now sees their season start with the fragrant, scarlet, diamond-shaped *gariguette* in April and May, followed by a host of other varieties throughout the summer.

A handful of crops are particularly associated with one region, such as the mirabelle plum of Lorraine, *mâche* from the Loire, apricots from Roussillon and blackcurrants from Burgundy; or even one village, such as the fiery peppers from Espelette in the Pyrenees.

At the same time as new varieties are being developed, there has also been a revival in the cultivation of neglected

MUSHROOMS

One of the highlights of the autumn menu in France is wild mushrooms, which appear after a period of heavy rain in the damp woods, especially in oak, chestnut and pine forests. The main types are ceps (various members of the *boletus* family), *girolle* (chanterelle), *lactaire* (milk-cap mushroom) and *trompette-des-morts* (horn of plenty). Ceps are particularly prized, and are auctioned off at special markets, as are precious truffles *(see p323)*. In contrast *morilles* (morels) are usually found in open meadows in spring and summer.

Champignons de Paris are cultivated button mushrooms, most of which are grown in caves in the Loire valley *(see p189)*. A number of other varieties are now also successfully cultivated, such as shiitake and *pleurotte* (oyster mushroom).

Fresh northern vegetables on sale at Rouen market

fruit and vegetables, such as Jerusalem artichokes, parsnips, pumpkins and rhubarb, or in maintaining specific local varieties such as the *bonnotte* potato of the Ile de Noirmoutier (Loire Valley).

SEASONAL PRODUCE

Although imports, improved storage, cultivation under glass and new varieties all mean that many fruits and vegetables now seem to be present all year round, some remain seasonal or are only at their prime for a limited period.

In spring, look out for *légumes primeurs* from the Nantes region (Loire Valley), and for cherries from Céret in Languedoc, along with the first strawberries that appear in April around Carpentras in Provence. Asparagus also is abundant from April well into May, when *bonnotte* potatoes feature.

Summer is the peak time for peaches, apricots and soft fruit. Cavaillon melons are at their best in June, as are plums from July to September. Late August and September bring a glut of figs.

By September, apples and pears are starting to appear, along with fresh walnuts from the Périgord, globe artichokes from Brittany and *chasselas de Moissac* table grapes from the warm south.

Winter brings chicory from Le Nord, *mâche* from the Loire Valley and clementines from Corsica.

SALADS AND CRUDITÉS

Various types of lettuces including *laitue, batavia, feuille de chêne, romaine* and *frisée*, are all used in green salads, along with young spinach, beetroot leaves, *mâche* and rocket. *Mesclun*, a mixture of young salad leaves and fresh herbs, is particularly associated with Provence. Chicory, from Le Nord and Picardy, is popular in winter salads, often combined with blue cheese, beetroot, or chopped apples and walnuts. Cooked potatoes and lentils may also be served cold or lukewarm in a vinaigrette.

Generous mixed salads can make a lunch in themselves; typical combinations include *Auvergnate*, made with *jambon d'Auvergne*, Cantal cheese and walnuts; *Périgourdienne*, with foie gras, *magret de canard* and gizzards, or *Parisienne* with *jambon de Paris* and hard-boiled eggs.

An everyday menu in a café or simple bistro may well start with crudités: a plate of cold, essentially raw, vegetables, such as grated carrot, sliced tomatoes, *céleri rémoulade* (grated celeriac in mayonnaise), cucumber and beetroot.

Bread & Patisserie

The skills of French bakers and pastry chefs are held in the highest esteem worldwide, and although much copied are rarely matched. A trip to France brings the opportunity to sample breads and cakes of superlative quality.

BREAD AND BAKERIES

Bread has played a pivotal role in French history. Bread riots, following poor harvests that led to a hike in the price of a loaf, helped trigger the start of the French Revolution in 1789. Even today, the price of the basic baguette is still regulated by the state.

The quintessential "French bread" – the long, crispy baguette – is actually a relatively late Parisian invention. Before that larger, long or round loaves of *pain de campagne* (country bread) dominated. Other forms include the *ficelle* (a small, extra-thin baguette) and the *bâtard* (a thicker baguette).

Today, most French bread is made from white wheat flour, but there has been a recent revival in breads made either wholly or partly from wholewheat flour *(pain complet)* or rye flour *(pain au seigle)*. Some are made with organic flour *(pain biologique)* or use a natural rising agent *(pain au levain)*, and may include added whole grains *(pain aux céréales)* or bran *(pain de son)*.

Breads at Sarlat market

Other specialities include the softer, square-shaped *pain de mie*, which has very little crust and is often used for sandwiches; *pain au lait*, soft rolls made with milk and butter; and *pain aux noix* (walnut bread) as well as variants with raisins or apricots.

Today only a shop where the bread dough is prepared and baked on the premises is allowed to call itself a *boulangerie*; any other place that sells bread can only be called a *dépôt de pain*.

SANDWICHES AND CROQUES

The typical French sandwich served in a bar or café consists of a half-baguette filled with either ham or cheese or both *(une mixte)*, or perhaps with *rillettes* or *saucisson sec*. *Sandwicheries* and *pâtisseries* increasingly also add some mixed salad and mayonnaise. If you find a baguette too hard on the jaw, look out for sandwiches made with the softer *pain de mie* or brioche rolls, or for Italian-style toasted *panini*, which are also becoming popular.

A quintessential café snack in France is the *croque-monsieur* – essentially a toasted sandwich filled with Gruyère cheese and ham; the *croque-madame* is similar but with a fried egg on top, and more refined variants may include tomatoes, herbs or country ham on an open slice of *pain Poîlane (see p39)*.

THE BAGUETTE REVIVAL

Following a decline in the quality of the average baguette, many bakers, since the mid-1990s, have returned to traditional methods and the use of high-quality, stone-ground flours. These old-style baguettes are often sold under trade-marked names such as *Banette, Rétrodor, Tradition, la Croquante* or *Flûte Gana*. They tend to have a thicker chewier texture and last longer, although they are generally pricier. Avoid baguettes with a rounded base covered in tiny circles – an indication they were cooked in a rotary oven – as these usually have a woolly texture and go stale quickly.

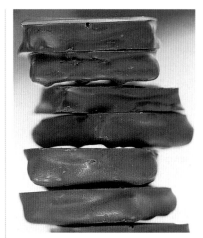
Mounds of Lyonnais chocolate

VIENNOISERIE

The range of flaky buttery "breads" – *croissants, brioches, pain au chocolat, pain aux raisins* – are known collectively as *viennoiserie*, supposedly because they were introduced to France from Vienna by the Austrian-born queen Marie-Antoinette. The *croissant* (the French word for crescent) was invented in 1686, when Austria was at war with Turkey, but gained its flaky texture in France.

PÂTISSERIE

Fresh fruit tarts made from seasonal fruits, such as apples, apricots, plums and cherries, are a French favourite. Most have a shortcrust (*pâte brisée*) or shortbread (*pâte sablée*) base, and the fruit may be combined with almond frangipane or whipped cream. They are usually eaten cold, although the *tarte fine*, which has a very thin flaky pastry base, is generally served hot or warm.

Luscious cakes include numerous sponge and mousse concoctions and rich chocolate gateaux, such as the *Opéra*. Favourites now found nationwide include *madeleines, financiers*

and chocolate or coffee *éclairs* and *réligieuses* (a large profiterole topped with a smaller one, which supposedly resembles a nun). Others remain more regional, such as *cannelés* (Aquitaine), *gaufres* (Le Nord) and *mirlitons* (Normandy).

CHOCOLATES

Paris, the Rhône Valley and French Alps region, and the Pays Basque (Pyrenees) are particularly noted for their chocolate makers. The main focus in France is on high-quality dark, bitter chocolate with a high proportion of cocoa solids. Rich ganache fillings are popular and may be flavoured with anything from alcohol to wild strawberries, herbs or spices.

Decadent cakes at Gérard Mulot

Cheese & Dairy Produce

Although President Charles de Gaulle once famously said, "how can you govern a country that produces 325 different cheeses", no-one appears to be quite certain as to exactly how many France produces. The precise number, however, is undoubtedly far in excess of that.

CHEESE

French cheeses are made from the milk of cows, goats and sheep. A few contain a mix from different animals and some are made with goats' milk in summer and sheeps' in winter. Although the milk is often pasteurized, the use of raw milk is increasing, which tends to result in greater character and depth of flavour. There is also a distinction made between *fromage fermier*, produced on a farm using its own milk, and *fromage laitier*, produced in a dairy using milk from several different farms.

Other factors can affect flavour too. Different producers will use different levels of salting for the same type of cheese. Many *appellation contrôlée* cheeses must be made from the milk of animals fed only on local pasture, without the addition of winter silage. Some breeds of animal, such as the *vache Normande*, the Montbéliard of Franche-Comté and the Salers of the Massif Central, are noted for the high quality and richness of their milk, qualities passed on to cheeses made from it.

Flavour also varies according to how long a cheese is left to mature and the conditions, such as the temperature and humidity, in which it is stored. Here the *fromagers-affineurs* (cheese shops which ripen cheese on their own premises) can

Savoie cheeses with their distinctive packaging

play a very important role. Fresh, young cheeses are generally mild, flavour becoming increasingly pronounced as a cheese matures. Sometimes the same type of cheese may be considered fit to eat at different ages, depending on the particular characteristics sought.

French cheeses are sometimes classified according to how they are made, although within each grouping there can be considerable differences in both form and flavour.

Maturing cheeses

Shelves of St-Nectaire cheese

Croûte fleurie After being moulded and drained, these cheeses develop a soft, velvety white rind. This group includes medium-fat varieties such as Camembert (Normandy) and Brie (Ile-de-France), full-fat Chaource (Champagne) and the triple cream Brillat-Savarin (Normandy).

Croûte lavée These cheeses have been washed with either brine, eau-de-vie, beer or grape marc, which imparts some of its flavour, and leaves the rind orange-coloured and feeling slightly damp and sticky. They often have a strong smell, although may have a milder taste than their odour suggests. Pungent Maroilles (Le Nord), Livarot (Normandy) and Epoisses (Burgundy) fall into this group, although milder Pont l'Evêque (Normandy) and Reblochon (the Alps) do as well.

Pâte persillée An injection of bacteria gives these cheeses their characteristic blue veining. They can be made from cows' milk, such as Bleu d'Auvergne and Fourme d'Ambert (Massif Central) and Bleu de Gex (Franche-Comté); goats' milk, such as Bleu Tarentais (the Alps); or sheeps' milk, such as Roquefort (Massif Central).

Pâte pressée Some cheeses are pressed in order to hasten the draining process. Hard, nutty varieties such as Cantal and Salers (Massif Central) are treated in this way, but so is the semi-soft St-Nectaire (Massif Central). There are also a number of *pâte pressée cuite* cheeses, such as Comté (Franche-Comté) and Beaufort (the Alps), where the milk used is first heated to "cook" the curds.

Fromage frais This term is used to describe both the fresh curd cheeses, such as Fontainebleau (Ile-de-France) and the Tomme Fraîche of Laguiole (Massif Central), as well as whey-based cheeses, such as Brousse (Provence) and Brocciu (Corsica).

Chèvre France produces a large range of *chèvre*, or goats' cheeses, both hard and soft. Soft *chèvre* is often rolled in herbs or ash, while other *chèvre* are left to develop a velvety *croûte fleurie* or even a natural crust.

MILK AND CREAM

Brittany and the Ile-de-France are important producers of fresh milk. Thick, luscious golden *crème fraîche* is skimmed off from whole milk so that it retains some of its natural ferments, which give it the extra "bite" absent from British double cream. *Crème fraîche d'Isigny* from Normandy has been awarded an *appellation contrôlée*.

BUTTER

Normandy, Brittany and Poitou are renowned for their high-quality butter. Most French butter is offered for sale unsalted, although you will find both fine *demi-sel* (slightly salted) and *salé* (salted) butters, mainly from Brittany and Poitou-Charentes, the home of the excellent *beurre d'Echiré (see p294)*.

The Cantal production process

Dining in France

The French consider eating well an essential part of their birthright, and eating out is France's most popular leisure activity. The choice of venues takes in all the options, from special occasion, haute cuisine restaurants to cafés and bistros offering simple cooking and conviviality.

Chefs outside a restaurant in Cassis

RESTAURANTS

The term encompasses everything from top-flight establishments, serving classical dishes, and trendy modern haunts with internationally inspired food, to simple rural eateries or seasonal seaside places. It is, however, generally used for more formal places than bistros or brasseries.

BISTROS

Bistros are the quintessential French eatery – small and relatively informal, with tables often tightly packed together. Grander bistros may have fine table linen; simpler ones often use paper place settings and may expect you to keep your knife and fork between courses. Generally they offer good, home-cooked, moderately priced meals. Modern bistros may be run by chefs who have

trained at top establishments, and there is a growing trend for bistro "annexes" of upscale restaurants.

BRASSERIES

Brasseries originated in Alsace as ale houses with breweries attached, but are now found all over France. Usually large and busy, with long opening hours, they typically serve shellfish platters, grills, and *choucroute garnie (see p119).* They offer beer on tap as well as wine.

CAFÉS

Cafés are part of the French way of life, ranging from celebrated literary and artists' haunts to local *café-tabacs.* Open as a rule from early morning to 10pm or so, they serve breakfast, snacks, simple meals and drinks throughout the day.

WINE BARS

At wine bars and *bistros à vins* you'll find a good choice of wines by the glass

Restaurant Square Trousseau

EATING OUT WITH CHILDREN

Most restaurants are happy to welcome well-behaved children, except for some very grand establishments or fashionable night-time haunts, and you'll often see French families of all generations dining out in brasseries and bistros, particularly at Sunday lunchtime. As an alternative, crêperies and cafés are usually good for a relatively speedy light meal. On the downside, most children's menus are disappointingly conventional, dominated by chicken, fish fillet, beefburger

or ham, with chips or pasta, and ice cream or mousse to finish. Don't be afraid to ask what else they can offer or, if you're with a small child, to ask for an additional plate and share your meal. Some places will come up with half-portions or prepare a simple dish with seasonal vegetables; another option is to choose a starter from the *carte*. You might instigate an early appreciation of good food!

as well as by the bottle. Some double as wine merchants. Food varies from sandwiches and plates of charcuterie or local cheeses to full-scale bistro cooking.

FOREIGN RESTAURANTS

Dining in France is becoming more and more international. North African restaurants, serving couscous and tagines, are very popular, reflecting former colonial links. Asian restaurants are widespread, but the quality varies hugely. Japanese and Italian restaurants are also plentiful.

MENUS AND COURSES

The basic menu consists of *entrées* (starters), *plats* (main courses), cheeses and desserts. Cheese is served as a separate course, before or instead of dessert. Many places offer a *plat du jour*, or daily special, often a good choice. In grander restaurants, the starter may be followed

Cafè culture, St-Tropez

by fish and then the meat course. Bread is provided free with a meal, as is tap water. In most places you can order *à la carte* or from set-price menus *(prix fixe* or *formule).* Lunch menus can be very good value; vegetarian menus are still rare.

PRACTICAL INFORMATION

Most restaurants serve from about noon to 2pm and around 7:30 to 10:30pm. The listings in this book give details of weekly or seasonal closures, but it is still advisable to phone ahead to check.

It is always best to book ahead, especially for grand or trendy places, or for remote country ones, though it can be worth trying last-minute for a cancellation or for lunch. Always phone to cancel.

Credit cards are widely accepted, but many small country restaurants accept cash only. Check when booking. Service (12.5–15 per cent) is included by law, but most people leave some small change in a café, 5 per cent or so elsewhere and up to 10 per cent when service is superb.

Dress code is generally relaxed except in top-flight places, but the French are habitually well turned-out and you may feel more comfortable if you are, too. Smoking is officially frowned upon but still very common in eating places.

Disabled access is often restricted; it is worth a word when booking to ensure that your needs can be accommodated.

Shops & Markets

Shopping for food and wine in France is an absolute delight. Supermarkets have made their mark, as they have everywhere in Europe, but the specialist food shops and busy local markets remain the best places to discover local produce and acquire culinary savoir faire.

BOULANGERIES AND PÂTISSERIES

A shop where the bread is not risen and baked on the premises cannot call itself a *boulangerie*, only a *dépôt de pain*. *Boulangeries* are often combined with *pâtisseries* selling *viennoiseries* (such as *croissants*) and cakes. Some are also *chocolatiers*, making their own chocolates. The price of a baguette is fixed by law.

FROMAGERIES

Good cheese shops not only have a wide range of cheeses but should also be able to select those that are perfectly ripe. A *fromager-affineur* matures cheeses on the premises. *Fromageries* are usually also a *cremerie* or *laiterie*, selling fresh cream, *fromage frais,* butter, and often eggs.

BOUCHERS AND CHARCUTERIES

French butchers are skilled in cutting and preparing meat, and good butchers will show the provenance of their meat, including which breed and even the herd of cattle. Many have a rôtisserie

Boulangerie delivery van

oven where you can buy spit-roasted chicken. Some are also charcuteries, preparing cooked and cured hams, terrines, pâtés and sausages such as *boudins*.

EPICERIES

The *épicerie* or *alimentation* (grocer) ranges from local corner shops, often useful for their long hours and sometimes Sunday opening, to upmarket chains such as Hédiard (see p42).

TRAITEURS

The French equivalent of a delicatessen sells a variety of ready-prepared salads, quiches, charcuterie and cooked dishes ready for heating up.

BUYING DIRECT

As you travel around France, you will often come across opportunities to buy direct from the producers at farms or at roadside stalls. Look out, too, for signs indicating food-themed routes. In Provence, olive oil can be bought direct from traditional mills and co-operatives in winter (generally Dec–Feb); sometimes you are able to watch the process. Most also have shops open all year round selling oil, olives and related products. In Périgord and Quercy you will find walnut oil mills, foie gras producers and farms making Rocamadour cheese. Some farms will let you take a look around and see the livestock, though hygiene regulations mean that it is not generally possible to see the cheese-making process unless it has been specially adapted for visitors. More unusual producers to seek out include snail farmers and sea salt harvesters.

Selection of cheeses at a Perigord market

SUPERMARCHÉS

Supermarkets have become an undeniable part of French life, ranging from city-based chains such as Franprix and Monoprix to out-of-town giants *(hypermarchés)* such as Carrefour, Leclerc and Intermarché, which stock everything from food and clothes to computers. Bigger branches usually have wet fish counters, butchers and cheese stands, displays of local produce and regional specialities from all over France.

OPENING TIMES

Most French shops open Monday to Saturday from about 9:30am to 7:30pm; food shops often close on Monday and open on Sunday morning instead. Many close around noon for lunch, sometimes until 3pm. Some supermarkets stay open

Display in a specialist charcuterie

until 10pm but are usually closed on Sunday. Bakeries tend to close around 1pm.

MARKETS

Bigger towns often have a covered market, called Les Halles, which may be open every day; some are built with beautiful old stone or cast-iron. Smaller towns and villages usually have an outdoor market once or twice a week. These generally operate only in the morning.

In many regions there are specialist markets (such as for foie gras or truffles) and, in tourist regions, evening farmers' markets in summer. At these you can meet, and sample the products of, local small-scale producers.

BUYING WINE

Wine can be tasted and bought at many individual châteaux or *domaines.* At local co-operatives you can buy in 5- or 10-litre containers *(en vrac)* as well as by the bottle. You will also find local wine shops, and chains such as Nicolas. Supermarkets have large wine selections, but do not always store wine in the best conditions, and will usually favour larger producers. If you know what you are looking for, the autumn *Foires au Vin* supermarket promotions can be the source of some bargain deals.

The Wines & Other Drinks of France

Wine is France's greatest liquid asset and vineyards carpet many regions. Elsewhere, the orchards of the north yield cider and Calvados, while mountain herbs flavour fascinating spirits and beer is made both on an industrial scale and in micro-breweries.

WINE

To many, France is the home of the world's greatest wines. Certainly it is one of the largest producers and has defined globally popular styles. Wine is integral to the culture and closely bound up with the fine art of eating. Some French wine and food matches are truly made in heaven.

TERROIR

The French claim that *terroir* is what makes a particular vineyard site unique and it is a concept that underpins the French system of wine classification. There is no one-word translation for *terroir*. It is a notion that covers several factors: principally the type of soil in a particular vineyard area, the topography and the prevailing climate.

WINE CLASSIFICATIONS

Appellation d'Origine Contrôlée (AOC) The French are extremely proud of this system that aims to guarantee that certain

criteria are respected in the production of wine. These criteria are laid down by the watchdog agency, the INAO (Institut National des Appellations d'Origine). The AOC system was first developed for wines, but it has since been extended to include a number of food products, especially cheeses *(see p11)*.

AOC guarantees that the wine is produced within a strictly defined geographical area. It also specifies the grape varieties, and sometimes the exact percentage of each one used to make the wine, together with the growing and vinification methods, planting density, pruning methods and permitted yields. A wine which does not fulfil the conditions is declassified or used for distilling.

AOC status is equated by many with quality and, theoretically, commands a higher price than other categories. But above all, the AOC seeks to consecrate time-honoured traditions, so that an area that has a long history of producing

Vineyard in Châteauneuf-du-Pape

Bronze sculpture of grape pickers

a particular wine will be far more likely to be given the precious title than one that does not.

VDQS Appellation d'Origine Vin de Qualité Supérieure, also governed by the INAO, comes immediately after AOC in status. Required alcoholic strength is lower than for AOC and yields at harvest may be higher. Only one per cent of all French wine is VDQS and many regions have now been promoted to full AOC.

Vin de Pays These "country wines" are subject to far less exacting specifications than AOC wines and are often excellent quality and good value. There are three types of *vin de pays*: regional (eg Vin de Pays du Jardin de la France, covering the whole Loire Valley), *départemental* (eg Vin de Pays du Gard) and local (eg Vin de Pays de la Cité de Carcassonne). Unlike most AOCs, the label may mention the grape variety.

Only a few years back, the French would have laughed at the idea that a quality wine could be anything other than AOC. But several leading wine-makers, unhappy with restrictions imposed by the AOC system, especially in Languedoc-Roussillon, have created great wines from the grape varieties

they themselves consider worthy, wines that stand outside any AOC guidelines but that have been embraced by the *vin de pays* classification.

Vin de table The bottom of the line as regards status, French *vin de table* is frequently vinegary, thin and just plain boring. Nearly all of it is sold in bulk and, thankfully, production is now steadily declining.

BUYING WINE IN FRANCE

From a caviste The majority of *cavistes* or wine retailers are passionate about wine. In contrast to the anonymity of a supermarket selection, a *caviste* will be able to advise on and talk about the wines they have selected.

Direct from the winemaker Many wine producers offer tastings and sell directly to the public. In such cases, there will be a sign somewhere near the estate announcing *"dégustation et vente à la propriété"*. Nothing quite beats the charm of buying wine direct, thus being able to regale friends with first-hand tales of the vineyard, the producer's colourful character and how they make their wine. Make sure, however, that you are as enthralled with the wine as you are with the folkloric attraction of the experience. Remember too that you will not be greeted with open arms at the time of the harvest or in the weeks immediately afterwards. Also, not all the regions welcome visitors gladly; the

Wine shop in Paris

Bordeaux vineyards are notorious for their cool reception and the Classed Growth châteaux will only accept visitors by previously arranged appointment. In Alsace, Burgundy and Beaujolais, however, there tends to be no such problem.

From a supermarket The average large supermarket may have an interesting selection of Bordeaux or of Beaujolais but rarely of Burgundies that are produced in small quantities and thus are sold at too high a price to interest the supermarkets. Good supermarkets will send their consultants and buyers to the bi-annual wine fairs *(foires aux vins).*

WINE IN RESTAURANTS

Top restaurants offer extensive wine lists, often with a breathtaking range of vintages, particularly for Burgundy and Classed Growth Bordeaux. Others will offer a restricted selection from several regions. However, very few offer any foreign wines. All restaurants either multiply the purchase price of their wines by at least three, or apply a margin. Generally, in the latter case, the choice of a more expensive bottle means better value.

WINE AND FOOD

The pairing of regional dishes with regional wines may seem obvious, but is nevertheless highly s u c c e s s f u l . Munster cheese with an Alsace G e w u r z t r a m i n e r , *boeuf bourguignon* with Gevrey-Chambertin, *cassoulet* with Madiran, a Crottin de Chavignol goats' cheese with Sancerre, *poulet aux morilles* and *vin jaune,* all seem made for one another.

However, it often pays to be adventurous. For example, instead of the hallowed ritual of Sauternes with foie gras, a combination that leaves the palate sticky and that is virtually impossible to follow with another wine, try a Tokay Pinot Gris Vendanges Tardives from Alsace, a Quarts de Chaume from the Loire or a vintage Champagne. Marry crudités with Alsace Pinot Blanc. Look to the Languedoc-Roussillon as well: try chocolate desserts with a glass of sweet Maury or Banyuls, oysters with a Picpoul de Pinet, or rump steak with a Faugères or Collioure.

Simple foods call for simple wines so you need not look any further than an Alsace Sylvaner or Pinot Blanc for

THE ROLE OF THE SOMMELIER

Many of the top French restaurants employ a specialist wine waiter, known as a sommelier, whose role is to advise diners on the wines that will best suit their budget and choice of dishes. The sommelier is responsible for managing stocks, recognizing which wines are ready for drinking, preparing the *cave du jour* (the current list) and sometimes, but not always, for buying the wine. A good sommelier is able to comment on the wine, the vintage and the producer and to demonstrate some knowledge about the AOC and region involved. He or she also needs to have some idea of customer psychology and be able to grasp what type of wine a customer really wants and, especially, what they are able to afford.

Oak barrels in the cellars of Château Palmer

quiche Lorraine, or a red Côtes du Rhône for shepherd's pie *(hachis Parmentier)*.

MAKING WINE

Red wine Most French reds are made from black-skinned grapes with clear juice that are crushed and destemmed before pressing (although some reds, such as Beaujolais, can be made by letting the whole bunch ferment). Fermentation, generated by yeasts on the grape or by cultivated yeasts, can be carried out in barrels, stainless steel or concrete-lined vats. As the skins, seeds and juice ferment, the grapes' natural sugar converts into alcohol by the action of yeasts. Red wines are fermented at higher temperatures than whites (28–30°C). Colouring matter in black grape skins contributes colour, flavour and tannin. Some reds are matured in stainless steel to emphasize fresh fruit flavours, while barrel-ageing promotes air contact and brings out new, more developed flavours and complexity.

White wine White grapes are crushed, destemmed and either pressed immediately without any maceration or are allowed some "skin contact" to extract maximum flavour and character. The grape juice is then separated from the solids. Alcoholic fermentation is carried out at a lower temperature than for red wine (usually 15–18° C). Some producers then decide to leave the wine in contact with its lees, which contributes flavour and a certain degree of freshness and sometimes a slight sparkle.

Sparkling wine In the traditional Champagne method, still white wine is bottled with sugar and yeast to provoke a second fermentation that creates the carbon dioxide bubbles. The sparkling wine is left to develop its flavour and bouquet for at least one year, in practice often longer. Before the Champagne is ready to leave the cellars the sediment created during fermentation is gathered in the bottle neck then removed by a process called *dégorgement*.

Oak barrels Barrel-making is an art that has been lost in many wine-producing countries, but France still has several thriving cooperage firms *(tonnelleries)*. Wood allows wine to "breathe" and develop as it comes into contact with oxygen. Tannin from the wood migrates into the wine contributing to the wine's aroma. Vanilla is the most common aroma. It comes from the vanillin which develops in oak as it is "toasted" by the barrelmaker. Oak can also bring hints of cocoa, roasted almond, liquorice, spice, smoke and mushroom. The great white Burgundies and top red Bordeaux and northern Rhône *crus* derive their depth of aroma partly from oak ageing.

Stainless steel Steel vats are increasingly common for fermentation in wineries as they are very hygienic and offer the considerable advantage of easy temperature control via a system of cooling coils or sheets. Also, stainless steel is inert and therefore contributes no extraneous odours or flavours to the wine.

Stainless steel fermentation vats

Copper tun in a brewery

BEER

Alsace is France's capital of beer, home to major industrial producers such as Kronenbourg and tiny local breweries alike. The local brewing traditions across the north all but disappeared in the wake of the two world wars, but have found a new lease of life over the last couple of decades. The majority of beer drunk across France is the Pilsner lager type, served well chilled in small glasses. For darker, hoppier brews with more depth of flavour, the new micro-breweries of Lille and other northern towns are leading the way (see p81).

The beer-making process begins by steeping barley in water until it germinates. The grains are roasted and transformed into malt then crushed into a type of rough flour and mixed with hot water to give the "mash". This is filtered to rid it of solid residue, such as the husk, and the clear liquid (called the "wort") is heated to 100°C at which point malt enzymes release soluble sugars from the starch. It is at this stage that hops come into play, determining the character and bitterness of the resulting beer. The next step is fermentation. Yeast transforms the sugar into alcohol and carbon dioxide. The beer matures for up to one or even two months, gradually gaining in sparkle.

CIDER

The orchards of Normandy and Brittany are powerhouses of cider production, with a wide variety of apples fermented to produce many different flavours (see pp147 and 170). More rustic styles are made in the Basque country of the Pyrenees (see p354). A number of regions are recognized by the AOC system.

EAUX-DE-VIE

Spirits are important throughout France, with many regional specialities. Norman cider can be distilled to make Calvados, the region's famous apple brandy that is

BOTTLED WATERS

The French are champion drinkers of bottled water. Annual consumption tops 6.7 billion litres, 84 per cent of which is still water and 16 per cent sparkling. Badoit from the Loire, Evian from the Alps and Perrier in its club-shaped bottles head the league tables. Other waters and their regions of origin are:
Arvie (Auvergne), **Carola** (Alsace), **Chateldon** (Puy-de-Dôme), **Contrex** (Vosges mountains), **Hepar** (Vosges mountains), **Orezza** (Corsica), **Quezac** (Cévennes hills), **St-Yorre** (Auvergne), **Salvetat** (Hérault), **Thonon** (Alps), **Vals** (Ardèche), **Valvert** (Ardennes), **La Vernière** (Cévennes hills), **Vichy Celestins** (Vichy), **Vittel** (Vosges mountains), **Volvic** (Puy-de-Dôme) and **Wattwiller** (Vosges mountains).

Beer and aperitifs at a Paris café

now highly regarded and recognized as an AOC *(see p146)*. Cognac, the world's most famous and revered eau-de-vie, begins life as grapes in the vineyards of the Cognac region north of Bordeaux. These grapes produce mean-tasting wine that is low in alcohol but it is an ideal base for distillation and the subsequent long barrel-ageing that gives Cognac its character *(see p301)*.

The Charente pot stills used for Cognac are made entirely of copper and are always heated over an open flame. Regulating the intensity of the fire requires experience as does the separation of the different parts of the first, cloudy distillate. The "heart", which contains about 30 per cent alcohol, undergoes a second distillation, the *bonne chauffe*, which further concentrates the spirit to 70 per cent. Armagnac, from the deep southwest, has many similarities, but the type of still used is different.

Fruit eaux-de-vie are one of Alsace's signature drinks *(see p122)*, made either by fermenting and distilling the fruit itself, or by macerating the berries in alcohol before the distillation process.

Courvoisier

LIQUEURS AND APERITIFS

Every region in France has its own liqueurs, digestifs or aperitifs. As with wine, it was the church that developed the liqueurs that are now famous throughout the world and often used for their medicinal properties, such as **Bénédictine** and **Chartreuse**. Citrus, especially orange, is the key to the flavour of two other celebrated liqueurs. **Cointreau** is a triple-sec or clear curaçao distilled from a blend of bitter and sweet orange peels dried in the sun. **Grand Marnier** marries Cognac with orange.

Pastis is the foremost of France's aniseed-based drinks, originally made with absinthe. Many liqueurs have regional origins, such as green **Izarra** from the Basque country, Corsica's **Cap Corse** or the verbena-infused **Verveine** from Le Puy-en-Velay. Fruit cream liqueurs such as **Crème de Cassis** are made with very ripe fruit, fermented and distilled or macerated in alcohol. Lower alcohol vermouths, made from white wine mixed with grape juice, alcohol and fruit zests, are led by **Noilly Prat.**

Where to Stay

France offers the visitor an array of hotel accommodation, from traditional, family-run establishments, simple farmhouse living and value-for-money chains, to grandiose châteaux and luxurious palace hotels.

SMALL FAMILY HOTELS

The small, traditional, family-run hotel is still the backbone of the hotel business in France. Often with only 20 rooms or less, facilities and standard of decoration vary enormously, as do cleanliness and service. Many of them, especially those in rural areas and small towns, have pleasant restaurants and bars.

SMALL CITY HOTELS

The city hotel ranges from the budget hotels that are often clustered around train stations to sleek designer dens and charming old-fashioned townhouses. Most have a breakfast room but often do not have a restaurant or salon.

PALACE HOTELS

Palace hotels, such as the Ritz and Plaza Athénée in Paris or the Negresco in Nice, are some of France's most glamorous hotels, with grandiose architecture and

Exquisite interior of the Hotel Meurice in Paris

sumptuous interiors. Among the select group of four-star luxe hotels, service can lay on every imaginable comfort, and the suites are often colossal. Most of these palaces boast cocktail bars, gourmet restaurants, gyms and beauty salons as well as an international, indeed often largely foreign, clientele.

CHÂTEAU HOTELS

Ranging from turreted medieval castles to 19th-century follies, France's château hotels are the chance to experience the country house lifestyle. They boast fine salons, grand rooms and period furnishings. Many have extensive grounds, that may include amenities such as swimming pools or golf courses, and good restaurants serving traditional cuisine.

CHAMBRES D'HÔTES

Chambres d'hôtes, the French equivalent of Bed-and-Breakfast, is growing in popularity, especially in Provence and Normandy. Settings are often in fine old farmhouses or even châteaux, with spacious, beautifully-decorated rooms and prices that rival a luxury hotel, although you should not expect the same degree of service. Limited to a maximum of five bedrooms, much of the charm is the sense of staying in a private house. Some offer a *table d'hôtes* (dinner) where you will be expected to dine and chat with your hosts and fellow guests.

APART-HÔTELS

Groups of studios and one-bedroom flats, these offer a combination of self-catering with some level of hotel servicing, such as breakfast or a bar. Although generally available from one night upwards, some require a minimum stay of three or more.

The extravagant Hotel de Paris, Monte-Carlo

ECONOMY CHAINS

Economy chains, such as Etap Hôtel, Formule 1, Première Classe and Mr Bed, tend to be clustered around motorway junctions and commercial centres on the edge of towns. Clean, modern and functional, many are unstaffed by night but you are able to check yourself in using a credit card.

BOOKING

It is advisable to book ahead if you are travelling in July or August or during public holidays. Paris, in contrast, risks being fully booked during spring and autumn when trade shows are on. Many hotels will take bookings over the phone with a credit card, others like to have confirmation by fax or by email. If you arrive somewhere without a reservation, the tourist office may be able to help; in busy periods they generally have lists of hotels which have vacancies.

HOTEL RATINGS

Hotels in France are rated from one to four stars and four-star luxe, with a few ungraded no-star hotels. Star ratings are based on room size and facilities such as private bathroom or a hotel lift and not necessarily on cleanliness or welcome. Ratings, however, can vary and were often set many years ago, before the days of modems or widespread air conditioning. They are, therefore, not always an accurate indication of facilities. Nonetheless, a four-star luxe is sure to be luxurious and a one star simple. Recently renovated two stars may well be better than non-renovated three stars.

BREAKFAST

The classic continental breakfast of tea or coffee, baguette with butter and jam and a croissant is still offered in most hotels but it is fast being caught up by the self-service buffet, generally offering cereals, a choice of breads and viennoiseries, cold ham, cheese, fresh fruit and yogurts. Eggs are sometimes included as well as fruit juices, tea and coffee. Breakfast is usually charged per person in addition to the price of the hotel room (except in *chambres d'hôtes*). Expect prices to go up proportionally with the category or price range of the hotel – from around 6 euros in a budget hotel to 25 euros in a luxury hotel. Most hotels will serve breakfast in bed but may make a small extra charge. Note that while the French generally drink black espresso coffee during the day, they often have *café au lait* (coffee with milk) for breakfast. Breakfast is also served at many cafés and brasseries; some offer cooked breakfasts while others will supply coffee and a croissant or buttered *tartine* at the bar, alongside locals off to work.

Luxurious interior of Hôtel de la Cité, Carcassonne

PRICES

Prices for a double room are for two people. Many hotels also have triple or quadruple rooms for families, or may be able to add a folding bed or cot *(lit bébé)* for an extra fee. Listed prices include TVA (value added tax), but not always the *taxe de séjour*, an additional local tax charged per person per night. Some Paris hotels put prices up during the main trade fairs but are cheaper in July and August, while seaside hotels are likely to be more expensive in high summer.

DEMI-PENSION

In high-season, many resort hotels insist on *demi-pension,* or half-board, which includes breakfast and dinner, or full pension (all meals). While this can often be good value, it does often mean that your menu choices are more limited than in a regular restaurant.

BON WEEKEND EN VILLE

This is an offer that gives you two nights for the price of one at weekends (either Fri and Sat nights, or Sat and Sun nights) in participating hotels in several main cities. In some less touristy or more business-oriented destinations, the offer lasts all year, but for most it runs from November to March. You must book at least 24 hours in advance, stating that you are making your reservation under the scheme. Tourist offices also offer gifts or discounts with the scheme.

LOGIS DE FRANCE

The federation of Logis de France is a France-wide organization with some 3,500 hotel-restaurants. The large majority of its member hotels are situated in rural villages or in small towns and most have restaurants focusing on regional cuisine. The group is renowned for its image of good-value, family-run hotels and has its own grading system of one, two or three chimneys (the majority are two chimneys). Some of its hotels are grouped according to themes; charm, peace, cycling, walking (staff can advise on local footpaths) and wine.

HOTEL GROUPS

HOTEL CHAINS AND FEDERATIONS

Various hotel chains are present in France. They range from the enormous Groupe Accor which comprises a variety of chains and price levels to small French groups or celebrated palace hotels belonging to luxury international groups such as the Dorchester Group or the Four Seasons.

Choice Hotels (0800 12 12 12; www.choice hotels.com) US-based franchise has 140 hotels in France from basic Comfort, via mid-range Quality to a few prestigious Clarion hotels.

Concorde Hôtels (freephone UK 0800 0289 880; freephone France 0800 05 00 11; www.concorde-hotels.fr) Luxury hotel group includes some of France's most famous palace hotels, such as the Hôtel du Palais in Biarritz and the Martinez in Cannes.

Groupe Accor (www.accorhotels.com) This French-owned hotel group is Europe's biggest and covers the whole range from the budget Formule 1 (modern boxes often near airports and motorway junctions) and Etap hotels (similar but slightly more comfortable) via mid-range Ibis (functional interiors, but efficient, good-value and often well placed), Timhôtel (a small Paris selection), Libertel (individually designed) to upmarket Novotel (modern, generally out of town) and Mercure (ranges from contemporary buildings and design to grand old urban hotels). Top-of-the-range are Sofitel hotels (luxury hotels with high-standard original decoration); Suite-hotels is a recently created chain of modular studios with kitchenettes.

Groupe Barrière (www.lucienbarriere.com) Luxury hotels and casinos in the coastal resorts of Cannes, Deauville, Dinard and La Baule, plus the spa town of Enghien-les-Bains.

Groupe Envergure (www.envergure.fr) Five hotel chains aimed at the bottom and middle of the market, from low-cost Nuit d'Hôtel and Première Classe, via purpose-built Campanile to Bleu Marine and Kyriad.

Hôtels de Paris (www.leshotelsdeparis.com) This recently created group has branched out beyond Paris' traditional upmarket districts with three- and four-star hotels with an emphasis on individual design and character.

Dorchester Group (www.dorchestergroup hotels.com) Luxury hotel group includes two of Paris' finest hotels, Hotel Meurice and Plaza Athénée.

Four Seasons Group (www.fourseasons.com) Canadian group with luxury hotels, resorts and resort clubs. Includes Four Seasons Resort Provence and the Hotel George V in Paris.

INDEPENDENT HOTEL GROUPINGS

These are associations of independently-owned, privately-run hotels, and often offer a centralized booking service. Look out also for hotels affiliated to the association *Table et Auberges de France* (www.francetaf.com), where the chefs have a commitment to regional produce in restaurants that range from traditional to gastronomic.

Best Western (France freephone 0800 90 44 90; www.bestwestern.fr or www.bestwestern.com) Worldwide group of independently owned hotels includes over 200, mainly three-star, hotels in France, ranging from beautiful period buildings to modern developments.

Châteaux et Hôtels de France (Central booking 01 55 34 16 16; www.chateauxhotels.com) Upmarket grouping of privately owned hotels often in fine settings, many with good restaurants; also a selection of *chambres d'hôtes* in private châteaux.

Golden Tulip / Tulip Inns (01 44 74 55 95; www.goldentulip.com) Dutch-owned consortium has a variety of hotels in city locations. Tulip Inns are comfortable mid-range, Golden Tulip hotels more upmarket.

Logis de France (01 45 84 83 84; www.logis-de-france.fr) France-wide federation of some 3,500 small, family-run hotels-restaurants situated in rural areas and small towns. Graded from one to three chimneys.

Relais et Châteaux (01 45 72 90 00; www.relaischateaux.com) Worldwide luxury group of rigorously vetted hotels, often in period châteaux, offering high levels of service, many with gastronomic restaurants.

Relais de Silence (01 44 49 79 00; www.silence hotel.com) Hotels chosen for their tranquil setting; many are in historic buildings.

PARIS & ILE-DE-FRANCE

Paris is not only the legendary home of the Louvre and the Eiffel Tower, it is also a great place to enjoy good food. Streetmarkets cohabit with glamorous food shops, and the choice of restaurants spans the globe. Surrounding it, beyond the suburbs, lie the pastures and forests of the Ile-de-France, the source of some truly fine cheeses and rich, hearty game.

The Flavours of Paris

Agriculture in the Ile de France has long been geared to feeding Paris, although modern transport means that a hugely expanded range of produce now arrives in its shops and markets daily from all over France and abroad.

BRIOCHE

When Marie-Antoinette naively told the hungry mob to eat cake, what she actually said was "let them eat brioche", a light, airy, golden, slightly sweet type of soft bread made with eggs and butter. The characteristic Parisian *brioche* is tall and flared, bursting out of the baking tin at the top. One story has it that the "brie-oche" was originally made with Brie cheese, not butter.

Brioche

CHEESE AND DAIRY

The Ile de France, as well as producing fresh milk, is the birthplace of one of France's oldest cheeses, Brie. Look out also for Fontainebleau, made by mixing whipped cream with *fromage frais*, which is often served with strawberries or other summer berry fruits.

FRUIT AND VEGETABLES

The Paris region was once renowned for its production of carrots, cherries and watercress. Even today, despite the encroachment of the ever-expanding surburban sprawl, as you head out of the city you'll see a mix of large-scale arable farming, producing huge quantities of wheat, and small-scale market gardening *(maraîchage)* for the Parisian market, notably of salads. Local *maraîchers* along with those from nearby Picardy are a visible presence at Paris street markets, including a growing number of organic producers.

Foodie Parisians themselves head out to the Fontainebleau forest in the autumn to look for wild mushrooms – but don't hold out too much hope, those in the know will probably have got there first.

BREAD AND CAKES

The culinary legacy of Paris is most visible in baking and pâtisserie. The long baguette, invented in Paris in the 19th century, has gradually been adopted all over

BRIE

The large white cartwheels of Brie have been made in the Ile de France for centuries, supplying the Paris market long before modern transport and refrigeration allowed other cheeses to reach the capital from the rest of France. The *croûte fleurie* cows' milk cheeses Brie de Meaux and rarer Brie de Melun have each been awarded an *appellation contrôlée (see p11)* and are made according to similar methods, although the Brie de Melun is smaller and thicker and matured for longer. Sold in triangular wedges, the cheese becomes runnier, yellower and tangier as it matures. Coulomniers is a smaller, thicker Brie-style cheese with 50 per cent fat content, but only the farm-produced versions made with raw milk have any real character.

Left Millefeuille in a Parisian pâtisserie **Right** Fontainebleau with succulent fruit

France. Before that people mainly ate large round, more durable *boules*. Likewise *viennoiseries* – such as *croissants, pain au chocolat* and *pain aux raisins* – have grown from regional specialities into national staples, and international treats.

A number of elegant gâteaux were also created for the sophisticated – and wealthy – Parisian market by the grand chef Carême, author of cookery treatises and chef to Napoleon, and some of Paris's historic *pâtissiers* still exist today, including Dalloyau, founded in 1802 (101 rue du Faubourg St-Honoré, 8e: 01 42 99 90 00), Pâtisserie Stohrer, founded 1730 (51 rue Montorgueil, 2e: 01 42 33 38 20) and Peltier (66 rue de Sèvres, 7e: 01 47 34 06 62) .

Typical Parisian cakes that you will find in many pâtisseries today include the *Paris-Brest*, an airy choux pastry ring filled with hazelnut cream and scattered with chopped nuts, which was named after a celebrated bicycle race; the *St-Honoré*, a ring of little choux pastries filled with cream and glazed with caramel; the many-layered flaky *millefeuille* pastry; the *Opéra*, a rich, square dark chocolate cake with shiny chocolate icing; and the *puits d'amour* (well of love), a type of vol-au-vent filled with *crème pâtissière* or jam and dusted with icing sugar, invented by Stohrer.

OTHER SPECIALITIES

Other specialities that originated in the Paris region include *jambon de Paris* (cooked ham or *jambon blanc*) and *champignons de Paris* (mushrooms), which were once cultivated in the city's quarries, though now largely come from the Loire region *(see p116)*. The cathedral town of Meaux just to the east of the capital still makes Moutarde de Meaux, an old-fashioned, coarse-grained mustard that is typically sold in attractive sealed earthenware pots.

SAUCE BÉARNAISE

The classic French hollandaise sauce with tarragon, delicious with grilled steak, most likely originated in the Ile de France at the imposing royal château at St-Germain-en-Laye, where it was created for much-loved monarch Henri IV, who was born in the Béarn capital, Pau.

Sandwiches made with *pain Poilâne*

PAIN POILÂNE

Master baker Lionel Poilâne revived an old family recipe to produce this chewy sourdough bread, made in large, flattish round loaves using stone-ground flour and baked in a wood-burning stove. His family continue to make the bread, which is popular in cafés for open *tartine* sandwiches or an upmarket *croque-monsieur*.

Eating Out in Paris

The choice of eating places in Paris is colossal – simple cafés and bistros, lively all-night brasseries, wine bars and salons de thé and a seemingly endless number of haute-cuisine, high-fashion and ethnic restaurants.

BEST PARIS BISTROS

Allard
6e *(see p50)*
Au Vin des Rue
14e *(see p63)*
Bistro d'Hubert
15e *(see p65)*
Chardenoux
11e *(see p62)*
Chez Paul
11e *(see p62)*
L'Epi Dupin
6e *(see p53)*
La Régalade
14e *(see p64)*
La Marlotte
6e *(see p52)*
Le Bistro d'à Côté
17e *(see p68)*
Square Trousseau
12e *(see p63)*
Ze Kitchen Galerie
6e *(see p54)*

Au Rocher de Cancale restaurant

It is in Paris that the bistro and brasserie took form. A wave of Alsatian migrants, after the Franco-Prussian war of 1870, brought the brasserie to Paris, while Auvergnat peasants from poor, mountainous central France opened many of the cafés. Breton *crêperies* are still concentrated around Gare de Montparnasse, where trains arrived from Brittany.

A typical bistro meal might start with crudités or a salad or terrine, followed by a grilled steak or a meat stew – perhaps a navarin of lamb or a *blanquette de veau* – or roast chicken, and finish up with apple tart, crème caramel or chocolate mousse. While these all remain favourites, a newer style of bistro – often opened either by young chefs trained in France's grand kitchens or by top chefs as a less formal offshoot – has modernized the regime. These tend towards modern, lighter dishes, bringing in influences from the regions and abroad, the menus changing with the seasons.

In the grand restaurants young chefs continue to innovate, whether in rediscovering forgotten regional produce or by creating new fusion dishes that combine French techniques with produce from all over the Mediterranean and Asia.

PARISIAN DISHES

Specifically Parisian dishes often reflected the needs of hungry market workers around the central market at Les Halles, the abattoirs at La Villette or the docks of

Modern interior at Ze Kitchen Galerie

Bercy. *Pot-au-feu* or *boeuf gros sel* is a traditional bistro dish made from brisket or topside of beef boiled in water with an onion and large chunks of carrot, turnip, leeks and celery. *Miroton de boeuf* is made with slices of leftover beef from a *pot-au-feu*, reheated gently in an onion reduction. *Entrecôte marchand de vin* is steak with a sauce of red wine, butter and shallots that originated at Bercy where wines were unloaded on the quays. Others that you might come across are *potage St-Germain*, a thick green pea soup, and *pommes Pont-Neuf*, long, matchstick potato chips, named after Paris's oldest bridge.

FOREIGN RESTAURANTS

An ever-growing number of foreign restaurants are opening in Paris. Asian and North African restaurants reflect the immigration from France's former colonies in Indochina, Morocco and Algeria. Asian restaurants often offer a pan-Asian tour, serving a selection of dishes that come from China, Thailand, Vietnam, Laos and Cambodia, arranged as a three-course meal. Authentic Vietnamese restaurants can be found in the 13e *arrondissement*, Paris's Chinatown. North African (Moroccan, Tunisian and Algerian) restaurants range from simple local cafés that serve couscous on Fridays to fashionable grand restaurants, frequently lavishly decorated in the Moorish style.

Japanese restaurants are concentrated around the rue Sainte-Anne and rue de Richelieu near the Palais-Royal, although there are now sushi and yakitori restaurants all over Paris. Italian usually means pizza or pasta, but recently there has also been a growth of excellent Sardinian restaurants.

Auvergnat café Le Nemrod

THE AUVERGNATS OF PARIS

Many Paris cafés and *tabacs* belong to Auvergnat families, a tradition that began when Auvergnats migrated to the city from the Massif Central to open up depots to supply coal and firewood, and reflected in dishes like *aligot* and *salade auvergnate* that are often found on café menus. Auvergnats still run the main companies supplying cafés with beer and coffee. Auvergnat-run cafés also include the ultra-chic haunts of the Costes brothers, including Café Beaubourg *(see p48)* and Georges *(see p48)*.

Salade Parisien

Shops & Markets of Paris

Every quartier *in Paris has its own local grocers, bakers, butchers, fishmongers and cheese shops, while the city's 78 markets form a vital element of local life and are often busy meeting places, especially at the weekends.*

GROCERS AND TRAITEURS

Da Rosa 62 rue de Seine, 6e (01 40 51 00 09). Jubago ham, olive oils, spices, wines and unusual pâtés.

Fauchon 26–30 place de la Madeleine, 8e (01 47 42 60 11). Beautiful terrines, mousses, charcuterie and salads, exotic fruits and veg.

La Grande Epicerie 38 rue de Sèvres, 7e (01 44 39 81 00). Fine breads, cheese and fish, Italian deli and a wide international range.

Hédiard 21 place de la Madeleine, 8e (01 43 12 88 88). Beautifully presented teas, spices, jams and honeys, fresh fruit and prepared dishes.

Rungis market

Hédiard exterior

CHEESE SHOPS

Barthélémy 51 rue de Grenelle, 7e (01 45 48 56 75). This small cheese shop is particularly famous for its Brie.

Dubois 80 rue de Tocqueville, 17e (01 42 27 11 38). Stocks an exceptionally large range of goats' cheeses.

Marie-Anne Cantin 12 rue du Champ-de-Mars, 7e (01 45 50 43 94). Cantin ripens wonderful, raw-milk farmhouse cheeses in her own cellars and supplies a large number of Paris restaurants.

SHOPPING DISTRICTS

A number of streets, sometimes semi-pedestrianized, have a good concentration of butchers, *fromagers*, and regional and foreign products. Among those worth heading for are rue du Buci/rue de Seine in the 6e *arrondissement*, rue Cler (7e), rue des Martyrs (9e), rue Daguerre (14e), rue de la Convention (15e) and rue Lepic (18e). Place de la Madeleine (1er/8e) is the venue for some of Paris's most upmarket *traiteurs* and specialists in caviar and truffles. Look for long queues to see which shops the Parisians most favour.

MARKETS

Stalls laden with farmhouse cheeses, glistening fresh fish on crushed ice, mounds of autumn mushrooms, countless varieties of olives, home-made jams and honeys tempt shoppers daily. Look for regional specialities like sausages from the Ardèche, hot dishes such as spit-roast chicken, paella or *choucroute*, and African, Caribbean, Lebanese or Far Eastern specialities, too.

Covered markets Covered market halls are generally open Tuesday to Saturday all day, closing for three hours at lunchtime, and on Sunday morning. Among those worth visiting are the vintage cast-iron Marché Beauvais (12e), with a particularly good cheese stall and Italian deli; the Marché St-Quentin (10e), a busy market near Gare du Nord, smart Marché de Passy (16e), and the Marché des Enfants-Rouge (3e), a recently renovated ancient market with regional specialities and a good wine bar.

Roving markets and market streets Roving markets vary from a handful of stalls to giants stretching for hundreds of metres. Many of the same stallholders will be found on different days at different markets. Head in particular for markets at Place Monge (5e: Wed, Fri, Sun), Boulevard du Port-Royal (5e: Tue, Thu, Sat), Avenue du Saxe (7e: Thu, Sat), Bastille (Boulevard Richard-Lenoir, 7e: Thu, Sun), Avenue Daumesnil (12e: Tue, Thu), Cours de Vincennes (12e: Wed, Sat), Boulevard Auguste-Blanqui (13e: Tue, Fri, Sun), Rue la Fontaine (16e: Tue, Fri), Boulevard de Grenelle (15e: Wed, Sun). Barbès (Bd de la Chapelle, 18e: Wed, Sat) has cheap goods and lots of ethnic produce. Marché Biologique Raspail (Bd Raspail, 7e: Sun) is Paris's longest-established organic market. Rue Mouffetard (5e) is a picturesque ancient market street frequented by both Parisians and tourists.

REGIONAL PRODUCE

Devoted specialists make it possible to take a gastronomic tour of the regions without leaving Paris. Auvergnat produce is delivered daily to Aux Vrais Produits d'Auvergne (111 rue Mouffetard, 5e: 01 47 07 10 40). At Pierre Orteiza (13 rue Vignon, 8e: 01 47 42 23 03) you can buy direct from one of the Basque country's main producers. Henri Ceccaldi (21 rue des Mathurins, 9e: 01 47 42 66 52) is a feast of all things Corsican, while Comptoir de la Gastronomie (34 rue Montmartre, 1er: 01 42 33 31 32) serves up south-western goodies. Genuine Bressane *quenelles* are available from the Paris outpost of Boutique Giraudet (16 rue Mabillon, 6e: 01 43 25 53 00).

Wine selection at Lavinia's

CAKES AND SWEET TREATS

A la Mère de Famille 35 rue du Fbg Montmartre, 9e (01 47 70 83 69). Vintage sweets, plus jams and more.
Christian Constant 37 rue d'Assas, 6e (01 53 63 15 15). *Traiteur* and *chocolatier* famed for its original Easter chocolate creations.
Gérard Mulot 76 rue de Seine, 6e (01 43 26 85 77). Beautiful cakes and fruit tarts draw a queue at this St-Germain pâtisserie.
La Maison du Chocolat 89 av Raymond-Poincaré, 16e (01 40 67 77 83). Luscious chocolate eclairs and cakes as well as unusual chocolates.
Pierre Hermé 72 rue Bonaparte, 6e (01 53 67 66 65). Fashionable designer cakes and biscuits.

WINE MERCHANTS

Les Caves Taillevent 199 rue du Fbg St-Honoré, 8e (01 45 61 14 09). The wine shop belonging to the same group as celebrated restaurant Taillevent has a wide choice ranging from everyday wines to the stuff of very grand occasions.
Lavinia 3–5 bd de la Madeleine, 1er (01 42 97 20 20). The spacious, modern wine shop stands out for its huge selection from every wine-producing country you could possibly imagine; there is also a restaurant and a wine bar upstairs.

Gérard Mulot's lavish window display

Where to Eat & Stay

1ER ARRONDISSEMENT
● Au Pied de Cochon
6 rue Coquillère, 75001 **Map** 15D3
☎ 01 40 13 77 00
FAX 01 40 13 77 09
w www.pieddecochon.com
✎ AE, DC, MC, V 🍴 €€€
One of the few places in Paris open 24 hours. Pig's trotters are the house speciality, alongside delightful onion soup and a delightful shellfish platter. Beautiful early-20th-century interior.

1ER ARRONDISSEMENT
● Au Rendez-Vous des Camionneurs
72 quai des Orfèvres, 75001 **Map** 14B5
☎ 01 43 54 88 74
✎ AE, DC, MC, V 🍴 €
There aren't many camionneurs (lorry drivers) on picturesque Ile de la Cité but this restaurant can satisfy the biggest appetite. Veal stew in white sauce is the house speciality, along with foie gras terrine and puff pastry filled with tomato, basil and mozzarella.

1ER ARRONDISSEMENT
● Barlotti
35 pl du Marché St-Honoré, 75001 **Map** 15D2
☎ 01 44 86 97 97
FAX 01 44 86 97 98
✎ AE, DC, MC, V
🍴 €€€€
From the creators of super-trendy Buddha Bar and Barrio Latino is this flash Italy-themed restaurant with its impressive atrium. Aubergine (eggplant) pasta, prawn risotto and cod satisfy the most delicate palates. Sunday brunch.

1ER ARRONDISSEMENT
● Café Marly
93 rue de Rivoli, 75001 **Map** 15D3
☎ 01 49 26 06 60
FAX 01 49 26 07 06
✎ AE, DC, MC, V 🍴 €€€€
Wonderful views of the Louvre and inventive French cuisine: carpaccio, caramel and coconut duck, outstanding salmon with spinach cream and for dessert, raspberry macaroons.

1ER ARRONDISSEMENT
● Carré des Feuillants
14 rue Castiglione, 75001 **Map** 14C3
☎ 01 42 86 82 82
FAX 01 42 86 07 71
✎ AE, DC, MC, V 🔵 Sun, Sat; Aug
🍴 €€€€€
Beautifully presented, innovative cuisine such as truffle-stuffed capon or fish in a lemon crust. Exceptional wine cellar to match. Elegant, pale-wood dining room with chandeliers and modern art.

1ER ARRONDISSEMENT
● Chez Pauline
5 rue Villédo, 75001 **Map** 15D3
☎ 01 42 96 20 70
FAX 01 49 27 99 89
✎ AE, MC, V 🔵 Sun, Sat L
🍴 €€€€
Huge mirrors give this 1900s bistro allure. The cuisine is also full of character: foie gras (in terrine, carpaccio or roasted), boeuf bourguignon (p217), calf's kidneys and fish with black olives.

1ER ARRONDISSEMENT
● Chez Vong
10 rue de la Grande-Truanderie, 75001 **Map** 15E3
☎ 01 40 26 09 36
FAX 01 42 33 38 15
✎ AE, DC, MC, V 🔵 Sun €€
Lavish restaurant offering Chinese and Vietnamese cuisine such as Peking-style chicken and beef sautéed with basil. Other specialities include prawns cooked in lotus leaf, a delight both for the palate and the eye.

1ER ARRONDISSEMENT
● Goumard
9 rue Duphot, 75001 **Map** 14C2
☎ 01 42 60 36 07
FAX 01 42 60 04 54
w www.goumard.fr
✎ AE, DC, MC, V 🔵 1st 2 wks Aug
🍴 €€€€
Opened in 1872 and still possessing many original features like glass chandeliers and inlaid wood panelling. Quality seafood on the menu including

bouillabaisse (p401) *and sea bass with oyster sauce as well as plenty of Champagne (over 150 vintages).*

1ER ARRONDISSEMENT
■ Hôtel Opéra Richepanse
14 rue du Chevalier de St-George, 75001 **Map** 14C2
☎ 01 42 60 36 00
FAX 01 42 60 13 03
✎ AE, DC, MC, V 🛏 (38) €€€€€
Beautiful Art Deco hotel with period guestrooms equipped with all mod cons.

1ER ARRONDISSEMENT
■ Hôtel St-Honoré
85 rue St-Honoré, 75001 **Map** 15D3
☎ 01 42 36 20 38
FAX 01 42 21 44 08
w www.parishotel.com
✎ AE, DC, MC, V 🛏 (29) €€€
Guestrooms are extremely well kept, making them very good value for money considering the location. A few rooms have been designed for families.

1ER ARRONDISSEMENT
▲ Il Cortile at Le Castille
37 rue de Cambon, 75001 **Map** 14C2
☎ 01 44 58 45 67
FAX 01 44 58 45 69
@ ilcortile@castille.com
✎ AE, DC, MC, V 🔵 Sun, Sat 🍴
€€€€€ 🛏 (107) €€€€€
Tjaco Van Eyken, a former disciple of superchef Alain Ducasse, mans the stoves at this Italian restaurant. Vitello tonnato (tuna with capers) and cannelloni with cuttlefish ink show his skill. Dinner served on the terrace by the fountain is truly la dolce vita. Upmarket guestrooms.

1ER ARRONDISSEMENT
▲ Il Palazzo at Hôtel Normandy
7 rue de l'Echelle, 75001 **Map** 15D3
☎ 01 42 60 91 20
FAX 01 42 60 45 81
✎ AE, DC, MC, V 🔵 Sun, Mon, Sat L; Aug 🍴 €€€€€ 🛏 (121) €€€€€
High-class venue with French and Italian cuisine: roast pigeon flambéed with Grappa with a mushroom fricassée

● Restaurant ■ Hotel ▲ Hotel / Restaurant

*and potato pancakes with asparagus
and truffle. Individually styled bedrooms.*

1ER ARRONDISSEMENT
● Joe Allen

30 rue Pierre Lescot, 75001 **Map** 15E3

☎ 01 42 36 70 13

FAX 01 42 36 90 80

W www.joeallenparis.com

AE, MC, V

● Aug 🍴 €€

*Some of the best burgers in Paris.
American menu of chicken wings, grilled
tuna with pesto and cheesecake. Chilled
but chic atmosphere, candlelit at night.*

1ER ARRONDISSEMENT
● La Muscade

36 rue Montpensier, 75001 **Map** 15D3

☎ 01 42 97 51 36

FAX 01 42 97 51 36

W www.muscade-palais-royal.com

AE, MC, V ● Sun D, Mon; 1 wk
Dec 🍴 €€

*The epitome of French classicism: a
Regency-style dining room nestled at
the heart of the Palais Royal gardens.
Mediterranean-inspired food such as
the orange, glazed tomatoes and veal
tagine. Tearoom in the afternoon, with
pastries such as fig pastilla (in filo).*

1ER ARRONDISSEMENT
La Potée des Halles

● 3 rue Etienne Marcel, 75001 **Map** 15E3

☎ 01 40 41 98 15

AE, MC, V

● Sun L, Sat L; Christmas 🍴 €€

*With its 100-year-old tiled frescoes,
this friendly bistro exudes the aura of a
bygone era. This continues to the food
with dishes such as boeuf bourguignon
(p217), and herrings with potatoes.*

1ER ARRONDISSEMENT
● La Robe et le Palais

13 rue des Lavandières Ste-Opportune,
75001 **Map** 15E3

☎ 01 45 08 07 41

AE, DC, MC, V

● Sun 🍴 €€

*A bistro with an exceptional wine list. A
touch of originality: anise fennel salad,
calamari risotto with Esplette pepper
or white chocolate quenelle.*

1ER ARRONDISSEMENT
● La Rose de France

24 pl Dauphine, 75001 **Map** 15D3

☎ 01 43 54 10 12

AE, MC, V

🍴 €€€

*Majestic setting, looking onto a 17th-
century square. The cooking updates
French classics, with specialities like
the John Dory with rhubarb, ginger
and basmati rice.*

1ER ARRONDISSEMENT
● La Victoire Suprême du Coeur

41 rue des Bourdonnais,75001 **Map** 15D3

☎ 01 40 41 93 95

W www.vscoeur.com

MC, V ● Sun; last 2 wks Aug 🍴 €

*Comforting vegetarian fare served in a
bright blue and white dining room.
Mushrooms are a speciality here, as in
mushroom pâté or roast mushrooms
with blackberry sauce. Desserts include
a locally famous berry crumble. No
alcohol served except cider.*

1ER ARRONDISSEMENT
● Le Bar à Soupes

5 rue Hérold, 75001 **Map** 15D3

☎ 01 45 08 49 84

FAX 01 45 08 49 84

W www.lebarasoupes.com

MC, V ● Sun, Mon–Fri D, Sat; Aug
🍴 €

*The sister venue to the Bar à Soupes
in the Bastille area. Just soup for the
main course, such as carrot and
coconut milk, lentils and sausage or
gazpacho. Cheese plates too.*

1ER ARRONDISSEMENT
● Le Fumoir

6 rue de l'Amiral Coligny, 75001 **Map** 15D3

☎ 01 42 92 00 24

FAX 01 42 92 05 05

AE, MC, V 🍴 €€

*Classy restaurant located opposite the
Louvre. Modern fare that follows the
seasons: lemon-flavoured chicken and
pan-fried tuna with crushed tomatoes.
Excellent Sunday brunch.*

1ER ARRONDISSEMENT
● Le Grand Véfour

17 rue Beaujolais, 75001 **Map** 15D3

☎ 01 42 96 56 27

FAX 01 42 86 80 71

@ grand.vefour@wanadoo.fr

AE, DC, MC, V ● Sun, Fri D, Sat; 1
wk Apr, Aug, last wk Dec

🍴 €€€€€

*Established in 1760, this is one of
Paris's oldest restaurants; Napoleon was
once a regular here. Today, the majestic
setting and cuisine are still worthy of an
emperor. The Prince Rainier pigeon is
stuffed with truffle and foie gras, and
ravioli is the house speciality.*

1ER ARRONDISSEMENT
▲ Le Meurice

228 rue de Rivoli, 75001 **Map** 14C3

☎ 01 44 58 10 10

FAX 01 44 58 10 15

W www.meuricehotel.com

AE, DC, MC, V

● Sun L, Sat L; Aug 🍴 €€€€€

🍷 (161) €€€€€

*Ultimate luxury in the lavishly decorated
dining room and the winter garden
tearoom with an impressive Art Nouveau
glass ceiling. Two-star Michelin chef
Yannick Alléno creates delightful Parisian
food. Eighteenth-century inspired rooms.*

1ER ARRONDISSEMENT
▲ L'Espadon at Hôtel Ritz

15 pl Vendôme, 75001 **Map** 15D2

☎ 01 43 16 30 80

FAX 01 43 16 33 75

W www.ritzparis.com

AE, DC, MC, V

🍴 €€€€€ 🍷 (162) €€€€€

*Gilded restaurant inside a luxury hotel.
An innovative take on French cuisine,
with spiced-up gourmet food: foie gras
in pepper jelly and cherries in sweet red
wine. Classic accommodation.*

1ER ARRONDISSEMENT
● Restaurant du Palais Royal

110 galerie de Valois, 75001 **Map** 15D3

☎ 01 40 20 00 27

FAX 01 40 20 00 82

AE, DC, MC, V

● Sun, Oct–Apr: Sat; Dec

🍴 €€€€

*Both simple and sophisticated dishes
such as lamb chops Provence-style,
prawns with truffles and red-berry*

*millefeuille. The terrace benefits from
the Palais Royal gardens' majestic setting.*

1ER ARRONDISSEMENT
● **Ristorante il Delfino**
74 quai des Orfèvres, 75001 **Map** 14B5
📞 01 43 54 16 71
🅾 MC, V
🌑 Mon, Sat L **🍴** €€

*Stylish Italian restaurant, complete with
fireplace and 17th-century cellar, and
well suited to a romantic dinner. Pasta,
tiramisu, and the Delfino escalope
(breaded veal cutlet) deserves its place
as house speciality.*

1ER ARRONDISSEMENT
● **Toraya**
10 rue St-Florentin, 75001 **Map** 14C2
📞 01 42 60 13 00
FAX 01 42 61 59 53
🅾 AE, DC, MC, V
🌑 Sun **🍴** €

*Dark wood contrasts with the vivid colours
of the leather armchairs. Beautifully
crafted Japanese pastries: red-bean or
green-tea-flavoured macaroons and
many authentic, delicate rice dishes.*

1ER ARRONDISSEMENT
● **Willi's Wine Bar**
13 rue des Petits-Champs, 75001
Map 15D2
📞 01 42 61 05 09
FAX 01 47 03 36 93
🅾 MC, V 🌑 Sun; 2 wks Aug
🍴 €€€

*Original wine posters cover the walls
and over 250 vintages are in the cellar.
The menu includes onion tart with a salad
topped with pine nuts, beef fricassée
with braised chicory (endive) and rosemary sauce, and bitter chocolate terrine.*

2E ARRONDISSEMENT
● **Aki**
2 bis rue Daunou, 75002 **Map** 15D2
📞 01 42 61 48 38
FAX 01 47 03 37 52
🅾 AE, MC, V 🌑 Sun, Sat L; 3 wks Aug
🍴 €€€

*Meaning "happiness" in Japanese, this
is an elegant and vibrant restaurant
with stylish velvet chairs and ochre
walls adorned with arabesques. The*

*chef prepares sushi, sashimi and other
Japanese classics like courgette tempura.*

2E ARRONDISSEMENT
● **Aux Crus de Bourgogne**
3 rue Bachaumont, 75002 **Map** 15E3
📞 01 42 33 48 24
FAX 01 40 26 66 41
🅾 AE, MC, V 🌑 Sun, Sat **🍴** €€€

*Quintessentially Parisian decor with bet-
ter than average bistro fare. Foie gras
and lobster are house specialities.*

2E ARRONDISSEMENT
● **Aux Lyonnais**
32 rue St-Marc, 75002 **Map** 15D2
📞 01 42 96 65 04
FAX 01 42 97 42 95
🅾 AE, MC, V 🌑 Sun, Mon, Sat L;
Aug, 1 wk Dec **🍴** €€€

*An institution, established in 1890, with
authentic 19th-century decor. Cuisine is
from Lyon; the gastronomic fare goes
beyond the classics and is perfectly
matched by local wine such as Beaujolais.*

2E ARRONDISSEMENT
● **Drouant**
18 pl Gaillon, 75002 **Map** 15D2
📞 01 42 65 15 16
FAX 01 49 24 02 15
🅾 AE, DC, MC, V 🌑 Sun, Sat; Aug
🍴 €€€€€

*Chef Louis Grondard maintains the
reputation of this venerable restaurant,
renowned both for its dazzling Art Deco
interior and its cuisine. Inventive uses of
the finest produce such as pasta with a
savoury truffle sauce. Sweetbreads are
cooked in wine, paired with asparagus.
A less formal café serves shellfish, beef
with Béarnaise sauce and grilled sole, in
a stunning Art Deco interior.*

2E ARRONDISSEMENT
● **Etienne Marcel**
34 rue Etienne Marcel, 75002 **Map** 15E3
📞 01 45 08 01 03
FAX 01 42 36 03 44
🅾 AE, MC, V
🍴 €€€

*Interesting French-American menu for
this 1970s-style spot. The menu offers
steak tartare, various carpaccio and
tomato cake. Massive juke box.*

2E ARRONDISSEMENT
● **Gallopin**
40 rue Notre-Dame des Victoires,
75002 **Map** 15D2
📞 01 42 36 45 38
FAX 01 42 36 10 32
🆆 www.brasseriegallopin.com
🅾 AE, DC, MC, V 🌑 Sun **🍴** €€€

*Impressive setting with a glass ceiling
from 1876. Great classics of brasserie
cuisine on the menu, from the shellfish
platters and flambéed pancakes to foie
gras and steak tartare.*

2E ARRONDISSEMENT
● **Gandhi Opéra**
66 rue Ste-Anne, 75002 **Map** 15D2
📞 01 47 03 41 00
FAX 01 49 10 03 73
🆆 www.gandhi.fr
🅾 AE, DC, MC, V **🍴** €€

*Reasonably priced, elegant Indian
restaurant complete with candles and
fine paintings. Special attention is paid
to the presentation of the dishes, which
include tandoori and curries.*

2E ARRONDISSEMENT
● **Grand Colbert**
2 rue Vivienne, 75002 **Map** 15D2
📞 01 42 86 87 88
FAX 01 42 86 82 65
🅾 AE, DC, MC, V **🍴** €€€€

*Elegant brasserie where the brass
shines and the potted palms soar to the
high ceilings. Shellfish platters and
salmon with sorrel are served.*

2E ARRONDISSEMENT
● **La Fontaine Gaillon**
1 rue de la Michodière, 75002 **Map** 15D2
📞 01 47 42 63 22
FAX 01 47 42 82 84
🅾 AE, DC, MC, V 🌑 Sun, Sat; Aug
🍴 €€€€

*In a 17th-century mansion, the menu
showcases John Dory, salmon with
sorrel purée and confit de canard (p326).*

2E ARRONDISSEMENT
▲ **Le Céladon at Hôtel Westminster**
15 rue Daunou, 75002 **Map** 15D2
📞 01 47 03 40 42
FAX 01 42 60 30 66
🆆 www.leceladon.com

● Restaurant ■ Hotel ▲ Hotel / Restaurant

🗝 AE, DC, MC, V ⬤ Sun; Aug
🍴 €€€€ 🍮 (112) €€€€€

Elegant dining room decorated with lots of celadon. Sea bass roasted in butter with potatoes and ceps and truffle-flavoured veal kidney demonstrate the chef's creativity. Comfortable rooms.

2E ARRONDISSEMENT
● **Le Domaine Léopold**
36 rue Léopold Bellan, 75002 **Map** 15E2
📞 01 45 08 45 83
🗝 MC, V ⬤ Sun, Sat L; Aug, last wk Dec 🍴 €

Wine bar where fine vintages can be sampled by the glass. Large salads and sausage confit with lentils.

2E ARRONDISSEMENT
▲ **Le Park at Hôtel Park Hyatt**
5 rue de la Paix, 75002 **Map** 15D2
📞 01 58 71 12 34
📠 01 58 71 12 35
🗝 AE, DC, MC, V ⬤ Sun, Sat L
🍴 €€€€ 🍮 (186) €€€€€

Sleek modern hotel with a circular dining room. Creative cuisine such as poached langoustines with vermicelli. High-tech amenities in chic guestrooms.

2E ARRONDISSEMENT
● **Le Tir Bouchon**
22 rue Tiquetonne, 75002 **Map** 15E3
📞 01 42 21 95 51
📠 01 43 91 72 37
🗝 MC, V ⬤ 3rd wk Dec 🍴 €€

The chef elaborates on various regional classics, adding a gourmet touch. Confit de canard (p326), prawns in puff pastry with saffron sauce and roast pigeon.

2E ARRONDISSEMENT
● **Le Vaudeville**
29 rue Vivienne, 75002 **Map** 15D2
📞 01 40 20 04 62
📠 01 49 27 08 78
🗝 AE, DC, MC, V 🍴 €€€

Impressive Art Deco interior where journalists lunch and theatregoers dine. Simple cooking: calf's head, truffled mashed potatoes and grilled cod.

3E ARRONDISSEMENT
● **Andy Walhoo**
69 rue des Gravilliers, 75003 **Map** 15E3

📞 01 42 71 20 38
🗝 AE, DC, MC, V
⬤ Sun 🍴 €€€

Pop-art take on North African motifs for the decor, but traditional recipes used for the cooking. El guassa is the house speciality: a large platter of Moroccan dips, salads and skewered meat.

3E ARRONDISSEMENT
● **Auberge Nicolas Flamel**
51 rue de Montmorency, 75003
Map 15E3
📞 01 42 71 77 78
📠 01 48 04 58 36
🌐 http://nicolasflamel.parisbistro.net
🗝 AE, MC, V ⬤ Sun, Sat L 🍴 €€€

Housed in Paris's oldest building (1407) and named after the famous alchemist. The speciality here is gigot de sept heures (p191) following a medieval recipe.

3E ARRONDISSEMENT
● **Chez Jenny**
39 bd du Temple, 75003 **Map** 15F3
📞 01 44 54 39 00
📠 01 44 54 39 09
🌐 www.chez-jenny.com
🗝 AE, DC, MC, V 🍴 €€€

Intricate marquetry work for the decor at this Alsatian ambassador. Sauerkraut is the uncontested star of the menu, and the Alsatian whites complement the shellfish platters perfectly. Valet parking.

3E ARRONDISSEMENT
● **L'Ambassade d'Auvergne**
22 rue du Grenier-St-Lazare, 75003
Map 15E3
📞 01 42 72 31 22
📠 01 42 78 85 47
🌐 www.ambassade-auvergne.com
🗝 AE, MC, V 🍴 €€€

Famous for its substantial dishes. Good selection of regional wines, the perfect accompaniment to specialities such as the aligot (p247). Rustic interior, with whole hams hanging from the beams.

3E ARRONDISSEMENT
● **Clos de Vertbois**
13 rue Vert Bois, 75003 **Map** 15E2
📞 01 42 77 14 85
🗝 AE, MC, V
⬤ Sun D, Mon, Sat L; Aug 🍴 €€

Authentic Parisian bistro offering friendly service and great food. Dishes include magret de canard, langoustine salad, grilled scallop brochettes and a hearty boeuf bourguignon (p217).

4E ARRONDISSEMENT
● **Au Petit Fer à Cheval**
30 rue Vieille du Temple, 75004 **Map** 15E3
📞 01 42 72 47 47
🌐 www.cafeine.com
🗝 MC, V 🍴 €€

Named for its vintage horseshoe-shaped bar, behind which is tucked a tiny dining room. Those in the know delight in confit de canard (p326), andouille and various salads. Small outdoor terrace.

4E ARRONDISSEMENT
● **Au Pied de Chameau**
20 rue Quincampoix, 75004 **Map** 15E3
📞 01 42 78 35 00
📠 01 42 78 00 50
🌐 www.aupieddechameau.fr
🗝 AE, MC, V 🍴 €€

Moroccan crafts decorate the dining room. Interesting traditional dishes are on the menu such as the lamb, prune and almond tagines, and meatball cous-cous. Belly dancers entertain. Nightclub in the basement.

4E ARRONDISSEMENT
● **Aux Vins des Pyrénées**
25 rue Beautreillis, 75004 **Map** 15F4
📞 01 42 72 64 94
📠 01 42 72 76 15
🗝 MC, V ⬤ Sat L, Jul–Aug: Sun L; last 2 wks Aug 🍴 €€

Antique dolls on display and red-and-white chequered tablecloths. Menu includes steak tartare, fish with basil and tomato and decadent chocolate cake.

4E ARRONDISSEMENT
● **Bofinger**
5–7 rue de la Bastille, 75004 **Map** 15F4
📞 01 42 72 87 82
📠 01 42 72 97 68
🗝 AE, DC, MC, V 🍴 €€€

Impressive Art Nouveau interior including a stained-glass ceiling in one room. Grilled lamb with a tomato tarte Tatin (p191), seafood sauerkraut and vanilla and blackcurrant vacherin.

For key to symbols see back flap

4E ARRONDISSEMENT
● **Café Beaubourg**

43 rue St-Merri, 75004 **Map** 15E3

☎ 01 48 87 63 96

FAX 01 48 87 81 25

💳 AE, DC, MC, V 🍴 €€€

With views of the animated piazza of the Beaubourg museum, this elegant contemporary café serves simple yet reliable, if slightly overpriced, fare such as a variety of tartares, grilled meats or fish and even a Thai salad.

4E ARRONDISSEMENT
● **Georges**

19 rue Beaubourg, 75004 **Map** 15E3

☎ 01 44 78 47 99

FAX 01 44 78 48 93

💳 AE, DC, MC, V ● Tue

🍴 €€€€

On the top floor of the Pompidou Centre, and with stunning views. Light and inspired cuisine such as cherry tomato and goat's cheese cake, sole meunière, lamb with chutney and macaroons.

4E ARRONDISSEMENT
● **Hiramatsu**

7 quai de Bourbon, 75004 **Map** 15E4

☎ 01 56 81 08 80

FAX 01 56 81 08 81

w www.hiramatsu.co.jp

💳 AE, DC, MC, V ● Sun, Mon; Aug

🍴 €€€€€

Where zen culture and French haute cuisine meet. Extreme refinement: frog consommé with morel sauce and ginger vegetables. Booking essential.

4E ARRONDISSEMENT
■ **Hôtel Acacias Hôtel de Ville**

20 rue du Temple, 75004 **Map** 15F3

☎ 01 48 87 07 70

FAX 01 48 87 17 20

w www.acacias-hotel.com

💳 AE, DC, MC, V 🥄 (33) €€€

In Le Marais, and not far from Notre Dame. Solid wooden furniture and fine prints make for a charming atmosphere in the rooms.

4E ARRONDISSEMENT
■ **Hôtel de la Bretonnerie**

22 rue Ste-Croix de la Bretonnerie, 75004 **Map** 15E3

☎ 01 48 87 77 63

FAX 01 42 77 26 78

w www.bretonnerie.com

💳 MC, V 🥄 (29) €€€€

In a 17th-century town house in the centre of historic Le Marais. Exposed stone, canopied beds (in some of the rooms) coupled with all mod cons.

4E ARRONDISSEMENT
■ **Hôtel St-Merry**

78 rue de la Verrerie, 75004 **Map** 15E3

☎ 01 42 78 14 15

FAX 01 40 29 06 82

w www.hotelmarais.com

💳 AE, MC, V 🥄 (12) €€€€

Formerly the presbytery of the church of St-Merri. Gothic style throughout with two exceptional rooms: number 9, which is located above the nave and features buttresses; and a top-notch suite.

4E ARRONDISSEMENT
● **La Chaise au Plafond**

10 rue du Trésor, 75004 **Map** 15E3

☎ 01 42 76 03 22

w www.cafeine.com

💳 MC, V 🍴 €€

At the heart of trendy Marais, but with a terrace that looks onto a quiet street. Simple fare: salads, charcuterie, steak tartare and savoury tarts.

4E ARRONDISSEMENT
● **Le Colimaçon**

44 rue Vieille du Temple, 75004 **Map** 15E3

☎ 01 48 87 12 01

w www.lecolimacon.com

💳 AE, MC, V

● Tue; 3 wks Aug 🍴 €€

Le Colimaçon (snail) refers to the restaurant's centrepiece: a corkscrew staircase. Snails are also on the menu along with gigot de sept heures (p191).

4E ARRONDISSEMENT
● **Les Philosophes**

28 rue Vieille du Temple, 75004 **Map** 15E3

☎ 01 48 87 49 64

w www.cafeine.com 💳 MC, V 🍴 €€

Classy bistro on one of Paris's most picturesque streets. Excellent traditional cuisine such as confit de canard (p326).

4E ARRONDISSEMENT
● **Maison Rouge**

13 rue des Archives, 75004 **Map** 15E3

☎ 01 42 71 69 69

FAX 01 42 71 04 08

w www.maisonrouge.fr

💳 MC, V 🍴 €€€

Extremely trendy, with a geometric, fluorescent decor inspired by Mondrian and pop art. The cuisine mixes fine influences from France and Asia.

4E ARRONDISSEMENT
● **Nos Ancêtres les Gaulois**

39 rue St-Louis en l'Ile, 75004 **Map** 15E3

☎ 01 46 33 66 07

FAX 01 43 25 28 64

w www.nosancetreslesgaulois.com

💳 AE, DC, MC, V

● Mon–Sat L 🍴 €€

Catering to big appetites in a jolly atmosphere. Only one set menu, which includes assorted salads, a buffet of cooked meats, one grilled meat, cheeseboard, fruit, dessert and plenty of wine.

4E ARRONDISSEMENT
● **Piccolo Teatro**

6 rue des Ecouffes, 75004 **Map** 15E3

☎ 01 42 72 17 79

💳 AE, MC, V 🍴 €

Established in the 1970s and one of Paris's first vegetarian restaurants. Tasty cuisine with a Mediterranean accent such as moussaka, lasagne and stuffed aubergines (eggplant).

4E ARRONDISSEMENT
● **Trésor**

5–7 rue du Trésor, 75004 **Map** 15E3

☎ 01 42 71 35 17

💳 AE, DC, MC, V 🍴 €€€

A decor of a contemporary elegance with a touch of kitsch. Lasagne, grilled steak in wine sauce and tiramisu show the blend of French and Italian cooking.

5E ARRONDISSEMENT
● **Aarapana**

6 rue du Petit-Pont, 75005 **Map** 14B5

☎ 01 46 33 55 10

FAX 01 46 33 55 10

💳 AE, DC, MC, V 🍴 €€

Exotic wooden furniture and coloured silks give this Indian restaurant a chic, modern twist. Some traditional curries, along with some unusual dishes: salmon tikka and pickled quail tandoori.

5E ARRONDISSEMENT
● Bistrot Côté Mer

15 bd St-Germain, 75005 **Map** 14C5

☎ 01 43 54 59 10

FAX 01 43 29 02 08

🗲 AE, MC, V ● 1 wk mid-Aug

🍴 €€€

Breton seafood restaurant serving grilled sea bass with ginger curried vegetables and other fish and shellfish with exotic spices. For dessert, try chocolate soufflé or pancakes flambéed with Grand Marnier.

5E ARRONDISSEMENT
● Café Panis

21 quai Montebello, 75005 **Map** 14C5

☎ 01 43 54 19 71

FAX 01 43 29 34 97

🗲 MC, V 🍴 €€

Steps from Notre-Dame, this bright and airy dining room looks onto the Seine. Bistro fare: confit de canard (p326) and steak-frites, plus massive salads.

5E ARRONDISSEMENT
● Fogon St-Julien

10 rue St-Julien Pauvre, 75005

Map 14B5

☎ 01 43 54 31 33

FAX 01 43 54 07 00

🗲 MC, V ● Mon, Tue–Fri L; 1st 2 wks Jan, last 3 wks Aug 🍴 €€€

Authentically Spanish. The elegant straw-coloured interior, with wrought iron accents, does credit to the fine cuisine. Savoury tapas and all sorts of paella.

5E ARRONDISSEMENT
● La Rôtisserie du Beaujolais

19 quai de la Tournelle, 75005 **Map** 15E4

☎ 01 43 54 17 47

FAX 01 56 24 43 71

🗲 MC, V ● Mon 🍴 €€€

Bistro by the Seine serving Lyonnaise specialities such as tête-de-veau and coq au vin (p217). Run by Claude Terrail, also behind neighbour La Tour d'Argent.

5E ARRONDISSEMENT
● La Tour d'Argent

15 quai de la Tournelle, 75005 **Map** 15E4

☎ 01 43 54 23 31

FAX 01 44 07 12 04

w www.latourdargent.com

🗲 AE, DC, MC, V ● Mon, Tue L

🍴 €€€€€

Haute cuisine on the sixth floor with a breathtaking view of Notre Dame. Exceptional cellar, the oldest vintage dating back to 1858. The speciality is canard à l'orange.

5E ARRONDISSEMENT
● L'Atelier Maître Albert

1 rue Maître Albert, 75005 **Map** 14C5

☎ 01 56 81 30 01

FAX 01 53 10 83 23

🗲 AE, MC, V

● L; Sun 🍴 €€€

The antique fireplace is decorative, yet dishes from the rotisserie are this restaurant's speciality. Menu varies, but focuses on traditional cuisine.

5E ARRONDISSEMENT
● Le Balzar

49 rue des Ecoles, 75005 **Map** 14B5

☎ 01 43 54 13 67

FAX 01 44 07 14 91

🗲 AE, DC, MC, V 🍴 €€€

Classy vintage 1930s brasserie, popular with the Sorbonne university crowd. Traditional cuisine: foie gras, pepper steak, steak tartare and skate.

5E ARRONDISSEMENT
● Le Cercle

1 rue Gay Lussac, 75005 **Map** 15D4

☎ 01 46 34 63 98

🗲 MC, V 🍴 €€

Facing the Luxembourg gardens, this is a contemporary café complete with leather armchairs and bistro fare. Provençal influence on the menu, which includes stuffed vegetables, snails and confit de canard (p326). Snacks such as pancakes, salads and sandwiches are served all day long.

5E ARRONDISSEMENT
● Le Coupe Chou

11 rue de Lanneau, 75005 **Map** 15E4

☎ 01 46 33 68 69

FAX 01 43 25 94 15

w www.lecoupechou.com

🗲 AE, MC, V ● Sun L 🍴 €€€

French classics: duck terrine with black-currant and onion marmalade and dill salmon. The perfectly romantic decor, offering a succession of tiny rooms, justifies this slightly pricey bistro fare.

5E ARRONDISSEMENT
● Le Grenier de Notre Dame

18 rue de la Bûcherie, 75005 **Map** 14C5

☎ 01 43 29 98 29

w www.legrenierdenotredame.com

🗲 MC, V 🍴 €

Opened in the 1970s and still exuding its original hippie atmosphere. Filling meals such as fish gratin, vegetarian casserole or meat-free escalope.

5E ARRONDISSEMENT
● Le Petit Pontoise

9 rue Pontoise, 75005 **Map** 15E4

☎ 01 43 29 25 20

🗲 AE, MC, V 🍴 €€€

Popular neighbourhood venue. Inventive use of spices: pan-fried quail with honey, dried fruits and nuts and prawns Provençal. Reservations recommended.

5E ARRONDISSEMENT
● Les Bouchons de François Clerc

12 rue de l'Hôtel Colbert, 75005

Map 14C5

☎ 01 43 54 15 34

FAX 01 46 34 68 07

w www.lesbouchonsdefrancoisclerc.com

🗲 AE, MC, V

● Sun, Sat L 🍴 €€€

Vintages, offered at wine growers' prices, complement dishes like marrow-flavoured roast beef with potato gratin and morello cherry soufflé.

5E ARRONDISSEMENT
● Les Quatre et Une Saveurs

72 rue du Cardinal Lemoine, 75005

Map 15E4

☎ 01 43 26 88 80

FAX 01 43 26 90 07

🗲 AE, MC, V

● Mon; 3 wks in Aug 🍴 €

High-class macrobiotic, organic and (mostly) vegetarian food. Inventive soups are flavoured with butternut squash or cinnamon; mains include fish bento or seitan (gluten) curry. Good choice of organic wines, plus fruit cocktails.

5E ARRONDISSEMENT
● **Mavrommatis**

42 rue Daubenton, 75005 **Map** 15E5

☎ 01 43 31 17 17

W www.mavrommatis.fr

✉ AE, MC, V ● Mon; mid-Aug–mid-Sep 🍴 €€€€€

This elegant restaurant serves Greek specialities: roast lamb and moussaka. The Hellenic excursion continues with Greek yogurt and baklava for dessert.

5E ARRONDISSEMENT
● **Restaurant E Marty**

20 ave des Gobelins, 75005 **Map** 15E5

☎ 01 43 31 39 51

FAX 01 43 37 63 70

✉ AE, DC, MC, V 🍴 €€€

Authentic Art Deco interior but the cuisine steals the show. Hearty fare such as roast duck or rabbit casserole and seasonal dishes such as gazpacho. Excellent crème brûlée.

5E ARRONDISSEMENT
● **Symposium**

29 rue de la Huchette, 75005 **Map** 14B5

☎ 01 40 46 87 12

✉ AE, MC, V 🍴 €€

A rustic dining room where, alongside the traditional grilled steak and chicken with fries, interesting fondues (blue cheese, beer) are on offer.

6E ARRONDISSEMENT
● **A la Bonne Crêpe**

11 rue Grégoire de Tours, 75006 **Map** 14B5

☎ 01 43 54 60 74

● Sun 🍴 €

One of Paris's oldest Breton-style crêperies. Buckwheat galettes with savoury fillings and flour pancakes with sweet ones.

6E ARRONDISSEMENT
● **Alcazar**

62 rue Mazarine, 75006 **Map** 14B5

☎ 01 53 10 19 99

FAX 01 53 10 23 23

✉ AE, DC, MC, V 🍴 €€€

A chic modern brasserie, once a print shop and now Sir Terence Conran's first Parisian venture. Shellfish platters, English classics such as fish and chips

and spiced-up traditional French dishes such as magret de canard.

6E ARRONDISSEMENT
● **Allard**

41 rue St-André des Arts, 75006 **Map** 14B5

☎ 01 43 26 48 23

FAX 01 46 33 04 02

✉ AE, DC, MC, V ● Sun; 3 wks Aug 🍴 €€€

A retro venue with home-style cuisine including frogs' legs in garlic, sole meunière and the house speciality, olive duck.

6E ARRONDISSEMENT
■ **Atelier Montparnasse**

49 rue Vavin, 75006 **Map** 15D5

☎ 01 46 33 60 00

FAX 01 40 51 04 21

W www.l-ateliermontparnasse.com

✉ AE, DC, MC, V 🥐 (17) €€€€

At the heart of Montparnasse with an atmosphere evocative of its 1930s heydays: Art Deco furniture in the rooms.

6E ARRONDISSEMENT
● **Au Relais Louis XIII**

8 rue Grands-Augustins, 75006 **Map** 14B5

☎ 01 43 26 75 96

FAX 01 44 07 07 80

W www.relaislouis13.com

✉ AE, MC, V ● Sun, Mon; 3 wks Aug 🍴 €€€€€

In a 16th-century town house, the menu includes lamb with thyme vegetables and the classic vanilla millefeuille.

6E ARRONDISSEMENT
● **Au Vieux Colombier**

65 rue de Rennes, 75006 **Map** 14A5

☎ 01 45 48 53 81

FAX 01 45 44 27 49

✉ DC, MC, V ● Sun D 🍴 €€

A traditional Parisian bistro interior but the menu goes beyond the classics. Pepper steak, grilled salmon and steak tartare are familiar but you'll also find cheeseburgers and citrus soup.

6E ARRONDISSEMENT
● **Bar à Soupes et Quenelles**

5 rue Princesse, 75006 **Map** 14A5

☎ 01 43 25 44 44

FAX 01 43 25 07 87

W www.giraudet.fr

✉ MC, V ● Sun 🍴 €

Sister to Giraudet, a famous Lyonnaise deli, established in 1910. Only quenelles and soups on the menu, often with original combinations of ingredients such as beetroot, carrot and orange soup.

6E ARRONDISSEMENT
● **Barocco**

23 rue Mazarine, 75006 **Map** 14B5

☎ 01 43 26 40 24

✉ AE, MC, V

● Sun D, Mon, Tue L

🍴 €€€

Serving Brazilian cuisine: seijoada (black bean casserole), churrasco (grilled meat) and Portuguese-style cod. A chic and cosy interior, complete with a library.

6E ARRONDISSEMENT
● **Bouillon Racine**

3 rue Racine, 75006 **Map** 14B5

☎ 01 44 32 15 60

FAX 01 44 32 15 61

✉ AE, MC, V 🍴 €€€

Stuffed roast suckling pig, liquorice-flavoured lamb and seafood risotto are served at this Art Nouveau masterpiece.

6E ARRONDISSEMENT
● **Boulangerie Paul**

77 rue de Seine, 75006 **Map** 14A5

☎ 01 55 42 02 23

✉ MC, V ● Sun 🍴 €

Bakery and tearoom serving great patisserie: custards, fruit tarts and fromage frais. Full breakfast, and deli-style lunch such as quiches with salad.

6E ARRONDISSEMENT
● **Brasserie Lipp**

151 bd St-Germain, 75006 **Map** 14A5

☎ 01 45 48 53 91

FAX 01 45 44 33 20

W www.brasserie-lipp.fr

✉ AE, DC, MC, V 🍴 €€€

A Parisian institution cherished by an intellectual crowd since 1880. Traditional brasserie fare of a high standard: pig's trotters, sauerkraut and sole meunière. Baba au rhum (p119) and millefeuille for dessert. Dazzling interior.

● Restaurant ■ Hotel ▲ Hotel / Restaurant

6E ARRONDISSEMENT

▲ Brasserie Lutétia

45 bd Raspail, 75006 **Map** 14A5

📞 01 49 54 46 76

FAX 01 49 54 46 00

W www.lutetia-paris.com

🗇 AE, DC, MC, V

⬤ Sun, Sat; public holidays

🍴 €€€€€ 🥂 (230) €€€€€

Chic, retro hotel with a massive oyster bar. The menu also accommodates sole meunière and steak tartare. Staid, very traditional guestrooms.

6E ARRONDISSEMENT

⬤ Café Cassette

73 rue de Rennes, 75006 **Map** 14A5

📞 01 45 48 53 78

FAX 01 42 84 08 16

🗇 AE, DC, MC, V 🍴 €

Conical orange lamps and splashes of purple adorn this bistro. The cuisine is traditional but often bears foreign accents, as in duck with curried cauliflower. The atmosphere is convivial.

6E ARRONDISSEMENT

⬤ Café de Flore

172 bd St-Germain, 75006 **Map** 14A5

📞 01 45 48 55 26

FAX 01 45 44 33 39

W www.cafe-de-flore.com

🗇 AE, DC, MC, V 🍴 €€€

A surrealists' haunt in the 1930s and still a legendary place. Blue cheese and chicory (endive) salad and duck foie gras on the slightly overpriced menu.

6E ARRONDISSEMENT

⬤ Café des Délices

87 rue d'Assas, 75006 **Map** 15D5

📞 01 43 54 70 00

FAX 01 43 26 42 05

🗇 AE, MC, V ⬤ Sun, Sat; 3 wks Aug

🍴 €€€

Nothing seems too audacious for young chef Gilles Choukroun. Scallops with chocolate is one of his inventions. Dishes don't stay on the menu for too long except for the speciality citrus dessert. Casual chic atmosphere.

6E ARRONDISSEMENT

⬤ Café du Métro

67 rue de Rennes, 75006 **Map** 14A5

📞 01 45 48 58 56

🗇 MC, V ⬤ 1st 3 wks Aug 🍴 €

Established in 1920, this café serves tea in the afternoon and cocktails in the evening. Classic French cuisine such as large salads and grilled meats, and more traditional dishes like andouillette. Competitively priced set menu.

6E ARRONDISSEMENT

⬤ Café Six

19 rue des Canettes, 75006 **Map** 14A5

📞 01 43 26 44 27

W www.cafesix.com

🗇 AE, MC, V

🍴 €€

Zestful creativity, reflected in leopard-print furnishings. Elevated French cuisine: goat's cheese millefeuille, honeyed magret de canard and iced nougat.

6E ARRONDISSEMENT

⬤ Chez les Filles

64 rue du Cherche Midi, 75006

Map 14C4

📞 01 45 48 61 54

🗇 MC, V ⬤ D 🍴 €

Afternoons offer an exotic tea break in this Moroccan-run place. Tagines, salads and couscous on the lunch menu, and a Berber brunch is served on Sundays. Featuring wrought-iron work.

6E ARRONDISSEMENT

⬤ Coffee Parisien

4 rue Princesse, 75006 **Map** 14A5

📞 01 43 54 18 18

🗇 AE, MC, V 🍴 €€

With wooden panelling, punctuated with pictures of American presidents, this is one of the best places for brunch. American classics including one of the best burgers in Paris, eggs benedict and all sorts of pancakes and sundaes.

6E ARRONDISSEMENT

⬤ Fajitas

14 rue Dauphine, 75006 **Map** 14B5

📞 01 46 34 44 69

🗇 AE, MC, V ⬤ Mon 🍴 €

This excellent venue conveys the warmth of Mexico without being garish. The cactus salad is an interesting starter. Mains include fajitas, chilli con carne, enchiladas and burritos.

6E ARRONDISSEMENT

■ Grand Hôtel des Balcons

3 rue Casimir Delavigne, 75006

Map 14B5

📞 01 46 34 78 50

FAX 01 46 34 06 27

W www.balcons.com

🗇 AE, DC, MC, V 🥂 (50) €€€€

Art Nouveau features at this hotel. Most guestrooms enjoy a balcony.

6E ARRONDISSEMENT

■ Hôtel de l'Abbaye St-Germain

10 rue Cassette, 75006 **Map** 14A5

📞 01 45 44 38 11

FAX 01 45 48 07 86

W www.hotel-abbaye.com

🗇 AE, MC, V 🥂 (44) €€€€€

Steps from Le Jardin du Luxembourg, a 17th-century abbey with finely furnished guestrooms and apartments.

6E ARRONDISSEMENT

■ Hôtel du Globe

15 rue Quatre-Vents, 75006 **Map** 14B5

📞 01 46 33 62 69

FAX 01 46 33 62 69

🗇 MC, V ⬤ Aug 🥂 (15) €€€

A 17th-century building right by Le Jardins du Luxembourg, with excellent accommodation. Breakfast is brought to your room. Extremely popular, so book.

6E ARRONDISSEMENT

⬤ Jacques Cagna

14 rue Grands Augustins, 75006

Map 14B5

📞 01 43 26 49 39

FAX 01 43 54 54 48

W www.jacques-cagna.com

🗇 AE, DC, MC, V ⬤ Sun, Mon L, Sat L; Aug 🍴 €€€€€

A 17th-century house decorated with Flemish paintings. Classic cuisine from Challans duck in Burgundy wine to strawberries and raspberries with Szechuan pepper and avocado ice cream.

6E ARRONDISSEMENT

⬤ La Boussole

12 rue Guisarde, 75006 **Map** 14A5

📞 01 56 24 82 20

🗇 AE, MC, V 🍴 €

An imposing brass compass adorns the entrance, and the menu follows the spice trail, with a predilection for North African dishes: lemon chicken tagine, banana tart and spiced crème brûlée.

6E ARRONDISSEMENT
● **La Marlotte**
55 rue du Cherche Midi, 75006
Map 14C4
📞 01 45 48 86 79
FAX 01 45 44 34 80
🆆 www.lamarlotte.com
🍽 AE, DC, MC, V ⬤ Sun; 1st 3 wks
Aug 🏨 €€€
Quaint interior, including a collection of old keys. Features foie gras, lentil salad and sausages, as well as great seafood.

6E ARRONDISSEMENT
● **La Petite Cour**
8 rue Mabillon, 75006 **Map** 14A3
📞 01 43 26 52 26
FAX 01 44 07 11 53
🆆 www.la-petitecour.com
🍽 AE, DC, MC, V 🏨 €€€
Colourful dining room with Napoleon-II-style furnishings, a view of a leafy court-yard and flavourful cooking. Tarragon prawns and honey-roasted fish with soya and mango are highlights.

6E ARRONDISSEMENT
● **La Rôtisserie d'en Face**
2 rue Christine, 75006 **Map** 14B5
📞 01 43 26 40 98
FAX 01 43 54 22 71
🆆 www.jacques-cagna.com
🍽 AE, DC, MC, V ⬤ Sun, Sat L
🏨 €€€
Jacques Cagna's rotisserie, located opposite his eponymous gastronomic restaurant. Perfectly mastered traditional recipes on the menu: veal chop with morel sauce and mashed potato and pan-fried red mullet with capers, lemon and caramelized chicory (endive).

6E ARRONDISSEMENT
● **La Rotonde**
105 bd Montparnasse, 75006 **Map** 15D5
📞 01 43 26 68 84 / 01 43 26 48 26
FAX 01 46 34 52 40
🍽 AE, MC, V 🏨 €€€€
Late-night spot with plush velvet seats, shiny brass and wood panelling. Dishes such as pan-fried steak and grilled tuna.

6E ARRONDISSEMENT
● **La Table d'Erica**
6 rue Mabillon, 75006 **Map** 14A5
📞 01 43 54 87 61
FAX 01 43 54 87 61
🍽 AE, DC, MC, V ⬤ Sun L, Mon L
🏨 €
Wooden parrots decorate this tropical hangout. Creole specialities abound, such as prawns in coconut milk or kid steamed with Madras spices.

6E ARRONDISSEMENT
● **La Taverne Basque**
45 rue Cherche-Midi, 75006 **Map** 14C4
📞 01 42 22 51 07
FAX 01 45 44 34 21
🍽 AE, DC, MC, V
⬤ Sun, Sat L; 1st 3 wks Aug 🏨 €€
For Basque food including axoa, stuffed peppers and oeufs à la piperade (p353). The desserts are tempting; try the good gâteau Basque and cherry clafoutis (p247). Basque singers often spice up the quietly rustic atmosphere.

6E ARRONDISSEMENT
● **L'Arbuci**
25 rue de Buci, 75006 **Map** 14A5
📞 01 44 32 16 00
FAX 01 44 32 16 09
🆆 www.arbuci.com
🍽 AE, DC, MC, V 🏨 €€€
The Blanc brothers, owners of venerable institutions like Procope, experiment at this contemporary venue. Seafood, including shellfish platters; other dishes accommodate foreign flavours, as exemplified in the lemongrass tuna and pineapple kebabs.

6E ARRONDISSEMENT
● **Le Be-Bop**
8 rue Grégoire de Tours, 75006
Map 14B5
📞 01 43 29 24 52
FAX 01 43 29 24 52
🍽 MC, V ⬤ L 🏨 €€
Nightly piano-jazz. Confit de canard (p326), and goats' cheese salad on the menu.

6E ARRONDISSEMENT
● **Le Bergamote**
8 rue Montfaucon, 75006 **Map** 14A5
📞 01 43 26 50 56

🆆 www.bergamote.org
🍽 DC, MC, V 🏨 €
Herbs are king here: various pots of them adorn the walls and they take pride of place in the cooking. The caramelized onion tart comes with chive cream and the red mullet in tomato makes good use of basil.

6E ARRONDISSEMENT
▲ **Le Paris at Hôtel Lutétia**
43 bd Raspail, 75006 **Map** 14A5
📞 01 49 54 46 90
FAX 01 49 54 46 00
🆆 www.lutetia-paris.com
🍽 AE, DC, MC, V ⬤ Sun, Sat; Aug
🏨 €€€€€ 🛏 (230) €€€€€
Restaurant in a retro-style hotel. Pasta stuffed with black truffle and foie gras is just one divine dish. Art Deco rooms with plenty of mahogany and bright colours.

6E ARRONDISSEMENT
● **Le Petit Lutétia**
107 rue de Sèvres, 75006 **Map** 14C4
📞 01 45 48 33 53
FAX 01 45 48 74 59
🍽 AE, MC, V 🏨 €€€
Opened in the 1920s, the Art Nouveau decor has acquired a patina of age. The cuisine sticks to brasserie fare but in a high-class way: veal liver (the house speciality), cod in a lemon butter sauce and rabbit with mustard cream.

6E ARRONDISSEMENT
● **Le Petit Zinc**
11 rue St-Benoît, 75006 **Map** 14A5
📞 01 42 86 61 00
FAX 01 42 86 61 09
🍽 AE, DC, MC, V 🏨 €€€
Art Nouveau masterpiece with blown glass lamps and wrought iron work delineating booth seating. Brasserie fare: grilled sole, pan-fried calf's liver and beautiful shellfish platters.

6E ARRONDISSEMENT
● **Le Pré**
4 rue du Four, 75006 **Map** 14A5
📞 01 40 46 93 22
🍽 MC, V 🏨 €€
Hip late-night venue screening fashion TV. French-Italian dishes such as large ravioli filled with chive cream or foie

---

● Restaurant   ■ Hotel   ▲ Hotel / Restaurant

gras, and macaroni and goat's cheese gratin. Moroccan lounge downstairs.

6E ARRONDISSEMENT
● L'Epi Dupin

11 rue Dupin, 75006 **Map** 14C4

01 42 22 64 56

FAX 01 42 22 30 42

MC, V ● Sun, Mon L, Sat; Aug

€€

Most dishes betray a French influence, some go further afield: tempura prawns with ginger-pineapple chutney, crispy beef with mustard ice cream, and rhubarb and melon salad with lemon thyme. Reservations recommended.

6E ARRONDISSEMENT
● Les Bouquinistes

53 quai des Grands-Augustins, 75006

Map 14B5

01 43 25 45 94

FAX 01 43 25 23 07

www.guysavoy.com

AE, DC, MC, V ● Sun, Sat L

€€€€

Subtle and modern, with dishes such as prawn tempura with avocado purée and a mango-coriander (cilantro) dressing.

6E ARRONDISSEMENT
● Les Deux Magots

6 pl St-Germain des Prés, 75006

Map 14A5

01 45 48 55 25

FAX 01 45 49 31 29

www.lesdeuxmagots.com

AE, DC, MC, V €€€

Hemingway used to be a regular. Chic bistro furniture and savoury bites: carpaccio, foie gras, smoked salmon platters and an excellent hot chocolate.

6E ARRONDISSEMENT
● L'Espadon Bleu

25 rue des Grands Augustins, 75006

Map 14B5

01 46 33 00 85

FAX 01 43 54 54 48

www.jacques-cagna.com

AE, DC, MC, V ● Sun, Mon; Aug

€€€

Naturally, espadon (swordfish) is on the menu, along with a great deal of other seafood. Traditional dishes include

mushrooms stuffed with snails and garlic butter, meat with rosemary sauce and aubergine (eggplant) with smoked salmon and Parmesan.

6E ARRONDISSEMENT
● L'Horizon

120 rue de Rennes, 75006 **Map** 14A5

01 45 48 03 20

MC, V €€

A true Parisian bistro complete with a collection of old advertisements. Provides tasty fare: pepper steak, large salads, tarte Tatin (p191) and chocolate mousse. Ice cream and pancakes in the afternoon.

6E ARRONDISSEMENT
● Marmitte et Cassolette

157 bd Montparnasse, 75006 **Map** 15D5

01 43 26 26 53

FAX 01 43 26 43 40

MC, V ● Sun, Sat L; last 2 wks Aug €€€

Cassoulet (p326), confit de canard (p326), foie gras and snail casserole are superbly prepared at this bistro.

6E ARRONDISSEMENT
● Polidor

41 rue Monsieur Prince, 75006

Map 14B5

01 43 26 95 34

FAX 01 43 26 22 79

€

Once frequented by Verlaine and Rimbaud, this is bohemian Paris incarnate. Traditional cuisine at rock-bottom prices. Grilled steak, daube de boeuf (p401) and Marengo veal (slow cooked with tomatoes). Various tarts such as chocolate, lemon or apple.

6E ARRONDISSEMENT
● Procope

13 rue de l'Ancienne Comédie, 75006

Map 14B5

01 40 46 79 00

FAX 01 40 46 79 09

www.procope.com

AE, DC, MC, V €€€€

Opened in 1686, Paris's oldest café welcomed literary and political figures such as Voltaire and Diderot. Nowadays, it's still a hub for the intelligentsia, who sit alongside those curious about this

historical monument. Coq au vin (p217) is the speciality. Shellfish platters, too.

6E ARRONDISSEMENT
● Restaurant Collation

17 rue Grégoire Tours, 75006 **Map** 14B5

01 46 33 50 45

DC, MC, V ● Sat L €

At the heart of St-Germain-des-Prés, this unpretentious little bistro knows its classics, such as onion soup or thick steak with French fries. No frills, but it's difficult to ask for more at such prices.

6E ARRONDISSEMENT
● Restaurant Orestias

4 rue Grégoire de Tours, 75006

Map 14B5

01 43 54 62 01

● Sun €

For French-Greek cuisine: meats from the grill or specialities such as octopus, Greek yogurt and baklava. Bargain prices for simple food since 1928.

6E ARRONDISSEMENT
● Salon de Thé Gnaouia

18 rue Princesse, 75006 **Map** 14A5

01 43 29 05 50

FAX 01 43 29 05 50

MC, V €€

Chic ethnic venue with a large selection of interesting tagines: lamb with prunes or artichoke, and chicken with glazed lemons or raisins and honey. For dessert, try the Moroccan pastries.

6E ARRONDISSEMENT
● Strapontin Café

12 rue Princesse, 75006 **Map** 14A5

01 43 26 79 95

agcafe@hotmail.com

AE, DC, MC, V

€€

Red walls, chandeliers and strapontins (theatre seats) give a baroque feel. Classics such as steak tartare, along with peppered ostrich and a large choice of exotic salads with ingredients like prawns and pineapple.

6E ARRONDISSEMENT
● Vagenende

142 bd St-Germain, 75006 **Map** 14A5

01 43 26 68 18

FAX 01 40 51 73 38
W www.vagenende.fr
AE, DC, MC, V
● 3 wks Aug 📋 €€

Art Nouveau brasserie. The cuisine is also evocative of a bygone era: spiced suckling pig and pepper steak, alongside classic platters of shellfish.

6E ARRONDISSEMENT
● Villa Médici chez Napoli

11 bis rue St-Placide, 75006 **Map** 14C4
01 42 22 51 96
FAX 01 45 48 47 57
W www.villa-medici.com
AE, DC, V ● Sun 📋 €€

With its trompe l'oeil frescoes, the dining room may seem a bit kitsch but, when it comes to food, it's the real thing: pizzas, pasta and some fine Italian dishes such as scallops with balsamic vinegar. Comprehensive selection of wines. An institution established in 1975.

6E ARRONDISSEMENT
● Yugaraj

14 rue Dauphine, 75006 **Map** 14B5
01 43 26 44 91
FAX 01 46 33 50 77
W www.yugaraj.com
AE, DC, MC, V ● Mon, Thu L; Aug
📋 €€€

Some of Paris's best Indian food: chicken in mint, cardamom and almond cream, great tandooris and desserts such as thène (Ceylon tea-flavoured cream).

6E ARRONDISSEMENT
● Ze Kitchen Galerie

4 rue des Grands Augustins, 75006
Map 14B5
01 44 32 00 32
FAX 01 44 32 00 33
AE, DC, MC, V ● Sun, Sat L
📋 €€€

Trendy place with sleek lines, modern art and an open kitchen. Fusion food that bans butter and cream in favour of herbs and spices: try poached plaice served with vegetable tempura.

7E ARRONDISSEMENT
● Au Sauvignon

80 rue des Sts-Pères, 75007 **Map** 14A5
01 45 48 49 02

MC, V ● Sun 📋 €€

This restaurant revolves around wine. Walls are plastered with posters of the beverage, and the wine list boasts fine vintages. Savoury snacks such as cheese or smoked salmon toast accompany. Sweets include puff pastry with apple, plum or other seasonal fruit.

7E ARRONDISSEMENT
● Casual Restaurant

29 rue Surcouf, 75007 **Map** 14B3
01 45 50 36 20
FAX 01 45 50 36 75
AE, MC, V ● Sun, Sat L; 3 wks
Aug 📋 €€

A still life by Miguel Macaya, of a table subdued by a dimly lit background, is central to the sober interior here. Stir-fried chicken with sesame seeds and honey, saffron-scented pike and stir-fried fruits flambéed with Armagnac are the stars on the menu.

7E ARRONDISSEMENT
● Chez Françoise

Aérogare des Invalides, 75007 **Map** 14C3
01 47 05 49 03
FAX 01 45 51 96 20
W www.chezfrancoise.com
AE, DC, MC, V 📋 €€€

Art Deco meets minimalism at this restaurant. Catalan-style cod with olive-oil mashed potatoes precedes desserts such as an assortment of cream pots (praline, chocolate and vanilla).

7E ARRONDISSEMENT
■ Eiffel Park Hôtel

17 bis rue Amélie, 75007 **Map** 14B3
01 45 55 10 01
FAX 01 47 05 28 68
W www.eiffelpark.com
AE, DC, MC, V ● (36) €€€€

Charming hotel offering individually designed guestrooms: intricate wallpaper in some, exotic furniture in others. On the top floor is a breakfast terrace.

7E ARRONDISSEMENT
● Ferme St-Simon

6 rue de St-Simon, 75007 **Map** 14C3
01 45 48 35 74
FAX 01 40 49 07 31
W www.fermestsimon.com

AE, DC, MC, V ● Sun, Sat L; 1st 2 wks Aug 📋 €€€€

Relaxed country-style house in the heart of a chic neighbourhood. In autumn, game is on offer. Lighter fare the rest of the year, with Mediterranean food such as grilled fish with stuffed courgette (zucchini) and prawns on an onion tart.

7E ARRONDISSEMENT
■ Grand Hôtel Levêque

29 rue Clerc, 75007 **Map** 14B3
01 47 05 49 15
FAX 01 45 50 49 36
W www.hotel-leveque.com
AE, MC, V ● (50) €€€

On a street with a quaint fruit-and-vegetable market, close to the Eiffel Tower. The great location isn't the only attraction: guestrooms are well kept.

7E ARRONDISSEMENT
■ Hôtel Lenox

9 rue de l'Université, 75007 **Map** 15D3
01 42 96 10 95
FAX 01 42 61 52 83
W www.lenoxsaintgermain.com
AE, DC, MC, V ● (34) €€€€

Tribute paid to the 1930s and days of luxurious travel, which finds its peak at the Lenox Bar featuring club armchairs. Guestrooms are plush.

7E ARRONDISSEMENT
● Jules Verne

Tour Eiffel, 75007 **Map** 14A3
01 45 55 61 44
FAX 01 45 05 29 41
AE, DC, MC, V 📋 €€€€€

On the second floor of the Eiffel tower, and with breathtaking views. Rabbit stuffed with truffle and foie gras and langoustine tartare are just two of the chef's classic dishes.

7E ARRONDISSEMENT
▲ La Cantine des Gourmets at Hôtel La Bourdonnais

111–113 ave de la Bourdonnais, 75007
Map 14B4
01 47 05 47 96
FAX 01 45 51 09 29
AE, DC, MC, V 📋 €€€€€
● (60) €€€€

The interior is average but the cooking

is unexpected. Gastronomic cuisine such as prawns with crab meat and coral dressing. Guestrooms are well equipped.

7E ARRONDISSEMENT
● L'Arpège

84 rue de Varenne, 75007 **Map** 14C4

☎ 01 45 51 47 33

FAX 01 44 18 98 39

w www.alain-passard.com

🍴 AE, DC, MC, V ⬤ Sun, Sat

ⵏⵏ €€€€€

Contemporary and elegant restaurant located near the Rodin museum. Chef Alain Passard creates masterpieces from simple vegetables picked from his own garden, although dishes are not exclusively vegetarian. Cherry tomatoes served with a dozen spices make a unique dessert.

7E ARRONDISSEMENT
● Le Bellecour

22 rue Surcouf, 75007 **Map** 14B3

☎ 01 45 51 46 93

FAX 01 45 50 30 11

🍴 AE, DC, MC, V ⬤ Sun, Sat l; Aug

ⵏⵏ €€€

Named after Lyon's main square, this restaurant serves the specialities of that city: tablier de sapeur (p368) and pike quenelle, alongside less hearty and more creative dishes such as Challans duckling with lime and ginger.

7E ARRONDISSEMENT
● Le Divellec

107 rue de l'Université, 75007 **Map** 14C3

☎ 01 45 51 91 96

FAX 01 45 51 31 75

🍴 AE, DC, MC, V ⬤ Sun, Sat; mid-Jul–Aug, 1 wk around Christmas

ⵏⵏ €€€€€

One of the best seafood restaurants in Paris, with a refined atmosphere. Great barely cooked oysters with seaweed and pressed lobster are the house specialities.

7E ARRONDISSEMENT
● Le Récamier

4 rue Récamier, 75007 **Map** 14A5

☎ 01 45 48 86 58

FAX 01 42 22 84 76

w www.lerecamier.com

🍴 AE, DC, MC, V

⬤ Sun **ⵏⵏ** €€€€

Serving Burgundian specialities such as boeuf bourguignon (p217), pike mousse and Grand Marnier soufflé. Tucked away in a pedestrian street, its terrace is one of the best in Paris.

7E ARRONDISSEMENT
● Le Violon d'Ingres

135 rue St-Dominique, 75007 **Map** 14B3

☎ 01 45 55 15 05

FAX 01 45 55 48 42

w www.leviolondingres.com

🍴 AE, MC, V ⬤ Sun, Mon

ⵏⵏ €€€€€

After working at luxury hotels such as the Ritz and Crillon, Chef Christian Constant wanted to imprint his very personal touch: a dining room inspired by the work of Ingres, and a creative cuisine, with signature dishes such as grilled pigeon with vegetables.

7E ARRONDISSEMENT
● Les Olivades

41 ave Ségur, 75007 **Map** 14B4

☎ 01 47 83 70 09

FAX 01 42 73 04 75

🍴 DC, MC, V ⬤ Sun, Mon l, Sat l; Aug **ⵏⵏ** €€€€

This chic restaurant makes good use of olive oil, featured in dishes such as lemon and thyme lamb with potato gratin and scampi served with a papaya marmalade. Comprehensive wine list with rare vintages.

7E ARRONDISSEMENT
● Nabuchodonosor

6 ave Bosquet, 75007 **Map** 14B3

☎ 01 45 56 97 26

FAX 01 45 56 98 44

w www.nabuchodonosor.net

🍴 AE, MC, V ⬤ Sun, Sat l; 1st 3 wks Aug **ⵏⵏ** €€€

This elegant bistro is an epicurean's paradise. Excellent regional cuisine: roasted tuna with ratatouille (p400) and pan-fried foie gras with a sherry-flavoured duckling marmalade.

7E ARRONDISSEMENT
● Sip Babylone

46 bd Raspail, 75007 **Map** 14A5

☎ 01 45 48 87 17

FAX 01 45 49 91 87

@ sallysa@club-internet.fr

🍴 MC, V ⬤ D **ⵏⵏ** €

Close to Le Bon Marché, great for a tasty shopping break. Tea and pastries are served all day long in the elaborate dining room. For lunch, try the cheese platters, bacon and Parmesan salad or a plate of smoked salmon, taramasalata and aubergine (eggplant).

7E ARRONDISSEMENT
▲ Thoumieux

79 rue St-Dominique, 75007 **Map** 14B3

☎ 01 47 05 49 75

FAX 01 47 05 36 96

w www.thoumieux.com

🍴 AE, MC, V

ⵏⵏ €€€ 🍽 (10) €€€€

Dazzling 1930s interior with mirrors reflecting the velvet wall seats. A southwestern menu: confit de canard (p326) to Andalucian gazpacho and cassoulet (p373). Bright bedrooms are quietly contemporary.

8E ARRONDISSEMENT
● Asian

30 ave George V, 75008 **Map** 14B2

☎ 01 56 89 11 00

FAX 01 56 89 11 01

w www.asian.fr

🍴 AE, DC, MC, V ⬤ Sat l **ⵏⵏ** €€€

Modern and creative Asian cuisine: "fight of the dragons" (very delicate lemon-scented raw tuna and salmon) or the more traditional chao chao pork (marinated then caramelized). DJ, trendy zen-chic interior complete with small bamboo forest and the work of Asian artists on display.

8E ARRONDISSEMENT
● B*fly

49–51 ave George V, 75008

Map 14B2

☎ 01 53 67 84 60

FAX 01 53 67 84 67

🍴 AE, DC, MC, V **ⵏⵏ** €€€

Urban loft chic in a former newspaper depot, offering global flavours. From Asian cooking such as sushi or tuna with sesame seeds to tried-and-true French dishes such as beef with morels. The strawberry tiramisu is a classic.

8E ARRONDISSEMENT
● Brasserie la Lorraine

2 pl des Ternes, 75008 **Map** 14A1

C 01 56 21 22 00

FAX 01 56 21 22 09

W www.brasserielalorraine.com

E AE, DC, MC, V **❚❚** €€€€

Shiny brass fixtures, uniformed waiters and red wall seats: this brasserie exudes a chic retro feel. First and foremost a shellfish specialist (with take-away available). Also brasserie fare such as pan-fried calf's liver with cider vinegar and beef entrecôte.

8E ARRONDISSEMENT
● Buddha Bar

8 rue Boissy d'Anglas, 75008 **Map** 14C2

C 01 53 05 90 00

FAX 01 53 05 90 09

W www.buddhabar.com

E AE, DC, MC, V ● Sun L, Sat L

❚❚ €€€€

A temple for the fashion crowd. Pan-Asian cuisine: Thai chicken salad, Japanese sushi and tempuras, and Korean-style frogs' legs. Jet-set party atmosphere in the evenings.

8E ARRONDISSEMENT
▲ Café Faubourg at Hôtel le Faubourg Sofitel

15 rue Boissy d'Anglas, 75008 **Map** 14C2

C 01 44 94 14 24

FAX 01 44 94 14 28

W www.sofitel.com

E AE, DC, MC, V ● Aug

❚❚ €€€€ 🍽 (174) €€€€€

Slightly baroque, comfortable dining room. Southwestern flavours: piquillos (peppers) casserole, grilled tuna and chocolate cake with pistachio-flavoured cream. Upmarket guestrooms.

8E ARRONDISSEMENT
● Cap Vernet

82 ave Marceau, 75008 **Map** 14A2

C 01 47 20 20 40

FAX 01 47 20 95 36

W www.guysavoy.fr

E AE, DC, MC, V ● Sun, Sat L

❚❚ €€€

Nautical decor with a brass and wood interior. Celebrated chef Guy Savoy serves up refined, exotic fish dishes: ahi

in vanilla, cod with celery mousse and anise-flavoured sea bass.

8E ARRONDISSEMENT
● Caviar Kaspia

17 pl de la Madeleine, 75008 **Map** 14C2

C 01 42 65 33 32

FAX 01 42 65 66 26

W www.kaspia.fr

E AE, DC, MC, V ● Sun; 2 wks Aug

❚❚ €€€€€

Located above the eponymous boutique, this small dining room is dedicated to the tiniest and finest of delicacies: caviar. Other savoury tastes include smoked salmon served with blinis, foie gras and a few Russian specialities.

8E ARRONDISSEMENT
● Chez Catherine

3 rue Berryer, 75008 **Map** 14B2

C 01 40 76 01 40

FAX 01 40 76 03 96

E AE, DC, MC, V ● Sun, Sat; 1st wk May, Aug, Dec, public holidays

❚❚ €€€€

Catherine Guerraz prepares beautiful, experimental cuisine such as tuna with mango and mushrooms, veal chops and kidneys with Parmesan cream and a good assortment of red berry desserts.

8E ARRONDISSEMENT
● Chiberta

3 rue Arsène Houssaye, 75008 **Map** 14B2

C 01 53 53 42 00

FAX 01 45 62 85 08

W www.lechiberta.com

E AE, DC, MC, V ● Sun, Sat L; Aug

❚❚ €€€€€

The intimate and minimalist interior contrasts with the complex cuisine, including dishes such as black truffle cooked in Champagne and served with toast.

8E ARRONDISSEMENT
● Copenhague

142 ave des Champs-Elysées, 75008 **Map** 14A2

C 01 44 13 86 26

FAX 01 44 13 89 44

W www.restaurantfloradanica.com

E AE, DC, MC, V ● Sun, Sat; Aug, public holidays **❚❚** €€€€€

Located inside the House of Denmark, this restaurant is a proud ambassador. Danish interior design of sleek lines and vibrant colours, with Nordic gastronomy on the menu. Salmon, reindeer and even rodgrod (red berry jelly).

8E ARRONDISSEMENT
● Dragons Elysées

11 rue de Berri, 75008 **Map** 14B2

C 01 42 89 85 10

FAX 01 45 63 04 97

E AE, DC, MC, V **❚❚** €€€

A gigantic aquarium serves as the floor at this original Asian eatery. Thai lemongrass and prawn salad and Chinese beef with spicy sauce are on the menu.

8E ARRONDISSEMENT
● Farnesina

9 rue Boissy d'Anglas, 75008 **Map** 14C2

C 01 42 66 65 57

FAX 01 42 66 69 85

E AE, DC, MC, V ● Sun, Sat L; 2 wks Aug **❚❚** €€€€

Elegant Florentine Renaissance-style decor with marble tables and elaborate frescoes. Carefully sourced mozzarella, truffle risotto (one of the specialities) and inventive combinations for pastas.

8E ARRONDISSEMENT
● Fermette Marbeuf 1900

5 rue Marbeuf, 75008 **Map** 14B2

C 01 53 23 08 00

FAX 01 53 23 08 09

W www.fermettemarbeuf.com

E AE, DC, MC, V **❚❚** €€€€

Popular for its Art Nouveau interior as much as for chef Gilbert Isaac's fine dishes such as steak with morels and olive duck. For dessert, the crêpes suzette and Grand Marnier soufflé are considered to be classics.

8E ARRONDISSEMENT
● Findi

24 ave George V, 75008 **Map** 14B2

C 01 47 20 14 78

FAX 01 47 20 10 08

W www.findi.net

E AE, DC, MC, V

❚❚ €€€

Fine Italian cuisine served in a modern-style palazzo: salmon carpaccio with pesto

---

● Restaurant ■ Hotel ▲ Hotel / Restaurant

and pine nuts, chicken lasagne with truffle butter and black pasta with scampi and tomatoes. Takeaway available at the deli counter. Brunch on Sundays.

8E ARRONDISSEMENT
● Flora

36 ave George V, 75008 **Map** 14B2

📞 01 40 70 10 49

FAX 01 47 20 52 87

💳 AE, MC, V

🌙 Sun, Sat L; 2 wks Aug

🍴 €€€€€

Gastronomic cuisine with a Provençal influence: lobster ravioli in lemon broth and sole with truffle butter and chestnut purée. The period furnishings mixed with a contemporary atmosphere are in tune with the quiet modernity of the cuisine.

8E ARRONDISSEMENT
● Flora Danica

142 ave des Champs-Elysées, 75008 **Map** 14A2

📞 01 44 13 86 26

FAX 01 44 13 89 44

🌐 www.restaurantfloradanica.com

💳 AE, DC, MC, V

🍴 €€€€

On the ground floor of the House of Denmark, this venue is more relaxed and less pricey than Copenhague upstairs. Danish specialities such as grilled salmon and exquisite strawberries with mulled wine.

8E ARRONDISSEMENT
● Fouquet's

99 ave des Champs-Elysées, 75008 **Map** 14B2

📞 01 47 23 50 00

FAX 01 47 23 50 55

💳 AE, DC, MC, V 🍴 €€€€€

Established in 1899, with a plush Belle Epoque interior. Classic brasserie fare includes fish with baked potato and tartar sauce, and more elaborate dishes such as scampi with asparagus and mushrooms served with a green tea prawn sauce. The terrace gives onto France's most famous avenue.

8E ARRONDISSEMENT
● Garnier

111 rue St-Lazare, 75008 **Map** 14C2

📞 01 43 87 50 40

FAX 01 40 08 06 93

💳 AE, DC, MC, V

🌙 Aug 🍴 €€€

Large shellfish platters and grilled fish as well as duck and grilled lamb. Stylish, Art Deco dining room.

8E ARRONDISSEMENT
■ Hôtel Franklin Roosevelt

18 rue Clément Marot, 75008 **Map** 14B2

📞 01 53 57 49 50

FAX 01 53 57 49 59

🌐 www.hroosevelt.com

💳 AE, MC, V

🛏 (48) €€€€€

Chic interior throughout, complete with period furniture, old paintings and a fireplace in the lounge. The bedrooms are generally very large. Cosy atmosphere at the Lord's bar, though the cafés of the Champs-Elysées are also nearby.

8E ARRONDISSEMENT
■ Hôtel Queen Mary

9 rue Greffulhe, 75008 **Map** 14C2

📞 01 42 66 40 50

FAX 01 42 66 94 92

🌐 www.hotelqueenmary.com

💳 AE, DC, MC, V

🛏 (36) €€€€€

Hotel famous for its quaint, old-England atmosphere. The colourful guestrooms are well equipped.

8E ARRONDISSEMENT
● La Cantine du Faubourg

105 rue du Faubourg St-Honoré, 75008 **Map** 14C2

📞 01 42 56 22 22

FAX 01 42 56 35 71

🌐 www.lacantine.com

💳 AE, DC, MC, V

🌙 Sun L, Sat L

🍴 €€€€

Big screens show conceptual art, and the kitchen serves classics such as pot-au-feu, or novel creations such as cumin and pumpkin cappuccino.

8E ARRONDISSEMENT
● La Maison du Caviar

21 rue Quentin Bauchart, 75008 Map 14B2

📞 01 47 23 53 43

FAX 01 47 20 87 26

🌐 www.caviarvolga.fr

💳 AE, MC, V 🍴 €€€€€

Run by caviar importer, Volga, in a prime location off the Champs Elysées. All sorts of caviar feature, as well as gourmet versions of Eastern European dishes such as lamb skewers with aubergine (eggplant).

8E ARRONDISSEMENT
● La Poele d'Or

37 rue de Miromesnil, 75008 **Map** 14C2

📞 01 42 65 78 60

FAX 01 49 24 96 17

💳 AE, MC, V

🌙 Sun, Sat; Aug, last wk Dec, public holidays 🍴 €€€€€

Modern-style, elegant bistro. Fine cuisine with subtle Provençal accents. Pan-fried red mullet with a basil-squid purée is a typical springtime dish; mushroom wheat risotto in winter.

8E ARRONDISSEMENT
● Ladurée

16 rue Royale, 75008 **Map** 14C2

📞 01 42 60 21 79

FAX 01 49 27 01 95

🌐 www.laduree.fr

💳 AE, DC, MC, V

🌙 mid-Jul–mid-Aug: Sun 🍴 €

Elegant tearoom, famous for its Renaissance-style interior and for its macaroons, which come in all sorts of inventive flavours such as anise, caramel, chestnut, lime and basil.

8E ARRONDISSEMENT
● L'Alsace

39 ave des Champs-Elysées, 75008 **Map** 14B2

📞 01 53 93 97 00

FAX 01 53 93 97 09

🌐 www.restaurantalsace.com

💳 AE, DC, MC, V 🍴 €€€€

Round-the-clock Alsatian food on Paris's most famous avenue. On the menu: sauerkraut, spaetzle and Alsatian wine. Stunning wooden brasserie interior.

8E ARRONDISSEMENT
● L'Angle du Faubourg

195 rue Faubourg St-Honoré, 75008 **Map** 14C2

📞 01 40 74 20 20

FAX 01 40 74 20 21

W www.taillevent.com

AE, DC, MC, V ● Sun, Sat; Aug; late Jul–late Aug ¶¶ €€€€

An offshoot of the renowned Taillevent, modernity is the key here. Classics are reinterpreted using California-style cooking, resulting in dishes such as five-spice rare tuna. Stylish, minimalist decor featuring abstract paintings.

8E ARRONDISSEMENT
● L'Appart

9 rue du Colisée, 75008 **Map** 14B2

☎ 01 53 75 42 00

FAX 01 53 75 42 09

W www.l-appart.com

AE, MC, V ¶¶ €€€

Paintings and a library set this eatery apart. Great classics such as veal with potato gratin and mustard sauce. Excellent Sunday brunch.

8E ARRONDISSEMENT
● Lasserre

17 ave Franklin Roosevelt, 75008
Map 14B2

☎ 01 43 59 53 43

FAX 01 45 63 72 23

AE, DC, MC, V ● Sun, Mon–Wed L, Sat L ¶¶ €€€€€

Chef Jean-Louis Nomicos updates the classics: sea bass with glazed lemons in the spring and macaroni stuffed with a truffle and foie gras mousse in the autumn. Neo-classical interior.

8E ARRONDISSEMENT
● L'Atelier Renault

53 ave des Champs-Elysées, 75008
Map 14B2

☎ 01 49 53 70 70

FAX 01 49 53 70 71

W www.atelier-renault.com

AE, DC, MC, V ¶¶ €€€

A huge space showcasing Renault's latest cars as well as fine, inventive cuisine such as crisped salmon with spinach, lamb tagine and chicken au gratin.

8E ARRONDISSEMENT
● Laurent

41 ave Gabriel, 75008 **Map** 14B2

☎ 01 42 25 00 39

FAX 01 45 62 45 21

W www.le-laurent.com

AE, DC, MC, V ● Sun, Sat L
¶¶ €€€€€

Restaurant nestled in the Champs-Elysées gardens. Such a setting does credit to Alain Pégouret's sophisticated classics and unusual creations: spider crab in jelly or braised veal with chanterelles, ceps and asparagus.

8E ARRONDISSEMENT
● L'Avenue

41 ave Montaigne, 75008 **Map** 14B2

☎ 01 40 70 14 91

FAX 01 40 70 91 97

AE, DC, MC, V ¶¶ €€€€

Nestled between couture houses, with a designer chic interior. Extremely trendy cuisine includes lettuce and crab mille-feuille, crispy duck, roast prawns and a divine chocolate gâteau.

8E ARRONDISSEMENT
● Le Bistrot du Sommelier

97 bd Haussmann, 75008 **Map** 14C2

☎ 01 42 65 24 85

FAX 01 53 75 23 23

@ bistrot-du-sommelier@noos.fr

AE, MC, V ● Sun; Aug, Dec
¶¶ €€€€€

Excellent wine service from Philippe Faure-Brac, voted World's Best Sommelier in 1992. Inventive cuisine such as roasted quail with apple crumble.

8E ARRONDISSEMENT
● Le Boeuf sur le Toit

34 rue du Colisée, 75008 **Map** 14B2

☎ 01 53 93 65 55

FAX 01 53 96 02 32

W www.flobrasseries.com

AE, DC, MC, V

¶¶ €€€

This venue exemplifies the classic Paris Art Deco brasserie. The changing menu can include sole meunière, snails, foie gras and crème brûlée.

8E ARRONDISSEMENT
▲ Le Bristol at Hôtel Bristol

112 rue du Faubourg St-Honoré, 75008
Map 14C2

☎ 01 53 43 43 00

FAX 01 53 43 43 01

W www.lebristolparis.com

AE, DC, MC, V

¶¶ €€€€€ ◇ (175) €€€€€

In a luxury hotel, elegant dining and exquisite cuisine: chicken cooked in a wine sauce and macaroni stuffed with foie gras, truffle and artichoke. Period furniture and chandeliers in the rooms. State-of-the-art fitness centre.

8E ARRONDISSEMENT
▲ Le Cinq at George V

31 ave George V, 75008 **Map** 14B2

☎ 01 49 52 70 00

FAX 01 49 52 71 81

W www.fourseasons.com

AE, DC, MC, V

¶¶ €€€€€ ◇ (245) €€€€€

Inside one of the grandest hotels in Paris, an exquisite and high-end dining room serving langoustines fricassée, lobster stew and roasted duck with horseradish mousse. Luxurious rooms.

8E ARRONDISSEMENT
▲ Le W at Hôtel Warwick

5 rue de Berri, 75008 **Map** 14B2

☎ 01 45 63 14 11

FAX 01 43 59 00 98

W www.warwickparis.com

AE, DC, MC, V ● Sun, Sat; Aug
¶¶ €€€€€ ◇ (147) €€€€€

In the dining room, modern art and sleek lines. The chef plays inventively with seasonal produce such as roasted John Dory with artichoke and glazed lemons. Original touches such as zebra print in the guestrooms.

8E ARRONDISSEMENT
● L'Envue

39 rue Boissy d'Anglas, 75008 **Map** 14C2

☎ 01 42 65 10 49

FAX 01 40 17 09 28

AE, DC, MC, V ● Sun
¶¶ €€€€

Urban chic interior with waitresses wearing corset-like uniforms. Traditional cuisine: pastis-flavoured sea bass, veal medallions and crème brulées.

8E ARRONDISSEMENT
▲ Les Ambassadeurs at Hôtel Crillon

10 pl de la Concorde, 75008 **Map** 14C3

☎ 01 44 71 16 16

FAX 01 44 71 15 02

● Restaurant ■ Hotel ▲ Hotel / Restaurant

W www.crillon.com

AE, DC, MC, V

€€€€€ 🍷 (147) €€€€€

Formal dress is required if you wish to dine in the 18th-century ballroom here. The menu provides a regional tour of France: roast pigeon from the Vendée, lamb with Niçoise-style vegetables, or duckling with pear and apple chutney. Guestrooms reflect the pinnacle of glamour and indulgence.

8E ARRONDISSEMENT
● L'Obélisque at Hôtel Crillon
10 pl Concorde, 75008 **Map** 14C3

01 44 71 15 15

FAX 01 44 71 15 02

AE, DC, MC, V

● Aug €€€€

The second and less formal restaurant at the 18th-century luxury hotel Crillon. Essentially traditional cuisine: veal kidney fricassée and rabbit with apples and prunes as well as some lighter, more exotic dishes like prawns roasted and spiced with ginger.

8E ARRONDISSEMENT
● Lucas Carton
9 pl de la Madeleine, 75008 **Map** 14C2

01 42 65 22 90

FAX 01 42 65 06 23

W www.lucascarton.com

AE, DC, MC, V

● Sun, Mon L, Sat L; 1 wk Feb, Aug, Christmas–New Year's Eve

€€€€€

Chef Alain Senderens' signature is the perfect combination of food and wines: Banyuls accompanies steamed duck with ginger and mango. Located in an Art Nouveau masterpiece.

8E ARRONDISSEMENT
● Luna
69 rue du Rocher, 75008 **Map** 14C1

01 42 93 77 61

FAX 01 40 08 02 44

AE, MC, V ● Sun; Aug

€€€€

Renowned for its pioneering seafood dishes: fish with ginger steamed in a banana leaf, lobster stew with smoked ham. The baba (yeast cake), from a Zanzibari recipe, is one of Paris's best.

8E ARRONDISSEMENT
● Maison Blanche
15 ave Montaigne, 75008 **Map** 14B2

01 47 23 55 99

FAX 01 47 20 09 56

W www.maison-blanche.fr

AE, MC, V ● Sun L, Sat L

€€€€€

A prestigious location and fabulous panorama from the roof of the Théâtre des Champs-Elysées. Stylish, novel cuisine, including tuna with asparagus and olive-stuffed lamb with aubergine (eggplant) gratin.

8E ARRONDISSEMENT
● Man Ray
34 rue Marbeuf, 75008 **Map** 14B2

01 56 88 36 36

FAX 01 42 25 36 36

W www.manray.info

MC, V ● L

€€€€

French-Asian fusion in a Buddha-filled room: citrus and ginger tuna and wok-fried scampi with oyster mushrooms. Great selection of sushi.

8E ARRONDISSEMENT
● Marcande
52 rue Miromesnil, 75008 **Map** 14C2

01 42 65 19 14

FAX 01 42 65 76 85

W www.marcande.com

AE, V ● Sun, Sat L; 2 wks Aug, 3rd wk Dec–1st wk Jan €€€€

The patio, an oasis of peace and green-ery, is the sought-after seating here. On the thoughtful menu are lime-flavoured fish tagine, Normandy veal pan-fried with mushrooms and peaches poached in lemon verbena.

8E ARRONDISSEMENT
● Maxim's
3 rue Royale, 75008 **Map** 14C2

01 42 65 27 94

FAX 01 42 65 30 26

W www.maxims-de-paris.com

AE, DC, MC, V ● Sun, Mon, Sat L

€€€€€

A monument of Belle Epoque design founded in 1893. Perfectly mastered classics include lamb and foie gras with truffle sauce, roast duck and pea purée

and sole meunière. Refined atmosphere with a touch of celebrity – owner-designer Pierre Cardin likes to gather his VIP friends around a table here.

8E ARRONDISSEMENT
▲ Pierre Gagnaire at Hôtel Balzac
6 rue Balzac, 75008 **Map** 14B2

01 58 36 12 50

FAX 01 58 36 12 51

W www.pierre-gagnaire.com

AE, DC, MC, V ● Sun L, Sat L, Aug: L, Sat D

€€€€€ 🍷 (56) €€€€€

"Respectful of the past, but looking to the future" is how chef Pierre Gagnaire defines his approach. On the menu, spider crab with asparagus and beetroot topped with caviar and white radish. Minimalist interior punctuated with contemporary works of art.

8E ARRONDISSEMENT
▲ Plaza Athénée
25 ave Montaigne, 75008 **Map** 14B2

01 53 67 65 00

FAX 01 53 67 65 12

W www.alain-ducasse.com

AE, DC, MC, V ● Sun, Mon–Wed L, Sat; mid-Jul–mid-Aug

€€€€€ 🍷 (143) €€€€€

At the heart of a four-star hotel, chef Alain Ducasse's exquisite restaurant. Truffles and foie gras, langoustines with caviar and lemon or vanilla chocolate. Exceptional wine list. Art Deco and classically styled guestrooms.

8E ARRONDISSEMENT
● Poona Lounge
25 rue Marbeuf, 75008 **Map** 14B2

01 40 70 09 99

FAX 01 40 70 09 88

@ poonalounge@wanadoo.fr

AE, DC, MC, V ● Sun L, Sat L

€€

Steps from the Champs-Elysées, a stylish French-Asian fusion restaurant. On the menu are tuna with sesame seeds, fish in a banana leaf and chicken skewers with cheese naan bread.

8E ARRONDISSEMENT
▲ Relais Plaza at Hôtel Plaza Athénée

25 ave Montaigne, 75008 **Map** 14B2

☎ 01 53 67 64 00

FAX 01 53 67 66 66

W www.plaza-athenee-paris.com

✆ AE, DC, MC, V ● Aug

🍴 €€€€ 🍽 (188) €€€€€

Luxurious experience in a beautiful Art Deco setting. On the menu are sole meunière and beef in a Béarnaise sauce with fried potatoes. Guestrooms combine 18th-century-style furnishings and 21st-century amenities.

8E ARRONDISSEMENT
● **Rue Balzac**

3 rue Balzac, 75008 **Map** 14B2

☎ 01 53 89 90 91

FAX 01 53 89 90 94

✆ AE, MC, V

● Sun L, Sat L; 2 wks Aug

🍴 €€€€

Chef Michel Rostang and rock singer Johnny Hallyday have joined forces to create this colourful, baroque venue serving grilled fish, olive pasta and millefeuille made of layers of crab and dried aubergines (eggplant).

8E ARRONDISSEMENT
▲ **Senso at Hôtel La Trémoille**

14 rue de la Trémoille, 75008 **Map** 14B2

☎ 01 56 52 14 00

FAX 01 40 70 01 08

W www.hotel-tremoille.com

✆ AE, DC, MC, V

🍴 €€€€ 🍽 (88) €€€€€

Sir Terence Conran's second Parisian venture. Inventive cuisine: braised sardines with piperade, crab with avocado cream and quail's eggs and grilled lamb with basil and crunchy vegetables. The lounge bar serves lighter fare. Contemporary, stylish lodgings.

8E ARRONDISSEMENT
● **Spicy Restaurant**

8 ave Franklin Roosevelt, 75008 **Map** 14B2

☎ 01 56 59 62 59

FAX 01 56 59 62 50

W www.spicyrestaurant.com

✆ AE, MC, V 🍴 €€€

French cooking using seasonings from around the globe: sea bass with caramelized fennel and star-anise cream.

8E ARRONDISSEMENT
● **Spoon Food and Wine**

14 rue de Marignan, 75008 **Map** 14B2

☎ 01 40 76 34 44

FAX 01 40 76 34 37

W www.spoon.tm.fr

✆ AE, DC, MC, V ● Sun, Sat; mid-Jul–mid-Aug 🍴 €€€€€

Another of superchef Alain Ducasse's places. Diners compose their own meal by choosing which sauce and vegetables accompany their choice of meat or fish. One possibility is grilled tuna with Thai peanut sauce. Vibrant modern interior.

8E ARRONDISSEMENT
● **Stella Maris**

4 rue Arsène Houssaye, 75008 **Map** 14B2

☎ 01 42 89 16 22

FAX 01 42 89 16 01

✆ AE, DC, MC, V ● Sun, Mon L, Sat L

🍴 €€€€€

Chef Tateru Yoshino reinvents French classics, producing dishes such as slow-cooked tête-de-veau (p268).

8E ARRONDISSEMENT
● **Taillevent**

15 rue Lamennais, 75008 **Map** 14B2

☎ 01 44 95 15 01

FAX 01 42 25 95 18

✆ AE, DC, MC, V ● Sun, Sat; Aug

🍴 €€€€€

The pinnacle of French cuisine. Chef Alain Solivérès adds sophistication to the classics: try fennel-flavoured Brittany lobster pudding. Exceptional wine cellar.

8E ARRONDISSEMENT
● **Tanjia**

23 rue de Pontieux, 75008 **Map** 14B2

☎ 01 42 25 95 00

FAX 01 42 25 95 02

✆ AE, MC, V ● Sun L, Sat L

🍴 €€€€

Glossy Moroccan restaurant. Authentic food: the Tanjia tagine is cooked with 25 spices for no less than ten hours. After dinner, there is water-pipe smoking.

8E ARRONDISSEMENT
● **Villa Mauresque**

5 rue du Commandant Rivière, 75008 **Map** 14B2

☎ 01 42 25 16 69

W www.villamauresque.com

✆ AE, DC, MC, V ● Jul–Aug: Sun, Sat L 🍴 €€€

Minimalist Moroccan restaurant with Moorish accents. The cuisine includes a traditional assortment of starters to be shared with papita (bread), fish pastilla (in filo), and couscous with chicken, spicy sausage and meatballs.

8E ARRONDISSEMENT
● **Yvan**

1 bis rue Jean Mermoz, 75008 **Map** 14B2

☎ 01 43 59 18 40

FAX 01 42 89 30 95

✆ AE, DC, MC, V ● Sun, Sat L

🍴 €€€

Comfortable burgundy velvet armchairs and Flemish cuisine such as fish waterzooï (p79).

8E ARRONDISSEMENT
● **Zo**

13 rue Montalivet, 75008 **Map** 14C2

☎ 01 42 65 18 18

FAX 01 42 65 10 91

W www.restaurantzo.com

✆ AE, MC, V ● Sun L, Sat L; 1 wk Aug 🍴 €€

Two fine chefs, one French and one Japanese, create a global menu. Goat's cheese salad and sushi feature. Balinese wooden statues and rattan chairs evoke exotic distant lands.

9E ARRONDISSEMENT
● **Au Petit Riche**

25 rue Le Peletier, 75009 **Map** 15D2

☎ 01 47 70 68 68

FAX 01 48 24 10 79

W www.aupetitriche.com

✆ AE, DC, MC, V ● Sun, mid-Jul–Aug: Sat 🍴 €€€

The tiny dining rooms with turn-of-the-century decor are popular for business lunches and post-theatre dinners. The menu is split between traditional cuisine, such as pork with lentil salad and dishes of the moment like fish with Vouvray wine.

9E ARRONDISSEMENT
● **Barramundi**

3 rue Taitbout, 75009 **Map** 15D2

● Restaurant ■ Hotel ▲ Hotel / Restaurant

01 47 70 21 21
FAX 01 47 70 21 20
AE, DC, MC, V
Sun, Sat L; 1 wk mid-Aug
€€€€

The classy decor wavers between Asia and Africa and an exotic touch is evident in the Mediterranean cuisine. Roasted chicken with thyme, honey and wok-style vegetables and salmon with braised lettuce are highlights.

9E ARRONDISSEMENT
● Bistrot Papillon

6 rue Papillon, 75009 **Map** 15E2
01 47 70 90 03
FAX 01 48 24 05 59
AE, DC, MC, V Sun, Sat L, Oct–Apr: Sat D; 1 wk May, Aug
€€€

Elegant bistro. The menu is resolutely traditional but the chef does let his creativity run free: duck foie gras, veal kidneys with mushroom sauce, but also orange-flavoured sole and rum cake with summer berries.

9E ARRONDISSEMENT
● Charlot le Roi des Coquillages

12 pl du Clichy, 75009 **Map** 14C1
01 53 20 48 00
FAX 01 53 20 48 09
AE, DC, MC, V €€€€

Self-proclaimed "king of shellfish". Large oyster platters and other seafood specialities such as bouillabaisse (p401), which is served with an excellent aïoli (p400). The decor illustrates the transition between Art Nouveau and Art Deco.

9E ARRONDISSEMENT
● La Taverne

24 bd des Italiens, 75009 **Map** 15D2
01 55 33 10 00
FAX 01 55 33 10 09
w www.taverne.com
AE, DC, MC, V €€

Antique clocks punctuate the decor at this late-night brasserie. Shellfish, sauerkraut and fish brochettes. Most wines are from Alsace.

9E ARRONDISSEMENT
● La Tradition

2 rue de Budapest, 75009 **Map** 14C2

01 48 74 37 33
MC, V Sun, Aug €€
Charming, authentic bistro complete with small tables topped with chequered tablecloths. Uncomplicated, traditional cuisine such as pepper steak.

9E ARRONDISSEMENT
● Le Grand Café

4 bd des Capucines, 75009 **Map** 15D2
01 43 12 19 00
FAX 01 43 12 19 09
w www.legrandcafe.com
AE, DC, MC, V €€€

Dazzling Art Nouveau brasserie, open round the clock. Alongside the traditional shellfish platters, more globally influenced fare: ginger fish and chicken tagines.

9E ARRONDISSEMENT
● Le Paprika

28 ave Trudaine, 75009 **Map** 15D1
01 44 63 02 91
FAX 01 44 63 09 62
w www.le-paprika.com
MC, V €€

Gourmet Hungarian cuisine and live gypsy music (October–April and June). A dish such as the csáky bélszin (beef with morels and foie gras) is familiar to the French palate, but desserts such as apple and cinnamon strudel offer a taste of Central Europe.

9E ARRONDISSEMENT
● Les Comédiens

7 rue Blanche, 75009 **Map** 15D1
01 40 82 95 95
FAX 01 40 82 96 95
AE, MC, V Sun, Sat L
€€€

Modern bistro at the heart of the theatre district. Classics include the grilled beef from Salers, sole meunière and iced nougat, as well as a fish of the day, such as tuna ratatouille (p400).

9E ARRONDISSEMENT
● No Stress Café

2 pl Gustave Toudouze, 75009 **Map** 14D1
01 48 78 00 27
AE, MC, V Mon €€
A bohemian fusion restaurant. Dishes include spicy grilled tuna, or Peking-style pork with pineapple. Complete

your dining experience with a shiatsu massage at the restaurant.

9E ARRONDISSEMENT
● Omnibus Café

13 bis pl Pigalle, 75009 **Map** 15D1
01 45 26 82 04
AE, DC, MC, V €

Burgundy tones and leopard prints compose a contemporary interior. However, cuisine here is resolutely traditional: sauerkraut or stuffed cabbage followed by apple tart or crème brûlée. Lighter and good-value lunches.

10E ARRONDISSEMENT
● Chez Prune

36 rue Beaurepaire, 75010 **Map** 15F2
01 42 41 30 47
FAX 01 42 00 42 20
DC, MC, V 1 wk Dec €
The terrace has a wonderful view of Canal Saint-Martin. Top spot for brunch on Sundays, with a choice of smoked salmon or ham with croissants. Upmarket cuisine for lunch: saffron and lime fish and three-cheese ravioli.

10E ARRONDISSEMENT
● Flo

7 cour des Petites Ecuries, 75010 **Map** 15E2
01 47 70 13 59
FAX 01 42 47 00 80
@ prussino@groupeflo.fr
AE, DC, MC, V €€€€

All stained glass and green leather, this historic restaurant was established in 1886. Traditional cuisine, with a predilection for Alsatian specialities. Sauerkraut is on the menu: the formidable version comes with pork and sausages from Morteau.

10E ARRONDISSEMENT
■ Hôtel Allety

4 bis bd Bonne Nouvelle, 75010 **Map** 15E2
01 48 24 94 54
FAX 01 45 23 90 10
w www.hotel-allety-hugot.com
AE, DC, MC, V (18) €€

A bargain hotel steps from Opéra Garnier and Paris's theatreland. Bedrooms are small with a personal touch.

10E ARRONDISSEMENT
■ **Hôtel Apollo**

11 rue de Dunkerque, 75010 **Map** 15E1

📞 01 48 78 04 98

FAX 01 42 85 08 78

🖥 www.hotel-apollo-paris.com

💳 AE, DC, MC, V 🍽 (45) €€€

Early 20th-century charm for this hotel near Gare du Nord. Period features include mirrors, mouldings and an old tiled floor in the lounge; colonial-style ceiling fans in the bedrooms.

10E ARRONDISSEMENT
● **Julien**

16 rue du Faubourg St-Denis, 75010 **Map** 15E2

📞 01 47 70 12 06

FAX 01 42 47 00 65

💳 AE, DC, MC, V 🍽 €€€

Uniformed waiters and the dazzling Art Nouveau interior, complete with an impressive mahogany bar. Sole meunière or à la plancha (grilled), cassoulet (p373) or pan-fried foie gras.

10E ARRONDISSEMENT
● **Terminus Nord**

23 rue de Dunkerque, 75010 **Map** 15E1

📞 01 42 85 05 15

FAX 01 40 16 13 98

💳 AE, DC, MC, V 🍽 €€€

Facing Gard du Nord, among many cheap eateries: a wonderful vintage 1930s interior, crisp linen, and satisfying brasserie fare. Shellfish platters, tasty sauerkraut and bouillabaisse (p401).

11E ARRONDISSEMENT
● **Bistrot du Peintre**

116 ave Ledru Rollin, 75011 **Map** 15F4

📞 01 47 00 34 39

FAX 01 47 00 34 39

💳 MC, V 🍽 €€

The beautiful Art Nouveau decor, punctuated with old paintings and large mirrors, matches the cuisine. Pike lasagne, calf's liver fricassée, foie gras and glazed orange tart are on the menu.

11E ARRONDISSEMENT
● **Blue Elephant**

43 rue de la Roquette, 75011 **Map** 15F4

📞 01 47 00 42 00

FAX 01 47 00 45 44

💳 AE, DC, MC, V

● Sat L 🍽 €€€

An island of refinement in the trendy Bastille area, with a tropical decor of lush plants, gurgling fountains and Thai woodwork. Superbly presented Thai cuisine: som tam (green papaya, dried shrimp and lime salad) and cashew nut chicken served in a fresh pineapple. Excellent Sunday brunch.

11E ARRONDISSEMENT
● **Boca Chica**

58 rue de Charonne, 75011 **Map** 15F4

📞 01 43 57 93 13

FAX 01 43 57 04 08

🖥 www.labocachica.com

💳 AE, DC, MC, V 🍽 €€

Funky decor, trendy tunes and Spanish fare. Tapas, grilled sardines, pork ribs and gâteau Basque on the menu.

11E ARRONDISSEMENT
● **Chardenoux**

1 rue Jules Vallés, 75011

📞 01 43 71 49 52

💳 AE, MC, V 🍽 €€

Archetype of the 1900s Parisian bistro, featuring Art Nouveau stained-glass windows and great wines. The new proprietor-chef continues the tradition of classic cuisine and refined elegance.

11E ARRONDISSEMENT
● **Chez Paul**

13 rue de Charonne, 75011 **Map** 15F4

📞 01 47 00 34 57

FAX 01 48 07 02 00

💳 AE, DC, MC, V 🍽 €€€

At the heart of the trendy Bastille, a monument to retro style. Tasty traditional recipes include the rustic tête-de-veau and a traditional grilled steak. More inventive is the rabbit with mint and pungent goats' cheese.

11E ARRONDISSEMENT
● **Chez Prosper**

7 ave du Trône, 75011

📞 01 43 73 08 51

💳 MC, V 🍽 €€

A truly Parisian bistro with quaint, well-preserved charm and a terrace. Great classics: thick grilled steak, bountiful salads and top-notch chocolate cake.

11E ARRONDISSEMENT
● **La Scène**

2 bis rue des Taillandiers, 75011

Map 15F4

📞 01 48 06 50 70

FAX 01 48 06 57 07

🖥 www.la-scene.com

💳 AE, DC, MC, V ● Sun, Mon L, Sat L; Aug 🍽 €€

Trendy bar, concert hall and restaurant all in one. A fusion of European cuisines in the intimate dining room: Spanish-style tuna and steak with Béarnaise sauce.

11E ARRONDISSEMENT
● **Mansouria**

11 rue Faidherbe, 75011

📞 01 43 71 00 16

FAX 01 40 24 21 97

💳 MC, V ● Sun, Mon L, Tue L; 1 wk Aug 🍽 €€€

Stylish Moroccan restaurant, where white linen contrasts with gold-embroidered fabrics. The fare is more elaborate than the standard couscous and tagines, with dishes such as pigeon pastilla (in filo) or tchicha (barley couscous).

11E ARRONDISSEMENT
● **Pause Café**

41 rue de Charonne, 75011 **Map** 15F4

📞 01 48 06 80 33

FAX 01 43 57 63 78

💳 AE, MC, V 🍽 €€

Much appreciated for its terrace and tarts. Inventive bistro cuisine includes tuna with Provençal vegetables and a twist on a warm goat's cheese salad.

11E ARRONDISSEMENT
● **Waly Fay**

6 rue Godefroy-Cavaignac, 75011

📞 01 40 24 17 79

FAX 01 43 73 68 02

💳 MC, V ● Sun; 1 wk Aug

🍽 €€

Full-bodied flavours of Africa at this subdued little spot. Mafé (beef cooked in peanut butter) and yassa (lemon-flavoured chicken) on the menu. Chilled music but a truly warm welcome.

12E ARRONDISSEMENT
● **Au Trou Gascon**

40 rue Taine, 75012

● Restaurant   ■ Hotel   ▲ Hotel / Restaurant

█ 01 43 44 34 26
FAX 01 43 07 80 55
AE, DC, MC, V ● Sun, Sat; Aug
██ €€€€

*Classy dining room with southwestern
cuisine. Try* cassoulet (p373), confit de
canard (p326) *and prune ice cream.*

12E ARRONDISSEMENT
● Barrio Latino

46 rue du Faubourg St-Antoine, 75012
Map 15F4
█ 01 55 78 84 75
FAX 01 55 78 85 30
@ barrio-latino@wanadoo.fr
AE, DC, MC, V ██ €€€

*Three floors of exuberant and luxurious
South American decor. Exotic food
includes guacamole, quesadillas (grilled
cheese-filled tortillas), Brazilian grilled
pork and Uruguayan-style scallops on a
skewer with salsa.*

12E ARRONDISSEMENT
● Chai 33

33 cour St-Emilion, 75012
█ 01 53 44 01 01
FAX 01 53 44 01 02
AE, DC, MC, V ██ €€€

*Former wine warehouse turned eatery
and wine bar complete with sommelier.
Rich menu offering four fine styles of
cuisine: "authentic", "contemporary",
"vegetarian" and "seasonal".*

12E ARRONDISSEMENT
● China Club

50 rue de Charenton, 75012 **Map** 15F4
█ 01 43 43 82 02
FAX 01 43 43 79 85
W www.chinaclub.cc
AE, DC, MC, V
● mid-Jul–mid-Aug ██ €€€

*Chinese restaurants can be kitsch, but
this one is revolutionary in an extremely
glamorous way. Colonial chic decor
along with superior Asian cuisine such
as five-spice crispy pigeon and sautéed
sole with ginger-plum sauce.*

12E ARRONDISSEMENT
■ Corail Hôtel

23 rue de Lyon, 75012 **Map** 15F4
█ 01 43 43 23 54
FAX 01 43 43 82 55

W www.corail-hotel.fr
AE, DC, MC, V ● (50) €€€
*Simple furnishings and a stylish use of
colour. Rooms are all well equipped, but
only the first-floor has air-conditioning.*

12E ARRONDISSEMENT
● Le Pataquès

40 bd de Bercy, 75012
█ 01 43 07 37 75
FAX 01 43 07 36 64
AE, MC, V ● Sun ██ €€

*The antique tiled floor contrasts with
the contemporary lighting fixtures at this
classy bistro. Provençal menu includes
tuna and aubergine (eggplant) cream,
millefeuille with black olive and fine
rosemary-scented beef brochettes.
Beautiful terrace adorned with a fig tree.*

12E ARRONDISSEMENT
● Le Train Bleu

Pl Louis Armand, Gare de Lyon, 75012
Map 15F5
█ 01 43 43 09 06
FAX 01 43 43 97 96
W www.le-train-bleu.com
AE, DC, MC, V ██ €€€€

*Buffet with a profusion of gilded panels,
built in 1901 for the World's Fair and
housed in the Gare de Lyon train station.
Specialities from Lyon such as pistachio
sausages and pike quenelle.*

12E ARRONDISSEMENT
● Les Grandes Marches

6 pl de la Bastille, 75012 **Map** 15F4
█ 01 43 42 90 32
FAX 01 43 44 80 02
W www.lesgrandesmarches.com
AE, DC, MC, V ● Aug
██ €€€€

*Loft-style dining room featuring a lot of
steel. Roast scampi with piperade, and
foie gras in a Jurancon-wine jelly are
typical menu items.*

12E ARRONDISSEMENT
● L'Oulette

15 pl Lachambeaudie, 75012
█ 01 40 02 02 12
FAX 01 40 02 04 77
W www.l-oulette.com
AE, DC, MC, V ● Sun, Sat
██ €€€€

*Broad southern influences on the menu:
aubergine (eggplant) cake and duckling
with stewed lemons and olives. Colourful
dining room with plants and curios.*

12E ARRONDISSEMENT
● Square Trousseau

1 rue Antoine Vollon, 75012
█ 01 43 43 06 00
FAX 01 43 43 00 66
AE, MC, V ● Sun, Mon; 1st 3 wks
Aug, 3rd wk Dec–1st wk Jan ██ €€

*Huge, beautiful 1900s bistro, favoured
by a fashionable professional crowd.
Trendy cooking includes pumpkin soup
and chicken pastilla (in filo). Carefully
selected wine list with many organic
choices. Terrace in summer.*

14E ARRONDISSEMENT
● Au Vin des Rues

21 rue Boulard, 75014 **Map** 15D5
█ 01 43 22 19 78
FAX 01 43 27 74 11
MC, V ● Sun, Mon ██ €€

*Retro-style bistro par excellence with
red seats, ancient tiled floors and
accordion music on Thursdays. Lyon-
style fare including pistachio-stuffed
sausage and steak with mushroom sauce.*

14E ARRONDISSEMENT
● Aux Petits Chandeliers

62 rue Daguerre, 75014 **Map** 14C5
█ 01 43 20 25 87
FAX 01 43 27 87 38
W www.aux-petits-chandeliers.fr
AE, DC, MC, V ██ €

*Unpretentious bistro, established in
1962 and still featuring the small
chandeliers after which it was named.
This was the first restaurant in Paris to
serve cuisine from the island of Réunion.
On the menu are Creole-style pudding,
and coconut-and-vanilla punch.*

14E ARRONDISSEMENT
● Bistro 7

7 rue Campagne Première, 75014
Map 15D5
█ 01 43 20 93 04
● Sun ██ €€

*The menu at this bistro is resolutely
traditional: confit de canard (p326), steak
tartare and salads with goats' cheese or*

gizzards. Good selection of wine from the Lyon area, such as Beaujolais.

14E ARRONDISSEMENT
■ Hôtel Apollon Montparnasse

91 rue Ouest, 75014 **Map** 14C5

C 01 43 95 62 00

FAX 01 43 95 62 10

W www.apollon-montparnasse.com

AE, DC, MC, V ◇ (33) €€€

Grecian statues, fine furnishings and tons of peach at this hotel. Guestrooms are well equipped and guests have access to private parking.

14E ARRONDISSEMENT
■ Hôtel Delambre

35 rue Delambre, 75014 **Map** 14C5

C 01 43 20 66 31

FAX 01 45 38 91 76

AE, MC, V ◇ (30) €€€

Steps from Montparnasse cemetery. This hotel mixes the modern and the classical. Simple, well-equipped guestrooms.

14E ARRONDISSEMENT
■ Hôtel du Parc Montsouris

4 rue du Parc Montsouris, 75014

C 01 45 89 09 72

FAX 01 45 80 92 72

AE, MC, V ◇ (35) €€€

Nothing lavish but attention has been paid to the decor. One attraction of this hotel is its location next to a leafy park.

14E ARRONDISSEMENT
▲ Justine at Hôtel Méridien Montparnasse

19 rue du Commandant Renè Mouchotte, 75014 **Map** 14C5

C 01 44 36 44 00

FAX 01 44 36 49 03

W www.lemeridien-montparnasse.com

AE, DC, MC, V

☰ €€€€€ ◇ (953) €€€€€

The glass ceiling brings a lot of light into this rattan-furnished dining room that overlooks a winter garden at the heart of this luxury hotel. Buffets for every meal with cooked meats, seafood and desserts. Deluxe guestrooms.

14E ARRONDISSEMENT
● La Bretonne

56 rue du Montparnasse, 75014

Map 14C5

C 01 43 20 89 58

AE, DC, MC, V **☰** €

A little piece of Brittany, complete with antique furniture. Tasty pancakes such as Provençal (mushrooms and snail butter), Guémènée (with chitterling sausages), and a choice of flambéed desserts.

14E ARRONDISSEMENT
● La Cagouille

10 pl Constantin Brancusi, 75014

Map 14C5

C 01 43 22 09 01

FAX 01 45 38 57 29

W www.la-cagouille.fr

AE, MC, V **☰** €€€

Maritime-themed restaurant. Simple dishes including cod steak with a sweet garlic sauce and seared king scallops.

14E ARRONDISSEMENT
● La Closerie des Lilas

171 bd du Montparnasse, 75014

Map 15D5

C 01 40 51 34 50

FAX 01 43 29 99 94

@ closerie@club-internet.fr

AE, DC, MC, V **☰** €€€€€

Large terrace with comfortable booth seating inside Paris's oldest literary café. High-class brasserie cuisine such as pan-fried prawns in saffron sauce and magret de canard with mussel cream.

14E ARRONDISSEMENT
● La Coupole

102 bd du Montparnasse, 75014

Map 15D5

C 01 43 20 14 20

FAX 01 43 35 46 14

AE, DC, MC, V **☰** €€€

An artists' hub in the 1930s with an impressive stained-glass ceiling. On the menu, classics such as onion soup, sauerkraut and grilled cod with mashed potatoes.

14E ARRONDISSEMENT
● La Régalade

49 ave Jean Moulin, 75014

C 01 45 45 68 58

FAX 01 45 40 96 74

MC, V ● Sun, Mon L, Sat; Aug

☰ €€

Gourmet fare is a bargain at this traditional bistro. Foie gras casserole and pan-fried cod with leek vinaigrette are main courses. Grand Marnier soufflé is the speciality dessert. Reserve ahead.

14E ARRONDISSEMENT
● Le Bal Bullier

22 ave l'Observatoire, 75014 **Map** 15D5

C 01 43 21 06 06

AE, DC, MC, V ● Sun D; last 2 wks Aug **☰** €€

A collection of Toulouse-Lautrec-like posters give this bistro a turn-of-the-century feel. Classic brasserie cooking with large salads, leg of lamb and fish. Tearoom in the afternoon.

14E ARRONDISSEMENT
● Le Bar à Huîtres

112 bd Montparnasse, 75014 **Map** 15D5

C 01 43 20 71 01

FAX 01 43 20 52 04

W www.lebarahuitres.com

AE, DC, MC, V **☰** €€€

Seafood – especially oysters – is king here. Enjoy them warm as a starter or raw in a shellfish platter. Those dining alone may appreciate the conviviality of the circular oyster bar. Other delicacies include a lobster menu or magret de canard with crayfish tails.

14E ARRONDISSEMENT
● Le Dôme

108 bd Montparnasse, 75014 **Map** 14C5

C 01 43 35 25 81

FAX 01 42 79 01 19

AE, DC, MC, V ● Aug: Sun–Mon

☰ €€€€€

A Parisian institution, loved for its quintessential Art Deco interior and for the quality of its seafood. Sole meunière, bouillabaisse (p401) or fried John Dory.

14E ARRONDISSEMENT
● Le Plomb du Cantal

3 rue de la Gaîté, 75014 **Map** 14C5

C 01 43 35 16 92

FAX 01 43 35 16 92

MC, V **☰** €

Named after the highest mountain in Auvergne, this restaurant serves regional specialities: truffade (p246), aligot (p247) and excellent Auvergne-style flan (with

*raisins and a brioche-like dough). Good
local wines such as Côtes d'Auvergne.*

14E ARRONDISSEMENT
● L'Echanson
89 rue Daguerre, 75014 **Map** 14C5
📞 01 43 22 20 00
FAX 01 43 22 20 00
💳 MC, V ● Sun, Mon L 🍴 €€
*Quintessential Parisian bistro serving
cuisine that couldn't be more French, yet
the chef shows creativity by reinventing
classics, such as magret de canard with
peaches, or poached fish with orange
cream and spinach-filled pasta.*

14E ARRONDISSEMENT
▲ Montparnasse' 25 at Hôtel
Méridien Montparnasse
19 rue du Commandant Renè
Mouchotte, 75014 **Map** 14C5
📞 01 44 36 44 36
FAX 01 44 36 49 00
W www.lemeridien-montparnasse.com
💳 AE, DC, MC, V ● Sun, Sat;
Jul–Aug 🍴 €€€€€
◐ (953) €€€€€
*This modern building hosts a black
lacquered dining room where Chef
Christian Moine's exquisite cuisine is
served. This restaurant is well known
for its impressive selection of cheeses.
The guestrooms are more colourful and
most have panoramic views.*

14E ARRONDISSEMENT
● Natacha
17 bis rue Campagne Première, 75014
Map 15D5
📞 01 43 20 79 27
FAX 01 43 22 93 97
@ restaurantnatacha@wanadoo.fr
💳 AE, MC, V ● Sun D; 1 wk Aug
🍴 €€
*Long curtains at the entrance and theatre
seats bring drama to an otherwise simple
interior. A hint of the exotic on the menu:
chicken terrine with pistachios and
glazed kumquats and steamed fish with
herb dressing. Brunch on Sundays.*

14E ARRONDISSEMENT
● Restaurant Produits du Sud-Ouest
21–23 rue d'Odessa, 75014 **Map** 14C5
📞 01 43 20 34 07

FAX 01 45 38 53 95
💳 MC, V ● Sun, Mon 🍴 €
*Rich produce from southwest France, at
the take-away deli counter or in the
restaurant with its half-timbered walls
and rugby paraphernalia. Confit de
canard (p326), cassoulet (p326) or prune
tart with Armagnac made with ingredients
direct from the owner's farm estate.*

15E ARRONDISSEMENT
● Beurre Noisette
68 rue Vasco de Gama, 75015
📞 01 48 56 82 49
FAX 01 48 56 82 49
💳 AE, MC, V ● Sun, Mon; Aug
🍴 €€
*Quietly contemporary decor and cuisine:
foie gras poached in red wine and
spices, pan-fried fish with Greek-style
vegetables and rice with strawberries
and foamy coconut milk.*

15E ARRONDISSEMENT
■ Hôtel de l'Avre
21 rue de l'Avre, 75015 **Map** 14A4
📞 01 45 75 31 03
FAX 01 45 75 63 26
W www.hoteldelavre.com
💳 AE, DC, MC, V ◐ (26) €€€
*Located on a quiet street, some of the
guestrooms look onto the garden where
breakfast is served in fine weather.
Extremely neat, well-equipped rooms.*

15E ARRONDISSEMENT
● La Folletterie
34 rue Letellier, 75015 **Map** 14A4
📞 01 45 75 55 95
💳 MC, V ● Sun, Mon, Sat L; 3 wks
Aug 🍴 €€
*Mixed influences on an ever-changing
menu at truly competitive prices. Roast
mullet with beetroot and oyster vinaigrette,
and poppy-seed chocolate cake.*

15E ARRONDISSEMENT
● La Gauloise
59 ave de la Motte-Picquet Grenelle,
75015 **Map** 14B4
📞 01 47 34 11 64
FAX 01 40 61 09 70
💳 AE, MC, V 🍴 €€€
*Classy bistro with pictures of VIPs
covering the walls. Satisfying fare*

*includes roast leg of lamb with haricot
beans, beef carpaccio and rotisserie
specialities. Booth seating.*

15E ARRONDISSEMENT
● La Villa Corse
164 bd de Grenelle, 75015 **Map** 14B4
📞 01 53 86 70 81
FAX 01 53 86 90 73
💳 AE, MC, V ● Sun 🍴 €€€
*Corsica's strongly flavoured traditional
cuisine is on the menu here: wild boar
stew, olive veal, Brocciu cheese and
chestnut bread, a speciality from the
city of Bonifacio.*

15E ARRONDISSEMENT
● Le Bistro d'Hubert
41 bd Pasteur, 75015
📞 01 47 34 15 50
FAX 01 45 67 03 09
W www.bistrodhubert.com
💳 AE, DC, MC, V ● Sat L
🍴 €€€
*Pale wooden furniture gives a modern
touch to this bistro. Black pudding
(blood sausage) fried with apples and
potatoes; spiced pork roll in port; and
spinach-stuffed salmon and leek patties.*

15E ARRONDISSEMENT
● Le Ciel de Paris
33 ave du Maine, 75015 **Map** 14C5
📞 01 40 64 77 64
FAX 01 43 21 48 37
💳 AE, DC, MC, V 🍴 €€€€€
*Europe's fastest lift will take you in
seconds to Europe's highest restaurant,
perched atop the Montparnasse tower.
The view is breathtaking. Chef Jean-
François Oyon's Mediterranean-inspired
cuisine does credit to the setting: lobster
risotto, nage (broth) of snails and red
berries topped with mascarpone cheese.*

15E ARRONDISSEMENT
● R
6 rue de la Cavalerie, 75015 **Map** 14B4
📞 01 45 67 06 85
FAX 01 45 67 55 72
💳 AE, DC, MC, V ● Sun 🍴 €€€
*Designer chairs made of wire echo the
Eiffel Tower, which is on view from this
eighth-floor restaurant. Pasta stuffed
with foie gras is comforting fare.*

16E ARRONDISSEMENT
● **6 New York**
6 ave de New York, 75016 **Map** 14A3
📞 01 40 70 03 30
FAX 01 40 70 04 77
💳 AE, DC, MC, V 🌙 Sun, Sat L; 3 wks Aug 🍴 €€€
Marrying pale wood and soft tones of grey, this is a fashionable venue with rather traditional cuisine: pig's trotters, Niçoise sole and vegetable risotto.

16E ARRONDISSEMENT
● **Auberge du Mouton Blanc**
40 rue d'Auteuil, 75016
📞 01 42 88 02 21
FAX 01 45 24 21 07
💳 AE, DC, MC, V
🌙 mid-Jul–Aug 🍴 €€€
Once frequented by the celebrated writers Racine and La Fontaine. Rustic dining room serves pistache de mouton (p326) and tapenade (p400).

16E ARRONDISSEMENT
■ **Costes K**
81 ave Kléber, 75016 **Map** 14A2
📞 01 44 05 75 75
FAX 01 44 05 74 74
💳 AE, DC, MC, V 🌐 (83) €€€€€
Steps from the Eiffel, a piece of modern art by architect Ricardo Bofill. Cool Asian interiors for the guestrooms.

16E ARRONDISSEMENT
● **Fakhr El Dine**
30 rue de Longchamps, 75016
Map 14A3
📞 01 47 27 90 00
FAX 01 53 70 01 81
🌐 www.fakhreldine.com
💳 AE, DC, MC, V 🍴 €€
Lebanese specialist, the mezze appetizer assortment is a meal in itself.

16E ARRONDISSEMENT
● **Faugeron**
52 rue de Longchamp, 75116 **Map** 14A3
📞 01 47 04 24 53
FAX 01 47 55 62 90
@ faugeron@wanadoo.fr
💳 AE, MC, V 🌙 Sun, Sat; Aug, 1 wk Dec 🍴 €€€€€
Chef Henri Faugeron is a gifted purist: simple recipes turn into gourmet meals.

Try soft-boiled eggs with truffle purée and the layered lobster dish.

16E ARRONDISSEMENT
■ **Hameau de Passy**
48 rue de Passy, 75016 **Map** 14A3
📞 01 42 88 47 55
FAX 01 42 30 83 72
💳 AE, DC, MC, V 🌐 (32) €€€€
In a private lane, which is an oasis of greenery. Rooms overlook the garden.

16E ARRONDISSEMENT
■ **Hôtel du Bois**
11 rue du Dôme, 75016 **Map** 14A2
📞 01 45 00 31 96
FAX 01 45 00 90 05
🌐 www.hoteldubois.com
💳 AE, DC, MC, V 🌐 (41) €€€€
Behind a typically Parisian façade, an interior exuding British charm: Georgian furniture in the lounge; thick patterned carpeting and fine prints in the bedrooms.

16E ARRONDISSEMENT
● **Jamin**
32 rue de Longchamps, 75116 **Map** 14A3
📞 01 45 53 00 07
FAX 01 45 53 00 15
💳 AE, DC, MC, V
🌙 Sun, Sat; 1 wk Feb, I wk May, 1st 3 wks Aug, 4th wk Dec 🍴 €€€€€€
The emphasis is on produce: scampi ravioli with chervil stew, and poultry from Bresse. Delightful presentation; simple, welcoming decor.

16E ARRONDISSEMENT
● **La Butte Chaillot**
110 bis ave Kléber, 75116 **Map** 14A2
📞 01 47 27 88 88
FAX 01 47 27 41 46
💳 AE, DC, MC, V
🌙 Sat L; Aug 🍴 €€€
Purists go to Guy Savoy's eponymous venue, whereas those happy with a miniature – and less pricey – Savoy experience will be delighted by this place. Salad of pan-fried prawns with sesame seeds, olive-crusted sea bass and crispy leg of lamb are on the menu.

16E ARRONDISSEMENT
● **La Gare**
19 chaussée la Muette, 75016

📞 01 42 15 15 31
FAX 01 42 15 15 23
🌐 www.restaurantlagare.com
💳 AE, MC, V 🍴 €€€
Although this railway station isn't working anymore, the decor has been kept. Much tastier fare than at a usual railway eatery, such as rotisserie and fish steamed with ginger and saffron.

16E ARRONDISSEMENT
● **La Grande Cascade**
Allée de Longchamp, 75016
📞 01 45 27 33 51
FAX 01 42 88 99 06
🌐 www.lagrandecascade.fr
💳 AE, DC, MC, V
🌙 mid-Dec–1st wk Jan, 2 wks Feb
🍴 €€€€€
Circular dining room showcasing the surrounding Bois de Boulogne. Gourmet cuisine: macaroni stuffed with black truffle and foie gras, sole with shellfish sauce over potatoes.

16E ARRONDISSEMENT
● **L'Astrance**
4 rue de Beethoven, 75016 **Map** 14A3
📞 01 40 50 84 40
💳 AE, DC, MC, V
🌙 Sun, Sat; Aug
🍴 €€€€€
Vibrant ode to modernity: colourful yet minimalist interior, and flavourful cuisine. Crab meat, avocado and soft almond oil ravioli and milk "in all sorts of states" as ice cream, in jelly, and foamed for dessert. Comprehensive wine list.

16E ARRONDISSEMENT
● **Le Chalet des Îles**
14 chemin Ceinture du Lac Inférieur du Bois de Boulogne, 75116
📞 01 42 88 04 69
FAX 01 42 88 84 09
🌐 www.lechaletdesiles.net
💳 AE, MC, V
🌙 mid-Nov–Mar: Sun D 🍴 €€€
Idyllic setting, nestled on an island in the middle of a lake. The country-style interior suits the bucolic environment, but the cuisine showcases a modern approach: pan-fried sole with a Creole-style sauce, and coconut and lemon chicken with red rice.

16E ARRONDISSEMENT
● Le Pré Catelan

Route de Suresnes, Bois de Boulogne, 75016

☎ 01 44 14 41 14

FAX 01 45 24 43 25

w www.lenotre.fr

AE, DC, MC, V ● Sun, Mon; 3 wks Feb €€€€€

Gastronomic cuisine in a Napoleon III-style pavilion, there is the feel of the countryside and a sense of relaxation here. On the menu is pigeon poached in a spicy stew and sole with mango.

16E ARRONDISSEMENT
● Prunier

16 ave Victor Hugo, 75116 **Map** 14A2

☎ 01 44 17 35 85

FAX 01 44 17 90 10

AE, DC, MC, V ● Sun; Aug

€€€€€

Founded in 1925 and featuring a dazzling Art Deco interior. Wonderful seafood including smoked salmon and caviars.

16E ARRONDISSEMENT
● Seize au Seize

16 ave Bugeaud, 75116 **Map** 14A2

☎ 01 56 28 16 16

FAX 01 56 28 16 78

AE, DC, MC, V

● Sun, Mon; Aug

€€€€€

Dishes such as fricasséed frogs' legs with garlic cream, mushrooms and parsley juice. Rich materials and simple lines in the dining room.

16E ARRONDISSEMENT
● Table du Baltimore

1 rue Léo Delibes, 75016 **Map** 14A3

☎ 01 44 34 54 34

AE, DC, MC, V ● Sun, Sat; Aug

€€€€

An up-to-the-minute outlook on food and decor lends this Michelin-starred restaurant a real buzz. Dishes include Breton-style seafood and seaweed, roasted rabbit with herbs, and fennel-flavoured ice cream.

16E ARRONDISSEMENT
● Tsé

78 rue d'Auteuil, 75016

☎ 01 40 71 11 90

FAX 01 40 71 11 99

AE, MC, V €€€€

Asian antiques and subdued lighting define the elegant atmosphere at this French-Asian fusion restaurant. Pan-fried langoustines with coconut milk, coriander (cilantro) tuna steak with wasabi (a hot mustard) and leg of lamb with mint are typical offerings.

16E ARRONDISSEMENT
● Tse Yang

25 ave Pierre 1er de Serbie, 75016 **Map** 14A2

☎ 01 47 20 70 22

FAX 01 49 52 03 68

w www.tseyang.fr

AE, DC, MC, V €€€€

Paris's most exclusive Chinese restaurant. Luxurious decor and very fine cuisine: mandarin-flavoured beef, stuffed crab claws and tea-scented poultry.

16E ARRONDISSEMENT
▲ Zebra Square

3 pl Clément Ader, 75016

☎ 01 44 14 91 91

FAX 01 45 20 46 41

w www.zebra-square.com

AE, DC, MC, V

€€€ (22) €€€€€

Part of the Hotel Square complex, a modern building with minimalist decor spiced up by splashes of zebra prints. Equally modern fare: crab cakes, aubergine (eggplant) carpaccio and salmon tartare. Stylish rooms done up in rich, soothing colours. A hit with the fashion and media crowd.

17E ARRONDISSEMENT
● Balthazar

73 ave Niel, 75017 **Map** 14A1

☎ 01 44 40 28 15

FAX 01 44 40 28 30

AE, MC, V €€€

Menu of updated French classics such as thyme-scented grilled sea bass and T-bone veal steak. Modern interior of dark wood and colourful lamps.

17E ARRONDISSEMENT
● Cai'us

6 rue Armaillé, 75017 **Map** 14A1

☎ 01 42 27 19 20

FAX 01 40 55 00 93

AE, DC, MC, V ● Sun, Sat L; 3 wks Aug €€€

Tartan fabrics and pale oak panelling lend a British aura to this restaurant serving French regional cuisine including Burgundy snails and caramel meringue.

17E ARRONDISSEMENT
● Dessirier

9 pl du Maréchal Juin, 75017 **Map** 14A1

☎ 01 42 27 82 14

FAX 01 47 66 82 07

w www.michelrostang.com

AE, DC, MC, V €€€€

Dedicated to seafood since 1883, this is one of Paris's best-known fish restaurants. Oyster risotto, whole grilled sea bass and langoustine salad feature.

17E ARRONDISSEMENT
● Guy Savoy

18 rue Troyon, 75017 **Map** 14A2

☎ 01 43 80 40 61

FAX 01 46 22 43 09

w www.guysavoy.com

AE, DC, MC, V ● Sun, Mon, Sat L; mid-Jul–mid-Aug €€€€€

Guy Savoy's love of art shows on the walls of this minimalist restaurant. On the menu are roast veal and truffled mashed potatoes, or steamed fish with shellfish and citrus-infused asparagus.

17E ARRONDISSEMENT
■ Hôtel Niel Élysées Arc de Triomphe

11 rue Saussier Leroy, 75017 **Map** 14A1

☎ 01 42 27 99 29

FAX 01 42 27 16 96

w www.hotelnielelysees.com

AE, DC, MC, V

(36) €€€

Right by the Arc de Triomphe, stylish guestrooms at a bargain price.

17E ARRONDISSEMENT
● La Braisière

54 rue Cardinet, 75017 **Map** 14B1

☎ 01 47 63 40 37

FAX 01 47 63 04 76

AE, DC, MC, V ● Sun, Sat L; Aug

€€€€

All soft colours and subdued lighting. Flavourful cuisine: foie gras and potato

cakes and piquillos *(peppers) stuffed*
with squid and pig's trotters.

17E ARRONDISSEMENT
● Le Ballon des Ternes

103 ave des Ternes, 75017 **Map** 14A1

[C] 01 45 74 17 98

FAX 01 45 72 18 84

[@] leballondesternes@wanadoo.fr

[≡] AE, MC, V [●] Aug [11] €€€€

Engraved glass partitions, ancient tiled
floor, and red wall-seats compose a
beautiful retro dining room. The menu
boasts a lot of shellfish as well as rabbit
terrine, fish soup and steak tartare.

17E ARRONDISSEMENT
● Le Bistro d'à Côté – Flaubert

10 rue Gustave Flaubert, 75017
Map 14B1

[C] 01 42 67 05 81

FAX 01 47 63 82 75

[W] www.michelrostang.com

[≡] AE, DC, MC, V [11] €€

Charming bistro. Season dependant, the
menu includes liver terrine, rabbit with
foie gras and tuna with lobster gratin.
For dessert, the small pots of chocolate
cream are the house's signature dish.

17E ARRONDISSEMENT
● Le Clou

132 rue Cardinet, 75017 **Map** 14B1

[C] 01 42 27 36 78

FAX 01 42 27 89 96

[≡] AE, DC, MC, V [●] Sun, Sat L; 2
wks Aug, Dec [11] €€€

Traditional bistro, complete with a
collection of old advertisements and
blackboard menus. Scallops, grilled beef
and desserts such as glazed nougat and
chocolate cake never leave the menu.

17E ARRONDISSEMENT
● Le Stübli

11 rue Poncelet, 75017 **Map** 14A1

[C] 01 42 27 81 86

FAX 01 42 67 61 69

[W] www.stubli.com

[≡] MC, V [●] Mon, Tue–Sun D [11] €

A little corner of Austria complete with a
patisserie, deli and tearoom. For lunch,
great classics such as sauerkraut. In the
afternoon, apple strudel, Linzertorte and
authentic Viennese hot chocolate.

17E ARRONDISSEMENT
● Le Troyon

4 rue Troyon, 75017 **Map** 14A2

[C] 01 40 68 99 40

FAX 01 40 68 99 57

[≡] AE, MC, V [●] Sun, Sat; Aug, Dec
[11] €€€

Convivial bistro. Constantly evolving
cooking from this pioneering chef.
Spiced swordfish and roasted lamb with
herb marmalade and carrots.

17E ARRONDISSEMENT
● Restaurant Michel Rostang

20 rue Rennequin, 75017 **Map** 14B2

[C] 01 47 63 40 77

FAX 01 47 63 82 75

[W] www.michelrostang.com

[≡] AE, DC, MC, V [●] Sun, Mon L, Sat
L; 1st 3 wks Aug [11] €€€€€

Chef Michel Rostang is a perfectionist.
The menu includes a wide array of
lobster and truffle dishes and conveys
a love of the rare and the precious,
such as quail eggs in sea urchin shells.

17E ARRONDISSEMENT
● Verre Bouteille

85 ave des Ternes, 75017 **Map** 14A1

[C] 01 45 74 01 02

FAX 01 47 63 07 02

[W] www.leverrebouteille.com

[≡] AE, DC, MC, V [11] €€€

Proof that simple can be tasty. The
house speciality is steak tartare, but
goat's cheese ravioli, foie gras and
chocolate cake are also superb.

18E ARRONDISSEMENT
● Au Grain de Folie

24 rue de la Vieuville, 75018 **Map** 15D1

[C] 01 42 58 15 57

[11] €

Paris has few vegetarian restaurants,
and this one has a truly cosy feel. Main
courses consist of salads of vegetables
and grains (most of which are organic).
The apple crumble is recommended.

18E ARRONDISSEMENT
● Au Pied du Sacré Coeur

85 rue Lamarck, 75018 **Map** 15D1

[C] 01 46 06 15 26

FAX 01 55 79 02 31

[≡] AE, MC, V [●] Mon L [11] €€

Contemporary interior and modern
cooking such as oeufs cocotte (eggs
baked with cream, salmon and chives)
and chicken suprême stuffed with prawns.

18E ARRONDISSEMENT
● Chao Ba Café

22 bd de Clichy, 75018 **Map** 15D1

[C] 01 46 06 72 90

FAX 01 42 51 81 02

[≡] AE, MC, V [11] €€

Exotic, chic restaurant in a seedy but
safe area. French-Vietnamese cuisine
such as pancakes stuffed with prawns.
Rattan chairs and ceiling fans.

18E ARRONDISSEMENT
■ Hôtel des Arts

5 rue Tholozé, 75018 **Map** 15D1

[C] 01 46 06 30 52

FAX 01 46 06 10 83

[W] www.arts-hotel-paris.com

[≡] AE, DC, MC, V [◇] (50) €€€

Curios, Persian carpets and paintings by
artists working on nearby Place du
Tertre, all give this hotel an individual
feel. State-of-the-art guestrooms.

18E ARRONDISSEMENT
● La Marmite

2 bd de Clichy, 75018 **Map** 15D1

[C] 01 42 55 83 42

FAX 01 42 55 83 42

[≡] MC, V [11] €

Mediterranean restaurant with very
competitive prices: magret de canard
with garlic potatoes and salmon with
sorrel and tagliatelle star.

18E ARRONDISSEMENT
● Le Templier de Montmartre

9 rue des Abbesses, 75018 **Map** 15D1

[C] 01 42 54 88 64

[≡] MC, V [11] €

Friendly fondue (both meat and cheese)
specialist. Lighter fare such as fish
baked en papillote and apple crumble
are also served. Small terrace looking
out onto a lively street.

18E ARRONDISSEMENT
● Le Wepler

14 pl de Clichy, 75018 **Map** 14C1

[C] 01 45 22 53 24

FAX 01 44 70 07 50

● Restaurant ■ Hotel ▲ Hotel / Restaurant

AE, DC, MC, V

🍴 €€€

*Retro-style brasserie open until late into
the night. Good for afternoon tea, early
evening cocktails and pre- or post-show
suppers. Large shellfish platters as well
as sauerkraut, andouillette and confit
de canard (p326). A venerated Parisian
institution, established in 1892.*

18E ARRONDISSEMENT
● L'Oriental

76 rue des Martyrs, 75018 **Map** 15D1

📞 01 42 64 39 80

FAX 01 42 64 39 80

W www.loriental-restaurant.com

AE, MC, V ● Sun, Mon; late
Jul–late Aug 🍴 €€

*Gurgling fountains and rich fabrics at
this chic Moroccan restaurant. Gourmet
North African cuisine: remarkably fine
seafood tagines, salmon with anise and
dates, or saffron cod with potatoes.*

18E ARRONDISSEMENT
● Musée de la Halle St-Pierre

2 rue Ronsard, 75018 **Map** 15D1

📞 01 42 58 72 89

FAX 01 42 64 39 78

● D 🍴 €

*Formerly a covered market, this venue
now hosts a library, the Max Fourny
primitive art museum and a restaurant.
Popular spot for afternoon tea and
pastries. At lunch, the menu is more
substantial with quiche, pies and tarts.*

18E ARRONDISSEMENT
■ Regyn's Montmartre

18 pl des Abbesses, 75018 **Map** 15D1

📞 01 42 54 45 21

FAX 01 42 23 76 69

W www.regynsmontmartre.com

AE, MC, V ◇ (22) €€€

*Near Sacré-Coeur, this is an impeccably
kept hotel. Top-floor guestrooms have
views of the Eiffel Tower.*

20E ARRONDISSEMENT
● Café Noir

15 rue St-Blaise, 75020

📞 01 40 09 75 80

MC, V ● L 🍴 €€

*An old-fashioned café, overlooking a tiny
and picturesque paved street, with a*

*collection of old dolls and copper utensils.
Traditional French cuisine with gourmet
touches, such as beef with foie gras,
and gingerbread for dessert.*

20E ARRONDISSEMENT
■ Hôtel Armstrong

36 rue de la Croix St-Simon, 75020

📞 01 43 70 53 65

FAX 01 43 70 63 31

W www.armstrongparis.com

AE, DC, MC, V

◇ (61) €€€

*Elegant, Haussmann-style building with
a colourful, modern lounge. Bedrooms
have flowery, traditional interiors.*

20E ARRONDISSEMENT
● La Boulangerie

15 rue des Panoyaux, 75020

📞 01 43 58 45 45

W www.restaulaboulangerie.com

MC, V ● Sun, Sat L, Aug: L;
2 wks Aug 🍴 €€

*A converted bakery with a beautiful
mosaic floor. Poached fish with balsamic
vinegar and pecans, leg of lamb with
figs, and strawberry tart with lime and
kiwi coulis show the creative approach.
The menu changes every three months.*

20E ARRONDISSEMENT
● La Mère Lachaise

78 bd de Ménilmontant, 75020

📞 01 47 97 61 60

MC, V 🍴 €

*Friendly bistro with a split personality. A
great terrace and two dining rooms, one
traditional and the other plastered in
aluminium. Uncomplicated food like
asparagus and citrus fruit salad, beef
with potato gratin, charcuterie and
crumble with seasonal fruit.*

20E ARRONDISSEMENT
● Piston Pélican

15 rue de Bagnolet, 75020

📞 01 43 70 35 00

MC, V 🍴 €€

*A long bar, wooden benches and a
collection of old advertisements adorn
this quaint venue. Salads served in
hollowed-out bread, salmon tartare with
sesame oil and caramel chocolate cake
exemplify the menu's twist on classics.*

20E ARRONDISSEMENT
● Ritals et Courts

1 rue des Envierges, 75020

📞 01 47 97 08 40

FAX 01 47 97 58 22

DC, MC, V ● Sun D, Mon

🍴 €€

*This unpretentious bistro with an arty
atmosphere has a wonderful view of the
city. Italian fare: Parma ham ravioli,
lasagne and grilled meat with Gorgonzola.*

ANGERVILLE
▲ Hôtel de France

2 pl du Marché, 91670 **Map** 3E5

📞 01 69 95 11 30

FAX 01 69 95 39 59

W www.hotelfrance3.com

AE, MC, V 🍴 €€ ◇ (20) €€€

*Exposed stonework, beamed ceilings
and period furniture throughout: a place
with character. Chef and owner Anne-
Marie Tarrene-Faucheux prepares duck,
fish with watercress sauce and red berry
soup. Comfortable guestrooms.*

ASNIERES-SUR-SEINE
● Le Van Gogh

2 quai Aulagnier, 92600 **Map** 2B1

📞 01 47 91 05 10

FAX 01 47 93 00 93

W www.levangogh.com

AE, DC, MC, V

● Sun, Sat; Aug, Dec

🍴 €€€€€

*The fireplace crackles in winter and in
summer the terrace offers great views
of the Seine. Lobster in puff pastry, veal
kidneys and duck terrine on the menu.*

ASNIERES-SUR-SEINE
■ Wilson Hôtel

10 bis rue du Château, 92600 **Map** 2B1

📞 01 47 93 01 66

FAX 01 47 33 74 98

W www.hotelwilson.com

AE, DC, MC, V ◇ (62) €€

*In a quiet residential suburb, yet the
centre of Paris is within easy reach.
Tastefully decorated rooms. Pleasant
garden, where breakfast can be taken.*

AULNAY-SOUS-BOIS
● Auberge des Sts Pères

212 ave de Nonneville, 93600 **Map** 2C1

C 01 48 66 62 11
FAX 01 48 66 67 44
⊘ AE, MC, V ● Sun, Wed D, Sat; Aug
❙❙ €€€€

This large townhouse is renowned for Chef Jean-Claude Cahagnet's pioneering gourmet cuisine: foie gras and ceps flan with pistachio cream sauce and gingerbread and lamb in chocolate with sweet potato and coffee-milk gratin.

AUVERS-SUR-OISE
▲ Hostellerie du Nord

6 rue Général de Gaulle, 95430 **Map** 3E4
C 01 30 36 70 74
FAX 01 30 36 72 75
⊘ AE, DC, MC, V
● Sun; 2 wks Aug (hotel)
❙❙ €€€€ **☞** (8) €€€€

A 17th-century coaching inn. In the kitchen, Chef Joël Boilleaut delivers gastronomic fare such as tempura of ginger-marinated chicken wings. Room designs honour famous painters.

BARBIZON
▲ Hôtellerie du Bas Bréau

22 rue Grande, 77630 **Map** 3F5
C 01 60 66 40 05
FAX 01 60 69 22 89
W www.bas-breau.com
⊘ AE, MC, V
❙❙ €€€€€ **☞** (20) €€€€€

A former coaching inn. In the wood-panelled dining room, game and fine regional cheeses complete the offering. The rooms exude a pastoral feel.

BOULOGNE-BILLANCOURT
▲ Les Quatre Saisons at Hôtel Tryp Paris Boulogne

20–22 rue des Abondances, 92100
Map 2A2
C 01 48 25 80 80
FAX 01 48 25 33 13
W www.tryp.hotel.paris.boulogne.com
⊘ AE, MC, V
● Sun, Sat; Aug
❙❙ €€€€ **☞** (75) €€€

Close to all the action, yet in a quiet residential area. The seasonal menu is best appreciated by the open fire in winter, and on the terrace in fair weather. Grilled steak and fish with steamed vegetables. Quiet accommodation.

BRIE-COMTE-ROBERT
▲ A la Grâce de Dieu

79 rue Général Leclerc, 77170 **Map** 2C2
C 01 64 05 00 76
FAX 01 64 05 60 57
W www.gracededieu.com
⊘ AE, DC, MC, V ● Sun D
❙❙ €€ **☞** (18) €€€

A 17th-century coaching inn with simply furnished guestrooms that have original features such as exposed beams. Classics such as duck, foie gras and scallops.

CHAUMES-EN-BRIE
▲ La Chaum'Yerres

Pont de l'Yerres, 77390 **Map** 3F5
C 01 64 06 03 42
FAX 01 64 06 36 15
W www.chaumyerre.fr
⊘ AE, DC, MC, V
● Sun D, Mon; 1 wk Jan, 2 wks Nov
❙❙ €€€ **☞** (9) €€€

Mansion covered with ivy. In the dining room, copperware hangs on the walls. On the menu are dishes such as foie gras with prunes. Guestrooms are rustic.

CHAUMONTEL
▲ Château de Chaumontel

21 rue André Vassord, 95270 **Map** 3F4
C 01 34 71 00 30
FAX 01 34 71 26 97
W www.chateau-chaumontel.fr
⊘ AE, DC, MC, V
● Sun D; 2 wks Aug
❙❙ €€€€ **☞** (18) €€€€

Once a hunting lodge for the Princes of Condé, this 18th-century castle has allure. Inventive cooking includes warm foie gras with chutney and balsamic vinegar and grilled fish tournedos with cream. Comfortable guestrooms.

CORBEIL-ESSONNES
● Aux Armes de France

1 bd Jean Jaurès, 91100 **Map** 3F5
C 01 64 96 24 04
FAX 01 60 88 04 00
W www.auxarmesdefrance.com
⊘ AE, DC, MC, V
● Sun, Sat L **❙❙** €€€

Inventive combinations such as soft-boiled egg with a cep crust or rosemary duckling. The dining room features hunting trophies and silver cutlery.

DAMPIERRE
▲ La Table des Blot at Auberge du Château

1 Grande Rue, 78720 **Map** 3E4
C 01 30 47 56 56
FAX 01 30 47 51 75
⊘ MC, V ● Sun D, Mon, Tue; 1 wk Aug, 1 wk Feb
❙❙ €€€ **☞** (10) €€€€

Half-timbered house near a forest. The food goes beyond the classics: traditional yet refined and perfectly mastered. Rustic chic guestrooms.

ENGHIEN-LES-BAINS
▲ Hôtel du Lac

89 rue du Général de Gaulle, 95880
Map 2B1
C 01 39 34 11 00
FAX 01 39 34 11 01
W www.lucienbarriere.com
⊘ AE, DC, MC, V ● Sat L
❙❙ €€€€€ **☞** (109) €€€

At the heart of the spa resort. The terrace overlooks the lake. High quality traditional cuisine, and contemporary guestrooms.

ENGHIEN-LES-BAINS
▲ L'Aventurine at Grand Hôtel

85 rue Général de Gaulle, 95880
Map 2B1
C 01 39 34 10 00
FAX 01 39 34 10 01
⊘ AE, DC, MC, V ● Mon
❙❙ €€€€€ **☞** (49) €€€€€

A hint of exoticism such as poached raspberries with vanilla. Tearoom in the afternoon. Guestrooms have a colonial feel.

FONTAINEBLEAU
▲ Le Beauharnais at Grand Hôtel de l'Aigle Noir

27 pl Napoléon Bonaparte, 77300
Map 3F3
C 01 60 74 60 00
FAX 01 60 74 60 01
W www.hotelaiglenoir.fr
⊘ AE, DC, MC, V
● Mon, Tue, Wed–Sat L
❙❙ €€€€€
☞ (53) €€€€€

Imperial style throughout for this mansion in front of Fontainebleau castle. Such a majestic setting does credit to Chef Rémy Bidron's cuisine. Bresse chicken

*in a truffle-oil bouillon and roast sea
bass are menu stars. Luxurious rooms.*

FONTAINEBLEAU

▲ Le Montijo at Grand Hôtel de
l'Aigle Noir

27 pl Napoléon Bonaparte, 77300
Map 3F5

C 01 60 74 60 00

FAX 01 60 74 60 01

W www.hotelaiglenoir.fr

AE, DC, MC, V

🍴 €€€ 🍷 (53) €€€€€

*A first-class hotel-restaurant. Less
culinary sophistication than at sister
venue Le Beauharnais, but still the same
impeccable service and carefully selected gourmet produce. The speciality is
lobster roulade. Top-class guestrooms.*

HOUDAN

● La Poularde

24 ave de la République, 78550
Map 3E4

C 01 30 59 60 50

FAX 01 30 59 79 71

W www.alapoularde.com

AE, MC, V ● Sun D, Mon, Tue; 1
wk Feb, 2 wks Aug **🍴** €€€

*In a mansion nestled in an oasis of
greenery. Poularde (fattened hen) is
undoubtedly Sylvain Vandenameele's
speciality. Try it cooked en papillote or
stuffed with white truffles.*

ISSY-LES-MOULINEAUX

● River Café

146 quai de Stalingrad, 92130 **Map** 2B2

C 01 40 93 50 20

FAX 01 41 46 19 45

W www.lerivercafe.net

AE, DC, MC, V ● Sat L

🍴 €€

*Barge moored on the Seine, with a
colonial-style dining room. European
classics with exotic twists: salmon
tartare and superb magret de canard
with ginger fried noodles.*

LA FERTE-GAUCHER

▲ Hôtel du Sauvage

27 rue de Paris, 77320 **Map** 3F4

C 01 64 04 00 19

FAX 01 64 04 02 50

W www.hotel-du-sauvage.com

AE, DC, MC, V ● Sun D, Mon L,
Fri D **🍴** €€€ 🍷 (23) €€

*Half-timbered house with a restaurant
serving light dishes such as poached
eggs with Brie and apple tart. Covered
swimming pool and reading salons add
to the place's comfort. Spacious rooms.*

LA VARENNE-ST-HILAIRE

▲ Le Château des Iles

85 quai Winston Churchill, 94210
Map 2C2

C 01 48 89 65 65

FAX 01 42 83 06 63

W www.chateau-des-iles.com

AE, MC, V ● Sun D

🍴 €€€€ 🍷 (12) €€€

*Occupying a veranda, the dining area ben-
efits from the surrounding greenery.
Tomato and crab millefeuille, pan-fried
pigeon with tripe and foie gras and a raspberry tart with pistachio mousse feature.*

LE PERREUX-SUR-MARNE

● Les Magnolias

48 ave de Bry, 94170 **Map** 2C2

C 01 48 72 47 43

FAX 01 48 72 22 28

W www.lesmagnolias.com

AE, DC, MC, V ● Sun, Mon L, Sat
L; Aug **🍴** €€€€

*Exquisite cuisine, each dish being a
marvel of culinary sophistication: duckling
and vegetable crumble with lime-scented
papaya and rice is a fine example.*

LES LOGES-EN-JOSAS

▲ Le Relais de Courlande

23 rue de la Division Leclerc, 78350
Map 2A2

C 01 30 83 84 00

FAX 01 39 56 06 72

W www.relais-de-courlande.com

AE, DC, MC, V

🍴 €€€€ 🍷 (53) €€€€

*In a massive park, a gourmet restaurant
serving country cuisine, such as pig's
trotters with foie gras and crisp oyster
mushrooms and braised lobster with
crystallized fennel. Stylish lodgings.*

LEVALLOIS-PERRET

▲ Le Bouchon at La Champagne Hôtel

20 rue Baudin, 92300 **Map** 2B1

C 01 47 48 96 00

FAX 01 47 58 13 29

W www.lachampagnehotel.com

AE, MC, V ● Sun, Sat; 3 wks Aug

🍴 €€€ 🍷 (30) €€€

*On the outskirts of Paris yet exuding the
conviviality and tranquillity of a country
inn. The emphasis is on simple cooking:
bacon and goats' cheese toast is one of
the house specialities. Charming rooms.*

LEVALLOIS-PERRET

● Le Petit Poucet

4 rond-point Claude Monet, 92300
Map 2B1

C 01 47 38 61 85

FAX 01 47 38 20 49

W www.le-petitpoucet.net

AE, DC, MC, V **🍴** €€

*On an island in the Seine, once an
open-air café (established 1910), now
a modern-style bistro featuring a bright
and airy dining room, a terrace and a
patio. On the menu are sea bass with
fennel and cucumber millefeuille.*

LISSES

▲ Espace Léonard de Vinci

Ave des Parcs, 91090 **Map** 3F5

C 01 64 97 66 77

FAX 01 64 97 59 21

W www.leonard-de-vinci.com

AE, MC, V

🍴 €€€€ 🍷 (74) €€€€€

*Relaxation offered in the spa, including
a state-of-the-art fitness centre. Three
restaurants on site. The best is Le Vinci,
serving dishes such as beef fillet with
foie gras. Basic rooms.*

MONTIGNY-LE-BRETONNEUX

▲ Auberge du Manet

61 ave du Manet, 78180 **Map** 2A2

C 01 30 64 89 00

FAX 01 30 64 55 10

W www.aubergedumanet.com

AE, DC, MC, V

🍴 €€€€ 🍷 (35) €€€

*Once the offices of an agricultural firm,
restored to offer well-equipped rooms
and a restaurant. Both vegetarian and
Provençal menus available.*

NEAUPHLE-LE-CHATEAU

▲ Domaine du Verbois

38 ave de la République, 78640 **Map** 3E4

For key to symbols see back flap

01 34 89 11 78
FAX 01 34 89 57 33
AE, DC, MC, V
Sun D; 2 wks Aug, last wk Dec
€€€€ (22) €€€

Stylish 19th-century mansion. Period furniture throughout, and a huge park. Traditional cuisine with a modern twist: roast sea bass with baby vegetables and pesto, and beef fillet in a puff pastry. Individually decorated guestrooms.

NEUILLY-SUR-SEINE
● Café de la Jatte
60 bd Vital-Bouhot, 92200 **Map** 2B2
01 47 45 04 20
FAX 01 47 45 19 32
@ cafejatte@club-internet.fr
AE, DC, MC, V ● €€€

The dining room here is so vast that it accommodates an impressive dinosaur skeleton, which hangs from the ceiling. Rich menu including both native and international classics such as fennel salad, cod curry and pistachio ice cream.

NEUILLY-SUR-SEINE
● Chez Livio
6 rue de Longchamp, 92200 **Map** 2B2
01 46 24 81 32
FAX 01 47 38 20 72
AE, MC, V
Sun, Sat; Aug ● €€

Patio restaurant offering Italian fare: rich ravioli filled with cheese and spinach or beef with rocket (arugula), Parmesan and cherry tomatoes. Exceptional tiramisu.

NEUILLY-SUR-SEINE
● La Guinguette de Neuilly
12 bd Georges Seurat, Ile de la Jatte, 92200 **Map** 2B2
01 46 24 25 04
FAX 01 47 38 20 49
W www.laguinguette.net
AE, MC, V ● €€€

Set on a verdant island on the Seine, the traditional decor and old-fashioned cooking such as pot-au-feu and cod with mashed potatoes revive the spirit of the guinguette (1930s open-air café).

NEUILLY-SUR-SEINE
● La Truffe Noire
2 pl Parmentier, 92200 **Map** 2B2

01 46 24 94 14
FAX 01 46 24 94 60
AE, MC, V
Sun, Sat; Aug
€€€€€

Black truffles can be sampled here all year long, as the restaurant receives harvests from various regions of France. Fish mousseline with buttery sauce is the house speciality.

NEUILLY-SUR-SEINE
● Le Bistrot d'à Côté
4 rue Boutard, 92200 **Map** 2B2
01 47 45 34 55
FAX 01 47 45 15 08
W www.michelrostang.com
AE, DC, MC, V
Sun, Sat L; 1 wk Aug
● €€€

Classy yet authentic Parisian bistro, with a collection of antique coffee grinders adding to its character. Tradition is respected with dishes such as kidneys, fish quenelle and hake with Niçoise-style vegetables. For dessert, the small pots of chocolate cream are a must.

NEUILLY-SUR-SEINE
● Sébillon
20 ave Charles de Gaulle, 92200
Map 2B2
01 46 24 71 31
FAX 01 46 24 43 50
AE, DC, MC, V
€€€€

High-class 1900-style brasserie, famous for its leg of lamb, carved at the table. Shellfish and other traditional dishes are also on the menu. Boasts a cigar box and fine wine cellar.

NOGENT-SUR-MARNE
▲ Le Canotier at Mercure Nogentel
8 rue du Port, 94130 **Map** 2B2
01 48 72 70 00
FAX 01 48 72 86 19
W www.accor-hotels.com
AE, DC, MC, V
Sun D
€€€€ (60) €€€

Venue overlooking the harbour. The cuisine uses a great deal of fine herbs: fish in a crust with herb-flavoured foamy milk sauce and calf's liver with a peach

and verbena infusion. Contemporary, but quite pleasant, guestrooms.

PROVINS
▲ Aux Vieux Remparts
3 rue Couverte, 77160 **Map** 3F5
01 64 08 94 00
FAX 01 60 67 77 22
W www.auxvieuxremparts.com
AE, DC, MC, V
€€€ (32) €€€€

At the heart of the medieval part of town this building hosts two restaurants and a hotel. Traditional cuisine at Le Petit Ecu and gastronomic fare at its eponymous restaurant where dishes such as prawns with aubergine (eggplant) caviar and a lemon and tomato dressing grace the gourmet menu. Tastefully decorated guestrooms, some with period furniture.

ROLLEBOISE
▲ Château de la Corniche
5 route de la Corniche, 78270 **Map** 3E4
01 30 93 20 00
FAX 01 30 42 27 44
W www.chateaudelacorniche.com
AE, DC, MC, V
Sep–Apr: Sun D; mid-Dec–
1st wk Jan €€€€
(35) €€€€

The restaurant at this 19th-century mansion has views of the Seine. On the menu, sole meunière and raspberry vinegar duck. Old-fashioned rooms.

RUEIL-MALMAISON
▲ Le Victor Hugo
4 ave Victor Hugo, 92500 **Map** 2A2
01 47 51 21 82
FAX 01 47 51 21 82
W www.hotelvictorhugo.com
MC, V
Sun, Sat, public holidays
€€€ (16) €€

Honest fare with plenty of classics such as steak-frites. Though simply furnished, the guestrooms are well equipped.

ST-CLOUD
▲ La Villa Henri IV
43 bd de la République, 92210 **Map** 2A2
01 46 02 59 30
FAX 01 49 11 11 02
W www.villahenri4.com

● Restaurant ■ Hotel ▲ Hotel / Restaurant

AE, DC, MC, V

Sun D

€€€€

(36) €€€€

Elegant town house with a beamed ceiling in the dining room, where such delights as veal with almonds and foie gras are served. Louis XVI-style furniture in the bedrooms

ST-GERMAIN-EN-LAYE

▲ **Cazaudehore at La Forestière**

1 ave Kennedy, 78100 **Map** 2A1

01 30 61 64 64

FAX 01 39 73 73 88

www.cazaudehore.fr

AE, DC, MC, V

Mon; Nov–mid Feb

€€€€€ (30) €€€€€

Nestled in an oasis of greenery, this large residence offers comfortable guestrooms, most of which follow a country theme. On the menu are sea bass with vegetable confit *and a Bayonne ham-flavoured sauce and prawns with almond-milk polenta.*

ST-MAUR-DES-FOSSES

● **Le Jardin d'Ohé**

29 quai de Bonneuil, 94100 **Map** 2C2

01 48 83 08 26

FAX 01 42 83 81 14

www.jardindohe.fr

AE, MC, V ● Sun D, Mon, Tue; 2 wks Apr, 2 wks Nov €€€€

Charming country feel at this inn on the banks of the Marne. Southwestern influence for the foie gras marinated in wine, and inspiration from Brittany for the lobster ravioli.

ST-OUEN

● **Le Coq de la Maison Blanche**

37 bd Jean Jaurès, 93400 **Map** 2B1

01 40 11 01 23

FAX 01 40 11 67 68

www.coqdelamaisonbl.com

AE, DC, MC, V ● Sun

€€€

Elegant yet comfortable venue, steps from the St-Ouen flea market and just a short drive from the Stade de France. Impressive shellfish platters, sea bass in a salt crust, game terrine and roasted leg of lamb with broad (fava) beans.

ST-OUEN

● **Le Soleil**

109 ave Michelet, 93400 **Map** 2B1

01 40 10 08 08

FAX 01 40 10 16 85

AE, MC, V

Sun–Wed D

€€€

Near the St-Ouen flea market, a funky bistro with a big sun adorning the ceiling. Menu includes gazpacho with prawn tails and spicy duck with black rice. Booking is essential.

SURESNES

● **Five**

5 quai Marcel Dassault, 92150 **Map** 2A2

01 45 06 55 55

FAX 01 41 38 68 40

www.lefive.com

AE, DC, MC, V

Sun, Sat L

€€€

Colourful barge, moored on the Seine, serving a rich menu of food from all over the globe such as king prawns with sautéed potatoes and tomatoes or rabbit rosemary stew.

TREMBLAY-EN-FRANCE

▲ **Restaurant Primevère at Comfort Inn**

141 ave Gilbert Berger, 93290 **Map** 2C1

01 49 63 96 00

FAX 01 48 60 14 10

www.tremblayenfrance.comfort-inn.fr

AE, DC, MC, V

€€€ (42) €€

Lying at the heart of Tremblay forest, this large mansion offers veal in a mushroom sauce and fish in a courgette crust, alongside some all-you-can-eat buffet menus. Neat and colourful rooms.

VERSAILLES

▲ **Trianon Palace**

1 bd de la Reine, 78000 **Map** 2A2

01 30 84 50 00

FAX 01 30 84 50 01

AE, DC, MC, V

Sun, Mon; Aug

€€€€€

(192) €€€€€

On the edge of the Château de Versailles, a luxurious, Regency-style

hotel and restaurant. Flavourful cuisine features dishes such as wild snail and vegetable stew with garlic mayonnaise. Formal dress required. Gorgeous guestrooms provide a welcome haven.

VILLE-D'AVRAY

▲ **Les Etangs de Corot**

53 rue de Versailles, 92410 **Map** 2A2

01 41 15 37 00

FAX 01 41 15 37 99

www.sodexho-prestige.fr

AE, DC, MC, V

Sun, Mon; Aug

€€€€ (49) €€€

Romantic setting by the lovely lakes immortalized by Impressionist painter Corot. Three restaurants, including Les Paillottes, by the waterside. Creative cuisine: spicy duck and chocolate dishes are some of the house specialities. Classically styled guestrooms.

VILLEPINTE

▲ **Hôtel Mercure Paris Villepinte**

54 ave des Nations, 95971 **Map** 2C1

01 48 63 26 10

FAX 01 48 63 28 01

www.hotel-le-patio.com

AE, DC, MC, V

€€€

(85) €€€

A convenient if lacklustre location near Roissy Airport and the Villepinte Exhibition Centre. High-quality cooking: duck with cranberry sauce and scallops in puff pastry with mixed diced vegetables. Guestrooms are pleasant and quiet.

YERRES

▲ **Château du Maréchal de Saxe**

Ave du Domaine de la Grange, 91330 **Map** 2B2

01 69 48 78 53

FAX 01 69 83 84 91

www.chateaudumarechaldesaxe.com

AE, DC, MC, V

€€€€€

(18) €€€€€

White stone and red brick 17th-century castle. A setting and cuisine worthy of a king with dishes such as red mullet tournedos with glazed cherry tomatoes and black olives. Period furniture in the comfortable, quiet guestrooms.

LE NORD
& PICARDY

Though its image is of industry and flat expanses, the landscape here ranges from the Baie de Somme marshes to the verdant pastures of the Avesnois and the gentle hills of Flanders, with dynamic Lille and the Gothic cathedrals of Amiens, Beauvais and Laon adding vibrancy and culture. Food is hearty and rustic, and beer the drink of choice.

The Flavours of Le Nord & Picardy

A northerly climate suits the hardy winter vegetables that form the backbone of this region's robust cuisine. The bounty of the North Sea is also much prized, along with game, marsh-reared lamb and beer-washed cheeses.

ENDIVES AND CHICORÉE

Chicory *(endive)*, also known locally as *witloofs* or *chicon*, was introduced from Belgium in the 19th century, and the north of France is now the world's leading producer. It is initially grown outdoors in fields, then the shoots are replanted and forced in the dark to ensure their white colour. *Chicorée à café* is a member of the same family, of which the bitter root is roasted and ground like coffee. It has connotations of wartime rationing, when it was used as a substitute for real coffee, but remains a popular breakfast drink in northern France.

Spectacular array of Boulogne-caught fish

MEAT AND CHARCUTERIE

Today agriculture is no longer dominated by the sheep that once made the fortune of the great wool towns, though they still graze on the salt marshes of the Baie de Somme, producing a delicate *pré-salé* lamb. Cows are mainly kept for dairy produce.

The best chickens come from Licques, where they and guinea fowl have a *label rouge (see p11)*. Colvert ducks are raised on the Somme wetlands. Bred from wild strains, they are smaller, leaner and more gamey than other farmed ducks.

The best known charcuterie is the jellied, white-meat terrine *potjevleesch (see p78)*. *Langue Lucullus*, smoked ox tongue studded with foie gras, is a speciality of Valenciennes. Cambrai and Arras are known for their *andouillettes* and Amiens for its *andouillette de canard*.

FISH AND SHELLFISH

Boulogne is France's leading fishing port. Pride of the catch is herring, which is smoked in numerous forms: kippers, buckling, *bouffi*, *gendarme* and *craquelot*. Seafood includes tiny grey North Sea shrimps.

Inland, wooden *anguillères* traps are laid across canals to catch eels, while other freshwater fish include trout, pike and carp.

CHEESE

Le Nord calls itself "the land of strong cheeses". Pungent Maroilles AOC is a thick, square, unpressed cheese with

Fresh chicory (endive)

Left Maturing cheeses, Philippe Olivier **Right** Jars of *potjevleesch*

Market at Boulogne-sur-Mer

an orangey brine-washed rind. It has a powerful smell and a delicious, complex flavour. It is one of France's oldest cheeses, supposedly invented by a monk in 962. Most other northern cheeses are its descendants. They include Vieux Lille (nicknamed *gris puant*: smelly grey), which is washed in brine and beer, Rollot and Coeur d'Arras. Conical red Boulette d'Avesnes and dolphin-shaped Dauphin are both made from fresh Maroilles flavoured with pepper and herbs. Two exceptions are Mimolette, a deep orange Gouda-like cheese often eaten matured until cracked and almost brick-hard, and Mont des Cats, a mild, monastery-produced cheese.

FRUIT, VEGETABLES AND CEREALS

Large expanses of wheat and sugar beet, and fields of potatoes, beans, peas, chicory and carrots contrast with small-scale market gardening around St-Omer, Laon and in the *hortillonnages* of Amiens – created on the dried-out marshy bed of the Somme and surrounded by a network of canals, along which vegetables are transported in flat-bottomed boats. Laon is known for its artichokes, Soissons for its beans. Other typical regional produce includes chicory, beetroot, watercress and rhubarb. The north is France's main producer of potatoes, and varieties include *bintje*, favourite for purées and *frîtes*, and the little, elongated, yellow-fleshed *ratte du Touquet*, perfect steamed, boiled or in salads. Wild samphire *(salicorne)* is gathered in the salt marshes around St-Valéry-sur-Somme in the Baie de Somme.

BAKED GOODS AND SWEETS

Regional baked specialities include *gâteau Carpeaux* from Valenciennes, made with *marrons glacés*, *cramique*, a brioche-like cake with raisins, and Amiens' honey and almond *macarons*. The best-known sweets are *Bêtises de Cambrai*, striped mint-and-caramel bonbons.

Pâtisserie Meert in Lille

Regional Dishes

The north of France is often unduly neglected as one of France's gastronomic regions. It has contributed some classic dishes, such as carbonnade de boeuf *and* potage Crécy, *and its brasserie cuisine is a source of huge pride.*

ON THE MENU

Anguille au vert Eel baked with green herbs and potatoes
Coq à la picarde or **à la bière** Cockerel cooked in beer with onions and juniper
Endives gratinées au jambon Chicory rolled in ham, baked in béchamel sauce
Flamiche aux poireaux Leek tart
Hochepot flamand Mixed meat and vegetable hotpot
Macquereau à la boulonnaise Poached mackerel with mussels
Potjevleesch Rabbit, pork, chicken and veal terrine in jelly
Lapin aux pruneaux or **à la flamande** Rabbit with prunes
Soupe à la bière or **flamande** Soup of eggs, beer and cream
Potage Crécy Carrot soup
Tarte aux rhubarbe Rhubarb tart
Tourte au Maroilles Maroilles cheese pie
Turbot rôti à la bière Roast turbot in beer with mushrooms
Velouté de potiron Cream of pumpkin soup

Ficelle picarde

THE NORTHERN MENU

The cuisine of Nord-Pas-de-Calais is a Franco-Flemish amalgam. Beer is the drink of choice, and its use in cooking is a northern culinary feature. As well as restaurants and brasseries, *estaminet (see p81)*, often serve regional dishes to accompany their brews.

As well as *waterzooï*, other fish stews and soups abound. Mounds of mussels are served with piles of *frites*. (At the Grande Braderie de Lille each September, a prize is given to the brasserie with the highest mound of mussel shells piled up outside at the end.) Herrings are pickled, rolled, soused, grilled or smoked, and tiny North Sea shrimps are fried and eaten whole.

Beef is probably the favourite meat, with oxtail often the key ingredient of *hochepot*. Chicken is served in *waterzooï*, braised in beer, roast with smoked garlic or stuffed with juniper. Sautéed leeks, or chicory, braised, baked as a gratin or as salad, accompany many dishes.

Picardy's market gardens furnish numerous soups including *soupe des hortillons* made with leeks, cabbage, potatoes, peas, lettuce and herbs. Duck is made into pies and terrines, while eels are served smoked as a starter or baked with herbs, cream and potatoes.

Northern desserts feature a whole range of sweet tarts and waffles. Chicory gets in here too, as ice cream or as flavouring for crème brûlée. Coffee will usually be accompanied by sugar-and-spice *speculoos* biscuits.

Flamiche aux poireaux

FICELLE PICARDE

This rich dish is an old-fashioned family favourite that features as a starter on many menus. A mixture of sautéed mushrooms, onions and cubes of ham, bound in a sauce of crème fraîche, is spooned on to pancakes which are rolled up and arranged in a gratin dish. More sauce is poured over, then the dish is sprinkled with grated cheese and browned in the oven.

WATERZOOÏ

This Flemish soup-like stew can be made with chicken or fish. For the latter, a variety of fish is used, such as sole, turbot and monkfish; some recipes add mussels. Leeks and carrots are sautéed in butter, then the fish fillets are added and poached in simmering stock until just cooked. The fish and vegetables are arranged in deep plates, while the liquid is reduced and thickened with egg yolks and cream and then poured over the top.

CARBONNADE DE BOEUF

An example of the northern taste for beer and sweet-savoury flavours. Sliced braising steak is browned in butter, then removed. Sliced onions are caramelized in the remaining fat with brown sugar and vinegar. Both are layered in a casserole, then covered with beer and topped with mustard-coated bread. The dish is then covered and oven-cooked slowly for three hours.

TARTE AU SUCRE

This is typical of northern home-cooking. Sweet, short pastry is glazed with egg, sprinkled with brown sugar, drizzled with cream and baked until crisp and golden.

REGIONAL DINING

The following restaurants are among those serving regional dishes at reasonable prices:

A l'Enfant du Pays
Bully-les-Mines (see p84)

Auberge de la Dune
Le Crotoy (see p88)

Auberge Sire de Créquy
Fruges (see p87)

Dame Journe
Noyon (see p90)

La Belle Porte
Vailly-sur-Aisne (see p93)

La Table de Picardie
Amiens (see p82)

Le Central
Roye (see p91)

Le Huteau
Plomion (see p90)

Le Tchiot Zinc
Amiens (see p82)

Le Verbois
St-Maximin (see p92)

L'Ecume des Mers
Lille (see p89)

Relais Charlemagne
Samoussy (see p91)

T'Kasteelhof
Mont-Cassel (see p89)

Left Fish waterzooï **Right** Carbonnade de boeuf

Regional Spirits & Beers

The north is too cold for growing grapes but is rich in cereals – oats, barley, rye and wheat – raw materials for the region's brewers and distillers. Since the collapse of the mining industry, production has become an artisanal affair, with the focus on quality and individuality.

Genièvre from Distillerie Persyn in Houlle

BEER TYPES

There are four main styles of beer brewed in the north, from simple thirst-quenchers to the darker styles for more thoughtful drinking.

Blonde Light, thirst-quenching and low in alcohol, these lager-type beers are fermented at low temperature (6–11°C).

Blanche Brewed with pale wheat malt, "white" beer is only partially filtered, resulting in a cloudy appearance and yeasty taste.

Brune Dark beer with a bitter aftertaste is made with heavily roasted malt and contains a high proportion of hops.

Ambrée This russet-coloured ale is made with toasted malt and fermented at temperatures of 15–25°C. The heat generates tumultuous fermentation, causing the yeasts to rise to the top. The brewer can then skim them off the surface.

GENIÈVRE (JUNIPER GIN)

The Dutch and Belgians had already been making *jenever*, a highly aromatic juniper-flavoured gin, for over two centuries when distilleries began to open in northern France. By 1810 there were 72 distilleries supplying rough juniper spirit to the thousands of bars catering for the region's miners. Emile Zola, in his graphic descriptions of the industrialised north during the 20th century, called these bars *assommoirs* – literally, places that deaden the senses. Today only three distilleries are left, in Houlle, Loos and Wambrechies. The *genièvre* they produce is of very high quality, appreciated as a regional speciality.

The distilled spirit is flavoured with a small amount of juniper berries or sometimes with oil of juniper. The mixture is then left to mature either in vats for a clear spirit or in oak barrels for a coloured, more rounded gin, and then blended to achieve the final taste.

Juniper gin is a superb accompaniment to smoked fish, particularly mackerel and salmon. Marvellous as an ice-cold aperitif, it can also be made into a sorbet. Top producer, Distillerie Persyn in Houlle, suggests dousing passion-fruit sorbet with its *genièvre* and serving with crunchy juniper berries or bilberries.

BEERS

The people of northern France rarely miss an occasion to enjoy their region's beer. Whether it be at the fabulous springtime carnival in Dunkirk, or at Lille's free-for-all September street sale, or simply at a get-together with family and friends, the beer flows as freely as wine does in the rest of France.

In 1900, there were still more than 2,000 breweries in northern France but the region was left

Hop plants

Hops ready for use in a brewery

SPECIAL BEERS

Bière de Noël This traditional style of beer, typically at 6–7% alcohol, is fermented at high temperature. The fully toasted malt gives this "Christmas beer" its intense flavour.
Bière de Mars Before the advent of refrigeration, brewers were obliged to make their beer in winter when it could ferment and mature slowly in cool cellars until spring. "March beer" was the first brew of the year and was reputed to be the best quality.

devastated after the two world wars and traditional beer-making almost came to an end. The revival began when the Duyck family launched their unpasteurized, pure malt beer, fermented at high temperatures for depth of flavour. They named it after the little village of Jenlain, near Valenciennes. Their success has encouraged other small breweries and the region is once again known for producing beers that have distinctive character and flavour.

Beer is made by fermenting malted barley. Hops determine the character and bitterness of the beer. The beer matures for up to one or even two months, gradually gaining in sparkle. Some brewers filter before bottling, but many now offer traditional-style, unfiltered beer with superior flavour.

ESTAMINETS

These small taverns are typical of the villages that line the border with Belgium. At one time they were the only places for local people to meet up and play a traditional game of darts, cards or billiards. Interest in these old taverns has recently revived and several have reopened, attracting both nostalgic locals and tourists hungry for folklore.

Micro-brewery

REBIRTH OF THE MICRO-BREWERIES

In the past, hundreds of the breweries in northern France were small-scale, family-run businesses and their beer was sold to local customers directly on the premises. This ancient tradition, however, gradually died out. Then, in the 1980s, Les Trois Brasseurs opened in Lille, specializing in beers brewed on site that were both unfiltered and unpasteurized. Their success inspired others to follow suit. Les Trois Brasseurs, 22 pl de la Gare, Lille (03 20 06 46 25).

Copper vat for fermenting beer

Where to Eat & Stay

ABBEVILLE

● **Auberge de la Corne**

32 chaussée du Bois, 80100 **Map** 3E2

📞 03 22 24 06 34

FAX 03 22 24 03 65

💳 AE, DC, MC, V

🌙 Sun, Fri D, Sat L 🍴 €€

The chef plunders the greengrocers'
and the fish market, creating scallops
in truffle juice with celery purée, and
monkfish with Granny Smith apples.

AGNETZ

● **Auberge de Gicourt**

466 ave de la Forêt de Hez Gicourt,

60600 **Map** 3E3

📞 03 44 50 00 31

FAX 03 44 50 42 29

💳 MC, V 🌙 Sun D, Mon, Wed D; 1st
wk Jan 🍴 €€

A quiet inn on the edge of the forest
where straightforward food drawn from
the surrounding countryside – like foie
gras and duck with ceps – is served.

AIRE-SUR-LA-LYS

▲ **Les Trois Mousquetaires**

Château du Fort-de-la-Redoute, RN43,

62120 **Map** 3E1

📞 03 21 39 01 11

FAX 03 21 39 50 10

@ phvenet@wanadoo.fr

💳 MC, V 🌙 mid-Dec–mid-Jan

🍴 €€€ 🛏 (33) €€€€€

A 19th-century mansion set in a park on
the edge of a forest. Sample the sole in
red wine, or guinea fowl in beer. Rooms
are simple. Book well in advance.

AMIENS

● **Au Relais des Orfèvres**

14 rue des Orfèvres, 80000 **Map** 3E3

📞 03 22 92 36 01

FAX 03 22 91 83 30

💳 DC, MC, V 🌙 Sun, Tue, Sat L

🍴 €€

A noted spot among locals and French
tourists. Dishes like fresh cod and
vegetable tartare with aïoli (p400), and
sweet and sour piccata of pork with
fennel show the chef's flair. Succinct,
well-selected wine list.

AMIENS

● **La Petite France**

118 rue Béranger, 80000 **Map** 3E3

📞 03 22 89 64 73

FAX 03 22 89 64 73

💳 AE, DC, MC, V 🌙 Sun D, Mon, Sat
L; mid-Jul–mid-Aug 🍴 €€

A heady mix of the Mahgreb and local
ingredients. Couscous, tagines and
paellas are all top quality and top value.

AMIENS

● **La Table Picarde**

24 pl Parmentier, 80000 **Map** 3E3

📞 03 22 92 57 54

FAX 03 22 72 35 65

@ la.table.picarde@wanadoo.fr

💳 MC, V 🌙 Sun D, Mon D; 1st 2 wks
Feb, last 2 wks Oct 🍴 €

Remarkable quality, even in a town
blessed with so many excellent restau-
rants. The menus are particularly good
value with a wide-ranging choice of
Picardy recipes. The beer list is good.

AMIENS

● **Le Bouchon**

10 rue Alexandre Fatton, 80000 **Map** 3E3

📞 03 22 92 14 32

W www.lebouchon.fr

💳 MC, V 🌙 Aug–Sep: Sun, SepJun:
Sun D 🍴 €€€

The cooking is a cut above typical bistro
fare: oxtail with potatoes, quite tangy
andouillette and baked foie gras.

AMIENS

● **Le T'chiot Zinc**

18 rue de Noyon, 80000 **Map** 3E3

📞 03 22 91 43 79

FAX 03 22 80 78 71

💳 MC, V 🍴 €€

This Art Deco building houses a Picardy
institution, cherished for more than a
century. Small wonder: the cuisine is
consistently good, particularly the
flamiche aux poireaux (p78) and catcquse.

AMIENS

● **Le Vivier**

593 route de Rouen, 80000 **Map** 3E3

📞 03 22 89 12 21

FAX 03 22 45 27 36

💳 AE, DC, MC, V 🌙 Sun, Mon;
2nd–3rd wks Aug, last wk Dec

🍴 €€€€

A rare sense of mission. The results are
dishes like sparkling fresh sole, grilled
turbot and swordfish encrusted with salt.

AMIENS

● **Les Bouchées Doubles**

11 bis rue Gresset, 80000 **Map** 3E3

📞 03 22 91 00 85

FAX 03 22 92 27 19

💳 MC, V 🍴 €

A neighbourhood favourite. Try the
huge steaks, tarts (adequate for two)
and princely desserts. The backdrop is
a former butcher's shop.

AMIENS

● **Les Marissons**

68 rue Marissons, 80000 **Map** 3E3

📞 03 22 92 96 66

FAX 03 22 91 50 50

💳 AE, DC, MC, V 🌙 Sun, Sat L

🍴 €€€

An old shipwright's shop on the banks
of the Somme. Discerning dishes like
minced foie gras with sea salt, and
monkfish roasted with apricots.

APREMONT

▲ **Le Grange aux Loups**

8 rue 11 Novembre 1918, 60300 **Map** 3F4

📞 03 44 25 33 79

FAX 03 44 24 22 22

W www.lagrangeauxloups.com

💳 MC, V 🌙 Sun, Sat L; 1st 2 wks
Jan 🍴 €€€ 🛏 (4) €€€

Chic offerings like partridge with a wild
mushroom and port sauce, and foie gras
served with prunes and Armagnac. The
wine list is strong. Cosy, beamed rooms.

ARRAS

● **La Faisanderie**

45 Grand Place, 62000 **Map** 3F2

📞 03 21 48 20 76

FAX 03 21 50 89 18

💳 AE, DC, MC, V 🌙 Sun D, Mon, Tue
L; 1st wk Jan, mid-Feb–1st wk Mar, Aug

🍴 €€€

● Restaurant ■ Hotel ▲ Hotel / Restaurant

A 17th-century home overlooking the Arras city square. Modern menu includes baked langoustine tails in vanilla oil, and sea bass in white beer.

AUTHUILLE
● **Taverne du Cochon Salé**
29 rue d'Albert, 80300 **Map** 3F2
(03 22 75 46 14
MC, V
Mon, Tue; mid-Aug–mid-Sep, last wk Dec–Jan €€
The bounty of the land appears in this former forester's cottage. Savour stuffed pig's trotters, whipped foie gras cake, and giblets prepared family-style. Excellent value for money.

BAMBECQUE
● **La Vieille Forge**
38 rue Principale, 59470 **Map** 3F1
(03 28 27 60 67
MC, V Sun D, Mon (except public holidays), Tue D, Wed D, Thu D (out of season) €€
Don't miss the fricassée of sole and lobster with fresh basil pasta, and young pigeon wings and thighs.

BAVAY
● **Bagacum**
2 rue d'Audignies, 59570 **Map** 4A2
(03 27 66 87 00
FAX 03 27 66 86 44
AE, DC, MC, V Sun D, Mon €€
A traditional restaurant in a converted barn in a sleepy village near the Belgian border. Dishes include basil-marinated scallop salad and turbot in pastry.

BAVAY
● **Le Bourgogne**
11 porte de Gommeries, 59570 **Map** 4A2
(03 27 63 12 58
FAX 03 27 66 99 74
AE, MC, V Sun D, Mon, Wed D (except public holidays); 2nd and 3d wks Feb, 1st 3 wks Aug €€€
The trans-regional menu stretches from gazpacho with large sautéed prawns to a confection of quail and duck. An exceptional, unusual dining experience. Enough Belgian and Flemish brews to charm any beer enthusiast.

BEAUVAIS
● **Le Bellevue**
3km (2 miles) on RN1 from Allonne, 60000 **Map** 3E3
(03 44 02 17 11
FAX 03 44 02 54 44
w www.restaurantlebellevue.com
MC, V Sun, Sat; mid 2 wks Aug €€
Highlights include salmon with dill, tête-de-veau, and cassoulet *(p373). Follow up with the sinfully enjoyable caramelized pear* millefeuille *for dessert.*

BELLE-EGLISE
● **La Grange de Belle-Eglise**
28 bd Rene Aimee Lagabrielle, 60540 **Map** 3E4
(03 44 08 49 00
FAX 03 44 08 45 97
MC, V Sun D, Mon, Tue L; mid-Feb–1st wk Mar, mid 2 wks Aug €€€€
One of France's finest chefs, Marc Duval, thrills guests with saffron lobster salad, langoustine basil ravioli and caramelized pears, all in the stylish, converted country barn.

BERCK
● **La Verrière**
Pl du 18 Juin, 62600 **Map** 3E2
(03 21 84 27 25
FAX 03 21 84 14 65
MC, V €€€
Gaze out to sea while enjoying mullet in tomato compote with aubergines (eggplants), or ravioli with courgettes (zucchini) and mascarpone.

BERGUES
● **Au Cornet d'Or**
26 rue Espagnole, 59380 **Map** 3F1
(03 28 68 66 27
MC, V Sun, Mon €€€
Remarkable for the purity of its approach, with a simple, exquisite menu including turbot mousseline, sole pan-fried in butter, slow-cooked veal cutlets and guinea fowl.

BERGUES
● **Le Bruegel**
1 rue de Marché-aux-Fromages, 59380

Map 3F1
(03 28 68 19 19
FAX 03 28 68 67 12
MC, V 25 Dec–2 Jan €
Savour Flemish dishes in a gracious 16th-century Spanish-style home. Wash down pork cheeks and lentils with an excellent blonde Escquelbecq.

BERRY-AU-BAC
● **La Côte 108**
1 rue Colonel Vergezac, 02190 **Map** 4A3
(03 23 79 95 04
FAX 03 23 79 83 50
AE, MC, V Sun D, Mon, Tue D; last wk Dec–1st 2 wks Jan, mid 2 wks Aug €€€
Roadside inn near the gateway to Champagne. Excellent classic cuisine: Provençal-style baked mullet, turbot with peaches, and young pigeon in rosé sauce. Well-selected wine list.

BETHUNE
▲ **Le Meurin**
15 pl de la République, 62400 **Map** 3F2
(03 21 68 88 88
FAX 03 21 68 88 89
@ marc.meurin@le-meurin.fr
AE, DC, MC, V Sun D, Mon, Tue L; 2 wks Jan, 2 wks Aug
€€€€ (7) €€€€
Superlatives abound: from the perfectly roasted sea bass to the exquisite pan-fried foie gras with rhubarb and gingerbread. Belle Epoque rooms.

BEUVRY-LA-FORET
● **La Chaumière**
685 rue Henri Fievet, route from Orchies-Marchiennes, 59310 **Map** 3F2
(03 20 71 86 38
FAX 03 20 61 65 91
AE, DC, MC, V Sun D, Mon; Feb €€
Dishes such as scallops with wild asparagus and duck with honey, have kept this lovely little spot prospering for over 20 years. The desserts, especially speculoos *or* tarte au sucre *(p79), end the meal on a high note.*

BLENDECQUES
▲ **Le St-Sébastien**
2 pl de la Libération, 62575 **Map** 3E1

C 03 21 38 13 05
FAX 03 21 39 77 85
✉ MC, V ● Sun D, Mon
🍴 €€ 🍴 (7) €€
A perfect mid-route stop, favoured by business travellers (a good sign). Small touches elevate this menu – from fricasséed pig's trotters with snails to veal liver with juniper berries, and a delectable chocolate caramel dessert.

BOLLEZEELE
▲ **Hostellerie Saint-Louis**
47 rue d'Eglise, 59470 **Map** 3E1
C 03 28 68 81 83
FAX 03 28 68 01 17
w www.hostelleriesaintlouis.com
✉ AE, MC, V ● Sun D, Mon–Sat L; last wk Dec–3rd wk Jan
🍴 €€ 🍴 (27) €€
Once home to a religious order, the site now welcomes diners and guests to its tidy rooms. Try the Maroilles cheese brioche, rhubarb tart or gaufres.

BOULOGNE-SUR-MER
▲ **La Matelote**
80 bd Ste-Beuve, 62200 **Map** 3E1
C 03 21 30 17 97
FAX 03 21 83 29 24
w www.la-matelote.com
✉ AE, DC, MC, V ● Sun D, Thu L; mid-Dec–mid-Jan
🍴 €€€ 🍴 (29) €€€€
Legendary chef turns out tuna carpaccio and turbot steak in a setting of discreet Louis XVI elegance. The wine list is worthy of long perusal, especially the whites. Rooms sport splashy colours.

BREMES-LES-ARDRES
● **La Faisanderie**
Chemin des Conduits, 62610 **Map** 3G
C 03 21 35 77 45
✉ MC, V ● Wed **🍴** €€
Enjoy rich, earthy dishes in a restored 17th-century barn. Highlights include waterzooï (p79), prawn fricassée with asparagus, and crêpes suzettes.

BRETEUIL
▲ **Taverne Picardie de Beauvoir**
18 Folie de Beauvoir, 4km (2.5 miles) from Breteuil, on D916 towards Creil, 60120 **Map** 3E3

C 03 44 07 03 57
✉ MC, V ● Sun D, Wed D; 1st 2 wks Jan, 1st 2 wks Mar, mid-Aug–1st wk Sep **🍴** €€ 🍴 (7) €€
Highlights include scallops in a cider cream sauce and roast chicken stuffed with medieval-style spices accompanied by a concise yet tempting wine list. This former village café provides comfortable and well-furnished guestrooms.

BULLY-LES-MINES
▲ **A l'Enfant du Pays**
152 rue Roger Salengro, 62160 **Map** 3F2
C 03 21 29 12 33
✉ MC, V ● Sun D, public holidays: D
🍴 €€ 🍴 (18) €
The "ch'ti" – native Northerners – pride themselves on their cooking. There's no better place to try waterzooï (p79), roast beef and exemplary beers. Simple rooms.

CALAIS
● **La Pléiade**
32 rue Jean Quéhen, 62100 **Map** 3E1
C 03 21 34 03 70
FAX 03 21 34 03 13
w www.lapleiade.com
✉ AE, DC, MC, V
● Sun, Mon; mid-Feb–1st wk Mar, last 3 wks Aug **🍴** €€
The waves – and daily catch – inspire dishes like sea bass steamed in anise. The wine list is long and thoughtful.

CALAIS
▲ **Le Petit George**
36 rue Royale, 62100 **Map** 3G
C 03 21 97 68 00
FAX 03 21 97 34 73
w www.georgev-calais.com
✉ AE, DC, MC, V ● Sun, Sat L; mid-Dec–mid-Jan **🍴** € 🍴 (39) €€
Convivial bistro atmosphere. Consistently fine fare, including salads, snails and hearty lamb steak with Maroilles cheese. Small, nicely-turned-out rooms.

CAMBRAI
▲ **Château de la Motte Fénelon**
174 allée St-Roch, 59403 **Map** 3F2
C 03 27 83 61 38
FAX 03 27 83 71 61
w www.cambraichateaudelamotte.com
✉ MC, V **🍴** €€ 🍴 (40) €€€

An innovative young chef turns out grilled scallops on toast with fine herbs, and caramelized beef with acacia honey. The brisk, modern feeling extends to the 150-year-old building's guestrooms.

CAULIERES
● **Auberge de la Forge**
14 rue du 49ème BCA, 80290 **Map** 3E3
C 03 22 38 00 91
FAX 03 22 38 08 48
w www.aubergedelaforge.fr.st
✉ MC, V ● Sun D, Wed D **🍴** €€
A perfect place to stop between Amiens and Neufchatel. Dishes like generous seafood platter, or lamb with sweet garlic sauce, assuage hunger.

CHANTILLY
● **La Belle Bio**
22 rue du Connétable, 60500 **Map** 3F4
C 03 44 57 02 25
FAX 03 44 58 03 34
✉ MC, V ● Mon D, Tue D, Wed D
🍴 €€
An unusual spot serving flavourful, zesty organic cuisine such as foie gras carpaccio on a bed of peppers, and beef with Tomme cheese. Excellent eco-friendly wines to complement.

CHANTILLY
▲ **La Carmontelle Dolce Chantilly**
Route from Apremont, Vineuil-St-Firmin, 60500 **Map** 3F4
C 03 44 58 47 77
FAX 03 44 58 50 11
w www.dolcechantilly.com
✉ AE, DC, MC, V
🍴 €€€€ 🍴 (225) €€€€€
Enjoy tasteful guest rooms and refined meals like foie gras with caramelized muscat sauce, or crispy baked striped sea bass, served in a lobster bouillon.

CHATEAU-THIERRY
● **Auberge Jean de la Fontaine**
10 rue des Filoirs, 02400 **Map** 4A4
C 03 23 83 63 89
FAX 03 23 83 20 54
✉ AE, MC, V ● Sun D, Mon; 1st 2 wks Jan, 1st 3 wks Aug **🍴** €€€
In a town which was once a battle-ground stands this peaceful, welcoming inn. Specialities include monkfish with

● Restaurant ■ Hotel ▲ Hotel / Restaurant

olive tapenade (p400), *John Dory with spice bread, and cuttlefish-ink rice.*

CHAUNY

▲ La Toque Blanche

24 ave Victor Hugo, 02300 **Map** 3F3

☎ 03 23 39 98 98

FAX 03 23 52 32 79

🗌 MC, V ⬤ Sun D, Mon, Sat L; 1st wk Jan, last 2 wks Feb, Aug

🍴 €€€ 🍽 (6) €€€

Beautiful bourgeois mansion in the heart of a park. Inspired cuisine, including quail with duck foie gras and truffle. Good wine list. Tidy, comfortable rooms.

CHELLES

● Le Relais Brunehaut

3 rue d'Eglise, 60350 **Map** 3F3

☎ 03 44 42 85 05

FAX 03 44 42 83 30

🗌 MC, V ⬤ Mon, Tue; mid-Feb–mid-Mar 🍴 €€

Bons vivants *favour this rising star, charmed by the chicken suprême with mushrooms and beef infused with truffles in foie gras sauce.*

COINCY

● Auberge de Coincy

4 route de Rocourt, 02210 **Map** 4A4

☎ 03 23 71 25 34

🗌 MC, V ⬤ Mon; Sep 🍴 €

Delectable duck terrine, scallops in Alsatian wine, and a hearty, flavourful veal liver in port. Succinct wine list.

COMPIEGNE

▲ Hostellerie du Royal-Lieu

9 rue de Senlis, 60200 **Map** 3F3

☎ 03 44 20 10 24

FAX 03 44 86 82 27

🌐 www.hostellerie-du-royal-lieu.com

🗌 AE, DC, MC, V ⬤ Sun D, Mon L

🍴 €€€ 🍽 (15) €€€

Savour fish from nearby rivers and mushrooms from the bordering forest. Or try the lamb sweetbreads braised in port, followed by a moelleux *(dark chocolate dessert). Classic guestrooms.*

COMPIEGNE

● Le Bistrot des Arts

35 cours Guynemer, 60200 **Map** 3F3

☎ 03 44 20 10 10

FAX 03 44 20 61 01

🗌 MC, V ⬤ Sun, Sat L 🍴 €€

Considered the best bistro in town by locals. Highlights include perfectly roasted swordfish, and lamb shanks braised with fresh figs.

COMPIEGNE

● Rive Gauche

13 cours Guynemer, 60200 **Map** 3F3

☎ 03 44 40 29 99

FAX 03 44 40 38 00

🗌 MC, V ⬤ Mon, Tue 🍴 €€€

An immaculate setting with a sterling reputation for dishes like rabbit sausage, minestrone, and sole with young fennel.

CORBIE

● La Table d'Agathe

6 rue Jean-et-Marcellin Truquin, 80800 **Map** 3F3

☎ 03 22 96 96 27

FAX 03 22 48 13 63

🗌 MC, V ⬤ Sun D, Mon, Tue D; 1st 2 wks Feb, 1st 2 wks Jul 🍴 €€

Somme Valley standards include fresh inventive salads, tournedos of salmon with bacon and Champagne sauce, and lamb in a creamy garlic sauce.

COUDEKERQUE-BRANCHE

● Le Soubise

49 route Bergues, 59210 **Map** 3F1

☎ 03 28 64 66 00

FAX 03 28 25 12 19

🗌 MC, V ⬤ Sun, Sat; 1st wk Apr, 1st 3 wks Aug, last 2 wks Dec 🍴 €€€

This former post house now has a distinctive wine cellar. Choices include snails with garlic, casseroled young Flemish pigeon, and gaufres.

COURCELLES-SUR-VESLES

▲ Château de Courcelles

8 rue du Château, 02220 **Map** 4A4

☎ 03 23 74 13 53

FAX 03 23 74 06 41

🌐 www.chateau-de-courcelles.fr

🗌 AE, DC, MC, V

🍴 €€€€ 🍽 (18) €€€€€

A Relais Château with a top chef cannot fail to charm. Try the langoustines with aubergine *(eggplant) confit, or turbot steaks smothered in chives and glazed onions. Excellent regional red wines.*

COYE-LA-FORET

● Les Etangs

1 rue Clos-des-Vignes, 60580 **Map** 3F4

☎ 03 44 58 60 15

FAX 03 44 58 75 95

🗌 AE, MC, V ⬤ Mon (except holidays), Tue; mid-Jan–mid-Feb 🍴 €

Robust rural cuisine is the order of the day here: Bordeaux-style pike-perch steak on a bed of lentils, and feuilleté (pastry) of caramelized pears.

CRISOLLES

● Auberge de Crisolles

44 les Usages, 60400 **Map** 3F3

☎ 03 44 09 02 32

🗌 MC, V ⬤ Sun D, Mon; last wk Jan

🍴 €€

A family-style inn, very popular with the locals. Equal in quality but with lower prices than its competitors. Cooking steeped in custom: local sausages and roast flank of veal with fresh vegetables.

CUVILLY

● L'Auberge Fleurie

64 route de Flandres, 60490 **Map** 3F3

☎ 03 44 85 06 55

🗌 MC, V ⬤ Sun D, Tue D, Wed; last wk Feb–1st wk Mar, last 2 wks Aug

🍴 €€

From seafood to freshwater fish via products of farm and field, it's all delightful and good value.

DOUAI

▲ La Terrasse

36 terrasse St-Pierre, 59500 **Map** 3F2

☎ 03 27 88 70 04

FAX 03 27 88 36 05

🗌 AE, MC, V 🍴 €€€ 🍽 (26) €€

One of the region's best wine cellars, with more than 1,000 varieties. Inspired dishes include smoked salmon stuffed with asparagus and grilled scallops with boudin noir. Welcoming rooms.

DOURLERS

● Auberge du Châtelet

3 RN2 from Avesnes-sur-Helpe, 59440 **Map** 4A2

☎ 03 27 61 06 70

FAX 03 27 61 20 02

🗌 MC, V ⬤ Sun D; 2 wks Jan, 1 wk Aug 🍴 €€

Comfort food like flammenkueche (p119). Game, calf's sweetbreads, lobster in whisky sauce and speculoos desserts are also served. Good wine list.

DREUIL-LES-AMIENS
● **Le Cottage**
385 ave Louis Pasteur, 80470 **Map** 3E3
🄲 03 22 54 10 98
🅜 MC, V ● Sun D, Mon; 1st 2 wks
Aug 🍴 €
Sample the fricassée of gizzards, a fiery pepper steak, or sauces like fine beurre blanc. Eclectic wines.

DUNKERQUE
● **L'Estouffade**
2 quai de la Citadelle, 59140 **Map** 3E1
🄲 03 28 63 92 78
🅜 MC, V ● Sun D, Mon; mid-
Aug–mid-Sep 🍴 €€€
Stunning sea views – and specialties to match, such as the turbot. Desserts include baked pineapple with Szechuan pepper and violet sorbet.

DURY
● **L'Aubergade**
78 route Nationale, 80480 **Map** 3F2
🄲 03 22 89 51 41
🅵🅰🅇 03 22 95 44 05
🅜 AE, DC, MC, V ● Sun, Mon
🍴 €€€€
The chef's efforts include marbled foie gras, baked scallops with swede (rutaba-ga) and pumpkin and notable cheeses.

EECKE
● **Brasserie St Georges**
5 rue de Caestre, 59114 **Map** 3F1
🄲 03 28 40 13 71
🅵🅰🅇 03 28 40 27 06
🅜 MC, V ● Mon L, Tue D 🍴 €
This out-of-the-way spot draws beer enthusiasts with over 100 brews. The open-fire grill specialities and cheeses – like Maroilles and Mont de Cats – are excellent. Worth seeking out.

ELINCOURT-ST-MARGUERITE
▲ **Château De Bellinglise**
A1 exit 11, 60157 **Map** 3F3
🄲 03 44 96 00 33
🅵🅰🅇 03 44 96 03 00
🅦 www.chateau-bellinglise.fr

🅜 AE, MC, V
🍴 €€€€ ◇ (35) €€€€€
Elegantly appointed 16th-century Renaissance manor. Delights include lobster salad in truffle oil with a saffron potato terrine, and baby rabbit stuffed with truffles. Superlative wine list.

ERMENONVILLE
▲ **Château d'Ermenonville**
Rue René Girardin, 60950 **Map** 3F4
🄲 03 44 54 00 26
🅵🅰🅇 03 44 54 01 00
🅦 www.chateau-ermenonville.com
🅜 MC, V 🍴 €€ ◇ (49) €€€€
A solid range of unpretentious dishes on offer, from game to seafood. Rooms are lovely, as befits the château where Rousseau spent his final days.

ERONDELLE
● **Auberge du Temps Jadis**
12 route Liercourt, D901, 80580 **Map** 3E2
🄲 03 22 27 92 27
🅵🅰🅇 03 22 27 92 27
🅜 MC, V ● Mon–Thu; Sep, last wk
Dec–mid-Jan 🍴 €€
Try the pork shins roasted in a wood oven, or pike-perch in herbs and saffron. The wine list is surprisingly good.

ESTAIRES
▲ **La Queneque**
1822 rue de l'Epinette, 59940 **Map** 3F1
🄲 03 28 40 84 69
🅜 MC, V
🍴 €€ ◇ (4) €€€€
This farmhouse turned hotel-restaurant still celebrates the harvest with rabbit and prunes, plus Flemish-style grilled meats. Simple, tidy rooms.

ESTREE
● **Le Relais de la Course**
15 rue de la Course, 62170 **Map** 3E2
🄲 03 21 06 18 04
🅵🅰🅇 03 21 06 57 92
@ lerelaisdelacourse@wanadoo.fr
🅜 MC, V ● Jul–Sep: Mon, Oct–Jun:
Sun D & Mon &Wed; 1st wk Feb 🍴 €€
A charmingly restored cottage in the rolling, sylvan countryside. Chicken with Camembert sauce is a typical offering, as well as snail ragout. The wine list is brief, affordable and apt.

ETAPLES
● **Aux Pêcheurs d'Etaples**
Bd Impératrice, 62630 **Map** 3E2
🄲 03 21 94 06 90
🅵🅰🅇 03 21 09 79 90
🅜 MC, V ● Sep-Jun: Sun D
🍴 €€
It's hard to get fresher than a restaurant-cum-fish-market. Offering a wine list perfectly matched for seafood – white, white and more white.

ETOUY
● **L'Oree de la Foret**
255 rue de la Forêt, 60600 **Map** 3E3
🄲 03 44 51 65 18
🅵🅰🅇 03 44 78 92 11
🅜 AE, DC, MC, V ● Sun D, Fri, Sat L,
D (public holidays); 1st 2 wks Jan, 1st
wk Aug–1st wk Sep 🍴 €€€€
A river runs through the parkland setting. Try the Breton lobster with fruit chutney and ham, followed by a heavenly vanilla millefeuille. Inspired wine list.

ETREAUPONT
▲ **Le Clos du Montvinage**
8 rue Albert Ledent, 02580 **Map** 4A3
🄲 03 23 97 40 18
🅵🅰🅇 03 23 97 48 92
🅦 www.clos-du-montvinage.fr
🅜 AE, DC, MC, V ● Sun D, Mon L;
1st wk Jan, 2nd wk Aug, last wk Dec
🍴 €€ ◇ (20) €€€
Finely restored bourgeois home with an acclaimed restaurant, L'Auberge du Val d'Oise. Dishes include scallops with lobster, and beef with Maroilles cheese sauce. Vegetarian menu. Lush velvet enlivens the guest chambers.

FAVIERES
● **La Clé des Champs**
13 pl Frères Caudron, 80120 **Map** 3E2
🄲 03 22 27 88 00
🅵🅰🅇 03 22 27 79 36
🅜 AE, DC, MC, V ● Mon, Tue (except
public holidays); mid-Feb–1st wk Mar,
last wk Aug–1st wk Sep 🍴 €€
The ocean, forest and countryside unite in this 19th-century farmhouse. Distinctive plates include the turbot with ginger and peppers, crab ravioli with fennel, and double-baked guinea fowl with dried fruits. Plentiful desserts.

● Restaurant ■ Hotel ▲ Hotel / Restaurant

FERE-EN-TARDENOIS
▲ Château de Fère
Route from Fisnes, 02130 **Map** 4A4
☎ 03 23 82 21 13
FAX 03 23 82 37 81
AE, DC, MC, V ● Feb–Mar &
Nov–Dec: Mon L (except public holidays);
1st 2 wks Feb
€€€€ ◆ (25) €€€€€
Quiet, sumptuous guestrooms. Style and skill blend perfectly in the langoustines with aubergine (eggplant) cake.

FLEURINES
● Auberge du Vieux Logis
105 rue Général Gaulle, 60700 **Map** 3F4
☎ 03 44 54 10 13
FAX 03 44 54 10 13
AE, DC, MC, V ● Sun D, Wed; 1st
2 wks Jan, 1st wk Aug €€€
Pure duck foie gras, and fillet of monkfish with medallions of bacon in truffle juices show the culinary imagination.

FONTENOY
● Auberge du Bord de l'Eau
1 rue du Bout-de-Port, 02290 **Map** 3F3
☎ 03 23 74 25 76
FAX 03 23 74 25 76
MC, V ● Wed; last 2 wks Jan, last
2 wks Sep €€
Straightforward, top-rank cooking near the Aisne River. Don't miss the duck foie gras or langoustines and scallops gratin.

FRUGES
● Auberge Sire de Créquy
Route de Créquy, 62310 **Map** 3E2
☎ 03 21 90 60 24
FAX 03 21 86 27 72
MC, V ● Sep–Jun: Sun L & Mon
& Tue–Sat D €
Carbonnade de boeuf (p79), potjevleesch (p76) and veal in beer served in the heart of the northern countryside.

GAMACHES
● Auberge du Double Six
24 pl Maréchal Leclerc, 80220 **Map** 3E2
☎ 03 22 26 11 39
MC, V ● Tue D, Wed D, Sep–Jun:
Mon; 1st 2 wks Jan, last wk Sep–1st
wk Oct €
A little-known gem tucked off the highway in fertile countryside. Gourmets and

truckers alike detour here for reasonably priced stuffed sole, tart with cod, and Maroilles cheese.

GOSNAY
▲ La Chartreuse du Val St-Esprit
1 rue de Fouquières, 62199 **Map** 3F2
☎ 03 21 62 80 00
FAX 03 21 62 42 50
W www.lachartreuse.com
AE, DC, MC, V
€€€ ◆ (69) €€€€
This ornate mansion hides an excellent restaurant. Dishes include foie gras with artichokes, fricasséed snails with bacon and turbot steak. A wine cellar worth nights of exploration. Luxurious rooms.

GOUVIEUX
▲ Pavilion St-Hubert
Ave de Toutevoie, 60270 **Map** 3F4
☎ 03 44 57 07 04
FAX 03 44 57 75 42
AE, MC, V ● mid-Jan–mid-Feb
€€ ◆ (18) €€
In a graceful setting on the banks of the l'Oise, try time-honoured Northern dishes like boudin noir on flaky pastry with warm apples, and sweetbreads with morels. Comfortable rooms.

GOUVIEUX
▲ Château de Montvillargenne
Ave Francois Mathet, 60270 **Map** 3F4
☎ 03 44 62 37 37
FAX 03 44 57 28 97
@ chateau@montvillargenne.com
AE, DC, MC, V
€€€€ ◆ (126) €€€€€
A château in the manner of Picardy's past, grand without overindulgence, comfortable in its heritage. The philosophy continues at the table with brisket of lamb with courgette (zucchini), or sole with tapenade (p400). Luxurious rooms.

HARBONNIERES
▲ Le Logis du Santerre
2 rue Raoul Defruit, 80131 **Map** 3F3
☎ 03 22 85 80 17
FAX 03 22 85 85 82
W www.logisdusanterre.com
MC, V €€ ● Sun D ◆ (15) €€
Tempting countryside cooking: scallops in cider with sweet potatoes and pike-

perch fresh from local streams. First-rate beer list. Basic but comfortable rooms. Full- and half-board available.

HARDELOT-PLAGE
▲ Hôtel du Parc
111 ave François 1er, 62152 **Map** 3E1
☎ 03 21 33 22 11
FAX 03 21 83 29 71
AE, DC, MC, V
€€€ ◆ (82) €€€€
A textbook example of a modern up-market resort: vast buildings overlooking a park, with lovely rooms and a stellar menu. Try the tuna carpaccio with sesame mousse.

HAZEBROUCK
● Auberge St. Eloi
60 rue d'Eglise, 59190 **Map** 3F1
☎ 03 28 40 70 23
FAX 03 28 40 70 44
DC, MC, V ● Sun D, Mon; mid 2
wks Aug €€
Dishes like frogs' leg fricassée with tomato confit, or young pigeon with bacon. The beer list, too, is well grounded.

LA CHAPELLE-EN-SERVAL
(SENLIS)
▲ Château Hôtel Mont Royal
Route from Plailly, 60520 **Map** 3F4
☎ 03 44 54 50 50
FAX 03 44 54 50 21
W www.chateau-mont-royal.com
AE, DC, MC, V
€€€€ ◆ (100) €€€€€
Elegant rooms offer the perfect place to retire after a meal at Le Stradivarius restaurant. Indulge in braised milk-raised veal with tender chicory (endive) and rhubarb. Expensive, but worth it.

LA MOTTE-AU-BOIS
▲ Auberge de la Forêt
La Motte Au Bois, 59190 **Map** 3F1
☎ 03 28 48 08 78
FAX 03 28 40 77 76
MC, V ● Sun D, Mon, Oct–Mar:
Sat L; 4th wk Aug, last wk Dec–3rd wk
Jan €€ ◆ (12) €€
Simple fare: rascasse or thick-sliced roasted tuna. The rooms are tidy, adequately sized and nicely kept. Set in a quiet location near a forest.

LAON
▲ Hôtel de la Bannière de France
11 rue Franklin Roosevelt, 02000
Map 4A3
[C] 03 23 23 21 44
FAX 03 23 23 31 56
AE, DC, MC, V ● mid-Dec–mid-Jan ‖ €€ ◇ (11) €€€
A 17th-century post house with time-tested cuisine such as sole and foie gras in balsamic vinegar. An extensive wine list.

LAON
● La Petite Auberge
45 bd Brossolette, 02000 **Map** 4A3
[C] 03 23 23 02 38
MC, V ● Sun (except public holidays), Sat L; 1 wk Feb, 1 wk Apr, 2 wks Aug ‖ €€€
Saffron spices up langoustines, while Arborio risotto nicely anchors cod with mustard sauce. Desserts are first-rate, especially the rice pudding and apple tart.

LAON
● Les Chenizelles
1 rue du Bourg, 02000 **Map** 4A3
[C] 03 23 23 02 34
MC, V ● Sun D, Mon ‖ €
Pure Northern ambience in the village centre. Famous for salads – from salade niçoise) to quirky seafood selections – plus carbonnade de bœuf (p79) and waterzooï (p79). Superb Belgian beers.

LAVENTIE
● La Cerisier
3 rue de la Gare, 62840 **Map** 3F1
[C] 03 21 27 60 59
FAX 03 21 27 60 87
[W] www.lecerisier.com
MC, V ● Sun, Mon, Sat L; mid-Feb–1st wk Mar, Aug ‖ €€€
Creativity shines in the foie gras with French toast and mango, crisped sole with potato compote, and brill with onion and spice bread. Finish with lemon tart.

LE CATELET
● Auberge La Croix d'Or
68 rue du Général Augereau, 02420
Map 3F2
[C] 03 23 66 21 71
MC, V ● Sun D, Mon; 1st wk Jan, Aug ‖ €€

Fresh, agreeable atmosphere. This inn specializes in smoked duck with celery, beef with green peppers, and salmon. Finish with a soft meringue in custard.

LE CROTOY
▲ Auberge de la Dune
36 rue de la Dune, 80550 **Map** 3E2
[C] 03 22 25 01 88
FAX 03 22 25 66 74
MC, V
● Tue D, Wed; 1st 2 wks Mar
‖ € ◇ (11) €€
Near a wildlife sanctuary. The menu offers plenty of local favourites such as ficelle picarde (p79), flamiche aux poirraux (p78), and an enviable lamb. Choose a Brouilly wine. Cosy rooms.

LE CROTOY
▲ Les Tourelles
2–4 rue Pierre Guerlain, 80550 **Map** 3E2
[C] 03 22 27 16 33
FAX 03 22 27 11 45
[W] www.lestourelles.com
MC, V ● 3rd wk Jan
‖ €€ ◇ (27) €€
Time-honoured fish and meat classics, artfully prepared. The wine list is well suited to the fruits of the sea. Cosy rooms should you tarry by the shore.

LE TOUQUET-PARIS-PLAGE
● Flavio
1 ave du Verger, 62520 **Map** 3E2
[C] 03 21 05 10 22
FAX 03 21 05 91 55
[W] www.flavio.fr
AE, DC, MC, V
● Sun D, Mon; mid-Jan–1st wk Feb
‖ €€€€
Beyond a favourite, this is an institution. Flavio's daughter keeps the magic alive, offering foie gras with Sauternes and roast lobster with tarragon butter.

LE TOUQUET-PARIS-PLAGE
▲ Le Pavilion at Le Westminster
5 ave du Verger, 62520 **Map** 3E2
[C] 03 21 05 48 48
FAX 03 21 05 45 45
AE, DC, MC, V ● L, Tue D; Jan–Feb ‖ €€€ ◇ (115) €€€€
Up-to-date menu with star dishes such as langoustines tempura, tuna carpaccio

with sardine tart, and duck foie gras grilled with cherries. Lively modern decor in dining and guestrooms.

LENS
● L'Arcadie
13 rue Decrombeque, 62300 **Map** 3F2
[C] 03 21 70 32 22
FAX 03 21 70 32 22
MC, V ● Sun D, Mon, Tue D, Wed D, Sat L, public holidays: D; mid-Feb–1st wk Mar, Aug ‖ €€
Refresh your palate with monkfish in Creole sauce, salmon with three sauces, and crème brûlée. Excellent value.

LIGNY-EN-CAMBRESIS
▲ Le Château de Ligny
2 rue Pierre Curie, 59191 **Map** 4A2
[C] 03 27 85 25 84
FAX 03 27 85 79 79
AE, MC, V ● Mon; Feb
‖ €€€€ ◇ (26) €€€€
This Renaissance château, with huge sumptuous rooms and a park setting, makes for a grand experience. The kitchen puts a Mediterranean twist on dishes such as striped mullet in rosemary and Tuscan grilled rabbit ravioli.

LILLE
● A L'Huitrière
3 rue des Chats-Bossus, 59000 **Map** 3F2
[C] 03 20 55 43 41
FAX 03 20 55 23 10
[W] www.huitriere.fr
MC, V ● Sun, D (all public holidays); last wk Jul–last wk Aug
‖ €€€€€
Famous across France, Chef Jean Proye showcases his skill with sole and lobster cooked with foie gras in bouillon, and turbot pot-roasted in beer. World-class wine cellar. Fabulous Art Deco decor.

LILLE
▲ Alliance Couvent des Minimes
17 quai du Wault, 59000 **Map** 3F2
[C] 03 20 30 62 62
FAX 03 20 42 94 25
AE, DC, MC, V ● last 2 wks July
‖ €€€€ ◇ (83) €€€€€
Red-brick,17th-century convent serving simple, traditional food. Highlights include chicken with Maroilles cheese

● Restaurant ■ Hotel ▲ Hotel / Restaurant

and a very good potjevleesch (p76).
Rooms have modern decor.

LILLE
● **Brasserie de la Paix**
25 pl Rihour, 59000 **Map** 3F2
📞 03 20 54 70 41
FAX 03 20 40 15 52
🔲 www.brasserielapaix.com
🔲 AE, MC, V ● Sun 🍴 €€
A local favourite, prized for its 1930s
decor and convivial atmosphere. Sample
the langoustine salad, choucroute
(p119) and tournedos Rossini (filet
mignon topped with duck liver mousse).
The beer list is almost unrivalled.

LILLE
● **Le Sébastopol**
1 pl Sébastopol, 59000 **Map** 3F2
📞 03 20 57 05 05
FAX 03 20 40 11 31
🔲 www.restaurant-sebastopol.fr
✉ AE, DC, MC, V ● Sun D, Mon L,
Sat L; 2 wks Aug 🍴 €€€€
Exemplary, even among Lille's abundance
of excellent restaurants. Highlights
include langoustines with asparagus,
sea bass with fennel, and beef ravioli
with morels. Outstanding beer and wine.

LILLE
● **Le Varbet**
2 rue de Pas, 59000 **Map** 3F2
📞 03 20 54 81 40
FAX 03 20 57 55 18
✉ MC, V ● Sun, Mon; public holidays,
mid-Aug–mid-Sep, last wk Dec–1st wk
Jan 🍴 €€€€
The foie gras, turbot and poultry dishes
are fabulously varied. Simple, classic
dishes, expertly executed.

LILLE
● **L'Ecume des Mers**
10 rue de Pas (across from the
convention centre), 59000 **Map** 3F2
📞 03 20 54 95 40
FAX 03 20 54 96 66
✉ AE, DC, MC, V ● Sun D; 1 May,
1st 3 wks Aug 🍴 €
Fish is best here, with notable choices
such as scallop carpaccio with truffle oil.
However, the duck with peppers and red
wine holds its own. A lively brasserie.

LILLE
● **L'Esplanade**
84 façade Esplanade, 59000 **Map** 3F2
📞 03 20 06 58 58
🔲 AE, DC, MC, V ● Sun, Sat L
🍴 €€€€
The sublime cuisine attracts international
gastronomes. Try the tender, perfect
scallops awash with truffles. The wine
list is worthy of such cooking, with
Bergerac vintages standing out.

LOOS
● **L'Enfant Terrible**
25 rue du Maréchal Foch, 59120
Map 3F1
📞 03 20 07 22 11
FAX 03 20 44 80 16
✉ MC, V ● Sun D, Mon D, Sat L; last
2 wks Aug 🍴 €€€
Plain decor: the focus here is on fine ingredients. Witness the swordfish with morels,
beef in beer sauce and the delectable
chicken in Maroilles cheese sauce.

LUMBRES
▲ **Moulin de Mombreux**
Route from Bayenghem, 62380 **Map** 3E1
📞 03 21 39 62 44
FAX 03 21 93 61 34
✉ AE, DC, MC, V ● last wk Dec–1st
wk Jan 🍴 €€€ 🍽 (24) €€€
A memorable experience, from the
master chef's menu to the guestrooms,
snuggled inside an 18th-century watermill. Duck foie gras roasted with brioche
and sea bass in wine are a credit to
the superb setting.

MARCELCAVE
● **Le Banneton**
29 rue de l'Hirondelle, 80720 **Map** 3F3
📞 03 22 42 30 78
FAX 03 22 42 30 78
✉ MC, V ● Sun, Mon; Aug 🍴 €
The bucolic setting doesn't hamper
creativity in the kitchen. Witness the
snails cooked with nettle tips and the
veal liver with caramelized apples.

MARCQ-EN-BAROEUL
● **Auberge de la Garenne**
17 Chemin de Ghesles, 59700 **Map** 3F1
📞 03 20 46 20 20
FAX 03 20 46 32 33

✉ AE, MC, V ● Sun D, Mon, Sep–
May: Tue; Aug 🍴 €€€
Expect Breton oysters on the half shell,
waterzooï (p79) gratin, and flambéed
veal liver with broad (fava) beans.

MARQUISE
● **Le Grand Cerf**
34 ave Ferber, 62250 **Map** 3E1
📞 03 21 87 55 05
FAX 03 21 33 61 09
🔲 www.legrandcerf.com
✉ DC, MC, V ● Sun D, Mon D, Thu D
🍴 €€
True passion and a fresh approach to
cooking. Highlights: cool cucumber soup
with oysters, tomatoes stuffed with crab,
and breaded tandoori langoustines with
fennel. Genteel and convivial.

MONAMPTEUIL
● **Auberge du Lac**
1 ham Moulinet, facing the lake on RN2,
02000 **Map** 4A3
📞 03 23 21 63 87
FAX 03 23 21 60 60
✉ MC, V ● Sun D, Mon, Tue D; 1st 2
wks Feb, last wk Aug–mid-Sep 🍴 €€
Bucolic setting in the green hills above
the River Ailette. Enjoy Provençal baked
frogs' legs, lamb shanks in a creamy
garlic sauce, or pike-perch with sorrel.

MONT-CASSEL
● **T'Kasteelhof**
Across from the windmill, Cassel exit
from A25, 59670 **Map** 3F1
📞 03 28 40 59 29
✉ MC, V ● Mon, Tue, Wed; 3rd wk
Jan, 1st 2 wks Oct 🍴 €
A perfect example of an estaminet –
defined as "not a restaurant, but you eat
here: a home away from home". Flemish
foods reign supreme: chicken in beer,
huge plates of sausages and speculoos
ice cream. Superb views.

MONTREUIL-SUR-MER
▲ **Château de Montreuil**
4 chausée des Capucins, 62170 **Map** 3E2
📞 03 21 81 53 04
FAX 03 21 81 36 43
✉ AE, DC, MC, V
● Mon, Tue L, Thu L; mid-Dec–Jan
🍴 €€€€ 🍽 (12) €€€€€

For key to symbols see back flap

A treasure of the Opal Coast. This château serves mullet with oysters, and fine veal double-baked with ginger. Encyclopaedic wine list. Beautiful rooms.

NEUFCHATEL-SUR-AISNE
● Le Jardin
22 rue Principale, 02190 **Map** 4A3
🄲 03 23 23 82 00
FAX 03 23 23 84 05
🄴 MC, V ⬤ Sun D, Mon, Tue; mid-Jan–1st wk Feb, 1st wk Sep
🍴 €€€
Light in winter, overrun with flowers in summer. Relax over beef and tender morels. The wine list has a few rough spots: discuss choices with the staff.

NEUVILLE-ST-AMAND
▲ Hostellerie Le Château
Rue Fontaine, 3km (2 miles) southeast of St-Quentin on D12, 02100 **Map** 4A3
🄲 03 23 68 41 82
FAX 03 23 68 46 02
🄴 AE, DC, MC, V ⬤ Sun D, Mon L, Sat L; last wk Dec, 1st 3 wks Aug
🍴 €€€ 🍽 (15) €€€€
Opulent manor house and lavish culinary creations to match, including eggs with truffles, scallops with lobster and fresh pasta, and beef tournedos with a three-pepper cream sauce. Quiet rooms.

NOEUX-LES-MINES
● Carrefour des Saveurs
94 rue Nationale, 62290 **Map** 3F2
🄲 03 21 26 74 74
FAX 03 21 27 12 14
🄴 MC, V ⬤ Sun D, Mon, Wed D; last 2 wks Jan, 1st 3 wks Aug 🍴 €€
Locals flock here for bountiful, creatively prepared staples, like five kinds of bread or five different garnishes on each plate. The flaky pastry stuffed with langoustines is superb, as is spice-crusted young pigeon. Finish with chicory-laced parfait.

NOUVION-EN-THIERACHE
▲ Hôtel de la Paix
37 rue Jean Vimont, 02170 **Map** 4A2
🄲 03 23 97 04 55
FAX 03 23 98 98 39
🄴 MC, V ⬤ Sun D, Sat L; last 2 wks Mar, mid-Aug–1st wk Sep
🍴 €€ 🍽 (15) €€

A perfect roadside break. Delicious Flemish specialties, like waterzooi (p79), charcuterie and flammenkueche (p119). Typical Northern decor, done with a discerning eye. Pleasant rooms.

NOYON
● Dame Journe
2 bd Mony, 60400 **Map** 3F3
🄲 03 44 44 01 33
FAX 03 44 09 59 68
🄦 www.damejourne.fr
🄴 AE, MC, V ⬤ Sun D, Mon, Wed D; 1st wk Jan, 1st 2 wks Aug 🍴 €€
Rare value for money. Both the menu and decor (Louis XVI) are classic. Savour fresh mixed white and green asparagus, perhaps accompanied by scallops.

NOYON
▲ Hôtel St-Eloi
81 bd Carnot, 60400 **Map** 3F3
🄲 03 44 44 01 49
FAX 03 44 09 20 90
🄦 www.hotelsainteloi.fr
🄴 AE, DC, MC, V ⬤ Sun D
🍴 €€ 🍽 (18) €€€
Time-tested cuisine in a 19th-century building decorated in Louis XV style. Highlights include mesclun salad with farm-raised chicken, langoustines and mussels, and mullet in a red-pepper sauce. Cosy rooms with period decor.

OGNES
● Relais St. Sébastien
26 ave de la Liberté, 02300 **Map** 3F3
🄲 03 23 52 15 77
FAX 03 23 39 91 52
🄴 MC, V ⬤ Sun D, Mon–Thu D, Sat L; 1st wk Feb, 1st wk Aug 🍴 €€
This tranquil, family-run inn is a fine stop between Laon and points west. Classics include lamb shanks in thyme and salmon smoked to a family recipe.

ORRY-LA-VILLE
▲ Relais d'Aumale
37 pl des Fêtes, 60560 **Map** 3F4
🄲 03 44 54 61 31
FAX 03 44 54 69 15
🄦 www.relais-aumale.fr
🄴 AE, DC, MC, V ⬤ Sun D (winter); 3rd wk Dec–1st wk Jan
🍴 €€€€ 🍽 (24) €€€€€

Once the hunting lodge for the Duke of Aumale. The forest still comes to the table in tender chateaubriand steak with Béarnaise sauce and Roussillon apricots. Excellent desserts. Intimate rooms.

PERONNE
▲ Hostellerie des Remparts
23 rue Beaubois, 80200 **Map** 3F3
🄲 03 22 84 01 22
FAX 03 22 84 31 96
🄴 MC, V 🍴 €€ 🍽 (16) €€
Excellent poultry and fish. Consult with the staff about the day's best options. Modest guestrooms.

PERONNE
▲ Le Provençal
15 Faubourg Bretagne, 80200 **Map** 3F3
🄲 03 22 84 06 16
🄴 MC, V ⬤ Mon
🍴 € 🍽 (7) €
Southern dishes include mussels stuffed with garlic, tangy sardine salad, and tête-de-veau. Snug, modest rooms.

PLOMION
● Le Huteau
Pl de l'Eglise, 02140 **Map** 4A3
🄲 03 23 98 81 21
FAX 03 23 98 81 21
🄴 MC, V ⬤ Sun D, Mon, Wed; mid-Jul–1st wk Aug 🍴 €€
An oasis of quality food, reasonably priced yet delicious. Options include scallops with mushrooms and a note-worthy foie gras. Worth a midday detour.

PONCHES-ESTRUVAL
● Ferme Auberge la Table de Ferme
Hameau d'Estruval, 80150 **Map** 3E2
🄲 03 22 23 54 02
🄴 MC, V
⬤ Aug: Sun L & Thu, Sep–Jul: Sun L & Sat D; Dec–Feb 🍴 €
An 18th-century farm in the Authie River valley that influenced generations of artists. Simple, delicious dishes also inspire: chicken with cider, guinea fowl and rich rhubarb tart.

PONT-DES-BRIQUES
▲ Hostellerie de la Rivière
17 rue de la Gare, 62360 **Map** 3G
🄲 03 21 32 22 81

● Restaurant ■ Hotel ▲ Hotel / Restaurant

FAX 03 21 87 45 48

AE, MC, V ● Sun D, Mon, Tue L; mid-Jan–mid-Feb, last wk Aug–mid-Sep

TI €€€ ◆ (8) €€

Tranquil garden and grounds. The menu shows similar refinement in dishes like baked lobster with foie gras and market-fresh fruits, and turbot with potato tart. Snug, welcoming rooms.

PRECY-SUR-OISE
● Le Condor

14 rue Gaston Watteau, 60460 **Map** 3E4

C 03 44 27 60 77

FAX 03 44 27 62 18

W www.le-condor.fr.st

AE, MC, V ● Tue, Wed; last 2 wks Feb, mid-Jul–mid-Aug **TI** €€

On the banks of the Oise River. Dishes include skate with capers, baked frogs' legs, and magret de canard *with peaches.*

PREMESQUES
● Le Châlet de Premesques

RN 641, 59840 **Map** 3F1

C 03 20 08 81 10

FAX 03 20 08 64 63

AE, DC, MC, V ● Sun D, Mon, Tue D, Sat L; mid-Aug–1st wk Sep **TI** €

A local favourite, especially among business types hoping to make an impression. The menu spotlights dishes like hot foie gras millefeuille *with julienne ham. Desserts – particularly* gaufres *and* speculoos *– are tempting.*

QUAEDYPRE
● Taverne de Westhoek

2 route from Wylder, 59380 **Map** 3F1

C 03 28 68 68 14

MC, V

● Mon D, Thu D, Sun L **TI** €

Smacks of an Irish pub outside, but the tavern's interior is pure Flemish. An impressive beer choice and dishes like potjevleesch (p76) *and Bergues sausage.*

RAISMES
● La Grignotière

6 ave Jean Jaurès, 59590 **Map** 4A2

C 03 27 36 91 99

FAX 03 27 36 74 29

MC, V ● Sun D, Mon, Tue D, Wed D; last wk Jan–1st wk Feb, last 2 wks Aug **TI** €€

Expect value for money. Highlights include scallops in ginger and chicory (endive) fondue, and char in mushroom butter with peppers. Overlooks a forest.

RANCOURT
▲ La Prieuré

24 RN17, 80360 **Map** 3F2

C 03 22 85 04 43

FAX 03 22 85 06 69

W www.leprieure-hotel.fr.st

AE, DC, MC, V

TI €€ ◆ (27) €€€

Hospitality in grand style at a graceful stone and brick country mansion. The large, agreeable menu has memorable salads and cheese. Well-appointed, reasonably priced guestrooms.

RETHONDES
● Alain Blot Restaurateur

21 rue Maréchal Foch, 60153 **Map** 3F3

C 03 44 85 60 24

FAX 03 44 85 92 35

AE, DC, MC, V ● Sun D, Mon, Tue, Sat L; 1st 2 wks Jan, 1st 2 wks Sep

TI €€€€

Alain Blot is celebrated by gourmets worldwide for his careful approach, leavened with experimentation. The grilled bass with onions, or the stuffed pigeon, stand as examples. The best desserts are on the all-chocolate menu.

REUILLY-SAUVIGNY
▲ Auberge le Relais

2 rue de Paris, 02850 **Map** 4A4

C 03 23 70 35 36

FAX 03 23 70 27 76

W www.relaisreuilly.com

AE, DC, MC, V ● Tue, Wed; Feb, mid-Aug–1st wk Sep

TI €€€€ ◆ (7) €€€

Menu highlights include foie gras with green apple and Banyuls sauce, and John Dory with carnaroli rice, broad (fava) bean and basil sauce. Superior Champagnes. Quiet, cosy rooms.

ROYE
● La Flamiche

20 pl Hôtel de Ville, 80700 **Map** 3F3

C 03 22 87 00 56

FAX 03 22 78 46 77

W www.flamiche.fr

AE, DC, MC, V ● Sun D, Mon, Tue L; mid-Aug–Sep, last wk Dec–1st wk Jan **TI** €€€€

Known across France for its refinement and expertise. Delight in the Treport sea bass with green asparagus, caramelized lemon salad with almonds, lamb with aubergine (eggplant), or caviar compote with cherries. Intense wine cellar.

ROYE
▲ Le Central

36 rue d'Amiens, 80700 **Map** 3F3

C 03 22 87 11 05

FAX 03 22 87 42 74

W www.leflorentin.com

AE, DC, MC, V ● Sun D, Mon; 1st 2 wks Aug, last wk Aug

TI €€ ◆ (8) €€

A graceful home with golden bedrooms that invite long naps. Restaurant Le Florentin impresses with its langoustine salad with foie gras vinaigrette and truffles, and sea bass with pistou.

SAMOUSSY
● Relais Charlemagne

4 route de Laon, 3km (2 miles) from Laon on A26, 02840 **Map** 4A3

C 03 23 22 21 50

MC, V ● Sun D, Mon, Wed D; last 2 wks Feb, 1st 3 wks Aug **TI** €€€

Classic, conservative – but never dull. Sample the scallops in Noilly vermouth with peppers; veal grenadine with morels; or thin slices of duck with a celery and chestnut mousse.

SARS-POTERIES
▲ Auberge Fleurie

67 rue Général de Gaulle, 59216 **Map** 4A2

C 03 27 61 62 48

FAX 03 27 61 56 66

AE, DC, MC, V ● Sun D, Mon; last 2 wks Jan, last 2 wks Aug **TI** €€€

◆ (8) €€€

Flower-filled gardens form the perfect backdrop. Experience the chef's skill with pike-perch on a bed of cabbage and bacon. Varied wines. Amply sized rooms.

SECLIN
▲ Auberge de Forgeron

17 rue Roger Bouvry, 59113 **Map** 3F2

03 20 90 09 52
FAX 03 20 32 70 87

MC, V ● Sun, Sat L; last wk
Jul–3rd wk Aug, 25 Dec–2 Jan

€€€ ◇ (18) €€€

Creative approach to Northern cooking.
Chef Philippe Belot, one of the famed
Sup de Co, produces dishes like pepper
mousse and roasted sea bass with
smoked herring. Agreeable rooms.

SENLIS

● Le Scaramouche

4 pl Notre Dame, 60300 **Map** 3F4

03 44 53 01 26
FAX 03 44 53 46 14
W www.le-scaramouche.fr
AE, DC, MC, V ● Tue, Wed; 1st 2
wks Feb €€€

In a grand house nestled near Notre
Dame cathedral. Innovations include
crab and mullet in Chartreuse liqueur,
and a delicious pig's trotter tart.

SOUASTRE

● Le Gourmet Champêtre

14 rue de Bienvillers, 62111 **Map** 3F2

03 21 22 69 87
FAX 03 21 22 28 13
W www.fermedesouastre.com
MC, V € €

Affordable yet indulgent meals in a
rustic setting, once a stable. Countryside
delights include farmer's soup, chicken
in cider, and a delectable tart with
libouili milk (like clotted cream).

ST-JEAN-AUX-BOIS

▲ Auberge A la Bonne Idée

3 rue des Meuniers, 60350 **Map** 3F4

03 44 42 84 09
FAX 03 44 42 80 45
W www.a-la-bonne-idee.fr
AE, MC, V ● Nov–Feb: Sun D &
Mon €€€ ◇ (23) €€€

The young chef serves turbot with
cream cheese, Anjou pigeon with wild
mushrooms, and warm chocolate tart
with orange marmalade. Guestrooms
are cosy and nicely appointed.

ST-MAXIMIN

● Le Verbois

Route d'Apremont, RN16, 60740 **Map** 3F4

03 44 24 06 22

FAX 03 44 25 76 63
W www.leverbois.com
AE, MC, V ● Sun D, Mon; 1st 2
wks Jan, last 2 wks Aug €€€

Once a postal inn, now home to a fine
establishment serving monkfish carpaccio and game. The chocolate fondant
makes a perfect dessert.

ST-QUENTIN

● Le Vert Gouteille

80 rue d'Isle, 02100 **Map** 3F3

03 23 05 13 25
FAX 03 23 05 13 27
AE, MC, V ● Sun, Sat D; 1st 2
wks Jan, Aug €€€

Locals flock here for a change of pace.
Juicy pistachio sausages and delicate
pike fillets prove they're on to something.
For dessert, the small chocolate pastries.

ST-VALERY-SUR-SOMME

● Relais de Quatre Saisons

2 pl de la Croix l'Abbé, 80230 **Map** 3E2

03 22 60 51 01
FAX 03 22 60 97 47
MC, V ● Sun D, Mon, Tue; Jan,
1st wk Sep €€

Highlights include tasty skate with
Camembert, and calf's liver with cider.
Desserts benefit from the chef's subtlety.

ST-VALERY-SUR-SOMME

▲ Relais Guillaume de Normandy

46 quai Romerel, 80230 **Map** 3E2

03 22 60 82 36
FAX 03 22 60 81 82
AE, DC, MC, V ● Tue; mid-
Dec–mid-Jan €€ ◇ (14) €€€

A gorgeous building on a leafy quayside,
this is an unabashedly traditional venue.
Nothing's too flashy, including the monkfish in cider vinegar, and rack of lamb
Bay of Somme style. Rooms are equally
solid and comfortable.

STE-PREUVE

▲ Château de Barive

6km (4 miles) southwest of Ste-Preuve
on D977, 02350 **Map** 4A3

03 23 22 15 15
FAX 03 23 22 08 39
AE, MC, V
● Jan €€€
◇ (14) €€€€

Delicacies include sole with tomatoes
and thyme, and duck in port. This countryside gem has tranquil surroundings and
comfortable guestrooms.

TERGNIER

● La Mandoline

45 pl Herment, 02700 **Map** 3F3

03 23 57 08 71
FAX 03 23 57 08 71
MC, V ● Sun D, Mon; last wk Feb,
mid-Aug–3rd wk Sep €€

Dishes are sensitively prepared, without
flights of fancy or trendy gimmicks.
Highlights include the foie gras baked
with Armagnac and prunes, and sole
with cream of caviar. The wine list is
also thoughtfully chosen.

TILQUES

▲ Château de Tilques

12 rue du Château, 62500 **Map** 3E1

03 21 88 99 99
FAX 03 21 38 34 23
W www.chateautilques.com
AE, DC, MC, V

€€€ ◇ (53) €€€€

The impetus is modern here, despite the
19th-century château, from the renovated
public areas to the menu, with items like
poached turbot and rosettes of duckling
with hop flowers. Choice wine selections.
Guestrooms have period furniture.

TOURCOING

● Le Plessy

31 ave Alfred Lefrançois, 59200 **Map** 3F1

03 20 25 07 73
FAX 03 20 25 43 24
MC, V
● Sun D, Mon; 1st wk Aug €€

The wine cellar is the big draw here,
though the cuisine more than matches it
in value for money. Tantalizing dishes in
the modern style: prawn in vanilla with
pears and ginger, and leg of lamb with
frogs' legs. Traditional desserts.

URCEL

● Hostellerie de France

2 rue Eglise, village centre on RN2,
02000 **Map** 4A3

03 23 21 60 08
FAX 03 23 21 60 08
MC, V ● Mon D, Tue D, Wed;

● Restaurant ■ Hotel ▲ Hotel / Restaurant

mid-Feb–1st wk Mar, last wk Aug–1st wk Sep **11** €€

Best choices include prawn salad, the mixed fish selection with saffron, and veal in mustard sauce. The building, once the village café, is pleasantly updated.

VAILLY-SUR-AISNE

● La Belle Porte

49 rue du Fouborg-de-Sommecourt, 02370 **Map** 4A3

C 03 23 54 67 45

FAX 03 23 54 67 45

⊗ AE, MC, V ● Sun D, Mon, Sat L

11 €€€€

Historical atmosphere and recipes, although the food will suit modern palates. Try langoustines on a bed of angel-hair pasta, soissoulet (bean stew) with monkfish, and lobster bisque.

VALENCIENNES

▲ Grand Hôtel Valenciennes

8 pl de la Gare, 59300 **Map** 4A2

C 03 27 46 32 01

FAX 03 27 29 65 57

⊗ AE, DC, MC, V

11 €€€ **⊘** (97) €€€

Brasserie menu – executed with verve and style – in an Art Deco environment. Sea bass in orange butter and Valenciennes-style lamb make this an address sought out by locals. The wine list is concise but carefully chosen. Guestrooms echo the 1930s theme.

VALENCIENNES

● La Planche à Pain

1 rue d'Oultreman, 59300 **Map** 4A2

C 03 27 46 18 28

FAX 03 27 30 98 01

⊗ AE, DC, MC, V ● Sun L, Mon; last wk Apr, 1st 3 wks Aug **11** €€

Large inn with a comprehensive stock of wine and beer. Flavour and imagination dazzle in dishes like prawn salad with foie gras, and baked scallops.

VERBERIE

● Auberge de la Normandie

26 rue de la Pêcherie, 60410 **Map** 3F4

C 03 44 40 92 33

FAX 03 44 40 50 62

⊗ MC, V ● Sun D, Mon; mid-Jul–1st wk Aug **11** €

Seasonal menus stretch to paillarde (thinly sliced and quickly sautéed) salmon with chanterelles, and pig's trotters stuffed with St-Nectaire cheese. The wine list complements the menu perfectly with mid-range chilled whites to hearty reds from across France.

VERVINS

▲ La Tour de Roy

45 rue Général Leclerc, A26, exit 13, RN2 towards Vervins, 02140 **Map** 4A5

C 03 23 98 00 11

FAX 03 23 98 00 72

w www.latourduroy.com

⊗ AE, DC, MC, V ● Mon L, Tue L

11 €€€€ **⊘** (22) €€€€€

A 17th-century former prison, serving without doubt the best food ever to be eaten there. Enjoy skate wings with polenta and smoked bacon, and sample the divine wine. The comfortable, artfully furnished rooms are a far cry from the original cells as well.

VIEUX-MOULIN

● Auberge du Daguet

25 rue Pillet Will, across from the church, 60350 **Map** 3F3

C 03 44 85 60 72

FAX 03 44 85 61 28

⊗ MC, V ● Mon D, Tue; 2nd & 3rd wks Jan, 2nd & 3rd wks Jul **11** €€

This former country tavern still has a medieval feel. Fare has moved on from roast haunches though: cheese soufflé glazed with foie gras, truffles and peaches, and turbot with carrots, mushrooms and a lemon butter sauce. Good choice of local beers and ciders.

VRON

● Hostellerie du Clos du Moulin

1 rue du Moulin, 80120 **Map** 3E2

C 03 22 29 60 60

FAX 03 22 29 60 61

@ restaurantleclosdumoulin@wanadoo.fr

⊗ AE, DC, MC, V

● Sun D, Mon; Jan **11** €€

Cuisine well adapted to the ingredients and style of the moment, in a restored 16th-century farm. Dishes like half-cooked foie gras with spice bread, monkfish stew and fillet of beef with smoked salmon echo that solidity.

WIERRE-EFFROY

● Ferme-Auberge de la Raterie

744 hameau de la Maloterie, 62720 **Map** 3E1

C 03 21 92 80 90

w www.ferm-auberge-laraterie.com

⊗ MC, V ● Sun D, Mon **11** €

Taste the bounty of farm, including terrine of duck and chicken liver, roast chicken with young vegetables and truly tender rack of lamb. The massive beer list reflects the Northern passion for the brew.

WIMEREUX

▲ La Liégeoise at L'Atlantic

Digue de Mer, 62930 **Map** 3E1

C 03 21 32 41 01

FAX 03 21 87 46 17

w www.atlantic-delpierre.com

⊗ AE, DC, MC, V ● Sun D, Mon L; Feb **11** €€€ **⊘** (18) €€€

Overlooking the sea at Wimereux beach. Specialities include scallop and oyster casserole with creamed fennel, and grilled sea bream on potatoes. Don't miss the Caribbean chocolate cream infused with star anise. Rooms are tidy and quite comfortable.

WIMEREUX

● L'Epicure

Rue Carnot, 62930 **Map** 3E1

C 03 21 83 21 83

FAX 03 21 33 53 20

⊗ MC, V ● Sun, Wed D; last wk Dec–1st wk Jan **11** €€

Spontaneous and sassy, rising chef Philippe Carrée turns out sherried mullet with a compote of onions and potatoes, and croquettes of potatoes, rosemary, aubergines (eggplant) and foie gras. Impressive dessert cart.

WIMILLE

● Relais de la Brocante

2 rue Ledinghen, 62126 **Map** 3E1

C 03 21 83 19 31

FAX 03 21 87 29 71

⊗ AE, MC, V ● Sun D, Mon

11 €€€

Classic seaside cuisine. Fish and seafood hold sway, with dishes like terrine of sole. Finish with pears in vanilla syrup and caramel ice cream.

For key to symbols see back flap

CHAMPAGNE

Spreading eastwards from the Ile-de-France up to the Belgian border, the region of Champagne takes in the arable plains and vineyards of the wide, lazy Marne valley, the pastoral countryside around the well-preserved medieval city of Troyes and the wooded uplands of the Ardennes. Freshwater fish, along with game, charcuterie and some fine cheeses are treats to enjoy here, but food takes second place to... Champagne, of course!

The Flavours of Champagne

While vineyards and vast plains of cereal and beet cover much of the landscape, the forests of the Ardennes provide plentiful game, and the rivers an abundance of fish. Charcuterie *is also of highest quality here.*

BEST MARKETS

Aix-en-Othe Designated *un marché d'exception*, held in a 19th-century cast-iron market hall. Wed & Sat am
Bar-sur-Aube Lively market selling local produce, Sat am. Wine fair, 2nd Sun Sep
Brienne-le-Château Market selling regional fare, Thur. Choucroute & champagne fair, 3rd weekend Sep. Cheese fair, 3rd weekend Jun & Oct
Troyes Colourful fruit and vegetable market, Daily. Champagne fair, 12–20 Jun

MEAT AND CHARCUTERIE

This region is mainly known for its charcuterie and ham, and for game. Wild boar, deer, rabbit, hare, quail partridge and woodcock are all found in the wooded valley of the Meuse in the Ardennes, They find their way into game pâtés (baked in pastry), terrines and *rillettes*, as well as roasts and stews. Farmed poultry includes pigeons and the rare *rouge d'Ardennes* turkey.

The Ardennes town of Rethel is known for *boudin blanc*. The recipe – involving finely minced pork, ham, breadcrumbs, milk and eggs – is closely guarded by the *confrérie* of producers. The Ardennes is also noted for its fine quality smoked ham, while *jambon de Reims* is a cooked ham, made from pork shoulder seasoned with Champagne, mustard and Reims vinegar.

Andouillettes, or chitterling sausages, are found in many parts of France, but the best known are those from Troyes. Made from chopped pig's stomach and intestines mixed with seasoning, onion, herbs and spices, their chewy texture is something of an acquired taste. Look for those labelled AAAAA – a seal of approval granted by the Association Amicale des Amateurs d'Andouillette Authentique. *Andouillettes* are generally grilled and served with fried onions or a white wine and shallot sauce, but can also be baked in a wine and cream or mustard and cream sauce.

Left Jambon de Reims **Centre** Pigs' trotters **Right** Boudin blanc

FISH

The area to the east of Troyes is known locally as the "wet Champagne", and is dotted with small lakes in which there are plentiful pike and carp. Trout are fished in the clear streams of the Ardennes.

CHEESE AND DAIRY PRODUCE

The two principal cheeses in the Champagne region are Chaource and Langres. Chaource AOC, which comes from the Aube *département*, is a rich, high-fat, smooth, soft white cheese with white *croûte fleurie* rind. Eaten young, it has a mild flavour with a distinctive aftertaste. Strong smelling Langres AOC cheese is similar to Epoisses from nearby Burgundy *(see p215)*, with a sticky, damp orange rind that is washed in Champagne or marc de Champagne. Other varieties from this region include Soumaintrain, Troyen, Carré de l'Est and Cendrée de Champagne or Cendrée d'Argonne.

Langres cheese, in perfect condition

FRUIT AND VEGETABLES

If the *côtes* of the Marne are devoted to the precious vineyards, the region's once arid chalk plateaus are now the domain of large expanses of wheat, sugar-beet, barley and maize, as well as sunflowers and colza that are cultivated for their oil. Potatoes and onions, along with white and green cabbages, are also grown, including the large white cabbages that are used in *choucroute*, a speciality around Brienne-le-Château. Apple orchards are common around Rethel and also in the Pays d'Othe, to the south of Troyes, which was once renowned for its cider-making.

PÂTISSERIE AND CHOCOLATE

The speciality of Reims is the *biscuit rose de Reims*, a sweet, crunchy, boudoir-style pink biscuit, created for dunking into a flute of Champagne – the colouring was originally added to hide the brown flecks of vanilla pod that flavour it.

Needless to say, the Champagne theme also makes its way into *confiserie*, with the *bouchon champenois*, a Champagne-cork-shaped chocolate filled with marc de Champagne. A much older local tradition is the making of *pain d'épices*, or spice bread, made here long before Dijon claimed it *(see p215)*. This sticky, dense and delicious cake is made using a base of rye flour, flavoured with honey and spices.

Local cabbages

FROM POVERTY TO PLENTY

Until the Champagne method was discovered in the 17th century, this was a poor region, where many people lived on a subsistence diet – even vine leaves were eaten – although the region was also an important hub for international trade thanks to the great medieval fairs of Troyes, Bar-sur-Aube and Provins.

REIMS MUSTARD & VINEGAR

Reims is known for its mustard and wine vinegar, both often flavoured with Champagne.

Gift presentation from Reims

Regional Dishes

Today the cuisine of Champagne essentially breaks down into the rustic peasant fare that dates back to before the invention of Champagne, and the whole gamut of dishes that use it in their preparation, plus those that have managed to combine the two in perfect harmony.

ON THE MENU

Cassolette de petits gris Snails in Champagne sauce

Choucroute au Champagne Sauerkraut cooked in Champagne

Coq au Bouzy Cockerel stewed in Bouzy red wine

Côtes de veau à l'ardennaise Veal chops with ham

Ecrevisses au Champagne Crayfish in Champagne

Matelote champenoise Freshwater fish stewed in Champagne

Poulet au Champagne Chicken in a Champagne, cream and mushroom sauce

Truite à l'ardennaise Trout stuffed with breadcrumbs and finely chopped Ardennes ham

Sorbet au marc de Champagne Refreshing sorbet made with marc de Champagne, served with marc-soaked raisins

Salade de pissenlits aux lardons

THE CHAMPAGNE MENU

If the number of dishes specifically associated with Champagne is limited, the region has proved adept at adapting those of its neighbours, Picardy, Alsace, Burgundy and Belgium. Thus you'll find *choucroute* as in Alsace (though made with Champagne rather than white wine) and Picardy-style cheese and leek tarts, using local Chaource. A number of creative chefs and gastronomic restaurants also thrive in the presence of the grand Champagne houses, notably Gérard Boyer at Les Crayères, in Reims *(see p109)*.

Ardennes ham may be served as a starter, but also features in several dishes, stuffed in trout or cooked with rabbit or wild boar. While Champagne features in many dishes, you'll also come across local red Bouzy in *coq au Bouzy* or with wild boar. Other main courses include *andouillette* cooked with onions or gratinéed with mustard, *potée champenoise*, and poultry cooked with Reims mustard. Game dishes are widespread in autumn and winter, while the tradition of game pies is also seen in dishes like *pigeon en croûte* (in a pastry case). Desserts might include *sabayon au Champagne* (a froth of egg yolks and sugar, like Italian *zabaglione* but with Champagne replacing marsala) and *sorbet au marc de Champagne*, as well as creamy fruit charlottes made with *biscuits roses de Reims (see p97)*.

Truite à l'ardennaise

Left Pieds de porc à la Sainte-Menehould **Right** Marcassin à l'ardennaise

REGIONAL DINING

The following restaurants are among those serving regional dishes at reasonable prices:
Debette
Aubrives *(see p102)*
Le Cellier aux Moines
Bar-sur-Aube *(see p102)*
Le Chapon Fin
Epernay *(see p106)*
Le Jardin
Chaumont *(see p105)*
Le Val Fleurie
Charleville-Mézières *(see p104)*
L'Etoile
Troyes *(see p112)*
Tarantella
Langres *(see p107)*

Interior of Gérard Boyer's Les Crayères in Reims

PIEDS DE PORC À LA SAINTE-MENEHOULD

The delicacy of pigs' trotters cooked so slowly that the bones become soft and can be eaten was invented at the Auberge du Soleil d'Or in Ste-Menehould. Here they were appreciated by Charles VIII in 1435 and Louis XVI (as he tried to flee the country) in 1791, as well as by Alexandre Dumas and Victor Hugo. The trotters are simmered in white wine with carrots, shallots, garlic, herbs and cloves for about four hours. When cold they are halved lengthways, egg-and-breadcrumbed and grilled until golden, then served hot with mustard.

SALADE DE PISSENLITS AUX LARDONS

Young dandelion leaves (at their best in springtime) are topped with crisp *lardons* of bacon, then the bacon juices are deglazed in the pan with wine vinegar and a spoon of mustard to make a hot dressing. Chopped hard-boiled egg or warm, sliced new potatoes are sometimes also added for a more substantial dish.

MARCASSIN A L'ARDENNAISE

Another dish from the Ardennes uses the young wild boar that roam its forests. Cutlets are browned in butter with onions, then simmered in red wine and stock. Tomato purée, mustard and juniper berries are added to the juices to make a rich, dark sauce.

POTÉE CHAMPENOISE

Hearty stews are popular in the north of France. Here smoked Ardennes ham, bacon and sausages are cooked slowly with white beans, potatoes, carrots, turnips and cabbage. Sometimes chicken is added. The stock is served separately from the meat and vegetables as a soup.

Regional Wines

*The wine of partying, the wine of celebration, the wine of dreams...
Whatever the billing, no other sparkling wine in the world can rival the
prestige of Champagne. While the big Champagne houses in Reims, Epernay
and Ay are the glamorous draw, still wines add interest to a visit.*

Winter frosts at the village of Monthelon in the Côte des Blancs

BEST PRODUCERS

Billecart-Salmon, Bollinger, Deutz,
Duval-Leroy, Pierre Gimmonet,
Gosset, Charles Heidsieck,
Jacquesson & Fils, Krug, Laurent-
Perrier, Moët & Chandon, Perrier-
Jouët, Philipponnat, Pol Roger,
Pommery, Roederer, Ruinart,
Jacques Selosse, Taittinger, Veuve
Cliquot Ponsardin

Historic tun at Mercier

Champagne lies on the northernmost and coldest edge
of France's vineyards. Ripening is therefore limited and
the grapes produced have high acidity levels, ideal for
the making of sparkling wine. The famously fine bubbles are created by starting a second fermentation in
the bottle *(see p29)*.

Almost all Champagne is white but well-made rosé,
such as the magnificent Laurent-Perrier Rosé, can be a
delight to the eye and tastebuds. On the label "brut"
indicates a dry Champagne, "extra dry" less so. "Sec" is
sweeter, and "demi-sec" sweeter still. Traditionally, the
French love to bring out a bottle of Champagne with
dessert. This is a throwback to the era when most
Champagne was sweet and therefore an excellent
match for cake or sugary fare. Try a dessert style such
as Duval-Leroy's Lady Rosé.

Blending is one of the great skills of the Champagne
houses, who bring together wines from different vineyards and different vintages to create the house style.
Elegant Blanc de Blancs Champagne is made entirely
from Chardonnay, while sturdier Blanc de Noirs comes
from dark-skinned Pinot Noir and Pinot Meunier.

THE VINEYARDS

Of the three major vineyard regions, the Montagne de
Reims is renowned for Pinot Noir, which gives the
Champagne body and power, while the Côte des

Blancs is so called because it is the realm of the delicate white grape, Chardonnay. In the Vallée de la Marne, Pinot Meunier is the main grape.

Lavishly packaged prestige bottles like Dom Pérignon, Roederer Cristal and Taittinger Comtes de Champagne are invariably made with grapes from selected top vineyards. These are classified in a hierarchy of Grands and Premiers Crus, which deliver Chardonnay with extra finesse and bouquet and Pinot Noir with more body and greater definition.

STILL WINES

Still wines are made under the Coteaux Champenois appellation. Reds from Bouzy in the Montagne de Reims are some of the best. The rare Rosé des Riceys from the southern Aube has a spicy bouquet and goes very well with exotic food, particularly mild curries or scented Thai dishes, although the *Ricetons* drink it with their ash-coated cheese, Cendré des Riceys. Ratafia de Champagne is a liqueur wine similar to Pineau des Charentes *(see p301)*.

VINEYARDS OF CHAMPAGNE

KEY

- Aube Vineyards
- Côte des Blancs
- Côte de Sézanne
- Montagne de Reims
- Vallée de la Marne

— Delimited AOC region of Champagne

···· *Département* boundary

DOM PERIGNON

Dom Pérignon is popularly thought to be the inventor of Champagne, but this is not strictly true. He was the cellarmaster at the Benedictine abbey at Hautvillers and his innovations and expertise in blending earned him the title "Father of Champagne". Moët & Chandon's prestige cuvée, launched in 1936, is named after him. Abbey and museum visits by appointment: Moët & Chandon, 18 ave de Champagne, Epernay (03 26 51 20 20), Apr–mid-Nov: daily; mid-Nov–Mar: Mon–Fri.

Statue of Dom Pérignon

CHAMPAGNE CELLARS

The vineyards are planted in a deep chalky soil. Subterranean galleries dug since Roman time enjoy a constant temperature of around 11°C and high levels of humidity which mean they are ideal for storing wine.

Cellars at Taittinger

Where to Eat & Stay

AMBONNAY
▲ **Auberge St-Vincent**
1 rue St-Vincent, 51150 **Map** 4A4
📞 03 26 57 01 98
FAX 03 26 57 81 48
W www.auberge-st-vincent.com
🍽 MC, V ⬤ Sun D, Mon; Feb, 2nd wk
Aug 🍴 €€€ 🛏 (10) €€
Vegetables take centre stage here, where the only meat served is snails. Wild mushrooms, beetroot, seeds and eggs top pastas and salads. Quaint, old-fashioned country-inn guestrooms.

ARSONVAL
▲ **Hostellerie de la Chaumière**
On RN19 between Chaumont and Vendeuvre, 10200 **Map** 4B5
📞 03 25 27 91 02
FAX 03 25 27 90 26
🍽 MC, V ⬤ Mon; mid-Dec–end Jan
🍴 €€ 🛏 (11) €€€
Rural retreat with outdoor dining in balmy weather. Unusual – but utterly successful – ingredients such as raspberries jazz up sea bass, duck, scallops and game. Gracious rooms overlook the gardens.

AUBRIVES
▲ **Debette**
Pl Louis Debette, 08320 **Map** 4B2
📞 03 24 41 64 72
FAX 03 24 41 10 31
W www.hotel.debette.com
🍽 MC, V ⬤ Sun D, Mon L
🍴 €€ 🛏 (16) €€€
Countryside restaurant worth seeking out for the game terrine, veal with scallops, pike and frogs' legs. Pride of place goes to the wild boar. Comfortable rooms lack inspiration.

BAR-SUR-AUBE
■ **Hôtel le St Nicolas**
2 rue Général de Gaulle, 10200 **Map** 4B5
📞 03 25 27 08 65
FAX 03 25 27 60 31
🍽 MC, V ⬤ (27) €€
Attractive exposed-stone building, two minutes' walk from the railway station. Several beamed guestrooms feature

Provençal blue furniture. This place scores highly with tourists because of its outdoor swimming pool and sauna.

BAR-SUR-AUBE
⬤ **La Toque Baralbine**
18 rue Nationale, 10200 **Map** 4B5
📞 03 25 27 20 34
FAX 03 25 27 20 34
🍽 MC, V ⬤ Sun D, Mon; Jan
🍴 €€€
One of two gastronomic restaurants in town. Flavourful fish selections: pike-perch with mushrooms, tuna with a tangy tomato sauce and scallops with Champagne. Game, particularly pigeon, is available most days. Limited wines.

BAR-SUR-AUBE
⬤ **Le Cellier aux Moines**
13 rue Général Vouillemont, 10200 **Map** 4B5
📞 03 25 27 08 01
FAX 03 25 01 56 22
🍽 AE, MC, V ⬤ Sun–Thu D, Tue
🍴 €€€
Elevated cooking style. Expect fish marinated in Champagne with sauerkraut, and meats in red wine. Occasional game, as well as the famed andouillette de Troyes. Local cheeses abound.

BAR-SUR-AUBE
⬤ **Le Jardin des Délices**
124 rue Nationale, 10200 **Map** 4B5
📞 03 25 27 33 92
🍽 MC, V 🍴 €€
Novel offerings like prawns in whisky sauce. Also recommended: Provençal-style frogs' legs and sirloin with wild mushrooms, bacon and potatoes. Calvados lights up the steak flambées. Pleasant outdoor terrace.

BAR-SUR-AUBE
⬤ **Le Rocher**
53 rue Général de Gaulle, 10200 **Map** 4B5
📞 03 25 27 15 86
⬤ Sun 🍴 €
An experience. Step back in time at this authentic roadside eatery with its

ancient wooden tables and old signs. One daily set menu featuring hearty, traditional food and that's it.

BAZEILLES
▲ **Auberge du Port**
Chemin de Remilly, 08140 **Map** 4B3
📞 03 24 27 13 89
FAX 03 24 29 35 58
W www.auberge-du-port.fr
🍽 AE, DC, MC, V
⬤ Fri L; Apr–Oct: Sun D, Sat L;
Nov–Mar: Fri D; 20 Dec–5 Jan
🍴 €€€ 🛏 (20) €€
Fantastic fish, from baked pike-perch with seafood to monkfish soup and a spicy salmon steak. Regional meats include wild boar, calf's liver and venison with chestnuts and apple. Quaint rooms.

BAZEILLES
▲ **Château de Bazeilles**
Chemin de Remilly, 08140 **Map** 4B3
📞 03 24 27 09 68
FAX 03 24 27 64 20
🍽 AE, DC, MC, V
⬤ Restaurant: L; public holidays
🍴 €€€€ 🛏 (20) €€€
Elegant offerings under a beamed roof: saffron lobster casserole, pike-perch in Champagne and classic sea bass with fennel. Modern, romantic guestrooms have magnificent garden views.

BOURBONNE-LES-BAINS
▲ **Des Sources**
Place Bains, 52400 **Map** 8C1
📞 03 25 87 86 00
FAX 03 25 87 86 33
🍽 MC, V
⬤ Wed D, Sat D
🍴 €€€ 🛏 (23) €€
Traditional French restaurant serving frogs' legs, mussel cassoulet (p373) and a selection of tarts. Guestrooms are clean and bright though somewhat basic.

BREVONNES
▲ **Au Vieux Logis**
1 rue de Piney, 10220 **Map** 4B5
📞 03 25 46 30 17
FAX 03 25 46 37 20

⬤ Restaurant ■ Hotel ▲ Hotel / Restaurant

@ annick.baudesson@worldonline.fr

AE, MC, V ● First 3 wks Mar, first wk Dec 🍴 €€€€ 🍷 (5) €€€
Cuisine so good that this restaurant doubles as a cooking school. Snails, scallops and local Chaource cheese serve as appetizers. Rooms inside this converted lodge face the gardens.

CHALONS-EN-CHAMPAGNE
● Au Carrillon Gourmand
15 pl Monseigneur Tissier, 51000
Map 4B4

📞 03 26 64 45 07

FAX 03 26 21 06 09

MC, V ● Sun, Mon, Wed D
🍴 €€
The building is bland, but the seafood is legendary. Curried fish, the vegetable gazpacho soup and aubergine (eggplant) caviar are just a few of the creative dishes. Beef with mustard is also popular.

CHALONS-EN-CHAMPAGNE
● Auberge du Cloitre
9 pl Notre-Dame, 51000 **Map** 4B4

📞 03 26 65 68 08

FAX 03 26 66 11 12

MC, V ● Mon D, Tue 🍴 €€
This is not a good option for vegetarians as beef and duck star at this restaurant. Pig's trotters are available, and the seafood menu is crowned by red mullet in parsley. Solid array of red Burgundy.

CHALONS-EN-CHAMPAGNE
● Le Chaudron Savoyard
9 rue des Poissoniers, 51000 **Map** 4B4

📞 03 26 68 00 32

FAX 03 26 21 77 89

MC, V ● Mon, Sat L 🍴 €€
Sample rustic raclette (p268). Charcuterie options include platters of Ardennes and Champagne ham, and the menu has plenty of filling tarts and salads.

CHALONS-EN-CHAMPAGNE
● Le Petit Pasteur
42 rue Pasteur, 51000 **Map** 4B4

📞 03 26 68 24 78

FAX 03 26 68 25 97

MC, V ● Mon L, Sat L; Aug
🍴 €€€
Foie gras abounds in this region, but not all pâtés are equal. Detour to sample

this melt-in-the-mouth delicacy. Roasted goat's cheese and carpaccio of salmon are also on the imaginative menu. Five rather expensive wines.

CHALONS-EN-CHAMPAGNE
▲ Le Renard
24 pl de la République, 51000 **Map** 4B4

📞 03 26 68 03 78

FAX 03 26 64 50 07

w http://le-renard.com

AE, MC, V ● Sun D, Sat L; Christmas 🍴 €€€ 🍷 (35) €€€
Stunning gastronomic display, especially the chic set menu. Try the red mullet with pistachio nuts, fruit and vegetables. Spacious guestrooms have bright bedspreads and are somewhat dated. Private parking in town centre.

CHALONS-EN-CHAMPAGNE
● Pré St Alpin
2 rue Abbé Lambert, 51000 **Map** 4B4

📞 03 26 70 20 26

FAX 03 26 68 52 20

MC, V ● Sun D 🍴 €€€
Gorgeous setting, but the food doesn't entirely live up to the elegance. The cooking is superb but predictable. Opt for the beef carpaccio, duck or scallop and prawn brochettes. Over 40 wines.

CHALONS-EN-CHAMPAGNE
● Restaurant de l'Avenue
86 ave de Ste-Menehould, 51000
Map 4B4

📞 03 26 68 04 44

FAX 03 26 21 60 71

MC, V ● Sun D 🍴 €€
The bright yellow façade matches the cheery, experimental cuisine that roams the globe, from New Zealand's hoki fish to kangaroo. The set menus are more down to earth, featuring Burgundy snails.

CHALONS-EN-CHAMPAGNE
▲ Restaurant Jacky Michel
at Hôtel D'Angleterre
19 pl Monseigneur Tissier, 51000
Map 4B4

📞 03 26 68 21 51

FAX 03 26 70 51 67

AE, MC, V ● Sun, Mon L, Sat L; last 2 wks July

🍴 €€€€ 🍷 (25) €€€€

Opulent hotel, near the Notre Dame church, with a refined dining room serving gourmet seafood and local produce. Highlights are the langoustine salad and foie gras with truffles. Good wine list and individually styled rooms.

CHALONS-EN-CHAMPAGNE
● Restaurant les Ardennes
34 pl de la République, 51000 **Map** 4B4

📞 03 26 68 21 42

FAX 03 26 21 34 55

AE, MC, V ● Sun D, Mon D
🍴 €€
Simple, straightforward dishes with minimal trimmings. Meat is the focus here: steak, veal and lamb chops with shallots, mushrooms and thyme. Seafood platters are a popular summer preference, as are oysters in season.

CHARLEVILLE-MEZIERES
● Cigogne
40 rue Dubois-Crancé, 08000 **Map** 4B3

📞 03 24 33 25 39

MC, V ● Sun D, Mon 🍴 €€
Inspired starters. Enjoy the andouillette brochettes, rabbit in Chardonnay or oyster fricassée. Select from lightly cooked crab, snails, prawns and lobster. Extensive rotisserie assortment.

CHARLEVILLE-MEZIERES
● Clef des Champs
33 rue du Moulin, 08000 **Map** 4B3

📞 03 24 56 17 50

FAX 03 24 59 94 07

AE, DC, MC, V

● Sun D; 25 Dec
🍴 €€€
Some of the town's finest meals unfold in an 18th-century interior. Foreign recipes, like Japanese fish soup and fish with basmati rice star alongside French standards. Crustaceans are a speciality. Desserts are also exotic, and include a passion fruit and liqueur sorbet.

CHARLEVILLE-MEZIERES
● La Cave du Dépôt-Vente
8 rue Noël, 08000 **Map** 4B3

📞 03 24 59 21 28

● Sun 🍴 €
A traditional stone building houses this restaurant specializing in omelettes.

Milanese tomato sauce and herbs are used to flavour the meats, particularly veal, chicken and sides of beef.

CHARLEVILLE-MEZIERES
● La Côte à l'Os
11 cours Aristide Briand, 08000 **Map** 4B3
📞 03 24 59 20 16
FAX 03 24 59 48 30
💳 MC, V ⬤ Sun D 🍴 €€

Frequent specials are steak tartare and entrecôtes of lamb, pork and veal. Fish steaks are a fine option. Outdoor terrace.

CHARLEVILLE-MEZIERES
● Lard des Mets
71 rue Bourbon, 08000 **Map** 4B3
📞 03 24 32 38 07
💳 MC, V
⬤ Sun D, Mon 🍴 €

Whisky, port, wine or beer are used to flavour pike-perch, prawns, scallops and pork. Extensive charcuterie and crudités platters featuring excellent Ardennes ham, Chaource cheese and good sausages. Great value.

CHARLEVILLE-MEZIERES
● Le Manoir
Rue de Paquis Prolengée, 08000
Map 4B3
📞 03 24 33 43 20
FAX 03 24 37 12 25
💳 AE, MC, V
⬤ Sun–Wed D 🍴 €€

Set menus to suit all budgets under a tree-dappled terrace. Appetizers put Le Manoir in a class of its own. Roast rascasse, oysters, clams and Ardennes ham are highlights. Don't miss the rabbit with prunes.

CHARLEVILLE-MEZIERES
● Le Marrakech
17 rue de Petit Bois, 08000 **Map** 4B3
📞 03 24 33 21 26
💳 MC, V 🍴 €€

Authentic Moroccan restaurant with melt-in-the-mouth tagines. Chicken with lemon, lamb with honey and pigeon with nuts are slow-roasted inside earthenware. Savour them alone or atop couscous. Grilled aubergine (eggplant) to start. Bedouin tent decoration inside.

CHARLEVILLE-MEZIERES
▲ Le Relais du Square
3 pl de la Gare, 08000 **Map** 4B3
📞 03 24 33 38 76
FAX 03 24 33 56 66
[w] www.citotel.com
💳 MC, V ⬤ Aug (restaurant)
🍴 €€ 🛏 (49) €€

Pleasant guestrooms close to the train station. Wooden lobby and staircase are quite evocative, but rooms are more functional than fantastic. The restaurant serves basic French traditional dishes.

CHARLEVILLE-MEZIERES
● Le Rimbaud
11 bis cours Aristide Briand, 08000
Map 4B3
📞 03 24 59 19 53
FAX 03 24 59 19 53
💳 MC, V ⬤ Sun L 🍴 €

Steak-frites with beer is the popular choice in this cheerful brasserie-style establishment. Other dishes include an epic mixed grill with pork and sausage and five styles of moules-frites. Plenty of large salads, too.

CHARLEVILLE-MEZIERES
● Le Val Fleuri
25 quai Arthur Rimbaud, 08000 **Map** 4B3
📞 03 24 59 94 11
💳 AE, MC, V ⬤ Sun D, Mon, Sat L
🍴 €€

Beef in beer sauce comes wrapped in Ardennes ham. Also recommended: wild boar terrine, goat's cheese, Ardennes pâté and wonderful pike-perch. Pleasant riverside location.

CHARLEVILLE-MEZIERES
● L'Eau à la Bouche
30 rue du Moulin, 08000 **Map** 4B3
📞 03 24 32 35 70
💳 MC, V ⬤ Mon–Fri D 🍴 €€

Exceptionally elegant restaurant. Tiny menu of freshwater fish and meat dishes laced with mint, cumin and coriander (cilantro). Cooking styles from around France including Provence and Brittany. Lamb is the meat of choice.

CHARLEVILLE-MEZIERES
● Les Deux Bouchons
17 rue Irénée Carré, 08000 **Map** 4B3

📞 03 24 37 20 20
FAX 03 24 33 33 59
💳 MC, V ⬤ Sun D, Mon 🍴 €€€

Pretty restaurant in a quiet courtyard. Highlights include curried monkfish, salmon with avocado and a huge portion of rump steak. A few Spanish and Italian antipasti dishes too, like Serrano ham.

CHARLEVILLE-MEZIERES
● Les Glycines
7 rue d'Aubilly, 08000 **Map** 4B3
📞 03 24 55 58 37
💳 MC, V ⬤ Sun, Mon
🍴 €€

Ancient restaurant with a beamed ceiling. Begin with oysters, snails or Ardennes ham. Move on to a quality steak tartare, veal or fish, where the best ingredients shine. This is traditional French home cooking par excellence.

CHARLEVILLE-MEZIERES
● Sous la Voûte
9 rue Pierre Bérégovoy, 08000 **Map** 4B3
📞 03 24 59 38 48
💳 MC, V ⬤ Mon, Thu D 🍴 €€

It takes two to tackle the giant roasts here. Solo diners should opt for veal with Gorgonzola or Marsala sauces. Asparagus, capers and lots of other ingredients grace the pizzas here.

CHAUMONT
● Agora
11 ave des Etats-Unis, 52000 **Map** 4B5
📞 03 25 03 28 64
FAX 03 25 03 08 81
💳 MC, V ⬤ Sun, Sat L; Aug, Christmas & New Year 🍴 €€

Wide selection of grilled meats, like sirloin with Roquefort and veal with Marsala. Pizzas have a French feel, laden with smoked duck, parsley butter and scallops. Good wine list, which includes inexpensive carafes. Five-minute walk from the centre.

CHAUMONT
▲ Hôtel Brasserie St Jean
2 pl Aristide Briand, 52000 **Map** 4B5
📞 03 25 03 00 79
FAX 03 25 03 08 81
💳 AE, MC, V ⬤ Sun
🍴 € 🛏 (14) €€

● Restaurant　■ Hotel　▲ Hotel / Restaurant

Mussels are a house speciality: whether with cream, Roquefort or marinière (white wine, shallots and herbs). Outstanding John Dory with saffron. Over 20 wines, several available by the carafe. Pleasant, modern guestrooms.

CHAUMONT
▲ Hôtel de France
25 rue Toupot, 52000 **Map** 4B5
📞 03 25 03 01 11
FAX 03 25 32 35 80
W www.chaumont-hotel-france.com
AE, DC, MC, V
⬤ Restaurant: L; Sun
🍴 €€€ 🍽 (20) €€€€

Red mullet stars here, along with cold meats and crudités. Standard collection of lamb, beef and duck, all wonderfully cooked. Andouillette de Troyes and Burgundy snails available daily. Very modern guestrooms.

CHAUMONT
● Le Capri
31 rue Félix Bablon, 52000 **Map** 4B5
📞 03 25 03 72 85
FAX 03 25 01 27 67
MC, V ⬤ Sun L, Mon, Tue L
🍴 €€

Superb grilled meats, enhanced by just one flavour, like Gorgonzola sauce or an alcohol flambé. Pizzas are topped with goat's cheese and Parma ham. Just six incredibly inexpensive French wines.

CHAUMONT
▲ Le Grand Val
Route de Langres, 52000 **Map** 4B5
📞 03 25 03 90 35
FAX 03 25 32 11 80
W www.hotel-legrandval.fr
MC, V ⬤ last wk Dec
🍴 €€ 🍽 (52) €€

Hearty feasts of beef, veal, local sausage, lamb and freshwater fish. Basic guestrooms, some with balconies.

CHAUMONT
● Le Jardin
4 rue Félix Bablon, 52000 **Map** 4B5
📞 03 25 03 89 97
MC, V ⬤ Sun, Mon 🍴 €€

Brochettes of lamb, rump steaks and duck breast served with herbs, cheese

sauces and spices. Affordable set menus emphasize local ham and cheese, plus famed andouillette de Troyes. Good wines. Outdoor terrace on the street.

CHAUMONT
▲ Les Remparts
72 rue de Verdun, 52000 **Map** 4B5
📞 03 25 32 64 40
FAX 03 25 32 51 70
W www.hotel-les-remparts.fr
AE, DC, MC, V
🍴 €€€ 🍽 (18) €€€

You'll find the best wine list in Chaumont here, and a few 25-year-old vintages; there are more bottles than dishes on the tiny menu. The appetizers shine, especially the grilled scallops and duck foie gras. Charming guestrooms.

CHAUMONT
● Palmier
16 rue Victor Mariotte, 52000 **Map** 4B5
📞 03 25 32 67 22
🍴 €€

Expertly crafted pizzas loaded with goat's cheese and seafood plus a tiny range of simple grilled dishes. Eastern flavours creep in: Tunisian brik pastries, couscous and succulent tagines.

CHAUMONT
▲ Terminus Reine
Pl Charles de Gaulle, 52000 **Map** 4B5
📞 03 25 03 66 66
FAX 03 25 03 28 95
W www.relais-sud-champagne.com
AE, DC, MC, V ⬤ Sun D
🍴 €€€ 🍽 (63) €€€

Intricate recipes, rich with game, wild boar and lobster. Langres cheese and roasted fish also feature. Pizzas are superb, particularly with Roquefort cheese, local ham and capers. Spacious guestrooms, though slightly dated.

CHAUMONT
● Toscana
21 rue de Verdun, 52000 **Map** 4B5
📞 03 25 32 41 36
MC, V ⬤ Tue 🍴 €€

Great for ocean fare and plain grilled steaks. Opt for the mussels, seafood pasta or freshwater fish. Not the only pizzeria in town, but excellent.

COLOMBEY-LES-DEUX-EGLISES
▲ Auberge de la Montagne
17 rue de la Montagne, 52330 **Map** 4A5
📞 03 25 01 51 69
FAX 03 25 01 53 20
AE, MC, V ⬤ Mon, Tue
🍴 €€ 🍽 (8) €€€

Renowned, Michelin-starred restaurant in Charles de Gaulle's home town. Try tarts, Langres cheese, lobster, pike and trout, all delicately prepared. Extremely classy considering the rural location. Character-filled bedrooms.

CUMIERES
● Le Caveau
44 rue Coopérative, 51480 **Map** 4A4
📞 03 26 54 83 23
FAX 03 26 54 24 56
W www.restaurant-le-caveau.com
MC, V ⬤ Sun–Tue D, Wed
🍴 €€€

Ground-breaking menu laced with Ratafia, a sweet liqueur. Imaginative elements like Serrano ham, marmalade, Reims' vinegar, caramel and chickpeas (garbanzo beans). Seafood includes rascasse and monkfish. Strong selection of wines including notable local labels.

DOLANCOURT
▲ Moulin du Landion
Rue St Léger, 10200 **Map** 4A5
📞 03 25 27 92 17
FAX 03 25 27 94 44
MC, V 🍴 €€€ 🍽 (16) €€€

Charming Tudor-style country house complete with a water wheel and an attractive terrace. Chicken and pigeon feature alongside freshwater fish and andouillette de Troyes. Comfortable rooms and outdoor swimming pool.

DORMANS
● Table Sourdet
6 rue du Dr Moret, 51700 **Map** 4A4
📞 03 26 58 20 57
FAX 03 26 58 88 82
AE, MC, V ⬤ Mon; Christmas & New Year 🍴 €€€

Dormans' finest restaurant specializes in fish marinated in Champagne, liqueurs or wine. Game and poultry, mostly roasted and grilled, make up the meat selection.

ECLARON

▲ **Hostellerie Moulin**

3 rue du Moulin, 52290 **Map** 4B5

☎ 03 25 04 17 76

FAX 03 25 55 67 01

W www.hotellerie.moulin.free.fr

AE, MC, V ● Sun D, Mon L; Jan

€€ ◆ (5) €€

Authentic country style, from the fine seafood specials to the decor. Desserts include the scrumptious Grand Marnier soufflé, roast figs with almonds and local cheese. Reserve a luxurious room well in advance.

EPERNAY

● **Au Bacchus Gourmet**

21 rue Gambetta, 51200 **Map** 4A4

☎ 03 26 51 11 44

W www.aubacchusgourmet.com

MC, V ● 21 Dec–19 Jan

€€€

Innovative dishes, some with a foreign twist such as lobster carpaccio with Chinese noodles, guinea fowl tagliatelle, sea bass in olive pastry and grilled trout with Parmesan. Hundreds of wines.

EPERNAY

● **La Cave à Champagne**

16 rue Gambetta, 51200 **Map** 4A4

☎ 03 26 55 50 70

FAX 03 26 51 07 24

@ cave.champagne@wanadoo.fr

MC, V ● Wed D €€€

Awards blanket the wall outside this wonderful eatery. Savour local ham in puff pastry and cassoulet (p326) with scallops or perch in lobster sauce. Stacks of Champagne and fine wine.

EPERNAY

▲ **Le Chapon Fin**

2 pl Mendès-France, 51200 **Map** 4A4

☎ 03 26 55 40 03

FAX 03 26 54 94 17

W http://chaponfin.fr

MC, V ● 26 Feb–10 Mar, 20–27 Nov €€ ◆ (9) €€

Great-value brasserie renowned for its local ham, rabbit in a prune sauce and andouillette de Troyes. House specials are the one-kilogram (2lb) steak to share and a three-fish sauerkraut. Guestrooms are standard, some en suite.

EPERNAY

● **Le St Vincent**

22 rue de Reims, 51200 **Map** 4A4

☎ 03 26 51 80 42

FAX 03 26 51 66 22

MC, V ● Sun D, Mon D, Tue D

€€

Serious restaurant with two set menus. Lighter items include langoustines with aïoli (p400), seafood brochettes and lovely andouillette de Troyes. Heavier offerings range from the house cassoulet (p326) to simple slabs of beef.

EPERNAY

● **Le Théâtre**

8 pl Mendès-France, 51200 **Map** 4A4

☎ 03 26 58 88 19

FAX 03 26 58 88 38

AE, DC, MC, V ● Sun D, Tue D, Wed

€€€€

Multilingual staff preside over the classy menu in this renovated theatre. Veal with local mustard is a delicacy, as well as duck and game in season.

EPERNAY

▲ **Les Berceaux**

13 rue des Berceaux, 51200 **Map** 4A4

☎ 03 26 55 28 84

FAX 03 26 55 10 36

@ les.berceaux@wanadoo.fr

AE, DC, MC, V ● 3 wks Feb; last 2 wks Aug €€€ ◆ (29) €€€

Try the pig's trotters and local ham with artichokes, gazpacho, Breton galettes and sweet crêpes. Cosy guestrooms.

EPERNAY

● **Les Cépages**

16 rue de la Fauvette, 51200 **Map** 4A4

☎ 03 26 55 16 93

FAX 03 26 54 51 30

@ lescepages@wanadoo.fr

AE, MC, V ● Sun D, Wed D, Thu; 10 days Mar & Jul, 25–31 Dec

€€€€

Extravagant seafood, with sea bream in Champagne and John Dory with wild mushrooms. Vast wine cellar.

EPINE

▲ **Aux Armes de Champagne**

31 ave Luxembourg, 51460 **Map** 4B5

☎ 03 26 69 30 30

FAX 03 26 69 30 26

W www.aux-armes-de-champagne.com

AE, DC, MC, V ● Sun D; Nov–Easter: Mon; beginning Jan–mid Feb €€€€ ◆ (37) €€€€

Something to suit every taste, including vegetarian: aubergine (eggplant) with pine nuts, lobster with apricots and Limousin veal. Expect novel flavours like seaweed, grapes and courgette (zucchini) flowers. Some rooms have a Jacuzzi.

GIVET

▲ **Le Roosevelt**

14 quai des Remparts, 08600 **Map** 4B2

☎ 03 24 42 14 14

FAX 03 24 42 15 15

MC, V ● Fri €€ ◆ (8) €€

Light meals include savoury galettes and exquisite sweet crêpes. Cassoulet (p326), with both scampi and scallops, is a real speciality. Local cider and Belgian beers. Pretty riverside terrace. Dated, plastic furniture in the guestrooms.

GIVET

▲ **Le Val St Hilaire**

7 quai des Fours, 08600 **Map** 4B2

☎ 03 24 42 38 50

FAX 03 24 42 07 36

AE, DC, MC, V

● Sun D, Mon L; mid-Dec–mid Jan

€€ ◆ (20) €€

Delicious veal in a rich creamy sauce and sea bass in white wine. Starters include snails, prawns and langoustines. Riverside terrace. Large, comfortable guestrooms with a modern edge.

GIVET

● **Les Mouettes**

2 quai des Fours, 08600 **Map** 4B2

☎ 03 24 42 04 38

FAX 03 24 42 17 97

MC, V ● Mon €€

Outdoor terrace squeezed between the river and the road. Vegetables, fruit and herbs grace the salmon, sea bass, pike-perch and turbot. The wild boar pâté, frogs' legs and Rocroi cheese are highly recommended. Barbecues in summer.

GIVET

▲ **Rex**

16 pl Méhul, 08600 **Map** 4B2

03 24 42 07 58
MC, V ● Sat; last 2 wks Aug
🍴 € 🍷 (8) €€

A dreamy air of bygone times lingers here. Soak up the atmosphere or lounge in the square outside while delighting in sausages, pork chops and seasonal vegetables. Pleasant guestrooms.

JOINVILLE
▲ Poste
Pl de la Grève, 52300 **Map** 4A5
03 25 94 12 63
FAX 03 25 94 36 23
w http://hoteldelaposte52.com
AE, DC, MC, V ● Sun D; Jan
🍴 €€ 🍷 (10) €€

Unpretentious restaurant where you can rub shoulders with the natives, who enjoy the sea- and freshwater fish here. Other hits include lamb and chicken with thyme, bacon or citrus fruits. Unassuming bedrooms.

JOINVILLE
▲ Soleil d'Or
9 rue Capucins, 52300 **Map** 4A5
03 25 94 15 66
FAX 03 25 94 39 02
AE, DC, MC, V ● Sun D, Mon
🍴 €€€ 🍷 (17) €€€

Old-style charm at one of Joinville's finest. Quail, pigeon and trout top the menu, which is heavy on cinnamon, herbs and local vegetables. Alluring, large guestrooms with original stone and wooden features.

LA CHAPELLE-ST-LUC
● Le Sarrail
3 ave Roger Salengro, 10600 **Map** 4A5
03 25 74 62 40
FAX 03 25 74 65 52
w www.le-sarrail.com
MC, V ● Sun, Mon D 🍴 €€€

Hardly a vegetable in sight, except for a stray potato or onion. Pike-perch, crab and bream stand against an otherwise carnivorous feast. Duck and beef come in giant portions with pepper, cream and Béarnaise sauces.

LANGRES
▲ Auberge Jeanne d'Arc
24–26 rue Gambetta, 52200 **Map** 8C1

03 25 86 87 88
FAX 03 25 86 87 89
w www.aubergejeannedarc.com
MC, V 🍴 €€€ 🍷 (10) €€

Auberge menu concentrating on local meats, tarts and soups. Quite delicious breakfasts with ham, pastries and honey. Pleasant, welcoming guestrooms.

LANGRES
▲ Grand Hôtel de l'Europe
23 rue Diderot, 52200 **Map** 8C1
03 25 87 10 88
FAX 03 25 87 60 65
w www.relais-sud-champagne.com
MC, V ● Oct–Mar: Sun D
🍴 €€€ 🍷 (26) €€€

Elegant cooking grounded by a few hearty local dishes such as beef with roast potatoes. Highlights include lemon cream crab, scallops in saffron sauce, Madeira veal and duck with foie gras. Ample, if dated, guestrooms.

LANGRES
▲ Le Cheval Blanc
4 rue de l'Estres, 52200 **Map** 8C1
03 25 87 07 00
FAX 03 25 87 23 13
w www.hotel-langres.com
AE, MC, V ● last 2 wks Nov
🍴 €€€€ 🍷 (22) €€€

This is the finest option in Langres, a walled town on a hill. Wonderful set menus under an ancient beamed ceiling. Carpaccio of scallops with caviar and roast pigeon stand out, plus more exotic tastes like Szechuan beef with figs. Some rooms have medieval brickwork.

LANGRES
● Le Pignata
59 rue Diderot, 52200 **Map** 8C1
03 25 87 63 70
FAX 03 25 87 69 68
MC, V 🍴 €€€

Veal with Milanese tomato sauce gets top marks. Several pastas, including seafood tagliatelle, plus delectable pizzas. Well-priced set menus include wine.

LANGRES
● Le Square
2 rue Général Leclerc, 52200 **Map** 8C1
03 25 84 23 00

FAX 03 25 84 67 23
MC, V ● Mon 🍴 €€€
Opulent dining in an old stone town house by the church. Spectacular appetizers: carpaccio of duck and scallops, crab and prawn terrine and salmon and caviar tartare. Rabbit, veal, nuts and honey star on the set menu.

LANGRES
● Tarantella
10 rue Boulière, 52200 **Map** 8C1
03 25 88 57 50
MC, V ● Sun 🍴 €€

Fabulous grilled meats with beef forestière (wild mushrooms, bacon and potatoes) and cheese smothering some cuts. Andouillette de Troyes is served with Dijon mustard. Appetizers include frogs' legs, smoked ham, snails and excellent Langres cheese.

MARNAY-SUR-MARNE
▲ La Vallée
Signposted off the RN19, 6km (4 miles) northeast of the A31/A5 interchange, 52800 **Map** 8C1
03 25 31 10 11
FAX 03 25 03 83 86
w www.hotel-de-la-vallee.fr
MC, V ● Feb, 23 Dec–3 Jan
🍴 €€€ 🍷 (6) €€

Minced scallops, wild berry salmon and woodland mushrooms dazzle among the regional favourites. Wonderful terrace with flowers and trees. Bedrooms are utterly peaceful. Good local wine.

LE-MESNIL-SUR-OGER
● Le Mesnil
2 rue Pasteur, 51190 **Map** 4A4
03 26 57 95 57
FAX 03 26 57 78 57
w www.chez.com/mesnil
AE, DC, MC, V ● Mon D, Tue D, Wed; end Jan–early Feb, mid Aug–early Sep 🍴 €€€€

Sink your teeth into a delectable seafood or snail cassoulet (p326) or the speciality trout. Hare and quail also frequently appear on the small à la carte menu.

MONTCHENOT
● Grand Cerf
RN51, 51500

Map 4A4

📞 03 26 97 60 07

FAX 03 26 97 64 24

🌐 www.le-grand-cerf.fr

✉ AE, DC, MC, V ⬤ Sun D, Tue D, Wed

🍴 €€€€

Michelin-starred country restaurant serving regional meat dishes and exquisite seafood. Pig's trotters, veal, lobster and cod feature. Set menu dégustation makes a lavish feast.

PINEY

▲ Le Tadorne

1 pl de la Halle, 10220 **Map** 4A5

📞 03 25 46 30 35

FAX 03 25 46 36 49

🌐 www.le-tadorne.com

✉ AE, DC, MC, V ⬤ Oct–Mar: Sun D

🍴 €€€€ 🛏 (27) €€€

Timbered farmhouse with a distinctive air. Local Chaource cheese, crushed garlic and berries add a tang to meat dishes. Bedrooms are simple, but cosy, and there's a pool for guests.

REIMS

● Au Petit Comptoir

17 rue de Mars, 51100 **Map** 4A4

📞 03 26 40 58 58

FAX 03 26 47 26 19

@ au.petit.comptoir@wanadoo.fr

✉ AE, MC, V ⬤ 21 Dec–4 Jan; first wk Aug 🍴 €€€

Beef is the favourite, prepared with a little pepper, onion or delicious sauces; filet mignon and tuna tartare are regular specials. Good wine and Champagne selection. Snazzy outdoor seating.

REIMS

● Au Plat du Jour

217 rue du Barbâtre, 51100 **Map** 4A4

📞 03 26 85 27 60

✉ MC, V ⬤ Sun, Sat L 🍴 €€

An ever-evolving menu, as the name "dish of the day" suggests. Expect tarts, beef and salads topped with mussels and bacon. Seasonal seafood includes langoustines and pasta paella for two.

REIMS

● Brasserie du Boulingrin

48 rue de Mars, 51100 **Map** 4A4

📞 03 26 40 96 22

FAX 03 26 40 03 92

🌐 www.boulingrin.fr

✉ MC, V ⬤ Sun 🍴 €€

Elaborate interior and a fine street-side terrace. Emphasis on seafood with dishes including grilled fish and tuna tartare.

REIMS

● Chardonnay

184 ave Épernay, 51100 **Map** 4A4

📞 03 26 06 08 60

FAX 03 26 05 81 56

✉ AE, DC, MC, V ⬤ Sun D, Mon, Sat L; 3 wks from end Jul, 26 & 30 Dec

🍴 €€€€

Family-run, gourmet restaurant serving meat and seafood with delicious wine-based sauces. Specialities are the calf's sweetbreads millefeuille, pan-fried duck foie gras, and famed desserts, like baked peaches and a hot chocolate surprise.

REIMS

● Da Nello

39 rue Cérès, 51100 **Map** 4A4

📞 03 26 47 33 25

✉ MC, V ⬤ Sun, Mon L; Aug 🍴 €€

Pizzas with a large variety of toppings, including snails. Expect Italian wines, fish and cold meat platters with Parma ham. A handful of French vintages.

REIMS

● Flo

96 pl Drouet d'Erlon, 51100 **Map** 4A4

📞 03 26 91 40 50

FAX 03 26 91 40 54

✉ AE, DC, MC, V 🍴 €€€€

With one of the best terraces in town and a gigantic wine and Champagne list, it's hard to go wrong here. Try the Breton oysters or Limousin beef.

REIMS

▲ Grand Hôtel de l'Univers

41 bd Foch, 51100 **Map** 4A4

📞 03 26 88 68 08

FAX 03 26 40 95 61

🌐 www.ebc.fr/hotel-univers

✉ AE, DC, MC, V ⬤ Sun D

🍴 €€€ 🛏 (42) €€€

Wonderfully elaborate set and à la carte menus at restaurant Au Congrès. Try the pan-fried scallops with citrus fruit, lamb with rosemary or honey-roasted duck.

Spacious guestrooms come complete with desks. Private town-centre parking.

REIMS

● La Forêt Noire

2 bd Jules César, 51100 **Map** 4A4

📞 03 26 47 63 95

FAX 03 26 83 02 27

✉ MC, V ⬤ Sun, Mon D, Tue D; 2 wks Nov 🍴 €€

Alsatian cuisine with an emphasis on flammenkueche (p119) and wonderful salads with bacon, sausage and pork.

REIMS

● La Grange

Au Cul de Poule, 51100 **Map** 4A4

📞 03 26 47 60 22

✉ MC, V ⬤ Sun, Mon D 🍴 €

The food here compensates for the dated, dowdy interior behind a Tudor façade. On the menu is beef in pepper sauce, sliced Reims pork, steak tartare, beef with snails and scallops in a Provençal sauce.

REIMS

● La Vigneraie

14 rue de Thillois, 51100 **Map** 4A4

📞 03 26 88 67 27

FAX 03 26 40 26 67

🌐 www.francegourmande.fr

✉ AE, MC, V ⬤ Sun D, Mon, Wed L; 2 wks Feb & 3 wks Aug 🍴 €€€€

Menus to suit any purse. The chef's masterpiece is a medley of scallop carpaccio, tuna and salmon. Unusual meat dishes include steak with pistachio nuts and Basque sauces or citrus confit.

REIMS

● Le Continental

93 pl Drouet d'Erlon, 51100 **Map** 4A4

📞 03 26 47 01 47

FAX 03 26 40 95 60

🌐 http://le-continental.fr

✉ AE, DC, MC, V 🍴 €€€€

Incredible salads with truffle, foie gras and scallop toppings, and lots of seafood dishes. Fancy interior at the edge of Reims' pedestrianized zone.

REIMS

● Le Foch

37 bd Foch, 51100 **Map** 4A4

● Restaurant ■ Hotel ▲ Hotel / Restaurant

☎ 03 26 47 48 22
FAX 03 26 88 78 22
W www.lefoch.com
✉ AE, MC, V ● Sun D, Mon, Sat L;
2 wks Feb, Aug **11** €€€€€

One of Reims' best, with some great Champagnes. Top choices include rabbit, pigeon, red mullet with chorizo and roast scallops with fennel and orange.

REIMS
● **Le Jamin**
18 bd Jamin, 51100 **Map** 4A4
☎ 03 26 07 37 30
FAX 03 26 02 09 64
✉ AE, MC, V ● Sun D, Mon
11 €€€

An exciting eatery boasting more than 50 wines and regional beers. Affordable gourmet dishes include langoustines, sea bass, duck, beef and Burgundy snails.

REIMS
● **Le Millénaire**
4–6 rue Bertin, 51100 **Map** 4A4
☎ 03 26 08 26 62
FAX 03 26 84 24 13
✉ AE, DC, MC, V ● Sun, Sat L
11 €€€€

Stylish central restaurant serving award-winning seafood like a langoustine and turbot platter, and roasted sea bass with fennel and artichokes. Meat dishes are heavy on mustard, wine and seasonal vegetables. Expansive appetizer menu.

REIMS
● **Le Monté Cristo**
3 rue de l'Ecu, 51100 **Map** 4A4
☎ 03 26 88 99 01
● Sun **11** €

Local hangout with bar stools and a smattering of tables. Beef, sauerkraut and steak tartare are mainstays. Good tapas selection including Serrano ham, tomato and mozzarella salad and prawns.

REIMS
● **Le St Rémi**
4 bis esplanade Fléchambault, 51100
Map 4A4
☎ 03 26 09 79 57
● Sun, Mon D **11** €

Two unpretentious dining rooms, one for local labourers and one for visitors.

Inexpensive three-course menu includes sausages, sauerkraut and steak-frites. Wine by the jug.

REIMS
● **La Table Anna**
6 rue Gambetta, 51100 **Map** 4A4
☎ 03 26 89 12 12
FAX 03 26 89 12 12
✉ AE, MC, V ● Sun D, Mon **11** €€

Restaurant decorated with Champagne bottles and countless pictures. Duck and seafood dominate the menu, which is exquisite despite the price. Highlights include scallop brochettes, foie gras, prawn platters and seafood pot-au-feu.

REIMS
● **Les Charmes**
11 rue Brûlart, 51100 **Map** 4A4
☎ 03 26 85 37 63
FAX 03 26 26 21 00
✉ MC, V ● Sun, Sat L **11** €€€

Salmon and rabbit are the specialities. Scallops, langoustines, meats and fish are prepared with herbs and sauces.

REIMS
▲ **Les Crayères**
64 bd Henry Vasnier, 51100 **Map** 4A4
☎ 03 26 82 80 80
FAX 03 26 82 65 52
W www.gerardboyer.com
✉ AE, DC, MC, V
● Mon, Tue, first 2 wks Jan
11 €€€€€ ● (19) €€€€€

Reims' finest restaurant, with three Michelin stars. Vast menu offering lobster, langoustines, foie gras, duck and sea bass. Opulent guestrooms, some with racy leopard-print furnishings.

REIMS
● **Les Thiers**
22 rue Thiers, 51100 **Map** 4A4
☎ 03 26 40 23 48
11 € ● Sun; Aug

A simple out-of-town local favourite which doubles as a bar, serving hearty steak-frites, steak tartare and Breton galettes. Excellent value set menus.

REIMS
▲ **Mercure Reims**
31 bd Paul Doumer, 51723 **Map** 4A4

☎ 03 26 84 49 49
FAX 03 26 84 49 84
✉ AE, DC, MC, V ● Sun L, Sat L
11 €€€ ● (126) €€€€

Innovative dining in a rather commercial restaurant. Sample tuna with mint, seafood brochettes, duck cassoulet (p326) and beef carpaccio with Parmesan. Spotless, modern rooms.

REIMS
● **Vonelly**
13 rue Gambetta, 51100 **Map** 4A4
☎ 03 26 47 22 00
FAX 03 26 47 22 43
✉ AE, DC, MC, V ● Sun D, Mon,
Sat L; Aug & other school holidays
11 €€€€

Interesting cuisine in a fashionable dining room. Salmon and snails are best enjoyed with a glass of Champagne.

RETHEL
▲ **Au Sanglier des Ardennes**
1 rue Pierre Curie, 08300 **Map** 4B3
☎ 03 24 38 45 19
FAX 03 24 38 45 14
✉ MC, V ● 24–25 Dec
11 €€ ● (12) €€

Vast array of of salads and appetizers, including smoked salmon and the chef's terrine. A giant steak is for two diners to share. Generous guestrooms.

RETHEL
▲ **Le Moderne**
2 pl de la Gare, 08300 **Map** 4B3
☎ 03 24 38 44 54
FAX 03 24 38 37 84
✉ MC, V ● Nov–Mar: Sun D; 24–25
Dec, 31 Dec–1 Jan
11 €€€ ● (22) €€

Flambées, often fuelled by Armagnac, dazzle diners. Cassoulet (p373) is a popular dish. Time-warped, bright rooms.

ROCROI
▲ **Les Remparts**
10 rue des Remparts, 08230 **Map** 4B3
☎ 03 24 54 11 83
FAX 03 24 54 13 20
✉ AE, MC, V ● Mon, Sat L, first 2
wks Nov **11** €€ ● (7) €€

Pizzas cooked in a wood-fired oven. Ardennaise-style pizza comes with eggs

For key to symbols see back flap

and ham. Diced bacon, chorizo, peppers and mushrooms cover others. Basic bedrooms. Swimming pool.

ROMILLY-SUR-SEINE
▲ l'Auberge de Nicey
24 rue Carnot, 10100 **Map** 4A5
C 03 25 24 10 07
FAX 03 25 24 47 01
W www.denicey.com
S AE, DC, MC, V
H €€€ **S** (24) €€€

Sweet-and-sour foie gras hints at the imagination used in this gourmet kitchen. Favourites include herb-laden lobsters and scallops, and excellent straightforward lamb and beef with garlic butter. Wonderful wine list. Well-equipped, comfortable guestrooms.

SEDAN
● Au Bon Vieux Temps
1 pl Halle, 08200 **Map** 4B3
C 03 24 29 03 70
FAX 03 24 29 20 27
S AE, DC, MC, V **●** Sun D, Mon, Wed D; last 2 wks Feb, last wk Aug **H** €€
Superb seafood appetizers like lobster soufflé, salmon ravioli and langoustine gratin. Also noteworthy: rabbit with prunes and good Ardennes ham with melon. Set menus range from budget (humble Bordelaise sirloin) to splurge (elaborate scallop gateau).

SEDAN
● Crêperie du Château
10 pl Château, 08200 **Map** 4B3
C 03 24 22 08 49
FAX 03 24 22 08 49
● Mon, Thu; 2nd wk Nov **H** €
Charming, typically French interior and a wooden terrace. Liqueurs, apples and pears dominate the sweet crêpes; scallops, bacon and eggs the savoury galettes. Original mains such as sole in mussel sauce. Small selection of wine and excellent cider.

SEDAN
▲ Hôtel de l'Europe
2 pl de la Gare, 08200 **Map** 4B3
C 03 24 27 18 71
FAX 03 24 29 32 00
S MC, V **●** last wk Aug (restaurant)

H €€ **S** (25) €€
Two-star hotel with a great reputation. Guests benefit from the swimming pool, Internet access, a bar and private parking. Guestrooms have mod cons. Restaurant L'Europe dishes up fine quality, if a little standard, French fare.

SEDAN
▲ Le Luxembourg
4 rue Thiers, 08200 **Map** 4B3
C 03 24 27 08 52
FAX 03 24 29 02 96
S MC, V **●** Sun D, Mon L, Christmas & New Year **H** € **S** (15) €
Perfect cooking, though somewhat lacking in imagination. Try the goat's cheese, Chaource cheese, sausage or rabbit. Guestrooms among the town's simplest but are adequate.

SEDAN
● Le Médièval
51 rue de l'Horloge, 08200 **Map** 4B3
C 03 24 29 16 95
S MC, V **●** Tue D, Wed
H €€
Good showing of lighter items including oysters, mussels, local cheese and fine Ardennes ham. Other outstanding dishes include herb-sprinkled steaks, frogs' legs and salmon tartare. Quite gorgeous ancient interior.

SEDAN
● Le Ste-Barbe
3 rue Ste-Barbe, 08200 **Map** 4B3
C 03 24 29 62 75
S MC, V **●** Mon **H** €€
Despite the poor wine list and scruffy interior, this restaurant serves generous portions of local meat dishes. Local pâté and Ardennes ham feature on the good cold meat platters

SEDAN
● Les Halles
5 pl Halle, 08200 **Map** 4B3
C 03 24 29 42 42
S MC, V **●** Mon L **H** €€
This great pizzeria draws crowds of locals. Fantastically crisp pizzas with egg, artichoke and asparagus toppings. Cuts of pork and lamb dominate the meat menu, all simply cooked.

SEDAN
▲ St-Michel
3 rue St Michel, 08200 **Map** 4B3
C 03 24 29 04 61
FAX 03 24 29 32 67
W www.le-saint-michel.fr
S MC, V **●** Sun D; 3 wks Aug
H €€€ **S** (20) €€
Medieval-style decor with wild boars' head trophies. On the menu are expensive lobster and less pricey grilled lamb, perch, seafood platters, veal and pork marinated with cider or beer.

SEPT-SAULX
▲ Le Cheval Blanc
Rue du Moulin, 51400 **Map** 4B4
C 03 26 03 90 27
FAX 03 26 03 97 09
W www.chevalblanc-sept-saulx.com
S AE, DC, MC, V **●** Oct–Mar: Tue & Wed L; Feb **H** €€€€ **S** (25) €€€€
Start with scallops and langoustines, then savour frogs' legs, sweetbreads or guinea fowl with leeks, apple, fennel and turnip. Rooms are plain but comfortable. Tennis courts in the fine grounds.

SEZANNE
▲ Croix d'Or
53 rue de Notre Dame, 51120 **Map** 4A4
C 03 26 80 61 10
FAX 03 26 80 65 20
S AE, DC, MC, V **●** Sun D, Wed, 2nd wk Jan **H** €€€ **S** (13) €€€
Seafood and outstanding regional dishes. Try the veal from Sézanne, rabbit and foie gras. Several dishes are cooked with Champagne, including the turbot, and there's a decent cheeseboard. Rooms are rather standard but pleasant enough.

ST-DIZIER
● Aux Gourmet des Remparts
58 rue Docteur Mougeot, 52100
Map 4B5
C 03 25 56 56 96
FAX 03 25 55 48 29
S MC, V **●** Sun D, Thu D **H** €€
Don't expect innovative cuisine, but rather just tasty meat with a simple sauce or herbs. The seafood is a bit more interesting, like sole in mussel and prawn sauce. Distinctive desserts.

● Restaurant ■ Hotel ▲ Hotel / Restaurant

ST-DIZIER
● Gentilhommière
29 rue Jean Jaurès, 52100 **Map** 4B5

☎ 03 25 56 32 97

FAX 03 25 06 32 66

🎫 MC, V ● Sat L, Sun D, Mon; first 3 wks Aug, 1 wk Mar 🍴 €€€

Arguably the best restaurant in town. Delicious Champagnes, period decor and sophisticated fare. Delicious duck with chutney. Long list of inspired desserts. Reservations essential.

ST-DIZIER
● La Pierre Gourmande
39 rue Maréchal de Lattre, 52100 **Map** 4B5

☎ 03 25 56 41 99

🎫 MC, V ● Wed, Sat L 🍴 €€

Staggeringly large menu with 15 potato dishes alone. Veal, lamb and beef are served with tomato tagliatelle. Scores of wines. Uninspired façade and interior.

ST-DIZIER
● L'Arquebuse
11 rue de l'Arquebuse, 52100 **Map** 4B5

☎ 03 25 05 38 19

🎫 MC, V

● 2 wks Jan, 2 wks Aug 🍴 €€

Warm up with veal and steak in winter, then chill out with cold meat, melon and tomatoes in summer. Pizza toppings include seafood, capers and local ham.

ST-DIZIER
● Le Capri
17 rue Emile Giros, 52100 **Map** 4B5

☎ 03 25 06 32 27

🎫 MC, V

● Sat L, Sun; 22–29 Dec 🍴 €€

A wood-fired oven perfectly crisps beef and pizza, often loaded with eggs or artichokes. A dozen salads including seafood with scallops, clams and prawns.

STS-GEOSMES
▲ Auberge des 3 Jumeaux
17 route d'Auberives, 52200 **Map** 8C1

☎ 03 25 87 03 36

FAX 03 25 87 58 68

🎫 AE, DC, MC, V ● Sun, Mon, end Jan–end Feb 🍴 €€€ 🍽 (10) €€€

Classic eatery with a basic, unfussy fixed-price menu featuring snails, local

trout, coq au vin (p217) *and Langres cheese. The gourmet menu contains flambéed lobster, veal fricassée and in-season game. Thick stone walls in some of the bedrooms.*

TINQUEUX
▲ Assiette Champenoise
40 ave Paul Vaillant-Couturier, 51430 **Map** 4A4

☎ 03 26 84 64 64

FAX 03 26 04 15 69

W http://chaponfin.fr

🎫 AE, DC, MC, V ● Tue, Wed L, 25 Dec 🍴 €€€€ 🍽 (55) €€€€

One of the region's best. Try skillful combinations like lobster gnocchi and langoustines with Japanese hot mustard. Sides include wild rocket and vegetable confits. Superior rooms vary in price and comfort. Fantastic gardens.

TOURS-SUR-MARNE
▲ Touraine Champenoise
2 rue Magasin, 51150 **Map** 4A4

☎ 03 26 58 91 93

FAX 03 26 58 95 47

W www.touraine-champenoise.com

🎫 MC, V ● Thu; first 2 wks Jan

🍴 €€€ 🍽 (8) €€€

Start with scallops, a warm veal salad or omelette paysanne, *then tantalize your taste buds with sea bream or mackerel. Singular rooms and great breakfast.*

TROYES
● Au Jardin Gourmand
31 rue Paillot Montabert, 10000 **Map** 4A5

☎ 03 25 73 36 13

🎫 MC, V ● Sun, Mon L; 2 wks Sep & 2 wks Jan 🍴 €€€

Ten styles of andouillette de Troyes, *with wine, mustard, Champagne or cider sauces. Salmon with* tapenade (p400) *shines. Many fine wines from Moselle, Alsace, Burgundy and Champagne.*

TROYES
● Au Pêché Mignon
31 rue de la Cité, 10000 **Map** 4A5

☎ 03 25 80 58 23

FAX 03 25 80 58 23

🎫 MC, V ● Sun, Sat D 🍴 €€

Dishes include celery-laden sauerkraut and lovely andouillette de Troyes *with*

mushrooms, alongside excellent seafood with unusual flavours such as rhubarb and nuts. White linen and wood interior.

TROYES
● Café de Paris
63 rue Général de Gaulle, 10000 **Map** 4A5

☎ 03 25 73 08 30

FAX 03 25 73 58 18

🎫 AE, MC, V ● Sun D, Tue; 2nd wk Feb, last wk Jul & first 2 wks Aug

🍴 €€€

Gourmet set menu offering duck with peaches, andouillettes *with contrasting cabbage and beef in a Bordelaise sauce. Saffron, Champagne and fruits liven up pike-perch, sea bass and turbot. Classic if somewhat nondescript decor.*

TROYES
● Chez Edouard
10 rue Kléber, 10000 **Map** 4A5

☎ 03 25 80 51 05

FAX 03 25 73 32 34

🎫 MC, V ● Sun D, Sat L 🍴 €€€

Slightly old-fashioned but charming nevertheless. The kitchen turns out steaks, salmon and foie gras with rich sauces, tomatoes, asparagus and nuts, but it's the flambées which pull in the crowds. Wine by the carafe.

TROYES
● Grand Hotel Troyes
6 ave Maréchal Joffre, 10000 **Map** 4A5

☎ 03 25 75 61 52

FAX 03 25 78 48 93

W www.grand-hotel-troyes.com

🎫 MC, V ● Sun, Mon L 🍴 €€

Huge spread of seafood that doesn't cost the earth. Certain lobster dishes can put the bill into orbit, however. Most fish is simply grilled or diced into the hefty sauerkraut or couscous salad.

TROYES
● Grenadine
16 rue Louis Ulbach, 10000 **Map** 4A5

☎ 03 25 73 36 10

● Sun 🍴 €

Breton-style galettes with a smart local twist. Fillings include ham, Gruyère cheese, snails and eggs. Sweet crêpes feature honey, almonds and pears, and a number of flambées use Grand

Marnier and Calvados. Exposed beams inside, pleasant seating outside.

TROYES
▲ **Hôtel de la Poste**
35 rue Emile Zola, 10000 **Map** 4A5
☎ 03 25 73 05 05
FAX 03 25 73 80 76
W www.hotel-de-la-poste.com
☒ AE, DC, MC, V
🍽 €€€€ 🍷 (32) €€€€
Absolutely luxurious hotel. Pig's trotters, tapenade (p400) and mussel butter give extra kick to sole, monkfish and lobster. Exceptional seafood platters for two. Modern, bright but elegant dining room and bedrooms with exposed brickwork.

TROYES
● **La Marinière**
3 rue de la Trinité, 10000 **Map** 4A5
☎ 03 25 73 77 29
☒ MC, V ● Tue L 🍽 €
Functional and attractive untreated pine interior. At least 40 different styles of mussels, prepared with Roquefort, cider, Calvados or sauerkraut. Wonderfully inexpensive lunchtime deal of any mussel dish and dessert.

TROYES
● **Le Bistroquet**
10 rue Louis Ulbach, 10000 **Map** 4A5
☎ 03 25 73 65 65
FAX 03 25 73 55 91
☒ AE, MC, V ● Sun D 🍽 €€€
Gourmet dining at great prices. Sample curried lamb, seafood risotto, veal and steak tartare. Cool, modern interior with a few signs of the establishment's early 19th-century roots.

TROYES
● **Le Bourgogne**
40 rue du Général de Gaulle, 10000
Map 4A5
☎ 03 25 73 02 67
FAX 03 57 73 02 67
☒ MC, V ● Sun D, Mon 🍽 €€€€
Quality ingredients make this kitchen distinctive. Try beef fillet with truffles, raspberry foie gras or monkfish with saffron. Also recommended are roast langoustines, lobster salad and John Dory with Champagne.

TROYES
● **Le Carpaccio**
3 pl Langevin, 10000 **Map** 4A5
☎ 03 25 73 31 10
FAX 03 25 73 55 91
☒ MC, V 🍽 €€
Reputable Italian with a commercial edge. Pizzas have a typical French twist with toppings like Gruyère cheese, bacon pieces, olives, anchovies and egg.

TROYES
■ **Le Champ des Oiseaux**
20 rue Linard Gonthier, 10000 **Map** 4A5
☎ 03 25 80 58 50
FAX 03 25 80 98 34
W www.champdesoiseaux.com
☒ AE, DC, MC, V 🍷 (12) €€€€
Right by the cathedral, this is Troyes' most charming hotel. An aura of calm pervades every Mediterranean court-yard, every airy lounge and every bewitching guestroom. Snuggle into luxurious bedding among ancient brick-work, aged wood and medieval touches.

TROYES
● **Le Fleuriotte**
24 rue Louis Ulbach, 10000 **Map** 4A5
☎ 03 25 73 21 86
● Sun 🍽 €
Only a cheap three-course menu is served. That's just fine, as it's perfect. Start with ham, crudités or charcuterie. Follow up with andouillette and tasty sauerkraut or steak. Beer on draught.

TROYES
▲ **Le Royal**
22 bd Carnot, 10000 **Map** 4A5
☎ 03 25 73 19 99
FAX 03 25 73 47 85
W www.royal-hotel-troyes.com
☒ AE, DC, MC, V ● Sun, Mon L, Sat L
🍽 €€€ 🍷 (40) €€€€
Spiced-up crustaceans including curried langoustines and lobster with Parmesan. Meat and fish are transformed into exotic creations with use of dates, fresh and dried fruits and coconut. Classy guest chambers with marble bathrooms.

TROYES
● **Le Soleil de l'Inde**
33 rue de la Cité, 10000 **Map** 4A5

☎ 03 25 80 75 71
FAX 03 25 80 75 71
☒ MC, V ● Mon 🍽 €€
A feast for vegetarians and anyone who hankers after spicy food. Outstanding Indian curries, especially the prawn dishes. Tikka and biryani sauces spice up meat, fish and many vegetable mains.

TROYES
● **Le Valentino**
35 rue Paillot Montabert, 10000 **Map** 4A5
☎ 03 25 73 14 14
FAX 03 25 73 14 14
☒ AE, MC, V ● Sun D, Mon, Sat L;
first 2 wks in Jan & last 2 wks Aug
🍽 €€€€
Shellfish stars, in salads or gratins, and fish is flavoured with mint, mustard, rocket and spinach. Meats are served with cabbage, mushrooms and local cheese sauces. Canopied outdoor terrace.

TROYES
● **Le Vivien**
7 pl de St-Rémy, 10000 **Map** 4A5
☎ 03 25 73 70 70
FAX 03 25 73 70 90
☒ AE, MC, V
● Sun D, Mon; last 2 wks Sept
🍽 €€€
Elegant but slightly pretentious, this restaurant is known for its interesting and exotic flavours: Pacific fish crop up on the eclectic table and raisins and onion confit are used to flavour meats. Small list of rather expensive wines.

TROYES
● **Les Clefs de St-Pierre**
89 rue de la Cité, 10000 **Map** 4A5
☎ 03 25 81 01 99
FAX 03 25 80 29 58
W www.restosaintpierre.com
☒ MC, V ● Sun D, Tue D, Wed
🍽 €€
Refined spread includes Champagne-laced salmon, langoustine salad and lemon-dressed scallops. White linen, heavy wine glasses and beams decorate.

TROYES
● **L'Etoile**
11 rue Pithou, 10000 **Map** 4A5
☎ 03 25 73 12 65

● Restaurant ■ Hotel ▲ Hotel / Restaurant

Ⓔ MC, V
Ⓢ Sun, Mon D, Tue, Wed D 🔢 €€
*Solid, homespun, regional fare including
several variations on andouillette de
Troyes, platters of local cheese, herrings
and omelettes with ham and Gruyère.
The cellar contains some Alsace whites.*

TROYES
● Relais St Jean
4 ave Maréchal Joffre, 10000 **Map** 4A5
Ⓒ 03 25 79 90 90
Ⓕ FAX 03 25 78 48 93
Ⓦ www.grand-hotel-troyes.com
Ⓔ AE, MC, V Ⓢ Sun, Sat L 🔢 €€€
*Land and sea gastronomy. Some rare
classics include sea bass baked in sea
salt. The elegance continues with the
salmon tartare and Champagne snails.
Surprisingly small section of wines.*

TROYES
● Un Angolo d'Italia
48 rue Général Saussier, 10000
Map 4A5
Ⓒ 03 25 41 55 39
Ⓢ Sun, Oct–Apr: Mon 🔢 €
*Simple menu with pastas, pizzas and a
lovely range of seafood including squid
and prawn brochettes and spaghettis.
Almost all of the fish dishes, such as
the salmon, come grilled. Great
lunchtime specials. Tables outside.*

VILLEMOYENNE
● Parentèle
32 rue Marcellin Lévêque, 10260
Map 4B5
Ⓒ 03 25 43 68 68
Ⓕ FAX 03 25 43 68 69
Ⓔ AE, DC, MC, V Ⓢ Sun, Mon, Tue;
end Feb–mid Mar, end Jul–early Aug
🔢 €€€
*Michelin-starred restaurant with
wonderful pigeon and game. Other
favourites include lamb and foie gras.*

VITRY-LE-FRANCOIS
● Au Petit Bourguignon
21 rue du Pont, 51300 **Map** 4B4
Ⓒ 03 26 74 14 81
Ⓔ MC, V Ⓢ Sun, Mon D; last 2 wks
Aug, 24 Dec, 1 Jan 🔢 €€
*Try the snails, rabbit terrine or steak
tartare. Grilled lamb and veal also*

*recommended. A pot of local mustard
accompanies each dish; don't miss its
exquisite tangy bite.*

VITRY-LE-FRANCOIS
▲ Hôtel de la Cloche
34 rue Aristide Briand, 51300 **Map** 4B4
Ⓒ 03 26 74 03 84
Ⓕ FAX 03 26 74 15 52
Ⓐ chef.sautetdomicile@wanadoo.fr
Ⓔ AE, DC, MC, V Ⓢ Sat D 🔢 €€
Ⓑ (22) €€€
*Trinkets and art abound in this elegant,
very central establishment. Restaurant
Jacques Sautet serves andouillette de
Troyes, grilled veal and terrines.
Guestrooms are genuinely charming.*

VITRY-LE-FRANCOIS
▲ Hôtel Restaurant de la Poste
Pl Royer Collard, 51300 **Map** 4B4
Ⓒ 03 26 74 02 65
Ⓕ FAX 03 26 74 54 71
Ⓦ http://hotellaposte.com
Ⓔ AE, DC, MC, V
🔢 €€€ Ⓑ (29) €€€
*Ostentatious if slightly dated dining
room. All the usual suspects on the
menu, plus sole, trout and veal in red
wine. Well-appointed guestrooms shame
most of the competition in town. Some
even have a Jacuzzi.*

VITRY-LE-FRANCOIS
● La Grand Brasserie
22 grande rue de Vaux, 51300 **Map** 4B4
Ⓒ 03 26 62 19 99
Ⓕ FAX 03 26 62 19 95
Ⓔ MC, V Ⓢ Sun D
🔢 €€€
*Alsatian-inspired sauerkraut is the order
of the day, with five varieties on offer,
including potatoes, bacon and scallops.
Crustaceans are also expertly-handled.*

VITRY-LE-FRANCOIS
● Le Grillardin
14 pl d'Armes, 51300 **Map** 4B4
Ⓒ 03 26 74 18 97
Ⓔ MC, V Ⓢ 24–25 Dec & 31 Dec–
1 Jan 🔢 €€
*Don't be put off by the commercial
slickness – the food still holds its own.
Meat minimally trimmed with parsley, a
few almonds or Roquefort sauce.*

*Seafood options include squid, which
doubles as a tasty pizza topping.*

VITRY-LE-FRANCOIS
● Les Gourmet des Halles
11 rue des Soeurs, 51300 **Map** 4B4
Ⓒ 03 26 74 48 88
Ⓕ FAX 03 26 72 54 28
Ⓔ MC, V Ⓢ Tue D 🔢 €€
*Classy establishment opposite the
covered market. Prices suit any budget:
rock-bottom to special-occasion splurge.
Time-tested favourites such as veal,
mussels and prawns are interspersed
with surprises such as kangaroo steaks.*

VITRY-LE-FRANCOIS
● Restaurant de l'Hôtel de Ville
2 pl Hôtel de Ville, 51300 **Map** 4B4
Ⓒ 03 26 41 08 78
🔢 €
*Fabulous food without gourmet airs.
No-nonsense bar with ten daily dishes,
most served with fries. A big pot of
mustard is set down with every meal, to
be used with care. An older clientele.*

VITRY-LE-FRANCOIS
● Restaurant du Marché
5 rue Soeurs, 51300 **Map** 4B4
Ⓒ 03 26 73 21 98
Ⓔ MC, V
Ⓢ 24–25 Dec, 1 Jan 🔢 €€€
*Traditional eatery with a knack for fresh
seafood. Pike-perch, scallops and prawns
are flawlessly grilled or fried. Turkey,
duck and beef get the same treatment.*

VOUE
▲ Au Marais
39 route Impériale, 10150 **Map** 4A5
Ⓒ 03 25 37 55 33
Ⓕ FAX 03 25 37 53 29
Ⓦ www.au-marais.com
Ⓔ MC, V Ⓢ Sun L, Mon L, Sat L,
Sep–May: Sun D
🔢 €€€ Ⓑ (20) €€€
*Beef is the overwhelming favourite,
grilled and served with a delicious
Béarnaise sauce; grilled andouillette
de Troyes and duck form the rest of the
meat mainstays. Trout and salmon are
simply grilled or are the base for thick
stews. Adequate if somewhat charmless
rooms with modern furniture.*

ALSACE & LORRAINE

Alsace and Lorraine share a history of shifting frontiers between France and Germany; a past clearly reflected in their cuisines. Amid rolling pastures, plum orchards, vineyards and the steep, pine-clad mountains of the Vosges, elegant Nancy and urbane Strasbourg contrast sharply with the many perfectly preserved, half-timbered wine villages.

The Flavours of Alsace & Lorraine

Alsace-Lorraine's proximity to Germany has led to a diet rich in meat, particularly pork products. Its pine forests house the bees that produce the famous Vosges pine honey, whilst its rivers and lakes ensure plenty of freshwater fish.

Bergamotes from Nancy

Best Markets

Colmar Place de l'Ancienne, selling local fruit and vegetables as well as many organic products, Thu am
Metz Place St-Jacques, Tue, Thu & Sat am
Nancy Covered market at place Henri Mengin. All local produce, daily
Strasbourg Place de Bordeaux. Local fare, Tue

Meat and Charcuterie

Pork and charcuterie are an important Alsatian tradition and feature prominently in local specialities. These include *cervelas, saucisse de Strasbourg* or *knackwurst* (a sort of fat frankfurter), *bratwurst* (made from veal and pork), *lewerzurscht* (liver sausage), cooked hams and *presskopf*, a terrine of pigs' brawn in jelly. In Lorraine, Nancy is known for *boudin noir.*

Alsace also has a long tradition of raising geese for foie gras, attributed to the Jewish population which cooked with goose fat rather than forbidden pork. A speciality since the 18th century is goose *pâté de foie gras* (goose foie gras in pastry).

Cattle are mainly kept for dairying, but milk-fed veal is produced, while poultry includes the black turkey of Alsace, chickens, capons and poussins.

Fish

Trout, carp, pike, pike-perch, shad and freshwater crayfish are found in the rivers Rhine, Meuse, Moselle and their tributaries. Trout pâté is a speciality of the Lorraine.

Cheese and Dairy Produce

The principal cheese of Alsace-Lorraine is Munster AOC, a semi-soft cow's milk cheese with an orangey-yellow rind. It is often served with a saucer of cumin seeds. Géromé AOC from Gérardmer is a similar cheese to Munster. Dairy herds also produce *crème fraîche fluide* which is used in many local recipes.

Left Fois gras **Right** Saucisse de Strasbourg

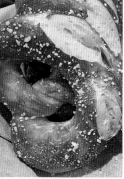

Left Brioche **Right** Bretzels

FRUIT AND VEGETABLES

Cabbages, potatoes, onions, carrots, turnips and asparagus are all grown in this region. Horseradish is a speciality of Mietesheim, while the white *quintal d'Alsace* cabbage, used for *choucroute,* is grown principally around Colmar and Krautergersheim. Harvested between September and November, it is packed with salt and left to ferment in barrels, with juniper berries, cumin seed and bay leaves, for around a month.

Fruit includes bilberries, quince, redcurrants, apples, pears and the mirabelle plums of Lorraine.

BREAD, BAKED GOODS AND SWEETS

Baked specialities include *kougelhopf* or *kouglof* (brioche with raisins and flaked almonds) and savoury bretzels. *Linzertorte* is a cinnamon flavoured sweet pastry lattice tart filled with raspberry jam.

Christmas cakes and biscuits include *lebkueche* (*pain d'épices* with honey, almonds, nutmeg, cloves and lemon) and *anisbredle* (aniseed biscuits). The region is also known for its dark rye bread (*pain de seigle*), its *bergamotes* of Nancy, made from honey and bergamot oil, and its *dragées*, sugared almonds, of Verdun.

PINE HONEY

Various types of honey are collected in Alsace-Lorraine, including acacia, chestnut, lime blossom and mixed flower, but it's particularly worth looking out for the *Miel de Sapin des Vosges* (Vosges pine honey), the first French honey to be awarded an *appellation contrôlée* in 1996. Sweet, dark brown and liquid with a resiny fragrance and taste of balsam, pine honey is technically made not from nectar but from *miellat,* or honeydew, collected by bees from pine trees in the Vosges. The honeydew is produced thanks to tiny aphids living under the bark.

PASTA AND SPAETZLE

You may be surprised to find pasta featuring on Alsatian menus, yet this is not a recent Italian importation, rather a tradition going back to the 15th century. Most often made in the form of wide, tagliatelle-style ribbons, Alsatian pasta is distinguished from Italian pasta by its high proportion of eggs – seven fresh eggs per kilo of durum wheat. *Spaetzle* are fresh noodles made from beaten eggs and flour, which are dropped in morsels into boiling water and then tossed in a pan with melted butter before serving.

THE MIRABELLE PLUM

These delicious, tiny, round, yellow plums flourish in the area between Nancy and Metz and have become one of the symbols of Lorraine. Golden-yellow with a slight pink blush, the mirabelle is fragile and easily bruised. It is found at shops and markets for only a very brief season, between July and early September.

Mirabelles can be eaten raw and are popular in tarts, candied or made into jam. Above all they are used to make Mirabelle *eau-de-vie.*

Regional Dishes

A history of changing nationalities between France and Germany has led to a distinctive Alsatian cuisine. Typifying this joint heritage is choucroute garnie, *a dish said to combine German heartiness with French refinement.*

ON THE MENU

Brochet au pinot noir Pike cooked in red wine

Carpe à la bière Carp cooked with onions and beer

Carpe frite Strips of carp, battered and deep-fried

Gâteau au fromage blanc baked cheesecake

Jambonneau rôti Roasted ham hock

Kougelhopf Fluted ring-shaped brioche with raisins and almonds

Omelette au boudin noir de Nancy Omelette with black pudding from Nancy

Potée Lorraine Casserole of salt pork cooked with cabbage, carrots and onions

Poularde au Riesling Hen cooked in white wine with cream and mushrooms

Rôti du porc aux quetsches Roast pork with damsons

Sandre au Riesling Pike-perch cooked in Riesling

Tarte à l'oignon Open onion tart

Tarte aux mirabelles Mirabelle plum tart

Tarte aux quetsches Damson plum tart

Truite au riesling Trout cooked in white wine

Choucroute garnie

THE REGIONAL MENU

A meal in Alsace will often start with onion tart, quiche Lorraine or goose foie gras, eaten in a pâté or terrine, or simply fried. As well as *choucroute garnie,* which is sometimes served with fish or game, another typical main course is *baeckeoffe.*

In both Alsace and Lorraine, pork is the most common meat, perhaps as a roast joint served with damsons and cabbage, or even a glazed roast suckling pig. Chicken is frequently cooked in beer or stewed in Reisling and served with a creamy sauce. *Boudin noir* from Nancy is popular fried and served with potato purée or cooked in omelettes. In winter, game stews abound, often accompanied by pasta or *spaetzle.*

Fish dishes are also plentiful. Trout is cooked in Riesling, and pike and pike-perch are grilled or roasted and served with a Pinot noir sauce. Carp is generally reserved for festive occasions, when it may be cooked in beer or stuffed; *carpe frite,* cut into strips, dredged in milk and flour and deep fried, is a speciality of the Sundgau area between Mulhouse and the Swiss border.

For the cheese course expect to find Munster cheese and for dessert, a wide variety of fruit tarts made with bilberries, damsons or mirabelle plums. Choices that are equally as tempting include apple strudel, cheesecake, Nancy chocolate cake and *baba au rhum.*

Carpe frite

CHOUCROUTE GARNIE

Typifying the Alsatian use of spices and love of charcuterie is this steaming platter of fragrant pickled cabbage, topped by a mound of sausages and hams. The ham hock and smoked pork belly are cooked slowly with the cabbage, juniper berries, white wine and onions. The smoked Montbéliard and Strasbourg sausages are added to the pot towards the end.

BAECKEOFFE

This layered casserole of assorted meats gets its name from "bake" and "oven". Beef, lamb, pork, and sometimes pig's trotters and oxtail, are marinated in herbs and white wine. The meat is arranged in layers along with thinly sliced potatoes and onions and the dish covered and sealed with a ring of pastry. It is baked for four hours.

QUICHE LORRAINE

This celebrated savoury tart consists of a short pastry base over which diced belly bacon is scattered and a mixture of eggs and cream poured. The tart is baked in the oven and served hot. The authentic version never contains cheese.

FLAMMENKUECHE

This crispy, flame-cooked tart is the Alsatian equivalent of pizza. The bread base is classically topped with diced bacon, *crème fraîche* and onions, though countless other ingredients can be added, from mushrooms to pineapple.

BABA AU RHUM

Babas, or dry, bready cakes, consist of flour, milk, sugar, raisins, eggs and butter. The dough is left to rise before being baked. The cake is then dunked in sugar syrup, doused with rum and served cold with whipped cream.

Le Chou restaurant, Strasbourg

REGIONAL DINING

The following restaurants are among those serving regional dishes at reasonable prices:
A la Couronne d'Or
Drusenheim (see p126)
A L'Etoile
Baldenheim (see p124)
Au Pont St-Martin
Strasbourg (see p134)
La Bonne Franquette
Ville (see p137)
Le Calmosien
Chaumousey (see p125)
Le Chou
Strasbourg (see p135)
Le Jamagne
Gerardmer (see p127)
Le Luth
Mirecourt (see p129)
Le Raybois
Le Puid (see p128)
Le St-Christophe
Neufchateau (see p131)
Les Agapes
Revigny-sur-Ornain (see p132)
Manoir St-Georges
Mommenheim (see p130)
Taverne Katz
Saverne (see p133)

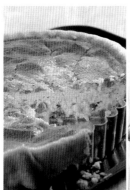

Left Quiche Lorraine **Right** Babas au rhum

Regional Wines & Spirits

Nowhere else in France do the vineyards present quite such picture-postcard charm as in Alsace. All along the 170-km (105-mile) wine route from Marlenheim to Thann the countryside is dotted with the ruins of ancient fortifications and immaculately kept medieval villages whose traditional drinks also include fruit eaux-de-vie and beers.

Grapes on the Rangen hillside

Although Alsace lies in the far northeast of France, the climate is well suited to grape-growing. The Vosges mountains protect the vineyards from the changeable weather conditions and rainfall is the second-lowest in the country. The long dry summers ensure the grapes ripen fully but slowly. Alsace is a geological mosaic, formed when the mountainous plateaux joining the Vosges to the Black Forest subsided 50 million years ago. Its diverse *terroirs* are home to a range of grape varieties and produce wines of great individuality.

Appellations of Alsace
Unlike other French appellations, Alsace wines, easily distinguishable in their slender flute bottles, are labelled by grape variety. Seven main grapes are used.
Riesling Considered the king of grapes by Alsace growers, Riesling produces classy, bone-dry wines. Floral in its youth, it can be steely and minerally. Certain Rieslings show much-sought-after petrolly aromas and are capable of prolonged ageing.
Pinot Gris Best when made from low-yielding vineyards, Alsace Pinot Gris has a complex honeyed, often smoky bouquet and opulent texture. It ages well and is a perfect match for Christmas dinner.
Muscat Two varieties, the spicy Muscat d'Alsace and elegant Muscat Ottonel, give beautifully aromatic, dry wines smelling and tasting of fresh grapes.

BEST PRODUCERS

Domaine Marcel Deiss, Domaine Kreydenweiss, Domaine Landmann, Domaine Mittnach-Klack, Domaine Muré, Domaine Ostertag, Domaine Trimbach, Domaine Weinbach, Domaine Zind-Humbrecht, Dopff & Irion, Kuentz-Bas, Gustave Lorentz
Best cooperatives Cave de Pfaffenheim, Cave de Turckheim, Cave de Kientzheim-Kaysersberg

EDELZWICKER

Edelzwicker is the only still wine in Alsace made from a blend of grapes. It is always a cheap, fun wine, sometimes with a zap of spice. Jugfuls of Edelzwicker wash down the hearty, pork-based fare served in *winstubs* and brasseries.

Rangen Grand Cru vineyard overlooking the village of Thann

VINEYARDS OF ALSACE

KEY

▦	Intensive vine-growing area
■	Vin de Moselle
○	Côtes de Toul
—	Delimited AOC region of Alsace
⋯	*Département* boundary
▬	International boundary

The ancient fortress of Château Haut-Kœnigsbourg

WINSTUBS

If ever there was a haven of snug contentment for the body and soul, the *winstub* is it. Originally, the "stube" was a small backroom in a farmhouse where friends would gather round a simple wooden table to enjoy a good chinwag. Often, the farmer had a few vines so the wheels of conversation would be oiled with copious amounts of white wine. During the various periods of annexation to Germany, producers began to transfer their *winstubs* from the countryside to the town. *Winstubs* were everything the brasseries were not: tiny, intimate bars serving local wine. Food was always a secondary consideration. Genuine *winstubs* are sparsely decorated, ensuring that the drinker's attention does not wander from the task at hand: lively conversation washed down with carafes of wine.

Gewurztraminer These rich wines, often showing notes of old English roses, soft spice and tropical fruit, are eminently suited to exotic and spicy dishes.

Sylvaner This grape produces refreshing thirst-quenchers with floral aromas.

Pinot Blanc Increasingly planted to replace Sylvaner, Pinot Blanc makes easy-drinking still wines and excellent fizz. Pinot Auxerrois is similar.

Pinot Noir The only red grape permitted in Alsace gives spicy red or rosé wines that often taste of cherries.

Confrérien in traditional costume

THE CONFRERIE DE ST-ETIENNE

The origins of this brother-hood, one of the oldest in France, date back to the 14th century. Every year, on 26 December, the town burghers of Ammerschwihr would get together to taste the new wines. After a period of decline, the tradition was revived last century and today the Confrérie de St-Etienne is based in the Château de Kientzheim near Kaysersberg. Its members now hold two major annual tastings during which they award a distinctive red seal of quality to wines that show typical character and meet strict quality requirements.

Vendange Tardive wines

The superior appellation Alsace Grand Cru represents a tiny percentage of all wines produced in Alsace. These must be made from one of the four noble grape varieties (Riesling, Gewurztraminer, Muscat and Pinot Gris) grown in one of the 50 named vineyard sites designated as Grand Cru, which will be mentioned on the label. Many of these vineyards are on dramatic, steep slopes overlooking the villages. A handful produce wines of world-class quality, including Goldert (near the village of Gueberschwihr), Rangen (Thann), Rosacker (Hunawihr), Pfersigberg (Eguisheim), Schoenenbourg and Sporen (Riquewihr), Steinert (Pfaffenheim), Vorbourg (Rouffach) and Zinnkoepflé (Soultzmatt).

Neighbouring Lorraine also produces wines but it is on the rainy side of the Vosges. The light reds from the Côtes de Toul and whites from the Vin de Moselle VDQS regions do not bear comparison with Alsace.

CRÉMANT D'ALSACE

These are sparkling wines produced by the traditional Champagne method of second fermentation in bottle. Grapes for *crémant* are always harvested before those destined for Alsace still wines, which ensures the levels of acidity required for the zing and freshness of sparkling wine. Much Crémant d'Alsace is good value for money and makes a good alternative to Champagne.

VENDANGE TARDIVE AND SÉLECTION DE GRAINS NOBLES

Vendange Tardive (VT) and Sélection de Grains Nobles (SGN) are not appellations in their own right, rather they are an extra designation that may be added to the generic or Grand Cru label.

VT wines are late-picked, sometimes but not always sweet and made only in exceptional years when a sunny autumn with low rainfall means that the grapes ripen beyond what might normally be expected. They pack all the aromatic intensity of the individual grape variety and can be cellared for many years.

SGNs are obtained by several successive pickings of grapes affected by noble rot *(see p300)*. These rare and expensive wines forfeit the expressiveness of the varietal in favour of an intense concentration of exotic aromas and a rare elegance. Their mellowness and rich bouquet mean they should be enjoyed alone, for their own sake, or at the end of a meal with dessert.

EAUX-DE-VIE

Fruit abounds in the Vosges mountains and on the plains of Lorraine. Williams pears, damsons and

Mirabelle plums

Mirabelle golden plums have long been made into eaux-de-vie, as have the many types of wild fruit: bilberries, wild strawberries, elderberries, cranberries, rosehips, rowanberries, sloes, myrtle and even holly berries. Raspberries have only been used for this purpose fairly recently, as the fragrant berries used to be destined exclusively for courtly tables the world over. Raspberry eau-de-vie is very delicate and should be drunk young, within two years of bottling. Cherry eau-de-vie (kirsch) is thought to be the original fruit eau-de-vie. It was created by a monk in the 17th century when it was named *kirschwasser* in the dialect of Alsace.

The lovely golden, red-speckled Mirabelle plum is the flagship fruit of Lorraine. Prized as a dessert fruit, it makes superb, intensely scented eaux-de-vie, renowned for their digestive virtues. Mirabelle eaux-de-vie are very sensitive to light, which alters their bouquet and clarity.

Bilberry eau-de-vie

BEER

The breweries in Alsace produce over 50 per cent of all beer made in France. The barley is still grown on the rich alluvial plain in the heart of the Ried area. The hops come from the softly rolling valleys of Kochersberg and Ackerland.

Just two of the six breweries in Alsace (Schutzenberger and Météor) are family-owned concerns that continue to make beer in the traditional way. Heineken has been in Alsace since 1972 and now controls Fischer in Schiltigheim. Giant Kronenbourg makes beer in Strasbourg-Cronenbourg and Obernai. Beer is also made in Lorraine.

BEST PRODUCERS

Distillerie Jean-Paul Metté This firm is recognized as one of the finest distillers in France, indeed in the world, and continues to produce eaux-de-vie that are a sublime expression of the fruits used. **Massenez** Raspberry and Williams pear are the two specialities from this distiller, established in Bassemberg in 1870.

EAU-DE-VIE AND LIQUEUR MUSEUM

This interesting little museum in the village of Lapoutroie near Colmar occupies an 18th-century coaching inn. 85 rue du Général Dufieux, Lapoutroie (03 89 47 50 26), open all year.

Schutzenberger Alsace beer

Where to Eat & Stay

AMNEVILLE-LES-THERMES

▲ **Restaurant La Forêt at Hotel Diane**

Centre Thermal et Touristique, Bois de Coulange, 57360 **Map** 5D4

☎ 03 87 70 34 34

FAX 03 87 70 34 25

✉ AE, DC, MC, V ● Sun D, Mon

🍽 €€€ 🍷 (47) €€€

Modern restaurant in the three-star Hotel Diane, one of a complex of three health-spa hotels in the woods around Amneville-les-Thermes. The light menu includes snails, foie gras and game. Comfortable, generously sized rooms.

ANDLAU

▲ **Au Canon**

2 rue des Remparts, 67140 **Map** 5E5

☎ 03 88 08 95 08

FAX 03 88 08 90 82

@ aucanon@aol.com

✉ MC, V ● Tue D, Wed

🍽 € 🍷 (10) €€

Delightful riverside restaurant, with a small terrace, in a picturesque wine village. Typical Alsatian fare and an extensive wine list featuring Rieslings from local vineyards. Period architecture ensures the hotel's enduring appeal.

BAERENTHAL

● **L'Arnsbourg**

18 Untermuhlthal, 57230 **Map** 5E4

☎ 03 87 06 50 85

FAX 03 87 06 57 67

🆆 www.relaischateaux.com

✉ AE, DC, MC, V ● Tue, Wed; Jan, 1st 2 wks Sep 🍽 €€€€€

Château-restaurant in the middle of the Northern Vosges. Menus with light dishes accompanied by Grand Cru wines.

BAINS-LES-BAINS

▲ **La Poste**

11 rue de Verdun, 88240 **Map** 9D1

☎ 03 29 36 31 01

FAX 03 29 30 44 22

✉ MC, V ● Sun L, Mon L; Oct–Mar

🍽 € 🍷 (14) €€

Riverside hotel-restaurant steps from most of the thermal baths. Light dishes include quiche Lorraine (p119), salads,

charcuterie and foie gras, plus some great desserts. Light and airy rooms.

BAINS-LES-BAINS

▲ **Le Parc**

15–17 ave du Docteur Mathieu, 88240 **Map** 9D1

☎ 03 29 30 40 00

FAX 03 29 30 46 99

✉ MC, V ● Dec–Jan

🍽 €€ 🍷 (23) €€

The terrace, library and health spa far exceed the two-star status. Plenty of diet and vegetarian options available. Basic guestrooms with big bathrooms.

BALDENHEIM

▲ **A l'Etoile**

14 rue de Baldenheim, Rathsamhausen-le-Haut, 67600 **Map** 5E5

☎ 03 88 92 35 79

FAX 03 88 82 91 66

✉ MC, V 🍽 € 🍷 (8) €€

Striking place with an outdoor pool and some of the best views in Baldenheim. Hearty dishes are served in the glass conservatory: flammenkueche (p119), and choucroute garnie (p119).

BALDENHEIM

▲ **Les Prés d'Ondine**

5 rue de Baldenheim, Rathsamhausen-le-Haut, 67600 **Map** 5E5

☎ 03 88 58 04 60

FAX 03 88 58 04 61

🆆 www.presdondine.com

✉ MC, V ● Sun D, Wed D

🍽 €€ 🍷 (12) €€€€

With such a modern exterior, the classical candlelit restaurant is a surprise. But don't be put off by the rigid table design as the menu is far from conventional.

BAN-DE-LAVELINE

▲ **Auberge Lorraine**

5 rue du 8 Mai, 88520 **Map** 5E5

☎ 03 29 51 78 17

FAX 03 29 51 71 72

✉ DC, MC, V ● Sun D, Mon D

🍽 € 🍷 (7) €€

In the heart of the Vosges, offering an air of tranquillity. Game dishes such as

wild boar and herb-roasted meats are popular. Basic but spacious rooms.

BARR

▲ **Château Landsberg**

133 rue de la Vallée, 67140 **Map** 5E5

☎ 03 88 08 52 22

FAX 03 88 08 40 50

🆆 www.chateau-landsberg.com

✉ MC, V ● Sun L, Mon–Thu, Fri L, Sat L 🍽 €€€ 🍷 (11) €€€€

Luxurious château with crenellated towers in the Vosges foothills, indoor pool (Apr–Dec), sauna, terrace and garden. The restaurant serves gourmet fare based on old-style Alsatian ingredients; seafood sauerkraut, baeckeoffe (p119) and potato gratin.

BARR

▲ **Maison Rouge**

1 ave de la Gare, 67140 **Map** 5E5

☎ 03 88 08 90 40

FAX 03 88 08 90 85

✉ MC, V ● Tue D, Wed; Feb

🍽 €€ 🍷 (11) €€

Named after its striking red-washed exterior. The country menu includes goose foie gras, charcuterie, meat stews and game. Sample the Gewürztraminer, Riesling and Tokay Pinot Gris.

BASSE-SUR-LE-RUPT

▲ **Auberge Haut du Roc**

Route touristique Vagney, La Bresse, 88120 **Map** 9D1

☎ 03 29 61 77 94

FAX 03 29 24 91 77

🆆 www.aubergehautduroc.com

✉ DC, MC, V ● Wed D; 1st 2 wks Oct 🍽 € 🍷 (10) €€

Countryside auberge serving grilled meats, flammenkueche (p119) and fruity desserts. Wooden furnishings and pastel linens in the guestrooms.

BAUDRICOURT

▲ **Auberge du Parc**

142 la Gare, 88500 **Map** 4C5

☎ 03 29 65 63 43

FAX 03 29 37 71 12

🆆 www.auberge-du-parc.fr

● Restaurant ■ Hotel ▲ Hotel / Restaurant

DC, MC, V

€ 🥢 (17) €€

An auberge with a choice of eateries: light bites in the bar, set menus in the brasserie, and innovative Alsatian cuisine in the Restaurant Gastronomic. The local speciality – mirabelle plum dessert – is served. Large, plush guestrooms.

BELLEVILLE
● **La Moselle**
1 rue Prosper Cabirol, 54940 **Map** 4C4

03 83 24 91 44

FAX 03 83 24 99 38

www.restaurant-la-moselle.com

AE, DC, MC, V ● Mon, Wed D

€€

Refined regional cuisine: salmon in the local Pinot Noir, sea bass with fennel cream, veal kidneys, and fruity desserts.

BERGHEIM
▲ **La Cour du Bailli**
57 Grand Rue, 68750 **Map** 5E5

03 89 73 73 46

FAX 03 89 73 38 81

www.cour-bailli.com

AE, MC, V ● Jan, 2 wks Nov

€€ 🥢 (24) €€

In a 15th-century winery, sample tasty Alsatian fare such as flammenkueche (p119) and baeckeoffe (p119).

BITCHE
▲ **Les Châteaux Forts**
6 quai Edouard Branly, 57230 **Map** 5E4

03 87 96 14 14

FAX 03 87 96 07 36

www.holigest.com/h-bitche.asp

MC, V

€€ 🥢 (30) €€

Two-star hotel isolated deep in the Vosgien forests. The restaurant has stunning views of the illuminated citadel at night. Foie gras, choucroute garnie (p119) and veal kidneys on the hearty menu. Rooms have small salon areas.

BUSSANG
▲ **Du Tremplin**
8 rue du 3ème RTA, 88540 **Map** 9D1

03 29 61 50 30

FAX 03 29 61 50 89

DC, MC, V ● Sun D

€€ 🥢 (16) €

In the heart of the regional natural park. To drink, try the sparkling mineral water from nearby Source Marie. Chalet-style guestrooms with shutters and flowers.

CHAMPENOUX
▲ **La Lorette**
52 rue St-Barthélémy, 54280 **Map** 5D4

03 83 39 91 91

FAX 03 83 31 71 04

www.lalorette-restaurant.com

DC, MC, V ● Sun, Mon, Sat L; 1 wk Feb, 2 wks Aug €€ 🥢 (10) €€

Colourful hotel-restaurant in a farmhouse. Snails and frogs' legs provide the entrée excitement. Modern guestrooms with narrow balconies.

CHAUMOUSEY
● **Le Calmosien**
37 rue d'Epinal, 88390 **Map** 5D5

03 29 66 80 77

FAX 03 29 66 89 41

MC, V ● Sun D, Mon €€€

Popular restaurant in a tiny village next to Lake Bouzey, offering veal kidneys with mustard sauce, roasted game, and butter-baked veal.

COLMAR
● **A la Ville de Paris**
4 pl Jeanne d'Arc, 68000 **Map** 5E5

03 89 24 53 15

FAX 03 89 23 65 24

www.sparisser-restaurant.com

MC, V ● Mon D, Tue L €

Atmospheric old winstub in central Colmar, within sight of the cathedral. Predominantly Alsatian dishes – goose foie gras, liver dumplings, baeckeoffe (p119), coq au Riesling – with local wines served by the jug.

COLMAR
▲ **La Maison des Têtes**
19 rue des Têtes, 68000 **Map** 5E5

03 89 24 43 43

FAX 03 89 24 58 34

www.la-maison-des-tetes.com

MC, V ● Sun D, Mon, Tue L

€€€ 🥢 (21) €€€€

In a beautiful 17th-century building. Top picks include roasted monkfish, fillet of turbot and the peach soup dessert. Wonderfully atmospheric guestrooms.

COLMAR
▲ **Restaurant A l'Echevin at Hostellerie Le Maréchal**
4–6 pl des Six Montagnes Noires, 68000 **Map** 5E5

03 89 41 60 32

FAX 03 89 24 59 40

www.hotel-le-marechal.com

MC, V €€€ 🥢 (30) €€€€

Hotel-restaurant constructed in the 16th century in Little Venice. The candlelit restaurant is famous for its fresh lobster and fish dishes such as pike-perch with dill. Classically decorated rooms.

CONTREXEVILLE
▲ **Villa Beauséjour**
204 rue Ziwer Pacha, 88140 **Map** 4C5

03 29 08 04 89

FAX 03 29 08 62 28

www.villa-beausejour.com

AE, DC, MC, V ● Oct–Mar

€€ 🥢 (30) €€

Unusual hotel-restaurant near the health spas serving low-fat cuisine. Modern bedrooms with great views over the park.

CORNIMONT
▲ **Le Géhan**
9 route de Travexin, 88310 **Map** 9D1

03 29 24 10 71

FAX 03 29 24 10 70

www.legehan-charlemagne.com

DC, MC, V

€ 🥢 (11) €€

Basic riverside hotel with a restaurant that specializes mainly in fish such as grilled trout in vin gris and a fluffy salmon terrine. Simple, modern rooms.

DABO-LA-HOUBE
▲ **Hôtel-Restaurant des Vosges**
41 rue de Forêt Brûlée, 57850 **Map** 5E4

03 87 08 80 44

FAX 03 87 08 85 96

www.hotel-restaurant-vosges.com

MC, V ● Tue D, Wed

€€ 🥢 (9) €€

In the middle of the tiny village, and with great views over Dabo's famous rock. The menu is at its best in early summer when it is crammed with wild boar and sauces made from wild mushrooms. Rooms vary between the modern and the traditional.

For key to symbols see back flap

DELME

▲ Hôtel a la XIIème Borne

6 pl de la République, 57590 **Map** 5D4

C 03 87 01 30 18

FAX 03 87 01 38 39

🖃 MC, V **🍽** €€ **🥄** (15) €€

The regional menu, "discovery" menu and gastronomic menu offer snails, foie gras, veal and beef. Basic, modern rooms.

DIEUE-SUR-MEUSE

▲ Château des Monthairons

Le Petit Monthairon, 12km (8 miles) south of Verdun on the D34, 55320

Map 4C4

C 03 29 87 78 55

FAX 03 29 87 73 49

W www.chateaudesmonthairons.fr

🖃 DC, MC, V **🍽** Sun D, Mon D; Jan–1st wk Feb

🍽 €€€€ **🥄** (18) €€€€

Four-star hotel-restaurant in a 19th-century château. Mouthwatering picks include foie gras pan-fried in cornmeal, veal kidneys infused with lavender, and rabbit with Meuse truffles. Plush rooms.

DRUSENHEIM

▲ A la Couronne d'Or

30 rue Général de Gaulle, 67410

Map 5E4

C 03 88 53 30 36

FAX 03 88 49 16 11

🖃 DC, MC, V **🍽** Sun D, Sat D

🍽 € **🥄** (12) €€

Small hotel with restaurant for guests only. The seafood sauerkraut, baeckeoffe (p119) and the flammenkueche (p119) are particularly tasty. Smart guestrooms.

DRUSENHEIM

▲ Auberge du Gourmet

4 route de Herrlisheim, 67410 **Map** 5E4

C 03 88 53 30 60

FAX 03 88 53 31 39

🖃 MC, V **🍽** Tue D, Wed, Sat L; mid-Feb–1st wk Mar **🍽** €€ **🥄** (11) €€

Popular auberge near to golf and tennis facilities. Expect baby rabbit, chocolate fondant and home-made ice cream. Fine, spacious, flower-filled guestrooms.

EGUISHEIM

▲ Auberge Alsacienne

12 Grand Rue, 68420 **Map** 5E5

C 03 89 41 50 20

FAX 03 89 23 89 32

🖃 MC, V **🍽** Sun D, Mon; Jan–mid-Feb

🍽 €€ **🥄** (19) €€

Large flower- and timber-covered restaurant on Alsace's wine route, with an outdoor terrace and Alsatian cooking. Spacious, characterful rooms.

EGUISHEIM

● Caveau d'Eguisheim

3 pl du Châteaux St-Léon, 68420

Map 5E5

C 03 89 41 08 89

FAX 03 89 23 79 99

🖃 MC, V **🍽** Mon, Tue; Jan–Feb

🍽 €€€

Great views over the château. Good range of lunch dishes. Book for a scenic table.

EGUISHEIM

▲ Hostellerie du Pape

10 Grand Rue, 68420 **Map** 5E5

C 03 89 41 41 21

FAX 03 89 41 41 31

W www.hostellerie-pape.com

🖃 MC, V **🍽** Mon, Tue; 1st wk Jan

🍽 €€ **🥄** (33) €€€

Known for its authentic and carefully crafted Alsatian cuisine. Simple rooms with views from vine-covered balconies.

ENTZHEIM

▲ Père Benoît

34 route de Strasbourg, 67960 **Map** 5E5

C 03 88 68 98 00

FAX 03 88 68 64 56

W www.hotel-pere-benoit.com

🖃 AE, MC, V **🍽** Sun, Mon L, Sat L; Christmas **🍽** € **🥄** (60) €€

Imposing 18th-century half-timbered farmhouse. Try the foie gras with a glass of Gewürztraminer. Tasteful guestrooms.

EPINAL

● Le Petit Robinson

24 rue Raymond Poincaré, 88000

Map 5D5

C 03 29 34 23 51

FAX 03 29 31 27 17

🖃 MC, V **🍽** Sun, Sat L **🍽** €€€

Restaurant in the heart of Epinal, with a menu of regional flavours. Reasonably priced set menu. Extremely traditional food such as tête-de-veau.

EPINAL

● Les Bouchons du Bretzel

7 pl de l'Atre, 88000 **Map** 5D5

C 03 29 35 47 25

🖃 MC, V **🍽** Mon **🍽** €

Fifteen set menus, which feature everything from choucroute garnie (p119) to Alsatian potato salad and local cheeses.

EPINAL

● Les Fine Herbes

15 rue de la Maix, 88000 **Map** 5D5

C 03 29 31 46 70

FAX 03 29 34 82 98

🖃 MC, V **🍽** Sun D, Mon **🍽** €€€

Fish restaurant with a menu as inventive as the decor. Reservations recommended.

FEY

▲ Les Tuileries

Route de Cuvry, 57420 **Map** 4C4

C 03 87 52 03 03

FAX 03 87 52 84 24

🖃 DC, MC, V **🍽** Sun D

🍽 €€€ **🥄** (41) €€

Expect pan-fried frogs' legs, seafood linguini, and a mango tarte Tatin (p119). Basic guestrooms are generous in size.

FLAVIGNY-SUR-MOSELLE

● Le Prieuré

3 rue du Prieuré, 54630 **Map** 5D5

C 03 83 26 70 45

FAX 03 83 26 75 51

🖃 AE, DC, MC, V

🍽 Sun D, Mon, Wed D **🍽** €€€

Dishes include mirabelle chutney tart with red cabbage, and pear and lemon confit with sorbet. Central fireplace.

FUTEAU

▲ L'Orée du Bois

Hameau Courupt, 55120 **Map** 4C4

C 03 29 88 28 41

FAX 03 29 88 24 52

🖃 AE, DC, MC, V

🍽 Sep-May: Sun D, Mon, Tue

🍽 €€€ **🥄** (14) €€€€

Quiet and peaceful rural location. Menu of seasonal local treats featuring fruit tarts and gratins. Spacious rooms.

GERARDMER

● A la Belle Marée

Les Bas Rupts, 88400 **Map** 5D5

● Restaurant   ■ Hotel   ▲ Hotel / Restaurant

03 29 63 06 83
FAX 03 29 63 20 76
MC, V ● Mon €
Mountain-top restaurant at its best
during its trout festival in May. The fish
is cooked with white wine and onions,
in beer or simply poached.

GERARDMER
▲ Auberge au Bord du Lac
166 chemin Tour du Lac, 88400
Map 5D5
03 29 63 44 98
FAX 03 29 63 21 21
w www.auberge-bord-lac.fr
DC, MC, V ● mid-Nov–mid-Dec
€€ ◇ (12) €€
Lakeside auberge with tasty regional
cuisine. Modern rooms with great views.

GERARDMER
▲La Jamagne
2 bd de la Jamagne, 88400 **Map** 5D5
03 29 63 36 86
FAX 03 29 60 05 87
MC, V ● mid-Nov–mid-Dec
€€ ◇ (48) €€€
Savour terrine de Montagne (house
recipe), veal kidneys in mustard, and
clafoutis (p247) with mirabelle plums.
Pale pastels and beams in the rooms.

GERARDMER
▲ Le Beau Rivage
Esplanade du Lac, 88400 **Map** 5D5
03 29 63 22 28
FAX 03 29 63 29 83
w www.hotel-beaurivage.fr
AE, DC, MC, V
€€€€ ◇ (46) €€€€
Luxury accommodation facing right onto
Gerardmer's famous lake. Haute cuisine.
Outdoor heated pool with sauna and
Jacuzzi. Romantic, red double rooms.

GERARDMER
▲ Le Chalet Fleuri
181 route de la Bresse, 88400 **Map** 5D5
03 29 63 09 25
FAX 03 29 63 00 40
w www.bas-rupts.com
AE, DC, MC, V
€€€€ ◇ (11) €€€€
A château with a gastronomic menu
and extensive wine list. Specialities

include foie gras salad, game, and
sweet desserts using the mountain
honey for which this area is known.
Wood-panelled walls in the guestrooms.

GERARDMER
▲ Le Grand Cerf & Le Coq
à l'Ane at Le Grand Hotel
Pl du Tilleul, BP12, 88401 **Map** 5D5
03 29 63 06 31
FAX 03 29 63 46 81
w www.grandhotel-gerardmer.com
AE, DC, MC, V
€€€ ◇ (68) €€€
A choice of two restaurants. Le Grand
Cerf is known for meat dishes such as
grilled pigeon with sesame seeds and
curried vegetables. Le Coq à l'Ane, the
nicer of the two, offers fish such as
salmon, whisky prawns and trout. Plush
accommodation, two pools and a disco.

GERARDMER
▲ Le Manoir au Lac
59 rue chemin de la Droite du Lac,
BP56, 88402 **Map** 5D5
03 29 27 10 20
FAX 03 29 27 10 27
w www.manoir-au-lac.com
AE, DC, MC, V ● 2 wks Nov
€€€ ◇ (12) €€€€€
Small, welcoming hotel with good views.
Tasty dinner (reservations recommended)
but most come for the afternoon tea.
Rooms are in a nearby wooden chalet.

GERARDMER
▲ Le Sommet du Holneck
Route des Crêtes, 88400 **Map** 5D5
03 29 63 11 47
FAX 03 29 63 11 47
DC, MC, V ● Nov–Apr
€ ◇ (7) €€
Mountain hotel-restaurant with Vosges
views. Choice of choucroute garnie
(p119), baeckeoffe (p119) and flammenkueche (p119). Simple guestrooms.

GERARDMER
▲ Les Liserons
5 bd Kelsch, 88400 **Map** 5D5
03 29 63 02 61
FAX 03 29 63 28 02
w www.lesliserons.fr
DC, MC, V ● 2 wks in Mar & Jun

€€ ◇ (11) €€
On the menu: foie gras in rhubarb wine,
duck andouillette, and veal kidneys.
Period guestrooms with wood walls,
exposed brickwork and large windows.

GERARDMER
▲ Les Loges du Parc
12–14 ave de la Ville de Vichy, 88400
Map 5D5
03 29 63 32 43
FAX 03 29 63 17 03
w www.leslogesduparc.com
AE, DC, MC, V ● Mar, Oct–Dec
€€ ◇ (30) €€
Three-star hotel with large lakeside
grounds. House specialities include pink
trout with almonds and foie gras with
mirabelle plums. Authentic guesthouse
feel, with locally produced furnishings.

GOMMERSDORF
▲ Auberge du Tisserand
28 rue de Cernay, 68210 **Map** 9E1
03 89 07 21 80
FAX 03 89 25 11 34
MC, V ● Mon, Tue; last 2 wks
Feb, Christmas € ◇ (8) €€
Sweet little auberge in a traditional
Alsatian family house. Hearty meat
stews and choucroute garnie (p119).
Sizeable guestrooms. Book early.

GRESSWILLER
▲ L'Ecu d'Or
12 rue Gutenberg, 67190 **Map** 5E5
03 88 50 16 00
FAX 03 88 50 15 11
w www.lecudor.fr
MC, V € ◇ (25) €€
Charming brasserie heavily influenced
by the local Riesling. The Ball family also
offer guided tours. Elegant guestrooms.

ILLZACH
● Le Parc de Modenheim
8 rue Victor Hugo, 68110 **Map** 9E1
03 89 56 61 67
FAX 03 89 56 13 85
w www.sehh.com
MC, V ● Sun D, Mon, Sat L
€€€
Gorgeous former hunting lodge on the
outskirts of Mulhouse. Classical but
inventive local dishes.

ITTERSWILLER

▲ Arnold

98 route des Vins, 67140 **Map** 5E5

📞 03 88 85 50 58

FAX 03 88 85 55 54

🌐 www.hotel-arnold.com

💳 AE, MC, V ● Sun D, Mon;
Nov–Apr 🍽 €€€ 🛏 (30) €€€

*Set in an 18th-century wine cellar with
original grape press. The superb foie
gras, venison and choucroute garnie
(p119) are best eaten on the terrace.
Lovingly decorated rooms.*

ITTERSWILLER

▲ Emmebuckel-Faller

2 route des Vins, 67140 **Map** 5E5

📞 03 88 85 50 24

FAX 03 88 85 51 56

🌐 www.emmebuckel-faller.com

💳 MC, V ● Thu 🍽 € 🛏 (7) €€

*In a gorgeous period country house.
The delicious cuisine includes presskopf
(chunky pork terrine), foie gras, roast
goose à pain d'épices (spiced bread),
and kougelhopf (p118) glacé au Kirsch.
Spacious rooms with old wood furniture.*

KAYSERBERG

▲ Chambard

9–13 rue du Général de Gaulle, 68240
Map 5E5

📞 03 89 47 10 17

FAX 03 89 47 35 03

🌐 www.chateauxhotels.com/chambard

💳 MC, V 🍽 €€€€
🛏 (20) €€€€

*Important stop on Alsace's famous wine
route, and linked to renowned local chef
Olivier Nasti. Rooms are modern and
funky with fake fur. Booking advised.*

KIENTZHEIM

▲ Hostellerie Schwendi

2 pl Schwendi, 68240 **Map** 5E5

📞 03 89 47 30 50

FAX 03 89 49 04 49

💳 MC, V ● Wed, Thu D
🍽 €€€ 🛏 (17) €€€

*Charming place with a terrace overflowing
on to the cobbled square. Menu of fine
seasonal game and meat hotpots. Book
early for the romantic top-floor bedroom
with a wooden-beamed slanted ceiling
and flower-covered window.*

LA BRESSE

▲ Du Lac des Corbeaux

103 rue du Hohneck, 88250 **Map** 5D5

📞 03 29 25 41 17

FAX 03 29 25 69 41

🌐 www.hoteldulac-dc.com

💳 DC, MC, V ● Wed D

🍽 € 🛏 (14) €

*Budget hotel-restaurant near the ski
slopes. Duck with bilberries and sliced
beef with Munster cheese feature
strongly. Good hiking trails in summer.
Chalet-like rooms with a tartan theme.*

LA BRESSE

▲ Les Chatelmines

41 route du Cornimont, 88250 **Map** 5D5

📞 03 29 25 40 27

FAX 03 29 25 64 83

🌐 www.leschatelmines.com

💳 AE, DC, MC, V

🍽 €€€ 🛏 (11) €€

*Two-star hotel, bar and restaurant. The
extensive menu features trout, duck,
beef and the chef's speciality of grilled
andouillette. Simple guestrooms.*

LA PETITE-PIERRE

▲ Auberge d'Imsthal

Route Forestiere, 67290 **Map** 5E4

📞 03 88 01 49 00

FAX 03 88 70 40 26

🌐 www.petite-pierre.com

💳 AE, MC, V 🍽 €€ 🛏 (23) €€€

*Tranquil auberge with an old farmhouse
feel in the Natural Park Vosges du Nord.
Specialities include local trout au bleu,
coq au Riesling and leg of boar.
Romantic rooms.*

LA WANTZENAU

▲ Relais de la Poste

21 rue Général de Gaulle, 67610
Map 5E4

📞 03 88 59 24 80

FAX 03 88 59 24 89

🌐 www.relais-poste.com

💳 MC, V ● Sun D, Mon, Sat L

🍽 €€€€ 🛏 (18) €€€

*Classy half-timbered restaurant with foie
gras or fried goose liver. Spacious rooms.*

LACROIX-SUR-MEUSE

▲ Auberge de la Pêche à la Truite

Route de Seuzey, 55300 **Map** 4C4

📞 03 29 90 15 08

FAX 03 29 90 16 88

🌐 www.aubergedelapechealatruite.com

💳 DC, MC, V ● Fri D

🍽 €€ 🛏 (6) €€

*Country inn in a converted mill with a
large trout and char fish-farming estate.
Guests are free to fish in any of the six
ponds and there's also horse riding,
water sports and trekking. Nautical-style
rooms with snug sleeping areas.*

LE MENIL-THILLOT

▲ Les Sapins

60 Grande Rue, 88160 **Map** 9D1

📞 03 29 25 02 46

FAX 03 29 25 80 23

💳 AE, MC, V ● last 2 wks Apr, last wk
Nov–3rd wk Dec 🍽 €€ 🛏 (22) €€

*Very reasonably priced hotel with a
panoramic terrace and generous servings
of charcuterie, andouillette and fruit
gratins. Plain but welcoming rooms.*

LE PUID

▲ Le Raybois

15 Le Haut du Village, 88210 **Map** 5E5

📞 03 29 41 05 39

FAX 03 29 41 05 81

@ ftboulange@free.fr

💳 AE, DC, MC, V ● Sun D, Mon D

🍽 € 🛏 (10) €

*Peaceful hotel-restaurant located in the
forest near mountainous Le Puid. Rustic
dishes befitting the rural location, with
game and wild mushrooms featuring
strongly. Brightly furnished guestrooms.*

LE THILLOT

▲ Le Perce Neige

Le Col des Croix, 88160 **Map** 9D1

📞 03 29 25 02 63

FAX 03 29 25 13 51

🌐 www.perce-neige.com

💳 AE, DC, MC, V ● Sun D, Mon

🍽 €€ 🛏 (10) €€

*Hotel with a creative gourmet menu
including bilberry tart and various frog-
based dishes. Pastel guestrooms.*

LE THOLY

▲ La Grande Cascade

24 route du Col de Bonnefontaine,
88530 **Map** 5D5

📞 03 29 66 66 66

● Restaurant ■ Hotel ▲ Hotel / Restaurant

FAX 03 29 66 37 17

AE, DC, MC, V ● 3 wks Dec

€ ● (30) €€

An old coaching inn with a changing set menu. Specialities include wild boar pâtés and sausages. Modern, pleasant rooms.

LE VALTIN

▲ Auberge du Val Joli

12 bis le Village, 88230 **Map** 5E5

03 29 60 91 37

FAX 03 29 60 81 73

www.levaljoli.com

AE, DC, MC, V ● Sun D, Mon D, Wed L €€€ ● (7) €€€€

Kitchen and hotel run by a father and son enthusiastic about traditional Lorraine cooking. Snug purple and blue rooms.

LONGUYON

▲ Mas et Hôtel Lorraine

65 rue Augistrou, 54260 **Map** 4C3

03 82 26 50 07

FAX 03 82 39 26 09

www.lorraineetmas.com

AE, DC, MC, V ● Mon; Jan, Christmas €€€ ● (14) €€€

Hotel-restaurant with a large flower-filled terrace and a top-notch wine cellar. The menu is dominated by salmon, sea bass and trout. Spacious modern rooms.

LUNEVILLE

▲ Château d'Adoménil

Adomenil, Rehainviller, 54300 **Map** 5D5

03 83 74 04 81

FAX 03 83 74 21 78

www.adomenil.com

AE, DC, MC, V ● Sun D, Mon, Tue €€€€ ● (13) €€€€€

Four-star hotel-restaurant in a stately 18th-century château. Classic cuisine: frogs' legs omelette, and roast pigeon with figs. Large, luxurious rooms with Jacuzzi and cosy sitting areas.

LUNEVILLE

▲ Des Pages

5 quai Petits Bosquets, 54300 **Map** 5D5

03 83 74 11 42

FAX 03 83 73 46 63

AE, DC, MC, V ● Sun D

€€ ● (30) €€

The menu is simple with quiche Lorraine (p119), charcuterie, and fresh cheeses.

Local fruits and berries such as Toul raspberries, Meuse blackcurrants and mirabelle plums make their mark on the dishes. Large, modern bedrooms.

LUTZELBOURG

▲ Hôtel des Vosges

149 rue Charles Ackermann, 57820 **Map** 5E4

03 87 25 30 09

FAX 03 87 25 42 22

www.hotelvosges.com

MC, V ● Sun D, Wed

€ ● (11) €€

In a peaceful valley with great views over the River Zorn. Expect poached trout, venison sausages and smoked wild boar. Guestrooms retain their traditional if cluttered feel.

MEISENTHAL

▲ Auberge des Mésanges

2 rue du Tiseur, 57960 **Map** 5E4

03 87 96 92 28

FAX 03 87 96 99 14

www.aubergedesmesanges.com

AE, MC, V ● Sun D, Mon

€ ● (25) €€

Auberge in the centre of the Parc Naturel des Vosges du Nord. Sporting menu of fish and game. Rooms filled with books and paintings.

MEREILLE

▲ La Maison Carrée

12 rue du Bac, 54850 **Map** 5D5

03 83 47 09 23

FAX 03 83 47 50 75

www.maisoncarree.com

DC, MC, V ● Christmas

€€ ● (23) €€€

On the banks of the River Moselle, reasonably priced cuisine with great views. The "Lorraine à deux" menu for two offers foie gras, duck, game and a plum dessert. Spacious guestrooms with large balconies and bright bathrooms.

METZ

● A la Ville de Lyon

7 rue des Piques, 57000 **Map** 5D4

03 87 36 07 01

FAX 03 87 74 47 17

AE, DC, MC, V ● Sun D, Mon; last wk Jul–3rd wk Aug €€€€

Popular restaurant in an atmospheric old house at the foot of Metz Cathedral. Mainly traditional menu, such as pigeon hotpot and fish stewed in rosé wine. The chocolate tarts are a Metz delicacy.

METZ

● Au Pampre d'Or

31 pl de Chambre, 57000 **Map** 5D4

03 87 74 12 46

FAX 03 87 36 96 92

AE, DC, MC, V ● Sun D, Wed, Thu L €€€€

One of Metz's best-known restaurants thanks to chef Jean-Claude Lamaze's big reputation. Jazzed-up versions of classic dishes using fish and game topped off by delicious red wine, wild-mushroom or beer sauces. Good cheeses.

METZ

● La Migaine

1 pl St-Louis, 57000 **Map** 5D4

03 87 75 56 67

MC, V ● Sun €

Small and slightly cramped tearoom renowned for its pastries. Savoury fare includes cheese or potato tarts, quiche Lorraine (p119) and salads. Must-eats include the lemon meringue tart.

METZ

● La Winstub

2 bis rue Dupont-des-Loges, 57000 **Map** 5D4

03 87 37 03 93

FAX 03 87 37 03 93

www.la-winstub.com

MC, V ● Mon €

Well-priced Alsatian cuisine in an authentic winstub. Menu treats include the flammenkueche (p119), choucroute garnie (p119) and baeckeoffe (p119). Wine list of Rieslings and Tokay Gris.

MIRECOURT

▲ Le Luth

Ave de Charmiec, 88500 **Map** 5D5

03 29 37 12 12

FAX 03 29 37 23 44

www.le-luth.fr

AE, DC, MC, V ● Fri D, Sat

€ ● (30) €

Eccentric hotel-restaurant with a fondness for pink. Remarkable seasonal desserts:

mirabelle plum gratin, clafoutis (p247) and soufflés. Good value half-board option. Rooms share the pastel theme.

MOMMENHEIM
▲ Manoir St-Georges
53 route de Brumath, 67670 **Map** 5E4
📞 03 88 51 61 78
FAX 03 88 51 59 96
💳 MC, V ● Sun L, Mon, Sat L
🍽 €€€ 🍴 (5) €€

Beautiful moss-covered auberge in a picturesque village. Expect duck terrine, snails, marinated salmon, red cabbage and fig jam. Atmospheric guestrooms, especially those in the tower.

MONT-ST-MARTIN
● Restaurant des Abattoirs
288 bd de Metz, 54350 **Map** 4C3
📞 03 82 23 20 74
FAX 03 82 25 67 20
💳 AE, DC, MC, V ● Sun, Mon
🍽 €€€

Popular eatery with a variety of menus. Foie gras and tête-de-veau remain standards. Desserts include chocolate mousse or gateau.

MORSBRONN-LES-BAINS
▲ Ritter Hoft
23 rue Principale, 67360 **Map** 5E4
📞 03 88 54 07 37
FAX 03 88 09 45 29
W www.morsbronn-les-bains.com
💳 MC, V
🍽 € 🍴 (16) €€

Quiet hotel-restaurant with a jam-packed wine cellar and very reasonably priced fresh, local cuisine. Simple yet comfortable old-fashioned guestrooms.

MULHOUSE
▲ Du Parc
26 rue de la Sinne, 68100 **Map** 9E1
📞 03 89 66 12 22
FAX 03 89 66 42 44
W www.hotelduparc-mulhouse.com
💳 AE, MC, V ● Aug
🍽 €€€ 🍴 (79) €€€€€

Large and imposing four-Michelin-star hotel-restaurant. Dishes include lemon-scented turbot and ricotta-stuffed ravioli. Expensive but worth it! Stylish rooms with sitting/reading areas.

MULHOUSE
● Winstub Henriette
9 rue Henriette, 68100 **Map** 9E1
📞 03 89 46 27 83
FAX 03 89 70 81 02
💳 DC, MC, V ● Sun 🍽 €€

One of the city's best-priced winstubs; reservations are recommended. Dishes like choucroute garnie (p119), baeckeoffe (p119) and flammenkueche (p119).

MUNSTER
▲ A la Verte Vallée
10 rue Alfred Hartmann, 68140 **Map** 5E5
📞 03 89 77 15 15
FAX 03 89 77 17 40
W www.vertevallee.com
💳 AE, DC, MC, V
🍽 €€ 🍴 (107) €€€

Pleasant country hotel with two cottages, a gym, two pools, sauna and Jacuzzi. The restaurant is acclaimed for its ever-changing set menus and comprehensive wine list. Vibrant, unusual guestrooms.

MUNSTER
▲ La Cigogne
4 pl du Marché, 68140 **Map** 5E5
📞 03 89 77 32 27
FAX 03 89 77 54 50
💳 MC, V ● Thu
🍽 €€ 🍴 (18) €€

Popular hotel-restaurant in a town house. Soups and stews in winter; light wines, salads and quiches in summer. Rooms are large and carefully decorated.

MURBACH
▲ Domaine Langmatt
Murbach Langmatt, 68530 **Map** 9E1
📞 03 89 76 21 12
FAX 03 89 74 88 77
W www.domainelangmatt.com
💳 MC, V ● Mon L
🍽 €€€ 🍴 (30) €€€€

Atmospheric hotel-restaurant in Vosges' Regional Park. The generous menu of hot filling stews is best sampled after a day spent trekking, horseriding or skiing. Walks to Murbach's Romanesque abbey are a must. Pleasant guestrooms.

MUTZIG
▲ La Poste
4 pl de la Fontaine, 67190 **Map** 5E5
📞 03 88 38 38 38
FAX 03 88 49 82 05
W www.hostellerie-la-poste.com
💳 MC, V ● Mon
🍽 €€ 🍴 (16) €€

A lovely country house on the outskirts of the Bruche Valley. The menu focuses on daily specials, featuring anything from game dishes to flammenkueche (p119) or choucroute garnie (p119).

MUTZIG
▲ L'Ours de Mutzig
Pl de la Fontaine, 67190 **Map** 5E5
📞 03 88 47 85 55
FAX 03 88 47 85 56
W www.loursdemutzig.com
💳 MC, V 🍽 €€ 🍴 (32) €€

Inviting child-, pet- and wheelchair-friendly hotel with a park and sports facilities. Favourites at the restaurant include flammenkueche (p119), potato, bacon and cheese galettes and roast meats. Moderately sized rooms.

NANCY
● Flo Excelsior
50 rue Henri Poincaré, 54000 **Map** 5D4
📞 03 83 35 24 57
FAX 03 83 35 18 48
W www.brasserie-excelsior.com
💳 AE, DC, MC, V 🍽 €€

One of Nancy's best-known brasseries, with a gorgeous stained-glass window. Refined brasserie fare with foie gras, truffles and choucroute garnie (p119).

NANCY
▲ Grand Hôtel de la Reine
2 pl Stanislas, 54000 **Map** 5D4
📞 03 83 35 03 01
FAX 03 83 32 86 04
W www.hoteldelareine.com
💳 DC, MC, V
🍽 €€€€ 🍴 (42) €€€€

Classy four-star hotel facing delightful Stanislas Square. Foie gras from Alsace, beef from the Vosges, and a celebrated sea bass dish. The large guestrooms are classic in feel with period furnishings.

NANCY
● Grenier à Sel
28 rue Gustave Simon, 54000 **Map** 5D4
📞 03 83 32 31 98

● Restaurant ■ Hotel ▲ Hotel / Restaurant

FAX 03 83 35 32 88
@ grenierasel@chez.com
DC, MC, V ● Sun, Mon 🍴 €€

Restaurant in one of Nancy's oldest houses (dating from 1714). Artfully crafted menu: foie gras, fresh lobster, trout and game. Booking recommended.

NANCY
● Le Capucin Gourmand
31 rue Gambetta, 54000 **Map** 5D4
📞 03 83 35 26 98
FAX 03 83 35 99 29
AE, DC, MC, V ● Sun D, Sat L
🍴 €€€

Restaurant-cum-contemporary art gallery under a stunning blown-glass chandelier. Rabbit with foie gras, roasted pigeon, and fish feature highly. Extensive wine list. Reservations required.

NANCY
● Les Pissenlits
25 rue du Pont, 54000 **Map** 5D4
📞 03 83 37 43 97
FAX 03 83 35 72 49
@ pissenlits@wanadoo.fr
DC, MC, V ● Sun, Mon;
1st 2 wks Aug 🍴 €€

Bistro famed for its Art Nouveau decor. On the menu: tête-de-veau, exquisite bouillabaisse (p401), baeckeoffe (p119) and roasted game. Reservations advised.

NANCY
● Mirabelle
24 rue Héré, 54000 **Map** 5D4
📞 03 83 30 49 69
FAX 03 83 32 78 93
DC, MC, V ● Sun, Mon D, Sat L
🍴 €€€€

Inviting restaurant near Place Stanislas serving fish and pasta dishes such as ravioli stuffed with wild mushrooms and perch poached in vin gris. Book ahead.

NATZWILLER
▲ Auberge Metzger
55 rue Principale, 67130 **Map** 5E5
📞 03 88 97 02 42
FAX 03 88 97 93 59
AE, DC, MC, V ● Sun D, Mon
🍴 €€€ 🍽 (16) €€

Delicious cuisine that's well worth the trip into the Vosges Mountains, a great

place to build up an appetite through walking, cycling and cross-country skiing. Try the best in regional flavour, including duck foie gras, choucroute garnie (p119) and pigeon. Lovely modern guestrooms.

NEUFCHATEAU
▲ Le St-Christophe
1 ave Grande Fontaine, 88300 **Map** 4C5
📞 03 29 94 38 71
FAX 03 29 06 02 09
DC, MC, V ● Sun D
🍴 €€ 🍽 (34) €€

Riverside hotel with a choice of eateries (restaurant, brasserie and bar). The brasserie serves wild boar sausages and quiche. Modern but atmospheric rooms.

NEUFCHATEAU
▲ L'Eden
Rue de la 1ère Armée Française, 88300 **Map** 4C5
📞 03 29 95 61 30
FAX 03 29 94 03 42
W www.leden.fr
AE, DC, MC, V ● Sun D, Mon L
🍴 €€€ 🍽 (27) €€€

Three-star hotel-restaurant. Creative takes on local cuisine: smoked salmon with langoustines, and duck foie gras pan-fried with pears and red wine. Guestrooms vary considerably from very basic to suites with Jacuzzis.

NIEDERSTEINBACH
▲ Cheval Blanc
11 rue Principale, 67510 **Map** 5E4
📞 03 88 09 55 31
FAX 03 88 09 50 24
W www.hotel-cheval-blanc.fr
MC, V ● Thu
🍴 €€ 🍽 (25) €€

Set in one of the loveliest villages in the North Vosges, among forest, lakes and castles. The menu includes the trout, wild boar and foie gras. Pleasant garden and outdoor pool, plus inviting rooms.

OBERNAI
▲ A la Cour d'Alsace
3 rue de Gail, 67210 **Map** 5E5
📞 03 88 95 07 00
FAX 03 88 95 19 21
AE, DC, MC, V ● Christmas
🍴 €€€ 🍽 (43) €€€€

Hotel in a former manor house and wine cellar. The two restaurants – Le Jardin des Remparts and Le Caveau de Gail Winstub – specialize in luxury Alsatian cuisine such as goose foie gras, seasonal game, Alsatian sausages and choucroute garnie (p119). A cosy bar in the courtyard.

OBERNAI
▲ Le Parc d'Obernai
169 route d'Ottrott, 67210 **Map** 5E5
📞 03 88 95 50 08
FAX 03 88 95 37 29
W www.hotel-du-parc.com
AE, DC, MC, V ● Sun D, Mon;
late-June–mid-July, Dec
🍴 €€€€ 🍽 (51) €€€€

Characterful, flower-covered restaurant with two eateries – La Stub for lunch (a typical Alsatian-style inn) and La Grande Table for more formal dining. Goose foie gras, grilled pike, and baeckeoffe (p119) appear. Many rooms are split-level.

OSTWALD
▲ Château de l'Ile
4 quai Heydt, 67540 **Map** 5E5
📞 03 88 66 85 00
FAX 03 88 66 85 49
W www.chateau-ile.com
MC, V
🍴 €€€
🍽 (62) €€€€€

Stately 19th-century château with a menu featuring foie gras and game. Guestrooms have half-timbered ceilings and terraces. Pricey but worth it.

OTTROTT
▲ Beau Site
Pl de l'Eglise, 67530 **Map** 5E5
📞 03 88 48 14 30
FAX 03 88 48 14 18
W www.hotel-beau-site.fr
AE, DC, MC, V ● Mon
🍴 €€€ 🍽 (18) €€€€

Gourmet winstub in the heart of Ottrott, overlooking the vineyards leading up Mont Ste-Odile. Choose à la carte or from three set menus offering dishes such as tangy choucroute garnie (p119), wild boar, goose or duck foie gras, rabbit in tarragon, or pike-perch with a Riesling sauce. Desserts include baba au rhum (p119). Unusual rooms with half-timbers.

For key to symbols see back flap

OTTROTT

▲ Hostellerie des Châteaux

11 rue des Châteaux, 67530 **Map** 5E5

📞 03 88 48 14 14

FAX 03 88 95 95 20

🍴 AE, DC, MC, V

🍽 €€€€ 🍷 (67) €€€€

Luxury country hotel with an indoor pool, sauna, Jacuzzi, gym and park. The colourful candlelit dining room offers goose foie gras flavoured with peach wine, and beef with a choucroute garnie (p119). Fine views from the guestrooms.

OTTROTT

▲ Mont Ste-Odile

Le Mont Ste-Odile, 67530 **Map** 5E5

📞 03 88 95 80 53

FAX 03 88 95 82 96

🔳 www.mont-sainte-odile.fr

🍴 MC, V 🍽 € 🍷 (140) €€

This mountain-top hotel and its eateries have something to suit everyone. Hearty regional fare has been satisfying local ramblers for centuries. Simple rooms reflect their former religious role.

PHALSBOURG

● Au Soldat de L'An II

1 rue de Saverne, 57370 **Map** 5E4

📞 03 87 24 16 16

FAX 03 87 24 18 18

🔳 www.an2.com

🍴 AE, MC, V ⬤ Sun L, Mon, Tue

🍽 €€€€

In the Vosges foothills, this little auberge serves especially good game. Pheasant and hare are roasted and served with vegetables in the traditional style. But a touch of chocolate or fruit in the sauce gives an original twist.

PHALSBOURG

▲ Hôtel-Restaurant Notre Dame

212 rue Bonne Fontaine, 57370 **Map** 5E4

📞 03 87 24 34 33

FAX 03 87 24 24 64

🍴 AE, MC, V

⬤ 3 wks Jan, 1st wk Feb

🍽 €€ 🍷 (34) €€

Simple luxury in the midst of a little wood. Restaurant serves choucroute garnie (p119), game, fish, and pâté lorrain (pork and veal pie). Good selection of Moselle wines. Small, basic guestrooms.

PLOMBIERES-LES-BAINS

▲ Le Strasbourgeois

3 pl Beaumarchais, 88370 **Map** 9D1

📞 03 29 66 00 70

FAX 03 29 66 01 06

🍴 AE, DC, MC, V 🍽 🍷 (20) €

Comfortable hotel-restaurant with plenty of salads, poached fish (especially local trout), and fresh fruit desserts. Fishing (reserved for hotel guests), mountain-biking and hiking facilities available.

PONT-A-MOUSSON

● L'Auberge des Thomas

100 ave Victor Claude, 54700 **Map** 4C4

📞 03 83 81 07 72

FAX 03 83 82 34 94

🍴 AE, DC, MC, V ⬤ Sun D, Mon, Wed D 🍽 €€

The decor may be on the kitsch side but the food is carefully presented. Try the house pâté lorrain (pork and veal pie) or caramelized plums served flambéed.

REHAUPAL

▲ Auberge du Haut-Jardin

43 bis le Village, 88640 **Map** 5D5

📞 03 29 66 37 06

FAX 03 29 66 22 81

🔳 www.gerardmer.net/fr/pages-hebergement/hotels/hautjardin.htm

🍴 MC, V 🍽 € 🍷 (8) €€

Cuisine includes a tasty Vosgien version of raclette (p268), grilled steaks and mirabelle plum desserts. Modern rooms with a Japanese feel.

REVIGNY-SUR-ORNAIN

▲ Les Agapes

6 pl Henriot du Coudray, 55800 **Map** 4B4

📞 03 29 70 56 00

FAX 03 29 70 59 30

🍴 AE, DC, MC, V ⬤ Sun D, Mon D, Sat L 🍽 €€ 🍷 (7) €€€

Picturesque restaurant with one Michelin star in a small hotel with original features. Delicately presented foie gras, roasted and grilled meats, and seafood sauerkraut with three kinds of fish appear on the menu. Carefully decorated guestrooms.

RIBEAUVILLE

▲ Le Clos St-Vincent

Route de Bergheim, 68150 **Map** 5E5

📞 03 89 73 67 65

FAX 03 89 73 32 20

🍴 MC, V ⬤ L, Tue D

🍽 €€€ 🍷 (24) €€€€

Hearty fare like rabbit in mustard sauce and beef fillet in a butter sauce. Spacious guestrooms have shared balconies.

RIQUEWIHR

▲ Au Cep de Vigne

13 rue du Général de Gaulle, 68340 **Map** 5E5

📞 03 89 47 92 34

FAX 03 89 73 30 34

@ hotel-cep-de-vigne@wanadoo.fr

🍴 MC, V ⬤ Mon 🍽 € 🍷 (7) €€

Gorgeous candlelit restaurant in the cellar. Think bubbling soups and hotpots, light green salads, and crisp local Riesling. Rooms are similarly enchanting.

RIQUEWIHR

● La Grappe d'Or

1 rue des Ecuries, 68340 **Map** 5E5

📞 03 89 47 89 52

FAX 03 89 47 89 52

🍴 MC, V ⬤ Wed, Thu L 🍽 €

Cute little restaurant with an entrance door hard to find for all the plants and flowers. Very reasonably priced menu, surprising for the quality and size of regional dishes on offer.

RIQUEWIHR

● La Table du Gourmet

5 rue de la 1ère Armée, 68340 **Map** 5E5

📞 03 89 49 09 09

FAX 03 89 49 04 56

🔳 www.jlbrendel.com

🍴 MC, V ⬤ Tue; Jan–mid-Feb

🍽 €€€€

One of Alsace's best-reputed restaurants. Expensive, but reasonably so due to the quality on offer. Ring to reserve.

ROUFFACH

▲ Château d'Isenbourg

Isenbourg, 68250 **Map** 9E1

📞 03 89 78 58 50

FAX 03 89 78 53 70

🍴 MC, V ⬤ Wed, Sat; Feb

🍽 €€€€ 🍷 (41) €€€€€

One of France's ten Grandes Etapes château-hotels, with a price tag to match its reputation and quality. Luxurious guestrooms.

● Restaurant ■ Hotel ▲ Hotel / Restaurant

ROUFFACH

▲ Ville de Lyon

1 rue Point-Carré, 68250 **Map** 9E1

C 03 89 49 65 51

FAX 03 89 49 76 67

DC, MC, V ● Mon, Wed

€€€ ◆ (43) €€€

Bustling establishment with service and quality of food far exceeding the very reasonable prices. Innovative Alsatian fare, such as rabbit with an oily aubergine (eggplant) dressing. Reserve ahead.

ROUFFACH

● Winstub de la Poterne

7 rue de la Poterne, 68250 **Map** 9E1

C 03 89 78 53 29

FAX 03 89 78 50 28

DC, MC, V ● Mon D, Tue €€

Small winstub that draws a mixed crowd of tourists and regulars. Dishes are as authentic as the atmosphere and you'll probably end up sampling (and loving) food you shied away from when you first arrived in Alsace, such as choucroute garnie (p119) and baeckeoffe (p119).

ROUVRES-EN-XAINTOIS

▲ Hôtel Burnel & La Clé des Champs

22 rue Jeane d'Arc, 88500 **Map** 4E5

C 03 29 65 64 10

FAX 03 29 65 68 88

W www.burnel.fr

AE, DC, MC, V ● Sun D

€€ ◆ (22) €€€

Little hotel-restaurant that creates original fish and game dishes. Rooms with mod cons and access to the sauna and gym.

RUPT-SUR-MOSELLE

▲ Du Centre

30 rue de l'Eglise, 88360 **Map** 9D1

C 03 29 24 34 73

FAX 03 29 24 45 26

DC, MC, V ● Sun D, Mon

€€€ ◆ (9) €€

In a picturesque building. Menus feature anything from quiche to hearty stews and fine trout cooked with beer or rosé wine. Simple accommodation.

SAND

▲ La Charrue

4 rue du 1er Décembre, 67230 **Map** 5E5

C 03 88 74 42 66

FAX 03 88 74 12 02

MC, V ● Mon–Sat L

€€ ◆ (24) €€

Next to forests, rivers and orchards perfect for a stroll or cycle-ride. The menu includes duck foie gras with figs, pike-perch on choucroute garnie (p119) and game. Vast, modern guestrooms.

SARREBOURG

▲ Hôtel de France

3 ave de France, 57400 **Map** 5E4

C 03 87 03 21 47

FAX 03 87 23 93 57

W www.hoteldefrancesarrebourg.com

AE, MC, V

€ ◆ (50) €€€

Great place for wood-fired pizzas, fine flammenkueche (p119), grilled meats and salads. Lively bar too. Basic rooms.

SARREBOURG

▲ Les Cèdres

Zone de Loisirs, Chemin d'Imling, 57400 **Map** 5E4

C 03 87 03 55 55

FAX 03 87 03 66 33

W www.hotel-lescedres.fr

MC, V ● Sun D, Sat L

€€€ ◆ (44) €€

Relaxing hotel on a picturesque lake, with one of the region's best-known gastronomic restaurants. Well-priced weekday menu. Specialities include foie gras, choucroute garnie (p119) and veal. Simple, spacious guestrooms.

SAVERNE

● Taverne Katz

80 Grand Rue, 67700 **Map** 5E4

C 03 88 71 16 56

FAX 03 88 71 85 85

W www.tavernekatz.com

MC, V €€€

Striking restaurant built in 1605. The menu includes pig's trotters, braised steak and duck. Or stick to old favourites such as quiche Lorraine (p119) or choucroute garnie (p119) with sausages.

SEINGBOUSE

▲ Diane

RN16, 57455 **Map** 5D4

C 03 87 89 11 10

FAX 03 87 89 53 25

W www.relais-diane.com

MC, V ● Sun D, Sat L

€ ◆ (15) €€

In an atmospheric forest, this little inn offers outdoor activities and delicious cuisine, especially fish caught in the nearby river and game from the forests. Charming, flower-filled guestrooms.

SELESTAT

▲ Auberge des Alliés

39 rue des Chevaliers, 67600 **Map** 5E5

C 03 88 92 09 34

FAX 03 88 92 12 88

W www.auberge-des-allies.com

MC, V ● Sun D, Mon

€€ ◆ (17) €€

Gastronomic fare so artful, dishes should be framed not eaten! Dressed lobster, quiche and charcuterie are just a few regional options on offer. Good selection of wines from local vineyards.

SOULTZ

▲ Château d'Anthes

25 rue de la Marne, 68360 **Map** 9E1

C 03 89 62 23 68

FAX 03 89 62 23 70

MC, V ● Sun D, Mon

€€€ ◆ (39) €€€

A large château within a pleasant park. Dishes accompanied by an impressive selection of local Rieslings, Pinot Gris and Gewürztraminers (tastings on request). Get a back room for views.

SOULTZMATT

▲ Klein

44 rue de la Vallée, 68570 **Map** 9E1

C 03 89 47 00 10

FAX 03 89 47 65 03

MC, V ● Mon; mid-Jan–mid-Feb

€€ ◆ (11) €€

Striking restaurant with whitewashed walls, flower-filled balconies and a tiny terrace. Specialities such as salmon on choucroute garnie (p119) with Munster cheese, and pig's trotters pan-fried with foie gras. Guestrooms are carefully furnished in a simple, rustic style.

SOULTZMATT

▲ Vallée Noble

BP17, 68570 **Map** 9E1

C 03 89 47 65 65

FAX 03 89 47 65 04

W www.valleenoble.com

MC, V ● Sun D, Sat L

€€€ ◇ (32) €€€

Named after the green valley it inhabits. The cuisine compensates for the modern architecture: try the snails in Provençal sauce and best seasonal produce. Basic yet comfortable rooms.

ST-AME
▲ **Lambert**
1 pl de la Mairie, 88120 **Map** 5D5

C 03 29 61 21 15

FAX 03 29 62 25 80

@ lambert8@wanadoo.fr

AE, DC, MC, V ● Sun D, Fri D

€€ ◇ (9) €€

Countryside auberge serving frogs' legs and asparagus in spring, game in autumn, and old favourites such as cold meats, stews, and fish year-round. Pale pastel guestrooms with wood furnishings.

ST-MAURICE-SUR-MOSELLE
▲ **Au Pied des Ballons**
39 rue de Lorraine, 88560 **Map** 9D1

C 03 29 25 12 54

FAX 03 29 25 87 74

W www.au-pied-des-ballons.com

AE, DC, MC, V

€€ ◇ (12) €€

Two-star hotel and large restaurant in one of St-Maurice's oldest buildings. House specialities: duck rillettes, rabbit terrine and grilled lobster. Long wine list. Luxurious furniture in the rooms.

ST-MAURICE-SUR-MOSELLE
▲ **Le Rouge Gazon**
St-Maurice-sur-Moselle, 88560 **Map** 9D1

C 03 29 25 12 80

FAX 03 29 25 12 11

W www.rouge-gazon.fr

DC, MC, V ● Tue D, Nov

€ ◇ (37) €€€

Piste-side hotel. Hearty meaty dishes, cheese plates and bilberry tart. Small, eclectic guestrooms with great views.

ST-NABORD
▲ **Les Prés Braheux**
1425 route de Fallières, 88200 **Map** 5D5

C 03 29 62 23 67

FAX 03 29 62 01 40

W www.les-pres-braheux.com

DC, MC, V ● Sun D, Mon

€€ ◇ (15) €€€

Countryside accommodation. On the menu: fish, game, quiches and stews. Good wine and beer list. Modern rooms.

ST-PIERREMONT
▲ **Le Relais Vosgien**
9 Grande Rue, 88700 **Map** 5D5

C 03 29 65 02 46

FAX 03 29 65 02 83

W www.relais-vosgien.fr

AE, DC, MC, V ● Fri D

€€€ ◇ (20) €€€€

Three-star hotel in a stunning village setting. Baeckeoffe (p119), choucroute garnie (p119) and seasonal game such as wild-boar sausages. Top selection of local wines. Guestrooms vary by cost: the cheapest are minimal but spacious, and the more expensive have leather furnishings and marble sculptures.

STRASBOURG
● **Ami Schutz**
1 Ponts Couverts, 67000 **Map** 5E5

C 03 88 32 76 98

FAX 03 88 32 38 40

W www.ami-schutz.com

AE, DC, MC, V €€

Well-reputed bierstub (beer tavern) at the fork of the River Ill, with original 18th-century features. Serves traditional Alsatian cuisine in the wooden-beamed interior and on the beautiful terrace, one of Strasbourg's nicest.

STRASBOURG
● **Au Bon Vivant**
7 rue du Maroquin, 67000 **Map** 5E5

C 03 88 32 77 81

FAX 03 88 32 95 12

MC, V ● Thu D, Fri €

Popular Alsatian winstub specializing in chicken (usually cooked in the local Riesling or Cognac), choucroute garnie (p119) and baeckeoffe (p119). The interior is painted with the story of local heroine, La Grenouille (the frog).

STRASBOURG
● **Au Coin des Pucelles**
12 rue des Pucelles, 67000 **Map** 5E5

C 03 88 35 35 14

FAX 03 88 35 35 14

MC, V ● Sun, Sat; public holidays

€

One of Strasbourg's oldest, smallest and latest-opening winstubs (it rarely closes before 1am). Highlights include pork knuckle, presskopf (chunky pork terrine), cheese dumpling, choucroute garnie (p119) and tarte alsacienne. Reserve.

STRASBOURG
● **Au Crocodile**
10 rue de l'Outre, 67000 **Map** 5E5

C 03 88 32 13 02

FAX 03 88 75 72 01

W www.au-crocodile.com

AE, DC, MC, V ● Sun, Mon; 1st wk Jan, last 3 wks Jul, last wk Dec

€€€€€

With a well-reputed gastronomic menu, this is one of Strasbourg's chicest and best-known Alsatian restaurants. The interior is as lavish as its innovative menu, which well deserves its three Michelin stars. Extensive wine list.

STRASBOURG
● **Au Pont du Corbeau**
21 quai St-Nicholas, 67000 **Map** 5E5

C 03 88 35 60 68

FAX 03 88 25 72 45

MC, V ● Sun D, Sat €€

This traditional Alsatian restaurant, named after one of Strasbourg's most impressive bridges, offers generous and delicious portions of popular choices such as charcuterie, flammenkueche (p119), and Alsatian sausages.

STRASBOURG
● **Au Pont St-Martin**
15 rue des Moulins, 67000 **Map** 5E5

C 03 88 32 45 13

FAX 03 88 75 77 60

W www.pont-saint-martin.com

MC, V €€

Very touristy but ideally located in a glorious old riverside building in Petite France. Good range of flammenkueche (p119), choucroute garnie (p119), and tasty fish and meat baeckeoffes (p119) will be the only things to pull you away from the delicious view. The Gewürztraminer sorbet is a must for dessert. Some musical evenings (extra charge).

● Restaurant ■ Hotel ▲ Hotel / Restaurant

STRASBOURG
● **Au St-Sépulcre**
15 rue des Orfèvres, 67000 **Map** 5E5

🄲 03 88 32 39 97

FAX 03 88 32 39 97

🍽 MC, V ● Sun, Mon 🍴 €€

Small, popular winstub *with a quite jovial atmosphere. Typical dishes include onion tart and presskopf (chunky pork terrine).*

STRASBOURG
● **Au Tire Bouchon**
5 rue des Tailleurs de Pierre, 67000
Map 5E5

🄲 03 88 22 16 32

FAX 03 88 23 10 73

🍽 MC, V 🍴 €€

Small, authentic Alsatian winstub *close to the cathedral, best for its inexpensive weekday plat du jour. House specialities include baeckeoffe (p119) au riesling, jarret de porc à la bière (knuckle of pork in beer) and knepfle (a kind of gnocchi).*

STRASBOURG
● **Aux Trois Brasseurs**
22 rue des Veaux, 67000 **Map** 5E5

🄲 03 88 36 12 13

FAX 03 88 24 24 05

🍽 MC, V 🍴 €

One of a chain of micro-breweries with a great selection of beers and bar snacks such as flammenkueche (p119). *Concerts on Fridays and Saturdays.*

STRASBOURG
● **Aux Trois Chevaliers**
3 quai des Bateliers, 67000 **Map** 5E5

🄲 03 88 36 15 18

🍽 MC, V ● Sun, Mon 🍴 €€

Popular winstub *with a terrace. Wide selection of local liqueurs, especially flavoured schnapps (raspberry, kirsch and the local* marc de gewürztraminer).

STRASBOURG
● **Buerehiesel**
4 parc de l'Orangerie, 67000 **Map** 5E5

🄲 03 88 45 56 65

FAX 03 88 61 32 00

🇼 www.buerehiesel.fr

🍽 AE, DC, MC, V ● Tue, Wed;
1st 2 wks Jan & Aug 🍴 €€€€€

Three-star Michelin restaurant in an ancient farmhouse. Chef Antoine

Westermann delivers brioche caramélisée à la bière *(brioche caramelized in beer). Reservations recommended.*

STRASBOURG
● **Fink Stuebel**
26 rue Finkwiller, 67000 **Map** 5E5

🄲 03 88 25 07 57

FAX 03 88 36 48 82

🍽 MC, V ● Sun D, Mon;
2nd & 3rd wk Aug 🍴 €

One of Strasbourg's best winstubs. *House specialities include onion tart,* spaetzle *(noodle dumplings) with foie gras, and* choucroute garnie (p119). *Pleasant terrace.*

STRASBOURG
● **HK**
12 rue du Vieux-Marché-aux-Grains,
67000 **Map** 5E5

🄲 03 88 32 11 05

🍽 MC, V ● Sun 🍴 €

Heineken bar popular with 20-some-things for its modern interior and bustling terrace. Well-priced menu of simple but tasty dishes with an Asiatic twist: salmon with lime and ginger, chicken satay, and ostrich kebabs.

STRASBOURG
● **La Chaîne d'Or**
134 Grand Rue, 67000 **Map** 5E5

🄲 03 88 75 02 69

FAX 03 88 32 11 06

🇼 www.chainedor.fr

🍽 AE, MC, V 🍴 €

This charming bistro has Alsatian menus with choucroute garnie (p119), baeckeoffe (p119) *and* flammenkueche (p119); *French menus offering steak tartare, fish, and foie gras; and "student" menus.*

STRASBOURG
● **La Choucrouterie**
20 rue St-Louis, 67000 **Map** 5E5

🄲 03 88 36 52 87

FAX 03 88 24 16 49

🇼 www.choucrouterie.com

🍽 MC, V ● Sun L, Sat L 🍴 €€

One of the best spots for choucroute garnie (p119), *this* winstub *– offers seven versions, including red cabbage, smoked duck and kosher. Must-eats include the* chouc *dessert with cinnamon ice cream.*

STRASBOURG
● **La Cloche à Fromage**
27 rue des Tonneliers, 67000 **Map** 5E5

🄲 03 88 23 13 19

FAX 03 88 32 99 60

🍽 DC, MC, V ● Tue 🍴 €€

Innovative restaurant serving over 200 varieties of French cheese – some rare and expensive. Its entrance is marked by a giant "cloche à fromage", mentioned in the Guinness Book of Records, *which gives an idea of the current seasonal produce. Reservations necessary.*

STRASBOURG
● **La Coccinelle**
22 rue Ste-Madeleine, 67000 **Map** 5E5

🄲 03 88 36 19 27

FAX 03 88 35 34 80

🇼 www.alsaweb.com/coccinelle

🍽 MC, V ● Sun, Sat L 🍴 €€

Small but animated winstub *popular for its generous portions of liver dumplings and Munster cheese gratin. Reservations are highly recommended.*

STRASBOURG
● **Le Clou**
3 rue du Chaudron, 67000 **Map** 5E5

🄲 03 88 32 11 67

FAX 03 88 75 72 83

🍽 AE, MC, V ● Sun, Wed L;
public holidays 🍴 €€

Ever-popular winstub *near the cathedral serving a classic onion tart,* choucroute garnie (p119) *and the ever-present* baeckeoffe (p119). *Reservations advised.*

STRASBOURG
● **Le Passeva**
2 quai des Bateliers, pl du Corbeau,
67000 **Map** 5E5

🄲 03 88 25 70 42

FAX 03 88 25 70 42

🍽 MC, V ● Sun, Mon 🍴 €

"Concept bar" – a cross between a restaurant and music bar – with dishes like flammenkueche (p119), *salads and pastas. Trendy at lunch and busy in the evenings when local DJs spin.*

STRASBOURG
● **Le Schutzenberger**
29–31 rue des Grandes Arcades, 67000
Map 5E5

C 03 90 23 66 66
FAX 03 90 23 66 67
@ leschutzenberger@wanadoo.fr
MC, V 🍴 €€

Trendy brasserie with a popular bar, a restaurant overlooking Place Kléber and a summer terrace. Innovative dishes includes anything from chicken and foie gras to fish, all marinated in beer.

STRASBOURG
▲ Maison Kammerzell

16 pl de la Cathédrale, 67000 **Map** 5E5
C 03 88 32 42 14
FAX 03 88 23 03 92
W www.maison-kammerzell.com
AE, DC, MC, V
🍴 €€€ 🛏 (9) €€€€

Hotel-restaurant in an atmospheric 16th-century landmark two paces from the cathedral. House specialities include seafood sauerkraut and fine baeckeoffe (p119). Modern rooms contrast with the ancient exterior.

STRASBOURG
● Munsterstuewel

8 pl du Marché aux Cochons de Lait, 67000 **Map** 5E5
C 03 88 32 17 63
FAX 03 88 21 96 02
W www.strasnet.com/munsterstub.htm
AE, DC, MC, V ◑ Sun, Mon
🍴 €€

Popular riverside Alsatian winstub. The house speciality is beef and vegetable stew. Terrace with delightful views of typical 15th-century Alsatian architecture.

STRASBOURG
● S'Thomas Stuebel

5 rue du Bouclier, 67000 **Map** 5E5
C 03 88 22 34 82
MC, V ◑ Sun, Mon 🍴 €€

Generous portions of local fare such as baeckeoffe (p119), and tasty desserts. Wood-beamed ceiling and whitewashed walls decorated with pots, pans and bronze engravings. Reserve a table. Young children not particularly welcome.

STRASBOURG
● Taverne de Sommelier

3 ruelle de la Bruche, 67000 **Map** 5E5
C 03 88 24 14 10

FAX 03 88 78 21 24
MC, V
◑ Sun, Sat 🍴 €€

Enchanting half-hidden tavern serving southern French cuisine to match the wines (mostly from the Rhone Valley and Languedoc). Reservations recommended.

STRASBOURG
● Zuem Ysehuet

21 quai Mullenheim, 67000 **Map** 5E5
C 03 88 35 68 62
FAX 03 88 36 50 67
MC, V ◑ Sun, Sat L; public holidays
🍴 €€

Famed bistro in a charming town house on the banks of the River Ill. Tasty dishes include crayfish marinated in lemon and virgin olive oil, veal kidney in mustard, and a good range of desserts. Booking recommended for alfresco dining.

STRASBOURG
● Zum Steckelburjer

8 rue des Tonneliers, 67000 **Map** 5E5
C 03 88 32 76 33
DC, MC, V ◑ Sun, Wed D 🍴 €€

Small, long-established winstub with a pleasant terrace, serving up jambonneau (ham knuckle), fleischschnecke (meat hash) and presskopf (pork terrine).

STRASBOURG
● Zum Wynhaenel

24 rue Sleidan, 67000 **Map** 5E5
C 03 88 61 84 22
MC, V
◑ Sun, Mon D; 1 wk Feb 🍴 €

One of Strasbourg's best winstubs, just off the tourist path. Diverse, innovative menu with onion tart and Munster cheese tartiflettes (p268). Extensive wine list, atmospheric terrace and regular concerts. Reservations recommended.

TENDON
▲ Auberge de la Poirie

67 route des Cascades, 88460 **Map** 5D5
C 03 29 66 66 99
FAX 03 29 66 66 98
W www.lapoirie.fr
DC, MC, V 🍴 € 🛏 (8) €€

Near the Tendon waterfalls, specializing in trout (cooked in vin gris or with cream and chopped bacon). Good game and

red wine stews and wild-mushroom dishes. Good value guestrooms.

THANN
▲ Du Parc

23 rue Kléber, 68800 **Map** 9E1
C 03 89 37 37 47
FAX 03 89 37 56 23
W www.alsacehotel.com
AE, MC, V ◑ Mon L, Tue L
🍴 €€ 🛏 (20) €€€

Classic restaurant and romantic hotel. The menu showcases snails, baeckeoffe (p119) and game. Traditional guestrooms.

THANNENKIRCH
▲ Auberge de la Meunière

30 rue Ste-Anne, 68590 **Map** 5E5
C 03 89 73 10 47
FAX 03 89 73 12 31
W www.aubergelameuniere.com
MC, V ◑ Jan–Mar
🍴 €€ 🛏 (25) €€

Charming little auberge with flower-filled balconies and views of the Black Forest. Hearty local cuisine with a good wine list. Rooms are modern but traditional.

THIONVILLE
▲ Le Concorde

6 pl du Luxembourg, 57100 **Map** 4C3
C 03 82 53 83 18
FAX 03 82 53 40 41
W www.hotel-le-concorde.com
AE, DC, MC, V ◑ Sun D, Mon, Sat L
🍴 €€ 🛏 (21) €€€

Three-star hotel-restaurant. Menus offer anything from prawns to snails but mostly feature fish and game. Adequate rooms, some with renovated bathrooms.

THIONVILLE
▲ L'Horizon

50 route Crève Coeur, 57100 **Map** 4C3
C 03 82 88 53 65
FAX 03 82 34 55 84
W www.lhorizon.fr
MC, V ◑ Mon L, Fri L, Sat L, Nov–mid-Mar: Sun D; Hotel: 3rd wk Dec–3rd wk Jan
🍴 €€€ 🛏 (12) €€€€

Three-star country inn. The menu always includes fish, duck and veal. Classy guestrooms, decorated in whites and pastels, with luxurious bathrooms.

● Restaurant   ■ Hotel   ▲ Hotel / Restaurant

TOUL

● **Auberge du Pressoir**

7 rue des Pachenottes, 54200 **Map** 4C4

☎ 03 83 63 81 91

FAX 03 83 63 81 38

🗺 DC, MC, V ● Sun D, Mon, Wed D

🍴 €€

Traditional restaurant in an old train station. Toul vin gris wine accompanies and Lorraine brandy follows.

TOUL

● **Le Dauphin**

65 allée Gaumiron, 54200 **Map** 4C4

☎ 03 88 43 13 46

FAX 03 88 43 81 31

@ christophe.vohmann@wanadoo.fr

🗺 AE, DC, MC, V ● Sun D, Mon, Wed D 🍴 €€€€

Haute cuisine. Deftly presented dishes; foie gras and veal regularly appear. Regional wines (mostly Grand Crus). Booking recommended.

VENTRON

▲ **Les Bruyères**

9 route de Remiremont, 88310 **Map** 9D1

☎ 03 29 24 18 63

FAX 03 29 24 23 15

ⓦ www.lesbruyeres.com.fr

🗺 AE, DC, MC, V ● Sun D, Mon D

🍴 €€ 🍽 (19) €€

Riverside hotel with large grounds and an emphasis on sporting activities. Quiche, choucroute garnie (p119), and rich winter stews on the menu alongside flavoursome cheese platters and fruit desserts. Narrow, basic guestrooms.

VENTRON

▲ **Les Buttes**

Ermitage Frère Joseph, 88310 **Map** 9D1

☎ 03 29 24 18 09

FAX 03 29 24 21 96

ⓦ www.frerejo.com

🗺 DC, MC, V

🍴 €€€€ 🍽 (27) €€€€

In an isolated mountain location on the site of an atmospheric old hermitage. Good range of fish dishes and fruit desserts. Rooms enjoy attention to detail.

VERDUN

▲ **Hostellerie du Coq Hardi**

8 ave de la Victoire, 55100 **Map** 4C4

☎ 03 29 86 36 36

FAX 03 29 86 09 21

ⓦ www.coq-hardi.com

🗺 AE, MC, V ● Fri

🍴 €€€ 🍽 (37) €€€€

Three-star inn with a delightful range of regional dishes. One set menu includes smaller versions of the main courses. Comfy, wood-beamed guestrooms.

VILLE

▲ **La Bonne Franquette**

6 pl du Marché, 67220 **Map** 5E5

☎ 03 88 57 14 25

FAX 03 88 57 08 15

🗺 MC, V ● Sun D, Mon

🍴 €€€ 🍽 (10) €€

Stunning whitewashed hotel-restaurant with hanging baskets overflowing with blossoms. Restaurant fare varies by season but tends towards local rustic cuisine. Typical dishes include fish in Pinot Noir and beer, plus the ever-present choucroute garnie (p119). Basic rooms.

VITTEL

▲ **La Tuilerie**

Parc Thermal, 88800 **Map** 4C5

☎ 03 29 08 18 88

FAX 03 29 08 18 38

ⓦ www.latuilerie.com

🗺 AE, DC, MC, V ● mid-Dec– mid-Feb 🍴 €€€ 🍽 (9) €€€€

Four-star place in a forested thermal park on the edge of Vittel. Popular local standards include foie gras, roasted meats and charcuterie with seasonal extras such as truffles or game. Large wine cellar. Luxurious rooms and suites.

VITTEL

▲ **L'Orée du Bois**

L'Hippodrome de Vittel, 88800 **Map** 4C5

☎ 03 29 08 88 88

FAX 03 29 08 01 61

🗺 AE, DC, MC, V ● Christmas day

🍴 €€ 🍽 (39) €€

Woodland hotel-restaurant. Monkfish, salmon, and veal kidneys are typical dishes. Basic yet large guestrooms with exposed brickwork.

WISSEMBOURG

● **La Taverne de la Petite Venise**

3 rue de la République, 67160 **Map** 5E4

☎ 03 88 54 30 70

FAX 03 88 54 84 60

ⓦ www.la-taverne-wissembourg.com

🗺 MC, V ● Wed 🍴 €€

Charming riverside restaurant in the heart of the Little Venice district. Menu includes everything from stuffed mussels to ham on choucroute garnie (p119). Good flammenkueche (p119).

XONRUPT-LONGEMER

▲ **Auberge du Lac**

2887 route de Colmar, 88400 **Map** 5D5

☎ 03 29 63 37 21

FAX 03 29 60 05 41

🗺 DC, MC, V ● Mon, Wed L

🍴 €€ 🍽 (16) €€

Small two-star auberge serving meaty mountain dishes. The winter stew is especially good, and summer brings a range of lighter fish and charcuterie dishes. Charming guestrooms.

XONRUPT-LONGEMER

▲ **La Vallée**

2817 route de Colmar, 88400 **Map** 5D5

☎ 03 29 63 37 01

FAX 03 29 60 00 62

ⓦ http://perso.wanadoo.fr/hotel.la.vallee

🗺 AE, DC, MC, V ● 1st 2 wks Dec

🍴 €€ 🍽 (10) €€

Relaxing two-star country hotel. The food is influenced by mountain fruits and herbs, and there's a good range of savoury and sweet tarts (including one using Meuse redcurrants). Wood-clad bedrooms with navy-blue touches.

XONRUPT-LONGEMER

▲ **Le Collet**

9937 route de Colmar, 88400 **Map** 5D5

☎ 03 29 60 09 57

FAX 03 29 60 08 77

ⓦ www.chalethotel-lecollet.com

🗺 DC, MC, V ● Wed L, Thu L; 1st 2 wks Apr, last 2 wks Nov

🍴 €€€ 🍽 (21) €€€

Three-star chalet with a restaurant serving some of "grandmother's dessert recipes" and an imaginative take on vegetable choucroute garnie (p119). Wild boar and venison with rich red wine sauces plus rabbit with mirabelle plums. Good wine cellar. Relaxing, pastel-coloured guestrooms.

For key to symbols see back flap

NORMANDY

The land of William the Conqueror and the Impressionist painters is also a gourmet's delight. Inland, its lush, green, rolling countryside, with cow-dotted meadows, orchards and half-timbered farmhouses, is the source of delectable veal and poultry, cheeses, cream, apples and pears, cider and Calvados. Along its coastline, seaside resorts alternate with fishing ports that provide a huge variety of superb fish and shellfish.

The Flavours of Normandy

Normandy's lush pastures are home to the cows that give the creamy milk for the region's great cheeses (see pp142–3). Cider, Calvados and Pommeau are made from the fruit of its orchards, and the coastline offers a bounty of fine seafood.

BEST MARKETS

Alençon Plenty of local produce on place de la Madeleine, Thu & Sat am
Bayeux Place St-Patrice, Sat am
Dieppe Busy market on place Nationale and spreading up the Grand'Rue, Sat am
Dives-sur-Mer Held under the wooden vaults of a magnificent covered market hall, Sat am
Forges-les-Eaux Best of the Bray. All local produce, Thu am
Pont l'Evêque Buy direct from producers at this summer farmers' market. Jul & Aug, Sun am
Rouen Place du Vieux-Marché. A surprising modern building is part market, part church; there are also plenty of good food shops around the square, Tue–Sun am
Trouville Fabulous daily quayside fish market, held in a listed building

MEAT, POULTRY AND CHARCUTERIE

The positive side to Normandy's one disadvantage for the tourist – the damp climate – is that it has pasture second to none. The *bocage*, that mix of hedged green meadows and apple orchards, is perfect for the brown-and-white *vache Normande* (Normandy cow) which, as well as rich milk, also supplies excellent free-range veal. In the past they were used for beef, too, although today are often crossed with Charolais *(see p214)*.

Pork features in various dishes and charcuterie. *Andouille de Vire*, made from pig's tripe and stomach and smoked to give its distinctive flavour and black skin, is still handmade by many *charcutiers* in the town of Vire. Other pork produce includes hams, terrines, black pudding from Coutances and Mortagne-au-Perche and *andouillette* from Alençon.

Ducks (especially Duclair), chickens, turkey and geese are all part of Norman cuisine, too, and foie gras is a traditional regional product.

Andouille de Vire

The soil is generally too rich for sheep, a notable exception being in the Baie de Mont-St-Michel, where sheep raised on the iodine- and salt-rich marshes are the source of prized *agneau de pré-salé*.

Sheep grazing on the salt marshes of the Baie de Mont-St-Michel

Left Carrots from Créances **Right** Local oysters and giant prawns

FISH AND SHELLFISH

Normandy is an important fishing region. Sole, plaice, mackerel (in particular, baby ones called *lisettes*), skate and herrings are all part of the catch. As well as the main ports there are many smaller fishing villages where you can buy direct from the boats. Normandy is also rich in shellfish – 80 per cent of France's scallops are landed here, especially at Dieppe. Oysters are cultivated at St-Vaast-la-Hougue, Isigny-sur-Mer and Courseulles, while Barfleur is known for wild mussels. Other shellfish includes crabs, whelks, tiny clams, grey shrimps and large prawns dubbed *Demoiselles de Cherbourg*.

FRUIT AND VEGETABLES

Along with Camembert, the apple is pretty much the emblem of Normandy. As well as the varieties used to make cider, *pommeau* and Calvados *(see pp146-7)*, eating apples are also grown, such as *reine de reinette*, *boskoop* and *colleville*. Pears also thrive here, while cherries are an old speciality of Duclair and Jumièges.

Vegetable produce includes cabbages, cauliflower, carrots, leeks, potatoes, celery and celeriac. The leeks and carrots grown in the sandy soils around Créances both have a *label rouge (see p11)*.

Wild mushrooms thrive in the damp meadows and woodland; they include morels, ceps, chanterelles, field mushrooms and horn of plenty. This is also an area where button mushrooms *(champignons de Paris)* are cultivated, and they feature in many local recipes.

BAKED GOODS AND SWEETS

Needless to say, many of Normandy's baked goods feature apples, including *tarte Normande* and *bourdilot*. *Mirlitons*, little frangipane tarts, are a speciality of Rouen, as is *sucre de pomme*, long sticks of apple candy. Isigny-sur-Mer produces tasty butter caramels.

FISHING AND TRADING

Fishing has played a vital role in Norman life for centuries, as it still does today. Fécamp was the port from which fishermen once set off on months-long voyages to Newfoundland to fish for cod, and it is still a centre for the production of salt cod *(morue)*. It supplied Paris with fish via the Seine; Dieppe did so by a relay system of horses until the railways arrived in the 19th century. Dieppe's scallop shells were used as badges by pilgrims who set off from here on the route to Compostela. The merchants of Honfleur, meanwhile, were trading their salt cod in the East, in return for spices, including the cinnamon that pairs so well with Normandy apples in many dishes.

Sticks of *sucre de pomme*, from Rouen

Cheese & Dairy Produce

The white and brown-splashed vache Normande *is renowned for both the quantity and quality of its milk, which is made not only into Normandy's celebrated cheeses but also into thick* crème fraîche, *butter, yogurt,* fromage frais *and other goods such as sweets and jam.*

FROMAGERIES TO VISIT

Fromagerie Réaux 1 rue des Planquettes, 50430 Lessay (02 33 46 41 33; www.reaux.fr). Open by appointment Mon–Fri. This big dairy gathers milk from around 100 farms on the Cotentin peninsula for high-quality AOC Camembert sold under the *Réo* brand, which has often won prizes at the Salon de l'Agriculture. *Crème fraîche epaisse* and butter are also made. Visits allow you to see all the different stages of production through windows.

Domaine de Saint-Hippolyte 14100 St-Martin-de-la-Lieue (02 31 31 30 68). Open daily May–Sep; rest of year groups only. A dairy farm set around a beautiful Renaissance manor house. Learn about the *vache Normande*, see calves, and watch the afternoon milking, as well as seeing production (Mon–Fri am) of Livarot, Pont l'Evêque and Pavé d'Auge.

Fromager with a fine display of Normandy cheeses

Normandy cows, grazing on lush grass

CAMEMBERT

Marie Harel, a farmer's wife in the tiny village that bears its name, is credited with perfecting the recipe for Normandy's most celebrated cheese in 1791. It has been packed in wooden boxes since the end of the 19th century, beginning the tradition of decorative Camembert labels. Now widely imitated (Camembert, like Cheddar, is deemed a generic name), true Normandy Camembert has had an AOC *(see p11)* since 1985. Look for the label "Camembert de Normandie".

If buying at a specialist *fromagerie* or at a market stall, ask the stallholder to select a cheese for you – they will generally ask if you want it *plus ou moins affiné* (more or less ripe). If buying at a supermarket, don't be surprised to see customers opening the box, smelling the cheese (through the paper) and pressing it gently with a thumb to see how much "give" it has. Unripe, the cheese will be firm, with a chalky white interior; as it matures, the crust may develop reddish patches and the interior will start to turn more yellow, becoming runnier and smellier until cut edges literally ooze away. It is usually considered best for eating when it is runny around the edges but still has some of the chalkiness left in the centre.

LIVAROT AOC

Pungent Livarot is made only in a small southern area of the Pays d'Auge. It has a distinct whiff of the stable and a pronounced flavour. It is round, with an orange washed rind that becomes stickier as it ripens. The interior is springy, with small, evenly spaced holes.

PONT L'EVÊQUE AOC

Normandy's oldest cheese is a square, non-pressed, semi-soft cheese with a washed rind and slightly elastic interior with tiny holes. Although it gets stronger as it matures, it is milder and sweeter than Livarot.

NEUFCHÂTEL AOC

Made since the Middle Ages, its heart shape allegedly dates from the Hundred Years' War, when the women of Neufchâtel-en-Bray made them as tokens for their soldiers. A soft, mild, non-cooked, non-pressed cheese, with velvety white crust, it can be eaten young or aged.

PAVE D'AUGE

This ancient cheese from the Pays d'Auge is similar to Pont l'Evêque but with a slightly higher fat content, creamier texture and more pronounced taste. Many are still farm-made, although it does not have an AOC.

BRILLAT-SAVARIN

This is a rich, triple-cream cheese, invented in the 1930s and named after the 18th-century gourmet and politician Jean-Anthelme Brillat-Savarin.

PETIT-SUISSE

These tiny individual *fromage frais* are eaten with a spoon as dessert, sprinkled with caster sugar.

OTHER PRODUCE

Golden, unsalted butter and thick *crème fraîche* are key ingredients in Norman cuisine. *Confiture du lait*, or "milk jam", is another Normandy favourite.

Trays of fresh Camembert during the ripening process

CHEESE CIRCUITS AND MUSEUMS

Various routes cover Normandy cheese country. La Route du Camembert takes in a 50-km (30-mile) signposted circuit around Vimoutiers. Start from the Office de Tourisme, with its Musée du Camembert (02 33 39 30 29) giving explanations of Camembert making, and displaying tools and a huge collection of Camembert labels. There's another small museum in the nearby village of Camembert itself. Ask at the Offices de Tourisme of Neufchâtel-en-Bray and Livarot for leaflets on La Route de Neufchâtel and La Route de Livarot respectively. The making of Livarot is explained at the Musée du Fromage at Livarot (02 31 63 43 13).

Left Ripe Camembert **Centre** *Confiture du lait* **Right** Isigny butter

Regional Dishes

Normandy cuisine conjures up images of lashings of cream, butter and cheese, but, although these are indeed the pride of Normandy, the menu here is far more varied and not over-rich in the hands of a skilled chef. The region's seafood also makes delicious lighter dishes.

ON THE MENU

Beurré normand Apple and raisin cake
Bourdelot Pastry-wrapped apple dumpling
Côte de veau vallée de l'Auge Veal chop in mushrooms, cream and cider or Calvados
Gratin d'huîtres Oysters gratinéed with cider, cream and breadcrumbs
Maquereaux à la fécampoise Mackerel baked in cider with a mussel sauce
Marmite dieppoise Assorted fish stewed in cider or white wine with cream
Moules marinières Mussels in white wine and shallots
Raie au beurre Skate fried in butter, often with capers
Soupe à la graisse Vegetable soup with lard
Tarte aux cerises de Duclair Cherry tart on a whipped cream and flaky pastry base
Tarte normande Apple pie with frangipane
Teurgoule Creamy baked rice pudding with cinnamon

Sole Normande

THE NORMAN MENU

On the coast, you can feast on a vast platter of mixed shellfish or a simple plate of whelks or prawns. Oysters are usually eaten raw, but are sometimes gratinéed and served hot on the half shell. Scallops may be sauced with cream, sautéed with Calvados or served raw and thinly-sliced as "carpaccio". Countless restaurants serve *moules marinières* or *à la crème, raie au beurre* and *marmite dieppoise.* Mackerel can be soused in white wine or cider and served cold, or hot with a sauce of mussels. Sole may come *à la normande, meunière* (sautéed in butter) or just lightly grilled.

Chicken and veal appear frequently, often served *vallée de l'Auge* style. Rabbit, and ham or fish may be braised in cider and/or cream, while cream is also used in baked vegetable gratins or stirred into green beans or spinach just before serving. Superb Duclair duck is prepared *Rouennais* or simply roasted.

On Mont-St-Michel, La Mère Poulard draws visitors from the world over for its famous omelette. Farm-fresh eggs are beaten into a froth in huge copper pans before being cooked, so the result is thick and fluffy.

As with other Normandy cuisine, cream is a prominent feature. Apples appear in numerous guises, and you'll also find tarts and turnovers made with pears, as well as indulgent Duclair cherry tart and *teurgoule.*

Cinnamon-scented rice dessert *Teurgoule*

Left Duclair duck roasted with rosemary **Right** Tripes à la mode de Caen

Sole Normande

This grand fish dish combines all the best elements of Normandy's cuisine. Mussels are cooked with shallots, butter and white wine; oysters are poached; and sliced mushrooms are sautéed in butter. Sole fillets are baked in stock on a bed of chopped shallots, then removed and kept warm while the liquid is reduced and thickened with *crème fraîche* and egg yolks. The sole is served dressed in the sauce and garnished with the mussels, oysters, mushrooms and peeled prawns.

Canard Rouennais

This Rouen speciality is made with ducks from Duclair, which are strangled rather than bled. The duck is part-roasted, then jointed. The carcass is crushed to extract the blood and juices, which are blended with shallots and duck liver cooked in butter to make a rich, thick dark sauce, poured over the duck for the final roasting.

Tripes à la Mode de Caen

Caen-style tripe was supposedly created by a monk at Caen's beautiful Abbaye aux Hommes. Although it often features on menus, you can also buy it ready-made at many butchers. Strips of cows' stomach and intestine are cooked with calves' feet, onions or leeks, carrots, herbs and cider in a sealed casserole lined with slices of *couenne* (rind), in a very low oven for at least ten hours. It is usually served with boiled potatoes.

Poulet Vallée de l'Auge

Jointed chicken is browned in butter, then flambéed in Calvados. Shallots and cider are added and simmered gently. Thickly sliced mushrooms are sautéed in butter and poured, with their juices, into the pan, along with *crème fraîche* (some cooks insist this dish be made only with mushrooms and cream, not cider or Calvados).

Regional Dining

The following restaurants are among those serving regional dishes at reasonable prices:

Café de Paris
Cherbourg (see p151)
Domaine St-Paul
Lyons-la-Fôret (see p157)
Dormy House
Etretat (see p153)
La Bonne Marmite
Pont-St-Pierre (see p159)
La Gazette
Evreux (see p153)
La Mère Poulard
Mont-St-Michel (see p158)
Le Relais Gourmand
Pontorson (see p159)
Le Rouennais
Rouen (see p160)
La Villa des Houx
Aumale (see p148)
L'Escale du Vitou
Vimoutiers (see p163)
Wilson
Le Havre (see p156)

Preparing an omelette at La Mère Poulard

Regional Cider & Spirits

In springtime, when Normandy's nine million apple trees are in snowy white and pink blossom, the region surely resembles the Garden of Eden. Very few of these apples, however, are grown for eating; rather they are used for making either cider or Calvados.

Calvados bottles

BENEDICTINE

Based on a 16th-century elixir, Bénédictine liqueur is flavoured with 27 spices including cinnamon, hyssop, cardamom, myrrh, saffron, aloe and vanilla. The extravagant Bénédictine palace at Fécamp was built in 1882 by Alexandre le Grand and houses the distillery, a museum and an art gallery. 110 rue Alexandre le Grand, Fécamp (02 35 10 26 10), open daily early Feb to 31 Dec.

Benedictine château at Fécamp

CALVADOS

Normandy's famous apple brandy has not always enjoyed the reputation it has today. For a long time country folk would drink Calvados straight from the still or mix it with their morning coffee at the local bar. Meals in Normandy are notoriously copious and rich and many dishes are liberally doused with generous dollops of cream, so the custom of the *trou normand* remains an integral part of any gastronomic gathering in Normandy. It implies knocking back a shot of fiery, young Calvados in between courses, supposedly to make room for the next dish.

Calvados owes its complex flavour to the range of apples used to produce it. There are around 300 varieties in Normandy, of which 48 are used for Calvados. The secret of a successful blend lies in a combination of approximately 40 per cent sweet, 40 per cent bitter and 20 per cent sour apples. Calvados begins life as cider; it is then distilled in the spring following the harvest. However, cider destined to become Calvados, as opposed to drinking cider, is more difficult to make as it has to be perfectly dry. The spirit is left to age in oak barrels which have previously contained cider or, even better, sherry or port. Tannins in the wood will interact with this brandy, bringing roundness and colour, and tempering its fire until it becomes mellow with scents of spice, apple, vanilla, leather and caramel.

Cider apples

CALVADOS APPELLATIONS

Generic AOC Calvados may be made in an area extending from Cherbourg to north of Le Mans. Traditionally it is produced in a continuous still, like Armagnac. AOC Calvados du Pays d'Auge is more aristocratic. It must be made by the double distillation method used for Cognac, and the apples must be grown in the picturesque Auge countryside that radiates out from the chic seaside town of Deauville.

The region known as the Domfrontais has always been renowned for its abundance of pear trees. Cider used for distilling AOC Calvados du Domfrontais must contain a minimum of 30 per cent pears; in practice it often contains up to 70 per cent. It has a softer texture and a riper, rounder flavour than the other two AOCs.

Vintage Calvados

CALVADOS CATEGORIES

The quality of the finished product is determined not only by the blend and varieties of apples used, but also by how long the brandy is aged in wood. A minimum of two years is required for Calvados sold under the three-star, or three-apple, symbol (three years for Domfrontais). These are pale, sharp-edged spirits tasting of bitter apples. Three years in barrel earns it a *réserve* or *vieux* label; after four or five years it becomes *vieille réserve* or VSOP and after six, a range of honorific designations can be used, such as Extra, Napoléon or Hors d'Age. When a bottle shows an indication of age, then that must be the minimum age of the youngest spirit in the blend. If the bottle mentions a particular vintage, the Calvados has been distilled from a single harvest.

BEST PRODUCERS: CALVADOS

Adrien Camut (La Lande Saint-Léger), Les Chais du Verger Normand (Domfront), Château du Breuil (Le Breuil-en-Auge), Distillerie des Fiefs Ste-Anne (Coudray-Rabut), Roger Giard (Cambremer), Roger Groult (Saint Cyr-du-Ronceray)

CIDER

Half of all the apples grown in Normandy are used for making cider. The apples most suitable for Calvados are not necessarily those that make the best cider. Areas with clay or flinty soil are good for cider apples whereas those with silty soil will give superior fruit for Calvados. For more on cider, see Brittany *(pp170–71)*.

Cidre du Pays d'Auge was awarded AOC status in 1996. It is a pure juice, unpasteurized cider; the fermentation process must be entirely natural. Small producers tend not to filter their cider, so the presence of a light deposit is quite normal.

POMMEAU

Pommeau is made by adding Calvados to freshly pressed apple must, thereby stopping the fermentation process. It was a relatively obscure regional speciality until it was awarded appellation status in 1991. AOC Pommeau de Normandie has a rich, sweet apple flavour with balancing acidity. It can be drunk chilled as an aperitif or with cream- or apple-based dishes.

Typical Normandy orchard

Where to Eat & Stay

ALENCON
● **Au Petit Vatel**

72 pl Commandant Desmeulles, 61000
Map 2C5

📞 02 33 26 23 78
FAX 02 33 82 64 57
💳 AE, MC, V
🌑 Sun D, Wed 🍴 €€

*Don't be put off by the red neon over
the door! Hidden behind is an old stone
house with flowery balconies and good,
simple cooking like Camembert fritters
and Norman chicken legs with apples.*

ALENCON
● **Le Chapeau Rouge**

117 rue de Bretagne, 61000 **Map** 2C5

📞 02 33 26 57 53
💳 MC, V
🌑 Sun, Fri D, Sat L; 1 wk Aug,
2 wks Sep 🍴 €

*Appetizing fare with southern flair
makes for a change. Olive quiche and
rillettes are an excellent start, but the
desserts take the cake: poppy-seed tart
and Camembert-and-apple clafoutis
(p247). The hotel next door has the
same name but different management.*

ARGENTAN
▲ **La Renaissance**

20 ave de la 2ème Division Blindée,
61200 **Map** 2C4

📞 02 33 36 14 20
FAX 02 33 36 65 50
💳 AE, MC, V 🌑 Sun D, Mon; 2 wks
Aug 🍴 €€ 🍽 (12) €€

*Behind the prestigious name lies a
simple and busy establishment. Be sure
to book for a delicious dinner of beef
fillet in red wine sauce or choucroute
garnie (p119). Soft floral designs are a
sweet touch to the good-sized rooms.*

ARROMANCHES
▲ **La Marine**

Quai du Canada, 14117 **Map** 2B3

📞 02 31 22 34 19
FAX 02 31 22 98 80
🌐 www.hotel-de-la-marine.fr
💳 MC, V 🌑 mid-Dec–mid-Feb
🍴 €€ 🍽 (30) €€

*Family-run establishment with well-
equipped guestrooms and a very large
dining area. With oysters caught daily
just a few kilometres up the coast, it is
hard to find a fresher seafood platter.
Room 122 is the one to request.*

AUDRIEU
▲ **Château d'Audrieu**

On D158, 13km (8 miles) from Bayeux,
14250 **Map** 2B4

📞 02 31 80 21 52
FAX 02 31 80 24 73
🌐 www.chateaudaudrieu.com
💳 AE, MC, V
🌑 Mon, Tue–Fri L; mid-Dec–mid-Feb
🍴 €€€€€ 🍽 (29) €€€€

*Stunning 18th-century château with
heated pool. Warm andouille with tasty
sesame, onion and cider honey leads
into a nougat dessert with saffron.
Excellent guestrooms.*

AUMALE
▲ **Hôtel du Mouton Gras**

2 rue de Verdun, 76390 **Map** 3E3

📞 02 35 93 41 32
FAX 02 35 94 52 91
🌐 www.lemoutongras.com
💳 MC, V 🌑 3 wks Feb, end
Aug–mid-Sep 🍴 €€€ 🍽 (3) €€

*Excellent cuisine such as the memorable
steak with oyster sauce. A 17th-century
building complete with beams and a
courtyard, with guestrooms boasting
antique Norman furniture.*

AUMALE
▲ **La Villa des Houx**

6 ave Général de Gaulle, 76390 **Map** 3E3

📞 02 35 93 93 30
FAX 02 35 93 03 94
🌐 www.planete-b.fr/villa-des-houx
💳 MC, V 🌑 Oct–Apr: Sun D,
Mon L; Jan 🍴 € 🍽 (22) €€€

*For a refined taste of quintessential
Normandy, this old gendarmerie is
difficult to beat. The menu samples
the best of the region's cuisine, from
apricot foie gras for starters to Calvados
soufflé for dessert. The most comfortable
guestroom has a four-poster bed.*

AUNAY-SUR-ODON
▲ **Saint-Michel**

6–8 rue de Caen, 14260 **Map** 2B4

📞 02 31 77 63 16
FAX 02 31 77 05 83
💳 AE, MC, V 🌑 Mon L, Sep–Jun:
Sun D, Mon; mid-Jan–mid-Feb
🍴 €€ 🍽 (6) €€

*In the heart of Normandy, a roadside
restaurant serving lobster, the house
speciality, and seafood. The guestrooms
need refreshing, but are functional.*

AVRANCHES
▲ **La Croix d'Or**

83 rue de la Constitution, 50300
Map 2A4

📞 02 33 58 04 88
FAX 02 33 58 06 95
💳 AE, DC, MC, V 🌑 mid-Oct–Mar:
Sun D; Jan 🍴 €€€ 🍽 (28) €€

*Old stone cider press with decor from
days of yore. Guestrooms are simple
and look out on the flowered garden. Fine
seafood specialities in the dining room.*

BAGNOLES-DE-L'ORNE
● **Chez Marraine**

6 rue du Square, 61140 **Map** 2B5

📞 02 33 37 82 91
FAX 02 33 37 82 91
@ chez-marraine@wanadoo.fr
💳 MC, V
🌑 Wed; mid-Jan 🍴 €

*Everything is kept simple, friendly and
very traditional. Like the brawn (head
cheese) pâté, andouille salad and
rabbit terrine with apples and Calvados
and langoustines.*

BAGNOLES-DE-L'ORNE
▲ **Le Manoir du Lys**

Route de Juvigny, 61140 **Map** 2B5

📞 02 33 37 80 69
FAX 02 33 30 05 80
🌐 www.manoir-du-lys.fr
💳 AE, DC, MC, V 🌑 late Sep–May:
Sun D & Mon
🍴 €€€€ 🍽 (30) €€€€

*Andouille tarts, exquisite boudin noir
cappuccino, tomato mousse and spicy
blue lobster grilled to perfection make*

● Restaurant　■ Hotel　▲ Hotel / Restaurant

up the innovative menu at this former hunting pavilion. Contemporary rooms.

BALLEROY
● **Manoir de la Drôme**
129 rue Forges, 14490 **Map** 2B4
☎ 02 31 21 60 94
FAX 02 31 21 88 67
✉ AE, MC, V ● Sun D, Mon; 2 wks Feb, 1 wk Sep ⑪ €€€€
The manor has improved a lot in recent years, becoming a favourite spot for excellent meals. Try the terrine of foie gras with dried ham and the famous chocolate tart with sweet red wine sauce.

BARFLEUR
● **Du Phare**
42 rue St-Thomas Becket, 50760
Map 2B3
☎ 02 33 54 10 33
✉ MC, V
● Oct–Mar: Sun D, Mon
⑪ €
Quick service and excellent value make it well worth stopping off at the end of the D-Day route. Recharge with mussels, French fries and draught beer.

BARNEVILLE-CARTERET
▲ **La Marine**
11 rue de Paris, 50270 **Map** 2A3
☎ 02 33 53 83 31
FAX 02 33 53 39 60
✉ AE, MC, V ● Mar–Apr & Sep–Oct: Sun D & Mon; mid-Nov–Feb
⑪ €€€€ ◑ (29) €€€
The prices may seem high, but the location is worth it. So is the tripe, and the Grand Marnier soufflé. Guestrooms are decently decorated.

BAVENT
▲ **Hostellerie du Moulin du Pré**
Le Moulin du Pré, route de Gonneville en Auge, 14860 **Map** 2C4
☎ 02 31 78 83 68
FAX 02 31 78 21 05
✉ AE, DC, MC, V ● Sep–Jun: Sun D & Mon & Tue L; 2 wks Mar, Oct
⑪ €€€ ◑ (10) €€€
Remote old farm with rustic guestrooms. Duck thighs with preserves and chicken with mushrooms are just a few of the meats cooked over an open fire.

BAYEUX
▲ **Château de Sully**
Route de Port-en-Bessin, 14400 **Map** 2B4
☎ 02 31 22 29 48
FAX 02 31 22 64 77
@ chsully@club-internet.fr
✉ AE, DC, MC, V ● Mon–Wed L, Sat L; last wk Nov–first wk Mar
⑪ €€€€ ◑ (22) €€€€
Amazing attention to detail by the ever-present château staff. The menu features salmon tart with oysters and superb roasted blue lobster. Regal guestrooms.

BAYEUX
● **La Reine Mathilde**
47 rue St-Martin, 14400 **Map** 2B4
☎ 02 31 92 00 59
✉ MC, V ● Mon; 3 wks Nov ⑪ €
Old-fashioned bakery decked out in white Italian marble. Built in 1902, the murals and sculptures are magnificent. Tea served most days with plenty of pastries from which to choose.

BAYEUX
▲ **Le Lion d'Or**
71 rue St-Jean, 14400 **Map** 2B4
☎ 02 31 92 06 90
FAX 02 31 22 15 64
w www.liondor-bayeux.fr
✉ AE, DC, MC, V ● Sat L, Mon L; late Dec–Jan ⑪ €€€ ◑ (25) €€€€
For an upmarket experience, head to this old-fashioned hotel known for its quiet tranquillity. The ex-coaching inn serves locally raised suckling pig in a superbly decorated dining room. The guestrooms are perfectly peaceful.

BAZINCOURT-SUR-EPTE
▲ **Château Hôtel de la Rapée**
7km (4 miles) from Gisors, direction St-Denis-le-Ferment, 27140 **Map** 3E4
☎ 02 32 55 11 61
FAX 02 32 55 95 65
w www.hotel-la-rapee.com
✉ AE, MC, V
● Wed; last 2 wks Jan, Mar
⑪ €€€ ◑ (14) €€€€
An ideal country retreat and place to unwind while sampling some of Normandy's more unusual traditional recipes, such as stuffed lamb's trotters. Relaxing, comfortable guestrooms.

BEAUMESNIL
● **L'Etape Louis XIII**
Route Barre-en-Ouche, 27410 **Map** 3D4
☎ 02 32 44 44 72
FAX 02 32 45 53 84
✉ MC, V ● Tue, Sep–Jun: Wed; 2 wks Feb, last wk Jun
⑪ €€€
In a 1612 house, a fabulous dining experience. Complicated, gorgeous dishes such as pig's trotters galette with lobster sauce. Reserve a table well in advance at this popular eatery.

BELLEME
▲ **Domaine du Golf de Bellême**
Les Sablons, 61130 **Map** 3D5
☎ 02 33 85 13 13
FAX 02 33 73 00 17
w www.belleme.com
✉ AE, MC, V
⑪ €€€ ◑ (75) €€€€
Glitzy and glamorous restaurant set in a 16th-century priory. Sea bass in cream and cider sauce is delightful. The tastefully decorated guestrooms are perfect for a romantic retreat.

BENOUVILLE
● **Café Gondrée**
12 ave du Commandant Kieffer, 14970
Map 2C4
☎ 02 31 44 62 25
FAX 02 31 44 62 25
✉ MC, V ● Nov–Mar ⑪ €
The first building liberated by the allies, it is said the owner dug up 3,000 bottles of hidden Champagne to celebrate. The café now doubles as a small museum and souvenir shop. Don't miss the apple tart flambéed with Calvados.

BENOUVILLE
▲ **Manoir d'Hastings et la Pommeraie**
18 ave de Côte de Nacre, 14970
Map 2C4
☎ 02 31 44 62 43
FAX 02 31 44 76 18
✉ AE, DC, MC, V ● Sun D, Mon; last 3 wks Nov, 2 wks Feb
⑪ €€€€ ◑ (15) €€€
Exceptional food and accommodation in a 17th-century priory. Ingenious menu from appetizers to the tarte Tatin (p191).

BERNAY

● **Le Lapin Gourmand**

10 rue Gaston Folloppe, 27300 **Map** 3D4

℃ 02 32 43 42 32

◯ Sat D, Sun

🍴 €

A cross between a delicatessen and a bistro. Pull up a chair and choose from a menu that typically includes quiche, pastries and salads.

BERNIERES-SUR-MER

● **L'As de Trèfle**

420 rue Léopold Hettier, 14990 **Map** 2B3

℃ 02 31 97 22 60

FAX 02 31 97 22 60

◉ MC, V ◯ Mon, Oct–May: Sun D, Mon 🍴 €€€

Specialities include andouille with apples and Camembert cream, and sea bass with ratatouille (p400) and red mullet sauce. Save room for crème brûlée.

BEUVRON-EN-AUGE

● **Le Pavé d'Auge**

Pl du village, 14430 **Map** 2C4

℃ 02 31 79 26 71

FAX 02 31 39 04 45

ⓦ www.lepavedauge.com

◉ MC, V ◯ Jul–Aug: Mon, Sep–Apr: Mon,Tue; 1 wk Jul, Dec

🍴 €€€

A unique restaurant located in an old market hall. There's something for every palate, but the crab tart with aubergine (eggplant) steals the show.

BEUZEVILLE

▲ **Cochon d'Or**

1 pl Général de Gaulle, 27210 **Map** 2C3

℃ 02 32 57 70 46

FAX 02 32 42 25 70

ⓦ www.le-cochon-dor.fr

◉ MC, V ◯ Mon, Oct–Mar: Sun D; mid-Dec–mid-Jan

🍴 €€€ 🍽 (20) €€

Don't expect to be pampered. Here everything is kept simple (especially the guestrooms), but the food is great and comes in enormous portions.

BEUZEVILLE

▲ **Hôtel de la Poste**

60 rue Constant Fouché, 27210 **Map** 2C3

℃ 02 32 20 32 32

FAX 02 32 42 11 01

◉ AE, MC, V ◯ Thu, Tue L; Sep–Jun: Sun D 🍴 €€ 🍽 (15) €€

The archetypal French country retreat, with comfortable guestrooms, plus great sole meunière and pepper steak.

BEZANCOURT

▲ **Château du Landel**

10km (6 miles) southwest of Gournay on D316 and D62, 76220 **Map** 3D3

℃ 02 35 90 16 01

FAX 02 35 90 62 47

◉ AE, MC, V ◯ Mon L, Thu L, Sep–Jun: Sun D; mid-Nov–mid-Mar

🍴 €€€ 🍽 (17) €€€€

Today the castle boasts a pool, tennis court and delicious food such as haddock mousse and chocolate mousse cake. Large guestrooms with all the frills.

BOURGTHEROULDE-INFREVILLE

▲ **Auberge de la Corne D'Abondance**

6 pl de la Mairie, 27520 **Map** 3D4

℃ 02 35 78 68 01

FAX 02 35 78 50 41

@ la.corne.d.abondance@wanadoo.fr

◉ MC, V ◯ Sun D, Mon

🍴 €€ 🍽 (11) €€

Charming rooms. The unusual menu samples some of Normandy's forgotten favourites, such as cod with cider and snails baked in garlic.

BREHAL

▲ **Le Relais des Iles**

Coudeville-plage, 50290 **Map** 2A4

℃ 02 33 61 66 66

FAX 02 33 61 43 50

◉ AE, MC, V ◯ Nov–Mar

🍴 €€€ 🍽 (47) €€

The façade is lacking, but the guestrooms are bright and colourful and have views of the Chausey Islands. Seafood menu.

BRETEUIL-SUR-ITON

● **Le Grain de Sel**

72 pl Lafitte, 27160 **Map** 3D4

℃ 02 32 29 70 61

FAX 02 32 29 70 61

◉ MC, V ◯ Sun D, Mon, Tue D; 2 wks Aug 🍴 €

An intimate and unpretentious eatery. The varied menu changes each Friday; however, salmon is a favourite option.

BRICQUEBEC

▲ **Hostellerie du Vieux Château**

4 cours du Château, 50260 **Map** 2A3

℃ 02 33 52 24 49

FAX 02 33 52 62 71

ⓦ www.chateauxcountry.com

◉ AE, MC, V ◯ late Dec–Jan

🍴 €€ 🍽 (17) €€€

If you're spending the night in the castle, ask for room 2, where Queen Victoria once stayed. Medieval-style restaurant, with rustic cooking.

BRIONNE

▲ **Le Logis de Brionne**

1 pl St-Denis, 27800 **Map** 2D4

℃ 02 32 44 81 73

FAX 02 32 45 10 92

◉ AE, MC, V ◯ Sun D, Mon, Oct–Apr: Sat L; 2 wks Feb, 2 wks Aug

🍴 €€€ 🍽 (12) €€

A country guesthouse with gourmet meals like crayfish with fennel, and foie gras terrine with dates. The rooms are tastefully decorated with dark pine. Gather around the piano and fireplace.

BRIOUZE

▲ **Hôtel Sophie**

5 pl Albert 1er, 61220 **Map** 2C4

℃ 02 33 62 82 82

FAX 02 33 62 82 83

◉ MC, V ◯ Fri D, Sat L; mid-Aug–first wk Sep, last wk Dec

🍴 €€ 🍽 (9) €€

Savour the leg of lamb with mustard, roast beef with vegetables, grilled beef with mashed potatoes and plenty of fish. Just the right balance of flowers and pastels in the guestrooms.

CAEN

● **Le Bouchon du Vaugueux**

12 rue Graindorge, 14000 **Map** 2C4

℃ 02 31 44 26 26

◉ MC, V ◯ Aug 🍴 €

One of the best-kept secrets in the Vaugueux, this place may be small, but it packs a mighty culinary punch. The menu features snail cappuccino and rhubarb clafoutis (p247).

CAEN

● **Le P'tit B**

15 rue du Vaugueux, 14000 **Map** 2C4

● Restaurant   ■ Hotel   ▲ Hotel / Restaurant

C 02 31 93 50 76
FAX 02 31 93 29 63
@ leptitb@wanadoo.fr
€ DC, MC, V ● Sun, Mon; 2 wks
Jan, 2 wks Aug **11** €€€€
Adventurous food aficionados will relish
a visit to Michel Bruneau's restaurant.
Exposed stonework and wooden beams
set the scene. Perennial favourites
include tarte normande *with camembert.*

CAEN
● **Le Costa**
32 bis quai Vendeuvre, 14000 **Map** 2C4
C 02 31 86 28 28
W www.lecosta.fr
€ AE, MC, V ● Sun; 1 wk Aug
11 €€€
This designer restaurant is a great spot
for people-watching – and innovative
reworkings of traditional recipes.

CAEN
● **Le Pressoir**
3 ave Henri Chéron, 14000 **Map** 2C4
C 02 31 73 32 71
FAX 02 31 73 32 71
€ AE, MC, V ● Sun D, Mon, Sat L; 2
wks Feb, 3 wks Aug **11** €€€€
Don't let the overcrowded furnishings
detract from the masterful cooking. A
nice balance of meat, poultry and fish.

CAEN
● **Maître Corbeau**
8 rue Buquet, 14000 **Map** 2C4
C 02 31 93 93 00
FAX 02 31 94 26 33
€ MC, V ● Sun, Mon L, Sat L; 2 wks
Aug **11** €€
Each dish (even the desserts) contains
cheese. One the menu highlights is the
Roquefort steak. Reservations essential.

CAILLOUET-ORGEVILLE
● **Deux Tilleuls**
11 Grand Rue, 27120 **Map** 3D4
C 02 32 36 90 48
FAX 02 32 36 90 48
€ MC, V ● Mon D, Wed; last wk
Feb–Mar, last wk Aug–mid-Sep **11** €
Great value food and a friendly welcome
for travellers. The menu covers all the
Norman staples and is finished off with
a good selection of desserts.

CAILLY-SUR-EURE
▲ **Auberge des 2 Sapins**
Rue Abreuvoir, 27490 **Map** 3D4
C 02 32 67 75 13
FAX 02 32 67 73 62
W www.hoteldesdeuxsapins.fr
€ MC, V ● Rue de la Mairie
11 €€ ● (15) €€
The dining room looks out over well-
tended gardens. All the regional
favourites are represented, from foie
gras as a starter to apples and Calvados
for dessert. Light and airy guestrooms.

CAMBREMER
● **Au Petit Normand**
Pl de l'Eglise, 14340 **Map** 2C4
C 02 31 32 03 20
€ MC, V ● Mon; 2 wks Jan, 1st wk
Nov **11** €
From the atmosphere to the cooking,
everything is rustic. Highlights include
steak with Camembert and Calvados,
apple sorbet and cinnamon apples.

CAMETOURS
● **Auberge des Tisserands**
Le Bourg, 50570 **Map** 2B4
C 02 33 46 10 10
FAX 02 33 46 26 21
€ MC, V ● Sun D, Mon, Wed D
11 €€€
Alpine cookery dominates the menu with
dishes pairing potatoes with dried fruits
and meat. The house speciality is jambon
au foin *(ham cooked in hay).*

CAMPINGS
▲ **Le Petit Coq au Champs**
La Pommeraie Sud, 27500 **Map** 3D4
C 02 32 41 04 19
FAX 02 32 56 06 25
W www.lepetitcoqauxchamps.fr
€ AE, DC, MC, V ● Nov–Mar: Sun D,
Mon; Jan **11** €€€ ● (12) €€€€
Grilled langoustines, pigeon wrapped in
ham and crêpes stuffed with pears whet
your appetite. Cosy guestrooms in this
thatched country house.

CARENTAN
▲ **Auberge Normande**
11 bd Verdun, 50500 **Map** 2B3
C 02 33 42 28 28
FAX 02 33 42 00 72

€ AE, MC, V ● Mon, Sep–Jun: Sun
D, Wed D **11** €€€ ● (2) €€
Very rustic restaurant serving oysters
with scrambled eggs, lamb, and apple
sorbet with Calvados. Simple rooms.

CEAUX
▲ **Au P'tit Quinquin**
Les Forges, route de Courtils, 50220
Map 2A5
C 02 33 70 97 20
FAX 02 33 70 97 42
W www.au-petit-quinquin.com
€ MC, V ● Sun D, Sep–Jun: Mon;
Jan–mid-Feb **11** € ● (15) €
The food, not the guestrooms, is the
main attraction here. Try the flavourful
fish with lemongrass and cream.

CHAMPEAUX
▲ **Au Marquis de Tombelaine**
Route de Carolles, 50530 **Map** 2A4
C 02 33 61 85 94
FAX 02 33 61 21 52
€ MC, V **11** €€€ ● (6) €€
With impressive views of Mont-St-
Michel, this is a great spot to while
away an afternoon or watch the setting
sun. Linger over hot oysters in cider or
roasted sea bass. Uninspired rooms.

CHERBOURG
● **Café de Paris**
40 quai de Caligny, 50100 **Map** 2A3
C 02 33 43 12 36
FAX 02 33 43 98 49
€ AE, MC, V ● Oct–May: Sun D &
Mon; 2 wks Mar, 2 wks Nov **11** €€
A Cherbourg institution for fish and
enormous seafood platters. An ideal stop
for lunch before cruising the coastline.

CHERBOURG
● **Le Faitout**
25 rue de la Tour Carrée, 50100 **Map** 2A3
C 02 33 04 25 04
FAX 02 33 04 60 36
€ MC, V ● Sun, Mon L **11** €
Bistro culture par excellence. Family-
style cooking: veal kidneys with mustard
and cream, cod and grilled sardines.

CLECY
▲ **Hostellerie du Moulin du Vey**
Le Vey, 14570 **Map** 2B4

[PHONE] 02 31 69 71 08
[FAX] 02 31 69 14 14
[WWW] www.moulinduvey.com
[CARDS] AE, DC, MC, V [●] Nov–Mar: Sun D
& Mon L; Dec–Jan (except 31 Dec)
[EAT] €€€ [●] (12) €€€

*Gorgeous old wheat mill with romantic
guestrooms and well-kept gardens.
Beware when booking: there are two
annexes to the main building. Don't
miss the refreshing, regional cooking.*

COLLEVILLE-MONTGOMERY
● La Ferme St-Hubert
3 rue de la Mer, 14880 **Map** 2C4
[PHONE] 02 31 96 35 41
[FAX] 02 31 97 45 79
[CARDS] AE, DC, MC, V [●] Sep–Jun: Sun D
& Mon; late Dec–mid-Jan [EAT] €€€

*Amid grazing fields lies the best-kept
secret of the Côte de Nacre. Specialities
are sautéed foie gras and fresh fish, or
choose a lobster from the tank.*

CONCHES-EN-OUCHE
▲ Hôtel du Cygne
2 rue Paul Guilbaud, 27190 **Map** 3D4
[PHONE] 02 32 30 20 60
[FAX] 02 32 30 45 73
[CARDS] AE, MC, V [●] Sun D, Mon; Feb, 1
wk Oct [EAT] € [●] (13) €€

*With wonderful views overlooking the
river Rouloir, the guestrooms here are
the epitome of Norman style. Menu
favourites are duck and pistachio terrine,
venison, strawberries in red wine, and
caramelized apple mousse with Calvados.*

CONDEAU-AU-PERCHE
▲ Moulin et Château de Villeray
Villeray, 61110 **Map** 3D5
[PHONE] 02 33 73 30 22
[FAX] 02 33 73 38 28
[CARDS] AE, DC, MC, V
[EAT] €€€€ [●] (25) €€€€

*In summer, the restaurant occupies the
mill, and in winter it is located in the
castle. Duck and monkfish with garden
vegetables grace the menu. Some
rooms have four-poster beds, others
have extra-special bathrooms.*

CONNELLES
▲ Moulin de Connelles
40 route d'Amfreville sous les Monts,

27430 **Map** 3D4
[PHONE] 02 32 59 53 33
[FAX] 02 32 59 21 83
[WWW] www.moulindeconnelles.com
[CARDS] AE, DC, MC, V [●] Sun D, Oct–Apr:
Mon [EAT] €€€€ [●] (13) €€€€

*A popular hotel that's synonymous with
luxury. Sample bream with citrus and
ginger or duck in raspberry vinegar. Pool.*

CORMEILLES
▲ L'Auberge du Président
70 rue de l'Abbaye, 27260 **Map** 2C4
[PHONE] 02 32 57 80 37
[FAX] 02 32 57 88 31
[@] aubergedupresident@wanadoo.fr
[CARDS] AE, MC, V [●] Sun D, Jun–Sep:
Mon D, Oct–May: Mon; first 2wks Jan
[EAT] €€ [●] (13) €€€

*No-nonsense dishes include snails in
Camembert, whiskey-flambéed scallops
and chocolate fondue. Basic rooms.*

COSQUEVILLE
▲ Le Bouquet de Cosqueville
38 hameau Remond, 50330 **Map** 2A3
[PHONE] 02 33 54 32 81
[FAX] 02 33 54 63 38
[WWW] www.bouquetdecosqueville.com
[CARDS] MC, V [●] Tue, Sep–Jun: Tue, Wed;
Jan, 1 wk Feb, last wk Jun
[EAT] €€€ [●] (7) €€

*Fresh seafood in generous portions,
such as lobster cooked in cider, at this
elegant restaurant. Impressively long
wine list. Guestrooms have sea views.*

COUTANCES
● Le Vieux Coutances
55 rue Geoffroy Montbray, 50200 **Map** 2A4
[PHONE] 02 33 47 94 78
[CARDS] AE, MC, V [●] Sun D, Mon; 1 wk
Jan, 2 wks Nov [EAT] €

*Former post house with sought-after
cuisine, often called the best restaurant
in Coutances. The cod in pastry with
baby spinach with a light curry flavour is
a long-standing favourite of the owner.*

CREPON
▲ La Ferme de la Rançonnière
Route d'Arromanches, D22, 14480
Map 2B4
[PHONE] 02 31 22 21 73
[FAX] 02 31 22 98 39

[WWW] www.ranconniere.fr
[CARDS] AE, MC, V [●] 3 wks Jan
[EAT] €€€€ [●] (45) €€€

*A sleepy farmyard guesthouse that has
expanded to become a chic restaurant.
Savour pork with pear vinaigrette or
guinea fowl with citrus and peppers.
Charming stone walls in rooms.*

CRESSERONS
● La Valise Gourmande
7 rue de Lion, 14440 **Map** 2C4
[PHONE] 02 31 37 39 10
[FAX] 02 31 37 59 13
[CARDS] AE, MC, V [●] Sun D, Mon; 2 wks
Mar, 2 wks Oct [EAT] €€€€

*An 18th-century priory-cum-restaurant.
The tarte Tatin (p191) of andouille and
beef fillet with grapefruit and potato
gratin are memorable.*

CREVECOEUR-EN-AUGE
▲ Auberge du Cheval Blanc
44 rue St-Pierre, 14340 **Map** 2C4
[PHONE] 02 31 63 03 28
[FAX] 02 31 63 41 58
[CARDS] MC, V [●] Mon, Tue L; mid-
Jan–mid-Feb [EAT] €€€ [●] (6) €€

*Menu favourites are grilled meats, trout
with sorrel and tête-de-veau. Rooms are
small and overpriced.*

DEAUVILLE
● Ciro's
Planches de Deauville, Laies de Mer,
14800 **Map** 3D3
[PHONE] 02 31 14 31 31
[FAX] 02 31 98 66 71
[WWW] www.casino-deauville.fr
[CARDS] AE, DC, MC, V [●] Jan [EAT] €€€€

*With a wonderful waterfront panorama,
there's only one thing that can obscure
the view, and that's the mountainous
seafood platter. But this comes at a price.*

DIEPPE
● Bucherie
Rue Sygogne, Les Vertus, St-Aubin-sur-
Scie, 2km (1.5 miles) south of Dieppe
on N127, 76550 **Map** 3D3
[PHONE] 02 35 84 83 10
[CARDS] AE, MC, V [●] Sun D, Mon, Tue D; 1
wk Feb, 1 wk Aug, 1 wk Dec [EAT] €€€

*Attractive restaurant with an open fire in
winter and a large terrace for summer*

● Restaurant   ■ Hotel   ▲ Hotel / Restaurant

dining. It's a hit with fish lovers, who enjoy the simple but delicious grilled or baked cod and monkfish. Surprisingly, no shellfish is served.

DIEPPE
▲ Le Windsor

18 bd de Verdun, 76200 **Map** 3D3

📞 02 35 84 15 23

FAX 02 35 84 74 52

🇼 www.hotelwindsor.fr

💳 AE, DC, MC, V ⬤ Jan

🍴 €€€ 🍷 (48) €€

The multi-storey tower of lobster, crabs, oysters and shrimps, which constitutes the Plateau Wilson, is delicious. Guestrooms are basic; the only truly outstanding factor is the Channel view.

DIEPPE
● Méli Mélo

55 quai Henri IV, 76200 **Map** 3D3

📞 02 35 06 15 12 🍴 €

A short walk from the port, this is a great little bistro that specializes in a wide range of salads and tasty pastries. An ideal place to take children, and with a fast turnover and take-away service it makes for a perfect meal on the run.

DIVES-SUR-MER
● Chez le Bougnat

27 bis rue Gaston Manneville, 14160 **Map** 2C4

📞 02 31 91 06 13

FAX 02 31 91 09 87

🇼 www.chezlebougnat.com

💳 MC, V ⬤ Jul–Aug: Tue & Wed D, Sep–Jun: Fri D & Sat D 🍴 €

Crammed with antiques and bric-a-brac, this lively restaurant offers a convivial atmosphere. Expect good food, good wine and good conversation. Try the smoked trout with warm potato salad.

DOMFRONT
● Auberge du Grandgousier

1 pl de la Liberté, 61700 **Map** 2B5

📞 02 33 38 97 17

💳 MC, V ⬤ Mon D, Wed D, Thu; Feb, Oct 🍴 €

The speciality here is stuffed seafood. The gratin of cockles is a permanent menu fixture. Fresh pastries and a welcoming air round out the experience.

DOUDEVILLE
▲ Le Relais du Puits St-Jean

Rue Henri Delanos, 76560 **Map** 3D3

📞 02 35 96 50 99

FAX 02 35 95 61 82

💳 MC, V ⬤ mid-Feb–mid-Mar

🍴 €€ 🍷 (4) €€

A smart 19th-century town house in the French capital of linen; highly regarded. House specialities, such as pressed duck, cost a fraction of their Parisian counterparts. Luxurious guestrooms.

DUCEY
▲ Auberge de la Sélune

2 rue St-Germain, 50220 **Map** 2B5

📞 02 33 48 53 62

FAX 02 33 48 90 30

💳 AE, DC, MC, V ⬤ Oct–Mar: Mon; mid-Jan–mid-Feb

🍴 €€ 🍷 (20) €€

Growing popularity means it is often difficult to get a table. The menu has a steady focus on seafood. Simple but comfortable guestrooms.

EQUEURDREVILLE-HAINNEVILLE
● La Gourmandine

24 rue Surcouf, 50120 **Map** 2A3

📞 02 33 93 41 26

FAX 02 33 93 41 26

💳 AE, DC, MC, V ⬤ Sun D, Mon, Tue D; Jul, last 2 wks Dec 🍴 €€€

Garden dining in summer. The house speciality is oysters in Beaumes de Venise, a white dessert wine. A rare vegetarian menu is available.

ETRETAT
▲ Dormy House

Route du Havre, 76790 **Map** 2C3

📞 02 35 27 07 88

FAX 02 35 29 86 19

🇼 www.etretat.net/dormy-house

💳 AE, MC, V

🍴 €€€ 🍷 (61) €€€

Perched on a clifftop overlooking the rugged bay, the views from the terrace are rewarding. With the sea below, it's fitting that the menu boasts an impressive catch of seafood, and there's an inspired selection of local cheeses. Most of the nautically-themed guestrooms overlook the sea.

ETRETAT
▲ Le Donjon

Chemin St-Clair, 76790 **Map** 2C3

📞 02 35 27 08 23

FAX 02 35 29 92 24

🇼 www.ledonjon-etretet.fr

💳 AE, DC, MC, V

🍴 €€€€ 🍷 (11) €€€€€

Imposing castle towering over the town. Minute attention to detail in both food and accommodation. Beef fillet with thyme sauce and truffle oil is a delight. Guestrooms are individually furnished.

EU
▲ Le Domaine de Joinville

Route du Tréport, 76260 **Map** 3D2

📞 02 35 50 52 52

FAX 02 35 50 27 37

🇼 www.domainejoinville.com

💳 AE, DC, MC, V ⬤ Sep–Jun: Sun, Mon, Tue 🍴 €€€€ 🍷 (25) €€€€

A world of luxury: swimming pool, hot tubs, fitness centre and a superb restaurant. The chef turns out roasted scallops with asparagus and thyme sauce and gigot de sept heures (p191). Stylish, well-presented guestrooms.

EU
▲ Maine

20 ave de la Gare, 76260 **Map** 3D2

📞 02 35 86 16 64

FAX 02 35 50 86 25

🇼 www.hotel-maine.com

💳 AE, MC, V ⬤ Sun D; last 2 wks Aug–1st 2 wks Sep

🍴 €€ 🍷 (18) €€

A wonderful turn-of-the-20th-century setting and a menu that charms most gastronomes. Dishes such as mackerel with aubergine (eggplant) compote and the house speciality beef terrine with onion marmalade. Guestrooms show the owner's care and personal touches.

EVREUX
● La Gazette

7 rue St-Sauveur, 27000 **Map** 3D4

📞 02 32 33 43 40

FAX 02 32 31 38 87

💳 AE, MC, V ⬤ Sun, Sat L; 3 wks Aug 🍴 €€

You'd be hard pushed to find a better place than this. Everything on the menu, from bread to ice cream, is prepared in the kitchens. Dishes include boudin noir with cider, and Camembert fritters.

EVREUX

▲ **Normandy Hotel**

37 rue Edouard Feray, 27000 **Map** 3D4

📞 02 32 33 14 40

FAX 02 32 31 24 74

@ norman.hotel@wanadoo.fr

💳 MC, V ● Sun; 2nd wk Aug

🍴 €€ 🍷 (20) €€€

This former post house has an open fireplace. A fantastic menu complements the surroundings, especially the chef's favourite – beef fillet with Roquefort. Rustic Normand-style rooms.

FALAISE

● **Fine Fourchette**

52 rue Georges Clémenceau, 14700

Map 2C4

📞 02 31 90 08 59

FAX 02 31 90 00 83

💳 AE, MC, V ● Sep–Jun: Tue D; 2 wks Feb, 1st wk Mar 🍴 €€€

The chef regularly spends time in the kitchens of top Parisian restaurants then comes back to apply his knowledge. Duckling fillet with spiced honey and duck with apples are two highlights.

FECAMP

▲ **Auberge de la Rouge**

Route du Havre, St-Léonard, 76400

Map 2C3

📞 02 35 28 07 59

FAX 02 35 28 70 55

🌐 www.auberge-rouge.com

💳 AE, DC, MC, V ● Sun D, Mon; 1 wk Jan, 2 wk Feb

🍴 €€€ 🍷 (8) €€

An established favourite with locals, this auberge's reputation is built on good food and a lively atmosphere, especially at weekends. Ever-popular dishes include the grilled John Dory with asparagus. There's also a lengthy wine list. Modern design in the guestrooms.

FERMANVILLE

● **Le Moulin**

16 vallée des Moulins, 50840 **Map** 2A3

📞 02 33 54 27 28

💳 MC, V ● Mon 🍴 €

First-rate food at this crêperie serving pizzas, galettes and crêpes using fine regional products including seafood.

FLERS

● **Auberge des Vieilles Pierres**

Le Buisson Corblin, 2km (1.25 miles) on D924 direction Briouze, 61100 **Map** 2D4

📞 02 33 65 06 96

FAX 02 33 65 80 72

💳 AE, MC, V ● Mon, Tue; 2 wks Feb, 3 wks Aug 🍴 €€

Considered among the best in the area, this cute auberge serves salt cod with leeks, braised guinea fowl with cabbage and wild boar terrine with pistachios.

FORGES-LES-EAUX

▲ **La Paix**

15 rue de Neufchâtel, 76440 **Map** 3E3

📞 02 35 90 51 22

FAX 02 35 09 83 62

@ hotelapaix@wanadoo.fr

💳 AE, DC, MC, V ● Jul–Sep: Mon L, Oct–Jun: Sun D & Mon L

🍴 € 🍷 (18) €€

The desserts are where the chefs showcase their culinary flair, with everything from nougat ice cream with Benedictine liqueur to apple and Calvados omelettes. Dated decor in the spacious guestrooms.

FOURGES

● **Le Moulin de Fourges**

38 rue du Moulin, 27630 **Map** 3E4

📞 02 32 52 12 12

FAX 02 32 52 92 56

🌐 www.moulin-de-fourges.com

💳 AE, MC, V

● Sun D, Mon; Nov–Mar

🍴 €€€

Pretty watermill with a terrace and views of the river. Mixture of innovation and classics: tête-de-veau (p268), turbot with vanilla and an intriguing wine list.

FRICHEMESNIL

▲ **Au Souper Fin**

Place de L'Eglise, 76690 **Map** 3D3

📞 02 35 33 33 88

FAX 02 35 33 50 42

💳 MC, V ● Wed, Thu, Oct–Mar: Sun D 🍴 €€ 🍷 (2) €€

At this petite spot, you'll have a warm welcome and a friendly introduction to

this sleepy village. Whenever possible the chef indulges his passion for seafood.

GIVERNY

● **Les Jardins de Giverny**

1 rue du Milieu, 27620 **Map** 3E4

📞 02 32 21 60 80

FAX 02 32 51 93 77

🌐 www.jardins-giverny.com

💳 AE, MC, V ● Mar–Oct: Mon; Nov–Dec: Mon, Tue; Jan–Feb 🍴 €€€

A great place to stop and reflect on the treasures in nearby Monet's house. The menu displays as much creative flair as one of the great Impressionist's paintings. Expect traditional Norman recipes with an innovative and contemporary spin.

GOUPILLERES

▲ **Auberge du Pont de Brie**

Halte de Grimbosq, 14210 **Map** 2BA

📞 02 31 79 37 84

FAX 02 31 79 87 22

🌐 www.pontdebrie.com

💳 MC, V ● Feb–Mar: Sun D, Mar–Oct: Mon, Mar–Jun & Sep–Oct: Tue, Nov–Dec: Sat & Sun; mid-Dec–mid-Feb 🍴 € 🍷 (7) €€

An extremely good-value spot with a terrace. The fixed price menu du terroir includes foie gras, meat, cheese and a glass of Calvados. Basic guestrooms.

GRANDCAMP-MAISY

● **La Marée**

5 quai Henri Chévron, 14450 **Map** 2B3

📞 02 31 21 41 00

FAX 02 31 21 44 55

@ lamaree@wanadoo.fr

💳 AE, MC, V 🍴 €€€

Seafood restaurant where the house speciality is sole meunière with Isigny-sur-Mer butter. Prices are honest and the seaside decor pleasant.

GRANVILLE

● **La Citadelle**

34 rue du Port, 50406 **Map** 2A4

📞 02 33 50 34 10

FAX 02 33 50 15 36

🌐 www.restaurant-la-citadelle.com

💳 MC, V ● Oct–Mar: Tue & Wed; 3 wks Feb, 3 wks Dec 🍴 €€

The charm and reliable cooking are enough to draw anyone over the bridge

● Restaurant ■ Hotel ▲ Hotel / Restaurant

to the only place in town that guarantees 300g (slightly more than 8oz) of sole meunière on your plate. Try the sweet icy Calvados soufflé.

HAMBYE

▲ Auberge de l'Abbaye d'Hambye

5 route de l'Abbaye, D51 south of Hambye, 50450 **Map** 2A4

C 02 33 61 42 19

FAX 02 33 61 00 85

MC, V ● Sun D, Mon; 2 wks Feb, 2 wks Oct **¶¶** €€ ● (7) €€

Serenely calm abbey serving hearty, good-value meals. On the hotel side, a makeover is due, but guestrooms are comfortable with excellent views.

HAUTEVILLE-SUR-MER

▲ Chez Maryvonne

3 ave de l'Aumesle, 50590 **Map** 2A4

C 02 33 47 52 11

FAX 02 33 47 68 18

AE, MC, V ● Tue D; 2nd half Dec **¶¶** € ● (3) €

Friendly bistro serving simple seafood and poached fish in Béarnaise sauce. Perfect stop for a quick family lunch, just steps from the beach. Sea-themed rooms are neatly refurbished.

HEBECREVON

▲ Château de la Roque

Route de Périers, D77 6km (4 miles) west of St-Lô, 50180 **Map** 2B4

C 02 33 57 33 20

FAX 02 33 57 51 20

W www.au-chateau.com/Roque.htm

MC, V ● L; Oct–Apr: Sun **¶¶** €€ ● (15) €€€

Guestrooms suit the 16th-century manor. Booking essential; best tables are close to the chimney. Luxurious and tasty dishes, especially wood-roasted meats.

HERICOURT-EN-CAUX

● Saint Denis

2 rue St-Mellon, 76560 **Map** 3D3

C 02 35 96 55 23

MC, V ● Tue, Wed; 2 last wks Oct **¶¶** €€

Popular and often packed eatery. Good-value menu offering avocado mousse, grilled trout, a fine cheese platter and an imaginative rhubarb sorbet.

HEUGUEVILLE-SUR-SIENNE

● Le Mascaret

16 rue de la Sienne, 50200 **Map** 2A4

C 02 33 45 86 09

FAX 02 33 07 90 01

MC, V

● Sun D, Mon; Jan

¶¶ €€€

Gourmet restaurant in an old presbytery. The chef uses rare herbs, spices and flowers in his compositions. If you are hungry, try the seven-course menu.

HONFLEUR

▲ L'Absinthe

10 quai de Quarantaine, 14600 **Map** 2C3

C 02 31 89 39 00

FAX 02 31 89 53 60

W www.absinthe.fr

AE, DC, MC, V ● mid-Nov–mid-Dec **¶¶** €€€ ● (7) €€€€

Once the quarters of Honfleur's English guards, this renovated fisherman's house today provides much more salubrious lodging. Highlights include grilled langoustines, sea bass and turbot with orange and bacon.

HONFLEUR

▲ Les Maisons de Léa

Pl Ste-Catherine, 14600 **Map** 2C3

C 02 31 14 49 49

FAX 02 31 89 28 61

@ lesmaisonsdelea@wanadoo.fr

AE, MC, V **¶¶** € ● (30) €€€€

Stone walls covered in vines give a cottage-like feel. The tea room is a popular stop for thirsty travellers, serving good tea and a tasty apple crumble. Guestrooms are warm and cosy.

HOULGATE

▲ Au 1900

17 rue des Bains, 14510 **Map** 2C4

C 02 31 28 77 77

FAX 02 31 28 08 07

W www.hotel-1900.fr

AE, MC, V ● Jan, last wk Nov, 2 wks Dec **¶¶** €€ ● (16) €€€

A family-run hotel that whisks you back to the Belle Epoque. While the interior evokes nostalgia, the menu is distinctly contemporary, covering everything from lobster flambé to a superb selection of homemade sweets.

IGOVILLE

● Auberge du Pressoir

RN15, zi Fort, 27460 **Map** 3D4

C 02 35 23 27 77

FAX 02 35 23 28 73

@ aubergepressoir@aol.com

MC, V ● Sun D, Mon D, Sep–Mar: Wed D **¶¶** €

Once home to the local governor, this is a handsome venue with an exciting menu that has a creative approach to traditional Norman cuisine. You'll also find that your euros go a very long way.

ILES CHAUSEY

▲ Hôtel du Fort et des Iles

100m on left after ferry terminal, 50400 **Map** 2A4

C 02 33 50 25 02

FAX 02 33 50 25 02

AE, DC, MC, V ● Mon; Sep–mid-Apr **¶¶** €€ ● (8) €€€

The only hotel on the island. Half- or full-board is compulsory, and non-residents should book ahead for meals. All seafood is straight from the boat.

INGOUVILLE-SUR-MER

▲ Les Hêtres

24 rue des Fleurs, 76460 **Map** 3D3

C 02 35 57 09 30

FAX 02 35 57 09 31

W www.leshetres.com

AE, MC, V ● Mon, Tue; mid-Jan–mid-Feb

¶¶ €€€ ● (4) €€€€

The pretty, beamed 1627 house hides luxurious rooms. In the innovative restaurant, find Brittany langoustines with Chinese-style cabbage and quail with a beetroot and Parmesan cake.

ISIGNY-SUR-MER

▲ Hôtel de France

13 rue Emile Demagny, 14230 **Map** 2B3

C 02 31 22 00 33

FAX 02 31 22 79 19

W www.hotel-france-isigny.com

AE, MC, V ● Sep–Jun: Fri D, Sat, Sun D; mid-Nov–mid-Feb

¶¶ €€€ ● (19) €€

Renowned for its rich and creamy cuisine. Stuffed oysters, fish sauerkraut and veal are all cooked using cream and butter. The guestrooms are old-fashioned.

LA BOUILLE

● **Les Gastronomes**

1 pl du Bâteau, 76530 **Map** 3D3

📞 02 35 18 02 07

FAX 02 35 18 14 49

💳 MC, V ⬤ Wed, Thu; mid-Nov–end Dec, mid-Feb 🍽 €€

The great atmosphere plays second fiddle to the impressive menu and wine list. Everything is prepared here, from smoked salmon to tarte Tatin (p191).

LA CHAPELLE-MONTLIGEON

▲ **Le Montligeon**

Pl de l'Eglise, 61400 **Map** 3D5

📞 02 33 83 81 19

FAX 02 33 83 62 71

🌐 www.hotelmontligeon.com

💳 MC, V ⬤ Sep–Jun: Sun D & Mon; 2 wks Feb, 2 wks Nov 🍽 €€ 🍴 (12) €

More popular for food than lodging. Try the boudin noir (black pudding/blood sausage) in pastry with apples, and guinea fowl glazed with cider caramel. Rooms lack soundproofing

LA FERRIERE-AUX-ETANGS

● **Auberge de la Mine**

Le Gué-Plat, 61450 **Map** 2B5

📞 02 33 66 91 10

FAX 02 33 96 73 90

🌐 http://aubergedelamine.free.fr

💳 AE, DC, MC, V ⬤ Tue, Wed, Sun D; 3 wks Jan, 3 wks Sep 🍽 €€€

Former mine-workers' canteen in a large brick building. On the menu, foie gras, a beautiful cheese platter and almond ice cream with chocolate chips.

LA FERTE-MACE

▲ **Auberge du Clouet**

Le Clouet, 61600 **Map** 2C5

📞 02 33 37 18 22

FAX 02 33 38 28 52

@ aubergedeclouet@wanadoo.fr

💳 AE, MC, V ⬤ Sun D, Mon; 2 wks Nov 🍽 €€ 🍴 (6) €€

Picturesque inn with a stone house and a mill. Simple but abundant food such as lobster casserole, which is a real highlight. Well-presented guestrooms.

L'AIGLE

▲ **Dauphin**

Pl de la Halle, 61300 **Map** 3D4

📞 02 33 84 18 00

FAX 02 33 34 09 28

💳 AE, DC, MC, V ⬤ Sun D 🍽 €€ 🍴 (30) €€€

This former coaching inn has smartly decorated guestrooms. Modern cooking such as fish and beef carpaccio.

L'AIGLE

● **Toque et Vins**

35 rue Louis Pasteur, 61300 **Map** 3D4

📞 02 33 24 05 27

FAX 02 33 24 05 27

💳 MC, V ⬤ Sun, Mon D, Tue D 🍽 €

There aren't many good wine bars in Normandy, but this one is a winner. Quick service and low prices. Boudin noir with apples, Camembert fritters, smoked salmon and a top-notch wine list.

LE BENY-BOCAGE

▲ **Castel Normand**

Pl du Marché, 14350 **Map** 2B4

📞 02 31 68 76 03

FAX 02 31 68 63 58

🌐 www.lecastelnormand.com

💳 MC, V ⬤ Mon, Tue L; 2 wks Aug 🍽 €€€ 🍴 (5) €€

Guestrooms are in need of a makeover, but the cooking is close to perfection. Layers of andouille cooked in sweet apple liqueur, and monkfish stuffed with bacon are two appealing dishes.

LE BOURG-DUN

● **Auberge du Dun**

3 route de Dieppe, 76740 **Map** 3D3

📞 02 35 83 05 84

💳 MC, V ⬤ Sun D, Mon, Wed D; 2 wks Jan, 2 wks Sep 🍽 €€

Normandy is France's orchard, hence the menu featuring caramelized pear with foie gras and veal loin with apples.

LE BREUIL-EN-AUGE

● **Le Dauphin**

Le Bourg, 14130 **Map** 2C4

📞 02 31 65 08 11

FAX 02 31 65 12 08

💳 AE, MC, V ⬤ Sun D, Mon; 2 wks Nov, 2 wks Dec 🍽 €€€€

A modest façade and furnishings give no hint of the magnificent cuisine. Regional dishes include barbecued oysters with bacon, veal with cider and apple tart with cinnamon ice cream.

LE HAVRE

● **Aux Huit Viandes**

20 quai Michel Ferré, 76600 **Map** 2C3

📞 02 35 42 12 39

FAX 02 35 41 10 30

💳 AE, MC, V 🍽 €€

As the name (eight meats) suggests, this restaurant is designed to satisfy carnivorous cravings. There's a good selection of desserts to follow.

LE HAVRE

● **La Petite Auberge**

32 rue Ste-Adresse, 76600 **Map** 2C3

📞 02 35 46 27 32

FAX 02 35 48 26 15

💳 AE, MC, V ⬤ Sun D, Mon, Sat L; Aug, 1 wk Feb 🍽 €€€

Well worth booking in advance at this cosy auberge. The menu exploits the town's maritime location and focuses on fresh seafood complemented by an exhaustive wine list.

LE HAVRE

● **Wilson**

98 rue Président Wilson, 76600 **Map** 2C3

📞 02 35 41 18 28

💳 AE, MC, V ⬤ Mon, Sun D, Sat L; 2 wks Aug, 1 wk Sep 🍽 €

The menu boasts almost encyclopaedic coverage of the region's specialities, so catch a last taste before the ferry.

LE TREPORT

● **Le Homard Bleu**

45 quai François 1er, 76470 **Map** 3D2

📞 02 35 86 15 89

FAX 02 35 86 49 21

💳 AE, DC, MC, V ⬤ mid-Dec–mid-Jan 🍽 €€

As the restaurant's name suggests, lobster crowns the menu; however, if it's out of your price range, there's also plenty of good-value fish.

LES ANDELYS

▲ **La Chaîne d'Or**

27 rue Grande, 27700 **Map** 3D4

● Restaurant ■ Hotel ▲ Hotel / Restaurant

📞 02 32 54 00 31
FAX 02 32 54 05 68
W www.planete-b.fr/la-chaine-d-or
💳 AE, MC, V ● Sun D, Mon, Tue L;
Jan **🍴** €€€€ 🍽 (10) €€€€

Expect such delicacies as oysters in Champagne sauce and turbot with lobster coulis. Comfortable guestrooms are done up in pastels.

LES CHAMPEAUX-EN-AUGE
● La Camembertière

6km (4 miles) from Camembert on D196, direction Trun, 61120 **Map** 2C4
📞 02 33 39 31 87
FAX 02 33 67 20 32
@ lacamembertiere.resto2@tiscali.fr
💳 MC, V ● Oct–May: Sun D & Wed;
Jan, Feb **🍴** €€

Camembert is the main ingredient here. The menu also has smoked salmon, foie gras and thinly sliced beef in gravy. Reservations recommended.

LES MOITIERS-EN-BAUPTOIS
● Auberge de l'Ouve

Village Longuérac, 50360 **Map** 2A3
📞 02 33 21 16 26
FAX 02 33 41 83 61
💳 MC, V ● Sep–Apr **🍴** €

On the banks of the Ouve, amidst a field of horses. All-you-can-eat terrine and apple duckling are two good choices. Avoid the terrace in summer – there's a pig farm next door.

LILLEBONNE
▲ La P'tite Auberge

20 rue du Havre, 76170 **Map** 3D3
📞 02 35 38 00 59
FAX 02 35 38 57 33
W www.la-ptite-auberge.com
💳 AE, MC, V **🍴** €€ 🍽 (15) €€

There's a saying in France that "if it moves, they'll eat it". This fine menu illustrates that perfectly with veal sweetbreads with shallots, and poultry gizzards with pistachio salad. Tidy rooms.

LISIEUX
● Auberge du Pêcheur

2 bis rue Verdun, 14100 **Map** 2C4
📞 02 31 31 16 85
FAX 02 31 31 76 80
💳 MC, V ● Wed **🍴** €€

You might be a ways from the sea, but the fish are fresh. The pike-perch is cooked on a stone to seal in moisture.

LISIEUX
▲ Le Grand Hôtel de l'Espérance

16 bd Ste-Anne, 14100 **Map** 2C4
📞 02 31 62 17 53
FAX 02 31 62 34 00
W www.lisieux-hotel.com
💳 AE, DC, MC, V
🍴 €€€ 🍽 (100) €€€

Attention has been paid to every detail at this top spot. Luxurious restaurant serving refined cuisine. Guestrooms are comfortable and beautifully furnished.

LISIEUX
● Parc

21 bd Herbet Fournet, 14100 **Map** 2C4
📞 02 31 62 08 11
FAX 02 31 62 79 55
💳 AE, MC, V ● Sun D, Sat L; Jul
🍴 €€€

Neo-Gothic dining room. The prawn and crab mousseline with mushroom sauce and the delicious peach crumble demonstrate the chef's mastery.

LOUVIERS
● Le Tassili

8 rue François-le-Camus, 27400
Map 3D4
📞 02 32 50 65 83
FAX 02 32 40 07 93
W www.tassili-romantica.com
💳 MC, V **🍴** €

Find the perfect antidote to traditional Norman cuisine. The menu makes a whistle-stop tour of the Mediterranean, with dishes from Morocco, Greece, Italy and Spain. Children are welcome.

LOUVIERS
▲ Manoir la Haye le Comte

4 rue de Haye le Comte, 27400 **Map** 3D4
📞 02 32 40 00 40
FAX 02 32 25 03 85
💳 AE, MC, V ● Sun D, Mon; mid-Dec–mid-Jan **🍴** €€ 🍽 (16) €€€

Beautifully located in immaculate gardens, this 16th-century manor house serves foie gras with apples and Calvados. The guestrooms are clean and well-presented, making a pleasant stop.

LYONS-LA-FORET
▲ Domaine St-Paul

7 route St-Paul, 27480 **Map** 3E3
📞 02 32 49 60 57
FAX 02 32 49 56 05
W www.domaine-saint-paul.fr
💳 MC, V ● Nov–Apr
🍴 €€ 🍽 (17) €€€

Set deep in one of the country's finest beech forests, this former hunting lodge makes an idyllic rural getaway. Perennial favourites include deep-fried breaded Camembert and duck stew with cream. Wooden beams and stone walls add character to the guestrooms.

MACE
▲ Ile de Sées

Vandel, on D238, 61500 **Map** 2C5
📞 02 33 27 98 65
FAX 02 33 28 41 22
W www.ile-sees.fr
💳 MC, V ● Sun D, Mon; Nov–Feb
🍴 €€ 🍽 (16) €€

Good value food and accommodation. "Simple but plenty" could be their motto. The small-but-comfy guestrooms offer a peaceful postscript to a delicious meal.

MENESQUEVILLE
▲ Le Relais de la Lieure

1 rue Général de Gaulle, 27850 **Map** 3D3
📞 02 32 49 06 21
FAX 02 32 49 53 87
💳 V ● Sun D, Mon; end Dec–mid-Jan **🍴** €€€ 🍽 (16) €€€

At the heart of the Lyons Forest, it's fitting that everything is cooked over an open fire. Grilled meats form the backbone of the main menu, while even the sweetest tooth is catered for with a choice of more than 30 desserts. Very masculine decor in the guestrooms.

MERY-CORBON
● Le Relais du Lion d'Or

Lion d'Or Sud, 14370 **Map** 2C4
📞 02 31 23 65 30
FAX 02 31 23 65 30
💳 AE, MC, V ● Sun D, Mon; 2 wks
Jan **🍴** €€

Two stone dining rooms in a chalet-style building. Simple food is served, such as succulent chicken with cider or tripes à la mode de Caen (p145).

MESNIERES-EN-BRAY

● Auberge du Bec Fin

1 rue de la Gare, 76270 **Map** 3D3

☎ 02 35 94 15 15

FAX 02 35 94 42 14

🍽 MC, V ● Mon; last 2 wks Jan

🍴 €€

Next to the Renaissance-era castle, this venue is a perfect country cottage. The flowers, dark beams and copper pots on the walls lend a rustic feel. The cooking is traditional with innovative elements.

MESNIL-VAL-PLAGE

▲ Hostellerie de la Vieille Ferme

23 rue de la Mer, 76910 **Map** 3D2

☎ 02 35 86 72 18

FAX 02 35 86 12 67

🍽 AE, DC, MC, V ● Sun D, Nov–Mar: Mon; mid-Dec–1st wk Jan

🍴 €€€ 🛏 (34) €€

An Anglo-Norman hotel near the beach. Half-board is compulsory in summer. Classic fare, such as seafood platters. Romantic beamed ceilings and views.

MONTIGNY

▲ Le Relais de Montigny

273 rue du Lieutenant Aubert, 76380 **Map** 3D3

☎ 02 35 36 05 97

FAX 02 35 36 19 60

🍽 AE, DC, MC, V ● Sat L; last wk Dec–1st wk Jan

🍴 €€ 🛏 (22) €€€

The menu focuses on Norman favourites, and there's a well-stocked wine cellar. Guestrooms are modern and simple.

MONTREUIL-L'ARGILLE

● Auberge de la Truite

5 rue Grande, 27390 **Map** 2C4

☎ 02 32 44 50 47

FAX 02 32 44 00 66

🍽 MC, V ● Tue D, Wed; Jan, 1 wk Jun 🍴 €€

Inn full of musical instruments and mechanical organs that ensure the night often ends with dancing. The cooking remains rustic, and during winter the fireplace is used to grill meat.

MONT-ST-MICHEL

▲ Croix Blanche

16 Grand Rue, 50116 **Map** 1A5

☎ 02 33 60 14 04

FAX 02 33 48 59 82

w www.auberge-saint-pierre.fr

🍽 AE, DC, MC, V ● Sep–Jun: Sun D & Mon D 🍴 €€€ 🛏 (9) €€€

Incredible views can be had from this hotel-restaurant. A great venue for seafood; try the fish gratin or poached salmon with sorrel. Simple guestrooms.

MONT-ST-MICHEL

▲ La Mère Poulard

Grand Rue, 50116 **Map** 1A5

☎ 02 33 89 68 68

FAX 02 33 89 68 69

w www.mere-poulard.com

🍽 AE, DC, MC, V

🍴 €€€ 🛏 (27) €€€€

Annette Poulard has been a legend in Normandy since 1888 when she began preparing wood-fired omelettes. Today the walk-in kitchen, hung with brass and copper pots, retains much of the old-world charm, and the menu is still exceptional, if slightly overpriced. The comfortable rooms have great views.

MORTAGNE-AU-PERCHE

▲ Hôtel du Tribunal

4 pl du Palais, 61400 **Map** 3D5

☎ 02 33 25 04 77

FAX 02 33 83 60 83

🍽 AE, MC, V 🍴 €€€ 🛏 (21) €€

Well-kept 16th-century courtyard serving the local percheronne salad, made with melting cheese and boudin noir. Plush guestrooms with great baths.

MORTAIN

▲ Hôtel de la Poste

Pl des Arcades, 50140 **Map** 2B5

☎ 02 33 59 00 05

FAX 02 33 69 53 89

w www.hoteldelaposte.fr

🍽 AE, MC, V ● Mon, Tue; mid-Jan–mid-Feb 🍴 €€€ 🛏 (27) €€

The only decent establishment in town. Try dishes such as fine rabbit terrine with tomatoes, and cod risotto. Excellent wine list to match. Quiet guestrooms.

NEGREVILLE

▲ Le Mesnil Grand

8kms (5 miles) west of Valognes on D902, 50260 **Map** 2A3

☎ 02 33 95 09 54

FAX 02 33 95 20 04

🍽 AE, MC, V ● Sun D, Mon

🍴 €€€ 🛏 (8) €€€

A farm restaurant with rooms, serving upscale cooking: warm spinach and mushroom salad, pork in cream, and raspberry tart. Reservations essential. Cosy guestrooms.

NEUFCHATEL-EN-BRAY

▲ Le Grand Cerf

9 Grand Rue Fausse Porte, 76270 **Map** 3E3

☎ 02 35 93 00 02

FAX 02 35 94 14 92

@ grandcerf.hotel@wanadoo.fr

🍽 AE, DC, MC, V ● Oct–Mars: Fri, Sat L 🍴 € 🛏 (12) €€

Doubles as a hunting lodge during autumn. On the menu are duck with cider, pancakes with wild mushrooms, and Calvados tripe. Comfortable rooms.

NOCE

● Auberge des Trois J

1 pl du Docteur Gireaux, 61340 **Map** 3D5

☎ 02 33 73 41 03

FAX 02 33 83 33 36

🍽 AE, MC, V ● Sun D, Mon; 2 wks Jan, 2 wks Sep 🍴 €€€

The three J's are the owner and his sons. The youngest has mastered the farmhouse favourite poule au pot (p353). Indulgent cheese selection and delicious poached figs with honey ice cream.

NOTRE-DAME-DE-BONDEVILLE

▲ Les Elfes

303 rue Longs Vallons, 76960 **Map** 3D3

☎ 02 35 74 36 21

FAX 02 35 75 27 09

🍽 V ● Wed; mid-Jul–mid-Aug

🍴 € 🛏 (6) €

This family-run restaurant is not wildly attractive, but it should appeal to the bank balance. The food is tasty, well-prepared and great value, but some may find the atmosphere a little soporific. Nautical theme in rooms.

NOTRE-DAME-DU-HAMEL

● La Marigotière

Route Departementale 138, D12, 27390 **Map** 2C4

☎ 02 32 44 58 11

FAX 02 32 44 40 12

MC, V ● Sun D, Tue D, Wed

🍴 €€€€

In a wonderful setting in an old riverside mill, the food here more than lives up to the salubrious surroundings. The trio of foie gras is as good as it gets.

ORBEC
● **Au Caneton**

32 rue Grande, 14290 **Map** 2C4

☎ 02 31 32 73 32

FAX 02 31 62 48 91

AE, MC, V ● Sun D, Mon;
3 wks Sep 🍴 €€€

Duck dominates the menu with dishes such as grilled wild duck, duck breast cooked in cider, pâté and rillettes.

OUILLY-DU-HOULEY
● **Auberge de la Paquine**

Route Moyaux, 14590 **Map** 2C4

☎ 02 31 63 63 80

FAX 02 31 63 63 80

MC, V ● Tue D, Wed; Feb, 2 wks
Sep 🍴 €€€

Ingenious cuisine here such as skate and scallop terrine, duck with cherry sauce, and an apple and cinnamon tart. Lovely flower garden for summer dining.

PONT-D'OUILLY
▲ **Auberge St-Christophe**

St-Christophe, 2km (1.5 miles) on the D23 direction Thury-Harcourt, 14690 **Map** 2C4

☎ 02 31 69 81 23

FAX 02 31 69 26 58

AE, MC, V ● Sun D, Mon; last 3
wks Aug, 2 wks Feb 🍴 €€ 🍃 (7) €€

Discover a real local hangout. The pigeon with preserved shallots and garlic is a favourite and the climbing vines lend charm. Guestrooms are cosy.

PONT-L'EVEQUE
● **Auberge de l'Aigle d'Or**

68 rue de Vaucelles, 14130 **Map** 2C4

☎ 02 31 65 05 25

FAX 02 31 65 12 03

AE, MC, V ● Sep–Jun: Sun D &
Tue D & Wed; 2 wks Feb 🍴 €€€

The well-preserved Norman building and flowery courtyard make a pretty

backdrop for a good-value meal of duck pâté with pistachios, and free-range chicken cooked in local cider.

PONTORSON
● **Le Relais Gourmand**

15 rue de Tanis, 50170 **Map** 2A5

☎ 02 33 58 20 96

MC, V ● Thu L, Jun–Sep: Thu D;
last wk Dec 🍴 €

Cream, apples and cheese dominate the menu. On Wednesday, market day, lunch is served from 8am, including tripe and tête-de-veau.

PONT-ST-PIERRE
▲ **La Bonne Marmite**

10 rue René Raban, 27360 **Map** 3D4

☎ 02 32 49 70 24

FAX 02 32 48 12 41

W www.la-bonne-marmite.com

AE, DC, MC, V ● Sun D, Mon, Tue
L; end Feb–mid-Mar, last wk Jul–first
2 wks Aug 🍴 €€€ 🍃 (9) €€€

A former coaching inn serving what locals staunchly defend as "the best traditional cuisine in the Andelle Valley". Not to be outshone by the menu, the wine list offers more than 600 reds and 270 whites. The guestrooms, though well equipped, are unexceptional.

PORTBAIL
● **La Ferme des Mielles**

Portbail plage, on D15, 50580 **Map** 2A3

☎ 02 33 04 85 96

FAX 02 33 04 26 71

MC, V ● Mon, Sep–Jun: Tue

🍴 €

Next door to some stables. Tasty crêpes, galettes and smoked ham as well as the heartier fish stew.

PORT-EN-BESSIN
▲ **La Chenevière**

Escures-Commes, on D6, 14520 **Map** 2B3

☎ 02 31 51 25 25

FAX 02 31 51 25 20

W www.lacheneviere.fr

AE, DC, MC, V

🍴 €€€€ 🍃 (22) €€€€

Luxurious 18th-century manor house. Indulgence cooking: fish soup, poultry skewers with spicy caramel and

caramelized apple fondant with arabica essence. Large, floral-themed guestrooms.

PORT-EN-BESSIN
● **L'Ecailler**

2 rue de Bayeux, 14520 **Map** 2B3

☎ 02 31 22 92 16

FAX 02 31 22 90 38

AE, MC, V ● Sep–Apr: Tue, Wed;
Jan 🍴 €€€

The best place to splurge in Normandy. A superb seafood emporium, headed by a chef trained under Georges Blanc.

PORT-MORT
● **Auberge des Pêcheurs**

Grand Rue, 27940 **Map** 3D4

☎ 02 32 52 60 43

FAX 02 32 52 07 62

MC, V ● Sun D, Mon D, Tue; last
2 wks Aug 🍴 €

Beyond the fake beams and faded paint – good quality, inexpensive Norman food. Savour the duck mousse, fish with leek purée, stuffed pigeon and foie gras.

PUTANGES-PONT-ECREPIN
▲ **Le Lion Verd**

Pl de l'Hôtel de Ville, 61210 **Map** 2C4

☎ 02 33 35 01 86

FAX 02 33 39 53 32

AE, MC, V ● Sun D, Mon; late
Dec–Feb 🍴 € 🍃 (19) €€

The restaurant is vast, but the decor cosy. Sautéed sweetbreads and roasted langoustines are perfect examples of Norman cuisine. Guestrooms are small.

QUINEVILLE
▲ **Château de Quinéville**

18 rue de l'Eglise, 50310 **Map** 2B3

☎ 02 33 21 42 67

FAX 02 33 21 05 79

AE, MC, V ● Mon, Wed L;
Jan–Mar 🍴 €€€ 🍃 (20) €€€

This immense estate, once the residence of King James II, could have its decor touched up. Always an excellent meal and an enjoyable retreat for the weekend. Classic guestrooms.

RANES
▲ **St-Pierre**

6 rue de la Libération, 61150 **Map** 2C5

☎ 02 33 39 75 14

FAX 02 33 35 49 23

W www.hotelsaintpierreranes.com

AE, DC, MC, V ● Fri D

€€ ◆ (14) €€

Not really much of a town, but the restaurant is good for sweetbreads with asparagus, duck with cider and sea bass with sorrel. Welcoming atmosphere and refined comfort in the rooms.

REMALARD

● **Le Galion**

21 rue de l'Eglise, 61110 **Map** 3D5

02 33 73 81 77

FAX 02 33 73 81 77

AE, DC, MC, V ● Tue, Wed; 2 wks Jan, last wk Jun, last wk Sep €€

A surprising maritime interior in a remote village restaurant. Try the sausage and smoked salmon salad.

REVILLE

▲ **Au Moyne de Saire**

Hameau Eglise, 50760 **Map** 2B3

02 33 54 46 06

FAX 02 33 54 14 99

W www.au-moyne-de-saire.com

AE, MC, V ● Oct–Mar: Wed; Feb

€€ ◆ (12) €€

An ideal place to recharge your batteries, with comfortable and charming rooms stuffed with antiques, and a great menu. Specialities include foie gras with figs and crêpes served with apple mousse.

ROSAY-SUR-LIEURE

▲ **Château de Rosay**

4km (2.5 miles) from Rosay-sur-Lieure, 27790 **Map** 3E3

02 32 49 66 51

FAX 02 32 49 70 77

W www.chateau-de-rosay.fr

AE, DC, MC, V

€ ◆ (30) €€€€

This Louis XIII-style castle is the epitome of luxury, and it's such a popular hideaway that booking is essential. Pan-fried foie gras with apple juice is an excellent appetizer. Opulent guestrooms.

ROUEN

● **Au Temps des Cerises**

4 rue des Basnages, 76000 **Map** 3D3

02 35 89 98 00

MC, V

● Sun, Sat L, Mon L; 3 wks Aug

€

Dubbed "le plus fromage des restos Rouennais"(the cheesiest restaurant in Rouen), this place earns its reputation. Cheese is everywhere – even the dessert trolley isn't exempt.

ROUEN

● **Gill**

9 quai Bourse, 76000 **Map** 3D3

02 35 71 16 14

FAX 02 35 71 96 91

W www.gill.fr

AE, DC, MC, V

● Mon, Sun; 1 wk Apr, 3 wks Aug

€€€€€

Rouen's top gastronomic destination, this spot marries old-world sophistication with an excellent menu. Highlights include langoustine salad with pepper chutney, pigeon Rouennaise and a delicious vanilla millefeuille.

ROUEN

● **La Couronne**

31 pl du Vieux Marché, 76000 **Map** 3D3

02 35 71 40 90

FAX 02 35 71 05 78

AE, DC, MC, V €€€

Having assured itself a place in most guidebooks as the oldest auberge in France, this beautiful 14th-century inn continues to go from strength to strength.

ROUEN

● **Le Bistrot du Chef en Gare**

1st floor, Gare SNCF (train station), 76000 **Map** 3E3

02 35 71 41 15

FAX 02 35 15 14 43

AE, MC, V

● Sun, Mon D, Sat L; Aug €€

A lively and atmospheric bistro located in the train station. People now come here just to sample the cuisine.

ROUEN

● **Le Rouennais**

5 rue de la Pie, 76000 **Map** 3D3

02 35 07 55 44

FAX 02 35 71 96 38

MC, V ● Sun D, Mon €€€

One of the best places to take Rouen's pulse is the famous Place du Vieux

Marché. Unwind over delicious canard Rouennaise (p145).

ROUEN

● **L'Etoile d'Istambul**

21 rue Bons Enfants, 76000 **Map** 3D3

02 35 71 97 41

MC, V ● Sun €

Summery Turkish salads, spicy kebabs, grilled Mediterranean fish and syrupy desserts make a welcome change.

ROULLOURS

● **Manoir de la Pommeraie**

L'Auverre, 2.5km (1.5 miles) on D524, direction Flers, 14500 **Map** 2D4

02 31 68 07 71

FAX 02 31 67 54 21

AE, DC, MC, V ● Sun D, Mon; 2 wks Feb €€€

The Viroise speciality is cold andouille. In this 18th-century manor, it also comes with apples and potatoes.

ROUXMESNIL-BOUTEILLES

▲ **L'Eolienne**

20 rue de Croix de Pierre, 76370 **Map** 3D3

02 32 14 40 00

FAX 02 32 14 40 18

AE, DC, MC, V ● Sun D; 2 wks Feb, last wk Dec €€ ◆ (15) €€

Beautifully housed in a restored barn, the proprietor has managed to marry exceptional guestrooms with a charming rustic restaurant. The menu includes duck with blackcurrant and grilled steaks.

RUFOSSES

● **Levéziel**

On RN13, 7km (4.5 miles) north of Valognes, 50700 **Map** 2A3

02 33 40 46 67

MC, V ● Mon–Fri D, Sun; mid-Oct–mid-Dec €

One of the best-value meals in the area. Try the tuna salad, pig's trotters or pear tart. Menu changes daily. Reserve ahead.

SILLY-EN-GOUFFERN

▲ **Le Pavillon de Gouffern**

3km (2 miles) from Haras-du-Pin on RN26, 61310 **Map** 2C4

02 33 36 64 26

FAX 02 33 36 53 81

● Restaurant ■ Hotel ▲ Hotel / Restaurant

AE, DC, MC, V ● 24–25 Dec

€€€ ◇ (20) €€€

Guestrooms are refined, the terrace bright and the food deliciously in touch with Norman tradition. A park surrounds this former hunting lodge.

SOURDEVAL
▲ Le Temps de Vivre
12 rue St-Martin, 50150 **Map** 2B4

02 33 59 60 41

FAX 02 33 59 88 34

@ le-temps-de-vivre@wanadoo.fr

MC, V ● Mon; 2 wks Feb

€€ ◇ (6) €€

Aptly named "the time to live". Huge menu featuring chicken liver terrine and apple tart with Calvados. Great rooms.

ST-AUBIN-LE-VERTUEUX
▲ Hostellerie du Moulin Fouret
Route de St-Quentin des Iles, 27300
Map 3D4

02 32 43 19 95

FAX 02 32 45 55 50

W www.moulin-fouret.com

AE, MC, V ● Sep–Jun: Sun D,
Mon, Tue L; Jul–Aug: Sun, Mon

€€ ◇ (8) €€

A 16th-century mill with one of the most beautiful views of the Charentonne River. The flower-bedecked restaurant stars foie gras, various cheeses and Calvados. Guestrooms are functional.

ST-AUBIN-SUR-MER
▲ Le Clos Normand
6 promenade Guynemer, 14750 **Map** 2C3

02 31 97 30 47

FAX 02 31 97 30 41

AE, MC, V ● mid-Nov–mid-Mar

€€€€ ◇ (35) €€€

With the largest terrace in Normandy, enjoy the marriage between gourmet meals and beach fun. Excellent seafood, such as lobster salad. Light, airy rooms.

ST-AUBIN-SUR-MER
▲ Le Lighthouse
Digue Léon Favreau, 14750 **Map** 2C3

02 31 97 72 40

FAX 02 31 97 72 41

W www.lelighthouse.com

AE, MC, V ● Sun D, Mon L;
Nov–Apr €€ ◇ (5) €€

A great beachfront retreat modelled on a turn-of-the-century lighthouse. The menu offers a seafood platter, plus more adventurous dishes such as Moroccan-inspired seafood couscous. Quite cosy guestrooms, but some are small.

ST-DENIS-LE-GAST
▲ Saint Evremond
4 rue du Clos d'Egypte, 50450 **Map** 2A4

02 33 61 44 42

FAX 02 33 61 33 77

W www.hotel-saint-evremond.com

MC, V ● Mon; last wk Sep–3rd
wk Oct €€ ◇ (10) €€

Bright, inexpensive restaurant, where one of the best starters is the foie gras with onion marmalade. Children are catered for with a pint-sized dining room.

ST-DENIS-SUR-SARTHON
▲ La Normandière
Off the RN12, 61420 **Map** 2C5

02 33 27 30 24

MC, V ● Jan, Sep

€€ ◇ (3) €

As the name suggests, Norman food is plentiful: apples, cream, butter and Calvados are in every dish. Simple guestrooms ideal for a short stay.

STE-ADRESSE
▲ La Petite Rade
3 pl Clémenceau, 76310 **Map** 2C3

02 35 54 68 90

FAX 02 35 54 68 91

W www.lapetiterade.com

AE, MC, V €€ ◇ (17) €€

Nautical decor and enormous seafood platters. Try the Alsatian speciality, seafood sauerkraut. Colourful, bright guestrooms overlooking the sea.

STE-CECILE
▲ Manoir de l'Acherie
37 rue Michel L'Epinay, 50800 **Map** 2D4

02 33 51 13 87

FAX 02 33 51 33 69

W www.manoir-acherie.fr

AE, MC, V ● Mon, mid-Oct–Apr:
Sun D €€ ◇ (15) €€

Old-fashioned manor house where cream, apples and cheese feature prominently. Some rooms located in a converted chapel.

STE-MARGUERITE-SUR-MER
● La Buissonière
Route du Phare d'Ailly, 76119 **Map** 3D3

02 35 83 17 13

MC, V ● Sun D, Mon; Jan–Feb

€

Fabulous restaurant where the chef will gladly share her recipes. Set in a chalet-like bungalow surrounded by a garden.

ST-GERMAIN-DES-VAUX
● Le Moulin à Vent
Hameau Danneville, off D202 and D45,
after Joburg, 50440 **Map** 2A3

02 33 52 75 20

FAX 02 33 52 22 57

AE, DC, MC, V €€

Close to the cliff path that leads to the lighthouse on Normandy's westernmost point. On the menu, smoked Vire ham, tuna tartare and whole sea bass.

ST-GERMAIN-DU-CRIOULT
▲ Auberge St-Germain
Route de Vire, D512 direction Vire,
4.5km (3 miles) west of Condé-sur-
Noireau, 14110 **Map** 2B4

02 31 69 08 10

FAX 02 31 69 14 67

AE, MC, V

● Sep–Jun: Sun D, Mon

€ ◇ (9) €€

On the menu are haddock in Normandy sauce (cream, diced apples and cider), tripe with Calvados, and beef sautéed in cider. Simple, functional guestrooms.

ST-HILAIRE-DU-HARCOUET
▲ Le Cygne et Résidence
99 rue Waldeck Rousseau, 50600
Map 2B5

02 33 49 11 84

FAX 02 33 49 53 70

W www.hotellecygne.com

AE, DC, MC, V ● Sep–May: Sun
D, Fri D €€€ ◇ (30) €€

A tastefully decorated granite house. Try the local lamb here. Guestrooms are well presented, but some lack sunlight. The pool is particularly attractive.

ST-JAMES
▲ Normandie
Pl Bagot, 50240 **Map** 2B5

02 33 48 31 45

FAX 02 33 48 31 37

🍽 AE, DC, MC, V ● Sun D; late Dec–mid-Jan 🍴 €€ 🍃 (14) €€

A simple and respectable address to use as a stopover on the way to Brittany. Excellent sea bass with creamy cider. The wine list is affordable and well selected. Tidy and comfortable rooms.

ST-LO
● Bistro de Paul et Roger

42 rue de Neufbourg, 50000 **Map** 2B4

📞 02 33 57 19 00

FAX 02 33 05 52 46

🍽 MC, V ● Sun; 2 wks Jul 🍴 €

Football heaven. The owners support Caen FC and aren't afraid to show it. Locals come for the traditional cooking: beef bourguignon, tête-de-veau (p268) and tarte Tatin (p191). Expensive drinks.

ST-LO
● Gonivière

Rond point du 6 Juin, 50000 **Map** 2B4

📞 02 33 05 15 36

FAX 02 33 05 01 72

🍽 AE, MC, V ● Sun 🍴 €€€

Charming auberge. Mussel stew is a change from the typical local fare, but foie gras and andouille satisfy the need for regional delicacies.

ST-PATERNE
▲ Château de St-Paterne

On D311 direction Châtres, 3km (2 miles) south of Alençon, 72610 **Map** 2C5

📞 02 33 27 54 71

FAX 02 33 29 16 71

🌐 www.chateau-saintpaterne.com

🍽 MC, V ● mid-Jan–Mar

🍴 €€€€ 🍃 (8) €€€€

Henri IV's 15th-century love-nest is magnificent. The candlelit dining room is for hotel guests, but a smaller restaurant is open to all. Luxurious rooms.

ST-PIERRE-DE-SEMILLY
● Les Glycines

Le Calvaire, on D972, 7km (4.5 miles) from St-Lô, 50810 **Map** 2B4

📞 02 33 05 02 40

FAX 02 33 56 29 32

@ lesglycines@club-internet.fr

🍽 AE, MC, V ● Sun D, Mon, Sat L; 2 wks Feb, last wk Jul 🍴 €€€

Grilled oysters in Sauvignon, crispy fried bass, and hot-and-cold foie gras are highlights. A quiet garden.

ST-PIERRE-DU-REGARD
● Au Poisson Vivant

2km (1.25 miles) south of Condé-sur-Noireau on D962, 61790 **Map** 2B4

📞 02 31 69 01 58

FAX 02 31 69 01 58

🍽 MC, V ● Sun D, Mon, Tue D; 2 wks Jan, Sep 🍴 €€

A good-value restaurant. Copious portions of culinary surprises including andouille gratin and apple cinnamon crisp.

ST-QUENTIN-SUR-LE-HOMME
▲ Le Gué du Holme

14 rue des Estuaires, 50220 **Map** 2B4

📞 02 33 60 63 76

FAX 02 33 60 06 77

🍽 AE, DC, MC, V ● Sun D, Mon, Sat L; Feb school holidays; 2nd wk Nov

🍴 €€ 🍃 (10) €€€

Popular eatery in a stone cottage. Seafood is showcased on the menu and the creamy, luscious morel risotto is a masterpiece. Comfy guestrooms.

ST-ROMAIN-DE-COLBOSC
▲ Au Nom de Jésus

8 rue Abbé Palfray, 76430 **Map** 2C3

📞 02 35 20 04 79

FAX 02 35 20 87 98

🍽 MC, V ● Sun, Fri D, Sat D (reservations only) ; mid-Dec–1st wk Jan

🍴 €€ 🍃 (14) €€

Travellers once beseeched the local monks: "In the name of Jesus, I am seeking food and rest". The story explains the hotel's peculiar name. The regional fare includes St-Romain boudin noir. Modern guestrooms are simple in this family-run gem.

ST-VAAST-LA HOUGUE
▲ Les Fuchsias

20 rue Maréchal Foch, 50550 **Map** 2B3

📞 02 33 54 42 26

FAX 02 33 43 46 79

🍽 AE, DC, MC, V ● Sep–May: Mon, Tue; Jun–Sep: Mon L; mid-Jan–Feb

🍴 €€€ 🍃 (34) €€€

This conservatory dining room serves dishes such as warm oysters with cider,

whole sea bass with crab sauce and apple-and-Calvados puff pastry. Country-style rooms and a tasty breakfast buffet.

ST-VALERY-EN-CAUX
● La Passerelle

Le Perrey, 76460 **Map** 3D3

📞 02 35 57 84 11

FAX 02 35 57 84 12

🌐 www.casino-saintvalery.com

🍽 AE, MC, V 🍴 €€

Expect starters such as oysters and bouillabaisse (p268), before moving on to chunky fillets of sea bass with basil.

ST-VICTOR-DE-RENO
▲ Auberge de Brochard

Le Brochard, 5km (3 miles) south of Autheuil, direction Les Larry, 61290 **Map** 3D5

📞 02 33 25 74 22

FAX 02 33 83 95 37

🌐 www.aubergedebrochard.com

🍽 MC, V ● Sun D, Mon; last 2 wks Dec 🍴 €€ 🍃 (9) €€

Guestrooms are basic as the focus is on the kitchen. Copious portions elegantly presented: duck in honey and lavender, monkfish pastry with a cream sauce.

ST-WANDRILLE-RANCON
● Auberge Deux Couronnes

Pl de l'Eglise, 76490 **Map** 3D3

📞 02 35 96 11 44

FAX 02 35 56 56 23

🍽 AE, MC, V ● Sun D, Mon; 3 wks Jan 🍴 €€

Opposite the abbey gate, in an old stone house. Scallops with mushrooms and grilled meat are always on offer.

TANCARVILLE
▲ La Marine

At the foot of the bridge, on the D982, 76430 **Map** 2C3

📞 02 35 39 77 15

FAX 02 35 38 03 30

🌐 www.planete-b.fr/lamarine

🍽 AE, MC, V ● Sun D, Mon, Sat L; mid-Jul–mid-Aug

🍴 €€€ 🍃 (9) €€

Overlooking the Pont de Tancarville as it spans the Seine, this is one place where you're never quite sure what's going to be on the menu. The chef takes his lead

● Restaurant   ■ Hotel   ▲ Hotel / Restaurant

from what's freshest at the fish market that day, then prepares innovative, original and still distinctly French dishes. Flowery guestrooms with soft furnishings.

THURY-HARCOURT

▲ Relais de la Poste

7 rue de Caen, 14220 **Map** 2B4

📞 02 31 79 72 12

FAX 02 31 39 53 55

@ lerelais@nol.fr

AE, MC, V ● Sun D, Nov–Mar: Mon; last wk Dec–1st wk Jan

€€€€ 🍽 (12) €€

The vaulted dining room in this long-established restaurant is an attraction in itself. Lobster flambé and langoustines are perfect. Lovely wine list to suit any palate. Louis XV and XVI-style in the guestrooms decorated with plenty of richly patterned fabrics.

TRELLY

▲ La Verte Campagne

Le Hameau au Chevalier, 1.5km (1 mile) southwest on D539, 50660 **Map** 2A4

📞 02 33 47 65 33

FAX 02 33 47 38 03

MC, V ● Oct–May: Mon, Tue; 2 wks Jan, 1 wk Mar, 2 wks Oct

€€€ 🍽 (7) €€

Climbing roses make this historic farmhouse irresistibly charming. The chef-owner is passionate about Norman cooking. There are only two rooms with private bathrooms.

TROUVILLE-SUR-MER

▲ Carmen

24 rue Carnot, 14360 **Map** 2C3

📞 02 31 88 35 43

FAX 02 31 88 08 03

www.hotelrestaurantcarmen.com

AE, MC, V ● Sep–Jun: Wed

€€ 🍽 (17) €€€

Pass by the tourist restaurants in the street and head straight to this one. The John Dory fillet with cider zabaglione, rabbit in pastry and warm Calvados soufflé are a perfect introduction to Norman produce. Plenty of family rooms.

VALMONT

● L'Agriculture

9 rue d'Estouteville, 76540 **Map** 2C3

📞 02 35 29 84 25

FAX 02 35 29 45 59

AE, MC, V ● Mon

€€

Fine ingredients prepared passionately and presented beautifully. Even better is that it's good value for money, especially if you time your visit for a weekday lunch.

VALOGNES

▲ Grand Hôtel du Louvre

28 rue des Religieuses, 50700 **Map** 2A3

📞 02 33 40 00 07

FAX 02 33 40 13 73

MC, V

● Oct–May: Sun D, Mon L

€€ 🍽 (20) €€

Inn established in 1700. The menu changes monthly, but fish and seafood are a priority. Old-fashioned rooms.

VARAVILLE

● Au Pied de Cochon

26 ave Président Cotty, 14390 **Map** 2C4

📞 02 31 91 27 55

FAX 02 31 91 86 13

MC, V ● Mon, Sep–Jun: Tue; 2 wks Dec, 1st wk Jan €€

An old farmhouse with such a generously proportioned menu that you could spend days deciding what to order. The seaside location accounts for much of the kitchen's output, while local produce and traditional recipes fill in any gaps.

VERNEUIL-SUR-AVRE

▲ Hôtel du Saumon

89 pl de la Madeleine, 27130 **Map** 3D4

📞 02 32 32 02 36

FAX 02 32 37 55 80

www.hoteldusaumon.fr

MC, V

● mid-Dec–Jan

€€ 🍽 (29) €€

The hotel's name is a giveaway as to what's on the menu. However, alongside salmon, the menu also offers lobster, plenty of grilled meats and a selection of regional classics. Cosy, romantic guestrooms with attractive furnishings.

VERNON

▲ Hôtel d'Evreux

11 pl d'Evreux, 27200 **Map** 3E4

📞 02 32 21 16 12

FAX 02 32 21 32 73

www.hotel-d-evreux.bigstep.com

AE, DC, MC, V ● Sun

€€ 🍽 (12) €€

Once the pre-revolutionary home of the Count of Evreux, today this charming hotel belongs to the visiting public. The restaurant is locally renowned for its fresh approach to traditional cooking at a price that most can afford. Sunny guestrooms with large windows.

VILLERS-BOCAGE

▲ Les Trois Rois

2 pl Jeanne D'Arc, 14310 **Map** 2B4

📞 02 31 77 00 32

FAX 02 31 77 93 25

AE, DC, MC, V ● Sun D, Mon, Tue L; Jan, last wk Jun

€€€€ 🍽 (14) €€

Flaunting all the hallmarks of an archetypal Norman restaurant, expect well-prepared traditional dishes served in huge quantities. The guestrooms are basic but comfortable.

VIMOUTIERS

▲ L'Escale du Vitou

Centre de Loisirs, route d'Argentan, 61120 **Map** 2C4

📞 02 33 39 12 04

FAX 02 33 36 13 34

www.ifrance.com/gite-en-france

MC, V ● Sep–Jun: Sun D & Mon & Tue L; Jan € 🍽 (17) €€

Creamy Norman cuisine with a delicious apple and duck foie gras, skate in Camembert sauce, rib-eye with Pont l'Evêque cheese sauce and a good old-fashioned apple and meringue tart. Guestrooms are simple and clean, but could do with refurbishing.

YERVILLE

▲ Hostellerie des Voyageurs

Rue Jacques Ferny, 76760 **Map** 3D3

📞 02 35 96 82 55

FAX 02 35 96 16 86

MC, V ● Sun D, Mon

€€€ 🍽 (10) €€

The hearty cuisine is a cross between regional specialities such as seafood and foie gras and classic French recipes such as terrine. Modern rooms, a pretty garden and private parking.

BRITTANY

Prehistoric remains, Celtic culture and Arthurian legends combine to make Brittany a fascinating and unique region. Its windswept granite headlands, sandy bays and myriad islands typify a land that has always looked seawards, sending mariners out into the wild Atlantic. Not surprisingly, its fish and seafood, notably oysters, are among the great pleasures of Breton dining – along, of course, with the omnipresent crêpe.

The Flavours of Brittany

With 1,700 km (1,055 miles) of coastline, Brittany is a major seafood supplier, its oysters being especially noted for their high quality. Charcuterie also features strongly on the menu here, as this is France's main pig-rearing area.

OUESSANT LAMB

One of the best places in France to experience the wonderful flavour of *pré-salé* lamb is on the Ile de Ouessant, off the windswept coast of Finistère. Reared on the marshy fields, the local breed of tiny, black-fleeced sheep have to be tied together and tethered to stone walls to protect them from the strong, salty sea breezes that flavour the pastures they feed on.

Local charcuterie of smoked ham and terrine

MEAT AND CHARCUTERIE

Brittany is France's main pig-rearing region. Look out for *porc fermier*, from pigs raised in the open on a cereal-based diet, and for some superb charcuterie, including *andouille de Guémené*, a smoked sausage made from pigs' intestines. Other fine charcuterie includes cooked and smoked hams, garlic sausage, *boudin noir* and *pâté breton*, a coarsely textured pork terrine.

Pré-salé lamb is raised on the marshy fields along the coast. Most cows are kept for dairying, especially the black and white *pie noire* breed, but there are also beef cattle, usually Charolais or Charolais crosses.

FISH AND SHELLFISH

Fishing is a major industry in Brittany. The ports of Guilvinec and Concarneau supply fishmongers and restaurants all over France. Loctudy is a centre for mackerel and langoustines, langoustes are found at Audierne while Erquy and Loguivy-de-la-Mer are home to the scallop. Canning factories for sardines and tuna can be found at Quiberon, Douarnenez and Concarneau.

As well as lobster and langoustines, there is plenty of other shellfish to fill the huge seafood platters popular in local restaurants: various types of crab and clam, cockles, prawns, scallops, shrimps and whelks. There are also 12 recognized "grands crus" of Breton oyster, each with a subtly different taste. Flat round *belons* are

MOULES À BOUCHOT

The practice of cultivating mussels on stout oak posts goes back for hundreds of years. One story has it that this method was invented by a shipwrecked Irish monk in 1235. Today the practice is used particularly in the Vilaine estuary, the Baie de Beaussais, near Dinard, and the Baie de Cancale, where the mussels thrive on the mix of fresh and salt water. Mussel larvae settle on ropes that are twisted around the oak posts; the posts are covered by water at high tide and exposed at low tide. It takes approximately two years for the mussels to grow to the required size and, although they are often smaller than wild mussels, they are usually considered to have a finer flavour.

Left Buying oysters at the local market **Right** Freshly caught sardines

reared at Riec-sur-Belon in the south and at Cancale on the north coast, and the more common, crinkled *creuse* oysters at Cancale, the Baie de Quiberon and the Golfe de Morbihan. *Moules à bouchot* are raised in the Vilaine estuary and the Baie de Cancale.

Butter and Dairy Produce

Salted butter is a Breton speciality and is excellent on rye bread to accompany oysters. It also goes into many Breton delicacies from sauces and cakes to salt butter caramels and ice cream. Look for butter labelled *beurre de baratte*, traditionally made by allowing the cream to mature for several hours before being churned.

Brittany is also an important producer of fresh milk, as well as a slightly fermented milk known as *lait ribot*. Curiously, cheese production here is small-scale and includes goats' cheese, St-Paulin, a mild, semi-soft cheese made with pasteurized milk, and the related cheeses Campénéac and Timadeuc.

Fruit and Vegetables

Brittany's mild, damp winters make this an important area for early and winter vegetables. The *Prince de Léon* artichoke is grown here from October to May and most of the country's cauliflower produce comes from north Finistère. Other principal crops include onions, shallots, haricot beans, asparagus, broccoli, potatoes and tomatoes. Strawberries are cultivated at Plougastel.

Baked Goods

An array of baked goods is found here including *Kouign-aman* (buttery sweet bread), shortbread or *sablé* biscuits, *quatre-quarts*, a type of pound cake, and *crêpes dentelles*, thin sugary pancakes, rolled up in tight layers and baked until crispy.

Best Markets

Dinard Offers a lively mix of regional produce and general goods, Tue, Thu and Sat am

Pont-l'Abbé Daily covered market, spreading to main town square on Sat

Rennes An extensive market gathering the region's riches on place des Lices, Sat am

St-Pol-de-Léon A busy market outside the cathedral in the artichoke capital, Tue

Vannes A traditional market in the well-preserved medieval quarter, Wed & Sat

Cancale A great market for seafood located in this Breton oyster port, Wed & Sat am

Saint Malo Traditional market with colourful and varied fare, in a walled seaside town, Wed am

Fresh bread for sale in a Breton market

Regional Dishes

Breton cuisine is most often associated with the simple crêpe, but you will also find far more gastronomic fare based on the region's fine seafood and vegetables. Meat also plays its part in the form of charcuterie *and hearty stews while cider and Muscadet wines are used to flavour.*

ON THE MENU

Bisque de homard Lobster soup

Feuilleté aux fruits de mer Shellfish in puff pastry

Fricassée de pétoncles Clams and leeks fricasséed with white wine and cream

Gigot à la bretonne Leg of lamb with white haricot beans, tomatoes and garlic

Homard à l'armoricaine Lobster in herby tomato and onion sauce

Kig ha farz Meat and vegetable hotpot with buckwheat dumpling

Palourdes farcies Stuffed clams

Roulade sévigné Roulade of guinea fowl, apples and ham, speciality of Vitré

Tourteau farci Stuffed crab

Homard à l'armoricaine, its herby sauce enriched by eau-de-vie

THE BRETON MENU

Meals often start with fish or shellfish, such as oysters, *moules marinières* or crab or lobster bisque or fish soup, served with croûtons, *rouille* and grated cheese. Clams and scallops come stuffed, gratinéed or prepared as a fricassée with leeks in a creamy sauce. Cockles and other tiny shellfish are served in a puff-pastry case.

Dressed crab with mayonnaise or splendid shellfish platters – a bed of crushed ice and seaweed topped with crabs, oysters, clams, periwinkles, langoustines and prawns – make a meal in themselves. Fresh fish may be grilled, baked in sea salt or braised in cider. Lobster, squid, monkfish and all manner of other things can be prepared in a herby tomato sauce *à l'armoricaine*. The best known fish stew is *cotriade*.

Meat dishes include local roast pork and the hearty *kig ha farz* stew. Lamb is served *à la bretonne*, with haricot beans, or the larger white *cocos de Paimpol* beans, prepared with onions, shallots and tomatoes. Breton-style beans also accompany other meats or fish, as may a garnish of artichoke hearts. Apples, puréed or sliced and sautéed in butter accompany *boudin noir* or *roulade sévigné*. Cauliflowers are cooked in gratins or with prawns and little buckwheat *galettes* often replace potatoes.

Desserts might include crêpes, *far aux pruneaux*, strawberries from Plougastel – perhaps served on a butter shortcake biscuit or macerated in wine – and delicious salted butter ice cream.

CRÊPES AND GALETTES

Crêpes probably weren't originally specifically Breton but they have become part of the Breton identity. Buckwheat is used for the savoury pancakes known as *galettes*, while white wheat flour is used for the sweet dessert pancakes known as crêpes. Savoury *galettes* usually contain a combination of egg, ham and cheese. Other fillings include *andouille*, sausage, mushrooms and spinach. Sweet crêpe fillings range from simple butter or sugar and lemon to a wide range of choco-late, nut, soft fruit and cream concoctions.

Left Cotriade **Right** Far aux pruneaux

REGIONAL DINING

The following restaurants are among those serving regional dishes at reasonable prices:

Amadeus
St-Brieuc *(see p183)*

Au P'tit Rafiot
Quimper *(see p180)*

Hotel Kastell an Daol
Ile Molene *(see p177)*

Hotel le Cadoudal
Auray *(see p172)*

Le Buccin
Concarneau *(see p175)*

L'Armoire
Carnac-Ville *(see p174)*

Pen Duick
Dinard *(see p176)*

St-Ex
Brest *(see p173)*

Moules marinières, freshly cooked in their soupy, wine sauce

COTRIADE

The ingredients of this traditional fish stew vary according to the day's catch. Assorted fish, such as eel, mackerel, wrasse, sea bream and whiting, or small whole fish such as baby mackerel or small red mullet, can all be used. Onions and thickly-sliced potatoes are half cooked before the fish is added to the pot. The firmest varieties of fish should be added first followed by the more fragile fish at the end. The soup, poured over slices of toast, is eaten first, followed by the fish and potatoes accompanied by a herb vinaigrette.

MOULES MARINIÈRES

This quintessential way of preparing mussels is found pretty much anywhere that mussels are eaten. Before cooking, the mussels should be thoroughly cleaned and the beard removed. Any which are not firmly shut should be discarded. The mussels are cooked in a large saucepan, along with a dry white wine (such as Muscadet), chopped shallots, parsley and butter, until the shells have opened to reveal the orangey-pink mollusc inside. Any mussels that fail to open during cooking should be discarded.

The fleshy mollusc is eaten directly from its shell; the empty shell providing a useful "spoon" to scoop up the delicious liquor with at the end.

FAR AUX PRUNEAUX

Fars or *farz*, both sweet and savoury are, like the crêpe, part of a long peasant tradition. The pudding consists of a thick batter made with whole eggs, sugar, flour and milk that has been infused with a vanilla pod. Prunes that have been soaked in tea, drained and macerated in apple *eau-de-vie* or rum are scattered evenly over the surface of the batter. This is then baked in a medium hot oven until brown on top.

Regional Cider, Beer & Spirits

The Bretons share their heritage with the Celts, rather than the wine-producing French to the east and further south. Here you will find cider, mead, even whisky, as well as the beginnings of a revival in brewing inspired by a mix of the Breton heritage and British real ale.

Breton cider and apple orchard

CHOUCHEN

Chouchen, *hydromel* and *chemillard* are the Celtic equivalents of Saxon mead – honey wine. It was once seen as an elixir of life and an aphrodisiac, and was presented as an offering to the gods. Most producers are also bee-keepers and make *chouchen* on a small scale for the family or to sell to passing tourists.

Chouchen

Cider

Cisera, as the Gauls called their fermented apple juice, featured in the stories of the Round Table, but it was only in the 16th century, when bitter, tannin-rich varieties of apple were brought to Brittany from the north of Spain, that Breton cider could be kept for any length of time and could therefore be exported outside the region. The fermentation process was also improved and these drinks were to become celebration ciders, taking precedence over wine on grand occasions.

Unlike Normandy, the granitic soils of Brittany lack copper, which is essential to the cultivation of apple trees, so the orchards were confined to those few areas where the soil contained the precious mineral. Breton ciders are made from apples with high acidity and traditional cider *(fermier)* has a distinctive tart flavour. Certain varieties are typical of particular areas: Guillevic around Vannes, Rouget in Dol, Petit Jaune in Châteaubriant and Kermerrien in Cornouaille.

Cornouaille, and particularly Fouesnant, have long enjoyed a reputation for outstanding cider. The cider route runs from Le Faou to Rédené, sometimes following the coast, sometimes winding inland over a strip of land just 20 km (12 miles) wide that was a favourite haunt of the artist Gauguin. Cidre de Cornouaille was awarded AOC status in 1996 and growing and production methods must now conform to stringent regulations. Cidre de Cornouaille is bitter-sweet with scents of ripe apples, flowers and summer fruits.

No self-respecting crêperie in Brittany would dream of omitting cider from its menu. Drunk from large, earthenware bowls, it used to be traditional for the *bolée* (bowlful) to be downed in three. That was before World War I, when they held half a litre; nowadays cider drinking is a more leisurely affair, and the bowls are a lot smaller!

BEER IN BRITTANY

Beer is traditionally known as *cervoise* in Brittany. A huge brewing industry sprang up in the 16th century to supply the French navy, and in the 19th century hundreds of small breweries were operating in the region. Gradually all of these disappeared and by the 1980s the only ones left were the giant lager distributors of eastern France.

However, the tradition has been revived by two small breweries whose owners are passionate about beer. Christian Blanchard and Jean-François Malgorn learned how to brew real ale in England. Their brewery, Deux Rivières, was established at the confluence of the rivers Jarlot and Queffleuth. Their unfiltered, unpasteurized and unrefrigerated beer, Coreff, contains a high proportion of hops.

The Manoir de Guermahia brewery, located in the land of the Arthurian legends, is owned by a former beekeeper. Unsurprisingly, his Cervoise Lancelot contains a dose of honey, as did the *cervoise* of the ancient Gauls. It also carries a secret combination of seven aromatic plants grown within the region.

Armorik whisky

BRETON WHISKY

Like their neighbours in Normandy, the Bretons make *pommeau* by adding eau-de-vie to sweet fermenting cider and itinerant distillers turn out *lambig*, Brittany's answer to Calvados. Much more of a curiosity in apple country is Breton whisky. Based on barley and wheat, WB is a blended whisky aged for three years in oak in the cellars of the Warenghem distillery in Lannion. Armorik is the same producer's single malt whisky.

Cider press

Where to Eat & Stay

AURAY
● **Capucine**

6 rue St Sauveur, 56400 **Map** 1C4

📞 02 97 56 35 53

🍴 €

Locally recommended crêperie with andouille galettes. Sirloins, fish soups and large salads also feature. Plentiful sweet crêpe selection: Grand Marnier, Calvados, Armagnac and rum fuel the flambées. Limited wine list or the decent house wine by carafe.

AURAY
● **Crêperie St Michel**

33 rue Belzic, 56400 **Map** 1C4

📞 02 97 24 06 28

🍴 MC, V ● Tue D, Wed 🍴 €

Galettes by the dozen available in this charming little crêperie. The four savoury andouille fillings come with mustard, tomatoes and herbs or cheese and eggs. Specialist crêpes include the forestière with mushrooms, eggs and smoked game, and the coralline with salmon, lemon and crème fraîche.

AURAY
■ **Hotel le Cadoudal**

9 pl Notre Dame, 56400 **Map** 1C4

📞 02 97 24 14 65

FAX 02 97 50 78 51

🍴 MC, V ● Oct–Apr: Sun except during school holidays 🍽 (14) €€

Fine old town house with pretty stone walls and outdoor terrace. Very modern rooms with polished wood. Popular bar.

AURAY
● **La Chaumière**

1 rue Abbé Philippe Gall, 56400 **Map** 1C4

📞 02 97 50 77 75

🍴 AE, MC, V ● Tue D, Wed 🍴 €€€

Set menus cater to discerning diners with a range of budgets. The less expensive option contains such delights as langoustines fricassée and superb duck brochettes. There's a massive seafood platter for two, which includes everything from sea bream to lobster and delectable crab.

AURAY
● **Le Frégate**

11 rue du Petit Port, 56400 **Map** 1C4

📞 02 97 50 71 95

🍴 MC, V ● Thu 🍴 €€

Galette specialist: the Breton crêpe comes with andouille, egg and cheese, the Norman crêpe comes with bacon, leek and onions. Other fillings include Camembert, anchovies and seafood. The galettes can be served individually or as part of a set menu.

AURAY
● **L'Eglantine**

10 St Goustan, Port d'Auray, 56400 **Map** 1C4

📞 02 97 56 46 55

🍴 MC, V ● Jul–Aug: Wed L, Sep–Jun: Wed 🍴 €€€

Stunningly located in sight of the old clipper in the enchanting harbour area. Sole and turbot – simple but delicious – and sea bass and monkfish medallions with elaborate sauces. Exquisite seafood platters. Meat dishes include pigeon and excellent steak.

BADEN
▲ **Gavrinis**

Toulbroch, 56870 **Map** 1C4

📞 02 97 57 00 82

FAX 02 97 57 09 47

🍴 AE, DC, MC, V ● Mon; Nov–Feb 🍴 €€€ 🍽 (18) €€€€

Large rooms and magnificent grounds, popular with golfers. The restaurant serves scallops with mandarin butter and guinea fowl pot-au-feu.

BREST
● **Amour de Pommes de Terre**

23 rue Halles St Louis, 29200 **Map** 1A2

📞 02 98 43 48 51

FAX 02 98 43 61 88

🍴 MC, V 🍴 €

Restaurant dedicated to the humble potato. Baked options come topped with cheeses, seafood or herbs. A range of Northern European beers is served. Characterful domed interior and outdoor terrace in the centre of town.

BREST
● **Brasserie de Siam**

12 rue de Siam, 29200 **Map** 1A2

📞 02 98 46 05 52

FAX 02 98 46 59 37

🍴 MC, V 🍴 €€

Monkfish, lobster and sea bass are on the seafood-studded menu at this modern eatery. Giant seafood platters feature grilled fish, prawns, langoustines and half a lobster.

BREST
■ **Citôtel de la Gare**

4 bd Gambetta, 29200 **Map** 1A2

📞 02 98 44 47 01

FAX 02 98 43 34 07

🍴 AE, MC, V 🍽 (38) €€

A modern hotel with views stretching over the Bay of Brest from the well-appointed guestrooms. Best in its class.

BREST
● **Crêperie Ar-Milin**

3 rue Louis Pasteur, 29200 **Map** 1A2

📞 02 98 80 21 29

🍴 MC, V ● Sun 🍴 €

Delightful town-centre crêperie with a typically Breton feel. Squid, ratatouille (p400), chorizo and andouille feature in the wide range of dishes. Sweet fillings include chestnut sauce, pears and Chantilly cream.

BREST
● **Crêperie Moderne**

34 rue Algésiras, 29200 **Map** 1A2

📞 02 98 44 44 36

FAX 02 98 80 58 32

🍴 MC, V ● Sun L 🍴 €

Over 50 mouthwatering crêpes on offer. Savoury versions are stuffed with fish, mushrooms, goat's cheese or scallops. Sweet varieties come filled with apples, pears, cider sauce or chocolate.

BREST
● **La Fondue des Lys**

40 rue Lyon, 29200 **Map** 1A2

📞 02 98 43 42 77

🍴 MC, V ● Sun, Mon D, Sat L; 3 wks Aug 🍴 €€

● Restaurant ■ Hotel ▲ Hotel / Restaurant

*Diners dip fish, meat and mushrooms
into cheese, oil and wine fondues here.
Fish soup and scallop brochettes also
feature. Clarets on the wine list.*

BREST
● La Koutoubia
44 rue Amiral Linois, 29200 **Map** 1A2
📞 02 98 80 56 86
💳 MC, V ⬤ Sun 🍴 €€

*Moroccan specialities include steaming
mounds of couscous at this elegant
restaurant. Delicious lamb, chicken and
vegetable tagines (enclosed earthenware
pots with the contents slowly baked
inside) and lamb brochettes. Moroccan
and French wines.*

BREST
● Le Boeuf sur le Quai
2 rue Commandant Malbert, 29200
Map 1A2
📞 02 98 43 91 34
📠 02 98 46 61 29
💳 MC, V 🍴 €€

*Contemporary restaurant at the harbour.
Beef comes grilled, fried, as carpaccio
or tartare. Daily specials such as curried
pork lend variety to the menu.*

BREST
● Le Vatel
23 rue Fautras, 29200 **Map** 1A2
📞 02 98 44 51 02
📠 02 98 43 33 72
🌐 www.le-vatel.com
💳 AE, MC, V ⬤ Sun D, Mon, Sat L
🍴 €€€

*Innovative fine dining: duck carpaccio,
foie gras in fig sauce and stuffed quail.
Snails, scallops and monkfish are also
cooked to perfection.*

BREST
● Ma Petite Folie
520 rue Eugène Bere, 29200 **Map** 1A2
📞 02 98 42 44 42
💳 AE, DC, MC, V ⬤ Sun; 2 wks Feb,
3 wks Sep 🍴 €€€

*On an old fishing vessel with heaps of
charm, this is one of the best seafood
restaurants in the region. John Dory,
scallops and oysters are grilled, often
with herbs and fennel. Reservations are
essential, especially in summer.*

BREST
● Maison de L'Océan
2 quai de la Douane, 29200 **Map** 1A2
📞 02 98 80 44 84
📠 02 98 46 19 83
💳 AE, DC, MC, V 🍴 €€€€

*A popular spot for seafood, serving sea
bass, monkfish, John Dory and skate.
The harbour setting is complemented by
a covered terrace and solid wine list.*

BREST
▲ Océania
82 rue de Siam, 29200 **Map** 1A2
📞 02 98 80 66 66
📠 02 98 80 65 60
🌐 www.hotel-sofibra.com
💳 AE, DC, MC, V ⬤ Sat, Sun; mid-
Jul–mid-Aug 🍴 €€€ 🍽 (82) €€€

*Possibly Brest's most elegant restaurant.
The wine list is certainly one of the
finest in town, with scores of vintage
reds and a dozen Champagnes. John
Dory and pigeon are served along with
chutneys and pastas.*

BREST
● St-Ex
4 rue de Siam, 29200 **Map** 1A2
📞 02 98 46 33 53
💳 AE ⬤ First wk Jan 🍴 €€

*Scallop and langoustine specialist also
serving mussels, fish soup and seafood
terrines. Despite being a display feature
in the contemporary interior, the range
of wines is rather dull and expensive.*

BRIGNOGAN-PLAGES
▲ Hôtel Castel Régis
Plage du Garo, 29890 **Map** 1A2
📞 02 98 83 40 22
📠 02 98 83 44 71
💳 MC, V 🍴 €€€ 🍽 (21) €€

*Wide selection of seafood including
mussel dishes and scallops with oyster
mushrooms. Leisure facilities aside from
the lovely beach include a swimming
pool and sauna. Cottages can be rented
by the week. Fully equipped guestrooms.*

CAMARET-SUR-MER
▲ Thalassa
12 quai Styvel, 29570 **Map** 1A3
📞 02 98 27 86 44
📠 02 98 27 88 14

🌐 www.hotel-thalassa.com
💳 MC, V ⬤ Restaurant: Oct–Apr
🍴 €€ 🍽 (47) €€

*Traditional spot serving simply-cooked
fish and deliciously fresh oysters. Bright,
cheery guestrooms, plus a swimming
pool, seawater therapy centre, Turkish
bath and fitness centre, too.*

CANCALE
▲ Cancalais
12 quai Gambetta, 35260 **Map** 2A4
📞 02 99 89 61 93
📠 02 99 89 89 24
💳 MC, V ⬤ Sun D, Mon (except
during school holidays); Dec–Jan
🍴 €€€ 🍽 (10) €€€

*A delightful harbour restaurant. Lobster
is stuffed with herbs or served as a platter. The shellfish is delicately marinated
and the fish is superbly grilled.*

CANCALE
▲ Maison de Bricourt
1 rue Duguesclin, 35260 **Map** 2A4
📞 02 99 89 64 76
📠 02 99 89 88 47
💳 AE, DC, MC, V
⬤ Tue, Wed; mid-Dec–mid-Mar
🍴 €€€€€ 🍽 (17) €€€

*Pioneering seafood including lobster
and langoustines flavoured with Asian
spices, and scallops and John Dory
prepared with liqueurs or rich sauces.*

CARANTEC
▲ Restaurant Patrick Jeffroy at
L'Hôtel de Carantec
20 rue du Kelenn, 29660 **Map** IB2
📞 02 98 67 00 47
📠 02 98 67 08 25
💳 AE, MC, V ⬤ Mon L, Tue L; mid-
Sep–Jun: Sun, Mon, Tue L; last 2 wks
Nov, 3 wks Jan
🍴 €€€ 🍽 (12) €€€€

*Shellfish in abundance: langoustines in
cider, spicy scallops and crab. Intimate
modern hotel with luxurious, though
contemporary guestrooms.*

CARNAC
▲ Auberge de Ratelier
4 chemin du Douet, 56340 **Map** 1C4
📞 02 97 52 05 04
📠 02 97 52 76 11

AE, DC, MC, V ⬤ Oct–Apr: Tue, Wed (except during school holidays); Jan 🍴 €€ 🛏 (9) €€€€
Charmingly peaceful, this is one of the most intimate hotels in Brittany. Elegant menu, with turbot, bream and sea bass as prime features. Rabbit is stewed with vegetables. Extremely popular rooms, with modern touches like television sets.

CARNAC
⬤ Chez Marie
3 pl de l'Eglise, 56340 **Map** 1C4
📞 02 97 52 07 93
MC, V ⬤ May, Jun, Sep, Nov–Apr (except during school holidays): Tue L, Wed L 🍴 €
A wonderful shaded courtyard with a fading Grand Marnier sign, a liqueur that adds a spark to many of the sweet crêpes. Savoury galettes are the chef's forte; ham, three types of sausage, ratatouille (p400) and egg varieties all feature.

CARNAC
⬤ Chez Yannick
8 rue du Tumulus, 56340 **Map** 1C4
📞 02 97 52 08 67
FAX 02 97 52 60 94
MC, V ⬤ Sun, Mon D; Jan–Mar 🍴 €€
Lobster, langoustine and fish dishes as well as a wide variety of galettes with fillings such as seafood, bacon and liqueur flambées. Tranquil garden.

CARNAC
⬤ La Bavolette
9 allée du Parc, 56340 **Map** 1C4
📞 02 97 52 19 69
AE, MC, V ⬤ Apr–Jun: Tue & Wed, Jul–Aug: Tue & Wed L; Sep–Mar 🍴 €€€
A class above most eateries in Carnac-Plage. Fish brochettes and terrines of sardine and red mullet are favourites. The specialities are fish soup, flambéed langoustines and oysters. The few beef dishes are outnumbered by fish.

CARNAC
⬤ La Boucane
62 ave des Druides, 56340 **Map** 1C4
📞 02 97 52 73 19
MC, V ⬤ Dec 🍴 €€

Despite having its own tank, the large lobster dishes must be ordered in advance here. Mussels should be enjoyed with a rosé or nice Muscadet. The daily set menu mostly includes fish fondue and seafood soup.

CARNAC
⬤ La Brigantine
3 rue Colary, 56340 **Map** 1C4
📞 02 97 52 17 72
FAX 02 97 52 78 32
MC, V ⬤ Sun, Mon D; Jan 🍴 €€€
Three types of lobster served here: roasted Breton-style, flambéed with Calvados and grilled with butter. An extensive menu, with seafood pot-au-feu, bouillabaisse (p401) with lobster soup and scallop brochettes. Appetizers range from rascasse soup to langoustine ravioli and oysters by the half-dozen.

CARNAC
⬤ Le Jardin de Valentin
2 rue St-Cornély, 56340 **Map** 1C4
📞 02 97 52 19 12
MC, V 🍴 €€
Pleasant walled garden in the very centre of town. Snacks include tartines (toasted sandwiches) loaded with bacon pieces, goat's cheese, egg and ham. Heartier fare includes squid with chorizo, skate in caper sauce, and straightforward rabbit and duck dishes, too.

CARNAC
▲ Le Plancton
12 bd de la Plage, 56342 **Map** 1C4
📞 02 97 52 13 65
FAX 02 97 52 87 63
W www.hotel-plancton.com
AE, DC, MC, V
🍴 €€ 🛏 (23) €€€
Three-star luxury overlooking the long, sandy beach. Meals are nothing too adventurous, but consistently perfectly cooked. Seafood dominates, with lots of oysters and grilled fish. Modern rooms, seawater therapy and tennis courts.

CARNAC
⬤ Pieds dans l'Eau
3 ave Miln, 56340 **Map** 1C4
📞 02 97 52 18 44

MC, V ⬤ Sun, Mon 🍴 €€
A popular venue, steps from the beach, serving simply prepared meat dishes such as steak, andouille, duck tagliatelle and herb-encrusted lamb. The seafood cassoulet (p326) is a highlight. Snacks include fish brochettes and oysters.

CARNAC-PLAGE
⬤ Huitres du Rhoy
65 ave des Druides, 56340 **Map** 1C4
📞 02 97 52 24 14
MC, V ⬤ Nov–Mar 🍴 €
Great-value set menus with dishes such as moules-frites or a half-dozen oysters plus a glass of Muscadet. Mussels cooked in lobster soup are delicious. Light bites include grilled sardines, gazpacho, lamb brochettes and small platters of langoustines.

CARNAC-VILLE
▲ L'Armorie
53 ave de la Poste, 56340 **Map** 1C4
📞 02 97 52 13 47
FAX 02 97 52 98 66
MC, V 🍴 €€ 🛏 (25) €€€
Elegant dining area with a tried-and-true menu of classic beef and fish dishes. Excellent Bordelaise wines and cider. Light, bright guestrooms, a lovely garden and a seawater therapy centre.

CONCARNEAU
⬤ Aux Remparts
31 rue Théophile Louarn, 29900 **Map** 1B3
📞 02 98 50 65 66
W www.crêperie-les-remparts.com
MC, V ⬤ Sep–Jun: Mon 🍴 €
Wooden-terraced eatery offering scores of sweet crêpes such as pear, honey and caramelized banana, and savoury such as bacon and mushrooms. Grilled scallops and fish soup, too.

CONCARNEAU
⬤ Chez Armande
15 ave du Docteur Nicolas, 29900 **Map** 1B3
📞 02 98 97 00 76
AE, MC, V ⬤ Mid-Dec–first wk Jan 🍴 €€
Several grilled fish, seafood platters, crab mayonnaise and fish soup. The two

lobster dishes and the foie gras with cider sauce are highlights. Totally unoriginal but utterly tasty desserts include chocolate cake and fruit sorbets.

CONCARNEAU
● **Crêperie du Grand Chemin**
17 ave de la Gare, 29900 **Map** 1B3
📞 02 98 97 36 57
💳 MC, V ● Tue, Wed 🍴 €
Typical crêperie serving savoury galettes filled with salmon, andouille or ham. The campagne crêpe is stuffed with onions, mushrooms and a thick, creamy sauce. Over 40 sweet varieties, too, and a small wine selection.

CONCARNEAU
■ **Hôtel de France et d'Europe**
9 ave de la Gare, 29900 **Map** 1B3
📞 02 98 97 00 64
FAX 02 98 50 76 66
💳 AE, MC, V 🛏 (26) €€
Though the public lounge areas are slightly dated, the guestrooms are spacious at this centrally located hotel.

CONCARNEAU
● **Le Buccin**
1 rue Duguay Trouin, 29900 **Map** 1B3
📞 02 98 50 54 22
FAX 02 98 50 70 37
💳 AE, DC, MC, V ● Mon L, Oct–Jun: Sun D, Thu, Sat L; mid-Nov–first wk Dec
🍴 €€€
Enticing dishes at an exceptional restaurant: beef in Roquefort, roast game, prawn fricassée and tuna fondue. The quite expansive (not to mention expensive) seafood platter contains king prawns, crab, mussels and langoustines, and must be ordered 24 hours in advance. Small, superior wine list.

CONCARNEAU
● **Le Parvis des Halles**
1 rue Villebois Mareuil, 29900 **Map** 1B3
📞 02 98 97 50 65
💳 MC, V
● Sep–Jun: Wed L, Tue 🍴 €€
Red mullet, John Dory, Dover sole and turbot all feature on the long menu, in soups, seafood platters and set menus. Local game is also offered, and potato dishes as sides or mains.

CONCARNEAU
● **Le Penfret**
40 rue Vauban, 29900 **Map** 1B3
📞 02 98 50 70 55
FAX 02 98 60 53 53
💳 AE, MC, V ● Oct–Jan 🍴 €€
Rather adventurous dishes considering the restaurant's touristy location. Squid, steak, salmon and stuffed scallops feature alongside crab terrine. Decent selection of wine.

CROZON
▲ **Hôtel de la Plage**
42 bd de la Plage, 29160 **Map** 1A3
📞 02 98 16 02 16
FAX 02 98 16 01 65
💳 AE, MC, V ● Sun D
🍴 €€ 🛏 (9) €€
Restaurant with a wooden bar and stunning sea views. Seafood dominates, but several lamb and poultry dishes are also available. Large guestrooms.

DINAN
● **Chez la Mere Pourcel**
3 pl des Merciers, 22100 **Map** 2A5
📞 02 96 39 03 80
💳 AE, DC, MC, V
● Sun D, Mon; Dec–Mar: Tue
🍴 €€€€
One of Dinan's finest, serving gourmet fare amid medieval splendour. Locally sourced lamb and lobster are offered along with more avant-garde creations such as foie gras with rhubarb and excellent cod with truffles.

DINAN
● **Crêperie Ahna**
7 rue de la Poissonerie, 22100 **Map** 2A5
📞 02 96 39 09 13
💳 MC, V
● Sun; 2 wks Nov, 3 wks Mar 🍴 €
A vast grill menu including turkey, beef and duck is available at this crêperie. Lamb, turkey, andouille, smoked ham and mushrooms fill some of the galettes. Try the sweet flambéed crêpes.

DINAN
● **Crêperie des Artisans**
6 rue de Petit Fort, 22100 **Map** 2A5
📞 02 96 39 44 10
● Apr–Sep: Mon; Oct–Mar 🍴 €

Sweet and savoury crêpes on a truly wonderful vine-covered terrace in a pretty back street. The three-course set menu includes an andouille and cheese galette starter, a smoked ham and mushroom main course crêpe and a liqueur-based flambé for dessert.

DINAN
■ **Hôtel Arvor**
5 rue Pavie, 22100 **Map** 2A5
📞 02 96 39 21 22
FAX 02 96 39 83 09
💳 AE, MC, V
● Jan 🛏 (23) €€€
A modern hotel with contemporary guestrooms in a 17th-century building. A certain charm still pervades despite the up-to-the-minute decoration.

DINAN
● **La Courtine**
6 rue de la Croix, 22100 **Map** 2A5
📞 02 96 39 74 41
💳 MC, V ● Sun D, Wed 🍴 €€
A warm, cosy dining room serving the best value seafood spread in town. Pan-fried scallops in a creamy sauce, sauerkraut with three fish and steaks. Lobster soup, oysters and foie gras are excellent starters.

DINAN
● **La Goulette**
3 rue du Fossé, 22100 **Map** 2A5
📞 02 96 39 26 39
● Sun D, Mon, Sat L 🍴 €€
Flavours from the entire Mediterranean are on the menu here. Try Tunisian pastries with feta cheese and eggs, huge paellas with prawns and mussels, moussaka and various couscous dishes. Excellent wines from Algeria, Crete, France and Morocco.

DINAN
● **La Pergola**
5 rue de la Chaux, 22100 **Map** 2A5
📞 02 96 39 64 34
💳 AE, MC, V ● Wed 🍴 €€€
Gourmet dining with seafood dishes such as mackerel in Muscadet, salmon with tartare sauce and salt cod. Beef and rabbit dominate the meat section. Culinary experimentation includes the

fish cassoulet (p373) and sea bream with a dash of oriental spice.

DINAN
● L'Atelier Gourmand

4 rue du Quai, 22100 **Map** 2A5

[02 96 85 14 18

MC, V ● Sun D, Mon ¶¶ €€

Tartines (toasted sandwiches) are topped with everything from mozzarella to potatoes and ham, then served with large, leafy green salads. The mussel dishes include one with spicy chorizo. Rather nondescript wine list. Dine on the terrace overlooking the River Rance.

DINAN
● Le Cantorbery

6 rue Ste-Claire, 22100 **Map** 2A5

[02 96 39 02 52

AE, MC, V ● Wed ¶¶ €€€

The seafood menu here uses leeks in a number of its dishes: baked with fish, in the fish fondue and as a stuffing for oysters. Other offerings include grilled duck and beef, and shellfish such as scallops and langoustines. Good wine list, including a few superior Bordeaux.

DINAN
● Le Léonie

19 rue Rolland, 22100 **Map** 2A5

[02 96 85 47 47

MC, V ● Sep–Jun: Sun D, Mon, Thu D, Jul–Aug: Sun D, Mon; 1 wk Feb, 1 wk May, 3 wks Sep ¶¶ €€

A respite from the touristy town-centre fare. Modern French coastal cuisine: herby haddock, salmon with chives, mussels with Roquefort and seafood terrine. Small wine list.

DINAN
● Le St-Louis

9 rue de Léhon, 22100 **Map** 2A5

[02 96 39 89 50

MC, V ● Sun D, Wed ¶¶ €€

Giant buffet of marinated duck, seared salmon, chicken in mint and charcuterie. The decor smacks of a bygone age, with exposed stone and antiques.

DINAN
● Les Clarisses

8 rue Ste-Claire, 22100 **Map** 2A5

[02 96 85 42 57

MC, V ● Tue ¶¶ €

Simple, tasty menu of grilled steaks, loaded omelettes and really special galettes. The fillings range from mussels to scallops and fondued fish.

DINAN
● Relais Corsaires

7 rue du Quai, 22100 **Map** 2A5

[02 96 39 40 17

FAX 02 96 39 34 75

AE, DC, MC, V ● Sep–Jun: Mon D, Tue; mid-Nov–mid-Feb ¶¶ €€€

Charming exposed-stone restaurant with a huge riverside terrace. Excellent set menus with steak and Breton-style sea bass, moules marinières (p169) and peppered cod. The à la carte menu bursts with coastal flavours: scallops, fish soup and outstanding oysters.

DINARD
▲ Altaïr

18 bd Féart, 35800 **Map** 2A5

[02 99 46 13 58

FAX 02 99 88 20 49

AE, MC, V ● Sun D, Mon, Tue L, except Jul–Aug & school holidays

¶¶ €€€ 🍽 (22) €€€

Perfectly flavoured cuisine: sea bass and mushrooms, red mullet with chicory (endive) and thyme-flavoured lamb are zesty main courses. Charming guest- and public rooms brim with antiques.

DINARD
● Didier Méril

6 rue Yves Vernay, 35800 **Map** 2A5

[02 99 46 95 74

FAX 02 99 16 07 75

AE, DC, MC, V ● Wed, mid-Oct–Mar: Tue, Wed; first 2 wks Dec, first 2 wks Jan ¶¶ €€€

The most elegant eatery on the central rue Yves Verney. On the inventive menu, mixed shellfish in butter and Champagne, lobster dishes and Breton cheeses.

DINARD
▲ Du Prieuré

1 pl du Général de Gaulle, 35800 **Map** 2A5

[02 99 46 13 74

FAX 02 99 46 81 90

MC, V ● Sun D, Mon; Jan

¶¶ €€€ 🍽 (7) €€€

Arresting sea views and some of Dinard's finest seafood such as cod with tartare sauce, moules marinières (p169) and oysters. Great ice creams.

DINARD
▲ Hôtel Roche Corneille

4 rue Georges Clémenceau, 35800

Map 2A5

[02 99 46 14 47

FAX 02 99 46 40 80

W www.dinard-hotel-roche-corneille.com

AE, MC, V ● Restaurant: Nov–Mar

¶¶ €€ 🍽 (28) €€€

Lavish, contemporary dining room with white linen and pale wood. Dynamic menu of simple yet tasty dishes, such as roast duck, turbot with hollandaise sauce and Cancale oysters. A few of the modern, well-equipped guestrooms have pleasant sea views.

DINARD
● La Salle à Manger

25 bd Féart, 35800 **Map** 2A5

[02 99 16 07 95

MC, V ● Mid Oct–Apr: Sat L, Sun D, Mon; 2 wks Jan ¶¶ €€€

Smart interior showcasing delicious lobster dishes; grilled, in salads or Breton-style. Creative cuisine includes langoustine tempura and John Dory suprême. The cheese course features Breton cheeses served with prunes.

DINARD
● Pen Duick

28 rue Maréchal Leclerc, 35800

Map 2A5

[02 99 88 19 02

MC, V ¶¶ €

These outstanding galettes are filled with bacon, John Dory and cream, leeks, spinach and seaweed. Sweet crêpes include raspberry liqueur with sorbet, berries and lemon juice.

DINARD
● Têtes de Lard

14 rue Yves Verney, 35800 **Map** 2A5

[02 99 16 78 74

MC, V

● Sun, Mon; first 2 wks Dec ¶¶ €

● Restaurant ■ Hotel ▲ Hotel / Restaurant

No glitz at this great light-bites option serving moules-frites, country terrines and baked Camembert salad as starters. Brochettes of beef or fish are mainstays.

DOUARNENEZ
● Au Gouter Breton
36 rue Jean Jaurès, 29100 **Map** 1A3

📞 02 98 92 02 74

💳 MC, V ⬤ Sun, Mon (except during school holidays); last 2 wks Jun, last 2 wks Nov 🍴 €

Established but original crêperie serving seafood galettes, quality scallops and fish fondue. Local cider in ceramic mugs.

FOUGERES
● Le P'tit Bouchon
13 rue Chateaubriand, 35300 **Map** 2B5

📞 02 99 99 75 98

💳 MC, V ⬤ Sat D, Sun 🍴 €€

Traditional French fare in modern and stylish surroundings, with exposed brick and subtle lighting. Country food, with lots of beef, and sea-based dishes in equal measure. Outdoor terrace.

HENNEBONT
▲ Château de Locguénolé
Route de Port-Louis en Kervignac, 56700 **Map** 1B3

📞 02 97 76 76 76

FAX 02 97 76 82 35

💳 AE, DC, MC, V

⬤ Mon–Sat L, Oct–May: Mon

🍴 €€€€€ 🛏 (22) €€€€€

One of Brittany's finest. Lobster is the house speciality, and is served as a carpaccio, in a sausage or simply with Parmesan. The game, lamb and veal dominate the meat mains, and are spiced up with cinnamon, thyme and baked fruit. Shellfish, langoustines, red mullet and turbot come baked, pan-fried or tartare. Fantastic wine list and jaw-dropping desserts.

HUELGOAT
● Crêperie des Myrtilles
26 pl Aristide Briand, 29690 **Map** 1B2

📞 02 98 99 72 66

💳 MC, V ⬤ Nov–Jan: Mon 🍴 €

Attractive small eatery with long opening hours. Traditional crêpes come filled with local sausages, mushrooms and ham.

Sweet varieties include seasonal fruits, liqueurs and the obligatory, child-friendly chocolate concoctions.

ILE D'OUESSANT
▲ Roc'h ar Mor
Near Lampaul village centre, 29242 **Map** 1A2

📞 02 98 48 80 19

💳 MC, V

⬤ Sun D, Mon; end Nov–mid-Dec; Jan

🍴 €€ 🛏 (15) €€€

Seafood is king here, and most is simply grilled. Views stretch out over the bay. Snug guestrooms, some with balconies.

ILE D'OUESSANT
● Ty Korn
Lampaul village centre, 29217 **Map** 1A2

📞 02 98 48 87 33

🍴 €

Cosy, unpretentious bar and restaurant frequented mostly by locals. Simply prepared regional fare includes fine langoustines, sea bass and fish soup. Hearty set menu.

ILE MOLENE
▲ Hotel Kastell an Daol
Near the main harbour, 29259 **Map** 1A2

📞 02 98 07 39 11

FAX 02 98 07 38 64

💳 MC, V ⬤ mid-Jan–mid-Feb

🍴 €€ 🛏 (10) €€€

Seafood in a setting full of character. Lobster is the house speciality, stewed, cooked whole or incorporated into other dishes. Guestrooms have enough comfort to satisfy a two-star rating.

JOSSELIN
● La Sarrazine
51 bis rue Glatinier, 56120 **Map** 1C3

📞 02 97 22 37 80

💳 MC, V ⬤ Wed 🍴 €

Traditional crêperie serving tasty galettes filled with ham, mushrooms or andouille. Sweet options abound with fruit and liqueur fillings. Don't miss the Breton cider to drink.

LANNION
● Le Ville Blanche
Route de Tréguier, 22300 **Map** 1B2

📞 02 96 37 04 28

FAX 02 96 46 57 82

🌐 www.la-ville-blanche.com

💳 AE, DC, MC, V ⬤ Sun D, Mon, Wed D 🍴 €€€€

Perfect balance between the produce of land and sea, with some dishes, such as the scallop and herb salad, using both. The autumnal menu features pigeon. Interesting desserts: cherries with fennel ice cream and roasted exotic fruit.

LE CONQUET
▲ Ferme de Keringar
Lochrist (by the landing strip), 29217 **Map** 1A2

📞 02 98 89 09 59

FAX 02 98 89 04 39

🌐 www.keringar.com

💳 MC, V 🍴 € 🛏 (8) €€

Hearty Breton cooking using local cider and seaweed for flavour. Breton dish kig ha farz (p168) is the speciality of the house. Guestrooms are basic but quite comfortable and snug.

LE CONQUET
● Taverne du Port
18 rue St Christophe, 29217 **Map** 1A2

📞 02 98 89 10 90

💳 MC, V ⬤ Nov–Jan: Tue 🍴 €

Pubby atmosphere with a maritime theme. Oysters and langoustines regularly feature as starters. Main courses are more elaborate, with plates of scallops and seafood with sauerkraut. Cider and beer as well as wine.

LES-SABLES-D'OR – LES PINS
▲ La Voile d'Or
Allée des Acacias, 22240 **Map** 1C2

📞 02 96 41 42 49

FAX 02 96 41 55 45

💳 AE, MC, V ⬤ Mon L, Tue L; mid-Nov–mid-Mar 🍴 €€€€

🛏 (22) €€€€

Seafood eatery overlooking a lagoon. Lobster and scallops are the house specialities. Oysters, langoustines and foie gras terrine with pear chutney also served. Up-to-date guestrooms with lovely wooden bathrooms.

LORIENT
● La Taverne de Maître Kanter
23 pl Aristide Briand, 56100 **Map** 1B3

C 02 97 21 32 20
FAX 02 97 21 52 64
W www.tavernes-maitre-kanter.com
S MC, V **11** €€

The largest collection of fresh seafood in the region, in a somewhat commercial setting. Seafood platters, bowls of mussels, sea bass, John Dory, red mullet and giant lobsters for two. Duck, pigeon and steaks frequently appear.

LORIENT
● **Le Jardin Gourmand**
46 rue Jules Simon, 56100 **Map** 1B3
C 02 97 64 17 24
FAX 02 97 64 15 75
S AE, MC, V ● Sun, Mon
11 €€€

One of the best restaurants in town. Andouille, anchovy and courgette (zucchini) tarts for starters, and a fish or meat choice to follow. Fine Breton cheeseboard and over 40 wines.

LORIENT
● **Le Marrakech**
18 rue Maréchal Foch, 56100 **Map** 1B3
C 02 97 21 91 41
S MC, V ● Mon; Jul **11** €€

A stunning interior in the style of a Marrakech merchant's house, with exquisite tiles. Scores of tagines and couscous dishes as well as succulent lamb brochettes. Starters include Moroccan soup and Tunisian pastries with an egg in the middle. Interesting list of Moroccan wines.

LORIENT
● **Le Victor Hugo**
36 rue Lazare Carnot, 56100 **Map** 1B3
C 02 97 64 26 54
FAX 02 97 64 24 87
S AE, DC, MC, V ● Sun, Mon L; late Feb–early Mar; late Aug–mid-Sep
11 €€

The distinctly non-Breton dishes here include Catalan-style tuna, Provence-style grilled fish and Porto-style ham. Beef in Roquefort sauce, steaks and duck are also served.

LORIENT
■ **Les Pêcheurs**
7 rue Jean La Garde, 56100 **Map** 1B3

C 02 97 21 19 24
FAX 02 97 21 13 19
W www.chez.com/hotellespecheurs
S MC, V ● Sun ◇ (21) €

Friendly and traditional one-star hotel close to the marina in a quiet area of town. Slightly dated guestrooms and a lively in-house bar that is popular with the region's residents.

LORIENT
● **Route Gourmande**
10a quai des Indes, 56100 **Map** 1B3
C 02 97 21 21 13
S MC, V **11** €€

Portside establishment with a covered wood terrace and a rich wood interior. Favourite dishes include beef, mussels and tuna steaks, along with duck and Breton lamb. Salads are a huge pull, with fine Provençal, fish and seafood varieties. Small but adequate list of mainly French wines.

LORIENT
● **Trattoria la Sardegna**
30 rue Paul Guieysse, 56100 **Map** 1B3
C 02 97 64 13 05
FAX 02 97 21 46 43
S MC, V ● Mon **11** €€

Crispy pizzas and hearty pastas come laden with buffalo mozzarella, seafood, olives and capers. Italian-style grilled meats such as herb-encrusted pork. Authentic coppa salami and prosciutto di San Daniele. Italian wines, including several fine Chiantis, outnumber French.

MORLAIX
● **Crêperie L'Hermine**
35 rue Ange de Guernisac, 29600 **Map** 1B2
C 02 98 88 10 91
S MC, V ● Jun: Wed, Sun; 2 last wks Jan **11** €

Seaweed, squid and scallops fill the galettes at this cheery unpretentious crêperie with its pleasant wooden terrace. Savoury options include ham, sausages and eggs. Good wines, and better Breton cider.

MORLAIX
■ **Hôtel de l'Europe**
1 rue d'Aiguillon, 29600 **Map** 1B2

C 02 98 62 11 99
FAX 02 98 88 83 38
W www.hotel-europe-com.fr
S AE, DC, MC, V ● Last wk Dec
◇ (60) €€€€

Old-style sophistication in the heart of town. Public rooms feature aged wood, period furniture, chandeliers and a centuries-old staircase. Guestrooms are large, stylish and supremely comfortable; better still are the suites, with antiques.

MORLAIX
● **La Marée Bleue**
3 rampe St-Melaine, 29600 **Map** 1B2
C 02 98 63 24 21
S MC, V
● Sun D; Sep–Jun: Mon; Oct **11** €€

Veal with olives, lamb with garlic and seafood stew are highlights on the small menu here. Specialities include foie gras and seafood with asparagus.

MORLAIX
● **L'Argoat**
11 rue de Callac, 29600 **Map** 1B2
C 02 98 63 40 73
● Sun **11** €

Simple and unpretentious restaurant serving great food. Only one set menu is served each day, with a simple but hearty fish, meat or pasta dish followed by a choice of Breton cheeses.

MORLAIX
● **Le Sterne**
Quai de Léon, Port de Plaisance, 29600 **Map** 1B2
C 02 98 15 12 12
S MC, V **11** €€

On a boat in the harbour. Stunning seafood with an original twist: sea bass in Breton cider and langoustine stew. Oysters and mussels are also served. Reservations recommended.

MORLAIX
● **Les Bains Douches**
45 allée du Poan-Ben, 29600 **Map** 1B2
C 02 98 63 83 83
S AE, MC, V ● Sun D, Sat L
11 €€

One of the most original restaurants in town, housed in the former public baths, with beautiful tiles and original stained glass still intact. Typical northern French appetizers, from moules marinières (p169) to a seafood terrine and tripe with pears, and some less usual ones such as roast rabbit with wholegrain mustard and a rare duck carpaccio.

MORLAIX
● **Restaurant La Reine Anne**
45 rue du Mur, 29600 **Map** 1B2
📞 02 98 88 08 29
💳 MC, V ⬤ Mon 🍴 €
The fixed menus at this sedate eatery are almost all meat-based – a rarity in fish-rich Brittany. Try the flank steak, charcuterie with andouille, lamb chops or a simple, unadorned piece of beef, the most popular dish.

PAIMPOL
● **La Braise**
20 rue des Huit Patriotes, 22500
Map 1C2
📞 02 96 55 11 41
💳 MC, V ⬤ Sun L, Nov–Jan: Mon D
🍴 €
Grilled dishes such as beef and andouille. Seafood stew and Breton-style moules-frites (with a cider base) also available.

PAIMPOL
● **La Cotriade**
16 quai Armand Dayot, 22500 **Map** 1C2
📞 02 96 20 81 08
💳 MC, V ⬤ Mon, Fri D, Sat L; 2 wks Feb, end-Jun–mid-Jul, 1 wk Nov
🍴 €€
Simple preparations of lobster, squid, sea bream and bass. Try the mixed shellfish in butter or the lobster risotto.

PAIMPOL
● **Le Marché dans l'Assiette**
18 rue Huit Patriotes, 22500 **Map** 1C2
📞 02 96 55 15 90
⬤ Mon 🍴 €
Amazing value Breton cooking. Terrines and tartines (toasted sandwiches), salmon, pork and lamb. Tasty vegetable dishes include courgette (zucchini) mousse and potatoes with goats' cheese.

PAIMPOL
▲ **Le Repaire de Kerroc'h**
29 quai Morand, 22500 **Map** 1C2

📞 02 96 20 50 13
FAX 02 96 22 07 46
💳 MC, V 🍴 €€
🌙 (13) €€€€
Star anise, honey and fennel are used to flavour many of the fish dishes here. Meats are similarly treated and include duck with apricots, honey and prunes. Many of the individual guestrooms have parquet floors and harbour views.

PAIMPOL
● **L'Islandais**
19 quai Morand, 22500 **Map** 1C2
📞 02 96 20 93 80
FAX 02 96 20 72 68
💳 MC, V 🍴 €€
A popular crêperie overlooking the marina and serving traditional Breton galettes, oysters, lobster and quite fine langoustine dishes.

PERROS-GUIREC
▲ **Villa Ker Mor**
38 rue Maréchal Foch, 22700 **Map** 1C2
📞 02 96 23 14 19
FAX 02 96 23 18 49
🌐 www.hotel-ker-mor.com
💳 AE, MC, V 🍴 €€€
🌙 (32) €€€
Seafood prepared with a creative touch: curried scallops, fried tuna and a giant seafood platter that must be ordered a day in advance. Pleasant guestrooms benefit from views over the hotel gardens or the sea. Fantastic beach nearby.

PLUGUFFAN
● **La Roseraie de Bel Air**
Impasse de la Boissiere, 29700 **Map** 1A3
📞 02 98 53 50 80
FAX 02 98 53 43 65
💳 AE, MC, V ⬤ Sun D, Mon
🍴 €€€
Fabulously inventive use of seafood: galettes stuffed with savoury shellfish, lobster purée or fish. Main dishes include sea bass and baked turbot served with fig jam and crystallized lemons. Game and lamb also. Many wines from Languedoc-Roussillon.

PONT-AVEN
▲ **Le Moulin de Rosmadec**
Venelle de Rosmadec, 29930 **Map** 1B3

📞 02 98 06 00 22
FAX 02 98 06 18 00
💳 MC, V ⬤ Wed, Sep–Jun: Sun D
🍴 €€€€€ 🌙 (4) €€€€
Ancient country house with one of the very best restaurants in the region, serving black truffles, sweetbreads and tender lamb. Extensive use of rich butter and cream sauces. Wide selection of wines, including some of France's most famous labels. Charming guestrooms.

PONTIVY
● **La Petite Bretonne**
20 rue du Fil, 56300 **Map** 1C3
📞 02 97 25 73 49
⬤ Sun 🍴 €
Galettes are the speciality here with excellent fillings as diverse as fondued fish, andouille and potatoes, salmon and lemon or Roquefort and Gruyere. Sweet varieties mostly feature fruit and a generous drizzle of honey. Several ciders served.

PONTIVY
● **La Petite Marmite**
15 rue des Forges, 56300 **Map** 1C3
📞 02 97 27 94 71
💳 MC, V ⬤ Tue D, Wed; first wk Jan, first wk Sep 🍴 €€
Some of Pontivy's best traditional cuisine served in an old-fashioned venue. Small à la carte menu with several seafood dishes, rabbit stew with apples and grilled fish with onions.

QUIBERON
● **Capitainerie**
1 rue Conserveries, 56170 **Map** 1B4
📞 02 97 30 38 39
💳 MC, V 🍴 €€
Savoury galettes are the speciality at this traditional harbour establishment. Oysters, scallops and fish are popular fillings, served with lemon juice and crème fraîche. Seafood platters and grilled fish, too.

QUIBERON
● **Jules Verne**
1 bd Hoëdic, 56170 **Map** 1B4
📞 02 97 30 55 55
💳 AE, MC, V ⬤ Tue, Wed
🍴 €€€€

Pride of place goes to the many lobster dishes at this gourmet seafront eatery, one of Quiberon's best. The sea bream, sea bass, monkfish and scallops are excellent. Superb selection of wines.

QUIBERON
● **Port Maria**
42 rue Port Maria, 56170 **Map** 1B4
📞 02 97 50 17 68
FAX 02 97 30 45 03
💳 MC, V ● Sun D, Mon 🍴 €€€
Seafood specialist with two extensive set menus and an à la carte range. Lobster flambéed in Cognac, various mussel dishes, oysters, peppered duck and a choice of large salads.

QUIMPER
● **Au Port d'Antan**
22 quai de l'Odet, 29000 **Map** 1A3
📞 02 98 55 56 66
💳 MC, V ● Mon L, Thu D, Sat
🍴 €€
Set menus offer a choice for all budgets at this modern establishment. On the seafood menu: sardines and scallop brochettes. Duck and goats' cheese feature in some of the inland dishes. Small wine list from around the country.

QUIMPER
● **Au P'tit Rafiot**
7 rue de Pont l'Abbé, 29000 **Map** 1A3
📞 02 98 53 77 27
💳 MC, V
● Mon, Tue 🍴 €€
Stylish eatery serving French and Mediterranean seafood dishes, such as lobster stew, fish couscous, Breton bouillabaisse (p401) and delicious seafood cassoulet (p326). Lobster is the house speciality. Decent wine list.

QUIMPER
● **Cosy**
2 rue du Sallé, 29000 **Map** 1A3
📞 02 98 95 23 65
FAX 02 98 95 23 82
💳 MC, V ● Sun, Mon 🍴 €€
Some of the best wines in Quimper's town centre are found here, although none of them are more than a few years old. Tarts and grilled meats feature strongly, the former loaded with tomatoes,

smoked ham and salmon. A sign outside advertises a "no crêpes, no fries" policy.

QUIMPER
● **Crêperie Ty-Borledenn**
10 rue Guéodet, 29000 **Map** 1A3
📞 02 98 95 57 18
💳 MC, V ● Oct–May: Mon–Thu D, 2 wks Oct, 2 wks Mar 🍴 €
Giant selection of sweet and savoury crêpes within a delightful exposed-stone dining room. The paysanne crêpe includes leeks, potatoes and sausages. Liqueur-flambéed crêpes, too.

QUIMPER
■ **Hôtel Gradlon**
30 rue de Brest, 29000 **Map** 1A3
📞 02 98 95 04 39
FAX 02 98 95 61 25
W www.hotel-gradlon.com
💳 AE, DC, MC, V ● Dec–Jan
🍽 (22) €€€
Pleasant, peaceful hotel with all mod cons. Guestrooms feature lots of wood, and some look out over the hotel's gardens. Apartments available.

QUIMPER
● **La Fleur de Sel**
1 quai Neuf, 29000 **Map** 1A3
📞 02 98 55 04 71
💳 AE, MC, V ● Sun, Sat L
🍴 €€
The gourmet range of original dishes ranks this in a league above most of Quimper's other restaurants. The menu features red mullet with roast fennel, herbed roast duck, and langoustine and foie gras salads. A very solid, if small, collection of wines.

QUIMPER
● **La Krampouzerie**
9 rue du Sallé, 29000 **Map** 1A3
📞 02 98 95 13 08
💳 AE, MC, V ● Sun, Mon
🍴 €
Seafood, including scallops in pepper sauce, oysters and seaweed, fill the crêpes here. Varieties stuffed with sausages, cubes of bacon, mushrooms and eggs are a meal in themselves. Wines (all Vin de Pays) are great value. Convivial sun-blessed terrace.

QUIMPER
● **Le Restau à Vins**
3 pl du Styvel, 29000 **Map** 1A3
📞 02 98 52 15 52
FAX 02 98 90 37 86
💳 MC, V ● Sun; 2 wks Aug, 2 wks May, late Dec 🍴 €€
On the menu, goat's cheese, smoked duck and salmon as well as scallops steeped in Armagnac. Pork and fish feature on the Mediterranean and seafood menus, respectively. Unusual desserts include nougat ice cream.

QUIMPER
● **Le Flamboyant**
32 quai de l'Odet, 29000 **Map** 1A3
📞 02 98 52 94 95
💳 MC, V ● Sun L, Mon
🍴 €€
Creole creations from the Indian Ocean island of Réunion, including chicken and king prawns spiced with ginger. The inexpensive set menu offers a great opportunity to try a variety of dishes.

QUIMPER
● **Le Pélican**
2 rue de Pont l'Abbé, 29000 **Map** 1A3
📞 02 98 53 70 48
● D 🍴 €
Locals congregate to eat great food at low prices at the rustic tables here. Andouille de Troyes, Breton sausages and omelettes are some of the regular offerings. Apricot, kiwi fruit and walnut rums make delicious digestifs.

QUIMPERLE
● **Du Pont-Fleuri**
5 rue Ellé, 29300 **Map** 1B3
📞 02 98 96 19 35
FAX 02 98 39 11 51
💳 MC, V ● Sun L, Mon 🍴 €
Smoked ham, andouille and excellent Breton sausages fill several of the crêpes here. Salads include tuna, feta and warm goats' cheese. Hearty lamb or beef entrecôte, too.

QUIMPERLE
● **La Cigale Egarée**
5 rue Jacques Cartier, 29300 **Map** 1B3
📞 02 98 39 15 53
💳 MC, V ● Sun, Mon D 🍴 €€

Sheltered terrace, perfect for enjoying a carafe of wine and some rather intricate fare: salmon in tequila, scallops tartare with foie gras and seafood ravioli with whisky sauce. The Breton lamb with caramelized spices is particularly good.

QUIMPERLE
● L'Assiette de l'Isole
2 rue Isole, 29300 **Map** 1B3

C 02 98 96 10 70

**MC, V ● Mon Ⅱ €€

Stylish eatery serving simply prepared catch of the day and grilled sardines and scallops as well as more interesting meat dishes such as filet mignon in Armagnac or duck in local cheese sauce.

QUIMPERLE
● Le Bistro de la Tour
2 rue Dom Maurice, 29300 **Map** 1B3

C 02 98 39 29 58

FAX 02 98 39 21 77

@ bistrodelatour@wanadoo.fr

AE, DC, MC, V ● Sun D, Sat L

Ⅱ €€€

Dine in a spectacularly opulent setting, surrounded by Quimperlé's finest selection of wines. Lobster, langoustines and a catch of the day are constant features. Some of the fish dishes bear a faint Indian influence. The sommelier menu allows samples of a host of wines.

QUIMPERLE
■ Le Vintage
20 rue Brémond d'Ars, 29300 **Map**1B3

C 02 98 35 09 10

FAX 02 98 35 09 29

**AE, DC, MC, V ● (10) €€€

The best hotel in town: modern, Art Deco and gloriously dated all at the same time. Hand-painted murals in the individually styled, well-equipped rooms.

QUIMPERLE
● Ty Gwechall
4 rue Mellac, 29300 **Map** 1B3

C 02 98 96 30 63

MC, V ● Mon, Tue D (except during school holidays); first 2 wks Dec Ⅱ €

Mussels, scallops and squid fill the crêpes here. Sweet varieties are laced with Chantilly cream, rum or ice cream. There are four Breton beers on the

menu, including outstanding Cervoise and Duchesse Anne.

RENNES
● A la Ciboulette
33 rue Ste-Melaine, 35000 **Map** 2A5

C 02 99 87 50 25

MC, V ● Sun, Sat L Ⅱ €

Crêpes, large salads and a meat-based daily special in a cosy crêperie. Savoury galettes are outnumbered by sweet crêpes with chestnut jam, myrtle and various liqueurs. Lighter bites include smoked duck salad or omelettes.

RENNES
● Au Marchés des Lices
3 pl du Bas de Lices, 35000 **Map** 2A5

C 02 99 30 42 95

MC, V

● Sun; 3 wks Aug, 2 wks Jan Ⅱ €

Traditional crêperie serving Breton cider in lovely ceramic cups. Savoury galettes: the Niçoise is filled with ratatouille (p400) and chorizo. There are good-value grilled meat dishes at lunchtime.

RENNES
● Café Breton
14 rue Nantaise, 35000 **Map** 2A5

C 02 99 30 74 95

MC, V ● Sun Ⅱ €€

Local haunt serving house speciality tarts featuring goat's cheese, snails and ham. The charcuterie includes thinly sliced salami, Italian-style spicy mortadella and andouille. The enormous, tasty salads are worth sampling.

RENNES
● Chez Maman
15 rue de Penhoët, 35000 **Map** 2A5

C 02 99 79 20 97

MC, V ● Sun Ⅱ €€

Rustic restaurant serving salads, including Breton cheeses, avocado and melon, or artichokes, almonds and tasty Scandinavian fish, and grilled meats like filet mignon and herb-encrusted lamb.

RENNES
● Crêperie Ste-Mélaine
13 rue St-Melaine, 35000 **Map** 2A5

C 02 99 38 72 06

MC, V ● Sun, Mon D Ⅱ €

A cut above most crêperies, with fillings such as scallops, smoked salmon and ham in the galettes. Omelettes are filled with bacon, mushrooms and goat's cheese. Pretty terrace.

RENNES
● Des Souris et des Hommes
6 rue Nationale, 35000 **Map** 2A5

C 02 99 79 75 76

MC, V ● Sun

Ⅱ €€

One of the city centre's finest, serving sea bream with basil and red mullet with potatoes and nuts. Classic roasts of duck and lamb, too. Pretty terrace on a busy pedestrian street.

RENNES
■ Hotel des Lices
7 pl des Lices, 35000 **Map** 2A5

C 02 99 79 14 81

FAX 02 99 79 35 44

w www.hotel-des-lices.com

MC, V ● (45) €€€

Great location just off Place St-Michel and Place des Lices. Stylish guestrooms with lots of modern touches; many have balconies looking out over Rennes' most buzzing streets.

RENNES
● La Bonne Pâte
6 rue Derval, 35000 **Map** 2A5

C 02 99 38 88 87

MC, V ● 24, 25 Dec, Jan 1st Ⅱ €

Stylish crêperie with a spacious upstairs dining room. Original galettes: the highly recommended terroir is stuffed with potatoes and Camembert; the Basquaise with chicken and ratatouille (p400). Crêpes are filled with myrtle jam, cassis and baked banana fillings.

RENNES
● La Cantine Délices
16 rue Nantaise, 35000 **Map** 2A5

C 02 99 31 36 36

MC, V ● Sun, Mon

Ⅱ €€

All dishes are the same price at this stylish, relaxed town-centre option. Novel cuisine: langoustines with guacamole, risotto with mushrooms and saffron and steak in red wine.

RENNES

● **La Fontaine aux Perles**

96 rue de la Poterie, 35200 **Map** 2A5

☏ 02 99 53 90 90

FAX 02 99 53 47 77

w www.lafontaineauxperles.com

AE, DC, MC, V

◐ Aug: Sun, Mon ▮▮ €€€€

Gourmet cooking at a gorgeous country house on the outskirts of Rennes. Extravagant menu of mostly seafood, with scallop flan, langoustines with vegetables and Caribbean-style snails. Lamb and foie gras, too.

RENNES

● **Le Corsaire**

52 rue d'Antrain, 35700 **Map** 2A5

☏ 02 99 36 33 69

FAX 02 99 36 33 69

AE, DC, MC, V

◐ Sun D, Wed, Jul–Aug: Sun & Mon ▮▮ €€€€

Classic, upmarket, mirrored dining room. Interesting menu with fennel and orange turbot and lamb with garlic, and an inexpensive set menu offering a mix of beef and fine seafood.

RENNES

● **Le Gange**

34 pl des Lices, 35000 **Map** 2A5

☏ 02 99 30 18 37

w www.legange.com

AE, MC, V ◐ Sun

▮▮ €€

Top-notch Indian and Pakistani cuisine. Three-course lunchtime menus feature raita, naan, curried chicken with rice and a sorbet. Lamb and chicken are served in rich, exquisite sauces. Indian pistachio ice cream and Kingfisher beer, too.

RENNES

● **L'Escu de Runfao**

11 rue du Chapitre, 35000 **Map** 2A5

☏ 02 99 79 13 10

FAX 02 99 79 43 80

w www.escu-de-runfao.com

AE, MC, V ◐ Sun D, Sat L

▮▮ €€€€

One of the most luxurious restaurants in the city, with three exquisite dining rooms filled with period furniture as well as a small garden at the back. The very finest meats and fish, from sea bream and turbot to beef and lamb.

RENNES

● **L'Ouvrée**

18 pl des Lices, 35000 **Map** 2A5

☏ 02 99 30 16 38

FAX 02 99 30 16 38

@ louvree@dial.oleane.com

AE, DC, MC, V

◐ Sun D, Mon, Sat L

▮▮ €€€€

Fabulous array of foie gras, in a terrine or served with steak. Offers a superior and extensive selection of Champagnes and red wines.

ROSCOFF

▲ **Chardons Bleus**

4 rue Amiral Réveillère, 29680 **Map** 1B2

☏ 02 98 69 72 03

FAX 02 98 61 27 86

AE, MC, V ◐ Sep–Jun: Thu, Sun D; Feb ▮▮ € ⌂ (10) €€

Seafood-biased menu with just a few concessions to meat eaters, including pepper steak. Highlights include grilled lobster in butter with prawns, crab mayonnaise and, of course, the ubiquitous but satisfying seafood platter for two. Modern guestrooms are among the best deals in town.

ROSCOFF

● **La Moule au Pot**

13 rue Edouard Corbière, 29680 **Map** 1B2

☏ 02 98 19 33 60

MC, V ◐ Wed ▮▮ €

Chalkboards strung up all over the pretty façade of this very authentic Breton restaurant advertise seafood: mussels cooked in cider, huge portions of seafood lasagne and fish brochettes. Salads, too, are loaded with whelks and mussels. Breton kir as well as cider available for thirsty diners.

ROSCOFF

● **Le Surcouf**

14 rue Amiral Réveillère, 29680 **Map** 1B2

☏ 02 98 69 71 89

MC, V ◐ Tue, Wed; Jan ▮▮ €€

Stunning coastal food starting with plates of mussels, snails and a half-dozen oysters, and following on with more imaginative mains such as the pollack in mussel sauce or a seafood casserole. Young red wines to accompany.

ROSCOFF

▲ **Le Temps de Vivre**

19 pl Lacaze-Duthiers, 29680 **Map** 1B2

☏ 02 98 19 33 19

FAX 02 98 19 33 00

w www.letempsdevivre.net

AE, DC, MC, V

◐ May, Jun, Sep, Oct: Sun D, Mon, mid Nov–Apr: Sun D, Mon, Tue L; Oct, first 2 wks Jan

▮▮ €€€€ ⌂ (15) €€€€

Inspired, contemporary restaurant right on the seafront. Plain beef dishes, foie gras, oysters, salmon, snails and fine mussels grace the menu. Guestrooms have stylish furniture, ultra-modern bathrooms, white linen and black marble.

ROSCOFF

● **Les Mouettes**

Pl de la République (corner of rue Jules Ferry), 29680 **Map** 1B2

☏ 02 98 69 73 81

MC, V ◐ Sun ▮▮ €

Hearty, traditional cooking: grilled fish, seafood salads, scallop brochettes and plates of oysters. Small terrace.

ROSCOFF

● **Ti Saozon**

30 rue Gambetta, 29680 **Map** 1B2

☏ 02 98 69 70 89

MC, V ◐ L; Sun, Mon ▮▮ €

A traditional crêperie with a no-smoking policy. Savoury crêpes are filled with sausage, seaweed and artichokes, and more standard fillings such as egg, ham and Breton cheese. Simple list of ciders and reasonable wines.

ST-AVE

● **Le Pressoir**

7 rue de l'Hôpital, 56890 **Map** 1C4

☏ 02 97 60 87 63

FAX 02 97 44 59 15

AE, DC, MC, V

◐ Sun D, Mon, Tue

▮▮ €€€€

Delectable dishes from around France served in arty, modern surroundings. Try

the bold lamb in milk and potato with truffle, red mullet with rosemary-covered potatoes or turbot with andouille. A very excellent wine list.

ST-BRIEUC
● Amadeus
22 rue Gouët, 22000 **Map** 1C2
📞 02 96 33 92 44
FAX 02 96 61 42 05
📧 AE, MC, V
⬤ Sun, Mon
🍴 €€€

Elegant gourmet restaurant serving unique cuisine such as truffle-topped sea bass, tuna ratatouille (p400) and rabbit and potato galettes. Lovely Breton biscuits (cookies) with fruit and Amaretto chocolate cake are particularly special.

ST-BRIEUC
■ Hotel du Champ-de-Mars
13 rue du Général Leclerc, 22000
Map 1C2
📞 02 96 33 60 99
FAX 02 96 33 60 05
@ hoteldemars@wanadoo.fr
📧 MC, V 🛏 (21) €€

Two-star hotel close to the railway station. Guestrooms are well appointed and have charm.

ST-BRIEUC
● La Sicilia
12 rue Trois Frères Le Goff, 22000
Map 1C2
📞 02 96 33 58 02
📧 MC, V ⬤ Sun L, Wed, Sat L
🍴 €

Pasta, pizza and salads are served at this authentic Italian restaurant. Pasta dishes come with a variety of French toppings like eggs, local sausage or langoustines. Similarly, pizzas are topped with scallops, eggs and crème fraîche. Generous salad plates feature charcuterie and carpaccio.

ST-BRIEUC
● Le Madure
14 rue Quinquaine, 22000 **Map** 1C2
📞 02 96 61 21 07
📧 MC, V ⬤ Sun, Sat L 🍴 €

Traditional establishment serving barbecued beef, pork and lamb, minced beef

with shallots and lamb with Provençal herbs. Clarets and Loire wines feature.

ST-BRIEUC
● Le P'tit Bouchot
4 rue Houvenagle, 22000 **Map** 1C2
📞 02 96 61 58 66
⬤ Wed, Sat L, Sun L; 2 wks Sep 🍴 €

Inexpensive local seafood, with a fondue the signature dish. Also mussel dishes, many in a lobster or fish-based sauce, and a notable cassoulet (p373) loaded with mushrooms and scallops.

ST-BRIEUC
● Les Bains
5 rue St-François, 22000 **Map** 1C2
📞 02 96 33 24 36
📧 MC, V
⬤ Sat D, Sun; 2 wks Aug 🍴 €€

No-nonsense meat and fish specialist. Beef is the house forte and the many grilled cuts are served with simple sauces or just a few slices of tomato. Steak tartare and red mullet also served.

STE-MARINE
● L'Agape
52 rue de la Plage, 29120 **Map** 1A3
📞 02 98 56 32 70
FAX 02 98 51 91 94
📧 AE, DC, MC, V ⬤ Sun D, Mon, Tue L, Jul–Aug: Mon, Tue L; Jan–mid Feb
🍴 €€€€

Fantastic seafood and local game, including pigeon, in quaint, countrified surroundings. Fish dishes are rather elaborate and well presented. One set menu devoted to local Breton cuisine.

ST-MALO
● A la Duchesse Anne
5 pl Guy la Chambre, 35400 **Map** 2A4
📞 02 99 40 85 33
FAX 02 99 40 00 28
📧 MC, V ⬤ Oct–Apr: Sun D, Mon L, Wed, May–Sep: Mon L, Wed; Dec–Jan
🍴 €€€€

An institution serving outstanding seafood. Appetizers include gratinée or terrine of langoustines. Grilled fish, veal and pigeon terrine are popular mains. The expensive set menu offers foie gras or oysters and a choice of lobster dishes, served with Veuve Clicquot Champagne.

ST-MALO
● Bénétin
Chemin Rochers-Sculptés, Rothéneuf, 35400 **Map** 2A4
📞 02 99 56 97 64
📧 MC, V ⬤ Oct–Apr: Tue, Wed
🍴 €€€

Four kilometres (2.5 miles) down the coast towards Cancale from St-Malo. Seafood platters brimming with shellfish, langoustines and fish are the house speciality. The savvy chef takes a quite modern approach to the presentation of dishes and garnishes them liberally with fruit and vegetables.

ST-MALO
▲ Grand Hôtel de Courtoisville
69 bd Hébert, 35400 **Map** 2A4
📞 02 99 40 83 83
FAX 02 99 40 57 83
📧 AE, DC, MC, V
⬤ Jan; late Nov–Dec 26
🍴 €€€ 🛏 (44) €€€€

Market-fresh seafood platters, which must be ordered a day in advance, and lamb entrecôte. The refined dining room looks onto the gardens and gets extremely busy during the summer months. Huge guestrooms have giant beds and elegant furniture.

ST-MALO
▲ Hôtel de l'Univers
16 pl Chateaubriand, 35400 **Map** 2A4
📞 02 99 40 89 52
FAX 02 99 40 07 27
🌐 www.hotel-univers-saintmalo.com
📧 AE, MC, V
🍴 €€€ 🛏 (63) €€€

Superbly located just inside the city walls, and with modern guestrooms, this hotel is one of the best in town. The bar has stood the test of time, making it something of an institution in St-Malo. The restaurant does have a slightly kitsch air, although it is an excellent people-watching spot. A wide range of steaks, several salads and heaps of pasta make up the multilingual menu. Reservations essential.

ST-MALO
● La Brigantine
13 rue de Dinan, 35400 **Map** 2A4

📞 02 99 56 82 82

⭘ Tue, Wed (except during school holidays); last 2 wks Nov, 3 wks Jan 🍴 €

Seafood, including prawns, scallops and shellfish, fills many of the galettes at this old-town crêperie. The ice-cream crêpes are the house speciality.

ST-MALO
● **La Chalut**

8 rue de la Corne de Cerf, 35400 **Map** 2A4

📞 02 99 56 71 58

FAX 02 99 56 71 58

💳 AE, MC, V

⭘ Mon & Tue L, Sep–May: Mon & Tue D

🍴 €€€€

One of St-Malo's finest, with cuisine which is second to none. Sea bass, red mullet and monkfish are flavoured with basil, lobster sauce and asparagus. Foie gras and oysters to start and a short but fine wine list.

ST-MALO
▲ **La Porte St Pierre**

2 place de Guet, 35400 **Map** 2A4

📞 02 99 40 91 27

FAX 02 99 56 06 94

💳 AE, MC, V ⭘ Tue, Thu L, Jul–Aug: Tue; mid Nov–late Jan

🍴 €€€ 🛏 (24) €€€

One of La Porte St Pierre's most elegant restaurants. On the menu, excellent seafood such as lobster, langoustines, oysters and mussels. For meat-lovers there are simple meat dishes. Superb wine list. Tiny, comfortable rooms.

ST-MALO
● **Le Chasse Marée**

4 rue Grout de St-Georges, 35400 **Map** 2A4

📞 02 99 40 85 10

FAX 02 99 56 49 52

💳 AE, MC, V

⭘ Sun L, Sat L

🍴 €€

Stylish dining behind a fading red façade. Duck, beef and fish carpaccios; mussels and oysters are simply presented. For the main course, everything from steak to peppered duck and fondued fish. High-class wines from the Pouilly-Fuissé vineyards.

ST-MALO
● **Le Salidou**

5 rue Puits aux Braies , 35400 **Map** 2A4

📞 02 23 18 20 95

💳 MC, V ⭘ Sep–Jun: Sun, Mon (except during school holidays); Jan 🍴 €

The tiny à la carte menu has salmon, moules-frites and scores of crêpes. The Provençal galette comes with peppers, onions, ham and courgettes (zucchini), while the fermier is stuffed with goat's' cheese. Sweet crêpes are filled with a variety of ice creams, including a delicious nougat flavour.

ST-MALO
● **Restaurant Escales**

14 rue du Boyer, 35400 **Map** 2A4

📞 02 99 56 61 93

💳 MC, V ⭘ Sep–Jun: Tue & Wed

🍴 €

Restaurant with a great terrace on a busy pedestrian crossroads. Large brochette selection on offer, composed of scallops, prawns or lamb as well as deep-fried squid, grilled steak and many crisp, quality salads.

ST-POL-DE-LEON
▲ **Pomme d'Api**

49 rue Verderel, 29250 **Map** 1B2

📞 02 98 69 04 36

FAX 02 98 29 18 23

💳 AE, MC, V

⭘ Sun D, Mon, Tue, Sep–May: Sun L

🍴 €€€ 🛏 (12) €€€

The town's best restaurant, with a focus on meat, offering hearty, elaborate servings of lamb, beef and game. Guestrooms are set inside a centuries-old stone building.

ST-QUAY-PORTRIEUX
● **Fleur de Blé Noir**

9 rue du Commandant Malbert, 22410 **Map** 1C2

📞 02 96 70 31 55

💳 MC, V ⭘ Sun, Wed (except during school holidays); Jan 🍴 €

Two menus of fine galettes: de la terre (from the land) and de la mer (from the sea). Andouille, fish and ham feature in the former. Flambéed scallops with sardine fillets and sole fillet with Camembert star in the latter.

ST-QUAY-PORTRIEUX
▲ **Gerbot d'Avoine**

2 bd du Littoral, 22410 **Map** 1C2

📞 02 96 70 40 09

FAX 02 96 70 34 06

🌐 www.gerbotdavoine.com

💳 MC, V 🍴 €€

🛏 (20) €€€

Dishes include duck and foie gras terrine, steak, mussels, duck in cider sauce and veal with Muscadet. The rather dated bedrooms detract slightly from the stunning clifftop location.

ST-QUAY-PORTRIEUX
▲ **Hôtel St-Quay**

72 bd Maréchal Foch, 22410 **Map** 1C2

📞 02 96 70 40 99

FAX 02 96 70 34 04

💳 MC, V ⭘ Sun D, Mon; Jan

🍴 €€ 🛏 (7) €€€

Intimate town-centre hotel serving interesting dishes such as scallop carpaccio, langoustines in Muscadet and sea bass and squid cassoulet (p373). Guestrooms are slightly old-fashioned but full of character.

ST-QUAY-PORTRIEUX
▲ **Ker Moor**

13 rue de Près-le-Sénécal, 22410 **Map** 1C2

📞 02 96 70 52 22

FAX 02 96 70 50 49

🌐 www.ker-moor.com

💳 AE, DC, MC, V

🍴 €€€

🛏 (29) €€€€

Four set menus, the most impressive offering three lobster courses. Oysters, sardines, langoustines and whelks also feature. Most of the stylish, well-appointed rooms have sea views. Reservations essential.

VANNES
● **Atlantique**

16 pl Gambetta, 56000 **Map** 1C4

📞 02 97 54 01 58

FAX 02 97 54 08 21

💳 MC, V 🍴 €€

Large, maritime-themed establishment. Plates of clams, prawns and oysters for starters. Lobster cassoulet (p373) or pasta and roasted sea bass for the main

---

● Restaurant   ■ Hotel   ▲ Hotel / Restaurant

course. A windowed kitchen allows a view of the chef at work.

VANNES

● Brasserie des Halles

9 rue des Halles, 56000 **Map** 1C4

C 02 97 54 08 34

FAX 02 97 47 80 64

W www.brasserie-des-halles.com

E MC, V

● Sun D, Sat

Ⅱ €€

Well-prepared, unfussy cuisine at this side-street restaurant. Skate, sea bass and monkfish come together on the brochette océanne. Popular moules-frites, and a renowned set menu offering veal and andouille.

VANNES

■ La Marébaudière

4 rue Aristide Briand, 56000

Map 1C4

C 02 97 47 34 29

FAX 02 97 54 14 11

W www.marebaudiere.com

E MC, V

◇ (41) €€€

Just outside the town centre is this charmingly attractive white Breton house with modern guestrooms. Good hotel bar and pleasant grounds.

VANNES

● La Morgate

21 rue de la Fontaine, 56000 **Map** 1C4

C 02 97 42 42 39

FAX 02 97 47 25 27

E MC, V ● Sun, Mon

Ⅱ €€

Meat dishes dominate the à la carte menu, with beef sourced from Limousin. Steaks are topped with foie gras or grated Parmesan. Seafood includes oysters, salmon and lobster tagliatelle.

VANNES

● La Villa Valencia

3 rue Pierre René Roge, 56000

Map 1C4

C 02 97 54 96 54

FAX 02 97 47 00 16

E MC, V **Ⅱ** €€

Relaxed atmosphere in Vannes' town centre. Refined innovation on the menu

with dishes such as seafood lasagne, Gorgonzola veal and scallops with superb smoked duck.

VANNES

● Le Boeuf dans l'Assiette

6 rue Lesage, 56000 **Map** 1C4

C 02 97 47 09 66

E MC, V

● Sun, Mon; first 2 wks Jul **Ⅱ** €€

Restaurant specializing in beef, mostly grilled, with an extensive red-wine list to match the solid cooking. Besides hearty steak dishes, the menu also offers lamb, duck and foie gras.

VANNES

● Le Carré Blanc

28 rue du Port, 56000 **Map** 1C4

C 02 97 47 48 34

E MC, V

● Sun D, Mon D, Sat L

Ⅱ €€

The most adventurous restaurant in town. Modern French cooking: pesto-glazed salmon, sea bream in milk and a revolutionary pepper and avocado mousse. Several superior aged clarets.

VANNES

● Le Margot

12 rue Porte Poterne, 56000

Map 1C4

C 02 97 47 18 86

E MC, V ● Sun

Ⅱ €

Limited à la carte menu with local meats, including sausages, andouille and fine lamb, fish dishes and scallop brochettes, and an extensive range of pizzas, which are liberally topped with fine ham and seafood. Terrace looking out over the city's ramparts.

VANNES

● Régis Mahé

24 pl de la Gare, 56000 **Map** 1C4

C 02 97 42 61 41

FAX 02 97 54 99 01

E AE, DC, MC, V

● Sun, Mon; last 2 wks Nov, last 2 wks Feb, last wk Jun **Ⅱ** €€€

Michelin-starred restaurant with a truly exceptional menu. Roast sea bass in marmalade, veal with Parmesan,

Moroccan lamb tagine, foie gras and outstanding lobster.

VANNES

● Saladière

36 rue de Port, 56000 **Map** 1C4

C 02 97 42 52 10

FAX 02 97 47 85 73

E MC, V ● Sun, Wed D

Ⅱ €

Harbourside restaurant serving large salads and big bowls of mussels – some with unusual combinations such as Muscadet sauce and Parmesan. Colourful, flavourful salads with prawns and Parma ham. Loire and Bordeaux wines dominate the small list.

VANNES

● Table Alsacienne

21 rue Ferdinand le Dressay, 56000

Map 1C4

C 02 97 01 34 53

E MC, V ● Sun, Mon; Aug

Ⅱ €€

House specialities include flam-menkueche (p119) and large cuts of well-seasoned grilled meats. The seafood platter is also of note.

VITRE

● Pichet

17 bd de Laval, 35500 **Map** 2B5

C 02 99 75 24 09

FAX 02 99 75 81 50

E AE, MC, V ● Sun, Wed D, Thu D

Ⅱ €€€

Utter elegance, innovation and pure inspiration. Try the scallops stuffed with walnuts and foie gras with fried apple. Reservations essential.

VANNES

● Table des Gourmets

6 rue Pontois, 56000 **Map** 1C4

C 02 97 47 52 44

FAX 02 97 47 52 44

● Sun D, Mon, Sat L

E AE, DC, MC, V

Ⅱ €€€

Modern restaurant, close to the ramparts and the port, serving stuffed pigeon with foie gras, and a large range of seafood such as baked sea bass and sea bream meunière.

LOIRE VALLEY

France's longest river unites this vast region, stretching from the Atlantic into the heart of France. Its central area was a playground for the nobility, who built châteaux such as Blois, Chenonceaux and Chambord. From the pastures of Anjou and Berry, the coastal marshes of the Vendée and Guérande, the vineyards of Touraine, the arable plains of the Beauce and the forests of the Sologne come food and wine fit for kings.

The Flavours of the Loire Valley

This huge area can take pride in a truly diverse range of specialities, from the seafood of its Atlantic coast to the freshwater fish of its many rivers; from the game birds of its royal hunting forests to the tiny white mushrooms that flourish in the darkness of its caves.

BEST MARKETS

Amboise Large market beside the Loire, Wed, Fri & Sat
Angers Bustling outdoor street market, daily
Chartres Busy covered market, Wed, Thu, Fri & Sat
Loches In the medieval town, Wed and Sat am
Nantes Tue–Sun am
Tours Daily upmarket covered market, plus stalls outside on Wed and Fri

Potatoes for sale in Angers market

MEAT AND CHARCUTERIE

Free-range chickens, *poulet fermier Loué*, are raised in the Sarthe, Touraine and Orléanais, and Challans duck in the Vendée. Anjou and Mayenne are home to grass-fed cattle, and the Berry to hardy Berrichon sheep. The sandy forests and lakes of the Sologne are the domain of deer, wild boar, pheasant, partridge, hare and duck.

The main charcuterie is *rillettes*, shredded and potted slow-cooked pork, a speciality of the Sarthe *(rillettes du Mans)* and Tours (usually with pork liver as well). *Rillons* are large, crunchy chunks of fried salted belly pork. The Vendée produces excellent cured ham. Look out for terrines in the Sologne, game pie in Chartres, and *pâté Berrichon*, baked in pastry with hard-boiled eggs.

FISH

The ports of the Loire-Atlantique and Vendée produce a variety of fish and shellfish. La Turballe near La Baule is the main sardine port on the Atlantic coast. The Ile de Noirmoutier is known for line-caught fish, lobster and oysters, as well as farmed turbot. But best of all is the region's freshwater fish, including pike, pike-perch, shad, tench, salmon, eels and lampreys.

CHEESE

Along with Poitou, the Touraine and Berry are France's most important areas for goats' cheeses. Log-shaped, ash-covered Ste-Maure de Touraine AOC, with a straw

SEL DE GUÉRANDE

Top-quality salt is produced naturally by the evaporation of seawater in the shallow salt pans of the marais salant de Guérande. For more than 1,000 years it has been harvested by hand, with no treatment or additives. It is valued for both its culinary qualities and its high magnesium content. Most forms large crystals of grey-tinted salt or gros sel; more scarce is the finer, white fleur de sel, "flower of salt", which is said to have a violet flavour and is much-prized by chefs. The purity and quality of sel de Guérande is recognized by a label rouge (see p11).

Left Fresh hake **Centre** Ste-Maure cheese **Right** Butcher's shop selling Sologne game

CHAMPIGNONS DE PARIS

The *champignon de Paris*, or button mushroom, is so named because it was first grown for the Paris market. The damp caves in the tufa cliffs along the Loire, originally dug to quarry stone for construction, are ideal for their cultivation. Other varieties are now also grown. A local speciality is *galipettes* – large mushroom caps slowly roasted over a wood fire and filled with butter, garlic and parsley.

Champignonnière du Saut-aux-Loups, Montsoreau
(02 41 51 70 70).

Musée du Champignon,
St-Hilaire-St-Florent, Saumur
(02 41 50 31 55).

Mushroom crop growing in the tufa caves of the Loire

down the middle to hold its shape and aerate it, can be eaten fresh, or matured in damp cellars. Selles-sur-Cher AOC is a flat round, cindered mild cheese. Valençay AOC, a truncated, ash-covered pyramid, is firmer and with a more pronounced taste, and Pouligny-St-Pierre AOC is a narrower pyramid (nicknamed "Tour Eiffel"), mottled and blueish outside and white within. Crottin de Chavignol is a small round cheese matured until hard and dry.

Cows' milk cheeses include Feuille de Dreux, a flat, soft cheese with a chestnut leaf on the top, ash-covered Olivet, and washed-rinded Port-Salut and Curé Nantais.

FRUIT AND VEGETABLES

Thanks to the mild climate, winter vegetables thrive in the Nantes area. Virtually all of France's lamb's lettuce *(mâche)* is grown here, as well as watercress, peas, radishes, turnips, early leeks and carrots. Samphire is gathered from the salt marshes near Nantes, and the Ile de Noirmoutier is known for its new potatoes. The Sologne produces some of France's best asparagus and lentils are grown in the Berry.

The Beauce, around Chartres, is known as "the bread basket of France" for its prairie-like expanses of wheat. Orchards north of Tours and in the Sarthe are important for apples and pears; Comice pears originated near Angers. Other fruit includes plums of the Touraine and strawberries from around Saumur.

BAKED GOODS

Two of France's largest biscuit companies are based in Nantes: LU, maker of Petit-Beurre and Petits Ecoliers, and BN, creator of the smiley-faced BN biscuit. A speciality of Sablé-sur-Sarthe is the *petit sablé*, a thin shortbread. The *pithiviers* of the Sologne is made with flaky pastry and almond paste. Around Saumur look out for *fouaces*, small, flat rolls filled with goats' cheese or meat.

Regional Dishes

Many of the Loire's most typical dishes have now become classics, to be found all over France. Others are very much local treats, using local produce, to be sought out and savoured in the region's many fine restaurants.

ON THE MENU

Alose à l'oseille Shad in a sorrel hollandaise sauce

Canard nantais Roast duck served with Muscadet wine sauce

Citrouillat Pumpkin pie

Civet de marcassin Wild boar stew

Géline à la lochoise Géline hen in cream sauce

Lapin chasseur Wild rabbit cooked with mushrooms

Porc aux pruneaux Pork fillets cooked with prunes in wine and cream sauce

Potage d'asperges Asparagus soup

Prunes au Vouvray Plums stewed in Vouvray wine

Ragoût d'anguilles et cuisses de grenouille Eel and frogs' legs stew

Soupe à la citrouille Pumpkin soup

Tarte aux rillettes Open tart of potted pork, eggs and cream

THE LOIRE MENU

All manner of terrines and pâtés may start a meal here, notably the game terrines of the Sologne, or *rillettes*, spread thickly on bread. Soups include creamy *veloutés* of asparagus, pumpkin or *mâche*. On the coast, there are shellfish and grilled sardines, or the now rare and pricey *frîture* of *alevins* (tiny elvers).

Main courses include fish cooked in a salt crust or poached and served with *beurre blanc*, with sorrel or in a sauce of cream, white wine and mushrooms. Loire Valley wines go into a variety of dishes, such as *coq au Chinon*, *carpe au vin rouge*, or a Muscadet sauce to accompany roast duck. Superb free-range poultry may be simply roasted or prepared as a fricassée with cream and butter. Meat dishes include excellent Maine-Anjou beef and Berrichon lamb: look out for the potent, slow-cooked *gigot de sept heures*. From around November to March, game dishes dominate the menu in the Sologne, including blood-thickened civets or roast game served with wine-infused pears or a sauté of the wild mushrooms that also flourish in the forest.

Many desserts are fruit-based, including prunes in wine and *tarte Tatin*. *Crémets d'Anjou* are creamy hearts made of whipped cream, sugar and beaten egg white, dribbled with a coulis of red fruit. A cave-dwellers' curiosity is *pommes tapées*, whole peeled apples that have been dried in bread ovens in the tufa cliffs and then stewed in wine.

GIGOT DE SEPT HEURES

This flavourful method of slow-cooking lamb (or, more correctly, mutton) originates in the Berry and should ideally made with meat from the Berrichon sheep. A leg of lamb *(gigot)* and sliced carrots are browned. Then the bottom of a casserole is lined with pieces of bacon rind *(couennes)* and the *gigot* is placed on top, with the carrots, thyme, bay leaf, a little nutmeg, and an entire unpeeled head of garlic, sliced horizontally in half, then moistened with white wine. The pot is sealed (traditionally with a band of pastry), then the dish is cooked in a low oven for seven hours, until the meat is so tender that it falls off the bone.

Lapin chasseur, or "hunter's rabbit", from the Sologne

Left Gigot de sept heures **Right** Tarte Tatin

REGIONAL DINING

The following restaurants are among those serving regional dishes at reasonable prices:

Auberge le Relais
Le Perrier *(see p204)*

Brasserie la Cigale
Nantes *(see p206)*

Hôtel de France
La Chartre-sur-le-Loir *(see p203)*

La Bonne Etape
Amboise *(see p196)*

La Cotriade
Les Herbiers *(see p204)*

Le Champalud
Champtoceaux *(see p198)*

Les Délices du Château
Saumur *(see p209)*

Le Grand Sully
Sully-sur-Loire *(see p210)*

Orangerie
Villandry *(see p211)*

Interior of the famous Brasserie La Cigale, in Nantes

BEURRE BLANC SAUCE

According to local lore, this sauce was invented at the end of the 19th century by Clémence Lefeuvre, cook at a simple Loire-side inn (according to one version, it was invented by accident when a *sauce Béarnaise* went wrong). Finely chopped shallots are reduced with white wine vinegar, nutmeg and black pepper, double cream is added and then butter is beaten in bit by bit. *Beurre blanc* traditionally accompanies poached fresh-water fish, although it is also used for noble saltwater fish such as sea bass and turbot.

BAR EN CROÛTE DE SEL DE GUÉRANDE

In this grand classic of fish cooking, a whole sea bass is baked in a salt crust, which seals in the flavour and moisture. The fish is laid on, and totally covered in, a thick layer of salt (sometimes mixed with a little thyme) to totally enclose it. As the dish bakes, the salt forms a hard crust. The fish is served in its dish; when the crust is broken, the skin lifts off easily. Good served simply with lemon and new potatoes or with a *beurre blanc*.

TARTE TATIN

This caramelized upside-down apple tart was invented in the 19th century by the Tatin sisters who ran an inn at Lamotte-Beuvron in the Sologne, and it is now one of France's best-loved desserts. Eating apples are peeled, cored and sliced. A round baking dish is buttered and sprinkled with caster sugar. The apple pieces are laid neatly on top, with more butter and sugar over them, then the dish is baked very slowly, so that the sugar caramelizes but doesn't burn. It is then covered with pastry and returned to a moderate oven until cooked. The tart is turned out upside down on to a plate and served lukewarm. Purists insist on eating it plain, but it is particularly delicious with a dollop of *crème fraîche*.

Regional Wines

From breezy Nantes on the Atlantic coast to Bourges way inland, the river Loire links a vast array of appellations. Sprinkled with fairytale castles, France's "valley of the kings" is home to a range of grapes including the multi-talented Chenin and the famous Sauvignon of Sancerre.

BEST PRODUCERS: ANJOU-SAUMUR

Anjou and Anjou-Villages
Château de la Guimonière,
Château de la Roulerie,
Domaine Ogereau
Bonnezeaux Château de
Fesles
Coteaux du Layon Château
de Breuil, Château de la
Guimonière, Domaine Ogereau,
Domaine Jo Pithon
Quarts-de-Chaume Château
Bellerive
Savennières Château de
Chamboureau, Château
d'Epiré, Château de la Roche-
aux-Moines, Clos de Varennes,
Domaine des Baumard
**Saumur and Saumur-
Champigny** Château du
Hureau, Château de Villeneuve,
Domaine René-Noël Legrand,
Domaine des Roches Neuves

PAYS NANTAIS

Embracing the area southwest of Nantes, this coastal zone is undeniably Muscadet country. No seafood platter is complete without a bottle of this dry white, which at best will be crisply tart, with appley, fresh almond or floral flavours and carry a natural spritz of gas, as fresh as the ocean spray. Look for Muscadet bottled *sur lie* – the wine spends the winter on its lees, or sediment, giving freshness and a slight sparkle with more complexity. Best is Muscadet de Sèvre-et-Maine.

ANJOU-SAUMUR

In the minds of many, Anjou is still equated with easy-drinking, rather unexciting rosé. However, the star appellations in this area are the white wines made from Chenin, which include some of the world's most luscious sweet wines.

Muscadet sur lie

Eighty-year-old vines

Anjou and Anjou-Villages The generic appellation produces mostly undistinguished red, rosé and white wines. Anjou-Villages produces only red wines made from Cabernet Franc and Cabernet Sauvignon which tend to be deeply coloured and well concentrated, with deep fruit flavour. The best come from old vines around the village of Brissac, with velvety tannins and blackberry richness.

Coteaux du Layon Produced from superripe Chenin grapes, these sweet wines are long-lived. Layon producers are also the source of the best dry Anjou whites. Six villages are said to produce superior wines and have the right to append their names to the generic appellation. Coteaux du Layon-Chaume is a single-village appellation producing top examples of rich, amber-gold wines with candied fruit flavour from extremely low yields of Chenin. Quarts-de-Chaume is a small, south-facing vineyard with its own AOC producing luscious whites usually from very old vines. The lovely vineyards

MAJOR VINEYARDS OF THE LOIRE

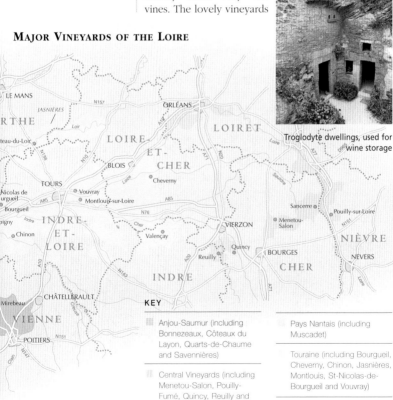

Troglodyte dwellings, used for wine storage

KEY

- Anjou-Saumur (including Bonnezeaux, Côteaux du Layon, Quarts-de-Chaume and Savennières)
- Central Vineyards (including Menetou-Salon, Pouilly-Fumé, Quincy, Reuilly and Sancerre)
- Haut-Poitou
- Pays Nantais (including Muscadet)
- Touraine (including Bourgueil, Cheverny, Chinon, Jasnières, Montlouis, St-Nicolas-de-Bourgueil and Vouvray)
- — Delimited VDQS regions
- ···· *Département* boundary

Bonnezeaux wines from
Château de Fesles

BIODYNAMISM

An oft-contested method of winemaking, the merits of which are the subject of much debate, biodynamism advocates a return to the ancient practice of cultivation according to the phases of the moon. Nicolas Joly, owner of Savennières Coulée de Serrant, is one of the most active and ardent defenders of this approach. Biodynamism refuses the use of weedkillers, chemical fertilizers and mechanical harvesting, preferring to "energize" the vines and the soil with natural products applied in homeopathic doses.

of Bonnezeaux lie on three south-facing slopes in the south of the Layon valley. The magnificent sweet wines will age gracefully for up to 30 years.

Savennières These dry whites are undoubtedly some of the best in the world. Extremely long-lived, supremely elegant with intense mineral notes, these wines are a magnificent expression of the Chenin grape.

Saumur and Saumur-Champigny Saumur is traditionally associated with sparkling reds, whites and rosés. The chalky *tuffeau* soil that is so typical of the whole region is particularly suitable for producing grapes with the right acidity for making sparkling wine.

TOURAINE

Radiating out from the genteel city of Tours, the vineyards of the Touraine are probably the best known for Chinon, Bourgeuil and Vouvray.

Touraine This all-encompassing appellation produces various styles of wine, including sparkling. Gamay and Cabernet Franc are the main sources for the fruity reds, and whites are essentially Sauvignon Blanc with a good nettle-like quality. Touraine-Mesland is a village appellation worthy of special note.

Chinon Cabernet Franc is the chief grape around the medieval fortified town of Chinon. Well-made Chinon reds can be an orgy of berry fruit flavour, sometimes mixed with ripe black cherry and tangy liquorice, and built to last; others can be mean-flavoured, with vegetal notes of green pepper. The hillsides give wines with firm structure and deep aroma whereas the gravelly terraces on the banks of the Vienne river produce light wines for drinking young.

Bourgueil and St-Nicolas-de-Bourgueil Delicious scents of raspberry, violet and red pepper characterize these neighbouring appellations on the north side of the river Loire.

Château de Cheverny

Hillside vineyards of Bourgueil

Vouvray No appellation exemplifies the widely differing styles of Loire whites as well as Vouvray. Rabelais christened Vouvray "taffeta wine", referring both to its shimmering golden colour and its quality. Overlooking the Loire just a few miles from Tours, Vouvray produces still and sparkling wines from Chenin that may be dry, semi-dry or very sweet depending on the vintage. The best sweet wines offer opulent scents of apricot, quince and beeswax and will age almost indefinitely.

Montlouis These whites come in the same styles as Vouvray, often acquiring a characteristic taste of almond after a few years.

Jasnières A tiny appellation, it produces delicious dry or sweet wines from Chenin. They are rarely found outside the area.

Vouvray

THE CONFRERIE DES ENTONNEURS RABELAISIENS

The French remember with great affection François Rabelais, the writer and gourmet born in Chinon in 1483. His revolutionary comical satires *Pantagruel* and *Gargantua* are celebrations of eating and drinking, Rabelais' favourite pastimes. Established in 1962, the Brotherhood of the Rabelaisian Songsters of Chinon celebrates its illustrious forefather's *joie de vivre* and love of wine. The brotherhood has thousands of members all over the world who have to swear to "fight those who abuse wine by adding water and who drink it unreasonably".

THE CENTRAL VINEYARDS

The vineyards at the heart of the Loire Valley, 200 km (125 miles) from Paris, are home to Sauvignon Blanc, an ideal partner for the local Crottin de Chavignol goat's cheese *(see p189)*, and some light Pinot Noirs.

Sancerre Sauvignon comes into its own here for whites with a scent of blackcurrant leaf that have been famous and fashionable for many a year now. The fact that the village itself, perched high above the vineyard, is picture-postcard pretty has obviously contributed to the wine's popularity. The best reds are excellent.

Pouilly-Fumé A smoky *(fumé)*, flinty flavour characterizes the Sauvignon from Pouilly's soils. AOC Pouilly-sur-Loire comes from the dull Chasselas grape.

Menetou Salon, Quincy and Reuilly Rich, moreish Sauvignons from Menetou marry well with food and can be very good value, as can crisp and very dry Quincy. Summer fruits come to mind with the fresh reds of Reuilly, whilst the whites cry out for a plate of seafood or shellfish.

Where to Eat & Stay

AMBOISE
▲ Chateau de Pray
Route de Chargé, D751, 37400 **Map** 7D2
📞 02 47 57 23 67
FAX 02 47 57 32 50
🖥 www.chateauxhotels.com
🅴 AE, DC, MC, V
⬤ Mon, Tue L; 2nd & 3rd wks Jan
🍴 €€€ 🍽 (19) €€€€

In a 17th-century fortress, this restaurant serves dishes like Touraine vegetables in a Champagne-foie gras bouillon, and pike-perch braised with shallots and vinegar. Antiques in the guestrooms.

AMBOISE
▲ Le Choiseul
36 quai Charles Guinot, 37400 **Map** 7D2
📞 02 47 30 45 45
FAX 02 47 30 46 10
🖥 www.choiseul.com
🅴 AE, DC, MC, V ⬤ last wk Dec–1st wk Jan 🍴 €€€ 🍽 (32) €€€€€

Views of the Loire from this 18th-century mansion with comfortably sized, tastefully decorated guestrooms, airy dining rooms and a flower-filled garden. A summer meal might include millefeuille of snails with potatoes in vinaigrette, or roast pike-perch with sorrel cream.

AMBOISE
⬤ La Bonne Etape
962 quai des Violettes, 37400 **Map** 7D2
📞 02 47 57 08 09
FAX 02 47 57 12 33
🅴 MC, V ⬤ Sun D, Mon, Wed; last wk Feb–1st wk Mar, last 2 wks Dec–1st wk Jan 🍴 €€

A reasonably priced spot with riverside views and a menu of classics, carefully prepared. The sandre au beurre blanc (p191) is excellent, as are the terrines.

ANCENIS
⬤ La Toile à Beurre
82 rue St-Pierre, 44150 **Map** 6B2
📞 02 40 98 89 64
FAX 02 40 96 01 49
🅴 AE, MC, V ⬤ Sun D, Mon, Wed D; 3rd wk Feb, last 2 wks Sep–1st wk Oct
🍴 €€

A dining room featuring exposed stonework, terracotta floors and a fine stone fireplace add to the draws of this restaurant. Selections include Loire lamprey or old-fashioned hare stew.

ANGERS
⬤ Auberge d'Eventard
Route de Paris, 49480 **Map** 6B1
📞 02 41 43 74 25
FAX 02 41 34 89 20
🅴 AE, MC, V ⬤ Sun D, Mon, Sat L; 1st 2 wks Jan, 1st wk early May
🍴 €€

Surrounded by tapestries and paintings, diners enjoy duck foie gras and pike-perch in an Anjou wine sauce. Saumur is the focus of the quality wine list.

ANGERS
⬤ La Boucherie
27 bd Maréchal-Foch, 49100 **Map** 6B1
📞 02 41 25 39 25
FAX 02 41 25 39 29
🅴 MC, V 🍴 €

As one might guess from the name (The Butcher's), meat dishes are the highlight at this busy place – the tender, perfectly cooked entrecôte with a rich pepper sauce is notable. Straightforward wine list.

ANGERS
▲ Le Salamandre
1 bd Maréchal Foch, 49100 **Map** 6B1
📞 02 41 88 24 82
FAX 02 41 87 22 21
@ info@hoteldanjou.fr
🅴 MC, V ⬤ Sun D
🍴 €€ 🍽 (53) €€€€

The salamander symbol of King Louis XI features in many of the Renaissance-themed rooms. Main dishes, such as smoked-salmon medallions, duck with courgette- (zucchini-) flower soufflé, reflect the chef's talent.

ARGENT-SUR-SAULDRE
▲ Le Relais de la Poste
3 rue Nationale, 18410 **Map** 7F1
📞 02 48 81 53 90
FAX 02 48 73 30 62
🅴 AE, MC, V

⬤ Sep–Jun: Sun D, Mon
🍴 €€ 🍽 (10) €€

Charming 15th-century postal inn with a menu laden with local specialities such as foie gras with grated strawberries and black pepper. Guestrooms are tidy and modestly appointed.

ARGENTON-SUR-CREUSE
▲ Le Cheval Noir
27 rue Auclert-Descottes, 36200 **Map** 7E3
📞 02 54 24 00 06
FAX 02 54 24 11 22
🅴 MC, V ⬤ Sep–May: Sun D
🍴 €€ 🍽 (20) €€

Charming, modest inn run by the Jeanrot family. Chef Christophe blends popular dishes such as soused pig's trotters in a Bordeaux sauce with more daring ventures such as millefeuille of crab with artichoke.

ARNAGE
⬤ Auberge de la Matfeux
289 ave Nationale, 72230 **Map** 6C1
📞 02 43 21 10 71
FAX 02 43 21 25 23
🅴 AE, DC, MC, V ⬤ Sun D, Mon, Tue D, Wed D; 1st 2 wks Jan, Jul–mid-Aug
🍴 €€€

Near the famous racetrack and a park, a renowned address serving modern dishes such as langoustines ravioli and chicken breast with lobster.

AZAY-LE-RIDEAU
⬤ Auberge du XIIème Siècle
1 rue du Château in Sache 8km (5 miles) east of Azay-Le-Rideau, 37190 **Map** 6C2
📞 02 47 26 88 77
FAX 02 47 26 88 21
🅴 MC, V ⬤ Sun D, Mon, Tue L; 1st 3 wks Jan, 1st 2 wks Jun, 1st wk Sep
🍴 €€

Half-timbered country house. The skills of Xavier Aubrun and Thierry Jimenez have gained a reputation in the area; find menu choices such as the delicate salad of pigeon and foie gras, roast langoustines with ginger, and a tempting range of chocolate desserts. Azay-le-

---

⬤ Restaurant   ■ Hotel   ▲ Hotel / Restaurant

Rideau and Chardonnay de Touraine
are on the wine list.

BANNEGON

▲ **Moulin de Chaméron**

2.5km (1.5 miles) south of Bannegon on
D76, 18210 **Map** 7F2

C 02 48 61 83 80

FAX 02 48 61 84 92

⊘ AE, MC, V **●** mid-Nov–mid-Mar;
restaurant: Mon L, Tue L, Mar–May: Mon
D **🍴** €€€ **🍽** (13) €€€

A converted 18th-century windmill.
Cuisine in the modern style: duck foie
gras with pear and red wine compote,
or roast pigeon with caramelized gravy.
Nicely tended rooms.

BEAUGENCY

▲ **L'Abbaye**

2 quai de l'Abbaye, 45190 **Map** 7E1

C 02 38 44 67 35

FAX 02 38 44 87 92

W www.chateauxhotels.com/abbaye

⊘ AE, DC, MC, V

🍴 €€€€ **🍽** (13) €€€€

A 17th-century abbey with a gourmet
restaurant specializing in beef and
freshwater fish; pike-perch with a
creamy mushroom sauce is the house
speciality. Guestrooms have parquet
floors and exposed medieval stone.

BEHUARD

● **Les Tonnelles**

12 rue Chevalier-Buhard, 49170 **Map** 6B2

C 02 41 72 21 50

FAX 02 41 72 81 10

⊘ MC, V **●** Sun, Mon, Oct–Dec:
Wed D; mid-Dec–mid-Feb **🍴** €€€€

On L'Ile de Béhuard and with a small
garden, this restaurant serves oyster
and cabbage crêpes and, for dessert,
roast pears. On the wine list, Loire
whites and sweet Andalusian wine.

BLERE

▲ **Le Cheval Blanc**

5 pl Charles-Bidault, 37510 **Map** 7D2

C 02 47 30 30 14

FAX 02 47 23 52 80

W www.lechevalblancblere.com

⊘ AE, DC, MC, V **●** Sun D, Mon L,
Fri L; Jan–mid-Feb

🍴 €€€ **🍽** (12) €€€

Chef Michel Blériot adroitly blends the
savoury produce of the market and the
rhythm of the seasons in this 17th-
century monastery. The pigeon stuffed
with foie gras and cabbage is amazing.

BLOIS

● **Au Bouchon Lyonnais**

25 rue des Violettes, 41000 **Map** 7D1

C 02 54 74 12 87

FAX 02 54 74 12 87

⊘ MC, V **●** Sep-Jun: Sun, Mon;
1st wk Sep, 1st wk Nov, 3rd wk
Dec–1st wk Jan **🍴** €€

Delicious dishes such as monkfish in
pepper sauce, and salmon in roasted
nut paste. Airy, light dining room.

BLOIS

● **L'Orangerie du Château**

1 ave Jean-Laigret, 41000 **Map** 7D1

C 02 54 78 05 36

FAX 02 54 78 22 78

W www.orangerie-du-chateau.fr

⊘ MC, V

● Sun D, Wed; mid-Feb–mid-
Mar, 3rd wk Aug, mid-Nov

🍴 €€€

A large, airy oak-beamed space in a
15th-century château. Traditional
approach to regional favourites: roast
pike-perch and aromatic andouillette. A
dependable, enticing wine list.

BLOIS

● **Au Rendez Vous Des Pêcheurs**

27 rue du Foix, 41000 **Map** 7D1

C 02 54 74 67 48

⊘ AE, MC, V **●** Sun, Mon L; 1st
2 wks Jan, 1st 3 wks Aug **🍴** €

Famed for seafood and fish creations
like crayfish flan with parsley and roast
bass with shallot confit Tatin.

BOISMORAND

▲ **Auberge Des Templiers**

Les Bézards, off A77, exit 19, 45290
Map 7F1

C 02 38 31 80 01

FAX 02 38 31 84 51

W www.lestempliers.com

⊘ AE, DC, MC, V **●** Feb

🍴 €€€€ **🍽** (30) €€€€€

Luxurious hotel with elegant and spacious
guestrooms, surrounded by wild but

tended parkland. Game dishes and
pike-perch with artichokes. Top-notch
Pouilly Fumé and Sancerre.

BONNEVAL

▲ **Hostellerie du Bois Guibert**

In Guibert on N10, 1km (0.62 miles)
from Bonneval, 28800 **Map** 3D5

C 02 37 47 22 33

FAX 02 37 47 50 69

W www.bois-guibert.com

⊘ AE, DC, MC, V

🍴 €€€ **🍽** (14) €€€

The restaurant is the heart of this 18th-
century building. Brilliant re-creations
of classic dishes like filet mignon with
cardamom and summer vegetables. The
guestrooms have a lovely period feel.

BOUIN

● **La Pêcherie**

Off D758, route from Bourgneuf, 85230
Map 6A2

C 02 51 68 69 14

⊘ MC, V **●** Tue D, Wed **🍴** €

A small fisherman's house, complete
with jaunty blue shutters, with dishes
such as pike-perch with smoked bacon
and a delicate scallop brochette. Try a
nicely chilled local white.

BOULAY-LES-BARRES

● **Relais De La Beauce**

49 route d'Orléans, 45140 **Map** 7E1

C 02 38 75 36 04

FAX 02 38 75 33 39

⊘ AE, DC, MC, V **●** Sun D, Mon; last
wk Mar, last wk Jul **🍴** €€€€

A half-timbered building tucked away in
a bucolic landscape. Curried John Dory
stands out, as does rich calf's liver.

BOURGES

▲ **Abbaye St-Ambroix**

60 ave Jean Jaurès, 18000 **Map** 7F2

C 02 48 70 80 00

FAX 02 48 70 21 22

⊘ AE, DC, MC, V **🍴** €€€€€

🍽 (59) €€€€

Renaissance-era chapel turned gourmet
restaurant serving roasted pigeon with
caramelized cassis and risotto. Reuilly
and Menetou-Salon vintages star on
the wine list. First-class guestrooms in
a 17th-century abbey.

BOURGES

● Bourbonnoux

44 rue Bourbonnoux, 18000 **Map** 7F2

☎ 02 48 24 14 76

💳 DC, MC, V ● Sep–Jun: Sun D, Fri; 2nd wk Feb, 3rd wk April, last two wks Aug ⊞ €€

A charming spot with sunny decor and creatively arranged presentations of classic dishes. All of the game, but particularly quail and hare, is excellent.

BRACIEUX

● Relais De Bracieux

1 ave de Chambord, 41250 **Map** 7E1

☎ 02 54 46 41 22

FAX 02 54 46 03 69

W www.relaisdebracieux.com

💳 AE, DC, MC, V

● Tue, Wed; mid-Dec–mid-Jan

⊞ €€€€€

Specialities like crispy lobster with dried tomatoes, or cushion of braised pork with Loire marc. Elegant tables.

BREHEMONT

▲ Le Castel de Bray et Monts

5km (3 miles) southwest of Azay-Le-Rideau on D57 and D16, 37190 **Map** 6C2

☎ 02 47 96 70 47

FAX 02 47 96 57 36

💳 AE, MC, V ● Last wk Nov–3rd wk Feb ⊞ €€€ 🍷 (10) €€€

This unusual hotel's rooms are carved out of the chalky river cliffs. Beyond the novelty bedrooms lay the delights of sophisticated dishes like salmon sausages.

BRINON-SUR-SAULDRE

▲ La Solognote

34 Grande Rue, 18410 **Map** 7E1

☎ 02 48 58 50 29

FAX 02 48 58 56 00

💳 MC, V ● Tue, Jul–Sep: Wed–Thu L, Oct–Jun: Wed; Feb–1st wk Mar, 3rd wk May, 2nd wk Aug

⊞ €€€ 🍷 (13) €€€

Warmly decorated village inn with tidy guestrooms. Local ingredients abound; turbot minestrone and pigeon in spiced bouillon soup are two favourites.

BRIOLLAY

▲ Château de Noirieux

26 route du Moulin, 49125 **Map** 6B1

☎ 02 41 42 50 05

FAX 02 41 37 91 00

W www.chateaudenoirieux.com

💳 AE, DC, MC, V

● Sun, Nov–mid-Apr: Mon; last 2 wks Feb–1st 2 wks Mar

⊞ €€€€ 🍷 (19) €€€€€

Specialities at this 17th-century château include spider crab lasagne with truffles, langoustines with fried artichokes and roast pigeon in Bonnezeaux wine sauce. Set in lush gardens, with deluxe rooms.

BRUERE-ALLICHAMPS

▲ Les Tilleuls

Route de Noirlac, 18200 **Map** 7E3

☎ 02 48 61 02 75

FAX 02 48 61 08 41

💳 MC, V ● Sun D, Mon, Fri D; 3rd wk Jan–early Mar, 3rd wk Jun, last 2 wks Dec ⊞ €€€€ 🍷 (11) €€

Refined traditional cuisine without frills: generous servings of potato terrine with pine-nut garnish and delicious veal in red Sancerre. A sleepy roadside location, with garden. Small, comfortable rooms.

BUZANCAIS

▲ L'Hermitage

Route d'Argy, 800m from the centre, 36500 **Map** 7D2

☎ 02 54 84 03 90

FAX 02 54 02 13 19

💳 MC, V ● Sun D, Mon; 1st 2 wks Jan, 2nd wk Sep

⊞ €€€ 🍷 (14) €€

Charming salon, washed in green tones that echo the surrounding countryside. The menu includes langoustine salad and turbot on a bed of tagliatelle.

CANDE-SUR-BEUVRON

▲ La Caillère

36 route des Montils, 41120 **Map** 7D1

☎ 02 54 44 03 08

FAX 02 54 44 00 95

💳 AE, MC, V ● Sun D, Mon, Sep–Jun: Thu D ⊞ €€€ 🍷 (14) €€

Dishes like balsamic vinegar-baked foie gras take classic ingredients to a new level. Comfortable rooms.

CHALLANS

● Chez Charles

8 pl du Champ-de-Foire, 85300 **Map** 6A2

☎ 02 51 93 36 65

FAX 02 51 49 31 88

💳 AE, DC, MC, V ● Sun D, Mon; last wk Dec–1st 3 wks Jan ⊞ €€

The chef here takes advantage of this area's top-quality duck, as well as other fresh farm fare. The duck foie gras and the Challandais duck are outstanding.

CHAMBORD

▲ Hôtel du Grand St Michel

103 pl St Michel, 41250 **Map** 7E1

☎ 02 54 20 31 31

FAX 02 54 20 36 40

💳 MC, V ● Dec–Mar: Wed; mid-Nov–3rd wk Dec

⊞ €€ 🍷 (38) €€€

Game, a selection of pâtés and terrines, and impressive desserts, especially the crème brûlée. Short but thoughtfully selected wine list. Simple guestrooms.

CHAMPTOCEAUX

▲ Le Champalud

Pl Chanoine Bricard, 49270 **Map** 6B2

☎ 02 40 83 50 09

FAX 02 40 83 53 81

W www.lechampalud.fr.st

💳 MC, V ● Oct–mid-Mar: Sun D

⊞ €€ 🍷 (13) €€

Offering good value for money, the menu includes sandre au beurre blanc (p191) and rillauds. Pastel rooms.

CHAMPTOCEAUX

▲ Les Jardins de la Forge

1 pl Piliers, 49270 **Map** 6B2

☎ 02 40 83 56 23

FAX 02 40 83 59 80

W www.jardins-de-la-forge.com

💳 AE, DC, MC, V ● Sun D, Mon, Tue; 1st 2 wks Mar, 1st 2 wks Oct ⊞ €€€

🍷 (7) €€€€

In a former forge overlooking château ruins, find seafood such as Loire pike-perch with oysters and fine lobster medallions. Comfortable rooms.

CHARTRES

● Au Petit Chaudron

11 pl des Epars, 28000 **Map** 3E5

☎ 02 37 21 23 72

FAX 02 37 21 23 72

💳 MC, V ● Sun D, Mon, Thu L; 1st 3 wks Aug ⊞ €

● Restaurant ■ Hotel ▲ Hotel / Restaurant

A modest façade in central Chartres is home to this bistro. Unique cuisine such as scallops in smoked salmon sauce.

CHARTRES
● La Vielle Maison

5 rue au Lait, 28000 **Map** 3E5

[☎] 02 37 34 10 67

[FAX] 02 37 91 12 41

[✉] MC, V [●] Sun D, Mon; 1st wk Aug

[¶] €€€

A rustic room with exposed beams and stonework. Masterfully executed classics like veal medallions in vegetable sauce.

CHARTRES
▲ Le Grand Monarque

22 pl des Epars, 28000 **Map** 3E5

[☎] 02 37 18 15 15

[FAX] 02 37 36 34 18

[w] www.bw-grand-monarque.com

[✉] AE, MC, V [●] Sun D, Mon

[¶] €€€ [◇] (55) €€€€

Magnificent hotel and restaurant. Flavourful treatments of lamb and a remarkable Loire eel with red mullet in a delicate vinaigrette. Simple rooms.

CHATEAU-D'OLONNE
● Cayola

76 promenade de Cayola, 85180

Map 6A3

[☎] 02 51 22 01 01

[FAX] 02 51 22 08 28

[@] info@domaine-cayola.com

[✉] MC, V [●] Sun D, Mon; 1st 3 wks Jan [¶] €€€

Set in a modern villa with a panoramic view of the ocean, this place offers superlative fish and seafood, like turbot.

CHATEAUBRIANT
● Le Poêlon d'Or

30 bis rue 11 Novembre, 44110 **Map** 6A1

[☎] 02 40 81 43 33

[FAX] 02 40 81 43 33

[✉] MC, V [●] Sun D, Mon; mid-Mar, 2 wks Aug [¶] €€€

The famed chateaubriand steak is this town's and restaurant's speciality. Here it stars with prunes and foie gras.

CHATEAUDUN
● Aux Trois Pastoureaux

31 rue Andre-Gillet, 28200 **Map** 3D5

[☎] 02 37 45 74 40

[FAX] 02 37 66 00 32

[w] www.aux-trois-pastoureaux.fr

[✉] AE, DC, MC, V [●] Sun D, Mon, Thu D; 2nd wk Jan–last wk Jan, 1st wk Aug

[¶] €€€

The oldest inn in Châteaudun, and a blend of rustic and Art Deco. Fresh salmon in beer sauce or rascasse in savoury wine sauce are highlights.

CHATEAUMEILLANT
▲ Le Piet a Terre

21 rue du Chateau, 18370 **Map** 7E3

[☎] 02 48 61 41 74

[FAX] 02 48 61 41 38

[✉] MC, V [●] Sun D, Mon, Sep–Jun: Tue; 1st wk Jul, 2nd wk Nov–Feb

[¶] €€€ [◇] (5) €€

Pleasantly surprising high-level cuisine, given the modest guestrooms, such as lasange with frogs' leg compote, and a caramel-perfumed juniper berry dessert.

CHATEAUNEUF-EN-THYMERAIS
▲ L'Écritoire

43 rue Émile-Vivier, 28170 **Map** 3D5

[☎] 02 37 51 85 80

[FAX] 02 37 51 86 87

[✉] MC, V [●] Sun D, Mon, Wed L; mid-Feb–1st wk Mar, last wk Oct–1st wk Nov [¶] €€€ [◇] (5) €€

A 16th-century post house. The quail fricassée and white prawns with five peppers and five spices is a good choice, as is the herb soup.

CHATEAUNEUF-SUR-SARTHE
▲ Hôtel de la Sarthe

1 rue du Port, 49330 **Map** 6B1

[☎] 02 41 69 85 29

[FAX] 02 41 69 85 29

[w] www.hotel-ondines.com

[✉] MC, V [●] Sun D, Mon D, Mar–Apr: Mon L, Oct–Feb: Tue D, Wed D

[¶] €€ [◇] (6) €€

A small, vine-covered inn on the banks of the River Sarthe. Dishes influenced by the river, such as sandre au beurre blanc (p191) or fried eel. Cosy guestrooms.

CHATEAUROUX
● La Ciboulette

42 rue Grande, 36000 **Map** 7E2

[☎] 02 54 27 66 28

[FAX] 02 54 27 66 28

[✉] MC, V [●] Sun, Mon; Aug, last 2 wks Dec [¶] €€

A well-known local choice, this is a quiet, convivial spot in old Châteauroux. The house speciality is a delectable caramelized magret de canard.

CHATILLON-SUR-INDRE
▲ Auberge de la Tour

2 route du Blanc, 36700 **Map** 7D2

[☎] 02 54 38 72 17

[FAX] 02 54 38 74 85

[w] www.aubergedelatour36.fr

[✉] MC, V [¶] €€€ [◇] (11) €€

A cute inn, with tidy little rooms. The restaurant has a straightforward menu, including sausage cooked in Muscadet wine. A solid list of vintages.

CHAUMONT-SUR-LOIRE
● La Chancelière

1 rue de Bellevue, 41150 **Map** 7D1

[☎] 02 54 20 96 95

[FAX] 02 54 33 91 71

[✉] MC, V [●] Wed, Thu; mid-Jan–1st wk Feb, 1st 2 wks Dec [¶] €€

A local haunt, steps away from the château, with a rustic dining room. Dishes like seafood with sauerkraut, feuillete of snails, and fine duck with cherries in fruit brandy.

CHENEHUTTE-LES-TUFFEAUX
▲ Le Prieuré

Prieuré, 49350 **Map** 6C2

[☎] 02 41 67 90 14

[FAX] 02 41 67 92 24

[w] www.prieure.com

[✉] AE, DC, MC, V [●] Jan, Feb

[¶] €€€ [◇] (36) €€€€€

Former priories overlooking the Loire. Pike-perch in spicy Chinon wine sauce and asparagus salad with langoustines in orange vinaigrette are recommended. Guestrooms with modern comforts.

CHENILLE-CHANGE
● La Table du Meunier

Bourg, in village centre, 49220 **Map** 6B1

[☎] 02 41 95 10 98

[✉] MC, V

[●] Sun D, Apr–Jun; Sep–Oct: Mon D, Tue, Wed; 1st wk Jan, Feb [¶] €€

For key to symbols see back flap

A former windmill on the banks of the Mayenne, where the cooking is notable. Wines include Saumur, Anjou and Brissac.

CHENONCEAUX
▲ La Renaudiere
24 rue Dr Bretonneau, 37150 **Map** 7D2
📞 02 47 23 90 04
FAX 02 47 23 90 51
@ gerhotel@club-internet.fr
💳 MC, V ● Mon–Fri L, Wed; 1st wk Dec–1st wk Feb 🍴 €€ 🛏 (15) €€
A respected menu: game and tasty pike-perch and eel. Sancerre, Saumur and Chinon are good wine choices and service is gracious. Simple, tidy rooms.

CHENONCEAUX
▲ Hôtel du Bon-Laboureur
et du Château
6 rue du Dr Bretonneau, 37150 **Map** 7D2
📞 02 47 23 90 02
FAX 02 47 23 82 01
W www.amboise.com/laboureur
💳 DC, MC, V ● 2nd wk Jan–2nd wk Feb 🍴 €€€ 🛏 (27) €€€
A park and enchanting garden surround this agreeable 18th-century country inn. Sea bass with baby vegetables, and Touraine tomato jelly with tapenade *(p400) are on the menu. Pleasant guestrooms.*

CHERISY
● Vallon de Chérisy
12 route de Paris 4km (2.5 miles) east of Dreux on N12, 28500 **Map** 3D4
📞 02 37 43 70 08
FAX 02 37 43 86 00
💳 MC, V ● Sun D, Tue D, Wed; mid-Jul–1st wk Aug 🍴 €
Lovely restaurant with Louise-Philippe-style furniture. One of the specialities is feuille de Dreaux (a pastry accompanied by a magnificent cheese platter), and the lobster in pistachio oil is also memorable.

CHEVERNY
▲ Hôtel Restaurant Saint Hubert
122 rue Nationale, 41700 **Map** 7E1
📞 02 54 79 96 60
💳 AE, DC, MC, V ● mid-Nov–mid-Mar: Sun D; Jan
🍴 €€ 🛏 (20) €€€
Inn with richly panelled and warmly lit main dining room. Renowned for fixed-price menus, offering a wide range of regional wine and cuisine. Tidy rooms.

CHEVERNY
● Restaurant la Rousselière
1km (0.62miles) south of Cour-Cheverny, route marked, 41700 **Map** 7E1
📞 02 54 79 23 02
💳 MC, V ● 25 Dec, 1 Jan
🍴 €€
Once a large, prosperous farm, today a restaurant serving patrons of the adjoining golf course. A classic menu with rillettes de Tours or prunes in Vouvray. Seasonal menu choices such as wild boar are excellent.

CHILLEURS-AUX-BOIS
● Le Lancelot
12 rue des Déportés, 45170 **Map** 3E5
📞 02 38 32 91 15
FAX 02 38 32 92 11
W www.restaurant-le-lancelot.com
💳 MC, V ● Sun D, Mon, Wed D; 1st 2 wks Aug 🍴 €
The roast sea bass in fennel leaves and wild herb cream sauce is notable, as is the roast calf's liver. Outstanding value at this rustic village house.

CHINON
● Au Plaisir Gourmand
2 rue Parmentier, 37500 **Map** 6C2
📞 02 47 93 20 48
FAX 02 47 93 05 66
💳 AE, DC, MC, V ● Sun D, Mon, Tue L; mid-Feb–mid-Mar 🍴 €€€
In one of Chinon's oldest quarters. Try young rabbit in game jelly, cold foie gras crème and red-wine braised oxtail. The wine list is among the region's best.

CHINON
▲ Gargantua
73 rue Voltaire, 37500 **Map** 6C2
📞 02 47 93 04 71
FAX 02 47 93 08 02
W www.hostelleriegargantua.com
💳 MC, V ● Wed D, Sep–May: Thu
🍴 €€€ 🛏 (8) €€€
Charming hotel and restaurant. Guestrooms are comfortable, albeit small. The star of the menu here is braised Chinon-style oxtail. The choice of Loire vintage wines is exceptional.

CHISSAY-EN-TOURAINE
▲ Hôtel Château de Chissay
Just outside the village, 41400 **Map** 7D2
📞 02 54 32 32 01
FAX 02 54 32 43 80
W www.chateaudechissay.com
💳 MC, V ● mid-Nov–mid-Mar
🍴 €€ 🛏 (21) €€€€
Lovely guestrooms with Louis XIII-style furniture and vaulted ceilings, befitting a château once frequented by royalty. Modern cuisine includes venison in barley risotto with chanterelles.

CLISSON
● La Bonne Auberge
1 rue Olivier de Clisson, 44190 **Map** 6A2
📞 02 40 54 01 90
FAX 02 40 54 08 48
💳 AE, DC, MC, V ● Sun D, Mon, Tue L, Wed D; last 2 wks Feb, last 3 wks Aug 🍴 €€€€
Hidden away in a comfortable house in the village centre. Dishes like foie gras lasagne with fillet of pigeon or the sea bass with truffle-infused potatoes.

COMBREAUX
● L'Auberge De Combreux
35 route de Gatinais, 45530 **Map** 7E1
📞 02 38 46 89 89
FAX 02 38 59 36 19
💳 AE ● Mon L; last 2 wks Dec–3rd wk Jan 🍴 €€
Duck in Chartreuse with cress and dried apricots features. The wine list is strong in local vintages. Terrace available.

COUDRAY
● L'Amphitryon
2 route Daon, 53200 **Map** 6B1
📞 02 43 70 46 46
FAX 02 43 70 42 93
@ lamphitryon@wanadoo.fr
💳 MC, V ● Sun D, Tue D, Wed; 2 wks Feb, 1st 2 wks Jul, last wk Oct–1st wk Nov 🍴 €
A 19th-century house with graceful rooms. A mixture of well-known dishes such as veal head and tongue in a cider sauce and duck foie gras with apple.

COURCAY
● La Couture
Rn 143 La Grande Couture, between

● Restaurant ■ Hotel ▲ Hotel / Restaurant

Tours and Loches, 37310 **Map** 7D2

C 02 47 94 16 44

FAX 02 47 94 12 84

E MC, V ● Sun D, Mon, Tue D, Wed D; 3rd wk Feb–1st wk Mar, 3rd wk Jul–1st wk Aug **H** €€

Stone walls, chimneys and oak beams. Cooking firmly rooted in the countryside, with dishes such as rabbit terrine with foie gras. Touraine wines feature.

CRAON

● **Ferme Auberge de la Borderie**
La Borderie, village centre, 53400 **Map** 6B1

C 02 43 06 26 67

E MC, V ● Sun D, Wed; 2 wks Feb, last wk Dec **H** €€

A sylvan farm amongst rolling hills. Specialities such as fricassée of guinea fowl and apple parfait, plus a shop.

DEOLS

● **L'Escale Village**
Route de Paris, on the N20, 36130 **Map** 7E2

C 02 54 22 03 77

FAX 02 54 22 56 70

E MC, V **H** €

Vibrant brasserie, known and loved for the quality and abundance of its seafood dishes. Locals come in droves to enjoy the seafood banquets.

DEOLS

▲ **Relais St Jacques**
Across from the airport, 5km (3 miles) north of Chateauroux on N20, Coings, 36130 **Map** 7E2

C 02 54 60 44 44

FAX 02 54 60 44 00

W www.relais-st-jacques.com

E AE, DC, MC, V ● Sun D

H €€ ◓ (46) €€

Though the hotel's exterior is modern, hospitality here is based solidly on tradition. Warm salad with Canadian bacon, and scallops in lemon-scented olive oil are particularly refreshing options. Efficient and courteous staff.

DOUE-LA-FONTAINE

▲ **Auberge Bienvenue**
104 route de Cholet, 49700 **Map** 6C2

C 02 41 59 22 44

FAX 02 41 59 93 49

W www.aubergebienvenue.com

E MC, V ● Sun D, Mon; 2nd & 3rd wks Feb **H** €€ ◓ (7) €€

This delightful inn makes a perfect stop on a visit to Doue Zoo. Favourites find their way into new preparations such as langoustines in saffron sauce or calf's liver in port and a five-pepper sauce. Small, nicely decorated guestrooms.

DREUX

● **Aux Quatre Vents**
18 pl Metezeau, 28100 **Map** 3D4

C 02 37 50 03 24

E MC, V ● D **H** €

Noteworthy for its affable welcome and all-round value. Meals are ample and simple, with an excellent buffet laden with seafood and a variety of regional favourites. The cheese plate with Montoire and Valencay is delicious.

ERNEE

▲ **Le Grand Cerf**
17–19 rue Aristide Briand, 53500 **Map** 2B5

C 02 43 05 13 09

FAX 02 43 05 02 90

E AE, MC, V ● Mon; last 2 wks Jan **H** €€ ◓ (8) €€

Dishes include roast langoustines and pig's trotters in pesto. A few small, pleasant guestrooms.

ERVAUVILLE

● **Le Gamin**
2 route Foucherolles, 45320 **Map** 7E5

C 02 38 87 22 02

FAX 02 38 87 25 40

E MC, V ● Sun D, Mon, Tue; 1 wk Feb, 1 wk Jun **H** €€€€

A 17th-century building that was once the village grocer's. Refined, traditional approach: veal fillets with fricassée of chanterelles; cherry clafoutis (p247) with caramel ice cream. The wine list is strong in Chablis and Menetou-Salon.

EVRON

● **La Tocque des Coevrons**
4 rue des Pres, 53600 **Map** 2B5

C 02 43 01 62 16

E MC, V ● Sun D, Mon, Wed D

H €€

A long, low farm building has been transformed into this convivial bistro. Sample the bounty of the area with dishes like salad of black pudding (blood sausage), potted duck with apples and garlic and, for dessert, clafoutis (p247).

EVRON

▲ **Relais du Gué de Selle**
Route de Mayenne, 53600 **Map** 2B5

C 02 43 91 20 00

FAX 02 43 91 20 10

@ relaisduguedeselle@wanadoo.fr

E MC, V

● Sun D, Mon L, Oct–Jun: Mon L, Fri D; last wk Dec–1st wk Jan

H €€ ◓ (32) €€€

The menu includes warm pigeon salad with foie gras, and an aromatic sea bass fillet. An open fire in the dining room and a tranquil lakeside garden. Quiet guestrooms, neatly furnished.

FLERE-LA-RIVIERE

● **Relais du Berry**
2 route de Tours, 36700 **Map** 7D2

C 02 54 39 32 57

E MC, V ● Sun D, Mon, Tue; Jan

H €€

Fresh, varied and in harmony with the seasonal produce of the surrounding countryside. Recommendations include roast pigeon in a shallot sauce.

FONTENAY-LE-COMTE

● **Aux Choans**
6 rue des Halles, 85200 **Map** 6B3

C 02 51 69 55 92

FAX 02 28 13 02 08

E MC, V ● Sun D, Mon; 2nd wk Jan, 2 wks Mar, last wk Aug–1st wk Sep

H €€

In a medieval building in Fontenay's old quarter, the menu here features game, such as venison and hare, as well as fish. A wide variety of Loire reds and whites are also on offer.

FONTEVRAUD-L'ABBAYE

▲ **Le Prieuré Saint-Lazare**
Rue St-Jean-de-l'Habit, 49590 **Map** 6C2

C 02 41 51 73 16

FAX 02 41 51 75 50

W www.hotelfp-fontevraud.com

E AE, DC, MC, V ● 1st wk Nov–last

wk Mar **11** €€€

🍽 (35) €€€

Once the cloister of a royal abbey, the surroundings are noteworthy. Try the spiced roast guinea fowl and pan-fried foie gras. Contemporary guestrooms.

FONTEVRAUD-L'ABBAYE

● **Licorne**

31 rue Robert d'Arbrissel, allée Ste-Catherine, 49590 **Map** 6C2

☎ 02 41 51 72 49

FAX 02 41 51 70 40

🍴 MC, V ● Sun D, Mon, Oct–May: Wed D; 2nd wk Dec–3rd wk Jan

11 €€€€

An alluring terrace and a Louis XIV-decorated dining room. The menu includes creations like monkfish and Chinon wine stew and veal ribs in garlic and rosé sauce. First-rate Loire wines.

GIEN

▲ **La Poularde**

13 quai Nice, 45500 **Map** 7F1

☎ 02 38 67 36 05

FAX 02 38 38 18 78

🍴 AE, MC, V ● Sun D, Feb: Mon L, Dec: Mon; 1st 2 wks Jan

11 €€€ 🍽 (9) €€

A classic riverside restaurant with ample-sized, tasteful guestrooms. Dishes include crispy langoustines and pike-perch in Chinon with mushrooms.

GUERANDE

▲ **Les Remparts**

14 bd du Nord, 44350 **Map** 1C4

☎ 02 40 24 90 69

🍴 MC, V ● Sep–Jul: Sun D, Mon; 1st wk Jan, 1 wk Feb, 1 wk Jun

11 €€ 🍽 (8) €€

This small hotel and restaurant are worth the effort to find. Seafood dishes, including scallops, are highlights. Well-appointed, cosy guestrooms.

ILLIERS-COMBRAY

● **Le Florent**

13 pl du Marche, 28120 **Map** 3D5

☎ 02 37 24 10 43

FAX 02 37 24 11 78

@ leflorent@aol.com

🍴 MC, V ● Sun D, Mon, Tue, Wed

11 €€€

A former ironmonger's shop in the shadow of a church beloved by Marcel Proust. The foie-gras-crusted bass, with scallops in foie gras and chestnut sauce, is known throughout the region.

ISSOUDUN

▲ **La Cognette**

Hotel: 26 rue Minimes; Restaurant: 6 bd Stalingrad, 36100 **Map** 2C5

☎ 02 54 03 59 59

FAX 02 54 03 13 03

W www.la-cognette.com

🍴 AE, MC, V ● Mon, Oct–May: Sun D, Tue L; Jan

11 €€€€ 🍽 (14) €€€

The refinement and selection of the wine list here is nationally known. In the kitchen: cannelloni with oysters and cucumber with cream of green lentils suffused with truffles. Grand guestrooms.

JAVRON-LES-CHAPELLES

● **Restaurant de la Terrasse**

30 Grand Rue, 53250 **Map** 7D2

☎ 02 43 03 41 91

FAX 02 43 04 49 48

🍴 MC, V ● Tue, Wed (except public holidays); 2 wks mid-Feb

11 €€€

An exceptional selection of modern main course favourites in a setting of sleek elegance. The chef's inspiration shows in dishes like the salad of seasonal greens topped with rillettes du Mans, duck foie gras and jambon cru (raw ham). Well-chosen wine list.

JOUE-LES-TOURS

▲ **Château de Beaulieu**

67 rue de Beaulieu, 37300 **Map** 7D2

☎ 02 47 53 20 26

FAX 02 47 53 84 20

🍴 AE, MC, V ● 24 Dec D

11 €€ 🍽 (19) €€€

A modest, graceful château opening onto a lovely small park. Period guestrooms. The restaurant offers pan-fried foie gras on spiced bread with raspberry vinegar, and delectable pike-perch roasted in a Loire red wine sauce.

LA BAULE-ESCOUBLAC

▲ **Castel Marie-Louise**

1 ave Andrieu, 44500 **Map** 1C4

☎ 02 40 11 48 38

FAX 02 40 11 48 35

W www.relaischateaux.com/marielouise

🍴 AE, DC, MC, V ● Sep–Jun: Mon–Sat L; mid-Nov–3rd wk Dec

11 €€€€ 🍽 (31) €€€€€

An early 20th-century mansion with ocean views and well-kept gardens. Turbot, sea bream and sardines are highlights. Belle Epoque guestrooms.

LA BAULE-ESCOUBLAC

▲ **Le Ruban Bleu**

14 esplanade Lucien Barrière, 44500 **Map** 1C4

☎ 02 40 60 24 86

FAX 02 40 42 03 13

W www.hotelmajestic.fr

🍴 AE, DC, MC, V

11 €€ 🍽 (66) €€€€

A place beside the sea, with a nautical theme reminiscent of the great ocean liners. Delicacies include langoustines grilled with aubergine (eggplant) and local herbs. The wine list is strong in Loire and local whites. Comfortable, slightly dated guestrooms.

LA BAULE-ESCOUBLAC

● **Barbade**

Bd René Dubois, 44500 **Map** 1C4

☎ 02 40 42 01 01

FAX 02 40 42 09 83

🍴 MC, V ● Oct–May: Tue–Wed; Nov–Feb **11** €

Right on the beach, serving remarkable oysters, moules-frites and plenty of other exquisite fish and shellfish.

LA BAULE-ESCOUBLAC

▲ **Eden Beach**

5 esplanade Lucien Barrière, 44500 **Map** 1C4

☎ 02 40 11 46 16

FAX 02 40 11 46 45

W www.lucienbarriere.com

🍴 AE, DC, MC, V ● Nov–Mar; restaurant: Jan–Feb: Sun D & Mon; last wk Nov–3rd wk Dec

11 €€€ 🍽 (212) €€€€

Bistro with a lively atmosphere and panoramic ocean views. The sea bass and turbot au beurre blanc are exemplary. The hotel, called the Hermitage, offers elegant guestrooms.

● Restaurant ■ Hotel ▲ Hotel / Restaurant

LA CHARTRE-SUR-LE-LOIR

▲ **Hôtel de France**

20 pl de la République, 72340 **Map** 7D1

[02 43 44 40 16

FAX 02 43 79 62 20

@ hoteldefrance@worldonline.fr

MC, V ⬤ Sun D, Sep–Jun: Mon; Feb

€ ⬤ (24) €€

An early 20th-century mansion serving a delicious variation on the ubiquitous sandre au beurre blanc (p191), plus the unusual matelot d'anguille (freshwater eel in seafood sauce). Some rooms have original period decor; others are modern.

LA CHATRE

▲ **Château de la Vallée Bleue**

Saint Chartier, Route de Verneuil, 36400 **Map** 7E3

[02 54 31 01 91

W www.chateauvalleebleue.com

AE, MC, V ⬤ Mar–May & Sep–Nov: Sun D, Mon; mid-Nov–mid-Mar €€ ⬤ (15) €€€€

In a 19th-century mansion once owned by a doctor whose patients included George Sand and Chopin, this restaurant is a gem. The pike-perch in red Loire sauce is notably delectable. Vast, well-tended gardens. Spacious guestrooms.

LA FERTE-BERNARD

● **Restaurant du Dauphin**

3 rue d'Huisne, 72400 **Map** 7D5

[02 43 93 00 39

FAX 02 43 71 26 65

MC, V ⬤ Sun D, Mon; 2 wks Mar, last 2 wks Aug €€€

Local hot spot and a sleek setting for innovative dishes such as fricassee of rabbit liver and a truly delectable lamb brochette. The wine list is eclectic.

LA FERTE-IMBAULT

▲ **Auberge à La Tête de Lard**

13 pl des Tilleuls, 41300 **Map** 7E2

[02 54 96 22 32

FAX 02 54 96 06 22

W www.aubergealatetedelard.com

MC, V ⬤ Sun D, Mon, Tue L; Jan–mid-Feb, 2 wks Sep

€€€ ⬤ (11) €€€

The fare reflects the enthusiasm of local hunters; pheasant, wild boar, rabbit, hare and even partridge are available in

season. The terrine of leeks is not to be missed. Small, country-style guestrooms.

LA FERTE-ST-AUBIN

● **La Ferme De La Lande**

Route de Marcilly, 45240 **Map** 7E1

[02 38 76 64 37

FAX 02 38 64 68 87

W www.fermedelalande.com

AE, MC, V ⬤ Sun D, Mon, Wed D; last wk Jan–1st wk Feb, 2 wks Oct, 1 wk Nov €€€

A vine-covered, oak-beamed brick farmhouse. Butterflied langoustine tails in beetroot purée and Bresse chicken with crayfish tails are representative.

LA FERTE-VIDAME

● **Auberge de la Trigalle**

68 pl de la gare, Route de Verneuil, 28340 **Map** 7D5

[06 12 97 82 00

MC, V ⬤ Mon, Tue; Jan, mid-Oct–mid-Apr (except D by reservation)

€€

Eclectic decor, heavy oak beams melding harmoniously with Chinese art. Excellent wine list, with noted Loire vintages and Bordeaux. The menu offers choices like slow-cooked suckling pig in honey.

LA PLAINE-SUR-MER

▲ **Anne de Bretagne**

Port de Gravette Nord-Ouest, 44770 **Map** 1C4

[02 40 21 54 72

FAX 02 40 21 02 33

W www.annedebretagne.com

AE, MC, V ⬤ Mon, Tue; Jan–mid-Feb €€€€ ⬤ (22) €€€€

Sleek, contemporary dining room. The menu includes roast monkfish in crab bouillon, or crushed crab in tomato confit. Ample-sized guestrooms, many with sea views.

LA ROCHE-SUR-YON

● **Le Rivoli**

31 bd Aristide Briand, 85000 **Map** 6A3

[02 51 37 43 41

FAX 02 51 46 20 92

AE, MC, V ⬤ Sun, Mon D, Sat L; Aug €€

The freshest catches make their way to the table in the form of dishes such as

spiced millefeuille of haddock in Nantais fennel butter. Meat options also on offer such as grilled loin of lamb.

LA TRANCHE-SUR-MER

▲ **Les Cols Verts**

48 rue de Verdun, 85360 **Map** 6A3

[02 51 27 49 30

FAX 02 51 30 11 42

W www.hotelcolsverts.com

AE, MC, V ⬤ Sep–Jun: Tue–Fri L; Oct–Mar

€€€ ⬤ (35) €€€€

Delectable dishes such as red shrimp casserole and scallops flambéed in Cognac. Vendée vintages are highlights. Rooms are cosy, with ocean views.

LA VILLE-AUX-CLERCS

▲ **Manoir de la Forêt**

Le Fort Girard, just outside village centre, 41160 **Map** 7D1

[02 54 80 62 83

FAX 02 54 80 66 03

W www.manoirdelaforet.fr

AE, MC, V ⬤ Oct–Mar: Sun D, Mon €€€ ⬤ (18) €€€

Once the hunting lodge for the Duke of Rochefoucauld, this is a beautiful Renaissance château. Wise choices are the lobster fricassée with prawns or the calf's liver. Elegant guestrooms.

LAVAL

▲ **La Gerbe de Blé**

83 rue Victor-Boissel, 53000 **Map** 2B5

[02 43 53 14 10

FAX 02 43 49 02 84

W www.gerbedeble.com

AE, MC, V ⬤ Sun, Mon L (except public holidays); 1st 3 wks Aug

€€€ ⬤ (8) €€€

A restaurant with a warm feel, serving dishes like sea bass fillet with chorizo, or Champagne and strawberry soup. Very spacious, comfortable rooms.

LAVAL

● **Le Bistro de Paris**

67 rue Val de Mayenne, 53000 **Map** 2B5

[02 43 56 98 29

FAX 02 43 56 52 85

@ bistro.de.paris@wanadoo.fr

AE, MC, V ⬤ Sun, Mon, Sat L; last 3 wks Aug €€€

For key to symbols see back flap

Outstanding food at reasonable prices at this chic bistro, with dishes such as cod and sea bass with wild mushrooms or sole fillet in lobster sauce.

LAVENAY
● **La Petite Auberge**
12 rue Val-de-Braye, Bessé-sur-Braye, 6km (4 miles) north of Lavenay on D303, 72310 **Map** 7D1
📞 02 43 44 45 08
FAX 02 43 44 18 57
🖻 MC, V ● Tue D, Wed; 2 wks Feb
🍴 €€

Affordable, quality menu, with a wine list to match, in a renovated farm building. Dishes include veal with hazelnuts.

LE BLANC
▲ **Domaine de L'Etape**
Route de Belabre, 5km (3 miles) south-east of Le Blanc on D10, 36300 **Map** 7D3
📞 02 54 37 18 02
FAX 02 54 37 75 59
🖻 AE, DC, MC, V
🍴 €€€ 🍃 (35) €€€

Nestled in a park, this Victorian-era home serves sea bass crusted with aubergine (eggplant) and pistou.

LE BLANC
● **Le Cygne**
8 ave de Gambetta, 36300 **Map** 7D3
📞 02 54 28 71 63
🖻 MC, V ● Sep–May: Sun D, Mon, Sep–Jun: Tue; 1st 2 wks Jan, last 2 wks Jun, last wk Aug 🍴 €€

Traditional restaurant offering excellent value for money. Try the oysters or a tasty fillet of beef with morels.

LE CROISIC
▲ **Fort de l'Océan**
Pointe du Croisic, 44490 **Map** 1C4
📞 02 40 15 77 77
FAX 02 40 15 77 80
🖻 AE, DC, MC, V ● Jul: Mon–Thu L, Mon D, mid-Sep–mid-Jun: Tue; 1st wk Jan–mid-Feb; mid-Nov–mid-Dec
🍴 €€€ 🍃 (9) €€€€€

Seventeenth-century ramparts surround this enchanting shoreline hotel; the fortress's chambers form comfortable guestrooms. Serves scallops with quail eggs in Graves wine sauce.

LE LUDE
● **La Renaissance**
2 ave de la Libération, 72800 **Map** 6C1
📞 02 43 94 63 10
FAX 02 43 94 21 05
W www.renaissancelelude.com
🖻 AE, DC, MC, V ● Sun D, Mon; 2 wks Feb, 2 wks Oct 🍴 €€

Agreeable little restaurant. Creative dishes, such as the rabbit with honey-infused sauerkraut confit. Excellent value.

LE MANS
▲ **Auberge de la Foresterie**
Foresterie route Laval, 72000 **Map** 6C1
📞 02 43 51 25 00
FAX 02 43 28 54 58
🖻 AE, DC, MC, V
🍴 €€€ 🍃 (41) €€€€

An inn with modern dishes like cream of aubergine (eggplant) and grilled tomato compote. The pepper steak is notable. Standard, comfortable hotel rooms.

LE MANS
● **Le Beaulieu**
24 rue Ponts Neufs, 72000 **Map** 6C1
📞 02 43 87 78 37
FAX 02 43 87 78 27
W www.jre.net
🖻 AE, DC, MC, V
● Sat, Sun; 1st wk Mar, Aug
🍴 €€€€

A pre-Renaissance, oak-beamed house in the midst of the old quarter, where the chef offers dishes such as roast sea bass, crème brûlée and apple tart.

LE MANS
● **Rascasse**
6 rue Mission, 72000 **Map** 6C1
📞 02 43 84 45 91
FAX 02 43 85 01 89
🖻 AE, MC, V ● Sun D, Mon, Sat L; 1 wk Feb, Aug 🍴 €€€

Try the mullet with a caramel and basil tapenade (p400) or shredded duck fillet. The dining room is replete with Art Deco furniture and has a grand fireplace.

LE PERRIER
▲ **Auberge le Relais**
Le Pré Boursier, route from Challans, 85300 **Map** 6A2
📞 02 51 68 32 28

FAX 02 51 93 81 73
🖻 MC, V ● Sep–May: Sun D, Mon; 1st 2 wks Feb, 1st 2 wks Oct
🍴 €€ 🍃 (20) €€

On the menu: duck, quail, river eel and even snails from the nearby marshes. Guestrooms are attractively decorated.

LE PETIT-PRESSIGNY
● **La Promenade J Dallais**
11 rue du Savoureulx, 37350 **Map** 7D2
📞 02 47 94 93 52
FAX 02 47 91 06 03
🖻 DC, MC, V ● Sun D, Mon, Tue; Jan, Aug–Sep 🍴 €€€€

Roast pigeon with foie gras is an old favourite but, in Jacky Dallais' hands, becomes superlative.

LE TREMBLAY
● **La Touche**
Just outside Tremblay centre to the west, 49520 **Map** 6B1
📞 02 41 94 22 45
FAX 02 41 94 21 27
🖻 MC, V ● Sun D, Mon, Oct–Mar: Tue–Thu D; Jan–Feb 🍴 €

In an attractive 17th-century farmhouse, this little-known gem celebrates local flavours in dishes like fresh duck pâté and guinea fowl in cider. Excellent value.

LES HERBIERS
▲ **La Cotriade**
18 rue de Saumur, 85500 **Map** 6B2
📞 02 51 91 01 64
FAX 02 51 67 36 50
🖻 MC, V ● Sun D, Mon, Fri D, Sat L
🍴 €€ 🍃 (26) €€

Here the essence of the Vendée; shellfish casserole and medallions of venison in thyme butter are highlights. The wine list features hearty local reds.

LES ROSIERS-SUR-LOIRE
▲ **Jeanne de Laval Les Duc d'Anjou**
54 route Nationale, 49350 **Map** 6C2
📞 02 41 51 80 17
FAX 02 41 38 04 18
🖻 AE, DC, MC, V ● Jan–Apr: Mon L; May–Oct: Mon D; 2nd wk Nov–last wk Dec 🍴 €€€ 🍃 (10) €€€

A handsome country home with a delightful garden. Famed for its beurre blanc. Guestrooms with period furniture.

● Restaurant ■ Hotel ▲ Hotel / Restaurant

LES SABLES-D'OLONNE

● Le Beau Rivage

1 bd Lattre de Tassigny, 85180 **Map** 6A3

📞 02 51 32 03 01

FAX 02 51 32 46 48

W www.le-beau-rivage.com

🍽 AE, DC, MC, V ● Sep–Jun: Sun
D–Mon, Jul–Aug: Mon D 🍴 €€€€

*Father and son chefs expertly prepare
seafood such as John Dory in onion
confit with dried tomatoes at this eatery
with sweeping coastal views.*

LES SABLES-D'OLONNE

● Fleur des Mers

5 quai Guiné, 85100 **Map** 6A3

📞 02 51 95 18 10

FAX 02 51 96 96 10

🍽 MC, V ● Mon, Jul–Aug: Tue

🍴 €€

*A relaxed yet polished setting, where
the sea inspires dishes such as roast
scallop tart with courgette (zucchini)
flowers. Don't miss the oxtail, roasted
for seven hours with foie gras.*

LEVROUX

● Relais St Jean

34 rue Nationale, 36110 **Map** 7E2

📞 02 54 35 81 56

FAX 02 54 35 36 09

🍽 AE, DC, MC, V ● Sun D, Wed,
Oct–May: Tue D 🍴 €€

*In the sunny-toned dining rooms of
an old house, taste sea bream with
aubergine (eggplant), garlic, onion, herbs
and tomato. Above average wines.*

LIGNIERES

▲ Hostellerie des 7 Soeurs

In Le Bourg-Touchay, 5km (3 miles)
south of Lignières on A71, 18160
Map 7E3

📞 02 48 60 06 77

FAX 02 48 60 06 77

🍽 MC, V ● Sun D, Mon, Oct–May:
Tue–Thu D; Feb 🍴 €€ 🍷 (7) €€

*Excellent value countryside gem. The
menu features sole medallions with
truffle sauce. The wine list features a
few well-selected bottles. Snug rooms.*

L'ILE-D'YEU

● Les Bafouettes

8 rue Gabriel-Guist'Hau, 85350

📞 02 51 59 38 38

🍽 MC, V ● Sun, Mon, Tue; 3 wks
Jan 🍴 €€€

*The Belgian chef here prepares delights
such as grilled monkfish in a lobster
sauce. Affordable for the quality on offer.*

LOUE

▲ Ricordeau

13 rue de la Libération, 72540 **Map** 6C1

📞 02 43 88 40 03

FAX 02 43 88 62 08

W www.hotel-ricordeau.fr

🍽 AE, MC, V ● Sep–Jun: Sun D
🍴 €€€ 🍷 (18) €€€€

*Famed for its poultry dishes like roast
pigeon with bacon and broad (fava)
beans. Charming guestrooms with
period features like beamed ceilings.*

LUCHE-PRINGE

▲ Du Port des Roches

On D214, 72800 **Map** 6C1

📞 02 43 45 44 48

FAX 02 43 45 39 61

🍽 MC, V

● Sun, Mon, Tue L; Feb, 1st wk Oct
🍴 €€ 🍷 (12) €€

*A cosy inn with pleasant rooms, a lovely
garden and a lively atmosphere. Local
favourites such as game and terrines.*

LUCON

● Mirabelle

89 bis rue du Président-de-Gaulle,
85400 **Map** 6B5

📞 02 51 56 93 02

🍽 MC, V ● Tue, Sep–May: Sun D;
Sep–Jun: Sat L; 2wks Feb, 1 wk Oct
🍴 €€€

*Fresh ingredients married to the perfect
wines. Typical dishes are curried snails
and freshwater eel in red wine.*

LUYNES

▲ Domaine de Beauvois

On route from Cléré-les-Pins, 37230
Map 6C2

📞 02 47 55 50 11

FAX 02 47 55 59 62

🍽 AE, DC, MC, V ● last wk Jan–1st
wk Mar 🍴 €€€ 🍷 (36) €€€€

*Renaissance manor house, flower-
bedecked grounds and top-notch cuisine
and wines. Luxurious rooms.*

MAISONNAIS

● La Table d'Orsan

Orsan, on D65, between Lignières and
Le Chatelet, 18170 **Map** 7E3

📞 02 48 56 27 50

FAX 02 48 56 39 64

🍽 MC, V ● Nov–Mar 🍴 €€

*The menu at this former priory features
chicken stuffed with nettles and herbs.
Dependable, fruity Loire reds dominate.*

MARCAY

▲ Château de Marçay

On D116, 7km (3.4miles) from Chinon,
37500 **Map** 6C2

📞 02 47 93 03 47

🍽 AE, DC, MC, V ● Mon L, Tue L,
mid-Apr–mid-Oct: Thu L, mid-Oct–mid-
Apr: Sun D & Mon D; mid-Jan–1st wk
Mar 🍴 €€€€ 🍷 (34) €€€€€

*Fortified 15th-century château with
beautifully appointed guestrooms. Try
the pike-perch in coriander (cilantro).*

MAYENNE

▲ Grand Hôtel

2 rue Ambroise-de-Loré, 53100 **Map** 2B5

📞 02 43 00 96 00

FAX 02 43 00 69 20

🍽 AE, MC, V ● Nov–Apr: Sun D; 1st
2 wks Aug, last 2 wks Dec

🍴 €€ 🍷 (24) €€€

*Dishes include thinly sliced andouille de
Vire with roast langoustines. A top-rank
cellar and well-kept rooms.*

MAYENNE

▲ La Croix Couverte

Route from Alençon, N 12 , 53100
Map 2B5

📞 02 43 04 32 48

FAX 02 43 04 43 69

🍽 MC, V ● Sun, Fri D; last two wks
Feb 🍴 € 🍷 (11) €€

*A retro-style dining room in a 100-year-
old house. Try the sandre au beurre
blanc (p191). Small guestrooms.*

MENESTREAU-EN-VILLETTE

● Le Relais De Solagne

63 pl de 8 Mai, 45240 **Map** 7E1

📞 02 38 76 97 40

FAX 02 38 49 60 43

🍽 AE, DC, MC, V ● Sun D, Tue D,
Wed; last wk Feb–mid-Mar 🍴 €€€

Inspired classics such as pan-fried duck foie gras with spice bread.

MESLAY-DU-MAINE
▲ Le Cheval Blanc
7 route du Laval, 53170 **Map** 6B1
📞 02 43 98 68 00
💳 MC, V
⬤ Sun D, Mon; 1st 3 wks Aug
🍴 €€ 🍽 (8) €

Dishes include Mayenne salad, pike-perch with shrimp, and Anjou sirloin in a chocolate sauce. Great value for money.

MEZIERES-EN-BRENNE
▲ Au Boeuf Couronné
9 pl de Gaulle, 36290 **Map** 7D2
📞 02 54 38 04 39
FAX 02 54 38 02 84
💳 MC, V ⬤ Sun D; 3rd wk Nov–Jan
🍴 €€€ 🍽 (8) €€

Dishes like minced carp in white butter, pistachio and Kirsch sauce. One of the region's best spots. Comfortable rooms.

MISSILLAC
▲ Hôtel de la Bretesche
La Breteshe, off the route between Nantes and Vannes, 44780 **Map** 6A1
📞 02 51 76 86 96
💳 AE, DC, MC, V ⬤ Mon L, Tue L, mid-Oct–mid-Apr: Sun D, Mon D, mid-Apr–early Jul & late Aug–mid-Oct: Mon D; mid-Jan–mid-Mar, 1 wk mid-Nov
🍴 €€€€ 🍽 (31) €€€€€

Stunning château with lovely guestrooms, set amidst an expansive park. Try the skate with creamed celery and artichoke.

MONTAIGU
⬤ Le Cathelineau
3 bis pl Champ-de-Foire, 85600 **Map** 6A2
📞 02 51 94 26 40
💳 AE, MC, V ⬤ Sun D, Mon; last wk Feb–1st wk Mar, 1st 3 wks Aug
🍴 €€€

From the kitchen of this eye-catching old house, excellent dugléré (sauce with tomatoes, shallots and white wine) and choron (Béarnaise sauce with tomatoes).

MONTARGIS
▲ De La Gloire
74 ave de Gaulle, 45200 **Map** 7F1
📞 02 38 85 04 69

FAX 02 38 98 52 32
💳 AE, MC, V ⬤ Tue, Wed; last 2 wks Feb–1st wk Mar, last 2 wks Aug
🍴 €€€€€ 🍽 (11) €€

An elegant place famed for both seafood and meat. Desserts make a grand appearance on a chariot. The guestrooms, though modest, are well appointed.

MONTBAZON
▲ Château D'Artigny
2km (1.2miles) west of Montbazon on D17, 37250 **Map** 7D2
📞 02 47 34 30 30
FAX 02 47 34 30 39
🌐 www.artigny.com
💳 AE, DC, MC, V ⬤ mid-Dec–Jan
🍴 €€€€ 🍽 (65) €€€€€

Though built in the 20th century, this hotel echoes the grandeur of the 18th. A splendid rotunda restaurant and sumptuous, Baroque guestrooms. A superior choice of wines and Armagnacs.

MOULAY
▲ La Marjolaine
Park of Le Bas-Mont, 53100 **Map** 2B5
📞 02 43 00 48 42
FAX 02 43 08 10 58
@ lamarjolaine@wanadoo.fr
💳 MC, V ⬤ Sun D, Mon L; 1st wk Jan, last wks Feb–mid-Mar
🍴 €€ 🍽 (18) €€€

A former farm serving warm oysters and stuffed pigeon with blackberries. Brief wine list. Nicely kept guestrooms.

NANTES
⬤ Brasserie La Cigale
4 pl Graslin, 44000 **Map** 6A2
📞 02 51 84 94 94
FAX 02 51 84 94 95
💳 DC, MC, V 🍴 €

An opulent Art Nouveau eatery, once the haunt of French literati and the great families of Nantes. Goats' cheese tart and peerless steak tartare on the menu.

NANTES
⬤ L'Atlantide
16 quai Ernest Renaud, 44100 **Map** 6A2
📞 02 40 73 23 23
FAX 02 40 73 76 46
💳 AE, MC, V ⬤ Sun, Sat L; mid-May, 4 wks Aug 🍴 €€€€

In a sleek office building, sample mullet fondue, or langoustine and bergamot bouillon. Nationally famous wine list.

NANTES
⬤ Lou Pescadou
8 allée Baco, 44000 **Map** 6A2
📞 02 40 35 29 50
FAX 02 51 82 46 34
💳 MC, V ⬤ Sun, Mon D, Sat L; Aug
🍴 €€€

House specialities include the excellent sole with bonotte de Noirmoutier (a type of potato).

NEUNG-SUR-BEUVRON
⬤ Auberge De La Croix Vert
1 rue du 8 Mai 1945, 41210 **Map** 7E1
📞 02 54 83 61 67
💳 MC, V ⬤ Sun, Thu; 1st 2 wks Mar, 1st 2 wks Oct 🍴 €€

Roadside inn with few equals in terms of value. Enticing pitchers of Touraine wine.

NOGENT-LE-ROI
⬤ Le Capucin Gourmand
1 rue de la Volaille, 28210 **Map** 3E5
📞 02 37 51 96 00
FAX 02 37 82 67 19
🌐 www.capucin-gourmand.fr
💳 MC, V ⬤ Sep–Jun: Sun D, Mon, Oct–May: Thu D; 2nd wk Jan, last wk Aug–1st wk Sep 🍴 €€

A 15th-century half-timbered house with roast rabbit, perfectly cooked veal and a wine list strong in Chinon and Borgeuil.

NOGENT-LE-ROI
⬤ Relais des Remparts
2 rue Marché Légumes, 28210 **Map** 3D5
📞 02 37 51 40 47
FAX 02 37 51 40 47
💳 AE, DC, MC, V ⬤ Sun D, Tue D, Wed 🍴 €

Charming and vivacious team led by Thierry Wagner. The seafood platter, with a fresh Loire white, is a reliable choice.

NOIRMOUTIER-EN-L'ILE
▲ Fleur de Sel
Rue des Saulniers, 85330 **Map** 1C5
📞 02 51 39 09 07
FAX 02 51 39 09 76
🌐 www.fleurdesel.fr
💳 AE, MC, V ⬤ Mon L, Sep–May: Tue

⬤ Restaurant   ■ Hotel   ▲ Hotel / Restaurant

L; 1st wk Nov–mid-Mar

🟥 €€€ 🍴 (35) €€€€

A Mediterranean-style garden with pool. Dishes include saffron brill and rabbit with polenta. Well-kept rooms.

NOIRMOUTIER-EN-L'ILE
● Le Grand Four

1 rue de la Cure, 85330 **Map** 1C5

🔵 02 51 39 61 97

FAX 02 51 39 61 97

🟢 AE, MC, V ⚫ Sun D, Sep–May: Mon; Dec–Jan 🟥 €€

A beautiful old island home where the chef's excellent creations include oven-baked wild turbot, and sole with delicious lamb sweetbreads and morels.

NOIRMOUTIER-EN-L'ILE
● Le Petit Bouchot

3 rue St-Louis, 85330 **Map** 1C5

🔵 02 51 39 32 56

FAX 02 51 35 86 00

🟢 MC, V ⚫ Jul–Aug: Mon; mid-Dec–mid-Jan 🟥 €€

A fresh approach, like monkfish baked in saffron, langoustines with fresh fruit and oysters seasoned with nutmeg. A simply decorated dining room near the old port.

NOIZAY
▲ Château de Noizay

Route de Chançay, 8km (5miles) east of Vouvray on D46 and D1, 37210 **Map** 7D2

🔵 02 47 52 11 01

FAX 02 47 52 04 64

🌐 www.chateaudenoizay.com

🟢 AE, DC, MC, V

⚫ Tue–Thu L; mid-Jan–mid-Mar

🟥 €€€€ 🍴 (19) €€€€€

Modern dishes such as scallop ravioli with Serrano ham, accompanied by local wines. Comfortable guestrooms.

OISLY
● Le Saint Vincent

Le Bourg, village centre, 41700 **Map** 7D2

🔵 02 54 79 50 04

FAX 02 54 79 50 04

🟢 MC, V ⚫ Tue, Wed; mid-Dec–end Jan 🟥 €€€

Deft use of spicy fragrances, like the langoustines gratin in green curry sauce. The wine list befits the restaurant's namesake, patron saint of winegrowers.

OLIVET
▲ Le Rivage

635 rue Reine Blanche, 45160 **Map** 7E1

🔵 02 38 66 02 93

FAX 02 38 56 31 11

🌐 www.relais-du-silence.com

🟢 AE, DC, MC, V ⚫ last wk Dec–3rd wk Jan 🟥 €€€ 🍴 (17) €€€

Dishes such as risotto with lamb and warm vegetables, in a riverside setting. Comfy guestrooms.

ONZAIN
▲ Domaine des Hauts de Loire

Route de Mesland, 41150 **Map** 7D1

🔵 02 54 20 72 57

FAX 02 54 20 77 32

🟢 AE, DC, MC, V

⚫ Mon, Tue; Dec–1st wk Mar

🟥 €€€€€ 🍴 (33) €€€€€

This former high-society hunting lodge retains its original grandeur. Signature cutting-edge or classic dishes include salad of crispy eel in shallot vinaigrette, and dark and white chocolate mousse with red fruits.

ORLEANS
● Eugène

24 rue de Ste-Anne, 45000 **Map** 7E1

🔵 02 38 53 82 64

FAX 02 38 54 31 89

🟢 AE, DC, MC, V

⚫ Sun, Mon L, Sat L; first wk May, 1st 2 wks Aug, last wk Dec 🟥 €€€

Hospitable bistro in the town centre. An affordable menu including lamb with sesame and red mullet with shellfish.

ORLEANS
● L'Epicurien

54 rue Turcies, 45000 **Map** 7E1

🔵 02 38 68 01 10

FAX 02 38 68 19 02

🟢 MC, V ⚫ Sun, Mon; last 3 wks Aug 🟥 €€

In an appealing riverside house. The chef's flair is evident in dishes such as caramelized asparagus tart and calf's liver in orange sauce.

ORLEANS
● Le Jardin de Neptune

6 rue Jean Hupeau, 45000 **Map** 7E1

🔵 02 38 62 45 64

🟢 MC, V

⚫ Sun, Mon; last 3 wks Aug 🟥 €€

A nautical theme adds to the fun in this convivial spot. Seafood delicacies – oysters, mussels, sea bass, turbot and monkfish – are exemplary. Chablis and Loire whites on the wine list.

ORLEANS
● Les Antiquaires

2 et 4 rue au Lin, 45000 **Map** 7E1

🔵 02 38 53 52 35

FAX 02 38 62 06 95

🌐 www.restaurantlesantiquaires.com

🟢 AE, MC, V ⚫ Sun, Mon

🟥 €€€

Gastronomic art is manifested in dishes like Sologne partridge casserole or an asparagus tart. The wine list is strong in Vouvray and Loire whites.

PIERREFITTE-SUR-SAULDRE
● Le Lion D'or

1 pl de l'Eglise, 41300 **Map** 7E2

🔵 02 54 88 62 14

FAX 02 54 88 62 14

🟢 MC, V ⚫ Mon, Tue, Oct–Apr: Wed D; 1st 3 wks Jan, 1st 2 wks Sep

🟥 €€€

Charming surroundings: a collection of fine china adorns timber-crossed walls. Try the sautéed langoustines with a confit of tomato on a bed of ginger tagliatelle.

PONTMAIN
▲ Auberge de l'Espérance

9 rue Grange, 53220 **Map** 2B5

🔵 02 43 05 08 10

FAX 02 43 05 03 19

🟢 MC, V

⚫ Nov–Mar: Sun D; last wk Dec–1st wk Jan 🟥 €€ 🍴 (11) €

This inn, teaching handicapped people the hotelier's trade, serves up affordable food in a cultivated setting. Straight-forward menu of terrines, pâtés and fresh fish. Well-tended guestrooms.

PORNIC
● Auberge La Fontaine aux Bretons

La Joselière rue Noëlles, 44210 **Map** 6A2

🔵 02 51 74 07 07

FAX 02 51 74 15 15

🌐 www.auberge-la-fontaine.com

🟢 MC, V ⚫ mid-Nov–Mar: Sun D

¶¶ €€€

A long stone house with a large fire-place, so many dishes are wood-smoked. From a tender organic roast chicken to the langoustines in gazpacho, devotees of both land and sea are well served.

PORNICHET
▲ Le Regent
150 bd des Océanides, 44380 **Map** 1C4

☎ 02 40 61 05 68

🗡 02 40 61 25 53

W www.le-regent.fr

🍴 AE, DC, MC, V ● Sun D, Fri; Dec–early Feb **¶¶** €€ 🍷 (22) €€€

The bounty of the sea is served: fine cod with a crumble of oats, and roast langoustines with peppers and smoked salmon. Guestrooms have a nautical theme with views of the sea.

POULIGNY-NOTRE-DAME
▲ Domaine des Dryades
D940 12km (7.5 miles) south of La Chatre, 36160 **Map** 7E3

☎ 02 54 06 60 60

🗡 02 54 30 10 24

W www.les-dryades.fr

🍴 AE, DC, MC, V

¶¶ €€€ 🍷 (85) €€€

The chef brings a novel approach to dishes such as scallops in lemon butter. The immaculate grounds, impressive furnishings and well-regarded cuisine draw a devoted clientele.

ROCHECORBON
▲ Les Hautes Roches
86 quai de la Loire, 37210 **Map** 7D1

☎ 02 47 52 88 88

🗡 02 47 52 81 30

W www.leshautesroches.com

🍴 AE, MC, V ● Apr–Oct: Mon L, Nov–Mar: Mon, Tue L, Wed L, Sat L

¶¶ €€€ 🍷 (15) €€€€

Bright dining room in a captivating spot on the river bank. Try the langoustine ravioli in chicken consommé, or sweet and sour Racan pigeon with dried fruits. Carved into the side of a stone cliff, the luxurious guestrooms are unique.

ROMORANTIN-LANTHENAY
▲ Auberge Le Lanthenay
9 rue Notre-Dame-du-Lieu, 41200

Map 7E2

☎ 02 54 76 09 19

🗡 02 54 76 72 91

🍴 AE, DC, MC, V

● Sun, Mon; last 2 wks Jul, last wk Dec–1st wk Jan

¶¶ €€€ 🍷 (10) €€

Tranquil surroundings in this picturesque hamlet. Dishes like gateau of poultry livers with crayfish, or fine catfish in Cheverny wine. Simple but cosy guestrooms.

ROMORANTIN-LANTHENAY
▲ Grand Hôtel du Lion D'Or
69 rue Georges Clemenceau, 41200

Map 7E2

☎ 02 54 94 15 15

🗡 02 54 88 24 87

W www.hotel-liondor.fr

🍴 AE, DC, MC, V ● Tue L; mid-Feb–Mar; 3rd wk Nov

¶¶ €€€€€ 🍷 (16) €€€€€

A Renaissance mansion, surrounded by formal gardens and broad terraces. On offer: roasted stuffed pigeon and an unmissable dessert selection such as cherry soup and tarte Tatin (p191).

RUAUDIN
● Auberge des Blés d'Or
29 rue principale, 72230 **Map** 6C1

☎ 02 43 75 79 33

🍴 MC, V ● Sun–Thu D, Mon; 1st 2 wks Feb, Jul **¶¶** €€

An acclaimed menu. Try the specialities such as sea bass with steamed aspara-gus or pan-fried foie gras.

SANCERRE
● Auberge de la Pomme d'Or
Pl de la Mairie, 18300 **Map** 7F2

☎ 02 48 54 13 30

🗡 02 48 54 19 22

🍴 MC, V ● Wed, Apr–Sep: Tue D, Oct–Mar: Tue; 1 wk Feb, 1 wk Oct

¶¶ €€€

Known as far away as Paris, Didier Turpin serves such delights as roast pike-perch with asparagus sauce.

SANCERRE
● L'Esplanade
17 Nouvelle Place, 18300 **Map** 7F2

☎ 02 48 54 01 36

🗡 02 48 54 17 52

🍴 MC, V ● Sep–Jun: Tue D, Thu D, Fri; last wk Feb-1st wk Mar, last wk Dec-1st wk Jan **¶¶** €

Young local chef, Pascal Lobjois, shows great promise in his approach: pike-perch in two Sancerre wines, or roast quail with Chavignol cheese.

SANDARVILLE
● Auberge de Sandarville
14 rue de la Sente-aux-Pretres, 28120

Map 3D5

☎ 02 37 25 33 18

🗡 02 37 25 35 18

🍴 MC, V

● Sun D, Mon; last 3 wks Jan, last 2 wks Aug **¶¶** €€€

Three countrified dining rooms in a Beauce farm dating from 1850. Favourites include the pig's trotters with foie gras and truffles, and a magret de canard a l'orange.

SAULGES
▲ L'Ermitage
3 pl St-Pierre, 53340 **Map** 6B1

☎ 02 43 64 66 00

🗡 02 43 64 66 20

W www.hotel-ermitage.fr

🍴 AE, DC, MC, V ● Sun D, Oct–mid-Apr: Mon; early Feb–early Mar

¶¶ €€ 🍷 (36) €€€

The chef's inspired approach to tradition shows in dishes like smoked pike-perch with green lentils and a shellfish salad. Spacious rooms with countryside views.

SAUMUR
● Auberge St Pierre
30 rue Tournelles, 49400 **Map** 6C2

☎ 02 41 51 26 25

🗡 02 41 59 89 28

🍴 AE, MC, V ● Sun, Mon; last 2 wks Mar, 2 wks Oct, last wk Dec **¶¶** €€

In a former 15th-century monastery, lovingly prepared dishes include chicken in Loire wine sauce and pike-perch fillet.

SAUMUR
▲ Hôtel Anne d'Anjou
32 quai Mayaud, 49400 **Map** 6C2

☎ 02 41 67 30 30

🗡 02 41 67 51 00

W www.hotel-anneanjou.com

🍴 AE, DC, MC, V

● Restaurant ■ Hotel ▲ Hotel / Restaurant

● Sun, Nov–Mar: Mon L
🍴 €€€ 🛏 (45) €€€€

A gem of a hostelry just across from Saumur's château. Specialities include Challans-style duck, pike-perch and freshwater eel. Unpretentious rooms.

SAUMUR
● Le 30 Février
9 pl de la République, 49400 **Map** 6C2
📞 02 41 51 12 45
💳 MC, V ● Sun L; mid-Sep–mid-May: Sun D, Mon; 2nd wk May, last 3 wks Sep, end Dec–early Jan 🍴 €

Pizza with a local twist. Try rillettes de Tours, eel, sardines or game toppings. A short, affordable wine list.

SAUMUR
● Les Délices du Château
Cour du Château, 49400 **Map** 6C2
📞 02 41 67 65 60
📠 02 41 67 74 60
@ delices.du.chateau@wanadoo.fr
💳 MC, V ● Oct–mid-Apr: Sun D, Tue D; mid-Dec–mid-Jan 🍴 €€€

A little restaurant in the courtyard of the château, serving standards such as fine rillettes of Tours, lovely game terrines and local duck pâtés.

SELLES-ST-DENIS
▲ Auberge De Cheval Blanc
Pl Mail, centre village, 14km (8.8 miles) east of Romorantin-Lanthenay on D724, 41300 **Map** 7E2
📞 02 54 96 36 36
📠 02 54 96 13 96
@ cheval.blanc.ssd@wanadoo.fr
💳 AE, MC, V
● Tue D, Wed; last 3 wks Feb, last 2 wks Aug, last wk Dec
🍴 €€€ 🛏 (6) €€

Contemporary cuisine such as white Sologne asparagus in a crab and grapefruit rémoulade. Cosy guestrooms.

SOLESMES
▲ Grand Hôtel
16 pl Dom-Guéranger, 72300 **Map** 6C1
📞 02 43 95 45 10
📠 02 43 95 22 26
💳 AE, DC, MC, V ● Nov–Feb: Sun D; last wk Dec–1st wk Jan
🍴 €€€€ 🛏 (32) €€€€

Former post house facing Abbaye St-Pierre. Main courses like snail casserole and pike-perch in sweet coffee cream. Superb wine list. Well-appointed rooms.

SOUVIGNY-EN-SOLOGNE
● Auberge De La Grange Aux Oies
2 rue Gâtinais, 41600 **Map** 7E1
📞 02 54 88 40 08
📠 02 54 88 91 06
💳 MC, V ● Mon D, Tue, Wed; mid-Mar, 1st 2 wks Sep, last wk Dec–mid-Jan 🍴 €€€

An 18th-century inn where all paintings and ornaments feature a goose theme. Try the young rabbit cooked in its own jelly with white Sancerre.

SOUVIGNY-EN-SOLOGNE
● La Perdrix Rouge
Rue Gâtinais, in village centre, 41600 **Map** 7E1
📞 02 54 88 41 05
📠 02 54 88 05 56
💳 AE, MC, V ● Mon–Tue; mid-Feb–1st wk Mar, 1st wk Jul, last wk Aug–1st wk Sep 🍴 €€€

This charming place is worthy of a detour. Dishes include millefeuille of white asparagus with a shellfish coulis.

ST-AMAND-MONTROND
● St-Jean
1 rue de l'Hotel de Dieu, 18200 **Map** 7E3
📞 02 48 96 39 82
🌐 www.restaurantsaintjean.com
💳 MC, V ● Mon, Wed, Thu; last 2 wks Sep, 1st wk Oct 🍴 €

A multiethnic, multicultural class of French cuisine such as smoked carpaccio with aubergine (eggplant) caviar.

ST-JEAN-DE-LINIERES
● Auberge de la Roche
Off N 23, 49078 **Map** 6B1
📞 02 41 39 72 21
💳 MC, V ● Sun D, Mon; 2 wks mid-Aug 🍴 €

A small, welcoming inn in a pretty village. Any of the game or fish dishes are a cut above average. Good value for money.

ST-JEAN-DE-MONTS
● La Quich'notte
La Davière, 200, route Notre Dame des Monts, 85200 **Map** 6A2
📞 02 51 58 62 64
💳 AE, DC, MC, V ● Mon, Tue L, Sep–May: Sat L; Nov–3rd wk Mar
🍴 €

Simplicity with no frills, the focus here is on the food: pan-fried foie gras with red fruits and frogs' legs are recommended.

ST-JEAN-DE-MONTS
● La Trattoria
1 ave Estacade, 85160 **Map** 6A2
📞 02 51 58 28 57
💳 MC, V
● Early Mar–mid-June & mid-Sep–mid-Nov: Mon–Fri; mid-Nov–early Mar 🍴 €

Time-honoured fare and dishes inspired by the Mediterranean. Specialities include mackerel with bacon and grilled vegetables and lamb with a mint confit.

ST-LYPHARD
▲ Les Chaumieres du Lac des Tymphas
Rue Vignonnet, facing the lake at St-Lyphard, 44410 **Map** 1A4
📞 02 40 91 40 30
📠 02 40 91 30 33
💳 AE, MC, V ● mid-Jun–mid-Sep: Mon L; mid-Jan–mid-Jun; mid-Sep–mid-Dec: Mon D; Tue, Tue D, Wed D; mid-Dec–mid-Jan
🍴 €€ 🛏 (20) €€

Lake views from the spacious rooms and cheery public spaces. On the menu: pan-fried veal mignon in a potato tart.

ST-NAZAIRE
▲ Au Bon Acceuil
39 rue Marceau centre-ville, 44600 **Map** 1C4
📞 02 40 22 07 05
📠 02 40 19 01 58
💳 AE, DC, MC, V ● Sun D; mid-Jul–1st wk Aug 🍴 €€ 🛏 (17) €€€

An enchanting little hotel serving dishes like hot oysters with steamed greens, and scallops. Modest guestrooms.

ST-OUEN
● La Vallée
34 rue Barré-de-St-Venant, 41100 **Map** 7D1
📞 02 54 77 29 93

FAX 02 54 73 15 51

AE, MC, V ● Sun D, Mon, Tue; 1 wk early Jan, 2 wks mid-Mar, 1 wk Oct

11 €

Tranquil establishment decorated in bright colours. Meals run along time-honoured lines: Nantaise scallops gratin and nougat ice cream with red fruit coulis.

ST-OUEN-LES-VIGNES

● L'Aubinière

29 rue Jules Gautier, 37530 **Map** 7D1

02 47 30 15 29

FAX 02 47 30 02 44

AE, MC, V ● Sun D, Tue D, Wed; mid-Feb–mid-Mar **11** €€€€

Rustic dining room and a flower-fringed terrace. Plentiful use of local ingredients: violet asparagus fricassée, or guinea fowl stuffed with veal. The best wines are Vouvray and Touraine-Mesland.

ST-PATRICE

▲ Château de Rochecotte

On N152, 37130 **Map** 6C2

02 47 96 16 16

FAX 02 47 96 90 59

www.chateau-de-rochecotte.fr

AE, MC, V ● Feb, 1st 2 wks Dec

11 €€€€ ◇ (34) €€€€€

Expansive grounds, perfect for an after-dinner stroll. Try the squid cannelloni with saffron, followed by fried banana dessert in cream sauce. Spacious rooms.

ST-SEBASTIEN-SUR-LOIRE

● Le Manoir de la Comète

21 rue de la Libération, 44230 **Map** 6A2

02 40 34 15 93

FAX 02 40 34 46 23

www.manoir-comete.com

AE, MC, V ● Sun, Sat L; last 2 wks Feb, 3rd wk Jul–3rd wk Aug

11 €€€€

A 1920s mansion with very comfortable rooms. Signature mains include grilled turbot Béarnaise with scallop roe.

ST-SYMPHORIEN-LE-CHATEAU

▲ Château d'Esclimont

Route de Gallardon, 28700 **Map** 3E5

02 37 31 15 15

FAX 02 37 31 57 91

www.esclimont.com

AE, DC, MC, V

11 €€€€€ ◇ (53) €€€€€

Grand Renaissance château offering coordinated luxury. Splendid dining room known for its Cordova leather interior. Traditional cuisine and a wine list of unusual breadth. Gorgeously appointed bedrooms.

SUCE-SUR-ERDRE

● Châtaigneraie

156 route Carquefou, 44240 **Map** 6A2

02 40 77 90 95

FAX 02 40 77 90 08

www.delphin.fr

AE, DC, MC, V ● Sun D, Mon, Tue; 3 wks Jan, 3rd wk Jul–1st wk Aug

11 €€€€€

In a fine 19th-century riverside mansion. Signature dishes include lobster gratin and millefeuille of rabbit with cabbage.

SULLY-SUR-LOIRE

▲ Le Grand Sully

10 bd Champ-de-Foire, 45600 **Map** 7E1

02 38 36 27 56

DC, MC, V ● Sun D, Mon; 1st 2 wks Mar **11** €€ ◇ (10) €€

A lovely house in a quiet village; time-honoured dishes such as pike-perch marinated in Saumur wine and veal gnocchi are served. Simple rooms.

TALMONT-ST-HILAIRE

● Le Cottage

60 ave du Luçon, 85440 **Map** 6A3

02 51 96 04 61

AE, MC, V ● Sep–May: Mon

11 €€

An inn serving oysters stuffed with garlic, sea bass in beurre blanc, and open-fire-roasted magret de canard.

TAVERS

▲ La Tonnellerie

12 rue des Eaux-Bleus, 45190 **Map** 7E1

02 38 44 68 15

FAX 02 38 44 10 01

www.tonelri.com

AE, MC, V ● Mon L, Sat L; last wk Dec–end Feb

11 €€€ ◇ (20) €€€€

A tastefully appointed manor house with specialities such as lobster couscous, or duck fillet in honey and rosemary. The

wine list is brief but worthy of mention, especially in its Touraine selections. Simple rooms overlook the gardens.

THORIGNE-SUR-DUE

▲ Hôtel Saint Jacques

Pl du Monument, 72160 **Map** 7D1

02 43 89 95 50

FAX 02 43 76 58 42

AE, DC, MC, V ● Sun D, Mon; last wk Dec–mid-Jan

11 €€€ ◇ (15) €€€

The chef here prepares quail salad with foie gras and a vinegar, Champagne and truffle sauce, and sautéed langoustines with apple and vanilla butter. Functional, comfortable guestrooms.

TOURS

● Charles Barrier

101 ave Tranchée, 37100 **Map** 7D2

02 47 54 20 39

FAX 02 47 41 80 95

AE, DC, MC, V ● Sun, Sat L

11 €€€€€

Highlights include crispy spiced langoustines, and roast John Dory with fennel, served in an airy, glass-canopied room in the heart of old Tours.

TOURS

▲ Jean Bardet

57 rue Groison, 37000 **Map** 7D2

02 47 41 41 11

FAX 02 47 51 68 72

www.jeanbardet.com

AE, DC, MC, V ● May–Nov: Mon L, Tue L, Sat L, Sep–May: Sun D; Nov–Apr **11** €€€€€

◇ (21) €€€€€

A garden surrounds this elegant mansion. Inspired cuisine includes tomato tartare with coriander (cilantro); or frogs' legs, sautéed lamb and chanterelles. Colourful guestrooms.

TOURS

● Les Tuffeaux

19 rue Lavoisier, 37000 **Map** 7D2

02 47 47 19 89

AE, MC, V ● Sun D, Mon L

11 €€€

In the historic part of Tours. Cooking flair much enjoyed by locals, displayed in dishes such as lamb medallions with

---

● Restaurant ■ Hotel ▲ Hotel / Restaurant

baby vegetables, as well as raspberry
millefeuille *with* fromage blanc.

TROO

▲ Le Cheval Blanc

Pl de Liberation, 6km (3.6miles) northwest of Montoire-sur-Loir on D917,
41800 **Map** 7D1

☎ 02 54 72 58 22

FAX 02 54 72 55 44

✉ MC, V ● Sun D, Mon, Tue L; mid-
Nov–mid-Dec 🍴 €€€ 🍷 (9) €€

*Local specialities such as quail salad
topped with foie gras. Tucked away in
a quiet riverside spot. Pleasant rooms.*

VAAS

▲ Le Vadequais

Pl de la Liberté, 72500 **Map** 6C1

☎ 02 43 46 01 41

FAX 02 43 46 37 60

✉ MC, V ● Sun, Mon D, Fri D; 1st 2
wks Feb, last wk Dec

🍴 €€€ 🍷 (12) €€

*A restaurant-hotel in a former village
school, with modern rooms and an
Internet café adjunct. Tradition reigns
in the dining room with dishes such as
chicken with morels and orchard-fresh
apple tart.*

VAILLY-SUR-SAULDRE

● Le Lièvre Gourmand

14 Grand Rue, 18260 **Map** 7F2

☎ 02 48 73 80 23

FAX 02 48 73 86 13

✉ MC, V ● Sun D, Mon, Tue; last
3 wks Jan, last wk Jun, 2nd wk Sep
🍴 €€€

*A brick building in the distinctive
Sologne style. Self-taught chef William
Page prepares roast turbot with puréed
potato, and fish dishes using saffron.*

VAUTORTE

● La Coutancière

Off N12 route Mayenne, 53500 **Map** 2B5

☎ 02 43 00 56 27

FAX 02 43 00 66 09

✉ MC, V ● Tue D, Wed D; mid-
Jul–1st wk Aug 🍴 €€

*On the outskirts of the famed Mayenne
forest, classic dishes prepared with flair.
Try the exceptional sandre au beurre
blanc (p191) or the chicken in cider.*

VELLURE

▲ Auberge de la Riviere

Rue Fouarne, 85770 **Map** 6B3

☎ 02 51 52 32 15

FAX 02 51 52 37 42

✉ MC, V ● Mon L, Oct–Jun: Sun D,
Mon D; last wk Dec–1st wk Mar

🍴 €€ 🍷 (11) €€€

*Flowers bedeck the small, comfortable
guestrooms of this rustic inn. Dishes like
hot oysters and pigeon in morel sauce.*

VENDOME

▲ Auberge De La Madeleine

6 pl de la Madeleine, 41100 **Map** 7D1

☎ 02 54 77 20 79

✉ MC, V ● Wed; Feb, 1st 2 wks Nov
🍴 €€ 🍷 (8) €€

*The game (especially wild boar and hare)
and river fish are recommended. Well-
appointed yet affordable guestrooms.*

VEUIL

● L'Auberge St Fiacre

Le Bourg, 6km (3.7 miles) southwest of
Valençay on D15 and D15a, 36600
Map 7E2

☎ 02 54 40 32 78

FAX 02 54 40 35 66

✉ MC, V ● Sun D, Mon 🍴 €€

*A 17th-century mansion. Menu selections
include minced duck with sour cherry,
and sea bass in saffron and chervil.*

VIBRAYE

▲ Le Chapeau Rouge

6 pl de l'Hôtel de Ville, 72320 **Map** 7D1

☎ 02 43 93 60 02

FAX 02 43 93 60 20

w www.le-chapeau-rouge.com

✉ MC, V ● Sun D, Fri D; 1st 2 wks
Jan, last wk Nov 🍴 €€ 🍷 (15) €€

*The chef keeps it simple, yet delicious –
the smoked salmon and duck pâté are
unmissable. Simple, cosy guestrooms.*

VIERZON

● Maison de Celestin

20 ave Pierre-Sémard, 18100 **Map** 7E2

☎ 02 48 83 01 63

FAX 02 48 71 63 41

✉ AE, MC, V ● Sun D, Mon, Sat L;
1st 2 wks Jan, 1st 3 wks Aug 🍴 €€€

*Two modern and tasteful dining rooms
within a lovely 19th-century home. An*

eclectic menu includes tomato sorbet
and sea bass with haricot beans.

VIGNOUX-SUR-BARANGEON

▲ Le Prieuré

2 route de St-Laurent 8km (5 miles) east
of Vierzon on N76, 18500 **Map** 7E2

☎ 02 48 51 58 80

FAX 02 48 51 56 01

✉ MC, V ● restaurant: Tue, Wed;
hotel: Oct–May

🍴 €€€€ 🍷 (7) €€€

*The langoustines on polenta with fresh
herbs and balsamic vinegar is marvellous.
Well-appointed guestrooms.*

VILLANDRY

▲ Cheval Rouge

9 rue Principale, 37510 **Map** 6C2

☎ 02 47 50 02 07

FAX 02 47 50 08 77

w www.lecheval-rouge.com

✉ AE, DC, MC, V ● Sun D, Nov–Apr:
Sun D & Fri D; last wk Dec–1st wk Jan

🍴 €€ 🍷 (35) €€€

*This century-old property offers small,
cosy guestrooms. The foie gras terrine is
excellent, as are the fish or meat served
straight from the wood-fired grill.*

VILLANDRY

● Orangerie

11 rue Principale, 37510 **Map** 6C2

☎ 02 47 43 56 26

FAX 02 47 43 56 26

✉ MC, V ● Mon; 24–25 Dec

🍴 €€

*Just beside what should be every keen
gardener's favourite château. Laudable
wood-fired pizza and a very noteworthy
French menu too. Solid value.*

VOVES

▲ Le Quai Fleuri

15 rue Texier-Gallas, 28150 **Map** 3E5

☎ 02 37 99 15 15

FAX 02 37 99 11 20

✉ AE, DC, MC, V ● Sun D, Nov–Apr:
Mon D; last wk Dec–1st wk Jan

🍴 €€ 🍷 (17) €€€

*Set in charming countryside. Try the
light pastry shell with langoustines and
rascasse. For dessert, French toast with
caramelized apples and caramel sauce.
Tidy, well-appointed guestrooms.*

BURGUNDY & FRANCHE-COMTE

The glorious wines of Burgundy (and the lesser-known ones of Franche-Comté) are well matched by the produce of their verdant pastures, orchards and rugged mountain areas: superb beef (in wine sauces, naturally), charcuterie, snails, poultry, wild fungi and fine cheeses.

The Flavours of Burgundy & Franche-Comté

Here you'll find not just superb wines to enjoy, but also great beef, charcuterie and fish, along with fine mustard, wild mushrooms, blackcurrants and formidable cheeses.

Shoppers making the most of Beaune market

MEAT AND CHARCUTERIE

Burgundy is renowned for its quality beef and poultry. Large, docile, creamy Charolais cattle originated around Charolles but are now widespread all over Burgundy. Bresse chickens are raised in the south *(see p266)*.

Pigs, especially in the Morvan and Franche-Comté, are made into a variety of charcuterie. In Burgundy look for dry-cured *jambon de Morvan*, and *jambon persillé (see p216)*. In the Jura mountains, the speciality is wood-smoked products, leading to its own architectural style centred on a huge, pyramid-shaped wooden chimney. Montbéliard sausage is made from pork flavoured with coriander, cumin and nutmeg, then salted and smoked. *Jésus de Morteau* is similar but plumper. Smoked sausages should always be cooked before being eaten. Smoked hams are also produced, as well as *Brésil*, a dried, smoked beef similar to Swiss *viande des Grisons*.

FISH

Trout, tench, pike, pike-perch and crayfish are found in the rivers Saône, Yonne and Doubs, and the lakes of the Jura. Frogs are also plentiful.

CHEESES

Franche-Comté is one of France's great cheese-producing regions, thanks to the milk-giving qualities of the Montbéliard cow and the abundant, varied flora of its

DIJON MUSTARD

Mustard has been used as a condiment since antiquity, and was a vital flavouring in the Middle Ages, when it was cheaper than imported spices. Although it was, and still is, made in other places, including Meaux and Reims, *moutarde de Dijon* was invented here, and the town's *moutardiers* had established their reputation as early as the 14th century. Originally, mustard seeds were crushed and soaked in *verjus* (the bitter juice of unripe green grapes), before being ground to a paste. *Verjus* has since been replaced by a mixture of white wine vinegar, water and salt. Today, virtually all the seed is imported, chiefly from North America, though there are attempts to resuscitate cultivation locally. As well as the classic strong, smooth variety, others include *moutarde à l'ancienne*, milder and coarse-grained, and mustards flavoured with tarragon, green peppercorns or blackcurrants.

Left Morvan ham producer **Centre** Morbier cheese **Right** Bouton de Culotte goats' cheeses

PAIN D'ÉPICES

A speciality of Dijon, this moist, slightly chewy cake is baked in blocks and novelty shapes. Makers all keep their own closely guarded secret recipe for *pain d'épices*, or spice bread, but the essentials are honey, flour and spices – though not necessarily ginger, as many people think.

Display of Dijon's traditional *pain d'épices*

SNAILS

The *helix pomatia*, or Burgundian snail, is bigger than the *helix aspersa*, or *petit gris*, found in most of France. Introduced by the Romans, and once found commonly in the vineyards, snails are now imported from eastern Europe, though they are also increasingly being farmed here.

mountain pasture. Comté AOC is a smooth, fruity Gruyère-type cheese made only from the raw milk of Montbéliard cows. The best has been aged for at least a year. Vacherin-Mont-d'Or AOC is a gooey winter treat, eaten straight out of its wooden box with a spoon or mopped up with a chunk of bread. Morbier AOC is a creamy-coloured, semi-soft cheese with a black stripe down the centre, made by running an ash-covered poker through it. Bleu de Gex AOC is a mild, dryish, crumbly cheese, with delicate greeny-blue veins. Franche-Comté is also the main producer of French Emmental.

Burgundy's most characteristic cheese is Epoisses AOC, a round, cow's milk cheese with an orange-red rind. It is at its best when washed with Marc de Bourgogne and served mature so that it is runny round the edges with a distinctive, tangy aftertaste. You may also find it served young (*fraîche*), when it is very mild with a soft, chalky texture. L'Ami du Chambertin, washed with Marc de Chambertin, is quite similar to Epoisses, while Cîteaux is a mild, monastic cheese. *Fromage blanc* is often served in Burgundy, seasoned as a starter or with fresh cream and sugar as a dessert. There is small-scale production of goat's cheeses, such as the Chevrotin de Mâcon, Charolles and the tiny Bouton de Culotte.

FRUIT AND VEGETABLES

The morel mushroom, or *morille*, with its spongy, black conical cap, appears in many dishes and sauces of Franche-Comté. Unusually, it is a spring variety.

Blackcurrants have been grown along the Côte de Nuits for centuries; bushes are often planted in amongst the vines. They are made into cassis liqueur (combined with white wine as the apéritif kir), but also feature in tarts, sorbets, jams and in *cassissines* sweets. Look out, too, for the Burgundy truffle, and cherries in Franche-Comté and the Yonne around Auxerre.

Regional Dishes

Burgundy's gastronomic reputation goes back to the feasts of medieval times, when the Burgundian court rivalled that of the French crown. Many of its recipes have become classics throughout France. Franche-Comté clings proudly to its local culinary traditions.

ON THE MENU

Côtes de porc à l'arboisienne Pork chops gratinéed in a cheese sauce

Croûtes comtoises aux morillles Morel mushrooms in cream sauce on toast

Ecrevisses au gratin Crayfish gratin

Escargots à la bourguignonne Snails stuffed with garlic and parsley butter

Gougère Cheesy choux pastry circle or bun

Jambon persillé Ham set in a parsley aspic

Jambon en saupiquet or saupiquet du Morvan Fried ham in a white wine and cream sauce

Lapin à la moutarde Rabbit baked with Dijon mustard and cream

Pôchouse Freshwater fish stew

Poire à la dijonnaise Pear poached in blackcurrant syrup

Rigodon Baked pudding of brioche with eggs and cream

Salade comtoise Salad with Comté cheese and smoked ham

Escargots à la bourguignonne, with garlic and parsley

THE REGIONAL MENU

A Burgundian meal will often start with an *amuse-gueule* of little cheesy *gougère* puffs to accompany an apéritif of kir, before getting down to the serious business of meat, cream and rich wine sauces. Typical starters include *oeufs en meurette*; a sizzling hot dish of snails in their shells oozing with melted garlic and parsley butter; or a thick slice of *jambon persillé*. A red wine sauce is a feature of many main courses, such as the celebrated *coq au vin* and *boeuf bourguignon*, or accompanies fish such as pike or pike-perch, or thick Charolais steaks. White wine goes into *saupiquet* sauce (with juniper berries and shallots) and *pôchouse*. Dijon mustard is cooked with rabbit and appears in vegetable gratins, while *pain d'épices* and blackcurrants go into numerous sauces, both sweet and savoury.

Desserts are often based on fruit combined with liqueur or wine – pears poached in Crème de Cassis (*see p220*) or in red wine, blackcurrant sorbet, and "soups" of strawberries or cherries in wine. As often as not you'll also be offered *fromage blanc* – soft, fresh white cheese – either before or instead of dessert, with sugar and thick fresh cream.

In Franche-Comté many dishes are marked by the unusual, sherry-like tones of its prized *vin jaune (see p223)*. Much use is also made of local cheeses, especially Comté, gratinéed over veal or pork chops, paired with Montbéliard sausage in tarts and pies, melted in thick sauces or warmed as a fondue with Kirsch. Morel mushrooms are a favourite dish, especially in springtime (though dried morels are also used out of season), piled generously into creamy sauces to accompany chicken or steaks, or served on *croûtes* (slices of toast) as a luxurious snack or starter. Fish is often prepared *à la vesoulienne*, with mousseron mushrooms, though you'll also find *pôchouse* fish stew here as well as in Burgundy. Franche-Comté is one of the few areas of France where native frogs are still relatively plentiful, and you may find them on the menu simmered with vegetables and *vin jaune* as a soup, or *en persillade*, sautéed in butter and parsley.

Left Boeuf bourguignon **Centre** Oeufs en meurette **Right** Coq au vin

REGIONAL DINING

The following restaurants are among those serving regional dishes at reasonable prices:

Bistro des Grands Crus
Chablis (see p229)

Hostellerie d'Aussois
Semur-en-Auxois (see p239)

Hôtellerie du Val d'Or
Mercurey (see p235)

Hôtel Mercure Pont de Loire Nevers (see p236)

La Belle Epoque
Le Creusot (see p234)

La Tête Noir
Autun (see p224)

Le Bougainville
Vezelay (see p241)

Le Gourmandin
Beaune (see p227)

Le Maxime
Auxerre (see p225)

Le Pré aux Clercs
Dijon (see p232)

Interior of Le Gourmandin
restaurant, Beaune

OEUFS EN MEURETTE

A *meurette* sauce is made with red wine, onions and a *bouquet garni*. Eggs are broken into a ladle or saucer and slid carefully one by one into the wine, where they are lightly poached, then removed and set aside. The sauce is reduced and thickened with a butter and flour paste. To serve, each egg is placed on top of a garlic-rubbed *croûte* and covered with the *meurette* sauce. Bacon *lardons* are often used to garnish.

BOEUF BOURGUIGNON

With its combination of choice Charolais beef and good red Burgundy, this dish is emblematic of Burgundian cuisine. Large cubes of beef, sliced carrots and onions are slow-cooked for at least two hours in beef stock and wine, with garlic and a *bouquet garni*. Snippets of bacon, tiny onions and sliced mushrooms are fried separately and stirred in at the end.

COQ AU VIN

A jointed cockerel (or chicken) is marinated overnight in wine with onion, carrots and a *bouquet garni*. Next day, the meat and vegetables are browned, with garlic, in a large casserole, the strained marinade is added, then it simmers, covered, until both sauce and meat are a deep purple, almost black. Bacon pieces are browned with whole pearl onions and button mushrooms, and are added to the dish just before serving.

POULET AU VIN JAUNE ET AUX MORILLES

This combination of cream, *vin jaune* and morel mushrooms epitomizes the cuisine of Franche-Comté. A jointed chicken is cooked gently in butter, then deglazed with the *vin jaune*. Thick *crème fraîche* is stirred in, followed by the morels, and simmered until the sauce is thick enough to coat the back of a spoon.

Regional Wines & Spirits

With its jigsaw-puzzle vineyards, its multitude of appellations and crus and wines that range from the truly sublime to sad disappointments, Burgundy is perhaps the most confusing of all France's wine regions. Just to the east, the less trumpeted but unique specialities of the Jura await the curious.

Chardonnay grapes

CHARDONNAY

Probably the most famous of all white grapes, Chardonnay grows happily in a wide range of conditions. However, it can produce some of the richest, most expressive wines in the world when grown in the cool, balanced climate of Burgundy's Côte d'Or and sagely dosed with oak. The wines have a distinctive golden colour with faint greenish tints and carry flavours of hazelnut and butter. The cooler vineyards of Chablis produce a steelier incarnation of the grape, often matured in steel tanks rather than oak to maintain a zesty freshness. Unoaked styles are also popular further south in the Mâconnais, where the many local cooperatives produce fresh, lemony wines.

Four major areas make up the Burgundian vineyards: Chablis and the vineyards of the Yonne, the world famous Côte d'Or, the Côte Chalonnaise and the Mâconnais. As far as grape varieties go, nothing could be simpler. All reds are made from Pinot Noir and almost all the whites come exclusively from Chardonnay. Sparkling *crémant* is mostly made from Chardonnay. Many are now of superior quality, and make a riper-tasting alternative to lesser Champagne. In terms of still wines, Burgundy has managed to persuade consumers that anything sporting its name is a guarantee of quality. This is certainly not always the case. Many vineyards are subdivided into numerous tiny plots, each with a different owner, and each producer has his own approach – sometimes obsessive, sometimes lazy, but always expensive.

CHABLIS AND THE YONNE

The sleepy, provincial town of Chablis has given its name to one of the most famous wines in the world. Chablis lies on an isolated pocket of land, northwest of the heart of Burgundy. The vineyards stand on the banks of the meandering river Serein and the best have a very particular type of clay and limestone soil called Kimmeridgian. Springtime frost protection is a vital part of the Chablis vineyard calendar.

There are four categories of Chablis organized in a hierarchy dominated by seven Grands Crus situated on an amphitheatre of hills overlooking the village. These

A layer of ice protects Chablis vines from severe spring frosts

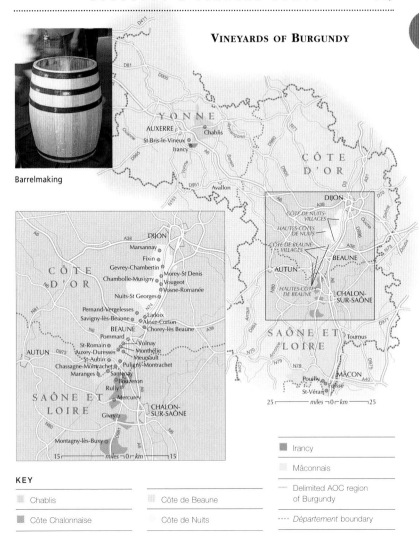

VINEYARDS OF BURGUNDY

Barrelmaking

KEY

Chablis

Côte Chalonnaise

Côte de Beaune

Côte de Nuits

Irancy

Mâconnais

— Delimited AOC region
of Burgundy

···· *Département* boundary

are the Chablis of fabled dry, minerally, buttery, hazelnut character that can be aged for ten years and have the wherewithal to stand oak maturation.

Premier Cru wines are made from 17 vineyard sites, which surround or lie opposite the Grand Cru sites. The very best plain Chablis offers everything one is entitled to expect from the appellation – dry, lemony, appley, minerally wine with steely acidity. Petit Chablis is the lowliest appellation, but occasionally it can prove to be very good value.

Irancy produces pleasant, fruity summertime reds, that are made from Pinot Noir and the unusual César grape. In Saint-Bris the main variety is Sauvignon, which is prohibited elsewhere in Burgundy.

BEST PRODUCERS: CHABLIS

Domaine Jean-Marc Brocard, La Chablisienne, Domaine René et Vincent Dauvissat, Daniel-Etienne Defaix, Domaine Jean-Paul Droin, Domaine Jean Durup et Fils, Domaine William Fèvre, Domaine Laroche, Domaine Long-Depaquit, Domaine Louis Michel, Domaine François Raveneau

Barrels of precious white Burgundy maturing in the cellars of the Château de Meursault

CREME DE CASSIS AND KIR

The blackcurrant plant *(cassis)* arrived in Burgundy several centuries ago and the region is now the world's premier producer of blackcurrants and source of the sweet blackcurrant liqueur, crème de cassis. Kir is a popular aperitif made by adding a little crème de cassis to white wine, preferably the sharp-tasting Aligoté. It was invented by Canon Félix Kir, a resolute Resistance fighter and later mayor of Dijon. When he first took office the blackcurrant producers were fighting for survival. By presenting the drink that was later named after him at official receptions, he managed to revive interest in the production of this liqueur.

A glass of kir

CÔTE D'OR, THE HEART OF BURGUNDY

As is often the case in viticultural France, vine-growing on Burgundy's 65-km (40-mile) Côte d'Or (golden slope) owes a lot to the church. Cistercian monks identified and cultivated the best vineyards of the area until their dispossession during the French Revolution. After 1789, estates were broken up and the region began to take shape as we know it today: an area of smallholdings, with tiny vineyard plots. The Côte d'Or has four categories of appellation – the regional wines, the villages, the Premiers Crus and the Grands Crus – and is traditionally divided into the Côte de Nuits, with its magnificent reds, and the Côte de Beaune, which is renowned for some of the world's greatest whites.

The Côte de Nuits stretches from Marsannay, south of Dijon, to Corgoloin north of Beaune, taking in the meaty, full-flavoured wines of Gevrey-Chambertin, the more elegant, fragrant reds of Morey St-Denis and Chambolle-Musigny, potent Vougeot and Vosne-Romanée, home to the legendary Domaine de la Romanée-Conti, and finally Nuits-St-Georges, with its full-throated rendering of the mercurial Pinot Noir grape. Within these villages the better *climats* (a specific Burgundian name for certain vineyards) are designated as Premiers Crus, whose names are added to the village name on the label, while the top sites are Grands Crus and hold appellations in their own names.

The hill of Corton announces the beginning of the Côte de Beaune, and is itself a Grand Cru for both red and white wines. Further south, the white Grands Crus of Puligny-Montrachet and Chassagne-Montrachet produce the richest, most concentrated, most perfectly balanced of all white Burgundies. Meursault possesses no Grands Crus but its golden, buttery, creamy-rich Chardonnays are no less popular for that. However, the bulk of the wine produced in the Côte de Beaune, from Beaune through Pommard to Volnay, is actually red. These reds are generally softer, easier and less concentrated than those from the Côte de Nuits.

There are 32 Grands Crus in all on the Côte d'Or, mostly red wine appellations in the Côte de Nuits, and over 450 different Premiers Crus. With most sites divided into small plots belonging to different domaines, this makes for a mind-boggling array of wines.

The N74 road runs right through the Côte d'Or and the better vineyard land is on western side of the highway, with the Grands Crus mid-way up the slopes. Higher up and across the wooded hilltops are the inferior but more affordable appellations of the Hautes-Côtes de Nuits and Hautes-Côtes de Beaune.

Côte Chalonnaise

Extending from Chagny to near Saint-Gengoux-le-National, the Côte Chalonnaise produces delicate, fresh white or red wines like Rully as well as tannic reds that will keep well, such as Mercurey (which constitutes the majority of production in the Côte Chalonnaise) and Givry. The village of Bouzeron produces the best white wine to be made entirely from the generally lean and acidic Aligoté grape.

The Mâconnais

White wines take the lion's share in the Mâconnais and pretty good value they can be too. Located in the hills to the west of Mâcon, these vineyards lie just north of those of Beaujolais *(see pp272–3)*. The most famous wines of the Mâconnais are the various Pouillys (Pouilly-Fuissé, Pouilly-Loché and Pouilly-Vinzelles), often made in a rich, oaky style. Then there are the often delicious, lemony whites of Saint-Véran. Fresh, simple whites go under the banner of Mâcon-Villages.

The village of Pernand-Vergelesses in the Côte de Beaune

BEST PRODUCERS: CÔTE D'OR

Alain Burguet, Louis Carillon & Fils, Chandon de Briailles, Bruno Clair, J-F Coche-Dury, Comte Georges de Vogüé, Domaine de l'Arlot, Domaine Leroy, Domaine de la Romanée-Conti, Domaine de la Vougeraie, Joseph Drouhin, Dujac, Joseph Faiveley, Jean-Noël Gagnard, Vincent Girardin, Jadot, Robert Jayer-Gilles, Michel Lafarge, Lafon, Domaine Leflaive, Méo-Camuzet, Ramonet, Georges Roumier, Armand Rousseau

Roof of the Hospices de Beaune

THE HOSPICES DE BEAUNE WINE AUCTION

The most famous wine auction in the world takes place on the third Sunday in November in magnificent former hospital of the Hospices de Beaune. This charitable institution possesses over 60 hectares (150 acres) of vineyards, mostly in the Côte de Beaune, and the fund-raising auction of the new wines sets the price parameters for the whole Burgundian vintage. The purchasers become responsible for maturing and bottling their wines

VINEYARDS OF THE JURA

KEY

- Arbois
- Château-Chalon
- Côtes de Jura
- L'Etoile
- ···· *Département* boundary
- ━━ International boundary

ABSINTHE AND ANIS

Pontarlier in the Jura was a great centre for absinthe production before its prohibition. Producers turned to another outlet and the pastis-like, aniseed-based Anis de Pontarlier soon became famous. According to locals, you should ask for a "Pon".

LOUIS PASTEUR

When in 1862 Napoleon III asked the scientist Louis Pasteur to find out why many of France's wines turned into vinegar, he naturally chose his native Jura as the place to carry out his experiments. Working at his father's house in Arbois, he found the *aceto-bacter* bacteria responsible and discovered that heating the wine – pasteurization – would kill it. The house is now a museum: 83 rue de Courcelles, Arbois (03 84 66 11 72), hourly tours 1 Apr–15 Oct.

The Pasteur house in Arbois

WINES OF THE JURA

Between Burgundy and the Swiss border, the vineyards of the Jura stretch 80 km (50 miles) north to south in an area called the Revermont. They are situated at an altitude of between 250 and 400 metres (800–1300 ft). Often highly underestimated, Jura wines can be delicious and some are extremely long-lived.

The regional Côtes du Jura appellation covers all types of wine produced in the Jura: dry whites, reds and rosés, *crémants* (white or rosé), *vin jaune, vin de paille* and *macvin*. Arbois, around the pretty town of Arbois, is a more specific appellation. Château-Chalon, from a village dominated by a beautiful castle, is the most prestigious appellation in the Jura and is wholly devoted to producing *vin jaune*. The wines of L'Etoile have very distinctive flint and hazelnut aromas.

GRAPE VARIETIES

Several grapes are unique to the area. Reds and most rosés come from the early-ripening Poulsard and carry delicious, smoky scents of liquorice, redcurrant and raspberry – a good partner for the region's Morteau sausage *(see p214)*. The red Trousseau grape is found mainly around Arbois, making gamey, spicy wines.

Savagnin is the most emblematic of the Jura's grapes, acquiring minerally scents and the flavour of apples, fresh walnuts, and roasted coffee beans. It produces wines with a sherry-like, resiny taste that you either love or hate.

Pinot Noir in the Jura is light and fruity with the slight bitterness of kirsch and the tang of blackberry. Chardonnay is the most widely planted white grape, here tasting of bitter almonds, citrus fruit and honey.

The castle at Château-Chalon

VIN JAUNE

Pungent *vin jaune*, named for its yellow or amber colour, is made from the Savagnin grape and has a unique character that is reminiscent of some of Spain's richest, nuttiest dry *fino* sherry. The six-plus years it spends in cask, under a protective film of yeast, determine its unique flavour.

Vin jaune is a traditional partner for Comté cheese *(see p215)* and the region's flagship dish, *poulet au vin jaune et aux morilles (see p217)*. It also makes an original match for spicy foods and for sushi.

Vin jaune in a clavelin bottle

VIN DE PAILLE

Rare and consequently expensive, sweet *vin de paille* (straw wine) is another of the Jura's extraordinary specialities. Its name comes from it being originally made from grapes that had been dried on straw mats.

Vin de paille is the colour of old gold, with unusual scents of dried tropical fruit and dates with hints of roasted coffee or cocoa beans. The texture is so thickly honeyed and rich that ideally it should be drunk fairly cool. It makes a truly amazing accompaniment to foie gras, or to chocolate- or apricot-based desserts.

MACVIN

A Jura curiosity, *macvin* is a *vin de liqueur*, made by mixing marc du Jura with grape must – hence the name: *marc* and *vin* – thereby arresting fermentation and retaining some of the grape's natural sugar.

THE CLAVELIN

Squat and broad-shouldered, the 62cl clavelin is modelled on a 16th-century bottle and is the only one authorized to contain *vin jaune*. The Château-Chalon bottle carries an engraved shield at the bottom of the neck.

BEST PRODUCERS

Château d'Arlay, Domaine Berthet-Bondet, Domaine Jean Maclé, Domaine Pierre Overnoy, Domaine de la Pinte, Domaine Jacques Puffeney, Domaine Rolet Père et Fils, Domaine André et Mireille Tissot, Domaine Jacques Tissot.

Grapes drying on straw for making *vin de paille*

Where to Eat & Stay

AILLANT-SUR-THOLON
▲ Domaine du Roncemay

Aillant-sur-Tholon, 89110 **Map** 8A1

☎ 03 86 73 50 50

FAX 03 86 73 69 46

🌐 www.roncemay.com

💳 AE, DC, MC, V

⬤ Oct–Feb, Sun D, Mon, Tue

🍴 €€€€ 🛏 (18) €€€€€

Large, beautiful estate with a Michelin star and a magnificent golf course, plus an organic orchard and herb garden. Sample the large, tasty Burgundy snails in a consommé, in ravioli or with a mushroom tartare. Follow with a slab of the region's famous Charolais beef. Very attractive rooms.

ANCY-LE-FRANC
▲ Hostellerie du Centre

34 Grand Rue, 89160 **Map** 8A1

☎ 03 86 75 15 11

FAX 03 86 75 14 13

💳 AE, MC, V ⬤ mid-Nov–mid-Mar

🍴 €€ 🛏 (22) €€

Ideally located for a visit to the Renaissance château surrounded by celebrated vineyards. Specialities include ham in Chablis sauce, chicken with mushrooms, or snails. Try a wine from Epineuil, Tonnerre or Molosmes. Simple but comfortable rooms.

ANOST
⬤ La Galvache

Grand Rue, 71550 **Map** 8A2

☎ 03 85 82 70 88

FAX 03 85 82 79 62

💳 MC, V ⬤ Dec–Mar 🍴 €€€

Simple place northwest of Autun, in the middle of Morvan's huge regional park. Generous helpings of traditional regional cooking such as red mullet salad, duck fillet with grapes and scallop salad.

APPOIGNY
▲ Hôtel Mercure

Le Chaumois, RN6, 89380 **Map** 8A1

☎ 03 86 53 25 00

FAX 03 86 53 07 47

💳 AE, DC, MC, V

🍴 €€€ 🛏 (77) €€€

In the heart of the Yonne Valley, this 1980s hotel-restaurant features a terrace, pool and spacious rooms. Standard but satisfying food in the restaurant.

ARNAY-LE-DUC
▲ Chez Camille

1 pl Edouard Herriot, 21230 **Map** 8B2

☎ 03 80 90 01 38

FAX 03 80 90 04 64

🌐 www.chez-camille.fr

💳 AE, MC, V 🍴 €€ 🛏 (11) €€

The food is filling and the setting, in a lush garden, is pleasant and relaxing. Mango and celery coq au vin (p217), smoked duck and shellfish vinaigrette are all highlights. Old-fashioned rooms.

AUTUN
⬤ Chalet Bleu

3 rue Jeannin, 71400 **Map** 8B2

☎ 03 85 86 27 30

FAX 03 85 52 74 56

⬤ Sun D, Mon D, Tue; mid-Feb–mid-Mar 🍴 €€

Traditional, reasonably priced rustic fare, such as thin slices of duck, have made this a popular place. Kitsch, but cheery.

AUTUN
▲ Hostellerie du Vieux Moulin

Porte d'Arroux, 71400 **Map** 8B2

☎ 03 85 52 10 90

FAX 03 85 86 32 15

💳 AE, MC, V ⬤ Sun D, Mon; Dec–Feb 🍴 €€€ 🛏 (16) €€

This lovely crêperie-grill is in an old mill that stopped operating in 1958; the sluice gates are still on the River Arroux. Grilled cuts of beef and veal are offered alongside a wide range of crêpes.

AUTUN
▲ Hôtel les Ursulines

14 rue de Rivault, 71400 **Map** 8B2

☎ 03 85 86 58 58

FAX 03 85 86 23 07

🌐 www.hotelursulines.fr

💳 AE, DC, MC, V

🍴 €€ 🛏 (43) €€€

Formerly a convent, this picturesque hotel has a lovely garden and mountain views. The restaurant serves hearty food and is known for its cheese plate. Pastel guestrooms with a rural feel.

AUTUN
▲ Hôtel St-Louis

6 rue de l'Arbalète, 71400 **Map** 8B2

☎ 03 85 52 01 01

FAX 03 85 86 32 54

🌐 www.amadeusprop.com

💳 AE, DC, MC, V ⬤ Sat L

🍴 €€€ 🛏 (44) €€€

Charming hotel that's been around for over 350 years. Rooms with modern comforts; several suites, the most expensive named after Napoleon, who is said to have stopped here on four occasions. The Charolais beef with mushrooms is a highlight.

AUTUN
▲ Hôtel-Restaurant du Commerce et Touring

20 ave de la République, 71400 **Map** 8B2

☎ 03 85 52 17 90

FAX 03 85 52 37 63

💳 MC, V ⬤ Mon; Jan

🍴 €€ 🛏 (20) €€

Convenient location opposite the train station. Locals flock to the restaurant to enjoy hearty portions. Comfortable rooms.

AUTUN
⬤ La Fontaine

6 pl du Terreau, 71400 **Map** 8B2

☎ 03 85 86 25 57

FAX 03 85 52 07 37

💳 MC, V ⬤ Tue, Wed 🍴 €€

Outdoor tables are laid out around the St-Lazare fountain. The menu offers œufs en meurette (p217) and excellent confit de canard (p326).

AUTUN
▲ La Tête Noire

3 rue de l'Arquebuse, 71400 **Map** 8B2

☎ 03 85 86 59 99

FAX 03 85 86 33 90

💳 MC, V ⬤ mid-Dec–mid-Jan

🍴 €€ 🛏 (31) €€€

Rooms at this rustic place are spread over three floors and have views of the

⬤ Restaurant ■ Hotel ▲ Hotel / Restaurant

*cathedral or the Morvan countryside.
Nourishment comes in the form of jambon
persillé (p216), Charolais beef, chicken
with morels and pike-perch.*

AUTUN
● Le Chateaubriant

14 rue Jeannin, 71400 **Map** 8B2

[03 85 52 21 58

FAX 03 85 52 04 54

W www.bourgogne-gourmande.com

MC, V ● Sun D, Mon, mid-Sept–
mid-May: Wed; 2 wks Feb, 3 wks Jul

€€

*Classic dining room offering regional
favourites such as œufs en meurette
(p217), frogs' legs and foie gras salad.*

AUTUN
● Le Petit Rolin

12 pl St-Louis, 71400 **Map** 8B2

[03 85 86 15 55

FAX 03 85 86 15 55

W www.bourgogne-gourmande.com

MC, V ● Tue, Nov–Mar: Mon

€€

*The Romanesque St-Lazare Cathedral
towers over this establishment. Dishes
include Morvan ham and jambon persillé
(p216). Stock up on other Burgundian
goodies such as Morvan honey and
gingerbread from its shop.*

AUTUN
● Relais des Ursulines

2 rue Dufraigne, 71400 **Map** 8B2

[03 85 52 26 22

FAX 03 85 86 23 07

AE, MC, V €€

*Buzzing place situated between the
cathedral and the ramparts. Traditional
snails and bœuf bourguignon (p217),
plus typical brasserie fare such as
Charolais beef, steak-frites and pizzas.*

AUXERRE
● Jardin Gourmand

56 bd Vauban, 89000 **Map** 8A1

[03 86 51 53 52

AE, MC, V ● Tue, Wed; 2 wks Feb,
2 wks June, 2 wks Nov €€

*A tranquil interior and pleasant garden
give off a spring-like glow year-round.
Attentive staff and light food such as
duck liver carpaccio add to the charm.*

AUXERRE
● La Belle Époque

26 rue Fécauderie, 89000 **Map** 8A1

[03 86 52 16 09

MC, V ● Sun, Mon

€€

*Check out the works of art on offer
opposite, while digging into the
Burgundy dish of your choice, such
as boeuf bourguignon (p217).*

AUXERRE
● La P'tite Beursaude

55 rue Joubert, 89000 **Map** 8A1

[03 86 51 10 21

FAX 03 86 51 10 21

W www.beursaudiere.com

AE, MC, V ● Sun D, Mon, Tue L;
last 2 wks Jan, last wk Jun, last wk Sep

€€

*Charmingly simple restaurant opposite a
theatre, down one of the spokes off
Place de l'Hôtel de Ville. Offerings
include oxtail salad and duck roasted in
cherry juice served with fresh pasta.*

AUXERRE
● La Salamandre

84 rue de Paris, 89000 **Map** 8A1

[03 86 52 87 87

FAX 03 86 52 05 85

AE, MC, V ● Sun, Sat L €€€

*Try the warm salmon fondant followed
by the large sole meunière with chive
butter; the apricot crumble is also highly
recommended. A sea of white wines.*

AUXERRE
● Le Bistrot du Palais

69 rue de Paris, 89000 **Map** 8A1

[03 86 51 47 02

MC, V ● Sun, Mon, last wk Dec

€€

*Photos adorn the walls of this small,
super-friendly bistro serving hearty
Lyonnaise meat specialities.*

AUXERRE
● Le Bounty

3 quai de la République, 89000 **Map** 8A1

[03 86 51 69 86

FAX 03 86 51 29 80

MC, V ● Tue, Wed; Nov €€

*A brasserie that's perfect for a spot of
lunch, particularly in summer when the*

*small terrace across from the Yonne can
be put to good use. On the menu you'll
find choices such as escargots à la
bourguignonne (p217), coq au vin (p217),
confit de canard (p326) and guinea fowl.*

AUXERRE
▲ Le Maxime

2 quai de la Marine, 89000 **Map** 8A1

[03 86 52 14 19

FAX 03 86 52 21 70

W www.auxerre.com

AE, DC, MC, V

● late Dec–mid-Jan

€€€ ◇ (22) €€€

*In medieval streets. Highlights include
escargots à la bourguignonne (p217),
jambon persillé (p216), braised turbot
with Irancy and veal kidneys in Chablis.
Some rooms overlook the River Yonne.*

AUXERRE
▲ Le Seignelay

2 rue du Pont, 89000 **Map** 8A1

[03 86 52 03 48

FAX 03 86 52 32 39

W www.leseignelay.com

AE, MC, V ● Mon; Oct–Jun: Sun
D; mid-Feb–mid-Mar

€€ ◇ (21) €€

*An 18th-century building with a flower-
filled courtyard. The menu teems with
œufs en meurette (p217), Morvan ham
and coq au vin (p217). Views of the
Romanesque tower from some rooms.*

AUXERRE
▲ Les Clairions

RN6, direction Paris, 89000 **Map** 8A1

[03 86 94 94 94

FAX 03 86 48 16 38

AE, DC, MC, V

€€€

◇ (66) €€€

*Hotel dating from the 1970s with a pool
and tennis courts. On the menu, sole fillet
in a saffron sauce, and pear and blackcurrant tart. Well-equipped bedrooms.*

AUXERRE
● Quai

4 pl St-Nicolas, 89000 **Map** 8A1

[03 86 51 66 67

FAX 03 86 51 31 99

MC, V €€

One-time stables for the horses that hauled riverboats down the Yonne, now a popular bar-restaurant.

AUXERRE
● Restaurant Barnabet

14 quai de la République, 89000 **Map** 8A1

■ 03 86 51 68 88

FAX 03 86 52 96 85

◆ MC, V ● Sun D, Mon, Tue L; 1 wk Dec, 1 wk Jan ■■ €€€€

Chef Jean-Luc Barnabet's skill with the finest cheeses, meats and wines have earned his restaurant a Michelin star. Try the pigs' trotters in shallot-vinegar sauce.

AUXERRE
▲ Moulin de la Coudre

2 rue Gravottes, 89290 **Map** 8A1

■ 03 86 40 23 79

FAX 03 86 40 23 55

w www.moulin-de-la-coudre.com

◆ MC, V ● Sun D, Mon; Jan

■■ €€ ◆ (7) €€

A former mill set among trees in a quiet valley. The dining room is simple, even rustic, in keeping with the surroundings. The roast pigeon is a menu highlight.

AUXONNE
● Restaurant Virion

34 rue Bizot, Aux Maillys, 21130

Map 8C2

■ 03 80 39 13 40

FAX 03 80 39 17 22

w www.ifrance.com/virionmailly

◆ MC, V ● Sun D, Mon ■■ €€€

Pleasant country house. On the menu: escargots à la bourguignonne (p216) and coq au vin (p217). The wine list includes Pinot Noir reds and Chardonnay whites.

AVALLON
▲ Château de Vault de Lugny

11 rue du Château, 89200 **Map** 8A1

■ 03 86 34 07 86

FAX 03 86 34 16 36

w www.lugny.com

◆ MC, V ● Wed; mid-Nov–Mar

■■ €€€ ◆ (11) €€€€€

Family-style dining where a wooden table in the cellar plays host to dinner guests. Great list of local wines. Quite elegant, pleasant guestrooms.

AVALLON
▲ Hostellerie de la Poste

13 pl Vauban, 89200 **Map** 8A1

■ 03 86 34 16 16

FAX 03 86 34 19 19

w www.hostelleriedelaposte.com

◆ AE, DC, MC, V ● Sun D, Fri L

■■ € ◆ (30) €€€€

Welcoming travellers since 1707, this stately inn offers guestrooms with old-world style and modern comforts. Good beef in wine sauce and veal dishes.

AVALLON
▲ Le Relais Fleuri

La Cerce, RN6, 89200 **Map** 8A1

■ 03 86 34 02 85

FAX 03 86 34 09 98

w www.relais-fleuri.com

◆ AE, DC, MC, V

■■ €€€ ◆ (48) €€€

Charming place with a pool. The rustic dining room serves Charolais beef, roast duck with celery and veal cutlets. Huge, relaxing guestrooms.

AVALLON
▲ Les Capucins

6 ave Paul Doumer, 89200 **Map** 8A1

■ 03 86 34 06 52

FAX 03 86 34 58 47

◆ AE, MC, V ● Tue, Wed; mid-Dec–mid-Jan ■■ €€ ◆ (8) €€€

Pleasant place with a lush garden and a terrace. The selection of hearty soups and cheeses is small but consistently good. Rooms are basic but comfortable.

AVALLON
▲ Moulin des Ruats

Vallée du Cousin, 89200 **Map** 8A1

■ 03 86 34 97 00

FAX 03 86 31 65 47

w www.moulin-des-ruats.com

◆ AE, DC, MC, V ● Sun D, Mon, Tue–Sat L; mid-Nov–mid-Feb

■■ €€ ◆ (25) €€€

A former flour mill set just beside the river, with a waterwheel turning outside the dining room window. The soups are especially flavoursome. Attractive rooms.

AVALLON
● Relais des Gourmets

45–47 rue de Paris, 89200 **Map** 8A1

■ 03 86 34 18 90

FAX 03 86 31 60 21

◆ AE, MC, V ● Oct–May: Sun D, Mon ■■ €€€

Lounge bar for pre-dinner drinks. Kick off with frogs' legs, accompanied by a great white Burgundy, then opt for the young Morvan pigeon in hazelnut oil, fillet of rabbit or Charolais beef.

BAUBIGNY
● Auberge du Vieux Pressoir

Evelle, 15km (9 miles) from Beaune, 21340 **Map** 8B2

■ 03 80 21 82 16

FAX 03 80 21 82 16

◆ MC, V ● L, Sun D; Jan ■■ €€

A cosy restaurant surrounded by vineyards. Foie gras is the reason for coming here. Other specialities include Charolais beef, coq au vin (p217). Very extensive wine list, particularly the reds.

BEAUNE
▲ Auberge Bourguignonne

4 pl Madeleine, 21200 **Map** 8B2

■ 03 80 22 23 53

FAX 03 80 22 51 64

◆ MC, V

● Oct–Mar: Mon; last 2 wks Feb, mid-Nov–mid-Dec

■■ €€€ ◆ (10) €€€

Two pretty houses. Over a leisurely kir, choose between Burgundian standards such as œufs en meurette (p217), jambon persillé (p216) and boeuf bourguignon (p401). Follow with a local cheese. Some rooms overlook the attractive square.

BEAUNE
● Auberge du Cheval Noir

17 bd St-Jacques, 21200 **Map** 8B2

■ 03 80 22 07 37

FAX 03 80 24 06 92

@ lechevalnoir@wanadoo.fr

◆ MC, V ● Tue D, Wed; mid-Feb–mid-Mar ■■ €€€

Located just outside the ramparts yet close to the magnificent Hôtel-Dieu, with a terrace for sunny days. Gourmet fish dishes feature on the menu.

BEAUNE
● Bernard Morillon

31 rue Maufoux, 21200 **Map** 8B2

☎ 03 80 24 12 06
FAX 03 80 22 66 22
☑ AE, DC, MC, V
◑ Mon; mid-Jan–end Feb **🍴** €€€
Romantic spot with one Michelin star. On the menu are beef and foie gras.

BEAUNE
▲ Bistro at Hôtel de la Poste
5 bd Clémenceau, 21200 **Map** 8B2
☎ 03 80 22 08 11
FAX 03 80 24 19 71
w www.hoteldelapostebeaune.com
☑ AE, DC, MC, V
🍴 €€ **🍽** (35) €€€€€
Like the hotel, the food is simple, elegant and classically French, like the fine smoked duck breast. Sophisticated rooms with an antique look.

BEAUNE
● Grilladine
17–19 rue Maufoux, 21200 **Map** 8B2
☎ 03 80 22 22 36
FAX 03 80 24 25 20
☑ MC, V **◑** Mon, Tue, Wed D
🍴 €€€
You'll find an abundance of regional dishes like boeuf bourguignon *(p217) and* escargots à la bourguignonne *(p216) and local wines at this popular establishment. Booking is advisable.*

BEAUNE
▲ Hostellerie de Levernois
Route de Verdun-sur-le-Doubs, 21200 **Map** 8B2
☎ 03 80 24 73 58
FAX 03 80 22 78 00
☑ AE, DC, MC, V **◑** Sun, Tue, Wed L; last wk Dec, first wk Jan
🍴 €€€€ **🍽** (16) €€€€€
Idyllic country setting and an 800-vintage-strong cellar. Snails with garlic and jambon persillé *(p216) on the menu.*

BEAUNE
▲ Hôtel Central
2 rue Victor Millot, 21200 **Map** 8B2
☎ 03 80 24 77 24
FAX 03 80 22 30 40
☑ AE, MC, V **◑** mid-Nov–mid-Dec
🍴 €€€ **🍽** (20) €€
Situated in the heart of Beaune. Its restaurant, Le Cheval Blanc, serves dish-

es such as guinea fowl with cassis and escargots à la bourguignonne (p216). Well-equipped, spacious bedrooms.

BEAUNE
▲ Hôtel Grillon
21 route de Seurre, 21200 **Map** 8B2
☎ 03 80 22 44 25
FAX 03 80 24 94 89
w www.hotel-grillon.fr
☑ AE, DC, MC, V **◑** Feb
🍴 €€€ **🍽** (18) €€€
A stately 19th-century mansion with an outdoor swimming pool. Modern rooms overlook the garden, where meals such as roast sea bass or veal with potatoes are served. Small, atmospheric cellar bar.

BEAUNE
▲ Hôtel Hostellerie Le Cèdre
12 bd du Maréchal Foch, 21200 **Map** 8B2
☎ 03 80 24 01 01
FAX 03 80 24 09 90
w www.lecedre-beaune.com
☑ AE, DC, MC, V **◑** Sun; 1st wk Jan
🍴 €€ **🍽** (40) €€€€
In the heart of Beaune, this luxurious hotel is ideally located for exploring the town. At the restaurant, duck is the star dish. Spacious pastel guestrooms.

BEAUNE
■ Hôtel La Villa Fleurie
19 pl Colbert, 21200 **Map** 8B2
☎ 03 80 22 66 00
FAX 03 80 22 45 46
w www.lavillafleurie.fr
☑ AE, MC, V **◑** Jan **🍽** (10) €€€
This pretty house, dating from the early 1900s, is surrounded by a flower-filled garden. Delightful breakfast room and relaxing lounge. Beautiful rooms.

BEAUNE
■ Hôtel Le Cep
25–33 rue Maufoux, 21200 **Map** 8B2
☎ 03 80 22 35 48
FAX 03 80 22 76 80
w www.hotel-cep-beaune.com
☑ AE, DC, MC, V **🍽** (57) €€€€€
Exquisite place comprising a number of interesting 14th- and 16th-century buildings decorated with rich antiques. Superb suites fit for the rich and famous.

BEAUNE
● La Ciboulette
69 rue Lorraine, 21200 **Map** 8B2
☎ 03 80 24 70 72
FAX 03 80 22 79 71
☑ AE, MC, V **◑** Mon, Tue; Feb, Aug
🍴 €
A delightful little bistro with a strong local following. Many wine merchants come here to enjoy the excellent wine list. Food is simple and hearty, such as steak with Époisses cheese.

BEAUNE
● Le Bénaton
25 faubourg Bretonnière, 21200 **Map** 8B2
☎ 03 80 22 00 26
FAX 03 80 22 51 95
@ le-benaton@libertysurf.fr
☑ MC, V **◑** Wed, Thu **🍴** €€€
A small, sunny place, out towards Autun, offering typical Burgundian fare and a wonderful chocolate gateau stuffed with blackcurrants. Reservations advised.

BEAUNE
● Le Caveau des Arches
10 bd Perpreuil, 21200 **Map** 8B2
☎ 03 80 22 10 37
FAX 03 80 22 76 44
☑ AE, MC, V **◑** Sun, Mon; 1st wk Jan, mid-Jul–mid-Aug **🍴** €€
An unusual place in a cave beneath Beaune, just outside the ramparts that surround the town. Specialities include smoked salmon, Charolais beef and very good tête-de-veau.

BEAUNE
● Le Fleury
15 pl Fleury, 21200 **Map** 8B2
☎ 03 80 22 35 50
FAX 03 80 22 21 00
w www.lefleury.com
☑ MC, V **◑** Dec–Feb: Sun D, Wed D, Thu **🍴** €€
Paintings adorn the dining room, and touches like gilded wood add opulence. There's West Indian perch stew with parsley cream on the menu.

BEAUNE
● Le Gourmandin
8 pl Carnot, 21200 **Map** 8B2
☎ 03 80 24 07 88

FAX 03 80 22 27 42

@ gourm1@aol.com

MC, V

¶¶ €€

A bistro offering plenty of duck. It's not fancy, but touches like the glass ceiling over an interior patio make it special. Unbeatable for the price.

BEAUNE

● Le Jardin des Remparts

10 rue de l'Hôtel-Dieu, 21200 **Map** 8B2

03 80 24 79 41

FAX 03 80 24 92 79

@ lejardin@dub-internet.fr

MC, V ◐ Sun, Mon; Feb ¶¶ €€

The elegant atmosphere and creative cuisine such as roast pike-perch with nuts and shellfish with fennel have earned this charming restaurant a Michelin star. Divine chocolate gateau.

BEAUNE

● L'Écusson

2 rue Lieutenant Dupuis, 21200 **Map** 8B2

03 80 24 03 82

FAX 03 80 24 74 02

AE, DC, MC, V ◐ Sun, Wed, Easter–Oct: Wed ¶¶ €€

The rather uninviting façade hides a charming dining room and a lovely terrace. Lamb shank in a delicate carrot sauce is just one of the dishes that attracts the crowds. Reserve.

BEAUNE

● Les Tontons

22 rue du Faubourg Madeleine, 21200 **Map** 8B2

03 80 24 19 64

FAX 03 80 22 34 07

MC, V ◐ Sun, Mon; first 2 wks Aug ¶¶ €€

Cosy bistro near Place Madeleine. Try their speciality creamy soups, coq au vin (p217) and whole roasted fruit desserts.

BEAUNE

● P'tit Paradis

25 rue Paradis, 21200 **Map** 8B2

03 80 24 91 00

MC, V ◐ Mon, Tue; 1st wk Mar, 1st wk Aug, mid-Nov–mid-Dec ¶¶ €€

Delightful, tiny place located in the town centre near the Musée du Vin de

Bourgogne. *Duck liver pâté, omelette with local cheese and foie gras all feature on the reasonably priced menu.*

BEAUNE

● Restaurant au Bon Accueil

La Montagne, 21200 **Map** 8B2

03 80 22 08 80

FAX 03 80 22 93 12

MC, V ◐ Mon D, Tue D, Wed; mid-Aug–1st wk Sep, last wk Dec–1st wk Jan ¶¶ €€

True to its name, you'll receive a good welcome at this local haunt. Try the pan-fried snails followed by the coq au vin (p217); in summer, head to a table on the wonderful tree-shaded terrace.

BESANCON

▲ Hôtel Castan

6 square Castan, 25000 **Map** 9D2

03 81 65 02 00

FAX 03 81 83 01 02

W www.hotelcastan.fr

AE, MC, V ◐ 3 wks Aug, last 3 wks Dec ¶¶ €€€€ ◒ (10) €€€€

An 18th-century mansion serving fine classics such as an excellent foie gras. The guestrooms are beautiful.

BEZE

▲ Auberge la Quatr'Heurie

Rue de Porte de Bessey, 21310 **Map** 8C1

03 80 71 30 13

FAX 03 80 75 32 72

W www.quatrheurie.com

AE, MC, V

¶¶ €€€ ◒ (22) €€€

Two good trout options here: one with morels, which also accompany the veal escalope, the other cooked à la meunière. The accompanying bread is baked on site. Romantic four-poster beds.

BLENEAU

▲ Blanche de Castille

17 rue d'Orléans, 89220 **Map** 7F1

03 86 74 92 63

FAX 03 86 74 94 43

AE, MC, V ◐ 1 wk Sep, Jan

¶¶ €€ ◒ (13) €€

In the heart of the beautiful Puisaye in southwest Yonne. Traditional cuisine such as fish and snail soup, terrines and sardines served. Individually styled rooms.

BLIGNY-SUR-OUCHE

▲ Hostellerie des Trois Faisans

2 route d'Arnay, 21360 **Map** 8B2

03 80 20 10 14

FAX 03 80 20 08 68

W www.troisfaisans.fr

AE, DC, MC, V ◐ Wed, Sep–Jun: Tue; Jan–Feb, 1st wk Nov

¶¶ €€€ ◒ (6) €€

At the Three Pheasants, you can enjoy an apéritif in the garden beside the River Ouche while perusing the traditional menu. Comfortable guestrooms and flats.

BOUILLAND

▲ Hostellerie du Vieux Moulin

1 rue de la Forge, 21420 **Map** 8B2

03 80 21 51 16

FAX 03 80 21 59 90

AE, MC, V ◐ Sun D, Mon; mid-Jan–Mar ¶¶ €€ ◒ (26) €

Former mill, just outside of town. A menu highlight is frogs' leg lasagne. Well-kept, cosy guestrooms.

BOUZE-LES-BEAUNE

● La Bouzerotte

On D970, 21200 **Map** 8B2

03 80 26 01 37

FAX 03 80 26 09 37

MC, V

◐ Mon, Tue; end Feb–early Mar ¶¶ €

Small-town feel at this restaurant serving big portions of simple fare alongside a truffle menu with risotto and pigeon.

BUXY

▲ Hôtel-Restaurant Le Relais du Montagny

Pl du Rond Point, 71390 **Map** 8B3

03 85 94 94 94

FAX 03 85 92 07 19

AE, MC, V ◐ Fri D, Oct–Mar: Sun D; 1st wk Jan, 1st wk Dec

¶¶ €€€ ◒ (30) €€

The restaurant, Giardot, is just down the road from the hotel and offers regional dishes such as duck foie gras or pike-perch with snails. Functional, identical rooms. Outdoor swimming pool.

BUXY

● Restaurant aux Années Vins

2 Grand Rue, 71390 **Map** 8B3

03 85 92 15 76

● Restaurant ■ Hotel ▲ Hotel / Restaurant

FAX 03 85 92 12 20

MC, V ● Tue L, Wed L; 3 wks Jan, 2 wks Sep **€€€**

Large, romantic cave with a stone fire-place and an unusual terrace beneath the arches. Excellent creative cooking involving firm favourites foie gras and escargots à la bourguignonne (p216), as well as specialities such as salmon tartare and veal with truffles.

CHABLIS

● Au Vrai Chablis

6 pl Général de Gaulle, 89800 **Map** 8A1

03 86 42 11 43

FAX 03 86 42 14 57

www.auvraichablis.fr

MC, V ● Tue D, Wed **€€**

Restaurant-bar with five rooms, five menus and a great location on the main square. A good place to try the famous succulent andouillette served with mustard or Chablis sauce, best accompanied by a young Chablis.

CHABLIS

● Bistrot des Grands Crus

8–10 rue Jules Rathier, 89800 **Map** 8A1

03 86 42 19 41

FAX 03 86 42 17 11

www.hostellerie-des-clos.fr

AE, MC, V

● last wk Dec–Jan

€€

Bistro owned by Michel Vignaud, chef at Hostellerie des Clos a few doors down. Snails make an appearance in a fine casserole and renowned escargots à la bourguignonne (p216) with parsley sauce. Try Chablis by the prominent wine grower, William Fevre, whose shop is next door.

CHABLIS

▲ Hostellerie des Clos

18 rue Jules Rathier, 89800 **Map** 8A1

03 86 42 10 63

FAX 03 86 42 17 11

www.hostellerie-des-clos.fr

AE, MC, V

● mid-Dec–mid-Jan

€€ (26) **€€**

Chef Michel Vignaud makes memorable meals. Light dishes such as iced cream of lobster soup and sautéed shiitake mushrooms stand out. Refined rooms.

CHABLIS

▲ Hôtel Aux Lys

38 route Auxerre, 89800 **Map** 8A1

03 86 42 49 20

FAX 03 86 42 80 04

AE, DC, MC, V **€** (38) **€€**

In the midst of Chablis vineyards and offering fabulous opportunities for out-door activities. The no-frills restaurant focuses on a very few dishes such as scallops in Champagne sauce and salmon carpaccio. Modern guestrooms.

CHABLIS

● La Feuillette 132

8 rue des Moulins, 89800 **Map** 8A1

03 86 18 91 67

FAX 03 86 42 49 84

MC, V ● Sun D, Wed; mid-Dec–mid-Jan **€€**

Half-timbered place named after the now-rare diminutive 132-litre-capacity wine barrel used in Chablis and Burgundy. Stick with the theme and order jambon au Chablis.

CHABLIS

● Le Vieux Moulin de Chablis

18 rue des Moulins, 89800 **Map** 8A1

03 86 42 47 30

FAX 03 86 42 84 44

www.vieux-moulin-chablis.com

MC, V ● last wk Dec **€€€**

Enchanting setting in a 10th-century grain mill straddling the River Serein. Specialities include confit de canard (p326), oeufs en meurette (p217) au pinot noir and andouillettes. Strong wine list.

CHABLIS

● Syracuse

19 ave du Maréchal de Lattre de Tassigny, 89800 **Map** 8A1

03 86 42 19 45

FAX 03 86 42 42 54

MC, V

● Sun D, Mon; 2 wks Mar & Oct, 1st wk Dec **€€**

Across from Place Charles de Gaulle. To start try oeufs en meurette (p217) in St-Bris wine and follow with grilled andouillette au Chablis or ham in a Chablis wine and grape sauce. Don't miss the coupe Syracuse, a blackcurrant, lemon and passion fruit sorbet.

CHAGNY

▲ Hostellerie du Château de Bellecroix

RN6, 71150 **Map** 8B2

03 85 87 13 86

FAX 03 85 91 28 62

www.chateau-bellecroix.com

AE, DC, MC, V ● Wed, Thu L; Jan, 2 wks Feb, 2 wks Dec

€€€€ (20) **€€€€**

Delightful, turreted chateau close to both Beaune and Cluny. After relaxing by the pool, head to the restaurant for some classical French fare. Many guestrooms are huge, with four-poster beds, medieval stone walls and antiques.

CHAGNY

▲ Lameloise

36 pl d'Armes, 71150 **Map** 8B2

03 85 87 65 65

FAX 03 85 87 03 57

AE, MC, V ● Tue L, Wed, Thu L; end-Dec–mid-Jan

€€€€ (16) **€€€€**

Family owned for more than a century, Lameloise is known for its fine service and tasty French fare such as frogs' legs. The hotel is welcoming and quite elegant, with touches like wood-beamed ceilings and antique French furniture.

CHAILLY-SUR-ARMANCON

▲ Château de Chailly

Pouilly-en-Auxois, 21320 **Map** 8B2

03 80 90 30 30

FAX 03 80 90 30 00

www.chailly.com

AE, DC, MC, V ● Mon L; Nov–Apr

€€€€€ (37) **€€€€€**

Luxurious Renaissance place with a golf course, Turkish bath, jacuzzi, pool, tennis court and wine-tasting cellar. At its gourmet restaurant, The Armançon, choose a fine vintage wine and the jambon persillé (p216), duck foie gras, or pigeon with Dijon mustard.

CHALON-SUR-SAONE

▲ Hôtel-Restaurant St-Régis

22 bd de la République, 71100 **Map** 8B2

03 85 90 95 60

FAX 03 85 90 95 70

www.saint-regis-chalon.com

AE, DC, MC, V ● Sun D, Sat L

🍴 €€€ 🍷 (36) €€€€

*Charming hotel-restaurant complete
with a bar that's perfect for a leisurely
apéritif before tucking into the likes of
foie gras and John Dory fillet. Supremely
elegant guestrooms with rich fabrics.*

CHALON-SUR-SAONE

▲ Hôtel-Restaurant Le St-Georges

32 ave Jean Jaurès, 71100 **Map** 8B2

📞 03 85 90 80 50

FAX 03 85 90 80 55

W www.lesaintgeorges71.fr

🍷 AE, DC, MC, V ⬤ Sun D, Sat L;

3 wks Aug 🍴 €€ 🍷 (48) €€€

*Conveniently located for the adjacent
train station. Sunny Neo-Classical dining
room offering a wide selection of dishes
such as tomato and aubergine (eggplant) gazpacho, grilled langoustines,
mussels with frogs' legs and duck foie
gras. Well-equipped guestrooms.*

CHARETTE-VARENNES

▲ Hôtel-Restaurant Doubs Rivage

8 rue de la Chapelle, 71270 **Map** 8C2

📞 03 85 76 23 45

FAX 03 85 72 89 18

🍷 MC, V ⬤ Mon, Sep–Jun: Sun D;

1st wk Jan, Feb, 1st wk Jun, 1st wk Dec

🍴 €€€ 🍷 (10) €€

*Menu inludes fish specialities like the
popular local dish pôchouse (p216).
Basic, comfortable rooms.*

CHASSAGNE-MONTRACHET

⬤ Le Chassagne

4 impasse Chenevottes, 21180 **Map** 8B2

📞 03 80 21 94 94

FAX 03 80 21 97 77

🍷 MC, V ⬤ Sun D, Mon, Wed D;

1st 2 wks Aug, mid-Dec–mid-Jan

🍴 €€€

*The quality at this bright and friendly
restaurant far outweighs its price. On
the menu, scallops with foie gras, roast
John Dory, cod, caviar and local cheese.*

CHASSEY-LE-CAMP

▲ Auberge du Camp Romain

Le Bourg, 71150 **Map** 8B2

📞 03 85 87 09 91

FAX 03 85 87 11 51

🍷 MC, V ⬤ Jan; 2 wks Feb

🍴 €€€ 🍷 (35) €€€

*Head here for some traditional lunchtime
fare such as coq au vin (p217), escargots
à la bourguignonne (p216) and frogs'
legs. Nice guestrooms; some balconies.*

CHASSEY-LE-CAMP

⬤ Le Relais du Gaulois

Nantoux, 71150 **Map** 8B2

📞 03 85 87 33 00

FAX 03 85 87 02 30

W www.relaisdugaulois.fr.st

🍷 MC, V 🍴 €€€

*From a table with a vineyard view,
choose wine from one of the five local
Côte Chalonnaise wine villages,
Bouzeron, Givry, Mercurey, Montagny or
Rully. Bouzeron wine also makes an
appearance in a pike-perch fillet dish.*

CHATENOY-EN-BRESSE

⬤ Les Pieds dans l'Eau

7 rue de Vertembeau, 71380 **Map** 8B2

📞 03 85 96 51 42

FAX 03 85 96 51 42

🍷 MC, V

⬤ Mon L, Tue L, May & Sep: Mon D &

Tue D, Apr & Oct: Mon–Fri; Nov–Mar

🍴 €€

*Those travelling by boat on the Saône
can pull up right outside this restaurant.
The chicken and crayfish dish is one of
its many culinary highlights.*

CHATILLON-SUR-SEINE

▲ Restaurant de la Cote d'Or

2 rue Charles Ronot, 21400 **Map** 8B1

📞 03 80 91 13 29

FAX 03 80 91 29 15

🍷 AE, DC, MC, V

🍴 €€ 🍷 (10) €€

*The morel fondue is a popular choice.
Cosy, if dated, guestrooms.*

CHEVANNES

▲ Chamaille

4 route Boiloup, 89240 **Map** 8A1

📞 03 86 41 24 80

FAX 03 86 41 34 80

@ la.chamaille@wanadoo.fr

🍷 AE, MC, V ⬤ Mon, Tue, Nov–Feb:

Sun D; 2 wks Jan

🍴 €€€€ 🍷 (3) €€

*Head here for dishes such as escalope
of duck foie gras with mango and pain
d'épices (spice bread) and the chocolate*

*gateau with marinated raisins. Pleasant,
if basic, guestrooms.*

CHOREY-LES-BEAUNE

▲ Ermitage de Corton

Route de Dijon, RN74, 21200 **Map** 8B2

📞 03 80 22 05 28

FAX 03 80 24 64 51

@ ermitagecorton@wanadoo.es

🍷 AE, DC, MC, V ⬤ Sun D, Mon,

Tue L; mid-Jan–Feb

🍴 €€€€ 🍷 (10) €€€€€

*Restaurant known for its creative
combinations of ingredients and for its
extensive wine list. Duck liver foie gras
with green asparagus, roast suckling
pig, several lamb and duck dishes are
on the menu. Guestrooms are plush and
comfortable. Satisfying breakfasts.*

CLOS-DE-VOUGEOT

▲ Château de Gilly

Gilly-les-Cîteaux, 21640 **Map** 8B2

📞 03 80 62 89 98

FAX 03 80 62 82 34

W www.chateau-gilly.com

🍷 AE, DC, MC, V

🍴 €€€€ 🍷 (48) €€€€€

*A former monastery, this château is
palatial in its splendour. Guestrooms are
each uniquely designed, but the dining
room in a converted cellar is the most
impressive. On the menu, quails' eggs
and fish in a Pinot Noir wine sauce.*

CLUNY

▲ Hôtel de l'Abbaye

14 ter ave Charles de Gaulle, 71250
Map 8B3

📞 03 85 59 11 14

FAX 03 85 59 09 76

🍷 AE, MC, V ⬤ Sun D, Mon;

Jan–Feb 🍴 € 🍷 (12) €€

*The best bet at this hotel's restaurant is
the fixed-price menu. Hearty meals, like
pan-fried beef or grilled duck with arabica
coffee sauce, match the atmosphere of
this small place. Cosy guestrooms.*

CLUNY

▲ Hôtel-Restaurant de Bourgogne

Pl de l'Abbaye, 71250 **Map** 8B3

📞 03 85 59 00 58

FAX 03 85 59 03 73

W www.hotel-cluny.com

⬤ Restaurant ■ Hotel ▲ Hotel / Restaurant

AE, MC, V ● Tue, Wed; Dec–Jan
TI €€€ ⊘ (16) €€€€

On the menu, Burgundian dishes with goat's cheese, pike-perch, Charolais beef and red Mâcon wine. Rooms have garden or Cluny abbey views.

COSNE-COURS-SUR-LOIRE
▲ **Restaurant le St-Christophe**
Pl de la Gare, 58200 **Map** 7F2
03 86 28 02 01
FAX 03 86 26 94 28
AE, MC, V ● Sun D, Fri; 1st wk Jul, 3 wks Aug, mid-Dec–1st wk Jan
TI €€ ⊘ (8) €€

Conveniently located for the station opposite, with simple cooking that's popular with the locals. Small rooms; those at the back are quieter.

COSNE-COURS-SUR-LOIRE
▲ **Le Vieux Relais**
11 rue St-Agnan, 58200 **Map** 7F2
03 86 28 20 21
FAX 03 86 26 71 12
W www.le-vieux-relais.fr
AE, MC, V ● Sun D, Fri D, Sat L; 2 wks Jan **TI** €€ ⊘ (11) €€€

A quaint stone building on an attractive street. The fixed-price menus offer the best value and feature char with broad (fava) beans and veal medallions with mushrooms. Simple, small guestrooms.

CUISERY
▲ **Bressane**
56 route de Tournus, 71290 **Map** 8B3
03 85 32 30 66
FAX 03 85 40 14 96
W www.hostellerie-bressane.fr
MC, V ● Wed, Thu L; 17 Dec–3rd wk Jan **TI** €€€ ⊘ (13) €€€

Cordon-bleu restaurant in the small town of Cuisery. Be sure to order a Bresse chicken dish. Fine rooms.

DIGOIN
▲ **Hôtel de la Gare**
79 ave du Général de Gaulle, 71160
Map 8A3
03 85 53 03 04
FAX 03 85 53 14 70
W www.hoteldelagare.fr
MC, V ● Sun D, Oct–Mar: Wed; Jan
TI €€€€ ⊘ (13) €€€€

Located near the Canal du Centre and the impressive stone aqueduct over the Loire, the restaurant serves Charolais beef grilled, pan-fried and braised. Quite spacious rooms.

DIGOIN
▲ **Hôtel-Restaurant le Merle Blanc**
36 route de Gueugnon, 71160 **Map** 8A3
03 85 53 17 13
FAX 03 85 88 91 71
MC, V ● Sun D, Mon L
TI €€€ ⊘ (16) €€

Poached bass, grilled salmon and Charolais beef feature strongly on the menu. For dessert, a refreshing choice of sorbets and ice creams.

DIGOIN
▲ **Hôtel-Restaurant Les Diligences**
14 rue Nationale, 71160 **Map** 8A3
03 85 53 06 31
FAX 03 85 88 92 43
W www.les-diligences.com
AE, DC, MC, V ● Mon, Tue; Dec
TI €€€ ⊘ (6) €€

Dishes at this smart 17th-century inn include veal kidneys with mustard sauce, Charolais beef, and sea bream with red Mâcon wine. There's also a summer terrace. Guestrooms overlook the Loire; three have private balconies.

DIJON
▲ **Best Western Chapeau Rouge**
5 rue Michelet, 21000 **Map** 8B2
03 80 50 88 88
FAX 03 80 50 88 89
W www.bourgogne.net/chapeaurouge
AE, DC, MC, V
TI €€€ ⊘ (30) €€€€

Traditional spot serving excellent snails and pigeon. Guestrooms are plush with colourful Provençal-style linens.

DIJON
● **Billoux**
13 pl de la Libération, 21000 **Map** 8B2
03 80 38 05 05
FAX 03 80 38 16 16
AE, DC, MC, V
● Sun D, Mon; 1 wk Aug **TI** €€

Sumptuous local wines, fresh and unique French cuisine, and a charming dining area. Chef Jean-Pierre Billoux has

a modern take on traditional Burgundy cooking, such as caramelized lamb.

DIJON
● **Bistro des Halles**
10 rue Bannelier, 21000 **Map** 8B2
03 80 49 94 15
MC, V ● Sun D **TI** €

This casual bistro hangs in the balance between country charm and Parisian café. The famed snails are not to be missed. Well-priced and reliable menu.

DIJON
● **Cézanne**
38 rue Amiral Roussin, 21000 **Map** 8B2
03 80 58 91 92
AE, DC, MC, V
● Sun, Mon L **TI** €€

Provençal-style dishes are served at this bright and cheery family restaurant. The prices are reasonable.

DIJON
■ **Hôtel des Ducs**
5 rue Lamonnoye, 21000 **Map** 8B2
03 80 67 31 31
FAX 03 80 67 19 51
W www.hoteldesducs.com
AE, MC, V ⊘ (38) €€€

Unbeatable location in an area steeped in history. Early in the day the courtyard serves as a breakfast area; later it becomes a pleasant extension to the bar. The utterly comfortable rooms are worth that little bit extra.

DIJON
■ **Hôtel le Jacquemart**
32 rue Verrerie, 21000 **Map** 8B2
03 80 60 09 60
FAX 03 80 60 09 69
W www.hotel-lejacquemart.fr
AE, DC, MC, V ⊘ (34) €€€

A big plus for this 17th-century place is its city-centre location, with Dijon's key sights all close by. Well-equipped rooms.

DIJON
▲ **Hôtel Sofitel La Cloche**
14 pl Darcy, 21000 **Map** 8B2
03 80 30 12 32
FAX 03 80 30 04 15
W www.sofitel.com
AE, DC, MC, V

🍽 €€€€€ 🥄 (68) €€€€€

A grand hotel in the centre of town. Two restaurants: the formal Les Jardins and the bistro-style Les Caves. Don't miss the snails, cabbage and pigeon pastry or the foie gras with prune chutney. Rooms are plush and extremely comfortable.

DIJON

● La Côte St-Jean

13 rue Monge, 21000 **Map** 8B2

📞 03 80 50 11 77

FAX 03 80 50 18 75

💳 MC, V ⬤ Tue, Wed L, Sat L; end-Dec–early Jan, end Jul–mid Aug

🍽 €€€

Try pain d'épices ((spice bread) followed by the stuffed rabbit at this restaurant, but leave room for the cheese platter.

DIJON

● La Dame d'Aquitaine

23 pl Bossuet, 21000 **Map** 8B2

📞 03 80 30 45 65

FAX 03 80 49 90 41

💳 AE, DC, MC, V ⬤ Sun, Mon L

🍽 €

Restaurant in a 13th-century crypt, serving duck and foie gras. The food is delicious but even better is the ambience: stone walls, stained-glass windows and the smell of great French food. Rooms have old-world charm.

DIJON

▲ La Musarde

7 rue des Riottes, 21121 **Map** 8B2

📞 03 80 56 22 82

FAX 03 80 56 64 40

💳 AE, DC, MC, V

⬤ Sun D, Mon

🍽 €€€ 🥄 (11) €€€

Lovely mansion located in the country-side just north of Dijon. Traditional hearty fare includes roast sea bass and seafood terrine. Guestrooms have an intimate feel with many antique touches.

DIJON

● Le Chabrot

36 rue Monge, 21000 **Map** 8B2

📞 03 80 30 69 61

💳 MC, V ⬤ Sun 🍽 €€€

Excellent selection of local wines at this classy restaurant. The menu offers plenty

of twists on traditional recipes – try the pain d'épices (spice bread) ice cream. Regional specialities also on the menu.

DIJON

● Le Clos des Capucines

3 rue Jeannin, 21000 **Map** 8B2

📞 03 80 65 83 03

FAX 03 80 67 37 00

🖥 www.closdescapucines.com

💳 MC, V ⬤ Sun, Mon L, Sat L

🍽 €€€

A medieval setting and full-bodied food and wine are on the menu here. A high-light is the cassis-flavoured mustard.

DIJON

● Le Pré aux Clercs

13 pl de la Libération, 21000 **Map** 8B2

📞 03 80 38 05 05

FAX 03 80 38 16 16

💳 AE, DC, MC, V

⬤ Sun D, Mon; Feb 🍽 €€

Stylish artful food: langoustines in a sherry vinaigrette and pain d'épices (spice bread) ice cream. Quite wonderful location on a central square.

DIJON

● Les Deux Fontaines

16 pl de la République, 21000 **Map** 8B2

📞 03 80 60 86 45

💳 MC, V

⬤ Sun, Mon 🍽 €€

Pleasant split-level bistro-style place with two interior fountains, hence the name. On the menu, duo of salmon and sole and trout escalope.

DIJON

▲ Philippe Le Bon

18 rue Ste-Anne, 21000 **Map** 8B2

📞 03 80 30 73 52

FAX 03 80 30 95 51

🖥 www.hotels-exclusive.com

💳 AE, DC, MC, V ⬤ Sun, Aug: L

🍽 €€€ 🥄 (32) €€€

Named after a Valais duke. Superb cuisine in the elegant medieval dining room or in the garden in summer. Try the young rabbit flavoured with marc de bourgogne followed by the gratin of perch. Leave room for the crème brûlée or pain d'épices (spice bread) ice cream. Book a room with a rooftop view.

DIJON

▲ Restaurant de la Porte Guillaume at Quality Hôtel du Nord

Place Darcy, 21000 **Map** 8B2

📞 03 80 50 80 50

FAX 03 80 50 80 51

🖥 www.bourgogne.net/hotelnord

💳 AE, DC, MC, V

🍽 €€€ 🥄 (27) €€€

Gourmet dishes on the menu include salmon roasted in Noilly Prat, salmon carpaccio with lemon and herbs, and beef on a courgette (zucchini) cake. Well-chosen wines. Rooms are basic.

DIJON

● Stéphane Derbord

10 pl Wilson, 21000 **Map** 8B2

📞 03 80 67 74 64

FAX 03 80 63 87 72

🖥 www.restaurantstephanederbord.fr

💳 AE, DC, MC, V ⬤ Sun, Mon, Tue L

🍽 €€€

A combination of local and international flavours have earned this cosmopolitan restaurant a Michelin star. Inventive dishes such as roast fish with walnuts pair well with local wines.

DIJON

■ Tulip Inn Le Jura

14 ave Foch, 21000 **Map** 8B2

📞 03 80 41 61 12

FAX 03 80 41 61 13

💳 AE, DC, MC, V ⬤ mid-Dec–mid-Jan 🥄 (79) €€€

Great location in the city centre between the TGV station and the tourist office. Two options for breakfast: continental-style in your room or the hot and cold buffet downstairs. Comfortable standard guestrooms, some overlook the garden.

DIJON

● Au Bon Pantagruel

20 rue Quentin, 21000 **Map** 8B2

📞 03 80 30 68 69

FAX 03 80 30 40 69

💳 AE, MC, V ⬤ Sun D, Mon 🍽 €€

Named after Rabelais' famous fictional character and facing the covered market which comes to life every Tuesday, Thursday, Friday and Saturday. Try the duck terrine or the millefeuille of snails and frog's legs.

● Restaurant ■ Hotel ▲ Hotel / Restaurant

DONZY

▲ Restaurant le Grand Monarque

10 rue de l'Étape, 58220 **Map** 7FZ

🄲 03 86 39 35 44

FAX 03 86 39 37 09

🅰 AE ⬤ Oct–Apr: Sun D, Mon; Jan

🍽 €€ 🍂 (11) €€€

Old stone place in the sleepy town of Donzy. Lovely rustic dining room where typical regional fare is dished up, such as andouillettes, œufs en meurette (p217) and sole soufflé. A handsome 16th-century spiral staircase leads to the simple yet spacious rooms.

DRUYES-LES-BELLES-FONTAINES

▲ Auberge des Sources

4 pl Jean Bertin, 89560 **Map** 8A1

🄲 03 86 41 55 14

FAX 03 86 41 90 31

🅦 www.auberge-des-sources.fr

🅰 MC, V ⬤ Mon, Tue D; 3 wks Jan, 2 wks Feb 🍽 €€€ 🍂 (15) €€

Château ruins serve as a backdrop here. At its restaurant, choose fish from the on-site tank, prepared in a variety of ways. The rooms are a rustic delight.

DUN-LES-PLACES

▲ Auberge Ensoleillée

Route du Vieux Dun, 58230 **Map** 8A2

🄲 03 86 84 62 76

FAX 03 86 84 64 57

🅰 V 🍽 €€ 🍂 (12) €€

There is an informal café in front, but for both elaborate dishes like stuffed veal roulade and simpler fare like creamy fresh cheese, head to the formal dining room behind the bustling café. Simple but comfortable guestrooms.

FONTANGY

● Ferme Auberge de Fontangy

Précy-sous-Thil, 21390 **Map** 8B2

🄲 03 80 84 33 32

⬤ Sat, Sun; mid-Dec–Mar 🍽 €

This working farm supplies many of its own ingredients for dishes like chicken liver salad and the fruit desserts. The dining room is in a converted barn, evoking the countryside experience.

GEVREY-CHAMBERTIN

▲ Aux Vendanges de Bourgogne

47 route de Beaune, 21220 **Map** 8B2

🄲 03 80 34 30 24

FAX 03 80 58 55 44

🅦 www.hotel-bourgogne.com

🅰 MC, V ⬤ Sun, Mon; mid-Dec–mid-Jan 🍽 €€ 🍂 (14) €€

Vendanges means grape harvest, and this place is ideal for exploring Gevrey-Chambertin wine cellars and world-famous vineyards. The menu offers jambon persillé (p216), snails in parsley butter, joue de bœuf (beef in Burgundy wine). Rooms are small, quiet and simple.

GEVREY-CHAMBERTIN

● Chez Guy

3 pl de la Mairie, 21220 **Map** 8B2

🄲 03 80 58 51 51

FAX 03 80 58 50 39

🅦 www.hotel-bourgogne.com

🅰 MC, V ⬤ Tue, Wed 🍽 €

Good service at a good price at this agreeable little place. Simple menu serving classics such as coq au vin (p217). Well-chosen, fairly priced wine list.

GEVREY-CHAMBERTIN

● Les Millésimes

25 rue de l'Église, 21220 **Map** 8B2

🄲 03 80 51 84 24

FAX 03 80 34 12 73

🄰 lesmillesimes@lesmillesimes.fr

🅰 AE, MC, V ⬤ Sun L, Tue L, Wed L; mid-Dec–mid-Jan

🍽 €€€€€

Dine at this cave-turned-restaurant – its staggering wine list befits the location in a prestigious wine village. The Charolais beef takes pride of place. Expensive but well worth it.

GEVREY-CHAMBERTIN

● Rôtisserie du Chambertin

Rue du Chambertin, 21220 **Map** 8B2

🄲 03 80 34 33 20

FAX 03 80 34 12 30

🅰 MC, V ⬤ Sun D, Mon, Wed L

🍽 €€€€

There's a small wine museum at the entrance to this dining room offering classics such as coq au vin (p217) and a long list of Burgundy wines including a superb selection of Chambertins. For a more relaxed atmosphere, try its dining room, Le Bonbistrot, serving steak-frites and other bistro favourites.

GIVRY

▲ Hôtellerie de la Halle

2 pl Halle, 71640 **Map** 8B2

🄲 03 85 44 32 45

FAX 03 85 44 49 45

🅦 www.restaurant-la-halle.com

🅰 MC, V ⬤ Sun, Mon; 3rd wk Dec–1st wk Jan 🍽 €€€ 🍂 (2) €€

Former convent on the wine route from Dijon to Macon. Modern dishes at the dignified restaurant include snail ravioli, smoked herring and poached haddock with leeks or braised monkfish with noodles. Bright bedrooms.

GUEUGNON

▲ Hôtel-Restaurant du Centre

34 rue de la Liberté, 71130 **Map** 8A3

🄲 03 85 85 21 01

FAX 03 85 85 02 67

🅰 AE, MC, V ⬤ Sun D

🍽 €€ 🍂 (20) €€

Practical stop in the historic town of Gueugnon in Saône-et-Loire, with three dining rooms offering traditional dishes such as oeufs en meurette (p217), beef fillet with five peppers, and crème brûlée. Functional guestrooms.

IGE

▲ Hôtel-Restaurant le Château d'Igé

Mâcon, 71960 **Map** 8B3

🄲 03 85 33 33 99

FAX 03 85 33 41 41

🅦 www.relaischateaux.fr/ige

🅰 AE, DC, MC, V ⬤ Mon–Thu L; Jan–Mar 🍽 €€€€ 🍂 (8) €€€€

Luxurious hotel-restaurant set in a beautiful garden. A perfect location to taste wines from the surrounding Mâcon vineyards while enjoying terrines, a mushroom and snail platter or sea trout fillet. Attractive guestrooms.

JOIGNY

▲ La Côte St-Jacques

14 faubourg de Paris, 89304 **Map** 8A1

🄲 03 86 62 09 70

FAX 03 86 91 49 70

🅰 AE, DC, MC, V ⬤ 2 wks Jan

🍽 €€€€€ 🍂 (32) €€€€

This classy and refined hotel-restaurant oozes luxury. Inventive cuisine such as red tuna and smoked salmon is presented with great flair. Minimalist rooms.

JOIGNY

▲ Le Paris Nice

Rond point de la Résistance, 89300
Map 8A1

📞 03 86 62 06 72

FAX 03 86 62 56 99

MC, V ● Sun D, Mon; 2 wks Jan
& Sep, 1 wk Feb 🍴 €€ 🛏 (10) €€

*On the Paris–Nice cycling-race route.
Entrées include a grand buffet with 16
different appetizers. Choice dishes
include roast pork with honey or salmon
with frogs' legs. Traditional guestrooms.*

JOIGNY

▲ Le Rive Gauche

Chemin du Port au Bois, 89300 **Map** 8A1

📞 03 86 91 46 66

FAX 03 86 91 46 93

W www.hotel-le-rive-gauche.fr

AE, MC, V ● Sun D, Mon; Feb
🍴 €€€ 🛏 (42) €€€

*Contemporary place in a wonderfully
peaceful setting. Well-equipped and
tastefully designed rooms. Relax on the
terrace with a kir, then begin your meal
with the rabbit terrine.*

JOIGNY

▲ Modern'Hôtel

Rue Robert Petit, 89300 **Map** 8A1

📞 03 86 62 16 28

FAX 03 86 62 44 33

W www.modern-hotel.com

AE, DC, MC, V ● restaurant: Sun
D, Mon; Feb 🍴 €€€ 🛏 (21) €€€

*Hotel-restaurant with pool, conveniently
located near the train station. Highlights
include snail casserole with mushrooms.
Guestrooms overlook the hotel grounds.*

LA CELLE-ST-CYR

● La Fontaine aux Muses

Route de la Fontaine, 89116 **Map** 7F1

📞 03 86 73 40 22

FAX 03 86 73 48 66

W www.fontaine-aux-muses.fr

MC, V ● Mon, Tue D 🍴 €€

*A restaurant for all seasons with alfresco
dining in summer. If you're lucky, the
chef-cum-saxophone player might play
some tunes once his talents are no
longer required in the kitchen. On the
menu, lobster ragout, bœuf bourguignon
(p217) and foie gras.*

LADOIX-SERRIGNY

▲ Hôtel et Caves des Paulands

RN74, 21550 **Map** 8B2

📞 03 80 26 41 05

FAX 03 80 20 47 56

MC, V ● Mon L, Oct–Mar: Tue L;
mid-Dec–mid-Jan

🍴 €€€ 🛏 (20) €€€

*Wonderful vineyard views, and poolside
dining too. Select a vintage Burgundy,
and fine escargots à la bourguignonne
(p217) and boeuf bourguignon (p216),
Fine rooms (where dinner can be served).*

LADOIX-SERRIGNY

● Les Coquines

RN74, Buisson, 21550 **Map** 8B2

📞 03 80 26 43 58

FAX 03 80 26 49 59

MC, V ● Wed, Thu 🍴 €€€

*Intimate and welcoming, this small
restaurant bases its seasonal menu on
the dishes that go best with local wines.*

LE CREUSOT

▲ Hostellerie de la Petite Verrerie

4 rue Jules Guesde, 71200 **Map** 8B2

📞 03 85 73 97 97

FAX 03 85 73 97 90

W www.hotelfp-lecreusot.com

AE, MC, V

● Sun, Sat L; 2 wks Aug, 1 wk Dec
🍴 €€€ 🛏 (43) €€€

*Small, distinguished château with well-
equipped rooms. At the restaurant meat
lovers should order the mixed plate of
ham followed by Charolais beef steak.
The Museum of Anthropology & Industry
and a theatre are also on site.*

LE CREUSOT

▲ La Belle Epoque

7 pl Schneider, 71200 **Map** 8B2

📞 03 85 73 00 00

FAX 03 85 73 00 10

MC, V ● Sun

🍴 €€ 🛏 (10) €€

*Expect to try traditional cuisine such as
pork with ceps at this restaurant on the
town's main square. Tucked-away tables
for two and a summer terrace.*

LIGNY-LE-CHATEL

● Auberge du Bief

2 ave de Chablis, 89144 **Map** 8A1

📞 03 86 47 43 42

FAX 03 86 47 48 14

MC, V ● Sun D, Mon, Tue D;
1 wk Aug 🍴 €€

*Situated next to the church. Dishes
include local meat pies, duck with
potatoes and platters of local cheese.*

LIGNY-LE-CHATEL

▲ Relais St-Vincent

14 Grand Rue, 89144 **Map** 8A1

📞 03 86 47 53 38

FAX 03 86 47 54 16

AE, DC, MC, V ● 3rd wk Dec–
1st wk Jan 🍴 €€ 🛏 (15) €€

*Traditional restaurant in a 17th-century
half-timbered house. Huddle near the
fire or enjoy the peaceful, flower-filled
courtyard. On the menu are sautéed
veal and duck. Modern rooms.*

L'ISLE-SUR-SEREIN

▲ Auberge du Pot d'Étain

24 rue Bouchardat, 89440 **Map** 8A1

📞 03 86 33 88 10

FAX 03 86 33 90 93

W www.potdetain.com

MC, V ● Sep–Jun: Sun D & Mon;
1 wk Oct 🍴 €€€ 🛏 (9) €€€

*Former coaching inn situated in the
Serein Valley near Nitry and Avallon.
There are three dining rooms and a
terrace at the restaurant. Choose the
potato cake and andouillette cooked in
Chablis followed by the Irancy oxtail
sausage. Comfortable guestrooms.*

LOUHANS

▲ Hôtel-Restaurant Moulin de
Bourgchâteau

Route de Chalon, 71500 **Map** 8C3

📞 03 85 75 37 12

FAX 03 85 75 45 11

AE, MC, V ● Mon; 2nd wk Jan
🍴 €€ 🛏 (17) €€

*Former flour mill, built in 1778 and
converted into a hotel and restaurant in
1973. The food, such as Dover sole and
grilled veal, is very good. The gurgling
millstream is audible from the cosy
guestrooms overlooking the Seille river.*

MACON

▲ Hôtel-Restaurant Bellevue

416–420 quai Lamartine, 71000 **Map** 8B3

📞 03 85 21 04 04
FAX 03 85 21 04 02
🌐 www.ila-chateau.com/bellevue
💳 AE, MC, V ⬤ 1st 2 wks Dec
🍴 €€ 🛏 (25) €€€

A quaint hotel in a charming spot along the Saône, with somewhat out-of-date furnishings. Try the beef fillet or veal cutlets in cream sauce paired with a wine from the excellent list. Guestrooms are luxurious and look onto the market.

MACON
● Restaurant Pierre

7–9 rue Dufour, 71000 **Map** 8B3
📞 03 85 38 14 23
FAX 03 85 39 84 04
🌐 www.restaurant-pierre.com
💳 AE, DC, MC, V ⬤ Sun D, Mon;
1 wk Feb, 3 wks Jul 🍴 €€€€

Situated on a small, central street near the Saône, this beautiful, softly-lit restaurant serves frogs' legs, crayfish and freshwater fish. An array of fruit showers the dessert menu. In summer try for a table on the flower-filled patio.

MAGNY-COURS
▲ La Renaissance

2 rue Paris, 58470 **Map** 7F2
📞 03 86 58 10 40
FAX 03 86 21 22 60
🌐 www.hotel-la-renaissance.fr
💳 AE, MC, V ⬤ Sun D, Mon; Feb,
2 wks Aug 🍴 €€€ 🛏 (9) €€€

Regional fare at fair prices. The crème brûlée is outstanding. Charming rooms.

MAREY-LES-FUSSEY
● Maison des Hautes Côtes

Route Villiers, 21700 **Map** 8B2
📞 03 80 62 91 29
FAX 03 80 62 96 79
💳 MC, V ⬤ Sun D, Mon
🍴 €€€

Countryside setting, three dining rooms and a shaded terrace. One menu specializes in cassis. Impressive wines.

MARSANNAY-LA-COTE
● Les Gourmets

8 rue Puits de Tet, 21160 **Map** 8B2
📞 03 80 52 16 32
FAX 03 80 52 03 01
💳 MC, V

⬤ Sun D, Mon, Tue L; 1st 2 wks Aug
🍴 €€€

This informal restaurant sometimes tries a little too hard to impress. However, the food is tasty and the wine list (with 500 labels) is sure to please.

MERCUREY
▲ Hôtellerie du Val d'Or

140 Grande Rue, 71640 **Map** 8B2
📞 03 85 45 13 70
FAX 03 85 45 18 45
🌐 www.le-valdor.com
💳 AE, MC, V ⬤ Mon, Tue L; last 2
wks Dec 🍴 €€€ 🛏 (12) €€€

Home-style charm is the hallmark of this restaurant and inn. The menu features oeufs en meurette (p217). Guestrooms are decorated in clean-looking pastels.

MEURSAULT
● Le Bouchon

Pl de l'Hôtel de Ville, 21190 **Map** 8B2
📞 03 80 21 29 56
FAX 03 80 21 29 56
💳 AE, MC, V ⬤ Sun D, Mon;
mid-Nov–mid-Dec 🍴 €€

Small bistro located in the famous white-wine village of Mersault. Try filet mignon and prawns with seafood sauce.

MEURSAULT
▲ Le Chevreuil

Pl de l'Hôtel-de-Ville, 21190 **Map** 8B2
📞 03 80 21 23 25
FAX 03 80 21 65 51
💳 MC, V ⬤ Tue L, Thu L
🍴 €€€€€ 🛏 (17) €€€€€

Choose how you'd like your oeufs en meurette (p217), either with red or white wine. Don't miss the millefeuille that combines pain d'épices (spice bread) and cassis. Comfortable guestrooms.

MONTAGNY-LES-BEAUNE
■ Hôtel le Clos

22 rue des Gravières, 21200 **Map** 8B2
📞 03 80 25 97 98
FAX 03 80 25 94 70
💳 MC, V ⬤ 1 wk Nov, 2 wks Jan
🛏 (24) €€€

Converted 18th-century farmhouse complete with a terrace and garden for balmy summer days and a roaring fire to fend off the cold. Attractive rooms.

MONTAGNY PRES-LOUHANS
● Restaurant Le Rustique

30 rue de l'Église, 71380 **Map** 8C3
📞 03 85 72 16 41
💳 MC, V 🍴 €

An ideal stop for a simple midday meal such as pizza or a salad. At dinner, dip into a more substantial dish such as the classic fondue savoyarde (p269).

MONTBARD
▲ Hôtel de l'Écu

7 rue Auguste Carré, 21500 **Map** 8B1
📞 03 80 92 11 66
FAX 03 80 92 14 13
@ snc.coupat@wanadoo.fr
💳 AE, DC, MC, V ⬤ Tue L; 2 wks Feb
🍴 €€€ 🛏 (23) €€€

A 17th-century house that is an ideal base for visiting the fascinating Abbey of Fontenay. The snail and quail dishes are specialities. Well-equipped guestrooms.

MONTIGNY-LA-RESLE
▲ Le Soleil d'Or

RN77, 89230 **Map** 8A1
📞 03 86 41 81 21
FAX 03 86 41 86 88
🌐 www.lesoleildor.fr
💳 AE, DC, MC, V
🍴 €€€ 🛏 (16) €€

Specialities at this country inn include foie gras with exotic fruits in caramel, sea bream in crayfish sauce and suckling pig with honey. Well-equipped, pretty bedrooms with white furnishings.

MONTMELARD
▲ Hôtel-Restaurant le St-Cyr

Le Bourg, 71520 **Map** 8B3
📞 03 85 50 20 76
FAX 03 85 50 36 98
🌐 www.lesaintcyr.com
💳 MC, V ⬤ Mon D, Tue; 2 wks Feb
🍴 €€€ 🛏 (7) €€

Where better than Montmelard itself to try some of this goats' cheese? Roast duck, gratin of salmon, crab and prawns, are all on offer. Guestrooms have countryside views.

MONT-ST-JEAN
● Le Médieval

Place de la Halle, 21320 **Map** 8B2
📞 03 80 84 34 68

FAX 03 80 84 38 21

MC, V ● Mon ❚❙ €€€

This place serves up dishes with an exotic twist, like Tahitian-style mahi mahi and pineapple with ginger ice cream.

MOREY-ST-DENIS

▲ Castel de Très Girard

7 rue de Très-Girard, 21220 **Map** 8B2

03 80 34 33 09

FAX 03 80 51 81 92

AE, DC, MC, V ● Sun, Mon L, Sat L; mid-Feb–mid-Mar

❚❙ €€€€ 🍴 (9) €€€€

Pretty 18th-century château, with an outdoor pool. Traditional dishes and hundreds of wine choices. Extremely lovely rooms with vineyard views.

NEVERS

▲ Hôtel Mercure Pont de Loire

Quai de Médine, 58000 **Map** 7FZ

03 86 93 93 86

FAX 03 86 59 43 29

AE, DC, MC, V

❚❙ €€€ 🍴 (59) €€€

Restaurant Le Côté Loire, the terrace and bar here are all blessed with views. Not all the rooms are so lucky though. Try escargots à la bourguignonne (p216), Morvan ham and Charolais beef.

NEVERS

▲ Hôtel-Restaurtant La Folie

Route des Saulaies, 58000 **Map** 7FZ

03 86 57 05 31

FAX 03 86 57 66 99

AE, MC, V ● Fri, Sat; Nov–Feb

❚❙ €€ 🍴 (37) €€

Complete with pool and tennis court. Book ahead for the restaurant, where tables on the flower-filled terrace enjoy a distant view of the Loire. On the menu, Charolais beef and coq au vin (p217). Contemporary guestrooms.

NEVERS

● Jean-Michel Couron

21 rue St-Etienne, 58000 **Map** 7FZ

03 86 61 19 28

FAX 03 86 36 02 96

MC, V ● Sun D, Mon, Tue; Jan, mid-Jul–Aug ❚❙ €€€

Housed in a medieval church, the food here is anything but old-fashioned. The

overall effect is wonderful. Both the tomato tart with goats' cheese and the roast beef are beautifully presented.

NOLAY

▲ Hôtel-Restaurant du Parc

3 pl de l'Hôtel-de-Ville, 21340 **Map** 8B2

03 80 21 78 88

FAX 03 80 21 86 39

MC, V ● Nov–mid-Mar

❚❙ €€€ 🍴 (14) €€€

This building dates from the 16th century. Specialities at the restaurant include snail casserole with Chablis and rabbit in a red wine. Small, simple rooms.

NOLAY

● Le Burgonde

35 rue de la République, 21340 **Map** 8B2

03 80 21 71 25

FAX 03 80 21 88 06

W www.nolay.net/restaurant.htm

AE, MC, V ● Tue, Wed; mid-Feb–mid-Mar ❚❙ €€€

One-time village market near the town hall. Try a speciality such as shoulder of Nolay pork with ginger or pike-perch and leek millefeuille with pain d'épices (spice bread). Reasonably priced wines.

NUITS-ST-GEORGES

● Au Bois de Charmois

Route de la Serrée, 21700 **Map** 8B2

03 80 61 04 79

MC, V

● Mon; 2 wks Feb ❚❙ €

For good value, there's no beating this quaint restaurant with its small outdoor patio. The menu highlight is the big portions of frogs' legs. Decent wine list.

NUITS-ST-GEORGES

▲ Hostellerie la Gentilhommière

13 vallée de la Serrée, 21700 **Map** 8B2

03 80 61 12 06

FAX 03 80 61 30 33

AE, DC, MC, V

● Tue, Wed, Sat L; mid-Dec–mid-Jan

❚❙ €€€ 🍴 (39) €€€

In a picturesque converted hunting lodge, the restaurant serves up crayfish from the hotel's lake. Sea bass, frogs' legs and fillet of beef with black pepper are also highlights. Modern guestrooms with themes such as an African safari.

NUITS-ST-GEORGES

▲ Hôtel St Georges

Carrefour de l'Europe, 21700 **Map** 8B2

03 80 62 00 62

FAX 03 80 61 23 80

W www.le-saint-georges.fr

AE, DC, MC, V

❚❙ €€ 🍴 (47) €€

Not as charming as its neighbours but solid quality nonetheless. Dishes such as snail casserole. Guestrooms are equipped with modern amenities.

NUITS-ST-GEORGES

▲ L'Alambic Hostellerie St Vincent

Rue Général de Gaulle, 21700 **Map** 8B2

03 80 61 14 91

FAX 03 80 61 24 65

AE, DC, MC, V

● Sun D, Mon L; mid-Nov–mid-Mar

❚❙ € 🍴 (23) €€€

Ambience is everything at this small restaurant. Dining rooms are in a dark cellar, built with stones from an old prison. On the menu, rabbit and green lentil salad in a balsamic vinegar reduction. Contemporary guestrooms.

ORMES

● Restaurant le Vieux Port

Port Ormes, 71290 **Map** 8B3

03 85 40 20 31

FAX 03 85 40 20 31

@ mariefrancoise.leduc@free.fr

MC, V ● Sep–Jun: L; mid-Nov–Apr ❚❙ €€€

Riverside location. On the menu, fillet of sole, Charolais beef grilled duck breast. Impressive variety of goat's cheese offered.

PARAY-LE-MONIAL

▲ Grand Hôtel de la Basilique

18 rue de la Visitation, 71600 **Map** 8A3

03 85 81 11 13

FAX 03 85 88 83 70

AE, MC, V

● 3 wks Mar, Nov–Feb

❚❙ €€ 🍴 (56) €€

Family-run place located between the Basilique du Sacré-Coeur and the Renaissance town hall. The three set menus feature market-fresh fish and Charolais beef. Guestrooms are simple and quite colourful.

● Restaurant ■ Hotel ▲ Hotel / Restaurant

PARAY-LE-MONIAL
▲ Hostellerie des Trois Pigeons

2 rue Dargaud, 71600 **Map** 8A3

☎ 03 85 81 03 77

FAX 03 85 81 58 59

w www.h-3-p.com

AE, DC, MC, V

Dec–Feb

€€€ (44) €€

A charming place offering apple sorbet with Calvados, escalope of duck foie gras, and langoustines. The rooms overlooking the road are soundproofed.

PARAY-LE-MONIAL
▲ Hôtel Terminus

27 ave de la Gare, 71600 **Map** 8A3

☎ 03 85 81 59 31

FAX 03 85 81 38 31

w www.terminus-paray.fr

MC, V

L, Sun, Fri, Sat; 1st wk Jan, 2 wks Nov, last 2 wks Dec

€ (16) €€

A big terrace and spacious guestrooms decorated in floral motifs make this a wonderful place. The brasserie serves good fare from a limited menu.

PARAY-LE-MONIAL
▲ Hôtel-Restaurant aux Vendanges de Bourgogne

5 rue Denis Papin, 71600 **Map** 8A3

☎ 03 85 81 13 43

FAX 03 85 88 87 59

w www.auxvendangesdebourgogne.fr

AE, MC, V Sep–Jun: Sun D; 2 wks Jan, 2 wks Feb

€€€ (15) €€

At the restaurant, choose a regional speciality such as Charolais beef or the snail tart with bacon. Guestrooms are rather elaborate with lots of pine.

PARAY-LE-MONIAL
▲ Hôtel-Restaurant Le Val d'Or

La Beluze, Volesvres, 71600 **Map** 8A3

☎ 02 85 81 05 07

FAX 03 85 81 46 05

w www.hotel-levaldor.com

MC, V Wed

€€ (14) €€

Try the famous Bresse chicken, among other delights. Extremely basic rooms. Fantastic terrace.

PEROUGES
▲ Ostellerie du Vieux Pérouges

Pl du Tilleul, 01800 **Map** 8C4

☎ 04 74 61 00 88

FAX 04 74 34 77 90

w www.ostellerie.com

AE, MC, V

€€ (28) €€€

Flower-filled window boxes cover the front of this hotel. Charming French specialities on the menu like la galette de Pérouges (a cream and sugar tart). Small, cosy guestrooms.

PLANCHEZ
▲ Hôtel-Restaurant le Relais des Lacs

Ave François Mitterrand, 58230 **Map** 8A2

☎ 03 86 78 49 00

FAX 03 86 78 49 09

w www.morvan-gourmand.fr

AE, MC, V Sep–Jun: Mon; Jan, mid-Nov–mid-Dec

€€€ (36) €€

Situated between two lakes in the Morvan Regional Park and an ideal base for outdoor activities. At the restaurant try duck foie gras, crayfish flambéed with whisky, and superb pigeon with sherry. Extremely stylish guestrooms.

PONTAUBERT
▲ Les Fleurs

Route Vézelay, 89200 **Map** 8A1

☎ 03 86 34 13 81

FAX 03 86 34 23 32

MC, V Wed, Thu; 1 wk Oct, mid-Dec–mid-Feb

€€€ (7) €€

Opt for the trout terrine and then the veal kidneys with cassis mustard at this rustic place in the village centre. Most guestrooms overlook the garden.

PONT-DE-PANY
● L'Auberge de Pont de Pany

170 rue de Ste-Marie, 21410 **Map** 8B2

☎ 03 80 49 77 79

FAX 03 80 49 73 79

MC, V Sun D, Mon, Tue; Dec–Feb €€€

An estate with a rustic dining room and a large terrace. Try the monkfish with Époisses cheese and marc de bourgogne or the roast duck.

POUILLY
▲ Hostellerie du Château

Châteauneuf-en-Auxois, 21320 **Map** 8B2

☎ 03 80 49 22 00

FAX 03 80 49 21 27

w www.hostellerie-chateauneuf.com

AE, DC, MC, V

Sep–May: Mon & Tue; Dec–Jan

€€ (17) €€

Sumptuous delicacies like truffles and foie gras are menu highlights. The charming ambience of a castle-like country château adds to the experience. Guestrooms have stone walls.

POUILLY-SUR-LOIRE
▲ Hôtel-Restaurant le Relais de Pouilly

Quai de Loire, 58150 **Map** 7FZ

☎ 03 86 39 03 00

FAX 03 86 39 07 47

w www.relaisdepouilly.com

AE, DC, MC, V

€€€ (24) €€€

Situated in the very west of Burgundy in the Loire Valley, with the Pouilly-sur-Loire vineyards close to hand. On the menu, grilled or roasted local meats. There's a summer terrace and play area outside to keep the kids amused. Quiet rooms with lovely views.

POUILLY-SUR-LOIRE
▲ Hôtel-Restaurant l'Espérance

17 rue René Couard, 58150 **Map** 7FZ

☎ 03 86 39 07 69

FAX 03 86 39 09 78

MC, V

Sun D, Oct–Mar: Mon; 2 wks Jan €€ (3) €€

Roadside location close to the Pouilly vineyards, a wonderful abbey, and the forest. Try the foie gras or andouillette and choose from over 150 wines.

POUILLY-SUR-LOIRE
▲ Le Relais Fleuri

42 ave de la Tuilerie, 58150 **Map** 7FZ

☎ 03 86 39 12 99

FAX 03 86 39 14 15

AE, DC, MC, V Oct–Apr: Tue, Wed; mid-Dec–mid-Jan

€€€ (11) €€€

Try crayfish soup flavoured with Pouilly wine and star anise, or roast pigeon with honey and coriander (cilantro). Consider a glass or two of Pouilly Fumé, made from the Sauvignon Blanc grape. Four of the guestrooms have a balcony.

PRENOIS
● **Auberge de la Charme**
12 rue de la Charme, 21370 **Map** 8B2
📞 03 80 35 32 84
FAX 03 80 35 34 48
💳 AE, MC, V ● Sun D, Mon, Tue L; 1st 2 wks Aug 🍴 €€€

Creative French cuisine has made this modern restaurant one of Prenois' claims to fame. The pigeon breast with snails and various rabbit dishes have earned it a Michelin star.

PULIGNY-MONTRACHET
▲ **La Chouette**
3 rue Creux de Chagny, 21190 **Map** 8B2
📞 03 80 21 95 60
FAX 03 80 21 95 61
🌐 www.la-chouette.fr
💳 MC, V 🍴 €€€ 🛏 (6) €€€

This small château set in a quiet forested area looks and feels like a private home. The restaurant is for guests only. The menu changes every week, but can feature dishes such as roast pigeon, lamb fillet and frogs' legs.

PULIGNY-MONTRACHET
● **La Table d'Olivier Leflaive**
Pl du Monument, 21190 **Map** 8B2
📞 03 80 21 37 65
🌐 www.olivier-leflaive.com
💳 MC, V
● Dec–Feb 🍴 €€€

A wonderful spot to combine a wine-tasting session with some light Burgundian fare. Try a cold platter of chicken, local ham or cheeses. After lunch, tour the wine cellar below.

PULIGNY-MONTRACHET
▲ **Le Montrachet**
Pl des Marronniers, 21190 **Map** 8B2
📞 03 80 21 30 06
FAX 03 80 21 39 06
💳 AE, DC, MC, V
● Dec
🍴 €€€ 🛏 (31) €€€€

Renowned for its excellent wine list. On the menu, turbot with artichoke hearts,

mushrooms and bacon, and escargots à la bourguignonne (p216).

QUARRE-LES-TOMBES
▲ **Auberge de l'Âtre**
Les Lavaults, 89630 **Map** 8A2
📞 03 86 32 20 79
FAX 03 86 32 28 25
🌐 www.auberge-de-latre.com
💳 AE, DC, MC, V
● Tue D, Wed; Feb
🍴 €€€ 🛏 (7) €€€

Savoury creations in a stone farmhouse include delicious wild mushroom dishes. Period furniture in the guestrooms.

QUETIGNY
▲ **Cap Vert**
1 rue du Cap Vert, 21800 **Map** 8C2
📞 03 80 48 55 00
FAX 03 80 48 55 01
🌐 www.capvert.fr
💳 MC, V 🍴 € 🛏 (40) €€

Great family place with a water park (Sep–Jun), a gym, beauty centre and squash courts. At the grill, try the king prawn brochette or the andouillette. Stylish, contemporary bedrooms.

ROMANECHE-THORINS
▲ **Les Maritonnes**
Route de Fleurie, 71570 **Map** 8B3
📞 03 85 35 51 70
FAX 03 85 35 58 14
🌐 www.maritonnes.com
💳 MC, V ● Jan
🍴 €€€ 🛏 (20) €€€

A country house in the midst of vineyards with great duck and meat dishes on the pioneering menu. Guestrooms have antiques and there's a pool.

RULLY
▲ **Le Vendangerot**
6 pl Ste-Marie, 71150 **Map** 8B2
📞 03 85 87 20 09
FAX 03 85 91 27 18
💳 MC, V ● Tue, Wed; first 2 wks Jan
🍴 €€ 🛏 (13) €€

Traditional hotel-restaurant with tranquil, old-fashioned guestrooms. Specialities in the restaurant include duck foie gras with grapes, pigeon confit with cabbage, rich stews in winter and hearty desserts such as the dark chocolate cake.

SANTENAY
● **Le Terroir**
19 pl du Jet d'Eau, 21590 **Map** 8B2
📞 03 80 20 63 47
FAX 03 80 20 66 45
@ restaurant.le.terroir@wanadoo.fr
💳 MC, V
● Sun D, Thu, Nov–Mar: Wed D; mid-Dec–mid-Jan
🍴 €€€

Take the opportunity to sample some Santenay wine at this place with two sunny dining rooms on the village square. Value-for-money local dishes include coq au vin (p217) and fish.

SAULIEU
▲ **Hostellerie de la Tour d'Auxois**
Square Alexandre Dumaine, BP53, 21210 **Map** 8B2
📞 03 80 64 36 19
FAX 03 80 64 93 10
🌐 www.tourdauxois.com
💳 AE, DC, MC, V
🍴 €€€ 🛏 (35) €€€

Comfortable hotel with sauna and outdoor pool. At its bistro, it would be remiss not to try the famed Morvan ham or the lamb with cassis.

SAULIEU
▲ **Hôtel de la Poste**
1 rue Grillot, 21210 **Map** 8B2
📞 03 80 64 05 67
FAX 03 80 64 10 82
🌐 www.hotel-de-la-poste.fr
💳 AE, DC, MC, V
🍴 €€€ 🛏 (38) €€€

A 17th-century coaching inn with a Belle Epoque dining room. The menu includes snails in red wine and garlic, fried lobster with Szechuan pepper, and Charolais beef fillet in truffle juice. The rooms are spacious.

SAULIEU
▲ **La Borne Impériale**
14–16 rue d'Argentine, 21210 **Map** 8B2
📞 03 80 64 19 76
FAX 03 80 64 30 63
💳 MC, V
● Mon D, Wed; 3 wks Jan
🍴 €€€ 🛏 (7) €€

A lovely old inn. Serious specialities include lobster entrées and, if ordered

● Restaurant ■ Hotel ▲ Hotel / Restaurant

in advance, steamed Bresse chicken with wild morels. Book a room with a gorgeous garden view.

SAULIEU
▲ **La Côte d'Or**
2 rue Argentine, 21210 **Map** 8B2
☎ 03 80 90 53 53
FAX 03 80 64 08 92
✦ AE, DC, MC, V ● Jan
🍴 €€€€€ ✦ (33) €€€€€

The restaurant remains one of France's best. White peaches with sorbet is a great dessert. Guestrooms have a fireplace or balcony.

SAULON-LA-RUE
▲ **Château de Saulon la Rue**
Route de Seurre, 21910 **Map** 8B2
☎ 03 80 79 25 25
FAX 03 80 79 25 26
✦ AE, DC, MC, V ● Sun D, Mon L; Feb, 1 wk Mar
🍴 €€€ ✦ (30) €€€

Coq au vin (p217) and lots of Burgundian specialities are served at this enchanting 17th-century château surrounded by woodland. Guestrooms have a sweet character and are individually styled.

SAVIGNY-LES-BEAUNE
▲ **Hôtel-Restaurant L'Ouvrée**
54 route de Bouilland, 21420 **Map** 8B2
☎ 03 80 21 51 52
FAX 03 80 26 10 04
✦ MC, V ● Feb, 2 wks Mar
🍴 €€ ✦ (22) €€

Located in the wine-producing village of Savigny, in a deep valley. Try the duck salad followed by veal liver with pears. Basic, welcoming guestrooms.

SAVIGNY-LES-BEAUNE
● **La Cuverie**
5 rue Chanoine Donin, 21420 **Map** 8B2
☎ 03 80 21 50 03
FAX 03 80 21 50 03
✦ MC, V ● Tue, Wed 🍴 €€€

Perfect for a spot of lunch before touring the vineyards. Try a glass of Savigny red wine and the beef roulade.

SEMUR-EN-AUXOIS
▲ **Hostellerie d'Aussois**
Route de Saulieu, 21140 **Map** 8B1

☎ 03 80 97 28 28
FAX 03 80 97 34 56
ⓦ www.hostellerie.fr
✦ AE, MC, V ● mid-Jan–mid-Feb
🍴 €€€ ✦ (43) €€€

At the restaurant, Le Mermoz, you'll find Burgundian favourites such as œufs en meurette (p217), snails, and coq au vin (p217). Poolside dining in summer. Well-equipped guestrooms.

SEMUR-EN-AUXOIS
▲ **Hôtel du Lac**
Rue du Lac, Pont-et-Massène, 21140 **Map** 8B1
☎ 03 80 97 11 11
FAX 03 80 97 29 25
ⓦ www.hoteldulacdepont.com
✦ AE, MC, V ● Sun D, Mon, Tue L
🍴 € ✦ (20) €€

This hotel-restaurant earns big points for the views alone. Specialities such as tête-de-veau with vinegar and shallot sauce are served. Guestrooms are simple and not very elegant.

SEMUR-EN-AUXOIS
● **Les Minimes**
29 rue de Vaux, 21140 **Map** 8B1
☎ 03 80 97 26 86
✦ MC, V ● Sun D, Mon 🍴 €€

Wonderfully plain and simple cooking, and a dining room to match. A taste of the famous Époisses cheese is a must here since the village where it's made is just down the road.

SENS
● **Auberge de la Vanne**
176 ave de Sénigallia, 89100 **Map** 3F5
☎ 03 86 65 13 63
FAX 03 86 65 90 85
✦ AE, DC, MC, V ● Sun D, Tue, Wed D; 2 wks Nov 🍴 €€€

On the banks of the Vanne River, south of the town centre. Feast on standards such as steak-frites and fillet of sole either in the panoramic dining room or among the weeping willows in the garden.

SENS
▲ **Hôtel de Paris et de la Poste**
97 rue de la République, 89100 **Map** 3F5
☎ 03 86 65 17 43
FAX 03 86 64 48 45

ⓦ www.hotel-paris-poste.com
✦ AE, DC, MC, V ● Sun D, Mon; 2 wks Aug 🍴 €€€ ✦ (30) €€€

Stylish property that's had the same owners since 1980. A third-generation Godard is chef at restaurant Le Sénon. Try the dozen snails followed by roast pigeon or sea bass. Spacious, modern rooms; four apartments.

SENS
● **La Madeleine**
1 rue d'Alsace-Lorraine, 89100 **Map** 3F5
☎ 03 86 65 09 31
FAX 03 86 95 37 41
ⓦ www.restaurant-lamadeleine.fr
✦ AE, DC, MC, V ● Sun, Mon, Tue L
🍴 €€€

This elegant bearer of two Michelin stars is named after its small courtyard chapel and not the small cakes. Specialities include foie gras with cassis, sea bass, and chocolate mousse with raspberry juice. Yonne wines include Chablis, Irancy, Sauvignon St-Bris and Chitry.

SENS
● **La Potinière**
51 rue Cécile de Marsangy, 89100 **Map** 3F5
☎ 03 86 65 31 08
FAX 03 86 64 60 19
✦ MC, V ● Sun D, Mon D, Tue
🍴 €€€

Across the river from most of the sights. Excellent choices include foie gras with port, flambéed veal kidneys and sole meunière. Try for a table on the pretty, shaded riverbank. Landing dock.

SENS
● **Le Clos des Jacobins**
49 Grande Rue, 89100 **Map** 3F5
☎ 03 86 95 29 70
FAX 03 86 64 22 98
✦ AE, MC, V ● Sun D, Tue, Wed D; mid-Aug–Sep 🍴 €€

A classy restaurant serving traditional French cuisine and fantastic soups. Touches like leather chairs lend a refined air to this hidden gem.

STE-SABINE
▲ **Hostellerie du Château Ste-Sabine**
D970, 21320 **Map** 8B2

C 03 80 49 22 01

FAX 03 80 49 20 01

W www.ifrance.com/chste-sabine

€ MC, V ● Jan–Feb

11 €€€€ ◇ (30) €€€€

Seventeenth-century castle with a pool, set in a wildlife park. Take a seat in the dining room, with its magnificent views of the lake and Châteauneuf Valley, or the medieval stone vault. The menu features fish and includes John Dory terrine and pike-perch. Rustic rooms.

ST-FARGEAU

● Auberge les Perriaux

La Gare, 89170 **Map** 7F1

C 03 86 74 16 45

FAX 03 86 74 08 27

W www.lesperriaux.com

€ MC, V ● Mon–Fri L

11 €€

This farm's been in business since 1959. Unsurprisingly, dishes revolve around duck, chicken, ham and eggs. Don't leave without trying their cider and some Puisaye cheese.

ST-LEGER-SOUS-BEUVRAY

▲ Hôtel du Morvan

Pl de la Mairie, 71990 **Map** 8A2

C 03 85 82 51 06

FAX 06 77 79 57 89

€ MC, V ● Mon, Tue; mid-Dec– mid-Jan **11** €€ ◇ (7) €€

An ideal base for the magnificent Morvan. Try Burgundy favourites oeufs en meurette (p217) or escargots à la bourguignonne (p216). Very basic rooms.

ST-LOUP-DE-VARENNES

● Restaurant Le St-Loup

13 RN6, 71240 **Map** 8B3

C 03 85 44 21 58

FAX 03 85 44 21 58

€ MC, V ● Sun D, Tue D, Wed; 2 wks Feb, 3 wks Jul, 1 wk Oct **11** €€

Ideal after visiting the house of Nicephore Niépce (inventor of photography). The menu includes Bresse chicken.

ST-PERE-SOUS-VEZELAY

▲ L'Espérance

On D957 from Vézelay, 89450 **Map** 8A1

C 03 86 33 39 10

FAX 03 86 33 26 15

€ AE, DC, MC, V ● Tue, Wed L; Feb

11 €€€€€ ◇ (34) €€€€

Regional flavours: foie gras, local wines and meat dishes. Cosy guestrooms.

ST-PIERRE-LE-MOUTIER

▲ La Grande Chaumière

On RN7, 58240 **Map** 7FZ

C 03 86 90 94 44

FAX 03 86 90 94 43

€ MC, V ● Sun, Mon

11 €€€ ◇ (5) €€€

This little restaurant is in a round, thatched-roof house, with a big stone fireplace in the centre. Cheery rooms.

ST-REMY

● Moulin de Martorey

Chemin de Martorez, 71100 **Map** 8B2

C 03 85 48 12 98

FAX 03 85 48 73 67

€ AE, MC, V ● Sun D, Tue L, Mon; 3 wks Jan, 2 wks Aug **11** €€€€

One of the best upscale restaurants in the area, this gorgeous converted mill serves modern food.

ST-SEINE-L'ABBAYE

▲ Hôtel-Restaurant de la Poste

17 rue Carnot, 21440 **Map** 8B1

C 03 80 35 00 35

FAX 03 80 35 07 64

€ MC, V ● Tue, Wed L; mid-Jan–Feb, mid-Dec–1st wk Jan

11 €€ ◇ (15) €€

Fruity choices off the menu here include the duck with morello cherries and the red-fruit gratin. Lovely shaded garden, a luxury suite and large guestrooms.

TONNERRE

▲ Auberge de Bourgogne

Route de Dijon, 89700 **Map** 8A1

C 03 86 54 41 41

FAX 03 86 54 48 28

€ AE, DC, MC, V ● Sun D, Mon; 2 wks Dec, 1 wk Jan

11 €€ ◇ (40) €€€

Choose between specialities like the snail brioche or the pôchouse (p216). Guestrooms offer wonderful views.

TONNERRE

● Le St-Père

2 rue Georges Pompidou, 89700 **Map** 8A1

C 03 86 55 12 84

FAX 03 86 55 12 84

€ MC, V ● Sun D, Mon; 2 wks Mar, 3 wks Sep **11** €

A pleasant, rustic establishment that's ideal for a bite before a visit to the nearby Fosse Dionne spring and Hôtel-Dieu.

TOURNUS

▲ Aux Terrasses

18 ave du 23 Janvier, 71700 **Map** 8B3

C 03 85 51 01 74

FAX 03 85 51 09 99

€ MC, V

● Sun D, Mon; Jan

11 €€ ◇ (18) €€€€

One of the best places in town, with a charming restaurant that is popular with locals. The speciality is monkfish ravioli. Old-fashioned, characterful guestrooms.

TOURNUS

▲ Hôtel-Restaurant de la Paix

9 rue Jean Jaurès, 71700 **Map** 8B3

C 03 85 51 01 85

FAX 03 85 51 02 30

W www.hotel-de-la-paix.fr

€ MC, V ● Oct–June: Tue, Wed L; 3 wks Jan, 1 wk Feb, 1 wk Oct

11 €€€ ◇ (24) €€

Mains on the menu include roast sea bass, frogs' legs and lamb with pain d'épices (spice bread); try the prunes with red wine and Armagnac for dessert. Book a guestroom in the quieter annexe.

TOURNUS

▲ Hôtel-Restaurant le Sauvage

Pl du Champ de Mars, 71700 **Map** 8B3

C 03 85 51 14 45

FAX 03 85 32 10 27

W www.le-sauvage-tournus.com

€ AE, DC, MC, V

11 €€€€ ◇ (30) €€€

Specialities at this old establishment include foie gras terrine or snails in their shells to start followed by plates starring frogs' legs and Bresse chicken. Classy rooms with dated furnishings.

TOURNUS

▲ Le Rempart

2–4 ave Gambetta, 71700 **Map** 8B3

C 03 85 51 10 56

FAX 03 85 51 77 22

● Restaurant ■ Hotel ▲ Hotel / Restaurant

[w] www.lerempart.com

[MC] MC, V [11] €€€ [symbol] (32) €€€

A hotel built into the city's medieval ramparts. The bistro serves good but uninspired dishes. The formal restaurant offers classic dishes like coq au vin (p217). Charming, well-furnished rooms.

TOURNUS
● Restaurant au Bon Accueil

31 rue Chaney, 71700 **Map** 8B3

[tel] 03 85 51 12 18

FAX 03 85 51 33 13

[MC] MC, V [symbol] Apr–Nov: Sun, Sep–Jun: Sat [11] €€

Head to the terrace on sizzling summer days; on colder days, dine inside on hearty veal stew. The cheeseboard features superb Époisses cheese.

TOURNUS
● Restaurant le Charles VII

Place de l'Hôtel de Ville, 71700 **Map** 8B3

[tel] 03 85 32 16 84

FAX 03 85 51 39 13

[w] www.le-charles-7.com

[MC] MC, V [11] €€€

Top-notch local dishes fit for a king, like the Bresse chicken garnished with prawns or the roast pigeon. Those wishing to indulge in apple pie need to order it at the start of their meal.

VAULT-DE-LUGNY
● Auberge des Chenêts

RN6, Valloux, 89200 **Map** 8A1

[tel] 03 86 34 23 34

FAX 03 86 34 21 24

[MC] MC, V [symbol] Sun D, Mon; 2 wks Apr [11] €€

Small country inn in a village lying between Avallon and Sermizelles. Delightful food such as langoustines with grapefruit sauce, duck foie gras and scallops with ceps. Non-smoking.

VERDUN-SUR-LE-DOUBS
▲ Hostellerie Bourguignonne

2 ave Président Borgeot, 71350 **Map** 8B2

[tel] 03 85 91 51 45

FAX 03 85 91 53 81

[MC] AE, MC, V [symbol] Tue, Wed L; Jan [11] €€ [symbol] (9) €€€

What this quaint country inn lacks in modernity it makes up for in charm.

Terrines, mussels and frog's legs all feature. Basic, antique guestrooms.

VERDUN-SUR-LE-DOUBS
▲ Moulin d'Hauterive

St-Gervais-en-Valliere, 71350 **Map** 8B2

[tel] 03 85 91 55 56

FAX 03 85 91 89 65

[MC] AE, MC, V [symbol] Oct–Jun: Sun D, Mon [11] €€€ [symbol] (20) €€€€

The old vine-covered château is the very definition of French charm. Tempting contemporary cooking. Modern rooms.

VEZELAY
● Auberge de la Coquille

81 rue St-Pierre, 89450 **Map** 8A1

[tel] 03 86 33 35 57

FAX 03 86 33 37 84

[MC] MC, V [11] €€

Ideal for a lunchtime crêpe. Also on the menu are boeuf bourguignon (p217), duck with honey, and pear gateau. Wines: Vezelay Pinot Noirs and Blancs.

VEZELAY
● La Dent Creuse Vézelay

Pl de la Foire, rue St-Etienne, 89450 **Map** 8A1

[tel] 03 86 33 36 33

FAX 03 86 33 36 34

[MC] MC, V [symbol] Jan [11] €€

Beneath the brasserie with its wonderful panoramic terrace you'll find a more refined restaurant. Try the fillet steak in a strong Époisses cheese sauce and the delicious apples drizzled in marc de bourgogne.

VEZELAY
● Le Bougainville

26 rue St-Etienne, 89450 **Map** 8A1

[tel] 03 86 33 27 57

FAX 03 86 33 35 12

[MC] MC, V [symbol] Tue, Wed; mid-Nov–mid-Feb [11] €€

Beautiful building, with a fine old fireplace, where terrine of Époisses cheese, Morvan ham and great chicken cooked in white Vézelay wine are served. Excellent value for money.

VEZELAY
● Le St-Étienne

39 rue St-Etienne, 89450 **Map** 8A1

[tel] 03 86 33 27 34

FAX 03 86 33 34 79

[MC] AE, DC, MC, V [symbol] Wed, Thu; Jan, Feb [11] €€€

Eighteenth-century place with pretty, beamed interior. Specialities include foie gras, trout and Charolais beef.

VILLARS-FONTAINE
● Auberge du Coteau

Village centre, 21700 **Map** 8B2

[tel] 03 80 61 10 50

FAX 03 80 61 30 32

[MC] MC, V [symbol] Tue D, Wed; 2 wks Feb, mid-Aug–mid-Sep [11] €€

Country inn. Try fondue bourguignonne, accompanied by a local wine from the vineyards of the Hautes-Côtes.

VILLENEUVE-SUR-YONNE
▲ Auberge La Lucarne Aux Chouettes

7 quai Bretoche, 89500 **Map** 4AZ

[tel] 03 86 87 18 26

FAX 03 86 87 22 63

[w] www.lesliecaron-auberge.com

[MC] AE, MC, V [symbol] Sun D, Mon

[11] €€ [symbol] (4) €€€€

This inn sits among the trees and flowers of the surrounding garden. Snails and wild-mushroom salad are on the menu.

VINCELOTTES
▲ Auberge les Tilleuls

12 quai Yonne Vinvelottes, 89290 **Map** 8A1

[tel] 03 86 42 22 13

FAX 03 86 42 23 51

[MC] MC, V [symbol] Wed; Oct–Easter: Thu; end Dec–mid-Feb [11] €€ [symbol] (5) €€

Alongside the Yonne River, this tiny place serves great game dishes and is an idyllic spot. Simple rooms are well presented.

VITTEAUX
● Vieille Auberge

19 rue de Verdun, 21350 **Map** 8B2

[tel] 03 80 49 60 88

FAX 03 80 49 68 14

[MC] AE, MC, V [symbol] Sun D, Mon, Tue D; 1 wk Jan, 1 wk Jun, 3 wks Nov [11] €€

Pleasant village inn with two rooms and a small terrace. The modern cooking includes turbot with bacon, beans and Szechuan pepper, and beef tournedos.

THE MASSIF CENTRAL

The heart of France, from the pastoral Limousin to the eerie, volcanic Auvergne, is a region where man is far outnumbered by beasts. Meat and game feature strongly, along with hearty lentil and vegetable dishes to bolster against the chill of winter. Roquefort, France's "King of Cheeses", and the region's mineral waters are world famous.

The Flavours of the Massif Central

The Massif Central is a major producer of beef, veal, lamb and also cheese, including the world-famous Roquefort. The forests and mountains are the source of wild mushrooms and fruit, while cultivated specialities include lentils from Le Puy and hardy root vegetables.

Fresh herbs at Brive-la-Gaillarde's busy market

BEST MARKETS

Brive-la-Gaillarde Busy covered market, plus a *marché au gras* (foie gras) in winter, Tue, Thu & Sat am
Limoges Covered market on Place de la Motte, daily
Le Puy-en-Velay Farmers' market on Place du Plot, Sat am
Villefranche-de-Rouergue Authentic market in an old *bastide* town, Thu am

MEAT AND GAME

Beef production is the principal agricultural activity of the Limousin. The orangey-red Limousin cattle are reputed for their finely marbled beef and also for veal. In the Auvergne, the robust deep red, lyre-horned Salers is raised for both cheese (Cantal and Salers) and for its superb lean beef. The golden-brown, doe-eyed Aubrac of the Aveyron and Lozère in the south of the Massif Central provides milk for Laguiole cheese.

Limousin farmers of milk-fed free-range lamb are grouped under the Baronet label. In the Allier, look for high-quality *agneau Bourbonnais*, while to the south, huge flocks range the dry limestone Causses.

In the Auvergne pigs are often kept alongside dairy cows, fed on the whey that is a by-product of cheese-making. In the Limousin, the free-range black and pink Cul Noir pig roams the meadows and woodland around St-Yrieix-la-Perche, feeding on potatoes, chestnuts and acorns, and has been awarded a *label rouge (see p11)* for its pork.

Ducks in the Corrèze are fattened for foie gras, as in the neighbouring Dordogne. Game in the Limousin forest includes wild hare, partridge, pheasant, venison and wild boar.

Left Ceps on a market stall **Right** Jambon d'Auvergne

ROQUEFORT

Moist, salty Roquefort is France's most celebrated blue cheese. It is produced using raw milk from sheep that graze the high limestone Causses plateaux of the Lozère *département*, principally the Lacaune, a hardy breed renowned for its milk. The cheese is matured for around five months in the damp limestone caves that surround the village of Roquefort-sur-Soulzon. The limestone is cut through by deep fissures that let air enter and allow the growth of the bacteria *Penicillium roqueforti* that is specific to these caves and responsible for the cheese's distinctive blue veining. The mould is first encouraged to grow on rye bread and then injected into the cheeses. You can visit the Société des Caves de Roquefort, Roquefort-sur-Soulzon (05 65 59 93 30), open all year.

AUVERGNAT CHARCUTERIE

The Auvergne produces some of France's finest charcuterie. *Jambon sec d'Auvergne* is a lightly salted cured ham. A seemingly infinite variety of dried sausages ranges from *naturel* – consisting just of minced pork, fat and saltpetre, a natural preservative – to varieties with peppercorns, rolled in herbs or ashes, or studded with cep mushooms or Roquefort.

CHEESES

Cantal is one of France's oldest cheeses. A strong, hard, nutty cheese made in large round *tommes*, it may be sold *jeune* (matured at least 30 days), *entre-deux* ("between the two", matured for two to six months) or *vieille* (matured more than six months), deepening in colour and strengthening in flavour as it ages. Laguiole and Salers are similar. Bleu d'Auvergne is like Roquefort but made using cow's milk, as is Bleu des Causses. Fourme d'Ambert is a milder, creamier blue cheese. St-Nectaire from the Puy-de-Dôme has a delicate hazelnut aroma. Other Auvergnat cheeses include the rarer Bleu de Laqueuille, the semi-soft Chambérat and Gaperon, a dome-shaped soft cheese flavoured with pepper and garlic.

FRUIT AND VEGETABLES

Long, harsh winters mean that it is root vegetables which dominate, including carrots, potatoes, swedes and turnips, pink garlic and onions, plus hardy green and red cabbages. Fruit includes apples and cherries cultivated in the Limousin and bilberries on the mountains of the Auvergne. In autumn, the forests of the Limousin abound in ceps, *girolles*, *mousserons*, *trompette-des-morts* and other wild mushrooms.

Lentils and grains for sale in Le Puy-en-Vélay

LENTILLES DE PUY

Lentils were cultivated in the fertile volcanic soils of the Puy-en-Velay basin as far back as Roman times. Today appreciated for its firm, nutty texture and nutritional benefits (low in fat, rich in proteins, fibre, vitamin B and iron), the dark greeny-blue Puy lentil benefits from an AOC and is still cultivated using traditional methods, with no artificial fertilizers or irrigation. A festival to celebrate the new season's lentils is held in Le Puy-en-Velay every August. Puy lentils are typically served cold as a salad or warm with cooked sausage or a knuckle of ham.

Regional Dishes

Hearty, rustic fare characterizes the mountainous Massif Central. But this does not necessarily mean that the robust dishes created here lack subtlety; this region is also the birthplace of smooth vichyssoise *soup.*

ON THE MENU

Canard duchambais Duck with cream, vinegar, apples and shallots

Carottes Vichy Glazed carrots

Cèpes farcis Cep mushrooms stuffed with ham, parsley and garlic, bound with egg

Chou farci Cabbage stuffed with pork and herbs

Falette Veal stuffed with ham, chard and breadcrumbs, then braised in white wine

Farçous Light egg, herb, chard and prune patties, sometimes with sausage meat

Flognarde or **flaugnarde** *Clafoutis*-like baked batter dessert with apples or pears

Gigot brayaude Leg of lamb baked on a bed of sliced potatoes and lardons

Pâté aux pommes de terre Potato, cream and bacon tart

Pounti Loaf of minced pork, herbs, onion and egg, sometimes with raisins and prunes

Salade auvergnate Salad of cubes of jambon d'Auvergne, Cantal cheese and walnuts

Petit salé aux lentilles

THE REGIONAL MENU

Staples such as pork, chestnuts, cabbage, potatoes, swedes, pulses (legumes) and cereals, supplemented by berries, mushrooms and game from the forest, have long characterized the frugal cuisine of this region. They find their way into hearty stews like *potée auvergnate*, the meatloaf-like *pounti* and tasty stuffed cabbage or warming potato dishes, such as *aligot* and *truffade*. Lentils are paired with everything from salted pork to delicate pike-perch.

Top-quality Limousin or Salers beef is often simply grilled (broiled) and lamb from the Allier or the Causses roasted or baked with potatoes as *gigot brayaude,* or served with a creamy purée of pink Auvergne garlic. Pork may be teamed with apples and red cabbage, or cooked with red wine and chestnuts. Dried sausages are usually eaten cold, and the excellent cooking sausages are used in stews or served with *aligot*.

As in neighbouring Périgord, duck dishes and foie gras feature strongly. Creamy *canard duchambais* is a speciality of the Bourbonnais.

The region's fine cheeses make a delightful course in their own right, as well as featuring in sauce to accompany steaks and dishes such as *aligot* and *soupe au Laguiole*. The ubiquitous dessert in the Limousin is *clafoutis* or its cousin the *flognarde*. Many cafés use a selection of regional produce to offer filling salads, such as *salade auvergnate*.

Carottes Vichy, sprinkled with fresh parsley

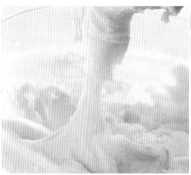

Left Aligot **Right** Cherry *clafoutis*

PETIT SALÉ AUX LENTILLES

The *petit salé* – a term used for various cuts of salted pork, such as knuckle and belly – is partnered with lentils to create a warming, nutritious casserole. After soaking overnight, the pork is simmered gently, while green Puy lentils are cooked separately with onions, carrots, herbs and cloves. The cooked meat is then cut into thick slices and heated through with the lentils and a little of their cooking stock before serving.

ALIGOT

This glistening garlicky cheese and potato purée is an Auvergnat institution. It is a frequent accompaniment to chunky Auvergne sausages and steaks, or even comes by itself as a warm starter. Potatoes are mashed and mixed vigorously into melted butter or pork dripping and minced garlic. Fine slivers of fresh *tomme* cheese (Cantal or Laguiole) are then beaten in with a wooden spoon. Showman chefs and waiters draw out the melting skeins in long strands.

PÔTÉE AUVERGNATE

Most regions seem to have a version of *potée*, a sustaining hotpot of stewed meat and vegetables. That of the Auvergne is composed of assorted cuts of salt pork, a pig's head and sausages, boiled with chunky vegetables, including onions, green cabbage, carrots, potatoes, and possibly leeks and turnips. *Potée limousine* is similar, but uses only salt pork and no sausages.

CLAFOUTIS

The favourite Limousin dessert of fruit baked in batter resembles a sweet toad-in-the-hole, although the eggy batter has a much more flan-like consistency. The authentic version is made with unstoned black *guignes* cherries, although plums, pears and apples are also used (when it is more strictly called a *flognarde*).

REGIONAL DINING

The following restaurants are among those serving regional dishes at reasonable prices:

Amphitryon
Limoges *(see p255)*

Auberge de la Vallée
Crozant *(see p254)*

Auberge du Barrez
Mur-de-Barrez *(see p258)*

Chez Camillou
Aumont-Aubrac *(see p250)*

Chez Francis
Brive-La-Galliarde *(see p252)*

Hôtel du Midi
St-Jean-du-Bruel *(see p261)*

Le Nautilus at Hôtel les Messageries
St-Flour *(see p260)*

Le Relais
Montemart *(see p257)*

Regional Wines, Waters & Spirits

Long gone are the days when the "volcano vineyards" were the third largest in France, shipping oceans of wine to the capital's tables by water, but they are undergoing a revival. Also springing from the volcanic soils are fine mineral waters and aromatic plants used in the local liqueurs.

VOLCANO WATERS

People have been coming to take the waters in the volcanic region of Auvergne since Roman times. With its 30 hot springs, Vichy is still the largest thermal spa centre in Europe. The resort became world famous thanks to the patronage of Napoleon III and his empress Eugénie. Volvic, located a few miles north of Clermont-Ferrand, is the region's most popular mineral water, sourced from a valley that was filled in by the ashes and lava from a nearby volcano, the layers of which now provide a huge natural filter for the water. Almost three million bottles are produced per day. Chateldon is an upmarket water first favoured by Louis XIV. Other waters are salty-tasting Vichy Célestins, and mineral-rich Arvie and St-Yorre, all reputed to help with particular ailments.

The Corent plateau with vineyards on volcanic basalt soil

WINES

Over the last few years the vineyards of the Auvergne have been revived by a handful of dedicated young producers, such as Vincent Tricot. The wines of the Côtes d'Auvergne VDQS are light, supple reds made from local variants of Gamay or Pinot Noir. Chanturgue near Clermont-Ferrand is the best known of five *crus* and the Auvergnats claim that this purple-hued, slightly tannic wine, with its scents of late-season raspberries, was the wine used in the original recipe for *coq au vin (see p217)*.

Although grape-growing dates back to the Middle Ages, Châteaumeillant is today a very obscure VDQS making only light-bodied red and rosé wines. Up and coming St-Pourçain VDQS is making dynamic efforts towards quality with juicy, medium-bodied reds, increasingly showing character. Whites have the toasty, hazelnut notes of Chardonnay, the zip of Sauvignon or the tartness of the local Tressalier.

The Côte Roannaise and Côtes du Forez are AOCs proper, in the upper reaches of the Loire valley. Here Gamay is made in a similar style to Beaujolais *(see pp272–3)*, although sharper and sometimes with added mineral fire from the volcanic soils of the Forez. Modernizing producers are also experimenting with white wines sold as *vins de pays*. Robert Sérol is the leading grower in the wooded hills of the Roannaise and produces a special house wine for the revered Maison Troisgros restaurant in Roanne.

St-Yorre mineral water poster

VINEYARDS OF THE AUVERGNE AND UPPER LOIRE

Verveine de Velay

KEY

▓ Châteaumeillant	
▓ Côtes d'Auvergne	▓ St-Pourçain
▓ Côtes du Forez	— Delimited VDQS regions
▓ Côte Roannaise	···· *Département* boundary

30 ⌐————— *miles* ¬0⌐ *km* ————⌐30

SALERS GENTIAN LIQUEUR

Created in 1885, Salers is the oldest brand of gentian liqueur sold in the Massif Central, taking its name from the Renaissance village of Salers. The gentian is a mountain plant that takes over 20 years to grow fully, flowering only once every two years. It is so rare that it is now a protected species. Only the twisted roots of yellow gentian that is at least 35 years old are used to make the liqueur. The roots are left to infuse in neutral alcohol for several months until they disintegrate, resulting in a yellow juice.

VERVEINE DE VELAY

In 1859, the herbalist Joseph Rumillet-Charretier invented the formula for Verveine de Velay liqueur by distilling the juices of 32 plants. The exact recipe remains a closely guarded secret to this day, although the main ingredient is of course verbena *(verveine)* from Velay. Harvested before the first frosts of autumn, the verbena leaves are left to dry in the open air, then macerated in alcohol before distillation and sweetening. Verveine de Velay may be served neat or in a cocktail. Green and yellow versions are available.

Wooden vats and copper stills for making Verveine de Velay

Where to Eat & Stay

ALLEYRAS

▲ Le Haut Allier

Pont d'Alleyras, 43580 **Map** 8A5

 04 71 57 57 63

FAX 04 71 57 57 99

@ hot.rest.hautallier@wanadoo.fr

 AE, MC, V Mon–Tue L;
Oct–Jun: Sun D; mid-Nov–mid-Mar

 €€€ (14) €€

Deep in the verdant Allier gorge and well worth seeking out for its creative cuisine. Tuck into plates of beef heaped with mushrooms, or crayfish. Rooms are smallish but have decent amenities.

AMBERT

▲ Les Copains

2 bd Henry IV, 63600 **Map** 8A4

 04 73 82 01 02

FAX 04 73 82 67 34

 MC, V Sun D, Sat; late
Feb–early Mar, mid-Sep–mid-Oct

 €€ (11) €€

Specialities include a delicious rabbit dish with crème fraîche, shallots, white wine and cheese. Smallish guestrooms.

ANDELAROCHE

▲ La Marguetière

Rue de la Marguetière, 03120 **Map** 8A3

 04 70 55 20 32

 AE, DC, MC, V Nov–Mar: Sun D, Mon L; 2 wks Jan, 2 wks Nov

 €€ (10) €€

Hotel with its own forest with a private lake, and comfy, well-appointed rooms. Good selection of local wines.

ARGENTAT

▲ Hôtel Fouillade

11 pl Gambetta, 19400 **Map** 7E5

 05 55 28 10 17

FAX 05 55 28 90 52

 www.fouillade.com

 DC, MC, V mid-Nov–mid-Dec

 €€ (14) €€

The Fouillade family concentrates on regional dishes, such as roasted lamb with puréed celeriac, and the atmosphere is relaxed and informal. The individually designed guestrooms are all classically decorated and welcoming.

AUMONT-AUBRAC

▲ Chez Camillou

10 route Languedoc, 48130 **Map** 12A1

 04 66 42 80 22

FAX 04 66 42 93 70

 www.hotel-camillou.com

 DC, MC, V Nov–Apr

 €€ (39) €€€

Superb leisure facilities, with a pool and health club, and a good restaurant. Guestrooms combine fresh, bright walls with eccentric fabrics. Menu highlights include duck foie gras with cep fricassée, and Aubrac beef with aligot (p247).

AUMONT-AUBRAC

▲ Le Compostelle at Grand Hôtel Prouhèze

Ave Gare, 48130 **Map** 12A1

 04 66 42 80 07

FAX 04 66 42 87 78

 www.prouheze.com

 AE, DC, MC, V Sun D,
Oct–Jun: Mon; Nov–late Mar

 €€€€ (25) €€€

Bold, colourful seats and inviting, elegant surroundings distinguish this space. On the menu: langoustines, cod and scallops alongside kid, beef and veal. Guestrooms have a fresh character.

AUMONT-AUBRAC

● L'Ousta Bas

Couffinet, RN9, Ste-Colombe-de-Peyre, 48130 **Map** 12A1

 04 66 42 87 44

FAX 04 66 42 90 10

 MC, V Tue D, Wed; 2 wks Oct

 €€

Coaching inn serving wholesome favourites including a five-meat hotpot and some tasty Auvergne ham. The cheese platter has some unique and renowned Massif Central varieties like Laguiole and Cantal.

AURILLAC

▲ Delcher

20 rue Carmes, 15000 **Map** 7F5

 04 71 48 01 69

FAX 04 71 48 86 66

 AE, DC, MC, V Sun D;

2 wks Jul, mid-Dec–mid-Jan

 € (23) €€

Reliable, no-frills accommodation. The guestrooms are comfy and quiet, and the restaurant prepares all the best-loved local dishes like steak with truffles.

AURILLAC

▲ Hostellerie du Château de Salles

Vézac, 15130 **Map** 7F5

 04 71 62 41 41

FAX 04 71 62 44 14

 www.salles.com

 AE, DC, MC, V Jan–Apr

 €€ (26) €€€€

An impressive baronial pile where antiques abound. The lavish interior opens onto lovely gardens, while the elegant dining room is filled with the aromas of roast veal and baked trout.

AURILLAC

● La Reine Margot

19 rue Guy de Veyre, 15000 **Map** 7F5

 04 71 48 26 46

 MC, V

 Sun D, Mon, Sat L €€

A cosy restaurant filled with wooden furniture and deep earthy colours. Try tripe with red cabbage, various meats and game, and a handful of vegetarian options. Excellent house wine.

AURILLAC

▲ Le Pommier d'Amour at Grand Hôtel St-Pierre

16 cours Monthyon, 15000 **Map** 7F5

 04 71 48 00 24

FAX 04 71 64 81 83

 www.ac-hotel.com

 AE, DC, MC, V

 €€ (35) €€€

Modest guestrooms and a grand dining room. The menu lives up to the salubrious surroundings, and includes favourites such as beef carpaccio, roast duck with mushrooms, and tarte Tatin (p191).

AURILLAC

● Quatre Saisons

10 rue Jean Baptiste Champeil, 15000 **Map** 7F5

● Restaurant ■ Hotel ▲ Hotel / Restaurant

(04 71 64 85 38
MC, V ● Sun D, Mon; 2 wks Aug
€€€

A relaxed and traditional old château. There's a wicked dark chocolate feuilleté with orange coulis for dessert, and a well-stocked cheeseboard.

BANASSAC
▲ Le Calice du Gévaudan
La Mothe, 1km (0.6 miles) north on RN9, 48500 **Map** 11F1
(04 66 32 94 18
FAX 04 66 32 98 62
W www.hotelcalicegevaudan.com
DC, MC, V ● Sun D; late Oct–early Nov **€€** 🍴 (29) €€

In a light-filled contemporary space, dine on tripe, cured local meats, and a crisp apple tart. Modern, minimalist bedrooms and a children's playground.

BEAULIEU-SUR-DORDOGNE
▲ Hôtel Fournié
4 pl du Champ de Mars, 19120 **Map** 7E5
(05 55 91 01 34
FAX 05 55 91 23 57
DC, MC, V ● mid-Sep–Jun: Tue; mid-Nov–May **€€€** 🍴 (23) €€

The location, on the Limousin Riviera, helps to attract the visitors, but others come for the tasty, no-nonsense fare. An attractive hotel with large guestrooms.

BEAULIEU-SUR-DORDOGNE
▲ Le Turenne
1 bd St-Rodolphe de Turenne, 19120 **Map** 7E5
(05 55 91 10 16
FAX 05 55 91 22 42
AE, DC, MC, V ● Mon L; Jan **€€€** 🍴 (15) €€€

Dating from the 12th century, this former Benedictine abbey covers the gastronomic spectrum from regional to gourmet.

BEAULIEU-SUR-DORDOGNE
▲ Les Charmilles
20 bd St-Rodolphe de Turenne, 19120 **Map** 7E5
(05 55 91 29 29
FAX 05 55 91 29 30
W www.auberge-charmilles.com
AE, DC, MC, V ● Wed **€€** 🍴 (8) €€€

Great classic dishes in a quintessential village along one of France's best-loved rivers. This is a cosy little hotel with good-sized rooms.

BEAUZAC
▲ L'Air du Temps
Confolent, 4km (3 miles) east on D461, 43590 **Map** 8A5
(04 71 61 49 05
FAX 04 71 61 50 91
W www.airdutemps.fr.st
AE, MC, V ● Sun D, Mon; Jan, 1st wk Sep **€€** 🍴 (8) €€

A calming, light-filled interior, plus excellent dishes like quail, and a rich biscuit with refreshing mint sorbet. Bright and fresh guestrooms.

BELCASTEL
▲ Le Vieux Pont
Le Bourg, 12390 **Map** 11E1
(05 65 64 52 29
FAX 05 65 64 44 32
W www.hotelbelcastel.com
AE, DC, MC, V ● Sun D
€€€€ 🍴 (7) €€€€€

Slumbering on the banks of the river Aveyron, this soporific little hotel is a great place to unwind. First-class service and simple and tasty dishes in the restaurant, such as sea bream with fennel and grapefruit. Spacious, light and airy guestrooms have modern furnishings.

BELLAC
▲ Hôtel les Châtaigniers
Route Poitiers, 87300 **Map** 7D4
(05 55 68 14 82
FAX 05 55 68 77 56
AE, MC, V ● Oct–May: Sun D, Mon, Tue L; Dec **€€** 🍴 (27) €€

Wonderful establishment, deep in the green pastures of Limousin. The menu includes locally reared bison and lamb. Extensive wine list. Guestrooms have a fresh feel and good facilities.

BENEVENT-L'ABBAYE
▲ Hôtel Restaurant du Cèdre
Rue Oiseau, 23210 **Map** 7E4
(05 55 81 59 99
FAX 05 55 81 59 98
MC, V ● Oct–Jan: Sun D, Fri, Sat L; Feb **€€** 🍴 (16) €€€

Fine 18th-century building set in verdant gardens. One of many menu highlights are the langoustines served with poached egg and asparagus.

BLESLE
▲ La Bougnate
Pl Vallat, 43450 **Map** 7F5
(04 71 76 29 30
FAX 04 71 76 29 39
W www.labougnate.com
MC, V
€€ 🍴 (12) €€€

Beyond the cheery creamy-white facade are inventive cuisine, elegant guestrooms, and an on-site gourmet shop.

BOUDES
▲ Le Boudes-la-Vigne
Pl Mairie, 63340 **Map** 7F5
(04 73 96 55 66
FAX 04 73 96 55 55
MC, V ● Mon D, Wed
€€ 🍴 (7) €€

For exquisite Puy-de-Dôme food, head to this charming address in Boudes' attractive square. Menu mainstays include roast catch of the day and a salmon crêpe with goat's cheese. Compact, very good value rooms.

BOUSSAC
● Le Relais Creusois
40 Maison Dieu, route de la Châtre, 23600 **Map** 7E3
(05 55 65 02 20
MC, V
● Sep–May: Tue D, Wed; Jan, Feb
€€€

Located near the handsome Château de Boussac, in a beautiful valley. Dishes like rabbit kidneys with curry and turbot with fruit conserve. Classic regional wines.

BRIOUDE
▲ La Sapinière
Ave Paul Chambriard, 43100 **Map** 8A5
(04 71 50 87 30
FAX 04 71 50 87 39
AE, DC, MC, V ● Sun D, Mon–Sat L, Feb **€€** 🍴 (11) €€€

Great-value, quality dishes at this modern hotel. Guestrooms have fresh, decorative touches and most have fine bathrooms. There are plenty of spaces for relaxation, including an indoor pool, Jacuzzi and tranquil leafy terrace.

BRIOUDE
▲ **Poste et Champanne**
1 bd Docteur Devins, 43100 **Map** 8A5
📞 04 71 50 14 62
FAX 04 71 50 10 55
💳 MC, V ⬤ Sun D, Mon; Feb
🍽 € 🍽 (14) €€
Classic regional specialities are served up to a loyal clientele at this great little eatery. Comfortable accommodation.

BRIVE-LA-GAILLARDE
⬤ **Chez Francis**
61 ave de Paris, 19100 **Map** 7E5
📞 05 55 74 41 72
⬤ Sun, Mon; 2 wks Aug, 1 wk Feb
🍽 €
One of the region's best-value dining experiences. Dishes are kept simple, such as spit-roasted pigeon and lemonade sorbet, and the house wine is good.

BRIVE-LA-GAILLARDE
▲ **La Crémaillère**
53 ave de Paris, 19100 **Map** 7E5
📞 05 55 74 32 47
FAX 05 55 74 00 15
💳 DC, MC ⬤ Sun D, Mon
🍽 €€ 🍽 (9) €€
This archetypal French bistro comes alive at night, when filled with animated conversation and laughter. Guestrooms are comfortable and full of character.

BRIVE-LA-GAILLARDE
⬤ **La Potinière**
6 bd Puyblanc, 19100 **Map** 7E5
📞 05 55 24 06 22
FAX 05 55 24 06 22
💳 AE, DC, MC ⬤ Sep–Jul: Sun D
🍽 €€
The service is impeccable, with waiting staff taking well-concealed delight in second-guessing your every need.

BRIVE-LA-GAILLARDE
⬤ **Périgourdine**
15 ave Alsace-Lorraine, 19100 **Map** 7E5
📞 05 55 24 26 55
FAX 05 55 17 13 22
💳 AE, DC
⬤ Sun D, Mon; 2 wks Sep 🍽 €€

The genteel atmosphere created by the refined decor is reflected in a subtle menu, including the inventive use of chicory (endive), violet, fennel and anise.

BRIVE-LA-GAILLARDE
▲ **Truffe Noire**
22 bd Anatole France, 19100 **Map** 7E5
📞 05 55 92 45 00
FAX 05 55 92 45 13
🌐 www.la-truffe-noire.com
💳 AE, DC, MC, V
🍽 €€ 🍽 (27) €€€
Dating from the late 19th century, this stately hotel has three dining rooms (including one in the cellar) and a terrace for summer dining. Seafood and traditional cuisine are served. Colourful guestrooms have enormous beds.

BUSSEAU-SUR-CREUSE
▲ **Le Viaduc**
9 Busseau Gare, Ahun, 23150 **Map** 7E4
📞 05 55 62 57 20
FAX 05 55 62 55 80
🌐 www.restaurant-leviaduc.com
💳 MC, V ⬤ Sun D, Mon; Jan
🍽 €€ 🍽 (7) €€
This flowery, vine-covered building offers truffle sauces and morels with meat and fish. Guest rooms have a '70s feel.

CALVINET
▲ **Puech at Hôtel Beauséjour**
Le Bourg, 15340 **Map** 11F1
📞 04 71 49 91 68
FAX 04 71 49 98 63
💳 AE, DC, MC, V
⬤ Mon, Oct–Feb: Sun D, Mon, Tue
🍽 €€€ 🍽 (12) €€
A beautifully restored farmhouse. The kitchen produces refined dishes like caramelized duck and chestnut chicken.

CHAISE-DIEU
▲ **L'Echo et Abbaye**
Pl de l'Echo, 43160 **Map** 8A5
📞 04 71 00 00 45
FAX 04 71 00 00 22
💳 AE, DC, MC, V ⬤ Oct–Jun: Wed;
mid-Nov–Apr 🍽 €€€ 🍽 (10) €€
Make a pilgrimage to this eatery in the shadows of a 14th-century abbey. Revered for its rabbit with hazelnuts. Guestrooms have good facilities.

CHAMALIERES
▲ **Le Radio**
43 ave Pierre Curie, 63400 **Map** 7F4
📞 04 73 30 87 83
FAX 04 73 36 42 44
🌐 www.hotel-radio.fr
💳 AE, DC, MC, V
⬤ Sun, Mon L, Sat L; Jan
🍽 €€€ 🍽 (26) €€€
An elegant Art Deco interior. Radio relics dot the mosaic-floored salon. Creative gourmet fare. Cool, contemporary rooms.

CHAMBON-SUR-VOUIEZE
▲ **Les Estonneries**
41 ave Georges Clémenceau, 23170 **Map** 7F3
📞 05 55 82 14 66
FAX 05 55 82 14 11
💳 MC, V 🍽 € 🍽 (14) €€
Century-old pine trees abound in the tranquil gardens. Culinary offerings include freshwater fish such as perch and pike-perch. Rooms are traditional.

CHAMPS-SUR-TARENTAINE
▲ **Auberge du Vieux Chêne**
34 route des Lacs, 15270 **Map** 7F5
📞 04 71 78 71 64
FAX 04 71 78 70 88
💳 AE, DC, MC ⬤ Sun D, Mon;
Nov–Mar 🍽 €€ 🍽 (15) €€€
A beautiful dining terrace and a creative kitchen. Dishes include trout with bacon and Puy lentils, and caramelized duck. Rooms have old-world charm.

CHATEAUNEUF-DE-RANDON
▲ **Hôtel de la Poste**
L'Habitarelle, 1.5km (1 mile) south on D988, 48170 **Map** 12A1
📞 04 66 47 90 05
FAX 04 66 47 91 41
💳 MC, V ⬤ Fri D, Sat L; last wk Dec,
first 3 wks Jan 🍽 € 🍽 (16) €€
A reliable hotel in a renovated barn near the Parc National des Cévennes. Dishes include local trout and nougat ice cream served with Lozère honey. Rooms can be a little dark and tired.

CHENERAILLES
▲ **Le Coq d'Or**
7 pl Champ de Foire, 23130 **Map** 7E4
📞 05 55 62 30 83

FAX 05 55 62 95 18

DC, MC, V ● Sun D, Mon, Wed D;
2 wks Jan, last wk Jun, 2 wks Sep
11 €€ ◇ (5) €€

*Flavoursome favourites include a feuilleté
with potatoes and local cheese, and foie
gras with rhubarb. Basic bedrooms.*

CHEVAGNES
● **Le Goûts des Choses**
RN12, 03230 **Map** 8A3

04 70 43 11 12
FAX 04 70 43 17 88

AE, DC, MC, V ● Sun D, Wed
11 €€

*Everything on your plate has a rich and
distinct taste, which is made that much
better when eaten on the terrace.*

CHIRAC
▲ **Les Violes**
Les Violes, 7.5km (5 miles) east of
Chirac, 48100 **Map** 12A1

04 66 32 77 66
MC, V ● Tue **11** € ◇ (6) €€
*Experience the Massif Central rural idyll
at this wonderful farmhouse. Tuck into
tender lamb from local Lozère Elovel and
wash it down with a bottle of St-Leger
or Meissonnier. Guestrooms are basic.*

CLERMONT-FERRAND
● **Anglard Gérard**
17 rue Lamartine, 63000 **Map** 7F4

04 73 93 52 25
FAX 04 73 93 29 25

AE, MC, V ● Sun, Sat; 2 wks Aug
11 €€€

*The salubrious dining room has a whiff
of the 1940s, or dine in the characterful
courtyard. Stylish Clermontois cuisine
includes the fried duck liver with cabbage.*

CLERMONT-FERRAND
● **Brasserie Daniele Bath**
6 pl St-Pierre, 63000 **Map** 7F4

04 73 31 23 22
FAX 04 73 31 08 33

DC, MC, V ● Sun, Mon; school
holidays in Feb **11** €€

*Informal bistro ambience makes for
extra-relaxing dining. Highlights include
a scallop and black truffle tart, and a
delicious rhubarb dessert. Lots of good-
value young bottles on the wine list.*

CLERMONT-FERRAND
● **Clavé**
12 rue St-Adjutor, 63000 **Map** 7F4

04 73 36 46 30
FAX 04 73 31 30 74

AE, MC, V ● Sun; late Aug–early
Sep **11** €€€

*A Clermentois institution in the elegant
Quartier Juridique. Try the langoustines
with green beans and tomatoes.*

CLERMONT-FERRAND
● **Emmanuel Hodencq**
6 pl St-Pierre, 63000 **Map** 7F4

04 73 31 23 23
FAX 04 73 31 36 00

www.hodencq.com

AE, DC, MC, V ● Sun, Mon
11 €€€€

*Trademark dishes include truffle risotto
and a crunchy chocolate dessert with
wild strawberries. Book a table.*

CLERMONT-FERRAND
● **Le Cinq Claire**
5 rue Ste-Claire, 63000 **Map** 7F4

04 73 37 10 31
FAX 04 73 36 49 12

MC, V ● Sun, Mon; 2nd half Feb,
Aug **11** €€

*An elegant interior at a popular address.
Exquisite, creative fare includes roast
sea bream with a hint of curry, and
smooth chocolate and morello cherry
gateau served with pistachio ice cream.*

CLERMONT-FERRAND
▲ **Le St-Emilion at Inter Hôtel
République**
97 ave de la République, 63100 **Map** 7F4

04 73 91 92 92
FAX 04 73 90 21 88

AE, DC, MC, V ● Sun, Sat L
11 €€ ◇ (55) €€

*Comfortable accommodation and
superb-value dining. Renowned for
game. Menu highlights include pig's
trotter stew with local cheese.*

CLERMONT-FERRAND
● **Le Terroir**
16 rue de la Préfecture, 63000 **Map** 7F4

04 73 37 47 13

AE, MC, V
● Sun, Mon D;

1st wk Jun, late Oct–early Nov, late
Dec–early Mar **11** €

*Tuck into pôtée auvergnate (p247) and
tripe on the terrace or in the intimate
dining room. Wines include reds like
Madargue, Châteaugay and Boudes.*

COMMENTRY
● **Michel Rubod**
47 rue Jean Jacques Rousseau, 03600
Map 7F3

04 70 64 45 31
FAX 04 70 64 33 17

AE, DC, MC, V

● Sun D, Mon; 3 wks Aug, Christmas
11 €€€€

*A market-inspired menu, always with a
balanced choice, typically including a
light fish dish and good desserts.*

COMPREIGNAC
● **Le Moulin de Margnac**
Margnac, 6km (4 miles) east on D5,
87140 **Map** 7D4

05 55 71 30 70
FAX 05 55 71 31 95

MC, V ● Sun D **11** €

*The adventurous menu includes frogs'
legs cooked in aniseed. In winter, crêpes
are cooked in the old fireplace.*

CONQUES
▲ **Domaine de Cambelong**
Le Moulin, 12320 **Map** 11F1

05 65 72 84 77
FAX 05 65 72 83 91

www.moulindecambelong.com

AE, DC, MC, V ● Tue, Wed;
Nov–early Jan

11 €€€€ ◇ (10) €€€€

*A lovingly renovated mill on the banks of
the River Dourdou, with a pool and
sunny dining terrace. Old-fashioned,
charming guestrooms.*

CRAPONNE-SUR-ARZON
▲ **Moulin de Mistou**
Pontempeyrat, 43500 **Map** 8A5

04 77 50 62 46
FAX 04 77 50 66 70

AE, DC, MC, V ● Mon–Sat L;
late Oct–late Apr

11 €€€ ◇ (14) €€€€

*In this former watermill amid green
pastures on the banks of River Ance,*

you'll find regional fare with a dash of Provençal colour. Highlights include the trout pot-au-feu with salted crayfish. The bedrooms vary in size and decor.

CROZANT
● **Auberge de la Vallée**
Le Bourg, village centre, 23160 **Map** 7E3
📞 05 55 89 80 03
FAX 05 55 89 83 22
🗭 DC, MC, V
⬤ Mon D, Sep–Jun: Tue; Jan 🍽 €
An intimate dining room. Traditional fare is served by staff dressed in the local Marchois costumes. For the adventurous gourmet there are dishes like snail millefeuille, and rabbit with mushrooms.

CROZANT
▲ **Hôtel du Lac**
Le Pont de Crozant, 23160 **Map** 7E3
📞 05 55 89 81 96
🗭 MC, V ⬤ Sun D, Mon, Wed; Feb
🍽 €€ 🍴 (9) €€
Set beside a serene lake, near the Crozant archaeological sites and bridle-ways. Menu mainstays include foie gras, and quails with vinaigrette. Basic rooms.

DURTOL
● **Bernard Andrieux**
Route Baraque, 63830 **Map** 7F4
📞 04 73 19 25 00
FAX 04 73 19 25 04
@ andrieuxBe@wanadoo.fr
🗭 AE, DC, MC, V ⬤ Sun D, Mon, Sat L; early May, late Jul–late Aug
🍽 €€€
This elegant, renowned restaurant, with its Art Nouveau decorative flourishes, lies near the famous Vulcania exhibition. Highlights include wild boar sausages cooked with woodland mushrooms and Cognac, plus a suitable wine list.

FLORAC
▲ **La Lozerette**
Cocurès, 4km (2.5 miles) east on D998, 48400 **Map** 12A1
📞 04 66 45 06 04
FAX 04 66 45 12 93
🗭 DC, MC, V ⬤ Tue, Jul–Sep: Wed L
🍽 €€ 🍴 (21) €€
Charming environment and first-class food. Try the flavoursome mushroom

risotto or Aubrac beef washed down by some Minervois. Traditional rooms.

FLORAC
● **La Source du Pécher**
Rue Remuret, 48400 **Map** 12A1
📞 04 66 45 03 01
FAX 04 66 45 28 82
⬤ Sep–Jun: Wed; Easter 🍽 €€
Fantastic little eatery with ever-changing fish and meat dishes, including Aveyron duck with honey. Regional wine list.

FONTANGES
▲ **Auberge de l'Aspre**
Le Bourg, 15140 **Map** 7F5
📞 04 71 40 75 76
FAX 04 71 40 75 27
🖳 www.auberge-aspre.com
🗭 AE, DC, MC, V ⬤ Oct–May: Sun–Tue; 1st wk Feb, 1st wk Dec
🍽 €€€ 🍴 (8) €€€
A cheerful farmhouse where brightly coloured rooms, striking views and a lovely pool create a happy atmosphere. Try the Salers beef or milk-fed veal.

GLENIC
▲ **Moulin Noyé**
Route de Châtre (D940), 23380 **Map** 7E3
📞 05 55 52 81 44
FAX 05 55 52 81 94
🗭 MC, V ⬤ May–Aug: Sun D; 3 wks Jan, 2 wks Oct 🍽 €€ 🍴 (18) €€€
Idyllic spot with fabulous views of the luxuriant Gorges de la Creuse. Expect foie gras, Limousin beef, and quality fish. Guestrooms have flowery touches.

GOUZON
▲ **Hostellerie du Lion d'Or**
Route Montluçon, 23230 **Map** 7E3
📞 05 55 62 28 54
FAX 05 55 62 21 63
🗭 MC, V ⬤ Oct–Mar: Sun D, Fri D
🍽 € 🍴 (12) €€
Traditional cuisine at an intimate village establishment. Tuck into a hearty plateful of duck thighs or trout with almonds. Guestrooms vary in size – all have country-style fabrics and furnishings.

GUERET
● **Le Coq en Pate**
2 rue Pommeil, 23000 **Map** 7E3

📞 05 55 41 43 43
FAX 05 55 41 43 42
🗭 MC, V ⬤ Mon D 🍽 €€€
In an elegant building, find traditional dishes with innovative twists: goat's cheese with leek and walnuts, and lobster flambéed with whisky.

GUERET
● **Les Touristes**
1 pl Mairie, Ste-Feyre, 23000 **Map** 7E3
📞 05 55 80 00 07
🗭 MC, V ⬤ Sun D, Mon, Wed
🍽 €€
Robust yet charming 19th-century building with light-filled dining rooms and wonderful conservatories. Savour Limousin beef with foie gras, and perch with leek and cumin.

ISPAGNAC
● **Le Lys**
Molines, 1.5km (1 mile) west on D907, 48320 **Map** 12A1
📞 04 66 44 23 56
⬤ Oct–early Apr 🍽 €€
Imaginative regional recipes in a superb little auberge. Wide choice, including grilled mullet with a vegetable ragout and pastis-infused buttery sauce.

ISSOIRE
▲ **Le Parc**
2 ave Gare, 63500 **Map** 7F4
📞 04 73 89 23 85
🖳 www.leparc-hotel-issoire.com
🗭 DC, MC, V ⬤ Sat L
🍽 €€ 🍴 (7) €€
Beyond the modern concrete façade is a great value eatery. Expect regional cuisine like beef with green peppers. Traditional guestrooms.

LA MALENE
▲ **Château la Caze**
Route Gorges du Tarn, 48210 **Map** 12A1
📞 04 66 48 51 01
FAX 04 66 48 55 75
🗭 AE, DC, MC, V ⬤ Wed L, Thu L; Nov–Mar 🍽 €€€ 🍴 (10) €€€
A very special 15th-century fairytale château on the banks of the River Tarn. Wonderfully prepared fish and meat dishes dominate. Warm and stylish guestrooms and suites.

● Restaurant ■ Hotel ▲ Hotel / Restaurant

LA MALENE

▲ **Manoir de Montesquiou**

La Malène, 48210 **Map** 12A1

📞 04 66 48 51 12

📠 04 66 48 50 47

🖥 www.manoir-montesquiou.com

✉ MC, V ⬤ late Oct–Apr

🍴 €€ 🍽 (12) €€€

The 15th-century manor is an evocative setting for a sophisticated experience. Feast on succulent lamb with subtle spices and the nougat cream with a hot forest-fruit sauce. Elegant bedrooms.

LA ROCHE-L'ABEILLE

▲ **Moulin de la Gorce**

Moulin de la Gorce, 87800 **Map** 7D4

📞 05 55 00 70 66

📠 05 55 00 76 57

✉ AE, DC, MC, V ⬤ Mon L, Tue L, Wed L; early Nov–early Apr

🍴 €€€ 🍽 (9) €€€

This 16th-century watermill looks onto a serene stretch of water – bring your fishing rod but ask for permission to use it. For dessert, try one of their fabulous crêpes filled with vanilla-infused butter and fruit sorbet. Cheery guestrooms.

LA SOUTERRAINE

▲ **La Porte St-Jean**

2 rue Bains, 23300 **Map** 7E3

📞 05 55 63 90 00

📠 05 55 63 77 27

✉ AE, DC, MC, V ⬤ Jan–May

🍴 €€ 🍽 (37) €€

Great hotel with bags of rustic character and some very decent food, including wild mushrooms and juicy red fruits, and Limousin beef served with peppers.

LAGUIOLE

▲ **Michel Bras**

Route de L'Aubrac, 12210 **Map** 11F1

📞 05 65 51 18 20

📠 05 65 48 47 02

🖥 www.michel-bras.com

✉ AE, DC, MC, V ⬤ Mon, Sep–May: Wed L & Thu L

🍴 €€€€€ 🍽 (15) €€€€

Geometric interiors and cutting-edge design place this hotel firmly in the 21st century. Similarly, the gourmet kitchen pushes all the boundaries of taste, texture, aroma and presentation.

LAGUIOLE

▲ **Relais de Laguiole**

Espace les Cayres, 12210 **Map** 11F1

📞 05 65 54 19 66

📠 05 65 54 19 49

🖥 www.relais-laguiole.com

✉ AE, DC, MC, V ⬤ Sep–Jun: Mon

🍴 € 🍽 (33) €€€

Guestrooms are bright and breezy; dinner is a chance to sample a local culinary speciality, aligot (p247).

LANGEAC

▲ **Auberge de l'Ile d'Amour**

Ile d'Amour, 43300 **Map** 8A5

📞 04 71 77 00 11

✉ MC, V ⬤ Oct–May: Sun D, Mon, Sat, Jun–Sep Mon L, Tue L; Christmas

🍴 €€ 🍽 (10) €€€

Relaxing inn with a serene terrace overlooking the water. Try one of their superb beef dishes. Spacious, comfortable rooms.

LE BLEYMARD

▲ **La Remise**

Le Bourg, village centre, 48190 **Map** 12A1

📞 04 66 48 65 80

📠 04 66 48 63 70

🖥 www.hotel-laremise.com

✉ MC, V ⬤ Mon D; last wk Dec, first 3 wks Jan 🍴 € 🍽 (20) €€

Old coaching inn near the Parc National des Cévennes. Dine on trout with almonds and truffles in the wooden-beamed dining room. Small guestrooms.

LE MONT-DORE

▲ **Le Panorama**

27 ave Libération, 63240 **Map** 7F4

📞 04 73 65 11 12

📠 04 73 65 20 80

✉ MC, V ⬤ early Mar–early May, early Oct–late Dec

🍴 €€€ 🍽 (39) €€€

Tranquil hotel nestled on verdant slopes of the Volcans d'Auvergne national park. Guestrooms are rather plain but cosy – many have stunning views. Traditional cuisine is served. There's an indoor pool and wonderful gardens.

LE PUY-EN-VELAY

● **Lapierre**

6 rue Capucins, 43000 **Map** 8A5

📞 04 71 09 08 44

✉ MC, V

⬤ Sun, Sat; mid-Dec–Jan 🍴 €€

Chef Estelle Thivillier adds some subtle feminine touches to the excellent fare served at this smoke-free zone. Notable dishes include veal and liver, and very inventive savoury mousses.

LE PUY-EN-VELAY

● **Tournayre**

12 rue Chénebouterie, 43000 **Map** 8A5

📞 04 71 09 58 94

📠 04 71 02 68 38

🖥 www.restaurant-tournayre.com

✉ MC, V ⬤ Sun D, Mon; Jan

🍴 €€€

An evocative 16th-century gothic building in the medieval quarter. Feast on lamb, beef, and expertly executed seafood dishes. There's a large cheese platter.

LEZOUX

▲ **Les Voyageurs**

2 pl Mairie, 63190 **Map** 8A4

📞 04 73 73 10 49

✉ MC, V ⬤ Fri D; Nov–May: Sun D, Mon; early Jan, late Aug–mid-Sep

🍴 €€ 🍽 (9) €€

Classic regional specialities served in copious amounts in a large, bright dining room. Try goose with a soft and spicy Auvergne cheese. Tidy guestrooms.

LIMOGES

● **Amphitryon**

26 rue Boucherie, 87000 **Map** 7D4

📞 05 55 33 36 39

📠 05 55 32 98 50

✉ DC, MC, V ⬤ Sun, Mon L, Sat L; 3 wks Aug, 1 wk Feb, 1 wk Apr 🍴 €€€

This ex-butcher's in the heart of old Limoges has been transformed into a contemporary dining space with a warm ambience. Dishes include asparagus and langoustines with apple vinaigrette, and roast veal with a coffee sauce.

LIMOGES

● **Chez Alphonse**

5 pl Motte, 87000 **Map** 7D4

📞 05 55 34 34 14

✉ MC, V ⬤ Sun, Mon D 🍴 €

Superb-value fare in a relaxed setting harking back to those dark-wood bistro

days. They do a fine range of savoury and sweet crêpes, hearty portions of meat and fish such as red mullet.

LIMOGES
● **Les Petits Ventres**

20 rue Boucherie, 87000 **Map** 7D4

℃ 05 55 34 22 90

FAX 05 55 32 41 04

AE, DC, MC, V ● Sun, Mon; 2 wks May, 2 wks Sep, 1 wk Jan ♦ €€

This fascinating 15th-century building lies in Limoges' old market quarter. Highlights include stuffed Provençal-style peppers, grilled salmon with potato purée, and crème brûlée with melon.

LIMOGES
● **L'Escapade du Gourmet**

5 rue 71ème Mobiles, 87000 **Map** 7D4

℃ 05 55 32 40 26

FAX 05 55 32 11 95

AE, DC, MC, V

● Sun D, Mon, Sat L; Aug

♦ €€€

Panache and quality ooze from every pore of this Belle Epoque brasserie. Sophisticated cuisine to match the Art Deco flourishes: duck liver infused with a hint of truffles; fine pork and veal.

LIMOGES
● **Philippe Redon**

3 rue d'Aguesseau, 87000 **Map** 7D4

℃ 05 55 34 66 22

FAX 05 55 34 18 05

DC, MC, V

● Sun, Mon L, Sat L; 1 wk Nov

♦ €€€

A spacious restaurant near the old marketplace. Look out for lobster in salted butter, millefeuille with savoury fillings, and some rather fine desserts.

LUZILLAT
● **Auberge de Vendègre**

Vendègre, 63350 **Map** 8A4

℃ 04 73 68 63 24

V ● Mon, Tue ♦ €€

Excellent-value fare make this auberge well worth visiting. Book a table in the cosy dining room or outside under a large canopy overlooking the lush garden. Dishes include canard à l'orange and Salers rib steak.

MAGNAC-BOURG
▲ **Fusade at Hôtel des Voyageurs**

16 RN20, 87380 **Map** 7D4

℃ 05 55 00 80 36

FAX 05 55 00 56 37

MC, V ● Sep–Jun: Sun D, Tue D, Sat; 2 wks Jan, 2 wks Jun, 3 wks Sep ♦ €€ ♦ (7) €€

Within the old walls loyal patrons sip glasses of the region's bold-tasting wines between bites of beautifully prepared Limousin beef.

MAGNAC-LAVAL
● **La Ferme du Logis**

Thibarderie, 87190 **Map** 7D3

℃ 05 55 68 57 23

FAX 05 55 68 52 80

W www.resa-france.com

DC, MC, V ● Sun D, mid-Sep–mid-May: Mon; Jan–mid-Feb

♦ €€

Outstanding dishes include foie gras with apples, and grilled Limousin beef. Delicious regional cheeses include Bleu d'Auvergne and Cantal.

MALEMORT-SUR-CORREZE
▲ **Auberge du Vieux Chênes**

31 ave Honoré de Balzac, 19360 **Map** 7E5

℃ 05 55 24 13 55

FAX 05 55 24 56 82

AE, DC, MC, V ● Sun

♦ €€ ♦ (12) €€

On the road to Aurillac, this hotel is a favourite with travellers. Guestrooms are more than adequate, and the restaurant is worth the journey in its own right. Foie gras is the speciality, alongside several grilled meats such as veal and beef.

MARVEJOLS
● **Viz Club**

Route Nord, 48100 **Map** 12A1

℃ 04 66 32 17 69

MC, V ● Sun D; Jan ♦ €€

Make a beeline for this attractive eatery set in flowery gardens. Enjoy a fine apéritif and try the trademark perch cooked in thyme and lemon.

MAURIAC
▲ **Voyageurs**

Pl de la Poste, 15200 **Map** 7E5

℃ 04 71 68 01 01

FAX 04 71 68 01 56

AE, DC, MC

● Sun, Mon; mid-Dec–mid-Jan

♦ € ♦ (19) €€

Cheery while maintaining a distinctly romantic air. The menu covers all the inland favourites, such as perch beurre blanc, and veal with mushrooms. Simple, bright guestrooms.

MAZAYES
▲ **Auberge de Mazayes**

Mazayes Basses, 63230 **Map** 7F4

℃ 04 73 88 93 30

FAX 04 73 88 93 80

MC, V ● Tue L; Oct–May: Mon; mid-Dec–late Jan ♦ ♦ (15) €€

Feast on superb local cuisine while sipping some very fine regional wine at this old farmhouse deep in Auvergne's volcano country. Cosy guestrooms have names reflecting their individual decor.

MEYRUEIS
▲ **Le Mont-Aigoual**

34 quai de la Barrière, 48150 **Map** 12A2

℃ 04 66 45 65 61

FAX 04 66 45 64 25

W www.hotel-mont-aigoual.com

AE, DC, MC, V ● mid-Dec–mid-Mar ♦ €€ ♦ (30) €€

Beyond the attractive façade with its large windows and director-style seating outside, you'll find an elegant dining room and some decent if unspectacular accommodation. Try the succulent lamb and subtly prepared fish dishes.

MEYSSAC
▲ **Le Relais du Quercy**

Ave de Quercy, 19500 **Map** 7E5

℃ 05 55 25 40 31

FAX 05 55 25 36 22

AE, DC, MC, V ● mid-Nov–mid-Dec ♦ €€ ♦ (14) €€

From the cosy rooms, squeezed into the attic, to the lively local bar, this hotel has bags of character and a deservedly loyal clientele. Expect favourites such as trout with wild mushrooms, and duck confit.

MILLAU
● **Auberge de la Borie Blanque**

La Borie Blanque, route de St-Germain,

● Restaurant   ■ Hotel   ▲ Hotel / Restaurant

12100 **Map** 11F2

C 05 65 60 85 88

E DC ● Wed **II** €€€

A no-nonsense restaurant that's popular with locals and visitors. Favourites include rib steak stuffed with juniper, fragrant lamb encrusted with herbs, and a slow-cooked gâteau à la broche (spit-roasted cake) with quince brandy.

MILLAU
▲ Hotel International

1 pl de la Tine, 12100 **Map** 11F2

C 05 65 59 29 00

FAX 05 65 59 29 01

E AE, DC, MC, V ● Sun, Sat (brasserie only)

II €€€€ ● (102) €€

The hotel's concrete façade may lack architectural finesse, but inside it's comfortable, and the service impeccable.

MILLAU
▲ La Musardière

34 ave de la République, 12100 **Map** 11F2

C 05 65 60 20 63

FAX 05 65 59 78 13

E DC, MC, V ● Nov, Feb

II €€€ ● (14) €€€€

Buried in the countryside, this Is a charming château. Guestrooms have parquet flooring. Enjoy a breakfast of fouace (orange-flower cake), and a din-ner of Charolais beef with mustard.

MILLAU
● La Table d'Albanie

23 rue du Pont de Fer, 12100 **Map** 11F2

C 05 65 59 16 87

FAX 05 65 59 44 92

E AE, DC, MC, V ● Tue D, Wed

II €€

Tasty regional favourites such as seared beef with garlic and haricot beans, and bitter chocolate fruit fondue.

MONTLUCON
▲ Château St-Jean

Parc St-Jean, 03100 **Map** 7F3

C 04 70 02 71 71

FAX 04 70 02 71 70

W www.chateaustjean.net

E AE, DC, MC, V

II €€€€ ● (20) €€€

Something to appeal to everyone: serenity, exclusivity, great food and bags of history. The restaurant occupies the former chapel of the Knights of St John, and the exquisite gourmet cuisine is appropriately heavenly. Guestrooms are elegant and spacious.

MONTLUCON
▲ Le Grenier à Sel

10 rue Ste-Anne, pl des Toiles, 03100 **Map** 7F3

C 04 70 05 53 79

FAX 04 70 05 87 91

W www.legrenierasel.com

E AE, DC, MC, V ● Sun D, Sep–Jun: Mon & Tue L; last 2 wks Oct

II €€€ ● (7) €€€€

Despite its popularity, much of this 16th-century château's allure lies in its discretion. Guestrooms are well furnished with large bathrooms. Try sole with duck foie gras, langoustines with a peanut sauce, and Charolais beef.

MONTLUCON
● Le St Trop'

15 rue Grande, 03100 **Map** 7F3

C 04 70 05 77 95

E DC, MC, V

● Mon, Sat L; 1 wk Nov

II €€

The menu has a strong seafood bias, with dishes including catfish with crab and mussels with lentils. The interior is sleek, and the service slick.

MORTEMART
▲ Le Relais

1 pl Royale, 87330 **Map** 7D4

C 05 55 68 12 09

E MC, V ● Tue, mid-Jul–Sep: Wed

II €€ ● (5) €€

Generous portions of traditional Haute-Vienne specialities are served to the loyal clientele. Try the excellent scallops with local ceps and pigeon in pastry with foie gras. Delightful rooms have wood beams and light colour schemes.

MOUDEYRES
▲ Le Pré Bossu

Le Bourg, 43150 **Map** 8A5

C 04 71 05 10 70

FAX 04 71 05 10 21

W www.leprebossu.fr.fm

E AE, DC, MC, V ● Nov–mid-Apr

II €€€ ● (10) €€€€

An old thatched cottage with access to the luxuriant Jardin du Curé where vegetables and herbs are grown for use in dishes like crayfish with artichokes. Vegetarians even have their own menu – a rare treat in France! Elegance and rusticity meet in the dining room; guestrooms offer warmth and luxury.

MOULINS
● Cours

36 cours Jean Jaurés, 03000 **Map** 8A3

C 04 70 44 25 66

FAX 04 70 20 58 45

E AE, DC, MC, V ● Wed; 2 wks Feb, 3 wks Jul **II** €€€

The chef experiments with unusual flavours, such as rabbit cooked in Chardonnay, and scallops with apple.

MOULINS
▲ Hôtel du Paris Jacquemart

21 rue de Paris, 03000 **Map** 8A3

C 04 70 44 00 58

FAX 04 70 34 05 39

W www.hoteldeparis-moulins.com

E AE, DC, MC, V ● Sun D, Mon, Sat L; 2 wks Jan, 3 wks Aug

II €€€ ● (27) €€€

Guestrooms are quite large and the restaurant serves juicy langoustines – a pleasant change so far inland.

MOULINS
● La Toquée

97 rue Allier, 03000 **Map** 8A3

C 04 70 35 01 60

E DC, MC ● Sun, Mon, Sat L; first wk Jan **II** €€€

This lively restaurant may be small, but their contemporary approach to local cuisine packs a culinary punch.

MOULINS
▲ Le Chalet

Coulandon, 03000 **Map** 8A3

C 04 70 46 00 66

FAX 04 70 44 07 09

E AE, DC, MC, V ● Dec–Jan

II €€€ ● (28) €€

Surrounded by flower-filled gardens, and with a pool, this is a great place to

unwind. The rooms are old fashioned, but forgivably so. Good food, such as foie gras and fillets of locally caught fish, plus good wine.

MURAT

● **Jarrousset**

Route Clermont-Ferrand, 15300 **Map** 7F5

📞 04 71 20 10 69

FAX 04 71 20 15 26

💳 DC, MC ⬤ Mon, Sep–Jun: Tue; mid-Nov–mid-Jan 🍴 €€

Just east of Murat, this small country house takes great pride in the reputation of its cooking. Specialities include roast pigeon and salmon carpaccio.

MUR-DE-BARREZ

▲ **Auberge du Barrez**

Ave du Carladez, 12600 **Map** 11F1

📞 05 65 66 00 76

FAX 05 65 66 07 98

🌐 www.aubergedubarrez.com

💳 AE, DC, MC, V ⬤ Sun

🍴 €€ 🍷 (18) €€

During the summer months evenings are spent on the terrace, choosing from an inventive menu that includes chou farci (p246) and duck with pears. Rooms are large and bright if dated.

NANTIAT

● **Le Relais des Etangs**

4 pl Mothe, 87140 **Map** 7D4

📞 05 55 53 51 50

FAX 05 55 53 51 50

💳 MC, V ⬤ Sun D, Mon 🍴 €€

Take a seat on the lovely terrace or in the intimate dining room of this superb eatery. Lip-smackingly good Limousin favourites include lamb with ceps and vanilla meringue rings with raspberries.

NIEUL

▲ **La Chapelle St-Martin**

33 St-Martin du Fault, 87510 **Map** 7D4

📞 05 55 75 80 17

FAX 05 55 75 89 50

💳 AE, DC, MC, V ⬤ Sun D, Mon, Tue D; Jan–Feb 🍴 €€€€ 🍷 (13) €€€€

An elegant dining room is the setting for exquisite offerings. One of the trademark dishes is fried Limousin beef with shallots. Lovely guestrooms and flats.

NOUZERINES

▲ **La Bonne Auberge**

1 rue Lelas, Le Bourg, 23600 **Map** 7E3

📞 05 55 82 01 18

💳 MC, V ⬤ Sun D, Mon; 3 wks Jan–Feb, 2 wks Oct 🍴 €€ 🍷 (7) €

Cosy little auberge just outside Boussac. Tuck into roast langoustines followed by figs filled with quinces. Over 70 different wines to choose from. Bedrooms are very clean and a fair snip at the price.

OLEMPS

▲ **Les Peyrières**

22 rue Peyrières, 12510 **Map** 11F1

📞 05 65 68 20 52

FAX 05 65 68 47 88

🌐 www.hotel-les-peyrieres.com

💳 AE, DC, MC, V ⬤ Sun D, Mon

🍴 €€ 🍷 (50) €€

A modern villa with a relaxed air. While away the afternoons by the pool. House specialities include beef carpaccio and sweet roasted pigeon.

ONET LE CHATEAU

▲ **Hostellerie de Fontanges**

Rue de Conques et de Marcillac, 12850 **Map** 11F1

📞 05 65 77 76 00

FAX 05 65 42 82 29

🌐 www.hostellerie-fontanges.com

💳 AE, DC, MC, V ⬤ Sun D, Sat L

🍴 €€ 🍷 (43) €€€

This beautiful 14th-century château watches over the city of Rodez. Rooms have a simple elegance and great views of the Aveyron hills; dining is a much grander affair. Favourite local dishes, such as foie gras and l'Aubrac beef, are served beneath huge chandeliers.

PANAZOL

● **Domaine de la Gresle**

La Gresle, 87350 **Map** 7D4

📞 05 55 06 27 82

FAX 05 55 06 38 10

🌐 www.domainedelagresle.com

💳 AE, MC, V ⬤ Oct–Jun: Sun D

🍴 €€

Simple country cooking in a sprawling old estate building just outside Limoges. Soak up the aristocratic air of the dining room while enjoying mullet and scallop dishes and feuilleté specialities.

PERIGNAT-LES-SARLIEVE

■ **Hostellerie St-Martin**

Allée de Bonneval, 63170 **Map** 7F4

📞 04 73 79 81 00

FAX 04 73 79 81 01

🌐 www.hostellerie-st-martin.com

💳 AE, DC, MC, V 🍷 (34) €€€€

This 16th-century ecclesiastical building once belonged to the Bourbons and Medici. Belle Epoque touches in the dining room, where superb Auvergne cuisine is served. Warm rooms with superb facilities. The wonderful grounds have a pool and tennis court.

PIERRE-BUFFIERE

▲ **La Providence**

Pl Adeline, 87260 **Map** 7D4

📞 05 55 00 60 16

FAX 05 55 00 98 69

💳 MC, V ⬤ mid-Oct–Easter: Sun D; early Jan–early Feb

🍴 €€€ 🍷 (14) €€

A great little place in the tranquil village of Pierre Buffiere near the River Briance. Seafood connoisseurs are well catered for – ask about the catch of the day. Decent wine list. Bright guestrooms.

PONT-DU-CHATEAU

● **Auberge du Pont**

70 ave du Dr Besserve, 63430 **Map** 7A4

📞 04 73 83 00 36

FAX 04 73 83 36 71

💳 MC, V ⬤ Sun D, Sat L; 2 wks at end of school summer holidays 🍴 €€

Contemporary dining rooms with delights such as grilled meats with bilberries and herbs, fried fish, frogs' legs with parsley, and a chocolate cinnamon gateau.

PONTGIBAUD

▲ **Hôtel de la Poste**

Pl de la République, 63230 **Map** 7F4

📞 04 73 88 70 02

FAX 04 73 88 79 74

💳 AE, MC, V ⬤ Sun D, Mon, Oct–Jun: Tue; Jan–Feb, 2 wks Oct

🍴 €€ 🍷 (9) €€

A riverside hotel in the stunning Parc des Volcans. Local Auvergne produce is used. Expect tasty fish and meat dishes, including trout, rabbit and lamb, and savoury mousses. Guestrooms are compact and simply furnished.

● Restaurant ■ Hotel ▲ Hotel / Restaurant

RIOM-ES-MONTAGNES

▲ **Le Saint-Georges**
5 rue Capitaine Chevalier, 15400
Map 7F5
📞 04 71 78 00 15
FAX 04 71 78 24 37
🖥 www.hotel-saint-georges.com
💳 AE, DC, MC, V ● Sun D; Nov
🍴 € 🛏 (14) €€

*A handsome building with smart rooms.
The menu stars pork with Puy lentils
and crème brûlée with myrtle soufflé.*

RODEZ

● **Goûts et Couleurs**
38 rue de Bonald, 12000 **Map** 11F1
📞 05 65 42 75 10
FAX 05 65 42 75 10
💳 AE, DC, MC, V ● Mon; Jan,
Apr–mid-May, 2nd half Jul 🍴 €€€

*Nouvelle cuisine like figs stuffed with foie
gras served with a pumpkin mousse,
and pigeon with peanuts and citrus.*

RODEZ

● **Le Kiosque**
Ave Victor Hugo, jardin publique, 12000
Map 11F1
📞 05 65 68 56 21
💳 AE, DC, MC, V ● Sun D 🍴 €€

*Overlooking the public gardens, this is a
great spot for people-watching. The
enormous seafood platters, salads and
roasted fish are all fresh and delightful.*

RODEZ

● **Les Jardins de L'Acropolis**
Rue d'Athènes, 12000 **Map** 11F1
📞 05 65 68 40 07
FAX 05 65 68 40 67
💳 DC, MC, V ● Sun D, Mon; Aug
🍴 €€€

*Light tempuras and scallops enlivened
by Chinese pepper sit alongside more
familiar local dishes, and there's a good
selection of accompanying wines.*

RODEZ

● **Restaurant Le Saint Amans**
12 rue Madeleine, 12000 **Map** 11F1
📞 05 65 68 03 18
● Sun D, Mon; Mar
🍴 €€

*Named after the patron saint of hoteliers.
The intimate atmosphere and subdued*

*lighting make it a perfect spot for a
romantic meal. Lamb with Roquefort,
and the chocolate millefeuille with
Crème-de-Menthe sauce recommended.*

RODEZ

■ **Tour Maje**
Bd Gally, 12000 **Map** 11F1
📞 05 65 68 34 68
FAX 05 65 68 27 56
🖥 www.hotel-tour-maje.com
💳 AE, DC, MC, V ● Hotel: mid-
Dec–mid-Jan 🛏 (42) €€€€

*This hotel's 14th-century tower forms
part of the city's ramparts. Within walking
distance of the best restaurants and
bars. Warmly decorated guestrooms.*

ROMAGNAT

● **Le Montrognon**
RN89, Saulzet-le-Chaud, 63540 **Map** 7F4
📞 04 73 61 30 51
FAX 04 73 61 55 40
🖥 www.le-montrognon.com
💳 DC, MC, V ● Sun D, Mon; Jan, 2
wks Aug 🍴 €€

*Handsome building near the Plateau de
Gergovie offering excellent Auvergne
fare. Highlights include mountain trout
with green lentils and roast lamb.*

ROYAT

▲ **Belle Meunière**
25 ave Vallée, 63130 **Map** 7F4
📞 04 73 35 80 17
FAX 04 73 29 95 18
🖥 www.la-belle-meuniere.com
💳 DC, MC, V ● Sun D, Mon, Sat L;
mid-Feb–early Mar, late Oct–late Nov
🍴 €€€ 🛏 (7) €€

*Classic Auvergne specialities are expertly
prepared by renowned chef Jean-Claude
Bon. Mainstays include foie gras with
mushrooms and lobster served with
ham. Guestrooms in Napoleon-III-style
have excellent facilities.*

SARPOIL

● **Le Bergerie de Sarpoil**
Sarpoil, St-Jean-en-Val, 63490 **Map** 8A4
📞 04 73 71 02 54
FAX 04 73 71 02 54
🖥 www.bergerie-de-sarpoil.com
💳 MC, V ● Sun D, Mon; 3 wks Jan,
Jul–Aug 🍴 €€€

*The expertly crafted food is served in a
refined space, which opens out on to a
pretty terrace. Perennial winners include
salmon with crayfish and woodland
mushrooms, and exotic desserts.*

SEREILHAC-LES-BETOULLES

▲ **Relais des Tuileries**
Les Betoulles, 87620 **Map** 7E5
📞 05 55 39 10 27
FAX 05 55 36 09 21
💳 MC, V ● Sep–Jun: Sun D, Mon;
Jan, 2 wks Nov 🍴 € 🛏 (10) €€

*Set amid lush pastures, this low-rise
building has the feel of a rustic ranch.
Sample dishes like braised piglet in red
wine and the delicious veal sweetbreads
with basil. Small, simple guestrooms.*

ST-AFFRIQUE

▲ **Le Moderne**
Ave Alphonse Pezet, 12400 **Map** 11F2
📞 05 65 49 20 44
FAX 05 65 49 36 55
🖥 www.lemoderne.com
💳 AE, DC, MC, V ● Jan, last wk
Sep–1st wk Oct
🍴 €€€ 🛏 (28) €€

*Just a short drive from Roquefort, it
comes as no surprise that cheese
features on the menu here. The food is
undeniably good (especially the soufflés
and young stuffed chickens) and the
dining room has a charm of its own;
however, the modern guestrooms are
somewhat lacklustre.*

ST-ALBAN-SUR-LIMAGNOLE

▲ **La Petite Maison at Relais St Roch**
Château de la Chastre, 48120 **Map** 12A1
📞 04 66 31 55 48
FAX 04 66 31 53 26
💳 AE, MC, V ● Jan–mid-Apr
🍴 €€€ 🛏 (9) €€€€

*An imposing pink granite building, set
in lush parkland and offering superb
accommodation. Cosy restaurant with
surprise offerings, including interesting
lamb and trout dishes and American
bison. Warm-hued, elegant guestrooms.*

ST-ANTHEME

▲ **Au Pont de Raffiny**
Raffiny, St-Romain, 63660 **Map** 8A4
📞 04 73 95 49 10

For key to symbols see back flap

FAX 04 73 95 80 21
W www.hotel-pont-raffiny.com
MC, V ● Sun D, Mon; Jan–mid-Feb 🍴 €€ ◠ (11) €€

At nearly 274m (900ft) in the Vallée de l'Ance you'll find these small, tidy rooms and fine wooden chalets. Two main dining rooms, one with retro styling, the other rustic with a large open fireplace. Highlights include sea bream with fine artichokes and some tasty beef dishes.

ST-BONNET-LE-FROID
▲ Auberge et Clos des Cîmes
Le Bourg, 43290 **Map** 8B5
📞 04 71 59 93 72
FAX 04 71 59 93 40
AE, DC, MC, V ● Jun–Sep: Mon D; Oct–May: Tue, Wed; Jan–mid-Mar 🍴 €€€€ ◠ (10) €€€€

Fabulous restaurant, one of the region's best. Enjoy savoury and sweet treats prepared with the utmost savoir-faire. The wine list includes Hermitage and Condrieu, and there is a good cigar selection. Sumptuous rooms.

ST-BONNET-LE-FROID
● Chatelard André
Le Bourg, 43290 **Map** 8B5
📞 04 71 59 96 09
FAX 04 71 59 98 75
MC, V ● Oct–May: Tue–Thu D; Jun–Sep: Sun D, Mon; mid-Jan–mid-Mar 🍴 €€€

Duck with foie gras and walnuts, and bass with crispy vegetables are two of the highlights here. Book a table inside or on the quiet village street.

ST-CHELY-D'APCHER
▲ Château d'Orfeuillette
Exit 32 from A75, direction La Garde, 48200 **Map** 12A1
📞 04 66 42 65 65
FAX 04 66 42 65 66
W www.chateau-orfeuillette.com
AE, DC, MC, V ● early Jan–early Feb 🍴 €€€ ◠ (27) €€€

A 19th-century turreted château in beautiful grounds. The restaurant's dark wood panelling and handsome fireplace make dining here quite an event. Highlights include lamb with Lozère honey and apple parfait.

ST-CIRGUES-DE-JORDANNE
▲ Les Tilleuls
Le Bourg, 15590 **Map** 7F5
📞 04 71 47 92 19
FAX 04 71 47 91 06
W www.hotellestilleuls.com
AE, DC, MC, V ● Tue, 1st Sun of month; Nov–Mar 🍴 € ◠ (15) €€

A quirky hotel, and a fabulous place to relax and be looked after. Some rooms have storybook-style antique four-poster beds. Five rich menus offer a wide choice.

ST-DIDIER-EN-VELAY
▲ Auberge du Velay
17 Grand Place, 43140 **Map** 8B5
📞 04 71 61 01 54
FAX 04 71 61 15 80
MC, V ● Sun D, Mon, Tue; school holidays in Feb, late Aug 🍴 €€ ◠ (2) €€

Feast on hearty cuisine at this evocative 17th-century maison. Expect Haute-Loire classics like salmon with Puy lentils, and chocolate à la menthe. Cosy guestrooms with traditional furnishings.

ST-ETIENNE-DE-FURSAC
▲ Hôtel Nougier
2 pl Eglise, 23290 **Map** 7E3
📞 05 55 63 60 56
FAX 05 55 63 65 47
MC, V ● Sun, Mon D, Tue L, Jul–Aug: Mon L; mid-Dec–mid-Mar 🍴 €€ ◠ (12) €€

Spend an afternoon lounging around on the waterside terrace then dine on Limousin beef, truffles, fresh fish and snails. Clean, fresh guestrooms.

ST-FLOUR
▲ Auberge de la Providence
1 rue Château d'Alleuze, 15100 **Map** 7F5
📞 04 71 60 12 05
FAX 04 71 60 33 94
AE, DC, MC, V ● Mon; mid-Dec–mid-Jan 🍴 €€ ◠ (10) €€

Small hotel with a relaxed atmosphere, simple, fair-sized rooms, and an intimate dining room. The menu can include anything from frogs' legs to crayfish gratin.

ST-FLOUR
▲ Château de Varillettes
St-Georges, 15100 **Map** 7F5

📞 04 71 60 45 05
FAX 04 71 60 34 27
W www.chateaudevarillettes.com
AE, DC, MC, V ● Sep–Jun: Sun D 🍴 €€ ◠ (11) €€€€

Luxurious 14th-century château; four-poster beds and monumental fireplaces flaunt its credentials as one of the finest hotels in the region.

ST-FLOUR
▲ Grand Hôtel de l'Etape
18 ave de République, 15100 **Map** 7F5
📞 04 71 60 13 03
FAX 04 71 60 48 05
W www.hotel-etape.com
AE, DC, MC, V ● Sun D, Mon; Jan 🍴 €€ ◠ (23) €€€

The restaurant here overflows into the garden and serves some fine cuisine. Guestrooms are well cared for, if slightly uninspiring. Book in advance.

ST-FLOUR
▲ Le Nautilus at Hôtel les Messageries
23 ave Charles de Gaulle, 15100 **Map** 7F5
📞 04 71 60 11 36
FAX 04 71 60 46 79
W www.hotel-messageries.com
AE, DC, MC, V ● Nov–Mar 🍴 €€€ ◠ (18) €€€

A gem of a hotel, which seems to have it all: comfortable rooms, a relaxing pool and a great restaurant. The menu includes rabbit cooked in cider, and sausages with aligot (p247).

ST-GERVAIS-D'AUVERGNE
▲ Castel Hôtel 1904
Rue Castel, 63390 **Map** 7F4
📞 04 73 85 70 42
FAX 04 73 85 84 39
W www.castel-hotel-1904.com
MC, V ● Mon, Tue; mid-Nov–late Mar 🍴 €€€ ◠ (17) €€€

This imposing turreted château has been a hotel for 100 years. Public rooms are full of dark-wood antiques. Le Comptoir à Moustache offers country bistro food while the lovely main Château restaurant offers more refined, creative cuisine. Guestrooms have a cosy, traditional feel and there is an attractive vine-covered inner courtyard.

● Restaurant ■ Hotel ▲ Hotel / Restaurant

ST-GOUSSAUD

● Relais de St-Goussaud

Le Bourg, village centre, 23430 **Map** 7E4

📞 05 55 64 32 71

FAX 05 55 64 37 15

💳 MC, V ⚫ Sun D, Mon 🍴 €

Enjoy fabulous food accompanied by a glass of Anjou or Saumur on the terrace amid the forest foliage. Highlights include lamb cooked in its own juices.

ST-HILAIRE-LE-CHATEAU

▲ Hotel du Thaurion

Le Bourg, 23250 **Map** 7E4

📞 05 55 64 50 12

FAX 05 55 64 90 92

💳 AE, DC, MC, V ⚫ Sun D, Wed, Sep–Jun: Thu L; late Dec–late Feb

🍴 €€ 🍽 (8) €€

Dine on sophisticated cuisine amid handsome surroundings. Try the cool fish soup infused with verbena tea. Guestrooms are comfortable and tranquil.

ST-JEAN-DU-BRUEL

▲ Hôtel du Midi

Le Bourg, 12230 **Map** 12A2

📞 05 65 62 26 04

FAX 05 65 62 12 97

🌐 www.hotel-midi-papillon.com

💳 AE, DC, MC, V ⚫ mid-Nov–Mar

🍴 €€ 🍽 (19) €€

There's no better sausage cassoulet (p326). Desserts include gâteau a la broche (spit-roasted cake) and clafoutis (p247).

ST-JULIEN-AUX-BOIS

▲ Auberge de St-Julien-aux-Bois

Le Bourg, 19220 **Map** 7E5

📞 05 55 28 41 94

FAX 05 55 28 37 85

💳 AE, MC, V ⚫ Tue D, Wed; last 2 wks Feb 🍴 €€ 🍽 (7) €€

Popular partly due to its location. The hotel is small but surrounded by lovely gardens, and guestrooms are surprisingly large. Excellent food includes scallops with couscous, duck with apples, and beef with ceps. Good wine cellar.

ST-JULIEN-CHAPTEUIL

▲ Le Barriol

Pl du Marche, 43260 **Map** 8A5

📞 04 71 08 70 17

FAX 04 71 08 74 19

@ lebarriol@aol.com

💳 MC, V ⚫ Sun D, Mon; Jan

🍴 € 🍽 (11) €€

A 19th-century building set in the tranquil main village square. Highlights include bourride (p373) and a wonderful verbena tea-flavoured ice cream. Guestrooms are rather plain but pretty good value.

ST-JULIEN-CHAPTEUIL

● Vidal

Pl Marché, 43260 **Map** 8A5

📞 04 71 08 70 50

FAX 04 71 08 40 14

🌐 www.restaurant-vidal.com

💳 AE, MC, V ⚫ Sun D, Mon D; Sep–Jun: Tue; mid-Jan–Feb 🍴 €€€

A stunning backdrop of extinct Auvergne volcanoes and sleepy village streets. The sprawling interior has warm hues and the food is first class; try the tasty pork dishes accompanied by snails and vegetables, and the crème brûlée.

ST-LEONARD-DE-NOBLAT

▲ Hôtel du Grand St-Léonard

23 ave Champ de Mars, 87400 **Map** 7E4

📞 05 55 56 18 18

FAX 05 55 56 98 32

💳 AE, DC, MC, V ⚫ Mon D, Tue L; Oct–May: Mon L; late Dec–Feb

🍴 €€€ 🍽 (13) €€

Head to this imposing coaching inn for a memorable dining experience. Dishes include foie gras, and turbot with ceps. Guestrooms brim with rustic charm.

ST-MARC-A-LOUBAUD

● Le Mille Sources

Le Bourg, 23460 **Map** 7E4

📞 05 55 66 03 69

FAX 05 55 66 03 69

💳 DC, MC, V ⚫ Oct–Jun: Sun D, Mon; Dec–mid-Feb 🍴 €€

Feast on roast meats like Limousin lamb at this popular eatery. Eat in the cosy dining area or outside on the terrace.

ST-MERD-DE-LAPLEAU

▲ Rendez-vous des Pêcheurs

Pont du Chambon, 19320 **Map** 7E5

📞 05 55 27 88 39

FAX 05 55 27 83 19

💳 AE, DC, MC, V ⚫ last 2 wks Jan, mid-Nov–mid-Dec 🍴 €€ 🍽 (8) €€

The restaurant serves dishes such as fried foie gras with toast and mango chutney. Guestrooms are large and well equipped, though somewhat dated.

ST-NECTAIRE

▲ Relais Mercure

St-Nectaire-le-Bas Est, 63710 **Map** 7F4

📞 04 73 88 57 00

FAX 04 73 88 57 02

💳 AE, DC, MC, V ⚫ Mid-Dec–Easter

🍴 €€€ 🍽 (71) €€

St-Nectaire has a thermal spa to soothe those aches and pains. Find epicurean delights here, plus gourmet food and comfortable lodging in modern rooms. Leisure facilities include in- and outdoor swimming pools, sauna and Jacuzzi.

ST-PARDOUX-LA-CROISILLE

▲ Le Beau Site

Le Bourg, 19320 **Map** 7E5

📞 05 55 27 79 44

FAX 05 55 27 69 52

🌐 www.hotel-lebeausite-correze.com

💳 AE, DC, MC, V ⚫ Tue L, Wed L; mid-Oct–mid-May

🍴 €€€ 🍽 (28) €€€

This old hotel is a popular retreat for outdoor types. Attractive guestrooms, and some great local dishes.

ST-SERNIN-SUR-RANCE

▲ Carayon

Pl du Fort, 12380 **Map** 11F2

📞 05 65 98 19 19

FAX 05 65 99 69 26

🌐 www.hotel-carayon.fr

💳 MC, V ⚫ Sun D, Mon, Tue L

🍴 €€€ 🍽 (60) €€

Modelled on a Swiss chalet, this hotel has everything you need for a relaxing break. Guestrooms are bright, with large windows. Hearty appetites are satisfied with well-prepared seasonal dishes.

ST-YRIEIX-LA-PERCHE

▲ La Tour Blanche

74 bd Hôtel de Ville, 87500 **Map** 7D4

📞 05 55 75 18 17

FAX 05 55 08 23 11

💳 DC, MC, V ⚫ Sun; late Feb–Mar

🍴 €€ 🍽 (10) €€

The culinary delights served in this lovely turreted building are well worth

stopping off for. Masterpieces include Limousin beef in Bergerac wine, and mullet with aubergine (eggplant). Guestrooms have warm, pastel shades.

ST-YRIEIX-LA-PERCHE

● **Le Cheval Blanc**

19 pl Marché, 87500 **Map** 7D4

📞 05 55 75 01 46

FAX 05 55 08 25 11

💳 DC, MC, V

🌑 Sun D, Mon D 🍽 €€

A charming higgledy-piggledy facade and a leafy terrace greet visitors to this solidly reliable eatery. Try the area's famous pork meat, porc cul noir, here accompanied by flavoursome ceps.

TENCE

▲ **Hostellerie Placide**

Ave de la Gare, 43190 **Map** 7E5

📞 04 71 59 82 76

FAX 04 71 65 44 46

💳 AE, MC, V 🌑 Mon, Oct–Jun: Sun D & Tue; mid-Nov–mid-Mar

🍽 €€ 🍴 (15) €€€

Charming vine-covered establishment nearly 900m (2,950ft) above sea level. Public areas and bedrooms are bright and cheery, mixing modern touches with the Belle Epoque. After dinner, lounge in one of the old club chairs and enjoy a cigar and a glass of Armagnac.

THIERS

● **La Ferme Trois Canards**

Biton route Maringues, Pont-de-Dore, 63920 **Map** 8A4

📞 04 73 51 06 70

FAX 04 73 51 06 71

🌐 www.alainroussingue.com

💳 DC, MC, V 🌑 Sun D, Tue D, Wed; 3 wks Jan 🍽 €€

Set in the green heart of the Parc des Volcans. Dine on lobster and scallops with morels, and the chocolate dessert called croustillant guanaja.

TULLE

▲ **Bon Accueil**

10 rue du Canton, 19000 **Map** 7E5

📞 05 55 26 70 57

FAX 05 55 20 29 73

💳 MC, V 🌑 Sun, Sep–Jun: Sat D

🍽 € 🍴 (12) €€

Next to Tulle's magnificent cathedral, this little hotel is clean, comfortable and good value. Families enjoy the reliable food and indulgent dessert menu.

TULLE

▲ **La Toque Blanche**

29 rue Jean Jaurès, 19000 **Map** 7E5

📞 05 55 26 75 41

FAX 05 55 20 93 95

🌐 www.hotel-latoqueblanche.com

💳 DC, MC

🌑 Sun D, Sat L; Feb

🍽 €€€ 🍴 (8) €€

As with many top restaurants, the hotel here feels like an afterthought. However, the rooms are pleasant and tidy, and the menu shows why this place is on the culinary map. Specialities are typically French and include stuffed pig trotters. Booking is essential.

TULLE

● **Le Central**

10 rue de la Barrière, 19000 **Map** 7E5

📞 05 55 26 24 46

FAX 05 55 26 53 16

@ r-pumier@internet19.fr

💳 MC, V 🌑 Sun, Sat D; 1st 2 wks Aug 🍽 €€€

Widely considered to be one of the best restaurants in Corrèze. Seafood is the speciality, with langoustines in butter and roast fillet of sole. Lengthy wine list and good selection of whiskies.

USSAC

▲ **Le Petit Clos**

Le Pouret, 19270 **Map** 7E5

📞 05 55 86 12 65

FAX 05 55 86 94 32

💳 MC, V 🌑 Sun, Mon; mid-Feb–mid-Mar, 1 wk Aug

🍽 €€ 🍴 (7) €€€

Buried deep in Correze's countryside. Start the evening with a poolside apéritif, but make sure you book a table as they quickly fill up. Guestrooms are neutrally decorated and have bathrooms.

VARETZ

▲ **Château de Castel Novel**

Route Objat, 19240 **Map** 7D5

📞 05 55 85 00 01

FAX 05 55 85 09 03

🌐 www.castelnovel.com

💳 AE, DC, MC, V 🌑 Sun D, Mon L–Fri L, Sat D; mid-Oct–Apr

🍽 €€€€ 🍴 (32) €€€€€

This magnificent 14th-century château is an ideal place to sample the finer side of life. The menu includes foie gras with veal, and mountains of truffles. Rooms are all finished to a high standard.

VEBRON

● **La Cardinale**

Racoules de Vebron, 48400 **Map** 12A1

📞 04 66 44 00 20

💳 MC, V 🌑 Mon

🍽 €€

Reasonably priced, hearty dishes like chestnut soup and mushroom omelette, as well as tripe and snail creations. The modern building has a tranquil leafy garden – a great place to bring children.

VERGONGHEON

● **La Petite Ecole**

Rilhac, 3km (2 miles) southeast on D174, 43360 **Map** 8A5

📞 04 71 76 00 44

FAX 04 71 76 90 94

💳 AE, MC, V 🌑 Sun D, Mon, Oct–Apr: Tue D; late Jun, 1 wk early Sep

🍽 €

Marvellous little eatery in a former schoolhouse with good prices. Look out for their trademark duck dishes, washed down with an interesting regional wine.

VICHY

▲ **Aletti Palace**

3 pl Joseph Aletti, 03200 **Map** 8A3

📞 04 70 30 20 20

FAX 04 70 98 13 82

💳 AE, DC, MC, V

🍽 €€ 🍴 (133) €€€€

Built during the Belle Epoque, this stately hotel was once home to Vichy France's Ministry of War. Today the atmosphere is much more relaxed, with cool and airy rooms. Fine cuisine and desserts.

VICHY

● **Brasserie du Casino**

4 rue du Casino, 03200 **Map** 8A3

📞 04 70 98 23 06

FAX 04 70 98 53 17

💳 AE, DC, MC, V 🌑 Tue, Wed;

● Restaurant ■ Hotel ▲ Hotel / Restaurant

mid-Feb–mid-Mar, mid-Oct–mid-Nov
Ⅱ €€
Art Deco restaurant with photographs of the musician guests. An interesting menu, with dishes including foie gras with pears and beef with truffles.

VICHY

● **Colombière**
Route de Thiers, Abrest, 03200 **Map** 8A3
Ⅽ 04 70 98 69 15
FAX 04 70 31 50 89
@ lacolmbiere@wanadoo.fr
AE, DC, MC ● Sun D, Mon;
mid-Jan–mid-Feb, 1 wk Aug **Ⅱ** €€
Oozing nostalgia, this refined restaurant has an unmistakable flavour of the 1950s. Waiters move swiftly and silently, serving dishes from the gourmet menus, and the well-prepared French classics suit the ambience. Lovely terrace too.

VICHY

▲ **Hôtel du Rhône**
8 rue de Paris, 03200 **Map** 8A3
Ⅽ 04 70 97 73 00
FAX 04 70 97 48 25
@ hoteldurhonevichy@hotmail.com
AE, DC, MC, V
Ⅱ €€ ◆ (30) €€€
Napoleon first put Vichy on the map back in the 19th century, and this stylish hotel is a testament to the city's heyday. There's a lovely garden for alfresco dining. Large, opulent guestrooms.

VICHY

● **La Table d'Antoine**
8 rue Burnol, 03200 **Map** 8A3
Ⅽ 04 70 98 99 71
FAX 04 70 31 11 39
AE, DC, MC, V ● Sun D, Mon;
1 wk Mar, Nov **Ⅱ** €€€
Frequented by the region's beautiful people, this urbane restaurant is one of Vichy's most desirable places to be seen. The varied menu covers the culinary spectrum, from sea bass with saffron to rabbit with berries.

VICHY

● **L'Alambic**
8 rue Nicolas Larbaud, 03200 **Map** 8A3
Ⅽ 04 70 59 12 71
FAX 04 70 97 98 88

AE, DC, MC, V ● Sun D, Mon, Tue;
3 wks Aug, 3 wks Feb **Ⅱ** €€€
This intimate restaurant is one of the most popular places in Vichy, so booking is essential. Highly praised though very traditional cuisine, but the chic modern interior makes it seem new and fresh.

VICHY

● **L'Aromate**
9 rue Bresse, 03200 **Map** 8A3
Ⅽ 04 70 32 13 22
FAX 04 70 32 13 22
AE, DC, MC, V
● Sun D, Tue–Wed D; mid-Jul–
mid-Aug **Ⅱ** €€
A Belle Epoque treasure, this grand mirrored dining room was a favourite of Napoleon's. Interesting uses of herbs and flowers in the dishes.

VICHY

● **L'Envolée**
44 ave Eugène Gilbert, 03200 **Map** 8A3
Ⅽ 04 70 32 85 15
FAX 04 70 32 85 15
DC, MC, V ● Tue D, Wed;
last 2 wks Aug **Ⅱ** €€€
Located on a sleepy back street, this fashionable bistro attracts a diverse crowd, even if the service can be erratic.

VIC-LE-COMTE

● **Le Comté**
186 bd Général de Gaulle, Longues,
63270 **Map** 8A4
Ⅽ 04 73 39 90 31
FAX 04 73 39 24 58
DC, MC, V ● Sun D, Mon; late Jul
Ⅱ €€
Traditional Auvergne dishes cooked to perfection plus an amiable atmosphere pull in a loyal crowd. Try the potillou (snail and frog casserole) and apple tart in a caramel-and-almond sauce.

VIEILLEVIE

▲ **La Terrasse**
Le Bourg, 15120 **Map** 11F1
Ⅽ 04 72 49 94 00
FAX 04 71 49 92 23
AE, DC, MC, V ● Nov–Mar **Ⅱ** €€
◆ (26) €€
Dramatically set on a plateau surrounded by hills, this modest hotel makes the

best of its location. Afternoons are spent by the pool, evenings on the dining terrace. All the rooms have great views.

VILLEFORT

▲ **Hôtel Balme**
Pl Portalet, 48800 **Map** 12A1
Ⅽ 04 66 46 80 14
FAX 04 66 46 85 26
AE, DC, MC, V ● mid-Nov–
mid-Feb **Ⅱ** €€ ◆ (18) €€
An elegant restaurant famed for its British-empire-style interior and Michel Gomy's thoughtful cooking. Specialities include pig's trotters stuffed with chanterelles, and the remarkable crème brûlée. Charming, old-style guestrooms.

VILLENEUVE-SUR-ALLIER

▲ **La Chaumière**
Le Pont, 03460 **Map** 7F3
Ⅽ 04 70 43 30 35
FAX 04 70 43 32 36
DC, MC ● mid-Nov–mid-Mar
Ⅱ € ◆ (17) €€
The restaurant has a reputation for classic French cuisine, with dishes including veal cooked in cream, and lamb with a herb crust. Rooms vary, but are all of a high standard.

VITRAC

▲ **Auberge de la Tomette**
Le Bourg, 15220 **Map** 11E1
Ⅽ 04 71 64 70 94
FAX 04 71 64 77 11
Ⓦ www.auberge-la-tomette.com
AE, DC, MC, V ● mid-Nov–Mar
Ⅱ €€€ ◆ (15) €€€
This smart hotel makes a lovely country getaway. Rooms are large and en-suite. Favourites include loin of lamb with garlic and veal with chanterelles.

YSSINGEAUX

▲ **Le Bourbon**
5 pl Victoire, 43200 **Map** 7B5
Ⅽ 04 71 59 06 54
AE, MC, V ● Sun D, Mon,
Jul–Sep: Tue L, Sep–Jul: Fri D; Jan, late
Jun–early Jul; Nov–Mar
Ⅱ €€ ◆ (17) €€
A zesty, modern interior and equally imaginative menu. Bright guestrooms with superb facilities.

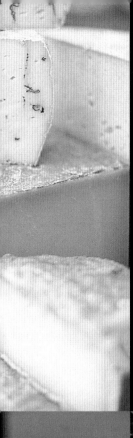

THE RHONE VALLEY & FRENCH ALPS

From snow-capped mountains to fertile plains, Alpine to Provençal climate, this region brings together the gentle hills of the Beaujolais, the crags of the Vercors and the wild forests of the Ardèche. At its heart, a bridge between north and south, lies Lyon, the "food capital of France".

The Flavours of the Rhône Valley & French Al

From the fertile plains of the Rhône Valley to the craggy peaks of the Haute-Savoie, this region is abundant in every way, with poultry, cheeses and charcuterie as its stars. No wonder that the capital, Lyon, is world-famous for the excellence of its markets and its restaurants.

POULET DE BRESSE

Bresse chicken, dubbed *poulet tricolore* for its blue feet, white plumage and red crest (the colours of the French *tricolore* flag), has been raised here since the 16th century and an *appellation contrôlée* since 1957. Free-range, with pale flesh and a superb flavour, it is generally considered to be France's finest poultry.

Poulet de Bressse, with its red, white and blue label

MEAT AND POULTRY

The Bresse area is renowned for farmed pigeon as well as for *poulet de Bresse*, and guinea fowl from the Drôme merit a *label rouge (see p11)*. Fine-quality lamb is produced in the Vercors and Baronnies mountains but cows, including the Tarentais, Abondance and Montbéliard breeds, are largely raised for dairying.

FISH AND FROGS

The region is important for its lake fish, both from the pond-dotted Dombes area and the large Alpine lakes. Char is especially prized, but other species include carp, perch, pike, trout and lake salmon. The Dombes is also rich in freshwater crayfish, ingredient of the famous *sauce Nantua (see p269)*, and frogs.

CHEESE

The lush summer alpine pastures are renowned for cows' milk cheeses. Fine textured, aromatic Beaufort AOC, made only with milk from Tarentaise or Abondance cows, has a mild flavour with a hint of hazelnut. Stronger Abondance matures for at least three months. Tomme de Savoie and Tomme de Montagne cover a range of smaller, semi-soft cheeses with granular, natural crusts

CHARCUTERIE

The Lyonnais are master *charcutiers* with a repertoire that includes dried sausages, cooking sausages and other *cochonailles*. The dried variety includes *rosette de Lyon*, a long, salami-type sausage, *jésus de Lyon*, which is shorter, thicker and more coarsely minced, and the smaller, drier *saucisson de Lyon*. Cooking sausages include *cervelas*, finely minced and often studded with pistachios, and *sabodet*, which may be boiled, baked in brioche or stewed in Beaujolais with onions. Other charcuterie includes hams, brawn, *museau* (snout) and *grattons* (rind or stratchings).

Alpine charcuterie includes smoked, tiny *diot* and cumin-flavoured *longeôle* sausages. From the Ardèche come *caillettes*, caul-covered patties of minced pork and chopped chard or spinach.

Left Bauges cheeses **Centre** Picodon goats' cheese **Right** Lyon's Palet d'Or chocolate

and a relatively low fat content. Reblochon, made since the 13th century, is a flat disc with a slightly runny, elastic centre when mature. St-Marcellin, a small, disc-shaped cheese from the Chartreuse area, has a golden surface and white interior. Unripe, the interior is chalky but, when ready to eat, it becomes very liquid (and is hence often sold in a black plastic dish). St-Félicien is a creamy cheese resembling St-Marcellin but with a sharper flavour. Blue cheeses include Bleu du Vercors and creamy Bresse Bleu. Goats' cheese is made in the south of the region: Picodon in the Drôme provençale and eastern Ardèche; flat, rectangular Brique de Forez; rigottes de Condrieu; and small, hard, round, farm-produced Chevrotin. Persillé (or Bleu) Tarentais becomes streaked with green veins as it ages.

FRUIT AND VEGETABLES

The Rhône valley is second only to Provence for fruit, especially apricots and peaches. Apples and pears are grown on the Monts du Lyonnais, while Alpine areas are renowned for soft berry fruits. The heavily forested Ardèche is dominated by chestnuts, made into *marrons glacés* and *crème de marrons*, and the source of scented honey. Walnuts are grown along the Isère valley, to be used for wine and liqueurs, cakes, preserves and oil. The mild climate of Nyons makes it the most northerly European outpost of the olive, with its own black *tanche* olive producing a fruity, mild AOC oil. Vegetables include onions, chard and cardoons. Maize is grown in Savoie, and used in Italian-style polenta.

SWEETS AND CHOCOLATES

Lyon, Annecy and St-Etienne are all noted for their chocolates, including *palets d'or* (dark chocolate discs covered with gold leaf) and praline-filled *cloches d'Annecy*. Montélimar is synonymous with nougat.

LYON'S MARKETS

To truly appreciate this region's abundance of produce, from fresh fruit and root vegetables to charcuterie and cheeses, visit Lyon's fabulous markets. Every district has its own, but the biggest and best are the open-air market beside the river Saône on quai St-Antoine (Tue–Sun am); Croix-Rousse market (Tue–Sun am), atop the hill in the increasingly trendy old silkworkers' district; and the central covered market, Halles Lafayette (102 cours Lafayette, Tue–Sun). At the latter you'll find the renowned Charcuterie Sibilia, as well as Mère Richard, France's most celebrated *affineur* of St-Marcellin cheese.

Redcurrants and berries in a Lyon market

Regional Dishes

This region encompasses a panoply of different culinary traditions, from the haute cuisine of legendary chefs to the comforting cooking of Lyonnais bouchons; from sustaining Alpine fare to the Italian legacy of Savoie and the herby, olive oil-based dishes of the southern Drôme.

ON THE MENU

Cuisses de grenouilles sautées Sautéed frogs' legs

Gâteau de foie blond bressan Chicken liver mousse

Gratin dauphinois Potato and cream gratin

Gratin savoyard Potato and Beaufort cheese gratin

Péla Diced potatoes fried with onions and Reblochon cheese

Pommes lyonnaises Potatoes sautéed with onions

Potage Dubarry Cream of cauliflower soup

Potée savoyarde Hotpot of vegetables, chicken, ham and sausage

Poularde demi-deuil Bresse hen roasted with sliced truffles under its skin

Poulet au vinaigre Bresse chicken cooked in vinegar

Rapée Grated potato bake

Ravioles de Royans Tiny herb and cheese ravioli

Tablier de sapeur Tripe fried in egg and breadcrumbs

Tête de veau sauce gribiche Calf's brawn with a sauce of capers, hard-boiled eggs and mustard

Vacherin with cream and fresh berries

THE REGIONAL MENU

The quintessential Lyon restaurant is the *bouchon*, serving up dishes like onion soup, charcuterie, tripe, steaks and stews to hungry workers, and where the cooks were often women, the famous *Mères* (mothers). A typical meal might begin with *saladiers lyonnais*, assorted salads and cold meats including warm dressed potatoes with sliced *lyonnais* sausage. *Cervelle de canut* (silkworker's brain) is a starter of *fromage frais* with garlic and chives. In Savoie and Drôme, *ravioles* are cooked in chicken broth and served gratinéed.

Bresse poultry is cooked in numerous ways – with truffles, cream, vinegar or combined with crayfish, and the livers are often made into a flan-like gâteau.

The Alps are home to a range of warming dishes, such as *raclette* (melted cheese, poured over boiled potatoes), *tartiflette* (baked Reblochon, *lardons*, cream and potatoes) and savoyarde *péla*. Then there is unctuous *gratin dauphinois* and its cheesy cousin *gratin savoyard*, as well as numerous variants on potato *galettes*, such as *râpée*. Polenta is often served, a reminder that until 1860 Savoie was part of Italy. Pasta dishes include *crozets*, eaten with melted cheese. Steak is sometimes cooked *à la pierrade*, grilled on a flat, sizzling-hot stone.

Desserts might include *vacherin*, *rissoles* (baked fruit turnovers) or soufflé flavoured with Chartreuse liqueur.

Gratin dauphinois, with its layers of creamy potato

Left Quenelles de brochet, sauce Nantua **Right** Fondue savoyarde

GRATINÉE LYONNAISE (SOUPE À L'OIGNON)

The onion soup of the Lyonnais *bouchon* is served in individual tureens with a gratinéed crust. Onions are gently cooked to a rich caramel colour and then simmered in chicken or beef stock. The soup is ladled into bowls, covered with slices of grilled baguette, topped with grated Gruyère and browned under a hot grill.

QUENELLES DE BROCHET, SAUCE NANTUA

Pike is notoriously bony to eat, so it is best enjoyed as smooth *quenelle* dumplings. Filleted raw pike is blended with beaten egg whites, *panade* (a mix of flour, melted butter, hot milk and egg yolks) and *crème fraîche*, shaped into large lozenges and poached in water. *Sauce Nantua* is made with freshwater crayfish, flamed brandy, finely chopped carrot and onion, tomato purée, white wine and cream. The poached *quenelles* are laid in a gratin dish, then covered with sauce and baked until golden-brown.

FONDUE SAVOYARDE

The ultimate *après-ski* supper is more a social event than a dish. An earthenware fondue pot is rubbed with garlic, white wine is heated in it and grated hard Savoie cheese stirred in and warmed gently to form a smooth sauce. Kirsch and seasoning are added and the pot is placed on a burner at the table. Chunks of dryish bread are speared onto special forks and dunked in the cheese. Tradition has it that anyone who loses a bit of bread into the pot has to kiss everyone at the table!

VACHERIN

A truly indulgent dessert, this is made up of large rings of meringue filled with mixtures such as liqueur-flavoured cream or *crème Chantilly* topped with fresh fruit or berries, or chestnut purée and cream decorated with *marrons glacés*, or ice cream with strawberries.

REGIONAL DINING

The following restaurants are among those serving regional dishes at reasonable prices:

Auberge de Savoie
Annecy *(see p276)*

Auberge Napoléon
Grenoble *(see p281)*

Café des Fédérations
Lyon *(see p283)*

Daniel et Denise
Lyon *(see p283)*

Ferme de l'Adroit
Val-d'Isere *(see p289)*

La Tartine
Crest *(see p279)*

Mairie
Embrun *(see p280)*

Relais du Soleil
Chabeuil *(see p278)*

Senteurs de Provence
Montelimar *(see p285)*

Café des Fédérations, a typical Lyon *bouchon*

Regional Wine & Spirits

The wines of the northern Rhône now enjoy star billing amongst the world's wine elite, while Beaujolais remains a light, joyful drink for supping up young. The wines of Savoie are little known but this is the source of fine aperitifs and liqueurs including the renowned Chartreuse.

Syrah grapes

GRAPE VARIETIES: NORTHERN RHÔNE

Syrah The only red variety used in the northern Rhône, tannin-rich Syrah gives deep-coloured wines that are at home in new oak. Suitable for ageing, they have a distinctive bouquet recalling tar, smoke, raspberries, violets and pepper.

Viognier Reigning supreme in Condrieu and Château-Grillet, where it makes some of France's rarest whites, Viognier is difficult to grow, has good alcohol and shows distinctive aromas of apricots and honey. Viognier has traditionally been added to Côte-Rôtie to "soften" the Syrah, but nowadays it is used less frequently.

Roussanne This wonderful grape gives delicate, aristocratic whites with a bouquet of honeysuckle and iris, sometimes capable of long ageing. Difficult to grow, it gives good results on well-drained, stony ground.

Marsanne Vigorous Marsanne renders powerful wines. It is often blended with the more elegant Roussanne, as in white Hermitage or St-Joseph.

NORTHERN RHÔNE

The northern Rhône vineyards are planted along a narrow corridor from Vienne down to Valence with vines clinging to precipitous slopes.

Cornas Baking in a sun-worshipper's paradise, the south-facing vineyards of Cornas make dark, robust and virile reds that slowly develop scents of truffle, preserved fruit and cocoa: sublime with game in sauce.

Côte-Rôtie The northernmost Rhône *cru* begins just outside the little town of Vienne in the narrowest part of the valley. The vineyards are so steep that they command almost a bird's-eye view of the river. These aristocratic wines made from Syrah, perhaps with a dash of white Viognier, give a firework display of smoky raspberry and truffle scents and deep liquorice and blackcurrant flavours. Serve with game fowl laced with truffles.

Crozes-Hermitage The largest of the northern Rhône appellations is also the biggest producer. The Mistral wind batters the vineyards, cooling the grapes, so here the Syrah grape renders light, fruity reds to be drunk young, like the fleshy, hazelnutty whites.

Hermitage The heady, tannic reds of Hermitage need perhaps 20 years to fully release their tarry, smoky scents with hints of iris. Made from Roussanne and Marsanne, the whites are long-lived.

St-Joseph Sprawling over 40 km (25 miles) between Condrieu and Cornas, St-Joseph delivers reds that are deeply fruity with a hint of liquorice and best drunk young. The whites from Roussanne and Marsanne grapes smell prettily of meadow flowers.

The hermit's chapel on the hill of Hermitage

VINEYARDS OF THE NORTHERN RHÔNE

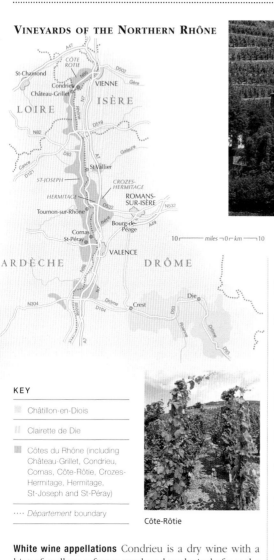

Château-Grillet

KEY

▨ Châtillon-en-Diois

▨ Clairette de Die

▨ Côtes du Rhône (including Château-Grillet, Condrieu, Cornas, Côte-Rôtie, Crozes-Hermitage, Hermitage, St-Joseph and St-Péray)

···· *Département* boundary

Côte-Rôtie

White wine appellations Condrieu is a dry wine with a hint of mellow softness produced exclusively from the low-yielding Viognier grape. Its bouquet is reminiscent of velvety apricots and peaches and spring blossom. The best vintages will age well but the rest should be drunk young with freshwater fish or the local goats' cheese, Rigotte de Condrieu. Château-Grillet is a tiny, single-estate appellation, a little way downriver from Condrieu, also using Viognier. St-Péray is the most southerly appellation of the northern Rhône, producing mainly light sparkling wines from Marsanne. The best wine from the banks of the Drôme is Clairette de Die, a delicious grapey fizz made from Muscat and Clairette grapes.

BEST PRODUCERS

Condrieu Gilles Barge, Yves Cuilleron, André Perret, Georges Vernay, François Villard

Cornas Thierry Allemand, A Clape, Jean-Luc Colombo, Domaine du Tunnel, Paul Jaboulet Aîné, Jean Lionnet, Noël Verset

Côte-Rôtie Gilles Barge, Bernard Burgaud, Delas, Domaine Clusel-Roch, Guigal (La Landonne, La Turque, La Mouline), Jean-Paul et Jean-Luc Jamet, René Rostaing, Tardieu-Laurent, Les Vins de Vienne

Crozes-Hermitage Bernard Ange, Chapoutier, Cave de Tain-l'Hermitage, Domaine Combier, Domaine des Remizières, Domaine de Thalabert, Alain Graillot

Hermitage Chapoutier, Jean-Louis Chave, J–L Grippat, Paul Jaboulet Aîné (La Chapelle red and Chevalier de Stérimberg white), Marc Sorrel

St-Joseph Cave de Tain l'Hermitage, Jean-Louis Chave, Pierre Coursodon, Jean-Louis Grippat

St-Péray Delas, Jean-Louis Thiers, Les Vins de Vienne, Alain Voge

VINEYARDS OF BEAUJOLAIS

KEY

- Beaujolais
- Beaujolais-Villages
- ···· *Département* boundary

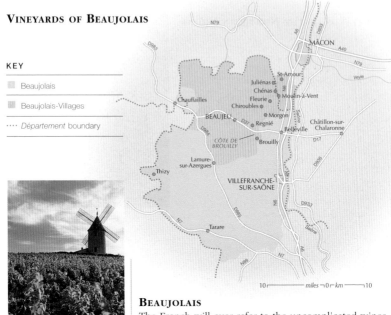

The windmill of Moulin-à-Vent

BEST PRODUCERS

Georges Duboeuf (especially Morgon Jean Descombes, Fleurie la Madone, Les Quatre Vents), Domaine Piron, Domaine des Terres Dorées, Domaine du Vissoux, Marcel Lapierre, Château Thivin

Beaujolais vineyards

BEAUJOLAIS

The French will ever refer to the uncomplicated wines of Beaujolais as the "third river in Lyon", a nickname based on the vast quantities of Beaujolais drunk in the town's *bouchons* (small bistros). With very few exceptions, Beaujolais is a wine for supping up soon; it will not age. These are light, simple, fruity wines with low acidity that are popular with some because they carry only a touch of tannin. The younger and fruitier they are, the cooler they should be drunk.

From Mâcon in the north to Lyon in the south, the Beaujolais vineyards ripple over an area of undulating countryside. The high-yielding Gamay is the only red grape used for the whole appellation and the wines are mostly made by the carbonic maceration method, a process that encourages the development of the grape's primary aromas and produces a wine with a bright ruby red colour and light tannins.

The southern half of Beaujolais covers the beautiful region of Pierres Dorées (literally, the golden stones). Generic Beaujolais, Beaujolais Supérieur (higher in alcohol, rather than better quality) and most Beaujolais Nouveau are made here. A tiny amount of white Beaujolais is produced in this area from Chardonnay.

The northern part of the region, right up to Villefranche-sur-Beaujolais, is on superior granite soils and includes the 37 villages entitled to the appellation of Beaujolais-Villages. These wines are often the best value for money, having much more character and more concentration than simple Beaujolais. This is also the land of the ten *crus*.

BEAUJOLAIS CRUS

The ten best villages in the northern Beaujolais have their own appellations and individual characteristics.

Brouilly The largest and southernmost of the *crus* is easy-drinking wine with red berry flavour.

Côte de Brouilly The blue granite soils on the Côte de Brouilly hillsides give the wines finesse. Typically, they smell of crushed fresh grapes combined with pretty hints of iris.

Chénas The smallest and rarest of the *crus* smells pleasantly of flowers, especially peony.

Chiroubles Chiroubles is the highest of the *crus*, situated between 250 and 450 m (800 and 1500 ft). Light and delicate, it shows characteristic scents of violet.

Fleurie Gentle and velvety, the wine with the beautiful name has hints of soft summer fruit, especially peach.

Juliénas Said to be named after Julius Caesar, this *cru* makes wines with a bouquet of peony and ripe white-fleshed peaches.

Morgon The wines found here are frequently compared to young red Burgundy *(see pp220–21)* for their lovely bouquet of kirsch and soft fruit and for their ability to mature well. The best soils lie on Le Py, the picturesque hill rising above the village.

Moulin-à-Vent Superb aromas of old roses typify this, one of the most powerful of the *crus*, which sometimes resembles a red Burgundy. The old windmill after which it is named was renovated in 1999.

Régnié The most recent addition to the *cru* club tastes of tangy raspberry and redcurrant.

St-Amour Wines from the northernmost *cru* are light but loaded with ripe red fruit flavour with touches of peach and apricot. Naturally, these wines do a brisk trade on St Valentine's day.

Beaujolais Nouveau

BEAUJOLAIS NOUVEAU

"Le Beaujolais Nouveau est arrivé" is a phrase that needs no translation. Released on the third Thursday in November, barely two months after the harvest, Beaujolais Nouveau is light, easy drinking, with the banana-like flavour of newly fermented wine. Originally aimed at Paris restaurants, it became a worldwide craze in the 1970s and, while its popularity may be waning now, Nouveau still accounts for almost 50 per cent of all the wine produced in the region. Nouveau is rarely of high quality and is seen by the more serious producers as damaging to the overall reputation of the region.

Grape harvest in Beaujolais

VINEYARDS OF SAVOIE

Terraced mountain vineyards

BEST PRODUCERS

Château de Ripaille, Domaine Dupasquier, Domaine Michel Grisard, Domaine André et Michel Quenard, Domaine Raymond et Pascal Quénard, Maison Mollex (sparkling Seyssel), Jean Perrier et Fils

KEY

- Crépy
- — Seyssel
- Vin du Bugey and Roussette du Bugey
- Vin de Savoie and Roussette de Savoie

···· *Département* boundary

— International boundary

Vin de Savoie wines from the Chignin *cru*

SAVOIE WINES

First-time visitors to the Alps are usually surprised to learn that Savoie is a wine-producing region. In fact, the vine has been at home in the valleys and along the lake and river sides of Savoie for 2,000 years or more. The vineyards are scattered in isolated pockets from around Lake Geneva all the way down to Albertville and located mainly in the *départements* of Savoie and Haute-Savoie. There are four appellations: Vin de Savoie (which may be followed by the name of one of the 17 *crus* such as Chignin, Ripaille, Jongieux or Apremont), Roussette de Savoie, Crépy and Seyssel. Three-quarters of all the wine produced here is white and is made from some twenty different grapes. The major white varieties are spritzy, floral Jacquère; high-alcohol Roussanne, with a magnificent bouquet of peach, hawthorn and hazelnuts; luscious, scented Roussette; and Chardonnay and Chasselas. Freshwater fish from the crystal mountain lakes make wonderful partners for these whites. The most interesting reds come from the native Mondeuse grape. Tannic, slightly bitter and peppery, it makes unusual wines that will often age quite happily and make a good match for game. Gamay and Pinot Noir also make gluggable reds. It can be difficult to find the better Savoie wines outside the region as supplies are quickly snapped up by holidaymakers. Bugey to the west in the Ain *département* specializes in light sparkling wines.

Savoyard aperitifs

SAVOYARD APERITIFS AND LIQUEURS

The mountains and meadows of the French Alps are treasure troves of aromatic herbs and plants that have been used for centuries to create tonics and aids to digestion. Savoie's speciality aperitifs, liqueurs and spirits are still made according to ancient recipes.

Bonal Grape juice and alcohol are blended together with roots of gentian and quinine. The resulting taste is bitter with subtle hints of Seville orange, pineapple, quince and honey.

Chambéryzette Vermouth with a strawberry liqueur.

Liqueur des Aravis Distilled Alpine plants, mainly gentian and genepy, with angelica, mint, cloves and others blended with Armagnac.

Liqueur de Génépi Golden liqueur made from the rare genepy plant combined with mint, verbena, hyssop and other herbs and spices.

Vermouth de Chambéry Delicately bitter and aromatic aperitif made from Jacquère grapes and an assortment of herbs including hyssop, wormwood, juniper, camomile, rose petals and cloves.

CHARTREUSE

Invented by Carthusian monks in the Grande Chartreuse monastery in the Dauphiné as a tonic, green Chartreuse was once widely used for medicinal purposes. The formula was nearly lost after the French Revolution, but eventually found its way back to the monastery. The secret recipe involves some 130 herbs, dried in wooden boxes at the monastery. Honey and golden syrup are added to sweeten the spirits after distillation. In 1838, the formula was adapted by Brother Bruno Jacquet to produce another sweeter liqueur with a lower alcohol content, yellow Chartreuse.

Green and yellow Chartreuse were all made in the pharmacy at the monastery until 1860. Nowadays they are made at Voiron near Grenoble.

The monastery has a musuem: La Grande Chartreuse, St-Pierre de Chartreuse (04 76 88 60 45); Apr–Oct: daily

The cellars and the distillery can also be visited: 10 blvd Kofler, Voiron (04 76 05 81 77); Apr–end Oct: daily; Nov–end Mar: Mon–Fri

Chartreuse distillery

Where to Eat & Stay

AIX-LES-BAINS
● Brasserie de la Poste
32 ave Victoria, 73100 **Map** 9D4
📞 04 79 35 00 65
💳 AE, MC, V ⬤ Sun D, Mon 🍴 €
Brasserie ideal for people-watching and an apéritif. Stewed beef and cheese fondue for hearty meals. Lighter fare includes vegetable soup and duck salad.

AIX-LES-BAINS
▲ Grand Hôtel du Parc
28 rue Chambéry, 73000 **Map** 9D4
📞 04 79 61 29 11
FAX 04 79 88 33 49
🖥 www.grand-hotel-du-parc.com
💳 MC, V 🍴 €€€ ⬤ (45) €€€
Victorian building offering simple accommodation with a pleasant outdoor space. Pigeon is just one of the dishes.

ALBERTVILLE
▲ Le Million
8 pl de la Liberté, 73200 **Map** 9D4
📞 04 79 32 25 15
FAX 04 79 32 25 36
🖥 www.hotelmillion.com
💳 AE, DC, MC, V ⬤ Sun D, Mon, Sat L; 1st 2 wks May, last wk Oct
🍴 €€€ ⬤ (26) €€€€
Also a cooking school, this restaurant serves sea bass with oysters, foie gras with apple chutney and rabbit ravioli. Antiques in the guestrooms.

ALBOUSSIERE
▲ Auberge de Duzon
Town centre, 07440 **Map** 8B5
📞 04 75 58 29 40
FAX 04 75 58 29 41
🖥 www.auberge-duzon.fr
💳 AE, MC, V ⬤ Sun D, Mon, Tue
🍴 € ⬤ (8) €€
This auberge has a colourful personality and daily changes to the regional menus. Rooms are named after flowers and are decorated in the hues of their namesake.

AMBERIEUX-EN-DOMBES
▲ Auberge des Bichonnières
Route to Ars, 01330 **Map** 8B4
📞 04 74 00 82 07

FAX 04 74 00 89 61
💳 AE, MC, V ⬤ Sun D, Mon, Tue L; mid-Dec–mid-Jan
🍴 €€ ⬤ (9) €€
Farm surrounded by lakes and ponds. Try the ravioles de Royans (p268), here combined with mussels in a flaky pastry with chives. Rooms are bright and cosy.

ANNECY
● Auberge de Savoie
1 St-François-de-Sales, 74000 **Map** 8D4
📞 04 50 45 03 05
FAX 04 50 51 18 28
🖥 www.aubergedesavoie.fr
💳 AE, MC, V ⬤ Tue, Wed; last wk Apr, 1st wk May, last 2 wks Aug
🍴 €€€
Informal and friendly setting with tasty lake treats including féra (lake salmon). Calm and cosy dining room and a small outdoor terrace.

ANNECY
● Bilboquet
14 fbg Ste-Claire, 74000 **Map** 8D4
📞 04 50 45 21 68
💳 AE, MC, V ⬤ Sep–Jun: Sun–Mon
🍴 €€
After a trip to the bustling market take your appetite to Bilboquet. The dining room of light wood and exposed stone is perfect for enjoying delicious lake fish.

ANNECY
● Croq en Bouche
9 fbg Ste-Claire, 74000 **Map** 8D4
📞 04 50 45 24 06
💳 AE, MC, V
🍴 €€
Country cottage-style surroundings with decidedly contemporary fare. Lovely sautéed foie gras on a carpaccio of fig. You can also try pela (p268), a type of tartiflette (p268) particular to the area.

ANNECY
■ Hôtel du Palais de l'Isle
13 rue Perrière, 74000 **Map** 8D4
📞 04 50 45 86 87
FAX 04 50 51 87 15
🖥 www.hoteldupalaisdelisle.com

💳 AE, DC, MC, V ⬤ (26) €€€
You'll be charmed by swan-filled canals and twisting streets where markets sell fresh seasonal produce. Spectacular views from your light-filled room.

ANNECY
● L'Atelier Gourmand
2 rue St-Maurice, 74000 **Map** 8D4
📞 04 50 51 19 71
FAX 04 50 51 36 48
💳 AE, DC, MC, V ⬤ Sun D, Mon, Tue L; 1st wk Jan, 1st wk Sep 🍴 €€€€€
Modern cuisine such as seafood lasagne. The tastiest dessert is the chocolate fondue with dried fruits.

ANNECY
▲ Le Belvédère
7 chemin du Belvédère, route du Semnoz, 74000 **Map** 8D4
📞 04 50 45 04 90
FAX 04 50 45 67 25
🖥 www.belvedere-annecy.com
💳 AE, DC, MC, V ⬤ Sun D, Tue D, Wed; mid-Jan–Mar
🍴 €€€ ⬤ (5) €€€€
Magical spot with spectacular views, offering fish from the lake, foie gras and potato purée with morels. This hotel stands out from the rest.

ANNECY
● Le Fréti
12 rue Ste-Claire, 74000 **Map** 8D4
📞 04 50 51 29 52
💳 MC, V 🍴 €
Tucked away under stone arches in the heart of the old town is this cheese shop of great repute. In the evenings diners are welcomed upstairs for Savoyard speciali-ties, including fondue savoyarde (p269), tartiflette (p268) and raclette (p268).

ANNECY
● Le Petit Zinc
11 rue du Port Morens, 74000 **Map** 8D4
📞 04 50 51 12 93
💳 AE, MC, V ⬤ Mon; mid-Jan–mid-Feb 🍴 €€
Country decor and pine furnishings create an appetizing environment for

● Restaurant ■ Hotel ▲ Hotel / Restaurant

risotto with wild mushrooms, grilled fish, and pormoniers (herb sausages).

ANNECY

▲ Les Terrasses

15 rue Louis Chaumontel, 74000
Map 9D4

C 04 50 57 08 98

FAX 04 50 57 05 28

✉ MC, V **▥** € **◔** (20) €€€

Escape the old-town bustle. Delicious lake fish feature prominently. Shaded terrace, lush gardens and spacious rooms.

ANNECY-LE-VIEUX

● Clos des Sens

13 rue Jean Mermoz, 74940 **Map** 9D4

C 04 50 23 07 90

FAX 04 50 66 56 54

✉ AE, DC, MC, V

◑ Sun D, Mon, Tue L; 1st 2 wks
Jan, Sep **▥** €€€

Inexpensive cuisine with nouvelle touches: prawns with smoked potatoes, beef with thyme, and rabbit with polenta. Good Chignin-Bergeron wines.

ANTHY-SUR-LEMAN

▲ Auberge d'Anthy

Rue des Écoles, 74200 **Map** 9D3

C 04 50 70 35 00

FAX 04 50 70 40 90

w www.auberge-anthy.com

✉ AE, DC, MC, V

◑ 1st 3 wks Jan

▥ €€ **◔** (16) €€

Fish is the speciality, with a perfect rendition of féra meunière. Excellent cheeses from Daniel Boujon and good sourdough bread. Savoyard pottery decorates bright, cheery rooms.

ANTRAIGUES-SUR-VOLANE

● La Remise

Pont de l'Huile, 07530 **Map** 12B1

C 04 75 38 70 74

◑ Sun, Sep–Jul: Fri; last wk Jun,
mid-Dec–1st wk Jan **▥** €

Once a barn and today a destination for tasting savoury home-made charcuterie, fresh from the market.

AUBENAS

● Le Chat Qui Pêche

6 pl de la Grenette, 07200 **Map** 12B1

C 04 75 93 87 49

FAX 04 75 93 87 49

✉ MC, V **◑** Wed, Sep–Jun: Tue;
Jan–Mar, last wk Oct **▥** €€€

The speciality is trout with chestnut butter. The seafood marmite is excellent. Children have their own menu.

AUSSOIS

▲ Les Mottets

6 rue des Mottets, 73500 **Map** 9E5

C 04 79 20 30 86

FAX 04 79 20 34 22

w www.hotel-lesmottets.com

✉ AE, MC, V **◑** May, Nov–mid-Dec

▥ € **◔** (25) €€

A central hotel with a merry Alpine feel and hearty cooking. Expect Beaufort cheese, meat, potatoes and vegetables – and plenty of red wine. Basic rooms that are great for families.

AVIERNOZ

▲ Auberge Camélia

Chef Lieu, entrance to town on D5,
74570 **Map** 9D4

C 04 50 22 44 24

FAX 04 50 22 43 25

w www.hotelcamelia.com

✉ AE, DC, MC, V

▥ €€ **◔** (12) €€€

Hotel run by a British couple. The restaurant serves delights from the French Alps. A great location for family fun around a wood-burning fireplace, skiing and lake activities.

BEAUJEU

▲ Anne de Beaujeu

28 rue République, town centre, 69430
Map 8B3

C 04 74 04 87 58

FAX 04 74 69 22 13

✉ MC, V **◑** Sun D, Mon, Tue L; 1st 2
wks Aug, mid-Dec–mid-Jan

▥ €€ **◔** (7) €€

This hotel-restaurant in the heart of Beaujeu provides comfortable lodging and such delights as scallops in puff pastry, pigeon with Chartreuse, and shrimp millefeuille with whisky vinaigrette.

BOURG-EN-BRESSE

● Chez Blanc

19 pl Bernard, 01000 **Map** 8C3

C 04 74 45 29 11

FAX 04 74 24 73 69

w www.georgesblanc.com

✉ AE, DC, MC, V **◑** Sun D, Mon

▥ €€

Chef David Pageau learned his craft under the region's favourite son and this restaurant's maître, Georges Blanc. Regional ingredients – Bresse chicken, frogs' legs – feature prominently.

BOURG-EN-BRESSE

■ Hôtel du Prieuré

49–51 bd de Brou, 01000 **Map** 8C3

C 04 74 22 44 60

FAX 04 74 22 71 07

@ hotel-duprieure@wanadoo.fr

✉ AE, DC, V **◔** (14) €€€

Though new, this hotel has all the charm of old France, including 500-year-old surrounding walls. In spring the smell of flowers is in the air from the forsythia, lilacs, roses and Japanese cherries. Spacious rooms with period furniture.

BRESSON

▲ Chavant

2 rue Emile Chavant, 38320 **Map** 8C5

C 04 76 25 25 38

FAX 04 76 62 06 55

w www.chateauxhotels.com

✉ AE, DC, MC, V **◑** Sun D, Mon, Sat L

▥ €€€€€ **◔** (7) €€€€€

A few Provençal treats, like stuffed vegetables, and mountain fare such as potato tartiflette (p268). Luxurious if slightly dated guestrooms.

BRIANCON

● Le Valentin

6 rue Mercerie (Petite Gargouille),
05100 **Map** 9D5

C 04 92 21 37 72

✉ MC, V **◑** Mon **▥** €€

Subdued lighting and a vaulted dining room make this a romantic spot. To eat: terrine with asparagus and scalloped potatoes or fromage blanc au miel (soft white cheese with honey).

BRIANCON

● Nano

Route d'Italie, 05100 **Map** 9D5

C 04 92 21 06 09

FAX 04 92 20 13 61

MC, V ● Sun D, Mon D; Jan, Easter, Nov 🍴 €€€

A renovated sheepfold with a vaulted ceiling and Alpine fare: foie gras, lamb in truffle sauce and iced nougat.

BRIANCON

● Péché Gourmand

2 route Gap, 05100 **Map** 9D5

📞 04 92 21 33 21

FAX 04 92 21 33 21

MC, V ● Sun D, Mon; last wk Dec 🍴 €€

Restaurant with an open kitchen where the tartiflette (p268) is outstanding.

BRIDES-LES-BAINS

● Grillade

Residence le Royal, 73570 **Map** 9D4

📞 04 79 55 20 90

FAX 04 79 55 20 90

MC, V ● Nov–2nd wk Dec 🍴 €

Many visitors come to Brides-les-Bains seeking help with health problems, so this little town-centre restaurant features both traditional and low-calorie offerings.

CHABEUIL

▲ Relais du Soleil

44 ave Romans, 26120 **Map** 8C5

📞 04 75 59 01 81

FAX 04 75 59 11 82

AE, DC, MC, V ● Oct–Feb: Sun; last wk Dec 🍴 €€ 🛏 (16) €€€

Chabeuil is famed for its caillettes, and equally celebrated bread. Sample them here. Comfortable rooms.

CHAMBERY

● Le Tonneau

2 rue St-Antoine, 73000 **Map** 8D4

📞 04 79 33 78 26

FAX 04 79 85 49 69

AE, DC, MC, V ● Sun D, Mon 🍴 €€€

A neighbourhood brasserie serving omelettes with morels, foie gras terrine, snails and gratin dauphinois (p268).

CHAMBERY

● L'Essentiel

183 pl de la Gare, 73000 **Map** 8D4

📞 04 79 96 97 27

FAX 04 79 96 17 78

w www.l-essentiel.com

AE, DC, MC, V ● Sun, Mon L, Sat L; 1st wk Jan 🍴 €€€€€

The building looks like a pyramid-shaped greenhouse. Try the duck with eight spices or venison terrine with pistachios. Roussette de Savoie wine.

CHAMBERY

● St-Réal

86 rue St-Réal, 73000 **Map** 9D4

📞 04 79 70 09 33

FAX 04 79 33 49 65

AE, DC, MC, V ● Sun, early Aug 🍴 €€€€

A 17th-century building with exposed stone and country furniture. The menu includes cheese fondue and pigeon.

CHAMONIX-MONT-BLANC

● Atmosphère

123 pl Balmat, 74400 **Map** 9D4

📞 04 50 55 97 97

FAX 04 50 53 38 96

w www.restaurant-atmosphere.com

AE, DC, MC, V 🍴 €€€€

This restaurant offers a nouvelle twist with salmon tartare, cured beef, or rabbit with dried fruit. Many fondues.

CHAMONIX-MONT-BLANC

▲ Auberge du Bois Prin

69 chemin de l'Hermine, Les Moussoux, 74400 **Map** 9D4

📞 04 50 53 33 51

FAX 04 50 53 48 75

w www.boisprin.com

AE, DC, MC, V ● Mon L, Wed L; mid-Apr–mid-May, Nov

🍴 €€€ 🛏 (11) €€€€

This family-run chalet has a panoramic view of the mountains from its terrace and some rooms. Good dairy dishes garnished with fresh garden herbs.

CHAMONIX-MONT-BLANC

▲ Hameau Albert 1er

119 impasse Montenvers, 74402 **Map** 9D4

📞 04 50 53 05 09

FAX 04 50 55 95 48

AE, DC, MC, V ● 2 wks May, mid-Oct–Nov 🍴 €€€€€

🛏 (42) €€€€€

The restaurant tempts with chanterelle ravioli, truffles with duck and artichoke

and cheese fondue. Some 20,000 bottles of wine. Luxurious accommodation.

CHAMONIX-MONT-BLANC

▲ Hôtel Jeu de Paume

705 route du Chapeau, 74400 **Map** 9D4

📞 04 50 54 03 76

FAX 04 50 54 10 75

w www.jeudepaumechamonix.com

AE, DC, MC, V

🍴 €€€ 🛏 (23) €€€€

Alpine architectural wonder with moose antlers over the fireplace, leather armchairs and a gourmet restaurant.

CHAMONIX-MONT-BLANC

▲ La Cabane at Hôtel Le Labrador

101 route du Golf, aux Praz-de-Chamonix, 74400 **Map** 9D4

📞 04 50 55 90 09

FAX 04 50 53 15 85

w www.hotel-labrador-chamonix.com

AE, DC, MC, V ● Mon, mid-Oct–mid-Nov: Tue & Wed D; mid-Nov–mid-Dec

🍴 €€€ 🛏 (32) €€€€

Savoyard log cabin built on a golf course with a stunning garden terrace. Menu eye-catchers include veal ribs, teriyaki sirloin, or strawberry soup. White-washed rooms with views of Mont Blanc.

CHAMONIX-MONT-BLANC

● Panier des Quatre Saisons

24 galerie Blanc-Neige, rue Paccard, 74400 **Map** 9D4

📞 04 50 53 98 77

FAX 04 50 53 98 77

AE, MC, V ● Wed, Thu L; mid-May–mid-Jun, mid-Nov–mid-Dec

🍴 €€

The menu usually includes fondue and tartiflette (p268). Also a good place for epogne (baked bread, cheese and ham).

CHAMONIX-MONT-BLANC

● Sarpé

30 pass Mottets, 74400 **Map** 9D4

📞 04 50 53 29 31

FAX 04 50 55 81 94

MC, V ● Mon; mid-May–mid-Jun, Nov 🍴 €€

An après-ski institution with cheese fondue and fried pork on the menu. This One of the area's most inviting spots.

● Restaurant ■ Hotel ▲ Hotel / Restaurant

CHARMES-SUR-RHONE

▲ Autour d'une Fontaine

15 rue Paul Bertois, 07800 **Map** 9B5

☎ 04 75 60 80 10

FAX 04 75 60 87 47

🏧 AE, MC, V ⬤ Sun D, Mon

🍴 €€ 🍽 (8) €€

All the rooms here open on to a patio overlooking the fountain. Dine on aubergines (eggplant) and tomato confit or rabbit with thyme. .

CLIOUSCLAT

▲ La Treille Muscate

Town centre, 26270 **Map** 12B1

☎ 04 75 63 13 10

FAX 04 75 63 10 79

🏧 MC, V ⬤ Wed; Jan–Feb

🍴 € 🍽 (12) €€€

Situated in a neighbourhood of potters' workshops and boutiques. Only one menu; recently pork cheeks with lemon and ginger. Rooms with modern baths.

COISE-ST-JEAN-PIED-GAUTHIER

▲ La Table du Baron

Château de Tour-du-Puits, 73800 **Map** 8D4

☎ 04 79 28 88 00

FAX 04 79 28 88 01

🏧 AE, DC, MC, V ⬤ Mon, Tue; Nov–2nd wk Dec

🍴 €€ 🍽 (8) €€€€€

This stately château serves specialities like matafans (a crêpe, some with potato). Individually decorated, grand rooms.

COLLONGES-AU-MONT-D'OR

● Paul Bocuse

40 quai de la Plage, 69660 **Map** 8B4

☎ 04 72 42 90 90

FAX 04 72 27 85 87

W www.bocuse.fr

🏧 AE, DC, MC, V 🍴 €€€€

Paul Bocuse is now simply considered an institution. Legendary lobster gratin and Charolais beef. Reserve far ahead.

COMBLOUX

▲ Aux Ducs de Savoie

253 route Bouchet, 74920 **Map** 9D4

☎ 04 50 58 61 43

FAX 04 50 58 67 43

🏧 AE, DC, MC, V ⬤ May, mid-Oct–mid-Dec 🍴 €€€ 🍽 (50) €€€€

Mont Blanc views from the terraces. Comfortable, modern hotel with a pool and excellent restaurant serving fondue.

CONFRANCON

▲ Auberge la Sarrasine

RN79, Le Logis Neuf, 01310 **Map** 8C3

☎ 04 74 30 25 65

FAX 04 74 25 24 23

🏧 AE, DC, MC, V ⬤ L; Jan (Oct–Easter, bookings only)

🍴 € 🍽 (9) €€€

Former farm situated between Burgundy and Bresse. Relax by the pool before heading to dinner (guests only). Rooms are warm and inviting, with rich fabrics.

CORDON

▲ Les Roches Fleuries

La Scie, 74700 **Map** 9D4

☎ 04 50 58 06 71

FAX 04 50 47 82 30

W www.rochesfleuries.com

🏧 AE, DC, MC, V

⬤ Apr–May, 3rd wk Sep–2nd wk Dec

🍴 €€€ 🍽 (21) €€€€

Take your pick from two excellent restaurants. At Boîte à Fromage, try matafans, charcuterie or fondue. The hotel's namesake serves rabbit cooked with mash and sage gravy. Guestrooms have mountain charm.

CORPS

▲ La Poste

Rue des Fossés, 38970 **Map** 9D5

☎ 04 76 30 00 03

FAX 04 76 30 02 73

🏧 MC, V ⬤ Jan–mid-Feb

🍴 €€ 🍽 (17) €€

As you walk in Napoleon's footsteps dine on turbot or tournedos of beef Rossini. After dinner recline in your own personal Jacuzzi (request ahead).

CORRENCON-EN-VERCORS

▲ L'Hôtel du Golf

Les Ritons, 38250 **Map** 8C5

☎ 04 76 95 84 84

FAX 04 76 95 82 85

🏧 AE, DC, MC, V ⬤ Apr, mid-Oct–mid-Dec 🍴 € 🍽 (12) €€€

After a day on the links you'll relish the menu at this hotel-restaurant just off the course. Expect the flavour of mountain

honey to feature on the dessert list. Guestrooms with nooks and mezzanines for tucking away the kids.

CREST

● La Tartine

10 rue Peysson, 26400 **Map** 12C1

☎ 04 75 25 11 53

FAX 04 75 25 30 73

🏧 MC, V

⬤ Mon, Wed D, Sat L; 1st wk Jul

🍴 €

Tartines (toasted sandwiches) satisfy diners seated under vaulted ceilings. Delights include snails and caillettes.

CREST

▲ Le Kléber

6 rue Aristide Dumont, 26400 **Map** 12C1

☎ 04 75 25 11 69

FAX 04 75 76 82 82

🏧 MC, V ⬤ Sun D, Mon–Tue L; 1st 2 wks Jan, 1st 2 wks Jul, last 2 wks Aug

🍴 €€ 🍽 (7) €€

The beef tenderloin Bordelaise is notable, as is the terrine of kid. After dinner climb the stone tower for a view of the Drôme countryside.

CRUSEILLES

▲ Château des Avenières

Route du Salève, Les Avenières, 74350 **Map** 9D4

☎ 04 50 44 02 23

FAX 04 50 44 29 09

W www.chateau-des-avenieres.com

🏧 AE, DC, MC, V

⬤ Mon, Tue; Nov–Feb Nov

🍴 €€€€ 🍽 (12) €€€€€

Fairytale château on the slopes of the Salève. Meals are luxe, from fish to venison and Savoyard cheeses.

CRUSEILLES

▲ L'Ancolie Chalet du Lac

1050 route Dronières, 74350 **Map** 9D4

☎ 04 50 44 28 98

FAX 04 50 44 09 73

🏧 AE, DC, MC, V ⬤ Sun D, Mon; 2nd wk Feb–1st wk Mar, 3rd wk Oct–1st wk Nov 🍴 €€ 🍽 (10) €€

An all-season favourite for well-priced and well-rounded fare. Try the rabbit with artichokes. Cosy guestrooms, some with forest and lake views.

DIVONNE–LES–BAINS
▲ Château de Divonne
115 rue des Bains, 01220 **Map** 9D3

C 04 50 20 00 32

FAX 04 50 20 03 73

W www.chateau-divonne.com

E AE, DC, MC, V ⬤ Jan

H €€€€€

⬤ (30) €€€€€

Luxury in a 19th-century manor with incredible views. Feast on trout and foie gras with green apples. Modern rooms accented with old-world touches.

DIVONNE–LES–BAINS
▲ Grand Hôtel
Avenue de Thermes, 01220 **Map** 9D3

C 04 50 40 34 34

FAX 04 50 40 34 24

W www.domaine-de-divonne.com

E AE, DC, MC, V

⬤ Sun D, Mon, Tue,

Sat L (restaurant only)

H €€€€€ ⬤ (133) €€€€€

Five-star resort with views of Mont Blanc, a pool, casino and five restaurants, including the area's finest, La Terrasse, managed by Dominique Roué. On the menu are crab, veal and langoustines tartare. Dine on gourmet offerings in the lavish winter garden or summer terrace. Eatery La Léman serves stuffed wild boar and traditional French fare in an Art Deco atmosphere. Elegant rooms with thoughtful touches, up-to-date after a 2002 renovation.

DUINGT
▲ Auberge du Roselet
RN508, 74410 **Map** 9D4

C 04 50 68 67 19

FAX 04 50 68 64 80

E MC, V ⬤ Nov–1st wk Jan

H €€ ⬤ (14) €€€

Enjoy Alpine fish like char – Lake Annecy is a protected habitat for the line-caught fish. Cheerful guestrooms.

EMBRUN
▲ Hôtel de la Mairie
Pl Berthelon, 05200 **Map** 13D1

C 04 92 43 20 65

FAX 04 92 43 47 02

W www.hoteldelamairie.com

E AE, MC, V

⬤ Dec–Apr: Mon; 3 wks May, Nov

H €€ ⬤ (24) €€€

Brasserie fare: foie gras, ravioli with morels and lamb stew. The front rooms can be noisy, but an outstanding location.

EMBRUN
▲ Mairie
Pl Barthelon, 05200 **Map** 13D1

C 04 92 43 20 65

FAX 04 92 43 47 02

W www.hoteldelamairie.com

E AE, MC, V ⬤ Jun & Sep: Mon L, Dec–Apr: Sun D & Mon; last 3 wks May, Oct, Nov **H** € ⬤ (24) €€

Local favourites such as foie gras, duck confit and ravioles de Royans (p268) with morels. Rooms have cheerful fabrics and wooden walls. Exceptional value.

ETOILE–SUR–RHONE
● Le Vieux Four
1 pl Léon Lérisse, 26800 **Map** 12B1

C 04 75 60 72 21

E MC, V ⬤ Mon, Tue; last wk Mar, 2nd wk Jun, mid-Aug–1st wk Sep

H €€€€

A sample: Drôme's guinea fowl is paired with olives and a tortilla of sun-ripened vegetables. Monthly cabaret night.

EVIAN–LES–BAINS
▲ Chez Tante Marie
2km (1 mile) past Evian-les-Bains on route 5 to Bernex, 74500 **Map** 9D3

C 04 50 73 60 35

FAX 04 50 73 61 73

E AE, DC, MC, V ⬤ May, mid-Oct–mid-Dec **H** €€ ⬤ (13) €€€

Elegant flower-draped chalet perched above the lake. Prawns in whisky as well as potato tartiflette (p268) are served. Farming objects decorate each bedroom.

EVIAN–LES–BAINS
▲ Hôtel Ermitage
Rive sud Lac de Genève, 74500 **Map** 9D3

C 04 50 26 85 00

FAX 04 50 74 65 62

E AE, DC, MC, V ⬤ mid-Nov–1st wk Feb **H** €€€€€ ⬤ (91) €€€€€

Discreet luxury in a 20th-century setting. Old-world menu from foie gras to lobster. Colourful patterns and very practical furnishings in the guestrooms.

EVIAN–LES–BAINS
▲ Hôtel Panorama
Ave Grande Rive, 74500 **Map** 9D3

C 04 50 75 14 50

FAX 04 50 75 59 12

E AE, MC, V ⬤ Oct–mid-Apr

H €€ ⬤ (29) €€€

Breathtaking views of Lake Geneva from the guestrooms. Cuisine includes foie gras and salmon. A verdant setting.

EVIAN–LES–BAINS
▲ Hôtel Royal
Rive sud lac de Genève, 74501 **Map** 9D3

C 04 50 26 85 00

FAX 04 50 74 65 62

E AE, DC, MC, V ⬤ Dec–1st wk Feb

H €€€€€ ⬤ (154) €€€€€

The height of luxury in a Belle Epoque setting. Several gourmet restaurants, a heliport and a golf course.

EYBENS
▲ Château de la Commanderie
17 ave d'Echirolles, 38320 **Map** 8C5

C 04 76 25 34 58

FAX 04 76 24 07 31

W www.commanderie.fr

E AE, DC, MC, V ⬤ Sun L, Mon, Sat L

H €€€ ⬤ (25) €€€€

Small château with Aubusson carpets and a swimming pool. Try the rabbit with spinach. Richly decorated guestrooms.

FLEURIE
● Le Cep
Pl de l'Eglise, 69820 **Map** 8B3

C 04 74 04 10 77

FAX 04 74 04 10 28

E AE, DC, MC, V ⬤ Sun, Mon; 1st wk Aug, mid-Dec–mid-Jan **H** €€

Notable are free-range chicken with wine and redcurrants, and frogs' legs. Beaujolais stars on the wine list.

FONTANIL–CORNILLON
● La Queue de Cochon
1 route Lyon, 38120 **Map** 8C5

C 04 76 75 65 54

FAX 04 76 75 85 76

E AE, MC, V ⬤ Sun D, Mon

H €€

In the comfort of a garden, this eatery has a satisfying lunch buffet and a vast selection of grilled meats and vegetables.

● Restaurant ■ Hotel ▲ Hotel / Restaurant

GAP

● Le Pasturier

18 rue Pérolière, 05000 **Map** 13D1

☎ 04 92 53 69 29

FAX 04 92 53 30 91

AE, MC, V ● Sun, Sep–Jul: Mon L; mid-1st wk Jan–mid-Jan, 1st 2 wks Jul

€€

An ambience as warm as the Provençal sun. The chef crafts delicacies such as crab gratin or pork cheeks with onions.

GAP

● Le Patalain

2 pl Ladoucette, 05000 **Map** 13D1

☎ 04 92 52 30 83

FAX 04 92 52 30 83

AE, DC, MC, V ● Sun, Mon; 1st 3 wks Jan €€

Two restaurants, one with bistro fare and the other gastronomic cuisine. Both offer exceptional value.

GEX

● Auberge Gessienne

7km (4 miles) south on D984c in Chevry, 01170 **Map** 9D3

☎ 04 50 41 01 67

FAX 04 50 41 01 67

MC, V ● Sun D, Mon; 1st 3 wks Aug €€

Popular with French locals and Swiss border-hoppers for the food, especially the sublime gratin dauphinois (p268).

GEX

▲ Hôtel Mainaz

Route de col de la Faucille, RN5, 01173 **Map** 9D3

☎ 04 50 41 31 10

FAX 04 50 41 31 77

AE, DC, MC, V ● Sun D, Mon; last wk Apr–mid-May

€€€ ⬤ (22) €€€

They make their own cheese here, which can be enjoyed at different stages of aging. Chalet-style rooms with views.

GLEIZE

▲ Château de Chervinges

69400 **Map** 8B4

☎ 04 74 65 29 76

FAX 04 74 62 92 42

AE, MC, V ● Apr–Sep: Sun D & Mon

€€€ ⬤ (15) €€€€

Use this medieval farmhouse as an elegant base while visiting the vineyards. Serene, luxurious rooms.

GRENOBLE

● Auberge Napoléon

7 rue Montorge, 38000 **Map** 8C5

☎ 04 76 87 53 64

FAX 04 76 87 80 76

AE, DC, MC, V ● L, Sun; last wk Aug–1st wk Sep €€€

Elegant, Empire-style dining area and equally upscale food: chicken with crayfish and rabbit ratatouille (p400).

GRENOBLE

● La Laiterie 1935

4 pl de Gordes, 38000 **Map** 8C5

☎ 04 76 44 81 22

DC, MC, V ● Mon €

Charming ambience and cheesy food on a fountain-splashed square. Not for the lactose intolerant.

GRENOBLE

● Le Mal Assis

9 rue Bayard, 38000 **Map** 8C5

☎ 04 76 54 75 93

MC, V ● Sun, Mon €€

Good, inexpensive food at a family-run eatery in the cathedral district. Excellent smoked ham starters.

GRENOBLE

● L'Escalier

6 pl Lavalette, 38000 **Map** 8C5

☎ 04 76 54 66 16

FAX 04 76 51 50 93

AE, DC, MC, V ● Sun, Mon L, Sat L; 2nd wk Aug €€€

Near the fine art museum. Magret de canard in spring, grilled tuna in autumn, and mushroom ravioli in winter.

GRENOBLE

▲ Park Hôtel

10 pl Paul Mistral, 38000 **Map** 8C5

☎ 04 76 85 81 23

FAX 04 76 46 49 88

AE, DC, MC, V

● Sun L, Sat L, 3 wks Aug

€€€€€ ⬤ (52) €€€€€

Unbeatable gratin dauphinois (p268) or morel ravioli. Some guestrooms overlook the park at this central location.

GRENOBLE

● Villa Marie

16 pl Notre Dame, 38000 **Map** 8C5

☎ 04 76 44 22 25

MC, V ● Sun €

No alcohol here but rabbit confit is a refreshing change from duck. Shellfish steamed with tea brings an Asian touch.

GRIGNAN

● Le Poème

Montée du Tricot, 26230 **Map** 12B1

☎ 04 75 91 10 90

MC, V ● Tue, Wed €

Like a poem, this little restaurant flanked by booksellers has a rhythm. Singled out for attention has been the snail cassolette.

GRIGNAN

▲ Manoir de la Roseraie

Route de Valreas, 26230 **Map** 12B1

☎ 04 75 46 58 15

FAX 04 75 46 91 55

W www.manoirdelaroseraie.com

AE, DC, MC, V ● Tue, Wed D; Jan–mid-Feb, 1st 2 wks Dec

€€€ ⬤ (21) €€€€€

Fruits and vegetables from the garden in the delicious dishes. Sumptuous rooms in this rose-filled château.

GUILHERAND-GRANGES

● Auberge des Trois Canards

565 ave la République, 07500 **Map** 8B5

☎ 04 75 44 43 24

FAX 04 75 41 64 48

AE, DC, MC, V ● Sun D, Mon

€

On the right bank of the Rhône is this little restaurant dedicated to duck.

JOYEUSE

▲ Les Cèdres

La Glacière, 07260 **Map** 12B1

☎ 04 75 39 40 60

FAX 04 75 39 90 16

AE, DC, MC, V ● mid-Oct–mid-Apr

€ ⬤ (40) €€

Superb chestnut honey duck and nougat with bilberries. Rooms have mezzanines. There's a pool for working off calories.

JULIENAS

▲ Chez la Rose

Marketplace, 69840 **Map** 8B3

[C] 04 74 04 41 20
[FAX] 04 74 04 49 29
[card] AE, DC, MC, V [clock] Mon, Tue L; last
3 wks Feb, 2nd wk–25 Dec
[fork] €€€ [key] (10) €€
Good food – coq au vin (p217),
Burgundy snails, Brittany lobster – plus a
hotel discount for diners. Rustic rooms.

LA CHAPELLE-D'ABONDANCE
▲ **Les Cornettes**
Town centre, 74360 **Map** 9D3
[C] 04 50 73 50 24
[FAX] 04 50 73 54 16
[W] www.lescornettes.com
[card] MC, V [clock] last 2 wks Apr, 2nd wk
Oct–3rd wk Dec [fork] €€ [key] (60) €€
Meals feature the charcuterie of Savoie,
including lovely herb and pork sausages.
Generously proportioned rooms.

LA CLUSAZ
▲ **Hôtel Beauregard**
Le Bossonet, 74220 **Map** 9D4
[C] 04 50 32 68 00
[FAX] 04 50 02 59 00
[card] AE, DC, MC, V [clock] Nov
[fork] € [key] (100) €€€
Perfectly located at the bottom of the
slopes. Fondue and raclette (p268) are
the specialities. Guestroom have views.

LA CLUSAZ
▲ **Hôtel Carlina**
La Perriere, 74220 **Map** 9D4
[C] 04 50 02 43 48
[FAX] 04 50 02 63 02
[W] www.hotel-carlina.com
[card] AE, DC, MC, V [clock] mid-Apr–3rd wk
Jun, 1st wk Sep–1st wk Dec
[fork] €€€ [key] (39) €€€€
Favourites include cabbage salad with
warm chicken livers, and caramelized
pears with honey. Cosy panelled rooms.

LA CLUSAZ
▲ **Les Chalets de la Serraz**
Route du Col des Aravis, 74220 **Map** 9D4
[C] 04 50 02 48 29
[FAX] 04 50 02 64 12
[card] AE, DC, MC, V [clock] May, Oct
[fork] € [key] (10) €€€€
Simple dishes using lake fish and the
delicious herb and pork sausages that
are the backbone of Savoyard cuisine.

Alpine-style rooms or split-level chalet
apartments provide refuge.

LA GRAVE
▲ **La Meijette**
RN91, 05320 **Map** 9D5
[C] 04 76 79 90 34
[FAX] 04 76 79 94 76
[card] MC, V [clock] mid-Sep–mid-Feb
[fork] €€ [key] (18) €€€€
Attractive wooden balconies and views
of the Massif de le Meije. Excellent potato
pancakes. Simple, comfortable rooms.

LA ROSIERE
▲ **Relais du Petit St-Bernard**
Montvalezan, 73700 **Map** 9E4
[C] 04 79 06 80 48
[FAX] 04 79 06 83 40
[W] www.petit-saint-bernard.com
[card] MC, V [clock] mid-Apr–Jun, Sep–Nov
[fork] €€ [key] (20) €€€
At the base of the ski slopes with a
restaurant celebrated for cheese fondue,
raclette (p268) and good wine. Simple
pine furniture in the guestrooms.

LA TOUR-DE-SALVAGNY
● **La Rotonde**
200 ave du Casino, 69890 **Map** 8B4
[C] 04 78 87 00 97
[FAX] 04 78 87 81 39
[W] www.lyonvert.com
[card] AE, DC, MC, V [clock] Sun D, Mon, Tue
L; last wk Jul–last wk Aug [fork] €€€
The best of French cuisine – rabbit with
potato millefeuille, snail ravioles (p268)
and tender frogs' legs.

LATHUILE
▲ **Châtaigneraie**
RN508, Chaparon, 74210 **Map** 9D4
[C] 04 50 44 30 67
[FAX] 04 50 44 83 71
[W] www.hotelchataigneraie.com
[card] AE, DC, MC, V [clock] May–Sep: Sun D
& Mon; Feb–Nov
[fork] €€ [key] (25) €€€
The setting invites relaxation, with gardens
and a pool. Always delicious, traditional
food. Comfortable rooms low on style.

LE BESSAT
▲ **La Fondue "Chez l'Père Charles"**
Grande Rue, 42660 **Map** 8B5

[C] 04 77 20 40 09
[FAX] 04 77 20 45 20
[card] AE, MC, V [clock] Sun D, Mon L; mid-
Nov–mid-Mar [fork] € [key] (8) €€
Savour the mijotés (slow braised stews)
that are the house speciality. Then rest
in one of the clean, simple rooms.

LE BOURGET-DU-LAC
● **Auberge Lamartine**
Route Tunnel du Chat, RN504, 73370
Map 8C3
[C] 04 79 25 01 03
[FAX] 04 79 25 20 66
[W] www.lamartine-marin.com
[card] AE, DC, MC, V [clock] Sun D, Mon, Tue
L; last 2 wks Dec [fork] €€€€
Warm and elegant decor: fireplaces,
flowers and wine bottles. The menu
stars duck caramelized in port and
salmon tartare with a ginger sauce.

LE BOURGET-DU-LAC
● **Bateau Ivre**
Route Tunnel, 2km (1 mile) north on
N504, 73370 **Map** 8C3
[C] 04 79 25 00 23
[FAX] 04 79 25 25 77
[card] AE, DC, MC, V [clock] Mon, Tue L, Thu
L; Nov–Apr [fork] €€€€€
Haute cuisine with views of Lac du
Bourget and the mountains. The house
speciality is frogs' legs with cream and
garlic. Excellent veal roasted in lard.

LE BOURGET-DU-LAC
● **La Grange à Sel**
La Croix Verte, 73370 **Map** 8C3
[C] 04 79 25 02 66
[FAX] 04 79 25 25 03
[card] AE, DC, MC, V [clock] Sun D, Wed; Jan
[fork] €€€
Picturesque ivy-covered restaurant
located in a former salt warehouse.
Divine yet reasonably priced meals:
poached eggs with truffle, pork fillet with
mozzarella, and a polenta crêpe soufflé.

LE COTEAU
▲ **Artaud**
133 ave de la Libération, 42120 **Map** 8A4
[C] 04 77 68 46 44
[FAX] 04 77 72 23 50
[card] AE, DC, MC, V [clock] Sun, Mon; Aug
[fork] € [key] (24) €€

Delicious dishes, like chicken with chanterelles, and a lovely room with garden view. Guestrooms lack pizzazz.

LE COTEAU
● Auberge Costelloise
2 ave de la Libération, 42120 **Map** 8A4
[04 77 68 12 71
FAX 04 77 72 26 78
AE, MC, V ● Sun, Mon; 3 wks Aug, 26 Dec–4 Jan **||** €€

Diners are pleasantly surprised by the new chef's talent with fish in a beef region. Enjoy wines from Côte Roanne.

LE MONETIER-LES-BAINS
▲ Alliey
11 rue Ecoles, 05220 **Map** 9D5
[04 92 24 40 02
FAX 04 92 24 40 60
w www.alliey.com
MC, V ● L, Sun D booking only; 3rd wk Apr–3rd wk Jun, Sep–3rd wk Dec **||** € ● (22) €€

Two stone houses built in 1873. Rustic cuisine prevails. Bright, woodsey flats with all amenities.

LE MONETIER-LES-BAINS
▲ Auberge du Choucas
17 rue de la Fruitière, 05220 **Map** 9D5
[04 92 24 42 73
FAX 04 92 24 51 60
MC, V ● 3 wks May, Nov–mid-Dec **||** €€€ ● (12) €€€€

A charming 18th-century inn. Draws ingredients from the quaint garden and inspiration from the mountains. Sweet, artistically styled rooms.

LE MONETIER-LES-BAINS
● Chazal
Les Guibertes rue Milieu, 05220 **Map** 9D5
[04 92 24 45 54
MC, V ● Mon; last 2 wks Jun, mid-Nov–mid-Dec **||** €€

For appetizers, epogne (baked bread, ham and cheese) and herb sausages. Also, foie gras and onion soup on offer.

LE TERTENOZ
▲ Au Gay Séjour
Signs from Faverge, 74210 **Map** 9D4
[04 50 44 52 52
FAX 04 50 44 49 52

w www.hotel-gay-sejour.com
AE, DC, MC, V ● Sun D, Mon; mid-Nov–mid-Dec
|| €€€ ● (11) €€€

A 17th-century Savoyard farm in the Bauges National Park. Sample cheese from the local abbey and lake fish. Rooms have clean, rustic charm.

LES GETS
▲ La Marmotte
61 rue du Chêne, 74260 **Map** 9D3
[04 50 75 80 33
FAX 04 50 75 83 26
w www.hotel-marmotte.com
AE, DC, MC, V ● Apr–Jun, Sep–3rd wk Dec
|| €€€€€ ● (48) €€€€€

Families appreciate this large chalet near the slopes. Expect tartiflette (p268), fondue savoyarde (p269) and raclette (p268) in winter and charcuterie in summer. Children enjoy the Little Marmott Club.

LES GETS
▲ Le St-Laurent
266 route du Léry, 74260 **Map** 9D3
[04 50 75 80 00
FAX 04 50 79 87 03
w www.labrador-hotel.com
AE, DC, MC, V ● 2nd wk Apr–3rd wk Jun, 1st wk Sep–3rd wk Dec
|| €€ ● (23) €€€€

Honey-coloured wood gleams in rooms and cowbells hang from the rafters. Try perch cooked in vanilla, or a fricassée of scallops and forest mushrooms.

LES SAISIES
▲ Le Calgary
Rue Perios, 73620 **Map** 9D4
[04 79 38 98 38
FAX 04 79 38 98 00
MC, V ● last wk Apr–last wk Jun, 2nd wk Sep–mid-Dec
|| €€ ● (40) €€€

Outings are organized for the little ones, and adults enjoy sumptuous cuisine. The chocolate cake with apricot sauce is fantastic. Spacious, balconied rooms.

LYON
● Café des Fédérations
8 rue du Major Martin, 69001 **Map** 8B4
[04 78 28 26 00

FAX 04 72 07 74 52
w www.lesfedeslyon.com
MC, V ● Sun, Sat; Aug
|| €

Taste traditional working-man's fare. Begin in the cave with an apéritif, then tablier de sapeur (p268), a menu staple.

LYON
■ Carlton
4 rue Jussieu, 69002 **Map** 8B4
[04 78 42 56 51
FAX 04 78 42 10 71
w www.libertel-hotels.com
AE, MC, V ● (83) €€€

A retro-style hotel perfectly situated for discovering Lyon. The cage elevator sets off the purple and gold decor.

LYON
● Chez Léa
11 pl Antonin Gourju, 69002 **Map** 8B4
[04 78 42 01 33
FAX 04 78 37 36 41
AE, MC, V ● Sun **||** €

Faintly feminine decor and gracious welcome. Be sure to try Léa's legendary quenelles in crayfish sauce.

LYON
● Comptoir du Boeuf
3 pl Neuve-St-Jean, 69005 **Map** 8B4
[04 78 92 69 27
FAX 04 78 42 26 02
AE, MC, V **||** €€

A terrine of wild game with onion marmalade is excellent, and the house-smoked salmon has inspired a following. Also known for its wine list.

LYON
● Daniel et Denise
156 rue de Créqui, 69003 **Map** 8B4
[04 78 60 66 53
FAX 04 78 60 66 53
● Fri, Sat; Aug **||** €

Veal is used judiciously – tablier de sapeur (p268), liver with vinegar sauce, kidneys en cocotte, tête-de-veau (p268).

LYON
● Fedora
249 rue Marcel Mérieux, 69007 **Map** 8B4
[04 78 69 46 26
FAX 04 72 73 38 80

For key to symbols see back flap

AE, MC, V ● Sun, Mon D, Sat L
🍴 €

Take your charcuterie-weary palate to this small bistro and rejuvenate with pesto shrimps or gazpacho soup.

LYON
● **Garet**
7 rue Garet, 69002 **Map** 8B4
📞 04 78 28 16 94
FAX 04 72 00 07 84
AE, MC, V ● Sun, Sat
🍴 €

Fans of French cinema might recognize this bistro's interior from the films of Bertrand Tavernier, who filmed here with star Philippe Noiret. Classic Lyonnais dishes include chicken with vinegar, plates of charcuterie and tripe.

LYON
● **La Commanderie des Antonins**
30 quai St-Antoine, 69002 **Map** 8B4
📞 04 78 37 19 21
W www.commanderie-antonins.fr
MC, V ● Sun, Mon L; Jul–Aug
🍴 €€

In the heart of this medieval hospital is a wood-burning oven. The ambience is ancient, with vaulted stone ceilings illuminated by candlelight.

LYON
▲ **La Cour des Loges**
4–6 rue du Boeuf, 69005 **Map** 8B4
📞 04 72 77 44 44
FAX 04 72 40 93 61
W www.courdesloges.com
AE, DC, MC, V ● Sun, Mon; Aug
🍴 €€€€ 🍷 (62) €€€€€

This UNESCO-protected Renaissance hotel houses, in its inimitable lobby, a crown prince of French cuisine, the young Nicholas Le Bec. His cuisine sparkles – foie gras with cocoa beans, Provençal artichokes in eucalyptus and rabbit in tobacco leaf. Rooms are the epitome of good taste and luxury.

LYON
● **Le Bouchon Lyonnais**
12 rue Pizay, 69001 **Map** 8B4
📞 04 78 28 10 94
FAX 04 78 28 10 94
MC, V ● Sun, Sat; Aug 🍴 €

Fare is classic bouchon with offerings like charcuterie, chicken in vinegar, salads, Beaujolais and runny St-Marcellin cheese.

LYON
● **Le Nord**
18 rue Neuve, 69002 **Map** 8B4
📞 04 72 10 69 69
FAX 04 72 10 69 68
AE, DC, MC, V 🍴 €

In this downtown brasserie, Paul Bocuse set out to deliver traditional cuisine. There's pepper steak with Charolais beef, Bresse chicken in tangy vinegar, salade niçoise with Nyons olives and tripe with Normandy cider.

LYON
● **Le Sud**
11 pl Antonin Poncet, 69002 **Map** 8B4
📞 04 72 77 80 00
FAX 04 72 77 80 01
AE, DC, MC, V 🍴 €

Look for exotic touches to elevate the palate: excellent Bresse chicken tagine, saffron fish soup and thyme coffee.

LYON
● **Le Théodore**
34 Franklin Roosevelt, 69006 **Map** 8B4
📞 04 78 24 08 52
FAX 04 72 74 41 21
● Sun; 2nd wk Aug, 22–25 Dec, 29 Dec–1 Jan 🍴 €€

A kitchen in a smart neighbourhood that turns out house-smoked salmon. The children's menu is surprisingly good.

MARNAND
▲ **La Terrasse**
Le Bourg, 69240 **Map** 8B4
📞 04 74 64 19 22
FAX 04 74 64 25 95
MC, V ● Sep–Jun: Sun D & Mon; Feb, 3rd wk Oct–1st wk Nov
🍴 €€ 🍷 (10) €€

Formerly a textile factory, now a hotel-restaurant with a rare vegetarian menu. Rooms are perfumed by the aromatic plants after which they're named.

MEGEVE
▲ **Chalet du Mont d'Arbois**
447 chemin la Rocaille, 74120 **Map** 9D4
📞 04 50 21 25 03

FAX 04 50 21 24 79
AE, MC, V ● May–mid-Jun, Nov–mid-Dec
🍴 €€€ 🍷 (24) €€€€€

Après-ski haunt decked out in untreated pine. At weekends the place turns into a bubbly jazz club. Feast on bacon confit, the wild turbot and clam risotto or Grand-Marnier soufflé.

MEGEVE
▲ **Ferme de Mon Père**
367 route Crêt, 74120 **Map** 9D4
📞 04 50 21 01 01
FAX 04 50 21 43 43
W www.marcveyrat.fr
AE, DC, MC, V ● Mon; Nov
🍴 €€€€€ 🍷 (6) €€€€€

One of France's greatest culinary talents, chef Marc Veyrat dazzles at this three-star Michelin restaurant. On the menu: foie gras, potato tartiflette (p268) and fried perch. Pleasant rooms are secondary to the exceptional kitchen.

MEGEVE
● **Flocons de Sel**
75 rue St-François, 74120 **Map** 9D4
📞 04 50 21 49 99
FAX 04 50 21 68 22
MC, V ● Tue D, Wed; Jun, Nov
🍴 €€€€

Inside a 19th-century farm, this rustic eatery serves scallops with truffle sauce, and langoustines with a corn and coriander (cilantro) sauce. An old wood-burning oven and views of peaked roofs.

MEGEVE
▲ **Lodge Park**
100 rue d'Arly, 74120 **Map** 9D4
📞 04 50 93 05 03
FAX 04 50 93 09 52
AE, DC, MC, V ● 2nd wk Apr–3rd wk Jun, 2nd wk Sep–1st wk Dec
🍴 €€€ 🍷 (50) €€€€€

Reminiscent of the grand lodges of America's national parks. Discover sesame-crusted shrimp, sea bream in lime leaves, and nems (hot rolls) of chocolate. Wood-panelled guestrooms.

MEGEVE
● **Vieux Megève**
58 pl de la Résistance, 74120 **Map** 9D4

● Restaurant ■ Hotel ▲ Hotel / Restaurant

[04 50 21 16 44
FAX 04 50 93 06 69
MC, V ● mid-Sep–mid-Dec
€€

This 1880 chalet has fairytale appeal.
The menu touches all the basics such
as fondue savoyarde (268) and raclette
(p268). Excellent bilberry tart.

MERIBEL
▲ Chaudanne

Rond-point des pistes, 73550 **Map** 9D5
[04 79 08 61 76
FAX 04 79 08 57 75
www.chaudanne.com
MC, V ● L
€€ ◆ (76) €€€€

A three-star hotel at the télécabines
station. Rustic decor with wine barrels,
St-Bernard dog photos and snow
sledges, plus classic Savoie dishes.
Chalet-style guestrooms.

MERIBEL
▲ Hôtel Alba

Route de Belvédère, rond-point des
pistes, 73550 **Map** 9D5
[04 79 08 55 55
FAX 04 79 00 55 63
www.meribel-hotel-alba.com
MC, V €€€ ◆ (20) €€€€

Massive wooden structure at the heart
of Meribel's skiing world. On the table:
cheeses, potatoes and meats in regional
dishes. Comfortable pine guestrooms.

MERIBEL
▲ Hôtel Allodis

Le Belvédère, BP43, 73552 **Map** 9D5
[04 79 00 56 00
FAX 04 79 00 59 28
www.hotel-allodis.com
AE, DC ● May–Jun, Sep–Nov
€€€ ◆ (44) €€€€€

Take a fireside seat and enjoy pigeon
stuffed with foie gras. Updated chalet-
style guestrooms; fireplaces in the suites.

MOLINES-EN-QUEYRAS
▲ L'Équipe

Route de St-Véran, 05350 **Map** 13E1
[04 92 45 83 20
FAX 04 92 45 81 85
www.lequipedemolines.com
AE, DC, MC, V ● Sep–Jun: Sun D

& Mon; Apr–May, Oct–Nov
€ ◆ (22) €€

Warm up with raclette (p268) in winter;
try pierrade (meat or fish cooked on a
hot stone) in summer. Chalet-style rooms
with panoramic views from the balconies.

MONTAILLEUR
▲ La Tour de Pacoret

Grésy-sur-Isère, 73460 **Map** 9D4
[04 79 37 91 59
FAX 04 79 37 93 84
www.hotel-pacoret-savoie.com
MC, V ● Tue, Wed; Nov–May
€€ ◆ (10) €€€

Bright summer terrace with regional
specialities and vintage wines. Pastel
rooms reflect their flowery namesakes.

MONTBONNOT
● Les Mésanges-Alain Pic

876 rue Général De Gaulle, RN90,
38330 **Map** 8C5
[04 76 90 21 57
FAX 04 76 90 94 48
www.restaurant-alain-pic.com
AE, MC, V ● Sun D, Mon, Sat L;
2nd wk Aug €€€€

Culinary nirvana: lobster medallion risotto,
and ham with fig jam. The flower-filled garden could be an Impressionist's painting.

MONTBOUCHER-SUR-JABRON
▲ Château du Monard

Domaine de la Valdaine, 26740
Map 12D1
[04 75 00 71 30
FAX 04 75 00 71 31
www.domainedelavaldaine.com
AE, DC, MC, V ● Oct–Mar: Sun D
€€ ◆ (35) €€€€

A 16th-century château enjoying its
renaissance into an elegant hotel with
golf, pool, tennis and a fabulous
restaurant. Daily truffle menu.

MONTELIMAR
● La Petite France

34 rue Raymond Daujat, 26200
Map 12B1
[04 75 46 07 94
MC, V ● Sun, Mon; mid-Jul–mid-
Aug, 24–28 Dec €

Once home to an Alsatian restaurant but
today serving regional fare prepared by

a chef who trained with Guy Savoy.
Simplicity reigns, with dishes such as
young quail and roasted duck breast.

MONTELIMAR
▲ La Table des Pins

148 route de Marseille (RN7), 26200
Map 12B1
[04 75 01 15 88
FAX 04 75 51 09 40
www.hostelleriedespins.com
AE, MC, V ● Nov–Mar: Sun D
€ ◆ (43) €€

A good place to get acquainted with the
Arab-influenced flavours of Marseille. Try
the "modern" couscous with lamb.
Bungalow accommodation is available.

MONTELIMAR
● Senteurs de Provence

202 route Marseille (RN7), 26200
Map 12B1
[04 75 01 43 82
FAX 04 75 51 32 88
MC, V ● Sun D, Tue D, Wed; 2nd &
3rd wk Feb, 2nd & 3rd wk Aug €€

Popular with locals for the ravioles de
Royans (p268). Lively and often noisy,
but worth enduring for the nougat glacé
– an ice-cream-like version of the town's
famous confection. Make a reservation.

MONTREVEL-EN-BRESSE
▲ L'Aventure at Hôtel le Pillebois

Route de Bourg-en-Bresse, Malafretaz,
01340 **Map** 8C3
[04 74 25 48 44
FAX 04 74 25 48 79
www.hotellepillebois.com
MC, V ● Sun, Mon
€€ ◆ (32) €€

So good and such good value that it's
earned critical acclaim and a loyal
following. Poolside restaurant. Pastel
rooms luminescent with country light.

MORANCE
● Auberge du Pont de Morancé

2680 route les Chères, 69480 **Map** 8B4
[04 78 47 65 14
FAX 04 78 47 05 83
MC, V ● Tue, Wed; Feb
€€

Unwind under the shelter of century old
trees and try the sautéed frogs' legs.

NANTUA

▲ L'Embarcadère

13 ave du Lac, 01130 **Map** 8C3

📞 04 74 75 22 88

FAX 04 74 75 22 25

📧 MC, V ● 3rd wk Dec–1st wk Jan

🍴 €€ 🛏 (49) €€

Chef Bernard Jantet is maître cuisinier de France (a distinction awarded to a handful of the best). Try quenelles de brochet sauce Nantua (p269). Small rooms undergoing renovation.

NYONS

● Charrette Bleue

La Bonté route to Gap, Condorcet, 26110 **Map** 12C1

📞 04 75 27 72 33

FAX 04 75 27 76 14

📧 MC, V ● Wed, Sep–Jun: Tue, mid-Dec–Jan 🍴 €€€

Along with Nyon olives you'll find Drôme's guinea fowl, sometimes with apricots and mushrooms. Excellent wine list.

NYONS

■ La Bastide des Monges

Quartier des Monges, 26110 **Map** 12C1

📞 04 75 26 99 69

FAX 04 75 26 99 70

🌐 www.bastidedesmonges.com

📧 AE, MC, V ● mid-Oct–mid-Apr

🛏 (8) €€€

Escape the midday sun by dipping into the pool, or relax on a shaded terrace and admire the view of Mont Ventoux. Rooms – each named after a type of wine – are gorgeous and well-appointed.

PONT-DE-L'ISERE

▲ Michel Chabran

29 ave 45ème Parallèle, 26600 **Map** 8B5

📞 04 75 84 60 09

FAX 04 75 84 59 65

📧 AE, DC, MC, V ● Wed, Apr–Sep: Fri L, Oct–Mar: Sun L

🍴 €€€€ 🛏 (12) €€€€

House-cum-hotel at the foot of the Hermitage vineyards. The chef works culinary magic with millefeuille of lobster and pigeon.

PONT-DE-VAUX

▲ Raisin

2 pl Michel Poisat, 01190 **Map** 8B3

📞 03 85 30 30 97

FAX 03 85 30 67 89

📧 AE, DC, MC, V ● Sep–Jun: Sun D; 1st wk Jan–2nd wk Feb

🍴 €€ 🛏 (18) €€

Wine is taken seriously here and there's a beautiful list. The cuisine is likely to include freshwater fish, Bresse chicken, fine crayfish and frogs' legs. Quiet and spacious rooms, especially at the back.

QUINCIE-EN-BEAUJOLAIS

▲ Mont-Brouilly

Pont des Samsons, 69430 **Map** 8B3

📞 04 74 04 33 73

FAX 04 74 04 30 10

🌐 www.hotelbrouilly.com

📧 AE, MC, V ● Oct–Mar: Sun–Mon D; Feb, last 2 wks Dec

🍴 €€ 🛏 (29) €€

Children can play on the swings or swim in the pool while parents visit nearby vineyards and tasting caves. Enjoy coq au Beaujolais or veal sweetbreads.

REGNIE-DURETTE

● Auberge Vigneronne

Le Bourg, 69430 **Map** 8B3

📞 04 74 04 35 95

FAX 04 74 04 34 47

📧 AE, MC, V ● Mon; 20 Jan–20 Dec

🍴 €€

This "house of the winemaker" is ideal for lunch on the terrace, washed down with a glass or two. Regional food with Lyonnais specialities.

RENAISON

● Jacques Coeur

15 route de Roanne, 42370 **Map** 8A4

📞 04 77 64 25 34

FAX 04 77 64 43 88

📧 AE, MC, V

● Sun D, Mon, Thu D 🍴 €

Old building of aged stone and modern furniture. Rooms continue the blend of modern and traditional. Classic cuisine.

RILLIEUX-LA-PAPE

● Larivoire

26 chemin des Iles, 69140 **Map** 8B4

📞 04 78 88 50 92

FAX 04 78 88 35 22

📧 AE, MC, V ● Sun D, Mon D, Tue; last 2 wks Aug 🍴 €€€

Take a seat on the shady terrace where a fountain splashes gaily. Refined versions of Lyonnais fare include lamb's trotters; classics include lacquered duck.

RIORGES

▲ Marcassin

16 rue Jean Plasse, 42153 **Map** 8A4

📞 04 77 71 30 18

FAX 04 77 23 11 22

📧 AE, MC, V ● Sun D, Fri D; Aug

🍴 €€ 🛏 (9) €€

A father-and-son team transform local products – poultry, pork, fish – into lovely dishes. Simple, adequate guestrooms.

ROANNE

L'Astrée

17 bis cours République, 42300 **Map** 8A4

📞 04 77 72 74 22

FAX 04 77 72 72 23

📧 DC, MC, V ● Sun, Sat; 2nd & 3rd wk Feb, mid-Jul–mid-Aug 🍴 €€

A comfortable, contemporary bistro with paintings from local artists. Families will appreciate the children's menu.

ROANNE

● Le Central

20 cours la République, 42300 **Map** 8A4

📞 04 77 67 72 72

FAX 04 77 72 57 67

🌐 www.troisgros.fr

📧 MC, V

● Sun, Mon; 1st 3 wks Aug 🍴 €€

Small-scale but incredibly chic place to sample the modern French cuisine that has earned Michel Troisgros three Michelin stars. A combination foodshop-café in a 1920s-era hotel. Reserve.

ROANNE

● Relais Fleuri

Quai Pierre Sémard, 42300 **Map** 8A4

📞 04 77 67 18 52

FAX 04 77 67 72 07

🌐 http://perso.wanadoo.fr/lerelaisfleuri

📧 MC, V ● Sun D, Tue D, Wed; Feb

🍴 €€

Look for lake fish here – perhaps done en friture (small, fried strips) – and beef from Charolais. In summer, enjoy your meal under the greenhouse-like dome that opens on to the flowering garden. Charming dining room in winter.

● Restaurant ■ Hotel ▲ Hotel / Restaurant

ROANNE

▲ Troisgros

1 pl Jean Troisgros, 42300 **Map** 8A4

📞 04 77 71 66 97

FAX 04 77 70 39 77

🌐 www.troisgros.fr

🍽 AE, DC, MC, V ● Tue, Wed; 3 wks
Feb, 1st 2 wks Aug **🍴** €€€€€
🍷 (18) €€€€€

*Michel Troisgros – perhaps the world's
best chef – uses Charolais beef, lamb
from Quercy, veal from the Roanne
countryside, Bresse chicken and Forez
cheese to create the best meal you'll
ever eat. Gourmets will appreciate the
hotel's specialized food library. Tasteful
guestrooms with soft colours.*

ROMANS-SUR-ISERE

● La Fourchette

8 rue Solférino, 26100 **Map** 8C5

📞 04 75 02 12 94

FAX 04 75 05 07 61

🌐 www.romansinfoline.com

🍽 MC, V ● Sun D, Mon, Fri D; 2 wks
Feb **🍴** €

*Dine in the shade of 100-year-old trees.
This is a popular place for family meals.
Fish and foie gras are specialities.*

RUY-MONTCEAU

▲ Laurent Thomas

54 Vie-de-Boussieu, 38300 **Map** 8B4

📞 04 74 93 78 00

FAX 04 74 28 60 90

🍽 AE, DC, MC, V ● Sun D, Mon, Tue
L; Aug **🍴** €€€ 🍷 (5) €€€€

*Ancient sequoias surround this hotel-
restaurant. The roasted goose liver
crusted in walnuts recently won rave
reviews. Rooms with shady park views.*

SAMOENS

▲ Edelweiss

La Piaz, 74340 **Map** 9D3

📞 04 50 34 41 32

FAX 04 50 34 18 75

🌐 www.hoteledelweiss.fr

🍽 MC, V **🍴** €€ 🍷 (20) €€€

*This pine chalet has thousands of alpine
plants in its carefully manicured garden,
many are herbs used in the menu. Pork
sausage in white wine, trout with
almonds and duck with blackberries.
Pine theme in the guestrooms.*

SCIEZ

▲ Château de Coudrée

Bonnatrait, 74140 **Map** 9D3

📞 04 50 72 62 33

FAX 04 50 72 57 28

🌐 www.coudree.com

🍽 AE, DC, MC, V ● Wed, Thu L,
Sep–Jun: Tue; last wk Jan–1st wk Mar,
Nov **🍴** €€€€ 🍷 (16) €€€€€

*Stunning 12th-century castle by the
lake, radiating classic elegance. French
classics like rabbit or roasted chicken.*

SCIEZ

▲ Hôtellerie Château de Coudrée

Domaine de Coudrée, 74140 **Map** 9D3

📞 04 50 72 62 33

FAX 04 50 72 57 28

🌐 www.coudree.com

🍽 AE, DC, MC, V ● Sep–Jun:
Tue–Wed; Nov

🍴 €€€€ 🍷 (19) €€€€

*Don't miss cheese from local legend
Daniel Boujon. A summer midday buffet
is served on the lakeside. Elegant rooms.*

SEREZIN-DU-RHONE

▲ Bourbonnise

45 ave du Dauphiné, 69360 **Map** 8B4

📞 04 78 02 80 58

FAX 04 78 02 17 39

🌐 www.labourbonnaise.com

🍽 AE, DC, MC, V

🍴 €€ 🍷 (39) €€€

*A relaxing alternative with rooms
arranged around a calm courtyard. The
chef creates dishes such as quail with
grapes or a gateau of artichoke.*

SERRIERES

▲ Schaeffer

34 quai Jules Roche, 07340 **Map** 9B5

📞 04 75 34 00 07

FAX 04 75 34 08 79

🍽 AE, MC, V ● Sep–Jul: Sun L &
Mon; Jan, 1 wk Nov

🍴 €€€ 🍷 (11) €€

*Game is the house speciality, closely
followed by desserts. The chocolate with
chicory and pistachio ice cream is earn-
ing a cult following. Functional rooms.*

SERVOZ

▲ Gorges de la Diosaz

Le Bouchet, 74310 **Map** 9D4

📞 04 50 47 20 97

FAX 04 50 47 21 08

🌐 www.hoteldesgorges.com

🍽 MC, V ● Sun D, Wed; May, Nov

🍴 €€ 🍷 (6) €€€

*Pine chalet covered in blooming flowers.
Try the fish fillet with pistou or duck.
Cosy, comfortable guestrooms.*

SEVRIER

▲ L'Arpège

823 route d'Albertville, 74320 **Map** 9D4

📞 04 50 19 03 69

FAX 04 50 52 49 42

🌐 www.restaurant-arpege.com

🍽 DC, MC, V ● Sun D, Mon L; mid-
Oct–mid-Nov, end Dec–1st wk Jan

🍴 €€ 🍷 (27) €€€

*Lake Annecy shimmers just off the
terrace of this elegant hotel-restaurant.
The chef is a fish expert. Bright rooms.*

ST-AGREVE

▲ Domaine de Rilhac

Lieu-dit-Rilhac, 07320 **Map** 9B5

📞 04 75 30 20 20

FAX 04 75 30 20 00

🍽 AE, DC, MC, V ● Tue, Wed;
Jan–Feb **🍴** €€€ 🍷 (7) €€€

*The chef at this farm turns out creamy
crayfish soup and roasted kid. Try the
nougat glacé. Provençal-style rooms.*

ST-CLEMENT-SOUS-VALSONNE

▲ St-Clément

Pl de l'Europe, 69170 **Map** 8B4

📞 04 74 05 17 80

FAX 04 74 05 17 80

🌐 www.le-saint-clement.com

🍽 MC, V ● Sep–Jun: Mon D; 3rd wk
Jan–2nd wk Feb **🍴** € 🍷 (9) €€

*If rooms are a bit austere, they're also
pleasantly inexpensive, as is your meal.
Try an entrée of halibut with local lentils.*

ST-DISDIER

▲ Auberge la Neyrette

La Neyrette, 05250 **Map** 13D1

📞 04 92 58 81 17

FAX 04 92 58 89 95

🍽 AE, MC, V ● 2nd & 3rd wks Apr,
mid-Nov–mid-Dec

🍴 €€ 🍷 (12) €€

*Surrounded by grassy prairies and over-
looked by the Dévoluy peaks you'll work*

up an appetite for generous portions of regional cuisine while fishing for trout in the hotel pond, hiking, biking or playing pétanque. Rooms profit from the view.

ST-DONAT-SUR-L'HERBASSE
▲ Chartron
1 ave Gambetta, 26260 **Map** 8C5
☏ 04 75 45 11 82
FAX 04 75 45 01 36
w www.restaurant-chartron.com
✉ AE, MC, V ● Sep–Jul: Tue–Wed;
1st wk Jan, 1st wk May, 1st 3 wks Sep
🍴 €€€€ 🍷 (7) €€

The place to go to indulge yourself with truffles. Chartron and his white labrador take to the hills to excavate them, and from December to March your whole menu might be composed of subtle variations on the truffle theme. Tender kid and local vegetables can also be savoured. Contemporary guestrooms.

ST-DONAT-SUR-L'HERBASSE
● Mousse de Brochet
6 ave Commandant Corlu, 26260
Map 8C5
☏ 04 75 45 10 47
FAX 04 75 45 10 47
✉ MC, V ● Sun D, Mon, Dec–Feb:
Tue–Sat D; 23 Jan–14 Feb, 20 Jun–12
Jul 🍴 €€

As the name implies, pike brochette is the house speciality. It's a light and airy dish – suitable as you approach Provence and the temperature rises. If you prefer, make an advance order for bouillabaisse (p401) or a platter of fine, savoury shellfish, heaped high.

STE-CROIX
▲ Chez Nous
Town entrance, 01120 **Map** 9C4
☏ 04 78 06 60 60
FAX 04 78 06 63 26
w www.hotel-cheznous.com
✉ MC, V
● Sun D, Mon, Tue; Jan
🍴 € 🍷 (29) €€

After a generous meal, abundant in the region's flavours, you'll be glad of the short walk across the street back to your finely turned-out hotel room. There are ample choices on the menu and a nice wine list.

ST-FORGEUX
● Taverne du Chasseur
Place del Bon, 69490 **Map** 8B4
☏ 04 74 05 60 15
FAX 04 74 05 90 40
w www.restaurant-michelroche.com
✉ MC, V ● Mon, Wed D; Feb, Aug
🍴 €

If you're on the hunt for regional products – fresh saucisson, wine or Puy lentils – stop for lunch at this tavern/foodshop just outside Lyon on the road to Roanne. Join the locals at the bar for a digestif.

ST-JACQUES-EN-VALGODEMAR
▲ Hôtel Loubet
Bas Séchier, 05800 **Map** 8D1
☏ 04 92 55 21 12
FAX 04 92 55 32 72
w www.hotel-loubet.fr
✉ MC, V ● mid-Sep–mid-Jun
🍴 € 🍷 (23) €€

Using regional products and fresh fruit and vegetables from the hotel garden the Loubets prepare dishes such as oreilles d'âne (potato cake stuffed with spinach and covered in cream) – they've been following Grandmother Loubet's recipe for decades! Large groups can order the marmite, a giant stockpot. Comfortable, restful guestrooms.

ST-MARTIN-DE-BELLEVILLE
▲ La Bouitte
Village of St-Marcel, 73440 **Map** 9D5
☏ 04 79 08 96 77
FAX 04 79 08 96 03
w www.la-bouitte.com
✉ AE, MC, V ● 3rd wk Apr–Jul,
Sep–mid-Dec
🍴 €€€ 🍷 (5) €€€€

In the patois of the region bouitte means "little house". This charming name is matched by the elegant but simple decor – which remains true to rustic Savoyard roots – and by the food, which is equally tied to tradition. The rack of lamb is a highlight but equally delicious are braised rabbit with polenta or chestnuts with Tomme. Reserve one of the fantasy log-cabin guestrooms.

ST-NIZIER-SOUS-CHARLIEU
● Moulin de Rongefer
Route to Pouilly, 42190 **Map** 8A3

☏ 04 77 60 01 57
FAX 04 77 60 33 28
✉ MC, V ● Sun D, Tue D, Wed; mid-
Aug–1st wk Sep 🍴 €

In the mountain villages of this part of the Alps, cuts of slowly braised meat are the order of the day. They're fitting fare after you've exerted yourself amid the savage scenery of the Pilat but there are plenty of lighter alternatives created from the offerings of farms clustered below the heights.

ST-PAUL-LES-ROMANS
▲ Karène Hôtel
RN92, Quartier St-Vérant, 26750
☏ 04 75 05 12 50
FAX 04 75 05 25 17
✉ AE, DC, MC, V ● Nov–Easter: Sat;
20 Dec–6 Jan 🍴 € 🍷 (23) €€

Expect a cheerful welcome at this colourful restaurant. Traditional cuisine includes the town's famous ravioles (p268). Situated away from the road, rooms are quiet and attractive.

ST-PIERRE-DE-CHARTREUSE
▲ Auberge de l'Atre Fleuri
Le Morinas, route du Col de Porte,
38380 **Map** 8C5
☏ 04 76 88 60 21
FAX 04 76 88 64 97
@ atrefleuribd@aol.com
✉ MC, V ● Sun D, mid-Oct–mid-
Nov: Mon–Tue D
🍴 €€ 🍷 (7) €€€

Flower-filled inn, great for a post-hike lunch. Inspired by Roy Andries De Groot's famous cookbook Auberge of the Flowering Hearth, this wood-panelled restaurant serves fresh bread, mountain hams and cheese. Excellent guestrooms.

ST-PONS
● Hostellerie Gourmand "Mère Biquette"
Allignols, 07580 **Map** 12B1
☏ 04 75 36 72 61
FAX 04 75 36 76 25
@ merebiquette@europost.org
✉ AE, MC, V ● Oct–Mar: Sun D &
Mon L; Dec–Jan 🍴 €€

The parents of the current owners were cheesemakers, and today there's a thoughtful selection of cheeses available.

The menu reflects Ardéchoise cuisine, with olives and honey, game, herbs and other sunny flavours. During summer you'll appreciate the shaded terrace. Rooms are calm, quiet, spacious and tidy.

TAIN-L'HERMITAGE

▲ Pavillon de l'Ermitage

69 ave Jean Jaurès, 26600 **Map** 9B5

📞 04 75 08 65 00

FAX 04 75 08 66 05

w www.pavillon-ermitage.com

💳 AE, DC, MC, V ● Sun, Dec–Mar:
Sat 🍴 €€ 😊 (44) €€€

Relax with a glass of Côtes-du-Rhône and take in the clean, pure ambience of this streamlined restaurant. Try the pot-au-feu, which draws from the largesse of the nearby coast (fish and shellfish). Ravioles de Royans (p268) are also on the menu. Notable wine list. Ask for a pool-side room with sweeping views.

TALLOIRES

▲ Auberge du Père Bise

Lac d'Annecy, 74290 **Map** 9D4

📞 04 50 60 72 01

FAX 04 50 60 73 05

w www.perebise.com

💳 AE, DC, MC, V ● mid-Dec–mid-Mar 🍴 €€€€€ 😊 (25) €€€€€

Hotel with rare idyllic charm complete with an outdoor terrace and views of the mountains mirrored in a still lake. House specialities include Tatin de pommes de terre (rich potato cake) with a truffle and foie gras sauce, crêpes suzettes and a delicious soufflé. Newly renovated guestrooms are individually decorated in classic French style. Reservations are essential.

TALLOIRES

▲ La Villa des Fleurs

Route du Port, 74290 **Map** 9D4

📞 04 50 60 71 14

FAX 04 50 60 74 06

w www.hotel-lavilladesfleurs74.com

💳 AE, DC, MC, V ● mid-Nov–mid-Dec 🍴 €€€ 😊 (8) €€€

A quaint chalet, just a stone's throw from the lake. The cuisine focuses on fish from Lake d'Annecy and includes poached trout. Sun-drenched, charming guestrooms with lake views.

TALLOIRES

▲ L'Abbaye

Chemin des Moines, 74290 **Map** 9D4

📞 04 50 60 77 33

FAX 04 50 60 78 81

w www.abbaye-talloires.com

💳 AE, DC, MC, V ● mid-Nov–Jan
🍴 €€€€ 😊 (33) €€€€€

A 17th-century former abbey with a lively piano bar, spa and restaurant. Guestrooms are set around a picture-perfect cloister. The menu bénédictin includes lamb chops, fish carpaccio with a mixed salad or prawns with vinaigrette. For dessert, the gazpacho made with forest berries is to die for.

TIGNES

▲ Gentiana

Montée du Rosset, 73320 **Map** 9E4

📞 04 79 06 52 46

FAX 04 79 06 35 61

w www.hotel-gentiana.com

💳 MC, V ● mid-May–Jun, last wk
Aug–last wk Nov

🍴 €€ 😊 (40) €€€€

Established in 1946, the chalet retains some of the quaintness of a bygone era but has all the amenities (pool, sauna) you need after a day on the mountain, including balconies for enjoying the view. Come dinner, take the menu or pick and choose from the buffet. Bright, south-facing guestrooms have a view of the glacier.

TIGNES

▲ Le Ski d'Or

Val-Claret, 73320 **Map** 9E4

📞 04 79 06 51 60

FAX 04 79 06 45 49

💳 AE, MC, V ● May–Dec

🍴 €€€ 😊 (22) €€€€

Though the chef post at the chalet is notoriously in flux, the owners quite scrupulously pick new talent and have retained continuity in the excellence of the cuisine. Expect gastronomic fare mixed with Savoyard tradition, and a lavish dessert table. Wood-panelled guestrooms with Alpine atmosphere.

URIAGE-LES-BAINS

▲ Grand Hôtel

Pl Déesse Hygie, 38410 **Map** 8E5

📞 04 76 89 10 80

FAX 04 76 89 04 62

💳 AE, DC, MC, V ● Sun, Mon; Jan
🍴 €€€€ 😊 (42) €€€€€

A grand old resort hotel dating to 1870. Chef Philippe Bouissou specializes in very showy cooking: frothed avocado with tomato, almonds and hazelnut cream; Chinese duck; or pigeon terrine with foie gras and artichokes. Iron beds and original fixtures in some guestrooms.

VAL-D'ISERE

● Ferme de l'Adroit

0.5km (0.3 miles) from centre past the church, 73150 **Map** 9E4

📞 04 79 06 13 02

FAX 04 79 41 93 91

w www.fermedeladroit.com

💳 MC, V ● Sun D, Mon; Jun,
Sep–Nov 🍴 €€

This cheese specialist sells offbeat varieties like Milkidou, Grosse Tome de Montagne and Avallin. For a full meal, order tartiflette (p268) with Tomme cheese or chicken and rice. Flats for rent, too.

VAL-D'ISERE

▲ Hôtel Chamois d'Or

Le Joseray, 73150 **Map** 9E4

📞 04 79 06 00 44

FAX 04 79 41 16 58

w www.hotelchamoisdor.com

💳 AE, MC, V ● May, Jun, Sep–Nov
🍴 €€ 😊 (24) €€€

A creative menu. For "calcium", Reblochon cheese, Tomme de Savoie cheese or raclette (p268). For "carni-vores", steak or beef with peppercorns. For "morale", red fruit mousse or crème brûlée with vanilla. A fireplace dominates the dining room. Pleasant, unpretentious surroundings and rooms.

VAL-D'ISERE

▲ Hôtel Christiana

Follow signs to the ski slopes, BP48, 73152 **Map** 9E4

📞 04 79 06 08 25

FAX 04 79 41 11 10

💳 AE, DC, MC, V ● Dec–mid-Apr
🍴 €€€€ 😊 (69) €€€€€

Awesome display of starters and a colourful dessert table. Everyone knows this is the best buffet in town. Close to the ski slopes, with a plush dining room and an open fire. Stone, pine and fabrics lend character to the guestrooms.

VALENCE
● **La Ciboulette**
6 rue du Commerce, 26000 **Map** 8C5
[04 75 55 67 74
FAX 04 75 56 72 83
w www.laciboulette.com
MC, V ● Tue, Sat L; 1 wk Jan, 1 wk Aug 🍴 €€€€

Sit at one of the colourful tables, amid a spread of stemware awaiting your wine selection, and savour the restaurant's promise of a feast of regional products prepared with a flair for original tastes and textures. A fillet of Drôme's guinea fowl is here stuffed with boudin noir.

VALENCE
● **Le Bistrot des Clercs**
48 Grande Rue, 26000 **Map** 8C5
[04 75 55 55 15
FAX 04 75 43 64 85
AE, MC, V ● Sun L, Mon L
🍴 €€

History may well have drawn you to this lovely traditional bistro within a building where Napoleon once lived. White table-cloths, gleaming brass and dark wood provide ambience while you enjoy grilled Charolais beef or tasty ravioles de Royans (pXX). In summer a seat by the fountain is worthy of an emperor.

VALENCE
● **L'Epicerie**
18 pl St-Jean, 26000 **Map** 8C5
[04 75 42 74 46
FAX 04 75 42 10 87
AE, MC, V ● Sun, Sat L; 16–22 Feb, 1st wk May, 1st 3 wks Aug, mid-Dec–1st wk Jan 🍴 €€€

On a hot day the stone terrace over the market square is a cool and chic place. It draws a young crowd who adore its contemporary dishes, such as ravioles de Royans (p268) with crab and Nyons olives, or pigeon in a broth of morels. Excellent Côtes-du-Rhône wines.

VALENCE
● **Petite Auberge**
1 rue Athènes, 26000 **Map** 8C5

[04 75 43 20 30
FAX 04 75 42 67 79
@ la.petite.auberge@wanadoo.fr
AE, DC, MC, V
● Sun, Wed D; Aug
🍴 €€€

Situated outside the city centre, with a stylish and contemporary interior and a menu creatively marrying fish and other regional produce. For the harmonie gourmande the chef combines scallops, langoustines, truffles and foie gras.

VALLOIRE
▲ **Grand Hôtel de Valloire et du Galibier**
Rue des Grandes Alpes, 73450 **Map** 9D5
[04 79 59 00 95
FAX 04 79 59 09 41
w www.grand-hotel-valloire.com
AE, DC, MC, V ● mid-Sep–mid-Dec 🍴 €€ ◆ (44) €€€

Hotel facing the ski slopes with an enormous dining room and a central open fire pit. The menu tradition has salade campagnarde (bacon, cheese and nuts), or chicken with cream and mushrooms. The menu saveur tempts with foie gras or lobster with morels. Guestrooms with a 1970s feel.

VALLOIRE
▲ **Le Gastilleur**
Rue de la Vallée-d'Or, 73450 **Map** 9D5
[04 79 59 01 03
FAX 04 79 59 00 63
w www.la-setaz.com
AE, MC, V ● 3rd wk Apr–Jun, mid-Sep–mid-Dec
🍴 € ◆ (22) €€€

Probably Valloire's best restaurant and you'll be jubilant to discover the inexpensive menu. Savoyard specialities are well represented – dishes luxuriant with potatoes and cheese – plus there are several well-prepared fish dishes. The location at the foot of the Galibier Pass makes for good summer hiking or great winter sports. Bright guestrooms with wooden balconies.

VALS-LES-BAINS
▲ **Vivarais**
5 rue Claude Expilly, 07600 **Map** 12B1
[04 75 94 65 85

FAX 04 75 37 65 47
AE, DC, MC, V
● Sun D, Mon L; Feb
🍴 €€ ◆ (44) €€

Here you've an opportunity to discover the myriad incarnations and flavours of the chestnut – star product of the Ardeche. Chestnut flour forms a crêpe served with salmon, and chestnut honey crisps the skin of tender duckling. For dessert, savour the union of chestnut and chocolate. Rooms here look out over the Volane.

VARS
▲ **Caribou**
Les Claux, 05560 **Map** 13D1
[04 92 46 50 43
FAX 04 92 46 59 92
w www.villagesclubsdusoleil.com
MC, V
● Vas les Claux
🍴 € ◆ (37) €€

Near the Italian border in the Southern Alps and situated at an altitude of nearly 2000m (6560ft)! The mountain air and rigorous outdoor activity makes for hungry diners, who savour traditional cuisine before a steam in the sauna or a drink by the fire. Cosy Alpine-style rooms, great for unwinding.

VARS
● **Chez Plumot**
Résidence Seignon, 05560 **Map** 13D1
[04 92 46 52 12
FAX 04 75 56 72 83
MC, V
● May–Jun, Sep–Nov
🍴 €€

Traditional restaurant serving southern French specialities. Dishes include duck consommé with truffles, goose foie gras and delicate ravioli.

VEYRIER-DU-LAC
▲ **Auberge de l'Eridan**
13 vieille route des Pensières, 74290 **Map** 9D4
[04 50 60 24 00
FAX 04 50 60 23 63
AE, DC, MC, V
● L, Mon, Tue; mid-Nov–mid-Apr
🍴 €€€€€
◆ (11) €€€€€

● Restaurant ■ Hotel ▲ Hotel / Restaurant

With three Michelin stars, this is among France's greatest and most expensive restaurants. Chef Marc Veyrat prepares foie gras "in cubist form" with fig purée, risotto with capers, Parmesan and roasted chicory (endive) and chateaubriand in a crust. Equally luxurious accommodation.

VIENNE
▲ La Pyramide
14 bd Fernand Point, 38200 **Map** 8B4
04 74 53 01 96
FAX 04 74 85 69 73
www.lapyramide.com
AE, DC, MC, V ● Tue, Wed; Feb
€€€€€ ⌒ (24) €€€€€
Inventive, fine dining awaits you at La Pyramide, where dishes are created from the finest fresh ingredients. Recently a crab soufflé with artichokes won rave reviews. Spacious guestrooms.

VIENNE
● L'Estancot
4 rue de la Table-Ronde, 38200 **Map** 8B4
04 74 85 12 09
FAX 04 74 85 12 09
MC, V
● Sun, Mon; 1st 2 wks Sep €
Delicious, memorable food for a price that puts it squarely in the affordable category, which is why locals adore this little restaurant behind the church of St-André-le-Bas. This is the place to taste criques, a generous potato pancake with bacon, eggs and Gruyère cheese.

VILLARD-DE-LANS
▲ Hôtel Christiania
220 ave Prof. Nobecourt, 38250 **Map** 8C5
04 76 95 12 51
FAX 04 76 95 00 75
www.hotel-le-christiania.fr
AE, DC, MC, V ● mid-Apr–mid-May, Oct–mid-Dec €€ ⌒ (23) €€€
Modern chalet. Scallop carpaccio with tomato and pesto, rascasse, or the truly divine fromage blanc de campagne à la crème – a cheese-lover's dream come true. Most rooms have private balconies.

VILLARD-DE-LANS
● Les Trente Pas
16 rue Francs-Tireurs, 38250 **Map** 8C5
04 76 94 06 75

FAX 04 76 95 80 69
MC, V ● Mon; mid-Mar–1st wk Apr, mid-Nov–1st wk Dec €€
Near the town church, a gourmet restaurant with a new take on regional produce and specialities. Most customers are regulars, so the menu changes often. Try trout with ham and ravioles de Royans (p268) in a candied green nut sauce, foie gras with apple-cinnamon toast and chestnut tart with passion fruit sauce. Wood from floor to ceiling; paintings by a favourite local artist.

VINEZAC
▲ La Bastide du Soleil
Ancien-Château, 07110 **Map** 12B1
04 75 36 91 66
FAX 04 75 36 91 59
AE, DC, MC, V
● Mon, Tue, Wed L, Dec–Jan
€€ ⌒ (5) €€€
A sojourn at this 17th-century château will fulfil your fantasies about southern France. Dine on Provençal dishes, such as the magnificent clafoutis (p247) of olives and thyme, on the terrace with views of lavender fields, vineyards and olive groves. After dinner, climb the Renaissance staircase to your room.

VONNAS
▲ Georges Blanc
Pl du Marché, 01540 **Map** 8B3
04 74 50 90 90
FAX 04 74 50 08 80
www.georgesblanc.com
AE, DC, MC, V
● Mon, Tue, Wed L; Jan
€€€€€ ⌒ (48) €€€€€
Celebrities hire helicopters to dine at Georges Blanc's table. And when a golden-crisp Bresse chicken, cooked in a sea-salt crust, is presented you'll understand why. Eating here is about tradition, ceremony, and appreciation for the finer things in life. The price is high, but it will be a meal you'll never forget. Rooms strike a very gracious balance between luxury and tradition.

VONNAS
● L'Ancienne Auberge
Pl du Marché, 01540 **Map** 8B3
04 74 50 90 50

FAX 04 74 50 08 80
www.georgesblanc.com
AE, DC, MC, V ● Jan €€
Let it not be said that Georges Blanc's cuisine is too dear for your average diner! The grace here lies in the details – antique decor, sepia photographs, Eiffel-style covered terrace. And then, of course, the food – traditional Bresse cuisine – which includes succulent frogs' legs and Bresse chicken.

YVOIRE
▲ Hôtel Restaurant du Port
Rue du Port, 74140 **Map** 9D3
04 50 72 80 17
FAX 04 50 72 90 71
http://hotelrestaurant.port.online.fr
AE, MC, V ● 3rd wk Oct–1st wk Mar €€ ⌒ (7) €€€€
Lakeside charmer with flower- and vine-twined balconies and terraces that define Alpine romance. Overlooking Lake Léman. You'll appreciate the chef's creative use of flavours. Rooms are light-filled and airy.

YVOIRE
▲ Le Pré de la Cure
Pl Mairie, 74140 **Map** 9D3
04 50 72 83 58
FAX 04 50 72 91 15
www.lepredelacure.com
AE, MC, V ● mid-Nov–1st wk Mar
€€ ⌒ (25) €€€
Near the ramparts of this postcard-perfect medieval town, a charming inn with views of Lake Geneva. Michel Magnin and son Olivier are lake fish specialists. Wood-beamed guestrooms.

YVOIRE
▲ Le Vieux Logis
Rue Principale, 74140 **Map** 9D3
04 50 72 80 24
FAX 04 50 72 90 76
www.levieuxlogis.com
AE, DC, MC, V ● Sun D, Mon
€€ ⌒ (11) €€€
Ivy-covered 14th-century building. Rustic dining room serving specialities such as smoked ham, tuna carpaccio and lake fish. Fabulous stonework and flower-filled garden. Medium-sized contemporary rooms.

POITOU &
AQUITAINE

*Behind France's surf-washed Atlantic
seaboard lie the world-famous vineyards
of Bordeaux; the pine forests and lakes
of the Landes; marshlands of the Marais
Poitevin and the green pastures of Poitou.
Oysters here are the best in France, with
Landes poultry, Poitou beef, Pauillac
lamb, local goats' cheese, asparagus and
charentais melons also highly regarded.*

The Flavours of Poitou & Aquitaine

Above all, this coast is France's chief area for oyster production, but the ocean, estuaries and bassins turn up many other treats too, even caviar, while foie gras is the greatest luxury of the land. Dairy produce here is outstanding and goats are important for cheese.

A splendid array of Charentais melons

Meat, Poultry and Charcuterie

The pine forests of Les Landes are renowned for poultry rearing, both ducks and geese for foie gras (*see p324-5*) and free-range chickens. Look out also for the *boeuf de Chalosse*, from the area around Dax. The Poitou region provides excellent pasture, primarily for Limousin cattle and the now scarce Parthenais. In the Bordelais you'll find the prized Pauillac spring lamb. Charcuterie includes the chipolata sausages and small *crépinettes*, often served with oysters, and *grattons* (*rillette*-type potted pork).

Fish and Shellfish

Mussels are raised as well as oysters, and the Atlantic coast yields a great variety of fish, including *bar* (sea bass), red mullet, sole and *céteau* (a type of small sole) at La Rochelle. Royan is known for sardines. Small fishing boats from Arcachon gather green crabs, mainly used in soup. Lampreys, eels and sturgeon are all caught in the Gironde estuary.

Cheese and Dairy Produce

Dairy cows in Poitou-Charentes produce some of France's best butter. The salted *beurre d'Echiré* and the unsalted *beurre de Charentes-Poitou* (also sold as *beurre des Charentes* and *beurre des Deux-Sèvres*) both have an *appellation contrôlée*.

Oysters

The Atlantic coast is France's most important oyster-producing region. Today, the flat *gravette* or plate oysters, that are native to this coastline, have largely been replaced by the *creuse* or *huître japonaise*.

Many of the oysters spawned in the Bassin d'Arcachon go to supply beds in Normandy and Brittany. Others remain in the *bassin*, where saltwater mixes with fresh water from the delta. North of the Gironde estuary, in the shelter of the Ile d'Oléron, the oysters from the prime beds of Marennes-Oléron have been awarded a *label rouge (see p11)*. The particular species of blue algae that these oysters feed on give them a distinctive green colouring as well as their prized delicate flavour.

Left Torteau fromage **Centre** Chabichou goats' cheese **Right** Poitevin goats

Poitou-Charentes is one of France's main goat raising areas and even has its own variety of goat, the Poitevin, with long brown fur and a white belly, reputed for the high protein content of its milk. The best-known goats' cheese is the Chabichou du Poitou, a small, cylindrical cheese that can be eaten young and moist but is often matured, when the rind becomes a mottled grey-blue and the interior harder and drier with a more pronounced taste. Other goats' cheeses include Bougon, Parthenay and Ruffec, while Pigouille is a soft cows' milk cheese.

FRUIT AND VEGETABLES

Shallots, onions, leeks, chard, spinach, sorrel and green cabbage grown in the area all feature in many local recipes. Asparagus and carrots thrive in the sandy soil of the Landes. The Ile de Ré is renowned for its baby potatoes. Young green garlic shoots, known as *aillet*, feature at many markets in springtime and are cooked with lamb or in omelettes. In the Marais Poitevin, flat, white *mojette* beans are grown in summer and harvested before the winter floods arrive. Fruit includes the melon du Haut-Poitou, a juicy orange-fleshed charentais melon.

CAKES AND BISCUITS

Distinctive regional cakes include the black-domed, burnt-crust *tourteau fromage* cheesecake of Poitiers, made with goats' cheese, and cakes using the green angelica of Niort, such as the *galette saintongeaise*, a flat biscuity cake made with angelica, salted butter and Cognac. Almond macaroons are a speciality of St-Emilion. In Bordeaux, look out for small, deep rusty-brown *cannelés*. Made with a batter-type dough and flavoured with vanilla, they should be slightly sticky on the outside and moist and airy in the centre.

ANGELICA

Angelica was supposedly introduced to France during the Crusades and became valued in the Middle Ages as a remedy against the plague. Today it is candied for use in cakes and desserts or made into a green liqueur. The tall plant is suited to the damp environment of the Marais Poitevin, with production centred on the town of Niort.

Angelica growing in the Marais Poitevin

CAVIARE D'AQUITAINE

Caviar was first produced in Aquitaine in the 1920s, when the region supplied the luxurious Parisian restaurant Prunier with the precious "black pearls". The species of Siberian sturgeon farmed today produces eggs that are smaller, firmer and less salty than Iranian or Russian caviar.

Regional dishes

Poitou and Aquitaine boast a number of quite distinct cuisines: the coast is noted for its fish soups, mussels and oysters, inland Poitou is famed for its hearty, rustic fare, and the Landes and Aquitaine for their fine duck dishes.

ON THE MENU

Assiette fermière or assiette paysanne Mixed platter of duck meat appetizers

Cagouilles à la charentaise Snails with sausage meats, herbs and wine

Chaudrée saintongeaise Soup of eels, fish and prawns with white wine and garlic

Embeurrée de chou Buttered cabbage

Entrecôte à la bordelaise Entrecote steak in a sauce made with red wine, shallots and bone marrow

Feuilleté au fois gras Puff pastry tart, layered with sausage meat, magret de canard and slices of foie gras

Garbure Thick cabbage, ham and vegetable soup

Homard à la charentaise Lobster with cream and Cognac sauce

Lamproie à la bordelaise Lamprey cooked in red wine with leeks

Matelotte d'anguilles Eel stew

Rouquette Arcachon fish and crab soup

Salade landaise Salad with foie gras, gizzards and confit

Cèpes à la bordelaise

THE REGIONAL MENU

The cooking of Poitou-Charentes is based on the excellent local butter, while that of Aquitaine, which shares many recipes with Périgord and Gascony *(see p322)*, is more likely to use duck or goose dripping.

A meal might well start with oysters, a *garbure* soup, asparagus from the Landes or a duck-laced *salade landaise*. Fish soups include *chaudrée saintongeaise*, a cauldron-full of assorted fish, small *seiche* (cuttlefish) and prawns, cooked with white wine, garlic and shallots. The best known mussel preparation is *mouclade*, but mussels are also served grilled with herbs and breadcrumbs, barbecued over vine stumps or *à la marinière*. Snails also feature on many menus, known as *lumas* in the Marais Poitevin and *cagouilles* in the Charente area, where they are prepared with sausage meat, herbs and red wine. Charentais melons are also often served as a starter, filled with the local *vin de liqueur*, Pineau des Charentes *(see p301)*.

A Bordeaux speciality is the surprisingly good combination of raw oysters served with grilled chipolata sausages. Steaks may be accompanied by a red wine and shallot sauce or grilled and sprinkled with shallots and parsley. A rarer treat is lamprey, a long, eel-like fish from the Gironde estuary. Notoriously complicated to prepare, it is traditionally stewed with its own blood, red wine and leeks. The Bordeaux region is also famed for its cep mushrooms, which may feature

Salade landaise, a typical regional starter

Left Farci poitevin **Right** Mouclade

in omelettes, sautéed with shallots and garlic, cooked with potatoes or served as a sauce with duck.

The Marais Poitevin has a number of distinct dishes of its own, including a *matelotte* stew of eels and frogs, stuffed snails or the flat white *mojette* beans, which are cooked slowly with tomatoes in a terracotta pot and often served with grilled gammon. Although goats are mainly raised in Poitou for cheese production, you may also find kid (*chevreau*) on the menu.

MOUCLADE

This golden-coloured dish of mussels in a curry sauce is a reminder that La Rochelle was once a port on the spice route. The mussels are boiled with dry white wine and a bouquet garni and arranged in a dish on the half shell. For the sauce, onions are gently sweated then wetted with mussel liquor and thickened with *crème fraîche*, egg yolks, butter and curry powder. The dish is served steaming hot.

FARCI POITEVIN

The Poitevin version of stuffed cabbage mixes bacon and pork with the slightly bitter flavour of a combination of spinach, chard leaves and sorrel. The stuffing is layered with the leaves of a green savoy cabbage to recreate the cabbage shape. The *farci* is served cut into quarters either hot or cold. A related dish, *far charentais*, uses a similar mix of bacon, spinach, chard, leeks and eggs, without the cabbage, and is baked in a dish like a terrine and served cold.

CÈPES À LA BORDELAISE

Meaty cep mushrooms appear in late summer and early autumn. For this simple dish, the ceps are sautéed with garlic and shallots and served with a sprinkling of finely chopped parsley.

REGIONAL DINING

The following restaurants are among those serving regional dishes at reasonable prices:

Adour Hôtel
Aire-sur-l'Adour (see p302)

Bistrot d'Edouard
Bordeaux (see p303)

Chez Germaine
St-Emilion (see p317)

Hôtel de Talleyrand
Chalais (see p305)

Hôtel du Lac
Léon (see p310)

L'Oyat Lacanau-Océan
(see p309)

L'Etrier
Parentis-en-Born (see p313)

La Belle Poule
Rochefort (see p315)

La Goulue
Poitiers (see p314)

La Régula
La Réole (see p308)

La Table des Jacobins
St-Sever (see p319)

Le Binjamin
Dissay (see p307)

Le Vieux Port
Messanges (see p311)

Moulin de Cierzac
Cierzac (see p306)

Regional Wines & Spirits

The word Bordeaux conjures visions of stately châteaux, fine red wines and rare sweet whites – yet these Classed Growths only account for a tiny proportion of the wine produced in this powerhouse region. North of the Gironde estuary is Cognac, source of the world's most famous brandy.

GRAPE VARIETIES

Red Bordeaux is made from a blend of grapes; proportions vary from region to region.

Cabernet Sauvignon At home on the gravelly soils of the Médoc, stern Cabernet makes astringent wines which in time develop fine tannin and considerable finesse.

Merlot For plummy, up-front flavours, Merlot comes into its own in St-Emilion and Pomerol.

Cabernet Franc Most common in the Libournais, and in the Bourg and Blaye area, Cabernet Franc makes wines rich in alcohol.

Petit Verdot Less widely grown, this "seasoning" grape contributes colour and tannin.

Sauvignon Blanc The basis for many dry whites, particularly in Entre-Deux-Mers, has a characteristic smell of blackcurrant leaf.

Sémillon The main grape for sweet wines is also used for dry whites.

Château Margaux

Cabernet Sauvignon grapes

Bordeaux is the largest fine wine area in the world. Wines bearing the generic Bordeaux name may come from an area covering more than 100,000 hectares, (250,000 acres) which stretches out on either side of the Gironde and shares its boundaries with the *département* of the same name. They can be red or rosé, or dry, medium or sweet whites. The best reds have attractive earthy fruit, while dry whites from Sauvignon can have real zip.

Within this region are numerous more specific districts and the appellations of individual villages, each step in theory marking a rung up the quality ladder. At the very top are the globally acclaimed Classed Growth properties. The stardust fallout from these has enchanted the entire market, and many thousands of lesser properties have benefited from the reflected glory.

Overall, Bordeaux may be divided into six separate areas: the Médoc and the Graves are on the left bank of the Gironde and the Garonne rivers; the Libournais and the Blayais and Bourgeais are on the right bank; Entre-Deux-Mers sits in the middle; and the sweet wine vineyards, including Sauternes, are towards the south of the appellation zone.

MÉDOC AND GRAVES

No other vineyard area in the world can boast such a dense concentration of fine wines, celebrated in the classification of 1855. The flat terrain of the Médoc lies to the north of Bordeaux on the left bank of the

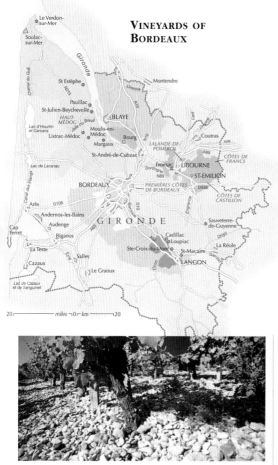

VINEYARDS OF BORDEAUX

KEY

- Barsac
- Cérons
- Côtes de Blaye
- Côtes de Bourg
- Entre-Deux-Mers and other AOC regions (including Premières Côtes de Bordeaux
- Graves
- Libournais (including Fronsac and Canon-Fronsac, Côtes de Castillon, Côtes de Francs and Lalande-de-Pomerol)
- Médoc (including Haut-Médoc, Listrac-Médoc, Margaux, Moulis, Pauillac, St-Estèphe and St-Julien)
- Pessac-Léognan
- Pomerol
- Sauternes
- St-Emilion
- Delimited AOC region of Bordeaux
- *Département* boundary

The gravel soils that give Graves its name

Gironde and produces only red wines. The best – aloof, tannic wines that need years to release their fine fragrance – come from the poor, gravelly soils of the Haut-Médoc, where the top Classed Growths are found in the renowned communes of St-Julien, Pauillac, Margaux and St-Estèphe. In the Graves, the best estates are in the Pessac-Léognan area. The Graves also produces some fabulous whites. The region's top properties were classifed in 1959, for both reds and whites.

LIBOURNAIS

The town of Libourne, from which this whole area takes its name, is of little interest to the tourist. Much better to press on to the spellbinding town of St-Emilion, basking in a sea of vines. The other major appellation of the Libournais is Pomerol. The Merlot grape really comes into its own in St-Emilion and

THE CLASSIFICATION OF 1855

In 1855 the Bordeaux wine merchants classified the region's wines so that the best might be presented at the Exposition Universelle in Paris. They drew up a five-tier ranking of Crus Classés (Classed Growths) for the top 60 wines in the Médoc, based simply on the prices commanded by the various properties at that time. The First Growths were Château Lafite-Rothschild, Château Latour and Château Margaux, with Château Haut-Brion added in from the Graves. The sole change since 1855 has been the promotion of Château Mouton-Rothschild to First Growth status in 1973.

Château d'Yquem

NOBLE ROT (BOTRYTIS CINEREA)

Grapes affected by *botrytis cinerea* may look to be good only for the bin but, for the makers of sweet wine, this unsightly fungus is always welcome. It earns the name noble rot because instead of ruining the grapes it concentrates the natural sugars whilst reducing the water content, thereby intensifying flavour and aroma. It develops in locations where autumn brings warm, humid weather, particularly morning mists and sunny afternoons. Yields are always small and the grapes must be picked selectively, so the wines always command a high price.

Botrytized grapes

Pomerol, producing succulent, ripe and fruity wines. The top wines of St-Emilion were first classified in 1954, divided into Grand Cru Classé, and Premier Grand Cru A or B. This classification is revised every ten years. The Libournais also includes outlying "satellites" of St-Emilion and Fronsac and Canon-Fronsac.

BLAYAIS AND BOURGEAIS

Some very good, predominantly red, fruity wines at reasonable prices come from Premières Côtes de Blaye, Blaye and Côtes de Bourg. These attractive vineyards follow the right banks of the rivers Dordogne and Gironde where the Malbec grape, Cabernet Sauvignon and Cabernet Franc are popular choices for producing reds, as are the Sauvignon Blanc and Colombard for white Côtes de Blaye. All these appellations have excellent potential for the future.

ENTRE-DEUX-MERS

The largest region in the Gironde is situated not between two seas (the literal translation of its name) but between the Garonne and the Dordogne rivers. This land of pretty villages, country manors and farmhouses is where the majority of straight Bordeaux and Bordeaux Supérieur is made and also, of course, the dry whites of the Entre-Deux-Mers appellation.

SWEET WINES

Sauternes and Barsac are the names that immediately spring to mind. The Sémillon grape, prone to developing noble rot as autumn mists swirl off the Garonne and the tiny River Ciron, is primarily responsible for producing these luscious offerings with their flavours of candied and tropical fruit, honey and spice. Nearby Cérons and several other appellations across the Garonne (Ste-Croix-du-Mont, Cadillac and Loupiac) also produce excellent sweet or very sweet wines.

KEY

▦ Grande Champagne

▦ Petite Champagne

▦ Borderies

▦ Fins Bois

▦ Bons Bois

CATEGORIES

Fine Champagne must contain a minimum of 50 per cent spirit from the Grande Champagne area, the rest from the Petite Champagne.

VSOP (Very Superior Old Pale) and **Reserve** apply to Cognacs that are at least five years old.

Napoleon indicates a Cognac that must have been aged in wood for a minimum of six years.

XO is aged at least eight years, but the best are much older.

COGNAC

The most famous eau-de-vie in the world was created by Dutch traders who were seeking a way of concentrating wine in order to be able to carry greater quantities of it in their ships. This they did by heating the wine over a direct flame. This *brandewijn* (burnt wine) came to be called brandy in English. The lovely Charente pot stills used for today's double-distillation process are made entirely of copper and continue to be heated over an open flame.

First-time visitors to the town of Cognac are likely to reflect on how dirty it looks. Roofs and walls are covered with a thick layer of black fungus that feeds on alcohol fumes (known as the "angels' share") rising from the thousands of barrels of spirit slumbering in the damp cellars along the Charente. The longer this ageing process goes on the more the Cognac gains complexity of flavour, elegance and notes of spice, fruit and oxidized *rancio* aromas.

The area producing wines to be distilled into Cognac is divided into six zones. Grande Champagne and Petite Champagne are the most prestigious (the term *champagne* refers to their chalky soils). They produce the finest, the most fragrant eaux-de-vie: the ones that will age best. Next comes Borderies, contributing fine bouquet and softness to the blend. The Fins Bois produce brandies that will age more quickly, while Bons Bois and Bois Ordinaires are of lesser quality.

Cognac cellars

PINEAU DES CHARENTES

Pineau des Charentes is made by adding one-year-old Cognac to grape juice, which prevents fermentation. The grapes must be grown in the Cognac region. It is aged for at least a year, sometimes for up to ten years, and the result is a clear, golden liquid with sumptuous flavour and fruit, retaining all the ripe sweetness of the fresh grape juice. Once a regional peculiarity, Pineau des Charentes is now an increasingly popular aperitif. Try it also with a dessert or with melon. It is produced in red styles too.

Premium XO Cognac

Where to Eat & Stay

AIRE-SUR-L'ADOUR

▲ **Adour Hôtel**

28 ave IV Septembre, 40800 **Map** 10B2

C 05 58 71 66 17

FAX 05 58 71 87 66

E AE, DC, MC, V

H €€ **S** (31) €€

This market town is famed for foie gras; sample it here. The salmon is also absolutely superb. Comfortable rooms.

AMOU

▲ **Au Feu de Bois**

20 ave de Pyrénées, 40330 **Map** 10B2

C 05 58 89 00 86

FAX 08 25 19 33 55

E MC, V **H** €€ **S** (16) €€

A small and friendly hotel with good guestrooms. Delicious, rich meat dishes, particularly during hunting season.

ANGLES-SUR-L'ANGLIN

▲ **Le Relais du Lyon d'Or**

4 rue d'enfer, route from Vicq, 86260 **Map** 7D2

C 05 49 48 32 53

FAX 05 49 84 02 28

W www.lyondor.com

E MC, V **●** Mon L, Tue L; Jan, Feb

H €€ **S** (11) €€€

Modern fusion cooking in a former post inn. Lunch choices include guacamole, tzatziki and hummus. Dinner brings salmon sashimi and andouille cake. Nicely appointed guestrooms.

ANGOULEME

● **La Chouc'**

16 pl du Palet, 16000 **Map** 6C4

C 05 45 95 18 13

E MC, V **●** Sun, Mon; Aug, Christmas, New Year's Eve **H** €€

Lively, convivial spot. Straightforward cuisine such as veal in ravigote (oil and vinegar dressing with shallots), and tripe cassoulet (p328) in Cognac.

ANGOULEME

● **La Ruelle**

6 rue des Trois-Notre Dame, 16000 **Map** 6C4

C 05 45 95 15 19

FAX 05 45 92 94 64

E AE, DC, MC, V **●** Sun, Sat L

H €€

Two ancient houses. Try the crusted brandade (p373) or the langoustines with asparagus risotto. First rate fruit desserts.

ANGOULEME

● **Le Terminus**

3 pl de la Gare, 16000 **Map** 6C4

C 05 45 95 27 13

FAX 05 45 94 04 09

E AE, DC, MC, V

● Sun, Mon; mid 2 wks Aug **H** €

Success stories include sea bass in olive oil, Spanish fricassée of monkfish, and langoustines with summer truffles.

ARCACHON

● **Le Grand Bleu**

30 bd de la plage, 33120 **Map** 10A1

C 05 56 54 92 92

FAX 05 57 52 01 84

E AE, DC, MC, V **●** Sep–Jun: Sun D; Mon **H** €€

Good example of the local crab and perch soup. Oysters are deep-fried and served au gratin, which makes for an interesting change, with a white Graves.

ARCACHON

● **Le Pavillon d'Arguin**

63 bd Géneral Leclerc, 33120 **Map** 10A1

C 05 56 44 59 72

E DC, MC, V **●** Sun, Mon L; Mar, Nov **H** €€

Don't leave Arcachon Bay without trying its oysters. This friendly beachside restaurant serves them with buttered bread and grilled crepinettes.

ASNIERES-SUR-NOUERE

▲ **Le Maine Brun**

La Vigerie, 8 km (5 miles) west of Angoulême on N141, 16290 **Map** 6C4

C 05 45 90 83 00

FAX 05 45 96 91 14

E AE, DC, MC, V **●** Sun, Mon (out of season); Nov–Jan

H €€ **S** (18) €€€€

Pleasant dining experience in an old windmill. Dishes include mullet lasagne,

spicy beef, and baked strawberries in balsamic vinegar. Tidy guestrooms.

AYTRE

● **La Nouvelle Maison des Mouettes**

1 route de la Plage, 17440 **Map** 6B3

C 05 46 44 29 12

FAX 05 46 34 66 01

W www.lamaisondesmouettes.fr

E MC, V **●** Sun D, Mon **H** €€€

Bold, imaginative efforts include lobster rigatoni and whole roasted veal kidney, paired with a daring wine.

BASSANNE

● **Le Moulin de Flaujagues**

1 Moulin Flaujagues, 33190 **Map** 10C1

C 05 56 71 08 62

FAX 05 56 61 18 75

E MC, V **●** Sun D, Mon **H** €€

Intimate restaurant with a wonderful garden. Specialities include fine duck terrines, prawns and millefeuilles laden with fruit. Reservations recommended.

BAZAS

▲ **Domaine de Fompeyre**

Bazas, 33430 **Map** 10B1

C 05 56 25 98 00

FAX 05 56 25 16 25

W www.domainedefompeyre.ue.st

E AE, DC, MC, V **●** Dec–Feb: Sun D

H €€€ **S** (50) €€€€

Hotel perched on a hillside opposite Bazas. The duck with wild cherries and duck liver with apples are both excellent. Rooms are split between two buildings.

BAZAS

● **Les Remparts**

Espace Mauvezin, 49 pl de la Cathedrale, 33430 **Map** 10B1

C 05 56 25 95 24

FAX 05 56 25 95 24

E MC, V **●** Sun D, Mon **H** €€€

Bazadaise beef originated in this town. The entrecôte à la bordelaise (p296) is highly recommended.

BEGLES

● **Le Châteaubriand**

89 ave Salvadorue Allende, 33130

● Restaurant ■ Hotel ▲ Hotel / Restaurant

Map 10B1
C 05 56 85 72 67
FAX 05 56 85 64 10
W www.le-chateaubriand.fr
E MC, V **II** €€€
*A fun, family-oriented place, popular on
summer evenings. Food ranges from
pigeon to a selection of Spanish tapas.*

BISCAROSSE
▲ La Forestière
1300 ave du Pyla, 40600 **Map** 10A1
C 05 58 78 24 14
FAX 05 58 78 26 40
W www.hotellaforestiere.com
E AE, DC, MC, V **●** Oct–Mar
II €€€ **○** (34) €€€
*Three-star hotel with a pool, close to
Lake Etang de Biscarosse. The menu
features foie gras with grapes, honey or
as a terrine. Rooms have balconies.*

BISCAROSSE-PLAGE
▲ Les Vagues
99 rue des Iris, 40600 **Map** 10A1
C 05 58 83 98 10
FAX 05 58 83 98 14
W www.lesvagues.com
E AE, MC, V **●** mid-Oct–mid-Mar
II €€€ **○** (29) €€€
*A lovely family hotel backing directly
onto the beach. Restaurant serves
lobster and shrimp, and meat grills.*

BLAYE
● Le Premayac
25 rue Prémayac, 33390 **Map** 6B5
C 05 57 42 19 57
FAX 05 57 42 37 71
E MC, V **●** Mon L **II** €€
*A little further afield than the usual wine
route. This place is well priced and has
lovely views over the vineyards. The fine
menu concentrates on meat grills.*

BONNEUIL-MATOURS
● Le Pavillion Bleu
Le Port, 86210 **Map** 6C3
C 05 49 85 28 05
FAX 05 49 21 61 94
E MC, V **●** Sun D, Mon; 2nd 2 wks
Oct **II** €€
*Tidy establishment with riverside charm,
refinement and verve. Savour the cold
nougat of scallops with oysters, the*

*pigeon brisket with thighs pastilla (filo-
wrapped) or the polenta with truffles.*

BORDEAUX
● Bistrot d'Edouard
16 pl du Parlement, 33000 **Map** 6B5
C 05 56 81 48 87
FAX 05 56 51 10 32
E AE, MC, V **II** €
*Downtown bistro, a great spot for people-
watching. Expect cheap, traditional fare
from entrecôte a la bordelaise (p296) to
some truly wonderful snails.*

BORDEAUX
● Café Louis
Pl de la Comédie, 33100 **Map** 6B5
C 05 56 44 07 00
FAX 05 56 81 23 55
E AE, DC, MC, V **II** €€€
*The Grand Theatre is a stately addition
to the city's façades and its restaurant
does not disappoint. Well-dressed waiters,
great seafood and Champagne.*

BORDEAUX
● Café Régent
46 pl Gambetta, 33000 **Map** 6B5
C 05 56 44 16 20
FAX 05 57 14 31 70
E AE, MC, V **II** €€
*Good-sized terrace overlooking the lively
pedestrianized Place Gambetta. All the
food is good but the walnut tart and the
fruit-laden meringue are legendary.*

BORDEAUX
● Chez Philippe
1 pl du Parlement, 33000 **Map** 6B5
C 05 56 81 83 15
FAX 05 56 89 19 36
E AE, DC, MC, V
● Sun, Mon; Aug **II** €€€€
*Expensive restaurant but worth it for a
special evening on the lovely Place du
Parlement. Lamprey stars – the fish is
so prized here that in 1170 the canons
of St Seurin of Bordeaux gave up their
property rights for 12 lampreys a year.*

BORDEAUX
● Il Bel Canto
20 allées de Tourny, 33000 **Map** 6B5
C 05 56 81 61 61
FAX 05 56 89 18 85

E AE, DC, MC, V
● Sun **II** €€
*One of the best Italian restaurants in the
Gironde. A wide range of pizzas, pastas
and meats. Opera singers from the
Grand Theatre perform most weekends.*

BORDEAUX
● La Crêpe d'Or
26 rue David Johnston, 33000 **Map** 6B5
C 05 56 48 29 03
FAX 05 56 51 31 19
E MC, V **II** €
*Follow the crowds to this popular
crêperie, next to the beautiful botanical
gardens. The cannelés de Bordeaux
(sponge cakes) are a speciality too.*

BORDEAUX
● La Table du Pain
6 pl du Parlément, 33000 **Map** 6B5
C 05 56 81 01 00
FAX 05 56 01 23 46
E MC, V **II** €
*A large and ever-changing range of
delicious breads and pastries, as well
as hip young staff, makes this one of
the city's finest brunch venues.*

BORDEAUX
● La Tupina
6/8 rue Porte de la Monnaie, 33800
Map 6B5
C 05 56 91 56 37
W www.latupina.com
E AE, DC, MC, V **II** €€€
*World-class bistro fare since 1968, from
hearty beef to delicate mushrooms and
asparagus. Outdoor seating.*

BORDEAUX
● Le Café Bordelais
15 allées de Tourny, 33000 **Map** 6B5
C 05 56 81 49 94
FAX 05 56 43 44 46
W www.le-cafe-bordelais.com
E AE, DC, MC, V **II** €€€
*An exceptional wine bar with over 190
vintages, many available by the glass.
Specialities like ceps in red wine sauce.*

BORDEAUX
● Le Café du Musée
Musée d'Art Contemporain, 7 rue
Ferrère, 33000 **Map** 6B5

📞 05 56 44 71 61
FAX 05 56 48 17 40
💳 AE, DC, MC, V 🍴 €€
In a wonderful art museum, this airy restaurant serves international cuisine, with one of the best sushi bars in town.

BORDEAUX
● Le Chapon Fin
5 rue Montesquieu, 33000 **Map** 6B5
📞 05 56 79 10 10
FAX 05 56 79 09 10
🌐 www.chapon-fin.com
💳 AE, DC, MC, V 🍴 Sun, Mon
🍴 €€€€€
Bordeaux's oldest restaurant and one of the most venerated. Early-19th-century surroundings and extravagant cuisine. Lobster gazpacho is the signature dish.

BORDEAUX
● Le Franchouillard
21 rue Maucoudinat, 33000 **Map** 6B5
📞 05 56 44 95 86
💳 AE, DC, MC, V 🍴 €€
Popular with students, the à la carte menu offers dishes from different French regions. Great atmosphere.

BORDEAUX
■ Les 4 Sœurs
6 cours de XXX Juillet, 33000 **Map** 6B5
📞 05 57 81 19 20
FAX 05 56 01 04 28
💳 AE, DC, MC, V 🛏 (34) €€€
Worth seeking out: the small rooms are basic but good value. Larger rooms overlook the square and the Grand Theatre.

BORDEAUX
● L'Oiseau Bleu
65 cours de Verdun, 33000 **Map** 6B5
📞 05 56 81 09 39
FAX 05 56 81 09 39
💳 AE, DC, MC, V 🍴 Sun, Sat L
🍴 €€€€
A must while you're in Bordeaux: a restaurant that really knows its wine. Chef Frederic Lafon, meanwhile, offers one of the town's most exquisite menus. Gastronomic dining at its finest.

BORDEAUX
● L'Olivier du Clavel
44 rue Charles Domercq, 33000

Map 6B5
📞 05 57 95 09 50
FAX 05 56 92 15 28
💳 AE, DC, MC, V 🍴 Sun, Mon, Sat L
🍴 €€€
With tables around an olive tree, the emphasis is on the Mediterranean: lots of olive oil, fresh tomatoes and white fish.

BORDEAUX
■ Petit Hôtel Labottière
14 rue Francis Martin, 33000 **Map** 6B5
📞 05 56 48 44 10
FAX 05 56 48 44 14
💳 AE, DC, MC, V 🛏 (2) €€€€€
Discreet but attentive service at this historic monument. An extensive, fine breakfast is included and cocktails and snacks are served in the elegant salons.

BOULIAC
● Café de L'Espérance
10 rue de l'Esplanade, 33270 **Map** 10B1
📞 05 56 20 52 16
FAX 05 56 20 52 16
💳 AE, DC, MC, V 🍴 €€
Bistro attached to the St James hotel. Service can be brusque but wonderful food is on offer. Lots of slow-roasted meats and a dessert trolley. Special wine list.

BOULIAC
▲ St James
3 pl Camille Hostein, 33270 **Map** 10B1
📞 05 57 97 06 00
FAX 05 56 20 92 58
🌐 www.saintjames-bouliac.com
💳 AE, DC, MC, V
🍴 €€€€ 🛏 (18) €€€€€
Designed by architect Jean Nouvel, this contemporary hotel is one of the best in Bordeaux. The pool overlooks vineyards and the city below. Two exceptional restaurants, as well as the Café de l'Espérance in the local village.

BOURG-CHARENTE
● La Ribaudière
Pl du Port, 2 km (1.2 miles) south on D158, 16200 **Map** 6C4
📞 05 45 81 30 54
FAX 05 45 81 28 05
💳 AE, DC, MC, V 🍴 Sun D, Mon, Tue L; last wk Feb–1st wk Mar, last 2 wks Oct 🍴 €€€

Standouts include the turbot fricasséed with capers and parsley and the veal kidney with saffron langoustines cooked in their shells. Thoughtful wine selection.

BOUTENAC-TOUVENT
▲ Le Relais de Touvent
4 rue de Saintonge, 17120 **Map** 6B4
📞 05 46 94 13 06
FAX 05 46 94 10 40
💳 AE, MC, V 🍴 Sun D, Mon; last wk Dec–1st wk Jan
🍴 €€€ 🛏 (12) €€€
The vineyards hint at the pleasures within this graceful countryside house. The very best of the menu: lobster salad with foie gras or magret de canard in vinegar and honey. Cosy, clean rooms.

BRESSUIRE
● Le Bouchon
9 rue Ernest-Pérochon, 79300 **Map** 6B2
📞 05 49 74 66 34
FAX 05 49 81 28 03
💳 MC, V 🍴 Sun, Mon; 2 wks Feb, last 4 wks Aug 🍴 €
Discover the terrine of poultry livers with confit of onion, the andouillette or the surprisingly complex beef casserole.

CADILLAC
▲ Châteaux de la Tour
On main D10 road Cadillac-Beguey, 33410 **Map** 10B1
📞 05 56 76 92 00
FAX 05 56 62 11 59
🌐 www.hotel-chateaudelatour.com
💳 AE, MC, V 🍴 Hotel: Apr–Oct Mon–Thu 🍴 €€€ 🛏 (32) €€€€
Overlooking the Château des Ducs d'Eperon. Regional cuisine, including a range of confits and grilled duck with ceps. Large, sumptuous guestrooms. Booking recommended.

CAMBES
● La Varenne
198 Esconac, 33880 **Map** 10B1
📞 05 56 21 85 69
💳 MC, V
🍴 Mon L, Sat–Wed D 🍴 €€
Well-priced restaurant on the banks of the Garonne. Some of the friendliest service in the area. The chef is known to be very inventive.

● Restaurant ■ Hotel ▲ Hotel / Restaurant

CANEJAN

● Chez Pascale

26 chemin Salvadore Allende, 33610
Map 10B1

C 05 56 89 18 57

FAX 05 56 89 18 57

W www.chez-pascale.com

⊘ AE, DC, MC, V **●** Sun, Sat L

¶¶ €€€

*A good culinary tour of the entire
Gironde region. Local specialities from
foie gras terrines to Chabichou cheeses.*

CAP-FERRET

▲ Hôtel De La Plage Chez Magne

1 rue des Marets, 33950 **Map** 10A1

C 05 56 60 50 15

⊘ MC, V **●** Jan **¶¶** € **⊘** (8) €€

*Simple hotel right by the beach, with
plentiful amounts of fish. The rooms
have a lovely rustic feel. Good value.*

CAP-FERRET

▲ La Maison du Bassin

5 rue des Pionniers, 33950 **Map** 10A1

C 05 56 60 60 63

⊘ MC, V **●** Jan–Feb

¶¶ €€ **⊘** (7) €€

*Teak wood, sand dunes, a relaxed
atmosphere and lashings of freshly
caught fish, plus a good cocktail bar.*

CAPBRETON

▲ Le Balcon

Pl de l'Hôtel de Ville, 40130 **Map** 10A2

C 05 58 72 11 76

FAX 05 58 72 11 76

⊘ MC, V **¶¶** €€ **⊘** (7) €€

*Chipirons a l'encre (squid cooked in its
own ink with Armagnac) is a popular
dish here. Strong Basque cider too.*

CARCANS-MAUBUISSON

● Café le Bord'eau

Pl du Pôle, 33121 **Map** 6B5

C 05 56 03 38 41

FAX 05 56 03 38 41

⊘ MC, V **¶¶** €

*Right on the water, this small, friendly
bar serves a mouthwatering array of ice
cream, sorbets, crêpes and galettes.*

CASTETS

● Ferme Auberge Lesca

428 chemin des tucs, 40260 **Map** 10A2

C 05 58 89 41 45

FAX 05 58 55 00 71

⊘ MC, V **●** Mon **¶¶** €€

*Farm restaurant. The meat dishes on the
menu here often make use of Chalosse
beef, famous for being tender and tasty.*

CELLES-SUR-BELLE

▲ Hostellerie de l'Abbaye

1 pl de Epoux-Laurant, 79370 **Map** 6C3

C 05 49 32 93 32

FAX 05 49 79 72 65

W www.hotel-restaurant-abbaye.com

⊘ MC, V **●** Sun D, Mon

¶¶ €€ **⊘** (20) €€

*Try the medallions of filet mignon, the
turbot and the fabulous French toast
dessert. Tranquil, well-appointed rooms.*

CHALAIS

▲ Hôtel de Talleyrand

18 pl Hôtel de Ville, 16210 **Map** 6B5

C 05 45 98 15 77

FAX 05 45 98 10 24

⊘ MC, V **●** Mon D, Tue; Feb, Nov.

¶¶ €€ **⊘** (4) €€

*Friendly faces and fine fare. The Anglo-
Dutch owners bring a new twist to
French classics, like foie gras with
strawberries or their tasty take on
Chalais' famous veal. Guestrooms are
spacious, some with elegant fireplaces.
Popular with locals, so book ahead.*

CHALAIS

● Le Relais du Château

15 rue du Château, 16210 **Map** 6B5

C 05 45 98 23 58

FAX 05 45 98 00 53

⊘ AE, MC, V **●** Sun D, Mon, Tue L;
Nov **¶¶** €

*Savour millefeuille of foie gras with fine
smoked magret de canard, turbot in
Champagne, and raspberry-orange crisp.*

CHARROUX

● Hostellerie Charlemagne

7 rue de Rochemeau, 86250 **Map** 6C3

C 05 49 87 50 37

⊘ AE, DC, MC, V **●** Sun D, Sep–Jun:
Mon **¶¶** €€

*Enjoy a timeless menu beside an abbey
erected in the time of Charlemagne.
Historical pride reflects in dishes like
feuilleté of snails with mushrooms, fresh*

*cod with caramel and spices, and beef
Limousin cooked in Charentes Pineau.*

CHATEAUBERNARD

▲ Château de l'Yeuse

65 rue de Bellevue, 16100 **Map** 6B4

C 05 45 36 82 60

FAX 05 45 35 06 32

W www.yeuse.fr

⊘ AE, DC, MC, V **●** Sun D (out of
season), Sat L; Jan

¶¶ €€€€ **⊘** (24) €€€€€

*A lovely mansion surrounded by flowers.
Let your taste buds bloom with the
crispy millefeuille and avocado mousse
or the cassoulette du marché de La
Rochelle. A wide cheese range and an
unmatched choice of Cognacs.*

CHATEAUBERNARD

▲ L'Echassier

72 rue de Bellevue, 16100 **Map** 6B4

C 05 45 35 01 09

FAX 05 45 32 22 43

W www.echassier.com

⊘ AE, DC, MC, V

¶¶ €€ **⊘** (24) €€€€

*Respect for the past marks the cuisine
here. Try the crêpes filled with Marennes
oysters, salmon and Aquitaine caviar, the
pork mignon with shellfish coulis or the
lamb in thyme. Tasteful rooms and pool.*

CHATELAILLON-PLAGE

▲ Acadie St-Victor

35 bd de la Mer, 17340 **Map** 6B4

C 05 46 56 25 13

FAX 05 46 56 25 12

@ stvictor@wanadoo.fr

⊘ AE, MC, V **●** Sun D, Mon (out of
season), Oct–Apr: Fri D; mid-Feb–1st
wk Mar, mid-Oct–mid-Nov

¶¶ €€ **⊘** (13) €€

*Modern cuisine in an up-to-date setting.
The wine list brims with first-rate whites
from Bordeaux producers. The beachside location adds allure to the rooms.*

CHATELAILLON-PLAGE

▲ Les Flots

52 bd de la Mer, 17340 **Map** 6B4

C 05 46 56 23 42

FAX 05 46 56 99 37

⊘ MC, V **●** Tue; mid-Dec–1st 3 wks
Jan **¶¶** €€ **⊘** (11) €€€

A regional favourite, beloved by the Rochelais. Outstanding creations like lemon-perfumed mackerel, and baked cuttlefish in crème of garlic illustrate the attraction. Cheery rooms by the sea.

CHATELLERAULT
▲ Grand Hôtel Moderne La Charmille
74 bd Blossac, 86100 **Map** 6C2
[C] 05 49 93 33 00
FAX 05 49 93 25 19
🗝 AE, DC, MC, V ⬤ Restaurant: Sun D, Mon; early Jan, mid Oct
🍽 €€€ 🍴 (24) €€€€
Calm, restful hotel with classic rooms. The grace continues in the kitchen with escabèche (spicy Spanish marinade) of goatfish with grapefruit gelatine, and tomato-orange confit. Broad wine list.

CHATELLERAULT
▲ La Taverne de Maître Kanter
10 ave Camille-Pagé, 86100 **Map** 6C2
[C] 05 49 02 18 19
FAX 05 49 02 01 79
🗝 MC, V 🍽 € 🍴 (72) €€
Casual bistro style but the cuisine here is great value for money. Oleron oysters, choucroute (p119) or flammenkueche (p119) prove the case. Adequate rooms.

CHENAY
▲ Les Trois Pigeons
Town centre, 79120 **Map** 6C3
[C] 05 49 07 38 59
FAX 05 49 07 37 82
[W] www.hoteldestroispigeons.fr
🗝 AE, MC, V ⬤ Sun D, Mon
🍽 €€ 🍴 (11) €€
Wise diners begin with duck foie gras cooked in Charentes Pineau then proceed to sautéed scallops with chanterelles and finish with a heavenly apricot tart. Guestrooms are tidy and attractive.

CIERZAC
▲ Moulin de Cierzac
St-Fort-sur-le-Né, 16130 **Map** 6B4
[C] 05 45 83 01 32
FAX 05 45 83 03 59
🗝 AE, DC, MC, V ⬤ Sun D, Mon (except Jul–Aug: D); last wk Jan–1st wk Feb 🍽 €€ 🍴 (9) €€€
Ancient recipes produce smoky Cognacs and fruity Pineau liqueur. The table here

is no less bountiful. Recommended plates include duck foie gras in brandy, langoustines with ginger, and local lamb with fresh garden mint. Pleasant rooms.

CLAM
▲ Le Vieux Logis
Le Bourg, 17500 **Map** 6B4
[C] 05 46 70 20 13
FAX 05 46 70 20 64
🗝 AE, DC, MC, V ⬤ Oct–Apr: Sun D, 1st wk Jan–1st wk Feb
🍽 €€ 🍴 (10) €€
Specialities include fricasséed scallops with mushrooms and the braised monk-fish with bacon and vegetable confit. Nicely decorated rooms.

COGNAC
▲ Les Pigeons Blancs
110 rue Jules Bresson, 16100 **Map** 6B4
[C] 05 45 82 16 36
FAX 05 45 82 29 29
🗝 AE, DC, MC, V ⬤ Sun D, Mon L; 1st 2 wks Jan 🍽 €€€ 🍴 (7) €€€
Immaculate grounds, gracefully decorated rooms and a gastronomic table. Inspired offerings like sea bass with Bourbon vanilla and nuts, with a glass of VSOP Cognac, or rack of lamb with rosemary. The wine and liqueur list is impressive.

CONDEON
▲ Le Bois de Maure
Town centre, 16360 **Map** 6C5
[C] 05 45 78 53 15
🗝 MC, V 🍽 € 🍴 (4) €€
Early-19th-century structure in the heart of Cognac country with a large lovely garden. The farm still produces foie gras and the menu reflects that. It's all about duck: magret, baked pâté with potatoes and giblet salad.

CONTIS-LES-BAINS
▲ Hôtel Neptune
Rue Avocettes, 40170 **Map** 10A2
[C] 05 58 42 85 28
FAX 05 58 42 44 47
🗝 MC, V ⬤ Oct–Feb
🍽 € 🍴 (16) €€
A good beachfront hotel. Great mussels and prawns and delicious fruit and vegetable dishes using asparagus and kiwis, grown locally and among the best

in Europe. Colours evocative of the coast fill the pretty rooms.

COULOMBIERS
▲ Le Centre Poitou
RN 39, 86600 **Map** 6C3
[C] 05 49 60 90 15
FAX 05 49 60 53 70
[W] http://centre-poitou.com
🗝 MC, V ⬤ Sun D, Mon (except Jul–Aug); 3rd wk Feb, 3rd wk Oct–1st wk Nov 🍽 €€€ 🍴 (12) €€€
A small countryside inn a cut above its fellows. Highlights include pastilla (filo-wrapped) lamb with marmalade, and turbot on a bed of seaweed. Rooms are well kept and amply sized.

COULON
▲ Le Central
4 rue d'Autremont, 79510 **Map** 6B3
[C] 05 49 35 90 20
FAX 05 49 35 81 07
🗝 AE, MC, V ⬤ Sun D, Mon
🍽 €€ 🍴 (5) €€
The chef turns out young pigeon with foie gras salad and truffles, plus monk-fish medallions with petis-gris (local snails), vinegar and veal sauce. Deftly chosen wine list. Reasonable rooms.

CREON
⬤ Le Lion d'Or
2 pl de l'Eglise, 33670 **Map** 10B1
[C] 05 56 23 90 23
FAX 05 56 23 90 80
🗝 MC, V ⬤ Sun D, Mon 🍽 €€
The locals come for the abundant portions of grills, terrines and well-chosen wines. Ask for the apples melted in red wine.

CREON
▲ Château Camiac
Route Branne D121, 33670 **Map** 10B1
[C] 05 56 23 20 85
FAX 05 56 23 38 84
🗝 AE, DC, MC, V
⬤ Restaurant: Nov–Mar
🍽 €€€€ 🍴 (10) €€€€€
One of the best château hotels in Bordeaux's wine region. Restaurant offering foie gras in Sauternes jelly, veal sweetbreads and chocolate desserts. The oak-beamed rooms nestle in the eves or turrets of the château.

⬤ Restaurant ■ Hotel ▲ Hotel / Restaurant

CURZAY-SUR-VONNE

▲ Château de Curzay La Cédraie

6 km northwest of Lusignan, 86600

Map 6C3

📞 05 49 36 17 00

FAX 05 49 53 57 69

w www.chateau-curzay.com

🗲 AE, DC, MC, V ⬤ mid-Apr–mid-Jun; Sep–mid-Nov: Mon L–Thu L; mid-Nov–mid Apr

🍽 €€€€ 🛏 (22) €€€€€

This château drew aristocrats in its heyday, the 18th century. Today all are welcome to dine on snail cassoulet (p326), langoustines with caviar, and artichokes. Ostentatious rooms. Immense park.

DANGE-ST-ROMAIN

⬤ Auberge la Crémaillère

56 ave de l'Europe, 86220 **Map** 7D2

📞 05 49 86 40 24

FAX 05 49 19 17 70

🗲 AE, DC, MC, V ⬤ Sun D, Wed

🍽 €€

Tucked away in sylvan surroundings. Indulge yourself with a terrine of liver, large prawn rounds with bacon, or tasty andouille gratin with onions.

DAX

▲ Jean le Bon

12/14 rue Jean Le Bon, 40100

Map 10A2

📞 05 58 74 90 68

FAX 05 58 90 03 04

🗲 AE, DC, MC, V 🍽 €€ 🛏 (27) €€

A small, good-value hotel with its own pool and a shuttle bus to the spas. Emphasis on healthy food like the salade jean le bon.

DAX

⬤ Le Sous Bois

70 ave St Vincent Paul, 40100 **Map** 10A2

📞 05 58 56 24 51

FAX 05 58 56 26 45

🗲 AE, DC, MC, V ⬤ Sun D, Mon, Sat L

🍽 €€

Pretty restaurant with seasonal options including flounder soufflé with shrimp in spring and lamb with basil in winter.

DAX

⬤ L'Estrope

Quai des arènes - Berges de l'Adour, 40100 **Map** 10A2

📞 05 58 56 03 41

FAX 05 58 56 03 41

🗲 MC, V ⬤ Sat L, Wed, Thu L

🍽 €€€

Herring, salmon and eels from the Landes rivers are the specialities at this barge eatery. Expect Spanish influences.

DAX

⬤ Lou Balubé

63 ave St Vincent Paul, 40100 **Map** 10A2

📞 05 58 56 97 92

FAX 08 25 18 88 05

🗲 AE, DC, MC, V ⬤ Sun 🍽 €€

A particularly charming place. Inexpensive fixed-price menu with dessert, coffee and wine included.

DISSAY

▲ Le Binjamin

RN10, 86130 **Map** 6C3

📞 05 49 52 42 37

FAX 05 49 62 59 06

w www.binjamin.com

🗲 AE, MC, V ⬤ Sun D, Mon, Sat L

🍽 €€ 🛏 (10) €€

Grand roadside establishment with a modern feel that extends from the sleek guestrooms to the table. Don't miss the large shrimp with caramel, sesame and ginger or the langoustine ravioli with saffron butter. Excellent desserts.

EUGENIE-LES-BAINS

▲ La Maison Rose

334 rue René Vielle (main road in Eugénie-les-Bains), 40320 **Map** 10B2

📞 05 58 05 06 07

FAX 05 58 51 10 10

🗲 AE, DC, MC, V ⬤ Jan–mid-Feb

🍽 €€€ 🛏 (27) €€€€

A wonderful hotel and spa In a town famed for its thermal baths. Known for its healthy food, this is French cooking at its best without excess calories or fat.

FRONSAC

⬤ Le Bord d'Eau

4 Poinsonnet, 33126 **Map** 6B5

📞 05 57 51 99 91

FAX 05 57 25 11 56

🗲 MC, V

⬤ Sun D, Mon, Wed D; Feb 🍽 €€

Fronsac and the slightly lesser-known La Lande-de-Fronsac wines feature at this

riverside restaurant. A good menu with freshwater fish and aromatic meat stews.

GABARRET

▲ Château de Buros

D656 northeast of Gabarret, 40310

Map 10C2

📞 05 58 44 34 30

FAX 05 58 44 36 53

w www.chateaudeburos.com

🗲 AE, DC, MC, V

🍽 €€€ 🛏 (20) €€€

Spectacular restaurant in a double-height oak-beamed room. The menu does not concentrate solely on south-western cooking but uses sources from all over France. Each guestroom is an interesting mix of antique and modern.

GAILLAN-EN-MEDOC

▲ Château Layauga

50 route Soulac, 33340 **Map** 6B5

📞 05 56 41 26 83

FAX 05 56 41 19 52

🗲 AE, DC, MC, V ⬤ Jan, Feb 🍽 €€€€ 🛏 (7) €€€€

A splendid four-star château hotel with an excellent restaurant. Recommended is the pigeon cooked in rolled poultry and stuffing. Good mix of antique and modern furniture in the rooms.

GIRONDE-SUR-DROPT

▲ Les Trois Cèdres

On main N113 road, 33190 **Map** 10C1

📞 05 56 71 10 70

FAX 05 56 71 12 10

🗲 AE, DC, MC, V ⬤ 1st 2 wks Jan

🍽 €€ 🛏 (10) €€

At the bottom tip of Entre deux Mers. Desserts are particularly good and make the most of the many fruits harvested in this rich agricultural area, such as the Brebis cheese with local cherry jam. Simple but large and airy guestrooms.

GRADIGNAN

▲ Le Chalet Lyrique bis

169 cours Général de Gaulle, 33170

Map 10B1

📞 05 56 89 11 59

FAX 05 56 89 53 37

w www.chalet-lyrique.fr

🗲 AE, DC, MC, V ⬤ Restaurant: Aug

🍽 €€€ 🛏 (44) €€€

Notable for its gourmet restaurant, this is a well-known, well-loved hotel. The genial family who run the place will offer you plenty of the local Graves wine to accompany food such as grilled sole, perfectly fresh and simple.

GRENADE-SUR-L'ADOUR
▲ Pain Adour et Fantasie

14–16 pls des Tilleuls, 40270 **Map** 10B2

☎ 05 58 45 18 80

FAX 05 58 45 16 57

🗐 AE, DC, MC, V ● Sun D, Mon L; 2 wks Feb 🍴 €€€ 🍽 (11) €€€

Elegant restaurant with a Michelin star. Favourites include chicken with foie gras and Bazas beef. Bedrooms are modern and elegant but balanced with some well-chosen antique pieces and lots of oak panelling. A riverside terrace makes for idyllic outdoor dining.

HAGETMAU
● Auberge du Conte

406 rue Carnot, 40700 **Map** 10B2

☎ 05 58 79 33 79

FAX 05 58 79 33 79

🗐 AE, MC, V ● 3 wks Aug

🍴 €€€

During hunting season (Oct–Feb) a choice dish is pigeon flambéed with duck fat and steamed in Armagnac. Good set menus.

HAGETMAU
▲ Les Lacs d'Halco

Route de Cazalis, 40700 **Map** 10B2

☎ 05 58 79 30 79

FAX 05 58 79 36 15

🌐 www.hotel-des-lacs-dhalco.com

🗐 AE, DC, MC, V

🍴 €€ 🍽 (24) €€

An unusual place with a restaurant affording views of the lake. Beef dishes are recommended: from flank steak to chateaubriand. Also a striking three-star hotel with stylish, modern guestrooms.

HOSSEGOR
▲ Le Rond Point

866 ave du Touring Club, 40150 **Map** 10A2

☎ 05 58 43 53 11

FAX 05 58 43 85 85

🗐 AE, MC, V 🍴 €€€ 🍽 (12) €€

Oyster cultivation began in Hossegor

around 1876. Eat them in the restaurant or take them away. Guestrooms are filled with lovely antique furniture.

HOSSEGOR
▲ Les Hortensias du Lac

1578 ave du Tour du Lac, 40150 **Map** 10A2

☎ 05 58 43 99 00

FAX 05 58 43 42 81

🗐 AE, DC, MC, V ● Nov–Mar: D

🍴 €€€ 🍽 (23) €€€€

The only four-star hotel in Hossegor, with a pool and near the lake. Great Champagne buffet, with a range of pastries, home-made conserves and plats chauds.

HOURTIN
● Chez Badine

27 rue de la Gare, 33990 **Map** 6B5

☎ 05 56 09 13 11

FAX 05 56 09 13 11

🗐 MC, V ● Thu D Sep–May 🍴 €

Inside a starkly modern building but with an emphasis on old-fashioned regional cuisine. A good range of freshwater fish.

ITEUIL
● Au Gardon Frais

Route de l'Ancienne-Gare, 86240 **Map** 6C3

☎ 05 49 55 00 04

FAX 05 49 30 13 34

🗐 MC, V ● Mon, Tue; 1st wk Jan, 1st wk Mar, 1st wk Aug, 1st wk Oct, 1st wk Nov 🍴 €

Basic, bubbly eatery with solid choices including pig's trotters stuffed with white string beans, salmon casserole with local sausage and delectable fish fritters.

JARNAC
● Le Château

15 pl du Château, 16200 **Map** 6C4

☎ 05 45 81 07 17

FAX 05 45 35 35 71

🗐 AE, MC, V ● Sun D, Mon, Wed D; last 2 wks Jan, last 3 wks Aug 🍴 €€

Seek out the millefeuille of foie gras with pear and turnip confit followed by a little ice cream with Cognac for dessert.

JONZAC
● Bistro 108

8 ave Mal-de-Lattre-de-Tassigny, 17500

Map 6B5

☎ 05 46 48 02 95

🗐 MC, V ● Sun D, Mon, Sat L

🍴 €€

The feisty conversation is as sought-after as the cooking. Delights include ratatouille (p400); thinly sliced, sautéed foie gras Lyon-style; and veal kidneys in a port sauce. Lively, light and simple.

LA CHAPELLE-ST-LAURENT
● La Petite Auberge

1 rue de la Basilique, 79430 **Map** 6B3

☎ 05 49 72 02 15

FAX 05 49 80 30 73

🗐 MC, V ● Sun D, Wed 🍴 €

The versatile kitchen offers pike-perch in Pineau liqueur or noisettes of lamb stuffed with goats' cheese. A lively spot.

LA HUCHET
▲ Maisons Marines d'Huchet

La Huchet (via Les Prés d'Eugénie), 40550 **Map** 10A2

☎ 05 58 05 06 07

FAX 05 58 51 10 10

🌐 www.michelguerard.com

🗐 AE, DC, MC, V ● Jan–Mar, last wk Nov–mid-Dec 🍴 €€ 🍽 (4) €€

Beach house spa. Good, simple cooking such as seafood flavoured with herbs and lightly grilled with lemon juice. Great cocktail bar. Teak wood in the rooms.

LA REOLE
● Le Régula

31 rue André Bénac, 33190 **Map** 10C1

☎ 05 56 61 13 52

FAX 05 56 61 13 52

🗐 MC, V ● Fri D; Jun–Jul: Wed, school hols except summer 🍴 €€€

Local cuisine served on a terrace over-looking the streets of this lovely town. One menu gives a culinary tour of the region with wine from Chateau Le Luc-Régula, just up the road.

LA REOLE
● Lou Cali

14 ave de la Victoire, 33190 **Map** 10C1

☎ 05 56 71 25 35

FAX 05 56 71 25 35

🗐 MC, V ● Oct–Apr 🍴 €

On the riverfront with lovely views. Crispy crêpes, both sweet and savoury.

LA ROCHELLE
● Chez Serge

46 cours des Dames, 17000 **Map** 6B3

C 05 46 50 25 25

FAX 05 46 50 25 34

W www.chezserge.fr

C AE, DC, MC, V ● Sun D, Mon (except mid-May–Sep) ** 11** €€€€

Flights of fancy include airy couscous in almond oil, tiny, oven-roasted monk-fish sausages, scallops with sabayon potatoes, and caramelized bananas.

LA ROCHELLE
● Comptoir des Voyages

22 rue St-Jean-du-Pérot, 17000 **Map** 6B3

C 05 46 50 62 60

FAX 05 46 41 90 80

W www.coutanceauonline.com

C DC, MC, V ● Sun D, Mon, Sat L **11** €€

Let your tongue travel with wok-fired cuttlefish in barbecue sauce or the fine magret de canard cooked crispy in its skin with olive marmalade and long macaroni gratin. Sophisticated wine list.

LA ROCHELLE
● Richard Coutanceau

Plage de la Concurrence, 17000 **Map** 6B3

C 05 46 41 48 19

FAX 05 46 41 99 49

W www.coutanceaularochelle.com

C AE, DC, MC, V ● Sun **11** €€€€€

Internationally known venue for bons vivants. Superlatives are heaped on this magical cuisine but the hyperbole is deserved. Recommended: ravioli of langoustines and courgette (zucchini), lobster salad with sea asparagus and Nice-style dumplings. Wise, witty staff.

LA ROCHE-POSAY
▲ Le St-Roch

4 cours Pasteur, 86270 **Map** 7D2

C 05 49 19 49 45

FAX 05 49 19 49 40

W www.larocheposay-shrp.com

C MC, V ● Last wk Dec–last wk Jan **11** € ● (39) €€€

This well-tended establishment lies in a quiet village on the banks of the Gartempe river. The judicious kitchen produces dishes like terrine of mullet

with wild herbs, and plaice with poppy seeds. Pleasantly broad wine list.

LA TREMBLADE
● Le Brise-Lames

2 ave de la Cèpe, 17390 **Map** 6B4

C 05 46 36 06 41

FAX 05 46 36 38 87

C MC, V ● Sun D, Mon (except Jul–Aug), Tue (out of season); Jan **11** €€

This seaside spot isn't explosive in its creativity but turns out thoughtful meals. The menu includes crab millefeuille, a delightful fricassée of lamb sweetbreads with lime and a confit of langoustines. Finish with the flaky apricot tart.

LABASTIDE-D'ARMAGNAC
● La Croûte de Pin

Rimbez, 40310 **Map** 10B2

C 05 58 44 94 02

FAX 05 58 44 91 40

C MC, V **11** €€

Idyllic rural spot just outside this well-preserved town. Generous amounts of country cuisine reflect the flavours of both Gascony and Les Landes.

LABOUHEYRE
▲ L'Aubergade

71 rue Bremontier, 40210 **Map** 10B1

C 05 58 07 00 78

FAX 05 58 04 52 17

C MC, V **11** € ● (9) €€

Two-star hotel and restaurant, excellent for the price. A large terrace affords great views and wonderful birdsong. Foie gras, duck salad and magret de canard are on the menu. Basic rooms upstairs – not the main draw.

LACANAU-OCEAN
▲ L'Oyat

Front de Mer, allée Ortal,33680 **Map** 6A5

C 05 56 03 11 11

FAX 05 56 03 12 29

@ oyat@lespiedsdansleau.com

C AE, DC, MC, V

● Nov–Mar

11 € ● (30) €€€

Reasonably priced, basic half-board accommodation right on the seafront with easy access to a range of water sports. The restaurant serves some of

the best food in town. Try the plentiful seafood platters, a true feast.

LANGON
▲ Claude Darroze

95 cours du General Leclerc, 33210 **Map** 10B1

C 05 56 63 00 48

FAX 05 56 63 41 15

C AE, MC, V ● Jan, mid-Oct–mid-Nov **11** €€€ ● (15) €€€€

Three-star 18th-century hotel with a four-star restaurant, offering beautifully prepared regional specialities. Notable dishes include young wild boar in red wine and veal kidneys in Sauternes. The large guestrooms are baroque in style.

LE BOIS-PLAGE-EN-RE
▲ L'Océan

172 rue St Martin, 17580 **Map** 6A3

C 05 46 09 23 07

FAX 05 46 09 05 40

W www.hotel-ocean.com

C AE, MC, V ● Wed; 2nd wk Feb–2nd wk Mar

11 €€ ● (26) €€€€

So close to the sea, it's no surprise to see dishes like sardines in a spicy Spanish marinade with tapenade (p400) or grilled sea bass in vanilla. Discerning wine list. Soothing pastel rooms over-looking the water.

LE GRAND-VILLAGE-PLAGE
● Le Relais des Salines

Port des Salines, 17370 **Map** 6A4

C 05 46 75 82 42

FAX 05 46 75 16 70

C MC, V ● Sun D, Mon; mid-Nov–3rd wk Mar **11** €

A warm, basic bistro. Fish, seafood and a finely tuned wine list are assured. Options include six hot oysters on a base of peppers in white butter and grilled sea bass au naturel.

LE GUA
▲ Le Moulin de Châlons

2 rue du Bassin Châlons, 17600 **Map** 6B4

C 05 46 22 82 72

FAX 05 46 22 91 07

W www.moulin-de-chalons.com

C AE, MC, V ● Sun D, mid-Oct–Apr:

Mon; 1st 3 wks Jan

🍴 €€ 🛏 (14) €€€

*In a former windmill at the juncture of
land, sea and river, enjoy dishes like
lightly baked duck foie gras or cod
cooked crispy with tomato and basil.*

LE PIAN-MEDOC

▲ **Le Pont Vernet**

Route du Verdon, 33290 **Map** 6B5

📞 05 56 70 20 19

FAX 05 56 70 22 90

W www.pont-vernet.fr

✉ AE, DC, MC, V ● 1st wk Nov

🍴 €€ 🛏 (18) €€

*Renowned restaurant with a variety of
gastronomic menus. In autumn, wood
pigeon is a favoured dish. Gracious,
comfortable and colourful rooms. English
and Spanish spoken. Dogs welcome.*

LE VERDON-SUR-MER

● **La Pêcherie**

2 allée Louis de Foix, 33123 **Map** 6B4

📞 05 56 09 60 32

FAX 05 56 73 70 16

✉ MC, V ● Mon–Thu D 🍴 €€

*Located at the end of the Gironde near
the mouth of the river. Seafood shines:
escabèche (marinated fried fish, served
cold) and many seafood platters.*

LE VIGEANT

▲ **Hotel Val de Vienne**

Port de Salles, 86150 **Map** 7D3

📞 05 49 48 27 27

FAX 05 49 48 47 47

W www.hotel-valdevienne.com

✉ MC, V ● Wed; Jan

🍴 €€ 🛏 (22) €€€

*Gaze out at the river as you dine on good
fricassée of frogs' legs with pecan nuts,
or wild sea bass with caramel and sweet
balsamic vinegar. Slick, motel feel but it
does have a swimming pool.*

LEGE-CAP-FERRET

● **Chez Hortense**

Ave du Sémaphore, 33950 **Map** 10A1

📞 05 56 60 62 56

FAX 05 56 60 42 84

✉ AE, DC, MC, V ● Sep–Mar

🍴 €€€

*Right at the end of the peninsula.
Imaginatively prepared seafood, and*

*oysters from Arcachon Bay, which is
France's fourth-largest oyster producer.*

LEIGNE-LES-BOIS

● **Bernard Gautier**

Pl de la Mairie, 86450 **Map** 7D3

📞 05 49 86 53 82

✉ MC, V ● Sun D, Mon; last wk
Feb–1st wk Mar; mid-Nov–mid-Dec

🍴 €€

*Fatted chicken in gelatine, salmon in
white butter, and spiced pigeons top the
menu. This village favourite has superb
desserts using fresh local fruit.*

LENCLOITRE

● **Le Champ de Foire**

18 pl du Champ-de-Foire, 86140
Map 6C2

📞 05 49 90 74 91

FAX 05 49 93 33 76

✉ MC, V ● Sun D, Mon, Tue D; 2
wks Feb 🍴 €€

*Fine tart of boudin noir, mesclun and
salmon tournedos in Saumur wine. Local
wines. No à la carte.*

LEON

▲ **Hôtel du Lac**

2 rue Berges du Lac, 40550 **Map** 10A2

📞 05 58 48 73 11

FAX 05 58 49 27 79

✉ MC, V ● Sep–Mar

🍴 €€ 🛏 (15) €€

*The coast of the southern Landes region
is often quiet and well worth a lazy few
days' drive. This small hotel makes full
use of the seafood that is delivered
fresh daily. Most rooms have balconies.*

LEON

● **La Pêche aux Moules**

1 pl de l'Eglise, 40550 **Map** 10A2

📞 05 58 49 26 85

FAX 05 58 49 21 78

✉ AE, DC, MC, V 🍴 €€€

*In an area known for its outdoor activities,
this is a restaurant famous for its oysters
and mussels, prepared in a variety of
classic ways, as well as, more unusually,
with Roquefort cheese. Pretty terrace.*

LEZIGNAC-DURAND

▲ **Château de la Redortière**

La Redortière, 16310 **Map** 7D4

📞 05 45 65 07 62

W http://perso.wanadoo.fr/redortiere

✉ MC, V ● Sun D, Mon

🍴 €€ 🛏 (15) €€€

*Even rare birds are attracted to this
Belle Epoque mansion in a vast park
with an avian preserve. Perhaps they are
intrigued by the nettle soup
or courgette (zucchini) tart.*

LIBOURNE

● **Grill de L'Etrier**

21 pl Decazes, 33500 **Map** 6B5

📞 05 57 51 26 99

✉ AE, DC, MC, V ● Sun–Mon D

🍴 €€

*This restaurant boasts both a traditional
and gourmet menu that include confit
de canard (p326) and foie gras dishes.*

LIBOURNE

● **Les Délices de la Mer**

21 rue Thiers, 33500 **Map** 6B5

📞 05 57 51 94 84

FAX 05 57 51 94 88

✉ MC, V ● Sun D, Mon 🍴 €€€

*A fish-lover's restaurant concentrating
on fresh seafood and offering a great
selection of fish kebabs. Look out for the
fried baby eels.*

LIT-ET-MIXE

▲ **Relais des Lacs**

105 rue de l'Eglise, 40170 **Map** 10A2

📞 05 58 42 83 36

FAX 05 58 42 43 28

✉ MC, V 🍴 €€ 🛏 (20) €€

*Plenty of freshwater fish plus shellfish,
from lobster to oysters, too. Meats include
jambon de Bayonne. The dish that really
stands out is the asparagus platter.
Rooms are simple, nothing flashy.*

LOUDUN

▲ **La Roue d'Or**

1 ave d'Anjou, direction Fontevraud,
86200 **Map** 6C2

📞 05 49 98 01 23

FAX 05 49 98 85 45

✉ AE, DC, MC, V ● Sun D, mid-
Oct–mid-Apr: Sat 🍴 €€ 🛏 (14) €€

*A wild blend of influences worth seeking
out. Discover osso bucco of monkfish
cooked with fennel and thyme, whole
roast Martaize pigeon with sweet wine*

● Restaurant   ■ Hotel   ▲ Hotel / Restaurant

glaze, and strawberries sabayon with Champagne sorbet. Neat guestrooms.

LUE

▲ Auberge de Biaudos

Rn117 Biaudos, 40390 **Map** 10B1

[C] 05 59 56 79 70

FAX 05 59 56 74 68

AE, MC, V ▮▮ €€ ◯ (7) €€

A small hotel with a restaurant that provides hearty portions of foie gras and freshwater fish. Great location at the confluence of Les Landes, Bearn and the Pays Basque. Bedrooms, some with small balconies, overlook parkland and the swimming pool below.

MAGESCQ

● Le Cabanon

1129 ave des Landes, 40140 **Map** 10A2

[C] 05 58 47 71 51

FAX 05 58 47 75 19

MC, V ◯ Sun D, Mon ▮▮ €€€

In the gastronomic heart of the Landes where you'll find a number of galleries and local craftsmen. This eatery claims the oldest collection of whiskies in Europe. Wood-fired cuisine.

MAGESCQ

▲ Relais de la Poste

24 ave de Maremne (off N10), 40140 **Map** 10A2

[C] 05 58 47 70 25

FAX 05 58 47 76 17

AE, DC, MC, V ◯ Mon, Sep–Jun: Tue; mid-Nov–mid-Dec

▮▮ €€€€ ◯ (10) €€€€

Excellent high-end local cuisine: foie gras with grapes, white asparagus and caviar d'Aquitaine (a nutty caviar from Russian sturgeon in the Gironde estuary). Booking recommended. Enormous, sleek and modern bedrooms.

MARGAUX

▲ Le Pavillon de Margaux

3 rue Georges Mandel (on main D2 road through Margaux), 33460 **Map** 6B5

[C] 05 57 88 77 54

FAX 05 57 88 77 73

AE, DC, MC, V

▮▮ €€€ ◯ (14) €€€

Plenty of classics. truffle-infused steak, foie gras terrine and an expensive but

thorough wine list. Guestrooms are all named after different châteaux, with bottles from the vineyards in each. Excellent value in a rather pricey area.

MARTILLAC

▲ Les Sources de Caudalie

Chemin de Smith Haut Lafitte, 33650 **Map** 10B1

[C] 05 57 83 83 83

FAX 05 57 83 83 84

W www.sources-caudalie.com

AE, DC, MC, V

▮▮ €€€€ ◯ (49) €€€€€

A spa hotel that perfectly reflects the spirit of the region with its range of wine-based treatments. The restaurant specializes in gastronomic yet healthy food. Service can be brusque.

MAUBUISSON-MONTAUT

● La Bécassière

18 bd du lac, 33121 **Map** 6A5

[C] 05 57 70 18 50

FAX 05 56 03 38 41

AE, DC, MC, V ▮▮ €€

A lovely restaurant with a terrace over-looking Lac d'Hourtin Carcans. A range of fish dishes is offered, from sardines to enormous seafood platters.

MAULEON

▲ L'Europe

15 rue de l'Hôpital, 79700 **Map** 6B2

[C] 05 49 81 40 33

FAX 05 49 81 62 47

MC, V ◯ Sun D, mid-May–mid-Sep: Mon L; 25 Dec–2 Jan

▮▮ € ◯ (12) €€

Respect for the past is this chef's bedrock but he still has fun. Playful items include terrine of morels, pollack in white butter, and veal with forestière sauce (mushrooms, bacon and potatoes). Bubbly company and comfortable rooms.

MAZEROLLES

● Auberge de Lapouillique

656 chem Pouillique, 40090 **Map** 10B1

[C] 05 58 75 22 97

MC, V ◯ Sun D, Mon L ▮▮ €€

Sometimes simple places are the best and this is certainly one of them. Good value for fish and local specialities, from roasted duck to wild boar.

MELLE

▲ L'Argentière

Route from Niort, D 948, 79500 **Map** 6C3

[C] 05 49 29 13 22

FAX 05 49 29 06 63

W www.largentiere.com

MC, V ◯ Sun D, Mon L

▮▮ €€ ◯ (18) €€

Since the time of the Romans, the people of this region have enjoyed their table. That tradition continues here with the half-duckling in sweet-sour honey and the sea bass with garlic sauce. Guestrooms are of equal quality.

MELLE

▲ Les Glycines

5 pl René-Groussard, 79500 **Map** 6C3

[C] 05 49 27 01 11

FAX 05 49 27 93 45

W www.paysmellois.com/lesglycines

AE, MC, V ◯ Sun D, Mon (except Jul–Aug); 2nd wk Jan, 3rd wk Nov

▮▮ €€ ◯ (7) €€

Impressive dining room with culinary creations to match. Offerings include baked pigeon with langoustine salad, tender kid with garlic sauce, and caramelized apples. Small, tidy rooms.

MESNAC

▲ Château de Mesnac

Pl de l'Eglise, 16370 **Map** 6B4

[C] 05 45 83 26 61

FAX 05 45 83 17 70

W www.dduveron.fr/hten

MC, V ◯ Sun D; Oct

▮▮ €€ ◯ (4) €€€

An 18th-century château snuggled among lush Charente vineyards. Dishes drawn straight from the land such as the hand-raised poultry in a Pineau liqueur sauce and goose flambéed in Cognac. Excellent Bordeaux. Spacious gue-strooms with period decor.

MESSANGES

● Le Vieux Port

Plage Sud, 40660 **Map** 10A2

[C] 05 58 48 19 00

FAX 05 58 48 30 26

MC, V ▮▮ €€

One of the best seafood restaurants in a coastal resort full of them. Wide-ranging menu with lobster, sole, oysters, mussels

and a catch of the day. Attached to a very welcoming and lively bar.

MIMBASTE
■ Maison Capcazal de Pachioü
C16 from Mimbaste, 40350 **Map** 10B2
📞 05 58 55 30 54
FAX 05 58 55 30 54
W www.maisonsudouest.com
🍽 (4) €€

A true find – a beautiful collection of antique furniture in the bedrooms and main areas of the house, put together thoughtfully and with style. Delicious breakfast of breads, conserves and fruits included, and evening meal on request.

MIMIZAN
▲ Au Bon Coin du Lac
34 ave du Lac, 40200 **Map** 10A1
📞 05 58 09 01 55
FAX 05 58 09 40 84
W www.jp-caule.com
🍴 AE, DC, MC, V
⬤ Sun D, Mon; Feb
🍽 €€€ 🍽 (8) €€€

Try the sole soufflé with langoustines or amazing seafood stew. Wonderful bedrooms also, generous and light, with views over the garden and lake. Large breakfasts. Booking advisable.

MIMIZAN
▲ L'Atlantique
38 ave Cote d'argent, 40200 **Map** 10A1
📞 05 58 09 09 42
FAX 05 58 82 42 63
🍴 AE, MC, V 🍽 €€ 🍽 (38) €€

Hotel by the beach, with good-sized rooms. In the restaurant, plenty of fish. During July and August the seafood reaches its heights, though you will find tasty southwestern food there all year.

MIMIZAN
⬤ Le Tropicana
Le Hameau du Lac, 407 route Dubord, Aureilhan, 40200 **Map** 10A1
📞 05 58 09 47 84
FAX 05 58 09 47 84
🍴 AE, DC, MC, V ⬤ Sep–Jun
🍽 €€€

Only open in high summer and a good bet for grilled seafood right on the lake

at Aureilhan, among palm trees and flower gardens. Children are made to feel very welcome and cherished.

MOLIETS
▲ Résidence Hôtelière du Golf
Ave du Tuc, 40660 **Map** 10A2
📞 04 79 65 07 65
FAX 05 58 49 16 29
🍴 AE, DC, MC, V
🍽 €€€ 🍽 (35) €€€

A golf spa resort offering luxury villas, each with swimming pool and private terrace. The restaurant offers a good range of fish dishes, one of the best being sea bream with aniseed.

MONCOUTANT
▲ Le St-Pierre
Route de Niort, 79320 **Map** 6B3
📞 05 49 72 88 88
FAX 05 49 72 88 89
🍴 DC, MC, V ⬤ Sun D, Sat L
🍽 €€€ 🍽 (30) €€

A current of fresh air runs through this spot, with new management in the kitchen. Menu innovations include the liver in spiced pocket bread and the beef with pepper and layers of foie gras. Bright and comfortable guestrooms.

MONTBRON
▲ Château Ste Catherine
30 km (19 miles) east of Angoulême on the route from Marthon, 16220 **Map** 6C4
📞 05 45 23 60 03
FAX 05 45 70 72 00
🍴 AE, DC, MC, V ⬤ Sun, Mon; Feb
🍽 €€ 🍽 (14) €€€

Cassoulette of petits-gris snails Charente-style, mignon of pork, and sausages of duck flambéed with Cognac are among the options. Agreeable mid-range wines from local vineyards.

MONT-DE-MARSAN
▲ Abor Hôtel
Route de Grenade Chemin de Lubet, St-Pierre du Mont, 40280 **Map** 10B2
📞 05 58 51 58 00
FAX 05 58 75 78 78
🍴 AE, DC, MC, V
🍽 €€€ 🍽 (68) €€€

On the outskirts of town, this three-star hotel has a large pool and well-equipped

rooms. Well-prepared Landaise cuisine. Light on atmosphere but a good bet for a comfortable stay.

MONT-DE-MARSAN
⬤ Chez Despons le Plumaçon
20 rue du Plumaçon, 40000 **Map** 10B2
📞 05 58 06 17 56
🍴 MC, V ⬤ D, Sun 🍽 €

Popular lunchtime place and always lively. There is no à la carte menu, just a dish of the day, a set menu and a buffet of charcuterie – but it all changes daily.

MONT-DE-MARSAN
⬤ Le Fournil Gourmand
13 rue Dominique de Gourgues, 40000 **Map** 10B2
📞 05 58 06 00 60
🍴 MC, V ⬤ Sun 🍽 €

A good find: this is an elegant eatery with an Art Deco feel, overlooking the pedestrianized heart of town. Lovely salon de thé with an outstanding range of delicate amuse-bouches. The house specialities are mixed grills, salade Landaise (duck salad) and buckwheat pancakes with confit de canard (p326).

MONTFORT-EN-CHALOSSE
▲ Aux Tauzins
Route Hagetmau, 547 rue Raphaël Lonné , 40380 **Map** 10B2
📞 05 58 98 60 22
FAX 05 58 98 45 79
🍴 AE, MC, V ⬤ Jan, early Oct
🍽 €€ 🍽 (16) €€

Plenty of good examples of Tursan and Chalosse wines at this two-star hotel and restaurant. The gourmet menu includes warm foie gras with apples and a salad with gizzards. Excellent fixed-price menus, and comfortable rooms.

MONTMOREAU-ST-CYBARD
⬤ Plaisir d'Automne
1 rue St-Denys, 16190 **Map** 6C5
📞 05 45 60 39 40
🍴 MC, V ⬤ Sun D, Mon; 2nd wk Feb, end Sep 🍽 €€

A subtle menu that employs the best ingredients. The terrine of oxtail is note-worthy, as is the fricasséed hand-raised chicken. Finish with a remarkable apple tart drizzled with crème de cassis.

MONTMORILLON

▲ Hôtel de France

4 bd de Strasbourg, town centre, 86500
Map 7D3

📞 05 49 84 09 09

FAX 05 49 84 58 68

W www.le-lucullus.com

💳 MC, V ⬤ Sun D, Mon

🍴 €€ 🍷 (10) €€

Restaurant Le Lucullus – honouring a connoisseur Roman general – serves dishes such as goat's cheese pressed with chives and stuffed rabbit. Bright fabrics in the spacious rooms.

MOSNAC

▲ Moulin du Val de Seugne

Town centre, 17240 **Map** 6C4

📞 05 46 70 46 16

FAX 05 46 70 48 14

💳 AE, MC, V

⬤ Oct–May: Mon, Tues L

🍴 €€€ 🍷 (10) €€€€

Once the Marcouze windmill. Today serving fresh, breezy meals like duck ballotine (boned, stuffed, rolled and bundled, then braised) with half-cooked foie gras, pear confit and leeks; and saddle of lamb infused with lavender. Tidy and comfortable guestrooms.

NERSAC

● Auberge du Pont de la Meure

La Meure, 10 km (6 miles) southwest of Angoulême on N10, 16440 **Map** 6C4

📞 05 45 90 60 48

FAX 05 45 90 91 07

💳 AE, DC, MC, V

⬤ Fri D, Sat; Aug

🍴 €€

An icon of consistency over the years. Savour the sweetbread salad with garlic confit or the lamb nuggets roasted in spices. The dessert tray groans with excellent choices. Enduringly popular so reservations are wise.

NEUVILLE-DE-POITOU

● Le St-Fortunat

6 rue Bangoura-Moridé, 86170 **Map** 6C3

📞 05 49 54 56 74

💳 MC, V ⬤ Sun D, Mon, Tue L; 2nd–3rd wks Jan, 1st 2 wks Aug 🍴 €

A simple twist redefines old standards like langoustines, foie gras and pigeons.

Fine options include the andouillette made with pig's trotters, and a very restrained magret de canard. Desserts vary but are consistently delicious.

NIEUIL

▲ La Grange aux Oies

Château de Nieuil, 1.5 km (1 mile) east on D739, 16270 **Map** 6C4

📞 05 45 71 81 24

FAX 05 45 71 46 45

💳 MC, V ⬤ Sun D, Mon, Tue (All Saints and Easter); 1st wk Apr, Nov

🍴 €€€ 🍷 (13) €€€€

One of the principal attractions of the Château de Nieuil. Fine cuisine like baked skate wing in butter and the magret of beef with tender new cabbage. Plentiful and varied desserts, including exquisite seasonal fruit dishes. Stylish rooms.

NIORT

● A La Belle Etoile

115 quai Maurice-Métayer, 79000
Map 6B3

📞 05 49 73 31 29

FAX 05 49 09 05 59

💳 AE, DC, MC, V ⬤ Sun D, Mon; 1st 2 wks Aug 🍴 €€€€

Flavour, freshness and finesse are all balanced here. Stunning efforts like the eel with smoked bacon or the entrecôte steak. Vàst selection of wines.

NIORT

● La Table des Saveurs

9 rue Thiers, 79000 **Map** 6B3

📞 05 49 77 44 35

FAX 05 49 16 06 29

💳 MC, V ⬤ Sun (except bank holidays)

🍴 €€

Nine flavours of foie gras, all deft and delicious. Also try the baked beef with potatoes, anchovies and Bordeaux wine followed by chocolate truffle with cookies in coffee sauce. Heavenly creations.

OIRON

● Relais du Château

Pl des Marronniers, 79100 **Map** 6C2

📞 05 49 96 54 96

FAX 05 49 96 54 45

💳 DC, MC, V ⬤ Sun D, Mon, bank holidays; D; mid-Feb–mid-Mar

🍴 €

This quiet village is a perfect spot to pause while visiting the château of Montespan. Menu high points include the langoustine ravioli with truffle oil and the sea bass with turmeric cream. Simple, well-constructed wine list.

ONDRES

● La Rose des Sables

63 promenade de l'Océan, 40440
Map 10A2

📞 05 59 45 32 59

FAX 05 59 45 32 81

💳 AE, DC, MC, V ⬤ Jan, Dec

🍴 €€

Great views over the Atlantic. Mussels, squid, swordfish and beautifully spicy clams star on the menu.

PARENTIS-EN-BORN

▲ L'Etrier

Ave Foch, 41060 **Map** 10B1

📞 05 58 78 42 62

FAX 05 58 78 48 97

💳 AE, DC, MC, V

🍴 €€€ 🍷 (10) €€

Clean, simple guestrooms and a well-loved restaurant, which is always full of locals feasting on regional fare, especially duck. Plenty of good walking in the area.

PARTHENAY

▲ Hôtel du Nord

86 ave du Général de Gaulle, 79200
Map 6C3

📞 05 49 94 29 11

FAX 05 49 64 11 72

W www.hotelnordparthenay.fr

💳 AE, DC, MC, V ⬤ Sun D, Sat; end Dec–early Jan 🍴 €€ 🍷 (10) €€

The simple, well-kept, pleasant façade reveals much about this eatery. The kitchen unveils quail with mesclun, vermouth plus mullet with lemon risotto in curry. Great cheeses.

PARTHENAY

● Le Fin Gourmet

26 rue Ganne, 79200 **Map** 6C3

📞 05 49 64 04 53

💳 MC, V ⬤ Sun D, Mon; 1st 4 wks Aug 🍴 €

The inspired work of Chef Thierry Guilbaut is causing a buzz with smoked sturgeon with peppered asparagus and

artichokes, and veal with goat's cheese. Local vintners light up the wine list.

PAUILLAC

● Brasserie Chez Johan

16 quai Léon Perrier, 33250 **Map** 6B5

C 05 56 59 08 68

FAX 05 56 59 67 58

W www.pauillac-medoc.com

✉ AE, DC, MC, V **🍴** €€

Brasserie with a view of the lovely quay and its fishing boats. Some of the finest examples of shad, lamprey, eel and white shrimp in the area.

PAUILLAC

▲ Château Cordeillan Bages

Route des Châteaux, 33250 **Map** 6B5

C 05 56 59 24 24

FAX 05 56 59 01 89

W www.cordeillanbages.com

✉ AE, DC, MC, V **●** mid-Dec–
mid-Feb **🍴** €€€€ **🍷** (29) €€€€

Halfway up the Route des Châteaux, this four-star hotel is a good choice for a special evening. Spacious, comfortable guestrooms, if a little sparsely chic for some. Renowned restaurant offering outstanding Pauillac lamb.

PELLEGRUE

● Chez Mireille

28 rue République, 33790 **Map** 10C1

C 05 56 61 30 11

FAX 05 56 61 30 66

✉ MC, V **●** Sun, Mon–Fri D, Sat
🍴 €€

Small restaurant specializing in traditional cuisine, with a particularly large range of duck dishes and grilled meats. Saturday and Sunday evenings for groups only; booking ahead is essential.

PERIGNAC

● Gourmandière

42 ave de Cognac, 17800 **Map** 6B4

C 05 46 96 36 01

FAX 05 46 95 50 71

✉ DC, MC, V **●** Sun D, Mon, Wed D
(except Jul–Aug) **🍴** €€€

A heady mix of southern, southwestern and Charentais cooking like John Dory roasted with fricasséed shellfish, or lamb with pimento and aubergine (eggplant). An establishment to watch.

PISSOS

▲ Le Café du Commerce

42 rue Pont Battant, 40410 **Map** 10B1

C 05 58 08 90 16

FAX 05 58 08 96 89

✉ MC, V **●** mid-Nov–early Dec

🍴 €€ **🍷** (5) €€

A beautiful, restful spot in the Haute Landes, surrounded by pine forests. Lovely restaurant with a shaded terrace. Comfortable guestrooms.

POITIERS

● La Goulue

2 rue de la Croix-Blanche, 86000
Map 6C3

C 05 49 88 92 33

✉ MC, V **●** Sun L **🍴** €

Fish standards revisited to great effect. Even the humble sardine and plaice receive novel handling. Enjoy a memorable repast paired with a moderately priced, excellent white wine.

POITIERS

● Le Poitevin

76 rue Carnot, 86000 **Map** 6C3

C 05 49 88 35 04

FAX 05 49 52 88 05

✉ MC, V **●** Sun; 2 wks Apr, 3 wks
Jul, end Dec–early Jan **🍴** €€

A bonne addresse whose reputation has spread among locals and travellers alike. Nothing complicated, just Poitevin cuisine in its essential forms, like mouclade (p297), compote of rabbit or kid in garlic. Wine lists brim with hearty selections.

POITIERS

● Les Trois Piliers

37 rue Carnot, 86000 **Map** 6C3

C 05 49 55 07 03

FAX 05 49 50 16 03

✉ AE, MC, V **●** Sun, Mon L, Sat L
🍴 €€€€

Poitiers is the epicentre of culinary activity in the region – and this spot is ground zero. Sensational plates include young pigeon ballotine (boned and bundled) and langoustine salad. The soufflé with Angelica liqueur makes a fine dessert.

POITIERS

● Maxime

4 rue St-Nicolas, 86000 **Map** 6C3

C 05 49 41 09 55

FAX 05 49 41 09 55

✉ AE, DC, MC, V **●** Sun, Sat (except
Mar–Oct: D); mid Jul–mid-Aug

🍴 €€€€

Even among its peers in Poitiers, this establishment shines. Highlights include hot oyster ravioli with herb butter, lobster in Thai vinaigrette, and langoustines with scallops in basil. Superb wines, especially the whites. Outstanding value for money.

POITIERS (CROUTELLE)

● La Chênaie

La Berlanderie, 7 km (4.2 miles) southwest by N10, 86240 **Map** 6C3

C 05 49 57 11 52

FAX 05 49 52 68 66

W www.la-chenaie.com

✉ AE, MC, V **●** Sun D, Mon (except
bank holidays); last wk Jan **🍴** €€€

An old farmhouse on the outskirts, where gourmets gather to enjoy dishes like oven-baked foie gras, monkfish medallions and dessert of pineapple millefeuille with Antilles rum sauce, prepared by a local master.

POITIERS (ST-BENOIT)

▲ Chalet de Venise

6 rue du Square, 4 km (2.4 miles) south
by D88, 86280 **Map** 6C3

C 05 49 88 45 07

FAX 05 49 52 95 44

W http://hotel-chaletdevenise.com

✉ AE, DC, MC, V **●** Sun D, Mon, Tue
L; 1st wk Jan, 2nd wk Feb, last wk Aug
🍴 €€€ **🍷** (12) €€

Savour warm veal sweetbread salad with langoustines, artichokes, capers and lemon; or lamb thrice-cooked with coriander (cilantro) and citrus fruits. This establishment has an equally strong reputation for lovely guestrooms.

POMAREZ

▲ Auberge du Châlet

47 route de Dax, 40360 **Map** 10B2

C 05 58 89 89 90

FAX 05 58 89 35 55

✉ MC, V **🍴** €€ **🍷** (9) €

One of the region's leading foie gras production centres, Pomarez is small but packed with places to sample this delicacy. A friendly, clean auberge.

● Restaurant ■ Hotel ▲ Hotel / Restaurant

PONDAURAT

● Auberge du Pont Duré

28 Le Bourg, 33190 Map 10C1

C 05 56 71 08 52

FAX 05 56 61 11 48

AE, DC, MC, V **€€**

Far-ranging menu: specialities include Grignols capon, magret de canard and plenty of home-grown vegetables.

PONS

▲ Auberge Pontoise

23 ave Gambetta, 17800 Map 6B4

C 05 46 94 00 99

FAX 05 46 91 33 40

MC, V Oct–Apr: Sun D

€€ (22) €

Consistently kind service and tasty food: roasted monkfish with herbs, young pigeon brisket crusted with capers and nuts, and a delicious lukewarm crêpes suzette to follow. Guestrooms are cosy.

PONS

▲ Hôtel de Bordeaux

1 ave Gambetta, 17800 Map 6B4

C 05 46 91 31 12

FAX 05 46 91 22 25

AE, MC, V Sun D, Mon, Sat L (except 1st wk Apr–Oct)

€€€ (15) €€

A grand name among local aficionados. Try the warm feuilleté of asparagus and crab, the sea bass with green clams or the guinea fowl with foie gras. A deep cellar. Large, breezy rooms.

PORT-DE-LANNE

▲ La Vieille Auberge

66 pl de Liberté, 40300 Map 10A2

C 05 58 89 16 29

FAX 05 58 89 12 89

AE, DC, MC, V

€€ (10) €€€

An 18th-century inn with a swimming pool. The food takes its cue from Gascony and the Gers, with plenty of Armagnac-soaked plums and hearty rustic dishes using goose fat. Robust breakfasts, supremely comfortable rooms and big apartments.

PYLA-SUR-MER

● Gérard Tissier

35 bd de l'Océan, 33115 Map 10A1

C 05 56 54 07 94

FAX 05 56 43 80 98

AE, DC, MC, V Sun D, Mon D

€€€

A great restaurant, with a terrace, serving traditional local dishes and Arcachon seafood. Lobster is the house speciality.

RIMONS

● Ferme Auberge Jauvry

1 Gauvry, 33580 Map 10C1

C 05 56 71 83 96

FAX 05 56 71 64 66

MC, V Sun D, Mon, Tue; early Jan **€€**

Farm restaurant serving up traditional meals such as onion and garlic soup with goose fat, foie gras and duck confits.

RIVEDOUX-PLAGE

● Auberge de la Marée

Rue Albert Sarau, 17940 Map 6A3

C 05 46 35 39 44

FAX 05 46 09 15 81

MC, V Sun D, mid-Apr–Nov: Tue L, Tue L, Nov–Apr: Wed; last 2 wks Jan

€€

Seafood shines in modest surroundings, although the ocean view is enchanting. Simple, time-honoured plates like sea bass and scallops are top-notch. Concise wine list. Good value for money thus very popular in summer.

ROCHEFORT

▲ La Belle Poule

Route de Royan, 17300 Map 6B4

C 05 46 99 71 87

FAX 05 46 83 99 77

AE, DC, MC, V Sun D, Fri (out of season); Nov **€€** (20) €€

Overlooking the legendary port (the terrace is almost in the water). Start with fricasséed snails then proceed to the crépinette (small, slightly flattened sausage) of pig's trotters.

ROCHEFORT

▲ La Corderie Royale

Rue Audebert, 17300 Map 6B4

C 05 46 99 35 35

FAX 05 46 99 78 72

www.corderieroyale-hotel.com

AE, DC, MC, V Sun D, Nov–Mar: Mon; Feb **€€€** (45) €€€€€

This 17th-century royal artillery battery fires only salvos of taste now. Its weapons include langoustine dariole with morels, fricasséed magret de canard with baked foie gras, and a dessert of dark chocolate tart with vanilla ice cream. Sumptuous rooms.

ROCHEFORT

● L'Escale de Bougainville

Port de Plaisance, quai de Louisiane, 17300 Map 6B4

C 05 46 99 54 99

FAX 05 46 99 54 99

MC, V Sun D, Mon (except public holidays) **€€**

Fronting the historic port, fabulous cuisine from starter to the final coffee. Choose the langoustines with goat milk, the monkfish cooked in a cocotte or lentils with lamb sweetbreads.

ROQUEFORT

▲ Hôtel le Columbier

105 rue Porte Lerang, 40120 Map 10B2

C 05 58 45 50 57

FAX 05 58 45 59 63

MC, V 1 May, Christmas

€€ (15) €€

One of the few places to stay in this quiet, beautiful 11th-century town. Great breakfast with plenty of pastries and breads, and decent rooms.

ROULLET-ST-ESTEPHE

▲ La Vielle Etable

Les Plantes, 12 km (7.5 miles) south-west of Angoulême by N10 and D42, 16440 Map 6C4

C 05 45 66 31 75

FAX 05 45 66 47 45

www.hotel-vieille-etable.com

MC, V Oct–May: Sun D; 1 May

€€ (29) €€€

Atmospheric rooms and restaurant in a rolling park. Highlights include scallops of sturgeon mousseline with saffron potatoes, duck foie gras in a Pineau (local liqueur) gelatine, and monkfish stew with asparagus tips.

ROYAN

● Le Relais de la Mairie

1 rue du Chay, 17200 Map 6B4

C 05 46 39 03 15

FAX 05 46 39 03 15

AE, DC, MC, V ● Sun D, Mon; mid-Nov–1st wk Dec 🍴 €€

No illusions of grandeur here, yet a true dedication to the delicacies of strand and land. Highlights include lobster salad in pepper vinaigrette, fish fry with ginger, and a surprisingly subtle rabbit dish with potatoes and mushrooms.

SABRES

▲ Auberge des Pins

Chemin départemental 327, 40630 **Map** 10B2

📞 05 58 08 30 00

FAX 05 58 07 56 74

W www.aubergedespins.fr

MC, V ● Jan

🍴 €€ 🍽 (24) €€

Farmhouse with individually furnished rooms and a really good restaurant. The peaceful setting and oak-lined dining room are the perfect accompaniments to the traditional fare. Ample cellar of Bordeaux wines, and a large collection of Armagnacs. Guestrooms range from airy white-and-blue rooms to cosier wooden dens. All are restful.

SAINTES

● La Ciboulette

36 rue de Pérat, 17100 **Map** 6B4

📞 05 46 74 07 36

FAX 05 46 94 14 54

W www.la-ciboulette.fr

AE, MC, V ● Sun, Sat L 🍴 €€

Classic and modern elements blended with skill. Don't miss the warm oyster salad with smoked brisket in balsamic vinegar, steamed plaice basted with ginger liqueur or the chateaubriand steak with caramel. The wine list is fittingly eclectic and satisfying.

SANGUINET

● Le Pavillon

519 ave de Losa, 40460 **Map** 10B1

📞 05 58 82 11 66

MC, V 🍴 €€

In the heart of Europe's largest pine forest is this long-established family-run restaurant specializing in wonderful galettes *filled with everything from seafood to smoked meats. Scallops are a highlight. The village runs traditional*

Landes entertainment evenings during the balmy summer months.

SANGUINET

▲ Le Relais de la Côte d'Argent

116 ave de la Côte d'Argent, 404 **Map** 10B1

📞 05 58 78 63 68

FAX 05 58 78 63 68

MC, V 🍴 €€ 🍽 (8) €€

A lovely hotel in a small village, where you can expect a warm welcome. Rooms and facilities are fairly basic but the kind owners are excellent guides to the area and serve plenty of healthy food.

SAUBUSSE

▲ Complexe Thermal

Les Bains Saubusse, 40180 **Map** 10A2

📞 05 58 57 40 00

FAX 05 58 57 37 37

AE, DC, MC, V ● Dec–Feb

🍴 €€ 🍽 (41) €€

Excellent for families and covering all budgets with a hotel, flats, caravans and pitches for tents. The restaurant, as befits a spa hotel, concentrates on healthy, low-fat cooking with plenty of fresh fruit and seafood salads.

SAUBUSSE

● Villa Stings

Rue Vieille, 40180 **Map** 10A2

📞 05 58 57 70 18

FAX 05 58 57 71 86

MC, V

● Sun D, Mon, Sat L 🍴 €€€

Gourmet seasonal food served in classic surroundings next to the River Adour. The Michelin-starred selection includes lobster, tête-de-veau and mountain lamb.

SAUTERNES

● Le Saprien

14 rue Principale, 33210 **Map** 10B1

📞 05 56 76 60 87

FAX 05 56 76 68 92

AE, DC, MC, V ● Mon D, Wed D

🍴 €€€

White truffles, liberally used when in season, are the perfect accompaniment to a glass of Sauternes and some pan-fried foie gras. Try the delicious regional rosé and claret wines. Booking are strongly advised at this popular spot.

SAUTERNES

● Les Vignes

23 rue Principale, 33210 **Map** 10C1

📞 05 56 76 60 06

FAX 05 56 76 69 97

MC, V ● Mon D; Sep–Jun: Wed D, Feb 🍴 €€

A country inn serving entrecôte cooked over vine branches, omelettes with mushrooms and truffles in season, and other local delicacies. Good range of desserts and local wine.

SAUVETERRE-DE-GUYENNE

▲ Le Guyenne

1 Pringis, 33540 **Map** 10C1

📞 05 56 71 54 92

FAX 05 56 71 62 91

AE, DC, MC, V

● Sun; end Dec–early Jan

🍴 €€ 🍽 (15) €€

One of the best value hotels in the region. The restaurant specializes in local cuisine such as duck rillettes and terrines. Basic rooms in a good location for nearby restaurants.

SEGONZAC

● Restaurant la Cagouillarde

18 rue Gaston Briande, 16130 **Map** 6C4

📞 05 45 83 40 51

FAX 05 45 83 12 99

MC, V ● Sun D, Mon 🍴 €€

Tranquil Mediterranean house in the heart of the Charente countryside. Try the stuffed snails, the terrine of goose liver or the grilled lamb with white string beans. Cognac snifters are first rate here.

SEIGNOSSE

▲ Chez Toton

Route Etang Blanc, 40510 **Map** 10A2

📞 05 58 72 80 15

FAX 05 58 72 80 15

W www.cheztoton.com

AE, DC, MC, V

🍴 €€ 🍽 (9) €€

Good views from the terrace. Interesting and unusual dishes include eel, roasted pigeon and perch in sorrel. Rooms are fine, if a little sparsely furnished.

SOULAC-SUR-MER

● La Pizza

6 rue Brémontier, 33780 **Map** 6B4

● Restaurant ■ Hotel ▲ Hotel / Restaurant

05 56 09 81 19
FAX 05 56 09 81 19
w www.chez.com/lapizza
AE, DC, MC, V ● Wed L €

This restaurant, at the mouth of the Gironde river, has been serving pizzas for almost 50 years. Great ice creams and a refreshing selection of Italian wines.

SOUSTONS
▲ Hôtel du Lac
63 ave de Galleben, 40140 Map 10A2
05 58 41 18 80
FAX 05 58 41 29 84
AE, DC, MC, V ● first wk Oct, end Dec–end Jan €€ (9) €€

Well loved in the area for its seafood and Landaise gastronomy. Specialities range from a variety of duck dishes to foie gras in fig sauce. Some of the bedrooms have balconies with lovely views. Quite friendly owners.

SOUSTONS
▲ Hôtel Restaurant Les Gourmandines
18 ave Galleben, 40140 Map 10A2
05 58 41 22 52
FAX 05 58 41 34 69
w www.lesgourmandines.com
AE, MC, V €€ (13) €€

The finest examples of country cooking: salmon or wonderful wild mushrooms and walnut dishes are on the menu. Guestrooms are simply furnished with a clean, modern finish.

SOYAUX
● La Cigogne
Impasse de la Cabane Bambou, 16800 Map 6C4
05 45 95 89 23
FAX 05 45 93 23 57
MC, V ● Sun, Wed D, Sat D; 1st 2 wks Aug, last 2 wks Dec €€€

Though surrounded by sylvan countryside, the menu resonates with sea and shoreline. Gourmets seek out the bass in vanilla-perfumed olive oil, the beef with morels or the remarkable rack of lamb. Chef Erick Bouix is a rising star.

ST-ANDRE-DE-CUBZAC
● Au Sarmant
50 rue Lande, 33240 Map 6B5

05 57 43 44 73
FAX 05 57 43 90 28
MC, V ● Sun D, Mon; 2 wks Aug, 2 wks Feb €€

Located in an old school house. Fish from the Dordogne river alongside plenty of seafood. A good place for lamprey.

ST-AUBIN-DE-BLAYE
■ Le Grand Moulin
La Champagne, 33820 Map 6B5
05 57 32 62 06
FAX 05 57 32 73 73
w www.grandmoulin.com
AE, DC, MC, V (3) €€

A rare chance to stay at a working château which exports its fine wine the world over. Warm and welcoming rooms, a wonderful mill on the river and, of course, the vines that surround the property make this a great experience. Plenty of fruit, croissants, brioches, conserves and local honey at breakfast.

ST-CLEMENT-DES-BALEINES
● Le Chat Botté
20 rue de la Mairie, 17590 Map 6A3
05 46 29 42 09
FAX 05 46 29 29 77
AE, DC, MC, V ● Mon (except Jul–Aug); Dec–Jan €€€€

A bonne addresse for aficionados. Chef Daniel Massé goes boldly where many chefs have gone before yet still impresses with oysters in Pineau liqueur sauce, and flaky sea bass in a pastry shell.

ST-EMILION
● Chez Germaine
13 pl du Clocher, 33330 Map 6C5
05 57 74 49 34
FAX 05 57 74 47 25
AE, DC, MC, V €€

A local institution, at the top of the steps leading down to the main square. The town's lightest macaroons, a speciality of St-Emilion, are on offer, as are rich meat dishes steeped in red wine sauces.

ST-EMILION
▲ Hostellerie Plaisance
5 pl du Clocher, 33330 Map 6C5
05 57 55 07 55
FAX 05 57 74 41 11
w www.hostellerie-plaisance.com

AE, DC, MC, V
€€€€ (14) €€€€€

One of the best hotels in this region. The restaurant, serving top-notch but expensive food, overlooks St-Emilion and the valley beyond. Sumptuous bedrooms with the biggest bathrooms in town.

ST-EMILION
● L'Huîtrier Pie
11 rue Porte Bouqueyre, 33330 Map 6C5
05 57 24 69 71
FAX 05 57 24 69 71
AE, DC, MC, V ● Nov–Mar: Wed €€€

This is a brasserie with a wide-ranging gourmet menu, a good bet for Quiberon and Marennes oysters throughout the year and Belon oysters in October. Amazing cheeseboard also; try their cabécou (goats' cheese with a sharp flavour). There are games to keep the little ones occupied and a good-value, pleasant children's menu.

STE-RADEGONDE
▲ Château de Sanse
1 Sanse, 33350 Map 10C4
05 57 56 41 10
FAX 05 57 56 41 29
w www.chateaudesanse.com
AE, DC, MC, V ● Feb
€€€ (16) €€€€

Chef Guillaume Depaire uses herbs and vegetables from the château's own garden, meaning generous portions of super-fragrant dishes. Eat by the fireplace in winter or out on the terrace on warm evenings. The majority of rooms have a balcony or terrace.

ST-GROUX
▲ Les Trois Saules
Le Bourg, 16230 Map 6C4
05 45 20 31 40
FAX 05 45 22 73 81
@ les3saules.faure@voilà.fr
MC, V ● Sun D, Mon L (out of season); 1st 2 wks Aug, last wk Oct–1st wk Nov, last 2 wks Dec
€€ (10) €€

An attractive riverside building. Sample the brochette of pike in white butter, the lamb with fresh garden herbs or the beef stew with Pineau liqueur sauce.

Tidy, if somewhat basic, reasonably priced guestrooms make a perfect overnight option for travellers.

ST-JEAN-DE-THOUARS
▲ Hôtellerie St-Jean

RN25 from Parthenay, 79100 **Map** 6C2

[C] 05 49 96 12 60

FAX 05 49 96 34 02

[W] www.hotellerie-st-jean.fr

[card] AE, MC, V ● Sun D, Wed (out of season); 1st 2 wks Feb

[dish] €€ [fork] (18) €€

The rhythm of village life hasn't changed much in modern times. Timeless rural menu including langoustine ravioli with tarragon, and John Dory with artichokes. Mid-range wines and fine rooms.

ST-JULIEN-BEYCHEVELLE
● Le St Julien

11 rue St Julien, 33250 **Map** 10B5

[C] 05 56 59 63 87

FAX 05 56 59 63 89

[card] AE, DC, MC, V [dish] €€€

A wine route village where you can be assured of a fine glass of cru bourgeois. This reputable seafood restaurant serves a wide range of locally landed fish. Trout meunière is always good here.

ST-JUSTIN
▲ Hôtel de France

Pl des Tilleuls, 40240 **Map** 10B2

[C] 05 58 44 83 61

FAX 05 58 44 83 89

[card] AE, DC, MC, V ● Sun D, Mon, Thu D

[dish] €€€ [fork] (8) €€

Simple bistro in an arcaded square shaded with linden trees. The fixed price menus are varied, with one focused purely on fish and another fine gourmet menu. Well-furnished guestrooms.

ST-JUSTIN
▲ Le St Georges

St-Justin, 40240 **Map** 10B2

[C] 05 58 44 69 84

[card] AE, DC, MC, V ● Sun

[dish] € [fork] (2) €

The daily menu covers all kinds of local delicacies: morels and truffles in autumn or freshwater fish in summer. Great relaxed atmosphere. The rooms are good but the tent pitches are a bargain.

ST-LAURENT-DE-BELZAGOT
▲ Champ Rose

Champ Rose, 16190 **Map** 6C5

[C] 05 45 60 20 75

FAX 05 45 24 02 75

[card] MC, V ● Mon (high season), Tue–Fri (low season)

[dish] €€ [fork] (12) €€

Dishes from a country kitchen hold true to their roots, though inside a Second Empire mansion. Witness the ham braised in Madeira, the fine magret de canard with capers or the salmon in sorrel sauce. Simple, comfortable guestrooms allow a refreshing pause.

ST-MACAIRE
▲ Le Pampaillet

5 rue de l'Eglise, 33490 **Map** 10C1

[C] 05 56 62 33 75

FAX 05 56 62 33 75

[W] www.feuilles-dacanthe.com

[card] MC, V ● 3rd wk Dec–3rd wk Jan

[dish] €€ [fork] (15) €€€

A 16th-century merchant's house. The restaurant is relaxed with a good selection of dishes from Spanish tapas and mixed grills to salads and crêpes. Bedrooms come with exposed stone walls and excellent views over the town below.

ST-MARTIN-DE-RE
● La Baleine Bleue

Quai Launay-Razilly, 17410 **Map** 6A3

[C] 05 46 09 03 30

FAX 05 46 09 30 86

[W] www.baleinebleue.com

[card] AE, DC, MC, V ● Mon, Oct–Mar: Tue; mid-Nov–mid-Dec [dish] €€€

This long-time favourite gazes on the picturesque port of St-Martin. Beloved for its langoustines in vanilla oil and a fabulous wine list. Cheese and dessert selections are creative and delectable.

ST-PALAIS-SUR-MER
▲ Auberge des Falaises

133 ave de la Grande-Côte, 17420
Map 6B4

[C] 05 46 23 20 49

FAX 05 46 23 29 95

[card] AE, MC, V ● mid-Nov–mid-Dec

[dish] €€ [fork] (12) €€€€

A little gem beside the sea. Superlative value for money in both dining room and

guest lodgings. At table the focus is on seafood including buccins (a local shellfish) tartare, or crispy langoustine tails with Szechuan pepper.

ST-PAUL-LES-DAX
▲ Hôtel Grill Campanile

1255 ave Résistance, 40990 **Map** 10A2

[C] 05 58 91 35 34

FAX 05 58 91 37 00

[card] MC, V [dish] €€ [fork] (47) €€

Perfect after a day at the many spas of St-Paul-les-Dax. Light, airy and romantic restaurant with a well-rounded menu and wine list. A great buffet of entrées, cheeses and desserts. Top-notch rooms.

ST-PAUL-LES-DAX
▲ Le Calicéo

Lac de Christus, 40990 **Map** 10A2

[C] 05 58 90 66 00

FAX 05 58 90 68 68

[W] www.caliceo.com

[card] AE, DC, MC, V

[dish] €€€ [fork] (196) €€€

A beautiful lake and plenty of water sports make this a fine base for a Landes holiday. This three-star hotel has a great spa and offers health breaks as well as day membership. The restaurant has a light menu and a traditional one, both of which change daily. All rooms have balconies; some have park views.

ST-PAUL-LES-DAX
● Le Moulin de Poustagnac

Poustagnac, 40990 **Map** 10A2

[C] 05 58 91 31 03

FAX 05 58 91 37 97

[card] MC, V ● Sun D, Mon [dish] €€

A fun and lively place with live folk and jazz bands. The chef uses Indian spices like turmeric and cumin imaginatively, and makes a great baba au rhum (p119).

ST-PIERRE-D'OLERON
● Auberge de la Campagne

Domaine du Fief-Norteau, RN 734, 17310 **Map** 6A4

[C] 05 46 47 25 42

FAX 05 46 75 16 04

[card] AE, MC, V ● Sun D, Mon (out of season); Jan–3rd wk Mar [dish] €€

This practical chef draws ingredients from next door, plucking vegetables from the neighbouring gardens and fish from the nearby port. Try the thinly sliced sea bass with caviar and aubergine (eggplant) on toast. Stellar wine list.

ST-PIERRE-D'OLERON
● Le Moulin du Coivre

10 ave Bel-Air, RD 734, 17310 **Map** 6A4

📞 05 46 47 44 23

FAX 05 46 47 33 57

MC, V ● Mon L (mid-Jul–Aug), Sun D, Mon; Tue D (rest of year)

€€

A former miller's house. The menu taps into the region's heartbeat with savoury standouts like tarragon langoustines, cabbage stuffed with shellfish and the lamb sweetbread casserole perfumed with thyme. Surprising wine list with many small, yet tasty, vintages.

ST-SEVER
● La Table des Jacobins

11 pl Verdun, 40500 **Map** 10B2

📞 05 58 76 36 93

FAX 05 58 76 06 28

MC, V ● Wed L €€

In one of the most beautiful villages in France, this is a popular small restaurant which can get crowded on sunny days. The cheerful owners serve carefully prepared regional dishes such as tourtiere (crispy pastry covering apples, sugar and plenty of Armagnac).

ST-SEVER
▲ Le Relais du Pavillon

Ave Gén de Gaulle, 40500 **Map** 10B2

📞 05 58 76 20 22

FAX 05 58 76 25 81

MC, V ● Jan

€€ (10) €€€€

In a town renowned for its gastronomy, this is a two-star hotel, well placed for the many restaurants but also with a great one of its own. Wide-ranging cheese course from Roquefort to Brebis. Charming bedrooms upstairs with small balconies and views over the park or the pleasant swimming pool.

ST-TROJAN-DES-BAINS
▲ Le Homard Bleu

10 bd Félix-Faure, 17370 **Map** 6A4

📞 05 46 76 00 22

FAX 05 46 76 14 95

AE, DC, MC, V ● Tue, mid-Jan–mid-Apr; Wed; Jan–mid Feb, Nov–25 Dec €€€ (20) €€€

The land and sea are inseparable in this small village, and the menu reflects that sweet harmony. Sample the mullet with a cream of fine herbs, and lobster, scallops and langoustines in a crème of chervil. Pleasant rooms.

TARTAS
▲ Le Marensin

146 rue du Docteur Calmette, 40400 **Map** 10B2

📞 05 58 73 40 83

FAX 05 58 73 40 83

● Sun D, Fri D

€€ (11) €€

Landes chicken stew with cream is the highlight here. The free-range chicken is deservedly popular as maize-fed poultry produces succulent, tasty meat. Guestrooms are very simple.

TRIZAY
▲ Les Jardins du Lac

Lac du Bois-Fleuri, 17250 **Map** 6B4

📞 05 46 82 03 56

FAX 05 46 82 03 55

w www.jardins-du-lac.com

MC, V ● Sun, Nov–Mar: Mon; 2 wks in Feb

€€€ (8) €€€

Lovely spot between a lake and forest. The wood-oven highlights include beef infused with pine nut oil, and Cotinière skate with ravigote (oil and vinegar dressing with shallots).

VIBRAC
▲ Les Ombrages

Route Claude-Bonnier, 16120 **Map** 6C4

📞 05 45 97 32 33

FAX 05 45 97 32 05

MC, V

● Sun D; Mon (off season); Christmas holidays

€€ (9) €€

A peaceful, riverside spot at the edge of the village. The rooms and menu both reflect a quiet pride in the region. Local sauces and liqueurs garnish meat, poultry, fish and seafood. A consistent and pleasurable experience.

VIELLE-ST-GIRONS
● Le Hillon

Route des Lacs, 40560 **Map** 10A2

📞 05 58 42 98 87

FAX 05 56 42 98 87

MC, V €€

Locally grown asparagus is a favoured seasonal ingredient at this popular place. A large terrace and games for children also make it a comfortable location to settle in for a few hours.

VIVONNE
● La Treille

10 ave de Bordeaux, 86370 **Map** 6C3

📞 05 49 43 41 13

FAX 05 49 89 00 72

MC, V ● Tue D, Wed D, Feb school holidays €€

Originality is the capstone of the menu, though crafted with basic ingredients. Seek out the crêpes with smoked salmon, and veal liver with rum-soaked grapes and lime. Try the excellent, sweet mandarin fondant for dessert.

VOUILLE
▲ Le Château de Périgny

La Chapelle, 86190 **Map** 6C3

📞 05 49 51 80 43

FAX 05 49 51 90 09

w www.chateau-perigny.com

AE, DC, MC, V

€€ (44) €€€€

Guests enthuse about the baked langoustines with tomato confit and broad beans, and milk-fed Poitou-Charente veal (complete with head and hooves), emerging from the kitchen. The spacious, beautifully appointed guestrooms also have a devoted following.

VOUZAN
▲ L'Orée des Bois

Town centre, 16410 **Map** 6C4

📞 05 45 24 94 38

FAX 05 45 24 97 51

AE, MC, V ● Sun D, Mon, Tue L; 1st 2 wks Mar, mid 2 wks Nov, 2nd wk Dec €€€ (7) €€

Catch it while it's hot: this establishment is hugely popular – and becoming more so. Enjoy the sea bass with tomatoes or the local lamb with lemon confit and fresh chèvre. Well-appointed rooms.

PERIGORD, QUERCY & GASCONY

Limestone plateaux, sun-baked valleys and oak forests, crossed by the Garonne, Dordogne and Lot rivers and dotted with historic towns – this is the setting for a cornucopia of summer fruits, autumn nuts and the great winter triumvirate of ceps, truffles and foie gras.

The Flavours of Perigord, Gascony & Quercy

Above all, the Périgord, Quercy and Gascony are associated with ducks and geese. The woodlands are a rich hunting ground for game and winter truffles alike, while summer brings abundant fruit. Garlic, saffron and walnut oil all add flavour and colour.

BEST MARKETS

Bergerac Local produce market at Place Nôtre-Dame, Wed & Sat

Cahors Market stalls set up outside the cathedral, Wed & Sat.

Martel Walnuts, foie gras and goats' cheeses on sale in an open-sided stone market hall, Wed & Sat.

Périgueux Poultry, cheese, fruit and veg direct from the farm at Place du Coderc, daily; plus a large general market, Sat

Sarlat The market fills the streets around the Renaissance town centre, Sat

Toulouse Colourful city market in Toulouse's grandiose main square, Mon–Sat am (biggest, Wed all day)

Villefranche-du-Périgord Farmers' market in the ancient covered market of this *bastide* town, Sat am

MEAT, GAME AND CHARCUTERIE

Ducks and geese, fattened to produce foie gras and a range of *confits (see pp324–5)* are of greatest significance, but you'll also find flavourful rosy *agneau de Quercy* lamb raised on the grasslands of the Causses de Quercy, and milk-fed veal *(veau sous la mère)*. Beef production is more important in the Gers. The woodlands of the Dordogne and Lot are rich in game, yielding *sanglier* (wild boar), *chevreuil* (roe deer), *lièvre* (hare), *perdrix* (partridge) and *faisan* (pheasant).

Charcuterie includes *saucisse de Toulouse*, a long fresh, meaty pork sausage, characteristically made in a single, long spiral; pork also features in the *boudin blanc* and *boudin noir* of the Quercy and is used in combination with duck or goose liver in foie gras.

ROCAMADOUR CHEESE

Long known as Cabécou, this small, creamy white goats' cheese was renamed Rocamadour, after the spectacularly sited pilgrimage town, when it gained its AOC in 1996. The goats are traditionally grazed on the rolling grassland of the Causses de Gramat, essential to

WALNUTS AND WALNUT OIL

Walnut trees are abundant in the Dordogne and Lot, where plantations hug the river valleys. For a few weeks following the harvest in mid-September, you may find moist, crunchy *noix fraîche* or *primeur* on sale, picked while the shell still has its green outer case. Walnuts are served raw with cheese, as well as going into numerous local recipes, from sauces to bread, cakes, tarts, liqueurs and aperitifs. Although there are only a handful of traditional oil mills still in operation, walnut oil is enjoying a revival, thanks to both its distinctive flavour and health benefits. Roughly two kilos of walnut kernels are required to make one litre of oil. In a highly ecological process, the pulp of crushed kernels is heated over a fire fuelled by the shells, while the thick circular blocks of pressed mass, known as *tourteaux*, are used as fodder for ducks and geese. Walnut oil is never used for cooking but is delicious simply dribbled over lettuce, perhaps with the scattering of a few walnut pieces.

Left Rocamadour cheese **Right** Crystallized violets from Toulouse

the particular flavour of the cheese. Rocadamour is best eaten when the exterior is still creamy white, the interior soft and slightly runny.

FRUIT

The fruit that best characterizes the region is the plum or, rather, two plums: the round, green *reine-claude* (greengage) and the larger, purple plums that become *pruneaux d'Agen*, succulent black prunes used in tarts and patisseries or enveloped in chocolate.

Another speciality is the golden yellow Chasselas de Moissac grape available in September and October. Other fruits include *fraises du Périgord* strawberries, which have been awarded a *label rouge (see p11)*, nectarines, apples, pears and cherries, as well as orange-fleshed cantaloup melons from the Montauban area, and a more recent arrival, the kiwi fruit. An ancient speciality of Toulouse is crystallized violets. Walnuts and hazelnuts also feature.

GARLIC

Gascony is a major producer of garlic, in particular the pink streaked garlic from Lautrec, which is sold in thick plaits. Recipes often feature garlic cloves pressed whole into cuts of meat or baked in entire heads.

TRUFFLES

The oak forests that cover much of the Périgord conceal one of the region's most prized treasures, the black truffle or *truffe du Périgord*, also dubbed the "black diamond", which goes to flavour many luxury dishes. Truffles grow on the roots of oak trees and are located with the help of trained pigs or dogs. During the season from November to March, truffles sell for astronomical prices at markets in villages such as Lalbenque and Limogne-en-Quercy.

SAFFRON

The saffron crocus has been cultivated in the Quercy since the Middle Ages, when it was France's most common spice, used not only in cooking, but also as a dye and for medicinal purposes. Cultivation virtually died out after World War I but has recently been revived, and now fields of purple crocus blooms are a common sight. The flowers are collected daily during October and November. The red pistils are removed by hand and dried carefully – it takes about 150 flowers to produce a single gram of dry saffron.

Basket of freshly-picked crocus blossoms for saffron

Ducks and Geese

Ducks and geese epitomize the cuisine of southwestern France, fattened for foie gras or used in a whole range of confits. *This area, along with the rest of Aquitaine, is now the main production area in France. Foie gras can be made from either duck or goose. Which is better is a matter of taste, although duck foie gras is richer and more powerfully flavoured.*

Fattened Toulouse geese

MARCHÉS AU GRAS

The fattened poultry and foie gras are generally sold at markets held between mid-November and mid-March. Look in particular for those at Périgueux, Montauban and Cahors.

The fattening process of *gavage*-style feeding

Foie gras stems from the natural tendency of geese or ducks to fatten in preparation for migration. Foie gras was consumed as long ago as ancient Egypt; the Greeks mixed it with a sort of flour gruel and the Romans fattened their geese on figs. It has been produced in Périgord and Quercy for several centuries.

Eighty per cent of foie gras produced is now duck, in part because it is less labour-intensive and therefore less expensive than producing it from geese, as ducks require less and shorter fattening time, but above all because of the demand for the duck meat, especially rich, meaty *magret*, which is produced at the same time.

The ducks or geese are first raised free-range on grass, corn, wheat and the *tourteau* of walnut oil pressings *(see p322)*. Then comes the period of *gavage* – hand-feeding with whole grains of maize forced down a funnel into the bird's stomach. This fattening process increases the size of the liver ten-fold. Although the funnels are now often electrically powered, rather than hand-turned, *gavage* remains a manual process and most duck or goose farming in the southwest is in small-scale units. Ducks are fed twice a day over a period of about two weeks, whereas geese have to be fed four times a day for a month.

Foie gras can be produced all year, but the main period is in autumn and winter, as a traditional Christmas and New Year food. As well as the liver, pretty much every part of the bird is used: legs and wings are preserved in fat as *confits* and the deep, red breast meat is sold as *magret* or fillet, either fresh, to be fried or grilled, or smoked or dried for use in salads. Gizzards are often also preserved as *confit*, while goose neck may be stuffed and its meat made into *rillettes*.

BUYING AND SERVING FOIE GRAS

When buying foie gras, look for a liver that is a pale creamy beige colour, flushed with pink, but avoid those with stains or obvious veins on the surface, and remember what the different labels mean. Raw foie gras is now available in vacuum packs. When buying *foie gras entier en terrine*, distinct lobes of liver should be visible, giving the foie gras a perceptible texture. Terrines are often flavoured with Armagnac *(see p329)*. All *blocs*, terrines and pâtés may be truffled.

As well as being cooked and served cold as a terrine or pâté, when it is often accompanied by toast and a salad and perhaps an onion chutney, there are numerous ways of cooking fresh foie gras – perhaps simply lightly fried, so that the liver goes slightly liquid, and served hot, cooked with peaches or other fruit, or accompanying beef tournedos.

PÂTÉ DE PÉRIGUEUX

The original pâté was a pastry case filled with all sorts of meat, poultry, fish or game, notably in Périgueux where *pâtissiers* (forerunners of *charcutiers*) would prepare a combination of truffled goose foie gras surrounded by charcuterie. Later the word pâté came to refer largely to the filling, and a pâté within a pastry case to be called a *pâté en croûte*. Recently various *charcutiers* and restaurants in Périgueux have revived the tradition to produce a truffled foie gras encased in a moulded flaky pastry case.

Whole fattened duck livers

FOIE GRAS LABELS

Bloc de foie gras
Reconstituted foie gras, with a smooth mushy texture
Canard Duck
Cru Raw
En conserve In a sterilized jar or tin, will keep several months
Foie gras entier en terrine
Whole liver seasoned and baked in a terrine
Frais Fresh and very lightly cooked, keeps only a few days
Mi-cuit Cooked, will keep several months in a refrigerator
Oie Goose
Pâté de foie gras Mixture of duck or goose liver with up to 50 per cent pork
Semi-conserve Partially conserved, will keep several months in a refrigerator
Sous vide In a sterilized jar or tin, will keep several months

Left Saucisses de canard **Centre** Foie gras de canard **Right** Escalope de foie gras

Regional Dishes

The Périgord's lavish bounty of foie gras, truffles and ceps features large on local menus, but the regional tradition spans both luxurious dishes such as lièvre à la royale, *and sturdy peasant fare, such as the* mique, confits *and bean stews.*

ON THE MENU

Cassoulet toulousain Stew of white beans, confit and sausages

Civet de lièvre Jugged hare

Confit de canard Preserved duck

Cou farci Goose neck stuffed with gizzards and foie gras

Enchaud de porc Pork roast in lard and left for several weeks, then served cold

Estouffade de poulet Stuffed chicken and vegetables cooked under a pastry lid

Magret aux cèpes Duck or goose fillet with cep mushrooms

Mique A thick dumpling served with soup or stews

Omelette aux truffes Omelette with truffles

Pistache de mouton Mutton with garlic and beans

Pommes sarladaises Potatoes sautéed in goose fat

Salade quercynoise Salad with foie gras, *magret* and gizzards of duck or goose

Tourtière gasconne

THE REGIONAL MENU

A meal might start with a soup, such as *tourin* or *soupe à l'Albigeoise*, a type of vegetable soup, but starter options will almost inevitably include duck or goose foie gras, perhaps served with an onion chutney or a jelly of sweet Monbazillac wine.

Salade quercynoise and *salade périgordienne* are variants on salad with foie gras, smoked *magret*, gizzard *confit* and perhaps stuffed goose neck, and can make a satisfying complete meal in a café or less formal bistro. Omelettes get particularly luxurious treatment here, prepared with ceps or shavings of truffle.

Main courses might include duck or goose *confit* cooked until nicely crisp, *magret* or Quercy lamb, roasted with garlic or baked in a herb crust, as well as game in winter. Steak or other meat may be served with a *sauce Périgueux* (onions, shallots, Monbazillac wine and truffle shavings) or *à l'Agennaise* (with prunes and Armagnac).

Almost everything may come accompanied by deeply indulgent *pommes sarladaises* – potatoes sliced and cooked slowly in goose fat, then sprinkled with chopped parsley before serving.

Further south, the bean, *confit* and sausage stew *cassoulet* is the signature dish of Toulouse, although *saucisse de Toulouse* is also served simply fried.

Rocamadour cheese is often served with a small green salad and drizzled with walnut oil. Desserts

Omelette aux truffes

typically make use of the abundant strawberries, plums and other fruit grown in the area and include the layered pastry *tourtière gasconne*.

TOURIN (OR TOURAIN)

Variations on this garlic and onion soup, a quickly made family stalwart, still hold their place on the menus of simpler restaurants. Finely chopped onions are cooked in goose fat until golden, then garlic, a few spoons of tomato purée and water or chicken stock are added. Just before serving, beaten egg yolks are stirred into the soup and it is poured over bread.

LIÈVRE À LA ROYALE

This grandiose hare preparation is one of the most sumptuous of all French game dishes. The hare is skinned, beheaded and its blood set aside, before deboning and marinating in the red wine of Cahors and Cognac, with onions, carrots and herbs. Next day, the meat is stuffed with foie gras and truffles and tied with string, then cooked slowly for as much as four hours in its marinade and more wine, until the meat is so tender it falls apart. At the end, the hare's blood is added to the strained sauce.

TOURTIÈRE GASCONNE (OR PASTIS GASCON)

This test of pastry-making skill is found under various names in Gascony. A very supple pastry is made using eggs, flour and oil, kneaded to acquire an elasticity and stretched out using the fingertips into a large, paper-thin sheet that covers an entire tabletop. The pastry is brushed with melted butter and sugar and folded to create several layers. The tart is filled with *pruneaux d'Agen* or sliced apples, doused with Armagnac and vanilla, and the layers of pastry folded in crinkly frills over the top.

Le 7 Place St-Sernin, Toulouse

REGIONAL DINING

The following restaurants are among those serving regional dishes at reasonable prices:
7 Place St-Sernin
Toulouse *(see p345)*
Auberge de la Salvetat
Cadouin *(see p332)*
Così Fan Tutte
Toulouse *(see p345)*
Jardin des Quatre Saisons
Albi *(see p330)*
La Bastide
Monpazier *(see p339)*
Le Grand Bois
Castillonnès *(see p333)*
Le Lion d'Or
Gramat *(see p336)*
Le Midi
Damazan *(see p334)*
Le Mylord
Bergerac *(see p331)*
Les Trois As
Le Bugue *(see p337)*

Left Lièvre à la royale **Right** Tourin

Regional Wines & Spirits

Wine and food from the same region often make for perfect harmony and this is particularly true of southwest France. Rich foie gras, succulent duck breast and earthy ceps have no trouble finding a soulmate in a feisty Cahors, a Madiran, an opulent Monbazillac or a Pacherenc du Vic-Bilh.

GRAPE VARIETIES

The Bordeaux grapes *(see p298)* are widely grown in Bergerac and the surrounding areas. Elsewhere, local varieties take over.

Côt Known as Malbec in Bordeaux, this red grape is rich in tannin and deep in colour.

Fer Servadou Thick-skinned Fer produces wines with deep berry flavours.

Gros and Petit Manseng Of the white varieties of Pacherenc du Vic-Bilh, Petit Manseng is the finest for making sweet wines.

Mauzac Planted widely in Gaillac, Mauzac makes wines with rustic, appley flavours.

Ondenc Clear, pleasantly flavoured yellow wine come from this low-yelding grape.

Ruffiac Flavours of pear and flint mark this white grape.

Tannat Traditionally this makes tough, tannic wines that need years to evolve into spicy, berry-flavoured specimens.

Madiran vineyards

WINES OF THE SOUTHWEST

Bergerac is often considered a poor cousin to Bordeaux. However, it does offer some decent value wines from the same varieties – Merlot, Cabernet Sauvignon and Sémillon and Sauvignon Blanc. Within its borders lies Monbazillac, which can rival some of the more illustrious sweet white wines, including Sauternes. East of the town of Bergerac, Pécharmant produces only reds. The Côtes de Duras follow the Bergerac pattern. Nearby Buzet is a surprisingly buzzing appellation on the fringes of Armagnac country, producing lively reds and some whites.

The Côt, or Malbec, grape is essential to Cahors, way up the Lot river from Bordeaux. Changing tastes and fashions have meant that the style of Cahors wines has evolved radically over the last few decades from tannic, treacly "black wines" to a lighter "wine-to-go" style ready to drink almost immediately. Gaillac, towards the historic city of Albi, is reviving its fortunes with a mix of traditional and Bordeaux grape varieties. The white wines can be dry, sweet or lightly sparkling. Most apple-fresh Gaillac Mousseux is now made using the traditional Champagne method.

Grown on spectacular terraces facing directly south towards the Pyrenees, the Tannat grape is the fierce power behind the deep purple wines of Madiran. Tannat is also the main grape of the Côtes de St-Mont. Whites from the Madiran region are sold as Pacherenc du Vic-Bilh. These dry or sweet wines display lots of fresh and rich fruit salad flavour with a touch of vanilla.

Pacherenc du Vic-Bilh

VINEYARDS OF SOUTHWEST FRANCE

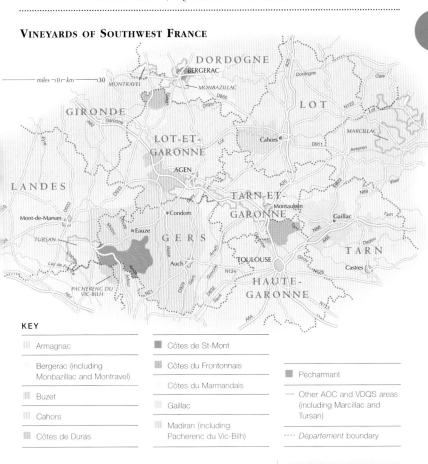

KEY

- ▦ Armagnac
- Bergerac (including Monbazillac and Montravel)
- ▦ Buzet
- ▦ Cahors
- ▦ Côtes de Duras
- ■ Côtes de St-Mont
- ■ Côtes du Frontonnais
- Côtes du Marmandais
- Gaillac
- ▦ Madiran (including Pacherenc du Vic-Bilh)
- ▦ Pécharmant
- — Other AOC and VDQS areas (including Marciliac and Tursan)
- ···· *Département* boundary

ARMAGNAC

Armagnac is France's oldest eau-de-vie. Wine from the region is distilled in the traditional continuous Armagnac still. Ageing in Gascon oak barrels completes the process and confers a roasted, coffee-like taste. The famous tawny soils of the Bas-Armagnac to the west of Eauze produce the finest eaux-de-vie. The full-bodied, rustic spirits of Ténarèze around Condom only reveal their full potential after long ageing.

Armagnac vineyards

BEST ARMAGNAC PRODUCERS

Domaine de Ravignan, Domaine de Boingnères, Francis Darroze, Domaines Laberdolive, Domaine de Lassaubatju, Château de Briat, Domaine d'Ognoas

FLOC DE GASCOGNE

Floc de Gascogne is to Armagnac what Pineau des Charentes is to Cognac. Young Armagnac is added to grape must, thereby stopping the fermentation process and retaining some of the natural grape sugar. The Floc is then aged for a minimum of nine months. White or rosé, Floc is delicious as an aperitif or with melon, foie gras or cheese.

Where to Eat & Stay

AGEN

● Fleur de Sel
66 rue Camille Desmoulins, 47000
Map 10C1

📞 05 53 66 63 70
💳 MC, V ⬤ Sun, Sat L 🍴 €€€
A richly decorated eatery serving classic
cuisine. Try the foie gras croustade,
tomato and chorizo gazpacho, or lamb
and pork casseroles.

AGEN

■ Hôtel Château des Jacobins
1 pl des Jacobins, 47000 **Map** 10C1

📞 05 53 47 03 31
FAX 05 53 47 02 80
W www.chateauxhotels.com/jacobins
💳 AE, DC, MC, V ➿ (15) €€€
Small, ivy-clad château with antique
furniture and crystal chandeliers. A lovely
base for exploring Agen. Many fine
restaurants are within walking distance.

AGEN

● Las Aucos
35 rue Voltaire, 47000 **Map** 10C1

📞 05 53 48 13 71
FAX 05 53 48 13 71
💳 MC, V ⬤ Mon D, Tue, Sat L
🍴 €€
Set in Agen's restaurant row, with its
friendly atmosphere, plentiful eating
spots and fair bills, a lively bistro.

AGEN

● Le Buffet de la Gare
1 pl Rabelais, 47000 **Map** 10C1

📞 05 53 66 09 40
FAX 05 53 66 09 40
💳 AE, DC, MC, V 🍴 €
Locals drop by the train station just to
eat entrecôte à la bordelaise (p216). For
good reason: the meat is tender, the
service quick and price is right.

AGEN

● Le Mariottat
25 rue Louis Vivent, 47000 **Map** 10C1

📞 05 53 77 99 77
FAX 05 53 77 99 79
💳 AE, DC, MC, V ⬤ Sun D, Mon, Sat L
🍴 €€€

Pruneaux d'Agen make up 65% of all
French prune production. This gourmet
restaurant makes the most of them; try
the five-course menu surprise.

AIGUILLON

▲ Jardin des Cygnes
Route de Villeneuve, 47190 **Map** 10C1

📞 05 53 79 60 02
FAX 05 53 79 61 94
W www.jardin-des-cygnes.com
💳 MC, V ⬤ Oct–May: Sat, Sun D;
end Dec–mid-Jan 🍴 €€ ➿ (23) €€
France's largest orchard provides fine
plums and prunes to accompany the
foie gras and confit de canard (p326)
here. Also try wild boar with Armagnac.
Rooms overlook the pool or gardens.

AIGUILLON

● Les Ecuries
Rue Fernand Sabaté, 47190 **Map** 10C1

📞 05 53 79 41 31
💳 MC, V ⬤ Sun, Mon 🍴 €
Popular with locals. The crêpe chef
incorporates generous portions of duck.
The crêpe complète, with succulent ham
and local cheeses, is a favourite.

ALBI

▲ Hostellerie St-Antoine
17 rue St-Antoine, 81000 **Map** 11E2

📞 05 63 54 04 04
FAX 05 63 47 10 47
W www.saint-antoine-albi.com
💳 AE, DC, MC, V ⬤ Sun, Mon; last
2 wks Feb 🍴 €€€ ➿ (44) €€€€
Fine establishment on the site of the
St-Antoine monastery. The dining room
offers a warm ambience and superb
regional food. Floral fabric guestrooms.

ALBI

● Jardin des Quatre Saisons
19 bd Strasbourg, 81000 **Map** 11E2

📞 05 63 60 77 76
FAX 05 63 60 77 76
💳 AE, DC, MC, V
⬤ Sun D, Mon 🍴 €€€
Gourmet restaurant whose specialities
are foie gras, roast pigeon and a
seafood pot-au-feu. Excellent wine list.

ALBI

▲ La Réserve
Route Cordes, 81000 **Map** 11E2

📞 05 63 47 60 22
FAX 05 63 47 63 60
💳 AE, DC, MC, V
⬤ Oct–Jun: Tue; Nov–Apr
🍴 €€€ ➿ (24) €€€€
Idyllic setting on the River Tarn. Unusual
dishes include pigeon with artichoke.
Guestrooms have comfort in abundance.

ANNESSE-ET-BEAULIEU

▲ Château de Lalande
57 route St-Astier, 24430 **Map** 6C5

📞 05 53 54 52 30
FAX 05 53 07 46 67
W www.chateau-lalande-perigord.com
💳 AE, DC, MC, V ⬤ early-Nov–
mid-Mar 🍴 €€€€ ➿ (18) €€€
Local specialities blended with Provençal
flavours. The innovative menu is nicely
complemented by the lovely ambience.
Guestrooms with parkland views.

ANTONNE-ET-TRIGONANT

▲ L'Ecluse
Route de Limoges, 24420 **Map** 7D5

📞 05 53 06 00 04
FAX 05 53 06 06 39
W www.ecluse-perigord.com
💳 AE, MC, V
🍴 €€€ ➿ (47) €€€
Wonderfully situated on an island, and
with bedrooms filled with character, this
hotel provides the perfect antidote to city
life. During the week, there's two menus
with regional delicacies such as foie
gras or truffles. Well-stocked wine cellar.

AUBIAC

▲ Château d'Aubiac
Salle des Côteaux de Gascogne, 47310
Map 10C2

📞 05 53 66 34 93
FAX 05 53 67 26 34
💳 MC, V 🍴 €€ ➿ (3) €€
Stunning views of the countryside.
Beautifully decorated, spacious rooms.
There's a choice of self-catering in the
gîte or an excellent array of traditional
dishes in the restaurant.

● Restaurant   ■ Hotel   ▲ Hotel / Restaurant

AUCH

▲ Hôtel de France

1 pl de la Libération, 32000 **Map** 10C2

📞 05 62 61 71 71

FAX 05 62 61 71 81

@ auchgarreau@intelcom.fr

🍴 AE, DC, MC, V ● Sun D

🍽 €€€ 🍽 (29) €€€

Superb food and refined rooms in an old coaching inn. Inventive masterworks such as four-flavoured foie gras, duck and tarte Tatin (p191) with Armagnac. Rooms and apartments have classic 19th-century decorative flourishes.

AUCH

● La Table d'Hôtes

7 rue Lamartine, 32000 **Map** 10C2

📞 05 62 05 55 62

🍴 AE, MC, V

● Sun, Wed; early Mar, early Jul, late Sep, late Dec 🍽 €

Superb value in an intimate, rustic, characterful eatery. Trademark treats include the famous Gascon hamburgers and tournedos of beef with morels.

AUVILLAR

▲ Hôtel de l'Horloge

Pl Horloge, 82340 **Map** 11D2

📞 05 63 39 91 61

FAX 05 63 39 75 20

🍴 AE, DC, MC, V

● Fri; Oct–Jun: Sat L; Dec

🍽 €€ 🍽 (10) €€

Dine on regional cuisine at this hotel on the handsome main square. Try lamprey cooked in wine or a truffle soufflé. Functional, simply furnished bedrooms.

BADEFOLS-SUR-DORDOGNE

▲ Lou Cantou

Le Bourg, 24150 **Map** 11D1

📞 05 53 27 95 61

FAX 05 53 27 22 44

🍴 MC, V ● Sun D, Oct–Mar: Mon

🍽 €€ 🍽 (12) €€

A welcoming eatery with good rooms. Perigord staples – foie gras, confit, duck with apples, veal, cheeses, sumptuous desserts – delivered in a relaxed setting.

BARBASTE

● La Table du Meunier

Moulin des Tours, 47230 **Map** 10C2

📞 05 53 97 06 60

FAX 05 53 97 06 60

🍴 AE, MC, V ● Mon, Tue; mid-Nov–Feb 🍽 €€

Casual dining in an underground mill near the 13th-century Moulin des Tours. Choose southwestern cuisine or light and luscious Gascon crêpes.

BARDIGUES

● Auberge de Bardigues

Le Bourg, 82340 **Map** 11D2

📞 05 63 39 05 58

🍴 MC, V ● Sat L, Mon; 3 wks Jan, 2 wks Sep 🍽 €

Dine on the shaded terrace or in the intimate dining room with curious art. Fish is served with inventive sauces, and vegetarians will love the savoury pastry.

BEAUMONT

▲ Hôtel des Voyageurs

Rue Romieu, 24440 **Map** 11D1

📞 05 53 22 30 11

🍴 MC, V ● Oct–Mar: Sat, Sun

🍽 €€ 🍽 (8) €€

Small guestrooms provide a lovely secluded getaway. The restaurant is particularly celebrated for its buffet table.

BELVES

▲ Le Belvédère de Belvès

1 ave Paul Campel, 24170 **Map** 11D1

📞 05 53 31 51 41

FAX 05 53 31 51 42

🍴 MC, V ● Nov–Mar

🍽 €€ 🍽 (20) €€

The medieval city of Belvès is truly exceptional, and this simple hotel is a good base. Treats include scallops with foie gras and veal with mushrooms.

BERGERAC

▲ La Flambée

153 ave Pasteur, 24100 **Map** 10C1

📞 05 53 57 52 33

FAX 05 53 61 07 57

w www.laflambee.com

🍴 AE, MC, V ● Sun D, Mon, Sat L

🍽 €€ 🍽 (21) €€

Worthwhile stop for seafood-lovers who are keen to try something a little different, such as filet de limande (dab), carpaccio d'étrilles gratinées (crab) or smoked salmon. Spacious guestrooms.

BERGERAC

▲ Le Mylord

Route de Bordeaux, St-Laurent-des-Vignes, 24100 **Map** 10C1

📞 05 53 27 40 10

FAX 05 53 27 40 19

w www.lemylord.com

🍴 MC, V ● €€ 🍽 (10) €€

A good find, not far from central Bergerac, with warmly decorated rooms. Notably good cellar with over 100 types of Bordeaux directly from the châteaux.

BERGERAC

● L'Imparfait

8 rue des Fontaines, 24100 **Map** 10C1

📞 05 53 57 47 92

FAX 05 53 58 92 11

w www.imparfait.com

🍴 MC, V ● Jan, Feb 🍽 €€

Beautifully set in a 12th-century building. An inspired (although limited) menu, with such dishes as partridge and pan-fried wild mushrooms.

BEYNAC-ET-CAZENAC

● Le Jardin d'Epicure

2 km (1.5 miles) east on D703, 24220 **Map** 11D1

📞 05 53 30 40 95

FAX 05 53 30 40 96

🍴 MC, V ● Wed, Thu L, Sat L

🍽 €€€

Owners Eric and Nathalie Jung have run restaurants all over France and picked up some great recipes. Mediterranean influences can be tasted in a range of smoked fish, while more hearty dishes have been borrowed from the Pyrenees, such as their duck casserole.

BOE

▲ Château St-Marcel

St-Marcel, Route de Toulouse, RN113, 47550 **Map** 10C2

📞 05 53 96 61 30

FAX 05 53 96 94 33

w www.chateau-saint-marcel.com

🍴 AE, DC, MC, V ● Sun D, Mon

🍽 €€€ 🍽 (25) €€€€

A 17th-century château. Ask for one of the period bedrooms. Wise to book, even for overnight guests. Specialities include creative interpretations of French classics, and enormous soufflés.

For key to symbols see back flap

BOUDOU

● **Auberge de la Garonne**
RN113, 82200 **Map** 11D2
📞 05 63 04 06 82
💳 MC, V ⬤ Sun D, Tue D, Wed
🍴 €€
Superb-value cuisine. Feast on hearty fish soup, fried turbot with polenta and mozzarella, and expertly prepared salmon.

BRANTOME

▲ **Domaine de la Roseraie**
Route d'Angouleme, D939, 24310
Map 7D5
📞 05 53 05 84 74
FAX 05 53 05 77 94
💳 AE, DC, MC, V ⬤ Oct–Mar
🍴 €€€€ 🛏 (10) €€€€
Chef Denis Roux's signature dishes include scrambled eggs with black truffles on puff pastry, and fresh scallops. Comfortable, unimaginative rooms.

BRANTOME

▲ **Les Frères Charbonnel**
57 rue Gambetta, 24310 **Map** 7D5
📞 05 53 05 70 15
FAX 05 53 05 71 85
💳 MC, V ⬤ Oct–Jun: Sun D, Mon; mid-Nov–mid-Dec
🍴 €€€ 🛏 (21) €€€
A vegetable garden ensures fresh produce, and local markets keep the larder well stocked. Outdoor dining in summer, and comfortable guestrooms.

BUZET-SUR-BAISE

● **Le Goujon qui Frétille**
Rue Gambetta, 47160 **Map** 10C1
📞 05 53 84 26 51
FAX 05 53 84 26 51
💳 MC, V ⬤ Tue D, Wed 🍴 €€
Good-value eatery with an outdoor terrace and southwestern cuisine. The local Buzet wine has improved. Try the red.

BUZET-SUR-BAISE

● **Le Vigneron**
20 bd de la République, 47160
Map 10C1
📞 05 53 84 73 46
FAX 05 53 84 75 04
💳 MC, V ⬤ Sun D, Mon 🍴 €€
Close to Lavardac, once a major Armagnac shipping port, they serve the

liqueur as an apéritif here. Light salads and vegetable dishes also available.

CADOUIN

▲ **Auberge de la Salvetat**
Route de Belves, 24480 **Map** 11D1
📞 05 53 63 42 79
FAX 05 53 61 72 05
💳 AE, DC, V ⬤ Oct–Mar late Nov
🍴 €€€ 🛏 (14) €€€
A beautiful spot with poolside dining and plenty of space for children. A highly inventive take on Perigordian beef and goose dishes. Guestrooms have lovely views over the surrounding countryside.

CAHORS

▲ **Le Balandre**
5 ave Charles Freycinet, 46000
Map 11D1
📞 05 65 53 32 00
FAX 05 65 53 32 26
w www.balandre.com
💳 AE, DC, MC, V ⬤ Sun, Sep–Jun: Mon; late Nov
🍴 €€€€ 🛏 (22) €€€
Refined 1930s ambience where you'll feel the urge to kick off your slippers, loosen your cravat and savour an after-dinner Armagnac. Try the roast Quercy lamb or the garlic flan covered in juniper berries. Rooms are rather ordinary.

CAHORS

● **Le Bateau au Fil des Douceurs**
90 quai Verrerie, 46000 **Map** 11D1
📞 05 65 22 13 04
FAX 05 65 35 61 09
💳 AE, DC, MC, V
⬤ Sun, Mon 🍴 €€
Stunning vistas from an anchored boat on the Lot. Fare features foie gras terrine with truffle salad, and sea bream. The owner is a pastry chef.

CAHORS

● **Le Rendez-Vous**
49 rue Clément Marot, 46000 **Map** 11D1
📞 05 65 22 65 10
FAX 05 65 35 11 05
💳 MC, V ⬤ Sun, Mon; 2 wks Easter
🍴 €€€
An ancient building with modern art. Try river fish such as perch and pike-perch as well as light pasta dishes and ravioli.

CAHUZAC-SUR-VERE

● **La Falaise**
Route Cordes, 81140 **Map** 11E2
📞 05 63 33 96 31
💳 DC, MC, V ⬤ Sun D, Mon, Wed L
🍴 €€
Feast on local classics in the rustic dining area or under boughs on the terrace. Subtle combinations of scallops with asparagus, and bold woodland flavours of veal fillet with ceps and chanterelles.

CAJARC

▲ **La Ségalière**
Route de Cadrieu, 46160 **Map** 11E1
📞 05 65 40 65 35
FAX 05 65 40 74 92
💳 AE, DC, MC, V ⬤ Sep–mid-Jul: L; early Nov–Mar 🍴 €€ 🛏 (18) €€
Great value and amenities, including a swimming pool. Foie gras, lamb and fish are beautifully crafted in the dining room, while warm colours and modern comforts grace the guestrooms.

CALES

▲ **Le Petit Relais**
Pl du Village, 46350 **Map** 11E1
📞 05 65 37 96 09
FAX 05 65 37 95 93
w www.le-petit-relais.fr
💳 DC, MC, V ⬤ Sat L; late Dec–early Jan 🍴 €€ 🛏 (13) €€
Abundant bonhomie and serenity in a rustic inn. Various foie gras creations lead into fish roasted in saffron butter, and chocolate fondant. Comfy rooms.

CANALS

● **Ancre Marine**
2020 RN20, 82170 **Map** 11D2
📞 05 63 02 84 00
FAX 05 63 02 84 01
w www.ancre-marine.com
💳 AE, DC, MC, V
⬤ Sun D, Mon, Sat L 🍴 €€
Charming blue-shuttered spot for some inventive seafood. Deftly prepared bites include langoustines with foie gras, and salmon cooked in Fronton wine.

CARMAUX

● **La Mouette**
4 pl Jean Jaurès, 81400 **Map** 11E2
📞 05 63 36 79 90

FAX 05 63 76 40 76

MC, V ● Sun D, Mon D; 1st wk Jan, 1st wk May, 1st wk Sep **††** €€

Frequented by colourful local characters who enjoy the hearty Tarn favourites on offer. Menu mainstays include chicken stuffed with herbs and some veal.

CASTELJALOUX
▲ La Vieille Auberge

11 rue Posterne, 47700 **Map** 10C1

05 53 93 01 36

FAX 05 53 93 18 89

MC, V ● Sun D, Wed L

†† € ◆ (3) €€

Casteljaloux claims an association with Cyrano de Bergerac, and you may find yourself passing through on the trail of Rostand's hero. Comfortable rooms above a lovely restaurant serving dishes made from the famous Aquitaine beef.

CASTELNAU-DE-LEVIS
● La Taverne

Le Bourg, 81150 **Map** 11E2

05 63 60 90 16

FAX 05 63 60 96 73

www.tavernebesson.com

DC, MC, V ● Mon; Feb–Mar

†† €€€

Fantastic restaurant, near the sprawling ruins of the Château de Castelnau de Lévis, offering some of the region's best food. Dishes such as red mullet terrine with ratatouille (p191). Big wine selection.

CASTERA-VERDUZAN
● Le Florida

Rue Principale, 32410 **Map** 10C2

05 62 68 13 22

FAX 05 62 68 10 44

DC, MC, V ● Sun D, Mon; French school holidays **††** €€

Gascon cuisine dominates at this exceptional eatery. Duck, pigeon, hare and wild mushrooms are the favoured delicacies around these parts. You may even get the chance to sample wood pigeon. Fine selection of Armagnacs.

CASTILLONNES
● Le Grand Bois

Grand Bois, RN21, 47330 **Map** 10C1

05 53 41 69 69

MC, V **††** €

Good, reliable food at very reasonable prices. Fine cheeseboard, well worth lingering over with a bottle of red.

CASTILLONNES
▲ Les Remparts

26–28 rue de la Paix, 47330 **Map** 10C1

05 53 49 55 85

FAX 05 53 49 55 89

AE, MC, V ● Sep–Jun:Sun D, Mon; 2 wks Jan, 2 wks Nov

†† €€ ◆ (7) €€

Small, 18th-century property with comfortable rooms and quality cooking at affordable prices. Duck appears with sweet Parmesan and black olives.

CASTRES
■ Hôtel Renaissance

17 rue Victor Hugo, 81100 **Map** 11E2

05 63 59 30 42

FAX 05 63 72 11 57

AE, DC, MC, V ◆ (20) €€€

This 17th-century courthouse retains its stone and timber charm; some rooms have fine antique furnishings.

CAUSSADE
● Le Clos Monteils

Gasherbes, Monteils, 82300 **Map** 11E2

05 63 93 03 51

FAX 05 63 93 03 51

● Sun D, Mon, Sat L, Nov–May: Tue; mid-Jan–mid-Feb **††** €€

Elegant touches fill the evocative former presbytery. Gastronomic epiphanies include langoustines with curried ceps, and ice cream in a violet liqueur.

CAUSSADE
▲ L'Hôtel Larroque

17 ave 8 Mai 1945, 82300 **Map** 11E2

05 63 65 11 77

FAX 05 63 65 12 04

AE, DC, MC, V ● Sun D, Sat L; Dec–mid-Jan **††** €€ ◆ (18) €€

Put on your Maurice Chevalier-style straw hat (which hails from this village) and revel in the laid-back atmosphere. Menu mainstays include pike served with conserves, and duck with grapes.

CAZAUBON
▲ Château Bellevue

19 rue Joseph Cappin, 32150 **Map** 10C2

05 62 09 51 95

FAX 05 62 09 54 57

www.chateaubellevue.org

DC, MC, V ● Jan–mid-Feb

†† €€ ◆ (23) €€€

Savour some of the southwest's favourite dishes, including magret de canard, cassoulet toulousain (p326) and foie gras, in this Napoleonic mansion with pool and gardens. Refined rooms.

CHAMPAGNAC-DE-BELAIR
▲ Le Moulin du Roc

Ave Eugène Le Roy, 24530 **Map** 7D5

05 53 02 86 00

FAX 05 53 54 21 31

www.moulinduroc.com

AE, DC, MC, V ● Oct–May: Mon–Wed; Jan

†† €€€ ◆ (14) €€€€

Idyllically located in a tiny verdant village. Wonderful, creative food like turbot with almond purée and walnut confit. Wine cellar stocked with the region's finest. Sumptuous rooms with comfortable beds.

CHANCELADE
▲ Hôtel Château des Reynats

Ave de Reynats, 24650 **Map** 7D5

05 53 03 53 59

FAX 05 53 03 44 84

AE, DC, MC, V ● Jan **††**

€€€€€ ◆ (37) €€€€

A constellation of stars (four for the hotel and five for the restaurant), lavish decor and one of the country's best chefs. Signature dishes include lasagne of pan-fried foie gras, and mushrooms with black truffle sauce.

CLAIRAC
● L'Ecuelle d'Or

22 rue Porte Pinte, 47320 **Map** 10C1

05 53 88 19 78

FAX 05 53 88 90 77

AE, DC, MC, V ● Sun D, Mon

†† €€€

Gourmet dining in the heart of a lovingly restored village. Sample the cassoulet (p326). Painting exhibitions enliven the tranquil, rustic setting.

COLOMIERS
● L'Amphitryon

Chemin Gramont, 31770 **Map** 11D2

☎ 05 61 15 55 55
FAX 05 61 15 42 30
w www.lamphitryon.com
☒ AE, DC, MC, V **▥** €€€€

Highlights here include fresh sardines with herring caviar, and a hot chocolate gateau with forest fruits.

COLY

▲ Manoir d'Hautegente

Haute Gente, 24120 **Map** 7D5
☎ 05 53 51 68 03
FAX 05 53 50 38 52
w www.manoir-hautegente.com
☒ AE, DC, MC, V **●** Mon L, Tue L, Wed L; Nov–Apr
▥ €€€ **◇** (15) €€€€

Half-board is mandatory here in high season but luckily the food is excellent. Wonderful, spacious bedrooms, well-tended gardens and a trout stream. The refined restaurant is open to non-guests by reservation only.

CONDAT

▲ Château de la Fleunie

Condat-sur-Vézère, 24570 **Map** 7D5
☎ 05 53 51 32 74
FAX 05 53 50 58 98
w www.lafleunie.com
☒ AE, DC, MC, V
● Sun D, Mon; Jan–Feb
▥ €€€ **◇** (33) €€€

Superb château near the busy town of Montignac. Most guestrooms offer views of the estate. The summer terrace is ideal for a romantic dinner.

CONDOM

■ Le Logis des Cordeliers

2 bis rue de la Paix, 32100 **Map** 10C2
☎ 05 62 28 03 68
FAX 05 62 68 29 03
w www.logisdescordeliers.com
☒ MC, V **●** Jan–early Feb
◇ (21) €€

Good modern hotel with swimming pool and verdant surroundings. Large windows fill rooms with light. Many have balconies overlooking the pool. Excellent value.

CORDES-SUR-CIEL

▲ Hostellerie du Parc

Le Bourg, Cabannes, 81170 **Map** 11E2
☎ 05 63 56 02 59

FAX 05 63 56 18 03
☒ AE, DC, MC, V
● Sun D, Mon; mid-Nov–mid-Dec
▥ €€€ **◇** (13) €€€

The handsome wooden panelling and grand marble fireplace evoke the Belle Epoque. Braised duck with foie gras is a perennial favourite. This 19th-century house also has modern guestrooms.

CORDES-SUR-CIEL

▲ Le Grand Ecuyer

Grand Rue Raymond VII, 81170
Map 11E2
☎ 05 63 53 79 50
FAX 05 63 53 79 51
w www.thuries.fr
☒ AE, DC, MC, V **●** mid-Oct–Mar
▥ €€€€ **◇** (13) €€€

Counts of Toulouse resided at this historic 18th-century address and many notables have stayed since, including Camus and De Gaulle. Yves Thuries was recently awarded Chef of the Year.

CORDES-SUR-CIEL

▲ Le Vieux Cordes

Rue St-Michel, 81170 **Map** 11E2
☎ 05 63 53 79 20
FAX 05 63 56 02 47
w www.thuries.fr
☒ AE, DC, MC, V **●** Nov–Apr: Sun D, Mon, Tue L; Jan **▥** € **◇** (21) €€€

Historic establishment in a former monastery. In summer sit outside on the leafy terrace. Regional bistro fare. Understated guestrooms.

COUFFOULEUX

▲ Manoir La Maysou

Manoir la Maysou, 81800 **Map** 11F2
☎ 05 63 33 85 92
FAX 05 63 40 64 24
w www.manoir-maysou.8m.com
☒ MC, V **●** L **▥** €€ **◇** (5) €€€

A fine, vine-covered 18th-century manor house. Highlights include mussel quiche, rabbit, their trademark St Valentin gâteau (heart-shaped pear and choco-late cake) and even mince pies. Rooms have attractive art. Bookings essential.

COURBIAC-DE-TOURNON

▲ Château de Rodié

Courbiac de Tournon, 47370 **Map** 11D1

☎ 05 53 40 89 24
FAX 05 53 40 89 25
☒ AE, MC, V **▥** €€ **◇** (5) €€€

A stunning yet modestly proportioned 16th-century château complete with bird sanctuary and a nature reserve in the pipeline. Meals are for guests only and are based on regional farmhouse produce. Delightful rooms in the towers.

CUQ-TOULZA

▲ Cuq en Terrasses

Cuq le Château, 81470 **Map** 11E2
☎ 05 63 82 54 00
FAX 05 63 82 54 11
w www.cuqenterrasses.com
☒ AE, DC, MC, V
● mid-Nov–mid-Mar
▥ €€€ **◇** (8) €€€€

A relaxing place, deep in the Cocagne region, with light and relaxing rooms. Tranquillity can be found in the beautiful gardens and by the pool. Food is simple yet sumptuous: try the red mullet.

DAMAZAN

● Le Midi

Bd du Midi, 47160 **Map** 10C1
☎ 05 53 79 40 20
FAX 05 53 84 48 09
☒ MC, V **●** D **▥** €

A good place for a leisurely repast with friends. Simple but well-chosen menu. Booking is advisable for larger groups.

DOMME

▲ L'Esplanade

Le Bourg, rue Pont Carral, 24250
Map 11D1
☎ 05 53 28 31 41
FAX 05 53 28 49 92
☒ AE, MC, V **●** Mon L, Tue L; mid-Nov–Mar **▥** €€€ **◇** (20) €€€

A romantic hotel in the heart of the medieval city, serving some of the region's best-loved and tastiest cuisine. Wild mushrooms, truffles and walnuts, as well as local wines and a glass or two of kir. Some guestrooms have canopied four-posters and great views.

DUNES

● Les Templiers

Pl Martyrs, 82340 **Map** 11D2
☎ 05 63 39 86 21

● Restaurant　■ Hotel　▲ Hotel / Restaurant

FAX 05 63 39 86 21
🍽 MC, V ● Sun D, Mon, Tue D, Sat L; 1st wk Oct 🍴 €€
Soak up the atmosphere of this 16th-century building while enjoying southwestern cuisine. Specialities include mullet with tomato and basil, roast veal, and a fine crème brûlée.

DURANCE
▲ La Palombière
Le Bourg, 47420 **Map** 10C2
📞 05 53 65 99 48
FAX 05 53 79 73 75
🍽 MC, V ● Wed 🍴 €€ 🛏 (4) €€
Surrounded by forests, this 13th-century bastide town is the place to sample local game in hunting season. The converted farmhouse serves wild boar and venison, with barbecues in summer. Rooms are simple and share a bathroom.

DURAS
▲ Hostellerie des Ducs
Bd Jean Brisseau, 47120 **Map** 10C1
📞 05 53 83 74 58
FAX 05 53 83 75 03
🌐 www.hostellerieducs-duras.com
🍽 MC, V ● Mon L, Sat L; Oct–Jun: Sun D, Mon D 🍴 €€ 🛏 (16) €€
Popular bastide town surrounded by the vineyards of Côtes-de-Duras, providing good quality reds, whites and rosés. Sample them alongside the robust menu. Amazingly quiet guestrooms.

EYMET
● Les Arcades
3 rue du Loup, 24500 **Map** 10C1
📞 05 53 23 90 05
🍽 DC, MC, V ● mid-Nov–mid-Mar 🍴 €€
Popular Italian restaurant. The menu covers all the basics, from hearty lasagnes and pizzas to mouthwatering tiramisu. Italian and French wines.

EYMET
● Plein Sud
14 bd National, 24500 **Map** 10C1
📞 05 53 27 32 57
FAX 05 53 22 94 11
🍽 MC, V ● Sun D, Mon 🍴 €
Conveniently located in Eymet's centre, this friendly bistro's menu provides

welcome respite from heavy traditional dishes. Beatrice, the delightful owner, is a fount of local knowledge.

FARGUES-SUR-OURBISE
● Prendin
Le Bourg, 47700 **Map** 10C1
📞 05 53 93 04 51
🍽 MC, V ● D 🍴 €€
Gourmet cuisine served at lunchtime only, making for a relaxed atmosphere. The daily menu might include oysters au gratin with prunes.

FENEYROLS
▲ Les Jardins des Thermes
Le Bourg, St-Antonin , 82140 **Map** 11E2
📞 05 63 30 65 49
FAX 05 63 30 60 17
🍽 MC, V ● Oct–Jun: Wed, Thu; mid-Nov–Feb 🍴 €€ 🛏 (5) €€
Stroll in the gardens and relax among the Roman spa ruins. Highlights include monkfish with ham and a sweet crab sauce. Guestrooms are a little worn.

FIGEAC
▲ La Château du Viguier du Roy
52 rue Emile Zola, 46100 **Map** 11E1
📞 05 65 50 05 05
FAX 05 65 50 06 06
🌐 www.chateau-viguier-figeac.com
🍽 AE, DC, MC, V ● late Oct–early Apr 🍴 €€€ 🛏 (16) €€€€€
Magical château with luxuries dating from the 12th century to the present. The cuisine, too, successfully blends old and new styles. Stunning glass-covered courtyard and period bedrooms. Relax in the spa, gardens, pool and cloisters.

FIGEAC
● La Cuisine du Marché
15 rue Clermont, 46100 **Map** 11E1
📞 05 65 50 18 55
🍽 AE, DC, MC, V ● Sun 🍴 €€
Dine under a converted wine cellar's arches. The foie gras escalope has a crunchy walnut coating and the Limousin veal is bathed in juniper juice.

FOURCES
▲ Château de Fourcès
Village centre, 32250 **Map** 10C2
📞 05 62 29 49 53

FAX 05 62 29 50 59
🌐 www.chateau-fources.com
🍽 AE, DC, MC, V
● Sep–Jun: Wed; Nov–late Mar
🍴 €€€ 🛏 (18) €€€€
For character and historic ambience, you can't beat a 12th-century château. Dine in style before retiring to your palatial suite, complete with four-poster bed. Delicacies include foie gras with figs, and guinea fowl stuffed with porcini.

FOURCES
■ Château du Garros
Fourcès, 32250 **Map** 10C2
📞 05 62 29 47 89
🌐 www.chateaudugarros.com
🛏 (3) €€€
Handsome small château run by a couple of Brits, set on a verdant estate. Rooms have geometric tiles and lavish frescoed ceilings.

FOURQUES-SUR-GARONNE
● Auberge de l'Escale
Pont des Sables, 47200 **Map** 10C1
📞 05 53 93 60 11
FAX 05 53 83 09 15
🍽 AE, DC, MC, V ● Sun D, Mon 🍴 €€
Specialities include duck with figs, scallops and ceps in pastry, and warm foie gras with apples. Book ahead.

FOURQUES-SUR-GARONNE
● Auberge des Pins
Pont des Sables, 47200 **Map** 10C1
📞 05 53 93 72 77
🍽 MC, V ● Sun 🍴 €€
A wide range of dishes to choose from on the not-so-fixed menu here, which specializes in local cooking. If they have it in, try their Floc (Gascon for "flower"), a delicious red wine-based apéritif.

FRANCESCAS
▲ Hôtel-Restaurant de la Paix
9 pl du Centre, 47600 **Map** 10C2
📞 05 53 65 41 41
🍽 AE, MC, V ● Nov–Mar: Sun 🍴 €€ 🛏 (13) €€
You'll find goose with a hint of Spanish influence here. One guestroom looks out over the square – worth an enquiry when booking (a good idea).

FRANCESCAS

● **Le Relais de la Hire**

11 rue Porte Neuve, 47600 **Map** 10C2

📞 05 53 65 41 59

FAX 05 53 65 86 42

💳 AE, DC, MC, V

🌙 Sun D, Mon, Wed L 🍴 €€€€

The chef has been called the "Rembrandt of the oven". Delicious osso bucco and a wonderful rendition of onion soup.

FRONTON

▲ **Lou Grel**

49 rue Jules Bersac, 31620 **Map** 11D2

📞 05 61 82 03 00

FAX 05 61 82 12 24

💳 AE, DC, MC, V 🌙 Sun D, Sat D, Mon; 1st wk Jan, 1st wk Sep

🍴 €€ 🛏 (12) €€

Savour sublime sea bream with porcini mushrooms or the veal à l'orange with fig chutney. Rooms with good facilities.

FUMEL

● **La Table aux Amis**

La Plaine du Caillou, 47500 **Map** 11D1

📞 05 53 40 97 78

FAX 05 53 70 74 04

💳 DC, MC, V 🌙 Sun 🍴 €

A modest routier, rather than a gourmet restaurant, but consistently good food. It's open pretty much around the clock and serves a wide range of soups, confit de canard (p326) and other favourites.

GAILLAC

▲ **La Verrerie**

1 rue Egalité, 81600 **Map** 11E2

📞 05 63 57 32 77

FAX 05 63 57 32 27

🌐 www.la-verrerie.com

💳 AE, DC, MC, V 🍴 €€ 🛏 (14) €€

Relaxing establishment with a wide choice of menus. Functional guestrooms. Lovely little pool in a tree-filled garden and a 19th-century bamboo grove.

GAILLAC

● **Les Sarments**

27 rue Cabrol, 81600 **Map** 11E2

📞 05 63 57 62 61

FAX 05 63 57 62 61

💳 AE, DC, MC, V 🌙 Sun D, Mon, Wed D; mid-Feb–mid-Mar, mid-Dec–mid-Jan

🍴 €€

High, arched, exposed brickwork ceilings add some drama here. Look out for the guinea fowl, pigeon, red mullet and sea bass. Desserts include roast figs with an apricot sauce.

GARIDECH

● **Le Club**

Route d'Albi, 31380 **Map** 11E2

📞 05 61 84 20 23

FAX 05 61 84 43 21

💳 AE, DC, MC, V 🌙 Sun D, Mon, Sat L; 1 wk Feb, 2 wks Aug 🍴 €€€

Start with duck foie gras with figs, or fish fricassée, followed by roast pigeon, with honey and spices. Leafy terrace.

GIMONT

▲ **Château de Larroque**

Route de Toulouse, 32200 **Map** 11D2

📞 05 62 67 77 44

FAX 05 62 67 88 90

🌐 www.chateaularroque.fr

💳 AE, DC, MC, V 🌙 Mon, Tue L; Nov

🍴 €€€ 🛏 (17) €€€€

Regional fare such as lamb or grilled pork, and apple and plum tart with Armagnac. Comfortable bedrooms, and a pool surrounded by trees.

GOURDON

▲ **Domaine du Berthiol**

On D704, 46300 **Map** 11D1

📞 05 65 41 33 33

FAX 05 65 41 14 52

🌐 www.hotelperigord.com

💳 DC, MC, V 🌙 Nov–Dec: Sun D, Mon; Jan–Mar 🍴 €€ 🛏 (29) €€€

Dine on hearty soups, tasty plates of fish – perch with white truffle vinaigrette – and divine white chocolate ice cream. Lush gardens, tennis court and pool. Bedrooms are gaudy for some tastes.

GRAMAT

▲ **Château de Roumégouse**

Rignac, 46500 **Map** 11E1

📞 05 65 33 63 81

FAX 05 65 33 71 18

💳 AE, DC, MC, V

🌙 Tue; Oct–Easter

🍴 €€€€ 🛏 (16) €€€€

Handsome fairytale château near the Compostella pilgrimage route. Exquisite in- or outdoor dining. The lamb and fish dishes are always inventive and satisfying. Guestrooms have ornate furnishings.

GRAMAT

▲ **Le Lion d'Or**

8 pl de la République, 46500 **Map** 11E1

📞 05 65 38 73 18

FAX 05 65 38 84 50

🌐 www.liondorhotel.com

💳 AE, DC, MC, V 🌙 Mon, Nov–Apr: Tue L; mid-Dec–mid-Jan

🍴 €€€ 🛏 (15) €€€

Ex-post office among cedars and spruce. Seasonal fare with a Mediterranean twist, served under vines on the terrace. Over 400 vintages, including the highly sought after Clos de Gamot 1918. Light and airy rooms with modern furnishings.

GRAMAT

▲ **Le Relais de Gourmands**

2 ave de la Gare, 46500 **Map** 11E1

📞 05 65 38 83 92

FAX 05 65 38 70 99

🌐 www.relais-des-gourmands.com

💳 DC, MC, V 🌙 Sep–Jun: Sun D, Mon; Feb 🍴 €€ 🛏 (15) €€

Chestnut trees create a popular shaded terrace. The chef recommends the calf's head and tongue. Modern guestrooms.

ISSIGEAC

● **Chez Alain**

Tour de Ville, 24560 **Map** 11D1

📞 05 53 58 77 88

FAX 05 53 57 88 64

🌐 www.chez-alain.com

💳 MC, V

🌙 Mon; mid-Jan–mid-Feb 🍴 €€

An excellent bistro with a Sunday brunch. The patron also owns a nearby vineyard, so take the chance to sample his wines.

LA COQUILLE

▲ **Hôtel des Voyageurs**

12 rue de la République, 24450 **Map** 7D4

📞 05 53 52 80 13

FAX 05 53 62 18 29

🌐 www.hotelvoyageurs.fr

💳 MC, V 🌙 Sep–Jun: Mon, Sat D

🍴 €€ 🛏 (9) €€

Great value for money with nice rooms much cheaper than you would expect. Specialities are scallop salad, foie gras, crème caramel and île flottante.

● Restaurant   ■ Hotel   ▲ Hotel / Restaurant

LA ROQUE-GAGEAC

● La Plume d'Oie

Le Bourg, 24250 **Map** 11D1

[05 53 29 57 05

FAX 05 53 31 04 81

MC, V ● Mon 🍴 €€€

Sandwiched between river and cliff, with a castle at each end of the village. House specialities include rack of lamb and game dishes. Reservations are essential.

LACABAREDE

▲ Demeure de Flore

106 Grand Rue, 81240 **Map** 11F3

[05 63 98 32 32

FAX 05 63 98 47 56

w www.hotelrama.com

DC, MC, V ● Jan

🍴 €€ 🥄 (11) €€€

The wholesome flavours of Provence and Italy can be sampled in imaginative dishes such as creamy carrot and grilled scallop soup. The hotel has wonderful gardens, a pool and very cosy bedrooms.

LACAPELLE-MARIVAL

▲ La Terrasse

Le Bourg, 46120 **Map** 11E1

[05 65 40 80 07

FAX 05 65 40 99 45

MC, V ● Sep–Jun: Sun D, Mon, Tue L; Jan, Feb 🍴 €€ 🥄 (13) €€

Mediterranean influence abounds in dishes like langoustines with woodland mushrooms and bass with artichokes. Cosy, well-maintained guestrooms.

LACAUNE-LES-BAINS

▲ Central Hôtel Fusiès

Rue République, 81230 **Map** 11F2

[05 63 37 02 03

FAX 05 63 37 10 98

AE, DC, MC, V ● Sun D, mid-Nov–mid-Apr: Fri D

🍴 €€ 🥄 (52) €€

The dining room is a gloriously over-the-top combination of Venetian red and murals. Head to the garden, pool or nearby casino for relaxation. Local dishes, including trout. Classic rooms.

LACAVE

▲ Le Pont de L'Ouysse

Pont de l'Ouysse, 46200 **Map** 11E1

[05 65 37 87 04

FAX 05 65 32 77 41

AE, DC, MC, V ● Mon L, Tue L; mid-Nov–early Mar

🍴 €€€ 🥄 (13) €€€€

Arguably the best restaurant in the Lot region, set in an idyllic country house near the River Ouysse. Dine indoors or out on duck liver and truffled vegetables. Guestrooms are full of warm hues.

LAGUEPIE

▲ Les Deux Rivières

Le Bourg, 82250 **Map** 11E2

[05 63 31 41 41

FAX 05 63 30 20 91

DC, MC, V ● Sun D, Mon, Fri D, Sat L; Feb 🍴 €€ 🥄 (8) €€

Verdant hills and immaculate gardens surround this imposing cream-coloured building. Expect classics like confit de canard (p326) and grilled fish.

LAMAGDELAINE

▲ Claude Marco

Le Bourg, 46090 **Map** 11E1

[05 65 35 30 64

FAX 05 65 30 31 40

AE, DC, MC, V ● Sun D, Mon, Tue L; Jan–early Mar, late Oct

🍴 €€€ 🥄 (5) €€€€

Undoubtedly one of the region's best culinary experiences. Whether you dine in the luxuriant garden or the vaulted 19th-century wine cellar, you'll be tempted with spicy foie gras and a heavenly rhubarb and shortbread dessert. Utterly peaceful guestrooms with modern, Spanish-style decor.

LAPLUME

▲ Château de Lassalle

Brimont, 47310 **Map** 10C2

[05 53 95 10 58

FAX 05 53 95 13 01

AE, DC, MC, V ● Oct–May: Sun D, Mon L 🍴 €€€ 🥄 (17) €€€€

Stylish 18th-century hotel offering exceptional hospitality. With luck your stay will coincide with cookery classes or wine and Armagnac tastings. Chic and inviting guestrooms.

LAUZERTE

▲ Le Luzerta

Lieu-dit "Vignals", 82110 **Map** 11D1

[05 63 94 64 43

FAX 05 63 94 66 67

w www.hotel-quercy.com

DC, MC, V ● Sun D, Tue; Nov–Mar

🍴 €€ 🥄 (20) €€

Look out for the delicate flavours of raw scallops with pear chutney and saffron. Excellent wine list. Uncluttered rooms.

LAVAUR

● L'Effet Boeuf

3 ave Pont St-Roch, 81500 **Map** 11E2

[05 63 58 53 80

FAX 05 63 58 37 44

MC, V ● Sun, Mon 🍴 €

Excellent-value Tarn cuisine. Menu mainstays include smoked salmon, a duck-beef fondue and crème caramel.

LE BUGUE

● Les Trois As

78 rue Paris, pl de Gendarmerie, 24260 **Map** 7D5

[05 53 08 41 57

DC, MC, V

● Tue, Wed; Feb

🍴 €€€

Serves delicious regional food with a twist, such as lobster cooked with vanilla, and pigeon with caramel and ginger.

LE BUGUE

▲ L'Oustalou at Domaine de la Barde

Route de Perigueux, 24260 **Map** 7D5

[05 53 07 16 54

FAX 05 53 54 76 19

AE, DC, MC, V ● mid-Oct–mid-Apr 🍴 €€€ 🥄 (18) €€€€

Manicured gardens and guestrooms crammed with antiques lend this luxury hotel a distinct whiff of pre-revolutionary France. The well-travelled chef puts a global spin on his menu.

LE BUGUE

▲ Royal Vézère

Pl de l'Hôtel de Ville, 24260 **Map** 7D5

[05 53 07 20 01

FAX 05 53 03 51 80

AE, MC, V ● Oct–Apr

🍴 €€ 🥄 (53) €€€€

Fairly large hotel in an attractive building and setting. The terrace and some rooms overlook the river. L'Oustalou restaurant is popular with locals.

LE BUISSON-DE-CADOUIN

▲ Manoir de Bellerive

Route de Siorac, 24480 **Map** 11D1

☎ 05 53 22 16 16

FAX 05 53 22 09 05

🍽 AE, DC, MC, V

⬤ Jul–Aug: Mon–Tue L

🛏 €€€€€ 🍴 (24) €€€€€

Wonderful bedrooms, with great views of the gardens and the Dordognet. The food, service and wine list are worthy of its one Michelin star, yet the atmosphere remains refreshingly unstuffy.

LE MAS-D'AGENAIS

⬤ Jean Champon

Grande Rue, 47430 **Map** 10C1

☎ 05 53 89 50 06

FAX 05 53 89 07 81

🍽 MC, V 🛏 €

A deceptively simple place to eat, hidden among the market stalls. Always busy, meaning the service could be friendlier. But you'll forgive and forget when you taste the results: great soups and quite excellent meat rillettes.

LE PASSAGE

⬤ L'Auteuil

3 route de Nérac, 47520 **Map** 10C2

☎ 05 53 96 78 67

🍽 MC, V ⬤ Mon 🛏 €

A good stop for a quick bite. Starters and main courses are especially good, quickly served and refreshingly inexpensive. A relaxed atmosphere.

LECTOURE

▲ Hôtel de Bastard

Rue Lagrange, 32700 **Map** 10C2

☎ 05 62 68 82 44

FAX 05 62 68 76 81

🌐 www.hotel-de-bastard.com

🍽 AE, DC, MC, V ⬤ Sun D, Mon D; late Dec–mid-Feb

🛏 €€€ 🍴 (29) €€€

Magnificent 18th-century mansion with sun deck and swimming pool. Menu mainstays include lamb with haricot bean purée, and a prune and Armagnac soufflé. Well-maintained guestrooms.

LES EYZIES-DE-TAYAC

▲ Le Centenaire

La Rocher de la Penne, 24260 **Map** 7D5

☎ 05 53 06 68 68

FAX 05 53 06 92 41

🍽 AE, DC, MC, V ⬤ Mon–Wed L, Fri L

🛏 €€€€€ 🍴 (24) €€€€€

Wonderfully large, airy guestrooms. Delicate flavours are deftly combined in snail ravioli with pan-fried morels and broad (fava) beans, or black truffle risotto.

MANCIET

▲ La Bonne Auberge

Pl du Pesquerot, 32370 **Map** 10C2

☎ 05 62 08 50 04

FAX 05 62 08 58 84

🍽 MC, V ⬤ Sun D, Mon; 2 wks Feb, 2 wks Nov 🛏 €€ 🍴 (14) €€

Small hotel-restaurant on a square where locals play pétanque. Creative southwestern dishes on the menu. Rooms are tiny yet comfortable.

MANCIET

▲ Le Moulin du Comte

Bourrouillan, 32370 **Map** 10C2

☎ 05 62 09 06 72

FAX 05 62 09 10 49

🍽 DC, MC, V 🛏 €€ 🍴 (10) €€€

An 18th-century water mill serving a solidly traditional menu. Children will love the magical location and the on-site pool. Loads of rustic charm.

MARMANDE

⬤ Auberge du Moulin d'Ané

Virazeil, 47200 **Map** 10C1

☎ 05 53 20 18 25

🍽 AE, DC, MC, V

⬤ Tue, Wed

🛏 €€€

Romantic setting in a converted mill, where the menu is renowned. Order something with Marmande tomatoes, the plumpest and juiciest around.

MARQUAY

⬤ L'Estérel

Marquay, 24620 **Map** 7D5

☎ 05 53 29 67 10

FAX 05 53 30 43 46

🍽 AE, MC, V ⬤ Nov–Mar 🛏 €€

Stop here after a visit to the prehistoric ruins at Marquay. The menu is kept simple (grilled freshwater fish with lemon) and tasty (warmed fois gras with apples and honey).

MASSAGUEL

▲ Auberge des Chevaliers

Pl de la Fontaine, 81110 **Map** 11E3

☎ 05 63 50 32 33

FAX 05 63 50 32 33

🌐 www.grand-sud.com/chevaliers

🍽 DC, MC, V ⬤ Mon D, Tue; 1 wk Mar 🛏 €€ 🍴 (2) €€

Fine little establishment looking onto the village square and its elegant fountain. Salmon, red mullet and fine perch for seafood-lovers. Excellent value rooms.

MAZAMET

▲ Hôtel Jourdon

7 ave Albert Rouvière, 81200 **Map** 11E3

☎ 05 63 61 56 93

FAX 05 63 61 83 38

🍽 DC, MC, V ⬤ Sun D, Mon; early Jan, 2 wks Aug 🛏 €€ 🍴 (11) €€

Smart little hotel in an early 20th-century building. Roast lamb and foie gras dominate the menu. Cosy guestrooms.

MEILHAN-SUR-GARONNE

⬤ Le Tertre

Ave Tertre, 47180 **Map** 10C1

☎ 05 53 93 57 23

🍽 MC, V ⬤ Sun D, Mon; 2 wks Jan

🛏 €€€

Excellent wild boar pasta and similar succulent fare. Good views of the Garonne. Booking is advisable.

MERCUES

▲ Château de Mercuès

Off the D911, 46090 **Map** 11D1

☎ 05 65 20 00 01

FAX 05 65 20 05 72

🍽 AE, DC, MC, V ⬤ Mon, Tue–Thu L; Nov–Easter 🛏 €€€€ 🍴 (24) €€€€€

Once home to the bishops of Cahors, feudal grandeur lives on in this château. Wild mushrooms, veal, foie gras, truffles, pigeon and lamb feature. Comfortable rooms.

MERCUES

▲ Le Mas Azemar

Rue du Mas de Vinssou, 46090 **Map** 11D1

☎ 05 65 30 96 85

FAX 05 65 30 53 82

🌐 www.masazemar.com

🛏 €€ 🍴 (5) €€€

⬤ Restaurant ■ Hotel ▲ Hotel / Restaurant

Delightful 18th-century home in the
Cahors vineyards. Bibliophiles will lose
themselves in the library's antique books
while the more active can jump into the
pool or stroll the lush gardens. Gourmet
dining – reservations essential.

MEZIN

▲ Le Relais de Gascogne
RN1, D656, 47170 **Map** 10C2
05 53 65 79 88
FAX 05 53 97 15 28
MC, V €€ (17) €€
To take advantage of the surrounding
pine and vine-clad hills, book a room
with a balcony at this unfussy hotel.
Typical Gascon kitchen serving every-
thing from game to locally cured hams.

MIRAMONT-DE-GUYENNE

● Le Chaperon Rouge
Lac du Saut du Loup, 47800 **Map** 10C1
05 53 20 99 85
FAX 05 53 93 65 22
AE, DC, MC, V Oct–May
€€€
Sunday lunches are popular for the set
gourmet menu, and there's often music
on Wednesday and Saturday nights.

MIRANDE

▲ Hôtel des Pyrénées
5 ave Etigny, 32300 **Map** 10C3
05 62 66 51 16
FAX 05 62 66 79 96
MC, V Sun D, Mon; 2 wks Feb,
1 wk Oct, 1 wk Christmas
€€ (26) €€
Pigeon and foie gras with pears and
wine are specialities. Try nougat ice
cream with peach. Cosy rooms.

MOISSAC

▲ Le Pont Napoléon
2 allées Montébello, 82200 **Map** 11D2
05 63 04 01 55
FAX 05 63 04 34 44
@ dussau.lenapoleon@wanadoo.fr
AE, DC, MC, V Sun D, Mon L,
Wed €€ (12) €€
The eye-catching, exposed-brickwork
façade hints at the refinement within.
Beautifully crafted creations such as
grilled foie gras with forest fruits. Small
guestrooms with no-frills furnishings.

MONBAZILLAC

● Le Grappe d'Or
Le Peyrat, 24240 **Map** 11C1
05 53 61 17 58
FAX 05 53 61 71 85
AE, DC, MC, V Mon, Oct–May:
Sun D, Mon, Tue €€
The excellent sweets are paired with
dessert wines from the local vineyard,
which produces some of France's most
celebrated bottles. Classic French all the
way: foie gras, duck, chateaubriand.

MONCORNEIL-GRAZAN

● Auberge d'Astarac
Village centre, 32260 **Map** 10C3
05 62 65 48 81
DC, MC, V
Sun D, Mon; mid-Nov–Jan €€
Top-quality Gascon fare like sturgeon with
capers and chervil. Excellent wine list.
Browse for goodies in the attached shop.

MONESTIER

▲ Chateau des Vigiers
on D18, 24240 **Map** 10C1
05 53 61 50 00
FAX 05 53 61 50 20
AE, DC, MC, V
€€€€ (47) €€€€
An exceptional hotel, surrounded by its
own golf course, with big fireplaces,
traditional floor tiles and canopied beds.
Restaurant Les Freques is quite rightly
considered one of the region's best.
Expect plenty of duck and beef dishes.

MONFLANQUIN

▲ Auberge du Bossu
Bossu, 47150 **Map** 11D1
05 53 36 40 61
FAX 05 53 36 40 61
www.auberge-du-bossu.fr
AE, DC, MC, V Oct–Apr
€€ (7) €€
Everything is sourced, plucked or
bottled by the owners. Expect pigeon
salami, cassoulet (p326), rabbit confit,
and fruit tarts. Comfortable guestrooms.

MONFLANQUIN

● Le Mercerie
Pl des Arcades, 47150 **Map** 11D1
05 53 36 48 74
MC, V Tue €€

Surrounded by the village's 13th-century
houses. The perfect setting for duck and
goose products, as well as delicious pork,
often cooked with prunes and wine.

MONPAZIER

▲ Edward 1er
5 rue St-Pierre, 24540 **Map** 11D1
05 53 22 44 00
FAX 05 53 22 57 99
www.hoteledward1er.com
AE, DC, MC, V mid-Nov–Feb
€€ (13) €€€
Elegant château includes guestrooms and
a swimming pool. The intimate restaurant
seats just 16, so book ahead. Suites
come with Jacuzzis or steam rooms.

MONPAZIER

● La Bastide
52 rue St-Jacques, 24540 **Map** 11D1
05 53 22 60 59
FAX 05 53 22 09 20
www.gerard-prigent.com
MC, V mid-Jan–mid-Feb: Mon
€€
Skilfully executed, old-school French
cookery. Nut-lovers should sample both
their pain aux noix (walnut bread) and the
gâteaux de noix.

MONTAIGUT-SUR-SAVE

▲ Le Ratelier
Route de Lévignac, 31530 **Map** 11D2
05 61 85 43 36
FAX 05 61 85 76 98
www.leratelier.fr
AE, DC, MC, V Tue
€€ (25) €€
Salads include tagliatelle with smoked
salmon and feta, and a tasty house version
with cheesy croutons. Well-kept rooms.

MONTAUBAN

● Au Fil de L'Eau
14 quai Docteur Lafforgue, 82000
Map 11D2
05 63 66 11 85
FAX 05 63 66 11 85
DC, MC, V Sun; Oct–May: Sun
D, Mon, Wed D; 2 wks Jul €€€
On the River Tarn's verdant banks, by an
old bridge. Specialities like roast pigeon
and fried foie gras are served. Finish with
a Cuban cigar and a glass of Armagnac.

MONTAUBAN

▲ La Cuisine d'Alain at l'Hôtel d'Orsay

29 ave Roger Salengro, 82000 **Map** 11D2

C 05 63 66 06 66

FAX 05 63 66 19 39

⊞ DC, MC, V ● Sun, Sat; Jul–Aug

⊞ €€€ ● (20) €€

Beyond the rather drab façade are a very fine restaurant and a popular, flowery, terrace-dining venue. Locals lap up dishes including pigeon stew with roast garlic, and seasonal game. Accommodation is a little characterless.

MONTAUBAN

● Les Saveurs d'Ingres

11 rue Hôtel de Ville, 82000 **Map** 11D2

C 05 63 91 26 42

FAX 05 63 66 28 92

⊞ MC, V ● Sat L, Sun D, Mon; 2 wks Jan, 3 wks Aug **⊞** €€€

An intimate dining room with vaulted ceiling. Creative dishes such as foie gras with apples and sorbet, and Breton monkfish. Excellent regional wines.

MONTAUT-LES-CRENEAUX

● Le Papillon

Route d'Agen, 32810 **Map** 10C2

C 05 62 65 51 29

FAX 05 62 65 54 33

⊞ DC, MC, V ● Sun D, Mon; 2 wks Feb, 2nd half Aug **⊞** €€€

Sophisticated restaurant. Fish is the chef's passion and langoustines or turbot with creamy sauces. Try the nectarine tart with honey ice cream.

MONTEGUT-ARROS

■ Domaine de l'Arros

Les Armands, 32730 **Map** 10C3

C 05 62 64 81 10

FAX 05 62 64 80 13

W www.domainedelarros.com

⊞ MC, V ● (8) €€€

Wonderfully restful place with comfortable guestrooms. Relax under the pergola or dip your toes in the river.

MONTETON

▲ Château de Monteton

Le Bourg, 47120 **Map** 10C1

C 05 53 20 24 40

FAX 05 53 20 21 96

www.chateaudemonteton.com

⊞ AE, DC, MC, V

⊞ €€ ● (35) €€

Worth visiting for the stunning setting, comfortable rooms with good views, and great fish dishes. Don't leave without tasting the house apéritif, takin, a blend of Sauvignon blanc, prunes and spices.

MONTIGNAC-LASCAUX

▲ Le Relais du Soleil d'Or

16 rue du 4 Septembre, 24290 **Map** 7D5

C 05 53 51 80 22

FAX 05 53 50 27 54

⊞ AE, DC, MC, V ● Nov–Mar: Sun D, Mon L; 1 wk Jan, 3 wks Feb

⊞ €€€ ● (28) €€€

Scope for relaxing in the surrounding gardens or by the poolside. The kitchen focuses on traditional Périgordian cuisine, from pan-fried steak to sautéed snails.

MONTPEZAT-DE-QUERCY

▲ Le Barry

Faubourg St-Roch, 82270 **Map** 11D1

C 05 63 02 05 50

FAX 05 63 02 03 07

⊞ € ● (5) €€€

Wonderful vine-covered building in a picturesque village notable for its old stone and timber housing. Rooms are full of dark-wood elegance and interesting artwork. Traditional fare is served in the simple dining room or flowery gardens.

MONTPON-MENESTEROL

● Auberge de l'Eclade

Route de Coudras, 24700 **Map** 6C5

C 05 53 80 28 64

FAX 05 53 80 28 64

⊞ AE, MC, V ● Tue L, Wed; 1st 2 wks Mar, Oct **⊞** €€

Good country fare with emphasis on the farmyard. No-nonsense creations, which range from beef and mutton dishes to pan-fried duck's liver.

MOULEYDIER

▲ Château les Merles

Les Merles, Tuilières, 24520 **Map** 10C1

C 05 53 63 13 42

FAX 05 53 63 13 45

W www.golf-lesmerles.com

⊞ AE, DC, MC, V ● 5 Jan–mid-Feb

⊞ €€€ ● (8) €€€

Many are drawn by the adjoining golf course. But the establishment warrants a visit in its own right. Apartments, plus light snacks during the day.

NONTRON

▲ Grand Hôtel Pélisson

3 pl Alfred Agard, 24300 **Map** 7D4

C 05 53 56 11 22

FAX 05 53 56 59 94

⊞ MC, V ● Oct–May: Sun D

⊞ €€€ ● (23) €€

A great hotel with guestrooms overlooking the handsome town square. The chef specializes in local cuisine and is well known for his sweet pastries.

PAILLOLES

▲ La Baptistine at Ferme Couderc

Pailloles, Castelnaud de Gratecambe, 47440 **Map** 10C1

C 05 53 41 15 24 / 05 53 01 14 05

FAX 05 53 01 56 76

⊞ MC, V ● Restaurant only: Oct–Apr

⊞ €€ ● (15) €€

La Baptistine is the sort of place that the French visit to remind themselves about their nation's cuisine. It specializes in all the region's favourite dishes, from tourtière gasconne (p327) to foie gras, confits and magrets. Simple guestrooms in the farm or self-catering gîtes nearby.

PENNE-D'AGENAIS

● La Maison sur la Place

10 pl Gambetta, Mounet, 47140 **Map** 11D1

C 05 53 01 29 18

FAX 05 53 01 29 18

⊞ MC, V ● Sun, Mon **⊞** €€

A pleasant stop, combining a Provence-style village with steep streets and medieval houses. Tasty meat, often marinated in local wines with shallots.

PERIGUEUX

● Le 8

8 rue de la Clarté, 24000 **Map** 7D5

C 05 53 35 15 15

⊞ AE, DC, MC, V ● Mon, Tue; 2 wks Feb, 2 wks Jul **⊞** €€€

This elegant restaurant is the town's best. The regional menu has some surprises such as boudin noir salad, and stuffed quails. Divine crème brûlée.

● Restaurant ■ Hotel ▲ Hotel / Restaurant

PERIGUEUX
● Le Rocher de l'Arsault
15 rue de l'Arsault, 24000 **Map** 7D5
📞 05 53 53 54 06
FAX 05 53 08 32 32
✉ MC, V ● 24 July–mid-Aug
🍴 €€
The rococo dining room provides an intimate setting for a romantic meal, and there's a well-rounded wine list.

PLAISANCE
▲ Hôtel Ripa Alta
3 pl 11 Novembre, 32160 **Map** 10C2
📞 05 62 69 30 43
FAX 05 62 69 36 99
✉ AE, DC, MC, V ● Oct–Jun: Sun D, Mon D; Jan 🍴 €€€ 🍽 (13) €€
Maurice Coscuella opened it in the late 1950s and is something of a local celebrity. His unusual creations include pig's trotters and edible pastry bowls. Small but comfortable bedrooms.

POUDENAS
▲ La Ferme de Boué
Le Boué, Ste-Maure-de-Peyriac, 47170
Map 10C2
📞 05 53 65 63 94
FAX 05 53 65 41 80
✉ MC, V ● Oct–Apr
🍴 €€ 🍽 (1) €€
Duck products abound, from foie gras to rillettes, on this farm-cum-restaurant. Fixed menus start with a fenelon (walnut liqueur) or kir apéritif and finish with Armagnac. Book ahead.

PUJAUDRAN
● Le Puits St-Jacques
Pl de la Mairie, 32600 **Map** 11D2
📞 05 62 07 41 11
FAX 05 62 07 44 09
✉ AE, DC, MC, V ● Sun D, Mon; late Feb–mid-Mar, late Aug–mid-Sep
🍴 €€€
Neo-rustic restaurant with a charming, sunny patio. The boudin noir is served with lobster in a ginger sauce. Also known for a tarte Tatin (p191), made from foie gras, brandy and cherries!

PUJOLS
● Auberge Lou Calel
Le Bourg, 47300 **Map** 11D1

📞 05 53 70 46 14
FAX 05 53 70 46 14
✉ MC, V
● Tue D, Wed L, Thu 🍴 €€€
Food-lovers throughout France flock to La Toque Blanche. Far fewer realize that in the annexe to the famous restaurant is this charming auberge with similarly wonderful but cheaper food.

PUY-L'EVEQUE
▲ Bellevue Côté Lot
Pl Truffière, 46700 **Map** 11D1
📞 05 65 36 06 60
FAX 05 65 36 06 61
✉ DC, MC, V ● Sun, Mon; 2 wks Feb, 2 wks Dec 🍴 🍽 (11) €€
The menu reveals an Italian influence in dishes such as porcini mushrooms with prosciutto and Parmesan. Superb desserts, wine list and cheese platter.

PUYMIROL
▲ Les Loges de l'Aubergade
52 rue Royale, 47270 **Map** 11D2
📞 05 53 95 31 46
FAX 05 53 95 33 80
W www.aubergade.com
✉ AE, DC, MC, V ● mid-Feb–mid-Mar
🍴 €€€€ 🍽 (10) €€€€€
Exquisite historic property, renovated into designer guestrooms and a gourmet restaurant. Wonderful wine list.

RABASTENS
▲ Le Pré Vert
54 promenades Lices, 81800 **Map** 11E2
📞 05 63 33 70 51
FAX 05 63 33 82 58
W www.leprevert.com
✉ AE, DC, MC, V 🍴 €€ 🍽 (12) €€
A fine little hotel in a gorgeous 17th-century building. Classic peasant dishes like quail with sheep's milk cheese plus exotic creations such as curried pork. Fantastic selection of cheeses and wine, plus tempting desserts. Some rooms have parquet floors and antique mirrors.

REALMONT
● Les Secrets Gourmands
72 ave Général de Gaulle, 81120
Map 11E2
📞 05 63 79 07 67
FAX 05 63 79 07 69

@ les-secrets-gourmands@wanadoo.fr
✉ AE, DC, MC, V ● Sun D, Tue; mid-Jan–Feb, 1st wk Aug 🍴 €€€
Regarded as one of the Tarn's best restaurants, with fabulous food and idyllic surroundings. Tantalizing favourites such as roast lamb with asparagus, and fennel tart with sorbet.

REALVILLE
● Le St-Marcel
Château St-Marcel, 82440 **Map** 11D2
📞 05 63 67 14 27
FAX 05 63 31 03 22
✉ MC, V ● Sun D, Mon; 2 wks Feb, 2 wks Oct 🍴 €€
Tradition and a dash of invention go into the menu here. Highlights include the flaky pastry filled with snails and mushrooms, foie gras with morello cherries, and saffron crème brûlée.

RIBERAC
● Le Chevillard
Gaynet, on Bordeaux road, 24600
Map 6C5
📞 05 53 91 20 88
✉ MC, V ● Mon, Tue 🍴 €
A taste of quintessential rural France. Portions are huge, everything is fresh (the region is known for its strawberries and nectarines) and there's a large garden for outdoor dining.

RIVIERES
▲ Le Domaine du Cèdre
Aiguelèze, 81600 **Map** 11E2
📞 05 63 81 53 25
FAX 05 63 81 52 95
@ sylvie.balzeau@wanadoo.fr
✉ MC, V ● Sun D, Sep–Jun: Mon
🍴 € 🍽 (2) €€
Alongside the foie gras with caramelized apples are dishes such as John Dory à l'orange, and pain d'épices (spice bread) with banana coulis. There is a bungalow available in the pretty garden.

ROCAMADOUR
▲ Beau Site
Cité médiévale, 46500 **Map** 11E1
📞 05 65 33 63 08
FAX 05 65 33 65 23
✉ AE, DC, MC, V ● early Nov–late Feb 🍴 €€€ 🍽 (40) €€€

For key to symbols see back flap

Hewn from the rocks, this magically medieval building has jaw-dropping views of the gorge. Exquisite fare with particularly delicious lamb and salmon. Guestrooms looking onto the cobbled street can be noisy.

ROCAMADOUR
▲ Hôtel du Château

Route du Château, 46500 **Map** 11E1

[C] 05 65 33 62 22

FAX 05 65 33 69 00

[W] www.hotelchateaurocamadour.com

[S] AE, DC, MC, V [●] early Nov–late Mar [11] €€ [S] (60) €€€

Foie gras is perfectly paired with fruits, and lamb comes with walnuts and aubergine (eggplant). Pool and garden.

ROUFFIAC-TOLOSAN
● 0 Saveurs

8 pl Ormeaux, 31180 **Map** 11E2

[C] 05 34 27 10 11

FAX 05 62 79 33 84

[W] http://o.saveurs.free.fr

[S] AE, DC, MC, V [●] Sun D, Mon, Sat L; late Feb, end-Aug [11] €€

Dine in the cream-and-cane dining room or outdoors on the village square. Monkfish is marinated in sherry vinegar and the rascasse is equally excellent.

RUFFIAC
▲ Château de Hautelande

Le Bourg, 47700 **Map** 10C1

[C] 05 53 93 18 63

FAX 05 53 89 67 93

[W] www.hotel-aquitaine.com

[S] AE, DC, MC, V [●] Restaurant: Oct–Apr [11] €€€ [S] (20) €€€

Moderately priced accommodation with stately bedrooms, a menu that is distinctly regional (foie gras, confits, prunes in Armagnac) and a wine list to match. The local wine – Marmandais, Buzet, Duras, Bordeaux, Bergerac, Montbazillac – is well worth the trip.

SAGELAT
▲ Auberge de la Nauze

Fongauffier, 24170 **Map** 11D1

[C] 05 53 28 44 81

[S] DC, MC, V [●] Oct–Jun: Mon D, Tue D, Sat L; 3 wks Dec

[11] €€ [S] (8) €€

Chef Etienne's reputation as one of the region's best means this establishment stands head and shoulders above most others. Discerning locals flock here for a mixture of traditional local cooking and an impressive seafood catch. Simple, old-fashioned spacious rooms.

SALIGNAC
▲ Hôtel Coulier

Laval de Jayac, 24590 **Map** 7D5

[C] 05 53 28 86 46

FAX 05 53 28 26 33

[W] www.hotelcoulier.com

[S] MC, V [●] Nov–early Feb

[11] €€ [S] (15) €€

A thoroughly unpretentious hotel with quiet and comfortable rooms. Expect duck, goose and truffle-based dishes.

SALIGNAC
● La Meynardie

Route Archignac, Paulin, 24590 **Map** 7D5

[C] 05 53 28 85 98

FAX 05 53 28 82 79

[S] MC, V [●] Wed; Oct–Jun: Tue L, Wed; mid-Nov–mid-Feb [11] €€

Excellent local meat and freshwater fish, but the desserts shine, especially le paulinoix, a wonderfully rich and moist walnut and chocolate cake that is a speciality of the area. Outdoor seating.

SARLAT-LA-CANEDA
▲ Le Domaine de Rochebois

Route de Montfort, Vitrac, 24200
Map 7D5

[C] 05 53 31 52 52

FAX 05 53 29 36 88

[W] www.rochebois.com

[S] AE, DC, MC, V [●] Nov–Mar

[11] €€€ [S] (40) €€€€

Set on an estate in Perigord's heart, it is little surprise that the menu indulges in truffles, foie gras and even caviar from the Dordogne's own sturgeon. Wonderful guestrooms, and a golf course.

SARLAT-LA-CANEDA
▲ Hôtel La Pagézie

Temniac, 24200 **Map** 7D5

[C] 05 53 59 31 73

FAX 05 53 59 30 53

[S] MC, V [●] mid-Nov–mid-Mar

[11] €€ [S] (11) €€

Attractive and reliable lodgings outside Sarlat. Guestrooms have great views of the surrounding countryside as do the dining room and terrace. The menu has a strong local bias, with an emphasis on duck and goose.

SARLAT-LA-CANEDA
● La Sarladerie

1 Côte de Toulouse, 24200 **Map** 7D5

[C] 05 53 59 06 77

FAX 05 53 59 06 77

[S] MC, V [●] Oct–Jun [11] €€

Praised by vegetarians for the impressive range of salads and their shady outdoor terrace, this is a lovely spot for a light meal in Sarlat's centre. Ever-popular dishes include confit de canard (p326) salad, and roasted vegetables.

SARLAT-LA-CANEDA
● Le Relais de Poste

Impasse de Vieille Poste, 24200 **Map** 7D5

[C] 05 53 59 63 13

FAX 05 53 59 63 15

[S] AE, DC, MC, V [●] Sun [11] €€€

A tasty traditional menu enhanced by a lovely plant-filled terrace. Regional staples, including duck and goose, with the addition of some more unusual dishes. Locals tend to start with tourin (p327) cooked with goose fat, before swilling the bowl out with a generous dash of red wine.

SAUVETERRE-LA-LEMANCE
● Le Cellier

Bonaguil, 47500 **Map** 11D1

[C] 05 53 71 23 50

FAX 05 53 71 23 50

[W] http://pro.wanadoo.fr/lecellier

[S] AE, DC, MC, V [11] €€

Delicate dishes with tempting twists await in the shadow of the château. Foie gras with apple, fish parcels with leek fondue, and crayfish flambéed in Armagnac. A wide range of ingredients, well combined and well presented.

SAUVETERRE-LA-LEMANCE
● Le Relais Fleuri

Le Bourg, 47500 **Map** 11D1

[C] 05 53 40 63 10

FAX 05 53 40 63 10

[S] MC, V [●] Sun D [11] €

● Restaurant ■ Hotel ▲ Hotel / Restaurant

Sauveterre is an interesting tourist stop
for its working castle on high. While in
town, drop in for a good-value meal,
simple and deftly prepared.

SEGOS
▲ Domaine de Bassibé
Bassibé, 8km (5 miles) south of
Aire-sur-Adour, 32400 **Map** 10B2
📞 05 62 09 46 71
FAX 05 62 08 40 15
W www.bassibe.fr
💳 AE, DC, MC, V ⬤ Oct–Jun:
Tue–Thu; Jan–mid-Apr
🍴 €€€ 🍽 (17) €€€€

Educate your palate and indulge your
lazy bones in this fine eating and sleeping
establishment. Innovative dishes include
young rabbit with apricots, or chicken
stuffed with chanterelle mushrooms.
Polish them off with Armagnac before
retiring to your faux-Regency bedroom.

SERIGNAC-SUR-GARONNE
▲ Le Prince Noir
Route Mont de Marsan, 47310 **Map** 10C1
📞 05 53 68 74 30
FAX 05 53 68 71 93
@ contact@le-prince-noir.com
💳 AE, MC, V ⬤ Sun D, Fri D, Sat D
🍴 €€ 🍽 (23) €€

Lot-et-Garonne is home to France's
largest orchards, and this former convent
near the riverbank makes full use of the
region's freshest fruits in its delicious
handmade prune pastries and peach-
pear-kiwi compote. Large guestrooms
overlook the pool or surrounding country.

SORGES
▲ L'Auberge de la Truffe
Le Bourg, N21, 24420 **Map** 7D5
📞 05 53 05 02 05
FAX 05 53 05 39 27
W www.auberge-de-la-truffe.com
💳 AE, DC, MC, V ⬤ Sun D, Mon L
🍴 €€ 🍽 (20) €€

Sorges is the centre of France's truffle
trade, and you'll find them on every
menu. This excellent hotel specializes in
black truffles; however, if your budget
won't stretch that far try a dish based
around less pricey wild mushrooms.
Book ahead and ask for a guestroom
that opens onto the garden.

SOUILLAC
▲ La Vieille Auberge
1 rue de la Recège, 46200 **Map** 7D5
📞 05 65 32 79 43
FAX 05 65 32 65 19
W www.la-vieille-auberge.com
💳 DC, MC, V ⬤ Jan–Apr: Sun D,
Mon, Tue L; early Nov–late Dec
🍴 €€€ 🍽 (19) €€€

Sophisticated ex-coach house brimming
with culinary delights. Revelational foie
gras creations. Light and simply furnished
guestrooms with good facilities. Two
terrific swimming pools (indoor and out)
and a health club.

SOUSCEYRAC
▲ Au Déjeuner de Sousceyrac
Le Bourg, 46190 **Map** 7E5
📞 05 65 33 00 56
FAX 05 65 33 04 37
💳 MC, V ⬤ mid-Oct–mid-Apr
🍴 €€ 🍽 (8) €€

Marking the confluence of the Dordogne
and the Lot, this is a cosy hotel in a very
popular area, and consequently booking
is near essential. The restaurant is a
celebration of regional produce; rich
dishes include a millefeuille of foie gras
with truffles. Rooms have attached baths.

ST-ANDRE-D'ALLAS
▲ Lo Gorissado
Village centre, 24200 **Map** 7D5
📞 05 53 59 34 06
FAX 05 53 31 08 60
💳 MC, V ⬤ Oct–Apr
🍴 €€ 🍽 (3) €€

Life on this farm revolves around the
kitchen, where generous rustic dishes
are prepared. Surrounded by chickens,
cockerels and rabbits, it's a great place
to get a real taste of country life. Book
ahead if you want to stay in the gîtes.

ST-BEAUZEIL
▲ Château de l'Hoste
L'Hoste, 82150 **Map** 11D1
📞 05 63 95 25 61
FAX 05 63 95 25 50
W www.chateaudelhoste.com
💳 DC, MC, V
🍴 €€ 🍽 (32) €€€

Wonderful château set in pristine, land-
scaped grounds with a lovely swimming
pool. Guestrooms vary in size but all are
full of individual warmth. The restaurant
serves traditional meat, poultry and fish
dishes amidst refined surroundings.

ST-CERE
▲ Les Trois Soleils de Montal
Les prés de Montal, St-Jean Lespinasse,
46400 **Map** 11E1
📞 05 65 10 16 16
FAX 05 65 38 30 66
💳 DC, MC, V
⬤ Oct–Jun: Mon–Wed L; Jan, Nov
🍴 €€€ 🍽 (30) €€€€

Renowned for serving some of the
region's best food, in a contemporary
building set in wooded parkland. Menu
mainstays include pig's trotters with ham
and porcini mushrooms, and Bourbon
vanilla ice cream. Guestrooms in zesty
colours with all mod cons.

ST-CERE
▲ Victor Hugo
7 ave de Maquis, 46400 **Map** 11E1
📞 05 65 38 16 15
FAX 05 65 38 39 91
W www.hotel-victor-hugo.fr
💳 MC, V ⬤ Sun D, Mon
🍴 €€ 🍽 (13) €€

The Irish are famed for their hospitality,
and the welcome at Tom Smyth's 16th-
century inn proves why. The kitchen
specializes in cuisine recherché, which
is a delicate approach to traditional
French cuisine (lighter sauces and more
vegetables and herbs). Attractive, bright
and airy guestrooms.

ST-CLAR
■ La Garlande
Pl de la Mairie, 32380 **Map** 11D2
📞 05 62 66 47 31
FAX 05 62 66 47 70
⬤ Dec–Mar 🍽 (4) €€

Beat the heat in the shady stone
arcades of this 18th-century guesthouse
constructed on the remains of a
medieval marketplace. Spacious, light-
filled rooms; some with parquet flooring,
and intriguing objets d'art.

STE-MAURE-DE-PEYRIAC
● Les Deux Gourmands
Le Bourg, 47170 **Map** 10C2

C 05 53 65 61 00

FAX 05 53 65 61 00

✉ MC, V **◐** Sun–Fri D, Sat **¶¶** €€

The popularity of this lunch spot makes you wonder why the rest of the country isn't covered with such traiteur à domicile (delicatessens where you can eat in or take away). The prix fixe menu changes daily but often features foie gras, lamb stew and andouille.

ST-EUTROPE-DE-BORN

▲ Château de Scandaillac

Off D153 & D257, 47210 **Map** 11D1

C 05 53 36 65 40

FAX 05 53 36 65 40

w www.scandaillac.com

✉ MC, V **◐** Mon; Nov–Mar

¶¶ €€ **🍴** (6) €€€

A warm welcome is guaranteed when visiting this wonderful 14th-century château. Rooms are filled with antique furniture and the kitchen prides itself on its generous portions of regional cuisine with a Mediterranean twist.

ST-JEAN-DE-COLE

● Auberge du Coq Rouge

Le Bourg, 24800 **Map** 7D5

C 05 53 62 32 71

✉ MC, V **◐** Wed; Oct–Easter

¶¶ €€

Difficult to find but worth it for the idyllic village surroundings alone. The English owner specializes in traditional Périgordian cooking, including delicacies such as freshwater crayfish, warmed goat's cheese, and magret de canard. It's a popular and well-priced place, hence booking is recommended.

ST-JULIEN-DE-CREMPSE

▲ Manoir du Grand Vignoble

Le Grand Vignoble, 24140 **Map** 6C5

C 05 53 24 23 18

FAX 05 53 24 20 89

w www.manoirdugrandvignoble.com

✉ AE, DC, MC, V **◐** mid-Nov–mid-Mar **¶¶** €€€ **🍴** (44) €€€

An impressive 18th-century building, surrounded by parkland. Favourites include lamb's lettuce salad, veal, and fresh strawberries with Monbazillac. Inside, oak-beamed rooms are tucked away in delightful corners.

ST-MARTIN-D'ARMAGNAC

▲ Auberge du Bergerayre

Bergerayre, 32110 **Map** 10C2

C 05 62 09 08 72

FAX 05 62 09 09 74

✉ MC, V **◐** Tue, Wed; Jan–Feb

¶¶ €€ **🍴** (12) €€€

Rural repose, with a dash of homespun refinement, amid the vineyards of St-Mont. Admire the collection of vintages while you savour cassoulet (p326) and other local treats. Simple bedrooms.

ST-MEDARD

● Le Gindreau

Le Bourg, 46150 **Map** 11D1

C 05 65 36 22 27

FAX 05 65 36 24 54

w http://perso.wanadoo.fr/le.gindreau

✉ AE, DC, MC, V **◐** Mon, Tue; 1st half Mar, mid-Oct–mid-Nov **¶¶** €€€€

Enchanting eatery that has won plaudits all over the southwest and beyond. Local mushrooms, truffles, lamb and fruits are presented like works of art. Try the Quercy lamb with a glass of Cahors.

ST-PIERRE-DE-CAUBEL

▲ Manoir Cabirol

Cabirol, 47380 **Map** 10C1

C 05 53 01 77 25

FAX 05 53 71 40 36

w www.manoir-cabirol.com

¶¶ €€ **🍴** (6) €€

Small hotel with bags of character. Guestrooms are individually decorated and have gorgeous countryside views. Menus typically include gizzard salad, confit de canard (p326), and prune tart.

ST-SULPICE-LA-POINTE

● Auberge de la Pointe

La Pointe, 81370 **Map** 11E2

C 05 63 41 80 14

FAX 05 63 41 90 24

w http://lapointe.free.fr

✉ MC, V **◐** Sep–May: Tue D, Wed; 2 wks Nov **¶¶** €€

There has been an Auberge de la Pointe on this site since the 17th century. The elegant dining room reflects this history with its dark wood character. Equally sophisticated food: favourites include salmon terrine with prawns, and fine langoustines with basil.

ST-SYLVESTRE-SUR-LOT

▲ Château Lalande

St-Sylvestre-sur-Lot, 47140 **Map** 11D1

C 05 53 36 15 15

FAX 05 53 36 15 16

w www.chateau-lalande.com

✉ AE, DC, MC, V

¶¶ €€€€ **🍴** (22) €€€€€

Exceptional quality in an exquisite setting. The luxury château features a Roman-style swimming pool and gourmet dining. The Surprise du Château menu is always worth sampling. Desserts may include good locally grown prunes stuffed with an Armagnac-cream filling. Beautiful, stylish rooms filled with rich fabrics and antiques.

TEMPLE-SUR-LOT

● La Commanderie

Pl des Templiers, 47110 **Map** 10C1

C 05 53 01 30 66

FAX 05 53 41 00 23

✉ AE, MC, V **◐** Sun D, Mon; 2 wks Jan **¶¶** €€

Regional dishes served up in a 12th-century Templar commandery, rebuilt in the 15th century, with round towers and mullioned windows. Plenty of palate-pleasing fish, including trout meunière.

TEMPLE-SUR-LOT

▲ Les Rives du Plantié

Route de Castelmoron, 47110 **Map** 10C1

C 05 53 79 86 86

FAX 05 53 79 86 85

w www.rivesduplantie.fr.st

✉ AE, DC, MC, V **◐** Mon; Nov

¶¶ €€ **🍴** (10) €€

Moderately priced hotel with a pleasant restaurant concentrating on the region's delights: warmed foie gras served with rustic bread, pork cooked in wine with prunes, and tempting fishcakes. Ask for a river-view bedroom.

TERRASSON-LAVILLEDIE

● L'Imaginaire

Pl du Foirail, 24120 **Map** 7D5

C 05 53 51 37 27

FAX 05 53 51 60 37

✉ AE, DC, MC, V **◐** Mon L; Sep–Jun: Sun D, Mon D **¶¶** €€€

Beautifully housed in converted stables and a favourite for gastronomes who

● Restaurant   ■ Hotel   ▲ Hotel / Restaurant

like their traditional cuisine prepared
with a modern spin. Dishes include rabbit
and walnut terrine, scallops with coriander
(cilantro), and passion fruit sorbet.

THIL

▲ Château Lagaillarde

Off D1, 31530 **Map** 11D2

☎ 05 61 85 76 72

FAX 05 61 85 70 60

W www.chateau-lagaillarde.com

✉ AE, DC, MC, V ☰ € ☕ (4) €€€

Elegant, fairytale château north of
Toulouse. Guestrooms are cool, spacious
and very comfortable. Stretch the legs in
the surrounding fields and swimming
pool. Dine on superb-value regional fare
in the very cosy dining room. Reserve.

TONNEINS

▲ Côté Garonne

36–38 rue de l'Yser, 47400 **Map** 10C1

☎ 05 53 84 34 34

FAX 05 53 84 31 31

W www.cotegaronne.com

✉ AE, MC, V

☰ 1 wk Jan

☰ €€€ ☕ (6) €€€€

One of the town's best-loved restaurants.
Charming bedrooms with balconies
overlooking the Garonne. The bar serves
tapas with a French twist, such as squid
with fresh rustic bread. The restaurant
serves bistro-style delicacies, including
salmon tartare and fresh asparagus.

TOULOUSE

● 7 Place St-Sernin

7 pl St-Sernin, 31000 **Map** 11D2

☎ 05 62 30 05 30

FAX 05 62 30 04 06

✉ AE, DC, MC, V ☰ Sun, Sat

☰ €€€

Sophisticated Toulousain dining awaits
behind an ivy-covered façade. The menu
mixes Mediterranean cuisine with local
specialities. Imaginative fish dishes such
as mullet à l'orange sit alongside classic
regional recipes. Excellent wine list.

TOULOUSE

▲ Au Pois Gourmand

3 rue Emile Heybrard, 31300 **Map** 11D2

☎ 05 34 36 42 00

FAX 05 34 36 42 08

W www.pois-gourmand.fr

✉ AE, DC, MC, V ☰ Sun L, Mon L,
Sat L; 1 wk Aug

☰ €€€ ☕ (4) €€€€

The 19th-century building overlooking
the Garonne sets a magical scene. Foie
gras, duck and fish are served in the
ornate salon and on the terrace.
Sumptuous guestrooms with curios.

TOULOUSE

● Brasserie Flo Les Beaux Arts

1 quai Daurade, 31000 **Map** 11D2

☎ 05 61 21 12 12

FAX 05 61 21 14 80

W www.brasserielesbeauxarts.com

✉ AE, DC, MC, V ☰ €€

Elegant dining on the banks of the
Garonne, once frequented by Matisse.
Refined Belle Epoque ambience and
food that is equally exquisite: rocket
and sesame salad, fish stockpot, and
Neapolitan-style pastries soaked in rum.

TOULOUSE

● Chez Emile

13 pl St-Georges, 31000 **Map** 11D2

☎ 05 61 21 05 56

FAX 05 61 21 42 26

✉ AE, DC, MC, V ☰ Sun, Mon L

☰ €€€

Elegance and warmth envelop visitors
to this much-loved eatery, established
in the 1940s. Regional dishes like
cassoulet (p326) are prepared in a simple
fashion to maximize the natural flavours.
Book a table on the wonderful patio.

TOULOUSE

● Cosi Fan Tutte

8 rue Mage, 31000 **Map** 11D2

☎ 05 61 53 07 24

FAX 05 61 53 27 92

✉ MC, V ☰ Sun, Mon; Aug, late
Dec–early Jan ☰ €€€

Arguably the best Italian in town, with
decor dedicated to opera. Traditional fare
sits alongside imaginative new dishes.
Specialities include fresh sardines with
lemon, and various risottos and pastas.
Excellent selection of Italian wines.

TOULOUSE

▲ Crowne Plaza Hotel

7 pl Capitole, 31000 **Map** 11D2

☎ 05 61 61 19 19

FAX 05 61 23 79 96

W www.crowneplaza-toulouse.com

✉ AE, DC, MC, V

☰ €€€ ☕ (162) €€€€€

Handsome top-class establishment on
the grand Place Capitole. L'Autantic
restaurant serves refined southwestern
cuisine and looks onto a Florentine-style
courtyard. Work off the calories in the
health club. Comfortable guestrooms
and suites with stunning views.

TOULOUSE

● Depeyre

17 route Revel, 31400 **Map** 11D2

☎ 05 61 20 26 56

FAX 05 61 34 83 96

✉ AE, MC, V ☰ Sun, Mon; 3 wks Aug

☰ €€

Cool yet evocative ambience and cuisine
that marries tradition with a dash of
eccentricity. Fabulous surprises await,
both savoury and sweet. Try cod stuffed
with delectable duck foie gras, and the
mint and chocolate cake.

TOULOUSE

▲ Grand Hôtel de l'Opéra

1 pl Capitole, 31000 **Map** 11D2

☎ 05 61 21 82 66

FAX 05 61 23 41 04

W www.grand-hotel-opera.com

✉ AE, DC, MC, V

☰ Sun, Mon; 3 wks Aug

☰ €€€€ ☕ (52) €€€€

Toulouse's swankiest address is actually
a 17th-century convent. Book a table at
gourmet restaurant Dominique Toulousy
and rub shoulders with the rich and
famous. Sumptuous food combining
southwestern ingredients and traditions
with haute cuisine flourishes. Chic, slick
guestrooms have interesting art.

TOULOUSE

■ Grand Hôtel Les Capitouls

29 allée Jean Jaurès, 31000 **Map** 11D2

☎ 05 34 41 31 21

FAX 05 61 63 15 17

@ hrp2@hrpromote.com

✉ AE, DC, MC, V ☕ (51) €€€€

A slice of 19th-century Toulousain
atmosphere with some contemporary
embellishments. The lobby has dramatic

exposed-brick walls, typical of this *ville rose*. Guestrooms have sleek furniture.

TOULOUSE

■ Hôtel Albert 1er

8 rue Rivals, 31000 **Map** 11D2

📞 05 61 21 17 91

FAX 05 61 21 09 64

🔲 www.hotel-albert1.com

🔳 AE, DC, MC, V 🍴 (50) €€

Great value and comfort in a typically Toulousain pink-brick building. A fresco greets you in the lobby, where elegant modern furniture complements bare-brick backdrops. Business-like rooms.

TOULOUSE

▲ Hôtel Capoul

13 pl Président Wilson, 31000 **Map** 11D2

📞 05 61 10 70 70

FAX 05 61 21 08 27

🔲 www.hotel-capoul.com

🔳 AE, DC, MC, V

🏨 € 🍴 (150) €€€€

Hotel with a cocktail bar and a very good brassiere serving Italian-influenced food in a sumptuous 1920s setting. Specialities include the catch of the day and huge seafood platters. Some guestrooms may lack character but all are light, comfortable and contemporary.

TOULOUSE

■ Hôtel des Beaux Arts

1 pl Pont Neuf, 31000 **Map** 11D2

📞 05 34 45 42 42

FAX 05 34 45 42 43

🔲 www.hoteldesbeauxarts.com

🔳 AE, DC, MC, V

🍴 (20) €€€€

Intimate and elegant hotel on the Garonne, near some magnificent Neo-Classical buildings. Breakfast is taken at the swank restaurant Le 19 just around the corner. Light, contemporary guestrooms; some with wonderfully scenic balconies and views.

TOULOUSE

■ Hôtel des Capitouls

22 descente Halle aux Poissons, 31000 **Map** 11D2

📞 05 34 31 94 80

FAX 05 34 31 94 81

🔲 www.hoteldescapitouls.com

🔳 AE, DC, MC, V

🍴 (14) €€€€

Chic boutique hotel in a narrow back street, a short walk from the river. Public areas have sleek furnishings and subtle lighting. Bedrooms have a calming, warm minimalist feel and are equipped with superb facilities, including Internet.

TOULOUSE

■ Hôtel Président

43 rue Raymond IV, 31000 **Map** 11D2

📞 05 61 63 46 46

FAX 05 61 62 83 60

🔲 www.hotel-president.com

🔳 AE, DC, MC, V 🍴 (31) €€

Hardly presidential but certainly excellent-value accommodation in the town centre. Behind the rather austere modern façade lie tidy, functional rooms. No doubt the best hotel in its price range.

TOULOUSE

▲ Hôtel St-Sernin

2 rue St-Bernard, 31000 **Map** 11D2

📞 05 61 21 73 08

FAX 05 61 22 49 61

🔳 MC, V 🏨 € 🍴 (18) €€

The area's most popular café, with great cathedral views. Grab a seat and watch the world go by while sampling the terrific snacks and drinks. Very refreshing iced coffee. Basic accommodation.

TOULOUSE

▲ Junior Hôtel

62 rue du Taur, 31000 **Map** 11D2

📞 05 61 21 69 67

🔳 AE, DC, MC, V 🍴 Sun

🏨 €€ 🍴 (15) €€€

Very good value for local dishes and pizzas, with a pleasant outdoor court-yard. Fine salads and fresh fish such as salmon carpaccio. The basic rooms can be noisy if on the street side.

TOULOUSE

● Le 19

19 descente Halle aux Poissons, 31000 **Map** 11D2

📞 05 34 31 94 84

FAX 05 34 31 94 85

🔲 www.restaurantle19.com

🔳 AE, MC, V 🍴 Sun, Mon L, Sat L; early Jan, 1 wk Aug 🏨 €€

Hugely atmospheric restaurant in the old fish market, with an air of relaxed sophistication matched by the inventive cuisine. Seafood dishes are delicately prepared with zesty flavours added, such as langoustines with ginger. Sublime desserts, wines and cheeses.

TOULOUSE

● Le Cantou

98 rue Velasquez, 31300 **Map** 11D2

📞 05 61 49 20 21

FAX 05 61 31 01 17

🔲 www.cantou.fr

🔳 AE, DC, MC, V 🍴 Sun, Sat; 2 wks Aug 🏨 €€€

Behind the rather unassuming farm façade lies a wonderful rose-filled garden. First-class cuisine where fresh seasonal produce is expertly crafted to create beautifully presented, flavoursome dishes such as veal with truffles and turbot with Parmesan. Thousand-label wine list.

TOULOUSE

● Le Palais du Dragon

189 ave St-Exupéry, 31400 **Map** 11D2

📞 05 61 34 82 73

🔳 DC, MC, V 🍴 Sun, Mon L 🏨 €€

Vegetarians and those craving exotic flavours will love this place. The exterior is somewhat drab but inside it's all red walls, dragon-filled artwork and oriental hanging lamps. Wash down the beautifully prepared, crisply textured bites with a pot or two of the excellent green tea.

TOULOUSE

● Le Pastel

237 route St-Simon, 31100 **Map** 11D2

📞 05 62 87 84 31

FAX 05 61 44 29 22

🔲 www.lepastel.com

🔳 AE, DC, MC, V 🍴 Sun, Mon; 1 wk Aug 🏨 €€€

Dine exquisitely in the parasol-shaded garden or the elegant 19th-century salon. Traditional southwestern recipes with a very personal touch. Flavourful favourites include turbot with black olives, and wild duckling.

TOULOUSE

● Le Sherpa

46 rue du Taur, 31000 **Map** 11D2

● Restaurant ■ Hotel ▲ Hotel / Restaurant

05 61 23 89 29

MC, V €

*Trendy boho café popular with artists
and students. Feast on fresh salads,
including the vast, mountainous salade
sherpa garnished with a zesty lemon
dressing. They also do crêpes.*

TOULOUSE

● **Le Verjus**

7 rue Tolosane, 31000 **Map** 11D2

05 61 52 06 93

Sun, Mon; Jul–Aug, late Dec €

*Great-value, authentic bistro where loyal
clientele enjoy classic southwestern
dishes like cassoulet (p326) and magret
de canard, and a tasteful wine list.*

TOULOUSE

● **Michel Sarran**

21 bd Armand Duportal, 31000
Map 11D2

05 61 12 32 32

FAX 05 61 12 32 33

www.michel-sarran.com

AE, DC, MC, V Sun, Sat L

€€€€

*Exceptional dishes that blend local
produce with exotic influences. Pigeon
brochette with sesame seeds in a light
curry sauce. The wine list includes Gaillac,
Jurancon and Côtes-du-Roussillon.*

TOULOUSE

● **Tantina de la Playa**

59 ave St-Exupéry, 31400 **Map** 11D2

05 61 54 59 59

FAX 05 61 80 26 98

MC, V

Sun, Sat L; 2 wks Aug €

*Sample the simply prepared yet fulsome
flavours of Basque cuisine. Cheery dining
room serving red peppers stuffed with
cod and some hearty main courses.*

TURSAC

▲ **Auberge du Pêche Lune**

Le Roc, 24620 **Map** 7D5

05 53 06 85 85

FAX 05 53 06 85 86

MC, V Wed–Thu L

€€ (26) €€

*Something of a gastronomic magpie,
chef Richard Cuevas borrows recipes
from all over the world. So, alongside*

*indigenous favourites such as foie gras
with morello cherries, you may find anything from Spanish paella to a Moroccan
tagine. Pleasantly eclectic guestrooms.*

VAISSAC

▲ **Terrassier**

Le Bourg, 82800 **Map** 11E2

05 63 30 94 60

FAX 05 63 30 87 40

AE, DC, MC, V Sun D, Fri D;
1 wk Nov, 1 wk Jan

€€ (12) €€

*A great place for kids as there is a large
pool and play area. Adults will adore the
food, which is served in a charming little
restaurant. Menu mainstays include fine
confit de canard (p326), foie gras and
apple pie. The rooms are slightly bland.*

VAREN

● **Le Moulin de Varen**

Le Bourg, 82250 **Map** 11E2

05 63 65 45 10

MC, V Sep–Jun: Sun D, Mon,
Tue; Dec–Feb €

*On the banks of the Aveyron at Varen,
this attractive former mill building houses
a very good eatery. Traditional cuisine
blends with the odd imaginative culinary
twist. Menu highlights include perch
with red peppers, and canard à l'orange.*

VILLECOMTAL-SUR-ARROS

▲ **Le Rive Droite**

1 chemin St-Jacques, 32730 **Map** 10C3

05 62 64 83 08

FAX 05 62 64 84 02

AE, DC, MC, V Mon–Wed; late
Oct–early Nov €€ (2) €€

*Much-loved riverside establishment
with deliciously light fish dishes and
laid-back charm. Sit on the terrace and
enjoy hake with tomatoes and Bourbon
vanilla. Simple, elegant guestrooms.*

VILLENEUVE-SUR-LOT

● **La Galerie**

38 bd le Marine, 47300 **Map** 11D1

05 53 71 52 12

FAX 05 53 71 52 12

MC, V Mon D, Tue €€€

*Gourmet restaurant with a good selection
of regional dishes. The "carte gastro"
combines a wonderful salad of duck*

*and foie gras with a scallop terrine.
Save room for the chocolate fondant.*

VILLENEUVE-SUR-LOT

● **La Toque Blanche**

Pujols, off D118, 47300 **Map** 11D1

05 53 49 00 30

FAX 05 53 70 49 79

ww.la-toque-blanche.com

AE, DC, MC, V

Sun D, Mon, Tue L; June

€€€€

*Plaudits have been heaped upon this
restaurant overlooking the Vallée du
Mail. Try wonderfully succulent meat
dishes, from rabbit to goose, a wide
array of fish, and the deliciously light
brie tart with cumin. Booking advised.*

VILLEREAL

● **Mondésir St-Roch**

1 rue St-Roch, 47210 **Map** 11D1

05 53 41 76 56

AE, MC, V €€

*Dining in the heart of this beautiful village
is always a delightful experience. Close
to the covered market, this restaurant
stands on 14th-century wooden piers.
Local delicacies include duck breast
with ceps, and confit de canard (p326).*

VILLETOUREIX

● **La Bergerie**

Domaine de Fayolle, 24600 **Map** 6C5

05 53 90 26 97

FAX 05 53 90 29 56

MC, V Sep–Jun: Tue & Wed

€€

*Picturesquely surrounded by cornfields,
it comes as something of a surprise to
find a distinct Asian accent to this menu.
Vegetarians are also well catered for.*

VITRAC

▲ **Hôtel La Treille**

Le Port, 24200 **Map** 11D1

05 53 28 33 19

05 53 30 38 54

MC, V Sep–Jun: Sun D, Mon;
mid-Nov–Feb €€ (8) €€

*Enjoy fine food on the terrace. Plenty of
confits and magrets on the menu but
also various salads and freshwater fish.
Stylish and well-decorated bedrooms
make this a good-value stop.*

THE PYRENEES

The Pyrenean range dominates this southwesternmost stretch of France, with lamb, tangy cheeses and hearty bean dishes on the menu, while the Bay of Biscay offers some of some of France's richest fishing waters, especially for fine tuna, anchovies and sardines. In the west, the Pays Basque shares its culture, language and cuisine with the Spanish Basque country over the border. Bayonne ham and spicy pimentoes feature strongly.

The Flavours of the Pyrenees

The mountains that dominate this region yield fine game, nutty-flavoured ewes' milk cheeses, and abundant trout from their fast-flowing streams. Down on the coast, tuna, superb hams from Bayonne, spicy peppers from Espelette, white beans, black cherries and rich chocolate are on offer.

PIMENTS D'ESPELETTE

Falling somewhere between the fieryness of Cayenne peppers and the flavour of capsicum or bell peppers, the *piment d'Espelette* was probably introduced to the area by the Conquistadors and is the only hot pepper grown in France. The peppers are harvested by hand in the autumn and then threaded onto strings and hung like decorative garlands from the gables of the half-timbered houses in the village of Espelette, until they turn from a bright scarlet to a deep, wine red. The dried peppers are often crumbled into a powder, but can also found as a paste or used to flavour olive oil.

MEAT AND CHARCUTERIE

The Pyrenees provide some of France's best lamb; in the Pays Basque, sheep and pigs reign supreme. In the Hautes-Pyrènèes and Ariège there are flocks of sheep and herds of creamy Blonde d'Aquitaine and tawny Gasconne cows. The principal game is pigeon, but there are also mountain deer, hare and partridge. The Pyrénées-Atlantiques produces *jambon de Bayonne*, France's most important cured ham. *Pâté basque* is a fine pork-liver pâté spiced with Espelette pepper, and you'll also find Spanish-style chorizo, *boudin* and *ventrèche* (belly bacon). Farms in the central Pyrenees make a range of artisanal charcuterie including sausages, *boudin noir* and pork liver sausage.

FISH

Many of the Basque coastal villages began as whaling ports, but today St-Jean-de-Luz is France's leading port for tuna. Germon (white), bonito and red tuna are all fished here beween May and October. Other fish include

Basque pigs and *jambon de Bayonne*

JAMBON DE BAYONNE AND JAMBON DE PORC BASQUE

Jambon de Bayonne is named for the port from where it used to be exported. The ham should be a deep pinky-red colour and tender to the bite. It is used in hot dishes as well as being eaten cold. Today, the pigs used are raised all over southwest France, although the curing process must take place in the Adour basin. Hams are salted and then hung to dry for seven to ten months. The mature hams are stamped with the Basque cross and the seal of Bayonne. Large-scale production means that quality is variable, so look out for those with the Ibaïona label.

More exclusive is *jambon de porc Basque*, made from the black and pink Basque pig which lives free-range in the meadows and woods of the Aludes valley, feeding on the chestnuts and acorns that give the ham its particularly fine and distinctive flavour.

Sheep on the mountain pastures of the Pyrenees

cod, hake, sea bream, anchovies, sardines, squid and elvers. Inland, wild salmon has become very rare, but brown trout are found in fast-flowing mountain streams.

CHEESE

Ossau-Iraty cheese is made of milk from the sheep that roam the mountain pastures of the Pays Basque and Béarn. Matured in damp cellars for three to six months, the cheese is delicate and slightly crumbly, with a distinctive nutty ewes' milk flavour, and is traditionally served with black cherry jam. The Route du Fromage AOC Ossau-Iraty indicates farms and *fromageries* where cheeses can be tasted and bought direct from the producers. Other varieties are also made in the Pyrenees, using cows' or ewes' milk and often simply known as Tomme de Pyrénées. Bethmale is a cows' milk cheese made in the area around Foix.

Ossau-Iraty cheese

FRUIT AND VEGETABLES

White *tarbais* and *haricot-maïs* beans feature in many Pyrenean dishes. Elongated white *trébons* onions are so mild that they are often used raw in salads. As well as Espelette peppers, a wide variety of other peppers and mild pimentoes are also grown. Fruit includes peaches, apricots, plums, figs and black cherries from Itxassou.

SWEETS AND BAKED GOODS

Among many delicious regional cakes are *gateau Basque*; *macarons*; praline-layered *russe*; orange-flower- or rum-flavoured *gâteau à la broche*, and aniseedy *pastis*.

CHOCOLATE

France's first *chocolatiers* were established in the city of Bayonne at the beginning of the 17th century, by Jews who had settled here after fleeing the Inquisition in Portugal. The Basque Country remains a place to come for excellent bitter, dark chocolate with a high cocoa content, made by such long-established *chocolatiers* such as Daranatz.

BEST MARKETS

Bagnères de Bigorre Plenty of local producers in this Pyrenean spa town, Sat am
Biarritz The covered Halles is half fish market, half fruit and vegetables and all things Basque. Daily
Mirepoix Pretty market on the main square of a small bastide town, daily
Pau Covered market at its best on Fri and Sat when local producers double its size. Daily
St-Jean-de-Luz Fish market, Tue & Fri
St-Jean-Pied-du-Port Big outdoor market along the main street, Mon
St Girons A colourful, hippy market, Sat am

Fish market at St-Jean-de-Luz

Regional Dishes

This cuisine of the Pyrenees is redolent of its coastline and mountains, and the Basque influence gives many of its rustic dishes some distinctly un-French-sounding names. Garlic and fiery little red Espelette peppers mean that some of the spiciest food in France is found here.

ON THE MENU

Achoa or **axoa d'Espelette** Tiny cubes of veal, cooked with onions and Espelette peppers
Chipirons à l'encre Baby squid cooked in their ink
Merlu a koskera Hake with asparagus, peas and mussels
Mounjetado Ariège version of *cassoulet*: bean, *confit* and sausage stew
Piquillos farcis/poivrons farcis à la morue Small red or green peppers stuffed with salt cod
Poulet à la basquaise Chicken pieces cooked with tomatoes, onions, peppers, garlic and Bayonne ham (can also be cooked with fish)
Salmis de palombe Wood pigeon flamed in Armagnac and cooked in red wine
Thon à la luzienne Tuna in a tomato, onion and pepper sauce
Ttoro Mixed fish and shellfish stew with potatoes, tomatoes and onions

Marmitako de thon

THE PYRENEAN MENU

In the Pays Basque, a meal might typically start with a plate of langoustines, a dish of *chipirons*, little peppers stuffed with spicy salt cod or simply a plate of high-quality *jambon de Bayonne*, sometimes with figs. Main dishes include *piperade*, *achoa d'Espelette* and *marmitako*. The cheese course will probably consist of thin slices of Brébis, traditionally accompanied by black cherry jam or quince paste *(pâte de coings)*. A meal often concludes with *gâteau basque* or a flaky apple or prune *tourtière*. Another common dessert is *mamia (caillé de brébis)*, junket-like ewes' milk curds eaten plain or with honey.

Béarnaise cuisine shares pigeon, lamb and ewes' milk cheese with the Basque country, but also has its own traditions. A meal may start (or even consist entirely of) a bowl of *garbure*, and duck appears in all its forms: foie gras prepared as a terrine or sautéed with peaches, *magret* and *confit*. In the central Pyrenees, dishes can be as sophisticated as *magret de canard* with ceps or as rustic as thick country sausage or *boudin noir* with potato purée and apples. Beans feature in many dishes, including the *garbure* of the Béarn and the *mounjetado* of the Ariège. Trout often features on menus in the Bigorre and Ariège. Look out, too, for chicken cooked with a melting mass of chopped, mild *trébons* onions, and pigeon cooked in a rich, dark *salmis* stew.

Chipirons (baby squid) cooked with peppers

GARBURE

Thick, stew-like *garbure* soup was the peasant staple of the Béarn. Cabbage, large white haricot beans and a ham bone are the key ingredients, to which are added other vegetables and bits of duck or goose *confit*. The tradition is to *faire chabrot* – pour a little red wine into the last of the soup and drink it straight from the bowl.

OEUFS À LA PIPERADE

Piperade is the quintessentially Basque combination of peppers, onions and garlic, stewed with tomatoes into a succulent sauce. At the end, beaten eggs are stirred in to give a consistency closer to scrambled egg than omelette. It is served with slices of warmed *jambon de Bayonne* draped on top as a sustaining rustic supper.

MARMITAKO DE THON

This speciality of St-Jean-de-Luz was originally prepared out at sea by tuna fishermen. Large cubes of skinned and boned fish are sautéed with garlic, onions, green peppers and Espelette peppers; potatoes, and sometimes tomatoes, are added, covered with white wine and simmered until the potatoes are cooked.

POULE AU POT BÉARNAISE

A hen, stuffed with a mix of chopped giblets, garlic, onion, parsley, breadcrumbs and egg, is simmered gently in water for about half an hour. Vegetables are added to the pot and all are stewed together until the chicken is tender. The broth is usually served first as a soup, before the hen, vegetables and sliced stuffing.

Poule au pot béarnaise

REGIONAL DINING

The following restaurants are among those serving regional dishes at reasonable prices:
Casa Juan Pedro
Biarritz *(see p358)*
Chez Maïté
Urrugne *(see p367)*
Chez Pierre
Pau *(see p364)*
Euzkadi
Espelette *(see p360)*
La Maison Sanbois
La Bastide-Clairance *(see p361)*
Le Cheval Blanc
Bayonne *(see p358)*
Phoebus
Foix *(see p360)*

Oeufs à la piperade, covered with slices of *jambon de Bayonne*

Regional Wines & Spirits

The rugged hills of the Pyrenees are a world away from the polished châteaux of Bordeaux and the wines here are as wild as the mountains. As in the Alps, fascinating herbs find their way into liqueurs, while orchard fruits make cider, the most traditional of Basque drinks.

BEST PRODUCERS

Jurançon Domaine Bru-Baché
(La Quintessence, Casterasses),
Clos Lapeyre (Vitatge Viehl),
Clos Uroulat (Cuvée Marie),
Domaine du Cinquau (Cuvée
Henri), Domaine Bordenave
(Souvenirs d'Enfance), Domaine
Cauhapé (Chant des Vignes
and Noblesse du Temps)
Irouléguy Domaine Arretxea
(Cuvée Haïtza), Domaine Brana
(the_"Domaine" wines),
Domaine Etxegaraya (Cuvée
Lehengoa), Domaine Ilarria
(Cuvée Bixintxo), Cave
Coopérative d'Irouléguy
(Mignaberry)

IROULÉGUY WINES

The wines of Irouléguy mirror the rough-hewn countryside that is the setting for the vertiginous vineyards of the Pyrenean foothills and echo the Basque language of the region. In the Middle Ages the abbeys and hospices along the road to Compostela provided sustenance for the pilgrims who would vaunt the virtues of the region's wines on their return home. After a long period of obscurity, the vineyards were revived last century by intrepid pioneers including Domaine Brana, Domaine Arretxea, Domaine Etxegaraya and Domaine Ilarria.

The wines are mainly red, made from the robust local Tannat grape doused with Cabernet Franc and Cabernet Sauvignon. These meaty reds show lots of red fruit flavour whilst the rosés are packed with scents of raspberry and blackcurrant. The rare whites are relative lightweights that go well with fish from the mountain torrents.

JURANÇON WINES

The term Jurançon usually refers to sweet wines whilst the crisp whites are labelled Jurançon Sec. Delicious but vastly underrated wines, they are starting to gain in popularity. The vineyards are located amongst woodland on the foothills on the Pyrenees. Luscious, sweet Jurançon is made from the fragrant Petit Manseng grape, which is often harvested as late as December when the warm days and cool nights enable the grapes to shrivel slowly on the vine thus concentrating the sugar. The result is waxy wines that offer the tang of peach, guava, cinnamon and honey with a supporting slash of lemon acidity. The supple dry whites come from the larger, more productive Gros Manseng. Both these white styles also carry a percentage of the local Courbu grape.

BASQUE CIDER

The Basques have been making cider (known here as *sagarnoa*) since at least the 14th century and today the region's producers still use age-old varieties of apple and traditional pressing techniques. Dry and decidedly

Irouléguy wine

VINEYARDS OF THE PYRENEES

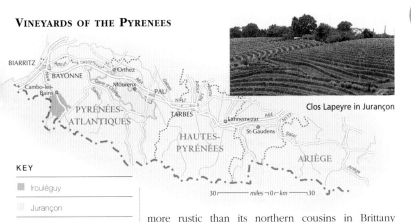

Clos Lapeyre in Jurançon

KEY

▦ Irouléguy

▦ Jurançon

▦ Delimited VDQS regions

···· *Département* boundary

— International boundary

30 ┌─────── miles ┐0┌ km ┌───── 30

IZARRA LIQUEUR

In the 19th century Joseph Grattau, a botanist from Bordeaux, bought the ancient recipe for a liqueur based on mountain herbs from two sisters in the village of Espelette. He used it to make Izarra, meaning "star" in Basque, from some 16 plants and spices combined with fruit (especially prunes), macerated in Armagnac and honey.

more rustic than its northern cousins in Brittany *(see pp170–71)* and Normandy *(see pp146–7)*, Basque cider is made from untreated apples. The art of cider making depends on blending different varieties so that the result attains just the right balance: neither too sour, too bitter nor too sweet. January is the time to taste the *txotx* (pronounced "chotch"), new cider taken straight from the barrel.

PEAR BRANDY FROM DOMAINE BRANA

Domaine Brana is justifiably famous for the quality of its pear brandy. The family orchard contains only top quality Williams pears. The

Pear brandy

trees are pruned severely so that each one produces only a small amount of fruit, thereby greatly increasing the aroma and flavour. The result is an exquisitely fragranced eau-de-vie that rounds off a meal with a touch of sophistication.

Irouléguy vineyards

Where to Eat & Stay

AINHOA
▲ **Ithurria**
Pl du Fronton, 64250 **Map** 10A3
📞 05 59 29 92 11
FAX 05 59 29 81 28
W www.ithurria.com
AE, MC, V
● Jun–Sep: Wed, Thu L; Nov–Apr
🍴 €€€ 🍽 (27) €€€€
A stop on the pilgrim route, this eatery serves Espelette peppers as well as seafood with the local dressing, a fine wine sauce. Desserts include cold Izarra (herb liqueur) soufflé. Flowery rooms.

ARGEIN
▲ **La Terrasse**
42 route Luchon, 09800 **Map** 11D3
📞 05 61 96 70 11
● mid-Nov–Mar 🍴 € 🍽 (6) €€
A small and well-maintained country inn that offers regional culinary delights such as trout wrapped in ham and rabbit cooked in a fragrant onion sauce. The rooms, which include two spacious suites, have good facilities.

ARGELES-GAZOST
▲ **Le Casaou at Le Miramont**
44 ave des Pyrénées, 65400 **Map** 10C3
📞 05 62 97 01 26
FAX 05 62 97 56 67
W www.hotelmiramont.com
AE, DC, MC, V ● Sep–Jun: Sun D & Wed D (except for guests); 1st wk Nov–mid-Dec
🍴 €€€ 🍽 (27) €€€
Le Corbusier-inspired, 1930s-style villa set amidst pristine gardens. In the Art Deco dining room, the cuisine of award-winning chef Pierre Pucheu: regional products like lamb and trout are mainstays. Bright, well-equipped guestrooms.

ARGELES-GAZOST
▲ **Les Cîmes**
1 pl d'Ourout, 65400 **Map** 10C3
📞 05 62 97 00 10
FAX 05 62 97 10 19
W www.hotel-lescimes.com
MC, V ● 1st wk Nov–3rd wk Dec
🍴 €€ 🍽 (31) €€

A 1950s building, set in the idyllic Vallée des Gaves. Classics, like cassoulet (p373) and confit de canard (p326) and desserts including delicious ice creams, sorbets and crème brûlée. Rooms are traditional.

ARREAU
▲ **Hôtel d' Angleterre**
Route de Luchon, 65240 **Map** 10C3
📞 05 62 98 63 30
FAX 05 62 98 69 66
AE, DC, MC, V ● Restaurant: Mon–Tue L; May, Jun, Sep: Sun D, Mon D; Oct–Apr 🍴 €€€ 🍽 (24) €€€
On the edge of sleepy Arreau, and beside the river Neste d'Aure. Highlights include a red pepper mousse and rabbit with olive oil with courgettes (zucchini). Bedrooms are small, modern and well kept. Staff can be a little reserved.

AUDRESSEIN
▲ **L'Auberge d'Audressein**
Village Le Bourg, 09800 **Map** 11D3
📞 05 61 96 11 80
FAX 05 61 96 82 96
@ aubergeaudressein@clubinternet.fr
DC, MC, V ● Sun D, Sep–Jun: Mon; Jan 🍴 €€ 🍽 (10) €€
Hidden in the Vallée de la Bellongue, with magical views from the veranda and superb regional cuisine. The chef has a creative approach to local produce, especially sauces used to dress fish and lamb. Small, well-maintained guestrooms.

AULON
● **Auberge des Aryelets**
Pl du village, 65240 **Map** 10C4
📞 05 62 39 95 59
MC, V ● Sun D, Mon, Tue; 2nd & 3rd wk Jun, 1st wk Nov–3rd wk Dec
🍴 €
A great-value retreat deep within the Hautes-Pyrénées. The dining area has a robust, rough-around-the-edges appeal. Favourites are garbure (p353), duck with bilberries and foie gras with prunes.

AULUS-LES-BAINS
▲ **Hostellerie de la Terrasse**
Village centre, 09140 **Map** 11D4

📞 05 61 96 00 98
FAX 05 61 96 01 42
MC, V ● Oct–May
🍴 €€€ 🍽 (12) €€€
Tranquillity and elegance define this spa town inn on the banks of the River Garbet. Sample beef with morels or roasted pigeon in port on the shady terrace. Guestrooms have good facilities.

AULUS-LES-BAINS
▲ **Les Oussaillès**
Village centre, 09140 **Map** 11D4
📞 05 61 96 03 68
FAX 05 61 96 03 70
@ jcharrue@free.fr
MC, V 🍴 € 🍽 (12) €€
Set within the grounds of a thermal bath, this historic turreted building affords some wonderful views of the valley from the terrace restaurant. Try the tuna with sautéed mangos, and duck with honey and Hypocras (a local liqueur). Guestrooms are simple.

AURIGNAC
▲ **Le Cerf Blanc**
Rue St-Michel, 31420 **Map** 11D3
📞 05 61 98 95 76
FAX 05 61 98 76 80
MC, V ● Sep–Jun: Sun
🍴 €€€ 🍽 (9) €€
One of the region's top gastronomic destinations. Wonderful views from the terrace, and the menu is inspired, with some notable fish and game dishes and a divine cep mousse. Guestrooms can feel a little cramped.

AUTERIVE
■ **La Manufacture**
2 rue Docteurs Basset, 31190 **Map** 11D3
📞 05 61 50 08 50
MC, V ● Nov–Apr 🍽 (5) €€€€
An 18th-century fabric factory turned elegant hotel. Guestrooms are crammed full of curios and antiques.

AX-LES-THERMES
▲ **L'Auzeraie**
1 ave Théophile Delcassé, 09110
Map 11E4

● Restaurant ■ Hotel ▲ Hotel / Restaurant

☎ 05 61 64 20 70
FAX 05 61 64 38 50 AE, DC, MC, V
Tue L; mid-Nov–late Dec €€
(33) €€€

Modern ambience with a faint whiff of the Belle Epoque. The inventive menu is geared towards meat- and fish-lovers, with salmon soaked in vodka and trout baked with almonds. Basic guestrooms, some with balconies.

AX-LES-THERMES
▲ Le Châlet
4 ave Turrel, 09110 **Map** 11E4
☎ 05 61 64 24 31
FAX 05 61 03 55 50
W www.le-chalet.fr
AE, DC, MC, V Sun D, Mon; Nov
€€ (10) €€

Award-winning hotel and restaurant in a wonderful location overlooking the river Ariège. Enjoy dishes such as roast turbot with asparagus. Delicious baba au rhum (p119 for dessert. Functional yet pleasant rooms, some with balconies.

AX-LES-THERMES
▲ L'Orry Le Saquet
20 route d' Espagne, 09110 **Map** 11E4
☎ 05 61 64 31 30
FAX 05 61 64 00 31
W www.auberge-lorry.com
AE, DC, MC, V Tue D, Wed; Jan
€€€ (15) €€

Amiable staff and a creative menu. Highlights include whiting with aubergine (eggplant) and wild mushrooms, and trout. Excellent guestrooms.

BAGNERES-DE-BIGORRE
● Le Jardin des Brouches
22 bd Carnot, 65200 **Map** 10C3
☎ 05 62 91 07 95
FAX 05 62 91 07 95
MC, V Sun, Mon €€

An intimate dining room with vibrant colours and an old fireplace. Adventurous salads and wonderful fish dishes are served. Southwest wines dominate the well-chosen wine list.

BAGNERES-DE-LUCHON
▲ Auberge de Castel Vielh
Castel Biel, route de Superbagnères, 31110 **Map** 10C4

☎ 05 61 79 36 79
FAX 05 61 79 36 79
MC, V Mar–Jul, Sep, Oct: Wed; Nov–Jan: Mon–Frib
€€ (3) €€

A modern chalet surrounded by fields. Save room for the apple and forest fruit dessert. Well-maintained guestrooms.

BAGNERES-DE-LUCHON
● Clos du Silène
19 cours Quinconces, 31110 **Map** 10C4
☎ 05 61 79 12 00
FAX 05 61 79 12 00
MC, V Wed, Oct–Jun: Tue
€€

A chic address with a surprisingly affordable menu, especially at lunch. Regional favourites, like foie gras, plus Mediterranean seafood dishes.

BAGNERES-DE-LUCHON
▲ Corneille
5 ave Alexandre Dumas, 31110
Map 10C4
☎ 05 61 79 36 22
FAX 05 61 79 81 11
W www.hotel-corneille.com
AE, DC, MC, V 3rd wk Oct–3rd wk Dec €€ (54) €€€

This 19th-century hotel has a distinct flavour of the Belle Epoque. Rooms have period touches, and there's a choice of two restaurants: Le Corneille and Le Gipsy, both serving good Pyrenean cuisine.

BAGNERES-DE-LUCHON
▲ Etigny
3 ave Paul Bonnemaison, 31110
Map 10C4
☎ 05 61 79 01 42
FAX 05 61 79 80 64
@ etigny@aol.com
MC, V Nov–May
€€ (58) €€€

Some rooms face the famous baths and gardens. The terrace bar is a relaxing way to begin the evening. Traditional fare.

BAGNERES-DE-LUCHON
● Gabriel Pène
12 ave Carnot, 31110 **Map** 10C4
☎ 05 61 79 00 39
FAX 05 61 79 52 08
AE, DC, MC, V €

Luchon's premier spot for chocoholics. The accompanying patisserie has an impressive selection of cakes, and is particularly well known for its chocolate and hazelnut cake.

BAGNERES-DE-LUCHON
● La Brioche au Beurre
21 allées d'Etigny, 31110 **Map** 10C4
☎ 05 61 79 20 79
Nov €

A wonderful patisserie on Luchon's elegant main shopping street. Both sweet and savoury pastries are available.

BAGNERES-DE-LUCHON
▲ Le Jardin des Cascades
Montauban de Luchon, 31110 **Map** 10C4
☎ 05 61 79 83 09
FAX 05 61 79 79 16
AE, DC, MC, V Oct–Apr
€€ (10) €€

Park on the main road and take the short walk to this idyllic getaway that's only accessible by foot. You'll be rewarded with wonderful views of the valley from the dining terrace, cosy guestrooms and generous portions of local cuisine.

BAGNERES-DE-LUCHON
● Les Caprices d'Etigny
30 bis allées d'Etigny, 31110 **Map** 10C4
☎ 05 61 94 31 05
DC Sep–Jun: Tue D, Wed D, Thu; first 2 wks Nov €

To make the most of the spectacular mountain views, book a table on the terrace. The menu concentrates on grilled meat and fish (notably trout).

BAGNERES-DE-LUCHON
▲ L'Esquérade
Castillon de Larboust, 31110 **Map** 10C4
☎ 05 61 79 19 64
FAX 05 61 79 26 29
W www.esquerade.com
AE, DC, MC, V Oct–Jun: Mon–Wed L; mid-Nov–mid-Dec
€€€ (14) €€

A handsome establishment which draws its culinary inspiration from traditions spanning the breadth of the Pyrenees. More than 180 regional vintages, as well as a well-stocked cigar selection. Immaculate guestrooms.

BARBAZAN

▲ L'Aristou

Route de Sauveterre, 31510 **Map** 10C3

[C] 05 61 88 30 67

FAX 05 61 95 55 66

AE, MC, V ● Sep–May: Sun D, Mon; early Dec–mid-Feb

€€ ● (7) €€

A converted 19th-century farmhouse with a stunning mountain views. A favourite is the pike-perch with crunchy vegetables. Rooms with period touches.

BARCUS

▲ Chilo

Bourg, 64130 **Map** 10B3

[C] 05 59 28 90 79

FAX 05 59 28 93 10

[W] www.hotel-chilo.com

MC, V ● Oct–Jun: Sun D, Mon, Tue L; Jan, 3rd wk Feb

€€€ ● (11) €€€

An inn with blue shutters and white-washed walls. On the menu, local dishes such as foie gras with a fine apple tart or a plate with three chocolate desserts. Luxurious guestrooms and a pool.

BAREGES

● Auberge du Lienz

Route Lienz, 65120 **Map** 10C4

[C] 05 62 92 67 17

FAX 05 62 92 65 15

MC, V ● 3rd wk Apr–1st wk May, Nov €

A mountain retreat with stunning views of Pic du Midi de Bigorre. Menu main-stays include trout, lamb stuffed with morels and a sumptuous soufflé.

BAYONNE

▲ Grand Hôtel

21 rue Thiers, 64100 **Map** 10A3

[C] 05 59 59 62 00

AE, DC, MC, V

● Nov–Apr: Sun, Sat; Dec–Feb

€€ ● (54) €€€€

The dining room, with pale cream walls and floral furnishings, is the perfect environment for the classic food and wines. Spacious, well-tended guestrooms.

BAYONNE

● Le Cheval Blanc

68 rue Bourgneuf, 64100 **Map** 10A3

[C] 05 59 59 01 33

FAX 05 59 59 52 26

AE, DC, MC, V ● Sep–Jul: Sun D, Mon L; Feb, 1 wk Jul €€

Fine Basque cuisine. Expect the freshest and most succulent seafood – the house speciality is a clam omelette. Try a glass of locally produced Jurançon.

BAYONNE

● Le Roy Leon

8 rue de Coursic, 64100 **Map** 10A3

[C] 05 59 59 55 84

FAX 05 54 59 55 46

DC, MC, V ● Sun L, Sat D

€€

Flame-grilled duck with sweet roasted red peppers is a highlight on the menu here. Top-notch but short wine list.

BAYONNE

● Pâtisserie Barrére

47 rue Port Neuf, 64100 **Map** 10A3

● Sun €

This chocolatier dates from the 1700s and is one of France's oldest. Look out for their famous discs of chocolate and the milky ganaches dusted with cinnamon – delicious with a strong coffee.

BEAUCENS

■ Eth Berye Petit

15 route de Vielle, 65400 **Map** 10C3

[C] 05 62 97 90 02

[W] www.beryepetit.com

● (3) €€

Charming 18th-century farmhouse run by a Basque couple. The spacious guestrooms have adequate facilities.

BIARRITZ

● Aloha

24 rue d'Espagne, 64200 **Map** 10A3

[C] 05 59 24 21 00

MC, V ● Mon; first 2 wks Mar

€€

Named in appreciation of the surfers who helped regenerate the city's once wobbly economy, Aloha draws an eclectic and vibrant crowd with its seafood.

BIARRITZ

● Bar Jean

5 rue des Halles, 64200 **Map** 10A3

[C] 05 59 24 80 38

FAX 05 59 22 09 93

AE, DC, MC, V

● Tue, Wed; Jan–Feb €

Across from Biarritz's fantastic market, this popular tapas bar has the best service in town. Tasty morsels are marinated, grilled, deep-fried or roasted.

BIARRITZ

● Casa Juan Pedro

Port des Pêcheurs, 64200 **Map** 10A3

MC, V ● Mon €

Excellent harbourside restaurant where seafood, from sardines to baby octopus to prawns, is simply grilled and served with frites. Good house wines and large jugs of sangria.

BIARRITZ

● Halles

Rue des Halles, 64200 **Map** 10A3

● Sun €

The local market is a lesson in Basque food, with stacks of preserves, foie gras, meats, chocolate, wine and cider. Pop into the superb Halles bar for mind-blowing coffee, crêpes and cakes.

BIARRITZ

▲ Hôtel du Palais

1 ave de l'Impératrice, 64200 **Map** 10A3

[C] 05 59 41 64 00

FAX 05 59 41 67 99

[W] www.hotel-du-palais.com

AE, DC, MC, V

€€€€ ● (156) €€€€€

The russet grandeur of the Hôtel du Palais is one of the most impressive sights along Biarritz's shoreline. Stately guestrooms, a huge pool and golf course. Inventive cuisine.

BIARRITZ

▲ Hôtel Plaza

10 ave Edouard VII, 64200 **Map** 10A3

[C] 05 59 24 74 00

FAX 05 59 22 22 01

AE, DC, MC, V ● Nov–May: Sun, Mon L, Sat L; Jun–Oct: Sun L

€€ ● (54) €€€

Enough original Art Deco fittings remain to counteract the drab 1970s-style rooms. The menu includes perfectly cooked pigeon in piperade, and sea bream with saffron and sherry.

● Restaurant ■ Hotel ▲ Hotel / Restaurant

BIARRITZ
● Les Ateliers du Chocolat
de Bayonne
1 rue Poste, 64200 **Map** 10A3
📞 05 59 24 47 05
💳 AE, DC, MC, V ● 1 May 🍴 €

Their bouquets de chocolats make great presents and they have rather interesting thin slabs of flavoured chocolate. Being French, the chocolate's mainly dark and contains 70% cocoa. Excellent café serving decadent sweet snacks.

BIARRITZ
● Mille et un Fromages
8 ave Victor Hugo, 64200 **Map** 10A3
📞 05 59 24 67 88
📠 05 59 22 22 57
🌐 www.milleetunfromages.fr
💳 MC, V ● Sun 🍴 €

Small shop full of gastronomic wonders and pungent smells. Look out for cheeses, like Garazi and Assau-Iraty, well-hung hams, Pyrenean sausages and wine shelves stacked with Basque standards Irouleguy and Jurançon. Quick meals of delicious deli food.

BIARRITZ
▲ Palacito
1 rue Gambetta, 64200 **Map** 10A3
📞 05 59 24 58 22
📠 05 59 24 33 43
🌐 www.hotel-palacito.com
💳 AE, MC, V ● Sun D
🍴 € 🍷 (27) €€

One of the few reasonably priced hotels in Biarritz. Simple, basic guestrooms. Pastries and crêpes in the salon.

BIDARRAY
● Auberge Iparla
Chemin de l'Église, 64780 **Map** 10A3
📞 05 59 37 77 21
📠 05 59 37 78 84
💳 AE, DC, MC, V ● Sep–Jun: Wed; Jan, Feb 🍴 €€

The beamed ceiling and wooden panels evoke a country kitchen. The menu is a bit random, but expect chunky Basque soup and squid stew.

BIDART
■ Irigoian Chambres d'Hôtes
Ave de Biarritz, 64210 **Map** 10A3
📞 05 59 43 83 00
📠 05 59 43 83 03
🌐 www.irigoian.com
💳 DC, MC, V 🍷 (5) €€€

Completely refitted, this 17th-century farmhouse is in the traditional, almost Alpine, style. Beautiful guestrooms.

BIDART
▲ La Table des Frères Ibarboure
Chemin de Ttaliénèa, 64210 **Map** 10A3
📞 05 59 54 81 64
📠 05 59 47 58 30
🌐 www.freresibarboure.com
💳 AE, DC, MC, V ● Oct–Jun: Sun D, Tue; Jul–Sep: Sun D
🍴 €€€ 🍷 (8) €€€€

Great Basque hospitality in luxurious surroundings. Rooms are well furnished. The pigeon, salmon and squid are tasty.

BIRIATOU
▲ Bakéa
Bourg, 64700 **Map** 10A3
📞 05 59 20 76 36
📠 05 59 20 58 21
🌐 www.basquexplorer.com/bakea.htm
💳 AE, DC, MC, V ● Mon L, Nov–Mar: Sun D, Apr–Oct: Tue
🍴 €€€ 🍷 (30) €€

In a mountain village near the sea, this imposing chalet, with shaded, lantern-lit terrace, has sublime views. Flavoursome Basque dishes include a gourmet salad. Cosy guestrooms, many with balconies.

BOUSSENS
▲ Hôtel du Lac
7 promenade du Lac, 31360 **Map** 11D3
📞 05 61 90 01 85
📠 05 61 97 15 57
💳 MC, V ● Nov–Apr: Fri, Sat L; mid-Feb–mid-Mar 🍴 €€ 🍷 (12) €€

A sleek, contemporary building set on a lakeside. Signature dishes include salmon with orange and a sublime crème brûlée with pistachios. Regional wines include Madiran and Tursan.

CADEAC
▲ Hostellerie du Val d'Aure
Route St-Lary Village, 65240 **Map** 10C3
📞 05 62 98 60 63
📠 05 62 98 68 99
🌐 www.hotel-valdaure.com

💳 MC, V ● Nov–mid-Dec
🍴 €€ 🍷 (23) €€

Perfect for both relaxation and play: extensive grounds, tennis courts and a pool. Dine on southwestern produce like trout or lamb in the rustic dining room or on the terrace. Basic, dated bedrooms.

CAMON
▲ Château Accueil
Château de Camon, 3 pl Philippe de Levis, 09500 **Map** 11E3
📞 05 61 68 28 28
📠 05 61688156
💳 AE, DC, MC, V ● Mon
🍴 €€€€ 🍷 (10) €€€€

This enchanting turreted château is set amidst immaculate gardens. New takes on old favourites include foie gras with ceps, and pigeon with honey. Baronial splendour in the guestrooms.

CASTAGNEDE
▲ La Belle Auberge
Bourg, 64270 **Map** 11D3
📞 05 59 38 15 28
📠 05 59 65 03 57
💳 DC, MC, V ● Sun, Mon; Dec–Jan
🍴 €€ 🍷 (15) €€

Pleasant hotel with a swimming pool, leafy surroundings and characterful rooms. The dining experience is full of surprises, with several dishes having Persian or Oriental touches.

CASTELNAU-MAGNOAC
▲ Manoir de la Grange
On D929, 65230 **Map** 10C3
📞 05 62 99 85 33
📠 06 89 10 00 73
💳 MC, V 🍴 € 🍷 (7) €€€

Large 16th-century manor with sprawling grounds, a swimming pool and stables. Some of the guestrooms have quirky fabrics and others exude 19th-century refinement. There's also a four-bedroom cottage. Set dinner served Sunday and Wednesday evenings to hotel guests.

CAUTERETS
▲ Hôtel Balneo Aladin
11 ave Général Leclerc, 65110
Map 10C4
📞 05 62 92 60 00
📠 05 62 92 63 30

w www.hotelbalneoaladin.com
🎫 DC, MC, V ● Apr–Jun, 3rd wk
Sep–3rd wk Dec 🍴 €€ 🍽 (70) €€€
*This modern hotel may lack character,
but the minimalist-style guestrooms are
well equipped. The restaurant buffet is in
a bright, modern dining hall. The health
centre has a pool, spa and sunbeds.*

CAUTERETS
▲ Lion d'Or
12 rue Richelieu, 65110 **Map** 11E3
📞 05 62 92 52 87
FAX 05 62 92 03 67
🎫 AE, MC, V ● 3rd wk Sep–3rd wk
Dec 🍴 € 🍽 (24) €€
*Victorian building near the spa of this
beautiful mountain resort. The intimate
restaurant serves tasty southwestern
fare. Guestrooms retain a quirky 19th-
century atmosphere.*

CHIS
▲ La Ferme St-Ferréol
20 rue Pyrénées, 65800 **Map** 10C3
📞 05 62 36 22 15
FAX 05 62 37 64 96
🎫 DC, MC, V ● Sep–Jun: Sat L, Sun
🍴 €€€ 🍽 (19) €€
*Large pink-hued building with a restful
courtyard for dining on scrumptious
southwestern offerings such as foie gras
with nettles. Cheery guestrooms.*

DURFORT
▲ Le Bourdieu
Off the D14 south of Durfort, 09130
Map 11D3
📞 05 61 67 30 17
FAX 05 61 67 29 00
w www.lebourdieu.com
● Sun D, Mon 🍴 €€ 🍽 (39) €
*Surrounded by rolling hills and wood-
land, this restaurant oozes rustic charm.
The hearty Pyrenean menu includes
trout, duck and chocolate profiteroles.
Simple chalets or camping are available.*

ESPELETTE
▲ Euzkadi
28 rue Karrika Nagusia, 64250 **Map** 10A3
📞 05 59 93 91 88
FAX 05 59 93 90 19
🎫 AE, MC, V ● Mon, Oct–Jun: Tue
🍴 €€ 🍽 (32) €€

*Rooms are quite small but have nice
big beds. Generous helpings of* garbure
(p353) *are on the menu.*

ESPELETTE
■ Irazabala
Quartier Le Ahar Keta, 64250 **Map** 10A3
📞 05 59 93 93 02
🎫 MC, V ● Mon, Tue; Nov–3rd wk
Dec 🍽 (2) €€
*Rooms are a little twee, but comfortable.
Children are welcome. The breakfast
alone is worth the stay.*

ESTAING
▲ Hôtel du Lac
Village centre, 65400 **Map** 10B3
📞 05 62 97 06 25
🎫 MC, V ● mid-Oct–May
🍴 € 🍽 (8) €€
*The dramatic mountain scenery more
than makes up for the guestrooms,
which are simple and a little cramped.
Sample lamb with lemon and bilberries
followed by a soup of forest fruits.*

FOIX
▲ Brasserie du XIX Siecle
at Hôtel Lons
Hotel: 6 pl Georges Duthil, brasserie:
2 rue Delcassé, 09000 **Map** 11E3
📞 Hotel: 05 61 65 52 44, Brasserie:
05 61 65 12 10
FAX 05 61 02 68 18
🎫 AE, DC, MC, V ● Sun, Fri D, Sat
L; May, 3rd wk Dec–3rd wk Jan
🍴 €€ 🍽 (38) €€
*Perched on a terrace over the river
Ariège, and noted for its fish (including
grilled salmon) and hors d'oeuvre buffets.
Comprehensive regional wine list. The
guestrooms have 1970s decor.*

FOIX
▲ La Charmille
25 quartier St-Antoine, St-Paul-de-Jarrat,
6km (4 miles) south on RN20 and D117,
09000 **Map** 11E3
📞 05 61 64 17 03
FAX 05 61 64 10 05
🎫 AE, DC, MC, V ● Mon; Oct–Jun:
Sun D, Tue; 1st wk Jul, first 2 wks Oct,
first 2 wks Feb 🍴 €€ 🍽 (10) €
*Sculptures and paintings fill the public
areas and there are jazz concerts. Tasty*

*local fare is available at the bar. Rooms
have sophisticated elegance.*

FOIX
● Le Jeu de l'Oie
17 rue Lafaurie, 09000 **Map** 11E3
📞 05 61 02 69 39
🎫 AE, DC, MC, V ● Sun 🍴 €€
*A great little restaurant in the centre of
town, offering confit de canard (p326)
and foie gras, or a wide choice of fish.*

FOIX
● Le Medieval
42 rue des Chapeliers, 09000 **Map** 11E3
📞 05 34 09 01 72
FAX 05 34 09 01 73
🎫 MC, V ● Sun D, Mon 🍴 €€
*In the heart of the town, near the
imposing Château de Foix, this old-world
restaurant has two dining rooms offering
plenty of atmosphere and intimacy.
Beautifully cooked fish, including mullet
and tuna, are livened up with Spanish
and Provençal influences.*

FOIX
● Le Sainte Marthe
21 pl Lazéma, rue Noël Peyrévidal,
09000 **Map** 11E3
📞 05 61 02 87 87
FAX 05 61 05 19 00
w www.le-saintemarthe.fr
🎫 AE, DC, MC, V ● Sep–Jun: Tue,
Wed; last 2 wks Jan 🍴 €€€
*Book to secure a table on the plant-filled
terrace here. Finish with Bethmale
cheeses and a glass of Margaux.*

FOIX
● Phoebus
3 cours Irénée Cros, 09000 **Map** 11E3
📞 05 61 65 10 42
FAX 05 61 65 10 42
🎫 AE, DC, MC, V ● Sat L, Mon;
mid-Jul–mid-Aug 🍴 €€
*Enchanting panorama over the river.
Run by an award-winning chef specializing
in inventive dishes such as pike-perch
cooked in Armagnac and caramel.*

FOIX
● Régis Amiel
Ave du Général Leclerc, route Espagne,
09000 **Map** 11E3

C 05 61 02 69 00

FAX 05 61 05 68 08

● Sun; 3rd wk Aug **11** €€

One of Ariège's most highly regarded patisseries. The secret lies in a lengthy kneading process for lush, smooth chocolate. Perfect for tea and a sweet.

GAVARNIE

▲ Grand Hôtel Vignemale

Chemin du Cirque, 65120 **Map** 10C4

C 05 62 92 40 00

FAX 05 62 92 40 08

W www.hotel-vignemale.com

✉ AE, DC, MC, V ● Oct–mid-May

11 €€€ 🍽 (24) €€€€

Handsome early-20th-century hotel near the Cirque de Gavarnie. Dishes include cassoulet (p373) and confit de canard (p326). Rooms have awe-inspiring views. Dinner served only for hotel guests.

GAVARNIE

▲ Le Marboré

Le Village, 65120 **Map** 10C4

C 05 62 92 40 40

FAX 05 62 92 40 30

✉ AE, DC, MC, V ● Nov–3rd wk Dec

11 € 🍽 (24) €€

Gavarnie's best-value hotel has a pub-restaurant, Le Swan. Specialities include veal with morels, prawn salad and magret de canard. Many of the guestrooms have breathtaking views.

GERDE

● L'Auberge Gourmande

4 pl 14 Juillet, 65200 **Map** 10C3

C 05 62 95 52 01

✉ DC, MC, V ● Tue, Wed; Nov

11 €€

Seafood-lovers will be in heaven: try the king prawns with pesto. The fine dessert list includes a delicious peach tart.

HOPITAL-ST-BLAISE

▲ Auberge du Lausset

Pl de L'Eglise, Bourg, 64130 **Map** 10B3

C 05 59 66 53 03

FAX 05 59 66 21 78

✉ MC, V ● Mon; mid-Oct–Jan

11 €€ 🍽 (7) €

Lovely rural farmhouse by a church in a peaceful, quiet location. Guestrooms are decorated with soft colours. The menu

includes steak with bilberries, and crêpes with cream cheese and spinach.

IBOS

● La Vieille Auberge

51 route de Pau, 65420 **Map** 10C3

C 05 62 31 51 54

FAX 05 62 31 55 59

✉ MC, V

● Sun D, Mon; last 2 wks Aug

11 €€

Try the Espelette peppers for a taste of the sun. Seafood, veal and lamb are menu mainstays. Quality wines.

JUILLAN

▲ L'Aragon

2 ter route Lourdes, 65290 **Map** 10C3

C 05 62 32 07 07

FAX 05 62 32 92 50

✉ AE, DC, MC, V ● Sun D; first 3 wks Aug, 3rd wk Dec–1st wk Jan

11 €€ 🍽 (12) €€

The langoustine salad and grilled beef fillet are menu mainstays. Desserts include tarte Tatin (p191) *with a rich Calvados cream, warm Grand Marnier soufflé and* baba au rhum (p119). *Some rooms are beguilingly eccentric.*

LA BASTIDE-CLAIRENCE

▲ La Maison Sainbois

Rue Notre Dame, 64240 **Map** 10A3

C 05 59 29 54 20

FAX 05 59 29 65 53

W www.sainbois.fr

✉ AE, DC, MC, V ● Sun, Mon L

11 €€ 🍽 (5) €€€€

An old inn with grand bedrooms and luxurious bathrooms. Dishes include tuna and marmitako (p352) *or* axoa, *a truly remarkable lamb and great Esplette pepper stew.*

LABARTHE-SUR-LEZE

● La Rose des Vents

2292 route du Plantaurel, 31860 **Map** 11D3

C 05 61 08 67 01

FAX 05 61 08 85 84

✉ AE, DC, MC, V ● Sun D, Mon, Tue; first wk Jan, mid-Aug–1st wk Sep

11 €€

Joël Lamothe has earned a reputation for himself by offering a refined interior

with a lovely terrace overlooking gardens, and a balanced menu that reworks traditional Pyrenean recipes.

LABARTHE-SUR-LEZE

● Poeion

Pl Vincent Auriol, 31860 **Map** 11D3

C 05 61 08 68 49

FAX 05 61 08 68 48

✉ MC, V ● Sun, Mon; 3rd wk Dec–1st wk Jan **11** €€€

Great surroundings – two old-world dining rooms – great food, using the freshest fish and game, and a great wine cellar.

LE BOSC

▲ Auberge Les Myrtilles

Col des Marrous, Le Bosc, 19km (11 miles) south on D17, 09000 **Map** 11D3

C 05 61 65 16 46

FAX 05 61 65 16 46

✉ AE, DC, MC, V ● Mon, Oct–Jul: Tue; Nov–Feb **11** € 🍽 (7) €€

Breathtaking views, excellent facilities and a chalet restaurant that specializes in hearty local dishes such as cassoulet (p373) and fresh trout. Indoor swimming pool, Jacuzzi and sauna complex. Well-kept accommodation with wooden beams lending Alpine charm.

LE FAUGA

● Le Château de la Mandre

3 rue Cazalères, 31410 **Map** 11D3

C 05 61 56 74 94

FAX 05 61 56 73 43

✉ AE, DC, MC, V ● Mon, Tue; 3 wks Aug **11** €€

A handsome building with an intimate restaurant. Favourites include foie gras and cassoulet (p326). Lengthy wine list and a great selection of local cheeses.

LESSCAR

▲ La Terrasse

1 rue Maubec, 64230 **Map** 10B3

C 05 59 81 02 34

FAX 05 59 81 08 77

✉ MC, V ● Sun, Sat L; Jan, 3rd wk Feb **11** €€ 🍽 (22) €€

A lovely little place with comfy, country-style guestrooms. Authentic Béarnaise food with interesting Italian twists, such as local sausage with polenta. The minty pea soup is deliciously sweet and fresh.

LONS

▲ Le Fer à Cheval

1 ave des Martyrs, 64140 **Map** 10B3

[C] 05 59 32 17 40

[FAX] 05 59 72 97 53

[w] www.leferacheval.com

[card] AE, MC, V ● Oct–May: Sat, Sun; Jun–Sep: Wed [11] €€ ◆ (8) €€

Set in beautiful grounds, this hotel offers peace and tranquillity near Pau. Rooms are light and airy with very big beds. The limited menu showcases the very best of Béarn, and food is well presented.

LORP-SENTARAILLES

▲ Horizon 117

Route de Toulouse (D117), 09190 **Map** 11D3

[C] 05 61 66 26 80

[FAX] 05 61 66 26 08

[w] www.horizon117.com

[card] AE, DC, MC, V ● Sun D, Sat L; 1st wk Nov [11] €€ ◆ (20) €€

A modern hotel with superb facilities and a jaw-dropping backdrop of peaks. The menu boasts confit de canard (p326) terrine, foie gras and Couserans pigeon, and the wine list spans Languedoc-Roussillon and Bordeaux.

LOURDES

▲ Grand Hôtel de la Grotte

66 rue Grotte, 65100 **Map** 10C3

[C] 05 62 42 39 34

[FAX] 05 62 94 20 50

[w] www.hotel-grotte.com

[card] AE, DC, MC, V ● Nov–Apr [11] €€€ ◆ (82) €€€

Grand 19th-century building with a clean, modern feel. Regional specialities in the restaurant and international dishes in the brasserie. Some rooms have Louis XVI-style furnishings.

LOURDES

▲ La Taverne de Bigorre

21 pl Champ Commun, 65100 **Map** 10C3

[C] 05 62 94 75 00

[FAX] 05 62 94 78 45

[@] albret.taverne.Lourdes@libertysurf.fr

[card] AE, DC, MC, V ● Sun D, Mon; 3rd wk Nov–1st wk Feb

[11] €€ ◆ (27) €€

Comfortable accommodation and good food served in a modern dining room.

Look out for the salmon in white wine, and foie gras with caramelized apple.

LOURDES

▲ Le Chalet de Biscaye

26 route du Lac, 65100 **Map** 10C3

[C] 05 62 94 12 26

[FAX] 05 62 94 26 29

[card] DC, MC, V ● Mon, Tue; Jan

[11] €€ ◆ (13) €€€

Cosy hotel surrounded by trees and near the lake. Seafood specialities include turbot in breadcrumbs. The terrace and swimming pool are tranquil havens.

LOURDES

● Le Magret

10 R4 Frères Soulas, 65100 **Map** 10C3

[C] 05 62 94 20 55

[card] AE, DC, MC, V

● Mon; last 3 wks Jan [11] €€€

Unpretentious southwestern food served in an intimate rustic setting. Highlights include lamb with white beans.

LOURDES

▲ Les Rocailles

Omex, 65100 **Map** 10C3

[C] 05 62 94 46 19

[FAX] 05 62 94 33 35

[card] MC, V ● first 2 wks Nov, Apr

[11] € ◆ (3) €€

Enchanting 17th-century house in the Basturguere valley. Spacious bedrooms with attractive wooden furniture. The hotel's vegetable garden provides many ingredients for the fabulous country cooking. Reservations essential.

LUDIES

▲ Château de Ludiès

On D511, 09100 **Map** 11E3

[C] 05 61 69 67 45

[FAX] 05 61 67 39 26

● Wed (restaurant); Jan

[11] €€ ◆ (6) €€€

Exposed brickwork, stone floors, antique ceramics and pastoral artworks imbue this 18th-century château with rustic charm. The menu focuses on local specialities, plus barbecues in summer.

MARTRES-TOLOSANE

▲ Castet

Ave de la Gare, 31220 **Map** 11D3

[C] 05 61 98 80 20

[FAX] 05 61 98 61 02

[card] AE, MC, V ● Sun D, Mon; 3rd wk Oct–1st wk Nov [11] € ◆ (10) €€

A traditional auberge with specialities that include snail casserole and beef ribs. The terrace is pleasant.

MAS-D'AZIL

▲ Le Jardin de Cadettou

Faubourg St-Féréol, 09290 **Map** 11D3

[C] 05 61 69 95 23

[w] www.cadettou.fr

[card] MC, V ● Sun, Mon, Sat L; Jan

[11] €€€ ◆ (3) €€

A much-loved village establishment with a terrace overlooking lovely gardens. Culinary highlights include salmon with sorrel, and sweet apple omelette. Spotless guestrooms with white walls.

MAZERES

▲ Maison Martimor

10 rue Martimor, 09270 **Map** 11E3

[C] 05 61 69 42 81

● Jan [11] € ◆ (5) €€

This grand 18th-century château is a great place to unwind, but reservations are a must. Cassoulet (p373) and wonderful fish dishes regularly grace the menu. Guestrooms are traditional.

MELLES

▲ Auberge du Crabère

Village centre, 31440 **Map** 11D4

[C] 05 61 79 21 99

[FAX] 05 61 79 74 71

[card] MC, V ● Tue D, Wed; 3rd wk Nov–mid-Dec [11] €€ ◆ (6) €€

Charming auberge serving pig's trotters with morels and a forest fruit tart. Good selection of wines and choice of cigars. Small, simple guestrooms.

MIREPOIX

■ La Maison des Consuls

6 pl Maréchal Leclerc, 09500 **Map** 11E3

[C] 05 61 68 81 81

[FAX] 05 61 68 81 15

[card] AE, DC, MC, V ◆ (8) €€€€

A beautiful 14th-century town house where guestrooms are filled with an eclectic array of antiques. Café des Maquignons serves breakfast and snacks. Reservations essential.

MIREPOIX

▲ Le Commerce

8 rue de l'Evêché, cours du Docteur
Chabaud, 09500 **Map** 11E3

🄲 05 61 68 10 29

FAX 05 61 68 20 99

🆆 www.le-commerce.fr

🅔 AE, DC, MC, V ⬤ Sep–Jun: Sat;
Jan, 3rd wk Nov

🕕 €€ ➲ (32) €€

*A charming coaching inn built around a
leafy courtyard. A no-nonsense menu
with* cassoulet (p373), *foie gras, and
monkfish cooked in a Pyrenean liqueur.
Rooms are well appointed.*

MIREPOIX

⬤ Les Ramparts

6 cours Louis Pons Tande, 09500
Map 11E3

🄲 05 61 68 12 15

🅔 AE, DC

⬤ Mon; Jul

🕕 €

*Locals flock here for the fresh trout
cooked with* Hyprocras, *a local liqueur.
The desserts and cigars are first-rate.*

MONTSEGUR

⬤ L'Occitadelle

12 village, 09300 **Map** 11E4

🄲 05 61 01 21 77

FAX 05 61 01 80 26

⬤ Tue; mid-Nov–Feb 🕕 €

*Enchanting dining in the former Cathar
stronghold of Château Montségur.
Dishes includes grilled liver sausage and
rabbit with prunes.*

MURET

▲ Il Paradiso

350 route de Rieumes, 31600 **Map** 11D3

🄲 05 61 56 39 73

FAX 05 61 56 39 73

🅔 AE, DC, MC, V

⬤ Sun D, Mon (restaurant); 3rd wk
Nov–mid-Dec

🕕 €€ ➲ (3) €€

*Surrounded by flower-filled gardens, this
converted farm serves the best Italian
food in the region. Enjoy classic
Neapolitan dishes such as aubergine
(eggplant) with mozzarella and
Parmesan, grilled fish and* tiramisu.
Swimming pool and charming rooms.

NAILLOUX-MONTGEARD

⬤ Ferme de Champreux

Champreux, 31560 **Map** 11E3

🄲 05 61 81 33 13

FAX 05 61 27 05 14

🅔 AE, DC, MC, V ⬤ Mon 🕕 €€

*Near a lake and nature reserve, this is a
great place to eat wholesome local food.
On the menu, cured meat salads and
grilled lamb, rabbit and beef.*

NALZEN

⬤ Les Sapins

Route de Foix, 09300 **Map** 11E4

🄲 05 61 03 03 85

FAX 05 61 03 03 85

🅔 AE, DC, MC, V

⬤ Wed 🕕 €€€

*Modern interpretations of classic Ariège
dishes grace the menu. Highlights
include quail with spinach and a devilish
chocolate* fondant *with vanilla sauce.*

NESTIER

▲ Relais du Castéra

Pl du Calvaire, 65150 **Map** 10C3

🄲 05 62 39 77 37

FAX 05 62 39 77 29

🅔 DC, MC, V ⬤ Sun D, Mon;
Oct–May: Tue; 3 wks Jan, 1st wk Jun

🕕 €€ ➲ (7) €€

The distinctive flavours include haricots
tarbais (white beans), *Gascon pork and
freshwater fish. An excellent wine list
and cheese selection. Cosy guestrooms.*

NIAUX

⬤ La Petite Auberge de Niaux

Village centre, 09400 **Map** 11E4

🄲 05 61 05 79 79

FAX 05 61 05 79 70

🅔 AE, MC, V ⬤ Sun D, Mon; last 2
wks Nov, last 2 wks Mar 🕕 €€

*Informal atmosphere. Enjoy salads and
pastries, rolled veal with pine nuts and
snails. Lovely terrace and garden.*

ODOS

▲ Le Concorde

61 ave Lourdes, 65310 **Map** 10C3

🄲 05 62 93 51 18

FAX 05 62 93 78 40

🆆 www.hotel-concorde-tarbes.com

🅔 AE, DC, MC, V ⬤ Sat, Sun; end
Dec–early Jan 🕕 €€ ➲ (42) €€

*Modern hotel with excellent creature
comforts including a swimming pool and
a piano bar. Traditional fare, including
pigeon. Functional guestrooms.*

OLORON-STE-MARIE

▲ Alysson Hôtel

Bd des Pyrénées, 64400 **Map** 10B3

🄲 05 59 39 70 70

FAX 05 59 39 24 47

🅔 AE, DC, MC, V ⬤ Oct–May: Fri,
Sat; Jan 🕕 €€ ➲ (32) €€€

*Hotel-restaurant on green plains fringed
by the Pyrenees. Rooms are small but
fresh and modern. Superb quality food
and service, and you can enjoy a
Cognac outside, under the stars.*

OUST

▲ Hostellerie de la Poste

Rue principale, le village, 09140
Map 11D4

🄲 05 61 66 86 33

FAX 05 61 66 86 33

🅔 DC, MC, V ⬤ Sun D, Mon, Tue L;
Nov–Apr 🕕 €€ ➲ (25) €€

*A peaceful village inn with a leafy
terrace and spacious dining room. The
menu has a bias towards meat dishes,
especially pork, lamb and pigeon. The
best guestrooms open onto the garden.*

PAMIERS

▲ Hôtel de La Paix

4 pl Albert Tournier, 09100 **Map** 11E3

🄲 05 61 67 12 71

FAX 05 61 60 61 02

🅔 MC, V

🕕 €€ ➲ (16) €€

*An 18th-century inn with a curious neo-
classical interior. The restaurant focuses
on regional specialities. Guestrooms are
decorated in warm colours.*

PAMIERS

▲ Le Roi Gourmand

21 rue Pierre Sémard, 09100 **Map** 11E3

🄲 05 61 60 12 12

FAX 05 61 60 16 66

🅔 AE, DC, MC, V ⬤ Sun D

🕕 € ➲ (20) €€

*In the heart of Pamiers. Innovative menu
boasting warm foie gras infused with
fragrant* Hyprocras *liqueur and a great
dessert list. Well-equipped guestrooms.*

PAU

● Best & British

26 bd des Pyrénées, 64000 **Map** 10B3

🅒 05 59 98 44 02

🍴 AE, DC, MC, V 🍽 €

Stylish deckchairs and wooden tables on the esplanade for taking in views of the Pyrenees. Inside the decor is all cool white. Simple Mediterranean food. Order cured hams, cheeses and salads.

PAU

● Chez Pierre

Rue Louis Barthou, 64000 **Map** 10B3

🅒 05 59 27 76 86

FAX 05 59 27 08 14

🍴 AE, DC, MC, V ● Sun, Mon L, Sat L; mid-Aug, first wk Jan 🍽 €€

Open since 1924, this is one of Pau's best restaurants. Each dish has a local flavour, like cod with esplette peppers.

PAU

● Chocolaterie de la Couronne

29 palais des Pyrénées, 64000 **Map** 10B3

🅒 05 59 82 83 77

🍴 AE, MC, V

● 20 Palais des Pyrénées 🍽 €

The oversized chocolates here are extremely popular. Their medailles Henri IV make wonderful presents, but the praline noisettes, shaped into huge half domes, weaken resolve. Coffee served.

PAU

▲ Hôtel Continental

2 rue du Maréchal Foch, 64000 **Map** 10B3

🅒 05 59 27 69 31

FAX 05 59 27 99 84

🍴 AE, DC, MC, V

🍽 €€ 🛏 (80) €€€

Pau isn't a great place for hotels, but this one is well situated in the heart of the city. Guestrooms are a decent size and well kept. The restaurant has good meals.

PAU

● Le Viking

33 bd Tourasse, 64000 **Map** 10B3

🅒 05 59 84 02 91

FAX 05 59 80 21 05

🍴 AE, DC, MC, V ● Sun D, Mon D, Sat L; 2 wks in Aug 🍽 €€

Superb, cheery eatery serving dishes such as beignets de fleur de courgette (p400), foie gras ravioli, and coconut with lime and rum.

PAU

● Les Pyrénées

9 pl Royale, 64000 **Map** 10B3

🅒 05 59 27 07 75

FAX 05 59 06 52 18

🍴 DC, V ● Sun 🍽 €€

Stylish wine-bar-cum-restaurant. Superb cheeseboard, pastries, salads and fine wines. Sit outside on the tree-lined square or on the smart mezzanine.

POUYASTRUC

● Aou Soum

15 route Bigorre, 65350 **Map** 10C3

🅒 05 62 33 24 60

FAX 05 62 33 24 60

🍴 MC, V ● Mon, Tue; 2 wks Aug

🍽 €€

The southwestern menu specializes in fish. The duck cooked in cider and served with apples is a favourite.

REVEL

▲ Auberge des Mazies

Route de Castres, 3km (2 miles) north of Revel on D622, 31250 **Map** 11C3

🅒 05 61 27 69 70

FAX 05 62 18 06 37

@ bievenue@maizes.com

🍴 AE, DC, MC, V

● Sun D, Mon; 3rd wk Oct–mid-Nov, 3rd wk Dec–3rd wk Jan

🍽 €€ 🛏 (7) €€

A fabulous auberge that's synonymous with fine dining and relaxation. The high quality of the regional cuisine, and the substantial wine list, are a strong draw.

REVEL

▲ Hôtel du Midi

34 bd Gambetta, 31250 **Map** 11C3

🅒 05 61 83 50 50

FAX 05 61 83 34 74

🍴 DC, MC, V ● mid-Oct–Apr: Sun D, Mon L; mid-Nov–early Dec

🍽 €€ 🛏 (17) €€

Comfortable 19th-century coaching inn with a bright and cheery dining room and a popular outside terrace. Starters include juicy pepper salad and tuna

tartare; mains are dominated by meat, with veal the house speciality.

REVEL

● Le Lauragais

25 ave Castelnaudary, 31250 **Map** 11C3

🅒 05 61 83 51 22

FAX 05 62 18 91 79

🍴 AE, DC, MC, V 🍽 €€

Behind an ivy-covered façade, Le Lauragais opens into a spacious warehouse. Seafood-lovers are well catered for, while other regional classics on the menu include poultry, game and stews.

ROQUEFIXADE

▲ Le Relais des Trois Châteaux

Palot, between Foix and Lavelanet on D117, 09300 **Map** 11E3

🅒 05 61 01 33 99

FAX 05 61 01 73 73

🆆 www.troischateaux.com

🍴 AE, DC, MC, V

● Sun D, Tue, Sat L; last 2 wks Nov; mid-Jan–early Feb 🍽 €€ 🛏 (7) €€

An amazing auberge, set in enchanting countryside, with a restaurant serving regional dishes. Well-appointed rooms, as well as a swimming pool and sauna.

SAUVETERRE-DE-COMMINGES

▲ Les Sept Molles

Gesset, 31510 **Map** 10C3

🅒 05 61 88 30 87

FAX 05 61 88 36 42

🍴 AE, DC, MC, V

● Oct–Mar: Tue, Wed L, Thu L; mid-Feb–mid-Mar

🍽 €€€ 🛏 (20) €€€€

Set around pristine gardens dotted with millstones (from which the hotel takes its name) and serving luxurious local cuisine. Swimming pool, clay tennis court and well-equipped guestrooms.

SEVIGNACQ-MEYRACQ

▲ Les Bains de Secours

Route Bains de Secours, 64260 **Map** 10B3

🅒 05 59 05 62 11

FAX 05 59 05 76 56

🍴 AE, DC, MC, V ● Sun D, Mon, Thu L; Jan 🍽 €€ 🛏 (7) €€

Small hotel, perfectly situated for visitors to the nearby thermal baths. Rooms

● Restaurant　■ Hotel　▲ Hotel / Restaurant

have bright flowery bedspreads and compact bathrooms. The menu features peasant-style food plus finer cuisine.

ST-BERTRAND-DE-COMMINGES
■ Comminges
Cathedrale St-Bertrand-de-Comminges, 31510 **Map** 10C3
📞 05 61 88 31 43
FAX 05 61 94 98 22
💳 DC, MC, V ● Nov–Apr
🍽 (14) €€

A charming converted convent with bags of character and an interior crammed with lovely antiques.

ST-BERTRAND-DE-COMMINGES
● Le Lugdunum
Valcabrère, 2km (1.2 miles) east on D26, 31510 **Map** 10C3
📞 05 61 94 52 05
FAX 05 61 94 52 06
W www.lugdunum-restaurant.com
💳 DC, MC, V ● Jul–Sep: Mon & Tue D
🍽 €€

Stunning views of the Romanesque cathedral. The cuisine of ancient Rome is on the seasonal menu, with meat dishes prepared in herbs and spices.

ST-FELIX-LAURAGAIS
▲ Auberge du Poids Public
Rue St-Roch, 31540 **Map** 11E3
📞 05 62 18 85 00
FAX 05 61 88 85 05
💳 AE, MC, V
● Sun D; Jan, 1st wk Nov
🍽 €€€ (10) €€€

Widely praised as being one of the best in the region, the restaurant has it all: a lovely terrace with views, great food and a first-class wine list. Guestrooms are decorated with flowery fabrics.

ST-FELIX-LAURAGAIS
● Baron de Roquette Buisson
Bordeneuve, 31540 **Map** 11E3
📞 05 61 83 02 23
FAX 05 62 18 91 93
W www.baron-de-roquette.com
💳 AE, DC, MC, V 🍽 €

The number one purveyor of regional delicacies in the mid-Pyrenees. Everything from foie gras and pâtés to confits and terrines line the shelves

here. Sit down for a sample of the foods with a glass of wine.

ST-GAUDENS
▲ Beaurivage
Bd Sommer, quart Pont de Valentine, 31800 **Map** 11D3
📞 05 61 94 76 70
FAX 05 61 94 76 79
💳 AE, MC, V ● Sun D, Mon
🍽 €€€ (10) €€

Quality ingredients include truffles, turbot, salmon and shellfish. Wooden beams lend a rustic feel and a sleek bar provides a modern edge. Spacious guestrooms.

ST-GAUDENS
▲ Hôtel du Commerce
Ave de Boulogne, 31800 **Map** 11D3
📞 05 62 00 97 00
FAX 05 62 00 97 01
W www.commerce31.com
💳 AE, DC, MC, V ● last 2 wks Dec
🍽 €€€ (50) €€

A modern hotel. The sophisticated kitchen concentrates on light dishes during the summer (such as salmon and turbot) and filling regional favourites in winter. Excellent guestrooms.

ST-GAUDENS
● La Connivence
Ave Foch, La Valentine, 31800 **Map** 11D3
📞 05 61 95 29 31
FAX 05 61 88 36 42
💳 AE, MC, V ● Mon, Sat L 🍽 €€

A rustic dining room, regional cuisine and live music at the weekends all conspire to create a quintessentially Pyrenean experience. Firm favourites with the loyal clientele include game with mushrooms and grilled fish.

ST-GAUDENS
▲ Les Cèdres
Rue Eglise, Villeneuve-de-Rivière, 31800 **Map** 11D3
📞 05 61 89 36 00
FAX 05 61 88 31 04
💳 AE, MC, V ● Oct–May: Sun, Mon L, Jun–Sep: Mon L, Tue L
🍽 €€€ (22) €€€

Immaculately kept and deservedly popular, this sophisticated hotel and restaurant are beautifully set in cedar-

filled grounds complete with swimming pool. Modern guestrooms.

ST-GIRONS
▲ Eychenne
8 ave Paul Laffont, 09200 **Map** 11D3
📞 05 61 04 04 50
FAX 05 61 96 07 20
W www.ariege.com/hotel-eychenne
💳 AE, DC, MC, V ● Sun D, Mon; Nov–Mar
🍽 €€€€ (44) €€€€

A beautifully renovated coaching inn. Rooms have a crisp Regency feel, and the dining room has a stately air. The menu includes duck liver, sole with ceps and classic French desserts.

ST-GIRONS
▲ La Clairière
Ave de la Résistance, 09200 **Map** 11D3
📞 05 61 66 66 66
FAX 05 34 14 30 30
W www.ariege.com/la-clairiere
💳 AE, DC, MC, V ● Sun D, Mon
🍽 €€€ (19) €€

Attractively set in parkland and even equipped with a swimming pool. Feast on Pyrenean favourites, such as lamb infused with thyme. Modern guestrooms.

ST-JEAN-DE-LUZ
● Le Petit Grill Basque
2–4 rue St-Jacques, 64500 **Map** 10A3
📞 05 59 26 80 76
💳 MC, V ● Wed; Dec–Jan 🍽 €€

For the best morro (fish soup) in town, this old restaurant hits the spot. Don't miss the rustic seafood, prepared in traditional Basque style.

ST-JEAN-DE-LUZ
● Pantxua
37 rue du Commandant Passicot, 64500 **Map** 10A3
📞 05 59 47 13 73
FAX 05 59 47 01 54
💳 DC, MC, V ● Sep–Jun: Mon, Tue; Jul–Aug: Tue; Nov–Feb 🍽 €€

Reservations are a must for this popular seaside restaurant. Expect flame-grilled king prawns in a tasty hot vinegar dressing, and sardines smothered in a garlicky tomato salsa. Sumptuous yet delicate sorbets too.

ST-JEAN-DE-LUZ
▲ **Parc Victoria**
5 rue Cépé, 64500 **Map** 10A3
[05 59 26 78 78
FAX 05 59 26 78 08
W www.parcvictoria.com
AE, DC, MC, V ● Wed; Nov–Mar
11 €€€€ ◒ (16) €€€€€

Outside of the busy centre, this grand white hotel has a swimming pool, a garden and relaxing guestrooms. The restaurant serves French classics, on the terrace during warmer months.

ST-JULIA
● **Auberge des Remparts**
Cers rue Vinaigre, 31540 **Map** 11E3
[05 61 83 04 79
AE, DC, MC, V ● Sun D, Mon D, Tue D **11** €

Deservedly popular for great-value food, this place is a quintessential medieval auberge. The menu is divided equally between the land (grilled meats) and the sea (red mullet salad and fresh scallops). The wine cellar is well stocked.

ST-LARY-SOULAN
● **La Grange**
13 route Autun, 65170 **Map** 11E3
[05 62 40 07 14
MC, V ● Tue D, Wed; 3rd wk Apr–May, mid-Nov–mid-Dec **11** €€

A wonderfully atmospheric dining room serving regional produce with a dash of Mediterranean flair. The flambés make a warming, wholesome winter snack.

ST-LARY-SOULAN
▲ **La Pergola**
25 rue Vincent Mir, 65170 **Map** 10C4
[05 62 39 40 46
FAX 05 62 40 06 55
AE, DC, MC, V ● 2nd wk Nov, first 2 wks Dec **11** €€€ ◒ (20) €€

Located in the spectacular Vallée d'Aure and near the thermal baths. L'Enclos des Saveurs offers a sophisticated gastronomic experience, and La Pergola serves excellent regional fare. Bedrooms are rather plain, but some sublime vistas.

ST-LARY-SOULAN
● **Le Garlitz**
Pl d'Adet, résidence Garlitz Altitude,

65170 **Map** 10C4
[05 62 97 44 09
FAX 05 62 97 44 09
MC, V ● Mar & May–Jun & Oct–Nov: D **11** €€

In picturesque Place d'Adet, this is one of the town's best-loved eateries. Dine on expertly prepared regional specialities while admiring expansive views of the surrounding mountains. Superb value.

ST-MARTIN-D'ARBERQUE
● **Auberge Goxoki**
Maison Elichabeheria, 64640 **Map** 10A3
[05 59 29 64 71
MC, V ● Sun, Mon L **11** €

Chef Margaret Lienhardt uses quirky – at least for this region – ingredients such as fennel and figs, and weaves them into dishes of duckling, pigeon and esplette peppers. A great wine list showcasing the best independent producers and the best years.

ST-LARY-SOULAN
▲ **Pergola**
25 rue Vincent Mir, 65170 **Map** 10C4
[05 62 39 40 46
FAX 05 62 40 06 55
W www.hotellapergola.fr
AE, DC, MC, V ● Dec–Mar: Mon L, Tue L **11** €€ ◒ (20) €€€

Set deep in the Aure valley, which offers numerous outdoor activities, a thermal spa and plenty of unspoilt mountain village charm. Guestrooms are modern, comfortable and reasonably priced. Choose from two restaurants: L'Enclos des Saveurs for a true gastronomic experience, and La Pergola for more robust regional specialities.

ST-SAVIN
▲ **Le Viscos**
1 rue Lamarque, 65400 **Map** 10C3
[05 62 97 02 28
FAX 05 62 97 04 95
W www.hotel-leviscos.com
DC, MC, V ● Sun D, Sep–Jun: Mon; 2 wks Jan
11 €€€ ◒ (12) €€

A wonderful auberge near the village square. The food is some of the region's finest. Dishes include lamb in a juniper-berry-infused pastry. Guestrooms vary in

size, from small attic rooms to more spacious suites.

ST-SULPICE-SUR-LEZE
● **La Commanderie**
Pl de l'hotel de ville, 31410 **Map** 11D3
[05 61 97 33 61
FAX 05 61 97 32 60
MC, V ● Tue, Wed; Oct **11** €€

This superb restaurant, occupying part of a 13th-century building in the town's enchanting main square, specializes in inventively reworking regional recipes. Expect duck with figs and cassoulet (p373) with confit de canard (p326).

TARBES
● **Bistrot Lafontaine**
2 rue Jean Pellet, 65000 **Map** 10C3
[05 62 93 37 95
MC, V ● Sun, Mon **11** €

Good-value bistro that serves excellent regional cuisine. Notable creations include liver with prawns, and the classic magret de canard with caramelized pears and raspberry vinegar. Excellent wine list and cheeseboard.

TARBES
● **L' Ambroisie**
48 rue Abbé Torné, 65000 **Map** 10C3
[05 62 93 09 34
FAX 05 62 93 09 24
AE, DC, MC, V ● Sun, Mon; 1st wk May, mid-Jun, 3rd wk Dec
11 €€€

Much-lauded eatery in a 19th-century presbytery offering familiar favourites with a few inventive twists. Outstanding dishes include roast pigeon stuffed with foie gras and vegetables in wine, and superb turbot with a delicate creamy leek and onion mousse.

TARBES
● **Le Fil a la Patte**
30 rue Georges Lassalle, 65000
Map 10C3
[05 62 93 39 23
FAX 05 62 93 39 23
DC, MC, V ● Sun, Mon, Sat L; 2nd & 3rd wk Aug **11** €

Fabulous restaurant near the cathedral, where regional produce is used in inventive ways. Dishes include lamb with sautéed aubergine (eggplant) and cumin. Superb wine list and cheeseboard.

TARBES
● Le Petit Gourmand
62 ave Bertrand Barère, 65000
Map 10C3
[05 62 34 26 86
FAX 05 62 34 26 86
⊘ AE, DC, MC, V ● Sun D, Mon, Sat L; Aug–Sep 🏮 €€
One of Tarbes' best restaurants. Spanish and Italian cusine influence this menu which features wild mushroom lasagne and marquise au chocolat dessert.

TOURTOUSE
● Sentenac
Village centre, 09230 **Map** 11D3
[05 61 96 43 25
● Mon; Dec 🏮 €
A good-value restaurant in a tranquil Pyrenean village. Classic local dishes such as foie gras, cassoulet (p326) and cabbage soup are on the menu. Fruit pies for dessert, and some fine local wines and cheeses complete this no-nonsense culinary experience.

URRUGNE
▲ Chez Maïté
Pl de la Mairie, 64122 **Map** 10A3
[05 59 54 30 27
⊘ AE, DC, MC, V ● Sun D, Tue, Jul & Aug: Mon, Sep–Jun: Wed
🏮 €€€ ⊘ (7) €€€
Staff here ensure that you learn a little about the Basque country. The restaurant serves mouth-watering duck and lamb, and an amazing ox in Béarnaise sauce. Delicious desserts made from local apples. Guestrooms in warm hues.

USSAT
▲ Le Parc
Ornolac, Ussat-les-Bains, 09400
Map 11E4
[05 61 02 20 20
FAX 05 61 05 55 99
@ thermes.ussat@wanadoo.fr
⊘ AE, MC, V ● Nov–1st wk Jan
🏮 €€€ ⊘ (49) €€€
A modern hotel complex, set in parkland, near the thermal baths. Facilities include a swimming pool, tennis courts

and mini-golf. The sleek, ambience belies the traditional menu.

VARILHES
● Auberge Marinette
1 pl du Vieux Pont, 09120 **Map** 11E3
[05 61 60 84 84
FAX 05 61 67 29 56
⊘ AE, DC, MC, V ● Tue D, Wed
🏮 €€€
Chef Michel Faure is known for his innovative approach to classic local dishes such as beef steak and chestnut flan, making this one of the best places to get a real flavour of the region's cuisine. Picturesque terrace and spacious dining rooms.

VIC-EN-BIGORRE
▲ Le Réverbère
29 rue de Alsace, 65500 **Map** 10C3
[05 62 96 78 16
FAX 05 62 96 79 85
⊘ AE, DC, MC, V ● Sun D, Mon L, Sat; 3rd wk Dec–1st wk Jan
🏮 €€ ⊘ (10) €€
Plant-filled bistro offering some of the town's finest southwestern cuisine. Exquisite seafood dishes, including fine roast perch cooked in Madiran wine, and many classic pork and lamb dishes. Guestrooms have a modern feel.

VIC-EN-BIGORRE
▲ Le Tivoli
Pl Gambetta, 65500 **Map** 10C3
[05 62 96 70 39
FAX 05 62 96 29 74
W www.hotel-resto-tivoli65.com
⊘ AE, DC, MC, V ● Mon
🏮 € ⊘ (27) €€
Reliable modern hotel offering good value. Southwestern specialities abound at the restaurant, such as liver with pears, caramelized chocolate soufflé and pistachio ice cream. Book a table on the large terrace. Guestrooms are spacious.

VILLEFRANCHE-DE-LAURAGAIS
▲ Hostellerie du Chef Jean
Montgaillard-Lauragais (off the N113), 31290 **Map** 11E3
[05 61 81 62 55
FAX 05 34 66 71 33
W www.hostellerie-chef-jean.com

⊘ AE, DC, MC, V
● Sep–Jul: Sun D, Mon, Tue L; Jan
🏮 €€€ ⊘ (14) €€
Pretty gardens, a swimming pool and a sauna make this a great place to relax. Find regional classics such as foie gras and cassoulet (p373), as well as bass flambéed with pastis.

VILLEFRANCHE-DE-LAURAGAIS
● La Marotte
Route Nailloux, Gardouch , 31290
Map 11E3
[05 61 27 19 46
FAX 05 61 81 74 37
⊘ AE, MC, V ● Sun, Mon 🏮 €€
This reliable restaurant dishes up traditional mid-Pyrenees fare in rustic surroundings. A loyal clientele chooses from an ever-changing menu that's dictated by the season's catch of seafood and game. The foie gras is very popular.

VILLENEUVE-D'OLMES
▲ Le Castrum
Le Laouzet, 09300 **Map** 11E4
[05 61 01 35 24
FAX 05 61 01 22 85
W www.lecastrum.com
⊘ AE, DC, MC, V
● 3 wks Jan
🏮 €€€€
⊘ (8) €€€€
A sleek, contemporary establishment with large windows gazing out over immaculate lawns and an alfresco dining terrace. Specialities such as langoustines with seaweed and summer fruits with pistachio coulis illustrate the kitchen's undeniable Mediterranean flavour. Guestrooms are bright, spacious and very comfortable.

VISCOS
▲ La Grange aux Marmottes
Le Village, 65120 **Map** 10C3
[05 62 92 88 88
FAX 05 62 92 93 75
W www.grangeauxmarmottes.com
⊘ DC, MC, V ● 2nd wk Nov–first wk Dec 🏮 € ⊘ (14) €€
A cosy, arch-roofed dining room in an old barn. House specialities include beef Wellington and salmon in Champagne. Guestrooms have rustic charm.

LANGUEDOC-ROUSSILLON

Inland lie the wild uplands of the Cévennes and the vines of Corbières and the Minervois, while on the Mediterranean coast sit a mix of salty lagoons, huge resorts and old fishing villages. Culinary influences from neighbouring Catalonia, Provence and Gascony are in evidence here, with the origin of traditional dishes such as cassoulet *fiercely defended.*

The Flavours of Languedoc-Roussillon

Mediterranean fish and seafood reign supreme in this region, notably the piquant anchovies of Collioure. At first glance, inland may seem covered in vines, but the mild winters and hot summers also help to contribute a bountiful crop of fruits and vegetables to local tables.

Display of rustic local bread

PÂTÉS DE PÉZENAS

Pâtés de Pézenas is one of the rare French confections to owe a culinary debt to Britain. The sweet and spicy covered mutton pie was introduced to the town by Clive of India, who stayed here in the 1760s on his return from Bengal, bringing his Indian cook with him. The cook taught local confectioners the Anglo-Indian combination of mutton, spices, brown sugar and lemon peel. After falling into disuse, the recipe was revived and is now prepared by numerous *pâtissiers* here.

UZÈS GARLIC FAIR

The garlic harvest has been celebrated at Uzès on 24 June *(Fête de la St-Jean)*, the traditional start of summer, ever since 1571. Producers set up stalls overflowing with garlic bulbs along the boulevards and streets of the old town.

MEAT AND CHARCUTERIE

Fine-quality lamb comes from the rocky *causses*, the Cévennes and the Pyrenean foothills. As elsewhere in the southwest, geese are raised. The Pyrénées-Orientales has a variety of charcuterie that is close to that of its Spanish neighbours; as well as *gambajo* (raw cured mountain ham), other specialities include *boutifarra* (black pudding), *chorizo* and *fouet*, a thin, dry sausage.

FISH AND SHELLFISH

Monkfish, tuna, sea bream, sardines and *langouste* (spiny lobster) are all in the catch at Sète, the largest fishing port on the French Mediterranean. Local fishermen also collect *tellines* (very tiny clams) and larger *palourdes*. Collioure is famed for its anchovies. The Bassin de Thau is a major centre for oyster and mussel cultivation, but the many lagoons that are dotted along the coastline also yield other species, such as eels.

CHEESE

The principal cheese of the Languedoc is Pélardon. The small, round cheese is made with the milk of goats raised on the sunbaked scrubland of the Cévennes, the Hautes Corbières and the Montagne Noire, whose

Bunches of fresh garlic

gorse, heather, chestnuts and herbs give its distinctive tang. Left to dry in wicker cages for two or three weeks, the crust turns an orangey colour. Look out also for Pérail, a mild, soft white sheeps' cheese.

FRUIT AND VEGETABLES

The sandy soil that extends along much of the coast is ideal for asparagus cultivation. Most is the green variety, which here is often roasted or sautéed rather than boiled. Wild asparagus grows on the hills around Uzès.

Vegetables compete with vast expanses of vines, but include tomatoes, aubergines (eggplants), beans, onions, garlic and potatoes. Good-quality olives and oil are produced around Nîmes, Uzès and Bize-Minervois. The warm winters of Roussillon make this a major area for early and delicate fruits. Rosy-hued apricots are available from mid-June and are delicious raw, as well as being used in tarts or made into jam, combined with local almonds. Early cherries also find their way into many dishes.

Pélardon cheese

BAKED GOODS AND SWEETS

Croquantes are jaw-achingly hard biscuits from Nîmes, made with sugar, eggs and roast almonds. A lighter touch infuses the orange-scented pastry *oreillettes* of Montpellier and lemony *rousquille* iced biscuits of Amélie-les-Bains. *Bunyettes* are deep-fried disks flavoured with lemon zest or rum. The *tourons* of Perpignan and Prades are nougat-like slabs of honey, grilled almonds, pine nuts and hazelnuts. Liquorice is grown around Uzès, home of one of the largest multinational sweet companies, Haribo.

BEST MARKETS

Béziers Excellent regional produce and wines in a pretty, cast-iron market hall. Pl Pierre Sémard, Tue–Sun am

Carcassonne Flowers and local produce are reason to explore the *ville basse* once you have visited the castle. Pl Carnot, Tue, Thu & Sat am

Nîmes Look for salt cod, olives and *charcuterie* at the busy central Halles. Daily, am

Perpignan Snails, seafood and other produce with a Catalan flavour. Pl de la République, Tue–Sun am

Pézenas Local fruit, vegetables and flowers in the elegant historic pl Gambetta, Sat am

St-Jean-du-Gard Lively market, Tue am. Also farmers' market, summer

Uzès Lots of local produce on the arcaded Place des Herbes, daily

Tourons on sale at a Perpignan patisserie

ANCHOVIES

Anchovies have been salted on the port of Collioure since the Middle Ages, and the brightly painted fishing boats that inspired the Fauve painters Matisse and Derain still sit on the beach, although most of the catch now comes from neighbouring Port-Vendres.

The fish are caught at night between May and October, lured to the boats by lanterns. The process of salting begins as soon as they are landed. The prepared fish are layered with salt in barrels and then left to mature for three months or more, before being packed into jars or tins. Reputed as the finest anchovies in France, they are used in many Catalan specialities or are served as an apéritif. Anchovy salting can be watched at Anchois Desclaux (04 68 82 05 25) and Maison Roque (04 68 82 04 99).

Regional Dishes

Culinary traditions range from the Catalan-accented food of Roussillon to the more Provençal flavours of the Gard, with other southwestern influences, too. This is a Mediterranean region, so olive oil and garlic appear in many dishes, along with tomatoes and anchovies.

REGIONAL DISHES

Aïgo boulido Garlic and bread soup

Boles de picolat Catalan meatballs in a spicy tomato and olive sauce

Canard aux cérises Duck with cherries

Cargolade Snails stuffed with bacon and garlic, and eaten with garlic mayonnaise

Civet de langouste Spiny lobster in a sauce of onions, tomato and garlic, thickened with langouste juices and coral

Crème catalane (crema catalana) Type of crème brulée

Escargots à la narbonnaise Snails in a sauce of almonds and egg yolks

Escargots à la catalane Snails with garlic and ham

Ouillade (ollada) Catalan pot-au-feu of ham hock, vegetables and dried beans

Pinyata Catalan stew of octopus, crabs, langoustine and assorted fish, cooked with garlic, olive oil and tomatoes

Poulet aux gambas Spicy Catalan chicken and giant prawn stew

Tielle à la sétoise Octopus and tomato pie

Trnixat cerdan Thick *galette* of fried cabbage, bacon and sausage

THE REGIONAL MENU

A meal might start with Catalan charcuterie, grilled skewered mussels, marinated anchovies, *brandade* or the rustic *aïgo boulido* soup. There are various snail dishes, including *escargots à la catalane, à la narbonnaise* and the traditional Easter dish of *cargolade*. At Port de Grau, tiny *telline* clams, cooked with white wine, shallots and garlic, might be served as an appetizer; other shellfish dishes include a gratin of *palourdes.*

As in Provence, there are countless fish soups and stews, including *bouillabaisse (see p401)* and *bourride*, particularly associated with Sète. Look out also for *pinyata* and *civet de langouste*, a speciality of Collioure. Ham, breadcrumbs and peppers are used to stuff sea bream or squid, and fish is also prepared with the local vermouth Noilly Prat, or grilled *a la plancha*. In Palavas, monkfish (sometimes here called *gigot de mer*) is baked with onions, peppers and garlic.

Carcassonne and Castelnaudry are renowned for *cassoulet*, and the use of goose fat is something the region has in common with the southwest. Local lamb is at its best simply roast with herbs. Cherries from Céret are cooked with duck, as are peaches, while sweet white Banyuls and Rivesaltes wines appear in many sauces.

Escargots à la catalane

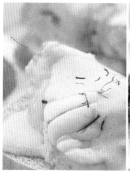

Left Bourride sétoise **Centre** Cassoulet de Castelnaudary **Right** Brandade de morue

Catalan traditions are evident in Perpignan and the Roussillon towards the Spanish border, which was part of the kingdom of Majorca until 1659. One characteristic is land-sea combinations, such as chicken with prawns, lamb with anchovies, and snails with prawns, ham or anchovies. The Catalan influence also shows in the use of rice and the adoption of paella and *tapas*.

BOURRIDE SETOISE

This garlicky, white fish stew has a sauce laced with *aïoli*. In Sète, it is usually made with monkfish, though two or three different fish may be used. Leeks, onions and carrots are cooked and sieved to form a sauce. Chunks of fish are fried briefly and then simmered gently in the sauce and, at the last minute, *aïoli* is stirred in.

BRANDADE DE MORUE

This is the signature dish of Nîmes. Sheets of dried salt cod are soaked in cold water for 24 hours, then gently simmered. Warmed olive oil and milk are beaten into the skinned and boned fish to form a thick purée, which is served hot with garlicky toasted baguette.

CASSOULET DE CASTELNAUDARY

Carcassonne, Castelnaudary and Toulouse all claim to be the true home of this hearty stew. Pork dominates in Castelnaudary, lamb or mutton is added in Toulouse, and mutton or partridge in Carcassonne. White haricot or *lingot* beans are cooked with pork rinds, *lardons*, garlic, carrots and an onion studded with cloves. Duck or goose *confit* is fried and the fat used to brown pieces of pork shin and shoulder and Toulouse sausage. Beans, *confit* and meat are layered in a casserole, starting and finishing with beans, with the sausage piled on top, and moistened with cooking liquor from the beans. The *cassoulet* is cooked gently in the oven, for as much as three hours; the crust that forms is pressed into the stew at intervals.

REGIONAL DINING

The following restaurants are among those serving regional dishes at reasonable prices:

Casa Sansa
Perpignan *(see p389)*
Chez Myou
Uzes *(see p392)*
Grand Sud
Le Grau-du-Roi *(see p383)*
L'Admiral
La Grande-Motte *(see p382)*
L'Angevis
Chusclan *(see p81)*
La Crèmerie
Beziers *(see p379)*
La Marina
Marseillan-Plage *(see p385)*
La Plancha Le Grau-du-Roi, Rive Gauche *(see p384)*
Le Chante Mer
Sete *(see p390)*
Le Fontaine due Temple
Nîmes *(see p387)*
Le Lezard Bleu Roquefort-des-Corbieres *(see p389)*
Le Paseo
Nîmes *(see p387)*
Maison du Cassoulet
Carcassonne-la-Cité *(see p380)*

Casa Sansa restaurant in Perpignan

Regional Wines

Over the last 10 to 15 years, the Midi has begun to realize its huge potential for quality, but it still has plenty of leeway. Robust reds and sweet wines are the aces but whites and the odd sparkler are useful wild cards.

GRAPE VARIETIES

The Languedoc makes good use of many internationally known grapes, introduced to improve quality, but gains its individuality from traditional varieties such as these.

Bourboulenc This ancient variety gives whites freshness.

Carignan The dominant red grape of the Midi can produce good juicy wines with modern winemaking methods and low-yielding old vines now fuel some heady, fascinating brews.

Cinsaut Fresh, light and fragrant red wines are typical of Cinsaut, which lightens up otherwise heavy blends.

Mauzac Also a major grape of the southwest and the Pyrenees, Mauzac gives fresh, appley whites.

Picpoul Oyster-loving Picpoul de Pinet is based on this zesty white grape.

Vineyards ouside the medieval Cité de Carcassonne

This is the largest vine-growing area in the world and produces approximately 35 per cent of all France's wines. The vineyard area stretches from Carcassonne in the west to Nîmes in the east and south to the Spanish border, forming a crescent that hugs the coast and faces the sea. Once notorious for producing oceans of woeful wine for the working-class cafés of the north, the flat plains still pump out unexciting *vin de table*, but more upmarket vineyards now occupy the hillsides and the whole region is committed to raising quality levels with better grape varieties, lower yields and improved winemaking techniques.

The Mediterranean summers are baking hot and inland winds such as the Tramontane make the climate seem even drier. In general, the reds are full, fleshy and structured, often virile and good with game or leg of lamb cooked with herbs. The rarer whites are dry and have the wild herby smell of the *garrigue* on a hot day. Sweet wines are a speciality.

COSTIÈRES DE NÎMES

This large area around Nîmes looks to the juicy, ripe, perfumy reds of the southern Rhône rather than the dustier, more muscular styles of its Languedoc cousins. The scented whites are very tasty.

CORBIÈRES

Wild and beautiful, the Corbières hills are home to one of France's largest appellations, focused almost entirely on red wines from a blend of Carignan and "improver" varieties such as Syrah, Grenache and Mourvèdre. The

Windmill in Faugères

VINEYARDS OF LANGUEDOC-ROUSSILLON

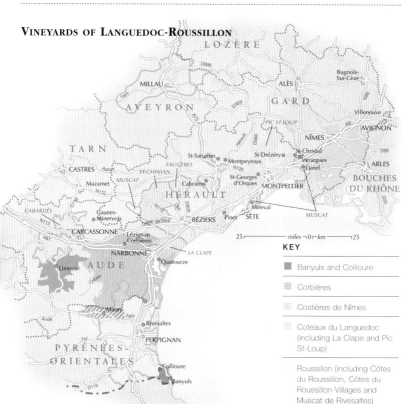

KEY

- Banyuls and Collioure
- Corbières
- Costières de Nîmes
- Coteaux du Languedoc (including La Clape and Pic St-Loup)
- Roussillon (including Côtes du Roussillon, Côtes du Roussillon-Villages and Muscat de Rivesaltes)
- Fitou
- Limoux
- Maury
- Minervois
- — Other AOC and VDQS regions (including Cabardès, Faugères, Muscat AOCs and St-Chinian)
- ···· *Département* boundary

New steel tanks in a modernized Languedoc cooperative

appellation has been divided into 11 *terroirs*, each with its own individual character, depending on whether it is close to the sea or situated more towards the dry, rocky interior. Boutenac, perhaps the best *terroir*, is highly suited to Carignan and Mourvèdre for reds with scents of game, liquorice, spice and berry fruit. The *terroirs* also reflect the region's history. Quéribus is the land of the Cathar castles. Here, the vines grow at an altitude of up to 400 m (1,300 ft), giving the red wines notes of cherry and roasted coffee beans. In Fontfroide, famous for its magnificent abbey, the well-drained soil is perfect for long-lived Mourvèdre.

Domaine Mansenoble wines

A vintage *vin doux naturel* from Mas Amiel

VIN DOUX NATUREL

The arid vineyard terraces and baking summers of the Roussillon are ideal for making the fortified sweet wines known as *vins doux naturels*. Banyuls, Maury and Rivesaltes, with their rich flavours of chocolate, fig, candied fruit, spice and caramel, are France's answer to port. Grenache Noir is the principal grape used. It is vinified according to the *mutage sur grains* method. Here, spirit alcohol is added to the semi-fermented grapes themselves, then the mixture is macerated for up to two months, producing a deep mahogany colour and plenty of tannin. *Rimage* or vintage wines are bottled young with plenty of fruit flavour. Older tawny styles are matured in wooden casks while oxidized *rancio* wines may be placed outside in demijohns, exposed partly to the air. Banyuls, Maury and Rivesaltes make wonderful partners for chocolate desserts, goat's cheese and game dishes prepared with fruit. They can all age very well, some for up to 30 years.

MINERVOIS

To the north of Corbières, Minervois is one of the oldest vineyards in the Mediterranean. The vineyards lie on a series of south-facing terraces on arid, hot and rocky terrain. Producers are making a concerted effort towards better quality wines, particularly in the vineyards of La Livinière, a sub-appellation within the Minervois. Many of the wines can be rather rustic but, with increased reliance on Syrah, Grenache and Mourvèdre grapes, the best are now showing much finer tannin, more fruit and a capacity for ageing. The commune of Saint-Jean-de Minervois produces magnificent sweet Muscat whites.

COTEAUX DU LANGUEDOC

The massive collective appellation of the Languedoc hills includes three *crus* with their own appellations (St-Chinian, Faugères and Clairette du Languedoc) and 12 *terroirs*, including La Clape and Pic-Saint-Loup, celebrated for their reds, and Picpoul de Pinet with its seafood-friendly whites. In the 19th century, the elegantly gutsy reds of St-Chinian were used in Parisian hospitals for therapeutic purposes. These are great-value wines, with a distinct fragrance of violets and smoke, and seem to be just made for drinking with game in sauce. Faugères lies in the foothills of the Cévennes in a typically Mediterranean climate. Its schistous soils produce rustic, spicy reds that smack of leather and liquorice.

LIMOUX

Sparkling wine is the tradition here, with records at the abbey of St-Hilaire dating back to 1531. Appley Blanquette de Limoux relies on the local Mauzac grape and is made by the traditional Champagne method. Wines made by the *méthode ancestrale* are light and refreshing. Crémant de Limoux is a more refined fizz

The rugged vineyard landscape of the Languedoc

Vineyards of Mas Amiel in the Roussillon

based on Chardonnay. The rich still Chardonnays are excellent, and reds with a high proportion of Merlot have now joined the appellation.

FITOU

Fitou was the region's first appellation for red wines. It is produced mainly from Carignan, blended with Syrah or Mourvèdre. The vineyards are divided into highland and maritime regions, with tough, savoury, herby wines coming from the mountains and a more voluptuous style emerging from the coastal strip.

ROUSSILLON

To the south of Corbières and towards the Spanish border, the Côtes du Roussillon and superior Côtes du Roussillon-Villages reds are based on Carignan, with Syrah and Grenache adding finesse to the better wines. Typical of the heady, mouth-filling wines of the sunny south, these wines are full of dust and spice. Collioure, with its picturesque port and terraced vineyards, produces some heady, great-value reds laced with notes of truffle, venison and leather, usually matured in oak. Banyuls and Maury are centres for *vin doux naturel*.

VINS DE PAYS AND VARIETALS

Historically Languedoc-Roussillon was the source of cheap bulk table wines with nothing but their low price and alcohol content to recommend them. Over the last decades of the 20th century, the region at last began to concentrate more on quality than quantity. Winemakers, often trained in Australia, brought new vinification techniques and helped the region's own winemakers take advantage of the *vin de pays* regulations which promise quality well above simple *vin de table* but allow greater flexibility than the AOCs, including labelling by grape variety and a wider range of internationally known grapes to choose from. The region-wide Vin de Pays d'Oc has become one of the best known names in French wine.

THE LANGUEDOC MUSCATS

Vins doux naturels can also be made from the beautifully fragrant Muscat à Petits Grains, giving attractive scents of beeswax, linden and honey with a slight apricot tartness. The Roussillon's Muscat de Rivesaltes is made mainly from coarser Muscat of Alexandria.

Muscat de Frontignan This coastal Muscat can be a *vin doux naturel* or a *vin de liqueur*, which means the alcohol is added to the grape juice before fermentation for an extra-sweet style.

Muscat de Lunel Delicate, apricotty wines hail from this small town northeast of Montpellier.

Muscat de Mireval Frontignan's inland neighbour is less famous but can be finer.

Muscat de St-Jean-de-Minervois From the Minervois hills, this is one of the best Muscats available, fine and sweet with a lovely apricot tang. It is a little lighter than the other three.

Old sign for Muscat de Mireval

MAS DE DAUMAS GASSAC

Aimé Guibert discovered a unique and ideal vine-growing soil at his home in the Hérault when the region was known for nothing but cheap wine. He set about producing a wine to rival the Classed Growths of Bordeaux and his Mas de Daumas Gassac, a Vin de Pays de l'Hérault, blazed a trail for quality wines from the Midi and showed the boundless possibilities of *vins de pays*.

Where to Eat & Stay

AIGUES-MORTES
● **Le Café de Bouzigues**
7 rue Pasteur, 30220 **Map** 12B2
📞 04 66 53 93 95
💳 AE, DC, MC, V ⬤ Tue D, Wed; mid-Jan–Apr 🍴 €
Traditional bistro with a small, light dining room and large patio. Menus change on a regular basis, but the house speciality is seafood, including oysters.

AIGUES-MORTES
▲ **Les Arcades**
23 bd Gambetta, 30220 **Map** 12B2
📞 04 66 53 81 13
📠 04 66 53 75 46
🌐 www.les-arcades.fr
💳 AE, DC, MC, V ⬤ Mon, Tue L
🍴 €€€ 🛏 (9) €€€€
Inside the city walls, a chic address with a rooftop pool. Guestrooms are done up in bright colours. The upscale restaurant is known for its excellent food: courgette (zucchini) flowers stuffed with seafood, lamb with tapenade (p400) and foie gras.

AIGUES-MORTES
▲ **Restaurant Auberge des Quatre Vents**
939 route Nîmes, 30220 **Map** 12B2
📞 04 66 53 71 50
📠 04 66 53 72 29
💳 AE, DC, MC, V ⬤ Jan
🍴 €€ 🛏 (44) €€
Modern hotel and restaurant with the added bonus of a decent pool. The large restaurant serves a huge selection of dishes ranging from seafood to the more meaty local dishes of the Gard, which means horse steak is often on the menu. Smallish but well-kept guestrooms.

AIGUES-MORTES
● **Restaurant la Camargue**
19 rue République, 30220 **Map** 12B2
📞 04 66 53 86 88
📠 04 66 53 72 69
@ restaurant-lacamargue@camargue.fr
💳 AE, DC, MC, V ⬤ Mon–Sat: L; Nov–May: Mon D 🍴 €€€
Very popular because of its Camargue-style flamenco performances. The setting

is imposing: an 18th-century building with a huge terrace right in the heart of the walled city. The extensive menu offers bull steak and rouille.

ALES
▲ **Restaurant and Hotel Le Riche**
42 pl Pierre Sémard, 30100 **Map** 12A2
📞 04 66 86 00 33
📠 04 66 30 02 63
🌐 www.leriche.fr
💳 AE, DC, MC, V ⬤ Aug
🍴 €€€ 🛏 (19) €€
An inviting, immaculately kept spot which oozes character. The restaurant is a step up from the hotel, serving duck foie gras and cod pan-fried with fennel. Guestrooms are great value.

ANDUZE
▲ **La Ferme de Cornadel**
Route de Générargues, 30140 **Map** 12A2
📞 04 66 61 79 44
📠 04 66 61 80 46
🌐 www.cornadel.fr
💳 AE, MC, V ⬤ Tue; Dec–Jan
🍴 €€ 🛏 (5) €€€
Next to the Gardon River, a farm serving regional country food, including pasta with local sausage, aubergine (eggplant) gratin and chicken stuffed with smoked ham and sage. Pretty guestrooms.

ANDUZE
● **La Paillerette**
1835 route de St-Jean-du-Gard, 30140 **Map** 12A2
📞 04 66 61 73 27
💳 MC, V ⬤ Sun 🍴 €
A vine-covered building and terrace provide the idyllic setting for a range of hearty dishes typical of this mountainous region. Freshwater fish and game served.

ARAGON
■ **Château Aragon**
Aragon, 11600 **Map** 11E3
📞 04 68 77 19 62
🌐 www.westland.ch/en/Aragon
💳 MC, V ⬤ Nov–Mar 🛏 (6) €€€
This impressive 16th-century château has Renaissance charm. Beyond the fine

porticoed entrance are cool, elegant interiors. Small courtyard pool.

ARGELES-SUR-MER
▲ **Auberge du Roua**
Chemin du Roua, 66700 **Map** 11F4
📞 04 68 95 85 85
📠 04 68 95 83 50
🌐 www.belle-demeure.com
💳 AE, DC, MC, V ⬤ Mon, Tue–Fri L; Nov–Mar 🍴 €€€ 🛏 (14) €€€
Converted 17th-century Catalan farmhouse set in tranquil grounds. Roussillon produce is expertly crafted into delicious fish and meat dishes. Guestrooms look out on the gardens, pool and Pyrenees.

ARGELES-SUR-MER
● **La Mariscada**
Résidence La Réale, 66700 **Map** 11F4
📞 04 68 81 59 87
💳 AE, DC, MC, V ⬤ Oct–Dec: Mon; Jan, Feb 🍴 €€
A favourite with the locals, this is the place to sample local seafood and shellfish, cooked in a traditional style and served up with plenty of charm. There's also a terrace overlooking the port.

BAGNOLS-SUR-CEZE
▲ **Jardins de Montcaud**
Combe route Alès, 30200 **Map** 12B2
📞 04 66 89 60 60
📠 04 66 89 45 04
🌐 www.relaischateaux.com
💳 AE, DC, MC, V ⬤ Nov–mid-Apr
🍴 €€€€€ 🛏 (22) €€€€€
Extravagant and totally breathtaking château in the Cevenne foothills. The restaurant fare pays tribute to the Mediterranean. The vast guestrooms are luxuriously appointed. Wonderful conservatory, pool and terrace too.

BANYULS-SUR-MER
▲ **La Littorine**
Plage des Elmes, 66650 **Map** 11F4
📞 04 68 88 03 12
📠 04 68 88 53 03
💳 AE, DC, MC, V ⬤ Tue L, Wed L; mid-Nov–mid-Dec
🍴 €€€ 🛏 (31) €€

Seaside retreat right on the Vermillion Coast. Fantastic seafood dishes and a first-rate wine list. Sleek bedrooms, many with sea views and balconies.

BARJAC
▲ **Le Mas du Terme**
Route de Bagnols-sur-Cèze, 30430 **Map** 12B2
☎ 04 66 24 56 31
FAX 04 66 24 58 54
W www.mas-du-terme.com
✉ MC, V **●** Nov–Mar
¶¶ €€ **◆** (23) €€€

Surrounded by vineyards and lavender fields, this farm has been transformed into a beautiful hotel and restaurant. Pleasant guestrooms and some small apartments. Menu standards include lamb, vegetable pâté and chicken with tarragon. Lunch by reservation only.

BEZIERS
● **La Crèmerie**
1 pl de la Madelaine, 34500 **Map** 11F3
☎ 04 67 28 54 26
✉ AE, DC, MC, V **●** Sun, Mon **¶¶** €€
Steaming tartiflettes (p268) and bubbling fondues are just some of the cheese dishes served here. Inside, a rustic atmosphere, and a small terrace outside.

BEZIERS
● **L'Ambassade**
22 bd de Verdun, 34500 **Map** 11F3
☎ 04 67 76 06 24
FAX 04 67 76 74 05
✉ DC, MC, V **●** Sun, Mon; 3 wks Jun
¶¶ €€€

Renowned chef Patrick Orly prepares classic Mediterranean-style dishes using seasonal produce. Chic dining room, with wood and a soothing ambience.

BEZIERS
● **Le Grilladin, le Carnivore et le Pêcheur**
21 rue Française, 34500 **Map** 11F3
☎ 04 67 49 09 45
FAX 04 67 49 20 84
✉ AE, MC, V **●** Sun, Mon **¶¶** €
A real favourite with locals. Mussels, sardines and sole feature in the house speciality stew. Beautiful courtyard complete with olive tree.

BIZE-MINERVOIS
▲ **La Bastide de Cabezac**
18 Hameau Cabezac, 11120 **Map** 11F3
☎ 04 68 46 66 10
FAX 04 68 46 66 29
W www.labastidecabezac.com
✉ MC, V **●** Sun D, Mon, Sat L
¶¶ €€€ **◆** (12) €€€

A handsome 18th-century coaching inn renowned for its tranquil atmosphere and superb restaurant. Mediterranean flair such as stuffed peppers and sea bream. Contemporary guestrooms.

BRISSAC
▲ **Mas de Coulet**
Route de Montpellier, 34190 **Map** 12A2
☎ 04 67 73 74 18
● Jan, Feb **¶¶** € **◆** (6) €
Twelfth-century stone farmhouse offering food and lodging to nature-lovers. Meals are served only to those staying overnight. Typical dishes include chicken with cornouille (a tart berry), veal with wild mushrooms and sheep's yogurt with honey and walnuts. Very simple dormitory accommodation.

CANET-PLAGE
● **La Rascasse**
38 bd Hippolyte Tixador, 66140 **Map** 11F4
☎ 04 68 80 20 79
✉ AE, DC, MC **●** Sep–May
¶¶ €€
Well known by locals as the place to eat by the sea in summer. Lots of seafood, including oysters and fresh fish. Good selection of regional wines.

CANET-PLAGE
● **Le Scoubidou**
5 rue des Cerisiers, 66140 **Map** 11F4
☎ 04 68 80 30 36
W www.lescoubidou.com
✉ AE, DC, MC, V **●** Oct–Mar
¶¶ €€
Catalonian-style grill that is practically all alfresco. Attached to a nearby campsite, it offers a huge selection of barbecued meats and fish.

CAP-D'AGDE
▲ **Hotel du Golf**
3 ave Passeur Challiès, 34300 **Map** 12A3
☎ 04 67 26 87 03

FAX 04 67 26 26 89
W www.hotel-du-golf.com
✉ MC, V **●** Jan
¶¶ €€€€ **◆** (50) €€€€
Stylish hotel near the port and golf course. Top-notch rooms have luxurious bathrooms. The chef focuses on fine Mediterranean and seafood dishes.

CAP-D'AGDE
● **La Madragde**
44 rue Gabelle, 34300 **Map** 12A3
☎ 04 67 26 23 90
FAX 04 67 01 35 24
✉ AE, DC, MC, V
● Sun D, Mon, Thu D **¶¶** €€€
Restaurants don't come much more refined than this on the Cap, a subtly opulent spot overlooking the port. Extensive set menu with foie gras, shellfish platters, brochette of scallops in butter and crème catalane (p372).

CAP-D'AGDE
● **La Manade**
15 pl Ste Clair, 34300 **Map** 12A3
☎ 04 67 01 23 91
✉ AE, MC, V **●** Wed **¶¶** €€
A vine-covered retreat in a quiet little corner away from the marina. The menu has a distinctly traditional feel, while emphasizing the area's Catalonian roots, with dishes like tuna in a spicy tomato sauce, seafood platter and squid stuffed with minced meat.

CAP-D'AGDE
● **Le Brasero**
Port Richelieu, rue Richelieu, 34300 **Map** 12A3
☎ 04 67 26 24 75
✉ AE, DC, MC, V **●** Jan **¶¶** €€
Overlooking the port and with a great reputation for good value seafood – oysters, squid, tuna and swordfish – as well as veal escalope in cream.

CAP-D'AGDE
● **Le Manhattan**
36 quai Jean Miquel, 34300 **Map** 12A3
☎ 04 67 26 21 54
✉ AE, DC, MC, V **¶¶** €€
An infinitely more appealing restaurant than the many surrounding it, and one of the best for super-fresh shellfish;

For key to symbols see back flap

huge platters make an ideal and good-value family meal. Full-length windows creating a light, airy ambience divorce the place from the surrounding kitsch.

CAP-D'AGDE

● **Les Copains d'Abord**
13 rue d'Estacade, 34300 **Map** 12A3
C 04 67 01 26 66
E AE, DC, MC, V ● Wed, Oct–Mar: Mon–Thu **11** €
Enjoy the sound of the lapping sea from the terrace. The Belgian owner makes his mark by offering moules-frites *alongside traditional seafood favourites.*

CARAMANY

● **Le Grand Rocher**
Rue Tresseres Eloi, 66720 **Map** 11F4
C 04 68 84 51 58
@ legrand.rocher@wanadoo.fr
E MC, V ● Mon; Jan–Feb **11** €
The terrace looks onto the surrounding vineyards. Highlights include spicy pork and the catch of the day.

CARCASSONNE

▲ **Hôtel de la Cité**
Pl de l'Eglise, 11000 **Map** 11E3
C 04 68 71 98 71
FAX 04 68 71 50 15
E AE, DC, MC, V ● Dec–mid-Jan
11 €€€€ ● (61) €€€€€
Hotel to the stars, enjoying one of the very few gardens in the entire city. Vast rooms, all decorated individually to a contemporary theme. Public spaces are more traditional. One restaurant is set in a splendid neo-gothic-style dining room and offers a selection of regional and traditional French gourmet dishes. The less formal Chez Saskia serves French breakfasts and light lunches.

CARCASSONNE

▲ **La Domaine d'Auriac**
Route St Hilaire, 11009 **Map** 11E3
C 04 68 25 72 22
FAX 04 68 47 35 54
E AE, DC, MC, V ● Nov–Apr: Sun D & Mon; Jan, 1 wk May, 1 wk Nov
11 €€€€€ ● (26) €€€€€
Elegant gardens and a fabulous pool in a haven of tranquillity just outside Carcassonne's medieval fortress. Superb

regional cuisine such as cassoulet (p373). Strong wine list and rather fine cigar selection. Flowery guestrooms.

CARCASSONNE

● **Le Languedoc**
32 allée d'iena, 11000 **Map** 11E3
C 04 68 25 22 17
E AE, DC, MC, V ● Sun D, Nov–Feb: Mon; last wk Jun, 1st wk Jul **11** €€€
Upmarket, staunchly traditional restaurant with the sort of attentive service that's becoming scarce. Try the ever-popular cassoulet (p373), foie gras or duck.

CARCASSONNE

● **Le Petit Couvert**
18 rue de L'Aigle-d'Or, 11000 **Map** 11E3
C 04 68 71 00 20
● Sun, Mon **11** €€€
Traditional dishes such as cassoulet (p326) abound, as do magret de canard, *steak tartare and fine desserts.*

CARCASSONNE-LA-CITE

● **Maison du Cassoulet**
6 rue Grand Puits, 11000 **Map** 11E3
C 04 68 47 61 03
E AE, DC, MC, V ● mid-Nov–Feb: Sun D, Mon–Fri, Sat D **11** €€
A shrine to cassoulet (p373). Set in the heart of the ancient city, this small restaurant enjoys a wealth of stone and beams, which lends a period feel to the proceedings. Expertly prepared cassoulet comes in various forms.

CARNON

● **La Rascasse**
Bât Le Solignac, rue Mistral, 34280 **Map** 12A3
C 04 67 68 37 17
E AE, DC, MC, V **11** €€
Selections include rouille Setoise *(cuttlefish in a spicy sauce of garlic, tomatoes and peppers), monkfish in green pepper sauce and a bucket of prawns.*

CARNON

● **La Traîne**
104 rue Mistral, 34280 **Map** 12A3
C 04 67 68 18 29
E DC, MC, V **11** €
Great food cooked right in front of you. House speciality is catigot aux gambas

(a variation on paella). Simple all-glass dining area overlooks the marina.

CARNON

● **Le j**
8 ave Grassion Cibrand, 34280 **Map** 12A3
C 04 67 50 34 99
FAX 04 67 68 08 56
E AE, DC, MC, V **11** €€
Minimalist decor and a terrace that runs to the beach. Traditional menu with a few twists: scallop and prawn brochette and tuna with aubergine (eggplant) gratin.

CASCATEL-DES-CORBIERES

● **Le Clos de Cascatel**
28 quai Berre, 11360 **Map** 11F3
C 04 68 45 06 22
FAX 04 68 45 06 22
E MC, V ● Tue; 2 wks Nov
11 €€
Set in beautiful vineyards. Favourites on the excellent menu include roast duck foie gras, steak and delicious desserts including a chocolate fondant tart.

CASTELNAUDARY

● **Au Petit Gazouillis**
5 rue de l'Arcade, 11400 **Map** 11E3
C 04 68 23 08 18
E AE, DC, MC, V ● Sep–Jun: Tue & Wed; mid-Dec–mid-Jan **11** €
A straightforward menu with simple, honest, local cuisine in portions big enough to satisfy the heartiest appetites. The house speciality is cassoulet (p373).

CASTELNAUDARY

▲ **Hôtel du Centre et du Lauragais**
31 cours de Republique, 11400 **Map** 11E3
C 04 68 23 25 95
FAX 04 68 94 01 66
W www.hotel-centre-lauragais.com
E AE, DC, MC, V **11** €€ ● (16) €€
Slightly upmarket family place with a large, light, open-plan dining room. Time-honoured cuisine like cassoulet (p373), foie gras and pigeon with ceps. Slightly dated but comfortable rooms.

CASTILLON-DU-GARD

▲ **Vieux Castillon**
Rue Turion Sabatier, 30210 **Map** 12B2

● Restaurant ■ Hotel ▲ Hotel / Restaurant

☎ 04 66 37 61 61
FAX 04 66 37 28 17
W www.relaischateaux.fr/vieuxcastillon
💳 AE, DC, MC, V ● Mon L, Tue L; Jan–mid-Feb
🍴 €€€€ 🛏 (32) €€€€€
Run by the Walser family, this is probably the finest establishment in the area. The dining hall overlooks the pool and courtyard and offers up exquisitely prepared Mediterranean fare. Incredible attention to detail and stylish decor; rooms enjoy views of the surrounding countryside.

CERET

▲ La Terrasse au Soleil
Route de Fontfrède, 66400 **Map** 11F4
☎ 04 68 87 01 94
FAX 04 68 87 39 24
W www.la-terrasse-au-soleil.com
💳 AE, DC, MC, V ● Mon–Fri L
🍴 €€€ 🛏 (31) €€€€
At this hilltop venue, Monsieur Perreau presents a menu brimming with classic dishes such as red mullet with herbs. Plain, slightly bland guestrooms.

CERET

▲ Les Feuillants
1 bd la Fayette (pl Picasso), 66400 **Map** 11F4
☎ 04 68 87 37 88
FAX 04 68 87 44 68
W www.feuillants.com
💳 MC, V ● Sun D, Mon; 1 wk Mar
🍴 €€€ 🛏 (6) €€€
A Belle Epoque mansion in a leafy area. The elegant dining room has warm-hued contemporary artwork which echoes the vibrancy and personality of the Catalan food served. The wine list is 600 strong. Modern, good-value bedrooms.

CHUSCLAN

▲ L'Angevis
Chemin du Cante Merle Abeilles, 30200 **Map** 12B2
☎ 04 66 90 03 15
💳 MC, V ● Sun, Mon; Sep
🍴 €€ 🛏 (6) €€
Beautiful views of the Cèze valley from this hotel-restaurant. Tapenade (p400), *tomato* confit *and grilled shrimp are on offer in the rustic dining room. Modern, simple, pleasing guestrooms.*

COLLIOURE

● Le Neptune
9 route Port-Vendres, 66190 **Map** 11F4
☎ 04 68 82 02 27
FAX 04 68 82 50 33
💳 AE, DC, MC, V ● Jul–Sep: Mon, Tue, Wed; Jan, 2 wks Dec 🍴 €€€
Views of the Mediterranean and the handsome Château Royal from the exceptionally beautiful gardens and terrace. Based in a port renowned for its fishing industry, expect some fine seafood dishes like lobster soup.

COLLIOURE

▲ Les Templiers
12 quai Amirauté, 66190 **Map** 11F4
☎ 04 68 98 31 10
FAX 04 68 98 01 24
W www.hotel-templiers.com
💳 MC, V ● Mon D, Tue, Jul–Sep; Nov–Jan 🍴 € 🛏 (56) €€
There are over 2000 works of art at this fabulous hotel-cum-eatery, once the haunt of Picasso, among other artists. Lots of Catalan food and flavoursome fish dishes. Modern guestrooms.

COLOMBIERS

● Restaurant du Château de Colombiers
1 route du Château, 34440 **Map** 11F3
☎ 04 67 37 06 93
FAX 04 63 37 63 11
💳 MC, V ● Oct–Mar: Mon, Sun-Thu D, Sat L; Jan 🍴 €€
Perched on the banks of the placid Canal du Midi, this 12th-century castle was built on a ruined Roman villa. Traditional cuisine under chestnut trees.

COMBES

▲ L'Auberge de Combes
4km (2.5 miles) west of Lamalou les Bains on D180, 34240 **Map** 11F2
☎ 04 67 95 66 55
FAX 04 67 95 63 49
💳 MC, V ● Mon; Jan
🍴 €€ 🛏 (2) €
Mountainside inn with gorgeous views of the Orb River valley from the terrace. Hearty regional food: pasta with clams and truffle butter, and pigeon with foie gras and port. Two guestrooms and a dormitory for budget travellers.

CONNAUX

▲ Le Bernon
Route Nationale 86, 30330 **Map** 12B2
☎ 04 66 82 00 32
FAX 04 66 82 92 20
💳 MC, V ● Sun D, Mon
🍴 €€ 🛏 (11) €€
Highly varied menu includes foie gras, beef fillet with morels and a wide range of fish dishes. Good-value rooms.

CORNILLON

▲ La Vieille Fontaine
Town centre, 30630 **Map** 12B1
☎ 04 66 82 20 56
FAX 04 66 82 33 64
W www.lavieillefontaine.net
💳 AE, DC, MC, V ● mid-Nov–Feb
🍴 €€€€ 🛏 (8) €€€€
Gorgeous hotel, surrounded by gardens, located in a tiny medieval hill town. Richly decorated guestrooms. The fine restaurant features dishes such as spicy mussels and soupe au pistou (p400).

CUCUGNAN

▲ Auberge de Cucugnan
2 pl de la Fontaine, 11350 **Map** 11F4
☎ 04 68 45 40 84
FAX 04 68 45 01 52
💳 MC, V ● Mar–May & Oct–Jan: Wed; Jan–Mar
🍴 €€ 🛏 (6) €€
Wonderful old village inn close to numerous Cathar castles. Wild boar, beef, rabbit and guinea fowl are menu mainstays. Small, simply furnished rooms.

FERRIERES-LES-VERRERIES

▲ L'Oustal de Baumes
Mas de Baumes – Chemin des Verriers, 34190 **Map** 12A2
☎ 04 66 80 88 80
FAX 04 66 80 88 82
W www.oustaldebaumes.com
💳 AE, MC, V ● Jan
🍴 €€ 🛏 (7) €€€
Imaginative modern furniture gives this 13th-century stone mansion an air of hip elegance. The menu reflects the decor: traditional dishes are dressed up in contemporary attire. Specialities include foie gras with fig jam, duckling stuffed with foie gras and veal with wild mushrooms. Live music in the restaurant.

FITOU
▲ **Auberge de la Tour**
Les Cabannes RN9, 11510 **Map** 11F4
☎ 04 68 45 66 90
FAX 04 68 45 65 97
@ daniel.auber@wanadoo.fr
MC, V ● Sun D, Mon, Jul–Sep:
Tue; Jan–mid-Feb
€€ ◇ (6) €€€
Beyond the sprawling exposed brickwork
façade of this auberge are pleasant
interiors filled with intriguing artwork.
Traditional dishes are complemented by
the locally produced Fitou wine. Salmon
and red mullet regularly feature. Well-
equipped guestrooms.

FLOURE
▲ **Château Hôtel de Floure**
1 allée Gaston Bonheur, 11800 **Map** 11F3
☎ 04 68 79 11 29
FAX 04 68 79 04 61
w www.chateau-de-floure.com
AE, DC, MC, V ● Nov–Apr
€€€€ ◇ (16) €€€€
An elegant dining experience complete
with lavish 18th-century paintings at
this wonderful ivy-covered château, set
in the midst of beautiful formal gardens.
On the menu, regional favourites with a
Mediterranean twist. Comfortable rooms.

FONTJOCOUSE
▲ **Auberge du Vieux Puits**
5 ave St Victor, 11360 **Map** 11F3
☎ 04 68 44 07 37
FAX 04 68 44 08 31
AE, DC, MC, V ● Sun D, Mon,
Jul–Sep: Mon L, Tue; Jan–Mar
€€ ◇ (8) €€€
Elegant dining and accommodation can
be enjoyed near the Lespinassse forest.
A gastronomic institution in these parts
– they even do cookery courses. Standout
dishes include roast salmon with herbs.

FRONTIGNAN
● **L'Escale**
Les Aresquiers, 34110 **Map** 12A3
☎ 04 67 78 14 86
FAX 04 67 78 14 26
MC, V ● Nov–Jan €€
A terrace right on the sea and excellent
service make a great dining experience.
Simple but exquisite seafood including

rascasse pan-fried in butter with fennel.
Traditional meat dishes too.

GOUDARGES
▲ **La Galantine**
Pl de la Mairie, 30630 **Map** 12B1
☎ 04 66 82 22 39
FAX 04 66 82 96 63
AE, DC, MC, V ● Sun D, Mon D;
last 2 wks Jan €€ ◇ (5) €€
Tiny place that feels more like a friend's
home. Meat dishes such as roast pork
cooked with apricots. Simple guestrooms.

HOMPS
▲ **Auberge de l'Arbousier**
50 ave Carcassonne, 11200 **Map** 11F3
☎ 04 68 91 11 24
FAX 04 68 91 12 61
MC, V ● Sun D, Mon, Tue L
€€€ ◇ (11) €€€
An old wine warehouse with a shaded
terrace that looks onto the Canal du
Midi towpath. Highlights include a light
asparagus mousse and beef with truffles.

LA GRANDE-MOTTE
● **Alexandre-Amirauté**
Esplanade Maurice Justin, 34280
Map 12B2
☎ 04 67 56 63 63
w www.alexandre-restaurant.com
AE, DC, MC, V ● Mon, Oct–Mar:
Sun D, Nov–Feb: Tue €€€
Swish place overlooking the port, and an
elevated terrace with unbeatable views.
Plenty of refreshing salads.

LA GRANDE-MOTTE
● **Bleu Marine**
446 quai Georges Pompidou, 34280
Map 12B2
☎ 04 67 56 55 53
FAX 04 67 56 68 20
AE, MC, V €€
Good view overlooking the marina. A
selection of local specialities includes
buffalo steak, plus seafood such as
king prawns in whisky.

LA GRANDE-MOTTE
■ **Hotel Azur**
Rue Casino, 34280 **Map** 12B2
☎ 04 67 56 56 00
FAX 04 67 29 81 26

w www.hotelazur.net/index.shtml
AE, DC, MC, V ◇ (20) €€€€
Overlooking the port, this small hotel is
immaculately kept and has a personal
touch in the service and the individually
decorated rooms. A large swimming pool
area provides a great place to sunbathe.

LA GRANDE-MOTTE
● **Imprévu**
Centre Commercial Le Miramar, ave
Robert Fages, 34280 **Map** 12B2
☎ 04 67 56 84 05
MC, V €
Totally unpretentious place overlooking
the marina and surrounded by greenery
and flowers. Extensive menu covering a
range of foods, but most interesting are
the seafood offerings: tuna fried with
basil and huge seafood platters.

LA GRANDE-MOTTE
● **La Voile Bleue**
Le Grand Travers (plage), 34280
Map 12B2
☎ 04 67 56 73 83
AE, DC, MC, V
● Nov–Apr €€
A beautiful peoples' hang out right on
the beach and with amazing sea views.
Seafood platters are the house speciality.

LA GRANDE-MOTTE
● **L'Amiral**
Ave Casino, 34280 **Map** 12B2
☎ 04 67 56 65 53
AE, DC, MC, V ● Mar–Oct: Tue
D & Wed €€€
Very traditional and extremely well-
presented restaurant. Light, breezy terrace
and a sumptuousl dining room. Large
menu offering seafood platters, frogs'
legs, sardines and bouillabaisse (p401).

LA GRANDE-MOTTE
● **Le Catamaran**
Les Boutiques du Couchant, 34280
Map 12B2
☎ 04 67 29 74 70
AE, DC, MC, V €
Great seafront eatery, featuring a huge
menu including sea snails in garlic,
oysters and the speciality, macaronade
(tagliatelle with shellfish). Quite superb
selection of ice cream desserts.

LA GRANDE-MOTTE
● L'Estrambord
Quai Pompidou, résidence Grand Pavois, 34280 **Map** 12B2

04 67 56 50 50

DC, MC, V ● Oct–May: Sun D & Mon €€€

Overlooking Port Pompidou, one of the most sophisticated spots in town. Lovely wooden terrace and interesting cave-like interior. Dishes include foie gras with muscat and a red onion compote, squid in lemon confit and local steak.

LA GRANDE-MOTTE
● L'Oasis
Motte du Couchant, 34280 **Map** 12B2

04 67 29 26 88

FAX 04 67 29 26 88

AE, DC, MC, V €

Good value family restaurant right on the seafront. Great selection of seafood. The fish platter consists of sole, king prawns, mussels and sea snails. Orchestra on Tuesday and Thursday nights.

LA GRANDE-MOTTE
● Restaurant Le Grand Bleu
Centre Neptune, pl de L'Epi, 34280 **Map** 12B2

04 67 56 60 97

FAX 04 67 56 26 63

AE, DC, MC, V ● Nov–Jan €€

A real favourite with the locals, firstly because of its fine position, right on the beach, and secondly because of its excellent fish. Traditional dishes include bream fried in butter with basil.

LA POMAREDE
▲ Château de la Pomarede
Château, 1400 **Map** 11E3

04 68 60 49 69

FAX 04 68 60 49 71

DC, MC, V ● Sun D, Mon, Nov–Apr: Tue; 3 wks Nov, last wk Mar, 1 wk Apr €€ (7) €€€

Atmospheric 11th-century fortress with a restaurant serving inventive fish and meat creations. Guestrooms retain some medieval grandeur.

LA SALVETAT-SUR-AGOUT
▲ Café de la Poste-La Pergola
Pl des Troubadours, 34330 **Map** 11F2

04 67 97 55 48

FAX 04 67 97 56 76

MC, V € (9) €€

Tiny brasserie offering basic fare: steak-frites, salads and sandwiches. Simple, inexpensive rooms. Evening concerts on the terrace in summer.

LAMALOU-LES-BAINS
▲ Hôtel Belleville
1 ave Charcot, 34240 **Map** 11F2

04 67 95 57 00

FAX 04 67 95 64 18

MC, V

€€ (55) €€

Traditional, well-presented, pretty little hotel with lots of attention to detail and first-class service. Rooms are small but well appointed. The menu emphasis is on Mediterranean seafood dishes.

LASTOURS
● Le Puits du Trésor
21 route Quatre Châteaux, 11600 **Map** 11F3

04 68 77 50 24

FAX 04 68 77 50 24

MC, V ● Sun D, Mon, Tue, Wed L; mid-Feb–mid-Mar €€€€

This newish eatery is gaining notoriety for classics like lamb with artichoke and rosemary and forest fruit soup.

LATTES
▲ Hôtel Restaurant Le Mejean
Ave Platanes, 34970 **Map** 12A3

04 67 99 79 00

FAX 04 67 22 36 64

W www.lemejean.com

AE, DC, MC, V

€€€ (50) €€€

Perfectly positioned between the coast and Montpellier. Most of the guestrooms overlook the garden and swimming pool. Regional specialities include marinated lobster and venison with bilberries.

LE GRAU-DU-ROI
▲ Grand Sud
45 quai Colbert, 30240 **Map** 12B3

04 66 53 03 63

FAX 04 66 53 03 59

W www.hotel-legrandsud.com

AE, DC, MC, V

€€ (17) €€

Impeccable place overlooking the river. Wicker tables and bright tablecloths add to the laid-back ambience. Specialities such as great monkfish bourride (p373), bouillabaisse (p401) and cod with peppers.

LE GRAU-DU-ROI
▲ Hôtel de la Plage
Bd Maréchal Juin, 30240 **Map** 12B3

04 66 51 40 22

AE, DC, MC, V €€ (28) €€

Deeply traditional. Dishes on offer include baked fillet of sole and rouille Setoise (cuttlefish in a spicy sauce of garlic, tomatoes and peppers), all served up by good-natured, obliging waiters. Guestrooms enjoy sea views.

LE GRAU-DU-ROI
● La Daurade
5 rue de la Rotonde, 30240 **Map** 12B3

04 66 51 52 11

MC, V ● Dec–mid-Jan €€

Bright, friendly spot with a great little terrace, shielded from the road by shrubbery. Menu includes local and Spanish dishes including zarzuela (Spanish fish stew), parillada (seafood mixed grill) and scallops in cream.

LE GRAU-DU-ROI
● La Table du Marché
20 rue Alsace Lorraine, 30240 **Map** 12B3

04 66 53 29 49

AE, DC, MC, V €€

Amazingly tiny place that is very inviting. So, too, is the menu, which might include grilled goats' cheese with almond flakes, salmon with paprika, or grilled sardines.

LE GRAU-DU-ROI
● Le Capriska
Bd du Boucanet, 30240 **Map** 12B3

04 66 51 46 33

DC, MC, V ● May–Sep: D €€

Very simple local place with a wonderful terrace overlooking the town and the sea beyond. On the menu, bouillabaisse (p401) and superb seafood platters. Unbeatable value for money.

LE GRAU-DU-ROI
▲ Oustau Camarguen
3 route Marines Pt Camargue Pge Sud, 30240 **Map** 12B3

☎ 04 66 51 51 65
FAX 04 66 53 06 65
✉ AE, DC, MC, V **●** Nov–Mar
∥ €€ **☕** (39) €€€

On the edge of town, but within walking
distance of the pretty marina. A tranquil
oasis is provided by well-kept gardens.
The restaurant, which overlooks the
swimming pool, serves local dishes with
plenty of seafood. Guestrooms have a
rustic feel with luxury touches.

LE GRAU-DU-ROI
● Restaurant du Port
44 Général de Gaulle, 30240 **Map** 12B3
☎ 04 66 51 41 96
✉ AE, DC, MC, V **∥** €€

Frill-free seafood restaurant with a
terrace over the river and sea views.
Huge selection of fish, plus favourites
such as duck in honey.

LE GRAU-DU-ROI, RIVE GAUCHE
● La Plancha
Rue du Commandant Marceau, 30240
Map 12B3
☎ 04 66 73 39 63
✉ MC, V **●** Nov–Jun: Wed **∥** €

Very simple place with an equally
straightforward menu. Intimate dining
room with a few tables on the terrace.
Bouillabaisse (p401) and grilled fish
are all prepared in front of patrons and
served up with enthusiasm.

LE SOULIE
▲ Ferme-Auberge Le Moulin
On D150 between La Salvetat and Le
Col de Cabaretou, 34330 **Map** 11F2
☎ 04 67 97 22 27
FAX 04 67 97 32 83
@ fa.lemoulin@wanadoo.fr
✉ MC, V **●** Dec–Apr
∥ € **☕** (2) €€

Authentic French country cooking at this
farmhouse restaurant on a cattle ranch.
The menu favours beef dishes, pâtés
and terrines. Try the veal with crayfish or
the wild mushroom omelette. Rooms are
in an adjacent stone building.

LES ANGLES
▲ Meissonnier l'Ermitage
30–34 ave de Verdun, 30133 **Map** 12B2
☎ 04 90 25 41 68

FAX 04 90 25 11 68
✉ DC, MC, V **●** Mon; Feb
∥ €€€€ **☕** (16) €€€

True haute cuisine at this top-rated
restaurant. Presided over by master
chef Michel Meissonnier, the menu lists
pleasures such as aubergine (eggplant)
cake with scallop petals, excellent rabbit
profiteroles with thyme flowers and
lavender honey and a wild strawberry
soufflé. Luxurious guestrooms.

LES COUDOULIERES
▲ La Begude Saint Pierre
Les Coudoulières, 30210
☎ 04 66 63 63 63
FAX 04 66 22 73 73
✉ AE, DC, MC, V **●** Sun D, Mon L,
Tue L; last wk Nov–mid-Feb
∥ €€€€ **☕** (23) €€€€

Upmarket country retreat with luxury
rooms and an exclusive restaurant. In
a restored 17th-century stone building,
the dining room and menu both evoke
the rustic feel of the area. Rascasse
with red rice and aubergine (eggplant)
chips is a highlight. Tranquil rooms.

LEZIGNAN-CORBIERES
▲ Restaurant Tournedos
et Hotel Tassigny
Pl de Lattre-de-Tassigny, 11200
Map 11F3
☎ 04 68 27 11 51
FAX 04 68 27 67 31
✉ AE, DC **●** Sun D, Mon; end
Jan–early Feb, end Sep–mid-Oct
∥ €€ **☕** (18) €€

The modern Tassigny has two stars for
its nondescript en-suite rooms. Try the
Cassoulet (p326) with Toulouse sausage.

LIMOUX
● La Maison de la Blanquette
46 proménade Tivoli, 11300
Map 11B3
☎ 04 68 31 01 63
FAX 04 68 31 20 59
✉ DC, MC, V **∥** €€

Affordable, traditional dishes are served
at this much-loved eatery. On the menu,
hearty meals such as creamy stew with
white beans and fine fish creations like
pike with a compote of grapes and
onions. Local labels on the wine list.

LIMOUX
▲ Moderne et Pigeon
1 pl Général Leclerc, 11300 **Map** 11E3
☎ 04 68 31 00 25
FAX 04 68 31 12 43
W www.grandhotelmodernepigeon.fr
✉ AE, DC, MC, V **●** Jul–Sep: Sun D,
Mon, Sat L; mid-Dec–Jan
∥ €€ **☕** (17) €€€

This wonderful 18th-century building
lies opposite the old market, on a quiet
side street. Well-crafted traditional cuisine
featuring duck is served in the lavish
dining room or else in the leafy courtyard.

LODEVE
▲ Hôtel Croix Blanche
6 ave Fumel, 34700 **Map** 12A2
☎ 04 67 44 10 87
FAX 04 67 44 38 33
W www.hotelcroixblanche.com
✉ MC, V **●** Dec–Mar
∥ €€ **☕** (31) €€

Set in the heart of Lodeve, this very neat
establishment offers quiet accommodation
and great food. The rich meaty dishes of
Languedoc Haute feature grilled lamb.

LODEVE
● Le Petit Sommelier
3 pl de la République, 34700 **Map** 12A2
☎ 04 67 44 05 39
✉ MC, V **●** Sun D, Mon; 1st wk Nov
∥ €

A little bit of bistro chic in this small
town serving classic food. Try the good
warm mussels with Banyuls.

LODEVE
▲ Le Sanglier
Domaine de Cambourras, St Jean de la
Blaquiere, 34700 **Map** 12A2
☎ 04 67 44 70 51
FAX 04 67 44 72 33
W www.logassist.fr/sanglier
✉ MC, V **●** Oct–Mar
∥ €€€ **☕** (10) €€€

Appealing countryside hotel with a lovely
pool and gardens. Charcoal-grilled meats
and fish are the speciality here, as well
as wild boar. Well-equipped rooms.

LUNEL
● Chodoreille
140 rue de Lakanal, 34400 **Map** 12B2

● Restaurant **■** Hotel **▲** Hotel / Restaurant

[C] 04 67 71 55 77

[FAX] 04 67 83 19 97

[E] AE, MC, V [●] Sun, Mon D; last 2
wks Aug [II] €€€

*Bullfighting is de rigueur in this town,
and the beasts show up on the menu at
this restaurant. The focus is on local
products, as is evident in Camargue
beef with apples and Calvados, or the
sole with rosehips and muscat.*

LUNEL
▲ Hotel Restaurant Pont de Lunel
113 pont de Lunel, 34400 **Map** 12B2

[C] 04 67 71 01 62

[FAX] 04 67 71 96 31

[W] www.monauberge.com

[E] AE, DC, MC, V

[II] €€ [🍴] (27) €€

*Cosy little hotel with a huge terrace
overlooking the riverbank. On the menu:
Bouzigues oysters, pan-fried squid salad
and sea bass with fennel. Simple rooms.*

LUSSAN
▲ La Petite Auberge de Lussan
Pl des Marronniers, 30580 **Map** 12B2

[C] 04 66 72 95 53

[W] www.auberge-lussan.com

[E] V [●] Nov–mid-Mar (restaurant)

[II] €€ [🍴] (10) €€

*A quaint 16th-century inn off the main
square. The restaurant serves country-
style meals such as brandade (p373).
Small but well-furnished guestrooms
are amazing value for money.*

MAGALAS
● Restaurant La Boucherie
Pl de l' Eglise, 34880 **Map** 11F3

[C] 04 67 36 20 82

[E] DC, MC, V [●] Sun, Nov–Mar: Mon;
Feb [II] €€

*A restaurant attached to a butcher's
shop. There's an emphasis on meat:
casseroles, charcuterie, steak tartare
or the speciality, tripe. Gaudy decor,
but the good food makes it forgivable.*

MARSEILLAN-PLAGE
▲ Hotel Le Richmont
48 allée Filliol, 34340 **Map** 12A3

[C] 04 67 21 97 79

[FAX] 04 67 21 99 51

[E] AE, DC, MC, V

[II] €€€ [🍴] (34) €€€

*Rooms here are of a high standard
and enjoy a view of either the sea or the
canal. The dining hall is not too formal
and the terrace offers great views.*

MARSEILLAN-PLAGE
● La Marina
Ave Medierannée, 34340 **Map** 12A3

[C] 04 67 21 82 93

[E] MC, V [●] Nov–Apr [II] €€

*Bright, lively, happy atmosphere at this
good value family restaurant. Huge
menu caters to all tastes, but features
in oysters and bouillabaisse (p401).*

MARSEILLAN-PLAGE
● Le Chalut
1 ave Méditerranée, 34340 **Map** 12A3

[C] 04 67 21 88 90

[E] AE, MC, V [II] €€

*Traditional seaside restaurant overlooking
the animated main street. The fine menu
includes scallop casserole, tasty bourride
(p401) and seafood stew.*

MINERVE
▲ Relais Chantovent
17 Grand Rue, 34210 **Map** 11F3

[C] 04 68 91 14 18

[FAX] 04 68 91 81 99

[E] MC, V [●] Sun D, Mon; mid-
Dec–mid-Mar [II] €€ [🍴] (10) €€

*Cosy restaurant offering quite tempting
regional fare as well as amazing views.
The town is entirely surrounded by deep
gorges; the restaurant peeks out over
the cliffs. The fine modern menu
includes asparagus tart and duck with
Minervois wine. Simple guestrooms.*

MOLITG-LES-BAINS
▲ Château de Riell
Les Thermes, 66500 **Map** 11F4

[C] 04 68 05 04 40

[FAX] 04 68 05 04 37

[E] AE, DC, MC, V

[●] Nov–Apr

[II] €€€ [🍴] (19) €€€€€

*A 19th-century turreted château with
views of snow-capped Mont Canigou.
Savour Catalan food in the baroque dining
room. Public rooms mix Art Deco, faux-
rustic and Victorian. The spacious rooms
also have eccentric style.*

MONT-LOUIS
▲ Lou Rouballou
Rue Ecoles Laïques, 66210 **Map** 11E4

[C] 04 68 04 23 26

[FAX] 04 68 04 14 09

[E] MC, V [●] Mon, Tue; May,
Nov–mid-Dec [II] €€ [🍴] (7) €€

*Small establishment offering a cosy
Catalan dining experience. Favourites
are served in the dining room filled with
eccentric artwork, rustic implements and
a fine old fireplace. Guestrooms have a
very similar charm.*

MONTPELLIER
● Brasserie du Théâtre
22 bd Victor Hugo, 34000 **Map** 12A2

[C] 04 67 58 88 80

[E] AE, DC, MC, V [II] €€

*Typical upmarket French brasserie,
set directly opposite the imposing opera
house. Wonderful enclosed terrace with
a delightful fountain. Seafood dominates,
with fresh Breton oysters the speciality,
plus meat and poultry dishes.*

MONTPELLIER
● Crêperie des 2 Provinces
7 rue Jacques Couer, 34000 **Map** 12A2

[C] 04 67 60 68 10

[E] AE, MC, V [●] Sun [II] €

*Typically Breton-style crêperie on the
edge of Place de la Comédie, with about
every conceivable crêpe combination.
Over 150 sweet and savoury varieties,
and plenty using regional ingredients.*

MONTPELLIER
■ Hôtel du Palais
3 rue du Palais, 34000 **Map** 12A2

[C] 04 67 60 47 38

[E] AE, DC, MC, V [🍴] (26) €€€€

*In one of the historic centre's prettiest
quarters, this ancient façade, dotted with
shutters and covered in crawling vines,
houses small, slightly faded rooms.*

MONTPELLIER
■ Hôtel Le Guilhem
18 rue Jean-Jacques-Rousseau, 34000
Map 12A2

[C] 04 67 52 90 90

[E] AE, DC, MC, V [🍴] (36) €€€

*In the heart of the old city, this hotel
consists of two 16th-century buildings.*

Small, well-appointed rooms with plenty of cosy touches. Perhaps the crowning glory is the courtyard and gardens, which provide a peaceful retreat.

MONTPELLIER

● **La Diligence**

2 pl Petraque, 34000 **Map** 12A2

[C] 04 67 66 12 21

[FAX] 04 67 66 80 41

[☑] AE, DC, MC, V

[●] Sun, Mon L, Tue L [☰] €€€

Chef Lombardo serves superb traditional, local dishes in this atmospheric eatery, complete with a vaulted stone ceiling. Menus are very meat and game oriented, with lamb, smoked duck and rabbit all playing star parts. Highly attentive and considerate service.

MONTPELLIER

● **Le Bouchon St Roch**

15 rue du Plan d'Agde, 34000 **Map** 12A2

[C] 04 67 60 94 18

[☑] AE, DC, MC, V [●] Sun [☰] €

Set within sight of Place St Roch and quintessentially French, right down to the red-chequered tablecloths. Quality chateaubriand steak, scallops and king prawns cooked in whisky feature.

MONTPELLIER

● **Le Floreal**

8 rue Alexandre Cabanel, 34000 **Map** 12A2

[C] 04 67 54 14 31

[☑] MC, V

[●] Sun; mid-Jul–mid-Aug [☰] €

A real hole-in-the-wall eatery in a back street in the historic town centre, serving a variety of duck, meat and fish dishes, which are fresh from the market daily.

● **Le Griffou**

5 rue Glaize, 34000 **Map** 12A2

[C] 04 67 60 92 63

[☑] MC, V

[●] Sun, Oct–May: D

[☰] €

Just a few tables inside and a terrace that spills out onto a very narrow street. Simple but accomplished food: cuttlefish in a sauce of oil, garlic and chillies, mushrooms and foie gras with pasta and an excellent paella.

MONTPELLIER

● **Les Bains**

6 rue Richelieu, 34000 **Map** 12A2

[C] 04 67 60 70 87

[☑] AE, DC, MC, V [●] Sun, Mon L

[☰] €€€

Super-chic oasis of tranquillity. This place serves up a range of modern and traditional Mediterranean dishes with a strong emphasis on seafood. Terrace.

MONTPELLIER

■ **New Hôtel du Midi**

22 bd Victor Hugo, 34000 **Map** 12A2

[C] 04 67 92 69 61

[FAX] 04 67 92 73 63

[w] www.new-hotel.com

[☑] AE, MC, V [☕] (47) €€€€

In a grand 19th-century building, this is the only hotel to border Place de la Comedie; try for one of the few rooms facing the square. An imposing entrance hall gives way to ample-sized rooms with modern decor.

MONTPELLIER

● **Roule Ma Poule**

20 pl Cargolle, 34000 **Map** 12A2

[C] 04 67 60 36 15

[☑] AE, DC, MC, V [☰] €

A gorgeous, wonderfully peaceful square provides the setting for unpretentious, traditional French cuisine. Brush shoulders with other diners in the tiny but appealing dining room, but head for the terrace whenever possible for dining al fresco.

MONTPELLIER, LES BEAUX-ARTS

▲ **Le Jardin des Sens**

11 ave Saint Lazare, 34000 **Map** 12A2

[C] 04 99 58 38 38

[w] www.jardindessens.com

[☑] AE, DC, MC, V

[☰] €€€€€ [☕] (12) €€€€€

Twin brothers Jacques and Laurent Pourcel have worked hard for three Michelin stars. Sophisticated menu offering traditional Mediterranean cooking with Asian and North African influences. Booking is strongly advised. Elegant and tranquil guestrooms.

MONTPELLIER, PORT-MARIANNE

● **Séquoïa**

148 rue Galata, 34000 **Map** 12A2

[C] 04 67 65 07 07

[☑] AE, DC, MC, V [●] Sun, Sat L

[☰] €€€

Overlooking a lake, this chic place looks spectacular at night. Menu includes king prawns in lemon sauce and minced duck with gnocchi.

NARBONNE

● **L'Estagnol**

5 bis cours Mirabeau, 11100 **Map** 11F3

[C] 04 68 65 09 27

[FAX] 04 68 32 23 38

[☑] MC, V [●] €€ [●] Sun, Mon D

Authentic dishes from the Mediterranean and the Languedoc served inside a very traditional dining room. Monkfish and sea bream are regular offerings.

NARBONNE

● **La Table St-Crescent**

Domaine St Crescent, 11100 **Map** 11F3

[C] 04 68 41 37 37

[FAX] 04 68 41 01 22

[☑] DC, MC, V [●] Sun D, Mon, Sat L

[☰] €€€

Magnificent yellow-hued building and serene garden. Claude Giraud's noted cuisine includes rabbit with sun-dried tomatoes and skate in olive sauce. Excellent Languedoc wines.

NARBONNE

● **Le Petit Comptoir**

4 bd de Marèchal-Joffre, 11100 **Map** 11F3

[C] 04 68 42 30 35

[FAX] 04 68 41 52 71

[☑] AE, DC, MC, V [●] Sun, Mon [☰] €

An imposing façade gives way to a surprisingly lavish dining room. Popular pasta, casserole and pastry dishes here.

NIMES

● **Courtois**

8 pl du Marche, 30000 **Map** 12B2

[C] 04 66 67 20 09 [☰] €

A truly historical cafés, this is a real Nîmes institution. Glorious mock-baroque interior. Light meals such as sandwiches and salads. Great pastries.

NIMES

● **Darling Café**

40 rue de la Madelaine, 30000

● Restaurant   ■ Hotel   ▲ Hotel / Restaurant

Map 12B2

04 66 67 04 99

AE, DC, MC, V Sun, Tue L

€€€

Wonderfully warm, atmospheric little place with exquisite food. Perfect examples of local cuisine; the regularly changing menu features foie gras, duck, veal and steak as well as frogs' legs.

NIMES

● Grand Café de La Bourse

2 bd Victor Hugo, 30000 **Map** 12B2

04 66 36 12 12

AE, DC, MC, V €

Café/bar with a huge wooden terrace overlooking the splendid Roman arena. Mixed menu offering everything from pizza and salads to traditional beef and fish dishes. There's even a student menu as well as an extensive selection of teas, desserts and patisserie.

NIMES

▲ Hôtel de Provence

5–7 square Couronne, 30000 **Map** 12B2

04 66 36 83 56

FAX 04 66 21 27 40

W www.hoteldeprovence.com

AE, DC, MC, V

€€ (33) €€

Interesting menu with a host of regional dishes and North African influences. Choose from fish lasagne, a selection of pâté, duck and plenty of beef. Bright dining hall, and meticulous and courteous service. Cosy guestrooms.

NIMES

■ Hôtel Imperator Concorde

Quai de la Fontaine, 15 rue Gaston-Bossier, 30000 **Map** 12B2

04 66 21 90 30

FAX 04 66 67 70 25

W www.hotel-imperator.com

AE, DC, MC, V (62) €€€€€

Overlooking the impressive Jardin de la Fontaine, this is one of the town's most scenic spots. Great terrace. Modern rooms with the right amount of luxury.

NIMES

● L' Escalafidou

7 rue Xavier Sigalon, 30000 **Map** 12B2

04 66 21 28 49

MC, V

Sun, Mon €€

Small, tranquil place with a refreshingly clutter-free decor. An interesting menu, with local flavour, includes snail tart, salmon steak in saffron and a range of brochettes. Good selection of sumptuous desserts as well as patisserie of the day.

NIMES

● La Flambée

3 rue Fresque, 30000 **Map** 12B2

04 66 67 53 61

MC, V Sun €

A dark but inviting crêperie. Savoury fillings include salmon, spicy vegetables, spinach and cheese. A host of sweet temptations are complemented by a range of ice creams.

NIMES

● La Fontaine du Temple

22 rue Curaterie, 30000 **Map** 12B2

04 66 21 21 13

FAX 04 66 67 92 48

W www.lafontaine-dutemple.com

AE, DC, MC, V Sun €€€

Run by the Randon family for generations, this restaurant enjoys a historic setting, with high vaulted ceilings and a glorious courtyard with fountain. Try the brandade (p373) mousse, tasty tartiflette (p268) and exquisite garlic soup.

NIMES

● Le Bouchon et L'Assiette

5 bis rue la Sauve, 30000 **Map** 12B2

04 66 62 02 93

FAX 04 66 62 03 57

AE, DC, MC, V Tue, Wed; 1st 2 wks Jan, 2nd wk Jul–3rd wk Aug

€€

Next to the Fontaine gardens, in a lovely old building, this is one of the most upmarket restaurants in Nimes. The food, such as the lightly grilled foie gras with caramelized peppers and grapes, brims with creativity.

NIMES

● Le Magister

5 rue Nationale, 30000 **Map** 12B2

04 66 76 11 00

@ le.magister@wanadoo.fr

AE, MC, V

Sun, Mon L, Sat L

€€€€

Light, comfy decor provides the setting for an eating experience to be savoured at this super-swish eatery boasting a host of restaurant awards. Regularly changing menu, typically including foie gras, salmon tartare, exquisitely prepared vegetables and a fine selection of wines.

NIMES

● Le Paseo

10 pl du Marche, 30000 **Map** 12B2

04 66 67 76 94

FAX 04 66 27 01 62

AE, DC, MC, V Sun €

The star attraction here is the pretty little terrace. Service is swift and the menu is a good mix of pastas, steak dishes and seafood. Dishes include salade Nîmoise (seafood salad) and cassoulet (p373).

NIMES

● Le Provencal

4 rue Ecole Vieille, 30000 **Map** 12B2

04 66 21 30 18

AE, DC, MC, V Sun, Wed

€€€

An intimate, happy, local restaurant. Formal but friendly, this is a good place to try pork brandade (p373), magret de canard and frogs' legs with parsley. A good selection of local wines is well presented by knowledgeable staff.

NIMES

● Le Taros

24 rue l'Etoile, 30000 **Map** 12B2

04 66 87 19 84

AE, DC, MC, V Sun €

Stylish little place with minimalist decor and a relaxing ambience. The menu includes tuna steak Provençal, entrecôte and a shellfish brandade (p373) as well as a few more adventurous offerings such as fine curried chicken tagliatelle.

NIMES

● Le Vintage Café

7 rue de Bernis, 30000 **Map** 12B2

04 66 21 04 45

AE, DC Sun, Mon, Sat L; 2 wks Aug €€

In the heart of the old town, with a terrace overlooking the tiniest square imaginable, complete with fountain. Inside, the dining area is compact and atmospheric. A variety of meat, seafood and poultry is served, with an emphasis on regional dishes.

NIMES

▲ Les 7 Collines

Esplanade Charles-de-Gaulle, 5 bd de Prague, 30000 **Map** 12B2

04 66 76 56 56

FAX 04 66 76 56 59

www.accorhotels.com

AE, DC, MC, V

€€€€ (119) €€€€

Good food and a splendid glass-covered terrace. A range of traditional French and regional dishes are on offer, with particular focus on meat dishes such as rack of lamb in garlic or pan-fried veal. Service is excellent. Simple guestrooms.

NIMES

● Les Milles Pattes

12 rue Condé, 30000 **Map** 12B2

04 66 67 37 38

AE, DC, MC, V €

Small locals' bar and restaurant with a selection of imaginative pasta dishes such as gnocchi with duck and garlic. Straw-matted floor, plants and earthy colours give the place a rural feel, while the small terrace enjoys pleasant views of the nearby church and square.

NIMES

● Los Piementos

24 bd Victor Hugo, 30000 **Map** 12B2

04 66 21 95 62

FAX 04 66 21 95 62

AE, DC, MC, V Sun €€

Small, popular family-friendly restaurant. Mixed set menus with interesting local dishes, including gratins, brandade (p373), and assiete Alizes (a mixture of bread, brandade, aubergine/eggplant caviar and goats' cheese).

NIMES

● Raphael's

12 rue Etoile, 30000 **Map** 12B2

04 66 36 85 98

AE, DC, MC, V Sun €€€

In an ancient stone building in the heart of the old town, and renowned for its Nîmoise dishes and incredibly smooth foie gras. The menu focuses on traditional meat dishes such as brandade (p373), with a smaller selection of fish. Good range of regional wines, too.

NIMES

● Restaurant Le Tango

6 rue Thoumayne, 30000 **Map** 12B2

04 66 67 40 77

AE, DC, MC, V Sun €€

Cheery little place comprised of a series of tiny dining rooms. Fish casserole, king prawns flambéed in whisky and great foie gras are on offer.

NIMES

● Le Pavillion de la Fontaine

9 quai Georges Clemenceau, 34000 **Map** 12B2

04 66 64 09 93

MC, V Sun €€

Contemporary dining room with a vast terrace overlooking the splendid Jardin de la Fontaine. A selection of fixed menus with brandade (p373), cassoulet (p373) and duck with green peppers.

NISSAN-LEZ-ENSERUNE

▲ Hôtel-Résidence

35 ave de la Cave, 34440 **Map** 11F3

04 67 37 00 63

FAX 04 67 37 68 63

MC, V L; Jan

€€ (18) €€

A typical 19th-century town house with a mix of old-style charm and modern elegance. Menu highlights include confit de canard (p326) with foie gras and onion jam, and scallop and leek tart. Good value for this level of quality. Cosy rooms boast period furniture.

OCTON

▲ La Calade

Pl de l'Eglise, 34800 **Map** 12A2

04 67 96 19 21

FAX 04 67 88 61 25

www.lacalade.com

AE, MC, V Tue, Sep–Jun: Wed; mid-Dec–Feb €€ (7) €€

On the edge of beautiful Lake Salagou, this unpretentious hotel-restaurant offers good food and spacious rooms as well as access to excellent fishing, hiking and biking. Specialities include crayfish casserole with ginger, lamb with garlic cream and goat's cheese with apples.

OLARGUES

▲ Domaine de Rieumégé

Route de St Pons, 34390 **Map** 11F3

04 67 97 73 99

FAX 04 67 97 78 52

www.tbsfrance.com/rieumege

MC, V L; Nov–Mar

€€€ (14) €€€€

Old farmhouse reborn as an upmarket bed-and-breakfast in the Parc Naturel du Haut Languedoc. Classy guestrooms with period furniture. Dishes feature specialities such as foie gras terrine, fig purée and chicken with crayfish.

ORNAISONS

▲ Le Relais du Val-d'Orbieu

Chemin départemental 24, 11200 **Map** 11F3

04 68 27 10 27

FAX 04 68 27 52 44

@ Relais.Du.Val.Dorbieu@wanadoo.fr

AE, DC, MC, V L, Nov–Mar: Sun D; mid-Nov–Jan

€€€ (20) €€€€

The terracotta tiles, Mediterranean plants and layout of this former mill have echoes of Italian villas and Spanish haciendas. Beautiful vegetables and exquisite fish dishes are a welcome change to meat-laden menus. Rooms have a cool, fresh feel.

PALAVAS-LES-FLOTS

● La Passerelle

Quai Paul-Cunq Rive Gauche, 34250 **Map** 12A2

04 67 68 55 80

MC, V Oct–Apr €

On the quieter side of the resort, a place for no-nonsense local seafood. Fish soup is the speciality. Better value would be hard to find around here, and the setting is wonderful – right on the edge of the gorgeous canal.

PERPIGNAN

● Banyols et Banyols

7 rue Cardeurs, 66000 **Map** 11F4

04 68 34 48 40

FAX 04 68 51 25 99

▓ MC, V ⬤ Sun, Mon

🍽 €€

Regional favourites are given imaginative treatment at this good-value bistro, run by a jovial father-and-son team. The gourmet menu hits all the right spots while the wine list includes local labels and Spanish vintages.

PERPIGNAN
⬤ Casa Sansa

2 rue Fabriques Nadal, 66000 **Map** 11F4

☎ 04 68 34 21 84

▓ AE, DC, MC, V 🍽 €

A big hit with the locals, this place serves authentic local food with an emphasis on good value. Hearty portions of tapas and traditional Catalan dishes, and intriguing decor with plenty of photos and pictures to muse over.

PERPIGNAN
■ Hôtel de la Loge

1 rue Fabriques d'en Nabol, 66000
Map 11F4

☎ 04 68 34 41 02

FAX 04 68 34 25 13

ⓦ www.hoteldelaloge.fr

▓ AE, DC, MC, V 🍴 (21) €€€

A delightful 15th-century mansion, this small, family-run hotel is ideally situated right in the town centre. Guestrooms are large, well equipped and comfortable; all have bathrooms and TV.

PERPIGNAN
⬤ La Soleillade

1 bd Kennedy, 66000 **Map** 11F4

☎ 04 68 50 25 25

FAX 04 68 50 38 73

▓ MC, V ⬤ Sun D, Mon, Sat L; 1st wk
Jan, mid-Jul–mid-Aug 🍽 €€

Catalan cuisine at this excellent eatery where chef's creations are arguably the best in town. Menu highlights include a fine melon and muscat grape tart and memorable tuna steak.

PERPIGNAN
⬤ Les Trois Sœurs

2 rue Frontfroide, 66000 **Map** 11F4

☎ 04 68 51 22 33

FAX 04 68 51 63 36

▓ AE, DC, MC, V ⬤ Sun, Mon L

🍽 €€

Three sisters run this contemporary restaurant that has views over a square and church. The menu offers a range of seafood together with traditional meat and poultry dishes, such as foie gras.

PEZENAS
⬤ Aprés le Déluge

5 ave Marechal Plantavit, 34120
Map 12A3

☎ 04 67 98 10 77

▓ AE, DC, MC, V ⬤ L 🍽 €€

Eat a piece of history at this restaurant, which takes its recipes from antique cookbooks. The Marquis de Sade's favourite cake is a menu standard, and heirloom vegetables are used in the kitchen. Weekly piano jazz concerts.

PONT-ST-ESPRIT
▲ Auberge Provençale

Route Bagnols, 30130 **Map** 12B1

☎ 04 66 39 08 79

FAX 04 66 39 14 28

▓ MC, V ⬤ Oct–Mar: Sun D; last wk
Dec–1st wk Jan 🍽 € 🍴 (14) €

Inexpensive family inn with simple guestrooms. Portions are generous and include favourites such as frogs' legs and steak tartare.

PORT-LA-NOUVELLE
▲ La Rascasse

8 ave de la Mer, 11210 **Map** 11F3

☎ 04 68 48 02 89

FAX 04 68 40 35 95

▓ MC, V ⬤ Sun D, Mon; Feb 🍽
€€ 🍴 (7) €€

Characterful dining room with views of the sea. Highlights include anchovy and red-pepper puff pastry and lots of good seafood. Rather fine ice creams too. Comfortable, sweet guestrooms.

PORT-VENDRES
⬤ La Côte Vermeille

Quai Fanal, 66660 **Map** 11F4

☎ 04 68 82 05 71

FAX 04 68 82 05 71

▓ AE, DC, MC, V ⬤ Sun, Mon;
Jan–Feb 🍽 €€€

A beguiling quayside spot in a charming fishing town. On the menu, langoustine salad, scallops cooked in Banyuls wine and lemon tart with apricot sauce.

PRATS-DE-MOLLO
▲ Le Bellevue

Pl Foiral, 66230 **Map** 11F4

☎ 04 68 39 72 48

FAX 04 68 39 78 04

ⓦ www.lebellevue.fr.st

▓ DC, MC, V ⬤ Tue, Nov: Wed;
Dec–mid-Feb

🍽 €€ 🍴 (18) €€

Excellent Catalan hotel-restaurant near the town's medieval ramparts. Standout creations include the lobster stewed in aged Banyuls wine. Amongst the divine desserts is the beautifully presented crème catalane (p372). Comfortable guestrooms with good facilities.

ROQUEFORT-DES-CORBIERES
⬤ Le Lezard Bleu

Rue de l'Eglise, 11540 **Map** 11F3

☎ 04 68 48 51 11

▓ AE, DC, MC, V ⬤ Oct–Jun

🍽 €€

In an ancient building at the heart of the old town, an interesting selection of modern art enlivens the tiny dining room. Small menu with a number of traditional dishes – many made with duck. Reservations recommended, especially at weekends.

SAILLAGOUSE
▲ L'Atalaya

Llo, 66800 **Map** 11E4

☎ 04 68 04 70 04

FAX 04 68 04 01 29

@ atalaya66@aol.com

▓ MC, V ⬤ Mon–Fri L; Nov–mid-
Dec, mid-Jan–Apr

🍽 €€€ 🍴 (13) €€€€

A handsome Catalan farmhouse building on a verdant hillside serving top-notch regional fare. Interiors marry dark-wood elegance with fresh decorative touches. Spotless guestrooms.

SAUVE
▲ Hôtel Restaurant La Magnanerie

Quai Evesque, 30610 **Map** 12A2

☎ 04 66 77 57 44

FAX 04 66 77 02 31

ⓦ www.lamagnanerie.fr

▓ AE, DC, MC, V 🍽 €€€ 🍴 (9) €€

A 17th-century mansion and an ideal retreat. The vaulted dining room provides an atmospheric setting and serves up fare including game as well as fruit and vegetables from the hotel's garden. Small but comfortable guestrooms.

SETE
● **Chez Massimo**
66 Grand Rue Mario Roustan, 34200 **Map** 12A3
(04 67 78 84 69
AE, MC, V
● Tue–Sun L, Mon **11** €
Bright, cheery place, adorned with lots of fresh flowers. Good-value menu with superb seafood stew, grilled fish and king prawns pan-fried in Cognac.

SETE
▲ **Hotel Port Marine**
Le Môle St-Louis, 34200 **Map** 12A3
(04 67 74 92 34
FAX 04 67 74 92 33
w www.roussillhotel.com
AE, DC, MC, V ● L
11 €€€ ◇ (42) €€€
Contemporary hotel and restaurant enjoying a prime spot overlooking the sea. The minimalist decor makes for a calming atmosphere. In the restaurant: fish soup or monkfish in saffron with ratatouille (p400). Rooms are nicely laid out, if small, and each has a terrace.

SETE
● **La Calanque**
10 bis quai Géneral Durand, 34200 **Map** 12A3
(04 67 74 28 37
AE, DC, MC, V **11** €€
Overlooking the canal and port, this place is as popular for its good-value seafood as for its meat-topped pasta dishes, a local speciality.

SETE
● **La Corniche**
Pl Edouard Herriot, 34200 **Map** 12A3
(04 67 53 03 30
MC, V ● mid-Nov–mid-Jan
11 €€
Traditional restaurant offering Sètoise dishes, including enormous seafood platters, big enough to feed a family and a change from the surrounding tourist traps. Small terrace.

SETE
■ **La Joie des Sables**
Route de la Corniche, 34200 **Map** 12A3
(04 67 53 11 76
AE, DC, MC, V ◇ (55) €€€
More exclusive than its neighbours, this three-star hotel has small, tastefully decorated rooms. Most have sea views.

SETE
● **La Marine**
29 quai Géneral Durand, 34200 **Map** 12A3
(04 67 74 30 03
FAX 04 67 74 38 18
AE, DC, MC, V **11** €€
A simple but upmarket seafood restaurant. Bouillabaisse (p401) and sardines and bourride (p373) feature.

SETE
● **La Péniche**
1 quai Moulins, 34200 **Map** 12A3
(04 67 48 64 13
AE, DC, MC, V ● Sat L **11** €
A delightful houseboat on a canal with simple, authentic French cuisine at a decent price. The menu includes crayfish and generous portions of profiteroles.

SETE
● **La Rotonde**
17 quai de-Lattre-de-Tassigny, 34200 **Map** 12A3
(04 67 74 86 14
AE, DC, MC, V
● Sun, Thu L, Sat L; last wk Dec–1st wk Jan **11** €€€
Originally part of the imposing Grand Hotel, this is a restaurant for a special occasion. The imposing baroque interior is offset by an imaginative menu. House specialities include roast pigeon with dried fruits and thyme and lamb chop with rosemary.

SETE
● **Le Bistrot Quai**
92 Grand Rue Mario-Roustan, 34200 **Map** 12A3
(04 99 04 99 90
MC, V ● Sun, Mon; 2 wks Jun **11** €€
Small, intimate eatery with an interesting menu; grilled cuttlefish and duck with

honey and grapes are two of the more unusual offerings. Fish a speciality.

SETE
● **Le Chante Mer**
16 promenade Jean Baptiste Marty, 34200 **Map** 12A3
(04 67 46 01 75
AE, DC, MC, V **11** €€
Extensive menu includes bouillabaisse (p401), tuna with tomatoes and macaroni with mussels. Also a huge selection of desserts such as fruit tarts and sorbets.

SETE
● **Le Flore**
21 Général de Gaulle, 34200 **Map** 12A3
(04 67 43 76 58
MC, V **11** €
Super-cheap traditional brasserie. A real locals' place that's great for a leisurely lunch. On offer is a selection of steaks, warm goat cheese salad, and mussels.

SETE
■ **Le Grand Hôtel**
17 quai de Tassigny, 34200 **Map** 12A3
(04 67 74 71 77
FAX 04 67 74 29 27
w www.sete-hotel.com
AE, DC, MC, V ◇ (43) €€€
Situated on the Ile Singulière, the town's oldest hotel is particularly good for those seeking a touch of good value luxury. The decor blends old and new – the public rooms are traditional while the bedrooms have a more modern theme.

SETE
● **Le Pat'Any**
39 quai Licciardi, 34200 **Map** 12A3
(04 67 74 38 37
AE, DC, MC, V
● Sun D, Mon
11 €€
Refreshingly contemporary restaurant with subtle nautical theme. A terrace overlooks the port. Huge seafood platters, grilled king prawns with fresh thyme and smoked duck cooked in green peppers.

SETE
● **Le Toit De Calou**
82 Grand Rue Mario Roustan, 34200 **Map** 12A3

● Restaurant ■ Hotel ▲ Hotel / Restaurant

🔲 04 67 74 40 24
🔲 AE, DC, MC, V
⚫ Tue 🔲 €€

There's a strong Spanish influence on the menu at this rustic restaurant. Service is relaxed and informal, to match the surroundings. Grilled fish dishes, including mackerel, seafood platters and spicy seafood salad. Live music most evenings.

SETE
● Le Véradier
1 promenade Jean Baptiste Marty, 34200 **Map** 12A3
🔲 04 67 74 49 70
🔲 AE, DC, MC, V
⚫ Fri 🔲 €€

Seaside restaurant serving up a huge variety of seafood such as the mixed fish grill. Grilled bream, prawns, oysters and mussels are also served. The glassed-over terrace has sea views.

SETE
● Palangrotte
Quai Général Durand, 34200 **Map** 12A3
🔲 04 67 74 80 35
🔲 04 67 74 97 20
🔲 AE, MC, V
⚫ Sep–Jun: Sun D, Mon 🔲 €€

An excellent seafood restaurant near the old port. Specialities include turbot in sea salt, bouillabaisse (p401), grilled monkfish and seafood platters.

SETE
● Restaurant de la Criée
11 quai Maximin Licciardi, 34200 **Map** 12A3
🔲 04 67 74 90 27
🔲 AE, MC, V ⚫ Mon 🔲 €€

Little restaurant right on the port. Small terrace and a cheery dining room. Huge selection of seafood dishes including oysters and snails from the Etang.

SETE
● Restaurant Isola Bella
32 rue Victor Hugo, 34200 **Map** 12A3
🔲 04 67 74 11 95
🔲 AE, DC, MC, V
⚫ Mon 🔲 €€

Cosy 1930s brasserie-style eatery offers classic Italian dishes and some French-Italian fusion. Specialities are tuna in a pepper and tomato sauce with seafood pâté and squid and scallops in a fine Provençal sauce. Small terrace.

SETE
● Restaurant La Mamounia
2 rue Palais, 34200 **Map** 12A3
🔲 04 67 46 12 25
🔲 MC, V ⚫ Mon 🔲 €

Tiny place with an equally small menu, offering traditional Moroccan dishes. Watch a variety of tagines and couscous dishes being prepared.

SETE
● Restaurant Les Flots d'Azur
Plage de la Corniche, Quartier Les Quilles, 34200 **Map** 12A3
🔲 04 67 53 01 52
🔲 04 67 51 24 26
🔲 AE, DC, MC, V 🔲 €€€

Tasteful, cool and breezy restaurant overlooking a long sandy beach. Careful attention to detail makes for first-class service. Seafood is the star, with a selection of shellfish from the Etang du Thau as well as Mediterranean fish.

SEYNES
▲ Restaurant Hôtel La Farigoulette
Le Village, 30580 **Map** 12A2
🔲 04 66 83 70 56
🔲 04 66 83 72 80
🔲 www.lafarigoulette.com
🔲 MC, V 🔲 €€ 🔲 (16) €€

Great family-oriented place on the edge of the Cevenne. A huge terrace and swimming pool provide a social focal point. The inviting stone and timber restaurant is famed throughout the region for its dishes such as smoked duck and steak tartare. Simple rooms.

SOREDE
● La Salamandre
3 route Laroque des Albères, 66690 **Map** 11F4
🔲 04 68 89 26 67
🔲 04 68 89 26 67
🔲 AE, DC, MC, V ⚫ Sun D, Mon, mid-Jul–mid-Sep: Tue L; Jan–mid-Mar, mid-Nov–Dec 🔲 €€

An intimate family-run restaurant serving simply prepared, traditional Catalan fare such as pork with apricots. Soak up the conviviality amid rustic surroundings.

ST-ANDRE-DE-ROQUEPERTUIS
● La Frigoulette
Le coureau, Rouvière, 30630 **Map** 12B1
🔲 04 66 82 21 26
🔲 AE, DC, MC, V ⚫ Sep–May: Sun
🔲 €€

Great-value restaurant with an informal country feel. Meat and fish are grilled over a wood fire. Other dishes include snails in herbs and butter as well an excellent roast lamb. Good local wine served by the pitcher.

ST-CYPRIEN
▲ Ile de la Lagune - L'Amandin
Bd de l'Amandin, Les Capellans, 66750 **Map** 11F4
🔲 04 68 21 01 02
🔲 04 68 21 06 28
🔲 AE, DC, MC, V ⚫ Mon, mid-Oct–mid-Apr: Tue; Feb, 1st wk Nov
🔲 €€€€ 🔲 (22) €€€€

Four-star beachside hotel with smart interiors and a fabulous restaurant. Seafood dishes such as red mullet, anchovies and caviar dominate. Very comfortable, well-equipped guestrooms.

ST-GERVAIS-SUR-MARE
● Ferme Piscicole du Pont des 3 Dents
Route de Castanet le Bas, 34610 **Map** 11F2
🔲 04 67 23 65 48
⚫ D, Mon L, Sep–Jun: Tue L; Jan
🔲 €

Fish farm with its own restaurant. Trout, salmon trout and crayfish are the highlights. If you feel like it, you can catch them yourself. If not, a fine menu featuring various takes on the trout-crayfish theme is available. Book ahead.

ST-GILLES
▲ Hôtel Restaurant du Cours
10 ave François Griffeuille, 30800 **Map** 12B2
🔲 04 66 87 31 93
🔲 04 66 87 31 83
🔲 AE, DC, MC, V 🔲 € 🔲 (34) €€

Set right at the edge of the Camargue, this hotel offers great value no-fuss rooms. The vast, formal dining room is bright, while trees provide a shady terrace. The menus feature a host of regional specialities including game.

ST-HILAIRE-D'OZHILHAN
▲ L'Arceau
1 rue de L'Arceau, 30210 **Map** 12B2

(04 66 37 34 45
FAX 04 66 37 33 90
✉ AE, DC, MC, V **●** Sun D, Mon L, Tue L; mid-Nov–mid-Feb
🍴 €€€ **🍽** (21) €€

Superb restaurant serving all the classics of the region, including warmed goose foie gras, lamb casserole and lobster. The restaurant and hotel take up part of an old stone house. Luxurious rooms.

ST-HILAIRE-DE-BRETHMAS
● Auberge de St-Hilaire
5 rue André Schenk, 30560 **Map** 12B2

(04 66 30 11 42
FAX 04 66 86 72 79
✉ MC, V
● Sun D, Mon **🍴** €€€€

Gastronomic elegance in a country setting. The wide-ranging menu includes foie gras and tete-de-veau and the wine list includes vintages from Bordeaux and Burdundy. Pretty outdoor terrace.

ST-HIPPOLYTE-DU-FORT
▲ Auberge Cigaloise
Route de Nimes, 30170 **Map** 12A2

(04 66 77 64 59
FAX 04 66 77 25 08
✉ MC, V **●** Dec–Feb
🍴 €€ **🍽** (10) €€

Delightful inn with a genuine family feel. The small restaurant concentrates on traditional meat dishes such as boar and lamb. Huge pool and terrace; bedrooms overlook the rolling countryside.

ST-HIPPOLYTE-DU-FORT
● Auberge de Valestalière
rue de Lasalle, 30170 **Map** 12A2

(04 66 85 45 79
FAX 04 66 85 45 79
✉ DC, MC, V
● Sun D, Mon, Tue; late Dec–early Feb **🍴** €€

A rustic dining room in an old school building. Local cuisine includes foie gras

and magret de canard. Views sweep over the valley from the outdoor terrace.

ST-JEAN-DE-VEDAS
▲ Yan's Hôtel
Mas de Grille, 93 rue Théophrase Renaudot, 34430 **Map** 12A2

(04 67 47 07 45
FAX 04 67 47 16 90
W www.yans-hotel.com
✉ AE, DC, MC, V
🍴 €€ **🍽** (40) €€

Set just off the A9, but in a nice, quiet leafy location. Well-proportioned rooms, most of which overlook the swimming pool and gardens. The restaurant offers French favourites such as foie gras and steak tartare. Good selection of wines from the local area, too.

ST-LAURENT-DE-CARNOLS
● La Ferme du Gubernat
Route de Salazac, 30200 **Map** 12B1

(04 66 82 21 27
FAX 04 66 82 70 90
● Jan, Jul **🍴** €€€

Built on the remains of a medieval mill, this family farm, a local institution, breeds ducks. Foie gras and confit de canard are presented in various guises and served with the farm's own Côtes-du-Rhône. Reservations required.

ST-LAURENT-DES-ARBRESSAINT
● Le Papet
2 pl de la Maire, 30126 **Map** 12B2

(04 66 50 34 54
✉ AE, DC, MC, V
● Sun D, mid-July–Aug: Mon, Wed
🍴 €€

Characterful little place just on the edge of the village, offering good value for money. Brandade de morue (p373) and seiche à la rouille (cuttlefish in oil, garlic and chillies) are served.

ST-MATHIEU-DE-TREVIERS
▲ L'Auberge du Cèdre
Domaine de Cazeneuve Lauret, 34270 **Map** 12A2

(04 67 59 02 02
W www.auberge-du-cedre.com
✉ AE, DC, MC, V
● Jan–Mar
🍴 €€ **🍽** (19) €€

A small auberge, part of an historic mansion house. Rooms are spacious and simple with a subtle contemporary style. Bathrooms are shared. The biggest draw is the restaurant, with its selection of top dishes such as brandade de morue (p373) and cassoulet (p373).

TORNAC
▲ Hotel restaurant les Demeures du Ranquet
Route St Hippolyte, 30140 **Map** 12A2

(04 66 77 51 63
FAX 04 66 77 55 62
✉ AE, DC, MC, V
● Tue, Nov–Mar: Wed
🍴 €€€€
🍽 (28) €€€€

Exclusive place with rustic charm and vast, luxurious rooms. Extensive gardens and a swimming pool lend a retreat-like feel. Master chef Ann Majourel provides an exquisite menu that draws on the flavours of the Cevennnes. She also holds top-notch cookery classes.

TORREILLES-VILLAGE
■ La Vieille Demeure
4 rue de Llobet, 66440 **Map** 11F4

(04 68 28 45 71
FAX 04 68 28 45 71
@ vignaud.christine@wanadoo.fr
✉ MC, V **🍽** (5) €€€

If you are seeking an intimate place with a truly special ambience, consider this 17th-century building a few miles from the coast. Rooms are sparsely furnished yet comfortable, and the overall effect is one of cool elegance. Relax on the Andalucian-style patio.

UZES
● Chez Myou
1 pl St-Etienne, 30700 **Map** 12B2

(04 66 22 59 28
✉ MC, V
● Mon; Nov **🍴** €€

Bright, jolly and very simple locals' restaurant with a terrace overlooking the church. Cassoulet (p373), smoked duck in honey and even truffles feature.

UZES
▲ Hôtel du Général d'Entraigues
8 rue de la Calade – Pl de l'Evêché,

30700 **Map** 12B2

C 04 66 22 32 68

FAX 04 66 22 57 01

W www.lcm.fr/savry/3.htm

E AE, DC, MC, V

H €€€ 🍴 (36) €€€

Smart hotel and restaurant next to an imposing cathedral in an extremely peaceful town centre location. Guestrooms have period furniture and exposed beams. The restaurant's menu provides classic cuisine with a few twists, like tuna with fennel and anise.

UZES

● **La Fontaine**

18 pl Albert 1er, 30700 **Map** 12B2

C 04 66 22 17 25

FAX 04 66 22 17 30

E MC, V

● Sun **H** €

A gracious outdoor café with a wide terrace and bubbling fountain. The menu offers simple fare such as steak and salade niçoise (p401). Arrive early on Saturdays for the farmers' market.

UZES

● **Le Bistrot Du Grézac**

Pl Belle Croix, 30700 **Map** 12B2

C 04 66 03 42 09

E MC, V

● Mon **H** €€

Cosy bistro in the heart of this medieval town. An eclectic menu offers a variety of bistro standards such as steak tartare and seafood platters, as well as some oddities like kangaroo steak with zesty honey and ginger sauce.

UZES

● **Les Trois Salons**

18 rue du Docteur Blanchard, 30700 **Map** 12B2

C 04 66 22 57 34

FAX 04 66 22 48 34

E MC, V

● Mon **H** €€€

Haunt of the local hip crowd. Three elegant, sleek dining rooms and a classy terrace with an ancient fountain. On the exquisite menu, tasty tarragon-infused artichoke gnocchi and lamb braised with apricots and fennel, or grilled skate with refreshing mint and lemon.

UZES

● **Terroirs**

5 pl aux Herbes, 30700 **Map** 12B2

C 04 66 03 41 90

FAX 03 66 22 58 83

@ terroirs-uzes@wanadoo.fr

E MC, V ● Mon; Feb, last 2 wks Nov

H €

On the main square, this is the perfect place for a light lunch. The solid menu features lots of inventive tartines (grilled sandwiches) and good cold salad plates. Impressive selection of wines, too.

VERS-PONT-DU-GARD

▲ **Hôtel de la Bégude Saint Pierre**

La Bégude, 30210 **Map** 12B2

C 04 66 63 63 63

FAX 04 66 22 73 73

W www.hotel-saintpierre.fr

E AE, DC, MC, V

● Dec–Feb: Sun D, Mon

H €€€€ 🍴 (20) €€€€€

Gorgeous 17th-century château, lovingly restored to its former glory. The top-class Mediterranean food such as veal with tapenade (p400), savoury fried aubergine (eggplant) chips and rascasse is all magnificently presented. The cosy rooms have beamed ceilings and sleek, contemporary fittings.

VEZENOBRES

▲ **Le Relais Sarrasin**

Route 106, 30360 **Map** 12B2

C 04 66 83 55 55

FAX 04 66 83 66 83

W www.le-relais-sarrasin.com

E AE, DC, MC, V

● Sun D, Mon, May–Sep: Wed

H €€ 🍴 (16) €€

Family-run hotel and restaurant ideally located at the foot of this interesting village. Regional cuisine is served on the poolside terrace or indoors. All the rooms in this former fire station are renovated to a high standard and offer plenty of comfort.

VILLEFRANCHE-DE-CONFLENT

● **Auberge St-Paul**

Pl de l'Eglise, 66500 **Map** 11F4

C 04 68 96 30 95

FAX 04 68 05 60 30

E DC, MC, V ● Sun D, Mon,

Oct–Apr: Tue; early Jan, 1st wk Jun, Nov–mid-Dec **H** €€€

Restaurant within the medieval ramparts. Menu mainstays include tasty deep-fried langoustines with herbs and the Landes duck brochettes. Roussillon labels and Bordeaux reds on the wine list.

VILLENEUVE-LES-AVIGNON

▲ **Les Cèdres**

39 ave Pasteur, 30400 **Map** 12B2

C 04 90 25 43 92

FAX 04 90 25 14 66

@ lescedres.hotel@lemel.fr

E MC, V ● Nov–Mar

H €€ 🍴 (21) €€€

Lovely hotel and restaurant in a country mansion surrounded by a private park, in a residential neighbourhood on the outskirts of town. Period furniture and modern amenities in the guestrooms. Restaurant offerings include regional cuisine such as lamb with basil.

VILLENEUVETTE

▲ **La Source**

3km (2 miles) west of Clermont l'Herault on D908, 34800 **Map** 12A2

C 04 67 96 05 07

FAX 04 67 96 90 09

W www.hoteldelasource.com

E MC, V

● mid-Nov–mid-Feb

H €€ 🍴 (13) €€

In part of what was once the royal textile mills, this fine hotel-restaurant respects the 17th-century ambience of this unique building. Guestrooms are furnished with period touches. Olive oil, local produce and fish are the solid foundations of the menu.

VIVES

▲ **L'Hostalet de Vivès**

Rue Mairie, 66490 **Map** 11F4

C 04 68 83 05 52

FAX 04 68 83 51 91

E MC, V

● Tue, Wed; mid-Dec–Feb

H €€ 🍴 (3) €€€

Wonderful building in a tranquil village, serving hearty Catalan food such as snails Catalan-style and crème catalane (p372). Guestrooms are small but well maintained, with a homely feel.

PROVENCE & THE COTE D'AZUR

The very names evoke France at its most glamorous and colourful. Olives, garlic, figs, melons and fragrant herbs head a panoply of ingredients that also includes succulent lamb from the hills and fish from the azure Mediterranean. This truly is the "cuisine of the sun".

The Flavours of Provence

The produce of this region is famed throughout France, and indeed the world. Olives, fruit, vegetables and herbs thrive in the glorious climate, complementing the fish docked at the ports along its Mediterranean coastline and the lamb and game that roam its hills and forests.

BEST MARKETS

Amost every town or village has its own market at least one day a week, and there are *Marchés Paysans* in summer, and winter truffle markets at Carpentras, Aups, Richerenches and Rognes
Aix-en-Provence Place Richelme. Chic shopping for fruit and veg, daily am
Apt Fabulous Luberon produce around the streets of the old town, Sat am
Arles This lively market is the place for olive oil and *saucisson d'Arles*. Wed, Sat am
Cannes Busy covered market in the old town. Tue–Sun am
Carpentras True local rendezvous sprawling along the boulevards. Fri am
Marseille fish market Flapping fresh fish sold straight from the boats. Daily am
Menton Fine local produce and fresh fish, in and around the covered market, daily am
Nice Fresh veg and flowers on cours Saleya, also fish on Place St-François. Tue–Sun am
Salernes Authentic village market in the town square. Wed, Sun am
Toulon Busy urban street market with fabulous vegetables. Daily am

Freshly caught Mediterranean sea bass

MEAT AND CHARCUTERIE

Lamb is the most important meat in these parts, notably *agneau de Sisteron*, which gets its prized flavour from grazing on herby mountain pasture. Few cattle are raised, the exception being the semi-wild black bulls of the Camargue. Game includes wild rabbit, hare and boar. Charcuteries feature *caillettes*, round patties of chopped pork liver and shoulder with spinach or Swiss chard and juniper berries, wrapped in caul and baked. Arles' *saucisson sec* was once made from a mix of pork and donkey, but now uses pork and Camargue beef.

FISH AND SEAFOOD

Quintessential Mediterranean species include rockfish, notably *rascasse* (scorpion fish), the larger *chapon de mer* and red mullet. The marine harvest also includes sea bass, sea bream, angler fish, john dory, monkfish, octopus and squid. Martigues produces *poutargue*, salted, pressed and dried grey mullet eggs. Around Nice, the main catch is sardines and anchovies. Shellfish include mussels from the bay of Toulon, tiny crabs *(favouille)* mainly used for soup, and the rarer violet or sea potato, with its tuber-like appearance and salty purple flesh. Sea urchins are gathered west of Marseille. Look out for trout from the Alpine streams north of Nice and freshwater eels in the Camargue.

Saucissons d'Arles

CAVAILLON MELONS

The juicy, sweet-scented, orange-fleshed Cavaillon melon is generally considered to be the best in France. Cultivation began here in the 12th century with the introduction of the canteloupe melon from Italy when the area was under the Avignon papacy. Production thrived thanks to the Canal St-Julien, which has been used to irrigate the melon fields since 1235. Early melons, grown in greenhouses, are available by April, but the best are harvested from open fields *(plein champ)* between June and early September. In choosing a melon, go for a heavy feel and a good perfume. Melons are classically eaten as a starter with cured ham or figs or as dessert, perhaps filled with Beaumes de Venise wine. In season, Cavaillon chef Jacques Prévôt serves an entire melon menu, with dishes such as melon and fish stew.

CHEESE

Provence is not a major cheese region, although you will find a variety of goats' cheeses of which the finest is unctuous Banon, a small round cheese wrapped in a brown chestnut leaf that imbues some of its flavour as the cheese matures, and tied with raffia. It is sometimes soaked in grape marc before being wrapped. Fresh goats' cheeses may be flavoured with summer savory or rolled in pepper; drier ones are sometimes preserved in olive oil. Brousse is a soft, fresh ricotta-like cheese, made with ewes' or goats' milk according to season and used in savoury and sweet dishes.

HERBS AND SPICES

Along with tomatoes, garlic and olive oil, herbs are one of the quintessential elements of Provençal cooking, and local terms such as *pebre d'ai* for summer savory and *farigoule* for thyme are reflected in countless restaurants' names. Rosemary, summer savory, thyme, bay, marjoram and sage grow wild in the sunny *garrigue* hills and woodland that covers much of Provence, although some species, such as basil and tarragon, are cultivated rather than wild. *Herbes de Provence* is the name given to commercially sold mixtures of herbs, though authentic Provençal recipes often use fewer varieties. Lavender, a major hill crop, is largely used for perfume and domestic products but is also used to aromatize grilled meats or flavour desserts, such as crème brulée. Look out also for juniper berries, fennel seeds and aniseed. The latter is a component of *pastis (see p402)*, but is also cooked with pork or used to flavour biscuits.

Provençal herb and spice stall

Left Glacéed mandarins **Centre** Tarte tropèzienne **Right** Fougasse breads

LES TREIZE DESSERTS

Provençal Christmas dinner, known as *le Grand Souper* and eaten on Christmas Eve, not Christmas Day, culminates in the 13 desserts, which symbolize Christ and the apostles at the Last Supper. The 13 are typically made up of *pompe à l'huile* (a biscuit of olive oil, honey and orange-flower water); white and dark nougat; *les quatre mendiants* (dried fruit and nuts) to signify the four mendicant orders (raisins for Dominicans, figs for Franciscans, hazelnuts for Augustinians, almonds for Carmelites); and fresh fruit. Local specialities such as *calissons d'Aix* or candied fruit may be substituted.

Almond- and melon-flavoured calissons d'Aix

FRUIT AND VEGETABLES

Tomatoes, courgettes (zucchini), peppers and aubergines appear in many typical Provençal dishes. Traditional produce also includes Swiss chard, cardoons, fennel, carrots and broad (fava) beans. Artichokes are mainly the small purple variety, which have virtually no choke.

The cornucopia continues with almost every summer and autumn fruit imaginable. Lemons are a speciality of Menton, but oranges are also grown, and orange-flower water is distilled in the perfume capital of Grasse.

Chestnuts are abundant in the wooded hills of the Maures, just inland from St-Tropez, and black truffles are found in the oak forests around Carpentras, Rognes and in the Var between November and March. The Camargue produces rice along the Grand and Petit Rhônes, a speciality being nutty red rice.

BAKED GOODS AND SWEETS

Fougasse is a flat, holey olive-oil bread, often studded with olives, *lardons* or anchovy, or flavoured with pine nuts, candied fruit or orange-flower water. The latter also flavours *oreillettes* ("little ears"), bits of light crispy pastry dredged in icing sugar, and the pastry *navettes* of Marseille, shaped like the boat that brought Mary Magdalene to Provence. The *tropézienne* is sponge cake filled with crème patissière, a speciality of St-Tropez.

Fruit has been candied in Apt since the Middle Ages. Other sweets include *calissons d'Aix*, made of ground almonds, melon and sugar; *pâtes de fruit* (square fruit jellies); stripey fruit-humbug-style *berlingots* from Carpentras; and light and caramelized dark nougat.

OTHER PRODUCE

Honey is scented with chestnut, heather, rosemary and lavender. Sea salt is harvested in the Camargue, where the Salins du Midi is one of Europe's largest producers.

OLIVE OIL

Olive oil is at the heart of Provençal cuisine. The olive brought to the region by the Phoenicians over 2,000 years ago is grown all over Provence, in terraces up to 600 m (2,000 ft) in altitude. Many varieties are grown in the region, notably *aglandou, manzanile, picholine,* the tiny pointed *cailletier (olive de Nice)* and the round black *tanche (olive de Nyons).* All olives begin green, turn browny-purple and finally turn black. The trees, with their silvery green leaves and gnarled trunks, can live for several hundred years – the celebrated *olivier millénaire* near Roquebrune Cap-Martin is thought to be over 1,000 years old.

Olive oil shop in Nice

Olive cultivation has declined since its peak in the early 20th century, but interest in the health benefits of a Mediterranean diet means that abandoned areas are again being planted with groves and traditional mills are being opened up.

The olive harvest begins in late September or early October, and olive oil pressing usually starts in early November. Around five kilos of olives are needed for a litre of oil. The resulting colour and taste will depend not only on the variety or varieties used but also whether they were picked young or mature. Look for *huile d'olive vierge extra, première pression à froid,* indicating a low acidity content and a product which has been naturally processed. Colour varies from golden yellow to deep green and flavours may be described as almond, citrus or truffle. At most mills or specialist shops you will generally be able to taste before you buy.

OLIVE OIL MILLS

Most are open for pressing only between November and February, but most have a shop selling oil and related products all year round (ring ahead to check).

Moulin à Huile Dauphin
Cucuron (04 90 77 26 17).

Moulin du Flayosquet
Flayosc (04 94 70 41 45).

Moulin à Huile Conti
Grasse (04 93 70 21 42).

Moulin à Huile Rossignol
Grasse (04 93 70 16 74).

Moulin de l'Olivette
Manosque (04 92 72 00 99).

Moulin Jean-Marie Cornille
Maussane-les-Alpilles
(04 90 54 32 37).

Left Olive trees **Right** Freshly picked ripe black olives

Regional Dishes

Ratatouille, bouillabaisse, salade niçoise, daube de boeuf...
*the traditional dishes of Provence – sometimes dubbed
the "cuisine of the sun" – have travelled the world, but
there's no better place on earth to taste them than here,
along with other less famous but no less delicious fare.*

ON THE MENU

Aïoli Garlic mayonnaise
Anchoïade Green olive,
anchovy and garlic purée
**Beignets de fleur de
courgette** Courgette
(zucchini) flower fritters
Bourride Soup of assorted
white fish and *aïoli*
Estocafinado Salt cod with
tomatoes, potatoes, garlic,
herbs and olives
Estouffade de boeuf Beef
stew with olives and tomatoes
Lapin/poulpe à la provençale
Rabbit/octopus with white
wine, tomatoes and herbs
Farçis niçois or **petits farçis**
Vegetables stuffed with minced
meat, rice and herbs
Pieds et paquets Sheep's feet
and tripe
Pissaladière Pizza-style
anchovy, olive and onion tart
Soupe au pistou Bean and
vegetable soup with basil sauce
Tapenade Olive, anchovy and
caper purée
Tian Gratin of vegetables
baked in a terracotta dish *(tian)*
Tourte de blettes Pie of chard,
raisins and pine kernels

Artichauts à la barigoule

THE PROVENÇAL MENU

A meal might start with *anchoïade* with *crudités*, baby
artichokes, fish soup or *caillettes*. In winter, look out
for scrambled eggs with truffles. While *bouillabaisse* is
Provence's most famous fish dish, a real treat at beachside restaurants is ocean-fresh fish simply charcoal-
grilled. Sea bass and bream are often matched with
fennel or artichokes. Meat dishes include lamb, grilled or
roasted with herbs; rabbit too may be roasted or baked
with wine. Also frequent are stews such as *daube de
boeuf*. Vegetable dishes include creamed Swiss chard
and cardoons, and all manner of gratins or *tians*.

There are few truly Provençal desserts, though the
abundant fruits are used in tarts and sorbets, while the
late summer glut will see figs roast, baked and stewed.

NIÇOISE CUISINE

This distinctive cuisine reflects the city's history as part
of Italian Piemont until 1860. Not surprisingly ravioli,
gnocchi, polenta and pasta dishes all feature. Sardines
and anchovies are the two favourite fish. *Nonats* are
tiny sardine and anchovy fry. Anchovies also feature in
pissaladière and *salade niçoise*, while sardines may be
marinated or stuffed with breadcrumbs and herbs. Nice
is also the home of *ratatouille* and *farçis niçois*.

Farçis niçois

Left Loup au fenouil **Right** Daube de boeuf

ARTICHAUTS À LA BARIGOULE

Small violet or poivrade artichokes are trimmed, halved and sautéd with onion, bacon, garlic, carrot and perhaps mushroom (a similar mix can be used to stuff them), then simmered in white wine and herbs until tender.

BOUILLABAISSE

Bouillabaisse is no longer a simple fisherman's stew, using the leftovers of the catch simmered in sea water. These days it is a costly, luxury dish that you may need to order 24 hours in advance. Some recipes use up to a dozen different types of fish, but the essentials are rascasse (scorpion fish), gurnard and conger eel, cooked in a saffron-scented fish stock with onion, leek, tomato, olive oil and dried orange peel. Potatoes are added shortly before serving. It is often eaten in two stages: first the golden broth, then the fish itself.

DAUBE DE BOEUF

This dish gets its name from the *daubière*, the terra-cotta casserole in which it is cooked. Large cubes of beef are marinated overnight with red wine, onions, garlic and a bouquet garni. Onions, carrots and bacon lardons, then the meat, are browned in olive oil and then stewed for three to five hours in the marinade, with tomatoes and a twist of orange peel, until the sauce has turned an almost blackish-brown. A very similar dish is made with lamb *(daube d'Avignon)* and, in the Camargue, with bull's meat *(gardiane de boeuf)*.

LOUP AU FENOUIL

Fennel's aniseed taste goes well with fish. A whole sea bass (or sea bream) is stuffed with a handful of stalks of fennel and baked with dry white wine. The fish can also be grilled over fennel twigs to impart flavour.

REGIONAL DINING

The following restaurants are among those serving regional dishes at reasonable prices:

African Queen
Beaulieu-sur-Mer *(see p406)*
Brunel
Avignon *(see p405)*
Cafè de Paris
Monte-Carlo *(see p417)*
Chez Simon
Nice (see p419)
L'Amphitryon
Aix-en-Provence *(see p404)*
Le Girelier
St-Tropez *(see p424)*
Le Poisson qui Marche
Marseille *(see p415)*
Le Mesclun
Cannes *(see p408)*
Tètou
Golfe-Juan *(see p412)*

NICOIS STREET FOOD

Nice has several tempting snacks that can be bought from stalls on cours Saleya or around the Vieux Port, including tasty *pissaladière. Socca* is a large chickpea *crêpe* baked in a flat circular iron dish and cut into pieces to be eaten with the fingers, while *panisses* are chickpea fritters dusted with icing sugar. *Pan bagnat* is a sort of *salade niçoise* in a bun – a round bread roll moistened with olive oil and stuffed with anchovies, tomato, egg and olives.

Regional Wines & Spirits

The vineyards of Provence and the Rhône Valley are probably the oldest in France, established in their current form by the Romans. The wines of Provence reflect the wild magnificence and the heady scents of the herb-strewn garrigue, the perfect complement to the region's colourful cuisine.

Bandol wines

Pastis in a shop window

PROVENÇAL WINES

Definitely one of France's finest reds, Bandol is a racy but punchy fistful of flavours such as olives, leather, morello cherries, blackberries, liquorice and truffles, and needs ageing. Mourvèdre is the hallmark grape, grown on a series of *restanques*, wide man-made terraces on a spectacular natural amphitheatre over-looking the coast. The spicy rosés are perfect with *bouillabaisse* whilst the simple whites, which sport scents of the wild fennel to be found all over the region, are a natural match for grilled fish.

The three tiny appellations of Bellet on the fringes of modish Nice, the wonderful little port of Cassis and inland Palette produce some interesting whites. Coteaux d'Aix-en-Provence, carrying the name of one of France's most elegant towns, stretches from the river Durance in the north down to the Mediterranean. Many of the reds are bouncy, liquoricy numbers with hints of leather. Its offshoot, from picturesque Baux de Provence, has juicy, herby reds. Coteaux Varois reds range from relatively powerful to easy-drinking. Côtes de Provence turns out vast amounts of thin, acidic "holiday" rosé with little regard for quality, but also some very decent reds.

SOUTHERN RHÔNE WINES

The southern Côtes du Rhône stretches from south of Montélimar to Avignon. Here the valley widens out and the grapes ripen on more undulating, less exacting terrain, contrasting with the northern area *(see pp270–71)* where the vines cling to steep slopes above the river. These vineyards, basking under the Mediterranean sun, are swept by the Mistral, the infamous north wind. Juicy, spicy reds are the signature here and in the surrounding regions. Seventeen communes claim to have superior vineyard conditions and have the appellation Côtes du Rhône-Villages.

World-renowned Châteauneuf-du-Pape owes its origins to the 14th-century popes of Avignon who built themselves a summer residence over the ruins of an old castle. No fewer than 13 grape varieties can be used to make Châteauneuf, led by Grenache, Syrah and Mourvèdre. The vineyard is overlain with large

VINEYARDS OF PROVENCE AND THE SOUTHERN RHÔNE

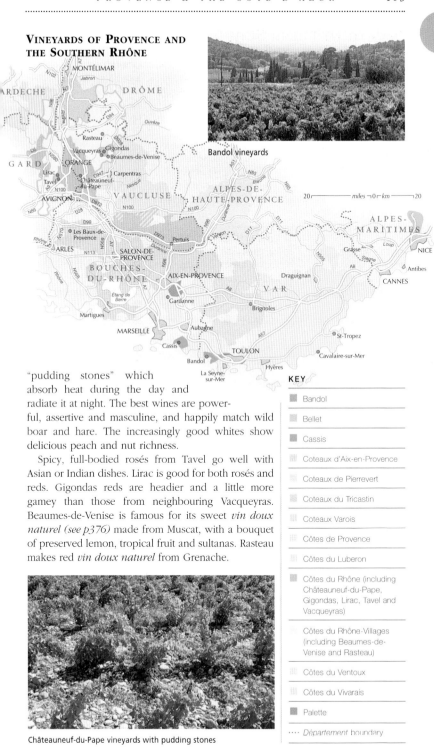

Bandol vineyards

"pudding stones" which absorb heat during the day and radiate it at night. The best wines are powerful, assertive and masculine, and happily match wild boar and hare. The increasingly good whites show delicious peach and nut richness.

Spicy, full-bodied rosés from Tavel go well with Asian or Indian dishes. Lirac is good for both rosés and reds. Gigondas reds are headier and a little more gamey than those from neighbouring Vacqueyras. Beaumes-de-Venise is famous for its sweet *vin doux naturel (see p376)* made from Muscat, with a bouquet of preserved lemon, tropical fruit and sultanas. Rasteau makes red *vin doux naturel* from Grenache.

Châteauneuf-du-Pape vineyards with pudding stones

KEY

- Bandol
- Bellet
- Cassis
- Coteaux d'Aix-en-Provence
- Coteaux de Pierrevert
- Coteaux du Tricastin
- Coteaux Varois
- Côtes de Provence
- Côtes du Luberon
- Côtes du Rhône (including Châteauneuf-du-Pape, Gigondas, Lirac, Tavel and Vacqueyras)
- Côtes du Rhône-Villages (including Beaumes-de-Venise and Rasteau)
- Côtes du Ventoux
- Côtes du Vivarais
- Palette
- ···· *Département* boundary

Where to Eat & Stay

AGAY-ST-RAPHAEL
▲ Sol e Mar
Le Dramont, 83530 **Map** 12A5
04 94 95 25 60
FAX 04 94 83 83 61
www.francehotelevasion.com
AE, DC, MC, V mid-Oct–Feb
€€€€ (50) €€€€
Some guestrooms overlook the Iles d'Or and two saltwater pools. Don't miss the fish and saffron stew and the delicate lamb and rosemary. The roof of the restaurant opens at night for starlit dining.

AIX-EN-PROVENCE
● La Vieille Auberge
63 rue Espariat, 13100 **Map** 12C2
04 42 27 17 41
FAX 04 42 26 38 35
DC, MC, V Mon L; 2nd & 3rd wks Jan €€
Abundant flavours, lovingly chosen wine list and a tranquil ambience. Dishes include lamb smoked with mountain herbs, and bass with new pea mousse.

AIX-EN-PROVENCE
● L'Amphitryon
2–4 rue Paul Doumer, 13100 **Map** 12C2
04 42 26 54 10
FAX 04 42 38 36 15
AE, MC, V Sun, Mon; mid-Aug–1st wk Sep €€
Start with a compote of courgette (zucchini) and pepper, rack of Sisteron lamb crusted with tapenade (p400), and fish. Save room for superb confections.

AIX-EN-PROVENCE
● Le Clos de la Violette
10 ave de la Violette, 13100 **Map** 12C2
04 42 23 30 71
FAX 04 42 21 93 03
www.closdelaviolette.fr
AE, MC, V Sun, Mon; 1st 2 wks Aug €€€€
The kitchen is the heart of this graceful château. Menu choices include langoustine tails roasted with onion and smoked bacon, and farm-raised pigeon infused with herbs. Convivial atmosphere but the cuisine is still taken seriously.

AIX-EN-PROVENCE
● Le Petit Verdot
7 rue d'Entrecasteaux, 13100 **Map** 12C2
04 42 27 30 12
www.lepetitverdot.com
DC, MC, V Sun L; Aug €
Discover a true estaminet (not quite an inn, not quite a restaurant: more like a family meal). This lively establishment serves charcuterie, foie gras with figs, and grilled mullet with Champagne sauce.

AIX-EN-PROVENCE (BOUC-BEL-AIR)
▲ L'Etape Lani
Route de Gardanne, 13320 **Map** 12C3
04 42 22 61 90
FAX 04 42 22 68 67
www.lani.fr
AE, MC, V Sun, Mon L, Jul: Sat L; 1st wk Jan, last wk Dec
€€ (32) €€
A memorable experience with charming public spaces, colourful guestrooms and a fine table. Selections include mesclun with summer truffles and asparagus tips, and rabbit with aubergine (eggplant).

ANNOT
▲ L'Avenue
Ave de la Gare, 04240 **Map** 13E2
04 92 83 22 07
FAX 04 92 83 33 13
MC, V Wed L, Fri L; Nov–Apr
€ (11) €€
Highlights include Provençal omelette in olive oil, and sea bream with bacon in a crêpe with chickpeas (garbanzo beans). Pleasant, brightly decorated rooms.

ANTIBES
● De Bacon
Bd de Bacon, 06600 **Map** 12B4
04 93 61 50 02
FAX 04 93 61 65 19
www.restaurantdebacon.com
AE, DC, MC, V Mon, Tue L; Feb–Oct €€€€
Overlooking the bay, this is Antibes' best seafood spot. Start with toast topped with olives or anchovies followed by rock lobster fricassée with tarragon butter.

ANTIBES
▲ Hôtel du Cap-Eden-Roc
Bd Kennedy, Cap d'Antibes, 06601 **Map** 12B4
04 93 61 39 01
FAX 04 93 67 76 04
www.edenroc-hotel.fr
mid-Oct–mid-Apr €€€€€
(123) €€€€€
They say more celebrities have stayed at this 1870 whitewashed pleasure palace than any other hotel in the world. Elegant restaurant serving traditional and international dishes. Flowery rooms.

ANTIBES
● Le Broc'en Bouche
Rue des Palmiers, 06600 **Map** 12B4
04 93 34 75 60
AE, MC, V Sun, Oct–May: Mon
€
Corsican fare is served at this venue that is equal parts art gallery, tearoom, antiques showcase and restaurant. Try the chicken parcel with ginger.

ANTIBES
● Le Brulot
3 rue Frédéric Isnard, 06600 **Map** 12B4
04 93 34 17 76
FAX 04 93 74 83 94
www.brulot.com
AE, MC, V
Sun; Aug, Dec €€
One of the friendliest spots on the Côte d'Azur, with a baker's oven converted into a barbecue. Excellent socca (thin chickpea flour pancake).

ANTIBES
● Le Sucrier
6 rue des Bains, 06600 **Map** 12B4
04 93 34 85 40
FAX 04 93 34 85 40
www.lesucrier.com
AE, MC, V Tue; Jan–Feb, 1st wk Nov €€€
Very special restaurant blending sweet and savoury in the same dish. On the menu are combinations such as lobster soup with coconut milk, duck with dried apricots, and cocoa veal.

● Restaurant ■ Hotel ▲ Hotel / Restaurant

ANTIBES
● Oscar's
8 rue du Docteur Rostan, 06600
Map 12B4

📞 04 93 34 90 14

FAX 04 93 34 90 14

W www.oscars-antibes.com

MC, V ● Sun, Mon; 1st 2 wks
Aug, 1 wk Dec 🍽 €€€

*A true gastronome's hideaway. The chef
prepares top-notch Italo-Provençal
cuisine such as truffle flan or sea bass.*

APT
▲ Auberge du Lubéron
8 pl Faubourg-du-Ballet, 84400
Map 12C2

📞 04 90 74 12 50

FAX 04 90 04 79 49

W www.auberge-luberon-peuzin.com

AE, DC, MC, V ● Oct–Apr: Mon &
Tue; 1st wk Nov–2nd wk Dec, last wk
Dec 🍽 €€€€ 🍷 (14) €€€

*A distinguished country inn. Highlights
include Luberon lamb with aubergine
(eggplant) confit, and mullet with
mini-vegetable confit. Simple rooms.*

APT
● Bernard Mathys
5km (3 miles) west on RN100, 84400
Map 12C2

📞 04 90 04 84 64

FAX 04 90 74 69 78

AE, MC, V ● Tue, Wed; mid-
Jan–mid-Feb 🍽 €€€€

*The menu includes baked scallops in
hazelnut oil, and kid with a ragout of
seasonal vegetables. The wine cellar is
bewilderingly complete.*

APT
● Le Carré des Sens
Cours Lauze-de-Perret, pl St-Martin,
84400 **Map** 12C2

📞 04 90 74 74 00

FAX 04 90 74 74 09

W www.carredessens.com

MC, V ● Oct–Mar

🍽 €

*Lively bistro, bar and art gallery. The
essentially modern menu spotlights
dishes like baked langoustines with
aubergine (eggplant), cumin and
coconut milk, and baby vegetable soup.*

ARLES
● La Charcuterie
51 rue des Arènes, 13200 **Map** 12B2

📞 04 90 96 56 96

MC, V ● Sun, Mon; mid-
Jul–mid-Aug 🍽 €€

*One of Arles' more elegant bistros. Fine
meat dishes dominate, especially the
excellent andouille, and superb Lyon hot
pistachio sausages.*

ARLES
● Le Jardin de Manon
14 ave des Alyscamps, 13200 **Map** 12B2

📞 04 90 93 38 68

FAX 04 90 49 62 03

AE, MC, V ● Wed, mid-Oct–mid-
Mar: Sun D & Thu D; 1st 2 wks Feb, last
wk Oct–1st wk Nov 🍽 €€

*A heady mix of colour and flavour in the
dishes such as cod brandade (p373)
with olive sauce, or stuffed guinea fowl
with aubergine (eggplant) and thyme.*

ARLES
● Lou Caléu
27 rue Porte-de-Laure, 13200 **Map** 12B2

📞 04 90 49 71 77

FAX 04 90 93 75 30

AE, DC, MC, V ● Sun D, Sep–Jun:
Mon; Jan 🍽 €

*The menu – based on the area's history
– suits this lovely 17th-century home.
Highlights include tiny red peppers
stuffed with Nîmes brandade (p373),
lamb bolognaise, and wild bull stew.*

ARLES
▲ Lou Marquès Jules César
9 bd des Lices, 13200 **Map** 12B2

📞 04 90 52 52 52

FAX 04 90 52 52 53

AE, DC, MC, V ● Mon L, Sat L;
Nov–last wk Dec

🍽 €€€ 🍷 (55) €€€€€

*Flame-cooked foie gras dazzles diners,
along with lobster risotto with red
Camargue rice and capers, and roast
lamb curry. The elegance carries on
from the table into the stately public
spaces and guestrooms.*

ARLES
▲ Mireille
2 pl St-Pierre, 13200 **Map** 12B2

📞 04 90 93 70 74

FAX 04 90 93 87 28

W www.hotel-mireille.com

AE, DC, MC, V ● 2nd wk Nov–1st
wk Mar 🍽 €€ 🍷 (34) €€€€

*A hidden gem, with an exterior that
qualifies it as a diamond in the rough.
Menu filled with Provençal standards.
Affordable, agreeable rosés. Tidy rooms.*

ARLES
▲ Nord-Pinus
14 pl du Forum, 13200 **Map** 12B2

📞 04 90 93 02 32

FAX 04 90 93 34 00

W www.nord-pinus.com

AE, DC, MC, V ● Tue, Wed L; Jan
🍽 €€€ 🍷 (26) €€€€€

*A classic menu in one of the town's
oldest corners. Exemplary dishes include
cod timbale and Provençal lamb with
garlic confit. Cosy, quaint guestrooms.*

AURONS
▲ Domaine de la Reynaude
Les Sonnaillets, 13121 **Map** 12C3

📞 04 90 59 36 35

FAX 04 90 59 36 06

AE, DC, MC, V ● Sun D; last 2
wks Dec 🍽 €€ 🍷 (32) €€€

*Modern approach despite the 16th-
century setting. Traditional meals such
as beef casserole or the vegetable gratin
with mullet and black olive tapenade
(p400). Comfortable, pleasant guestrooms.*

AVIGNON
● Brunel
46 rue de la Balance, 84000 **Map** 12B2

📞 04 90 85 24 83

FAX 04 90 86 26 67

MC, V ● Sun, Mon; mid-Dec–mid-
Jan 🍽 €

*A convivial bistro delivering dishes like
terrine of tomatoes with tapenade
(p400), and monkfish tail drizzled with
pistou, along with refreshing local wines.*

AVIGNON
● Christian Étienne
10 rue de Mons, pl du Palais-des-
Papes, 84000 **Map** 12B2

📞 04 90 86 16 50

FAX 04 90 86 67 09

W www.christian-etienne.fr

MC, V ● Aug–Jun: Sun & Mon
€€€€

*Don't miss the tomato tartare, alpine
pigeon, fennel sorbet and saffron custard.
Côtes-du-Rhône-Villages and Côtes du
Luberon are high notes of the wine list.*

AVIGNON

▲ Hôtel d'Europe

12 pl Crillon, city centre, 84000
Map 12B2

04 90 14 76 76
FAX 04 90 14 76 71
W www.hotel-d-europe.fr
AE, DC, MC, V ● Sun, Mon L;
middle 2 wks Jan, last 2 wks Aug–1st
wk Sep, last wk Nov (restaurant only)
€€€€€ ◇ (44) **€€€€€**

*The menu here includes tartare of
strawberries and tomatoes with basil.
Beautiful guestrooms.*

AVIGNON

● La Petite Pêche

13 rue St-Etienne, 84000 **Map** 12B2

04 90 86 02 46
@ lapetitepeche@wanadoo.fr
MC, V **€**

*Tucked away on a quiet street near
Place de l'Horloge. The very tranquil
surroundings belie the passion that
infuses the menu, from succulent local
octopus to cuttlefish and fish.*

BANDOL

▲ Ile Rousse les Oliviers

25 bd Louis Lumière, 83150 **Map** 12C3

04 94 29 33 00
FAX 04 94 29 49 49
W www.ile-rousse.com
AE, DC, MC, V
€€€ ◇ (55) **€€**

*Possibly the most beautiful undiscovered
gem on the French Mediterranean coast,
Bandol is graced by this charming
establishment with its well-kept, amply
sized rooms and a delightful menu. The
small fried mullets are a treat.*

BARCELONNETTE

● Le Poivre d'Ane

49 rue Manuel, 04400 **Map** 13D1

04 92 81 48 67
FAX 04 92 81 35 01
MC, V ● mid-Dec–mid-Apr: Sun &

Mon; mid-Apr–May, Nov–mid-Dec
€

*Sun-washed hills serve as backdrop
for the straightforward, delicious cuisine.
Start with a confit of carrots with wild
mountain honey, followed by lamb confit
in very fine goose jelly.*

BAUX-DE-PROVENCE

▲ La Cabro d'Or

Au Val-d'Enfer, 13520 **Map** 12B2

04 90 54 33 21
FAX 04 90 54 45 98
W www.lacabrodor.com
AE, DC, MC, V ● Tue L, Nov–Mar:
Mon; mid-Nov–mid-Dec
€€€ ◇ (31) **€€€€**

*The gorgeous cooking matches the
breathtaking château, lush flowerbeds
and the pastoral landscape complete
with a pond. A grand wine list – including
Coteaux d'Aix-en-Provence-les Baux
and Côtes de Provence – supports the
chef's masterpieces. Well-appointed
guestrooms open onto a beautiful garden.*

BAUX-DE-PROVENCE

▲ Oustau de Baumanière

Town centre, 13520 **Map** 12B2

04 90 54 33 07
FAX 04 90 54 40 46
W www.relaischateaux.fr/oustau
AE, DC, MC, V ● Nov–Mar: Wed
& Thu L; Jan–mid-Mar
€€€€€ ◇ (30) **€€€€€**

*One of France's finest options. Expect
ravioli with truffles and peppers, turbot
casserole with mussels and sea lettuce,
and rack of lamb. Graceful guestrooms.*

BEAULIEU-SUR-MER

● African Queen

Port de Plaisance, 06310 **Map** 12B4

04 93 01 10 85
FAX 04 93 01 28 33
MC, V **€€**

*Lively, jungle-inspired brasserie, popular
with celebrities. On the menu are a variety
of dishes such as bouillabaisse (p401),
African curry and pizza.*

BEAULIEU-SUR-MER

▲ Auberge du Soleil

44 ave de la Liberté, 06360 **Map** 12B4

04 93 01 51 46

FAX 04 93 01 58 40
AE, DC, MC, V ● Nov
€€€ ◇ (10) **€€€**

*Mediterranean dishes such as sweet red
peppers in anchovy sauce, oven-roasted
vegetables, grilled meats and aïoli (p400)
grace the menu. Guestrooms are modest.*

BEAULIEU-SUR-MER

▲ Hôtel La Réserve

5 bd Général Leclerc, 06310 **Map** 12B4

04 93 01 00 01
FAX 04 93 01 28 99
W www.reservebeaulieu.com
AE, DC, MC, V ● Nov–mid-Dec
€€€€€ ◇ (37) **€€€€€**

*A neo-Renaissance palace built in 1880
by an American publishing tycoon and
now one of the area's most exclusive
hotels and opulent dining rooms. The
chef has two Michelin stars and
prepares dishes such as salmon with
basil, lamb with thyme, and grilled sea
bass. Guestrooms are over-the-top.*

BEAULIEU-SUR-MER

▲ Le Métropole

15 bd Maréchal Leclerc, 06310
Map 12B4

04 93 01 00 08
FAX 04 93 01 18 51
W www.le-metropole.com
AE, DC, MC, V ● mid-Oct–mid-
Dec **€€€€** ◇ (40) **€€€€€**

*An opulent Italianate palace by the sea.
The restaurant offers dishes like asparagus tart and a vegetable platter with a
truffle vinaigrette. Guestrooms predominantly bright blue with Provençal fabrics
and painted wooden furniture.*

BEAULIEU-SUR-MER

● Les Agaves

4 ave Maréchal Foch, 06310 **Map** 12B4

04 93 01 13 12
W www.les-agaves.com
AE, DC, MC, V ● Mon L, Tue; Feb
€€€

*Located opposite the train station in a
yellow building known as the Palais des
Anglais. French and Provençal dishes
include ravioles (p268) with ceps, cream
and truffles; lobster and mango salad;
and lamb with a pine-nut crust.
Fabulous wine list.*

● Restaurant   ■ Hotel   ▲ Hotel / Restaurant

BEDOIN

● Le Mas des Vignes

Route from Mont-Ventoux, 84410

Map 12C2

🔇 04 90 65 63 91

🍴 MC, V ⚫ Mon, Tue L; Jul–Aug: L; Nov–Mar 🍴 €€€

Almost like sharing dinner with a quite distinguished Provençal family. Choices include fennel, prawn and scallop soup, and lamb crusted with herbs and risotto.

BIOT

● Auberge du Jarrier

30 passage du Bourgade, 06410

Map 12B4

🔇 04 93 65 11 68

FAX 04 93 65 50 03

W www.guide-gerard.com/gastro/jarrier

🍴 AE, MC, V ⚫ Mon L, Sat L

🍴 €€€

With stunning views, this is the most romantic veranda in town. Dishes include risotto with truffles and langoustines. Classy guestrooms.

BIOT

▲ Hôtel des Arcades

16 pl des Arcades, 06410 **Map** 12B4

🔇 04 93 65 01 04

FAX 04 93 65 01 05

⚫ Sun D, Mon

🍴 €€€ 🍷 (10) €€€

Known as Chez Mimi to locals. Service can be unfocused but the menu is perfect, with dishes such as roast lamb and all-you-can-eat goats' cheese. Some guestrooms have canopied beds.

BIOT

● Les Terraillers

11 rue du Chemin Neuf, 06410

Map 12B4

🔇 04 93 65 01 59

FAX 04 93 65 13 78

W www.lesterraillers.com

🍴 AE, MC, V ⚫ Wed, Thu L; Nov

🍴 €€€€

A 16th-century pottery-turned-restaurant. Stunning cannelloni, duck gratin, and sweet lemon and raspberry dessert.

BORMES-LES-MIMOSAS

● La Tonelle

Pl Gambetta, 83230 **Map** 13D3

🔇 04 94 71 34 84

FAX 04 94 01 09 37

🍴 AE, MC, V ⚫ Jan–May & Sep–Nov: Wed–Thu, Jul–Aug: L; mid-Nov–mid-Dec 🍴 €€€

Dine under a vine-covered pergola, far away from the crowds. Regional classics such as roasted chestnuts and veal with red peppers stuffed with goats' cheese.

CABRIS

▲ Le Vieux Château

Pl du Panorama, 06530 **Map** 12A4

🔇 04 93 60 50 12

FAX 04 93 60 58 47

W www.aubergeduvieuxchateau.com

🍴 AE, MC, V ⚫ Mon; mid-Jan–mid-Feb 🍴 €€ 🍷 (4) €€€

This castle-turned-picturesque hotel has charming guestrooms and a terrace with great views. Menu choices include prawns and pigeon stuffed with cabbage.

CABRIS

● Petit Prince

15 rue Frédéric Mistral, 06530 **Map** 12A4

🔇 04 93 60 63 14

FAX 04 93 60 62 87

🍴 AE, MC, V ⚫ Wed; mid-Dec–mid-Jan 🍴 €€

Quaint, rustic restaurant decorated in honour of The Little Prince. The menu features rabbit cooked in lavender.

CADENET

▲ Auberge la Fenière

Route de Cadenet, BP18, 84160

Map 12C2

🔇 04 90 68 11 79

FAX 04 90 68 18 60

W www.reinesammut.com

🍴 AE, DC, MC, V ⚫ Mon, Tue L; mid-Nov–Jan

🍴 €€€€ 🍷 (9) €€€€€

This country inn is more than just a beautiful place to stay, it's a star in Provence's culinary galaxy. Delight over braised artichokes, ravioli with feta cheese and tuna with herb salad.

CAGNES

▲ Le Cagnard

Rue Sous Bari, 06800 **Map** 12B4

🔇 04 93 20 73 21

FAX 04 93 22 06 39

🍴 AE, DC, MC, V

⚫ Nov–mid-Dec (restaurant)

🍴 €€€€€ 🍷 (14) €€€€€

The most luxurious accommodation in town, with painted ceilings and original Renaissance details. The 13th-century building is attached to the walls of the Grimaldi castle. Dinner specialities include grilled langoustines with young salad and olives, lasagne with black truffles, and duck with white asparagus.

CALLAS

▲ Gorges de Pennafort

Route from Muy, on D25, 83830

Map 12A4

🔇 04 94 76 66 51

FAX 04 94 76 67 23

🍴 AE, DC, MC, V ⚫ Sun D, Wed L, Jun–Aug: Mon L, Sep–May: Wed D; mid-Jan–mid-Mar 🍴 €€€€

🍷 (16) €€€€

Near the gorges and lush greenery of Verdon. Relax over a truffle ravioli with Parmesan or bass roasted with artichokes. Charming little guestrooms.

CANNES

● Astoux et Brun

27 rue Félix Faure, 06400 **Map** 12A4

🔇 04 93 39 21 87

FAX 04 93 39 74 27

W www.astouxbrun.com

🍴 AE, MC, V 🍴 €€

One of the best places for fish in town. The assortiment royale is a gargantuan seafood platter, a must for fans.

CANNES

● Bistrot des Artisans

67 bd de la République, 06400

Map 12A4

🔇 04 93 68 33 88

@ bistrot-des-artisans@wanadoo.fr

🍴 AE, MC, V

⚫ Sun; mid-Jul–mid-Aug 🍴 €€

Colourful and cosy bistro serving good food at great prices. The buffet is piled high with cheeses. Follow up with grilled steak and fries.

CANNES

▲ Carlton Inter-Continental

58 bd de la Croisette, 06400 **Map** 12A4

🔇 04 93 06 40 06

FAX 04 93 06 40 25

W www.interconti.com

AE, DC, MC, V

€€€€€ ❤ (326) €€€€€

The domed roofs of the Carlton are a Cannes emblem and La Belle Otero restaurant lives up to its tradition of high quality. Don't miss the sea bass crusted in Parmesan or the pigeon stuffed with foie gras. Plush guestrooms.

CANNES
▲ Hôtel Majestic Barrière

10 bd de la Croisette, 06407 **Map** 12A4

04 92 98 77 00

FAX 04 93 38 97 90

W www.lucienbarriere.com

AE, DC, MC, V

€€€€€

❤ (305) €€€€€

Cannes' finest dining experience, the Villa de Lys restaurant is presided over by legendary chef Bruno Oger, who brings exotic touches to the menu. The pigeon marinated in Rasteau wine is sublime and the wine list encyclopaedic. Guestrooms are tops, too.

CANNES
▲ Hôtel Martinez

73 bd de la Croisette, 06400 **Map** 12A4

04 92 98 73 00

FAX 04 93 39 67 82

W www.hotel-martinez.com

AE, DC, MC, V ● Mon, Tue; mid-Nov–mid-Dec

€€€€€ ❤ (390) €€€€€

Everything at this gourmet hideaway is picture perfect, from the Art Deco details to the impeccable food and luxurious rooms. Offerings have included beef fillet with tuna, potato marmalade, candied aubergines (eggplant), and wild strawberry casserole in orange butter.

CANNES
● La Cave

9 bd de la République, 06400 **Map** 12A4

04 93 99 79 87

FAX 04 93 68 57 69

W www.restaurant-lacave.com

AE, MC, V ● Sun, Sat L; Aug

€€

A lively place shielded from the glitz and glamour of Cannes. Daily specials often

include pistou soup, courgette (zucchini) flower fritters, chicken liver terrine and an apple omelette.

CANNES
● Le Farfalla

1 bd de la Croisette, 06400 **Map** 12A4

04 93 68 93 00

AE, MC, V €€€

Extremely trendy spot right in front of the Film Festival palace. If you get past the bodyguards on the door, have a steak and fries or just an apéritif and a look at the A-list crowd.

CANNES
● Le Festival de la Crêpe

29 rue Félix Faure, 06400 **Map** 12A4

04 93 39 34 93

€

Crêperie with 46 combinations of sweet or savoury fillings – everything from Brie to berries. Apple cider to drink.

CANNES
● Le Mesclun

16 rue St-Antoine, 06400 **Map** 12A4

04 93 99 45 19

FAX 04 93 47 68 29

@ lemesclun@wanadoo.fr

AE, MC, V ● Wed; mid-Nov–mid-Dec €€€

One of the most romantic restaurants in town, hidden among the charming labyrinth of old Cannes. This a good option for vegetarians.

CANNES
● Le Restaurant Arménien

82 bd de la Croisette, 06400 **Map** 12A4

04 93 94 00 58

FAX 04 93 94 56 12

W www.lerestaurantarmenien.com

DC, MC, V ● Christmas

€€€

World-class Armenian restaurant with hints of Turkish, Iranian and Azerbaijani cooking. Twenty different starters from stuffed vine leaves to kebabs. Vodka is the favoured drink here.

CAP-D'AIL
● L'Eden

Plage Mala, 06320 **Map** 12A4

04 93 78 17 06

MC, V ● Oct–Apr €€

Only accessible by yacht or by a footpath that clings to the Cap d'Ail coastline, this charming restaurant serves traditional cuisine and fresh seafood.

CAP-FERRAT
▲ Grand-Hôtel du Cap-Ferrat

71 bd Général de Gaulle, 06230 **Map** 12B4

04 93 76 50 50

FAX 04 93 76 50 76

W www.grand-hotel-cap-ferrat.com

AE, DC, MC, V ● Jan, Feb

€€€€€ ❤ (53) €€€€€

At the tip of one of the world's most expensive pieces of real estate lies this opulent Belle Epoque hotel. The modern cuisine includes foie gras with apples and raisins, ravioles (p268) with artichoke, and rascasse. Very luxurious guestrooms.

CAP-FERRAT
▲ Hôtel Belle Aurore

49 ave Denis Séméria, 06230 **Map** 12B4

04 93 76 24 24

FAX 04 93 76 15 10

W www.hotel-belleaurore-riviera.com

AE, DC, MC, V ● D

€€ ❤ (20) €€€

If you can't afford the Hôtel du Cap then this is a pleasant alternative, with bird's-eye views of the peninsula. Sample dishes at its poolside restaurant such as salads, grilled meats and fish. Comfy guestrooms with stunning sea views.

CAP-FERRAT
▲ La Voile d'Or

7 ave Jean Mermoz, 06230 **Map** 12B4

04 93 01 13 13

FAX 04 93 76 11 17

W www.lavoiledor.fr

AE, DC, MC, V ● mid-Oct–Mar

€€€€ ❤ (45) €€€€

A Florentine-style villa and gourmet restaurant with a terrace. Dishes include vegetable-stuffed squid, Mediterranean lobster in soy sauce, and beef with ham and figs. So-called "Venetian-style" guestrooms with marble bathrooms.

CAP-FERRAT
● Plage La Paloma

Route St-Hospice, 06230 **Map** 12B4

04 93 01 64 71

AE, DC, MC, V ● Oct–May

€€€

Cool off in the shaded restaurant when the sun is hottest. Grilled fish, salmon tartare, and pizza with seafood toppings.

CAP-FERRAT
▲ Royal Riviéra
3 ave Jean Monnet, 06230 **Map** 12B4

04 93 76 31 00

FAX 04 93 01 23 07

W www.royal-riviera.com

AE, DC, MC, V ● mid-Dec–mid-Jan €€€€ 🍽 (77) €€€€€

An architectural showcase with neo-Hellenic finishes; an elegant but informal restaurant and terrace. Try the fish risotto or the sea bass in basil. Very spacious, plush guestrooms.

CAP-MARTIN
▲ Monte Carlo Beach Hotel
Ave Princesse Grace, 06190 **Map** 12B4

04 93 28 66 66

FAX 04 93 78 14 18

W www.slh.com/montecarlo

AE, DC, MC, V ● mid-Nov–Mar

€€€€€ 🍽 (46) €€€€€

There are several dining options at this modern Italianate hotel. La Salle à Manger serves French contemporary cuisine in refined surroundings. Le Rivage offers salads, pasta and grilled meat and fish at its poolside tables. La Vigie has a relaxed atmosphere and a Provençal buffet. Comfortable, airy guestrooms with sea views.

CAP-MARTIN
▲ Vista Palace
1551 route de la Turbie , 06190
Map 12B4

04 92 10 40 00

FAX 04 93 35 18 94

AE, DC, MC, V ● Feb

€€€€€ 🍽 (68) €€€€€

Named "palace of views", this luxury hotel lies past the hairpin turns on the Grand Corniche. The gourmet restaurant is one of the area's best. Large guestrooms.

CAROMB
● Le Four à Chaux
2253 ave Charles de Gaulle, route from

Malaucène, 84330 **Map** 12C2

04 90 62 40 10

FAX 04 90 62 36 62

MC, V ● Sep–Jun: Mon & Tue; last wk Jun, Jul, last 2 wks Nov

€€€

Flowers of courgette (zucchini) stuffed with cod, beef baked in its juices with balsamic vinegar, and chocolate mousse with a strawberry sorbet are just a few attractions in this pleasant multi-level establishment with a welcoming terrace.

CARPENTRAS
▲ L'Hibiscus at Safari Hôtel
1 ave Jean Henri Fabre, 84200
Map 12C2

04 90 63 35 35

FAX 04 90 60 49 99

W www.safari-hotel.fr

AE, DC, MC, V ● Oct–Apr: Sun D

€€ 🍽 (42) €€€

Dishes such as brandade (p373), *and roast langoustines with sesame-curry sauce. Tidy, agreeable rooms.*

CASSIS
● La Presqu'ile
Quartier de Port-Miou, 13260 **Map** 12C3

04 42 01 03 77

FAX 04 42 01 94 49

W www.restaurant-la-presquile.com

AE, MC, V ● Mon, Sep–Jun: Sun D; mid-Nov–Feb €€

Sample sea bass, whisked from the waves in virgin olive oil and lemon, or the pigeon millefeuille *with courgette (zucchini) and aubergine (eggplant).*

CASSIS
● Nino
1 quai Jean Jacques Barthélemy, 13260
Map 12C3

04 42 01 74 32

FAX 04 42 01 74 32

AE, DC, MC, V ● Mon, Oct–Apr: Sun D; mid-Dec–2nd wk Feb €€€

A lively spot, soaked in the charm of coastal Provence, with a bright terrace. Try the grilled fish, bouillabaisse (p401) *and wines from nearby vineyards.*

CASTELLANE
▲ Nouvel Hôtel du Commerce
Pl de l'Eglise, 04120 **Map** 9D2

04 92 83 61 00

FAX 04 92 83 72 82

W www.hotel-fradet.com

AE, DC, MC, V ● Mon, Wed L; Nov–Mar €€ € 🍽 (35) €€

Experience the peace of Provence. Though no dishes leap out as stunning, the overall feeling – in the tidy lodgings and the dining room – is harmonious.

CASTILLON
▲ Hôtel La Bergerie
Quai St-Louis Streus, 06500 **Map** 12B4

04 93 04 00 39

FAX 04 93 28 02 91

AE, MC, V ● Sun D, Mon, Sep–Apr: Tue–Fri; Nov

€€ 🍽 (15) €€€

A rustic hideaway complete with a pool, lush garden and spacious rooms. In high season half-board is mandatory, making La Bergerie all the more attractive. The food is simple and tasty.

CAVALAIRE-SUR-MER
▲ Hôtel de la Calanque
Rue de la Calanque, 83240 **Map** 12A5

04 94 01 95 00

FAX 04 94 64 66 20

W www.hotel-la-calanque.com

AE, DC, MC, V ● Oct–Dec: Mon; Jan–mid-Mar

€€€€ 🍽 (28) €€€€€

One of the treasures of the Massif des Maures, despite its massive, modern architecture. The shaded terrace serves a fish-focused menu with bouillabaisse (p401), *and scallops with saffron. Most of the guestrooms have balconies.*

CERESTE
▲ Hostellerie l'Aiguebelle
Pl de la République, 04110 **Map** 12C2

04 92 79 00 91

FAX 04 92 79 07 29

MC, V ● Mon; mid-Nov–mid-Feb

€€ 🍽 (14) €€

Family-run country house with tidy guestrooms. Dishes include lamb with sea parsley and raviolis des Champsaur *(with potatoes, cheese and honey).*

CHATEAU-ARNOUX-ST-AUBAN
▲ La Bonne Étape
Chemin du Lac, facing the Château,

04160 **Map** 9D2

C 04 92 64 00 09

FAX 04 92 64 37 36

W www.bonneetape.com

⚡ AE, DC, MC, V **●** Dec–Apr: Mon &
Tue & Wed L & Thu D; Jan–mid-Feb,
last wk Nov–1st wk Dec

¶¶ €€€€ **◇** (18) €€€€€

One of the region's grand names. A
noble mansion with antique-furnished
guestrooms. The chef's skill shines:
mullet with tapenade (p400), a gratin of
cod, peppers and pistachio potatoes,
and roast rabbit with broad (fava) beans.

CHATEAU-ARNOUX-ST-AUBAN

● L'Oustaou de la Foun

On RN85, 04160 **Map** 9D2

C 04 92 62 65 30

FAX 04 92 62 65 32

⚡ AE, DC, MC, V

● Sun D, Mon; 1st wk Jan,
1st 2 wks Jul **¶¶** €€€

Once a Provençal farm, but now a
restaurant serving sautéed langoustines
or ratatouille (p400) cooked in shellfish
sauce with mussels and pesto. Tasty
local vintages on the wine list.

CHATEAUNEUF-DU-PAPE

▲ Château des Fines Roches

Route from Sourges, 84230 **Map** 12B2

C 04 90 83 70 23

FAX 04 90 83 78 42

W www.chateaufinesroches.com

⚡ AE, MC, V **●** late Nov–mid-Dec

¶¶ €€€€ **◇** (8) €€€€€

Relax among the golden turrets and
emerald topiary of this 19th-century
château surrounded by a vineyard.
Kitchen creations include timbale of crab
and lobster, and grilled bull. Many of the
guestrooms have lovely views.

COLLOBRIERES

● La Petite Fontaine

Pl de la République, 83610 **Map** 13D3

C 04 94 48 00 12

⚡ MC, V **●** Sun D, Mon; Feb

¶¶ €€

Hearty dishes such as rabbit with polenta
and wild mushrooms and lamb with
roasted garlic grace the menu. Local
wine is sold by the carafe, and antique
farm tools adorn the walls. This is the

country's capital of marrons glacés (tasty
candied chestnuts), so don't miss out.

CORRENS

▲ Auberge du Parc

Pl du Général de Gaulle, 83570
Map 13D3

C 04 94 59 53 52

FAX 04 94 59 53 54

⚡ MC, V **●** Tue, Nov–Mar: Sun–Thu
D **¶¶** €€€ **◇** (6) €€€

Owned by local gastronomic legend
Clement Bruno. Only one menu available,
which changes daily. The only constant is
the excellence. Small, colourful rooms.

CRILLON-LE-BRAVE

▲ Hostellerie de Crillion-le-Brave

Pl de l'Eglise, 84410 **Map** 12C2

C 04 90 65 61 61

FAX 04 90 65 62 86

W www.crillonlebrave.com

⚡ AE, DC, MC, V **●** Tue, Oct–Jun:
Mon; mid-Jan–mid-Feb, mid-Nov–mid-
Dec **¶¶** €€€€ **◇** (32) €€€€€

Riverside restaurant serving contemporary
cuisine such as baked foie gras with
French toast, and wild sheep with a
millefeuille of aubergine (eggplant)
polenta with Szechuan pepper. Large,
airy rooms with Provençal fabrics.

CUCURON

● La Petite Maison

Pl de l'Etang, 84160 **Map** 12C2

C 04 90 77 18 60

FAX 04 90 77 18 61

W www.la-petite-maison.com

⚡ AE, MC, V **●** Tue, Oct–Jun: Mon;
mid-Jan–mid-Feb **¶¶** €€€€

On the menu are Mediterranean mullet
dumplings and Alpine lamb with fresh
thyme and vegetables.

CUERS

● Le Lingousto

Route from Pierrefeu, 83390 **Map** 13D3

C 04 94 28 69 10

FAX 04 94 48 63 79

⚡ AE, DC, MC, V **●** Sun D, Mon
¶¶ €€€€

A vineyard surrounds this pretty nook in
the hills, where guests linger over
Provençal delicacies. Recommended:
salads and pigeon with foie gras.

DABISSE

● Le Vieux Colombier

La Bastide-Dabisse, on d4, 04190
Map 9D2

C 04 92 34 32 32

FAX 04 92 34 34 26

⚡ AE, DC, MC, V **●** Sun D, Wed; 1st
2 wks Jan **¶¶** €€€

A mix of the modern and traditional.
Try gazpacho with new peas, foie gras,
crispy prawns, and beef with quail ravioli
in a red wine sauce.

DIGNE-LES-BAINS

▲ Le Grand Paris

19 bd Thiers, 04000 **Map** 9D2

C 04 92 31 11 15

FAX 04 92 32 32 82

⚡ AE, DC, MC, V

● Sep–May: Mon, Tue L; Dec–Mar

¶¶ €€€€ **◇** (24) €€€€€

A former Trinitarian monastery. The heat
of the local thermal baths seems to
inspire this kitchen. Dishes like fillet of
pigeon and woodcock. Charming rooms.

DIGNE-LES-BAINS

● L'Origan

6 rue Pied-de-Ville, 04000 **Map** 9D2

C 04 92 31 62 13

FAX 04 92 31 62 13

⚡ AE, DC, MC, V

● Sun; 1st 3 wks Feb **¶¶** €€€

Chef Philippe Cochet's southern highlands heritage resonates in dishes like
sage pork stuffed with pistachios, and
lamb with chickpea (garbanzo bean)
purée and sesame garlic oil.

EYGALIERES

● Bistrot d'Eygalières Chez Bru

Rue de la République, 13810 **Map** 12C2

C 04 90 90 60 34

FAX 04 90 90 60 37

⚡ AE, MC, V **●** Mon, Jun–Sep: Tue
L, Oct–May: Sun D **¶¶** €€€

A dynamic and experimental kitchen in a
serene village. Enjoy the poached eggs
with truffles, fresh cod with onion confit,
and prawn tempura with green beans.

EZE

▲ Château Eza

Rue de la Pise, 06360 **Map** 12B4

C 04 93 41 12 24

FAX 04 93 41 16 64
W www.slh.com/eza
AE, DC, MC, V ● Nov–Mar
€€€€€ ◗ (10) €€€€€
A medieval castle complete with polished armoury and iron chandeliers. Romantic restaurant on a breathtaking terrace complete with mini "kissing balconies" for two. Guestrooms feature stone fireplaces and private balconies overlooking the sea or the mountains.

EZE
▲ La Chèvre d'Or
Rue du Barri, 06360 **Map** 12B4
C 04 92 10 66 66
FAX 04 93 41 06 72
W www.chevredor.com
AE, DC, MC, V ● mid-Nov–Feb
€€€€€ ◗ (33) €€€€€
Restaurant in a stunning mountain-top village, with excellent sea views. Duck with fresh peaches is a menu highlight. Guestrooms are luxuriously furnished.

EZE
● Le Nid d'Aigle
1 rue du Château, 06360 **Map** 12B4
C 04 93 41 19 08
FAX 04 93 41 19 08
AE, DC ● Wed D, early Jan–early Feb €€
Lively, informal appeal. The menu never strays far from Provençal favourites such as rabbit, potato, garlic and basil soup, and bream with pistou.

EZE
● Le Troubadour
4 rue du Brec, 06360 **Map** 12B4
C 04 93 41 19 03
MC, V ● Sun, Mon L; 1 wk Feb, 1st 2 wks Jul, Nov–Dec €€
Regional favourites on the menu include duck foie gras, courgettes (zucchini) stuffed with truffles, and outstanding Mediterranean lobster millefeuille.

EZE
▲ Les Terrasses d'Eze
Route de la Turbie, 06360 **Map** 12B4
C 04 92 41 55 55
FAX 04 92 41 55 10
AE, DC, MC, V
€€€€ ◗ (81) €€€€€

A modern hotel with an infinity pool and a cascade of private balconies offering beautiful views. Refined French and international cuisine such as crayfish salad with citrus fruit, pan-fried tuna with sun-dried tomatoes, and tiramisu.

EZE
▲ L'Hermitage
1951 ave des Diables Bleus, 06360 **Map** 12B4
C 04 93 41 00 68
FAX 04 93 41 24 05
AE, MC, V ● mid-Nov–mid-Dec
€€ ◗ (14) €€€
Country house with stunning seaside views. The cooking is Provençal and the portions are famously generous. Don't miss the rabbit stew. The small, rustic guestrooms overlook the sea or the mountains. Swimming pool and garden.

EZE
● Mas Provençal
243 ave Verdun, 06360 **Map** 12B4
C 04 93 41 19 53
FAX 04 93 41 08 00
@ mas.provencal@wanadoo.fr
AE, MC, V ● 1st 3 wks Dec
€€€
If you've just one night in Eze then head to this unique place. The floral decorations are spectacular: like fireworks, bouquets explode from ceiling hooks to create an unforgettably romantic gastronomic greenhouse. Succumb to suckling pig marinated in milk, or beef entrecôte.

FAYENCE
● Le Castellaras
Route from Seillans, 83440 **Map** 12A4
C 04 94 76 13 80
FAX 04 94 84 17 50
AE, DC, MC, V ● Mon, Tue; 2 wks Mar, last wk Jun–1st wk Jul, mid-Nov–mid-Dec €€
Restaurant in the hills of Provence serving regional fare. Sample the lobster stew with truffle risotto and the stuffed rack of lamb. The wine list is exemplary.

FLAYOSC
▲ La Vieille Bastide
306 route du Peyron, 83780 **Map** 13D2
C 04 98 10 62 62

FAX 04 94 84 61 23
W www.la-vieille-bastide.com
DC, MC, V ● Sun D, Mon, Nov–mid-Jan: Tue L; Apr, last 3 wks Dec
€€ ◗ (7) €€
A lively, convivial place serving pigeon braised in vegetable sauce and tasty John Dory with fennel and pepper. Attractive guestrooms and garden. Pool.

FONTVIEILLE
▲ Auberge la Régalido
118 rue Frédéric Mistral, 13990 **Map** 12B2
C 04 90 54 60 22
FAX 04 90 54 64 29
W www.laregalido.com
AE, MC, V ● Mon, Tue L, Sat L; Jan–Feb €€€ ◗ (15) €€€€€
Highlights include roast Provençal lamb, and Mediterranean sea bass with tomatoes and lemon oil. The wine list showcases Coteaux d'Aix-en-Provence-les-Baux and Châteauneuf-du-Pape. Guestrooms are colourful and charming.

FORCALQUIER
● Le Lapin Tant Pis
10 ave St-Promasse, 04300 **Map** 12C2
C 04 92 75 38 88
FAX 04 92 75 38 89
● L €€
An unusual approach: no à la carte, just one daily menu, like lamb puff pastry in garlic cream with tomatoes. Desserts are equally fresh and innovative.

FORCALQUIER
● Oliviers & Co
3 rue des Cordeliers, 04300 **Map** 12C2
C 04 92 75 00 75
FAX 04 92 75 01 00
W www.oliviers-co.com
AE, MC, V ● Tue; mid-Nov–mid-Dec €
The Mediterranean inspires creations like courgette (zucchini) stuffed with red Camargue rice and a tangy marinade of chickpeas (garbanzo beans) with aubergines (eggplants).

FREJUS
● El Salmon
Résidence Aigue-Marine, pl Port d'Hermès, 83600 **Map** 12A5

C 04 94 51 05 07
FAX 04 94 52 00 31
MC, V ● Sun D, Wed; Jan, Nov
❙❙ €€

*Dishes include smoked salmon topped
with coriander (cilantro), and poached
salmon with potatoes.*

FREJUS
▲ L'Aréna
145 rue Général Gaulle, 83600
Map 12A5
C 04 94 17 09 40
FAX 04 94 52 01 52
w www.arena-hotel.com
AE, DC, MC, V ● mid-Dec–mid-
Jan **❙❙** €€€ 🛏 (36) €€€€

*Considered the best Provençal restau-
rant on the Estérel Coast. Choices like
artichokes with coriander (cilantro), veal
with polenta an home-made ice cream.
Some guestrooms have terraces.*

FREJUS
● Le Mérou Ardent
157 rue de la Libération, 83600
Map 12A5
C 04 94 17 30 58
FAX 04 94 17 33 79
MC, V ● Mon, Sep–May: Thu L;
late Nov–mid-Dec **❙❙** €€

*Marine decor suits a seafood menu that
includes monkfish and prawns stewed in
curry, and grilled sea bass.*

FREJUS
● Les Potiers
135 rue Potiers, 83600 **Map** 12A5
C 04 94 51 33 74
MC, V ● Tue, Wed L; 1st
3 wks Dec **❙❙** €€

*Rustic ambience, friendly service and
hearty country cooking. Opt for the daily
special, which might be fish soup.*

GIENS
● Tire Bouchon
1 pl St-Pierre, 83400 **Map** 13D3
C 04 94 58 24 61
FAX 04 94 58 15 37
MC, V ● Tue, Wed; Oct **❙❙** €€

*The menu has possibly the world's best
calamari fricassée as well as sea bream
and spinach. As the name "corkscrew"
suggests, there is an excellent wine list.*

GIGONDAS
▲ Les Florets
Route des Dentelles, 84190 **Map** 12C2
C 04 90 65 85 01
FAX 04 90 65 83 80
AE, DC, MC, V ● Tue, Mar &
Nov–Dec: Mon D; 1st 2 wks Mar
❙❙ €€€ 🛏 (15) €€€

*Seek out the fricasséed snails with pig's
trotters and red wine sauce, and roast
sea bass in mussel soup with cream of
broad (fava) bean and fennel. Desserts
are outstanding as well. The guestrooms
are filled with country charm.*

GOLFE-JUAN
● Tétou
Bd des Frères Roustan, Plages du Soleil,
06220 **Map** 12B4
C 04 93 63 71 16
FAX 04 93 63 16 77
● Mon L, Wed; Nov–mid-Mar
❙❙ €€€€€

*A culinary institution since 1920, with
one Michelin star. New York-style spot
specializing in bouillabaisse (p401)
Mediterranean lobster, prawns, mussels,
crabs, and an array of fish.*

GORBIO
● Restaurant Beau Séjour
14 pl de la République, 06500 **Map** 12B4
C 04 93 41 46 15
MC, V ● Jul–Sep: Wed, Oct–Jun:
Wed D **❙❙** €€

*Visitors to the tiny hillside hamlet of
Gorbio come for June's Snail Festival
and for a taste of Italy. Specialities
include courgette (zucchini) flowers
stuffed with creamy mozzarella.*

GORDES
● Le Mas Tourteron
Chemin St-Blaise, 84220 **Map** 12C2
C 04 90 72 00 16
FAX 04 90 72 09 81
AE, MC, V ● Mon, Tue, Feb–Mar:
Sun D; mid-Nov–Feb **❙❙** €€

*Terrine of fromage frais and sea bass
with fresh fennel purée at this restaurant
that occupies an 18th-century silk farm.*

GORDES
▲ Les Bories
Route d l'Abbaye-de-Sénanque, 84220

Map 12C2
C 04 90 72 00 51
FAX 04 90 72 01 22
w www.hotelprestige-provence.com
AE, DC, MC, V ● Jan–Mar
❙❙ €€€€ 🛏 (37) €€€€€

*A lovely hillside inn with beautiful rooms.
The chef's masterpieces include
bugnes (yeast dough fritter) with olives
and fennel. Viognier du Vaucluse and
Côtes-du-Rhône Villages top the wine list.*

GRASSE
● Brasserie Les Arcades
23 pl aux Aires, 06130 **Map** 12A4
C 04 93 36 00 95
MC, V ● Oct–Mar: Mon **❙❙** €

*This inviting brasserie makes a perfect
lunch spot in the heart of France's city
of perfumes. Enjoy the scent of grilled
tuna with a red pepper sauce under
picturesque stone arches.*

GRASSE
● Café Arnaud
10 pl Foux, 06130 **Map** 12A4
C 04 93 36 44 88
AE, DC, MC, V
● Sun, Sat L; Jun **❙❙** €

*Friendly Mediterranean-style bistro with
tables scattered along the street. The
house speciality is a truly divine tomato,
mozzarella and basil tart. Or try the
assortment of finger foods featuring the
cook's fabulous anchoïade (p400).*

GRASSE
▲ La Bastide St-Antoine
48 ave Henri, 06130 **Map** 12A4
C 04 93 70 94 94
FAX 04 93 70 94 95
w www.jacques-chibois.com
AE, DC, MC, V
❙❙ €€€€€ 🛏 (11) €€€€€

*This 18th-century farmhouse-cum-inn
is a real Riviera favourite. Chef Jacques
Chibois, who has two Michelin stars,
creates dishes with Tuscan touches
such as lobster with basil purée, sweetbreads with millet and pigeon with broad
(fava) beans. Luxurious rooms.*

GRASSE
● Moulin des Paroirs
7 ave Jean XXIII, 06130 **Map** 12A4

● Restaurant ■ Hotel ▲ Hotel / Restaurant

🎧 04 93 40 10 40
FAX 04 93 36 76 00
💳 AE, MC, V ⬤ Sun, Mon D; Nov, Jan
🍴 €€€

Inside an 18th-century olive mill, cuisine and a romantic setting that is hard to top. Prawn casserole with vegetables, and lamb with onion jam are highlights. Excellent wine list, too.

GRAVESON
● Le Clos des Cyprès
Route de Châteaurenard, 13690
Map 12B2
🎧 04 90 90 53 44
FAX 04 90 90 55 84
💳 MC, V ⬤ Sun D, Mon 🍴 €€€

The outgoing Bertinelli family make this a warm haven. Sample the crusty foie gras baked in pears, or fine zabaglione gratin with lobster, celery and basil.

GREOUX-LES-BAINS
▲ Hôtel Villa Borghese
Ave des Thermes, 04800 **Map** 13D2
🎧 04 92 78 00 91
FAX 04 92 78 09 55
🌐 www.villa-borghese.com
💳 AE, DC, MC, V ⬤ mid-Nov–mid-Mar 🍴 €€ 🛏 (67) €€€€

Nestled in the hills of the Luberon country but mindful of the sea. Maritime delights include courgette (zucchini) stuffed with scallop risotto, and John Dory. Spacious guestrooms.

GREOUX-LES-BAINS
▲ La Crémaillère
Route Riez, 04800 **Map** 13D2
🎧 04 92 70 40 04
FAX 04 92 78 19 80
💳 AE, DC, MC, V ⬤ Jan–Feb
🍴 €€€ 🛏 (51) €€€

Ingredients drawn from the sun-drenched hills and bountiful Mediterranean. Dishes include mackerel tart with two onions and basil gratin, and John Dory cooked with bay leaves and orange juice.

GRIMAUD
● Les Santons
D558, 83310 **Map** 12A5
🎧 04 94 43 21 02
FAX 04 94 43 24 92
@ lessantons@wanadoo.fr

💳 DC, MC, V ⬤ Apr–Jun: Wed, Jul–Aug: L; Nov–mid-Mar 🍴 €€€€

Worth a trip just for the amazing collection of santons – hand-painted Christmas figurines made by local craftsmen. The menu includes fish stew, lamb with thyme, truffles and beef millefeuille.

HYERES
● Les Jardins de Bacchus
32 ave Gambetta, 83400 **Map** 13D3
🎧 04 94 65 77 63
FAX 04 94 65 71 19
🌐 www.les-jardins-de-bacchus.com
💳 AE, DC, MC, V ⬤ Mon; 2 wks Jan
🍴 €€€€

Lobster, ratatouille (p400) and cannelloni with pork complement the many wines on offer. Sugary classics like chocolate fondant and brownies for dessert.

ILE-DE-PORQUEROLLES
● Il Pescatore
Carré du Port, 83400 **Map** 13D3
🎧 04 94 58 30 61
FAX 04 94 58 35 53
💳 AE, MC, V ⬤ Nov–Feb 🍴 €€

Bouillabaisse (p401), swordfish carpaccio and sashimi at a lovely restaurant more Amalfi Coast than Côte d'Azur.

ILE-DE-PORQUEROLLES
▲ Mas du Langoustier
Chemin Langoustier, 3.5km (2 miles) from the port, 83400 **Map** 13D3
🎧 04 94 58 30 09
FAX 04 94 58 36 02
🌐 www.langoustier.com
💳 AE, DC, MC, V ⬤ Nov–Apr
🍴 €€€€ 🛏 (46) €€€€€

Hotel guests arrive by helicopter and then scoot about in golf carts. The restaurant serves warm foie gras and pigeon simmered in eucalyptus honey. Spacious, modern guestrooms.

ISLE-SUR-LA-SORGUE
▲ Mas de Cure Bourse
Route de Caumont-sur-Durance, 84800
Map 12C2
🎧 04 90 38 16 58
FAX 04 90 38 52 31
@ masdecurebourse@wanadoo.fr
💳 DC, MC, V ⬤ Mon, Tue L
🍴 €€ 🛏 (13) €€

Dine on a crumble of sun-dried tomatoes and Parmesan, followed by the day's best fish cooked with kumquat lasagne and ginger confit. Nicely sized, tidy rooms.

ISTRES
● Les Deux Toques
7–9 ave Hélène Boucher, 13800
Map 12C3
🎧 04 42 55 16 01
FAX 04 42 55 95 02
💳 AE, MC, V ⬤ Sun, Mon; last wk Aug–1st wk Sep, last wk Dec–1st wk Jan 🍴 €€€

Highlights include anchovy cake with sea salt, and Beauregard lamb cooked in a herb crust with a pistou glaze.

JAUSIERS
● Villa Morelia
Town centre, 04850 **Map** 13E1
🎧 04 92 84 67 78
FAX 04 92 84 65 47
🌐 www.villa-morelia.com
💳 MC, V ⬤ L, Sep–Jun: Sun D & Mon D; mid-Mar–mid-Apr, 1st wk Nov–mid-Dec 🍴 €€€

Gracious table in the highlands with ravioli of young rabbit with figs, rosemary sauce and pigeon roasted in rosé wine with a Parmesan cheese crust.

JOUCAS
▲ Le Mas des Herbes Blanches
Route de Murs, 6km (4 miles) east by D2 and D102, 84220 **Map** 12C2
🎧 04 90 05 79 79
FAX 04 90 05 71 96
💳 AE, DC, MC, V ⬤ Jan–Feb
🍴 €€€ 🛏 (19) €€€€€

Fabulous fine cuisine and world-class hospitality in a château. Delicacies include crab with mayonnaise, green apples and curry, and lamb with mint and coriander (cilantro). Good-sized guestrooms look out over the hills.

JUAN-LES-PINS
● Bijou Plage
Bd Guillaumony, bd du Littoral, 06160
Map 12B4
🎧 04 93 61 39 07
FAX 04 93 67 81 78
💳 AE, DC, MC, V ⬤ Tue D, Nov–Apr: Wed; last 2 wks Jan 🍴 €€

For key to symbols see back flap

The gem of Juan-les-Pins. Try breaded pork chops, lamb with truffle oil, rich pesto tomatoes and mussels with cream and saffron.

JUAN-LES-PINS
▲ Hôtel Juana
Ave Georges Gallice, La Pinède, 06160
Map 12B4
☏ 04 93 61 08 70
FAX 04 93 61 76 60
🍽 AE, MC, V ⚫ Sep–May: Tue & Wed D; mid-Nov–mid-Dec 🍴 €€€€€
🥢 (40) €€€€€
Celebrated luxury hotel opened in 1931, with a restaurant facing the sea. The lamb in terracotta is a menu highlight.

JUAN-LES-PINS
⚫ La Douce
10 bd Edouard Baudoin, 06160
Map 12B4
☏ 04 93 61 04 27
🍽 AE, DC, MC, V ⚫ mid-Dec–mid-Jan 🍴 €€
Dine with your feet in the sand and enjoy the area's best seafood salad, piled with grilled prawns and scallops.

JUAN-LES-PINS
⚫ Le Grill (Eden Casino)
15 bd Edouard Baudoin, 06160
Map 12B4
☏ 04 92 93 71 71
FAX 04 93 61 67 00
🖥 www.edencasino.fr
🍽 AE, DC, MC, V 🍴 €
Affordable gourmet lunch menus. On the menu are salads as well as grilled prawns with lemon and coriander (cilantro) sauce.

LA CADIERE-D'AZUR
▲ Hostellerie Bérard
Ave Gabriel Péri, 83740 **Map** 12C3
☏ 04 94 90 11 43
FAX 04 94 90 01 94
🖥 www.hotel-berard.com
🍽 AE, DC, MC, V ⚫ Mon L, Sat L; last wk Jan–1st wk Feb
🍴 €€€€€ 🥢 (37) €€€€€
The 11th-century buildings, bountiful vineyard and the kitchen all vie for high praise. Expect stuffed morels with sweet new peas and chicken. Well-kept, cosy guestrooms.

LA CIOTAT
▲ La Rif Chez Tania
Calanque de Figuerolles, 13600
Map 12C3
☏ 04 42 08 41 71
FAX 04 42 71 93 39
🖥 www.figerolles.com
🍽 MC, V 🍴 €€ 🥢 (10) €€
A joke nation – the Independent Republic of Figuerolles – was founded here in the 1950s. Though you can't pay with figs (the official currency), you can enjoy mullet, and sweet almond ice cream. Basic, comfortable guestrooms.

LA CROIX-VALMER
▲ Château de Valmer
Plage de Gigaro, 83420 **Map** 12A5
☏ 04 94 55 15 15
FAX 04 94 55 15 10
🖥 www.chateau-valmer.com
🍽 AE, DC, MC, V ⚫ Tue; mid-Oct–mid-Apr
🍴 €€€ 🥢 (42) €€€€€
Extremely hospitable and nicely appointed establishment with an extraordinary seaside location. Menu highlights include baked langoustine with thyme flowers, and lobster cassoulet (p373) in coral butter.

LA TURBIE
▲ Hôstellerie Jérôme
20 rue Compte Cessole, 06320
Map 12B4
☏ 04 92 41 51 51
FAX 04 92 41 51 50
🍽 MC, V ⚫ 1st 3 wks Dec
🍴 €€€€ 🥢 (5) €€€€
Gourmets will delight in the risotto with truffles, mushrooms and prawns, and the delicate pastry topped with fresh berries. Guestrooms are filled with artwork.

LA TURBIE
▲ Le Napoléon
7 ave de la Victoire, 06320 **Map** 12B4
☏ 04 93 41 00 54
FAX 04 93 41 28 93
🍽 AE, MC, V ⚫ Wed
🍴 €€ 🥢 (24) €€
Simple, economical meals and a bird's-eye view can be enjoyed at this top-floor restaurant. Salads, grilled meats and stuffed vegetables grace the menu. Guestrooms have splendid sea views.

LE LAUZET-UBAYE
▲ France
On D900, 04340 **Map** 13D1
☏ 04 92 85 54 55
FAX 04 92 85 59 84
🍽 MC, V ⚫ Sep–Jun: Tue D & Wed
🍴 € 🥢 (10) €
Straightforward, delicious and affordable: a perfect stop along the mountain highway between Gap and Barcelonette. Impressive pastry buffet, good beef Wellington, and rare bull casserole. Rooms are spartan and serene.

LE LAVANDOU
⚫ Le Sud
Ave des Trois Dauphins, Aiguebelle, 83980 **Map** 13D3
☏ 04 94 05 76 98
🍽 MC, V ⚫ Jun–Aug: Sun L
🍴 €€€€
Ratatouille (p400), pigeon with polenta, truffles and rabbit stewed in four herbs are all on the menu. Both the wine and dessert offerings are top-notch.

LE LAVANDOU
▲ Les Roches
1 ave des Trois Dauphins, Aiguebelle, 83980 **Map** 13D3
☏ 04 94 71 05 07
FAX 04 94 71 08 40
🍽 AE, DC, MC, V ⚫ Oct–Mar
🍴 €€€€ 🥢 (32) €€€€€
A little piece of seaside paradise. Luxury accommodation with pool, tennis courts and private beach. The restaurant blends the best ingredients like grated truffles with sun-dried tomatoes and Parmesan and pan-fried foie gras with Jerusalem artichoke sauce.

LE PARADOU
⚫ La Petite France
55 ave de la Vallée des Baux, 13520
Map 12C2
☏ 04 90 54 41 91
FAX 04 90 54 52 50
🍽 MC, V ⚫ Wed, Apr–Sep: Thu L, Oct–Mar: Thu; 1st wk Nov–1st wk Dec
🍴 €€
Menu offerings include ravioli with Corsican olives, the lamb cooked three ways, and the hot fondant of chocolate with a heavenly vanilla cream.

⚫ Restaurant ■ Hotel ▲ Hotel / Restaurant

LE ROVE

▲ Auberge du Mérou

3 chemin du Port, Calanque de Niolon,
13740 **Map** 12C3

📞 04 91 46 98 69

FAX 04 91 46 90 06

💳 MC, V ⬤ Mon D, Oct–Apr: Sun D

🍽 €€ 🍷 (5) €€

*Huge picture windows show off the
stunning coastline. Plenty of seafood:
sardines, bream, bouillabaisse (p401)
and paella. Basic, tidy guestrooms.*

LES ISSAMBRES

● Chante-Mer

Village Provençale, Calanque des
Issambres, 83380 **Map** 12A5

📞 04 94 96 93 23

FAX 04 94 96 81 79

💳 MC, V ⬤ Mon; mid-Dec–Jan

🍽 €€€

*Run by the same brothers as the Feu
Follet in Mougins, this dining room is
elegant. The menu includes foie gras,
scallop ravioli, and beef with morels.*

LES ISSAMBRES

▲ Villa Saint Elme

Corniche des Issambres, 83380
Map 12A5

📞 04 94 49 52 52

FAX 04 94 49 63 18

🌐 www.slh.com/saintelme

💳 AE, DC, MC, V

🍽 €€€€€ 🍷 (17) €€€€€

*The fashionably tanned flock to this
turn-of-the-century villa for luxury
pampering. For breakfast, the kitchen
makes its own bread and jams. Two
gourmet restaurants and a poolside grill.
Absolute luxury in the guestrooms.*

LOURMARIN

▲ Le Moulin de Lourmarin

Rue du Temple, 84160 **Map** 12C2

📞 04 90 68 06 69

FAX 04 90 68 31 76

💳 AE, DC, MC, V ⬤ Tue L, Wed;
early Jan–mid-Feb, mid-Nov–early Dec

🍽 €€€€€ 🍷 (19) €€€€€

*Try a taste of the Luberon hills with foie
gras and green tomatoes, monkfish with
poppy seeds, and a smooth chocolate
dessert. The wine list overflows with
first-rate choices. Rustic guestrooms.*

MANDELIEU-LA NAPOULE

● Bistrot du Port

Port La Napoule, 06210 **Map** 12A4

📞 04 93 49 80 60

FAX 04 93 93 28 50

💳 MC, V ⬤ Tue D, Wed; mid-
Nov–mid-Dec 🍽 €€

*Affordable portside eatery where the
daily specials are pulled straight from
the sea just hours before appearing on
your plate. Excellent mussels.*

MANDELIEU-LA NAPOULE

▲ Ermitage du Riou

26 ave Henry Clews, 06210 **Map** 12A4

📞 04 93 49 95 56

FAX 04 92 97 69 05

🌐 www.ermitage-du-riou.fr

💳 AE, DC, MC, V ⬤ mid-Dec–mid-
Jan 🍽 €€€ 🍷 (24) €€€€

*Nice rooms plus private beach and pool
nestled among the spectacular red rock
beaches. Retire to the dining room for
oysters and stuffed sardines followed by
pork saltimbocca or lamb with basil and
garlic-roasted potatoes.*

MANDELIEU-LA NAPOULE

● L'Armorial

198 bd Henry Clews, 06210 **Map** 12A4

📞 04 93 49 91 80

💳 MC, V ⬤ Wed 🍽 €€

*There's only one reason to come here:
bouillabaisse (p401). The seafood soup
is cooked with the shells – to add extra
texture and taste – and served with the
traditional toasted bread and rouille.*

MANDELIEU-LA NAPOULE

● L'Oasis

Rue Jean Honoré Carle, 06210 **Map** 12A4

📞 04 93 49 95 52

FAX 04 93 49 64 13

🌐 www.oasis-raimbault.com

💳 AE, DC, MC, V ⬤ Oct–Mar: Sun D
& Mon; Jan–mid-Feb 🍽 €€€€€

*The three Raimbault brothers share two
Michelin stars. One house speciality is
the veal chop cooked in milk. Fantastic
garden and a 400-label wine list.*

MANOSQUE

● Dominique Bucaille

43 bd des Tilleuls, 04100 **Map** 12C2

📞 04 92 72 32 28

FAX 04 92 72 32 28

💳 AE, MC, V ⬤ Sun, Wed D; mid-
Jul–mid-Aug 🍽 €€€

*Chef Dominique Bucaille is just begin-
ning a luminous career. Sample his
tartare of crisped vegetables and wild
herbs and lamb galette.*

MARSEILLE

● Carbone

22 rue Sainte, 13001 **Map** 12C3

📞 04 91 55 52 73

💳 MC, V ⬤ Sun, Mon; Aug 🍽 €€

*Wild unions of ingredients, like Thai
lobster, wok-fried prawns and bananas,
and duck baked with ginger. A bright,
colourful house hosts this lively eatery.*

MARSEILLE

● La Côte de Boeuf

35 cours Honoré d'Estienne d'Orves,
13001 **Map** 12C3

📞 04 91 54 89 08

FAX 04 91 54 25 60

💳 MC, V ⬤ last wk Dec–1st wk Jan

🍽 €€

*The real attraction is the wine cellar,
with more than 1,500 vintages. Tender
meat dishes from steak to entrecôte.*

MARSEILLE

▲ Le Petit Nice Passédat

17 rue des Braves, 13007 **Map** 12C3

📞 04 91 59 25 92

FAX 04 91 59 28 08

💳 AE, MC, V ⬤ May–Oct: Sun D &
Mon D, Nov–Apr: Sun & Mon

🍽 €€€€€ 🍷 (16) €€€€€

*One of the region's finest names, with
chic design. Bream with fish dumplings,
and a world-class bouillabaisse (p401).
The wine list alone merits a visit.*

MARSEILLE

● Le Poisson qui Marche

Chemin du Littoral, 13016 **Map** 12C3

📞 04 91 46 70 00

FAX 04 91 46 06 67

@ lepoissonquimarche@wanadoo.fr

💳 MC, V ⬤ Sun 🍽 €€€

*This lively spot, under a dynamic
young chef, serves affordable, top-rank
dishes like bouillabaisse (p401) and very
succulent langoustines. Heavy seafood
emphasis on the menu.*

For key to symbols see back flap

MARSEILLE

● **L'Épuisette**

156 rue du Vallon des Auffes, 13007

Map 12C3

04 91 52 17 82

FAX 04 91 59 18 80

AE, DC, MC, V Sun D, Mon, Sat
L; last 2 wks Feb, last 3 wks Aug

€€€

An intriguing blend of France, Asia and
Central America. Savour the lobster
carpaccio with nuoc man (Vietnamese
hot fish sauce), and the sea bass with
vegetables and morsels of chorizo.

MARSEILLE

● **Michel**

6 rue des Catalans, 13000 **Map** 12C3

04 91 52 30 63

FAX 04 91 59 23 05

AE, MC, V €€€€

A long-time local favourite serving a
terrific bouillabaisse (p401) and a
superb bourride (p401). A strong wine
list and a lively bistro atmosphere.

MARSEILLE

● **René Alloin**

8 pl de l'Amiral Muselier, 13008

Map 12C3

04 91 77 88 25

FAX 04 91 71 82 46

MC, V Sun D, Sat L €€

No over-the-top ingredients. This is
Provençal food for Provençal people,
though travellers are welcome. The
rabbit ravioli with wild herbs is a standout.

MAUSSANE-LES-ALPILLES

● **Ou Ravi Provençau**

34 ave de la Vallée des Baux, 13520

Map 12B2

04 90 54 31 11

FAX 04 90 54 41 03

AE, DC, MC, V Tue, Wed; 2nd
wk Apr, last wk Jun, early–mid-Dec

€€€

A truly delightful establishment serving
barigoule d'artichauts (braised artichokes), ham with onion confit, and
pigeon roasted with honey and lavender.

MENERBES

▲ **Hostellerie le Roy Soleil**

Le Fort, 84560 **Map** 12C2

04 90 72 25 61

FAX 04 90 72 36 55

www.roy-soleil.com

MC, V Dec–Mar

€€€€ (19) €€€€€

Even the Sun King – with his impossibly
high standards – would have approved.
A veritable banquet awaits: poached
lobster with truffle vinaigrette, delicate
little sorbets and a regal wine list.
Elegant guestrooms.

MENTON

● **Braijade Meridiounale**

66 rue Longue, 06500 **Map** 12B4

04 93 35 65 65

FAX 04 93 35 65 65

MC, V Sep–Jun: Wed; mid-
Nov–mid-Dec €€€

Rustic eatery just steps from Menton's
medieval centre. Steaks and brochettes
are cooked over an open fire and served
with delicious sauces and seasonal
vegetables. Wide-ranging wine list.

MENTON

● **Carnival**

29 quai de Monléon, 06500 **Map** 12B4

04 93 35 99 95

FAX 04 93 35 99 95

MC, V Mon, Tue L €€

A colourful place with a quite inventive
selection of tasty dishes such as chicken
salad with sesame and Parmesan, and
cooked cream topped with berries. The
wine list is better than most in town.

MENTON

▲ **Hôtel Aiglon**

7 ave de la Madone, 06500 **Map** 12B4

04 93 57 55 55

FAX 04 93 35 92 39

www.hotelaiglon.net

AE, DC, MC, V Nov–mid-Dec

€€€ (29) €€€

A perfect escape from the busy Riviera,
this proud 1800s hotel has a lush
garden, banana tree grove and a poolside restaurant. Foie gras and veal with
prunes in red wine feature on the menu.
Charming guestrooms.

MENTON

▲ **Hôtel des Ambassadeurs**

3 rue des Partouneaux, 06500 **Map** 12B4

04 93 28 75 75

FAX 04 93 35 62 32

www.ambassadeurs-menton.com

AE, DC, MC, V Sun, Mon L, Sat
L; mid-Nov–mid-Dec

€€€€ (49) €€€€

This centrally located Belle Epoque
hotel is the town's most glamorous.
Dishes such as red mullet with mangoes
and basil, pork with honey and pears,
and lamb with lavender grace the menu.
Guestrooms in traditional, local style.

MENTON

▲ **Hôtel St Michel**

1684 promenade du Soleil, 06500

Map 12B4

04 93 57 46 33

FAX 04 93 57 71 19

AE, DC, MC, V Nov

€ (18) €€€

A cute, modest hotel, decorated with
posters from local art exhibits. Colourful,
lively restaurant serving salads, pizzas
and curious Italo-Franco culinary hybrids
such as tagliatelle with pistou.

MENTON

● **La Boucherie**

7 rue des Marins, 06500 **Map** 12B4

04 93 35 74 67

AE, MC, V €€

Classic French cuisine with an
emphasis on various cuts of meat, as
the name suggests. Dishes include
boeuf bourguignon (p217), rib of beef,
entrecotes of lamb and pot-au-feu.

MENTON

● **La Riviera Restaurant**

1563 promenade du Soleil, 06500

Map 12B4

04 93 35 25 75

AE, MC, V Wed D, Thu €€

A waterfront eatery ideal for an elegant
repose from sporty beach activities. Try
the shrimp bruschetta, linguini with clams
and moules marinières (p145).

MENTON

● **La Tavernetta**

4 pl du Cap, 06500 **Map** 12B4

04 93 35 45 00

AE, MC, V

Tue, Oct–Mar: Wed; Nov €€

● Restaurant ■ Hotel ▲ Hotel / Restaurant

This is your best bet in Menton's centre. Italian menu of pasta dishes such as seafood penne and tagliatelle with squid.

MENTON
● **Le Nautic**
27 quai de Monléon, 06500 **Map** 12B4
04 93 35 78 74
AE, MC, V ● Mon ¶¶ €€€
Facing the Jean Cocteau Museum, this is the best place in town to eat raw fish. Don't miss the super-sized appetizer platter or the oyster combinations.

MENTON
▲ **Le Royal Westminster**
1510 promenade du Soleil, 06500
Map 12B4
04 93 28 69 69
FAX 04 92 10 12 30
www.vacancesbleues.com
AE, MC, V ● Nov
¶¶ €€€ ◇ (82) €€€
This Belle Epoque hotel, with a pétanque strip, attracts an older crowd. The Italian-inspired menu offers delicious light starters, such as grapefruit and crab, followed by an assortment of grilled fish. The big sunlit guestrooms overlook a pebble beach.

MENTON
● **Paris Palace**
1892 promenade du Soleil, 06500
Map 12B4
04 93 35 86 66
FAX 04 93 28 34 90
AE, MC, V ● Sep–May: Mon
¶¶ €
With tables sporting Hawaii-style umbrellas, this is a great place for smoked salmon or a salade mentonnaise with salmon, lemon and orange.

MENTON
● **Pistou**
9 quai Gordon Bennett, 06500 **Map** 12B4
04 93 57 45 89
AE, MC, V ● Sun D, Mon ¶¶ €€
Harbourside restaurant serving a wonderful range of seafood including hearty fish stew, bouillabaisse (p401), seafood platters and huge paellas. The speciality is the seafood soup, best eaten on the almost year-round terrace.

MENTON
● **Restaurant du Petit Port**
4 rue du Jonquier, 06500 **Map** 12B4
04 93 35 82 62
AE, MC, V ● Mon ¶¶ €€
A favourite with the locals, this tiny eatery has shaded outdoor tables and sits snug against picturesque buildings and balconies draped with drying laundry. Eye-catchers include paella, swordfish carpaccio, sardines and moules à la provençale.

MENTON
● **Utopia**
1360 promenade Soleil, 06500
Map 12B4
04 93 28 23 04
FAX 04 93 28 23 04
AE, MC, V ● mid-Sep–mid-Jun: Mon; 1st 2 wks Nov ¶¶ €
Toppings come with a French twist at this seaside eatery. Try the pizza paysanne with tomato, mozzarella, bacon, onion and egg; or the house special with ham, prawns and curry spices.

MISON
● **L'Iris de Suse**
Town centre, 04200 **Map** 13D1
04 92 62 21 69
MC, V ¶¶ €
Ravioli with sage and fresh goat's cheese, scallops, and a delightfully piquant young guinea fowl stuffed with figs. Brief but good wine list.

MONTE-CARLO
● **Bar & Boeuf**
Ave Princesse Grace, 98000 **Map** 12B4
00 377 92 16 60 60
FAX 00 377 92 16 60 61
www.alain-ducasse.com
AE, DC, MC, V ● Mon; Oct–mid-May ¶¶ €€€€
Philippe Starck furniture and panoramic views at this Alain Ducasse restaurant. The menu offers squid with smoked fish and fennel, aubergine (eggplant) and courgette (zucchini) tian.

MONTE-CARLO
● **Bice**
17 ave des Spélugues, 98000
Map 12B4

00 377 93 25 20 30
www.biceristorante.com
AE, MC, V ¶¶ €€
Despite being part of a chain, a flair for things Italian and its minimalist decor make this place popular. Try the aubergine (eggplant) piled high with cheese, squid, tuna tartare or bresaola.

MONTE-CARLO
● **Café de Paris**
Pl du Casino, 98000 **Map** 12B4
00 377 92 16 25 54
AE, DC, MC, V ¶¶ €€
This streetside café is the ultimate people-watching spot in town. On the menu are hearty steaks as well as salads with toppings such as goats' cheese, ham and red peppers.

MONTE-CARLO
▲ **Hôtel Columbus**
23 ave des Papalins, 98000 **Map** 12B4
00 377 92 05 90 00
FAX 00 377 92 05 91 67
www.columbushotels.com
AE, DC, MC, V
¶¶ €€€€€ ◇ (184) €€€€€
Hip and contemporary hotel that is a breath of fresh air. The bar is part-owned by Formula One driver David Coulthard, making it the "in" place during the Grand Prix, and the brasserie is one of the trendiest places to see and be seen. Large, bright guestrooms.

MONTE-CARLO
▲ **Hôtel de Paris**
Pl du Casino, 98000 **Map** 12B4
00 377 92 16 30 00
FAX 00 377 92 16 38 49
AE, DC, MC, V ● Tue, Wed L, mid-Aug–mid-Jun: Wed D
¶¶ €€€€€ ◇ (191) €€€€€
Of all Monaco's stars, this hotel, opened in 1865, shines the brightest. When Edward VII and a lady friend dined here their crêpes were accidentally set aflame, hence crêpes suzettes, named after his companion. First-class rooms.

MONTE-CARLO
▲ **Hôtel Hermitage**
Sq Beaumarchais, 98000 **Map** 12B4
00 377 92 16 40 00

FAX 00 377 92 16 38 52
w www.sbm.mc
AE, DC, MC, V
€€€€€ (263) €€€€€

A landmark hotel. Near Les Thermes de Monte-Carlo, the building is a sight worth seeing with its crystal chandeliers and Art Nouveau glass-and-steel dome by Gustave Eiffel. Sumptuous guestrooms.

MONTE-CARLO
▲ Hôtel Mirabeau Monte Carlo
1 ave Princesse Grace, 98000 **Map** 12B4
00 377 92 16 65 65
FAX 00 377 93 50 84 85
w www.hotelsdeluxe.com/mirabeau
AE, DC, MC, V
€€€€ (103) €€€€

Chef Michel de Matteis is the force behind this hotel's well-kept secret: a romantic, gourmet restaurant. Try the ravioles (p268), delectably stuffed with tender lobster, or the scallops with truffle shavings. Luxurious guestrooms.

MONTE-CARLO
● La Rose des Vents
Plage du Larvotto, 98000 **Map** 12B4
00 377 97 70 46 96
FAX 00 377 97 70 46 97
AE, MC, V €€€€

One of the principality's newest eateries. The menu features duck liver with mushrooms and roast veal.

MONTE-CARLO
● Le St-Benoit
10 ave de la Costa, 98000 **Map** 12B4
00 377 93 25 02 34
FAX 00 377 93 30 52 64
AE, MC, V
Mon, Oct–Mar: Sun D €€€

Memorable meals and an unforgettable view. The menu includes classic fish soup, oysters and a lemon tart.

MONTE-CARLO
● L'Hirondelle
2 ave Monte Carlo, 98000 **Map** 12B4
00 377 92 16 49 30
AE, DC, MC, V D; 1 wk Dec
€€€€

Part of Les Thermes Marins, this health-food restaurant delights diners with its vegetable pâté and veal cooked in broth.

MONTE-CARLO
● Loga Café
25 bd des Moulins, 98000 **Map** 12B4
00 377 93 30 87 72
AE, DC, MC, V Sun; last
2 wks Aug €€€€

Opulent if slightly stuffy brasserie offering traditional fare. Dishes include cod in olive oil, wine and tomatoes, Swiss chard pie and daube de boeuf (p401).

MONTE-CARLO
▲ Monte-Carlo Grand Hôtel
12 ave des Spélugues, 98007 **Map** 12B4
00 377 93 50 65 00
FAX 00 377 93 30 01 57
w www.montecarlograndhotel.com
AE, DC, MC, V
€€€€ (619) €€€€€

Casino, rooftop pool and restaurants complete with grand hotel. The 1975 building isn't particularly interesting but the rooftop terrace makes for prime Formula One viewing. Culinary options include Le Pistou for Italian fare, L'Argentin for meat over a charcoal pit, and picturesque Café Viennois for tea and pastries. Standardized luxury and private balconies for the guestrooms.

MONTE-CARLO
● Zebra Square
10 ave Princesse Grace, 98000
Map 12B4
00 377 99 99 25 50
AE, DC, MC, V €€€

Fantastic views, low lighting and oversized booths. On the menu, inventive cuisine such as goats' cheese salad with aromatic herbs, and monkfish with Parmesan.

MOUGINS
▲ La Terrasse à Mougins
31 bd Georges Courteline, 06250
Map 12A4
04 92 28 36 20
FAX 04 92 28 36 21
w www.la-terrasse-a-mougins.com
AE, MC, V mid-Dec–mid-Jan
€€€ (4) €€€€

A charming country house with views all the way to Cannes. Specialities are cooked on skewers, including veal, beef, pigeon and fish. Charming, spacious white rooms with classic local furnishings.

MOUGINS
● Le Feu Follet
Pl de la Mairie, 06250 **Map** 12A4
04 93 90 15 78
FAX 04 92 92 92 62
w www.feu-follet.fr
AE, DC, MC, V Mon; mid-Dec–mid-Jan €€€

Another piece of stellar real estate, with five dining rooms, a terrace and a garden. The ambitious chef dazzles with fromage de tête (brawn/head cheese), and salmon smoked on the premises.

MOUGINS
▲ Le Moulin de Mougins
424 chemin du Moulin, ave Notre-Dame-de-Vie, 06250 **Map** 12A4
04 93 75 78 24
FAX 04 93 90 18 55
w www.moulin-mougins.com
AE, DC, MC, V Mon; Dec–mid-Jan €€€€€ (3) €€€€€

Mougins is a culinary mecca, and this is the best of the best. Chef-author Roger Vergé presides over a 16th-century olive mill, where he also gives cooking lessons. The sautéed Breton lobster is superb. Authentic guestrooms with whitewashed walls and antiques.

MOUGINS
▲ Mas Candille
Bd Clément Rebuffet, 06250 **Map** 12A4
04 92 28 28 28
FAX 04 92 92 88 23
w www.lemascandille.com
AE, DC, MC, V Nov–mid-Dec
€€€€€ (40) €€€€€

An 18th-century farmhouse made into a super-luxury hotel with antiques, rich fabrics and balconies. The gourmet restaurant serves tarte Tatin (p191) of foie gras with Armagnac, sea bass steamed with shellfish, and veal with morels.

MOUSTIERS-STE-MARIE
▲ La Bastide de Moustiers
Chemin de Quinson, 04360 **Map** 9D2
04 92 70 47 47
FAX 04 92 70 47 48
w www.bastide-moustiers.com
AE, DC, MC, V Tue L, Wed, Thu;
mid-Dec–1st wk Jan
€€€ (12) €€€€€

● Restaurant ■ Hotel ▲ Hotel / Restaurant

Savour slices of spit-roasted turbot, pigeon with purple artichokes, or quince tart glazed with rum. Guestrooms are decorated with equal aplomb.

NICE
● **Au Pizzaiolo**
4 bis rue du Pont Vieux, 06300 **Map** 9D2
☎ 04 93 92 24 79
● Tue ⫘ €
Head here for traditional finger food including the sumptuous pissaladière (p400), served thicker than elsewhere. Also on the menu are farcis niçois (p400) and stuffed courgettes (zucchini) and lovely aubergines (eggplant).

NICE
● **Bar-Théâtre des Oiseaux**
5 rue St-Vincent, 06300 **Map** 9D2
☎ 04 93 80 27 33
FAX 04 93 80 21 93
☒ MC, V ● Sun L, Mon, Sat L; last wk Aug ⫘ €
Open since 1961, this eccentric live entertainment venue serves a menu including daube de boeuf (p401), anchoïade (p401) and ravioles.

NICE
● **Bistrot du Port**
28 quai de Lunel, 06300 **Map** 9D2
☎ 04 93 55 21 70
FAX 04 93 55 21 70
☒ MC, V ● Tue ⫘ €€
Friendly little bistro serving platters of local specialities such as fine stuffed vegetables, tapenade (p400) and pigeon.

NICE
● **Chez Simon**
275 route St-Antoine de Ginestière, 06200 **Map** 9D2
☎ 04 93 86 51 62
FAX 04 93 37 03 87
☒ AE, MC, V ● Sep–May: Sun D, Mon ⫘ €€€
Nestled in the hillside, this restaurant's façade is awash with flowers. Don't miss beignets with sardines or ravioles (p268) with daube de boeuf (p401).

NICE
● **Don Camillo**
5 rue des Ponchettes, 06300 **Map** 12B4

☎ 04 93 85 67 95
FAX 04 93 13 97 43
☒ AE, DC, MC, V ● Sun, Mon L
⫘ €€€€
A small, unpretentious restaurant serving duck salad with exotic fruits, lobster cream soup, Niçoise ravioles (p401), and prawns with gnocchi.

NICE
● **Fenocchio**
2 pl Rossetti, 06300 **Map** 12B4
☎ 04 93 80 72 52
● Nov–Mar ⫘ €
Said to be Nice's best gelateria, with 100 flavours spanning from pistachio to lavender. Servings on a baked waffle cone are copious.

NICE
● **Karr**
10 rue Alphonse Karr, 06000 **Map** 12B4
☎ 04 93 82 18 31
FAX 04 93 82 53 69
w www.karr.fr
☒ AE, MC, V ● Sun ⫘ €€€
Brasserie-bar-restaurant with minimalist decor and 1950s-diner-style bar stools. Try crêpes with smoked salmon and cream cheese; prawn and mint risotto; and poached salmon with spinach, almonds and coconut milk. Desserts include orange crème brûlée.

NICE
● **La Merenda**
4 rue de la Terrasse, 06000 **Map** 12B4
● Sun, Sat ⫘ €€€
The rustic restaurant serves cod, daube de boeuf (p401), pasta pistou, lightly fried courgettes (zucchini) and stuffed cabbage. It's small, so stop by to reserve ahead. The house rules: "no credit cards, no phone, no cheques, no smoking".

NICE
● **La Petite Maison**
11 rue St-François de Paule, 06300 **Map** 12B4
☎ 04 93 85 71 53
FAX 04 93 92 28 51
w www.lapetitemaison.net
☒ AE, MC, V ● Sun ⫘ €€
This tavern style eatery is popular for business lunches and pre-opera din-

ners, and serves a salade niçoise (p401), vegetable risotto and sea bass. It's also a great place to try pissaladière (p400).

NICE
● **La Porte des Anges**
17 rue Gubernatis, 06000 **Map** 12B4
☎ 04 93 62 69 80
FAX 04 93 62 69 80
☒ AE, MC, V ● Sun, Mon–Thu D
⫘ €€€
The Côte d'Azur is so focused on rosé that red wine is often overlooked. However, at this tiny bistro the owner and sommelier Olivier Labarde is a red wine aficionado. Traditional Niçoise fare.

NICE
● **La Toque Blanche**
40 rue de la Buffa, 06000 **Map** 12B4
☎ 04 93 88 38 18
FAX 04 93 82 54 29
☒ MC, V ● Mon, Tue L, 2nd wk Jan, 1st 2 wks Aug ⫘ €€
This restaurant has just a few tables and pleasant garden. Marinated sea bass, and duck salad are menu highlights.

NICE
● **La Véritable Socca**
4 rue St-François, 06000 **Map** 12B4
☎ 04 93 13 98 23
● Sun ⫘ €
Friendly spot serving tasty finger foods: socca (thin chickpea-flour pancake), fine pissaladière (p400) and beignets.

NICE
● **La Zucca Magica**
4 bis quai Papacino, 06200 **Map** 12B4
☎ 04 93 56 25 27
● Sun, Mon ⫘ €€
Popular, cavern-like vegetarian eatery decorated with dried gourds and strings of garlic. Excellent Italian food spans five sumptuous courses and you eat what the chef brings you. The aubergine (eggplant) rolls are excellent.

NICE
● **L'Auberge de Théo**
52 ave Cap de Croix, 06100 **Map** 12B4
☎ 04 93 81 26 19
FAX 04 93 81 51 73
w www.auberge-de-theo.com

📧 MC, V ⬤ Sun, Mon D; mid-Aug–mid-Sep 🍴 €€

One of the nicest dining patios in the Cimiez neighbourhood. Pizzas, as well as squid carpaccio, and courgette (zucchini) flowers stuffed with ricotta.

NICE

⬤ Le Grand Café de Turin

5 pl Garibaldi, 06000 **Map** 12B4

📞 04 93 62 29 52

FAX 04 93 13 03 49

📧 AE, MC, V 🍴 €€€

Your best option for fresh oysters, served with lemon or vinegar and shallots. Good fun but crowded; reservations aren't taken so expect a wait.

NICE

⬤ Le Pain Quotidien

3 rue Louis Gassin, 06300 **Map** 12B4

📞 04 93 62 94 32

W www.lepainquotidien.com

📧 AE, DC, MC, V 🍴 €€

This restaurant is part of a successful chain near the flower market in the centre of town. Try freshly baked bread, a salad and a glass of chilled rosé.

NICE

⬤ L'Univers de Christian Plumail

54 bd Jean Jaurès, 6300 **Map** 12B4

📞 04 93 62 32 22

FAX 04 93 62 55 69

W www.christian-plumail.com

📧 AE, MC, V ⬤ Sun, Mon L, Sat L 🍴 €€€

A simple and affordable Italian eatery serving thinly sliced artichoke with slivers of Parmesan and olive oil as well as gazpacho, foie gras and Breton duck.

NICE

▲ Négresco

37 promenade Anglais, 06000 **Map** 12B4

📞 04 93 16 64 00

FAX 04 93 88 35 68

W www.hotel-negresco-nice.com

📧 AE, DC, MC, V

🍴 €€€€€ 🍷 (150) €€€€€

The Négresco is more than a luxury hotel: its green dome and pink roof are symbols of Nice. The 18th-century-inspired dining room serves ravioles (pXX) stuffed with foie gras, and sea

bass with pesto. La Rotonde bistro has a whimsical interior complete with carousel horses and puppets. Themed yet quite luxurious guestrooms.

NICE

▲ Palais Maeterlinck

30 bd Maeterlinck, 06000 **Map** 12B4

📞 04 92 00 72 00

FAX 04 92 04 18 10

📧 AE, DC, MC, V ⬤ mid-Jan–mid-Mar

🍴 €€€€€ 🍷 (328) €€€€€

Guestrooms at this hotel have stunning views of the city and its colourful bay. Fantastic risotto with truffles and fish with artichoke hearts grace the menu.

NICE

⬤ Pâtisserie Cappa

7–9 pl Garibaldi, 06300 **Map** 12B4

📞 04 93 62 30 83

📧 MC, V ⬤ Mon; Sep 🍴 €

Famous tearoom and pastry shop, considered to be Provence's best. There's a decadent chocolate mousse but the house special is the torte de blettes *with Swiss chard and apple.*

NICE

⬤ Terres des Truffes

11 rue St-François de Paule, 06300 **Map** 12B4

📞 04 93 62 07 68

FAX 04 93 62 44 83

📧 AE, MC, V ⬤ Sun 🍴 €

A cross between a boutique and a bistro. Truffles are in everything: pâté, foie gras, in cheese and on potatoes. There are even truffle-based desserts.

NICE

⬤ Tire Bouchon

19 rue de la Préfecture, 06300 **Map** 12B4

📞 04 93 92 63 64

📧 AE, DC, MC, V 🍴 €€€

One of Nice old town's most elegant restaurants. Highlights include duck ravioles (p268), crab terrine and Moroccan lamb and apricot tagine. Try the vodka and lime sorbet. Varied wine list.

NICE

⬤ Villa d'Este

6 rue Masséna, 06000 **Map** 12B4

📞 04 93 82 47 77

FAX 04 93 82 09 06

W www.boccaccio-nice.com

📧 AE, DC, MC, V 🍴 €€€

This massive place is covered with frescoes and is one of Nice's best Italian restaurants. The pasta dishes are the main attraction and are as good as any across the border. Good wine list too.

NOVES

▲ Auberge de Noves

Route from Châteaurenard, 13550 **Map** 12B2

📞 04 90 24 28 28

FAX 04 90 24 28 00

W www.aubergedenoves.com

📧 AE, DC, MC, V ⬤ Mon L, Sat L, Oct–Apr: Tue L; Nov–mid-Feb

🍴 €€€€ 🍷 (23) €€€€€

Regal setting in a grand home. Dishes such as roast veal with truffle gnocchi, and strawberry gratin in Grand Marnier with Châteauneuf-du-Pape blanc or Lirac. Rooms with lovely views.

ORANGE

⬤ Le Parvis

3 cours Pourtoules, 84100 **Map** 12B2

📞 04 90 34 82 00

FAX 04 90 51 18 19

📧 AE, DC, MC, V ⬤ Sun, Mon; last 2 wks Nov, last 2 wks Jan 🍴 €

Refined but lively atmosphere. The chef taps into the area's long gourmet history, all the way back to Roman banquets. The tarte Tatin (p191) of mullet, and veal with sorrel are fit for an emperor.

PALUD-DE-NOVES

▲ La Maison du Domaine de Bournissac

Montée d'Eyragues, 13550 **Map** 12B2

📞 04 90 90 25 25

FAX 04 90 90 25 26

W www.lamaison-a-bournissac.com

📧 AE, MC, V ⬤ Mon, Tue L; Jan

🍴 €€€ 🍷 (13) €€€€€

New twists on old favourites. Options include lamb roasted with wild thyme, and a crumbly pastry shell filled with calamari. The exquisite cuisine is matched by the decor and scenery. Lovely guestrooms overlook the park and gardens.

⬤ Restaurant ■ Hotel ▲ Hotel / Restaurant

PEILLON

▲ Auberge de la Madone

2 pl Auguste Arnulf, 06440 **Map** 12B4

☎ 04 93 79 91 17

FAX 04 93 79 99 36

MC, V ● Wed; last 3 wks Jan, mid-Oct–mid-Dec

🍴 €€€ 🍷 (17) €€€

A family-run hotel, opened in 1946, with olive groves, fruit orchards and authentic country-house appeal. Outdoor tables are set in the shade. Classic Provençal food. Spacious rooms.

PERNES-LES-FONTAINES

● Dame l'Oie

56 rue du Troubadour Durand, 84210 **Map** 12C2

☎ 04 90 61 62 43

AE, DC, MC, V ● Mon, Tue; Feb

🍴 €

Charming countryside inn where diners tuck into roast duck with green lentils or sardine and sorrel pithviers (puff pastry).

PERTUIS

▲ L'Olivier at Hôtel Sévan

Route from Manosque, 84120 **Map** 12C2

☎ 04 90 79 08 19

FAX 04 90 79 35 77

W www.le-sevan.com

AE, DC, MC, V ● Mon, Sep–Jun: Sun D & Wed D; 1st wk Jan

🍴 €€ 🍷 (46) €€

On the menu are tuna carpaccio in hazelnut oil, and a lamb dish with rosemary sauce. Sweet guestrooms.

PIOLENC

▲ Auberge de l'Orangerie

4 rue de l'Ormeau, 84420 **Map** 12B2

☎ 04 90 29 59 88

FAX 04 90 29 67 74

W www.orangerie.net

MC, V ● Mon L, Oct–Apr: Sun D & Mon 🍴 €€ 🍷 (5) €€€

Relax in the Orange countryside, just as Roman senators did long ago. The allure continues, though the cooking's more up-to-date, with dishes like baked scallops, and veal with pâté. Lovely rooms.

PLAN-D'AUPS

▲ Lou Pébre d'Aë

Plateau de Ste-Baume, 83640 **Map** 12C3

☎ 04 42 04 50 42

FAX 04 42 04 50 71

AE, DC, MC, V ● Oct–Apr: Tue D & Wed; Jan–mid-Feb

🍴 €€€ 🍷 (12) €€

A warm, colourful spot, high on the plateau of St-Beaume. Recommendations include foie gras with figs, and fish with pistou. Comfortable rooms.

PORT-CROS

▲ Le Manoir d'Hélène

Ile de Port Cros, 83400 **Map** 13D3

☎ 04 94 05 90 52

FAX 04 94 05 90 89

AE, DC, MC, V ● Nov–Mar

🍴 €€€ 🍷 (23) €€€€

A remote and romantic hotel. On the menu: sun-dried tomato tart, and John Dory with prosciutto and Parmesan chips and a caramelized onion sauce.

PUYLOUBIER

● Les Sarments

4 rue Qui-Monte, 13114 **Map** 12C2

☎ 04 42 66 31 58

FAX 04 42 66 85 96

MC, V ● May–Sep: Mon, Oct–Apr: Mon–Thu & Fri L 🍴 €

Heritage and integrity make this kitchen distinctive. Try the simple fish soup, pieds et paquets (p400), and Provençal beef stew. Brief, robust wine list.

RAMATUELLE

▲ Château de la Messardière

Route de Tahiti, 83350 **Map** 12A5

☎ 04 94 56 76 00

FAX 04 94 56 76 01

W www.messardiere.com

AE, DC, MC, V ● L; Oct–Feb

🍴 €€€€ 🍷 (34) €€€€€

A favourite wedding venue, with cicadas singing in the pine forest. The menu includes beet carpaccio with red mullet fillets, and veal marinated in coconut milk. Large, romantic guestrooms.

RAMATUELLE

▲ La Figuière

Route de Tahiti, 83350 **Map** 12A5

☎ 04 94 97 18 21

FAX 04 94 97 68 48

AE, DC, MC, V ● Oct–Apr

🍴 €€€ 🍷 (40) €€€

Secluded, historic farmhouse, with a pool and tennis court, located in the middle of a beautiful vineyard. The outdoor restaurant specializes in local cuisine like daube de boeuf (p401), sea bass with aubergine (eggplant) purée, and apple tart. Simple white guestrooms.

ROGNES

● Le Korrigan

Pl de la Coopérative, 13840 **Map** 12C2

☎ 04 42 50 17 13

MC, V ● Sun, Mon; mid-Jul–mid-Aug 🍴 €€

Pair fresh goat's cheese – on grilled local bread – with any of the main dishes like entrecôte, duck or lamb.

ROGNES

● Les Olivarelles

Route du Bassin-St-Christophe, 13840 **Map** 12C2

☎ 04 42 50 24 27

FAX 04 42 50 17 99

AE, DC, MC, V ● Sep–Apr: Sun D & Mon–Thu 🍴 €€€

This large Provençal guesthouse has a huge terrace. Tempting dishes on the menu include foie gras, poached eggs with truffles, and pieds et paquets (p400).

ROQUEBRUNE

● Au Grande Inquisiteur

18 rue du Château, 06190 **Map** 12B4

☎ 04 93 35 05 37

AE, MC, V ● Mon, Tue L; Nov–mid-Dec 🍴 €€€

Charming, elegant dining room with stunning panoramic views. Point of pride is the cheese selection.

ROQUEBRUNE

● La Grotta

2 pl des Deux Frères, 06190 **Map** 12B4

☎ 04 93 35 00 04

● Wed; Nov 🍴 €

La Grotta (cave), carved from solid rock, offers a cool escape from the summer sun. The straightforward menu is accented by pizzas, goat's cheese salad, and salade niçoise (p401).

ROQUEBRUNE

▲ Les Deux Frères

Pl des Deux Frères, 06190 **Map** 12B4

C 04 93 28 99 00
FAX 04 93 28 99 10
W www.lesdeuxfreres.com
€ AE, DC, MC, V ● Jun–Sep: Mon L
& Tue L, Sep–May: Sun D & Mon D
‖ €€€ ● (10) €€€
With panoramic views of Monaco, this whitewashed hotel is perfect for lovers or honeymooners. The restaurant serves excellent sole, pigeon and raw seafood.

ROQUEFORT-LES-PINS
▲ Auberge du Colombier
D2085, 06330 **Map** 12B4
C 04 92 60 33 00
FAX 04 93 77 07 03
W www.auberge-du-colombier.com
€ AE, DC, MC, V ● Jan
‖ €€€€€ ● (20) €€€€€
Picture-perfect farmhouse with white-washed walls. On the menu are ravioli with wild mushrooms and walnuts, and foie gras with purple artichokes.

ROUGON
▲ Auberge du Point Sublime
Town centre, 04120 **Map** 13D2
C 04 92 83 60 35
FAX 04 92 83 74 31
€ MC, V ● Sep–mid-Jul: Wed & Thu
L; mid-Oct–mid-Apr
‖ € ● (14) €€
Tucked away in an eagle's perch over the famed Verdon gorges, with a menu featuring lamb. Plain, comfortable rooms.

RUSTREL
▲ Auberge de Rustréou
3 pl de la Fête, 84400 **Map** 12C2
C 04 90 04 90 90
€ MC, V **‖** € ● (7) €€
Livery inn with comforting, sensible food. Fill up on rabbit terrine with mustard, beef casserole, and cake filled with fruit cofit. Country-style rooms.

SALON-DE-PROVENCE
● La Salle à Manger
6 rue de Maréchal Joffre, 13300
Map 12C2
C 04 90 56 28 01
€ MC, V ● Mon, Oct–Jun: Sun D
‖ €
Even with its reputation on the rise, there has been no slacking of the focus

here. The menu includes daube de boeuf (p401), and sea bass with fennel.

SAULT
▲ Hostellerie de Val de Sault
Route de St-Trinit, 84390 **Map** 12C2
C 04 90 64 01 41
FAX 04 90 64 12 74
€ MC, V ● mid-Nov–Mar
‖ € ● (16) €€€
Hunters' bounty at table. The focus here is game and meat, with the added bonus of truffles in season. Hearty wines.

SEGURET
● Le Mesclun
Rue des Poternes, 84110 **Map** 12C2
C 04 90 46 93 43
FAX 04 90 46 93 48
€ MC, V
● Sun D, Mon; Jan **‖** €€
The food lives up to its lavish descriptions such as "lamb ravioli with black diamonds and pistachio emeralds". Great desserts and a substantial cellar.

ST-ANDIOL
▲ Le Berger des Abeilles
Quartier du Rabet, 13670 **Map** 12C2
C 04 90 95 01 91
FAX 04 90 95 48 26
€ AE, MC, V ● Mon–Fri L; Jan–2nd
wk Feb **‖** €€€ ● (8) €€
Even in a land known for lovely vistas, undiscovered pockets exist; this is one of them. Join locals in truffle ravioli and mullet and saffron risotto. Small, tidy guestrooms, some with garden views.

ST-CANNAT
▲ Mas de Fauchon
Quartier Fauchon, 13760 **Map** 12C2
C 04 42 50 61 77
FAX 04 42 57 22 56
W www.mas-de-fauchon.fr
€ AE, MC, V
‖ €€€ ● (16) €€€€
Travellers of old chose this roadside inn to rest and recuperate – and it still serves that purpose. Revitalize with roasted mullet and scallops.

ST-CHAMAS
● Le Rabelais
8 rue Auguste Fabre, 13250 **Map** 12C2

C 04 90 50 84 40
FAX 04 90 50 78 49
€ AE, MC, V ● Sun D, Mon, Sat L;
last 2 wks Feb, last wk Aug–2nd wk Sep
‖ €€€
This spot offers baked lamb sweet-breads with shrimp tails, crispy rack of Sisteron lamb, and a cool finisher of granita made with three seasonal fruits.

STE-AGNES
▲ Hôtel St-Yves
60 rue des Sarrasins, 06500 **Map** 12B4
C 04 93 35 91 45
FAX 04 93 35 65 85
€ AE, MC, V
● mid-Jan–mid-Feb
‖ €€ ● (17) €€
To escape from the Riviera head to this charming hotel for stunning seaside views and hearty fare such as ravioles (p268) stuffed with rabbit and herbs. Rustic guestrooms with beautiful views.

STE-AGNES
● Le Logis Sarasin
40 rue des Sarrasins, 06500 **Map** 12B4
C 04 93 35 86 89
FAX 04 93 35 65 85
€ AE, MC, V ● Mon, Sep–Jun: D;
mid-Oct–mid-Nov **‖** €€
A lively bistro with seaside views serving ham ravioles (p268), omelettes, trout, rabbit and grilled lamb brushed with fresh rosemary and rubbed with garlic.

STE-MAXIME
▲ Hostellerie de la Belle Aurore
5 bd Jean Moulin, 83120 **Map** 12A5
C 04 94 96 02 45
FAX 04 94 96 63 87
W www.belleaurore.com
€ AE, DC, MC, V ● Oct–Mar
‖ €€€€ ● (17) €€€€€
A romantic, pink, seaside hotel-restaurant. On the menu are sea bream, marinated sardines and stuffed vegetables. Rooms all have private balconies or terraces.

STE-MAXIME
● La Gruppi
Ave Charles de Gaulle, 83120 **Map** 12A5
C 04 94 96 03 61
FAX 04 94 49 16 86
W www.lagruppi.com

🖉 AE, DC, MC, V
⬤ Mon L; Dec 🍴 €€

Fish restaurant on the promenade. The bouillabaisse (p401) needs to be ordered a day in advance, but is worth the trouble.

STE-MAXIME
● L'Amiral
Galerie marchande port, 83120
Map 12A5
☎ 04 94 43 99 36
FAX 04 94 43 99 36
🖉 AE, MC, V ⬤ Sun D, Mon; mid-Nov–mid-Dec 🍴 €€€

A refreshing splash of modernity in the middle of the port area. Grilled seafood like fish and lobster. Crisp, cool wines.

STE-MAXIME
● Le Wafu
Pl Victor Hugo, 83120 **Map** 12A5
☎ 04 94 96 15 74
⬤ mid-Jan–mid-Feb 🍴 €

Order a cool pastis or a frothy beer and just watch the world go by. Good salade niçoise (p401) and sandwiches among other brasserie-style foods.

STES-MARIES-DE-LA-MER
● Hostellerie du Pont de Gau
Route from Arles, 13460 **Map** 12B3
☎ 04 90 97 81 53
FAX 04 90 97 98 54
🖉 AE, MC, V ⬤ mid-Nov–mid-Apr: Wed; 2nd wk Jan–2nd wk Feb 🍴 €

The best choices include cream of sole with goujonettes (small slices of deep-fried fish) and a bouillabaisse (p401).

STES-MARIES-DE-LA-MER
▲ Le Mas de Fouque
Route de Petit-Rhône, 13460 **Map** 12B3
☎ 04 90 97 81 02
FAX 04 90 97 96 84
🖳 www.masdelafouque.com
🖉 AE, DC, MC, V ⬤ Sep–Jun: Tue; Nov–mid-Mar
🍴 €€€ 🍽 (13) €€€€€

Try the langoustine risotto, and roast veal with vegetable broth. Lavish rooms.

ST-RAPHAEL
▲ Hôtel San Pedro
890 rue Colonel Brooke, 83700
Map 12A5

☎ 04 94 19 90 20
FAX 04 94 19 90 21
🖳 www.hotelsanpedro.fr
🖉 AE, DC, MC, V ⬤ last 3 wks Nov
🍴 €€ 🍽 (28) €€€

A country bastide set amidst a pine forest, with comfortable guestrooms, a pool and a good Provençal-style menu.

ST-RAPHAEL
● Jardin de Sébastien
599 ave des Golfs, Valescure, 83700
Map 12A5
☎ 04 94 44 66 56
FAX 04 94 44 66 56
🖳 http://jardindesebastien.free.fr
🖉 AE, MC, V ⬤ Sun D, Mon 🍴
€€€

The golf set flocks to this sunny terrace. Perfect for lunch on the links with hearty classics such as steak and excellent, filling Provençal-inspired pastas.

ST-RAPHAEL
● L'Arbousier
6 ave Valescure, 83700 **Map** 12A5
☎ 04 94 95 25 00
FAX 04 94 83 81 04
🖉 AE, DC, MC, V ⬤ Sun D, Mon L, Tue L 🍴 €€€

A gastronomic haven and a beautiful terrace off the beaten track. The menu is inspired by all things marine and Provençal, with dishes like langoustine carpaccio with a marjoram, mango and grapefruit vinaigrette, lobster tagine, and chocolate soufflé with Jamaican pepper.

ST-RAPHAEL
● Pastorel
54 rue de la Liberté, 83700 **Map** 12A5
☎ 04 94 95 02 36
FAX 04 94 95 64 07
🖉 AE, DC, MC, V ⬤ Sun D, Mon; Nov 🍴 €€

Inexpensive, friendly restaurant opened in 1922 and run today by the grandson of the founder. An aïoli (p400)-based menu: rich bourride (p373), marinated sardines and stuffed vegetables.

ST-REMY-DE-PROVENCE
● Alain Assaud
13 bd Marceau, 13210 **Map** 12B2
☎ 04 90 92 37 11

🖉 MC, V ⬤ Wed, Thu L, Sat L; mid-Nov–mid-Dec 🍴 €€

Freshness is key in dishes like galette with fresh tomatoes and basil, aïoli (p400) with fresh cod, and pot-au-feu with confit de canard (p326). Refreshing wines.

ST-REMY-DE-PROVENCE
● La Maison Jaune
15 rue Carnot, 13210 **Map** 12B2
☎ 04 90 92 56 14
FAX 04 90 92 56 32
🖳 www.franceweb.org/lamaison-jaune
🖉 MC, V ⬤ Sun D, Mon, Jun–Sep: Tue; Jan–Mar 🍴 €€€

Grilled sardines with lemon confit are a highlight. A lively spot that's surprisingly vivacious in spite of its regal 18th-century building. A local favourite.

ST-REMY-DE-PROVENCE
● Le Bistrot des Alpilles
15 bd Mirabeau, 13210 **Map** 12B2
☎ 04 90 92 09 17
FAX 04 90 92 38 15
🖳 www.bistrotdesalpilles.com
🖉 MC, V 🍴 €

A well-known local gem with a fresh approach. The menu includes dishes such as tagliatelle in bouillabaisse (p401), and steak with lemon thyme. Incredible vintages at reasonable prices.

ST-REMY-DE-PROVENCE
● Le Jardin de Frederic
8 bis bd Gambetta, 13210 **Map** 12B2
☎ 04 90 92 27 76
FAX 04 90 92 27 76
🖉 AE, MC, V ⬤ Wed, Thu L; mid-Jan–mid-Feb. 🍴 €

Dishes such as sea bass with artichokes and saffron sauce, and lamb with garlic cream and wild herbs. Refreshing rosés and hearty local reds on the wine list.

ST-REMY-DE-PROVENCE
▲ Le Vallon de Valrugues
Chemin de Canto-Cigalo, 13210
Map 12B2
☎ 04 90 92 04 40
FAX 04 90 92 44 01
🖉 MC, V ⬤ Jan–Feb
🍴 €€€ 🍽 (53) €€€€€

Options include mullet in vinaigrette, roasted pigeon with creamy polenta,

and a skewer of shiitake mushrooms.
18th-century-style beams in the rooms.

ST-TROPEZ
● Café de Paris
15 quai Suffren, 83990 **Map** 12A5
☎ 04 94 97 00 56
FAX 04 94 54 87 72
w www.cafe2paris.fr
💳 AE, MC, V ¶¶ €€

An elegant old bar with some modern
design touches. Drop in for a drink and
a snack and don't miss the sushi served
with a bottle of chilled rosé. This place is
so trendy it even hosts a live webcam.

ST-TROPEZ
● Chez Fuchs
7 rue des Commerçants, 83990
Map 12A5
☎ 04 94 97 01 25
💳 MC, V ◐ Oct–Mar: Mon & Tue;
mid-Jan–Feb ¶¶ €
Bistro serving plates piled high with
meat and potatoes. The beef stew is
divine. Also a bar and tobacconist.

ST-TROPEZ
● La Bouillabaisse
Plage de la Bouillabaisse, 83990
Map 12A5
☎ 04 94 97 54 00
FAX 04 94 97 54 00
💳 AE, MC, V ◐ mid-Nov–Feb ¶¶ €€
The bouillabaisse (p401) here is the best
in town but must be ordered a day
ahead. The fish soup is prepared
according to time-honoured tradition
and uses the very freshest the sea has
to offer. St-Tropez's friendliest service, too.

ST-TROPEZ
● Le Girelier
Quai Jean Jaurès, 83990 **Map** 12A5
☎ 04 94 97 03 87
FAX 04 94 97 43 86
w www.legirelier.com
💳 AE, DC, MC, V
◐ Nov–Feb
¶¶ €€€
Opened in 1956, a true relic from St-
Tropez's golden era. Feast on fish soup,
pistou Provençale, good stuffed mussels,
aubergine (eggplant) terrine, and snails.
Excellent fried squid, too.

ST-TROPEZ
● Leï Mouscardins
1 rue Portalet, 83990 **Map** 12A5
☎ 04 94 97 29 00
FAX 04 94 97 76 39
w www.leimouscardins.com
💳 AE, DC, MC, V ◐ Jul–Aug: L
¶¶ €€€€€
A restaurant with creative cooking and
harbour views. On the menu are good
barigoule d'artichauts (artichokes), baby
squid with balsamic vinaigrette, and
rabbit with aubergine (eggplant).

ST-TROPEZ
● Les Beaux Arts
Espace des Lices, 7 bd Louis Blanc,
83990 **Map** 12A5
☎ 04 94 97 02 25
FAX 04 94 97 87 71
💳 AE, DC, MC, V ¶¶ €€
A St-Tropez institution that has lost
some of its lustre but is still a trendy
haunt of the young and restless. If you
can eat to pulsing dance music, enjoy
the sea bass in truffle sauce and the
mussels in cream.

ST-TROPEZ
▲ Résidence de la Pinède
Plage de la Bouillabaisse, 83990
Map 12A5
☎ 04 94 55 91 00
FAX 04 94 97 73 64
w www.residencepinede.com
💳 AE, DC, MC, V ◐ Oct–mid-Apr
¶¶ €€€€€ 🍽 (35) €€€€€
Among the most elegant accommodation
in St-Tropez, with its own private beach.
For culinary delights there's tomato terrine,
gnocchi, and Grand Marnier soufflé. Spoil
yourself with Champagne and sea views.

ST-VALLIER-DE-THIEY
▲ Le Préjoly
5 pl Rouguière, 06460 **Map** 12A4
☎ 04 93 42 60 86
FAX 04 93 42 67 80
💳 AE, DC, MC, V ◐ Sep–Jun: Sun D,
Mon; mid-Nov–Jan
¶¶ € 🍽 (17) €€€
A good choice for simple rooms and
traditional country cooking. The restaurant
serves up superb salade niçoise (p401),
omelettes, grilled meats and vegetables.

THEOULE-SUR-MER
▲ Miramar Beach
47 ave de Miramar, 06590 **Map** 12A4
☎ 04 93 75 05 05
FAX 04 93 75 44 83
w www.mbhriviera.com
💳 AE, MC, V
¶¶ €€€€ 🍽 (57) €€€€€
Romantic gourmet hideaway with
stunning sea views. Mediterranean
menu highlights are the lobster with
saffron rice and the mussels sautéed
in white wine, garlic and parsley. The
swordfish carpaccio is also a tasty
temptation. Colourful modern rooms.

TOURTOUR
▲ Bastide de Tourtour
Route from Flayosc, 83690 **Map** 13D2
☎ 04 98 10 54 20
FAX 04 94 70 54 90
💳 AE, MC, V ◐ Sep–Jul: Mon–Fri L
¶¶ €€€ 🍽 (25) €€€€
A fabulous example of a welcoming yet
elegant Provençal country home, from
the graceful public spaces to the cooking.
Dishes include foie gras terrine with wild
herbs, and twice-cooked pigeon in rosé
wine sauce. Large guestrooms.

VAISON-LA-ROMAINE
● Le Moulin à Huile
1 quai Maréchal Foch, 84110 **Map** 12C2
☎ 04 90 36 20 67
FAX 04 90 36 20 20
💳 AE, MC, V
◐ Sun D, Mon; Feb
¶¶ €€€€
Powerful spices hold centre stage.
Startle your taste buds with foie gras
royale (truffles and cream) in crab jelly,
or lamb with ratatouille (p401).

VALBONNE
● La Pigeot
16 rue Alexis Julien, 06560 **Map** 12A4
☎ 04 93 12 17 53
💳 AE, MC, V
¶¶ €€
The best North African cuisine on the
Riviera. Family-run, with an unbelievable
selection of tagines, couscous, meat
and fish. Authentic decor means no
chairs, just plush carpets and cushions.
Reservations strongly advised.

● Restaurant ■ Hotel ▲ Hotel / Restaurant

VALBONNE

● Le Bois Doré

265 route Antibes, 06560 **Map** 12A4

☎ 04 93 12 26 25

FAX 04 93 12 28 73

w www.leboisdore.com

✉ AE, MC, V

◐ last wk Feb–1st wk Mar, mid-Oct–mid-Nov 🍴 €€€

A gorgeous country manor where careful attention is paid to every detail, from frescoed walls to fresh-cut roses. The nouvelle cuisine menu offers prawns in basil sauce and the rather artfully assembled lobster platters.

VALBONNE

● Lou Cigalon

4 bd Carnot, 06560 **Map** 12A4

☎ 04 93 12 27 07

✉ MC, V ◐ Sun, Mon; Jan

🍴 €€€

Guarding the entrance to the old village, Lou Cigalon tempts its guests with dishes such as the langoustine tempura and the roast sea bass with fresh herbs. Simple ingredients prepared with flair.

VALENSOLE

▲ Hostellerie de la Fuste

Route d'Oraison, 04210 **Map** 13D2

☎ 04 92 72 05 95

FAX 04 92 72 92 93

w www.lafuste.com

✉ AE, DC, MC, V

◐ Oct–mid-May: Sun D & Mon; mid-Nov–early Dec, early Jan–mid-Feb

🍴 €€€€€ 🍷 (14) €€€€€

Top-rank cuisine, but the ambience is the real draw. A lovely mansion surrounded by towering trees and lavender-scented breezes. Menu highlights include fine scrambled eggs with truffles and stuffed baby vegetables. Gorgeous guestrooms.

VALLAURIS

● La Gousse d'Ail

11 ave de la Grasse, 06220 **Map** 12B4

☎ 04 93 64 10 71

✉ AE, MC, V

◐ Sun D, Mon; 1st 2 wks Jul, Nov

🍴 €€

Tradition with a twist at this neighbourhood favourite that is close to the Picasso Museum. On the menu are

scallops with caramelized chicory (endive) and lasagne with foie gras.

VENASQUE

▲ Auberge La Fontaine

Pl de la Fontaine, 84210 **Map** 12C2

☎ 04 90 66 02 96

FAX 04 90 66 13 14

w www.auberge-lafontaine.com

✉ MC, V ◐ mid-Nov–mid-Dec

🍴 €€ 🍷 (5) €€€€

Almost a Zen approach: just the essentials presented with grace and passion. Experience the smoked duck with mesclun, Mediterranean swordfish with mushrooms, or lamb with courgette (zucchini) confit and truffles.

VERQUIERES

● Le Croque-Chou

Pl de l'Eglise, 13670 **Map** 12B2

☎ 04 90 95 18 55

✉ MC, V

◐ Oct–May: Sun D & Mon & Tue; last wk Dec–Mar

🍴 €€€

The chef draws inspiration from this tranquil village, surrounded by ancient vines. He delights diners with items like rabbit infused with sage, and sea bream roasted in red wine. Cellar highlights include Côteaux des Baux and Cairanne.

VILLEFRANCHE-SUR-MER

● La Mère Germaine

7 quai Amiral Courbet, 06230 **Map** 12B4

☎ 04 93 01 71 39

FAX 04 93 01 96 44

w www.meregermaine.com

✉ MC, V ◐ mid-Nov–mid-Dec

🍴 €€€

An institution serving all kinds of seafood such as red mullet, lobster, linguine with prawns, fish soup and good bouillabaisse (p401).

VILLEFRANCHE-SUR-MER

● La Trinquette

Ave Général de Gaulle, 06230 **Map** 12B4

☎ 04 93 01 71 41

◐ Wed, Dec–Jan

🍴 €€

A few steps from the harbour, the menu here lists more than 20 kinds of fish. There's also excellent bouillabaisse

(p401) and oven-roasted rascasse. Cups of aïoli (p400) accompany most dishes.

VILLEFRANCHE-SUR-MER

● Le Carpaccio

17 promenade des Marinières, 06230 **Map** 12B4

☎ 04 93 01 72 97

FAX 04 93 01 97 34

w www.restaurant-carpaccio.com

✉ AE, DC, MC, V 🍴 €€€

A port-facing seafood restaurant that relies on tried-and-true favourites such as monkfish with curry sauce, and lobster bisque. Try a chilled Bandol rosé from the excellent wine list.

VILLEFRANCHE-SUR-MER

▲ Le Versailles

7 bd Princesse Grace de Monaco, 06230 **Map** 12B4

☎ 04 93 76 52 52

FAX 04 93 01 97 48

w www.hotelversailles.com

✉ AE, DC, MC, V

◐ Sep–May: Mon; Oct–Feb

🍴 €€ 🍷 (46) €€€

Another favourite among sun-seekers. The restaurant's menu dégustation spans an amazing 11 courses and includes turbot fillet with asparagus purée, and roasted suckling lamb. For dessert try the excellent peach tart. Guestrooms have views of the old ramparts and the azure bay.

VILLEFRANCHE-SUR-MER

● Michel's

Pl Amélie Pollonnais, 06230 **Map** 12B4

☎ 04 93 76 73 24

w www.michel-s.net

✉ AE, MC, V ◐ Tue 🍴 €€€

This stone-vaulted dining room, with its Provençal landscape paintings, always attracts a lively crowd thanks to the restaurant's delicious grilled fish.

VILLENEUVE-LOUBET

● Le Caravanser

12 ave de la Libération, 06270 **Map** XX

☎ 04 93 20 89 53

✉ MC, V ◐ Mon 🍴 €€

North African dishes include couscous royale, tagines, lamb brochettes and small, sweet pastries.

CORSICA

The unspoilt landscapes of Napoleon's birthplace have earned it the appellation "island of beauty". It proudly preserves its identity, despite centuries of outside influences. The Greeks and Phoenicians introduced olives and vines; chestnuts arrived with the Genoese in the 16th century; clementines were first planted in the 20th. All now play a key role in the island's cuisine, along with semi-wild pigs, game, seafood and herbs.

The Flavours of Corsica

Climate, terrain, coastline and history all contribute to the wonderful produce found here, and its island status means that many Corsican specialities are unique and seldom found beyond its shores. In particular, Corsicans are rightly proud of their superb charcuterie and cheese.

SHOPS AND MARKETS

Ajaccio Outdoor market selling an arry of local produce, Tue–Sun am
Bastia Place du Marchè Colourful market, Tue–Sun am
Bonifacio Place du Marchè, Wed am
Calvi Lively market near the seafront, daily am

Ajaccio market

MEAT AND CHARCUTERIE

Flocks of sheep and goats are led into the mountains in June and taken to lower pasture in October, their milk used for cheese. Kid is a favourite meat. Pigs are raised for meat and charcuterie. There is also abundant game, including wild boar, rabbit, hare, pigeon and partridge.

The semi-wild black pigs that roam the uplands, foraging for nuts, roots, fruit, insects and grubs, often end up in a distinctive range of hams and sausages that has more in common with Italian than French charcuterie. *Prisutu* is a cured ham that is hung to dry for between one and two years; *salsiccia* and *salamu* are air-dried sausages made from minced pork. Round, marbled, red *coppa* is made from pork shoulder, and dark red *lonzu* from cured pork fillet with a strong peppery seasoning. Both are lightly smoked. The most unusual product is *figatelli*, a dark, U-shaped, smoked liver sausage which can be grilled or dried and eaten cold.

FISH AND SHELLFISH

The catch here includes red mullet, sea bass, swordfish, monkfish, John Dory, wrasse, sardines and anchovies, as well as spiny lobster, squid, sea urchins and spider crabs. Oysters and mussels are cultivated in the Etang de Diane on the eastern side of the island.

CHESTNUTS

One of the distinctive features of Corsican cuisine is its use of chestnuts. This is a legacy that goes back to the 16th century when plantations were established by the Genoese in the Castagniccia area on the eastern side of the island. As in the Ardèche, the chestnut tree was dubbed *l'arbre à pain* – the bread tree – because it provided the islanders with a form of flour for the staple bread, to supplement that from the limited wheat, rye and other cereals on the island. It was also a useful source of wood for furniture, wine barrels and fuel.

Today, chestnuts are found in numerous recipes for soups and stews as well as being roasted to accompany charcuterie and game and made into liqueurs. And they are still ground into flour, not just for bread, but also for crêpes, *fritelli* (fritters) and *pulenda*, a type of polenta.

Left Corsican fromagerie **Right** Local olive oil

CHEESE

A cheese you're sure to come across in one form or another on the island is Brocciu or Brucciu, a mild, white fresh cheese similar to Italian Ricotta or the Brousse of Provence. It is is made from whey and usually eaten fresh, within 48 hours, sprinkled with sugar or in many cooked dishes, although it can be left to mature into a hard, dry ball. The island's other cheeses mostly get their names, including Niolo, Venaco, Sartène and Bastelicaccia, from the area where they were first made; others are simply called Tome or Tomme, varying from mild semi-soft cheeses with washed rinds to hard, pressed cheeses which gain in strength as they age and may be matured until hard and crumbly. Newer varieties include Brin d'Amour, which is rolled in herbs, and Bleu de Corse, a Roquefort-like blue ewes' milk cheese.

FRUIT AND VEGETABLES

As well as all types of citrus fruit, including kumquats, grapefruit and *cédrat* or citron, you'll find exotic species such as barbary figs and the *arbousier* or strawberry tree. Clementines are one of the island's main crops, most of the harvest being exported to the mainland. The Corsican clementine is small and firm with a sharp, tangy flavour and thin, tightly-fitting skin.

Vegetables include aubergines (eggplants), courgettes (zucchini), beans, chard, tomatoes and peppers. Olives were introduced by the Greeks, and some of the trees in the south of the island are over 1,000 years old. The *maquis* scrub is the source of abundant herbs.

OTHER PRODUCE

The Corsicans seem to be able to make jam out of just about anything, while another typical island product is honey from bees that feed on the island's varied flora, *maquis* herbs and chestnut trees.

CHARCUTERIE CHECKLIST

Coppa Round sausage of smoked pork shoulder

Figatelli U-shaped smoked and cured liver sausage, flavoured with spices

Lonzu Air-dried salted pork fillet flavoured with wine, herbs and spices

Panzetta Cured streaky bacon, similar to Italian *pancetta*

Prisutu *Jambon cru* (cured, air-dried ham)

Salamu or **salsiccia** *Saucisson sec* (dried sausage)

Corsica's wide variety of charcuterie

Regional Dishes

Corsican cuisine reflects the island's dual Mediterranean and mountain habitats, in dishes perfumed with the herbs of the maquis *scrub, as well as the legacy of its former Italian rulers. It is, for the most part, hearty, tasty peasant food that makes the very best of island produce.*

ON THE MENU

Cannellonis au brocciu
Cannelloni filled with Brocciu cheese and spinach

Civet de sanglier aux châtaignes Wild boar stewed in red wine with chestnuts

Fêves au lard Broad (fava) beans with bacon

Fritelli Chestnut flour fritters

Lapin aux olives Rabbit with olives

Omelette aux oursins Omelette with sea urchins

Ragoût de cabri Kid stewed in red wine with onions

Ragoût de sanglier Wild boar stew

Rouget aux anchois Red mullet stuffed with anchovies

Sardines au brocciu Sardines stuffed with Brocciu

Stufatu Pork, beef, lamb and ham stewed with red wine, served with pasta

Tianu d'agneau aux olives Stewed neck of lamb, herbs and olives

THE CORSICAN MENU

A meal here will often start with *charcuterie*, perhaps accompanied by figs or roast chestnuts, aubergine (eggplant) gratinéed with Brocciu, or *soupe corse*.

Numerous pasta dishes testify to Corsica's Italian past: served with a simple fresh tomato sauce; macaroni with *stufatu* stew; ravioli and cannelloni tubes stuffed with Brocciu and fresh herbs or spinach; or wild boar lasagne. Brocciu crops up frequently, in a simple salad with tomato, in a *tourte* or omelette, or as the stuffing for courgettes (zucchini) or sardines.

Fresh fish is often simply grilled over charcoal at beachside restaurants; there is also a *bouillabaisse*-style fish soup called *aziminu*, and other specialities include squid baked in tomato sauce, red mullet stuffed with anchovies and sardines stuffed with Brocciu. Sea urchins scooped out with a spoon or bread are a winter treat.

Wild boar and kid are stewed or roast with herbs and garlic, lamb and suckling pig are superb roast simply with herbs, while lamb, rabbit or veal may be cooked with olives and tomato. Vegetable gratins of aubergines (eggplants), courgettes (zucchini) and tomatoes feature, and bean dishes encompass thick soups, a *cassoulet*-style stew, and fresh broad (fava) beans with bacon.

Left Rouget aux anchois **Right** Soupe corse

Left Cabri rôti **Right** Fiadone

REGIONAL DINING

The following restaurants are among those serving regional dishes at reasonable prices:
Agora
Ajaccio (see p434)
A Scudella
Corte (see p437)
Chez Anna
Porto-Vecchio (see p440)
Da Sergio
Bonifacio (see p436)
La Voute
Piana (see p439)
Ominanda
Corte (see p438)
Restaurant l'Oria
L'île-Rousse (see p438)
Santa Barbara
Sartene (see p441)
Sol et Mar
Bastia (see p435)
Terra Cotta
Propriano (see p441)
U Mare
Porto-Vecchio (see p440)

The best-known Corsican dessert is *fiadone*; others feature figs, clementines and oranges, chestnut fritters or pancakes made from chestnut flour. *Eaux de vie*, from the inevitable chestnut to heather and myrtle, find their way into soufflés, or are drizzled over Brocciu.

SOUPE CORSE

This soup is typical of Corsica's wild, sparsely populated interior, rather than its chic beach resorts. White beans, onions, carrots, potatoes and cabbage are gently simmered with marjoram and a ham bone for a couple of hours. Then chopped basil, garlic, diced ham and pasta are added and simmered until the pasta is cooked.

CABRI RÔTI

Roast kid is a celebratory dish in Corsica: long, lean shanks are spiked with slivers of garlic and rosemary, brushed with olive oil and then roasted until the meat is deep-red and crisp on the outside, tender and succulent within. Best served simply with a mound of potatoes, boiled in their skins and tossed in olive oil.

COURGETTES FARCIES

Long or round courgettes (zucchini) are blanched then cut in half lengthwise (or the top cut off round ones) and the interior scooped out. The pulp is fried in olive oil with chopped onion, garlic, tomato, parsley, minced meat and Brocciu. Beaten eggs are added, off the heat, and the mixture is used to stuff the courgettes (zucchini) which are then baked until golden.

FIADONE

For this cheesecake, fresh Brocciu cheese is drained and mixed with egg yolks, sugar and finely chopped lemon zest. Egg whites are stiffly beaten and folded into the mixture, which is baked in a round cake tin.

Regional Wines, Beers & Spirits

Rarely do wine lovers outside Corsica get the chance to taste the island's best wines as they are swamped by the majority, brilliantly marketed under the lyrical name Vin de Pays de l'Ile de Beauté. Native grapes have a major part to play and other drinks equally draw on indigenous plants including the 50 varieties of chestnut found on the island.

Vineyards in Patrimonio

Corsican wines

RAPPU

Rappu is made mainly in Patrimonio and Cap Corse from a blend of Grenache and Aleatico grapes left on the vine until they are gorged in sugar. They are macerated with their stalks in wooden casks before being fortified with spirit. Typically, mahogany-tinted Rappu tastes and smells of cocoa, caramel, liquorice, smoke and stewed fruit. Good with desserts or to end a meal.

Nearer to Italy than to France, the mountainous "beautiful island" lies on the same latitude as Rome. Over the last 20 years, a new generation of winemakers have put considerable effort into improving the quality and reputation of their wines by planting native vines and reviewing vinification techniques. Reds account for 60 per cent of all wines made; they are perfect with the island's winter game. Whites and rosés make a good match for Corsica's fish and seafood or one of the many variations on the theme of Brocciu *(see p429).*

MAJOR GRAPE VARIETIES

Sciacarello This is a true native Corsican. The name is onomatopoeic, translating as "crunchy". It produces fine, supple reds and peppery rosés.

Nielluccio Related to Italy's Sangiovese of Chianti fame, Nielluccio produces deep coloured wines with plenty of body, aromas of violet, animal fur and fruits of the forest and flavours of liquorice and spice.

Vermentino This is the aromatic Rolle of southern France. Producing lovely, dry whites, often high in alcohol, with a floral bouquet and a taste of almonds and sultanas.

Uva Muscatella This is the deliciously fragranced Muscat à Petits Grains.

WINES OF CORSICA

Corsica has four main appellations of which Patrimonio is probably the most prestigious. Made mainly from Nielluccio, the reds are beefy and tannic

Vineyards of Corsica

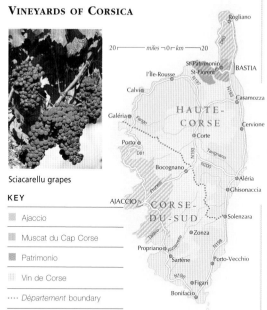

Sciacarellu grapes

KEY

▨ Ajaccio

▨ Muscat du Cap Corse

▨ Patrimonio

▨ Vin de Corse

···· *Département* boundary

PIETRÀ BEER

Created in the 1990s, Pietra beer is based on the island's most emblematic ingredient: chestnuts. Granulated chestnuts and malt are fermented at low temperature with Acqua Bianca spring water to make an original, rounded, rich-tasting but refreshing beer, popular in Corsica and on the mainland.

EAUX-DE-VIE AND LIQUEURS

The island's abundance of berries and citrus fruits has encouraged the Corsicans to become master distillers and liquorists. Perhaps the most typical eau-de-vie is made from chestnuts. Others include the following.

Myrtle liqueur Made from distilled myrtle berries, flowers or leaves, this liqueur is renowned for its digestive properties and can be colourless or purple-hued.

Bonapartine There are no prizes for guessing who this sweet liqueur made from mandarins and oranges was named after.

Cédratine Corsica is one of the few places to grow the rare citron *(cédrat)*. This aperitif has an exquisite aroma and a slightly tart, long-lasting flavour.

and age happily; the Vermentino whites are fruity and rich, a result of the chalky soil.

Ajaccio stretches from below Porto in the north to the Golfe de Valinco. Sciacarello is the chief variety, at home on the granitic soil producing rosés and raspberry-coloured reds with good ageing potential.

The Vin de Corse appellation applies to the whole island but these easy-drinking wines actually come mainly from the eastern plains. Quality takes an upward turn when the title is followed by one of five village names.

The sweet wines of Muscat du Cap Corse are made from the partially fermented juice of late-harvested Muscat grapes with added alcohol. Slightly chilled, they make a seductive aperitif wine with the fragrance of lemon flowers, roses, beeswax and honey.

Le Cap Corse

Louis-Napoleon Mattei first made what was to become his most successful invention in 1894. "Vin du Cap Corse au Quinquina", as he first called it, was invented to treat fever. This stimulating aperitif is made from more than 17 different natural ingredients including bilberries, cocoa beans, oranges, vanilla, cinchona bark (quinine) and gentian. Very successful during the Belle Epoque, Cap Corse is currently undergoing a popularity revival. Drink it chilled, without ice, or use it in cocktails.

Arbutus berries, used in liqueurs

Where to Eat & Stay

AJACCIO
● A Funtana
9 rue Notre-Dame, 20000 **Map** 13E5
04 95 21 78 04
AE, DC, MC, V
Sun D, Mon
€€€
The best and most expensive in town. Innovative dishes, akin to the informal, contemporary atmosphere and decor. One of the best wine lists in Corsica.

AJACCIO
● A Madunuccia
10 rue des Glacis, 20000 **Map** 13E5
04 95 50 16 90
MC, V Oct–Apr €€
Outdoor eatery serving seafood either sliced thinly and lightly cooked or grilled with fennel and herbs. Reservations are recommended in summer.

AJACCIO
● Agora
4 rue Emmanuele Arene, 20000
Map 13E5
04 95 20 36 83
MC, V Sun €€
One of the city's finest, with a stunning dark-wood 1920s interior. The owner believes that printed menus are an insult to good food. Seafood and grilled vegetables make up the half-dozen delicious dishes on the daily chalkboard.

AJACCIO
● Au Bec Fin
3 bis bd du Roi Jérome, 20000
Map 13E5
04 95 21 30 52
AE, DC, MC, V
Sun, Mon D; last 2 wks Dec; first 2
wks Jan €€
A classy Art Deco dining room with rustic outdoor seating. Carpaccio of salmon and tuna, sea bream and red mullet are on the seafood menu. Make reservations – and dress for dinner.

AJACCIO
● Café du Flore
33 rue Fesch, 20000 **Map** 13E5
04 95 21 13 87
Sun; Feb €
Spicy, hearty pasta dishes. Tasty toppings include meatballs, basil and mussels. Huge salads, with squid and Corsican cheese, and a classic salade niçoise (p401). Jugs of inexpensive vin de pays.

AJACCIO
● Chez Coco
Rue Bonaparte, 20000 **Map** 13E5
€
Traditional, stuccoed restaurant serving thin, crispy pizzas topped with squid and mussels, Corsican bouillabaisse (p401), tripe, snails and pasta with seafood.

AJACCIO
● Des Halles
4 rue des Halles, 20000 **Map** 13E5
04 95 21 42 68
FAX 04 95 21 49 92
DC, MC, V Sun €€
Serving seafood since 1927. Langoustines, scallops and sea bass are cooked with cream, wine and herbs, and steak tartare and lamb entrecôte also feature. A few Corsican wines and several Champagnes. Bustling terrace.

AJACCIO
■ Hôtel Kallisté
51 cours Napoleon, 20000 **Map** 13E5
04 95 51 34 45
FAX 04 95 21 79 00
MC, V (50) €€€
Old and new, perfectly combined, in a building dating back to 1864. Ancient stone walls are left exposed, and fine wrought-iron banisters lead up to the simple yet elegant rooms.

AJACCIO
● Le Bosco
10 rue Conventionnel Chiappe, 20000
Map 13E5
04 95 21 25 06
MC, V Oct–Apr €€
Chalkboards with a wealth of seafood including mussels, sardines and prawns. The pièce de résistance is the spaghetti with langoustines, crab and squid.

Lobster is boiled or fricasséed. Outdoor terrace on a quiet street.

AJACCIO
● Le Golfe
Quai Napoleon, 20000 **Map** 13E5
AE, DC, MC, V Oct–Mar
€€
Harbourside eatery with a terrace looking out at bright bobbing boats. Try the fine charcuterie and squid beignet appetizers, grilled fish with herbs, seafood and vegetarian pizzas and moules-frites.

AJACCIO
● Panini
2 pl Foch, 20000 **Map** 13E5
04 95 21 09 53
Feb–Mar €
One of the only cafés on the Place Foch in the town centre. The panini are named after Italian places: Roma, Napoli and Capri. Each is filled with produce native to that town, whether olives, basil, mozzarella or ham, then toasted to perfection and brought to your outside table. Excellent Illy coffee, along with local beers.

AJACCIO
● Pasta e Basta
8 pl Générale de Gaulle, 20000
Map 13E5
04 95 50 18 92
AE, DC, MC, V Sun €€
Pasta restaurant with fabulous sea views from the terrace. Several pestos, mussels, squid and crab. Pappardelle with mussels and basil is a favourite.

AJACCIO
● Rendez-vous
6 rue Roi de Rome, 20000 **Map** 13F5
04 95 21 84 84
FAX 04 95 21 84 85
MC, V Oct–May: Sun, Mon;
Jun–Sep: Mon €
One of Ajaccio's most fashionable bars, with a beautiful and well-stocked bar and outside seating. Salmon, spinach and wild boar terrines are served with Corsican cheeses and local chutneys.

● Restaurant ■ Hotel ▲ Hotel / Restaurant

ALGAJOLA

▲ **Hôtel de la Plage**

On the sea front, 20220 **Map** 13E4

📞 04 95 60 72 12

FAX 04 95 60 64 89

💳 AE, DC, MC, V

🍴 €€ 🍽 (36) €€

One vine-covered pavement terrace and one sea-facing. Corsican and Provençal dishes dominate. Rooms have traditional wooden furnishing, half overlook the sea. Slow service but charming owners.

ALGAJOLA

● **La Vieille Corse**

Rue Droite, 20220 **Map** 13E4

📞 04 95 60 70 09

FAX 04 95 60 70 09

💳 AE, DC, MC, V

🌑 Mar–Oct 🍴 €

Exotic flavours of ginger and lime are used alongside honey in some of the traditional seafood, steak and pork dishes. Rustic stone interior and a pretty terrace with hanging lights, huge candles and an ancient tree.

ALGAJOLA

▲ **Le Beau Rivage**

29 rue A Marina, 20220 **Map** 13E4

📞 04 95 60 73 99

FAX 04 95 60 79 51

🌐 www.hotel-beau-rivage.com

💳 AE, DC, MC, V 🌑 mid-Oct–mid-Apr 🍴 €€ 🍽 (36) €€

Lively terrace bar and restaurant balcony right on the sandy beach. Try carpaccio of fish or duck and local grilled seafood. Modern guestrooms have terraces with wonderful sea views.

ALGAJOLA

● **U Castellu**

10 pl Château, 20220 **Map** 13E4

📞 04 95 60 78 75

💳 MC, V 🌑 Oct–Apr 🍴 €€

Potted olive trees surround diners at this stone-walled restaurant with giant terrace next to Algajola's fort. Lunchtime tapas feature seafood. Wonderful desserts with lots of mint, lemon, ricotta and honey.

BASTIA

● **A Scaletta**

4 rue St-Jean, 20200 **Map** 13E3

📞 04 95 32 28 70

💳 MC, V 🌑 Wed 🍴 €€

Small fish-oriented à la carte selection and two full set menus, traditionally Corsican or exclusively seafood-based. Fish soups, grilled sardines and the beignets of Corsican cheese are fine mainstays. Magnificent views over the old harbour from the six balcony tables.

BASTIA

● **Chez Memé**

Quai des Martyrs de la Libération, 20200 **Map** 13E3

📞 04 95 31 44 12

💳 AE, DC, MC, V 🌑 Dec–Jan 🍴 €

Arguably the best, and certainly the busiest, of the lively Quai des Martyrs Libération promenade restaurants. Huge five-course seafood menu and a smaller three-course Corsican speciality menu. Delicious moules-frites. Corsican wines, plus Pietra beer, made from chestnuts.

BASTIA

■ **Hôtel Bonaparte**

45 bd General Graziani, 20200 **Map** 13E3

📞 04 95 34 07 10

FAX 04 95 32 35 62

💳 AE, DC, MC, V 🍽 (23) €€€

Situated right in the city centre. Large, modern reception and guest lounge with brimming bookshelves and heaps of natural light. Boat, bike or car rental.

BASTIA

■ **Hôtel Central**

3 rue Miot, 20200 **Map** 13E3

📞 04 95 31 71 12

FAX 04 95 31 82 40

🌐 www.centralhotel.fr

💳 MC, V 🍽 (14) €€

Unpretentious rooms with fans, solid wooden furniture and views onto the street below. Several self-contained attic rooms have ovens, fridges and views over Bastia's rooftops. Watch out for the amusingly brusque manner of the owner, a real character.

BASTIA

● **La Citadelle**

6 rue de Dragon, 20200 **Map** 13E3

📞 04 95 31 44 70

💳 DC, MC, V 🌑 Sun 🍴 €€€€

Elegant gourmet option high up in Bastia's citadel area. Tremendous choice of meat dishes with beef, pork, wild boar and lamb. Many of the well-chosen wines are displayed around the medieval-style room.

BASTIA

● **Le Caveau du Marin**

Quai des Martyrs Libération, 20200 **Map** 13E3

📞 04 95 31 62 31

FAX 04 95 30 67 48

💳 AE, MC, V 🌑 Mon 🍴 €€

Regional delicacies and fresh seafood at this superior restaurant. Pasta with boutargue, grilled meats and heaps of langoustines. Tiny, quiet terrace facing the promenade, and a rather stylish and elegant dining room.

BASTIA

● **Le Concorde**

5 bd Gén de Gaulle, 20200 **Map** 13E3

📞 04 95 31 04 64

FAX 04 95 31 88 47

💳 AE, DC, MC, V 🍴 €

One of the few Place St-Nicolas eateries serving full meals. Thin pizzas and fine grilled meats dominate. Enjoy an apéritif or one of several top-quality wines. A curious American-diner theme, complete with booth seating.

BASTIA

● **Sol et Mar**

Quai des Martyrs de la Libération, 20200 **Map** 13E3

📞 04 95 58 14 26

💳 MC, V 🌑 Feb 🍴 €€

Plentiful portions of squid, fish soups, mussels and other seafood. Wild boar charcuterie. Small, carefully selected range of Corsican wines. Intimate, rather refined terrace, pleasant for both lunch and dinner. Booking recommended.

BASTIA

● **U Marinaru**

Quai des Martyrs Libération, 20200 **Map** 13E3

📞 04 95 31 45 99

💳 AE, DC, MC, V 🌑 Sun L 🍴 €€

Fish platters with the daily catch, prawns, squid and mussels. Generous terrace but most prefer the ivy-covered dining room in a charming, weather-beaten Vieux Port building.

BONIFACIO
● Cantina Doria

27 rue Doria, 20169 **Map** 13F5

04 95 73 50 49

FAX 04 95 73 50 49

V Nov–Apr €

This place remains untouched by the rapid commercialization of many of Bonifacio's restaurants. Tripe, lasagne and risotto au figatelli (rice, parmesan and pork sausage) all brim with tasty local herbs. Aubergine (eggplant) dishes, Corsican cheeses and great regional charcuterie with fine wild boar. Pietra chestnut beer on draught.

BONIFACIO
● Da Sergio

Rue Fred Scamaroni, 20169 **Map** 13F5

04 95 73 19 85

@ da.sergio@wanadoo.fr

DC, MC, V Nov–Jan €

Corsican foods with a taste of Italy: crispy pizzas are topped with seafood, herbs and local vegetables. Penne with salmon, sea bass with fennel and lasagne with various Corsican cheeses all feature. Pietra and Serena beers.

BONIFACIO
▲ Hôtel le Royal

8 rue Fred Scamaroni, 20169 **Map** 13F5

04 95 73 00 51

FAX 04 95 73 04 68

MC, V € (14) €€€

One of the few hotels in the raised Haute Ville. Many rooms have views stretching for miles over the cliffs and sea. The hotel snack bar serves grilled sardines, vegetable gratins, lamb, and large salads such as caprese (mozzarella, tomato and basil, with olive oil).

BONIFACIO
● Kissing Pigs

15 quai Banda del Ferro, 20169 **Map** 13F5

04 95 73 56 09

MC, V Nov–Mar €

The extremely sociable young couple who run this spot call it a meeting place,

not a restaurant. Assorted charcuterie and a lengthy list of Corsican wines make this place an excellent bet. Fine wild boar sausages and huge salads with Corsican cheeses and fruit also feature. Wooden harbourside terrace.

BONIFACIO
● La Galiote

17 Bando di Ferro, 20169 **Map** 13F5

04 95 73 06 94

Oct–Mar €

A rustic restaurant popular with the locals. Good wild boar terrine, omelette paysanne, sea bream and seafood salads, with tarts for dessert. Great Corsican muscat and myrtle apéritifs.

BONIFACIO
● L'Albatros

47 quai Comparetti, 20169 **Map** 13F5

04 95 73 01 97

FAX 04 95 73 13 41

AE, DC, MC, V Nov–Mar €€

Seafood indulgence at a busy harbour-side restaurant. Great selection of fine lobster and shellfish. Mussels splashed in Champagne, rascasse and fisherman's soups are followed by grilled scallops, John Dory and sea bream. The fine wild boar charcuterie is among the few land-based additions. Book for dinner.

BONIFACIO
● Le Tiki

9 rue Palais, 20169 **Map** 13F5

04 95 73 14 39

Sun Oct–Mar €

Apéritifs include muscat, a sweet myrtle-based liqueur and the fiery Cap Corse. Seafood-based terrines with squid, anchovies, goats' cheese and mozzarella salads. Wild boar terrine and rascasse soup are regular specials.

BONIFACIO
● Le Voilier

81 quai Comparetti, 20169 **Map** 13F5

04 95 73 07 06

FAX 04 95 73 14 27

AE, DC, MC, V Oct–May: Sun D, Wed; Dec–Feb €

Classy marina restaurant offering seafood dishes with Italian inspiration.

Try John Dory, lobster, langoustines and big bowls of fish soup. Spaghetti with clams and squid salad nod to Naples. Reservations recommended.

BONIFACIO
● Les Terasses D'Aragon

21 rue Simon Varsi, 20169 **Map** 13F5

04 95 73 51 07

FAX 04 95 73 54 92

AE, DC, MC, V Nov–Mar €€€

Lonzu, carpaccio of tuna and excellent rascasse soup are mainstays; ten types of fish are always on offer or you can pick your lobster from a tank. Bonifacio's best and most extensive wine selection. Liqueurs made from nuts, figs and myrtle too. Views stretch for miles along the cliffs from the inspiring terrace.

CALACUCCIA
● Restaurant du Lac

Hameau Sidossi, 20224 **Map** 13F4

04 95 48 02 73

Oct–Mar €

Several excellent menus to fill up the hungriest of Corsica's mountain walkers. Casseroled wild boar and very tasty charcuterie. Duck, veal, lamb and a few fish dishes, cooked with local herbs and vegetables. A handful of Corsican and vin de pays wines, mostly red.

CALVI
● A Candella

9 rue St-Antoine, 20260 **Map** 13E4

04 95 65 42 13

Oct–Apr €

One of the unpretentious eateries amid the pretty stone streets around Calvi's citadel, with a great terrace and a narrow whitewashed dining room. Light meals include grilled local pork and lamb, and seafood salads with lots of squid. Small range of Corsican wines.

CALVI
▲ La Magnolia and Le Jardin

Rue Alsace Lorraine, 20260 **Map** 13E4

04 95 65 19 16

FAX 04 95 65 34 52

W www.hotel-le-magnolia.com

AE, DC, MC, V Wed L; Sep–May

€€ (11) €€€€

● Restaurant ■ Hotel ▲ Hotel / Restaurant

Intimate 19th-century town house, with balconied rooms, next to Santa Maria church. Choose lobster, langoustines, sea bass or John Dory at the restaurant. Quiet but central location with a terrace under the cover of an ancient magnolia, and a less exciting conservatory inside. Guestrooms are elaborate affairs; some have sea views.

CALVI
● L'Altu
Chajappata San Giovanni, 20260 **Map** 13E4

● Oct–Apr **11** €

Stunningly located below the giant Santi Ristiduta di Calenzana church, with views over Calvi's beach and harbour. Light meals include brochettes, tarts, tapas of cheese beignets, salads and grilled bread with local cheeses including Brocciu.

CALVI
● Le Plaisance
10 rue Joffre, 20260 **Map** 13E4

04 95 65 13 60

MC, V

● Nov–Mar **11** €€

Harbourside eatery with a focus on fresh seafood. Excellent Corsican menu with squid-based dishes, sumptuous French menu with wild boar ragout and foie gras. Most of the simple seating is outside on the sun-drenched terrace.

CALVI
● Le Tire Bouchon
15 rue Clemenceau, 20260 **Map** 13E4

04 95 65 25 41

MC, V ● Wed L; Dec–Mar **11** €

Scores of Corsican bottles by region – Calvi, Ajaccio and Cap Corse included. Daily chalkboard studded with carpaccio of beef and lonzu, and fine herb-laden grilled meats. Small terrace above pretty Rue Clemenceau. Wonderful antique fireplace warms diners inside.

CALVI
● Pizza Capuccino
Quai Landry, 20260 **Map** 13E4

04 95 65 11 19

MC, V ● Nov–Mar **11** €€

One of the classiest harbourside options, and one of the few with daily chalkboard specials. Dishes range from thin, crispy pizzas to seafood platters, soups and brochettes. The wide, partly shaded terrace is a great place for cocktails.

CALVI
▲ St Christophe
Pl Bell'Ombra, 20260 **Map** 13E4

04 95 65 05 74

FAX 04 95 65 37 69

www.hotel-saint-christophe.com

AE, DC, MC, V ● Nov–Mar

11 €€€ ◆ (48) €€€€

Modern hotel overlooking Calvi's stunning citadel. Balconies and swimming pool with superb views of the Mediterranean. Tuna carpaccio, wild boar with bilberries, and rascasse soup. Decent range of local Corsican wines.

CALVI
● U Caradellu
13 rue Clemenceau, 20260 **Map** 13E4

04 95 65 21 48

AE, V ● Nov–Mar **11** €€

Corsican specialities include salamu and cheese, carpaccio of lonzu and sea bass. Mussels are served with pasta and in seafood platters. Old-style interior; large terrace outside.

CARGESE
▲ Thalassa
Plage du Pero, 20130 **Map** 13E4

04 95 26 40 08

FAX 04 95 26 41 66

MC, V ● Oct–Apr

11 €€ ◆ (26) €€€

Dine by the water at this simple place. Fish dominates: grilled John Dory, red mullet and sea bream. Many of the traditional but quite spartan guestrooms overlook the Mediterranean.

CENTURI
● Le Langoustier
On the sea front, 20238 **Map** 13E3

04 95 35 64 98

MC, V ● Oct–Apr **11** €€

One of Centuri's finest dining options and a langoustine specialist. Charcuterie is followed by seafood; fish, especially sea bass, is baked, grilled or forms the base for rich soups. Delicious flambéed prawns; langoustines and bouillabaisse

(p401) must be ordered in advance. Look over the delightful port from the terrace.

CORTE
● A Scudella
2 pl Paoli, 20250 **Map** 13F4

04 95 46 25 31

MC, V ● Sep–Jun: Sun **11** €

Lovely views of the town square and the Pascal Paoli statue. Most opt for the set menus as the à la carte selection is minimal. Charcuterie and terrines are popular choices. Don't miss the tasty chestnut beer and Corsican wines.

CORTE
■ Hôtel de la Poste
2 pl Padoue, 20250 **Map** 13F4

04 95 46 01 37

● last 2 wks Dec ◆ (11) €€

Delightful old-style rooms, some with a shared terrace, with sturdy wooden furnishings, old marble tiles and aged objets d'art. Family rooms available.

CORTE
■ Hôtel du Nord
22 cours Paoli, 20250 **Map** 13F4

04 95 46 00 68

FAX 04 95 46 03 40

www.hoteldunord-corte.com

MC, V ◆ (16) €€€

Modern, centrally located rooms with ceiling fans and quaint, swinging shutters. Reception is in the Café du Cours next door, which is open all day. An Internet terminal and breakfast menu can also be found here.

CORTE
● La Riviere des Vins
5 ramps St-Croix, 20250 **Map** 13F4

04 95 46 37 04

● mid-Oct–Apr: L **11** €

Terrines, meat brochettes and figatelli (pork sausage): simply prepared meat dishes at this curious little eatery. A random assortment of wooden tables in the cobbled lane allows outdoor seating. Corsican wines, and liqueurs made from oranges and peaches available.

CORTE
● Le Gaffory
Pl Gaffory, 20250 **Map** 13E4

☎ 04 95 46 36 97

▨ AE, DC, MC, V

◐ Oct–Mar **▯** €

Busy restaurant, below Corte's citadel, where age-old solid wooden tables sit in shade. Wild boar in pies and sausages, with pasta and as charcuterie; trout and good pizzas too.

CORTE

● Ominanda

15 rue Scolicia, 20250 **Map** 13F4

☎ 04 95 46 05 10

▯ €

Peeling green paint, a fine unadorned terrace with quite rickety wooden tables and a traditional interior, but still some of the best value on the island. Most set menus include wild boar and other local dishes. Strong chestnut beer.

CORTE

● Osteria di u Castellu

5 quartier Calanches, 20250 **Map** 13F4

☎ 04 95 46 32 50

▨ MC, V **◐** Sep–May **▯** €€

Stunningly located by the Belvedere lookout point, this restaurant commands fine views over the valley below. Fig, palm and pine trees cover the outdoor dining area. Grilled meats, wild boar stew and charcuterie on offer, alongside several Corsican wines.

CORTE

● U Museu

Pl Poilu, 20250 **Map** 13F4

☎ 04 95 61 08 36

▨ MC, V **◐** Apr, May, Oct: Sun; Nov–Mar **▯** €€

Up the steps on Rampe Ribanelle to a wooden platform beneath the citadel. Herbs, Corsican cheeses and maquis honey feature at this wild boar specialist.

ERBALUNGA

● Restaurant le Pirate

Pl Marc Bardon, 20222 **Map** 13F3

☎ 04 95 33 24 20

FAX 04 95 331897

W www.restaurantlepirate.com

▨ AE, MC, V

◐ Jan–Feb **▯** €€

Shellfish boiled, grilled, in soups and heaped onto pasta. Several wines,

including one or two local labels. Views of the harbour from the dining area.

EVISA

▲ Scopa Rossa

Town centre, 20126 **Map** 13E4

☎ 04 95 26 20 22

FAX 04 95 26 24 17

▨ MC, V **◐** Nov–Mar

▯ €€ **◖** (25) €€€

Several sweet and savoury country-style dishes are flavoured with locally grown chestnuts. Hearty meat dishes, perfect for those visiting Evisa for hill walking. Slightly dated but nonetheless quite well-appointed, tranquil guestrooms.

LEVIE

▲ A Pignata

Route de Pianu, 20170 **Map** 13F5

☎ 04 95 78 41 90

FAX 04 95 78 46 03

W www.apignata.com

◐ Nov–Dec

▯ €€ **◖** (5) €€€

No-frills, hearty fare from the hills, including wild boar and entrecôtes of pork and lamb. Farmhouse with simple but comfortable rooms. Horse riding can be arranged. Great value but book ahead.

L'ILE-ROUSSE

▲ L'Escale

Rue Notre Dame, 20220 **Map** 13F3

☎ 04 95 60 27 08

FAX 04 95 60 14 33

▨ AE, MC, V

▯ € **◖** (12) €€

Buzzing first-floor terrace overlooking the town's main promenade and the sea. Specialities are mussels and a variety of delicious ice creams. Spacious rooms divided between the main building and an annexe. Most of the rooms have sea views.

L'ILE-ROUSSE

● L'Osteria

Pl Santelli, 20220 **Map** 13F3

☎ 04 95 60 08 39

FAX 04 95 60 25 95

▨ MC, V

◐ Last 3 wks Jan **▯** €

Serving up wild boar, sea bass and beef. Simple seating either in the large dining

room, outside in the shade, or in the sunny cul-de-sac nearby.

L'ILE-ROUSSE

● Restaurant la Cave

Pl Paoli, 20220 **Map** 13F3

☎ 04 95 60 33 41

▨ MC, V

◐ Jan **▯** €€

Several wonderful menus including Provençal, Corsican, children's and a daily special. John Dory, sea bass, mussels and brochettes of assorted seafood; thin, crispy pizzas and an enormous array of salads. Selection of Corsican wines.

L'ILE-ROUSSE

● Restaurant l'Oria

Plage l'ile Rousse, 20220 **Map** 13F3

☎ 04 95 62 03 06

FAX 04 95 62 03 36

W www.restaurant-loria.com

▨ AE, DC, MC, V

◐ Jan–Mar **▯** €€€

Elegant dining at the beach, with a piano bar. Seafood dominates: salmon tartare, tuna tart and carpaccio of John Dory to start; squid and sea bass as regular specials. Several Corsican wines.

LOZARI

▲ Auberge de Tesa

Lieu-dit Tesa route Regino, 20226 **Map** 13F3

☎ 04 95 60 09 55

FAX 04 95 60 44 34

W www.aubergedetesa.com

▨ MC, V **◐** L; Nov–Jan

▯ €€ **◖** (7) €€€

Elegant gastronomic dining: sautéed veal, duck with foie gras and duck with honey, plus freshly baked bread. Contemporary bedrooms.

MACINAGGIO

▲ Ricordu

Town centre, 20248 **Map** 13F3

☎ 04 95 35 40 20

FAX 04 95 35 41 88

▨ MC, V **◐** Nov–Mar (restaurant)

▯ €€ **◖** (54) €€€

Unfussy cuisine, including seafood and grilled meats, in chintzy surroundings. Lobster, John Dory and sea bass follow

the popular wild boar appetizer. Modern
guestrooms have a polished air. Relax in
the swimming pool.

OLETTA

● Auberge a Magina

Town centre, 20232 **Map** 13F3

📞 04 95 39 01 01

⬤ Mon; Oct–Apr 🍴 €€

Family-run village restaurant offering
country cuisine. Herbs, honey and fruit
flavour many of the lamb, duck and
pork dishes. Contemporary dining area
with a renowned terrace offering views
of the countryside below.

PARTINELLO

● U Caspiu

Plage de Caspiu, 20147 **Map** 13E4

📞 04 95 27 32 58

FAX 04 95 27 30 36

[W] www.leclosdesribes.com

MC, V

⬤ Oct–Apr 🍴 €€

Turn off from one of Corsica's best
drives, the Porto to Girolate route, to
reach this excellent beach shack.
Bouillabaisse (p401) teeming with fine
seafood flavours, and a spectacular
spread of grilled fish and shellfish such
as lobster, langoustines, red mullet and
sea bream are mainstays. Herb-laden
pork and lamb also on offer. If only all
beach bars were as good as this.

PIANA

● Auberge U Spuntinu

From Porto to Piana, 400m past the town
centre on the left, 20115 **Map** 13E4

📞 04 95 27 80 02

⬤ L 🍴 €

Fantastic food from the Corsican interior.
The owner keeps his own pigs and
goats and makes his own coppa. Try
lamb, pork and Brocciu cheese, often
flavoured with herbs, as well as wild
boar pâtés, charcuterie and good
terrines. Sample the tiny selection of
excellent local AOC Corsican wines.

PIANA

● Chez Jeanette

Town centre, 20115 **Map** 13E4

📞 04 95 27 84 98

⬤ Mon 🍴 €

Shellfish and fish from the Gulf of Porto
feature most days at this tiny restaurant.
Try the seafood brochettes and platters,
or grilled wild boar steak with myrtle

PIANA

■ Continental

From Porto to Piana, 100m past town
centre on the right, 20115 **Map** 13E4

📞 04 95 27 89 00

FAX 04 95 27 84 71

⬤ Oct–Mar 🛏 (17) €€

Wonderfully old-fashioned clifftop hotel
oozing old-world magic. Guestrooms are
quite basic but have lovely old furniture
and an aura of calm. Most of the rooms
have en-suite showers.

PIANA

● La Voute

Town centre, 20115 **Map** 13E4

📞 04 95 27 80 46 🍴 €

Traditional Corsican food in a rustic
building. Maquis-herb-flavoured red
mullet, sea bream, grilled meats and a
variety of large salads. Several Corsican
wines and local firewaters.

PIANA

▲ Les Roches Rouges

Follow the road to Porto 300m past
Piana; signposted down a lane on the
left, 20115 **Map** 13E4

📞 04 95 27 81 81

FAX 04 95 27 81 76

AE, DC, MC, V

⬤ Nov–Mar 🍴 €€ 🛏 (30) €€€

Stunning turn-of-the-century clifftop
palace. Fennel, nuts, fruits and wine
are woven into several of the dynamic
meat and seafood dishes. Fabulous
wooden balcony facing the ocean.
Beautiful guestrooms with antique
furnishings and some with sea views.
Very accommodating staff.

PIOGGIOLA

▲ Aghjola

Town centre, 20259 **Map** 13F4

📞 04 95 61 90 48

FAX 04 95 61 92 99

MC, V ⬤ Oct–Mar

🍴 € 🛏 (9) €€

Authentic fare from Corsica's interior.
Lamb, beef and pork are grilled, stewed

or served as charcuterie. Fine chestnut-
based produce abounds. Guestrooms
are cosy, traditional and full of character,
traits that carry through to the rest of
the intimate hotel.

PORTO

● La Mer

Porto marina, 20150 **Map** 13E4

📞 04 95 26 11 27

MC, V ⬤ Dec–Feb 🍴 €€€

Luxurious cooking with a hint of innovation: bouillabaisse (p401), rascasse soup
and tuna sashimi. Huge array of fish and
shellfish. Stunning views of the castle
and coast from the terrace.

PORTO

▲ Le Belvedere

Porto marina, 20150 **Map** 13E4

📞 04 95 26 12 01

FAX 04 95 26 11 97

[W] www.hotel-le-belvedere.com

AE, DC, MC, V

⬤ Nov–Mar (restaurant)

🍴 €€€ 🛏 (20) €€€

Tasty selection of beef, duck and pork.
Several prawn dishes and a daily range
of grilled fish. Rooms are comfortable,
spacious, and most have sea views.

PORTO

● U Pescador

Port de Porto Ota, 20150 **Map** 13E4

📞 04 95 26 15 19

⬤ Oct–Apr 🍴 €

Seafood dominates at this simple
but busy paillotte (beach shack).
Soups, langoustines and a variety of
fish are simply grilled with herbs and
vegetables. Good wild boar terrine and
pork entrecôtes also served. Several
AOC wines and Corsican vin de pays
by the jugful.

PORTO-VECCHIO

● A Tanna

Rue Borgo, 20137 **Map** 13F5

AE, DC, MC, V

🍴 €€

Luxurious seafood, including seared
tuna, prawns and bowls of mussels,
and a delicious wild boar lasagne.
Wonderful balcony with views over
the harbour and sea below.

PORTO-VECCHIO
● **Chez Anna**
Rue Docteur de Rocca Serra, 20137
Map 13F5
C 04 95 70 19 97
FAX 04 95 70 19 97
⊘ MC, V ● Sun L; Oct–Apr **◯** €€
A melting pot of Italian and Corsican
flavours. Pasta is topped with veal and
olives, pesto or aubergine (eggplant).
Simple interior and small wooden terrace.

PORTO-VECCHIO
● **Créperie les 4 Oémes**
Rue Borgo, 20137 **Map** 13F5
◯ €
Straightforward eatery with simple
wooden benches on the restaurant-filled
Rue Borgo. Wonderful, generous crêpes.
Savoury options include great coppa,
local cheeses, mint and basil. Sweets
feature Chantilly cream, honey and
bananas. Draught and bottled Pietra
chestnut beer and Torra lager spiced
with maquis herbs.

PORTO-VECCHIO
▲ **Grand Hôtel de Cala Rossa**
Rue de Cala Rossa, 20137 **Map** 13F5
C 04 95 71 61 51
FAX 04 95 71 6011
W www.hotel-calarossa.com
⊘ AE, DC, MC, V
● Jan–Mar
◯ €€€€ **⊘** (42) €€€€€
Modern hotel, just a short walk from
the beach, with extensive gardens and
terraces. Luxurious, individually styled
rooms. Innovative cuisine with native
flavours featuring Brocciu cheese, mint,
subtle mushrooms and maquis herbs.

PORTO-VECCHIO
● **La Vigie**
Rue Borgo, 20137 **Map** 13F5
C 04 95 70 32 33
⊘ AE, DC, MC, V ● Nov–Mar **◯** €
A Neapolitan chef presides over the
delectable Italian fare here. Pizzas
topped with coppa alongside pasta
with squid, mussels and prawns.

PORTO-VECCHIO
● **Le Grilladin**
Quai Paoli, 20137 **Map** 13F5

C 04 95 70 59 75
⊘ MC, V
◯ €€
Seafood is usually cooked on the wood-
fired grill here. Find red mullet, John
Dory and sea bass, fish terrine and
squid salad. Many Corsican wines and
several superior mainland vintages.

PORTO-VECCHIO
● **Le Roi Théodore**
Porte Genoise, 20137 **Map** 13F5
C 04 95 70 47 98
⊘ AE, DC, MC, V
● Sun L; Oct–Apr **◯** €€
Upmarket restaurant serving traditional
dishes. Coppa, a good soupe corse
(p431) and duck foie gras are followed by
herbed beef, fish and game in season.
Langoustines are a speciality. Corsican
apéritifs, digestifs and wines aplenty.

PORTO-VECCHIO
● **Le Troubadour**
13 rue Gal Leclerc, 20137 **Map** 13F5
C 04 95 70 08 62
⊘ MC, V ● Sun L **◯** €€
Classy surroundings where country-
based dishes – duck, lamb and
artichokes, and seafood dishes such
as herb-laden turbot, sea bass and
John Dory – are served. Expansive wine
list including Corsican and mainland
vintages. Folk bands play regularly here.

PORTO-VECCHIO
▲ **Moderne Hôtel**
10 cours Napoleon, 20137 **Map** 13F5
C 04 95 70 06 36
⊘ MC, V ● Oct–Apr **⊘** (22) €€
Tapas dishes of sardines, olives and
grilled aubergine (eggplant) are served
in the snack bar. Most of the simply
decorated rooms overlook a pretty
church. The top-floor rooms, with their
own private terraces, have stunning views.

PORTO-VECCHIO
▲ **Quatre Saisons**
Rue du 9 Septembre 1943, 20137
Map 13F5
C 04 95 70 9203
FAX 04 95 70 92 00
⊘ AE, DC, MC, V ● Nov (restaurant)
◯ €€€ **⊘** (43) €€€

Formal restaurant serving an extensive
range of gourmet fare. Fine fish soup,
rascasse and flambéed prawns on the
seafood menu. Chestnut-flour crêpes,
veal with olives and wild boar are
specials. Great selection of wines.

PORTO-VECCHIO
● **Sous la Tonnelle**
Rue Abbatucci, 20137 **Map** 13F5
C 04 95 70 02 17
● Sun D, Mon **◯** €€
Rustic yet elegant spot, covered in ivy,
with potted olive trees sitting either side
of the entrance. Nuts, cream and honey
are used in beautifully prepared pork,
aubergine (eggplant) and asparagus
dishes. Corsican wines are listed by
region. Local eaux de vie too.

PORTO-VECCHIO
● **Spuntino**
Rue Sampiero, 20137 **Map** 13F5
C 04 95 72 11 63
● Sun **◯** €
Exceedingly rustic locals' hangout with
a beach-bar-style terrace. Seafood is
king here; hand-painted menus tell of
grilled sardines, flambéed langoustines
and marinated squid. Huge salads are
topped with sausages, herbs and local
cheeses such as Brocciu cheese. A
single tasty AOC wine (produced down
the road) and one vin de pays.

PORTO-VECCHIO
● **U Mare**
Rue Borgo, 20137 **Map** 13F5
⊘ MC, V ● Nov–Mar
◯ €€
A rich, rustic restaurant. Brocciu cheese
with chutneys and fruit-filled desserts
are laid out on a battered table by the
door. An ancient dresser overflows
with fresh herbs and fragrant spices,
and a balcony overlooks the marina
below. Try the exquisite langoustines,
wild boar steaks, high quality flambéed
prawns and soupe corse (p431).

PORTO-VECCHIO
● **U Molu**
Quai Paoli, 20137 **Map** 13F5
C 04 95 70 04 05
⊘ DC, MC, V

● Restaurant   ■ Hotel   ▲ Hotel / Restaurant

🍽 mid-Nov–end Jan 🍴 €€

Along with Le Grilladen, this forms the pick of the marina-side restaurants. Several fish dishes are served carpaccio style. Try the langoustines, fruits de mer platters and moules-frites.

PROPRIANO
● **Le Cabanon**
Ave Napoleon, 20110 **Map** 13E5
📞 04 95 76 07 76
FAX 04 95 76 27 97
💳 AE, DC, MC, V
🍽 Dec–Mar 🍴 €€€

Kick off with carpaccio of salmon or the aubergine (eggplant) caviar at this classy waterside restaurant. Scallops, red mullet and sea bass are grilled or served with wine or cider sauces. Duck and Corsican cheeses are the only non-seafood items on this stellar menu.

PROPRIANO
● **Rescator**
11 ave Napoleon, 20110 **Map** 13E5
📞 04 95 76 08 46
💳 MC, V 🍽 Nov–Mar
🍴 €€€

Langoustines are grilled, boiled or heaped on spaghetti at this waterside eatery. Mussels, rascasse and crab soup are served in huge white bowls. Sea bass, sea bream and other fish are grilled or served in tagines.

PROPRIANO
● **Terra Cotta**
29 ave Napoleon, 20110 **Map** 13E5
📞 04 95 74 23 80
💳 MC, V 🍽 mid-Mar–May, Oct–Dec: Sun D, Mon; Jan–mid-Mar 🍴 €€€
Intimate restaurant with a stylish wooden terrace and a refreshingly small menu. Delicious seafood: John Dory with wild mushroom risotto; boiled langoustines.

PROPRIANO
● **U Pescadori**
13 ave Napoleon, 20110 **Map** 13E5
📞 04 95 76 42 95
FAX 04 95 76 42 95
💳 AE, DC, MC, V
🍽 Jan–Feb 🍴 €€€
Six generations of fishermen have run this rather elegant seafood restaurant.

They catch and cook the daily special; sea bream, rascasse, red mullet and lobster frequently feature alongside bouillabaisse (p401) and mussels. Reservations are highly recommended.

SARTENE
● **Chez Jean Noel**
Town centre, 20100 **Map** 13F5
💳 MC, V 🍽 Sun L, Mon 🍴 €€
Authentic country fare at this tiny eatery: soupe corse (p431), Sartene-style tripe and lamb and pork dishes. Massive desserts. Serena lager, Pietra beer and a few Corsican wines.

SARTENE
● **Santa Barbara**
2km (3 miles) past the Sartene city limit on the road to Propiano, 20100 **Map** 13F5
📞 04 95 77 09 06
🍽 Mon; Oct–Feb 🍴 €€
Sea bass, lobster and fish baked with citrus fruits compose the gastronomic seafood selection. Roast lamb, pork charcuterie and stuffed courgette (zucchini) too. Several Brocciu cheese dishes, including a dessert. Rustic dining area with delightful gardens.

SARTENE
● **U Passachju**
Rue des Fréres Bartoli, 20100 **Map** 13F5
🍴 €
Tables are laid out on a cobbled street in the quaint Santa Anna old town area. Charcuterie, veal with olives, tangy wild boar, hearty lasagne and Brocciu cheese with home-made fig jam.

ST-FLORENT
● **La Gaffe**
Port de Plaisance, 20217 **Map** 13F3
📞 04 95 37 00 12
💳 MC, V 🍽 Oct: Tue; Apr–Sep: Mon L, Tue L; Nov–Mar 🍴 €€
Sea bass, John Dory and scallops are served grilled or in hearty soups. Pasta is tossed with squid, fish and vegetables. Excellent range of local Corsican wines. Reservations essential in summer.

ST-FLORENT
● **Rascasse**
Rue Strada Nova, 20217 **Map** 13F3

📞 04 95 37 06 99
FAX 04 95 37 06 09
💳 AE, DC, MC, V
🍽 Oct–Mar
🍴 €€€

One of St-Florent's very best. Tasty squid, lobster, fish and shellfish served in soups, pastas and other tried-and-tested dishes. Great terrace facing the sea. A handful of wines.

VENACO
▲ **Le Torrent**
20250 **Map** 13F4
📞 04 95 47 00 18
🌐 www.letorrent.com
💳 AE 🍽 Nov–Jun
🍴 € 🛏 (21) €€

Charmingly rustic, slightly run-down hotel with somewhat spartan rooms. Traditional peasant dishes like hearty pastas, lasagne and grilled meats cooked with local herbs and Brocciu cheese. Local sausages and trout too.

VENACO
▲ **U Frascone**
Maison La Croix, 20231 **Map** 13F4
📞 04 95 47 00 85
FAX 04 95 47 06 21
💳 MC, V
🍽 Jan–Feb
🍴 € 🛏 (6) €€

Good-value set menus offering roast lamb and pork with maquis herbs. Other dishes include Brocciu cheese, wild boar and sausages. Outdoor terrace. Simple rooms, but reserve well in advance.

ZONZA
▲ **Hôtel Restaurant le Tourisme**
Route de Quenza, 20124 **Map** 13F5
📞 04 95 78 67 72
FAX 04 95 78 73 23
🌐 www.hoteldutourisme.fr
💳 DC, MC, V
🍽 Nov–Mar
🍴 €€ 🛏 (14) €€

Turn-of-the-century building with old-world charm and delightful guestrooms, each with a balcony. Several terraces for outdoor dining; try the trout, lobster, and omelette with Brocciu cheese. Excellent selection of Corsican wines.

REGIONAL MAPS

The key map below shows the 16 regions of France as featured in this guide, and the pages on which they can be found in the following map section. All important arterial roads and rail routes are shown, along with international airports.

Map references appear in all hotel and restaurant listings and, on the regional maps, each town or village that features in the listings is tinted grey. The map of central Paris on map pages 14–15 shows main sights and other useful information.

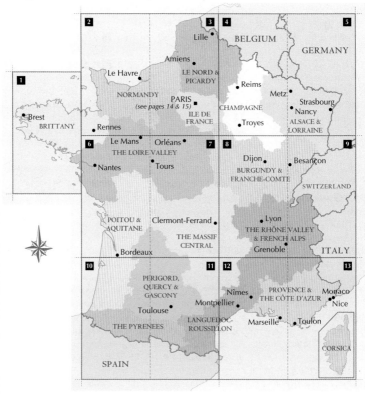

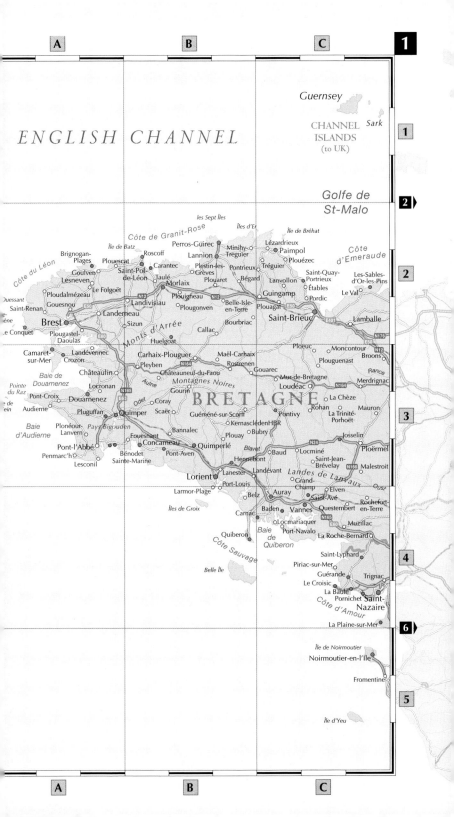

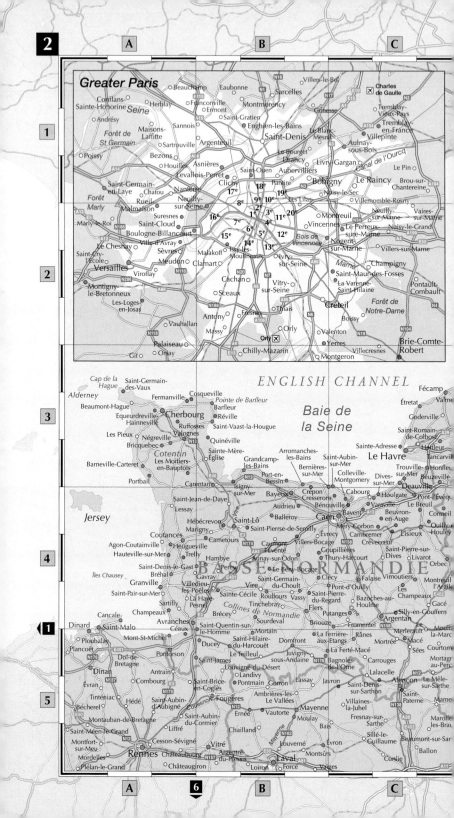

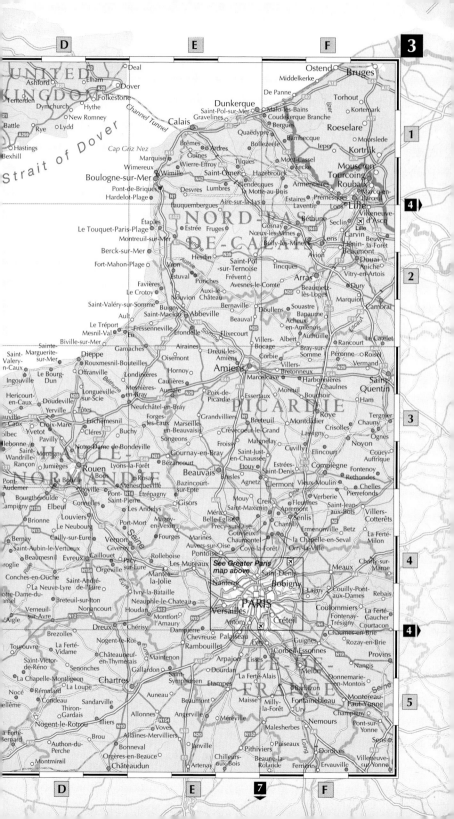

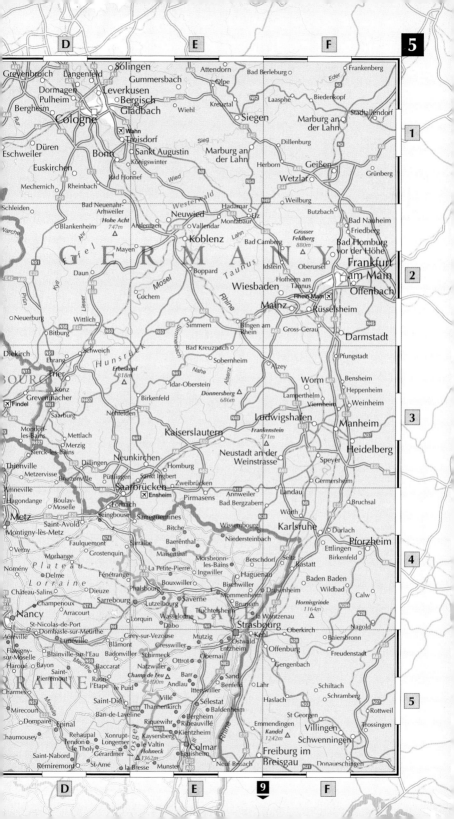

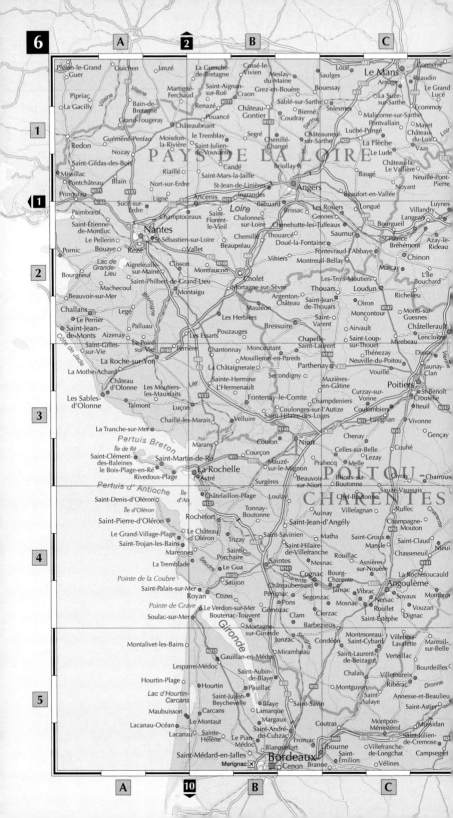

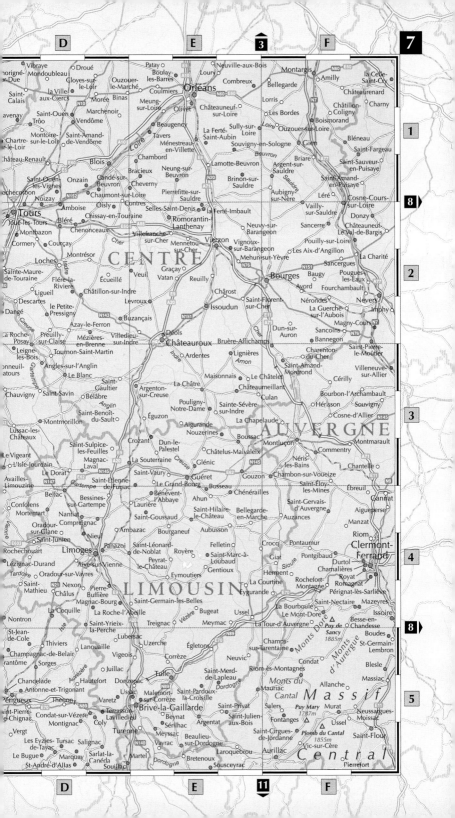

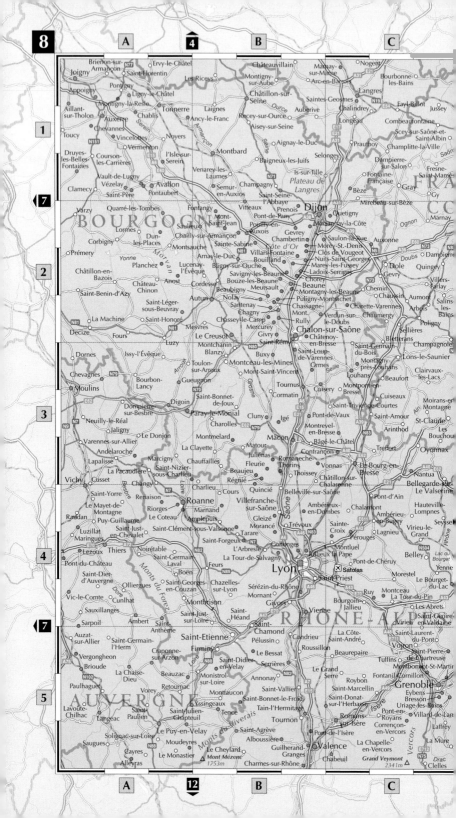

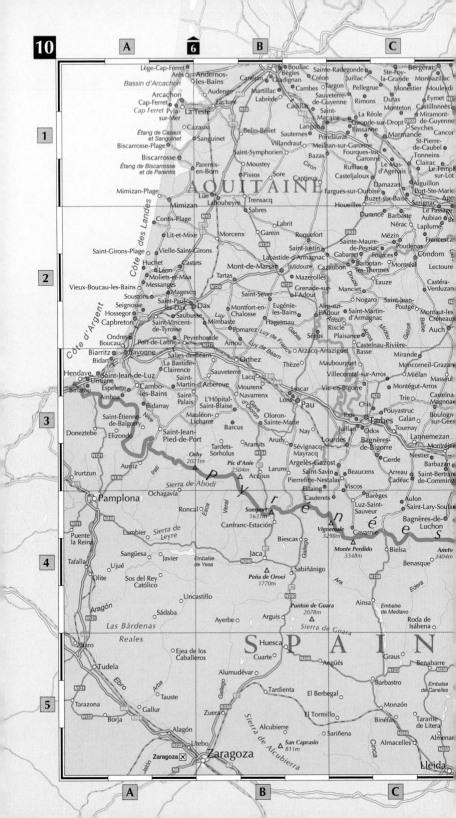

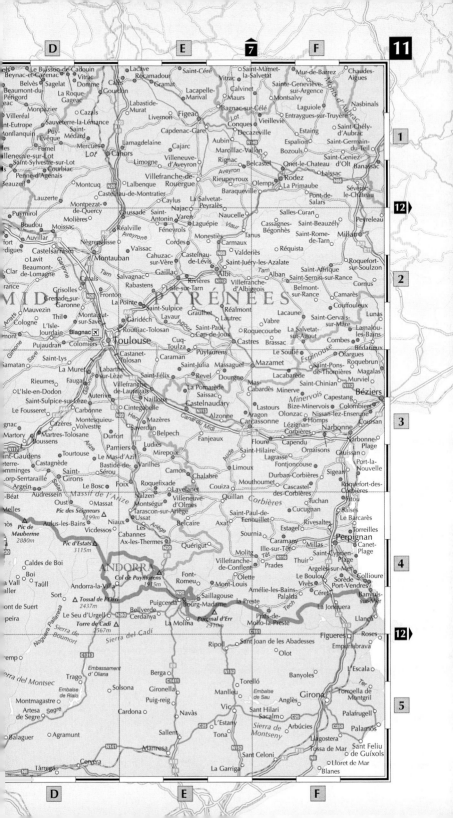

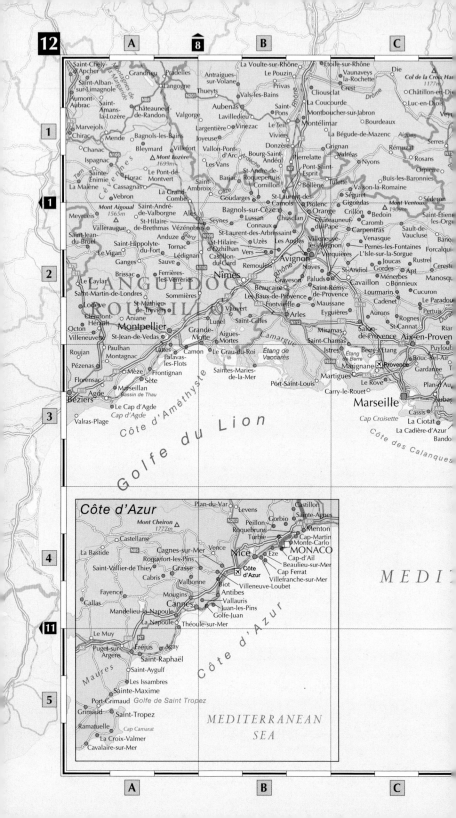

A   **8**   **B**   **C**

1

1

2

3

4

11

5

Saint-Chély-
d'Apcher
Grandrieu Pradelles
Saint-Alban-
sur-Limagnole
Langogne
Antraigues-
sur-Volane
La Voulte-sur-Rhône
Le Pouzin
Privas
Étoile-sur-Rhône
Die
Col de la Croix Hat
1171m
Vaunaveys-
la-Rochette
Crest
Châtillon-en-Di
Aumont-
Aubrac
Châteauneuf-
de-Randon
Valgorge
Thueys
Vals-les-Bains
Cliousclat
Drôme
Luc-en-Diois
Marvejols
Aubenas
La Coucourde
Bourdeaux
Chirac
Mende
Largentière
Le Teil
Montboucher-sur-Jabron
Montélimar
Aigues
Serres
Chanac
Bagnols-les-Bains
Joyeuse
Vinezac
Vivier
La Bégude-de-Mazenc
Rémuzat
Ispagnac
Bleymard
Villefort
Vallon-Pont-
d'Arc
Donzère
Grignan
Valréas
Rosans
Serres
Tarn
Sainte-
Enimie
Mont Lozère
1699m
Le Pont-de-
Montvert
Les Vans
Bourg-Saint-
Andéol
Pierrelatte
Nyons
Orpierre
La Malène
Cassagnas
Florac
Saint-
Ambroix
Bariac
St-André-
de-Roquepertuis
Pont-Saint-
Esprit
Tulette
Buis-les-Baronnies
Vebron
La Grand-
Combe
Cèze
Goudargues
Bollène
Vaison-la-Romaine
Séderon
Meyrueis
Mont Aigoual
1565m
Saint-André-
de-Valborgne
Cornillon
St-Laurent-des-
Carnols
Piolenc
Séguret
Mont Ventoux
1909m
Saint-Étienne-
les-Org
Vallerauge
St-Hilaire-
de-Brethmas
Vézénobres
Alès
Lussan
Connaux
Chusclan
Orange
Crillon
Gigondas
Bedoin
Saint-Jean-
du-Bruel
Anduze
St-Laurent-des-Arbresaint
Les Angles
Châteauneuf-
du-Pape
Carpentras
Caromb
Sault-de-
Vaucluse
Le Vigan
Saint-Hippolyte-
du-Fort
Tornac
St-Hilaire-
d'Ozilhan
Uzès
Vers
Villeneuve-
lès-Avignon
Vacqueyras
Venasque
Pernes-les-Fontaines
Forcalqu
Ganges
Lédignan
Remoulins
Avignon
L'Isle-sur-la-Sorgue
Rustrel
Cereste
Brissac
Sauve
Castillon-
du-Gard
Joucas
Gordes
Apt
Manosqu
Le Caylar
Ferrières-
les-Verreries
Nîmes
Noves
St-Andiol
Ménerbes
Bonnieux
Saint-Martin-de-Londres
Sommières
Beaucaire
Graveson
Paluds
Saint-Rémy-
de-Provence
Cavaillon
Lourmarin
Cucuron
Cadenet
Le Paradou
Loupe
St-Mathieu-
de-Tréviers
Les Baux-de-Provence
Fontvieille
Maussane
Eyguières
Aurons
Rognes
Pertuis
Dura
Clermont-
l'Hérault
Aniane
Vauvert
Lunel
Saint-Gilles
Arles
Miramas
Salon-
de-Provence
Aix-en-Proven
Octon
St-Jean-de-Vedas
Montpellier
Grande-
Motte
Aigues-
Mortes
Saint-Chamas
Istres
Puyloub
Villeneuvette
Paulhan
Lattes
Camon
Le Grau-du-Roi
Berre-
l'Étang
Étang
de Berre
Bouc-el-Air
Roujan
Montagnac
Palavas-
les-Flots
Étang de
Vaccarès
Marignane
Gardanne
Pézenas
Mèze
Frontignan
Saintes-
Maries-
de-Mer
Provence
Le Rove
Plan d'Au
Florensac
Sète
Port-Saint-Louis
Martigues
Carry-le-Rouet
ubal
Agde
Marseillan
Bassin de Thau
Cassis
Béziers
Le Cap d'Agde
Cap d'Agde
Marseille
La Ciotat
Valras-Plage
Côte d'Améthyste
Cap Croisette
La Cadière-d'Azur
Bando

LANGUEDOC
ROUSSILLON

Golfe du Lion

Côte des Calanques

Côte d'Azur

Mont Cheiron
1777m
Plan-du-Var
Levens
Castillon
Sainte-Agnès
Corbio
Peillon
Roquebrune
Turbie
Menton
Cap-Martin
Monte-Carlo
MONACO
Cap-d'Ail
Beaulieu-sur-Mer
Cap Ferrat
Villefranche-sur-Mer
Castellarre
Cagnes-sur-Mer
Vence
Nice
Eze
La Bastide
Roquefort-les-Pins
Grasse
Côte
d'Azur
Saint-Vallier-de-Thiey
Cabris
Valbonne
Biot
Villeneuve-Loubet
Fayence
Mougins
Antibes
Vallauris
Callas
Valbonne
Cannes
Juan-les-Pins
Mandelieu-la-Napoule
Golfe-Juan
La Napoule
Théoule-sur-Mer
Le Muy
Côte d'Azur
Puget-sur-
Argens
Fréjus
Agay
Saint-Raphaël
Maures
Saint-Aygulf
Les Issambres
Sainte-Maxime
Port-Grimaud
Golfe de Saint Tropez
Grimaud
Saint-Tropez
Ramatuelle
Cap Camarat
La Croix-Valmer
Cavalaire-sur-Mer

M E D I T

M E D I T E R R A N E A N
S E A

A   **B**   **C**

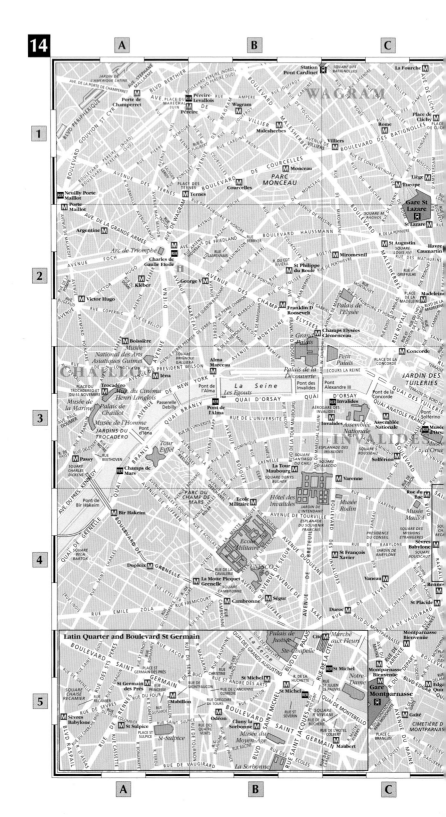

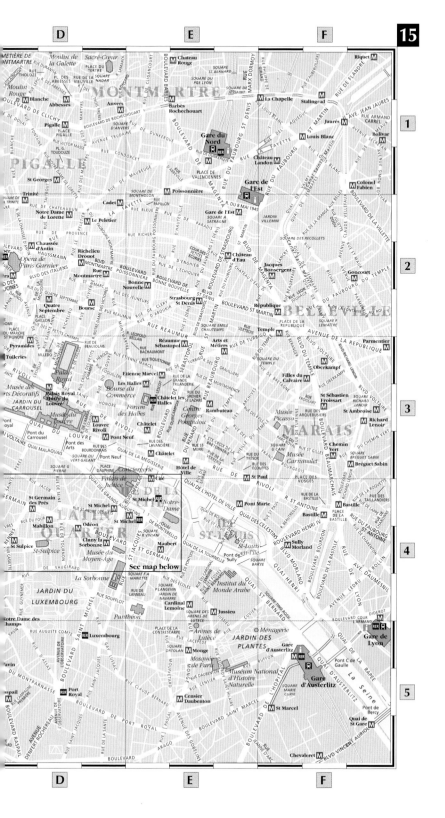

Phrase Book

IN EMERGENCY

Help!	Au secours!	oh sekoor
Stop!	Arrêtez!	aret-ay
Call a doctor!	Appelez un médecin!	apuh-lay uñ medsañ
Call an ambulance!	Appelez une ambulance!	apuh-lay oon oñboo-loñs
Call the police!	Appelez la police!	apuh-lay lah poh-lees
Call the fire department!	Appelez les pompiers!	apuh-lay leh poñ-peeyay
Where is the nearest telephone?	Où est le téléphone le plus proche?	oo ay luh tehlehfon luh ploo prosh
Where is the nearest hospital?	Où est l'hôpital le plus proche?	oo ay l'opeetal luh ploo prosh

COMMUNICATION ESSENTIALS

Yes	Oui	wee
No	Non	noñ
Please	S'il vous plaît	seel voo play
Thank you	Merci	mer-see
Excuse me	Excusez-moi	exkoo-zay mwah
Hello	Bonjour	boñzhoor
Goodbye	Au revoir	oh ruh-vwar
Good night	Bonsoir	boñ-swar
Morning	Le matin	matañ
Afternoon	L'après-midi	l'apreh-meedee
Evening	Le soir	swar
Yesterday	Hier	eeyehr
Today	Aujourd'hui	oh-zhoor-dwee
Tomorrow	Demain	duhmañ
Here	Ici	ee-see
There	Là	lah
What?	Quel, quelle?	kel, kel
When?	Quand?	koñ
Why?	Pourquoi?	poor-kwah
Where?	Où?	oo

USEFUL PHRASES

How are you?	Comment allez-vous?	kom-moñ talay voo
Very well, thank you.	Très bien, merci.	treh byañ mer-see
Pleased to meet you.	Enchanté de faire votre connaissance.	oñshoñ-tay duh fehr votr kon-ay-sans
See you soon.	A bientôt.	byañ-toh
That's fine.	Voilà qui est parfait.	vwalah kee ay parfay
Where is/are…?	Où est/sont…?	oo ay/soñ
How far is it to…?	Combien de kilomètres d'ici à…?	kom-byañ duh keelo-metr d'ee-see ah
Which way to…?	Quelle est la direction pour…?	kel ay lah deer-ek-syoñ poor
Do you speak English?	Parlez-vous anglais?	par-lay voo oñg-lay
I don't understand.	Je ne comprends pas.	zhuh nuh kom-proñ pah
Could you speak slowly. please?	Pouvez-vous parler moins vite s'il vous plaît?	poo-vay voo par-lay mwañ veet seel voo play
I'm sorry.	Excusez-moi.	exkoo-zay mwah

USEFUL WORDS

big	grand	groñ
small	petit	puh-tee
hot	chaud	show
cold	froid	frwah
good	bon	boñ
bad	mauvais	moh-veh
enough	assez	assay
well	bien	byañ
open	ouvert	oo-ver
closed	fermé	fer-meh

left	gauche	gohsh
right	droit	drwah
straight ahead	tout droit	too drwah
near	près	preh
far	loin	lwañ
up	en haut	oñ oh
down	en bas	oñ bah
early	de bonne heure	duh bon urr
late	en retard	oñ ruh-tar
entrance	l'entrée	l'on-tray
exit	la sortie	sor-tee
toilet	les toilettes, les WC	twah-let, vay-see
free, unoccupied	libre	leebr
free, no charge	gratuit	grah-twee

MAKING A TELEPHONE CALL

I'd like to place a long-distance call.	Je voudrais faire un interurbain.	zhuh voo-dreh fehr uñ añter-oorbañ
I'd like to make a collect call.	Je voudrais faire une communication PCV.	zhuh voodreh fehr oon komoonikah-syoñ peh-seh-veh
I'll try again later.	Je rappelerai plus tard.	zhuh rapel-eray ploo tar
Can I leave a message?	Est-ce que je peux laisser un message?	es-keh zhuh puh leh-say uñ mehsazh
Hold on.	Ne quittez pas, s'il vous plaît.	nuh kee-tay pah seel voo play
Could you speak up a little please?	Pouvez-vous parler un peu plus fort?	poo-vay voo par-lay uñ puh ploo for
local call	la communication locale	komoonikah-syoñ low-kal

SHOPPING

How much does this cost?	C'est combien s'il vous plaît?	say kom-byañ seel voo play
I would like …	je voudrais…	zhuh voo-dray
Do you have?	Est-ce que vous avez?	es-kuh voo zavay
I'm just looking.	Je regarde seulement.	zhuh ruhgar suhlmoñ
Do you take credit cards?	Est-ce que vous acceptez les cartes de crédit?	es-kuh voo zaksept-ay leh kart duh kreh-dee
Do you take traveler's checks?	Est-ce que vous acceptez les chèques de voyage?	es-kuh voo zaksept-ay leh shek duh wayazh
What time do you open?	A quelle heure vous êtes ouvert?	ah kel urr voo zet oo-ver
What time do you close?	A quelle heure vous êtes fermé?	ah kel urr voo zet fer-may
This one.	Celui-ci.	suhl-wee-see
That one.	Celui-là.	suhl-wee-lah
expensive	cher	shehr
cheap	pas cher, bon marché	pah shehr, boñ mar-shay
size, clothes	la taille	tye
size, shoes	la pointure	pwañ-tur
white	blanc	bloñ
black	noir	nwahr
red	rouge	roozh
yellow	jaune	zhohwn
green	vert	vehr
blue	bleu	bluh

TYPES OF SHOPS

antiques shop	le magasin d'antiquités	maga-zañ d'oñteekee-tay
bakery	la boulangerie	booloñ-zhuree
bank	la banque	boñk
book store	la librairie	lee-brehree
butcher	la boucherie	boo-shehree
cake shop	la pâtisserie	patee-sree
cheese shop	la fromagerie	fromazh-ree

dairy	la crémerie	krem-**ree**
department store	le grand magasin	groñ maga-**zañ**
delicatessen	la charcuterie	sharkoot-**ree**
drugstore	la pharmacie	farmah-**see**
fish seller	la poissonnerie	pwasson-**ree**
gift shop	le magasin de	maga-**zañ** duh
	cadeaux	kadoh
greengrocer	le marchand	mar-**shoñ** duh
	de légumes	lay-**goom**
grocery	l'alimentation	alee-moñta-**syoñ**
hairdresser	le coiffeur	kwafuhr
market	le marché	marsh-**ay**
newsstand	le magasin de	maga-**zañ** duh
	journaux	zhoor-**no**
post office	la poste,	pohst,
	le bureau de poste,	booroh duh pohst,
	le PTT	peh-teh-teh
shoe store	le magasin	maga-**zañ**
	de chaussures	duh show-**soor**
supermarket	le supermarché	soo pehr-**marshay**
tobacconist	le tabac	tabah
travel agent	l'agence	l'azhoñs
	de voyages	duh vwayazh

SIGHTSEEING

abbey	l'abbaye	l'abay-**ee**
art gallery	la galerie d'art	galer-**ree** dart
bus station	la gare routière	gahr roo-tee-**yehr**
cathedral	la cathédrale	katay-**dral**
church	l'église	l'ayg**leez**
garden	le jardin	zhar-**dañ**
library	la bibliothèque	beeb**leeo**-tek
museum	le musée	moo-**zay**
tourist	les renseignements	roñsayn-**moñ** too-
information	touristiques, le	rees-**teek**, sandee-
office	syndicat d'initiative	ka d'eenee-sya**teev**
town hall	l'hôtel de ville	l'oh**tel** duh veel
train station	la gare (SNCF)	gahr (es-en-say-ef)
private mansion	l'hôtel particulier	l'oh**tel** partikoo-**lyay**
closed for	fermeture	fehrmeh-**tur**
public holiday	jour férié	zhoor fehree-**ay**

STAYING IN A HOTEL

Do you have a	Est-ce que vous	es-kuh voo-**zavay**
vacant room?	avez une chambre?	oon shambr
double room,	la chambre à deux	shambr ah duh
with double bed	personnes, avec	pehr-**son** avek un
	un grand lit	groñ lee
twin room	la chambre à	shambr ah
	deux lits	duh lee
single room	la chambre à	shambr ah
	une personne	oon pehr-**son**
room with a	la chambre avec	shambr avek
bath, shower	salle de bains,	sal duh bañ,
	une douche	oon doosh
porter	le garçon	gar-**soñ**
key	la clef	klay
I have a	J'ai fait une	zhay fay oon
reservation.	réservation.	rayzehrva-**syoñ**

EATING OUT

Have you	Avez-vous une	avay-**voo** oon
got a table?	table libre?	tahbl leebr
I want to	Je voudrais	zhuh voo-**dray**
reserve	réserver	rayzehr-**vay**
a table.	une table.	oon tahbl
The check	L'addition s'il	l'adee-**syoñ** seel
please.	vous plaît.	voo **play**
I am a	Je suis	zhuh swee
vegetarian.	végétarien.	vezhay-**tehryañ**
Waitress/	Madame,	mah-**dam**,
waiter	Mademoiselle/	mah-demwah**zel**/
	Monsieur	muh-**syuh**
menu	le menu, la carte	men-**oo**, kart
fixed-price	le menu à	men-**oo** ah
menu	prix fixe	pree feeks
cover charge	le couvert	koo-**vehr**

wine list	la carte des vins	kart-deh vañ
glass	le verre	vehr
bottle	la bouteille	boo-**tay**
knife	le couteau	koo-**toh**
fork	la fourchette	for-**shet**
spoon	la cuillère	kwee-**yehr**
breakfast	le petit	puh-**tee**
	déjeuner	deh-**zhuh**-nay
lunch	le déjeuner	deh-**zhuh**-nay
dinner	le dîner	dee-**nay**
main course	le plat principal	plah prañsee-**pal**
appetizer, first	l'entrée, le hors	l'oñ-**tray**, or-
course	d'oeuvre	duhvr
dish of the day	le plat du jour	plah doo zhoor
wine bar	le bar à vin	bar ah vañ
café	le café	ka-**fay**
rare	saignant	**say**-noñ
medium	à point	ah **pwañ**
well-done	bien cuit	byañ **kwee**

NUMBERS

0	zéro	zeh-**roh**
1	un, une	uñ, oon
2	deux	duh
3	trois	trwah
4	quatre	katr
5	cinq	sañk
6	six	sees
7	sept	set
8	huit	weet
9	neuf	nerf
10	dix	dees
11	onze	oñz
12	douze	dooz
13	treize	trehz
14	quatorze	ka**torz**
15	quinze	kañz
16	seize	sehz
17	dix-sept	dees-**set**
18	dix-huit	dees-**weet**
19	dix-neuf	dees-**nerf**
20	vingt	vañ
30	trente	tront
40	quarante	karo**ñt**
50	cinquante	sañko**ñt**
60	soixante	swaso**ñt**
70	soixante-dix	swasoñt-**dees**
80	quatre-vingts	katr-**vañ**
90	quatre-vingt-dix	katr-vañ-**dees**
100	cent	soñ
1,000	mille	meel

TIME

one minute	une minute	oon mee-**noot**
ten minutes	dix minutes	dee mee**noot**
one hour	une heure	oon urr
quarter of an hour	un quart d'heure	kar dur
half an hour	une demi-heure	oon **duh**-mee urr
Monday	lundi	luñ-**dee**
Tuesday	mardi	mar-**dee**
Wednesday	mercredi	mehrkruh-**dee**
Thursday	jeudi	zhuh-**dee**
Friday	vendredi	voñdruh-**dee**
Saturday	samedi	sam-**dee**
Sunday	dimanche	dee-**moñsh**
January	janvier	**jon**vee-ay
February	février	fayvree-ay
March	mars	marss
April	avril	ahvreel
May	mai	meh
June	juin	jwan
July	juillet	jwee-ay
August	août	oo
September	septembre	septoñbr
October	octobre	oktobr
November	novembre	novoñbr
December	décembre	daysso**nbr**

Menu Guide

abats	offal
abricot	apricot
à emporter	to take away
agneau	lamb
aiguillette de bœuf	slices of rump steak
ail	garlic
aïoli	garlic mayonnaise
à la broche	roasted on a spit
à la jardinière	with assorted vegetables
à la normande	in cream sauce
alose	shad
amande	almond
ananas	pineapple
anchois	anchovies
andouillette	chitterling sausage
anguille	eel
à point	medium (cooked)
araignée de mer	spider crab
artichaut	artichoke
asperge	asparagus
aspic de volaille	chicken in aspic
assiette anglaise	selection of cold meats
au gratin	baked in a milk, cream and cheese sauce
au vin blanc	in white wine
avocat	avocado
baba au rhum	rum baba
banane	banana
bananes flambées	bananas flambéed in brandy
barbue	brill
bavaroise	light mousse
bavette	flank or skirt steak
béarnaise	with béarnaise sauce (thick sauce made with eggs and butter)
bécasse	woodcock
béchamel	white sauce, béchamel sauce
beignet	fritter, doughnut
betterave	beetroot
beurre	butter
beurre d'anchois	anchovy paste
beurre d'estragon	butter with tarragon
beurre noir	dark melted butter
bien cuit	well done (cooked)
bière	beer
bière à la pression	draught beer
bière blonde	lager
bière brune	bitter, dark beer
bière panachée	shandy
bifteck	steak
bifteck de cheval	horsemeat steak
biscuit de Savoie	sponge cake
bisque d'écrevisses	crayfish soup
bisque de homard	lobster soup
blanc de blancs	white wine from white grapes
blanquette de veau	veal stew
blette	Swiss chard
bleu	cooked extremely rare ("blue")
bleu d'Auvergne	blue cheese from the Auvergne
bœuf	beef
bœuf à la ficelle	beef cooked in stock
bœuf à la mode	beef braised in red with carrots and onions
bœuf bourguignon	beef cooked in red wine
bœuf braisé	braised beef
bœuf en daube	beef casserole
bœuf miroton	beef and onion stew
bolet	boletus (mushroom)
bouchée à la reine	veal vol-au-vent
boudin blanc	white pudding
boudin noir	black pudding
bouillabaisse	fish soup from the Midi
bouilli	boiled
bouillon	broth
bouillon de légumes	vegetable stock
bouillon de poule	chicken stock
boulette	meatball

bouquet rose	prawns
bourride	fish soup
braisé	braised
brandade	cod in cream and garlic
brioche	round roll
brochet	pike
brochette	kebab
brugnon	nectarine
brûlot	flambéed brandy
brut	very dry (Champagne)
cabillaud	cod
café	coffee (black)
café au lait	white coffee
café complet	continental breakfast
café crème	white coffee
café glacé	iced coffee
café liégeois	iced coffee with cream
caille	quail
cake	fruitcake
calamar/calmar	squid
calvados	apple brandy
camomille	camomile tea
canapé	small open sandwich, canapé
canard	duck
canard à l'orange	duck in orange sauce
canard aux cerises	duck with cherries
canard aux navets	duck with turnips
canard laqué	Peking duck
canard rôti	roast duck
caneton	duckling
cantal	cheese from Auvergne
carbonnade	beef cooked in beer
cari	curry
carotte	carrot
carottes Vichy	carrots in butter and parsley
carpe	carp
carré d'agneau	rack of lamb
carrelet	plaice
carte	menu
carte des vins	wine list
casse-croûte	snack
cassis	blackcurrant
cassoulet	bean, pork and duck casserole
céleri (en branches)	celery
céleri rave	celeriac
céleri rémoulade	celeriac in rémoulade dressing
cèpe	cep (mushroom)
cerfeuil	chervil
cerise	cherry
cerises à l'eau de vie	cherries in brandy
cervelles	brains
chablis	dry white wine from Burgundy
chambré	at room temperature
champignon	mushroom
champignon de Paris	white button mushroom
champignons à la grecque	mushrooms in olive oil, herbs and tomatoes, served hot or cold
chanterelle	chanterelle (mushroom)
chantilly	whipped cream
charcuterie	sausages, ham and pâtés; pork products
charlotte	dessert of fruit, cream and finger biscuits
chasseur	sauce or garnish of mushrooms and shallots
chausson aux pommes	apple turnover
cheval	horse
chèvre	goats' cheese
chevreuil	venison
chicorée	endive
chiffonnade d'oseille	seasoned sorrel cooked in butter
chocolat chaud/glacé	hot/iced chocolate
chocolat glacé	iced chocolate
chou	cabbage
chou à la crème	cream puff
choucroute	sauerkraut with sausages and pieces of smoked ham

chou-fleur	cauliflower
chou-fleur au gratin	cauliflower with cheese
chou rouge	red cabbage
choux de Bruxelles	Brussels sprouts
cidre	cider
cidre doux	sweet cider
citron	lemon
citron pressé	fresh lemon juice
civet de lièvre	jugged hare
clafoutis	baked batter pudding with fruit
cochon de lait	suckling pig
cocktail de crevettes	prawn cocktail
cœur	heart
coing	quince
colin	hake
compote	stewed fruit, compote
comté	hard cheese from the Jura
concombre	cucumber
confit de canard	duck preserved in fat
confit d'oie	goose preserved in fat
confiture	jam (jelly), preserve
congre	conger eel
consommé	clear soup made from meat or chicken
coq au vin	chicken in red wine
coque	cockle
coquelet	cockerel
coquille Saint-Jacques	scallops served in cream sauce
côte de porc	pork chop
côtelette	chop
cotriade bretonne	fish soup from Brittany
coulommiers	rich, soft cheese
coupe	dessert dish
court-bouillon	stock for poaching fish or meat
couscous	steamed semolina with meat and vegetable stew
crabe	crab
crème	cream; creamy sauce or dessert; white coffee
crème à la vanille	vanilla custard
crème anglaise	custard
crème chantilly	whipped cream
crème d'asperges	cream of asparagus soup
crème fouettée	whipped cream
crème pâtissière	rich thick custard
crème renversée	set custard
crème vichyssoise	cold potato and leek soup
crêpe	sweet pancake
crêpe de froment	wheat pancake
crêpes Suzette	pancakes flambéed with orange sauce
crépinette	small sausage patty wrapped in fat
cresson	cress
crevette grise	shrimp
crevette rose	prawn (large shrimp)
croque-madame	grilled cheese and ham sandwich with a fried egg
croque-monsieur	grilled cheese and ham sandwich
crottin de Chavignol	small goats' cheese
crudités	selection of salads, chopped raw vegetables
crustacés	shellfish
cuisses de grenouille	frogs' legs
cuissot de chevreuil	haunch of venison
dartois	pastry with jam
dégustation	(wine) tasting
déjeuner	lunch
digestif	liqueur
dinde	turkey
dîner	dinner
doux	sweet
eau minérale	mineral water
eau minérale gazeuse	sparkling mineral water
eau minérale plates	still mineral water
échalote	shallot
écrevisse	saltwater crayfish
écrevisses à la nage	crayfish in wine and vegetable sauce
endive	chicory (endive)
endives au jambon	endives with ham baked in the oven
en papillote	baked in foil or paper
entrecôte	rib steak
entrecôte au poivre	peppered rib steak
entrecôte maître d'hôtel	steak with butter and parsley
entrée	starter
entremets	dessert
épaule d'agneau farcie	stuffed shoulder of lamb
éperlan	smelt (fish)
épinards	leaf spinach
escalope à la crème	escalope in cream sauce
escalope de veau milanaise	veal escalope with tomato sauce
escalope panée	breaded escalope
escargot	snail
esquimau	ice cream on a stick
estouffade de bœuf	beef casserole
faisan	pheasant
farci	stuffed
fenouil	fennel
filet	fillet
filet de bœuf Rossini	fillet of beef with foie gras
filet de perche	perch fillet
fine	fine brandy
flageolets	green flageolet beans
flambé	flambéed
flan	custard tart
foie de veau	veal liver
foie gras	fattened goose or duck liver
foies de volaille	chicken livers
fonds d'artichauts	artichoke hearts
fondue bourguignonne	meat fondue
fondue savoyarde	cheese fondue
fraise	strawberry
fraise des bois	wild strawberry
framboise	raspberry
frisée	curly lettuce
frit	deep-fried
frites	chips
fromage	cheese
fromage blanc	cream cheese
fromage de chèvre	goats' cheese
fruité	fruity
fruits de mer	seafood
galette	round, flat cake or savoury crêpe
garni	with potatoes and vegetables
gâteau	cake
gaufre	wafer; waffle
gelée	jelly
génoise	sponge cake
Gewürztraminer	dry white wine from Alsace
gibelotte de lapin	rabbit stewed in white wine
gibier	game
gigot d'agneau	leg of lamb
gigue de chevreuil	haunch of venison
girolle	chanterelle (mushroom)
glace	ice cream
goujon	gudgeon (fish)
grand cru	vintage wine
gras-double	tripe
gratin	baked cheese dish with milk and cream
gratin dauphinois	sliced potatoes baked in milk, cream and cheese
gratinée	baked onion soup
grillé	grilled
grive	thrush
grondin	gurnard (fish)
groseille blanche	whitecurrant
groseille rouge	redcurrant
hachis parmentier	shepherd's pie
hareng mariné	marinated herring
haricots	beans
haricots blancs	haricot beans
haricots verts	green beans
homard	lobster
homard à l'américaine	lobster with tomatoes and white wine
hors-d'œuvre	starter
huître	oyster
îles flottantes	poached egg whites on top of custard
infusion	herb tea
jambon	ham
jambon au madère	ham in Madeira wine
jambon de Bayonne	smoked and cured ham
jarret de veau	shin of veal

julienne	matchstick strips of vegetables
jus	juice
kir	white wine with blackcurrant liqueur
kirsch	cherry brandy
kougelhopf	cake from Alsace
lait	milk
lait grenadine	milk with grenadine cordial
laitue	lettuce
langouste	freshwater crayfish
langoustine	scampi
langue de bœuf	ox tongue
langue de chat	long, thin crisp sweet biscuit
lapereau	young rabbit
lapin	rabbit
lapin à la Lorraine	rabbit in mushroom and cream sauce
lapin à la moutarde	rabbit in mustard sauce
lapin de garenne	wild rabbit
lard	bacon
léger	light
légume	vegetable
lentilles	lentils
lièvre	hare
limande	flounder, lemon sole
limonade	lemonade
livarot	strong, soft cheese from the north of France
longe	loin
lotte	turbot
loup de mer	sea bass
macédoine de légumes	mixed vegetables
mache	corn salad
mangue	mango
maquereau	mackerel
marc	grape brandy
marcassin	young wild boar
marchand de vin	in red wine sauce
marron	chestnut
massepain	marzipan
menthe	peppermint
menthe à l'eau	mint cordial
menu du jour	today's menu
menu gastronomique	gourmet menu
menu touristique	tourist menu
merlan	whiting
millefeuille	custard slice
millésime	vintage
morille	morel (mushroom)
morue	cod
mouclade	mussels in creamy sauce with saffron, turmeric and white wine
moules marinière	mussels in white wine
mousse au chocolat	chocolate mousse
mousse au jambon	light ham mousse
mousseux	sparkling (wine)
moutarde	mustard
mouton	mutton
mulet	mullet
munster	strong cheese
mûre	blackberry
Muscadet	dry white wine from Nantes
myrtille	bilberry
nature	plain
navarin	mutton stew with vegetables
navet	turnip
noisette	hazelnut
noisette d'agneau	small, round lamb steak
noix	walnut
nouilles	noodles
œuf à la coque	boiled egg
œuf dur	hard-boiled egg
œuf en gelée	egg in aspic
œuf mollet	soft-boiled egg
œuf poché	poached egg
œufs à la neige	poached egg whites on top of custard
œufs brouillés	scrambled eggs
œuf sur le plat	fried egg
oie	goose
oignon	onion
omelette au naturel	plain omelette

omelette aux fines herbes	omelette with herbs
omelette paysanne	omelette with potatoes and bacon
orange givrée	orange sorbet served in an orange
orange pressée	fresh orange juice
oseille	sorrel
oursin	sea urchin
pain	bread
pain au chocolat	chocolate puff pastry
palette de porc	shoulder of pork
palourde	clam
pamplemousse	grapefruit
panade	bread soup
parfait glacé	type of ice cream
pastis	anise-flavoured alcoholic drink
pâté de canard	duck pâté
pâté de foie de volaille	chicken liver pâté
pâte feuilletée	puff pastry
pâtes	pasta
paupiettes de veau	slices of veal, rolled up and stuffed
pêche	peach
perdreau	young partridge
perdrix	partridge
petit déjeuner	breakfast
petite friture	whitebait
petit pain	roll
petit pois	peas
petits fours	small fancy pastries
petit suisse	light, white cream cheese
pied de porc	pig's foot/trotter
pigeonneau	young pigeon
pignatelle	small cheese fritter
pilaf de mouton	rice dish with mutton
pintade	guinea fowl
piperade	Basque egg dish with tomatoes and peppers
pissaladière	Provençal dish similar to pizza
pissenlit	dandelion (leaves)
pistache	pistachio
plat du jour	dish of the day
plateau de fromages	cheese board
pochouse	fish casserole with white wine
poire	pear
poire belle Hélène	pear in chocolate sauce
poireau	leek
poisson	fish
poivre	pepper
poivron	red or green bell pepper
pomme	apple
pomme bonne femme	baked apple
pomme de terre	potato
pommes Dauphine	potato fritters
pommes de terre à l'anglaise	boiled potatoes
pommes de terre en robe de chambre/ en robe des champs	baked potatoes
pommes sautées	fried potatoes
pommes frites	chips
pommes paille	finely cut chips
pommes vapeur	steamed potatoes
porc	pork
porto	port
potage	soup
potage bilibi	fish and oyster soup
potage Crécy	carrot and rice soup
potage Esaü	lentil soup
potage parmentier	leek and potato soup
potage printanier	vegetable soup
potage Saint-Germain	split pea soup
potage velouté	creamy soup
pot-au-feu	beef and vegetable stew
potée	vegetable and meat stew
Pouilly-Fuissé	dry white wine from Burgundy
poularde	fattened chicken
poule au pot	chicken and vegetable stew
poule au riz	chicken with rice
poulet à l'estragon	chicken in tarragon sauce
poulet basquaise	chicken with ratatouille

poulet chasseur	chicken with mushrooms and white wine
poulet créole	chicken in white sauce with rice
poulet rôti	roast chicken
praire	clam
pré-salé	salt marsh, where top-quality lamb is raised
premier cru	vintage wine
provençale	with tomatoes, garlic and herbs
prune	plum
pruneau	prune
pudding	plum pudding
purée de marrons	chestnut purée
purée de pommes de terre	mashed potatoes
quatre-quarts	rich cake, similar to Madeira cake
quenelle	meat or fish dumpling
queue de bœuf	oxtail
quiche lorraine	quiche with bacon
râble de chevreuil	saddle of venison
raclette	alpine dish of melted cheese
radis	radish
ragoût	stew
raie	skate
raie au beurre noir	skate fried in butter
raifort	horseradish
raisin	grape
râpé	grated
rascasse	scorpion fish
ratatouille	stewed peppers, courgettes (zucchini), aubergines (eggplants) and tomatoes
ravigote	dressing with herbs
reblochon	strong cheese from Savoie
reine-claude	greengage (plum)
rémoulade	mayonnaise with herbs, mustard and capers
répas	meal
rigotte	small goats' cheese from Lyon
rillettes	potted pork or goose meat
ris de veau	veal sweetbread
rissole	meat pie
riz	rice
riz à l'impératrice	sweet rice dish
riz pilaf	spicy rice with meat or seafood
rognon	kidney
roquefort	blue cheese
rôti	roast
rouget	red mullet
rouille	spicy mayonnaise served with bouillabaisse
sabayon	egg yolks whipped with wine
sablé	shortbread
saignant	very rare ("bloody")
saint-honoré	cream puff cake
saint-marcellin	goats' cheese
saint-pierre	John Dory
salade	salad, lettuce
salade composée	mixed salad
salade niçoise	salad of olives, tomatoes, anchovies, tuna, hard-boiled eggs, peppers, lettuce and green beans
salade russe	salad of diced vegetables in mayonnaise
salade tiède	warm salad
salade verte	green salad
salmis	game stew
salsifis	oyster plant, salsify
sandre	pike-perch, zander
sanglier	wild boar
sauce aurore	white sauce with tomato purée
sauce béarnaise	thick sauce with eggs and butter
sauce blanche	white sauce
sauce gribiche	dressing with hard-boiled eggs
sauce hollandaise	rich sauce made with eggs, butter and vinegar
sauce Madère	Madeira sauce
sauce matelote	wine sauce
sauce Mornay	béchamel sauce with cheese
sauce mousseline	hollandaise sauce with cream
sauce poulette	sauce made with mushrooms and egg yolks
sauce ravigote	dressing with shallots and herbs
sauce rémoulade	mayonnaise with herbs, mustard and capers
sauce suprême	creamy sauce
sauce tartare	mayonnaise with herbs and gherkins
sauce veloutée	white sauce with egg yolks and cream
sauce vinot	wine sauce
saucisse	sausage
saucisse de Francfort	frankfurter
saucisse de Strasbourg	beef sausage
saucisson	salami-type sausage
saumon	salmon
saumon fumé	smoked salmon
sauternes	sweet white wine
savarin	crown-shaped rum baba
sec	dry (wine)
seiche	cuttlefish
sel	salt
service (non) compris	service (not) included
service 12% inclus	12% service charge included
servir frais	serve cool
sirop	cordial
sole bonne femme	sole in white wine and mushrooms
sole meunière	sole dipped in flour and fried in butter
sole véronique	sole in a wine sauce with grapes
soufflé	soufflé
soupe à l'oignon	French onion soup
soupe au pistou	thick vegetable soup with basil
soupe aux moules	mussel soup
soupe de poisson	fish soup
steak au poivre	peppered steak
steak frites	steak and chips
steak haché	minced meat, minced beef
steak tartare	raw minced beef with a raw egg
sucre	sugar
suprême de volaille	chicken breast in cream sauce
tanche	tench
tarte	tart, pie
tarte frangipane	almond cream tart
tartelette	small tart
tarte Tatin	baked apple dish
tartine	slice of bread and butter
tendrons de veau	breast of veal
terrine	pâté
terrine du chef	chef's special pâté
tête de veau	calf's head
thé	tea
thé à la menthe	mint tea
thé au lait	tea with milk
thé citron	lemon tea
thon	tuna
tilleul	lime tea
tomate	tomato
tomates farcies	stuffed tomatoes
tome/tomme de Savoie	white cheese from Savoy
tournedos	round beef steak
tourte	covered pie
tourteau	type of crab
tripes	tripe
tripes à la mode de Caen	tripe in spicy vegetable sauce
truffe	truffle
truite au bleu	poached trout
truite meunière	trout dipped in flour and fried in butter
vacherin	strong, soft cheese from the Jura
vacherin glacé	ice cream meringue
veau	veal
velouté de tomate	cream of tomato soup
vermicelle	vermicelli (very fine pasta used in soups)
verveine	verbena tea
viande	meat
vin	wine
vinaigrette	French dressing
vin blanc	white wine
vin de pays	local wine
vin de table	table wine
vin rosé	rosé wine
vin rouge	red wine
vinaigre	vinegar
volaille	poultry
VSOP	mature brandy
waterzooï	northern stew of chicken or fish with vegetables
xérès	sherry
yaourt	yoghurt

General Index

Acknowledgments

DORLING KINDERSLEY would like to thank the
following people whose contributions and
assistance have made the preparation of this book
possible.

MAIN CONTRIBUTORS

NATASHA EDWARDS moved to Paris from London in
1992 and since then has travelled widely around
France, exploring unknown corners and eating
and writing about food, culture, design and
tourism. Editor of *Time Out Paris*, she also writes
for *Condé Nast Traveller* and the *Independent*,
among other publications.

SHARON SUTCLIFFE is a wine and food writer based
in Paris. She is a regular columnist for *Rustica*
magazine and contributes to several restaurant
guides, including *Time Out Paris* and *Charming
Restaurants in France*. After settling in France,
she became chief editor of the *Guide des Vins des
Sommeliers*. Co-author of the reference book
Culinaria France, Sharon is also a translator in
the field of food and wine and has translated
several major works, notably the *Nez du Vin*
series.

PUBLISHER
Douglas Amrine

PUBLISHING MANAGERS
Fay Franklin
Kate Poole

SENIOR ART EDITOR
Marisa Renzullo

PRODUCTION
Melanie Dowland

DIGITAL CONTENT MANAGER
Nina Blackett

ADDITIONAL TEXT
Chris Barstow

ADDITIONAL PHOTOGRAPHY
Max Alexander, Philip Enticknap, Steve Gorton,
John Heseltine, Roger Hilton, Neil Lukas, Neil
Mersh, Roger Moss, Robert O'Dea, John Parker,
Roger Phillips, Kim Sayer.

DESIGN AND EDITORIAL ASSISTANCE
Nishi Bhasin, Anna Freiberger, Anjali Goel, Pooja
Huria, Rebecca Milner, Sangita Patel, Manjari Rathi,
Rachel Symons.

PROOFREADER
Stewart J Wild

INDEXER
Hilary Bird

SPECIAL ASSISTANCE
The authors would like to thank Jean-Pierre
Bordaz, Olivia Bordaz, Martine Bouchet of the
CDT du Lot; Corinne Russo of the Office de
Tourisme de Cavaillon; the CDT des Pyrénées
Atlantiques; Michèle Piron-Soulat, Communication
Vinicole Internationale (Maisons Laffitte) and
Laurent Courtial, N&N's (Lyon).

PHOTOGRAPHY PERMISSIONS
DORLING KINDERSLEY would like to thank the
following for their assistance and kind permission
to photograph at their establishments: Boucherie
Dumont, Paris; Château de Meursault; Château
Mansenoble; Château de Fesles; Château du Clos
de Vougeot; La Cigale, Nantes; Distillerie Dolin,
Chambéry; Distillerie du Velay, St-Germain Laprade;
Musée du Vin, Châteauneuf-du-Pape; Domaine de
Terrebrune, Ollioules; Magasin Jean-Luc Aegerter,
Beaune; La Maison du Chocolat, Paris; Paul Danjou,
Vire; Lavinia, Paris; Les Sources de Caudalie;
Taittinger C.C.V.C., Reims; Taverne de l'Ecu, Lille;
Le Train Bleu, Paris, and all other shops, markets,
hotels, restaurants, vineyards and producers too
numerous to thanks individually.

PICTURE CREDITS
t = top; tl = top left; tlc = top left centre; tc = top
centre; tr = top right; cla = centre left above; ca =
centre above; cra = centre right above; cl = centre
left; c = centre; cr = centre right; clb = centre left
below; cb = centre below; crb = centre right
below; bl = bottom left; b = bottom; bc = bottom
centre; bcl = bottom centre left; br = bottom right;
d = detail.

Every effort has been made to trace the copyright
holders and we apologize in advance for any
unintentional omissions. We would be pleased to
insert the appropriate acknowledgments in any
subsequent editions of this publication.

DORLING KINDERSLEY would like to thank the
following individuals, companies and picture
libraries for their kind permission to reproduce
their photographs:

CEPHAS PICTURE LIBRARY: Mick Rock 7b;

CORBIS: David Ball 114bl; Nathan Benn 23t;
Annebicque Bernard/Sygma 11tr; Georgina
Bowater 94bl; Michael Boys 76bl; Gary Braasch
427br; Michael Busselle 329bl; Jan Butchofsky-
Houser 18b; Julio Donoso/Sygma 273b; Owen
Franken 28br, 33br, 38cl, 245cr; Franz-Marc Frei

138-139t; Marc Garanger 94-95b, 348-349t; Farrell Grehan 94tl; Annie Griffiths Belt 186bl; Bill Howes/Frank Lane Picture Agency 74-75b; Jacqui Hurst 187br; Catherine Karnow 138bl; Kevin Morris 433br; Charles O'Rear 95br, 213br, 265br; Hamish Park 244bl; Jacques Pavlosvsky/Sygma 349br; Kim Sayer 74bl; Leonard de Selva, Advertisement for Vichy Mineral Water, 1895, Albert Guillaume (c) ADAGP, Paris and DACS, London 2003 248bl; Pamela Smith/Eye Ubiquitous 323br; James A. Sugar 74-75t; Sandro Vannini 426-427t; Adam Woolfitt 139br, 242bl, 242-243b, 245tl.

BILL EVANS: 375cl, 377cr.

GETTY IMAGES: Richard Passmore 31t; Andrea Pistolesi 2-3.

LEONARDO MEDIABANK: 34t; LOGIS DE FRANCE: 34br.

MARKA, MILAN: Nevio Doz 426tl.
SCOPE, PARIS: Balzer 428cl; Jean-Luc Barde 270tl, 273tr, 300b, 324bl, 355b, 432tr; Pascale Desclos 429tl, 429br; Michel Gotin 433tl; Jacques Guillard 100t, 218tl, 223br; Michael Guillard 298bl; Roland Huitel 428br, 429tr, 432cl; Francis Jalain 30br; Michel Plassart 218b, 299c; SYNDICAT D'INITIATIVE DES COMMUNES DE L'APPELLATION FAUGERES: 374bl.

JACKET
FRONT – ALAMY IMAGES: Peter Bowater bl; CORBIS: Bryan F. Peterson cr; DK IMAGES: cb; Ian O'Leary bc; IMAGES OF FRANCE: David Martyn Hughes main.
BACK – DK IMAGES: br; Leonardo MediaBank: tl.
SPINE – IMAGES OF FRANCE: David Martyn Hughes.

All otherimages c Dorling Kindersley. See www.DKimages.com for further information.

The Regions of France

THIS BOOK DIVIDES FRANCE into 16 regional sections, although officially the country comprises 22 *régions*. Each of the regional chapters has a colour code, shown on the map below and appearing throughout the book as "thumb tabs". Detailed maps of the whole of France, showing the locations of featured hotels and restaurants, along with a map of central Paris, can be found in a separate section starting on page 442.

GETTING AROUND

In spite of its size, France is relatively easy to travel around. There is a well-organized rail network, and travelling times are considerably shortened between towns with a high-speed TGV link. Most of France's excellent motorways *(autoroutes)* have expensive tolls but are fast and efficient for longer distances. City ring-roads are usually free, and some longer sections of motorway may also be free. Smaller roads are usually a more interesting way to discover the country's varied landscape and they are almost invariably well-maintained and signposted. Many of the hotels and restaurants featured in the listings are in places "off the beaten track".

KEY

— Motorway

— Major road

0 km	100
0 Miles	100

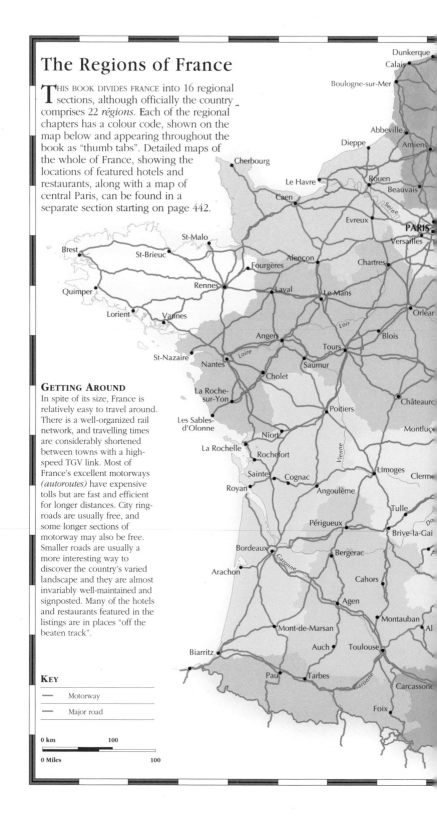